Fielding's EUROPE with CHILDREN

by

Leila Hadley

Fielding Travel Books
c/o William Morrow & Company, Inc.
105 Madison Avenue, New York, N.Y. 10016

For mothers, fathers, grandparents, children, and the young in heart and spirit!

For the children dearest to you and the children dearest to me: Caroline, Victoria, the two Matthews, Allison, Kip, my children's friends and my friends' children.

For Peter Matson, father of Emily, Elijah, Nyssa, Pamela, Sara, Tabitha.

For Eunice Riedel, a superb editor and a beloved friend, and the children who are dearest to her.

Library of Congress Catalog Card Number: 83-82819
ISBN: 0-688-02731-8 (pbk)

Printed in the United States of America
Second Revised Edition
3 4 5 6 7 8 9 10

CONTENTS

JUST BETWEEN US

You don't have to postpone your plans for foreign travel until "the children are older."

You don't have to worry about leaving your children behind while you're traveling.

You don't have to get in a swivet about moving abroad with the children for a job relocation or a sabbatical year.

And, if you do your homework, you won't even have to worry about how you can afford it. You can, even in a world of inflation, recession, and dithering dollars.

Traveling through Europe and around the world with four children, I've come to know that certain plans, procedures, and easy-to-follow advice are vital ingredients in happy, trouble-free travel. A little advance homework and an on-the-spot reference source are all that's necessary. Some parents see taking their children to Europe as a kind of penance to be lived through. They need another perspective. A European vacation should be fun for parents as well as children, and wonderful for the entire family.

Besides, did you know that traveling with children can be a great advantage? That traveling with children can be as easy—and far more rewarding—as traveling without them? And certainly infinitely preferable to not traveling at all? This book is your guide to all the details, a revised report on Europe for children—infants, toddlers, preteens, and teenagers—as complete, detailed, and up-to-date as I could possibly make it. Many of my concerns are the extras—fun trips, specialized interests such as riding, swimming, tennis, skiing, sailing, and fishing, the great parks, zoos, and animal preserves, the happily rewarding things you can do with children and that they can do on their own.

Besides reporting on entertainments, natural and handmade wonders, and other passions shared by people like us, my energies have been devoted to the practical, hard-to-track-down details vital to the peace of mind of traveling parents before they set off and while they are in Europe. What supplies should you carry abroad for your infant? What's a good skiing resort for a family? How do you order your toddler's applesauce in German? What size shoe does your 6-year-old wear in England?

At the same time, I have tried to look at Europe from your child's point of view (as I saw it as a child traveler and as I have watched my own children's reactions) to tell you about all the things I feel will make your trip wonderful for your children—whether they delight in horror chambers, or are interested only in horses or boats, or more interested in clowns than in cathedrals.

And, on the assumption that no matter how well and how much you love your children you will want some time away from them to pursue your own interests, I have supplied—country by country—the names of babysitters, kindergartens, and nurseries, children's companions, tours just for children, and other childcare facilities available by the hour, day, week, or month.

For those who are planning long stays, I have included schools.

Should you be unable to go to Europe yourself, but would like your child to have the experience, you'll also find descriptions of camps and holiday homes-away-from-home where your child may be safely sent on his own.

Finally, since I've traveled on my own with the children, and since there have been times when I've lived it up and times when I've squeaked by on a stringent budget, in these pages you'll find suggestions for every circumstance and every economic level of family travel. For those of you who needn't count pennies, I've included some pleasures for-the-rich-only. But, luckily, rewarding travel is more a matter of imagination, taste, and good sense than money, and my fondest hope is that this book will supply you with options for life-sweetening fun and delight at modest costs for value received at any time of year, as well as for extended stays in Europe.

THE "DRAWBACKS" OF TAKING CHILDREN WITH YOU The arguments generally advanced in favor of leaving the children at home are that (1) it is "too expensive" to take them with you; (2) parents need and deserve a vacation away from their children; (3) it's too much trouble to cope with children in the back seat of a car or in strange places; and (4) the children are "too young" to get "anything out of it" until they are at least 16, or 18, or 21.

Persuasive though these arguments may sound, they are far from the truth. First of all, the cost of transporting, housing, feeding, and entertaining children abroad can be a good deal less than getting in a housekeeper to look after them while you're away or the expenses of summer camp (that almost always add up to more than you think they will). If you are lucky enough to have friends or relatives who will take over all responsibility for your child's well-being while you are away, the financial cost may be less. On the other hand, that whopping obligation cannot be paid off in money but only in kind, and it's the sort of indebtedness that cannot easily be reciprocated. In either situation, no matter how ideal, if there is an ocean between you and your children, you are bound to worry either about your children's well-being or about yourself as a parent. Whatever you save, if you save anything at all, by not taking the children with you, is simply and swiftly canceled out by the emotional expense of leaving them behind. When a young child no longer sees something, he thinks it is gone forever. It's not surprising that children who are left behind are often upset. Older children can feel rejected or abandoned, and this may lead to serious problems with which neither they nor you should be burdened.

In answer to points 2 and 3, I couldn't agree more about parents occasionally needing a little rest and vacation away from the children. I might object that something as special as a trip to Europe properly ought to be exempted from this consideration, but it is not altogether necessary to do so. By taking the children with you, you can still be independent. Europe is beautifully organized for taking care of children. In the most civilized continent in the world it shouldn't be surprising that the tradition of caring for children is so deeply ingrained that for an hour, a day, or even a couple of weeks your child can be looked after with scrupulous and devoted attention, leaving you free to do all the resting or gallivanting you want. If you have trouble coping with your child at home, my guess is that he will be more of a problem for you and everyone else to worry about if you leave him at home. If you take him with you, you may be pleasantly surprised. If you aren't, at least you can rely upon wonderfully qualified help and childcare facilities (I've listed these for each country). As for the last point, this also depends somewhat on your child. Under 5, I honestly don't think a child would "get much" out of a trip to Europe. That is, he's not going to come back filled with facts and noticeably impressed. But almost certainly he will benefit from the travel experience itself. I think you'll find that it will be less worrisome and easier all around to take him with you. A 5-year-old can definitely gain from traveling abroad, and from 6 on, a child will gain a great deal. By 15 and 16, children will be going off more and more frequently on their own as exchange students or in youth groups, so don't put off going abroad with the children for too long, because they may soon be too old to go with you!

THE ADVANTAGES OF TAKING CHILDREN WITH YOU Apart from what seems to me to be the rather negative aspects of less emotional and financial strain, there are definite advantages to taking your children with you.

First, you will be granted a special gift of vision. You will see Europe with the fresh outlook of a child. More unusual, unexpected, and downright pleasant things happen when you travel with your children than when you travel alone. Children have a way of making friends unself-consciously both for themselves and for you. Their presence entitles you to fellowship in an internationally recognized club of good will. People everywhere go out of their way to be helpful and kind. And children will lead you toward all sorts of activities you probably wouldn't consider if they weren't along.

They safeguard you from overdoing formal sightseeing to the point of exhaustion. You go off on a boat trip or a picnic or to a country fair instead. With the children along, you can't dash from museum to museum, or go to every concert or festival, so you pick and choose with the greatest care what you will go to, and you enjoy it far more.

But the greatest of all advantages is that traveling together is an experience that you share perhaps more closely than any other with your children. This is a great opportunity for you to get to know each other, to accumulate together a fund of happy memories of shared pleasures.

Travel is a blue-chip investment for parents who want to enrich their children's lives. It helps a child to interpret his daily experiences at school and home, to develop more fully, to gain confidence by adapting to new and strange places, to become more outgoing and receptive. Above all, travel, as nothing else, can give new meaning to formal education. You can only go so far with books and talk. When London no longer is a spot on the map but a real place where you saw the Changing of the Guard or a debate in the House of Commons; or when you have sat in the shade of a cork tree in Portugal; or when you have visited Versailles or the Vatican; or when you have seen a real Viking ship—then geography and history come alive to you and you really understand your Western heritage of culture and tradition. Not only will your child see the connection between his present-day life and the fascinating past, but he will gain a better understanding of his own country as he explains himself and America to the people he meets.

The foregoing are advantages that the child absorbs more or less unconsciously, hardly aware even that they are advantages. What a child will know—if you plan your trip right—is that traveling abroad is the most fun, the most exciting, and the most wonderful adventure that ever happened!

THE TRAVELING PARENT

YOUR ITINERARY Whether you are going to limit yourself to one country or visit four, five, six or ten is really more a matter of preference than of time, whether you are traveling with or without children. Spending more time in a country does not necessarily mean you will know it better. During the first two or three days in a new place, your mind is receptive and your impressions will be clear and sharp. Within two weeks, it's astonishing how much will no longer surprise you, and will be overlooked or taken for granted. I'm not suggesting that you race like a lemming from one country to another—but there is no reason to feel that three weeks in one country would be ''better'' than visiting three or four lands in the same time. Fast change of scene doesn't bother children. One parent may still be signing the hotel register, the other may still be unsnapping the locks on the suitcases, but the children will have had sufficient time to be all set for a gondola ride with a gondolier whose name they already know.

As for the ridiculous prejudice against crisscrossing, or returning to a place you have already been, don't think your itinerary is ''wrong'' if you find this desirable or necessary. With children, a little crisscrossing is a satisfying prospect, because it means they will be returning to a familiar place, to a place they ''know,'' and probably back to ''their old hotel,'' where they will remember everyone's name, and where everyone will remember them.

If there is any pattern in family travel, it seems to be that travelers first go to many places to get an overall view; then they visit two countries or two islands on their second trip; then they revel in one area or one country; and, on their fourth trip, they spend little time sightseeing but go mainly to relax in their favorite spot.

There is a tradition that you go to Europe in the summer, during the high season as far as prices and transportation are concerned, but the children are also home on vacation during the off season for magnificent Christmas celebrations and toy fairs, winter sports, the opera, the London pantomimes and circus, the theater, and music. April and May are wonderful times to visit Europe: spring and Easter festivals and fairs everywhere; horse shows, sailing regattas, and general pageantry. May marks the beginnings of the *Son et Lumière* and music festivals, the blossoming of Europe's beautiful chestnut trees, and many special events. I have tried to list reasonably complete "Calendars of Events" of special family interest for each country.

PASSPORTS Passport applications are available from your travel agent, airline, local Post Office or, if your city has one, a Department of State Passport Agency. To file the application, you and your children over 13 should appear in person at your local Post Office, Passport Agency, or any U.S. District Court or State Court authorized by law to naturalize aliens. Bring with you two full-face, head-and-shoulders photographs (black-and-white or color) two inches square; proof of U.S. citizenship (original birth certificate or microfilm copy showing state seal) or, if born abroad, certificate of citizenship and consular report of birth abroad or naturalization certificate; an identification document bearing your signature, photograph and physical description (such as a driver's license or an industrial ID card). For the under 13 contingent, documents and photographs are necessary, but the children need not appear in person. Children 13 to 17 should apply for a passport in person; a letter of parental permission on your business or personal stationery may be adequate, but the presence of parent will greatly facilitate the application. Allow about six weeks for processing passport applications.

When your passport is mailed back to you, sign it, sign for your children if there is the slightest possibility that they might make an ink blot which can possibly invalidate their passports, and fill in the personal emergency information section in your passport and in those of your children under 12.

MONEY AND PRICES There are some maxims to remember about money. First, whatever your trip costs, it is worth every penny. The child who has been taught about the world through traveling has a start in life he never loses.

Second, although travel is worth every penny, don't think for a minute that "you get only what you pay for" or that the best necessarily is the most expensive. Traveling first class is unquestionably more luxurious than traveling economy class. Expensiveness is in no way an infallible guide to excellence. Too, it is always a good idea to change your money only at banks or at official money–exchange offices.

YOUR TRAVEL AGENT For your children's and your own travel pleasure, the conducted or escorted tour of Europe is out of the question; this field of travel simply does not cater to children's interests. Therefore, if you don't know precisely what's what from personal experience, you'll probably want to check with several sources, pencil in a tentative itinerary, and then drop in to see your nearest ASTA (American Society of Travel Agents) travel agent.

You pay no more to book through an agency. They receive a commission from the airlines and hotels. But the travel agent is there to sell you, so don't be pressured into spending more on accommodations than you should. European tourist information bureaus can suggest many inexpensive but comfortable and delightful accommodations. What are you looking for? What are the essentials for you? It's your travel agent's business, but remember that it's your holiday! For travelers who are strong on creature comforts, good taste, and the cultural benefactions of life and are subscribers to such periodicals as the *Wall Street Journal,* my recommendation for personalized loving care would be **Inverness Travel, Inc.** 770 Lexington Ave., New York, NY 10021 Tel: (212) 486–1800. Ask for its president, Mrs. Katherine Unger.

I like to feel free to do as I please, to stay as long as I want, then move on. I used to pride myself that I could arrive anywhere in any season and always find a convenient and charming place to stay. Traveling during the off season, you can usually manage to play things pretty much by ear—if you've got a well-tempered and well-trained ear. But traveling with children is different. *You* can skip dinner or wait until two in the morning for a snack. *You* can cope with snarls, disappointments, and upsets. But no matter how adaptable your children are, it's awfully difficult for everyone if you are in any way concerned or anxious about their well-being. More than discomfort, tension can raise havoc with everyone's enjoyment of a trip. That's why I recommend letting a travel agent make your basic arrangements.

If you would like to center your vacation around bicycling, fishing, music, art, folkloric festivals, riding, crafts, or whatever, a valuable source of information is the *Specialty Travel Index,* a publication available through many travel agents as well as by mail, if you send $3 plus a self-addressed, stamped envelope to Specialty Travel Index, 9 Mono Ave., Suite 4, Fairfax, CA 94930. Another valuable source of information is a quarterly newsletter, *Traveling With Your Children.* For information about this newsletter, get in touch with Ms. Dorothy Jordon at 80 Eighth Ave., New York, NY 10011.

▶ **Note:** When you and your travel agent have drawn up your itinerary, have several extra copies made for your children to distribute to their special friends or relatives who will be writing to them.

SINGLE, DIVORCED, WIDOWED PARENTS If you don't like the idea of traveling alone with your children, if you would like the services of an au pair, driver, translator, housekeeper, aide, or simply a traveling companion, try the **Traveling Companion Exchange,** Box 833, Amityville, NY 11701.

THE TRAVELING CHILD

Reading up on the countries you want to go to is obviously wise for any traveler who wants to telescope as much pleasure as possible into whatever time he has at his disposal. If you are planning to travel with children, background reading is as much of a "must" for them as it is for you. A child learns from participating in travel plans. If the children are 7 or older, knowing about the places they are going to visit gives them an opportunity months ahead of time to be on the lookout for information of interest. It's astonishing how much knowledge a child can store up if it *means* something to him. Teachers, friends, and neighbors—everyone you know—will rally round to suggest places to go, to tell your children where *they* went, and to fish out foreign knickknacks to show or give your children. It's one of the few occasions when children can practice and improve upon their relationships with older friends. Most of the time, grownups' conversation with children is limited to remarks such as: "How are you doing in school?" or "What are your favorite subjects?" It gives children a feeling of confidence and a desirable social poise to be able to talk with older people about a subject of mutual interest.

For younger children, who aren't such good readers or who are too young to read at all, there are books that you can read aloud and pictures for them to look at.

In all events, talk about the forthcoming trip and about the things a child can expect to see and do. Apart from other advantages, it eliminates embarrassing moments during your travels. What is strange and unfamiliar may make a child laugh, point, stare, or shriek: "Look at the funny men in those funny skirts!"

FREE TRAVEL INFORMATION The **European Travel Commission** (630 Fifth Ave., Suite 610, New York, NY 10111) will send you on request the addresses of all the European government tourist information offices and/or a calendar of this year's events in Europe. Include a self-addressed envelope with two stamps.

It is practical and interesting to have a look at the information that foreign travel information bureaus offer. Just write to indicate what sort of information you would like (see chapters on individual countries for the addresses of national tourist bureaus). Then sit back and wait for the glorious deluge to arrive.

Put your children's name rather than your own on the return address. Getting mail will make the children happy, and if mail is addressed to them, they will read it and become both informed and interested.

NATIONAL TRAVEL OFFICES Every country operates a tourist bureau with a head office and regional branches to serve you in its homeland, representation in major cities throughout the world to serve you on your travels, and main offices in New York (and other North American cities) to advise you. Their staffs are usually knowledgeable, cheerful, cooperative, ever ready to help you to plan your trip and provide solutions to special problems and difficulties. To get the most from their services, *always be specific*. Ask for information about anything that comes to mind from trout fishing to accommodations in a castle. Encourage your children to make a list of things they're interested in.

U.S. GOVERNMENT PUBLICATIONS Request from the Superintendent of Documents (U.S. Government Printing Office, Washington, DC 20402) a subject bibliography on foreign affairs and foreign countries. Once you have this list, booklets may be ordered by name and/or number.

U.S. ARMED FORCES BENEFITS If you write to the Public Affairs Office of any Army, Navy, or Air Force installation in the area in which you expect to travel, requesting information about the area, the base, and if you are interested, about the possibilities of visiting the base or station, you will receive a prompt reply.

Naval stations are located in Edzell, Scotland; Naples, Italy; Rota, Spain; and Keflavik, Iceland.

Air bases Wiesbaden, Rhein-Main, Hof Air Base, Germany; Athens, Greece; Torrejon, Spain; Aviano, Brindisi, Italy; Amsterdam, Holland; Oslo, Norway; High Wycombe, England.

Army bases Chièvres, Belgium; Harrogate, England; Leghorn, Italy; and in Germany, you are seemingly always near a base somewhere, from Ansbach to Zweibruecken. Berlin, Heidelberg, Stuttgart, Darmstadt are more suited for viewing than the giant complex at Frankfurt. The office of the Secretary of Defense (U.S. Army Headquarters, The Pentagon, Washington, DC 20301) will supply you with a complete list on request. Army bases often have recreational programs and facilities for children. Speak with the special services officer if you are resident in the area and would like your child to be included in the fun. Or, write the **Public Affairs Office,** Headquarters, U.S. Army Europe (A.P.O.,

NY 09403) for information about education and recreation opportunities for you and your children.

PROJECTS FOR SCHOOL AND HOME Confronted by a foreigner's imaginary America—Indians, Hollywood, detective-story violence, everyone a millionaire, lunar conquest, lunacy, and fascinating variations upon these themes—just how do you go about explaining the U.S. to Europeans? The "real America" seems to me to be impossible to locate materially in any one object, institution, or part of our country. I have given up trying. Instead, I have handed over to my children most of the pleasurable burden of explaining America to Europeans, and my children, I must say, did a far better job of it than I, because they came up with the scrapbook idea. One *Scrapbook to Take* is filled with pictures of themselves, their friends, school, activities, clubs, ourselves as their parents, descriptions and pictures of where we live and what we do, and a section about the U.S. in general, showing places of interest that they have seen and many that they have not seen but have heard about. The other scrapbook, a *Scrapbook to Make,* is a glorified travel diary illustrated with postcards, snapshots, maps, newspaper clippings, menus, pressed flowers, a pinch of sand from a beach preserved in a glassine envelope, a bird's feather, airline tags, travel folders, and anything else that is paper or portable—a scrapbook that can be outlined before you start off and filled in en route.

Our scrapbooks were home projects. Later, I discovered that the scrapbooks were ideally suited for school projects. Classmates could join in. It's a wonderful way to make schoolwork real and interesting.

PARENTS WITH HANDICAPPED CHILDREN If your child is blind, deaf, or otherwise physically handicapped, you may find some helpful suggestions in the admirable publication *Young Visitors to Britain,* available free from the British Tourist Authority, 680 Fifth Ave., New York, NY 10019. Also, Rehabilitation International—USA (1123 Broadway, New York, NY 10010) publishes an *International Directory of Access Guides* that provides addresses for obtaining copies. *Michelin Red Guides* indicate ramp access to major attractions, in their individual country guides. For access guides to cities in Great Britain and France write to the Royal Association for Disability and Rehabilitation (RADAR), 25 Mortimer St., London, W1, England. *Holiday Facilities for Handicapped Children* is available free from The Spastics Society, 16 Fitzroy Sq., London, W1, England. For *Vacances Pour Les Handicapés* write to the Centre d'Information et de Documentation Jeunesse, 101 quai Brandy, 75740 Paris, Cedex 15, France. *Urlaub, Ferien, Freizeit: Kuren und Erholung fur Familien mit Behinderten BZW, Kranken Kindern und Jugendlichen* is free from Bundesarbeitsgameinschaft, Hilfe fur Behinderte e.V., 4 Dusseldorf, Kirchfeldstrasse, 149, West Germany.

FOREIGN FRIENDS Most of us would like to go beyond the Baedeker attractions to meet Europe's people. Until fairly recently you had to depend upon letters of introduction to friends of friends who often weren't there when you arrived or else were there and proved to be just the sort of people you didn't want to meet.

I have therefore the highest regard for the hospitality programs offered to overseas guests by European hosts. Through these programs, your children will be able to meet young boys and girls who are the same age and share the same interests.

Consult the country-by-country listings for hospitality programs so that you can make any prior arrangements necessary.

PEN PALS Most countries' travel information bureaus can direct you to organized pen pal services, although I think children usually do better selecting their own pen pals by just making new friends. The following organizations will help your child find a European pen pal: **International Friendship League,** 22 Batterymarch St., Boston, MA 02109; **Letters Abroad,** 209 East 56th St., New York, NY 10022; **Student Letter Exchange,** Waseca, MN 56093; **The League of Friendship,** Box 509, Mount Vernon, OH 43050.

SPECIALIZED INFORMATION SOURCES **Forsyth Travel Library** (P.O. Box 2975, Shawnee Mission, KS 66201; Tel: (913) 384–0496) is an excellent source for all kinds of travel books. **The Traveller's Bookstore** (22 West 52nd St., New York, NY 10019; Tel: (212) 664–0995) also has a wonderful selection of relevant travel books for grown-ups and children.

WHAT TO TAKE—AND WHAT NOT TO TAKE

BAGGAGE ALLOWANCE ON AIRLINES Regulations, once standard, currently "deregulated," are complex, subject to frequent change, and vary from airline to airline. Some airlines go by the piece, some by the weight, and some take both into consideration in the computation of excess baggage charges which can run as much as 1% of your individual transatlantic fare for each excess kilo (2.2 lbs.). Sports gear is subject to other regulations and costs little to transport, whether skis, golf bag, or fishing rod. Tennis rackets can usually be handcarried free of charge. *Be sure to consult your airline before you start packing*. No baggage allowance is made for children under 2 who are traveling on the 10% fare.

Each person over 2 years of age is also allowed to carry free of charge a handbag, a doll or a "reasonable" amount of reading material, an extra overcoat, a raincoat, a camera, and a small hand case, parcel, or briefcase *you can stow beneath your seat on the plane* (8″ × 14″ × 21″).

When traveling with children, particularly with a baby or with two fairly young children, I have found that it is much easier to take one duffel bag or a canvas bag that comes with wheels rather than two smaller bags for the children's toys and equipment.

LUGGAGE The first rule of all sensible travelers, and particularly those traveling with children, is to take as little as possible. The less luggage you have, the more comfortable, efficient, speedy, and happy you'll be. First-time travelers, who are the most likely to take along excess baggage, almost always say—*Never again!* The next time they travel, they take only half the things they lugged the first time. So do whittle everything down to essentials. The ideal luggage is durable, serviceable, efficient, and lightweight. Rather one large bag than two or three small ones. Sammy the Seal (a stuffed animal) and Teddy (a bear that moos like a cow) happen to be essentials for which you may have, as family travelers, your own equivalents. Family travelers always have more luggage than other travelers. If you incline to panic when no porters are visible or when the porter tells you he'll meet you at the taxi rank with your luggage and you discover there are *two* taxi ranks, the sturdy Crown Fold-a-way luggage cart is an invaluable help.

If you are traveling with several children, continual packing and unpacking can become a whale of a nuisance (let no one tell you otherwise). I suggest you consider salesmen's sample cases. Fiber sample cases, they are called—but don't be misled by the name, which sounds awfully sleazy. They are wonders, virtually indestructible, and marvelously convenient—because they are made with trays that can be stacked one on top of the other, which makes it possible, for instance, to pack all the shoes in one layer, all the underwear in the next, and all the shirts in another. This, as you can imagine, makes everything a great deal easier to get to when you need it. These cases come in all lengths, widths, sizes, and shapes. The most popular model is one with three trays (30″ width, × 18″ length, × 2″ depth).

Some of them have locks, others come with leather lockstraps. Empty, they weigh less than other luggage of comparable size, yet are capable of holding more weight or bulk than any other sort of luggage when packed. Plain boxlike containers with lockstraps can, when necessary, expand to almost twice their depth, a feature I've found of considerable help when homeward bound with bulky packages. These salesmen's vulcanized fiberboard sample cases cost less for the space and convenience they offer than most ordinary luggage.

Drawbacks? Only one. They aren't beautiful. Rectangular, generally available only in black, they can by no means compete in appearance with the conventional sets of matched leather or fabric-covered luggage.

You can have luggage made to your specifications, too. Look in the classified section of your telephone book under the heading of Fiber Products or Sample Cases.

Take along a collapsible duffel bag for that inevitable collection of miscellany you always find yourselves encumbered with. Ideal for car, boat, bus, plane or train trips abroad, for trips to the beach, or just simply for stowing away last-minute things, this duffel bag can also double, if you are making the initial ocean hop by plane, for the two cabin bags your children are allowed to carry.

Be sure to supplement the duffel bag with a couple of book bags that you can slip into your suitcase when not in use, plus a roll-up shopping bag. Book bags, usually made of canvas or cotton twill, have waterproof linings and adjustable straps so that they can be carried or used as shoulder bags.

Whatever other luggage you decide upon, it's a blessing in plane embarkation to have your luggage not only tagged (this, of course, is *vital*) but also distinctly marked or covered. I mark my black fiberboard cases with a pale blue stripe and mark the trays and drawers with the corresponding initials of the children. This color-coding certainly gives the luggage a distinctive and easily identified charm. You can mark fabric-covered or leather luggage with adhesive tape or miracle tape, either by snipping your initials together or making some private little design. Porters can then spot your bags and whisk them out of the general pile while other travelers are still pointing and calling out, "No, no, not that one, *that* one!"

WHAT TO TAKE—INDISPENSABLES If you're wise and want to be prepared for any and all emergencies, the following list will probably be the *minimum* you'll find yourself carrying with you at all times in that huge handbag suggested in Chapter 4.

Medical supplies (see Ch. 9).

Johnson & Johnson moist towelettes or travel pack washcloths—as many as I have room for; also just the thing for sticky faces and hands—little babies may prefer a familiar wet washcloth (carried in a plastic bag).

A clean diaper for a towel.

A Chap-stick for dry lips.

Tube of shaving cream (to use instead of soap), or cake of soap in a container.

Toothbrushes and toothpaste.

Brushes and combs (several—they have a way of getting lost).

Kleenex purse-packs.

Scissors (manicure, sewing, and all-purpose).

A combination corkscrew, bottle/jar/can opener.

A lightweight clothes brush (Scotch tape is also useful for removing dust and lint).

Small sewing kit.

Nail kit.

Extra shoelaces for children's shoes.

Bundle of elastic bands.

Safety pins in assorted sizes.

Plastic bags in assorted sizes (small ones for washcloths, larger for soiled diapers and clothes).

Pens and pencils; felt pens such as Magic Markers in permanent colors for marking packages, luggage, tags; and water-color markers for drawing and notes.

Notebook and writing pad.

Travel literature, guidebooks, pocket phrasebooks.

A fabric tape measurer for measuring luggage, clothes and linens you might be buying.

Rolled-up cloth shopping bag.

Pocket flashlight, the kind that comes on a keychain, plus extra batteries—or, better yet, a Dispoz-a-lamp (guaranteed for 12 months or more, weighing 5½ oz., 2½″×4″). *Vital* for anyone like myself, who has difficulty reading microscopic city maps, telephone books in the dark, or amps in a moving car, is a combination flashlight and magnifying glass, plus extra batteries. If you have trouble finding a lighted magnifier, order from Hoffritz (515 W. 24th St., New York, NY 10011).

2 rolls dull finish Scotch tape (Magic Transparent); useful for everything from improvised paper dolls to taping reminders on suitcase lids.

Traveling alarm clock (transistor ones operate for a year on 1 flashlight battery).

If you have an electric appliance you can't live without, voltage converters for converting 220 volt AC foreign current to our 110 volt current are available at most department stores, or write to Hoffritz.

▶ **Note:** See also special lists in Chapter 5, Chapter 7 (if you'll be camping or caravaning), and Chapter 10 (if you're going by car).

WHAT TO TAKE—OPTIONALS This list may sound obvious. A seasoned traveler will see that most things listed here are available almost anywhere in Europe. But to locate any of them in a strange city takes time:

A source for travel accessories to save time, space, energy is Traveler's Checklist, Cornwall Bridge Rd., Sharon, CT 06069, Tel: (203) 364–0144. For improvised dentistry, an emergency kit is offered which includes everything you might need to cope with lost fillings, toothaches, and chipped teeth. There are many other items in the *Traveler's Checklist* catalog for which you'll have to send 50¢ in coin, unless you have children, in which case you get the catalog free.

Shampoo in plastic packets.

Plastic bottle of all purpose liquid soap.

A hand mirror, magnified on one side, regular on the other.

2 pairs of sunglasses.

Camera and film.

A few favorite books for yourself and the children.

2–3 wooden nipper-type clothespins for keeping correspondence and memoranda together.

2 shower caps.

A few packets of throw-away tissues impregnated with neutral leather polish, each good for several shines. (One brand is Miracle Instant Shine.) Good for maintenance of shoes, bags, camera cases.

A set of plastic cups in small case.

Calling cards—not with the children's names on them (an Americanism incomprehensible to Europeans), but with your own name and address on which the children's names can be written when the occasion arises as a prelude to correspondence.

1 carton of 20 foil-wrapped packages of the cold-water soap powder (Woolite).

Traveling clothesline, nylon string or rubber Flexoline, as long as possible.

12 plastic hook-type clothespins that you can use on the line or on towel racks.

▶ **Note:** You have no idea of the time and trouble you'll save by taking along extra buttons. Matching any button whatever is next to impossible. Except for antique buttons, European department stores have never provided a button I needed at the time. A small box of miscellaneous buttons is a time and temper saver.

TOYS AND DIVERSIONS A few days before departure, have the children select the toys they would like to take with them. If you explain about the limitations of space aboard a plane, and the inconvenience of lugging a space gun or a large doll across Europe, you will find that the children will cooperate by substituting smaller, more suitable toys. Children do rise to the occasion if given an idea of what to expect and an opportunity to share in travel plans. Specific suggestions about toys that offer variety, toys that involve the entire family, toys that quietly teach and inspire are included in two illustrated booklets, "Tips on Choosing Toys for a Car Trip" and "Tips on Choosing Toys for Plane Travel" available free of charge from *Toys to Grow On,* Dept. 10, 2695 East Dominguez St., P.O. Box 17, Long Beach, CA 90801. Also, Fisher–Price (620 Girard Ave., East Aurora, NY 14052) and Child Guidance (41 Madison Ave., New York, NY 10010) offer an excellent variety of toys that travel well. Write for their catalogs.

Baby toys: Something to hold onto, bathe with, cuddle, grip, push, pull, slide, turn, squeeze, bite, shake, look at, listen to.

Toys for toddlers: A most satisfactory one is Shake-and-Sort, a cylinder filled with colored balls and four platforms. Turn the cylinder on one end, and the colored balls swirl about. Turn and shake it, and the colored balls sort themselves through the holes in the platforms to fall into layers of matching colors. Too rattly for plane travel, but it delights children from one to four and me; under $5 from Child Guidance, 41 Madison Ave., New York, NY 10010, who tell me it teaches color and size concepts, and develops hand dexterity and visual discrimination. Substitute a cuddly animal for the plane, and keep this toy tied with a string to the stroller for airport fun. Also recommended is the Busy Puzzle, in Disney or Sesame Street patterns, no loose pieces, under $7, from Child Guidance.

For the 4–10 age group:

Pencil Fun Books—puzzles, games, mazes, connecting dot games and drawings, simple crossword puzzles, and pictures to color.
Electronic pocket games.
Colored pencil crayons—not the kind that turn into paint when wet.
Rand McNally Cards of Knowledge about stars, planets, animals.
Educards of Nature, Rocks and Minerals, Butterflies, Seashells.
Hand puppets.

Finger puppets.
Small—about 4 or 5″—stuffed animals with movable arms and legs.
Comic books and 1–2 real books for each child.
A couple of packages of pipe cleaners to make into people or animals or just to twist into circles.
An origami or paper-folding book, if you are a parent who can show your child how this can be done.
A book of simple riddles.
A box of bright-hued instant water-color markers, completely washable.
A magic designer (whirl the paper disc under the pencil held in adjustable arms to make thousands of geometric designs).
Choice of any of the Sesame Street educational games and books.
A small book of paper dolls and doll dresses and blunt scissors to cut them out.
A pack of children's playing cards, or card games. Since trays are provided, it is possible to play card games while flying.

For ages 10–14: Books, crossword puzzles, diaries, correspondence, and Electronic pocket games are usually all that is necessary. Around ten, girls develop a passion for small stuffed animals (some often not so small), and also seem to have endless patience with reading to their baby brothers and sisters. This keeps both them *and* the baby entertained.

PACKING I have a passion for lists and always Scotch-tape a list of the contents of each suitcase on the inside cover.

To simplify clothes-sorting and laundry checkups, I mark the toe tips of cotton socks with matching numbers for each pair—1 and 1, 2 and 2, 3 and 3. When traveling with more than one child, use different colored Magic Markers to do this so that the children will know that the red-marked things are theirs and the blue-marked things are their brother's or sister's. This system applies to underwear, shirts, dresses, pants, everything. A colored dot can be inked onto handkerchief corners as well.

A further help for keeping things together and in order is to put gloves, handkerchiefs, and underwear into plastic bags. Stuff shoes with socks and put shoes in plastic bags. Plastic freezer bags are very useful in keeping your bags organized, with everything separate yet available.

Lining suitcases and trays with pliofilm or plastic garbage bags keeps clothes dust and moisture free.

I've found, too, that packing dresses *with* their coat hangers is a great help and time-saver. Wooden coat hangers are too heavy to be practical and so, for that matter, are most plastic ones except those in children's sizes. These are so convenient that even though they may occasionally break (you can quickly repair them with adhesive or Scotch tape), I take along at least three for each child. For older children and adults I use wire hangers for everything you can possibly hang on them.

This ploy makes packing and unpacking a snap, and nicely arms you against the shortage of hangers in most European hotels. (See also "Crossing the Atlantic, Special Pointers for Air Travel.")

WHAT NOT TO TAKE It makes sense not to take along noisy toys.

The same approach applies to lollipops, sourballs, peanuts, bubblegum, popcorn, crackers, and chocolate bars. Lollipops are sticky. Sourballs and peanuts are dangerous (they can be swallowed whole by accident). Peanuts make a child thirsty, and those in the shell are unspeakably messy—as are popcorn and crackers. Chewing gum is permissible because it can relieve pressure on the ears at takeoff and landing.

To the list of things not to be taken abroad should be added any games that comprise many small pieces—such as Chinese checkers, checkers, jigsaw puzzles, marbles, beads or little plastic and wooden sticks or pegs. These little pieces inevitably get lost, spill, and may cause someone to fall. Colored wax and plasticine is another pretty messy and sticky proposition while traveling.

DO NOT BRING DRUGS!!! If anyone is caught buying, selling, carrying, or using any type of drug from hashish to heroin, marijuana to mescaline, it can mean prison. For drug offenses, consular officials cannot get offenders out of jail or out of the country.

CLOTHES FOR EVERYONE

Essentials for the entire family are your most becoming clothes, the best-fitting, the most comfortable, the most attractive, the ones that will look fresh and unwrinkled at the end of a day. Taking a well-coordinated wardrobe of a few things cuts down indecisions about what to wear, saves time in packing and unpacking, adds to everyone's sense of confidence and well-being, and lends a feeling of orderliness and tidiness to transient living.

Feet often swell during air travel, so be sure that all your family's shoes are roomy. It's not unusual to slip off your shoes in midair and be unable to put them back on when it comes time to land.

A wise mother takes along in her hand luggage, a cover–all to protect her own clothes or to wear instead, plus an extra change of clothing for her children—better yet, two for baby. Then, come wrinkles or spills, there is no need to worry. You may not need that extra change of clothes, but having it on hand makes for general relaxation all around.

Airports are always breezy, so long hair should be done up in a pony tail, braided, or simply caught back with a ribbon.

Remember to take sweaters. Though it may be hot as the Sahara on the landing field, up in the stratosphere, with the air conditioning on, it can get cool as an autumn day.

If you have an early walker or a very active little tot, you may want to bring along harness and leading strings for stand-up-and-totter-down-the-aisle times.

CLOTHES FOR MOTHERS Traveling with children, comfortable and relaxed clothes are a must. I like traveling "uniforms" and a uniform look so that I don't have to think or worry about what I'm going to wear. Coats or capes with matching skirts and dresses, coat linings and blouses that match, dresses with matching head scarves and cardigans work best. Rather than a raincoat, I take a traveling umbrella and some sort of turban. For cold and rainy weather, high-fitted vinyl or leather boots can turn pants into knickers and protect your legs from the hazards of puddle-jumping children. Comfortably wide and sturdy shoes with rubber or crepe soles are a must for walking, for cobbled streets, slippery decks, and museum floors.

CLOTHES FOR INFANTS The indispensable item, of course, is diapers. You won't have any trouble obtaining diapers, disposables, plastic liners, and waterproof pants in major cities. Information about where to find these is included in every individual country listing.

Your baby's comfort is the most important factor to be considered. Try diaper liners and disposable diapers for at least two weeks before your trip to be sure you can determine which type of liner and disposable diaper is best for your baby. Disposable diaper liners provide "social" insurance that loving laps won't be wet ones, and they do make for easier diaper washing. Disposable diapers have been greatly improved in the last ten years, but they can't double as regular diapers can for napkins, towels, bibs, lap covers, mothers' clothes protectors, pillow covers, or sheets.

If you prefer regular diapers to disposable ones, you can buy sterilized but not-quite-what-they-used-to-be diapers from a diaper service that you can afford to discard as you go along—just as if they were disposables.

TRAVELING WITH YOUR BABY

The infant's world goes with him. A baby used to his own crib may squawk with surprise and consternation if suddenly removed to a carrycot. Weeks before you leave, let your infant get adjusted to anything strange or new—especially if you feel *you* may be nervous. Happiness and contentment—or nervousness!—are easily transmitted from the mother to her child. Your being happy and contented means good health for your baby. That's why, when traveling, you owe it to yourself and your children to take it easy and indulge yourself as much as possible. Spare yourself laundry chores and avail yourself—as European mothers do—of trained help and assistance to keep you happy, refreshed, and rested. On your pediatrician's prescription, a little quieting medication en route might be in order to spare both you and your baby.

INDISPENSABLE SUPPLIES For infants to 9 months you'll need, apart from the medical supplies suggested in Chapter 9, a baby kit containing infant rectal thermometer, diaper pins, baby aspirin (know the proper dosage!), prescriptions for upset tummies, tranquilizers, an antinauseant or other calming medicine prescribed by your doctor, scissors, a good can opener and jar opener for baby food, six plastic spoons, vitamin drops, antiseptic, petroleum jelly, Kleenex, adhesive bandage, and, for older infants, a nasal aspirator for relieving the sniffles of nonnose-blowers.

A bath and toilet kit should contain oil, powder, soap, Q-tips, manicure scissors, brush, comb, cotton wool, washcloths, and bathtowels.

You'll also need a large plastic bag for laundry, wet bathing suits, etc.

Bedding for two weeks (pared to the minimum) should include:

1 warm blanket.

6 crib, car-bed, carriage, or playpen-size sheets.

1 plastic or quilted pad for changing baby on.

2 flannel-coated waterproof sheets.

For beds, infant carriers, transport and seating facilities, and food, see the special sections below.

FORMULA FOR YOUNG BABIES If your baby is four months or younger, chances are he's on a formula. According to one New York physician, "It is doubtful if many mothers would rely on breast feeding while traveling. She would certainly have to be ready for a cessation of the milk supply, with the necessity of a change to bottle feeding and the various difficulties that such a shift entails." If you do have to switch over to formula feeding before you travel, take heart, prepared infant formulas provide excellent nutrition. Some are available in convenient ready-to-use forms, in either bottles or cans, ready to feed to your baby with little preparation on your part so that your baby can go traveling tonguing cheerily away at the same formula he's been accustomed to having—no water change, no change at all.

Similac and Enfamil both come in ready-to-use 8 oz. cans, but only Enfamil comes already bottled (just put on a nipple and cap and you're all set). Warming is a matter of preference—not necessity! Reusable nipple units are available and may be sterilized by boiling. Those lucky families abroad with commissary or PX privileges will find Enfamil stocked, I'm told: Concentrated Liquid (13 oz.) in PXes and commissaries; Ready-To-Use (8 oz.) in PXes; and Nursette (8 oz. disposable nurser) in commissaries.

Unfortunately, these premixed and ready-to-feed formulas aren't yet available on the European local market. So far, all that is available is powdered Enfamil which you mix with water—and this is available only in England (for further information, write Bristol-Myers Co., International Division, 345 Park Ave. NY 10145). Adding water (distilled water from a pharmacy or the more expensive Evian or Fiuggi noncarbonated bottled water) gives the baby a change to cope with. The ideal solution, it seems to me, is to air freight (10 days or so in advance) all the Enfamil ready-filled, ready-to-feed Nursettes you need, to whatever airport you're headed for, with instructions to hold for your pickup. Your airline should attend to confirming cables and making absolutely sure that your baby's food supply is waiting for you on arrival. Then all you have to do is take the feeding supplies you'll need for him in flight plus a few extra emergency bottles. If you buy a 24-can case of Ready-To-Use Enfamil (all you do is decant a can into a bottle as you need it) or a 24-Enfamil Nursette case (to prepare a feeding, unscrew cap, attach any sterilized nipple unit and feed) tell your druggist to leave it in the case (a ready-made shipping container). Take along plenty of extra nipples. Be sure to consult your pediatrician about the possibility of using Enfamil as a formula while you travel. Unopened Nursette bottles need no refrigeration; warming is optional; there's nothing to mix or measure; just attach any standard sterile nipple; 4-, 6-, or 8-oz. sizes; a luxurious way to feed a traveling baby. Air freighting a couple of cases ahead to the airport of your destination may cost the price of a couple of steaks, but whatever makes your trip easier, simpler, and more fun is money well spent.

FEEDING HINT FOR AIRBORNE INFANTS AND CHILDREN During the ascent after takeoff and during the descent before landing, it is quite normal to feel a slight pressure in your ears. Most passengers and older children can clear their ears by swallowing, yawning, or by chewing gum or sucking candies, which the stewardess will pass around. Babies can't do this, but they will react by starting to cry, which will automatically clear their ears. So if your baby wants to cry, just let him. A little cry is good for him at takeoff and landing.

An additional help is a drink of water, milk, or fruit juice (don't mix juice and milk), which will naturally make the baby swallow. Swallowing will effect the necessary clearance. *Therefore, be sure to carry a small bottle of orange juice or water with you for immediate use after you board the plane and again for the last 25 minutes of flight when the most rapid pressure changes happen.* Since your baby must be held on your lap while the aircraft is taking off and descending, this is an ideal time to give him a cozy little drink to reassure him that all is well, and to clear his ears. Just holding your baby and feeding him at this time will help to get him off to a happy flying start.

IN-FLIGHT SERVICES FOR INFANTS If you are traveling with children under two, your most important considerations will probably be where your baby is going to sleep and what he is going to eat.

The baby supplies that airlines carry, even with advance notice that you and your baby will be aboard, is limited. Regard it simply as an emergency supply. *Never travel without your baby's food and clothing requirements, grooming, and medical necessities, no matter how short the flight.* Domestic American and European planes often *don't* carry baby supplies, and transatlantic carriers' supplies are meant for emergency use and convenience in case mothers forget or run short of some item.

First, check all the facts with your travel agent or airline. Alert the airline about food requirements and skycot reservations—*which should be made well in advance;* it's easiest to make these arrangements at the time you make your reservation.

All airlines provide skycots—or bassinets for babies 23″ (58 cm.) to 27½″ (70 cm.) in length—which vary slightly in size and construction from airline to airline; most of them are 8″ deep, and a little over 12″ wide. All are durable, waterproof, guaranteed to be hospital-clean and cellophane wrapped, and more important, outfitted with safety straps or zippered-cocoon arrangements so that your child is protected at all times. There is space for only three of these aboard a jet, and 14 aboard a 747, so make advance reservations for them early. But advance reservations *cannot* be made for the two 39″-long sleeping bags carried aboard as standard equipment for children too large to fit into skycots and which are provided for mothers sitting in front seats or adjacent to two unoccupied seats. If two mothers ahead of you latch onto these sleeping bags, you will be sitting there with your little one on your lap, a knee- and arm-numbing misadventure that just doesn't have to happen to you.

Although no baggage allowance is given for a baby, if you have an infant's carrycot or basket of your own, it will be transported free of charge along with any baby food, diapers, blankets, or clothing needed on the flight *if the weight of the cot and articles packed in it—minus the baby—doesn't come to more than 20 lbs.* on an American airline. Foreign carriers have a 10-kilo (22 lb.) regulation for westbound mothers (which they sometimes absentmindedly apply to eastbound travelers). If it isn't a very crowded plane, ground personnel will be tolerant. If you make an effort to conform more or less to the limit, most airline personnel will be inclined to overlook a couple of pounds. You may be able to get away with 5 lbs. extra, but excess baggage charges will probably be levied for anything over that.

If your carrycot does not exceed the standard size of 30″ long and 16″ wide by 8″ deep, you will probably be allowed to use this on board, if there's enough cabin space. To be acceptable, it has to be collapsible so that, if necessary, it can be packed flat and stowed away. In this event, all the contents will be decanted into a plastic sack that you can keep at your feet. If you are traveling with a portable wicker cradle, this will be stowed in the baggage compartment during the flight, but the contents, of course, will be transferred to a plastic sack. The same procedure applies to detachable baby-carriage tops that exceed standard carrycot measurements and aren't really collapsible.

If you are going to travel without a cot—that is, carrying your baby in your arms or in an aluminum and canvas piggyback carrier—the airlines will allow you a free baggage allowance of 10 lbs. (again, most jetliner personnel will give you the benefit of an extra pound or so). This is not to be confused with your baby's travel wardrobe; it's supposed to consist only of the blankets, clothing, diapers, and food that he needs in flight. Some baby carriers have storage room beneath where you can cache additional supplies. Airlines know that the carrier itself weighs only two lbs., so chances are rare that anyone is going to embarrass you by asking you to weigh it separately. If this sneaky ploy of mine offends your sense of honesty, my apologies. I rationalize it on the grounds that I weigh 120 lbs. and pay the same fare as a 180-lb. man.

Airlines do their darndest to see that mothers and babies are comfortably seated but, apart from making reservations early, I also recommend getting to the airport and the reception desk early, so that you can make absolutely sure that a front seat on a jet or specially positioned seat on a 747 is allotted to you. Ask for the services of a ground hostess to be sure that all this is checked out for you. Don't bypass your comforts because you are too nice and don't want to give anyone any trouble. You're not giving anyone any trouble if you double- or triple-check in advance. You are usually permitted to board first to avoid crowds. Ask the ground hostess about assisting you to do this.

If your baby needs special foods, it is best to prepare such food at home and bring it with you. Bottled milk or food can be stored in the refrigerator on the aircraft until it has to be heated. Whatever your airline, facilities will always be provided for heating food that you have brought with you. A baby meal of strained meat, vegetables, and dessert can be provided for you, free of charge, if you order at least 24 hours in advance of your flight, but I recommend bringing along some bottled milk and whatever baby food you will need in transit from plane to hotel—I always take along a few extra bottles and jars of food to be on the safe side.

Although the flight attendant can't feed your baby for you, she will always be happy to warm your baby's bottle and to follow your wishes as to when you would like the rest of your baby's food to be warmed and brought to you. But do please remember *not* to request bottles and baby food during regular passenger meals. Flight attendants are as busy as bees, beavers, and one-armed paperhangers immediately before, after, and during mealtime, so do try to time your infant's milk and other sustenance accordingly!

If you are nursing the baby yourself, the flight attendant can be counted upon to fix up a private place for you to do so.

To conserve energy, time, and effort, I'd recommend presterilized disposable nursers (see ''Formula for Young Babies'').

Remember: (1) Flight attendants may not be able to warm food for you at the moment your baby is hungry; (2) Bring baby's own spoon, because you may want to feed your child in the airport; (3) Use disposable diapers provided by the airline to conserve your own supply, but have enough on hand so that if the supply runs out you have enough. Should you run short, feminine hygiene pads and Kleenex plus rubber pants are adequate substitutes. The flight attendant has a supply of the first two items.

BABY CARRIERS You may prefer English prams, frilly bassinets and custom-made carrycots, but for convenience and simplicity of baby travel there is nothing like a sturdy combination of canvas carrycot and a wheeled frame with a regular pram handle. This does the job of a carrycot, bed, and baby-carriage. Clamped onto the frame, it's a baby-carriage or a stroller. When you unclamp the carrycot, you have a familiar resting place for your baby that can be most convenient in planes, trains, cars, ships, and hotels.

Backpacks and slings are the only thing if you are hiking, camping, or planning to do a good deal of walking with an infant or toddler. For train stations, airports, bus terminals, a backpack has the additional safety factor of leaving your hands free while you negotiate escalators, stairs, and climbing aboard. Obviously they are limited to casual, sporty attitudes and clothes, but I think they are great. The Snugli—a canvas sling without an aluminum frame—is sturdy, compact, well-made, yet easily rolled up and tucked into briefcase or purse. It supports the head of a day-old baby as a front pouch and carries a two-year-old (though not both at the same time) as one takes out tucks to allow room for growing child. It can be worn front or back and—as long as the shoulder straps are kept tight and weight kept off the small of the back—is very comfortable. The Snugli comes in corduroy cloth or denim. The corduroy cloth model is the stronger. Available from L. L. Bean, Inc. (Freeport, ME 04033). I also recommend a recliner-stroller carriage-bed (minus mattress) suitable for infants 2 months to 3 years. The most compact and lightweight stroller-carriage imaginable, as portable as an umbrella, it is sturdy enough to use as a shopping cart or hold-all (it can hold up to 100 lbs. with ease).

BABY TRANSPORT—ALOFT What you need with infants and toddlers:

A lightweight collapsible stroller.

A carrycot or car bed, unless you plan to make use of the bassinets many airlines provide (see ''In-Flight Services,'' above). You may prefer to take your own if you have the detachable portion of a baby-carriage that can be converted into a car bed.

BABY TRANSPORT—MOTORING What you need if you are planning on driving with infants and toddlers abroad:

For the teeny-tinies: a car bed, used as a crib on arrival; reclining seat with a safety belt, excellent for restaurant feeding, visiting, waking periods.

For infants who can sit up: automobile harness; a safety belt that no little nipper can wiggle out of; reclining seat; collapsible stroller; portable bed.

For creepers and crawlers: automobile harness; car seat; collapsible stroller; portable bed.

The stroller can be omitted if you have a demountable carriage that can be pressed into service as a car bed, crib, and bed, keeping the wheelbase in the trunk compartment until needed. For sleep and transport, a playpen and stroller are needed for any infant over 6 months (see ''Motoring,'' Ch. 10). If you want to hike rather than promenade, you can take along as a replacement for the collapsible stroller a sling or backpack (see ''Baby Carriers,'' above). Please don't overdo. Remember there's no replacement for *you* if you collapse piggybacking the babe!

BABY TRANSPORT—CAMPING AND HIKING What you need if you are planning to camp and hike with baby along (apart from a pioneering sense of adventure and a high degree of good cheer and fortitude):

A car bed for babies up to 8 months or so.

A collapsible playpen that can be used as a bed for older infants.

Mosquito nets for car bed and playpen.

A carrier, backpack, or sling.

CROSSING THE ATLANTIC

BY PLANE You get where you're going in the fastest way possible by air, and your vacation abroad can start as soon as you and your children can readjust yourselves to the shenanigans of the international clock. What this means in practical terms is that the night of your arrival, your children will go to bed and wake up, not in time for breakfast, but in time for lunch. Do not lose heart. By the greatest good luck it only takes a day or so to get used to this new time schedule. Returning home, the adjustment seems more difficult, because your children may be bright-eyed and clamoring for breakfast at 2 a.m. American time. If you are going to be an airborne traveler, do make note of these abrupt time changes and plan your first day abroad or your first day home with as simple and easy a schedule of activities as possible. Take it easy and all will be well.

Almost all international airlines provide free special meal options on any flight as long as you give them 48 hours' advance notice, and order the type of meal you require when you make a reservation or purchase a ticket. It's wise to check about 24 hours before take-off to be sure that the computer has logged your order for vegetarian, kosher, salt-free, low-carbohydrate meals, or fruit and cheese snacks should you prefer or need these in lieu of the regular airline fare. *Scandinavian Airlines* asks parents with small children to specify the children's ages because it offers different meals for infants, babies, and toddlers. *Pan American* will provide a child's birthday cake, free, with 48 hours' notice.

AIRLINE FARES The difference between calling at the last moment and booking first class, and making arrangements several weeks ahead to travel economy class or to take advantage of Super Saver rates can be *over $2000* on just one adult fare. Always try to book your flights a month or more in advance for the sake of security and to take advantage of extraordinary opportunities for savings. Check with your airlines and travel agent well ahead about this.

Charter flights, one-way and round-trip can save you wads of money. The problem with charter flights that used to bother me was that they might not take off when scheduled, leaving you and yours in a terrible fix. However, now you can take out insurance against this horror and be provided with transport on another airline if your charter flight doesn't wing away when it says it will. Over 3000 listings of charter flights with dates and prices to more than 80 destinations are listed in a monthly publication called *Jax Fax Travel Marketing Magazine,* subscribed to by travel agents and also available to individuals. For a subscription, which doesn't cost much, contact Jet Airtransport Exchange, Inc. (280 Tokeneke Rd., Darien, CT 06820).

CHILDREN'S AIRLINE FARES Children over 2 and under 12 pay half fare, children under 2 pay 10% of the adult fare if not occupying a seat. If a child under 2 occupies a seat, he comes under the half-fare regulation. If your under-2 child is too big to be happy in a carrycot, please don't make the sacrifice of thinking you can hold him in your lap all the way. In the Low season when the plane isn't booked to capacity, you may be able to put him in the seat next to you and let him ride as comfortably as any other half-fare child. But in the Peak season, your chances of getting away with this money-saving ploy are absolutely nil. Please spare yourself the misery of holding a child too big for a carrycot as an economy measure. That's one economy that isn't worth it in any circumstance. In the case of twins under 2 years of age, as long as both Papa and Mama are traveling with them, the fare remains 10% of the adult fare. You get this 10% infant fare on the basis of one adult and one infant. If Mama is traveling with twin infants or two children under 2 years of age, she will have to pay half fare for one of them.

AIRLINE SPECIALS Stopover plans, free transportation, sightseeing, discounts on admissions to a wide range of attractions and on car rentals, free overnight stays, food and beverage credits and many other arrangements that represent convenience and value are available from certain airlines. Most of these programs, particularly the stopover packages, must be booked in advance of departure. British Airways, KLM, Sabena, Lufthansa, Swissair, Air France, Scandinavian Airlines, and Pan Am all have "specials" well-worth inquiring about.

CHILDREN UNACCOMPANIED BY PARENTS Each airline has its own ruling about this, and the differences concern regulations for children under 8, with special limitations for children under 5.

At what age your child can be trusted to travel with an airborne babysitter is something only you can determine.

The official picture is that a child must be accompanied by a responsible adult until on the plane. Evidence must be furnished that the child is in good health, and that he or she will be met by a responsible adult when the plane lands.

It is important to make all arrangements as far as possible in advance: I'd recommend three weeks to a month. When you make the reservation, tell the reservations agent that your children will be traveling alone. Request all the necessary forms at this time. These are short, simple, to the point, and vital. When you take your child to the airport, go over the forms again with the passenger service manager. Your name, your address, your telephone number, special advice about the care, feeding, and handling of your child, the names, addresses, telephone numbers of the people meeting your child—be sure that everything is clear as crystal. The passenger service manager gives one form to the flight attendant and/or hostess. He then sends a message to his counterpart at the child's destination. On arrival, the flight attendant or hostess turns over your child and form to this person. If by chance no one arrives to meet your child, the passenger service agent calls the people who were supposed to be there on time, and holds onto your child, seeing that he or she is looked after until they arrive, really carefully looked after. Under no circumstances is your child ever surrendered to anyone else. British Airways, KLM and Swissair are particularly recommended for flights on which your child may be unaccompanied.

Remember that your unaccompanied child's welfare depends on in-flight attention. Cologne, trendy pantyhose or some other little token would be a nice gesture.

AIRPORT TERMINAL FACILITIES Did you know you could have a shower and the use of a private dressing room in an airport? Warm a baby bottle? Receive medical attention? Flake out in a reclining chair or a rocker? Board your pet? Expect to find telephones for the hard of hearing or the blind? Let your baby nap in a crib? These and many other services are available; some, like medical attention and facilities for the handicapped are standard operating procedure; others often can be found. Make your needs known! Seek and you may find many unexpected comforts!

NURSERY FACILITIES Many European and a few progressive U.S. airports have special nursery areas with changing tables, playpens, cribs, arm chairs, play equipment for toddlers, and special lavatories. These areas are usually located near the women's restrooms and a lounge area. Nursery areas may also be combined with "mothers' rooms" where a nursing mother can feed her baby in peace and privacy. These are your heavenly havens in case of a holdover, a missed connection, or simply as a convenience before or after flights. *Ask your travel agent, your airline, or at the airport for the location of these facilities.*

At Rome's Fiumicino Airport, in the domestic terminal, there are staffed and supervised rooms for babies and children, with toys, books, and cribs. *Amsterdam's Schiphol,* one of the world's finest airports, has a dozen cribs, sterilized potties, and baby baths. If you are a KLM passenger with children in arms or in tow, a groundhostess will drive you to the departure or exit gate in an electro-car; and, for a small charge, day rooms and showers are provided for the relaxation of family travelers. In *Brussels' International* you'll find a nursery with crib, toys and refrigerator. At *Zurich Airport* Terminals A and B have modern facilities—bedrooms with cots, baths and showers. Relaxation rooms are located in Terminal A. In Terminal B, only showers are available. At *Geneva's Airport,* nurseries are on the mezzanine floor and by the main waiting room. *Copenhagen's Kastrup Airport* has a new nursery with cribs and lots of toys. At *Gatwick, Aberdeen, Edinburgh, Stansted,* and *Prestwick,* you'll find nursing mothers' rooms; London's *Heathrow* has a nursery with babysitters available 8 a.m. to 8 p.m. Another facility in Europe is the *Airport Hotel (Aerohotel)* where, for a modest charge, you can have a shower or bath even if you don't book a room. Sometimes, day rooms and showers are available in the airport, sometimes free, generally for a small fee.

In the U.S., where even among top-ten rated airports, "nursery facilities" amount to a beat-up reclining chair and a table in a hard-to-find room, or an extra-wide "changing table" counter in the ladies' room, only three airports cater to the comfort and convenience of traveling families. *Miami International's Satellite Terminal* offers, on the arrival level, showers in the restrooms, a children's play area with foam-filled toys, special lavatories, changing room, kitchen with refrigerator, a pleasant nursery, color TV; an electric transit shuttle, as well as buses, operative between buildings; in the concourse of the main terminal is an arcade of coin-operated electronic games. *San Francisco's International North Terminal* has three nursery rooms with cribs, and rocking chairs for its domestic flights' passengers; there are similar facilities in its new *Central Terminal* for international passengers; changing table and comfy chairs in its *South Terminal.* At *New York's Kennedy Airport,* you'll find in Room 2113, 2nd floor, *International Arrivals Building,* a bottle warmer, a diaper disposal, changing table, and chairs; at *Pan Am's Worldport,* on the 3rd level, a coin-operated video gameroom near the lounge, a changing table in the ladies' room, a comfortable chair, table and basin in the mothers' room. If you are a *British Airways'* passenger, on the departure level in the *BA Terminal* there is a nursery for the use of BA passengers only. Ask at the BA counter for the key! Inside, there's a fully equipped kitchen with stove, utensils, refrigerator; a bathroom; a pleasant sitting room with subdued lighting, three cribs, a supply of blankets, disposable diapers, a playpen, a baby-feeding chair, comfortable chairs for mothers, a telephone, and a closed circuit TV that alerts you to the time you should board your plane. The best facility in Canada is in Toronto Airport's Terminal #2.

AIRLINE CLUB ROOMS: Most large airlines—Pan Am, TWA, United, American, Eastern, Delta, Northwest Orient—maintain clubs at major airports along their route systems in the U.S. and overseas. Your first year's initiation fee plus annual dues may cost about $100 (except for Northwest Orient's Top Flight Club, for which there's no membership fee). Application cards can be had by telephoning or writing to the airlines. Some of the benefits of joining an airline club are comfortable, quiet waiting rooms; free coffee and tea; cocktails, soft drinks, sandwiches served to you at your table; color TV; desk-typewriter-telephone cubicles for working parents and communicative teenagers; and the relaxation of luxury and privilege, away from crowds and confusion. Family privileges are extended to a card-holding member who is present and can vouch for "guests" and/or spouse who can receive complimentary membership on application. Club membership guarantees you first class on-the-ground privileges without paying first class fares, which is a saving blessing.

AIRPORT MEDICAL FACILITIES Federal regulations require every airport, domestic and foreign, to maintain a sophisticated medical facility with attending physicians on duty 24 hours. This seems to be one of the better-kept secrets of all time, but such facilities do exist and their staffs are first-rate at coping with all emergencies from scraped knees to cardiopulmonary resuscitation. Often, there are also pharmacies able to fill prescriptions.

AIRPORT ASSISTANCE TO THE HANDICAPPED For the blind, deaf, and those in wheelchairs, many airports in the U.S. and in Europe provide escort service, ramps, elevators; special facilities in diningrooms, restrooms, lavatories; and many other special services. Handicapped travelers should make reservations well in advance. For a detailed report on world-wide coverage of airport facilities for the handicapped, free of charge, updated annually by the Airport Operators Council International, write to Access America, Washington, DC 20202.

ANIMAL CARE FACILITIES You can trust the ASPCA to take loving care of your dog, cat, bird, horse, or hamster at an Animalport, of which the nation's largest and finest is at Kennedy Airport (Air Cargo Bldg. 189, Jamaica, NY 11430. Rates are reasonable. You can ship your pet here from another city or country for boarding until you arrive. If you want to travel now and have your pet join you later, the Animalport will ship your pet to you on the date and flight you request. Shipping crates that meet humane and airline requirements are available at the Animalport. A staff member can meet you outside any Kennedy airline terminal with your pet, or arrange for home pick-up or delivery. The Animalport at Kennedy is open 24 hours. The facilities are fine, and their staff can also help you with customs and public health clearances. ▶ **Note:** KLM is *the* airline specializing in both small and large animal transportation, with a specially-trained personnel corps to attend to them.

AIRPORT TRANSPORTATION Trains connect with many European airports. At Frankfurt and Zurich, you can just trundle your luggage cart from plane terminal to train station. London's Heathrow train connections are almost as simple. If you're bound for Germany, the Airport Express trains from Frankfurt to Düsseldorf, Bonn, and Cologne may be preferable to connecting flights—you get to see more of the countryside and, if you book ahead, the price is the same as airfare and more relaxing and comfortable. Lufthansa can give you details on this service. Subways and buses are often the best transport to and from airports. Taxi service is usually simple and easy. Being met by a car involves the driver and you finding each other and generates needless anxiety if the plane is late or arrival procedure is slow. Hiring a car and a driver to take you to the airport, however, makes for the most relaxing departure possible, and I'm for anything that does that!

MIRACLE PREFLIGHT DIET FOR CHILDREN Let's not mince words. If I see a child, mine or anyone else's, throw up, it is almost a foregone conclusion that I will too. Whether you share this reaction or not, you have to admit that a child throwing up is an unpleasant circumstance under any condition and particularly unpleasant for all concerned in a public transport such as a plane.

Motion sickness rarely occurs if people are rested and relaxed. To keep the butterflies out of the stomachs of children about to undergo flight, Dr. Samuel I. Fuenning, of the Univ. of Nebraska, has originated a miracle diet based on a simple explanation—in times of nervousness and fatigue, the digestive process of converting solid food to liquid is slowed down, and this can make anyone have nervous cramps or throw up. His diet, good for all members of the family except infants in arms, who are generally relaxed and therefore not susceptible to nervous cramps and nausea (except under the conditions mentioned in the preceding section), is as follows: Six hours before the flight, a little toast, coffee, tea, or one-half glass of milk, and some tinned peaches with heavy syrup; four hours before the flight, 8–16 oz. of any of the calorie-rich reducing liquid meals.

If everyone followed this diet, there would be no more need for those paper bags for use "in the event of motion sickness."

IN-FLIGHT SERVICES If you are traveling with a child under 2, see Chapter 5 for information on what services are available to you.

Most airlines will comply happily with a personalized meal service or special children's menu if requested at least 48 hours in advance of flight time. Some airlines are more imaginative than others, but typical children's fare proffered is a hotdog, hamburger, or peanutbutter sandwich; vanilla or chocolate milkshake; vanilla or chocolate ice cream.

Having your own cache of fresh fruit, brownies or other favorite munchies is often a benison.

IN-FLIGHT ENTERTAINMENT Movies are routinely offered, along with individual headphones on which to listen to a variety of programmed entertainment including a channel devoted to children's interest programs. The use of these, which are necessary to hear the sound of films, usually costs about $3. Children from 5 on usually find headsets and programs fun. Almost all airlines will give their junior passengers pins, badges, coloring books, or some little entertainment for free, but you should bring your own supply of toys, games, and reading material (see Ch. 3).

SPECIAL POINTERS FOR AIR TRAVEL No one should ever fly with a cold or with a stuffed-up nose. If it is essential, ask your doctor for a broad-spectrum antibiotic, such as penicillin or Aureomycin, and some antihistamines. If you or your children must fly with a cold or nasal congestion, take nose drops and an antihistamine a half-hour before takeoff and a half-hour before landing. Drink plenty of nonalcoholic liquids during flight. These simple procedures ward off ear pain and infections which may occur when the Eustachian tube, the inner ear's only channel to the outside, is blocked or narrowed by a cold or upper respiratory infection.

Passengers seated in front of children can, by tilting back their chairs, occasionally and accidentally cause minor mishaps by joggling a child's food tray. More often, a child can annoy a passenger seated ahead of him by accidentally kicking his chair seat. The additional space and freedom allowed by the front-seat spot is a real advantage. Conversely, the back seats have the least room and, in the economy section, the disadvantage of chairs that cannot be tilted all the way back for "reclining comfort."

Be sure to keep your children from trotting off to the john the moment the flight attendant begins serving meals.

Prolonged sitting sometimes slows down blood flow in the legs, causing "pins and needles" or achy, swollen feet. Rotating each foot at the ankle, tightening then relaxing calf muscles, pressing feet down hard on the floor are recommended exercises for adults. Most children are saved from discomfort by doing a bit of bouncing, wriggling, foot-swinging—just the sort of behavior parents often discourage. Don't encourage its happening on the plane, just let it happen without protesting! Happiness is a 747. On 747's, in first class, there is a spiral stairway twirling up to a sofa-lined lounge. In economy class, there is room to walk around.

Request aisle seats, rather than window seats, when traveling with children. It's easier to make your way to the aisle, you have more room, and, if your child is next to you, he can see out the window almost as well as if he were sitting by it.

Security precautions require that all handcarried baggage be x-ray screened before being allowed on board any and every plane, in the U.S. and in Europe. Don't expect any smiles or friendly faces during this process. Crowds and the need to concentrate lead to robot-like efficiency. You'll feel better, and so will the airlines, if you do your best not to cause any extra delays:

1) Try to arrive a little earlier than usual for your flight;

2) Bag everything possible in transparent plastic bags. That way it can be examined swiftly and you'll be spared exasperated looks from personnel and fellowpassengers;

3) Have your ticket envelope, boarding pass, and passport handy to show the agents;

4) Carry your camera and film separately. Don't pack them in the luggage that you check or carry them on you. Whatever electronic or x-ray eyes screen you and your luggage can do strange things to ordinary undeveloped film and can damage high-speed film. Make sure your film and camera won't be damaged. Tell the people at the check-in counter and search table about them.

Remember to take extra sweaters aboard. Planes sometimes are too cool for some children; nighttime temperatures when you disembark are often surprisingly chilly even in the middle of summer. You may never use a folding traveling umbrella at an airport, but for all the times I never used one, I felt quite compensated the one time it saved my children from being drenched when everyone around us was.

Above all, remember that whatever you carry on you will have to carry off. The less you have to carry, or the more you can wheel, the more carefree you will be.

CASTLES AND OTHER HAPPY FAMILY ACCOMMODATIONS

Singling out ideal places to stay with your children is simple only if you know exactly what you are looking for. Accommodations in Europe are just that: accommodating. You can have freedom and space and adventure without sacrificing material comforts. You can live like a beachcomber and still have the benefit of a babysitter. You can enjoy the best of country and city life. You can find many alternatives to just checking into a hotel. For instance, farmhouse accommodations in Austria, Britain, France, Germany, Ireland, and Scandinavia; countryside Bed-and-Breakfast guest houses in the British Isles—with reductions for children under 8!—are wonderful values; so are castle hotels and chateaux where you pay more money but get all sorts of extras. As alternatives to routine hotels, for each country I have listed possibilities to stir the heart and quicken the imagination.

PRICES Whatever price you are given, and whoever provides it in advance to you, double check. With exchange rates weakening and strengthening at a dizzying pace, the best I can do is to indicate fine values in the lowest cost, moderate and expensive categories.

Hotel managements have worked out pretty standard rates for adults, but when it comes to children, there seems to be a great deal of leeway. Unless established by a travel agent ahead of time, prices are variable. If you ask in advance or suggest to the manager that surely a more favorable price for the children can be arrived at—after all, they're just children—you'll be happily surprised by the cooperation and discounts you'll receive.

Depending on the season, the mood of the manager, your charm and appearance, the size and type of accommodation available, what you'll be charged for your children varies. A hotel which prefers an ambiance in which lonely singles can meet will undoubtedly not offer attractive rates for children. Even if a hotel advertises reduced rates for children, if your child has a tantrum on arrival in the lobby, or annoys other guests, the rates may turn out not so reduced as advertised owing to a new policy just put into effect five minutes before.

In general, babies in arms are usually free of charge. Most places have cots at the ready for children sharing their parents' room, and such children are given reduced rates. Rates for children occupying separate rooms varies. In hotels, farmhouses, manor houses, and castles, reduced rates may vary for babies in arms or for children under 2, 8, 12, or 16. If meals are included there may be children's small portions for half price or a discount.

HOTELS There is a tendency to think of hotels only in terms of price, renown and location, and to overlook the fact that in many places, in each class, from deluxe to fifth rate, there are many choices and variations.

In all major cities of the world, you will find a Great Hotel, a princely pleasure that may prove to be a financial Waterloo, but nonetheless a masterpiece of hotel-keeping that is justly celebrated as a discreetly opulent preserve of elegance, luxury, and style. Richly rewarding though all this may be for you, don't expect the children to react with sheer, unalloyed excitement. As far as the children are concerned, there's nothing particularly bewitching about a luxury hotel unless it has a swimming pool or some other outstanding recreational facility. At 16, their reaction may become a trifle more heart-warming, but until then, don't think of going to a luxury hotel for the children's sake. You might just as well fling the money out of the window.

You're better off, when traveling with children, to pause and consider the three *C*'s—comfort, cleanliness, and charm—and to choose places that are small enough to allow for a maximum of personal attention and that will have special appeal for your children.

In the country-by-country chapters which follow, I have mentioned only special hotels with particular attractions for families in large cities. What matters to me about a hotel is accommodating service; kitchenettes in your suite rather than crystal chandeliers in the foyer and celebrities at the bar; gardens and lawns; children's supervised playrooms; babysitters resident or easily available; interesting or charming interiors; services that will make your life easier; and an atmosphere that will be fun rather than restrictive for children. I've tried to pick hotels that are surrounded by attractions for children, or hotels where a babysitter can come to fix the children supper or where the children can play under supervision while you go out. With the children along, it makes much more sense to me to stay at a hotel with a children's playroom, even if it's less expensive than a well-known hotel where your room is the only playroom for your child.

CASTLES The enchantment of living in a castle used to be a private one, enjoyed only by the owners and their friends. But today there are a great number of castles that have let down their drawbridges and flung open their magnificent gateways to travelers who want pleasures that have all but disappeared from the world.

Castles, built as fortress-strongholds during the days of knighthood in the Middle Ages, were always built, for security reasons, to command the countryside—a happy circumstance today, because you know for certain that *every* castle will have a sweeping view.

It's awful to skip from romance to plumbing, but when I mention authentic medieval castles, don't think that modern amenities have been sacrificed. Far from it. All comforts are provided as well as many diversions, such as swimming, fishing, riding, hunting, and exploring the surroundings of the castle itself. Most castles are easy to get to, some are definitely off the beaten track. There are also imperial hunting lodges and country houses so fabulous that even though they are not, in the strictest sense of the word, castles—having been built as pleasure domes rather than noble fortresses—they are still very, very special indeed. Set in handsome parklands, they offer idyllic surroundings and accommodations.

Staying at a castle gives one an astonishing feel of history. I was glad to see that knights on horseback with falcons flying before them, serfs, vassals, liege lords and ladies also grabbed my children by the heartstrings.

Accommodations in castles or palatial houses usually require a stay of three days or more, and may be pricey, but Austria, Belgium, France, Germany, Great Britain, Ireland, the Netherlands, Portugal, Scandinavian countries, Scotland, Spain, and Wales have jewels you may find irresistible, and where you and your children will have a marvelous time.

PARADORES, POUSADAS, PENSIONES, PENSIONS, INNS, AND OTHER HOMES AWAY FROM HOME Comprising over 110 castles, monasteries, abbeys, villas notable for scenic charm and historic interest, *paradores* in Spain, and *pousadas* in Portugal are moderate in price and ideal for motorists. *Pensiones* are Italian boarding houses, some with immense charm, and I have a penchant for the charming French *pensions,* and for the enchanting inns to be found all over Europe. There is a tremendous range and variation in style, comfort, and food provided by these establishments. Less expensive than castle accommodations (although some paradores and pousadas *are* refurbished castles) accommodations in this grouping can be a life-enhancing experience for the same amount of money you might spend for impersonal and undistinguished hotel quarters. Most government travel information offices can provide illustrated booklets and brochures about their countries' offerings.

Historic manor houses, inns, and abbeys listed in France's *Relais de Campagne* are accommodations of distinction and charm, invaluable to motorists who aren't on a strict budget. Britain has a great variety of elegant, romantic manor-house accommodations, and both Austria and

Germany abound in rustic hunting castles and grand but cosy lakeside accommodations.

Private homes that take guests are everywhere in Europe, and most government travel information offices will provide lists of recommendations.

Bed-and-Breakfast accommodations (see individual country listings) are ideal for traveling families! Britain has inexpensive family accommodations in London and other cities and, in the country, guesthouses and Bed-and-Breakfast accommodations that are not only inexpensive but may be an adventure in themselves.

Farmhouse accommodations, where you usually have to stay at least a week, are another bargain, particularly if you have a car. You can use the farmhouse as a base from which to explore the countryside and still allow time for the children to croon over cows, sheep, piglets, and baby chicks. Britain has many such offerings; as do Austria, Denmark, Finland, France, and Sweden. Rooms are simple, clean, airy. Some have private bathrooms. Childrens' rates are generally half the adult rate for bed and breakfast or full board.

You can bunk in on a barge-hotel anchored in Paris. River-cruising is another alternative—though not necessarily cheap—that combines housing with transportation. France has many boat-charter programs. Germany has many charter possibilities along the Rhine and other rivers. Holland offers boat and houseboat rentals. And, Britain has all sorts of canalboat possibilities.

CLUB MÉDITERRANÉE If you're a single parent, a young-at-heart, an individualistic family, sociable and eager to broaden your horizons in the company of other freedom-loving families who like swimming, relaxing in the sun, playing with computers, mountain-climbing, riding, snorkeling, sailing, scuba-diving, yoga, tennis, miniature golf, or archery, what about the Club Méditerranée? Out of their eight dozen vacation villages emphasizing informality, reasonable prices, free-wheeling life-style and considerable charm, many are set up to take on the younger generation (yours!). This doesn't mean that Club Méditerranée has child-care facilities in ALL of its club resorts. Certain of its villages won't take children at all. The villages to seek out are those which operate Baby-Clubs, Mini-Clubs, and Kid's Clubs where attentive care is provided from 9 a.m. to 9 p.m., with optional evening baby-sitting, resident doctors and pediatricians, plus instruction by specially-trained counselors in sports such as swimming, skiing, riding; plus excursions, picnics, plays, musicals, and even circuses put on by the children themselves.

Some things to consider about Club Méditerranée: there are no telephones, no televisions, no newspapers, no radios, no room service. And no tipping! You pay cash up front, and all attractions and equipment is yours for the asking on a first-come basis. You pay for drinks, other than the wine served by the carafeful, with beads from a poppit necklace as carefree Polynesians once did. Some villages have neither electricity nor private bathrooms!

For babies, 4 months and older, Club Med offers *Baby-Clubs* with infants' nurses, smiling, tender, and loving, to change and feed your treasures at Don Miguel (Costa del Sol, Spain); Vittel (lovely wooded French Vosges countryside); Zinal (Swiss Alps); and Roussalka—for babies 1 year and up—in Bulgaria.

For children 4 to 8, there are *Mini-Clubs* with supervised meal-feeding, fun activities, play and game rooms, music, dance, and sports at: Caprera (Sardinia); Cargèse (Corsica); Chamonix (French Alps); Don Miguel (Costa del Sol, Spain); Donoratico (across from Elba, Italy); Grégolimano (on the sea, near Delphi, Greece); Kamarina (Sicilian coast near Agricento); Kos (Greek island in the Dodecanese group); Monêtier (French Alps); Pakostane (Yugoslavia), Pompadour (in Limousin, central France), Pontresina (Swiss Alps), Roussalka (Bulgaria), St. Moritz Victoria (Swiss Alps), Santa Giulia (Corsica), Santa Teresa (Sardinia), Thalassa (Rumania), Tignes Val Claret (French Alps), Valbella (Swiss Alps), Villars/Ollon (Swiss Alps), Vittel (French Vosges countryside), Wengen (Swiss Alps), and Zinal (Swiss Alps).

Where there are *Mini-Clubs,* there you will also find *Kid's Clubs,* for children 8 and older where they can learn judo, how to sail, swim, play tennis, ride, master various crafts, enjoy imaginative activities and entertainments, and have an absolutely glorious time with children their own age.

There are also Club Med vacation resorts where there are no facilities for younger children, but where there are *Kid's Clubs* at: Ipsos, Corfu (island, northwest of Greece), Otranto (on the Adriatic, Italy), Porto Petro (near Palma, Majorca), Puerta Maria (Cadiz, Spain), Les Restanques (near St. Tropez, France).

Other Club Med vacation resorts will accept children 6 years and older, 8 years and older, 12 years and older, but provide neither counselors nor special facilities for them. See chapters on individual countries for additional details. Membership to Club Med, open to all, is $25 with discounts for children. For prices and other information, get in touch with **Club Med,** Place de la Bourse, 75088 Paris.

SPECIAL!!!! Valbella, in the Swiss Alps, *is for children only* during the summer, and provides lake sailing, tennis, mountain hiking, camping out excursions, cooking classes, dancing, archery, photography, and manual arts workshops as well as a splendid camp experience for children from 4 to 13.

VILLA VACATIONS Holiday villas are a British convention. Anyone renting a villa anywhere in Europe will usually find that his landlord is not Portuguese, Greek, or French, but English. The British have always been great ones for living well in foreign countries, and their homes in the sun always come complete with maid service, part-time or full-time help who can shop, cook, babysit, houseclean, and do the laundry. Cribs can usually be rented—I'd recommend taking your own, though, because then you know that the sheets fit as will the mosquito netting, and the baby is used to his little world. Villas come furnished with cutlery, crockery, glassware, refrigerator, gas or electric stoves and cooking utensils, linens, and a reasonable amount of furniture, (usually locally made—comfortable, simple, sturdy). Once the preserve and the privilege of the very rich, European villa life remains as individual as ever, but within the reach of almost any family traveling abroad. For children, villas are wonderful, because they have the freedom of doing as they please—sleeping, eating, drinking, getting up, and going to bed, making noise without restrictions. If you have three or four lively children with you, it's not only fair to them, but fair to hotels to live in a villa.

You can pick a villa as you would a hotel or a resort. If you want an easily run, efficient place, pick a modern, contemporary-style villa. If you want something unusual, with atmosphere, or romantic, you can rent chateaux, little castles, farmhouses. Villas in Spain are among the cheapest and most numerous in Europe.

Fishing villages and fishermen in Portugal are a magnetic draw for most children. For a villa holiday with children 4 on up, I'd recommend the Algarve except in midsummer when the heat can be pretty shattering during the day. Nights are cool. Malta, Gozo, and Camino, set in the Mediterranean between Sicily and the North African coast and Corfu, the most northern of the Greek Ionian islands, are popular villa outposts for families with older children, families who have traveled extensively. For a child's first holiday abroad in a villa, I think families would be happiest in France, Spain, Portugal, or my first choice, Italy. Amalfi, Porto Santo Stefano, Ansedonia are paradises. Southern Italy, Sicily also have villas. Many, many villas to choose from in Italy. With low season, midseason, peak season rates to contend with, plus the spectrum of small and low-cost to large, swimming-pooled, high-cost luxury villas, working out expenses is just a matter of villa-power! For gregarious families, parties are simpler and less expensive in a villa than in a hotel. The English are unrivalled for their villa expertise. Read the Sunday travel sections of the London *Times* for suggestions. If you cannot get a copy locally, get in touch with the New York office at 210 South St., New York, NY 10002.

Other informational sources about villa and apartment holidays throughout Europe are these England-based firms: **Beach Villas Ltd.,** 8 A Market Passage, Cambridge, an organization specializing in villas for families with children; **OSL, OSL House,** Broxbourne, Hertfordshire; Villaguide Ltd., 168 Sloane St., London; **Holiday Villas,** 8 Barclay Rd., Croydon; **Continental Villas,** 38 Sloane St., London; **Villa Venture Ltd.,**

123 Gloucester Rd., London; **Starvillas Ltd.,** 25 High St., Chesterton, Cambridge and the *International Herald Tribune*.

SPECIAL TIPS ON RENTING COTTAGES, HOUSES, CASTLES Why not venture beyond the London *Times* as a source for villa rental information? For the best possible arrangements, *get out of the realm of tourism and take advantage of cottages, houses, and castles being offered for rent or for sale* to the local people in the region you want to visit. How? First, get a copy of the major Sunday newspaper in France, Italy, Germany, Switzerland, Greece, wherever you want a house. Check out the *advertisements for rentals intended for the local population*. Check out the house and castle sale offerings. Chances are the seller will be happy to *rent* their house-for-sale to you for a week. Through the newspapers, you can also get in touch with the *local* realtors. Tell them what you want and how much you are willing to pay. You don't need to speak French, German, Italian, or Greek fluently to work out what the advertisements are saying. Someone in your neighborhood can speak these languages and translate for you. An interpreter can be found who can translate your letter into Greek or Italian, which is a good idea, even though almost all realtors do have a knowledge of English. Once you familiarize yourself with the little rental vocabulary necessary, you'll do fine. Even if a house is offered for sale or for a term of rental longer than you require, *ask* and *negotiate*. This method can get you a castle, a house or a cottage with staff and swimming pool, or whatever your requirements are, *for the best possible price on the market*.

At Home Abroad, Inc. (405 East 56th St., New York, NY 10022) is a firm with years of experience locating villas, castles, palazzi, and cottages, towers by the sea, châlets, and farmhouses tailored to your individual requirements. Efficient, tireless Owner-President Claire Packman and her staff comb Europe for suitable establishments to make sure that their clientele will have all the comforts of home. She specializes in families with children of all ages, bless her heart. A $35 registration fee (no fee required if you consult by appointment) will supply you with color photographs and all details. Car and bicycle rentals easily arranged.

Miss Packman has inspected every place she offers and can answer all the questions that you must ask before renting a house where you will live with young children. ''Is pasteurized milk available? Is there a fence? Is there a pediatrician nearby? Is the water safe for drinking? Are there other children the same age nearby? How is the beach? Where can I find babysitters?'' Why Miss Packman doesn't tire of this catechism is a wonder. She genuinely cares. She wants families to be happy. She prides herself on finding babysitters, cooks, and maids, seeing that you are all settled in securely, with guest memberships in local country clubs.

Renting a house abroad sounds like an elephantine project, a jumbo chore. Not at all. You are simply stepping into a system that has worked and existed in Europe for years, and worked far more easily and simply than rentals do in America. Do try to make arrangements early. As the last of the Christmas tinsel is packed away, it is none too early to turn your thoughts to Italy, Portugal, Spain, France, Greece, and villas, villas, villas!

Villas Abroad (509 Madison Ave., New York, NY 10022) specializes in villas with swimming pools and staff in France, Italy, Spain. These other firms can make arrangements for you in Greece, Italy, France, Spain, Portugal: **Interhome** 297 Knollwood Rd., White Plains, NY; **Villas International Ltd./Interchange** 213 E. 38th St., New York, NY 10016; **Inqiline, Inc.** Cedar Rd., Katonah, NY 10536. When you write for information, state your dates and length of stay, number of people in your party, number of bedrooms you'd like and some idea of how much you wish to spend.

For further information see chapters on individual countries.

HOME EXCHANGE In recent years these services have boomed. **Vacation Exchange Club, Inc.** (350 Broadway, New York, NY 10013) now includes in their directory over 6000 listings in 40 countries, and is affiliated with Austria's Intervac, Belgium's Inter-Residentia, France's Vacances d'Echanges, Germany's and Switzerland's Holiday Service, Great Britain's Home Interchange, Italy's Scambio Casa, and Spain's Intercambios. Or, you can work out arrangements for your family to be the *guests* of a European family who, in turn, will be *your guests* when they vacation in the U.S., in an intercultural exchange program. Or arrange for your teenager to spend a month in Paris with a French family with a daughter her same age and then return with her to *your* house a month later.

For steeper fees, but still a terrific money-saver, convenience and comfort-provider, rendering all the paperwork and directory perusal obsolete by handling all the correspondence for you, is **Home Exchange International** (130 West 72nd St., New York, NY 10023), a fabulous service with offices in Los Angeles, London, Paris, Milan, and Sydney, that tries to match Americans seeking temporary homes abroad with their life-style counterparts in Britain, France, Italy, and Australia, with 80% of their registration comprising families. Home Exchange deals only with principals, does not have a directory, and can arrange an exchange given advance notice of a week–two months or more.

Home-swapping requires a good deal of detailed correspondence, human kindness, concern, and consideration. You might want to make an inventory of everything or you might want to lock away valuables and breakables. Houseswapping is a more personal operation than renting a house, but it involves just as much work and far more correspondence. However, for thoughtful, people-loving, adventurous individualistic families, with one member who has the patience and organizational ability to cope with all the necessaries, it might be just the ticket.

SINGLE PARENTS' SPECIAL According to Club Med statistics, some 60% of its members are single, divorced, or widowed, and almost the same number are between the ages of 30 and 60. Club Med, originally considered ''just for swinging singles,'' has now developed wonderfully attractive and charming vacation villages *ideal* for single parents. See aforementioned details.

CAMPING AND CARAVANING Anyone can go anywhere. It doesn't take money to travel. All it takes is a sense of humor, stamina, self-possession, and an ability to look on the bright side of any catastrophe. Right, campers? Children are natural campers and gypsies. Their discomforts are minimal. Although today's campers can travel in relative style and comfort, camping and caravaning require neat, organized, orderly, list-making, practical, and competent parents. If you qualify, Europe is a camper's paradise. Plenty of forests, pine woods, fields, and clear blue water. Campgrounds in Europe have modern, clean facilities, hot-water showers, lavatories, laundromats; many have swimming pools, shopping centers, snack bars, restaurants, wonderful children's playgrounds, and super recreational facilities. Although Britain now offers many similar comforts in some of its campsites—games and television rooms, indoor and outdoor swimming pools, fishing, golf, sailing, pony trekking, tennis—campsites on the Continent tend to have far more extensive facilities than those in England, Scotland, and Ireland. Britain, however, does offer bungalows, châlets, and cabins for hire on some sites, as well as static pitches, which are caravans without hitches to cars, some just parked on the site, some available for rent, overnight or longer.

Apart from the things you will need for emergencies, travel convenience, and recreation (see ''Motoring''), besides tenting equipment and bedding, folding chairs and tables, extra blankets, saw and axe for cutting up driftwood or deadwood for your campfire, you will need the following for outdoor meals:

cooler
insulated picnic jug
picnic or camp stove
2 saucepans, 1 heavy skillet
kettle
cutlery
detergent
plastic dishpan
flashlights
plastic bags
plastic pail
utility knives
storage bowls
coffeepot and/or teapot
heavy aluminum foil for cooking, lining pots
paper cups and plates
can and bottle opener (take an extra)
ice pick
paper towels
plastic sponges for bathing and cleaning up
cleansing powder
terrycloth towels

Emergency food supplies: powdered milk, instant orange drink, tea, coffee, and cocoa; dry soups; dried fruit; minute rice; sugar; salad dressing; minced garlic for salads, vegetables, and fish; canned fruit, vegetables, and all-in-one meals.

Pressure pump camping lanterns (bring along extra mantles, and either a stake or an iron hook for hanging) marvelous at night and invaluable in an emergency. A Coleman 2-mantle gasoline pressure lantern or, if you prefer, a lantern that uses liquefied petroleum in cans or kerosene, for which you need a small bottle of alcohol to preheat the generator before opening the fuel valve. But a lantern you should have; it's useful, it's romantic and it's a necessity.

A self-contained portable water purifier that kills bacteria and removes sediments, harmful minerals, suspended solids, and waste material, objectionable tastes and odors, and that will purify up to 20 gallons of water? It consists of tubing and reusable filter pads and maybe you can cope with it less sloppily than I can. It's called Porta-Pure, available from Gokey Co., Saint Paul, MN 55102.

Games and diversions for the children (see Ch. 3).

National Campers and Hikers Association (7172 Transit Rd., Buffalo, NY 14221) will supply you with a carnet, a convenient "passport" for camping, which will serve as an inter-club membership card in western European camps affiliated with the International Federation of Camping and Caravanning. Some campsites will only take those who have a carnet. When checking-in to a site, the carnet is held by the main office rather than the passport, thereby minimizing the chance of losing your U.S. passport. Up to 15 people are covered by any one carnet which also includes "Third Party" liability insurance and some discounts.

Much as I delight in recreational vehicles, they do use a lot of gasoline, and the price of gasoline is always higher in Europe than it is in the U.S. So consider this, plus rental cost plus the fees for the use of campgrounds. An alternative to investigate might be to rent a small car or minibus and take camping gear with you that you can buy or rent in major cities. The daily hire charges offered by Great Britain's Automobile Association for you to pick up at Dover, England, for sturdy equipment—frame tent, camp bed, table, chairs, cooker and grill, groundsheet, lantern and a roof-rack with cover to transport it all—are surprisingly low. Many users claim that you can't do better than trust AAA and its affiliated motoring organizations, whose book, *Camping and Caravanning in Europe,* is the best all-inclusive guide I've ever seen, complete with not only all sites, but information about passes and tunnels, necessary documents, maps, driving hints, and motoring regulations. Another excellent guide is available from the British Tourist Authority Bookstore in New York. Equally valuable is the *International Youth Hostel Handbook,* available from American Youth Hostels, Inc., 132 Spring St., New York, NY 10012. Youth hostels provide sleeping accommodations, washing and lavatory facilities, often cooking facilities; in many cases, the service of economical meals, from Austria to Yugoslavia. Write for membership information.

CAMPING EQUIPMENT TO TAKE ALONG? Mass-market camping gear is widely available in Europe. European camping stoves, lanterns, rucksacks (frameless packs), guns, optical goods, woolen blankets, stockings, sweaters, and all sports clothing are less expensive and often superior to those produced in the U.S. But when it comes to water-purifiers, compasses, flashlights, battery-lit magnifying glass, emergency kits, fishing equipment, insect repellents, tents, backpacks, and sleeping bags—American technology puts us way out in front. A never-failing source of information about camping equipment and clothes is L.L. Bean, Freeport, ME 04033.

MAGIC FAMILY HELPERS AND SERVICES

Childcare facilities and babysitters abroad really are superlative. There is just no comparison between the average babysitting types I've come across in this country, who, it seems to me, normally do just about as little as they possibly can, and the babysitters available abroad, who consider childcare an art and take pride in doing as much as they can.

BABYSITTERS AND COMPANIONS For infants to 14-year-olds, babysitters and companionable chaperons of exceptional merit are to be found in Austria, Belgium, Denmark, England, Finland, France, Germany, Holland, Iceland, Ireland, Norway, Scotland, Sweden, and Switzerland. In these countries—for an hour, a day or overnight—your children can be cared for or entertained to perfection. I don't use the word *perfection* lightly. Any qualified babysitter in these countries associated with an agency or recommended by a tourist information center or your hotel is, for reasons of national pride, handpicked or qualities of optimum virtue.

In Austria, Denmark, England, Finland, France, Germany, Holland, and Switzerland, excellent provisions have been made for your children to meet and play with others of their own age, or to go off on individual sightseeing tours.

A young girl student who will expect room and board, pocket money, and time off for study, but who will help with the children, run errands, and make herself generally useful is called an *au pair* girl. She is to be considered as part of the family. Employment agencies and international youth labor boards will direct you to agencies specializing in *au pair* girls. Often you will see advertisements in European papers placed by girls looking for *au pair* positions. The possibility of hiring a girl to travel with you if you have young children, and to act as an interpreter and guide, is well worth looking into if you can afford the extra traveling expense. These girls can be marvelous or they can be just not your type. I've loved the ones I've had, and hope you are as lucky.

If your travel arrangements are being handled by Thomas Cook & Son or by American Express, you can arrange to be met at your arrival point. Both organizations can, if advance plans are made, have a babysitter, children's companion, or guide waiting for you when you arrive, baby food prepared, diapers waiting, or whatever it is that you fancy. If you are working out your travel plans, reservations, and tickets with them (the use of their traveler's checks does not qualify you for special services), ask about camps, schools, or last-minute babysitters. Other travel agents also offer similar services.

CHILDREN'S COUNTRY CLUBS AND HOTELS These are a European specialty for parents who would like to take off on their own for a week to a couple of months, reassured that their children are being lovingly and expertly looked after and given the finest care.

In the mountains, by the sea, in parklike estates comprising gardens, fields and woods, there are hotels catering *solely* to infants and toddlers, and in many cases to their sisters and brothers up to the age of 12. Trained, experienced staff and medical care, balanced meals and special diets, winter sports, summer sports, indoor games and outside activities—these are the basic offerings of children's hotels, where the rates are as small as the young visitors from Europe and America. Compared with the color and clutter of the average American child's room, the majority of these European accommodations appear almost overwhelmingly clean, unadorned, and tidy.

This is not the time to particularize—that will come in later chapters—but perhaps these generalities will be helpful:

England, France, Germany, Holland, Italy, and Switzerland offer the widest choice for babies and the very young. Professional baby care in these countries is superlative. *Professional* sounds clinical. Don't be misled. Baby care in these countries is a deeply personal matter. When you put your baby into someone else's outstretched arms, he becomes a treasure on loan, a special charge to be loved and attended to with the greatest of care about every detail concerning his health, security, happiness.

For children from 4 up, Belgium, England, France, Germany, Italy, and Switzerland have a great many children's home-school-hotel facilities that offer, during the academic year, the European school curriculum and special courses for foreign children, as well as courses in handicrafts, art, music, and sports.

Although all children's hotels offer recreational facilities, in England, France, Holland, Italy, and Switzerland, children's hotels are generally country-clublike in atmosphere.

All children's hotels offer an international atmosphere and are set up to receive English-speaking children, but apart from the appeal of knowing that your children are having a heavenly time (it's a rare child that doesn't), there is, to me, an invaluable feature for young guests. This bonus—which children may not even be aware of at the time—is the experience of living with youngsters of other nations and accepting new customs and new languages as a part of their everyday life.

CHILDREN'S CAMPS—SUMMER AND WINTER All the foregoing advantages also apply to foreign summer and winter camps for the 8–14 set in France, Holland, Ireland, Italy, Norway, Spain, and Switzerland. There is, to be sure, nothing the matter with American camps—if you can overlook the fact that they are expensive, needlessly demanding about uniforms and camping equipment, and generally of little benefit culturally or spiritually—but it does seem to me to be more sensible, if your children want to go to camp and if you are going to Europe, to take the children with you and let them go to camp in Europe instead.

The International Camps in Switzerland combine American-style camps with the European way of living. At Camp Montana, a new, comfort-oriented camp for co-eds 8–17, no uniforms are required; high standards of accommodation, sanitation, health, supervision; and there is just about every sport you can think of.

For other children's camps see Switzerland.

For parents who feel their children would enjoy camping in woodsier, less elaborate camps, let me specially recommend the camps in Norway. The recreational facilities are wonderful. Prices of Norwegian camps are low to moderate, as are those in the Netherlands.

Besides American-style camps (where the administration, program, and campers are predominantly American) and the Continental-style (where the activities are centered around a sport), there are Swiss, Italian, Spanish, and French style get-togethers in châlets, villas, or private-school buildings with language lessons in the mornings and mountain climbing, sports, or sightseeing excursions in the afternoon. Some of these facilities are modest in price; all are reasonable.

British Activity Centres offer travel and adventure, and friendships with attractive British and continental youth. Standards are high and costs are reasonable. Though British-based (exposing campers to the surprises of cricket, theater, water sports, and geology), they also extend international options, such as canoeing in France, riding on the Riviera, or teenage group tours of many countries. For fuller details, see the camping section of the chapter on England, and, in this chapter, Holidays for Children on Their Own.

Several summer camps in Ireland are based on the campuses of private schools and colleges, and offer a rich mix of sports, cultural activities, and enjoyable learning experiences with excellent supervision.

For expert help in arranging European camping for your child, see "School and Camp Experts" (below).

Language problems? As a rule, children have no qualms about trying out foreign languages and pick them up with more ease than grownups. No parent, however, should send his youngster off to a European camp in the fond expectation he'll come back fluent in French or Danish. Phrases, yes. What he will come back with is an "ear" for languages. A child can always be counted upon to learn what he wants or needs to say. To this, I add the directive to my children that whatever else they learn, they should learn to express appreciation—"thank you" and "please" in every language. Manners are a fact of life, not an optional pleasantry. A European mother doesn't ask, "Did you have a good time?" but "Were you good?" Since children mirror their parents, your children may find that their European friends treat them with the courtesy they have been brought up to extend only to grownups. Another difference American children may notice is that European children may be more mature than they at first appear. Food may be a problem. Many American children find it difficult to adjust to snacks of apples, grapes, cheese, and fruit drinks instead of peanut butter, hot dogs, hamburgers, and Fritos. Coke is universal.

Teenage tours? Katherine Unger, President of **Inverness Travel** (770 Lexington Ave., New York, NY 10021) arranges chaperoned teenage and private school tours during winter and spring vacations. See also **American Institute for Foreign Study;** American Youth Hostels.

FOR TEENAGERS: THE BEST OF BOTH WORLDS A number of European travel, educational, and work programs for teenagers are sponsored by colleges and organizations such as American Field Service, Experiment in International Living, International Christian Youth Exchange, Youth for Understanding, American Heritage Association, American Friends of the Hebrew University, and American Youth Hostels. The best source of information is the nonprofit **CIEE—Council on International Educational Exchange**—(205 East 42nd St., New York, NY 10017) which functions as an informational clearinghouse for more than 180 member organizations, arranges low-cost transatlantic transportation for students, issues the money-saving student ID cards, publishes numerous helpful brochures, and programs the *Whole World Handbook,* a guide to study, work, and travel abroad for students, which is well worth the price. More information of value is found in CIEE's *Work, Study, Travel* catalog.

Most of the programs involve small work-and-study groups for volunteers and groups with common interests. If these programs interest your older children, they will probably travel to Europe in charter groups by air, or dormitory style by sea. Unless staying with a European family is part of the plan, they should expect the plainest accommodations and the simplest fare. Those 18 and older can earn pocket money waiting on tables, as clerks in banks and offices and other jobs. Careful perusal of the directory may turn up fruit-picking stints, architectural restoration, work on archaeological sites, and scientific research.

Also under the aegis of the **CIEE** is the School Exchange Service, wherein over 200 secondary schools in the U.S. are linked with partner schools in Britain and France for annual short-term exchanges of students. The sharing of experiences with host families is an essential component of the program with evenings and weekends free for informal activities. Brochures with more information are available from **CIEE.**

The **American Institute for Foreign Study** (102 Greenwich Ave., Greenwich, CT 06830) is the leading educational travel organization for highschool and college students, and adults who wish to join the groups. It offers a choice of over 100 itineraries ranging from one to five weeks including traveling, homestay, campus and cruise programs; mini ten-day winter, spring, summer discovery programs to college summer and academic year programs.

HOLIDAYS FOR CHILDREN ON THEIR OWN In England, as in most of Europe, you come to feel very secure about your children's well-being. There are many, many possibilities available. For over 25 years, PGL holidays, organized by Peter Gordon Lawrence, have been one of Europe's leading young people's holiday organizations for ages 6–18. PGL holidays include tennis coaching, pony trekking, riding, skiing and sailing holidays, canoeing, creative arts, and multiactivity adventures. These enjoyable experiences are offered in England, France, and Holland; prices are reasonable; separate centers are reserved for ages 6–8, 8–12, 12–15, and 16–18. Also, PGL is now expanding its programs of Family Holidays in Great Britain and France. Full details can be had from **PGL Young Adventure Ltd.** 850 Station St., Ross-on-Wye, England.

Pony trekking and riding holidays are another British specialty. You don't need to know how to ride to pony trek. All you do is sit on the back of a sturdy, surefooted pony and let it carry you through one of Britain's scenic areas in the company of a small pony-riding troop, stopping for lunch, tea or overnight breaks in some picturesque site in England, Scotland, or Wales. You, as well as your children, can enjoy this form of transport for an hour, a day, a week, or more. A full descriptive list of trekking and riding holiday centers is available from the **British Travel Bookstore,** 40 West 57th St., New York, NY 10019. Also, the British Horse Society publishes a list of BHS approved riding schools giving details of facilities and services of each. Write for this to **British Equestrian Centre,** Kenilworth, Warwickshire, England.

Excellent study programs for students 14–19 are offered by Choate Rosemary Hall (Box 788, Wallingford, CT 96492), for which students must have a working knowledge of Spanish or French, as they live in private homes, attend morning classes in language, history, and customs, and spend time in the cities and country of either France or Spain. St. George's School (Newport, RI 02840), offers total immersion in French culture for six weeks, (for which at least two years of French is recommended, though not mandatory). Woodberry Forest School (Woodberry Forest, VA 22989), has six-week study programs in either French or Spanish civilization, with morning seminars and afternoon excursions. All three schools have detailed brochures about their reasonably-priced summer offerings.

The **Experiment in International Living** (21 East 40th St., Suite

1307, New York, NY 10016) accepts children as young as 14, although 16 or 17 is more often the minimum age for its programs, in which participants travel to a host country in groups of about a dozen, then spend time living individually with a native family "not as a guest but as a member of the family," immersing themselves in the culture and language of their host country.

International Cultural Studies (John O'Connor, 57 Long Lots Rd., Westport, CT 06880) takes a group of about 30 13–17 year olds to France for four weeks of bicycling. The young can bring their own bicycles or rent new ten-speeds. Accommodation is in a boarding school just outside Valenciennes.

SCHOOL AND CAMP EXPERTS Although I have done my best to touch upon schools, camps, and holiday courses that welcome English-speaking children (aged 2 to teenagers) in all the countries covered in this book, it would take another book to list, much less describe, all possibilities. Every year brings new changes. I leave in-depth coverage of schools and holiday courses for children to those whose profession it is to devote themselves to a thorough knowledge of such matters. For a $125 consultation fee, you might wish to discuss the secondary school situation abroad with Mrs. Emily S. Lewis (150 East 72nd St., New York, NY 10021). A member of the Independent Educational Counselors Association (IECA), Mrs. Lewis has an in-depth knowledge of 300 schools in Austria, Britain, France, Germany, Italy, Spain, Switzerland, both day and boarding schools, English-speaking and foreign language curriculum as well as expertise in the academic and social requirements of private schools in the U.S. She matches children and schools with an expert and discriminating touch.

Although testing, collating school records and personal interviews with parents and child are involved, enrolling a child in a European school is a cinch compared to the convolutions necessary at home. Where the expertise enters the picture is in knowing which school would be best for your child. My daughter, for example, an A student when she's interested, a casual D when she isn't, had no trouble fitting into an intensified tutorial course in London to prepare her for Oxford, and felt she was working at her top potential for the first time in her school years. Mrs. Lewis, after an initial consultation, is agreeable either to advising you how to enroll your child in the best and most suitable school abroad for your child, or to attending to the enrollment details herself.

On the West Coast, marvelously knowledgeable Elizabeth V. Zierer heads up **Education Continentale** (5863 Birch Ct., Oakland, CA 94618). Her specialty is schools, camps, and placement in families as paying guests for young Americans, 6–20, who would like to spend a summer or winter abroad, learn a foreign language quickly and pleasantly, combine studies with recreation, travel, sight-seeing, and learn the customs and ideas of other students from many lands. Her forte is Switzerland, but she is also in touch with many schools and camps in Germany, England, France, and Austria. She recommends only places she knows personally, spends three months of every year in Switzerland checking up on facilities, and meticulously matches each child's personality with the character of camp, school, or home. Other services are a summer study tour for young people and Guests Continentale whereby (while your children are studying) parents and teachers can become members of French families in Lausanne and brush up on French while enjoying swimming, riding, tennis, bridge, and golf, or take courses in French literature, cuisine, or landscape or porcelain painting. Fees are $75 for standard counseling at her office; an additional $35 if you wish her to make arrangements with the school, camp, or family and include her personal recommendation *after* personal interview with parent and child. If distance prevents such an interview, a questionnaire must be filled in and returned with a $50 fee before "further action." Also highly recommended are John and Anne Holden (0353 N. Thomas Rd., Carbondale, CA 81623) as counselors for foreign schools and colleges. With 45 years of experience in the education field as faculty members and headmasters, they have a salutory wisdom about and interest in the European educational scene and are honorary members of IECA.

The **Independent Educational Counselors Association, Inc.,** Cove Rd., Box 125, Forestdale, MA 02644, is an organization whose members accept no fee from the schools they recommend. Their counselor members specialize in both U.S. and foreign secondary school and university placement. Write IECA for a free directory of their independent professional educational counselors.

YOUR CHILD AS A PAYING GUEST For years, families abroad have taken young girls and boys as paying guests, but these facilities have been arranged on a personal-contact level only and have been almost impossible to arrange unless you were lucky enough to have many close friends living abroad and who could advise you and make all arrangements.

So far, Great Britain is the only area where these facilities for children's accommodations are widely available. As part of the Meet the British program, services have been organized from Cornwall to the Orkneys to screen with care what might be described as expanded private homes, generally run by well-qualified couples with children of their own, who may take no more than four or five children as guests, providing them with a week to several months of family atmosphere and holiday recreation. Friends of mine have found these facilities ideal for younger children, 6 and older, who adapt better to a family environment than to camp life. The British Tourist Authority suggests you telephone their New York office (212) 581–4708), stating the locale you prefer so that you can then be advised which agency to get in touch with. If you aren't sure, and would like the complete list of child placement-in-host family services, region by region, write to the BTA, 40 West 57th St., New York, NY 10019.

Elizabeth V. Zierer of Education Continentale (described above) will also place your child as a paying guest with a European family.

FIRST AID FOR THE FRANTIC

Happily, children are the most hardy and healthy of travelers and generally far more adaptable to quick shifts of scene and circumstances than their parents. Europe has fine doctors and excellent public health officials, and for each country in this book I have a section titled ''Emergencies Made Easy'' which will guide you to proper help for anything you can't cope with on your own.

INOCULATIONS Though the U.S. requires no immunization for re-entry, the Public Health Service's Centers for Disease Control *strongly* recommends that you and your children be protected against diseases that may be common in countries you might visit. Some countries will not let you in without documentation that you have received certain vaccines. The most reliable source of immunization information is an annual Centers for Disease Control publication, *Health Information for International Travel* (Supt. of Documents, U.S. Government Printing Office, Washington, DC 20402; HHS Pub. No. CDC 80-8280). A call to any regional office of PHS will give you the latest immunization update required and *recommended*. No matter where you are going, you should have the basic immunizations. Primary immunizations are routinely administered for measles, mumps, rubella, diphtheria, pertussis, poliomyelitis, and tetanus. Boosters are needed every ten years. Also, ask your doctor about gamma globulin shots against viral hepatitis.

If you are going on to the Middle East, Far East, Africa, or visiting friends in the Peace Corps in undeveloped areas, Health Information for International travelers will advise about typhoid, yellow fever, malaria. ▶ **Note:** My pediatrician advised me to save the fees he would have to charge for immunization by taking advantage of services supplied free of charge by the U.S. Public Health Service. But for babies and very young children, your pediatrician may feel he would prefer to give the inoculations. Privately administered inoculations have to be validated (stamped) by the U.S. Dept. of Public Health office in your city.

MEDICAL SUPPLIES Pepto-Bismol is my choice (or whatever your doctor prescribes) for diarrhea; a tin of Band-Aids; a bottle of children's aspirin; a bottle of antihistamine pills to ward off colds and hay fever—these are about the only medical supplies I find are of immediate practical value to carry with me while traveling. And by "carry with me," I mean just that—in my handbag. For temporary effect and mysterious soothing power, a Band-Aid applied to a child's skinned knee seems to relieve pain instantly. The diverting and entertaining value of Band-Aids for children is considerable. I carry a thermometer in my handbag because it gets lost if it's anywhere else, and the only kind of thermometers available in Europe are marked on a metric scale (which means you have to convert Celsius temperature to Fahrenheit by multiplying by 9⁄5 and adding 32). At the crucial moment, this seems too complicated a procedure.

Naturally, if your children are allergic to penicillin or any other drug, or are diabetic or have any physical condition that might require emergency care, you should carry with you a note to this effect signed by your doctor, who may also recommend that you take along a copy of your children's medical records. To be on the safe side, I've always done this. The schools my children go to require annual medical information about them. I photostat these records, add information about allergies, and list their blood types. I take two copies for each child so that, if they are going to a baby hotel or a camp, either as part of the plan or as a spur-of-the-moment decision, all information is on hand, including our own doctor's name, address, and telephone number.

You can have emergency information engraved on specially designed bracelets or necklaces which are available from $7 to $25 from the nonprofit **Medic Alert Foundation,** P.O. Box 1009, Turlock, CA, 95381; in New York, at 777 UN Plaza, NY 10017.

Water and food are, for the most part, completely safe, but the *change* of diet and of water can lead to diarrhea. I'm not saying this is inevitable, but there's a good chance of it happening, particularly if your child is overtired or overexcited. Therefore, check with your doctor about what prescriptions are necessary. With children, recovery from diarrhea is rapid with hourly feedings, in a series, of tea, rice, applesauce. The U.S. PHS suggests: 8 oz. fruit juice, ½ tsp. honey or table sugar and a pinch of salt in 1 glass; in another 8 oz. water (boiled, or Perrier) mixed with ¼ tsp. baking soda. Drink alternately in frequent sips. Sounds odd, but it *does* work.

Almost all medical supplies are available in Europe, but by all means talk things over with your doctor and get whatever prescriptions he suggests filled a couple of weeks before your departure so that you can have them all on hand when it comes time to pack. Get an adequate supply as well as a prescription (using the drug's generic name, not its trade name) in case you need more. It's simple to have American prescriptions refilled at pharmacies and American or British hospitals in most capital cities of Europe. Keep drugs in their *original* containers, *unmixed,* so as not to confuse yourselves or arouse suspicions in customs officers who might confiscate your medication, particularly if carried by a teenager.

With all the wonderful possibilities of beaches and boat trips, do be careful about sunburn. Take your sunscreen with you.

Medical Kit for those traveling by yacht, small boat, car, or camping in the wilderness: Check with your doctor about these medications not requiring prescriptions: Ophthalmic irrigating solution in plastic squeeze bottle for help in removing foreign body in eye, also for use with conjunctivitis; Calamine lotion without phenol for itching skin, poison ivy, or insect bites; Neo-Synephrine nasal spray or drops for unblocking nasal passages; Marezine for airsickness or seasickness; Zinc oxide powder for temporary filling of tooth cavity; Eugenol or Oil of Cloves for toothache; Suntan lotion (RVP for those with unusual susceptibility to sunburn); Hypoallergenic dusting powder to avoid fungus infections of skin in moist contact areas; a laxative; syrup of ipecac for accidental poisoning. Prescription medications for emergencies when you are unable to obtain medical care. The choice of these should be left entirely up to your doctor, but to give you some idea of what you might need I have made a list of common emergencies and medications I have found useful in treating them: Allergic reactions, hay fever, itching, hives (Benadryl); Conjunctivitis (sodium sulfacetamide opthalmic solution); Persistent high fever with cough, earache, sore throat, or diarrhea (oral penicillin or tetracycline); Superficial skin infections, fungal or bacterial (Vioform); Severe asthma or allergic reaction to insect bites or medicines with difficulty in breathing and collapse (medihaler-Epi, an oral inhaler). Some of these medications produce allergic reactions in certain people, some doctors do not believe in handing out strong drugs for self-treatment and diagnosis, so again, let your doctor decide, he knows your medical history, allergies, and drug-tolerance.

IMPORTANT! North Americans do have medical idiosyncrasies. A drug, aminopyrine, formerly commonly dispensed in southern Europe as an aspirin-like painkiller, destroys the white blood cells of those of Anglo-Saxon extraction but is harmless to Latins. It was this discovery that led to the foundation of the **International Association for Medical Assistance to Travelers (IAMAT),** headquartered at 736 Center St., Lewiston, NY 14092. It costs nothing to join. Members are given a directory listing English-speaking physicians familiar with North American medical practice who will provide 24-hour care at reasonable fees, a world immunization and malaria-risk chart, and other literature. Just write to IAMAT's offices for membership. Although you can get the names of recommended doctors and dentists from the U.S. Embassy or American Consulate in European capitals, IAMAT's coverage includes 450 cities in 116 countries. Hurrah for this helpful service, whose aim is to make IAMAT members feel as if they are being treated by their family doctor even while in a foreign country.

Intermedic, 777 Third Ave., New York, NY 10017 also lists English-speaking doctors in more than 200 countries who have agreed to provide prompt service for fixed fees. Family membership $10.

Bats. Vanderbilt University's Dr. James P. Carter warns that large numbers of bats living together in caves can transmit rabies to human beings without biting—the virus is excreted in their urine. Therefore, keep young speleologists out of widely touted—but potentially hazardous—tourist attractions such as the Hercules Caves near Tangier, Morocco.

Mosquitoes. Dr. Carter recommends wearing light-colored clothing and staying indoors at dusk to avoid being bitten. Other Carter fiats: You should use repellents on your children even if you do not use them on yourself. Use of mosquito netting over baby's crib is recommended. Keep repellent out of the eyes.

MOTION SICKNESS Thanks to stabilizers on ships and smoother take-offs and landings by planes, motion sickness has gone out of fashion. Children almost never get seasick or airsick, which seems to bear out the theory it's 95% mental. Any discomfort is more likely to be caused by fatigue and excitement than by motion.

On planes, a mild tranquilizer for 9- to 12-month-olds *if prescribed by your doctor* is a possibility. A nasal aspirator which creates a gentle suction (available at any drugstore) is helpful in relieving the sniffles of nonnoseblowers. Ask your doctor about nose drops for older children.

If you're worried, check with your doctor about pills and lozenges such as Bonamine, Lergigan, and Bonadettes. Motion sickness, I gather, must exist for someone, but not you, I trust, because there's also Dramamine, Nautamine, Marezine, and Compazine! Capsules (only) of powdered ginger root, available in health food stores, are suggested by health-expert Jane E. Brody as helpful in combating motion sickness without the sleep-inducing effects of the usual medications. She is right!

If you follow the previously mentioned Miracle Preflight Diet (Ch. 6) and feeding hints for airborne infants, you won't have to worry.

If you fear your child might become carsick or airsick, a plastic bottle of white vinegar is handy for quick, deodorizing clean-up.

WATER To the extent that generalities are reassuring, in all capitals and large cities, tap water is pure and potable. Throughout the British Isles, water is fine. The purity of water in Switzerland, parts of Germany, France, Italy, and Austria is a worldwide attraction. Bottled water—in nonfizzy varieties (such as Evian and Fiuggi), almost flat types (such as Vichy and San Gemini), and sparklers (Perrier and San Pellegrino)—is drunk for its taste and the wide range of therapeutic qualities attributed to each brand. In the Netherlands, Switzerland, France, Belgium, and Germany, I follow right along with whatever the local customs are with regard to bottled water. In villages and rural areas, I'd advise that you and your children never drink any but bottled water.

MILK Milk, which looks so pure and simple, isn't. Meeting high standards involves inspection and checking of dairy herds, grazing and barn facilities, milking routine, storage, refrigeration, packaging, and delivery. The British Isles, the Netherlands, Scandinavia, Belgium, and Switzerland are subject to governmental controls similar to those in the U.S.; but even so, the decision about milk will vary with the location, as it does in America.

Outside countries where milk standards are governmentally controlled (or where imported milk from controlled countries is available), be wary of ice cream or milk unless you are certain that it has been boiled. It is wise to check out the situation with the local health department, the American Embassy, or to hear the opinions of American mothers living in the area.

For information on formulas for young babies, see Chapter 5. For the older baby on fresh milk, thorough cleaning of bottles and nipples is all that's generally required, since germs cannot multiply on clean, dry surfaces. Depending on your itinerary and plans, you may decide that powdered milk would be more convenient. Discuss with your doctor whether powdered milks (whole or skim) or canned milks (whole or condensed) would be a better choice. These milks should be diluted with potable water and prepared and stored in clean utensils and bottles. Some children accept the processed milk; some prefer fresh cow's milk boiled for three minutes. The time to work all this out is as far in advance as possible. Processed milks, powdered or tinned, are available everywhere in Europe.

PHARMACIES Night service is rotated among the European pharmacies which fill prescriptions, so that you'll have no trouble finding 24-hour service. Every pharmacy has a notice posted on its door indicating the 24-hour pharmacy open that night. The concierge at your hotel can also tell you which one it is, as can local giveaway guides and newspapers. Your concierge can act as interpreter if necessary (though many have English-speaking personnel). In fact, I've found service is *much* better in Europe in filling prescriptions at late hours than in New York.

TRAVEL INSURANCE Blue Cross and Blue Shield will reimburse you according to their fee schedules for medical costs abroad *if* an insurance form (which you must bring with you) has been properly filled out by the treating physician. It is infinitely wiser and cheaper to buy accident and illness insurance to cover your trip directly from private insurers or through your travel agent.

For a minimum of seven days, **International SOS Assistance, Inc.** (P.O. Box 11568, Philadelphia, PA 19116) provides hospital admittance fees, emergency evacuation in a special aircraft, lists of English-speaking doctors, and access to legal aid. Similar coverage is provided by **Health Care Abroad** (1511 K St. NW, Washington, DC), which has a minimum of 25 days. **Assist-Card** (745 Fifth Ave., New York, NY 10022), staffed 24 hours a day with multilingual service representatives, charges a tad more for a daily rate. Sentry Insurance is among the major companies to have a comprehensive travel plan offered by affiliates of the American Society of Travel Agents.

DOCTORS AND EMERGENCIES Don't try to cope with them on your own. Should any medical or dental care be necessary, telephone the American Consulate, Legation, or Embassy nearest to you (telephone numbers are listed under ''Emergencies Made Easy'' in each country). If for any reason the Consulate should be closed, call the residence of the chief Consular official, who can be relied upon to help you out of any emergency. Arrangements can even be made for an embassy or U.S. military plane to come to your rescue if necessary. But please bear in mind that unless it is a *serious* legal, medical or financial difficulty, our consuls do not offer their services on an unconditional or totally indulgent basis. Don't expect them to cash checks, act as travel agents or, as the Bureau of Consular Affairs informs wearily, ''search for missing luggage, or settle disputes with hotel managers.'' See also IAMAT and Intermedic, mentioned above.

Before you leave the U.S. you should check your medical insurance for extent of cover. Be sure to read Travel Insurance mentioned above, because, with rare exception, the U.S. government expects to be reimbursed and may require proof of ability to pay before any expense incurring services are rendered. However, as a liaison operation, which seems to be another well-kept secret, the U.S. State Department maintains the Overseas Citizens' Emergency Center (Department of State, Washington, DC 20520) to help with any complicated medical, financial or legal problems when traveling abroad. They will locate and notify close relatives at home, expedite the sending of private funds oversees, and gather and transmit medical information to overseas physicians. If you have difficulties with the local authorities or find yourself in a dispute which could lead to legal or police action, the U.S. consuls can provide lists of local attorneys and help you find adequate legal representation presentation.

CREDIT CARDS are a help, but if you should lose your American Express, Visa, or Mastercard, let's hope you have taken the wise precaution of registering them all with a credit card service bureau and have their number, address and your account number in a locket soldered around your neck, tattooed on the sole of your left foot or sensibly in the keeping of your lawyer, bank manager and a trusted friend—then, at least someone will be available if you don't have the information with you. There are many organizations who serve to prevent illegal or fraudulent use of the cards, as well as recording these impossible-to-remember numbers with which they are imprinted, but Credit Card Service Bureau (P.O. Box 1322, Alexandria, VA 22313) first comes to mind.

GETTING AROUND IN EUROPE

Don't just go somewhere—have fun getting there! Vary your transport. Your choices may interweave some or all of the following peripatetic approaches:

PLANES A round-trip ticket with open flight departures for cities you are visiting bought in the U.S. will cost you much less than buying air travel once you are abroad. If you are a V.I.P., by all means get a letter from your U.S. carrier introducing you to upper-echelon personnel in their foreign offices.

If any of your children are over 16, or if you yourself are a student 30 years old or younger, check with the CIEE (see the section for teenagers in Ch. 8) about eligibility requirements for the bargain student flights abroad.

PERSONAL GUIDE SERVICES **Take-A-Guide, Ltd.** (63 East 79th St., New York, NY 10021) with an office in London (see chapter on England) is the best guide service in Europe. Every guide is personable, university-educated, young, attractive, with expertise in fields ranging from antiques and backgammon to art, history, economics, and music. Without competitors in price, luxury or comfort, TAG offers station wagons, touring cars, and limousines to take you and your children, or just your children, on half-day, full day, or 3-day or longer specialized tours with itineraries adapted solely to your interests and your tastes or, if you aren't sure what attracts your interests, TAG has fascinating suggestions from classic highlights to the offbeat and esoteric. TAG will meet you on arrival; provide multilingual interpreters, escort you to the homes of your ancestors or Sherlock Holmes' private study; arrange for your stay in inns and castles; bring history to life for your children.

In England, Ireland, Scotland, Austria, Italy, Germany, France, you can enjoy the luxury of Take-A-Guide's unique sightseeing and touring service with door-to-door personal service. Guides, chosen for outstanding personalities and intelligence, are English but fluent also in foreign languages so that you can, if you wish, extend your trip to other countries. In Switzerland, the car service with the highest recommendations is **Welti-Furrer.**

HELICOPTERS Even for children who call a helicopter a ''heliplopper,'' rides in a whirlybird are an enthralling treat. You really have the sense of flying—of being a giant bird surrounded by other giant birds surveying a world grown as small as a miniature town. It's a sensation most children love. A few major European airports have helicopter services. Commercial inter-city, island, or sightseeing flights are the ones to ask about. They're much easier on the budget than charter flights. At Copenhagen's freshly modernized Kastrup Airport, for instance, the helicopter-over-the-city tour is great, a memorable $15 treat for a child!

BOATS If you agree with the remark in the *Wind in the Willows* that ''there is nothing—absolutely nothing—half so much worth doing as simply messing about in boats,'' Europe offers all sorts of possibilities. If I had only one week in Europe, I'd certainly try to squeeze in at least one boat trip. Here are some examples of trips described under the various countries.

The ***Rhine steamer excursions,*** of course, are the classic and most popular of all river excursions. The middle section of the Rhine, from Bonn upstream to Bingen, is singled out as the ''best'' portion of the romantic Rhine, with the loveliest scenery and the most castles. Though children will not enjoy the longest routes (see ''Germany''), I'd make the trip at least from Koblenz to Bingen.

The four-hour trip from Passau to Linz along the Danube in a paddlewheeler is equally scenic, and the novelty of sailing along in a large paddlewheeler seems to be interesting to children.

Lake Constance, lapping at the boundaries of Germany, Switzerland, and Austria, also offers excursions in beautiful white paddlewheelers. There are more lakes in Europe than you can shake an oar at, and there's always the chance of hiring a boatman to take you for a short sail or row. In many countries there are opportunities for you to paddle your own canoe. If you have a Eurailpass, you can sail from France to Ireland for only the price of a cabin accommodation, take a free ferry ride from Germany to Denmark, or travel at reduced rates by steamship from Venice to Piraeus.

You can charter a yacht or rent a sailboat in Athens and have a heavenly time sailing the Aegean from island to island.

If you are in Germany near Salzburg or Munich, don't miss the ***raft rides.*** These are not really rafts, but bargelike vessels, complete with cheery little brass bands.

You can cruise along canals and rivers in France, Germany, and Holland, or just laze in riverboats along the canals of Copenhagen and Amsterdam, drift through the canals of Venice in a gondola (there are motorboats in Venice, but no one who has an ounce of feeling about

Venice would dream of riding in one—at least, this is what I prefer to think). You can traverse the Seine and the Thames in a riverboat, but in Britain, my choice of water transport is by canal boat through any distance of Britain's 2000 miles of inland waterways.

You can navigate 65 locks in a much larger vessel if you take the three-day ***Göta Canal cruise,*** a fascinating 35-mile journey winding through lakes, forested rivers and canals from Gothenburg to Stockholm. You can tour the fjords of Norway or cruise for eight days through the labyrinthine lake country of Finland or have yourself skippered around in a private cabin cruiser through the waterways of the Netherlands.

If you can imagine a boat masquerading as a flying Venetian blind, you'll have a pretty good idea of what a ***Hydrofoil*** looks like. It's an absurd but exhilarating method of water travel.

N.B.: Greek Island cruises are like tours, a quick, superficial way of seeing the highlights, of checking out places you'd like to come back to. Shore excursions give you little time to look about, swim, to do anything more than follow a droning guide. Shopkeepers, knowing you are a bird of passage, often overcharge, or are just too swamped with customers to be friendly. You may find a few fellow cruise members compatible, but often you will not. Cruises tend to attract senior citizens, the less adventurous, the less individualistic. Few children ever turn up on cruises and most cruises have nothing planned for children except access to a swimming pool. Cruises are, however, a convenient way of seeing a good deal in a short time. What I did, when I went on a cruise of the Greek islands with the children, was to use not the tour buses ashore but the local buses and taxis available at all but minuscule ports, where you can just walk around by yourself anyway.

HOVERCRAFT Another larky way to travel is by Hovercraft, a vehicle which skims over the water on a self-produced cushion of air. Traveling over land and water, **Hoverspeed Hovercraft** service operates between England and France (Dover/Boulogne, Dover/Calais), Southhampton and Portsmouth to Cowes and Ryde on the Isle of Wight.

BUSES Despite all the reclining seats, handy plumbing, refrigerated refreshments, smiling hostesses, snack bars, radios, public-address systems, and sliding glass roofs offered by such bus companies at CIAT (in Italy) and Linjebuss and Europabus (which weave an intricate pattern all over Europe)—the Big Three bus companies, offering the most comfortable and commodious bus transportation—touring buses are not much fun for children. *Exception:* In Greece, clean and cheap bus transportation is far simpler and more convenient than train transport, for the most part. Greek bus drivers let you on and off when and where you want!

City buses are a fruit from another tree, however. The knowledge that you can get off when you want to obviously eases the strain all around. The double-decker buses of Great Britain's cities are always a treat, as are tram and trolley trips in many cities. Unlimited city bus and subway travel vouchers for London and Paris can be prebooked in the U.S. along with rail travel bargains. See *Trains* in following section.

TRAINS American trains and stations lack the charm, romance, sophistication, and many of the complexities of European trains. Making train reservations in America is as simple as giving the children a peanut-butter sandwich and milk for lunch. European trains are like having a dinner party—you have to do considerable advance planning for the best results.

The money-saving plans are dazzling, because they not only save money, but are time-saving conveniences as well. For travel on the Continent, your best bet is the *Eurailpass,* about which detailed information is available from the national tourist offices of the 16 participating countries: Austria, Belgium, Denmark, Finland, France, Germany, Greece, Holland, Ireland, Italy, Luxembourg, Norway, Portugal, Spain, Sweden, Switzerland. A single ticket good for unlimited first class rail travel throughout these countries, Eurailpass is also honored on many scheduled boat services on the Danube, the Rhine, steamers on Swiss lakes, ferries, and large riverboats, granting you free passage or fare reductions. Eurailpasses are issued for 15 days, 21 days, one, two, or three months. Children under 12 pay half fare. Under 4, they travel free. Eurail Youthpasses are for people 12 to 26 and entitle you to one or two months second class rail travel throughout the 16 participating countries, but the small initial savings in the lower rate of their cost is important only if you are really on bone-thin budget and don't plan to travel in a way that will take full advantage of the first class Eurailpass, which is infinitely preferable and costs so little and offers so much more that the extra expense is negligible. *You must buy the Eurailpass here in the U.S., because you cannot buy it abroad.* Your Eurailpass will become valid on the date you first use it, when you must have the validation slip bearing your name and passport number and the first and last days of your trip (which make it possible to have lost cards replaced at Eurail Aid offices abroad) filled in. Allow plenty of time to have your Eurailpass validated at a train information window. Then all you do is just board a train and flash the pass.

If you are going to spend most of your time in France, then *France Vacances,* good for first or second class unlimited rail travel in France for seven days, 15 days or one month, is a bargain package, entitling you to four or seven days of unlimited travel on the Paris Metro (subway) and bus system; a free roundtrip transfer from Orly Airport by train to various points in downtown Paris, or from Charles de Gaulle Airport by train to the Gare du Nord; a free admission to the Pompidou Museum; free transportation on the private Provence railroad between Nice and Digne; and, if you get a first class ticket, you get a car for one day with a 100 km. free allowance in one of 30 French cities, and with a one month France Vacances pass, you get two days with 200 km. free. Children 4 to 12 get about ⅓ deduction in rates. Children under 4 travel free. *The deal on the car rental*—you have to pay for the gas—requires also a valid credit card (American Express, Diner's Club or Visa), and *you have to return the car to the location from which you borrowed it.*

For travelers to England, Scotland, Wales, a *BritRail* pass which also includes *four days car rental for each week of the package,* allowing you to drop off the car at any of 250 Godfrey Davis Europcar rental offices, plus unlimited rail travel first class or economy, is an exceptionally good bargain for seven, 14 or 21 days. Your spouse, and half-fare children 5 to 15, just pay the regular prices for a BritRail Pass. You can pre-book cars to collect on your airport arrival or to meet trains, do as you please, or follow any of the suggested itineraries. Book your BritRail Pass at least three weeks ahead from BritRail Travel International Office, 630 Third Ave., New York, NY 10017. Offices also in Los Angeles, Chicago, Toronto, and Vancouver.

European railways offer all sorts of bargains on weekend and holiday roundtrip tickets, special excursions to places of interest, and family discounts. Be sure to investigate before your departure about each country's specials with the travel information offices, as many of these special tickets are not sold abroad.

In most countries, children under 4 travel free, and the half-fare age limit is 10 in the Netherlands and Germany; 12 in Scandinavia; 14 in Italy and Austria; and 16 in Switzerland. However, the age limits may vary on some of the discount tickets.

▶ **Note:** In Great Britain, the difference in quality between first- and second-class railway accommodations is more a matter of upholstery and prestige than anything else, but on the Continent, I would recommend traveling first class if possible.

SEAT RESERVATIONS AND SLEEPING RESERVATIONS: Some trains require compulsory seat reservations and are marked with an R enclosed in a square in timetables. All trains require compulsory reservations for sleepers. Your Eurailpass does not cover this nominal fee, nor does it guarantee you a seat during the peak vacation and holiday times. Advance reservations must be requested early. Sleepers are first-class compartments for single or double occupancy. Couchettes have four bunks in first class and six bunks in second class. You have berths with curtains in sleepers, and just open bunks in couchettes.

In Sweden, you're fined if you don't have a seat reservation and board a train where seat reservations are compulsory.

In Spain, you're not allowed to board express trains unless you have a reserved seat or get a boarding pass at the station and have this clutched in your hand.

Make a point of finding out, before you make your reservations, which trains offer observation cars, dining cars, the services of a stenographer, snack cars for quick pick-me-ups, or "Express Tray" service (meals served in your compartment). Remember to reserve both your compartment seats and your seats in the dining car when you purchase your passage.

Telephone reservations are accepted five days in advance; in person, from two months to a few hours before the train departs.

DINING-CARS AND PICNIC BASKETS Night trains, as a rule, do not have dining cars.

You can have a good meal aboard a train, even a very good meal. Wine, liquor, tea, coffee, soft drinks, sandwiches, and snacks of some sort are usually available rolling past on a cart or in a bar section, but European trains don't carry drinking-water. The best thing to do is always to take along a picnic basket.

An important point to remember in traveling with children on the train is that their attention span for scenery is appallingly short. Children like sleeping on trains and eating on trains; the smell, the feel, and the sound of trains. Therefore, take advantage of train travel for long, overnight journeys, or for two-hour journeys during which you can picnic in your compartment. Even if you do make use of the dining facilities on the rails, always bring along something extra to drink and eat when you are traveling with your children.

Come what may, be prepared should be your motto. A local diesel or a luxury express, it makes no difference, I climb aboard expecting that there will be no drinking water, no food, no toilet paper, no soap, and no towels. If my expectations turn out to be false, I'm delighted; if not, I'm prepared. During cold weather, British trains can be chilly enough to make a lap-rug worth lugging along. Lighting during the cold season can also be counted upon to be dim and occasionally nonexistent. My trusty flashlight-magnifying glass frequently had to double as a reading light on my last trip.

BAGGAGE: At many stations you can get a self-service luggage cart to take your luggage aboard by yourself if a porter isn't available. Suitcases no wider than 26 inches fit best in overhead racks and storage compartments.

Many stations have a forwarding desk that, for a small charge, will ship your luggage to another terminal a day before you arrive. Check with your hotel concierge about the proper procedures.

Boarding the right train car in the right class and taking your right seat if you have a reservation is important. Each car, especially on long-distance international trains, is its own entity, which means that a long line of cars will not necessarily remain coupled and together until a common destination is reached.

Remember never to discard your train ticket after it has been marked or punched by the conductor. Most European railroads require that you present your ticket in order to leave the station platform at your destination. If you toss your ticket away, you'll usually end up having to pay double.

Most travel information offices can supply you with free timetables, and timetables of *everything*—trains, boats, ferries—are listed in Thomas Cook's Continental Timetables, available from Forsyth Library (see Ch. 3).

AERIAL TRAMS, CABLE CARS, FUNICULARS These are all safe and easy, yet with the built-in thrill of an amusement park ride. Oenologists may be happy to know that children can swing across German vineyards in aerial trams. In Athens, thank heavens, there's a funicular up Lycabettus Hill where there are many attractions it's great not to have to climb to, and a funicular from the harbor up to the clifftop town of Thira on that beautiful island of Santorin. The Swiss have some of the most breathtaking rides. See individual country chapters for more suggestions about these entertaining transports.

HORSES AND PONIES Don't overlook horses as a particularly delightful means of transport. Not only the horse-drawn carriages in which you can be driven, spanking lightly along, harness jingling, tassels bobbing, through most of the major European cities, but also horses to ride across the heather in Scotland or over the Scandinavian countryside.

Ireland offers donkey rides along stretches of its long beaches of golden sand, and as far as the children are concerned, riding bareback on a shaggy, furry little donkey is an absolute must on every Irish holiday. For boys and girls—with or without riding experience—the Netherlands, England, Ireland, Wales, Scotland, and other countries offer pony trekking by the hour, day, or week.

Ireland, Wales, and the Netherlands also offer horse-drawn gypsy-like caravans, complete with mattresses, cooking, heating, and lighting facilities, and wash-up basins, that you can hire by the day or the week. "Previous experience with horses is not necessary," says one of the outfitters, "but is useful." For children under 8, I think this would be pretty tiring for more than a day, but for older children it might be a lot of fun.

MOTORING My theory and practice, when traveling with children, is to cover long distances by plane, boat, or train, and motor for short periods of time and distance only. A kilometer may be equal technically to ⅝ of a mile, but on some continental roads you will find that it will take you almost twice if not three times as long to negotiate 1 kilometer as it will a mile.

First, although it isn't mandatory, it's highly recommended to secure an International Driving Permit, for which you'll need a passport-sized photograph. The Automobile Association of America can help you with both of these, and let's hope you are a member of this organization because they can give you, just as advertised, a passport to carefree motoring overseas, and put you in touch with all their affiliated motoring organizations in Europe, whose names, services and branch offices are all listed in triple A's *Your Passport to Carefree Travel,* free to members. Your local AAA or the head office (8111 Gatehouse Road, Falls Church, VA 22047) will give you assistance and advice about motoring in Europe.

RENTING A CAR In some cases, you'll get a better car-rental rate by prepaying in dollars. Europacar tours stresses this angle. So does Avis. On the other hand, Hertz's Affordable Europe guarantees your car-rental rates in local European currencies if you reserve at least two weeks in advance. Cars with stick-shift equipment are always less expensive than automatic transmission. There are fly-and-drive packages offered by airlines; rail-and-ride packages offered by railways; rental, lease and purchase-cars-abroad plans. Raymond Chambers, public relations counsel *par excellence,* recommends going to a local used-car dealer in Europe and asking him to rent you one of his sale cars for a week or longer, and working out the pittance of the insurance cost with him. This route worked out wonderfully for Mr. Chambers, his wife and four children, and cost about a quarter of the regular car rental prices.

To save fuel, time, effort, I urge you also to take advantage of Europe's rail network and *special auto-train facilities.* Cars can be put aboard or taken off special trains, including long distance trains which carry you and your car together and on short distance hops, particularly in mountainous regions, and even to offshore islands. These auto-trains are popular with Europeans, so do check well in advance about their availability.

PROTECTION FOR INFANTS AND SMALL CHILDREN Ideally, try to get hold of a car with the safety feature of rear doors that open only when the front doors are opened. To prevent in-car accidents, check with whatever car agency you are dealing with in regard to safety belts for the car you rent, lease, purchase or drive in while you are in Europe. Make sure that the seat belt system in your vehicle will secure a rear-facing infant-style carrier or a forward-facing toddler-style or the convertible carrier for infant and toddler/preschooler which are convertible from a backward-facing infant position to forward-facing for a toddler, such as International Teddy Tot's Astroseat series, and Cosco/Peterson's Safe-N-Easy, Safe-N-Snug, Safe-T-Seat, Safe-T-Shield; or Collier-Keyworth's Bobby-Mac Champion Car Seat; Questor-Kantwet's Care Seat or their One Step; Strolee's Wee Care #597A or #599 series; Kolcraft's Hi-Rider (Shield) or Redi-Rider; Century's 100, 200, 300 series. A parent's lap is not a safe place to transport a child in a car, and infants should be transported only in an infant/child car safety seat. Remember that all "child restraint devices" manufactured after 1981 must be federally approved and meet with Federal Standard #213! If a safety seat is not available for a young child, a seat belt is better than nothing.

You can have your child's or children's safety seats all shipped ahead and arrange for it or them to be unpacked and placed in your car for delivery to you in Europe. American manufactured safety and booster seats are almost impossible to find in Europe.

Throughout Europe, Hertz offers European-manufactured safety seats, approved by governmental councils on safety, for rental cars. For these seats there is a non-refundable charge of $12–$30, and the seats must be returned to the same office from which they were rented. Reservations for these seats should be made a week in advance.

In Europe, concern with child safety while car passengers is such that there are mandatory regulations about the use of seat belts and children's seating in the back of the car. Please check out regulations with your local motoring club when abroad. They can tell you about keeping children safe while motoring according to the rules of their region.

Trouble with tots in the back seat often comes from boredom and restlessness; stop often. Children adore animals. Don't drive past that flock of goats or sheep or geese; let the children get out and admire them. Stop for a picnic at a beautiful place even if it isn't quite lunch-time or teatime. The picnic basket and thermos jug are lifesavers for motoring families.

One game for traveling is a variation of Roadside Cribbage. You come to a town-line: Bern, for example, The children start looking for objects beginning with *B*, the initial letter of Bern. "I see a bridge," counts as one. But "I see a bear," counts as two because the first two letters are used. "Berry" counts three and if anyone spies "Bernadette's" or "Bernstein's," he wins the piece of cheese or chocolate or tiny surprise hidden in the toy box.

An alternative is Who-Can-Translate-the-Road-Signs-First. For this you need the translations provided in touring maps or motoring guides. This may drive some driving Daddies dotty. You can be educational and see who can remember best the phrase pages given in this book; you can write down foreign words to look up later. Or see who remembers the most things about the town you were in yesterday.

Children should be provided with plastic bags or cloth pouch bags in which to collect pebbles, wild flowers, or bits of bark at every stop. These may seem useless to you, but don't discourage your children from magpie instincts. Collections can be sorted out in the evening, the "best" things saved.

A tape recorder is great to have along. Some parents are better than others at planning programs that can be played back with tremendous pleasure. A small cassette library can be fun.

Pencils, crayons, Magic Markers won't get lost and will zip back into place after use if attached to the ends of those little round-cased zip-out measuring tapes, which can be hung from the interior side hooks most cars are equipped with. Tie all baby toys to the car seat on a short piece of string (in which your baby can't possible get tangled) and so that you won't get clonked with them if your baby, as mine did, decides to throw them.

Cover the back seat with a plastic tablecloth (to be used also when picnicking) and cover that in turn with a sheet securely pinned to the upholstery. A sheet is cooler for children's bare legs than the leather or fabric upholstery which it protects at the same time.

Do encourage the children to read maps, translate road signs. Provided with magnifying glasses, children love "helping." Whether they actually do or not, they are participating and learning, and that's the main thing. Children enjoy and respect authority. By all means give assignments: "You will be in charge of unfolding and folding the maps. You are awarded custody of the thermos jug. You will handle the litter." This system does work, but remember that responsibility takes a long time to acquire!

Bottle warmers or other gadgets which plug into the 12-volt system of the cigarette lighter of your American car operate on all recent models of European cars. European cars built in the early 70's or before have 6-volt systems for which you need a special transformer-converter.

MUSEUMS CAN BE FUN

BEFORE YOU GO How can you help children 6 and older to respond to places of interest and to see museums with awareness? Obviously, creating interest ahead of time is a good idea. Let the children choose in advance what they think they would like to see. This may involve getting hold of a travel folder or a museum catalog in advance, but make the effort. It will pay off in quickening your child's anticipation and curiosity. Having time to sit down and look at the pictures, knowing which ones appeal to you beforehand, knowing who painted what, makes museum-going a happy tour of recognition for a child.

There is a nice sense of joy for a child in being familiar with art books and for yourself when you are happily able to say, "Ah, we'll see this Velasquez in the Prado in Madrid."

ON-THE-SPOT TIPS My suggestion is to go to the museum and find your way to the gallery your child either has said he was interested in seeing or to a gallery you think your child might be interested in.

If it's a gallery with pictures in it, you can ask your child to go off on his own—and it must be strictly on his own—and pick out the picture he likes best so that he can get a postcard or print of it to put in a scrapbook or send to his grandmother. You can try to guess after he has made his choice which picture he has selected. If you make the wrong guess, you can say, perhaps, that you'll treat him to a marionette show or some other sure-fire treat. Or say that you'll bet him a giant balloon that he cannot find a picture with a horse, peacock, dog, archway, apple, or boat in it—and make sure that you pick something that you are sure he will be able to find. Or, depending on your child's age, ask him to find a "sad" picture or a "happy" picture; a picture that would look well in the living room or in his room; or challenge him to find more than four Renoirs, three Titians, two Holbeins or whatever. The variations are many, and you'll be interested to see how carefully your children will look at pictures that they otherwise might just have walked past.

Children relate to drawings and watercolors because they do them themselves. Encourage this rapport which is the main thing, not the actual facts—i.e., when your child says enthusiastically or enviously, "That Mr. Durer draws awfully well. I wish I could draw fur like that on a rabbit," don't, as I heard one mother do, say, "He's dead."

Sometimes, I just sit down on a bench, say that I'm tired and that I'd be very grateful if my child would look around and let me know if he thinks there is anything I would be interested in looking at. If my child sits down on the bench and announces that he also is tired, we leave, although I usually point out just one thing before we go and ask my child to take a look at it for me, or tell me what the label says. Sometimes this leads to looking at more things, sometimes it doesn't, but the main point is to leave the museum before your child gets bored or your feet hurt.

Another reward for oneself and one's children is the How-Observant-Are-You game, which can be played almost anywhere a couple of times a day, no more. It's a big bore if overdone. From Close-your-eyes-and-tell-me-how-many-colors-there-are-in-the-stained-glass-window to I'll-bet-you-can't-tell-me-whether-that-church-we-just-saw-had-a-clerestory-or-not, this is a competitive game that can do a lot to make observant looking a habit. Whether you ask the children or they ask you the questions, this is a very enriching habit to acquire.

Identifying signs and symbols common in Christian art can turn a stony-eyed little klutz into an enthusiastic art lover within minutes. A handy dozen simple symbols might include the bird in the hands of the Christ Child (the winged soul); a butterfly (the Resurrection); coral (protection against evil); pearls (salvation); a peacock (immortality), the hundred eyes in its tail sometimes used to symbolize the all-seeing Church; the shell (pilgrimage); the cherry (the delights of the blessed); the pear (Christ's love for mankind); the palm frond (victory); the beehive (eloquence, as in "honeyed words"); the wheel (the rotating force of divine power); the leopard (sin, cruelty, the Devil and Antichrist).

SMALL MUSEUMS Your children should visit the great museums—such as London's National Gallery, the Louvre, the Prado, Rijksmuseum, and the Uffizi—but there are also small and generally overlooked museums in great cities that have a special flavor and may appeal to your children even more. Because they are small, a child can see art as a chance encounter in what was once an elaborate private house which retains the sense of past grandeur. *Beware of toy museums,* except ones like that in Edinburgh where the displays are the kind children can relate with and not feel covetous about. Most toy museums are for grownups.

TORTURE CHAMBERS Many museums display the iron maidens, spikes, thumb-screws, racks, wheels on which bones were broken and bodies pierced. **Madame Tussaud's Waxworks** in London has a Chamber of

Horrors with tableaux of the most famous persecutors and their victims, murderers and the murdered, including the Little Princes in the Tower. In Switzerland, England, Austria, France, Germany, Belgium, the Netherlands, Spain, Italy, Portugal, you come across these exhibits in museums and in castle dungeons. Some parents feel these are bad for children to see, not nice, that they are nightmare-producers. I disagree. I think exhibits of torture instruments and torture chambers are first-class attention getters and mnemonic devices for impromptu history lessons. How else could you better explain the strength of religious convictions, the ferocity of political convictions? History in books, a collection of facts to be memorized for an exam, suddenly becomes living, its importance real and understandable when a child sees a guillotine or an iron maiden with its cruel spikes. A child who sees how people were tortured is a lot more interested in knowing why they were tortured than a child reading a dreary listing of political, national, economic, and religious causes for something called the Inquisition, the Revolution, the Reformation, or persecution. Far from avoiding these exhibits, don't let your child miss seeing them.

GARDENS, BOTANICAL AND FORMAL Take the children to them. Greenhouses filled with tropical vegetation and jungley gardens give rise to what later may seem ancestral memories of the primitive and paradisaical. Topiary gardens, and the formal and elegant gardens nourish a sense of visual order and structure.

LET'S BE EUROPEAN

HOTELS Some of the out-of-the-way, low-priced hotels don't provide soap for their guests, so carry an emergency supply.

Hotel rooms often come furnished with antiques, marble-topped tables, and armoires in lieu of closets. Rooms with balconies are lovely to have and—although I always worry—safe, if you take every precaution with the children. Looking out from windows or balconies always interests children. Rooms that face on courts tend to be dark and quiet. Rooms facing the street tend to be bright and possibly noisy.

Always, if you don't like a room, speak up, ask for something else. Nicely, but firmly. If you want a room facing the Grand Canal, and this is what your travel agent said you could have, there is no point in being a martyr and shruggingly allowing yourselves to be put in a room facing a Venetian back street unless this is the only possible room available in the hotel. A discreet tip, as a last resort, may produce something else. I know this may be a racket, but if $10 is going to produce the room of my dreams on the spot, smiles and happiness all around, I won't feel anything but pleasure.

THE HALL PORTER OR CONCIERGE He is the man with the crossed keys on his lapel at the reception desk of your hotel. He is amenable to a generous tip for which he will do his utmost to get tickets for you, make reservations, get anything and everything repaired, tell you how to get everywhere and where to find everything. I think it's a good idea to tip the coincierge in advance. He is your key to happiness during your hotel stay.

FOOD As generalities go, food is generally wonderful in Europe and children love new things once they have tried them. They usually will try them if you do.

A mealtime simplifier is not to fight the system of the continental breakfast, which is usually included in the price of your room. If your children are egg lovers, have eggs for lunch—French eggs *en cocotte*, an English souffle, a Spanish tortilla (omelet) are always good choices, and other egg specialties in Europe are many and varied.

Children's portions (Kinderteller) are available in many restaurants and dining cars, cost less, and sometimes differ from adult fare. Europeans are appalled by wastefulness; leaving large quantities of food is considered a wild extravagance and somewhat rude. European waiters sadden noticeably when they see food not eaten. "Didn't you like it?" they ask sorrowfully, or gently reproach, "You didn't like it." To spare yourself these contretemps, ask for an extra plate and share your meal with the children or ask for a children's portion. Many restaurants have the admirable practice of giving you second helpings. The **Movenpick** chain, with restaurants mostly in Switzerland and Germany, is a Europeanized version of an ideal American family restaurant. The decor is lush, restful, charming, the food delicious, both adult and children's menus dazzling (the latter converts to an animal mask).

Meal hours in Europe often differ from ours. Lunch, for many Europeans, is the main meal of the day. For children used to the pattern of light lunch-early supper, requests for popsicles and milk-shakes can be answered by visits to the nearest equivalent of the *konditorei* or cafe wherever you are. Here you can have sandwiches, snacks, fruit juice, ice cream, coffee, tea, chocolate, pastries, cakes, pancakes. These usually are more pleasant for leisurely stops than the snack bars, milk bars, and ice cream parlors. Most Europeans take a coffee or tea break around 11 a.m. and follow the custom of the *gouter* or afternoon tea around 4 p.m. This is the time to feed the children in Spain—feed them *heavily,* because the dinner hour in Spain doesn't begin until around 9 p.m., often later.

Food seems to be incredibly good everywhere except in Germany, Luxembourg, Portugal, Greece, and Spain, where *what* you order can make the difference between a good meal and the unpalatable. From south to north, the standard continental breakfast of pastrylike rolls or hard rolls and coffee becomes heartier until it culminates in the lavish English breakfast and Scandinavian fare.

These random jottings will be expanded upon in the individual country listings. To cut costs in Austria, Germany, and Switzerland, besides the Kinderteller, there's also "Tellerservice" or plate service (each member of your family ordering the same meal and dessert for which reductions are often offered).

A special low-price menu for travelers, called the tourist menu, is available in France, Holland, and other countries. Most countries have moneysaving family and children's restaurant specials, such as Denmark's Danmenu, which offers a two- or three-course meal for much less than you'd pay for the same in the U.S.

Picnics: Europe is meant for picnics. Pop into the local bakery, fruiterer or supermarket; and bring along a paring knife. Swinging your locally bought basket or string bag, off you go to laze by rivers and castle ruins for as memorable an afternoon as one could possibly have. Whatever you do, please set aside one day somewhere for a picnic. (See also "Motoring" in Ch. 10.)

Station Buffets: These have surprisingly good food and quick service. There are first-class and second-class ones. Either are perfectly adequate.

Sharing restaurant tables: Although this practice is most common in crowded station buffets, it is also customary in snack bars and cafeterias, tables in the dining saloons of Channel ferries, tables in dining cars on trains, and often in inexpensive restaurants.

HOURS AND HOLIDAYS Shops, museums, palaces, and galleries keep regular but idiosyncratic hours. Most keep shorter hours on weekends and close one or more weekday afternoons. Many museums are open on Sunday but closed on Monday. The schedule for each place is different. Check in advance about small museums—many close without warning for repairs, as do castles and national monuments. If you make a list of things you want to see, the tourist board will tell you the regular hours these are open. Telephone anyway. Europeans always do.

In southern Europe, particularly in Spain, Portugal, and Greece, the shops, stores, offices all close their doors while everyone goes home for lunch to return several hours later. Forget shopping! This is the time to picnic in the park, look at the ruins, or have your hair done while a babysitter looks after the children.

Don't despair if a castle you want to see is closed or some out-of-the-way attraction is open only on Monday and you arrive on a Tuesday for four days. If you present your case to the tourist bureau, inquire about a suitable tip and add to it, doors will open in most cases. I leave it to you to project to yourself, your children, and the local tourist bureau that you don't for a moment suggest that anyone can be "bought" but rather that you are willing to reimburse whoever is concerned for his kindness and generosity in making available to you something that means a great deal. It is a nice gesture in such instances to send a postcard from America thanking the caretaker and signed with the names of all members of the family.

Don't be on a diet, dear parents, when in Europe. Especially in France or Italy, eat out and eat often because the food in these countries is really heavenly. Ask local residents where they eat. Cafes in France and Italy usually charge more if you sit at a table than if you stand at the counter.

Here is a list of items you cannot get abroad or which are extremely difficult or expensive to come by. Many of these items make wonderful presents both for American and European friends abroad: *Vermont maple syrup* (dehydrated maple sugar crystals, lighter in weight, can be obtained from Vermont Country Maple, Inc., Jericho Center, VT 05465).

Nestle's chocolate chips
Hershey's baking chocolate
Karo corn syrup
Sara Lee cheese cake
Thomas' English muffins
Oreo cookies
garlic powder
cream of tartar
canned tuna fish
Hellmann's mayonnaise
bagels
cornmeal
molasses
pecans
walnuts
cranberry sauce, cranberry jelly
jelly beans
pumpkin-pie mix
grape jelly
freeze-dried coffee
peanut butter
marshmallows
saltines
Fritos
canned corn beef

LANGUAGE English is understood in just about every large hotel, restaurant, shop, and sightseeing area abroad. However, do try to master and help your children learn some of the phrases listed for each country you are visiting. It's fun, and your hosts will appreciate it. Try to teach your children how to say please and thank you by saying them as often as you can. There's nothing to take the place of the old graces of courtesy and politeness in establishing open lines of communication based on those two words.

Off the beaten track, few people speak English. By all means brush up on your French, German, Greek, Portuguese, or Spanish, and take along a phrasebook. The trick is to have a little familiarity with a language, and then to try to speak and understand it with the willingness and open-mindedness of most children!

Great games for older children evolve from asking how names and things are spelled. Any telephone operator in America, for instance, would spell the name Anderson back for you as: *A,* Arthur; *N,* Nathan, and so forth. Depending on what country you're in, it can come out: *A,* Anton or Adolf or Adonis—to *Z,* Zoe or Zurich or Zenobia.

It's also fascinating to determine what sounds animals make in different countries. My 13-year-old collected these with great success. Listing origins of family names in German is another language-learning game. Meyer, Myer, Mier—farmhand; Schulz—deputy mayor; Ritter—knight; Hirschfeld—deerpark or deer field; Berg—mountain; Stein—stone; Grunwald—green forest. This can be played with any language, but works best with German, Dutch, the Scandinavian languages, and Icelandic.

Some children care about languages and are quick to play around with phrases. Some show interest only to communicate wants and needs. When a 6-year-old discovers that in Spain *dos* gets him two of something he likes, he'll learn enough Spanish to make his needs known.

CHURCHES There are American churches in almost all European capitals. Call the American Embassy for addresses and times of services, or consult local information booklets available from hotels or tourist offices. Some American churches have Sunday school programs; not all. Going to a European church can be a moving and beautiful experience. European children attend services with their parents, and perhaps your children would prefer to do this rather than go to Sunday school in an American church.

LAUNDRY AND DRY CLEANING For each country I have given details on how to handle the laundry and diaper problem. In general, laundry can be done anywhere in two days, one day, or even on a couple of hours' notice. In general, too, results are fine. However, no matter how articulate and detailed your directions may be, and no matter how reassuring the responses of laundresses or chambermaids, you're apt to find silk, shantung, jersey, linen, and drip-dries returned to you beautifully pressed but in a shrunken, permanently limp, discolored state. When in doubt, send things out to the drycleaner or do them yourself. Cottons and ginghams are done superbly. With the above exceptions, you'll have no laundry troubles if you make certain beforehand when and to whom the laundry should be given, how much it will cost, and when you can have it back. If no list is provided, or only a list in an unfamiliar language, just write out your list as you normally would—in English!

Don't feel you have to restrict your or your children's wardrobes to miracle fabrics. They are unbeatable in some combinations, but not all, and please remember that every wash-and-wear item is yours and yours alone to wash. Rinse out a few little things while your bath is running, if you feel like it, but remember that a vacation is a time to indulge yourself rather than doing the family wash in hotel bathrooms. However, you can hand over your personally hand-washed miracle fabrics for a touch-up pressing. Perhaps the first warning sizzle as the hot iron touches the fabric does the trick, but the clothes come back touched up to perfection.

Dry cleaning is a sometime thing. Sometimes the service is magically quick and done with old-world skill and perfection, but this is to be expected only if you are staying in first-class hotels or places where topflight cleaning services exist and someone can direct you to them.

If clothes are dusty and wrinkled, have them brushed or sponged instead of dry cleaned. Even in the most modest of accommodations, this service is readily available and usually takes no more than an hour or so.

Moral: Take as few clothes that have to be cleaned as you can. And don't overlook the old-fashioned trick of steaming clothes to remove wrinkles by hanging them above hot water.

BATHROOMS AND HOW TO FIND THEM When you say you want to go to the bathroom, many Europeans are puzzled. They think you want to have a bath. (There are facilities in many hotels where you can have a bath or shower even when you are not booked there.) Except in England, if you murmur some euphemism about wanting to powder your nose or go to the girl's room, you may be misunderstood. In large hotels, first-class restaurants, and other places where English is spoken you can discreetly ask for a ladies' room or men's room. Elsewhere, the word *toilette* (pronounced twah-let) or WC (scribbled on a piece of paper) will produce directions. In Spain, *servicio* is the operative word.

The phrase "spending a penny" is more aptly descriptive, although rarely understood outside of England (where it originated), because you should *always* have small change on hand for restrooms in restaurants, bars, hotels, gas stations, airports (!), train stations, department stores. If not vital to gain access into the toilets themselves, you'll need the pittance to tip the attendants.

Anent baths. Inexpensive hotel rooms in Europe come with a basin and running hot-and-cold water. The bath is down the hall and so is the john. You may have to put pennies into a slot to heat up the water or pay extra for using a public bath. A private bathroom about doubles the price of the room. If you're traveling with children, spend the money—have a private bathroom.

The bidet. Let's not mince words about it. It's an article designed for feminine hygiene commonly encountered in European bathrooms but virtually unknown in America. Pronounced bee-day, it looks vaguely like a john without a lid and the moment a child looks at his first bidet, he's bound to say, "What's that?" As far as I know, there is no evasive answer. Just say it's a bottom washer-offer. As long as you do not tell a child *not* to play with it, most children will fiddle around with it, be momentarily intrigued by a possible jetting fountain of water that may squirt up to the ceiling, and that probably will be the end of bidets as a topic of interest.

What to do when a small plaintive voice announces (a) in the middle of a strange city or (b) while driving along a foreign highway, "I have to go to the bathroom." I did not realize this was much of a problem until someone told me that she and her friends grabbed the nearest taxi and rushed either to American Express or the American Embassy "for lack of knowing what else to do." There are super-fastidious mothers who worry about strange john seats with which their children's bottoms may come in contact; and for them, I would recommend carrying around in their bags packets of disposable paper john-seat covers. Otherwise, the finding of a bathroom to me is no problem. I head for the nearest hotel, shop, cafe, child or children in tow, and ask if we can use their facilities.

Along highways, gas stations are not always happy to open up their restrooms to the family arriving with a full gas tank, having just filled up when a restroom was not in demand by the passengers. What to do? How do Europeans handle the "emergency" on the road? Same as we do at home. One gives the gas station attendant a tip, or an apple from the picnic basket can be proffered, and one uses the restroom.

On the road, if no cafe looms in sight, it's the field, the bush, the woods.

Europeans are more casual—less modest, if you will—about acceding openly to their children's needs than we are, with the exception of the British Isles and the Netherlands, where the bathroom functions of children are preferably always conducted out of public view. Elsewhere, no one seems to get uptight about this very natural circumstance.

SIGHTSEEING Divide your day into several parts for different activities. One day devoted solely to sightseeing is exhausting. If your children's interests and yours happen to conflict—you want to spend a few hours in a museum, while they prefer an amusement park—do avail yourself of the local babysitting, children's tour or young people's companion facilities. Be selective and do what you and your children really want to do. Think of sightseeing NOT as a list of things to get through, but as a directional guide that may lead you into seeing all sorts of other fascinating sights along the way. Your personal discoveries are just as special to you and your children as the place you may have set off to see. Walk! Explore! Enjoy! Be adventuresome!

From 8–14, children may be mildly interested in scenery. Under 8, scenery is remembered, but means little at the time. Under 5, scenery means almost nothing.

Do not expect your children to go into raptures about your own pet pleasures. Don't tell them what they should be enjoying. Ask them what they think of things. Don't, above all, confuse the learning process with misbehavior, i.e. when a child wants to play with the gravel in the driveway of a world-famed chateau and shows little interest in the chateau itself—or if a child wants to play with the squirrels or pick the flowers instead of looking at the horseshow, the zoo, the museum—don't drag him away crossly saying that he can play with the gravel and the squirrels at home. Children learn only when they play and explore, a process many parents find hard to understand. Children like to get their bearings in strange surroundings. A squirrel is less overwhelming than a castle or a hippopotamus; gravel feels good to touch. Children like to touch and see things at eye level before they can comprehend a larger milieu.

It is challenging to channel your child's interests. Try to extend them into your own. Encourage his interests and fantasies and you both will be rewarded at best by blissfully happy moments and memories of travel. At least, your child will be more receptive to looking and learning.

SHOPPING FOR YOUR FAMILY Most of the time, I've never quite had the courage *not* to bring a camera or *not* to go shopping, but both of these pursuits can be tiring to an extraordinary degree. I have, however, found that it is much better to buy only things *you* and *your family* want, unless you happen to see something completely and infallibly right in every way for someone else you love dearly. No long list of souvenir presents, please. These take up much too much time and effort. If you add shipping and excess-baggage charges and carfare to the cost of items bought abroad, you may be nettled to know that local stores at home often turn out to be the best places to stock up on Italian pottery or French gloves.

Things I would recommend buying are things to wear, such as sweaters; collectibles, such as dolls—even boys like character dolls, fishermen, soldiers; or things you will get the most daily use from, that will serve as continual reminders of your trip abroad, that your children can associate fondly with the countries they visited. And what might these things be?

Things for the table, perhaps. A cream jug and sugar bowl, figurines for a centerpiece, or a silver salt cellar. Whatever you choose, be sure it is something you will use. I buy pictures, books, boxes, baskets, things for the house, some antique, some contemporary. I have learned to buy only things that would be remarkable in America, things you would buy if you saw them in a store at home. If I truly love something and if the children love it, I buy it. What seems like an extravagance at the time may turn out to be something you will show to everyone and your children will rush to show their friends.

▶ **Note:** Check with your local passport office before you go for duty-free allowances and restrictions for you and your children.

SHOPPING FOR YOUR FRIENDS Giving is a lovely and generous habit. A child should be encouraged to give and realize the joy of giving. Tangible proof that one has been remembered in a far-off place is heart-warming to the recipient. The twinge of pain at not having brought back a souvenir to someone is not restricted to grownups. Children experience this distress as well. But presents for Granny and Grampa, the aunts and uncles, the doorman, teachers, classmates, friends, the cleaning woman, the football coach, the neighbors, and five more presents in case there are still more people to be remembered or whose birthdays in one's absence should be acknowledged? Souvenirs in the 25¢ bracket—some charming, most of them consume so much searching time that one becomes desperate and settles for the local little souvenir ghastlies—end up costing a lot more than you should waste on things that aren't worth the trouble of buying in the first place. Parents should come to the aid of their children in such matters.

When my children were smaller, I solved the problem by hoarding the individually packaged containers of jam provided with continental breakfasts (waiters were obliging about producing extras) in various countries and labeled in various languages. Other things foreign, bearing foreign labels, are the individually boxed samples of perfume; Italian nougat *(torrone)* in little decorated boxes; tiny rectangles of Swiss chocolate (wrapped with miniature postcard graphics); and Viennese chocolate yummies called Mozartkugeln, wrapped in foil with assorted pictures of Mozart indicative of the varieties.

As my children grew older, multiples of the same object didn't satisfy their earlier need just to give something. They wanted to give something special and personal, and came up with a solution agreeable to them and to me, a solution that has an infinity of variations that can be put together by children from 4 on. The basic ingredient is foreign matchboxes obtainable anywhere abroad with foreign labels, scenes, and decorations—perhaps lined with scraps of material or colored paper, perhaps the striking sides pasted over—to be filled with little objects: tiny-size, tiny value coins; sprigs of heather or alpine flowers; little seashells, stamps; charms; foreign words on a scrap of paper; a chip of quartz picked up on a mountain path; a baby pine cone; a glass animal; doll's forks and spoons; a brass button found in a hotel lobby—every object had a special meaning or an association. Simple or elaborate, as the boxes were filled with one or more objects, the recipients' names were written on the underside and the boxes stacked in a biscuit box. Assembled en route, or assembled at home with components collected while traveling (for emergencies, I bought extra chocolates and almond sugar babies), these matchbox surprises evolved as personalized, funny, endearing presents, objects of the heart.

CHILDREN'S CLOTHING AND SHOE SIZES ABROAD There are wonderful clothes for children abroad. In England, children's clothing is generally measured in terms of inches, and on the Continent children's clothing is classified by age, but sizes are far from being standardized.

European shoes are made on different lasts from American shoes, and while they are fine for children with C, D, and E widths, children with narrow feet are difficult to fit with ready-made shoes. If your children have any foot problems and you are planning to stay for several months or longer, do buy ahead. Mothers who have ever had the problem of lace-up baby shoes, will be delighted to find baby shoes that zip on and off distributed in many fine stores in northern Europe (Au Printemps, in Paris, has specially nice ones).

It is very hard to find any accurate list of conversions for children's clothes abroad, but I have done my best to prepare one from many sources of cross-checked information. Sizes vary so much from country to country that these statistics—although helpful, I feel—have in my experience varied by as much as one whole size in two shops on the same street. I can only say that for the best results you have to take along a list of measurements and a tape measure or—best of all—your children in tow.

England

Coats and ***dresses*** are measured by the length from collar to hem, in inches. An approximate gauge for the sizes in comparison to the age of the child is: 18″ = 2–3 years, 20″ = 3–4 years, 22″ = 4–5 years, the sizes going up two inches each time.

Sunsuits and ***trousers*** with tops to them are again measured in inches according to the length from shoulder or collar to the bottom of the trouser. An approximate gauge according to the age of the child would be: 27″ = 2–3 years, 30″ = 3–4 years, 33″ = 4–5 years, etc.

Socks are also measured by inches, but it is quite easy to find the size if the shoe size is known: 6″ = 6–7 shoe, 6½″ = 8–9 shoe, 7″ = 10–11 shoe, 7½″ = 12–13 shoe, 8″ = size 14 shoe. These cannot be gauged according to age.

Blouses and ***pullovers*** are measured according to the bust measurements, again in inches: 24″, 25″, and so forth. ***Shirts*** for boys, however, are not so easy, and unless the size is known the only guide is the age of the child: 000 = 2–3 years, 00 = 3–4 years, 0 = 4–5 years, size 1 = 5–6 years, 2 = 6–7 years, 3 = 7–8 years. 000 is called treble O.

Hats. If the actual size is not known, the measurement round the crown of the head in inches is enough: Size 6¼ = 20¼, 6⅜ = 20½″, 6½ = 20⅞″, 6⅝ = 21¼″, 6¾ = 21⅝″, 6⅞ = 22⅛″, 7 = 22⅜″.

Pajamas are sized according to the chest measurements only.

Nightgowns and ***dressing gowns*** are measured according to the length from collar to hem.

Undershirts are measured according to the length.

Blazers are sized according to the chest measurement.

Shorts for boys are measured the same way as shirts.

Skirts and ***trousers*** are measured according to the waist measurements in inches.

Junior misses' dresses and coats. American sizes 8, 10, 13 and 15 are equivalent to British sizes 7, 9, 10 and 12.

Teen-age girls' dresses, suit, and blouses. American sizes 10–32, 12–34, and 14–36 equal British sizes 32, 33, and 35.

Boys' suits, shirts, and ***overcoats*** are measured the same in England as they are in America—that is, from size 36 in suits and overcoats and from size 13 in shirts.

Shoes in England for children and for young girls and boys, although wider, sometimes run a size or two smaller in length than American shoes, and it is definitely advisable to try them on before buying.

Stockings are the same size in America as they are in England, with the only noticeable difference being that English stockings for girls have longer tops.

Continental Sizes

Shoes and Sandals for Children and Young Girls

American	3	4	5	6	7	8	9	10	11	12	13	1	2	3	4	5
Continental shoes	19	20	21	22½	23½	25	26¼	27½	28½	30	31½	32½	33½	34	35	36

Continental sandals	22	23	24	25	26	27	28	29	30	31	32	33

Teen-Age Boys' Shoes

American	1	2	3	4	5	6	7	8	9	10
Continental	34	35	36	37	38	39	40	41	42	43

(If you are buying shoes for friends at home, better trace the outline of their foot before you leave!)

Children's Dresses and Coats

American	2	4	6	8	10
Continental	2	3	5	7	9

Dresses and coats for junior misses are measured the same as English sizes.

Teen-Age Girls' Dresses and Suits

American	10–32	12–34	14–36
Continental	36	38	40

Teen-Age Girls' Blouses and Sweaters

American	32	34	36
Continental	38	40	42

Boys' Suits and Overcoats

American	36	38	40
Continental	46	48	51

Boys' Shirts

American	13	13½	14	14½
Continental	33	34	35–36	37

Socks and Stockings on the Continent?
Tell them your child's local foreign shoe size and let the salespeople figure it out for you.

In ***Germany,*** children's clothing sizes are reckoned by height in centimeters. There are approximately 2½ cm. to an inch.

Age (U.S. Size)	German
2	92
4	104
6	116
8	128
10	140
12	152
13	164

Teenagers should try small women's sizes:

7	34
9	36
11	38

THE CARE AND TRAINING OF YOUNG FINANCIERS If you give your child a weekly allowance, be sure to give him some money to spend in the local currency on arrival and departure in each country. Familiarizing your child with handling traveler's checks and foreign currency, letting him work out his own spending arrangements independently—he may want to get you a secret present (don't feel hurt if he doesn't't)—is the best possible training you can give him. If he loses his travelers' checks, see that he goes through all the motions necessary for their recovery.

HOBBIES AND COLLECTIONS From the age of 6 on, children are enchanted with collections that may be forgotten in a day or may eventually lead to lifetime hobbies, or just to being a contented pack rat like myself. If your child is interested in collections, your trip provides all sorts of possibilities. If your child hasn't shown any interest in collections, he may now decide to begin one. A few ideas for the beginnings of a valuable collection:

Dolls; foreign trains; miniature lead soldiers, knights in armor and heraldic trappings; doll's house furniture; miniature china, silver, pewter objects; wooden and china animals; foreign costumes; carved wooden figures; handcrafts. Or eclectic miscellany of subjective value, such as: Postcards; maps; stickers—luggage, airplane, hotel, boat; autographs; matchbooks and matchboxes; menu cards; foreign recipes; souvenirs; stamps; coins; badges and pins.

CULTURE SHOCK Some people deplore "the Americanization of Europe" in which the formal, charming, and graceful have been abandoned in favor of the efficient, comfortable, and practical. The homogeneity of airports is one example, the proliferation of hamburger bars and milkshake snackaterias another.

Others deplore the *lack* of Americanization. You won't always find total air conditioning even in the best hotels; hotel furniture may appear old-fashioned or not what it's like in the U.S. Elevator buttons may confuse you—R/C, for instance, is an abbreviation of *rez de chaussee,* or ground floor. The European way of writing the number one like a little tent may be confusing. Bills and service charges may be bewildering, as can be the order of street numbers and zip codes.

Culture shock at its simplest level is irritation or disappointment at other ways of doing things. It's supposed to happen to people who have stayed three or four months in a country. But one may be overwhelmed by culture shock in a day. It can happen anywhere. But everything works out wonderfully well if I make it a challenging game to set a good example for the children, to transcend all upsets and potential piques with as good a grace as possible. You will all be happier if you parents can remember that it's up to you to transmute clouds into silver linings. Try it, anyway. Just knowing you are doing the right thing does impart a nice sense of joy.

TELEPHONES Using the telephone in Europe can be expensive and/or frustrating. Here are a few tips for low-cost, keep-your-cool dialing. Some hotels belong to the *Teleplan* network which has fixed maximums for surcharges on overseas calls which otherwise can double or even triple the basic toll, but many do not belong to this AT & T program. Teleplan is operative throughout Ireland and Portugal; the Marriott and Hilton chains in Europe; the Comfort Hotels in Britain, France, and the Netherlands; Novotel Hotels in Austria and Germany; Golden Tulip Hotels in the Netherlands; and Inter-Hotels in Switzerland. Except in Portugal or West Germany, you can also minimize hotel surcharges by using your Bell credit card. You can eliminate hotel charges for international calls by using public telephone centers at post offices, airports, train terminals. The idiosyncrasies of new and old pay telephones for local and international calls will be mentioned in individual country chapters.

VALUE ADDED TAX Referred to as TVA in France, Mehrwertsteuer or MWSt. in Austria and Germany, BTW in the Netherlands, MOMS in Denmark, IVA in Italy, this is a sales tax, more commonly known as VAT. When leaving countries other than Greece, Iceland, Italy, Portugal, Spain, Switzerland, you and yours, 15 or older, as non-residents, are entitled to a refund on the tax applicable to manufactured goods you have bought within the country and are taking out of the country—anywhere from 6% on printed material bought in Germany to 35% on luxury items bought in Ireland. Some countries have a minimum amount required to be spent in a single store that will entitle you to a rebate. Others have no minimum. To be eligible for a refund, you must have tax-free receipts obtained when shopping to produce at the border point to show to special customs officials when leaving. Some countries, however, simply deduct the tax, as long as your purchases are sent directly to the airport or to your home address. Tax refunds are payable in cash when travelers leave Sweden, Austria, and France. If you charged your purchases to your credit card, you'll have to wait to get a tax-refund check. In France, if you pay by credit card, your refund is automatically deducted. Other countries will refund the tax money by check in the currency of the country in which you bought the goods. This process may require you to send forms stamped at your departure point back to the store where you purchased your goods. The process is slow. **Deak Perera Co.** (630 Fifth Ave., New York, NY 10111) can cash foreign checks promptly and usually charges less than most banks. Getting a rebate may be more trouble than it's worth. However, it is recommended that you find out from each country's National Travel Information office before you leave just what their system about VAT refunds is.

BE A GOOD GUEST The best guest is someone who, without losing his own identity, fits in, has a wonderful time and shows it. It's up to you to be an ambassador, your family a small traveling embassy of good will. If this sounds corny to you, it's only because I'm expressing myself badly. What I'm saying shouldn't sound trite.

The American Express News Bureau summed it up nicely by saying: "Every American man, woman or child in a foreign land is . . . an important representative of 200 million fellow citizens. . . . Safe advice is to be twice as polite as seems courteous at home." Hear! Hear! A corollary is that well-mannered children may appear to be oafs if they unwittingly don't observe certain niceties, e.g.: It is still customary abroad for young girls to stand whenever an older woman enters the room. Boys, of course, should also be reminded to stand up on such occasions!

Vacations are more public than home life. On a trip you are conscious of seeing your children through the eyes of other people. The more you love your children, the more concerned you are that other people like them. Vacations sometimes make you sterner about their behavior than you would be at home. Remember though, that it is your own sensitivity you sometimes have to guard against, not your children's behavior. Other people in hotels and restaurants have children too. Traveling, manners should be much as they are at home with a little more emphasis than usual on the comfort of other people. Ask other people to tell you if your children are disturbing them. You'll find you'll make many more friends for your children by saying, "Please tell me if they are bothering you," than with any number of apologies after the event.

People are so nice to you and your children that you may want to send them Americana; subscriptions to some of our better magazines; or pictorial calendars of our natural wonders. Sending flowers from your next stop, writing a note and then writing again from America, are gestures that constitute the best present of all—your thought and appreciation.

Please bear with me, for perhaps I have gone a long way round to say what you knew already—that you get from travel as much as you give to it.

Since this is a reference book written for you, the Europe-bound family traveler, I'd be very grateful for any suggestions or advice that you might have, and if you should have any special problems about traveling with your family abroad, do let me know.

In the meanwhile, this seems to be a good place to wish you and your family the happiest and most rewarding European holiday imaginable.

AUSTRIA

In Austria, land of *Gemutlichkeit,* even during the briefest visit you and your children will delight in the friendliness and joy of living in a country where the passport that will get you the furthest carries the identification "Occupation: Child." There is a childlike spirit here; everyone waves at trains, and church towers often flaunt cheerful colors—vermilion or green.

Austrians are fond of light wines, light-hearted dancing, and lots of music—so children who like music, and most do, find rapture here.

Austria is known for sports festivals, marionettes, and Tyrolean costumes. Children fancy the tall-feathered caps of Austrian hunters (considered the best rifle marksmen in Europe). For families who enjoy hunting and fishing, Austria is a fabulous game preserve. If you prefer to look at animals rather than hunt, you can explore wild game parks, lovely beyond words, with special dwarf donkeys to ride. In winter, skiing and skibobbing (rather like bicycling in the snow) are superb; in summer, you can sail on the Alte Donau, an arm of the Danube converted to a lake. You can also "sail" in the sky by taking up gliding. And wait until you see all those castles, many of which are simply super to stay in!

INFORMATION ABOUT AUSTRIA Before you go, contact the **Austrian National Tourist Office** (545 Fifth Ave., New York, NY 10036; Tel: (212) 697–0651 or 287–8742) or its branches in Chicago, Los Angeles, and Portland, for rafts of brochures. For art lovers, an invaluable free booklet is *Museums and Art Treasures in Austria*.

With no fee to you, **Dial Austria** (3 East 54th St., New York, NY 10022; Tel: (212) 838–9677, or outside New York State, toll-free 800–221–4980) a private company, books hotel reservations, and can secure tickets for *"everything except tickets for the Salzburg Music Festival which only can be done through the Austrian National Tourist Office or from the Ticket Bureau in Salzburg."*

The **Austrian National Tourist Office** (Hohenstaufengasse 3, A–1010 Wien 1 Austria) heads 9 provincial centers: **Vienna** (Wien) Fremdenverkehrsverband fur Wien, Kinderspitalgasse 5, A–1095 Wien

IX; Tel: (222) 43 16 08); **Burgenland** (Landesfremdenverkehrsverband fur das Burgenland, Schloss Esterhazy, A–7000 Eisenstadt; Tel: (2682) 3384); **Carinthia** (Kärnten) Landesfremdenverkehrsamt Karnten (Kaufmanngasse 13, A–9010 Klagenfurt; Tel: (4222) 80 5 11); **Lower Austria** (Niederosterreich) Niederosterreichische Fremdenverkehrsverbung (Paulandergasse 11, A–1040 Wien IV; Tel: (222) 56 55 18); **Upper Austria** (Ober Osterreich) Oberosterreichisches Landesfremdenverkehrsamt (Schillerstrasse 50, A–4020 Linz; Tel: (997) 66 30 21); **Salzburgerland** Landesverkehrsamt in Salzburg (Mozartplatz 1, A–5010 Salzburg; Tel: (6222) 43 2 64); **Styria** (Steiermark) Amt der steiermarkischen Landesregierung, Landesfremdenverkehrsabteilung (Herrengasse 16, Landhaus, A–8010 Graz; Tel: (316) 831 or (316) 22 87); **Tyrol** (Tirol) Tiroler Fremdenverkehrswerbung (Bozner Platz 6, A–6010 Innsbruck; Tel: (5222) 20 7 77 or (5222) 20 7 59); **Vorarlberg** Landesfremdenverkehrsamt Vorarlberg (Romerstrasse 7/I, A–6901 Bregenz; Tel: (5574) 22 5 25). Together, they have produced several booklets listing all local family services—ski kindergartens, daily kindergartens, the pensions, inns, and hotels that have reduced rates for children—as well as an astounding variety of activities available to tourists. For example, **Burgenland** has a booklet about special interests and *hobby courses (Hobbykurse)*. There are courses in pottery *(Topfern)*, cooking *(Kochen)*, glass engraving *(Glasritzen)*, making nativity figures *(Krippenfiguren herstellen);* doll handicraft *(Puppen basteln);* rustic painting *(Bauernmalerei);* painting glass in Tyrolean designs *(Hinterglasmalerei);* making paper-flower bouquets *(Blumengestecke aus Papier);* working with modeling clay *(Modellieren mit Knetmasse);* painting *(Malen)*, drawing *(Zeichnen);* macrame; wood carving *(Schnitzen);* ornithology, printing *(Druck)*, music *(Musisch)*, working with semi-precious stones *(Edelserpentinarbeiten)*. Or, the Tyrol has a booklet listing all their holiday hobby courses *(Hobby Urlaub)* including model airplanes *(Modellflugsport)*, weaving *(Handwebe);* and every known sports activity, including gliding *(Segelflug)* and hang-gliding, which is confusingly the same term used for kite-flying *(Drachenflug)*. Each province has a huge list of festivities *(Veranstaltungen)*.

Most of this information, classified as special interest, is in German.

For information in Austria, check with your hotel concierge or with the local tourist office. Every city has one, generally open 9 a.m.–6 p.m. daily; weekend service depends on the season and demand. Major sources are: in **Innsbruck, Fremdenverkehrsverband** (Burggraben 3; Tel: 25715); in **Salzburg, Stadtverkehrsburo** (Auerspergstr. 7; Tel: 74620). And in **Vienna, Austria Information,** (Margaretenstrasse 1; Tel: (0222) 57 57 14); Mon.–Fri., 9 a.m.–6 p.m.; Sat. 9 a.m.–1 p.m.; closed Sun.; don't forget to pick up the list of weekly attractions called *Diese Woche in Wien;* an information service is operative (daily 9 a.m.–7 p.m.) in the **Underground Opernpassage** (Tel: 431608); another at the **Airport** (daily 9 a.m.–10:30 p.m.), and still another at **Praterkai,** the landing point of the Danube steamers (9 a.m.–9 p.m.). For motorists, two bright-red railroad cars with information lettered on them are open 9 a.m.–9 p.m. from Apr.–Oct.; at the western autobahn exit to Vienna and on Highway 306 as you approach Vienna from the south. There is also an information counter at the railroad station in every town. And three Youth Info-Centers, with up-to-the-minute news on Vienna's many youth clubs, pop concerts, sports events, jazz festivals, movies, operas, concerts, plus counselors to solve all problems. Open weekdays from 11 a.m.–7 p.m. (Schlossbergasse 13, Tel: 821501; Geymullergasse 18, Tel: 471312; Schadeckgasse 1, Tel: 579131). *Information service for motorists?* The *Osterreichische Automobil-Motorrad Und Touring Club (OAMTC)* with headquarters in Schubertring 1–3, 1010 Vienna; Tel: (222) 72 99; and regional offices in Linz, Salzburg, Innsbruck, Dornbirn, Graz, Klagenfurt.

Reservations and tickets for the Bregenz, Salzburg, and Carinthian festivals and for the Salzburg Palace concerts and marionette performances must be arranged for separately in Dec. and Jan. (about six months ahead) through the tourist office.

HEALTH, WATER, AND FOOD Health standards are very high. Vienna has the cleanest air of any of the world's capitals. Water is safe throughout Austria and the tap water in Vienna is icy and delicious. But if you are subject to upsets or worried, drink bottled water when visiting small villages. Avoid unpasteurized milk.

Main-course specialties are *Wiener Schnitzel,* sauteed, breaded veal cutlet; *Naturschnitzel,* ordinary veal cutlet; *Wiener Backhuhn,* breaded, fried chicken; and *Knodeln* or *Nockerln,* dumplings or noodles. But Austria's true specialty is dessert. And everything preferably with "schlagobers," the Austrian word for whipped cream. You may get snow blind from those mountains of whipped cream, the sum total of calories may peak the Alps, but there is nothing like a *Konditorei,* the ultimate in pastry or bakery shops. These have many small tables at which you are served your choice of pastry and coffee, hot chocolate, or cocoa *(kakao).* There are *Palatschinken,* thin, rich pancakes filled with almonds and chocolate or apricot jam; *Kaiserschmarren* (imperial fluff), a slightly thicker pancake, shredded and mixed with fruit, jam, or cottage cheese and dusted with sugar; *Zwelschkenknodel,* a distinctive Viennese confection made of damson plums whose stones are replaced by sugar lumps and the fruit snuggled into a light dumpling overcoat; pastry boats filled with whipped cream and fragrant wild strawberries; melt-in-the-mouth *Strudel,* the flakiest of pastry filled with apple, cherry, sweetened cheese, or mincemeat; ice creams and cream puffs. There are *Torten: Sachertorte* (rich cake, layered with jam and iced with chocolate); *Linzertorte* (with almond paste); *Doboschtorte* (many layered); and *Kuchen* (plain cakes), like our coffee cake. *Guglhupf* is a light sponge cake. *Fasching-*

skrapfen, a fluffy, crispy apotheosis of our jelly doughnut, is a seasonal specialty during *Fasching,* the carnival season. You can also get all sorts of iced fruit juices in many *Konditoreien; Himbeersaft* (raspberry juice) is wonderful, so is *Apfelsaft* (apple juice).

The most celebrated of all pastry shops in **Vienna** is **Demel** (Kohlmarkt 14, near the Hofburg Palace gates). Open daily 11 a.m.–7 p.m.; on Sun. the choice is a bit more limited. Both **Demel** and **Sacher Confiserie** (Karntnerstrasse 38) will pack and airmail cakes for you which arrive in perfectly edible condition. You might also try **Lehman** (Graben 12); **Heiner** (Wollzeile 9) or its sister establishment (Karntnerstr. 21); or **Gerstner-Koberl** (Karntnerstr. 6). These yummeries also serve snacks. The **Hotel Sacher**'s coffee shop, the **Cafe Tirolerhof** in the Augustinerplatz, the **Cafe Landtmann** on the Ring are splendid for light refreshments. For dinner with your older children, there's the Palais Palffy (Josefsplatz 6), which houses the sumptuous **Spanish Riding School Restaurant,** named in honor of, but having no connection with the famous institution just around the corner. Also in the Palais Palffy are the **Palffy Keller,** a cozy, rustic nook, and the **Rotisserie,** planned for guests in a hurry. The **Weisser Schwan** (Nussdorferstr. 59) features Viennese specialties and venison, boar, hare, and other game dishes. The outdoor courtyard is most attractive and the White Swan's cuisine is really special. Filling, inexpensive, and therefore crowded at lunchtime is **Zum Laterndl** (12 Landesgerichtstrasse), near City Hall. Traditional cafes—where you can sit and read the newspapers provided, "jause" (snack) and just relax in dim, old-fashioned interiors, sipping *eiskaffee* (coffee with ice cream and whipped cream in an old-fashioned ice cream soda glass), or an *einspanner* (coffee, with powdered sugar, served hot in a tall glass with lots of whipped cream) or *kapuziner* (coffee with so much cream that it is the pale dun color of a monk's robe) and munching on bread, eggs, frankfurters, pastries at a marble-topped table—are simple, informal, stay open late, open early. Recommendations: **Cafe Museum** (Friedrichstrasse 6), daily 7 a.m.–11 p.m.); **Cafe Sirk** (Karntnerstrasse 53), daily 10 a.m.–midnight; **Kleines Cafe** (Franziskanerplatz 3) Tues.–Sun., 1 p.m.–2 a.m.; **Cafe Schwartzenberg** (Karntner Ring 17), daily 7 a.m.–1 a.m.; **Cafe Braunerhof** (Stalburggasse 1), Mon.–Fri. 7 a.m.–8 p.m., Sat., Sun. 7 a.m.–p.m.; concerts Sat. and Sun., 3 p.m.–6 p.m.; **Cafe Central** (Herrengasse 14) daily 7 a.m.–10 p.m.; closed Sun. and holidays; summertime terrace, closed in winter; **Cafe Tirolerhof** (Tegetthofstrasse 8), Mon.–Sat., 7 a.m.–9 p.m., Sun. 10:30 a.m.–8 p.m., close to the Spanish Riding School. In **Salzburg,** if the children haven't already foundered themselves on the tasty soufleed dumplings *(Salzburger Nockerln)* or the wafer-thin pancakes *(Palatschinken)* the outstanding place for snacks and sweetmeats is **Cafe Tomaselli,** overlooking the Alter Markt (Old Market Place). A ride up to **Cafe Winkler** on the Monchsberg is a must! Another fabulous establishment is **Kon-**

ditorei Zauner, in **Bad Ischl** (Pfarrgasse 7), although it needs an address no more than the Statue of Liberty.

BABY FOOD Wide assortment and variety of Nestle's, Hipp, and Felix vegetables, meat, fish, mixed meat, rice and vegetable dinners, fruits and fruit desserts in baby and junior foods. Available in pharmacies, drugstores, and supermarkets.

Nestle's, Pomil, Milupa, and Altemil milk powders; Dr. Rey's nutritional maltmilk; Nestle's farina, apple and milk porridge, Kathreiner's malt cereal, Hipp's *Vielkorn-Flocken* (corn flakes) and *Kindergriess* (children's semolina); Hipp's Vitamin A and C enriched vegetable and fruit syrups to mix with the formula, four varieties—*Karotten-Fruchte-Trank* (carrot-fruit-drink), *Baby-C-Trank, Karotten-Trank, Roter Fruchte-Trank* (red fruit drink, labeled *eisenhaltig* or iron-rich)—these are what you find most often. The white-lettered Hipp sign with its bright-red background and picture of a darling plump baby with jar of baby food captioned *meine Lieblingskost* (my favorite food) tops a display of food that one doesn't need much German to comprehend. That *Karotten* are carrots and *Spinat* spinach and *Fruchte* fruit and *Salat* salad and *Reiscreme* creamed rice and *Tomatenreis* tomato rice is pretty obvious. *Fruhstuck* is breakfast; *Brei* means puree; *Gemuse* is vegetables (as in *Gartengemuse* or garden vegetables), *Obst* is another word for fruit (as in *Obstsalat* or fruit salad); *Allerlei* means of all sorts (as in *Gemuse-Allerlei,* or mixed vegetables). *Menus* means just what it says—a menu or complete meal. *Leber* is liver; *Huhn,* chicken; *Kalbfleisch,* veal; and *Rindfleisch,* beef. *Fruchte-Dessert* contains mixed fruits. *Apfel mit Bananen* (apples and bananas), *Ananas* (pineapple), *Aprikosen* (apricots), *Pfirsiche mit Honig* (peaches with honey). That's the spectrum of baby food displayed with neatly labeled files telling you exactly at what age (usually a bit later than our pediatricians recommend) you can start your baby on whatever it is. The fruit and vegetable syrups, for instance, are labeled *Fur Babys ab 6. Woche* (for babies from 6 weeks), or *Fur Babys ab 6. Monat* (babies from 6 months). *Ab 8. Monat,* babies progress to Junior-Kost or Junior food. You see? You're reading German with no strain at all. For junior tykes, you have *Vanillecreme,* that needs no explanation. New additions are *mit,* or *m. Butter* (with butter), or *Rahm* (cream). An 8-month-old gets such goodies as *Rahmspinat m. Frischei* (creamed spinach and fresh egg), *Eiernudeln* (egg noodles), *Lammfleish* (lamb), *Krautersosse* (herb sauce—ah, those gourmets), *grune Bohnen* (green beans), and *Schinken* (ham). The Junior foods are plainly marked "Junior" on a blue-banded label running around the bottom of the jar. The Nestle's products may be labeled in French—if so, refer to the section on French baby food.

Nestle's, Felix, and Hipp all seem palatable to babies and equally digestible. American mothers report that their babies seem content with the European age-food correlations.

DIAPERS AND LAUNDRY The word for diaper is *Windel.* A disposable diaper is called *Papier Windel* (pronounced pap-peer win-dell—rhymes with a bell). Large pharmacies stock disposable diapers as do department stores, baby corners of supermarkets, and baby specialty shops (where you can get cloth diapers).

The most widely sold brand of ***Disposable Diapers*** is Molny's *Schwedenwindel,* imported from Scandinavia. They are adequate, but not in the same class, as Pampers. However, they are soft, inexpensive, and can be bought by the yard, rolled up in perforated triangle shapes that you can easily separate. You can buy Pampers in pharmacies if you want to spring for the extra cost.

There are no organized ***Diaper Laundries.*** If you have cloth diapers, ask your concierge for the nearest Laundromat *(Wascherei)* where you wash them or where you can get someone else to do them for you. *In either case, diapers must be rinsed!*

EMERGENCIES MADE EASY ***Pharmacies,*** or *Apotheken,* rotate evening and Sun. duties; if one is closed, it will have a notice indicating the nearest one open. The concierge can also tell you which pharmacies are open.

The **Gerstenberger** chain (Westbahnstrasse 26, Vienna; Tel: 933197) with branches everywhere, once came to my rescue, minutes after my telephone call, with baby food and baby bottles when my supplies had been lost.

Medical facilities are excellent. ***Doctors*** are listed in the telephone directory under ***Arzte,*** but you can call the American Embassy or Consulate any hour of the day or night for advice and information about English-speaking doctors and dentists particularly recommended for overseas visitors. In Vienna, the **Embassy** is at Boltzmanngasse 16 (Tel: (222) 315511); the **Consulate** is at Friedrich-Schmidt-Platz 2 (same Tel). In Salzburg and Innsbruck, telephone the Tourist Offices, or ask the hotel concierge. The new **Pediatric Clinic** (Lazarettgasse 14; Tel: 4800) is superb. An underground garage at **General Hospital** (Alser Str. 4–9; Tel: 4800).

MAGIC FAMILY HELPERS (see Information for good news about child care and entertainment facilities.) Informal but reliable babysitting arrangements can be made with the concierge of your hotel or with the local tourist office, which must, however, be given a day's notice. (Costs are about 80¢ to $1 an hour). If you are staying in a castle, you can book a babysitter at the same time that you make room reservations.

Vienna goes all out to make a mother's life carefree, with all sorts of reliable and well-organized facilities for children. ***Babysitters*** are available at the **Babysitter Center** (Tel: 652893) and at another student babysitting organization (Tel: 573525). Many students are willing to serve as companions and guides and to take the children to the magnificent Prater fun park or to the playgrounds (Kinderspielplatzen) in the city parks.

The ***kindergarten*** situation is admirable. Kindergartens with English groups or at which English is spoken feature games, ice-skating in winter, and rhythmic dancing. Some kindergartens have nursery facilities for day care of babies and toddlers. Fees (for half-days or full days) are extremely modest. There are many fine kindergartens, and the following in Vienna have special facilities for English-speaking children: **Alt-Wien** has a central information bureau at its kindergarten (Mariahilferstrasse 88 A; Tel: 930174), with 20 branch nurseries including those at: Salesianergasse 2 (Tel: 733194) near the Hilton and Intercontinental hotels; Strohgasse 9 (Tel: 7348752); Sechsschimmelgasse 5 (Tel: 3480384); and Martinstr. 69 (Tel: 4269944), where the restaurant is located. Fine nursery-kindergartens include **Christl** (Wasagasse 19; Tel: 3479434); **Cinderella,** in downtown Vienna (Neutorgasse 13/1; Tel: 6340265); **Dornroschen** (Lindengasse 47/2/9 A; Tel: 939376; **Schwarzenbergplatz** (Prinz Eugenstrasse 4; Tel: 6540924); and **Neubau** (Zieglerg 18; Tel: 936484). Neubau, just west of the city center, is open year-round and offers ski courses. Advance telephone booking is required.

In winter, children from 2 up can be accommodated in the children's ski schools, and ski kindergartens, located in all the larger ski centers (see ''Fun and Games'' and ''Information'').

Personalized Services: If you are in Vienna during Carnival time, Dec.–Feb., and don't have a costume for the children or yourselves, or if Dad didn't bring a dinner jacket for an opera premiere, reach for the telephone directory: Clothes and costume rental services are listed under *Kleiderleihanstalten.*

Instruction: Hobby courses in painting Tyrolean designs *(Bauernmalerei)* and painting rustic designs on glass *(Hinterglasmalerei)* are available throughout the year in many locations. For information: Freizeitborse, Bahnhofstrasse 23 Bregenz. If you're there in Sept.–Nov., you can sign up for a course in making nativity figures *(Krippenfiguren)* and doll handicraft *(Puppen basteln).* For information: Festspiel-und Kongresshaus, Bregenz.

The Fremdenverkehrsverband in **Lienz** (Tel: (4852)4747) can put you in touch with *model airplane makers and flyers.* At **Mayrhofen/Zillertal,** site of a fabulous *mountaineering school,* you can also travel on and learn how to operate a 1916 *steam locomotive* on summer Fridays and Saturdays. Ask at the Bahnhof for information about *Amateurlokfahrten* (Tel: (5285) 2362). In **Vorarlberg,** in the Arlberg region at Lech and at St. Anton, there are *Alpine schools.* For information, contact Alpinschule Arlberg, Walter Strolz, A–6580 St. Anton.

Riding instruction for beginners and advanced riders, show-jumping, dressage instruction, *trekking on Haflingers or Icelandic ponies* and many other courses are possible in *Amplfwang,* the "horseriders' village," 60 miles from Salzburg; with two indoor riding schools, a *children's pony school,* a night-riding paddock; also swimming, bowling, riflery; *gymnastics courses;* curling, sauna, and tennis.

In **Mondsee,** a town on the northwest shore of the lake in the Salzkammergut area of Upper Austria, the *Mondsee Sailing School* offers courses for children 8–16 in sailing and windsurfing. Details from Mondsee und Salzkammergut-Reisebetreuung, Rainerstrasse 11, A–5310 Mondsee, or directly from Segelschule, A–5310 Mondsee, Robert Baum-Promenade.

Worthy of special mention is the **Children's Ski School** at the mountain-top Tyrolean town of Mayrhofen, with 30 instructors, fluent in English, who specialize in classes for the littlest skiers, age 4 up. The program operates from 9 a.m.–4 p.m. For a 6-day program, lifts, child-care and lunch, or a 3-day program, the cost is modest. For older children and grown-ups, there are two 2-hour lessons daily, and the 6-day package price for this instruction is also inexpensive. The Austrian National Tourist Office can give you more details.

HOLIDAYS FOR CHILDREN ON THEIR OWN In one of those charming wood and stone mountain chalets in Styria, you'll find **Kinderpension Prabichl** (8794 Prabichl/Steiermark, Laufstrasse 59). This attractive family-style guesthouse for children takes in paying guests 3–15 for games, swimming, hiking, mountaineering, campfire evenings and nature studies. Elsewhere in Austria, there are ***Baby Pensions*** and ***Kinderheime*** which differ from *Kinderhotels* in preferring a two-week stay as a rule—although shorter stays can be worked out and longer stays of one, two, or three months are common.

When is a *Kinderheim* a holiday resort and when is it a convalescent home? You'll have to check to find out. The following *Kinderheime* are holiday resorts for children: In **Axams, Landeskinderheim** takes babies up to 2½; several weeks' stay required; open all year. In **Sankt Florian, Baby-Pension** (St. Florian 129) welcomes babies up to 2½; open year-round; telephone Mrs. Monika Heidlmair (404) for further details. In **Sankt Leonhard bei Freistadt, Privat-Kinderheim** takes boys and girls 3–14; minimum stay four weeks; open all year. And in **Schiltern,** children 4–12 are welcomed during July only at the **Institutum B.M.V. der Englischen Fräulein.** Lucky children get to stay at Schloss Schiltern, the town castle. All qualify under the high standards set for childcare facilities in Austria.

CHILDREN'S CAMPS *Students Abroad Summer Ski and Tennis Camps* for beginners or experts 12–19 are available in *Kaprun in Salzburgerland*. Language classes in French, German, Italian are also available, as are excursions in Austria and to Paris, London and Italian resorts. For information about travel, study and camping programs in Europe, contact *Ski/Tennis Camp Headquarters, Students Abroad, Inc.*, 179 North Fulton Ave., Mt. Vernon, NY 10552.

The Austrians entrust their children to less expensive camps with specialized interests—riding, tennis, sailing, summer skiing—located all over **Salzerburgerland.** These camps come under the aegis of **Young Austria** *(Osterreichisches Jugendferienwerk),* as does the International Junior Ski Camp, with Christmas and Easter sessions based in **Kaprun** and **Zell am See** and the **Kitzsteinhorn,** with programs for children 8–16. For the same age groups, there's also a riding and tennis camp based in **Abtenau** in Salzburgerland during the summer. Also, there's a children's *fat farm* for overweight children who want to shed pounds and inches during a three-week summer session at **Obertauern.** For information contact **Thayer-Sportcamp Organization, International Jugend-Ski Camp** and Young Austria, both at Alpenstrasse 108 a, A–5020 Salzburg, Austria.

For children 8–16, there's also the **Gloria-Felix Holiday School,** based in Chalet Gloria in **Lech/Arlberg** in **Voralberg,** with two-to-four week courses in intensive German, swimming, hiking, summer skiing, arts and crafts. For details, contact Summer Camp Program, Chalet Gloria, P.O. Box 44, A–6764 Lech/Arlberg.

Young Austrian friends tell me they enjoyed a riding camp in Lower Austria, with workshops in dancing, painting, music, rhythm and drama at the **Reitclub** A–3351 Weistrach 123.

CASTLES AND OTHER HAPPY FAMILY ACCOMMODATIONS Castles are an Austrian specialty. There are more castles, palaces, and monasteries to stay in than in any other country—each with its lovely heritage of paintings, art, and furniture—all authentic, many of intriguing medieval architecture. Comfortable, luxurious; fine food and personal service. Castle proprietors treat you and your children as their guests, rather on the order of an astonishingly pleasant house party. A *Schloss* is a residence of nobility. A *Lustschloss,* more innocent than it sounds, is an aristocrat's summer or winter palace away from home. A *Jagdschloss* is a hunting castle, timbered and rustic, with beamed ceilings and open fireplaces; marvelous armor, canopied beds, carved furniture, copper kitchen utensils, and lots of antlers are decorative specialties. A *Schlosspension* simply means that meals are included in the bill. *A Gastschloss* is another way of saying a castle-guesthouse.

There is great variation in the arrangements that can be made, depending on the time of year, the ages of your children, whether your children will be sleeping in a separate room, and the length of your stay. Most castle-hotels prefer that you stay two or three days. Not all are willing to take the responsibility of hiring a babysitter in advance, although on arrival satisfactory arrangements can generally be worked out.

But make sure all your arrangements and reservations are worked out well in advance. The Austrian National Tourist office has a lengthy list of castle hotels.

If you enjoy living legends, you will find a castle in **Aschach an der Donau,** reportedly built by the Devil for Dr. Faust in the space of a single evening and redone as a hotel in the sixties. **Faustschossl** (Tel: 245) has large, lovely gardens along the Danube, heated swimming pool, water sports, fishing, and tennis; open all year. Castle car will meet you at Linz.

Bad Hall: Schloss Feyregg (Tel: (7258) 2591 and 2427), with its own farmlands, barns, and wooded gardens, is an updated baroque castle. The furniture is a tasteful blend of antique and contemporary, the doors painted in the regional style; ceilings arched and vaulted; dining room warmed by a porcelain-tile stove; all rooms with TV, telephone, and private bath. Delicious meals and soothing rates. Transport around the area can be arranged. Riding, swimming, fishing, and tennis nearby.

In **Bernstein,** near the Hungarian border, is **Schloss Bernstein** (Tel: (03354)220) a real special. High on a forested crag with a view of four provinces, this authentic 12th-century castle-fortress conceals behind its massive walls not only a brilliantly imaginative garden, but a new baronial luxury—an Olympic-size swimming pool. Marvelous historical collections, a family ghost for the children to boast about braving, and even an ancestral torture chamber. Two dozen rooms, all with private bath. Attractive interior. Open Apr.–Dec.; do make reservations well in advance. Roebuck and wild-boar hunting are among the many specialties offered, along with trout fishing and exploring the castle grounds.

Looking for a Renaissance palace in **Braunau am Inn?** Try **Schloss Hagenau** (Tel: (07720) 3421), fronting the idyllic Stausee. Set in a handsome park offering troutfishing, swimming, and hunting; delicious food. Owned and operated by Baron Handel. **Durnstein** thought to be the loveliest village of all the Wachau, has **Hotel Thiery Zum Richard Lowenherz** (Durnstein an der Donau, Tel: (02711)212), an inn and restaurant dating back to the 13th century, backed by a steep crag on which the ruins of a medieval castle, in which Richard the Lion-Hearted was once imprisoned, are now crumbled. Charming guesthouse on the Danube, with heated swimming pool, sauna, solarium; moderate rates; excellent food and delicious wine from home-grown grapes!

If you're in **Frohnleiten,** you and your children should enjoy **Schloss Rabenstein** (Tel: (3126)2303). The oldest inhabited castle in a province of castles, it crowns the cliff above the Mur River. Built on the ruins of a Roman fort, all scarlet and gold and rococco and exhaling the substance of history. Only guests are privileged to explore it—no sightseers allowed. Beautifully furnished; all rooms have private bath. The armor and tapestry are magnificent; in its Knight's Hall, it even has a ghost—a happy ghost of a medieval princess whose life was saved by a pet raven that plucked from her mouth a piece of cake that had been poisoned by a disappointed beau! The only drawback as far as children are concerned is that dinner is served around nine o'clock in the vaulted dining room. Sigurt Reininghaus, the owner-architect-proprietor of the castle, and a most charming host, will send a car to meet you at the railway station of Bruck; and because he takes no more than a dozen guests at a time from mid-May–Sept., arrangements probably can be made for a babysitter. The maids wear Styrian festival costumes, all green and gold, and you can have breakfast on one of three vine-covered terraces overlooking the old Roman road that curves along the banks of the Mur. Note old church and village within walking distance. Swimming pool and golf-course nearby; chamber music concerts in June.

Fuschl: Schloss Hotel Fuschl (Tel: (06226) 253), is an entrancing 18th-century hunting lodge-castle crowning a gently sloping hill that curves to the edge of Fuschl Lake. Children can rowboat or motorboat on the lake, explore the beach, ride, or play tennis. Wonderful woods and parklands to explore on foot or by horse-drawn hunting cart. Hunting and fishing, summer, fall, and spring; skiing, sledding, skating in winter. Accommodations in a hunting lodge next to the main lodge-castle—I think the balcony room is the nicest—with gaily painted, cottagey furnishings; accommodations also on the lake. Splendid dining room, extremely fine meals.

High above Innsbruck, in **Igls,** is **Schlosshotel Igls** (Tel: (05222) 77217); enclosed swimming pool; sauna; massage; all winter and summer sports. In **Igls-Patsch,** on the old Roman road through a green valley near Innsbruck, is the family enclave of the Counts Thurn and Taxis, **Hotel Grunwalderhof** (Tel: (05222) 77304). Heated indoor and outdoor swimming pool, sauna, tennis, nearby ski runs and golf course; hearty welcome for American families; cosy chalet atmosphere. Get one of the 16 rooms with private bath. Open May–Sept.; Dec.–mid-May. At **Irdning,** in the heart of Styria, **Schloss Pichlarn,** white and turreted, is a world in itself with indoor and outdoor swimming pool, sauna, 9-hole golf course, tennis courts, riding horses and much more. In **Kapfenberg,** an interesting stopover between Vienna and Graz is **Burghotel Kapfenberg.** This fortressed residence looks about as welcoming as a three-story dungeon. Older children and adventurous parents may share my delight in this startling monster. The proprietor, Count Josef Stubenberg, has installed a fine kitchen and suites with private bath; reasonable. A supervised baby nursery and children's playroom are featured at **Kitzbuhel's Schloss Lebenberg** (Lebenbergstrasse 17; Tel: (5356) 4301). Enclosed swimming pool; sauna; sun terrace; skating on artificial ice; tennis courts. Direct connections from Innsbruck and Munich airports. For the same price, there's **Schlosshotel Munichau** (Reith bei Kitzbuhel; Tel: (5356) 2962), a 14th-century Bavarian hunting lodge, small and beautiful with outdoor pool. Open Dec. 18–Mar. 15, end of May–Sept. **Kuhtai: Alpenhotel Jagdschloss Kuhtai** (Tel: (05239) 201,225) is the 15th-century hunting lodge of Emperor Maximilian the

Great. In the mountains, it offers riding, fishing, shooting, swimming; in winter, horse sleighs and skiing. Directed by Count and Countess Stolberg; imperial luxury; 90-foot banqueting hall; accommodation for 90 people, but only 12 baths. Open July 1–Sept. 15; Dec. 20–Apr. 20. Moderate rates.

Lofer: Schloss Grubhof (Sankt Martin, Lofer; Tel: (6588)249), a princely manor with private swimming pool; architect owner; pillows for 56; all rooms with bath. Reasonable. In **Moosburg,** you might try the very special Carinthian pension, **Schloss Moosburg** (Tel: (4272)8206). Open June–Oct., this 15th-century castle has a private beach, miniature golf, hunting, fishing, tennis courts, indoor swimming pool and sauna, and water sports. All rooms with private bath.

In my opinion, the most exclusive and beautifully managed of all castle hotels is at **Neumarkt,** some 16 miles from Salzburg. The road may be slow, but the going is beautiful approaching **Schloss Sighartstein** (Neumarkt am Wallersee; Tel: (6216)251). Surrounded by a moat, this baronial mansion for 500 years has been the hereditary seat of the Counts Uiberacker. Wonderful collection of 15th-century armor, heraldic trappings, and hunting trophies. Beautiful grounds; swimming and fishing on the Wallersee. From Easter to late autumn the drawbridge is open to welcome guests—no more than 18 at a time.

Oberalm: About eight miles from Salzburg is the little 14th-century **Schloss Haunsperg** (Tel: (06245)2662). Antique (but comfortable!) furniture; huge family suites with wonderfully private and spacious sitting rooms; interesting Baroque chapel; estate park and garden; big music room with piano for young musicians only; tennis court; riding, swimming, fishing nearby. The owner is an amateur cellist who delights in arranging chamber music parties and can tell you everything about Salzburg's concerts and music festivals. Open year round. A charming country retreat is **Pinzgau's Jagdschloss Graf Recke** (Wald im Pinzgau; Tel: Neukirchen/Wald (06565) 417) originally a hunting lodge and now directed by the Count and Countess Recke. Near Jagdschloss Kuhtai and the beautiful Krimmler waterfalls, one of the highest in Europe, this schloss has heated swimming pool; mountain meadows, large garden; hunting, fishing, tennis, minigolf, riding, all winter sports (year-round skiing nearby), deer feeding, sauna, movies, and folklore evenings—offered either on the premises or in the little resort village five minutes away. Open late Dec.–mid-Jan.; late Feb.–Sept. Down-filled pillows for 40 heads; 15 rooms with private bath.

Portschach: Hotel Schloss Seefels (Portschach am Worthersee; Tel: (4272) 2377), set in a large park on the lake, has a private natural beach, a tennis school, nearby golf, riding, all water sports, and water-skiing school. Open May–Sept. Also (Tel. (04272) 2816) is **Schloss Leonstain,** a 15th-century castle offering three tennis courts, a tennis school, nearby golf, private beach, and all water sports, plus weekly chamber music commemorating Brahms in the castle courtyard. Open May–Sept.

If you aren't booked for one of the 57 rooms at the historic and exclusive **Goldener Hirsch Hotel** in **Salzburg,** try: **Hotel Fondachhof** (Gaisbergstr. 46, Salzburg; Tel: 20906), a serene site with vast park, swimming pool; open Mar.–Oct.; 22 rooms with private bath. **Gastschloss Monchstein** (Monchsberg 26; Tel: (06222) 41363), perched on a hill overlooking Salzburg, large garden; tennis court; open Apr. 1–Oct.; deluxe, small, all rooms with bath; breakfast only. **Schlosshotel Klessheim-Kavalierhaus** (Salzburg-Siezenheim; Tel: (06222) 31177), a seigneury with beautiful parklands, lovely view, swimming pool, 9-hole golf course, tennis court, and all the luxuries one would associate with the former winter palace of Archduke Ludwig Viktor; President Nixon slept here. **Schlosshotel St. Rupert** (Morzgerstr. 31; Tel: (06222) 43231), with sweeping views and parkland. All these are, literally, little palaces.

Sankt Donat bei Klagenfurt: Castle Hochosterwitz, crowning a steep, rocky cliff, is the most dramatic of Austrian fortress castles. Reached by a winding lane that passes through 14 successive tower gates, it dominates the landscape. "It is no wonder that Walt Disney used it as a model for the castle in his film of Snow White," says one guidebook, but I think you can take this with a grain of salz, because Disney's castles are as many and far afield as George Washington's beds.

Pleasant restaurant in the top courtyard with waiters in Carinthian folk costumes. The castle keep has a small museum and a collection of 16th-century armor. Medieval costume festival in Sept. Prince Franz Khevenhuller, whose family stronghold this is, has been known to accept a few house guests from time to time; perhaps a gracious letter of inquiry would get you past those 14 tower gates as guests rather than day trippers. It may be a slim chance, but the rewards are great.

For tranquillity and aristocratic charm in **Steinakirchen am Forst** try **Schlosspension Ernegg** (Tel: (07488) 214). An hour's drive from Vienna, this lovely manor house with arcaded court is the seat of the counts of Auersperg. Fronting the castle is a 1000-year-old linden tree, allegedly the oldest and largest in Austria. Private swimming pool, fishing, hunting, clay pigeon shooting, riding, and tennis. A car can meet you at Amstetten station, and you can also rent cars for local excursions. Open May–Sept. A dozen double rooms with private baths; rates, including delectable food.

Velden: Hotel Schloss Velden (Velden am Worthersee; Tel: (04274) 2655), a former stronghold and elegant country palace practically lapped by the sun-warmed waters of the Worthersee. Exalting gardens; moonlight sailing regattas for younger children to watch. Many travelers, among them the Princess Royal, have said they would never forget their stay there. The bathing enclosure, motorboats, sailboats, rowboats, and pedalboats are ideal for children; tennis, golf, riding, fishing, waterskiing. Excellent food in the cafe-restaurant built on a terrace overlooking the lake; a dower-house **Cavalier House** across the garden offers excellent accommodations. Open May–Oct. Hotel Schloss Velden itself has 150 rooms, about ⅓ of them with private bath; the best are in its four picturesque turrets. Reserve well ahead here; special and very popular.

Wolfnitz: you might try **Schloss Seltenheim** (Tel: (04358) 49218), a 13th-century Carinthian fortress castle, besieged during the early Turkish invasions but now reconstructed. Riding, hunting, fishing, and private beach. Open June–Sept., it offers only five apartments, each with two rooms that sleep four to five; fully equipped kitchen, bathroom; laundry and service included.

Would you like to **rent a house** in the Alps, near a lake, an apartment in Vienna? Simply contact the Austrian Tourist Office here, which will supply information and suggestions. Then write away to the Landesverkehrsamt or Landesreiseburo—being sure to send return airmail postage—asking for listings of *available* houses, apartments, or accommodations, stating exactly what you have in mind, the ages of your children, and the price you wish to pay and underscoring the word *available* in your letter (or you'll get listings of places perhaps already rented). If possible, negotiate rents through the tourist bureaus—you're more likely to pay the prevailing nontourist rates. Be sure, *very* sure, when making arrangements, to have put in writing all extra charges (tourist bureau fees, heat and light costs, taxes, telephone) and, when you arrive, to make a list of all existing damage so your children won't be blamed for it and yourselves charged extra. Such is the advice of friends who have spent four summers and two winter vacations in Austria with their three children. They recommend the experience as blissful and money-saving.

Farmhouse *(Bauernhof)* accommodations are singularly attractive in Upper Austria in **Attersee,** with its lake surrounded by little hamlets; in **Altmunster,** where there's a sailing and windsurfing school; in **St. Konrad,** near Gmunden in the Salzkammergut, near the Grunau game park, where **Bauernhof Etzeldorfer,** a large farm surrounded by meadows and pastures, offers delicious farm-fare; in **Scharnstein** in the Alm Valley; at the **Bauernhof Traxenbichl** in Muhldorf, with a windowbox at every window; in **Grunau** at the **Bauernhof Sieberer Karoline;** in **Hinterstoder** in the Pyhrn-Eisenwurzen region at **Pension Gressenbauerhof,** a secluded retreat near a beautiful Alpine village with many leisure-time facilities; in **Windischgarsten,** a valley resort with indoor tennis and squash courts, a summer tobogganing track *(Sommerrodelbahn),* a funicular railway, indoor and outdoor swimming pools, hobby courses and nature trails. N.B. **Pyhrn-Eisenwurzen,** an idyllic region in Upper Austria, specializes in Bauernhof accommodations featuring organic food (milk, vegetables, cider, fruit, home-made bread, home-cured bacon) and if you're a horse-lover, you can stay at **Reitergut Weissenhoff,** a stud farm with stables, indoor riding school, a network of bridle paths, and riding instruction on horses and ponies.

CAMPING AND CARAVANING Austria has hundreds of summer camping sites, some with swimming pools, some with beaches, many with restaurants and provision stores. An increasing number of winter facilities are also available. Consult the national and local tourist offices.

ATTRACTIONS FOR CHILDREN IN VIENNA Walt Disney made a film of *The Miracle of the White Stallions,* but the children can see it all for themselves at **The Spanish Riding School** (Hofburg). Marvelous performances by riding masters whose white Lipizzan stallions perform the pirouette, the capriole (an upward leap, all legs off the ground, with an outward kick of the hind legs at the height of the leap), the courbette, and other feats that must be seen to be appreciated. This medieval art of classical horsemanship has hardly changed for over 400 years, and is unique in Vienna. Performances in grand style with musical accompaniment at Hofburg Palace; Sun. at 10:45 a.m., Weds. at 7 p.m. and ½-hr performances Sats. at 9 a.m., Sept.–end of June. You can watch these cleverest of all horses being trained Tues.–Sat., 10 a.m.–12; the stalls can be visited from 2 p.m.–4 p.m. daily except Sun. Sun. performances, about 2 hrs. long, mid-Mar.–end of June, and from Sept.–mid-Dec.; training periods and stables open Sept.–end-June. Be sure to secure tickets in advance. Young horse lovers will also enjoy exploring the city by fiacre, or **horse-drawn carriage,** which can usually be found around the Ringstrasse. And it's fun to stop to listen to Austrian bands in regional dress playing in the Graben, a mall next to St. Stephen's Cathedral.

Vienna has more art treasures for its size than any other European area except the Vatican. For older children, the **Kunsthistorisches Museum** (main building, Maria-Theresienplatz), one of the greatest museums in Europe, is a must. See the paintings first. It has the world's largest collection of Brueghels; take a special look at his painting, *Kinderspielen* (Children's Games). The **Albertina** (Augustinerstr. 1) is the world's largest collection of engravings, drawings, and prints; a complete review of old masters and graphic art of the 20th century; unique collections of Klimt, Schiele, Kokoschka, and the mystical Alfred Kubin are often revelations to the young. Hours vary daily. (If you go around lunchtime, you can include the **Glockenspiel's** performance at Hoher Markt at noon.) The **Academy of Fine Arts** (3 Schillerplatz) has works of Cranach and Hieronymous Bosch whose imagination and clarity of detail children like. For special interests, there are museums featuring everything from fire-fighting equipment to dog-breeding to medical history; you name it. For a magnificent panoramic view of Vienna, children can climb the 365 steps up to the watchman's chamber in the *south tower* of 700-year-old **St. Stephen's Cathedral,** its structure slaked with wine rather than water, and open daily 9 a.m.–5:30 p.m. The *north tower* also has a fine view and is reachable by an elevator, thank goodness, and contains a huge bell, weighing 19.5 tons, which you can also see daily, 9 a.m.–5:30 p.m. The new **Coffee Museum,** only one of its kind in Europe, was planned with school children's interests in mind but is getting raves from parents. The Tourist Office will supply information.

The **Hofburg** (Imperial Palace of the Hapsburgs) has a fabulous storehouse of treasures. Small admission fee; hours subject to change. In order of interest, I'd suggest: **The Treasury** *(Schatzkammer),* with the jeweled crown of the Holy Roman Empire, imperial cross, and the entire Hapsburg collection of relics; the **Collection of Weapons and Old Musical Instruments,** containing Beethoven's pianoforte and pianos owned and played by Brahms and Lizst; the **Imperial Apartments** of Emperor Franz Joseph and Empress Elizabeth; the **Imperial Tableware and Silver Collection** (Hoftafel und Silberkammer); the **Austrian National Library** *(Nationalbibliothek),* superb Theater Collection; and the **Hofburg Chapel,** performances by the Vienna Boys' Choir (Sun., 9:30 a.m.); mid-Sept.–end of June only; secure tickets in advance from Wiener Sangerknaben (Hofburgkapelle, Schweizerhof, Hofburg), or from Dial Austria.

The **Uhrenmuseum der Stadt Wien** (Schulhof 2) in an old house; thousands of watches and clocks, all in perfect working order. Open 10 a.m.–1 p.m. Tues.–Fri., Sat. 2 p.m.–6 p.m.; Sun. and hols. 9 a.m.–1 p.m. Closed Mon.

Beethoven's house (Probusgasse 6), not to be confused with the Beethoven Museum at Molkerbastei, will delight young lovers of his music. The composer's home in the early 1800's, it is now a little museum.

A world music center, Vienna offers concerts, recitals, ballet performances, indoors or outdoors, every day through the summer: **symphony concerts** every Tues. and Thurs., at 8 p.m. in the arcaded courtyard of the neo-Gothic **City Hall;** every Wed. and Sat. at 8:15 p.m. in the **Schonbrunn Palace;** and every Fri. and Sun. in various palaces throughout the Inner City. Program listings available from the city tourist office in the underpass near the State Opera. The **Theater an der Wien** features light opera every Mon., Wed., Fri. and Sat. from mid-July to end of Aug. Comes Sept., and the **Vienna State Opera,** the city's concert halls and operetta theaters (Raimundtheater, Theater an der Wien, People's Opera) carry on with their fall-winter programs.

It would be worth going to Vienna just to see **Schonbrunn Park, Palace, Zoo, and Gardens.** Don't take the guided tour; just walk on your own through the 40-odd rooms (out of 1400) that are open and then wander through the park gardens. Operas in the private theater mid-July–mid-Aug.; evening concerts in the summer every Wed. at 7:30 p.m. in the Galerie des Glaces; pleasant cafe-restaurant in the courtyard; pheasant garden; and the climbable Gloriette colonnade—all delights to the young. Allow most of the day. Palace apartments shown daily. Nearby is the **Wagenburg**—a collection of royal coaches and sleighs—deserving a quick look.

Belvedere Palace and Park features a **Baroque Museum,** a museum of 20th-century paintings, medieval Austrian art, **Alpine Garden,** and **Son et Lumiere** spectacle of Austria's history on summer evenings. For children 8-and-over. Ask the City Tourist Information Center. The **Prater** and its **Volksprater** (Fun Fair), dominated by a huge Ferris wheel, are famous throughout Europe. You can explore the park by fiacre; stop at a lake and rent a boat by the hour; watch puppet shows; or cheer at the race track or sports stadium, six square miles of fun and frolic; cramjammed on Sun. **Donaupark,** its gardens massed with roses, is spread like a garland along the Danube. Chair lift; lilliputian train; and a lake with a stage performing light opera on summer evenings. **Revolving cafe** (one full turn every 20 min.), and **revolving gourmet restaurant** (one full turn every hr.), high up in an 850′ tower overlooking the Carpathian Mountains, the city, the Danube, and Schonbrunn Palace. For a nominal fee you can ride the elevator to the checkroom level, and walk down to the **viewing terrace** beneath the (expensive) gourmet restaurant. The upper-level cafe has better prices; for a snack, try off-hours. On ground level is a **minigolf course** and enchanting **playgrounds,** beautifully supervised, where children up to 12 can play happily and safely at penny-candy fees; also an **Indian Tepee Village,** a real playing ground of old-time trains, streetcars, and fire trucks; a pond for rowing; jungle jims, swings, and turntables. Sponsored as goodwill gestures by two local banks! A great first-time experience for children. The **Volksgarten** is where all the Viennese children and their nannies go. The new **Laaer Berg** park offers pollution-free cars, monorail, gardens, 10 restaurants and snack bars, 11 exhibition halls with constant entertainment, super children's playgrounds. In summer, teenagers like to dance at **Burgring,** a park club. The **Camera Obscura** in the Neubaugasse, Vienna-Neubau, has a tireless disc jockey and short films by young film-makers. These are the most way-out rendezvous for the young. Saner spots are the **Volksgarten-Dancing** in the Ringstrasse not far from the city center and **Jazz-Freddy,** in the Schottenfeldgasse in Vienna-Neubau, where you can hear every style of jazz. My children's teenage chums tell me I don't have to provide more than street addresses because "everyone *knows* where these discos are." Okay, so be it. The aquarium, **Haus des Meeres,** in the **Esterhazypark,** may not be as new or grand as Schonbrunn's, but I find the exhibits and atmosphere more interesting.

In summer, children adore the beach life—sailing, pedalo boats, canoeing—the sand-castle world along the Alte Donau, an arm of the Danube converted into a lake, lively with food and entertainment; two sparkling-clean swimming pools, (one with, and one without, artificial waves). From mid-May–Sept., the **Strandbad Gansehaufel** (Moissigasse 21) is *the* fun beach for children. Great poolside conviviality. Punch and Judy **open-air theater** on all but rainy days. (From Oct.–Apr., the Urania Punch and Judy puppets are playing at Uraniastr. 1. Even though all plays are in German, children usually enjoy them.) Children will also enjoy the **Ottakringer Marionette Theater** (Ottakringer Strasse 150); **Walcher's Marionette Theater** (Gurkgasse 34); and **"Arlequin" Marionette Theater** (Cafe Mozart, Maysedergasse 5). The **German Krone** and the **Rebernigg Circus** may be traveling your way. Ask the Tourist Office. From mid-Feb.–mid-Mar., the ATA Circus plays at the Stadthalle (Vogelweidplatz 14; Tel: 95490). City-sponsored walking tours through the Vienna woods, library and museum visits, games and other activities are programmed in summer for Vienna's children. The City Tourist Information Center has details. Mid-Sept.–June is the season for the **State Opera,** which has performances of children's interest, like "The Nutcracker"; the **Volksoper** includes in its repertoire matinee performances children will enjoy such as "Hansel and Gretel"; the **Vienna Boys' Choir** can be heard every Sun. at the Hofburg Kapelle.

ATTRACTIONS FOR CHILDREN IN SALZBURG The **Salzburg Music Festival** (July and Aug.), the **Salzburg Mozart Festival** (Jan.), the **Easter Music Festival, Salzburg Palace Concerts** of medieval and Renaissance music, and Baroque chamber music, from Apr.–Oct. and during the Christmas season, have to be experienced to be believed. Official festival program is released in December; Mailorder requests opened and filled by the first week in January, when you have the best chance of obtaining seats. Apply for tickets to the Austrian National Tourist Office or the Ticket Bureau, Salzburg Music Festival. A-5010, Salzburg.

The **Salzburg Marionettes** (Schwartzstrasse 24; Tel: 72406)—the famous puppet creations of Professor Hermann Aicher, whose family has been making and exhibiting marionettes for over 200 years—perform such things as the *Nutcracker Suite* and *Fledermaus* with great charm and appeal for all ages. From Apr.–late Sept. Flake out for coffee and pastry at **Tomaselli's** pastry shop in Getreidegasse; the **Cafe Konditorei** in the Alter Markt Square; or at **Cafe Glockenspiel** on Mozartplatz.

Schloss Hellbrunn and its gardens are filled with hidden fountains and waterpowered mechanical devices just waiting to drench you. Most children adore getting themselves and you wet. Guides will play up to the children and show them all the water tricks performed by statues. Also featured is the **Monatschlosschen,** a pleasant castle with a folklore museum; at the foot of Hellbrunn Hill is a zoo, dating back to the 15th century. Conducted tours in Apr., Sept., Oct. 9 a.m.–4:30 p.m.; May–Aug. 8 a.m.–6 p.m. In July and Aug., night visits on Mon. and Fri., 8:30 p.m. Best summer-evening display of illuminated fountains plus castle concert, July–Aug., Wed. and Sat., 8 p.m.

The **Carolino Augusteum** museum (Museumsplatz 6) displays Roman and Celtic treasures, folk art and handicrafts, musical scores and instruments; very special. **Haus der Natur** (Franz-Neumayr/Platz) freaks out all kids with its natural and unnatural history collections.

Folklore, folk-song, and **folk-dancing** evenings are well worth letting the children stay up past their bedtime for. Yodeling, zither music, singing saws, harps, and the rollicking Schuhplattler and other national dances. You and your children will be asked to join in during the intermission or after the last number. Summers at the **Stieglkeller** at 8:15 p.m. Mon. (mid-July–mid-Aug.), Wed., Sat. (June–mid-Sept.); at the **Fortress Restaurant** at 8:30 p.m., Tues., Thurs. and Fri. (June–Sept.); and at the **Sternbrau,** 8 p.m. Fri. (June–Sept.)

Half the fun with **Hohensalzburg Fortress** is in getting there—by funicular railway. With children, I'd skip the conducted tours, but do try to hear the 180-pipe barrel organ—the Bull or *Stier* of Salzburg. Don't miss the torture chamber—intriguing to children 8 and up. The railway leaves from Festungasse 4; 7:30 a.m.–11 p.m., every 10 minutes; winters, less often. **Schloss Mirabell** and the Castle gardens have Sun. morning band concerts, and sometimes folk dances. For hours, ask the Stadtverkehrsbuero (Tel: 74620). The performance of **Everyman** *(Jedermann)* on the Domplatz, in front of the baroque Cathedral takes place Sun. 5 p.m. during the Festival, and on Aug. 15. The **Cathedral's treasury** is also worth seeing.

You and your children will enjoy the conducted tours of the **Durnberg salt mines** near Hallein—a 2½ hour treat for the adventuresome; buses start from the Mirabellplatz. Wear sneakers or your stoutest shoes and most comfortable clothing. At the mine entrance you are given a protective coverall and fezlike hat. Then you walk straight into a mountain of salt, illuminated by the guide's lamp. The children will be intrigued to find that raw salt is not as white as they thought it was. The highlight of the expedition, which leads you through an other-worldly land of subterranean lakes and little caves, is a slide down a salt chute. You are provided with a backward leather apron (your own portable sled) and leather gloves for clinging to the guide ropes; then off you go whizzing through a dark tunnel to tumble out at the other end onto a mattress. A thrilling ride for 6-year-olds and up (younger children not allowed), but I walk down the stairs that are thoughtfully provided. Open May 1–Sept. 30, 8 a.m.–6 p.m. Check with the tourist bureau to see if a local **sword dance**—a specialty of the area and fun to watch—will be scheduled at the time of your visit. The **Hallstatt salt mine,** a 10-minute walk from the mountain station of the Salzberg cable railway, has been in operation for 2800 years, is the largest salt pit in Austria, has an interesting exhibit on salt mining but is less exciting to explore. The **Dachstein Ice Caves,** to which you are hoisted by the cable car, are freezing cold in midsummer, but I know children who think they're magnificent.

ATTRACTIONS FOR CHILDREN ELSEWHERE IN AUSTRIA The castle museum with alchemists' workshop, prehistoric and folkloristic collections in **Bernstein** is a standout. In **Bregenz,** the Festival on Lake Constance during July and Aug. is the big attraction. Operas, operettas, ballets, concerts, serenades, chamber music, and theater. You might also try the cable car ride up **Pfaender. Dalaas/Wald** in **Klostertal,** Vorarlberg offers a 435-mile train ride in miniature, replicating the round-trip from Salzburg to Vienna via Linz on its **Minieisenbahn's** 20-min. ride. **Feldkirch** features **Schattenburg,** a castle-fortress-museum, brass bands, and summer-resort attractions in a medieval setting. At **Gan-serndorf** (Tel: (02282)7261/7262) about 20 mi. from Vienna, a safari and adventure park with all the game you'd see in Africa, viewed from your own car or safari bus. Open daily from April–Oct., from 9 a.m. **Gerlos,** in the Tyrol, with forested mountains and waterfalls, has wind-surfing, sailing, a sailing school at the Durlassboden reservoir, high-altitude rainbow trout-fishing, and it is a skier's paradise in winter. The largest outdoor swimming pool in this tiny carved and painted village is at the **Hotel Kroller;** the **Oberwirt Hotel** serves home-grown produce, rents horsedrawn sleighs in winter and has horses and ponies for hire year-round. Not recommended for small children (no special kindergarten or childcare arrangements) but great for teenagers. For information: FVV, 6281 Gerlos, 1245 Austria. **Grunau: Cumberland Wildpark** with the **Schindlbach Marchenwald,** an Alpine Disneyland for children in its enclosure. The Frunau Fremdenverkehrsverband (Tel: (07616) 268) can supply you with other details for family pleasure in the area. **Gurk,** north of Klagenfurt, has a splendid cathedral of **frescoes** with a glittering gold altar and many art treasures. Napoleon once used the abbey as a barracks. In **Hallstatt,** a beautiful must-see village, close to Bad Ischl, you can be transported around the lake in gondola-like craft. **Hinter-bruhl bei Modling,** a small village 15 miles south of Vienna, features the **Seegrotte** (see Fun Trips).

In **Innsbruck,** folklore evenings of Schuhplattler dancing can be enjoyed at the **Hotel Europa.** The **Museum of Tyrolese Folk Art** (Universitatsstrasse 2) and the **Ferdinandeum Museum** (Museum-strasse 15) are easily absorbed and absorbing cultural attractions. There's also an **Alpine zoo,** with wolves, wildcats, wild boars, brown bears, and beavers. Two morning excursions outside of town are the cable car ride up **Patscherkofel,** or a ride in the narrow-gauge railways to the **Ziller valley** or the **Stubai.** A third cable car ride up **Hafelekar/Nordkette** leaves from the city center and soars you up the mountain peaks around town. **Kitzbuhel** is a wintertime favorite with skiers. There is a great ski school for both adults and children, as well as ice skating, sleigh rides, tobogganing, indoor tennis and other good non-ski alternatives. In summer there is fishing, golf, riding, hiking, climbing, squash, swimming, boating and water skiing. The **Aquarena,** the community spa, is open year round, with two swimming pools, saunas, tanning cubicles, masseurs, mud baths.

In **Klagenfurt,** don't miss **Minimundus,** a collection of miniature buildings—even a miniature White House—donated by countries all over the world. Rivers, cars, trains, and lights—all working. Admission money goes to Austria's children's welfare fund. Hard to find—be careful you don't find yourself in the City Dump, which is right alongside! Have a look at the **Celtic and Roman excavations** at Magdalensberg nearby. You can dine at the medieval 14-towered **Hochosterwitz Castle,** at a height of well over 2000′, near St. Veit an der Glan.

Korneuburg is a charming village at which to picnic on the way to **Burg Kreuzenstein,** a magnificently furnished, reconstructed castle. Parapets, drawbridge, and moat; lots of armor and a medieval kitchen. In **Linz,** there is the **Kindergalerie** (Pfarrplatz 1), with exhibits of children's drawings. Also, don't miss the **children's grotto railway** with fairy-tale scenes and dwarfs right out of the Nibelungenlied. Then take the ride up the nearby mountain train to the Postlingberg pilgrimage church, a sweeping view. Detailed information available from the Fremdenverkehrsverband, A 4010 Linz, Alstadt 17. Linz is also a fine take-off spot for **Danube and Salzkammergut lake excursions.** As a child, I saw the carved altar at the **Pfarrkirche** in **Maria Gail am Faaker See,** a very off-beat spot but forever memorable. **Mayrhofen** is the site of **Alpinschule Zillertal,** one of the finest mountaineering schools in the world. For information, write A–6290 Mayrhofen. The little **railway line** in **Murtal** is a dream spot for railway buffs. **Neustift/Stubai** is a *sportif* Tyrolean village, with an indoor pool and indoor tennis during the winter, miles of marked cross-country trails; climbing, hiking, tennis, riding, and summer skiing. The **Stubai Glacier** is the largest year-round ski center in the country. Apartments sleeping two to six are available at the **Sporthotel Neustift,** a small but well-equipped hostelry with a children's playroom, gym, sauna and prices like yesteryear's moneysavers. Only 16 mi. from Innsbruck by convenient and frequent bus service. Details from Fremdenverkehrsverband Neustift, A–6167 Neustift, Stubai, Tyrol.

Obertauern, near Radstadt, linked by bus service to Salzburg, is a tiny village with dandy skiing until May for advanced and intermediate levels. **Hotel Edelweiss** has an indoor pool, sauna, solarium; the **Berghotel** is nearest to the major lifts, and the **Kristall Hotel Garni** is a large bed-and-breakfast inn. Low hotel rates drop even lower after April 9. Taxis are available to take you to and from this lovely hamlet to the train station at Radstadt. **Petronell** features Roman ruins plus a castle museum by the Danube and is reachable from Vienna by bus; a few miles away **Carnuntum,** in Bad Deutsch-Altenberg, boasts a Roman villa—completely reconstructed. Lipizzan colts are bred at the federal stud farm in **Piber. Rattenberg** is a well-preserved medieval town in the Tyrol with a pleasant castle inn. **St. Christoph** is a romantic ski resort reachable from Zurich by the special bus called the **Arlberg Express.** Accommodations are available in chalet-style hotels on top of the Arlberg Pass. **St. Florian** near Linz, **St. Wolfgang im Salzkam-**

mergut are little treasuries of art goodies for older children. Plying from St. Wolfgang to St. Gilgen is the **Wolfgangsee Kinderschiff,** a round-trip boatride just for children 6–14, with an Austrian story-telling "Tante" aboard. In **Schenkenfelden,** near Bad Leonfelden in Upper Austria, there is a pleasant **Marchenwald** for children and a summer/winter recreational park for families. The **open-air museum** at **Stubing,** near Graz, lies in a flowering meadow. In **Zell-am-See, Schloss Ritzen,** by the lake, open Wed., Sat., Sun. from 2 p.m.–4 p.m., other times by appointment, has a superb collection of nativity scenes, folk art, and minerals.

ATTRACTIONS FOR CHILDREN—GAME RESERVES Austria has superb nature parks and wildlife reserves, some with animals from other lands. Children can stand right beside stags and deer, throw food to grunting wild boar, watch ibexes leap, and wait for gopherlike marmots to poke their heads out of hiding places. Great camera possibilities. Willow forests and reed-grown marshes with deer, herons, cormorants, and greylag geese can be found north of Linz around Altenberg, and in many of the Austrian **Wildparks,** including those in Upper Austria: **Wildpark Freinberg,** in the district of **Innviertel-Hausruckwald; Cumberland-Wildpark** at **Grunau im Almtal; Wildpark Hochkreut,** at **Altmunster** on the Traunsee in the Salzkammergut region; and at **Wildpark Altenfelden Muhltal,** northwest of Linz with Asiatic sambars, tarpan, deer, and exotic animals of all kinds. Game feeding at 3 p.m. and 5 p.m. Open all year.

Geras: the **Geras Nature Park** is stocked with deer, moufflon, and Caucasian mountain goat. Dwarf donkeys for children to ride; natural, 22-acre swimming pool; and game feedings. Open mid-March–Nov.; winters only on holidays and weekends. **Gussing:** the **Gussing Game Reserve,** where you can wander through a 17-acre castle park, or over 247 acres of the Punitz forest area. From lookout towers you can watch aurochs (a retrogressive breed of European bison), tarpan, Hungarian steppe cattle, stags from Korea, and Macedonian dwarf donkeys. Tickets available at the castle or at the forester's house in the Punitz reserve. Open year round.

Just a few miles from **Leoben,** the **Mautern Game Reserve** is reachable only by chair lift. Sacred Chinese deer (now extinct in Asia), Highland cattle, Shetland ponies, moufflon, wild boar, and mountain sheep. Chinese deer on view year round; the rest of the reserve is open May–Nov. Near **Marchegg,** the **Marhauen Wildlife Reserve** features deer, wild boar, a lynx, white storks, other birds. Two lookout towers. Open all year; late March–Oct.; recommended.

In **Mayrhofen, Hotel Alte Post** (Tel: 2204) has a private 15-acre mountain pasture game preserve for guests only. Mountain huts, Alpine flora, glaciers, and waterfalls, the 9000′ Zillertal Alps are the dramatic backdrop for chamois and marmots. A 45-minute drive by private road from the hotel. Just outside **Salzburg** is the 1500-acre **Salzburg Nature Park Untersberg.** The **Seewinkel Wildlife Reserve** has one of the most remarkable landscapes in Central Europe—a soda-and-salt-encrusted steppe, rather like Death Valley. A winter resting place for Nordic ducks and geese, and summer retreat for spoonbills, avocets, plovers, and silk and purple herons. Open year round; most interesting from March–Oct.

About ten minutes' drive from **Velden,** the **Rosegg Game Reserve** is overlooked by the ruins of an ancient castle; 75 acres of magnificent woodland along the Drau river at the foot of the Karawanken mountains. Shetland ponies, deer; Siberian wild camels; and American buffalo. Open all year. In the southwestern sector of **Vienna, the Lainzer Tiergarten,** some 6200 acres—originally part of the imperial hunting reserves—boasts deer, moufflon, tarpan, and auroch. The forests are inhabited by aurochs, hare, polecat, fox, and wild boar. A lovely place—networks of footpaths, a lookout tower, and plenty of benches. The Lipizzan horses of the Spanish Riding School summer here. Open Mar.–Oct., Wed.–Sun.; admission a pittance.

ATTRACTIONS FOR CHILDREN—CAVES AND MINES There are 4000 or so water caves, ice caves, caverns with waterfalls, stalactite caves, caves with beautiful crystal formations, caves with bone relics of Ice Age fauna. Guided tours of these take from 25 min.–3½ hours. The temperature of ice caves is around freezing point in midsummer; other caves, beautiful though they may be, are cold and damp. **Ice caves** at **Dachstein** near Obertraun and at **Werfen**—warm clothing, boots, gloves mandatory—rough going for kids under 14. Of the stalactite caves, the **Lurgrotte** between **Peggau** and **Semriach,** the **Grasslhohle** in **Durntal** near Weiz are recommended for 8's and over; the **Alland Stalactite cave,** in the Vienna Woods, takes only 25 minutes to tour and is open weekends and holidays from Easter until late autumn. Cave-loving families can also get in touch with the Association of Austrian Speleologists, Obere Donaustrasse 99/7/1/3, A-1020 Vienna.

There are also ore, gypsum (see Fun Trips), and salt mines on view; **salt mines** in **Altaussee, Bad Ischl, Hallein** and **Hallstatt** (see "Attractions for Children in Salzburg"). For more information, ask the Austrian National Tourist Office.

FUN TRIPS For about $4 you can have a 2½-hour **sightseeing excursion** in Vienna in an old time trolley car. Ask the City Tourist Office for details. The **Danube River Trip** has ships leaving Vienna five times a week, May 13–Sept. 16. Tickets and information are available at your travel agent, the local tourist information offices, or the offices of the steamship company—the Erste Donau Dampfschiffahrts-Gesell-schaft (DDSG; Hintere Zollamtsstr. 1, 1031 Vienna; Tel: 725141). One class only, remarkably inexpensive. You can spend the night aboard or in Linz and return the next day. Striking scenery on the four-hour passage from Passau to Linz and the two-hour passage from Melk to Krems. Music and restaurant service aboard. The stop before Krems is Durnstein, and I recommend getting off in the afternoon at Durnstein, spending the night and re-boarding the next day. **Boating and hydrofoil** fanciers can sail from the Alps to the Black Sea on a Russian tour, or whip along to Czechoslovakia and Hungary on a hydrofoil; visas vital, of course. Children 6–15 ride half-price; they can hydrofoil on the Vienna–Linz trip, stopping at Krems, Durnstein, Melk, and Grein. Contact DDSG. **City boat trips** that travel between the Danube River and the Danube Canal set off daily except Mon. from Schwedenbrucke. The 20-mi. excursion takes 3 hrs., too long a haul for children under 12.

Austria specializes in **Aerial Cableways,** often called suspension airways or basket locomotion (not, as they are sometimes termed, mountain railways). Perfectly safe, and a delight to children. One reaches Hunerkogel at the edge of the Dachstein glacier, where you can hail a tanklike glacier taxi for sightseeing rides at modest prices. **Sightseeing tours by plane** are offered over Vienna and Salzburg. Consult local or Viennese travel agents. Departure from Vienna Airport, Apr.–Oct. The **Seegrotte** (Hinterbruhl, Tel: 6364) formerly a gypsum mine, offers ¾-hour guided tours year round from 9 a.m. to noon, 1 p.m.–5 p.m.. The best part is a motor-boat trip across a subterranean lake. Admission fees minuscule.

FUN AND GAMES For sports-loving children, Austria is ideal. Check with the Austrian National Tourist Office for the best locales for swimming, fishing, waterskiing, canoeing, riding, bicycling, and playing ninepins—Austrians love bowling.

Gliding, an Austrian specialty, might interest older children. The minimum age for beginners is 16—but you might possibly get an unforgettable flight as a passenger. Contact **Gliding Centre Wien-Donauwiese** (Langenzerdorf; Tel: 262); ASKO-Zivilluftfahrerschule Wien (Hauslabgasse 24a, 1050 Vienna); **Alpine Segelflugschule** (Zell am See; Tel: 7225); or **Gliding School Spitzerberg** (Bad Deutsch-Altenburg).

Helicopters for skiers or just for pleasure can be obtained at moderate prices from **Firma Aircraft Innsbruck** (Flughafen Innsbruck; Tel: 81777).

The top **skiing** months are from Jan. to the beginning of Apr. Summer skiing at Ramsau-Dachstein is good for beginners. Year-round skiing at Neustift/Stubai. Many hotels and inns at Styrian Enns Valley gateway resort Schladming and Ramsau open year round. Summer skiing at Kaprun-Kitzsteinhorn, Hintertux-Gefrorene Wand, Hochgurgl-Wurmkogel recommended only for experts. Austria has every type of ski slope you could wish for. Here even 3-year-olds ski embarrassingly well. The ski schools accept beginning skiers from 6 on up; hours are usually 10 a.m.–noon, and 2 p.m.–4 p.m. The greatest institution for families is the ski kindergarten, which accepts children from 2½–5 or 6, with 7- or 8-year olds also welcome from 9 a.m.–4 p.m. Children will be given lunch, hot chocolate for snacks, and playtime on the slopes as well as ski instruction. When traveling with children from 2½–7, be sure there's a ski kindergarten at your ski resort or close by, or have a babysitter handy to bring your youngling to and from the ski school and supervise his lunch and optional nap. That way, the entire family has a marvelous time. **Ski kindergartens** I know of are in **Brand, Bundschuh, Ebensee,** the **Gastein Valley, Katschberg, Kirchberg** near Kitzbuhel, **Kotschach-Mauthen, Lech-Oberlech, Lungau, Mittendorf,** the **Nock Mountains, Radstadt,** and **Wildschonau,** among other places! See Information. For skibobbing, which any bicycle rider can learn, there are schools for children from 8 up, although even 6-year-olds can enjoy experimenting. There is also tobogganing, bobsledding, and curling, and skijoring (letting yourself be pulled on skis at your own pace by horses); great for beginners and children. You can also attach your own skijoring rig to a horse-drawn sleigh.

Swimming pools in Vienna? More than a dozen being upgraded and several new ones under construction. The **Diana Bath Building** (Untere Donaustrasse, Vienna 2), has four swimming pools, saunas, other amenities.

Sailing? Attersee, Mattsee, Traunsee are among the most popular lakes in the Salzburg area for small boats. The 11th-century fortress, Schloss Kammer (A-1862 Kammer Schorfling) has been converted into a sailing school, **Attersee-Yachtschule,** offering 13-day courses from late May–late Sept. Board, lodging, sailing, and instruction at moderate cost. Simple, clean, inexpensive, YMCA-like accommodations, but no meals except breakfast, available for parents or relatives of young people taking the courses, mostly German teenagers. Water sports, riding, summer concerts, but little English spoken.

Unless you plan to be in Austria for some time, **hunting** seems a bit impractical, because you need a government license and a short-term permit issued by the local police. Fees are set for every animal killed or wounded, and you'll often be asked to make a whopping bank deposit in advance. For information about angling, riding, or hunting write to **Heinrich Sewann** (International Travel Agency, Mariahilferstr. 86, Vienna; Tel: 934641). Accommodations in his lodge in hunting grounds.

SHOPPING WITH AND FOR CHILDREN Austria is bargain-hunting land. Best buys for boys and girls are the *Trachtenmode,* or authentic native costume, incredibly durable and very attractive. The local handcraft *(Heimatwerke)* shops in all the provincial capitals are musts. Dolls, stuffed animals, games, sports equipment, and apparel are all excellent buys. The firm, *Piatnik,* makes beautiful and inexpensive playing cards, featuring Lipizzan horses and other Austrian specials. Some stores close during lunch hour on weekdays; most close Sat. afternoons.

In **Vienna,** for clothing there are four major ***department stores:*** **Herzmansky, Stafa,** and **Gerngross** (all on Mariahilfestr.) and **Steffel** (on Karntnerstr.). Other fine shops for children's gear are: **Bertl Aschenbrenner** (Seilergasse 1); **Dohnal** (Mariahilferstr. 97), which carries baby carriages, children's furniture, and children's clothes (infants' to teenagers'); **Kindermoden Mary** (Mariahilferstr. 117; with a dozen branches, clothes for infants to 14-year-olds; **Lanz** (Karntnerstr, 10), internationally known for attractive children's clothing, carries charming girls' dresses, leather wearables for boys, Tyrolean hats, and Salzburg jackets. **Annabelle** (Seilergasse 10) is splendid for casual and leisure wear for teenagers. For puffy down quilts, pillows and linens, **Zur Schwabisch Jungfrau** in the Graben.

For toys, try Walter Bucherl's **Liliput-Spielwarenfabrikat** (Kalvarienberggasse 22), specializing in miniature trains, doll houses, and animals; **Josef Muehlhauser** (Karntnerstr. 28), for charming toys and games; and **Matador Haus** (Mariahilferstr. 62), specializing in mechanical toys. For hand-made Christmas tree ornaments, **Wilhelm Brauns** (Schwalbengasse 12) is very special. You can see rocking horses in the making, or order one custom designed, at the workshop of **Ferdinand Bauer** (Sautergasse 35) in the Ottakring district. In **Kitzbuhel,** try **Resi Hammeren** for clothing, *loden* style.

In **Salzburg,** for clothing try **Lanz** (Schwarzstr. 4) for eye-catching Alpine-style togs. For toys, try **Joseph Schatz** (Getreidegasse 3). The **Heimatwerke** shop (Residenzplatz) is fascinating.

In **Bregenz** and **Innsbruck,** the **Heimatwerke** will give you a fine idea of the variety of regional wearables and local handcrafts.

AUSTRIAN FRIENDS AND PEN PALS Although Austria has no formal, organized hospitality program, the local Austrian tourist office will make arrangements for your children to meet children of hospitable Austrian families. During the school year, the **Austro-American Institute of Education** (Operngasse 4, Vienna; Tel: 527720) offers children's English lessons from Oct.–June. American families are most welcome, and arrangements can be made for family and children's get-togethers. The **Austro-American Society** (Stallburgasse 2, Vienna; Tel: 523982) will also serve as liaison between American and Austrian families and set up the necessaries for correspondence between the young of both countries.

If you do go to someone's house, it's the Austrian custom—and a very pleasant one—to bring your hostess some flowers.

CALENDAR OF EVENTS The best advice here is to pick an interesting variety. You may never get your fill of operettas, for example, but to a child one operetta is far more memorable than three. Too many folk dances, too many musical performances will deaden the wonderful impression of one. Austrian tourist offices will provide detailed information about events.

Starting **Jan. 6,** and continuing for six weeks, *Carnival,* or Fasching, is celebrated in Vienna. Tyrol, Syria, and the Pongau area of Salzburg Province feature peasant processions and festivals (peasants parade with wooden masks in Tyrol). Parties, masked balls, and dancing everywhere. ***Ski races.*** In Feb., ***Fasching*** celebrations continue. **Mar.** brings ***spring fairs*** to Vienna.

Apr. and **May** feature ***racing events*** (horse, and automobile) and ***folk festivals.*** The first Sun. in May Gauderfest (Zill am Ziller) is a folk-festival featuring ***wrestling, folk dancing,*** and ***cock-fighting;*** another festival is at Bruck an der Mur. From **Apr.–Sept.** in Salzburg you'll find the *marionette theater* and *palace concerts;* and elsewhere, starting in **May,** local *passion plays.*

In **May** and **June,** on Whitmonday, there's a marvelous ***folk festival*** on horseback in Weitenfels and in Feistritz; parades and horse-drawn coaches decked with flowers in all cities. ***Corpus Christi*** features processions everywhere—special in Zederhaus, Traunkirchen, and Hallstatt; these last two feature ***lake processions*** with flower-decked boats and barges. Vienna parades ***flowered floats*** and features a ***battle of flowers*** in the Prater park. On Midsummer's Day (June 21) ***bonfires*** alight in nation-wide celebrations. ***Castle plays*** and ***folklore evenings*** swing into action. ***International Festival of Young Musicians*** in Vienna.

July and **Aug.** sound off with ***organ recitals*** at St. Stephen's Cathedral, ***brass bands*** in public parks; ***concerts*** by Mozart Choirboys, ***folklore shows*** in the new Folklore Theater; ***palace concerts*** in Vienna; ***music festivals*** in Salzburg and Bregenz; and ***folk festivals*** in Tyrol, Styria, and Carinthia (specials are in Innsbruck, Mayrhofen, Villach, Seefeld, and Velden). At the ***Feast of the Assumption, bonfires*** are set on mountain peaks. Aug. brings ***operetta*** performances in lake. Morbisch every Sat. and Sun. evening on the lake.

From **Sept. 1–June 30** the ***State Opera*** performs at the Vienna State Opera House. The first Sun. in **Sept.** boasts a ***medieval costume festival*** at Hochosterwitz Castle in Carinthia. ***Fall fairs*** in Vienna, Innsbruck, and Graz; ***music festival*** in Graz; and a ***folklore festival*** at Wels. ***Wine festivals*** from **Sept.–Nov.** celebrate the harvest On **Nov. 15,** a ***folk festival*** in Klosterneuberg, near Vienna, celebrates St. Leopold's Day.

Dec. 6, St. Nicholas' Day, is a children's holiday. The Dec. special is the Christkindlmarkt (Messeplatz, Vienna). A ***Christmas Fair;*** small amusement park, and many toys, cakes, and candies on sale. Beautiful creche. It's all very jolly, glittering, and happy.

LANGUAGE AND PHRASEBOOK Because English is mandatory in the national school system, Austrians seem far more adept than Germans at speaking English. For phrases your child can learn in German, see Germany.

BELGIUM

Belgium has a 43-mile coastline with vast, white beaches of fine sand and dunes, which is a children's paradise worth knowing about.

Belgium's carillons ring sweetly wherever you go; castles; caves and caverns; canals; and carnivals so spectacular that the word "binge" derives from Binche, a walled town whose annual pre-Easter carnival is one of the world's greatest costumed pageants. Belgians also go in for odd sports such as crossbowmanship, shrimping on horseback, and pigeon racing. And Brussels' famous Manneken-Pis (the statue of a small boy furnishing the water for a fountain in an uninhibited way) provides evidence of the tolerant attitude toward children that prevails. No great fuss is made about children here, but not many restrictions are imposed, either. To get the most fun from your stay, you really ought to plan your itinerary carefully to include the local folkore pageants and spectacular parades and processions. If Mardi Gras, the Rose Bowl floats, or Macy's Thanksgiving Day Parade delight your children, just wait until they see a festival procession in Belgium—wow!

INFORMATION ABOUT BELGIUM Before you go, for useful and interesting brochures, contact your nearest **Belgian Tourist Office** (BTO) (head office: 745 5th Ave., New York, NY 10151 Tel: (212) 758–8130). For general tourist information for the Flemish/Dutch-speaking provinces of Belgium (Antwerp, East and West Flanders, Limburg and the northern half of Brabant) see the **Commissariat Generaal voor Toerisme** (Grasmarkt 61, B–1000 Brussels). For the French-speaking provinces of Hainaut, Liege, Luxembourg-Belge, Namur and the southern half of Brabant, see the **Office de Promotion de la Comminaute Francaise de la Belgique (C.P.T.)** at 7 rue Stevens, B–1000 Brussels. If you want in-depth information about northern Brabant, write to the **Toeristische Federatie van de Provincie Brabant** (Grasmarkt 61, 1000 Brussels); southern Brabant, write to the **Federation Touristique de la Province de Brabant** (rue du Marche-aux-Herbes 61, 1000 Brussels). Schizophrenic Brussels happily integrates in its **City Tourist Office,** known as the T.I.B., where English, French and Flemish/Dutch are spoken. The TIB has information about everything in Brussels and its environs. There are information centers also at the Arrival Hall at Brussels National Airport (open 8 a.m.–8 p.m.); at the Gare du Midi and the Gare du Nord. For students there is **Infor-J** (for Jeunes) at 27 rue du Marche-aux-Herbes. Open daily 10 a.m.–7 p.m.; Sats. noon–7 p.m. There is a **Student and Youth Travel Center** (T.E.J) at 20 rue de la Sablonniere. The youth information center, **Jongerenadviescentrum,** (J.A.C.) has organizations in Antwerp, Brussels, Bruges, Ostend. A similar organization, **Jeugd-Info,** has bases in Antwerp, Brussels, Ghent. In Liege, there's a Centre "J".

For on-the-spot information consult the **City Tourist Office** (CTO), or the **Provincial Tourist Office** for advance or in-depth information.
Antwerp: Karel Oomstraat 11, 2000 Antwerpen.
East Flanders: Koningin Maria-Hendrikplein 64, 9000 Ghent.
Hainaut: Rue des Clercs 31, 7000 Mons.
Liege: Blvd. de la Sauveniere 77, 4000 Liege.
Limburg: Bokrijk Domain, 3600 Bokrijk (Genk).
Belgian Luxembourg: Quai de l'Ourthe 9, 6980 La Roche en Ardenne.
Namur: rue Notre-Dame 3, 5000 Namur.
West Flanders: Vlamingstraat 55, 8000 Brugge (Bruges).

For information about historical pageants and folkloric events, contact the **Brussels Ommegang Society** (Maison de Bellone, 46 rue de Flandre), open daily 8:30 a.m.–1 p.m.

The Provincial Tourist Office of Brabant collates a touristic and cultural calendar called the BBB (Brussels and Brabant in Belgium) Agenda which is published in *Le Soir* on Thursday, and in other periodicals.

The Societe de Transport Inter-Urban de l'Agglomeration Bruxelloise has information centers in the Gare du Midi premetro station and Porte de Namur (Tel: (02) 511 49 18) open 8 a.m.–5:30 p.m.; (02) 512 17 90 from 5:30 p.m.–8 a.m. They offer a 24-hr. unlimited travel pass for the metro (subway), premetro (the subway running along the surface before it tunnels underground), tram and yellow bus. Also, inquire at TIB or at the station information centers about reduced-fare excursion tickets on trains—"beautiful day" tickets which include free admissions to zoos, parks, museums, boat trips. Ask the SNCB (Societe Nationale Chemins-de-Fer Belge) about their many reduced railway fares for tourists. Convenient office also in **Antwerp** (Anneessenstraat 1–5).

For motorists, the well-spring of advice and help is the **Royal Automobile Club de Belgique** (53, rue d'Arlon; B 1040 Brussels), with a branche in **Antwerp** (Appelmansstraat 25, B–2000 Antwerpen). Also, there's the **Touring Club Royal de Belgique** (rue de la Loi, 44 B–1040 Brussels) and, in **Antwerp:** Quellinstraat 9, B-2000 Antwerpen.

The Bulletin, Belgium's news weekly in English (with offices at 382 Ave. Louise, 1050 Brussels), has an informative classified ad section, and an excellent guide to entertainment in Belgium, which is free from TIB.

HEALTH, WATER, AND FOOD Health standards are high. In tourist centers and major cities, the water is perfectly safe to drink. In rural areas, or if you are subject to upsets, drink bottled water. *Spa Monopole* is one of several excellent varieties available.

Belgian food, like the mother tongue, comes in two varieties: Flemish and French. *Waterzooi de poulet,* a Flemish specialty, is a sort of chicken stew that most children like; and you'll be happy to hear that steak and French-fried potatoes *(biftek et frites),* another favorite of almost all children who have mastered the art of chewing, is a favorite main course. *Tournedos,* the small filleted center cuts of beef, are the tenderest and nicest. Belgians are devoted to the first fruits of the season: the tiniest peas, the youngest carrots, baby new potatoes. Exceptions are enormous leeks and giant asparagus stalks, covered during the growing season so that they are ivory from the stem end to pale green at their tip. Children love the strawberries, peaches, apricots, cherries, and the Royal Black grapes.

Belgians' favorite vegetables—chicory and Brussels sprouts—have little appeal for most children's palates, nor does the smoked ham from the Ardennes, or the variety of sausages and seafood, as a sweeping generality. Cooks use butter and cream with a sumptuous hand, and generally the food is both wholesome and delicious.

An idea for your child's *Scrapbook to Make* is a list of cakes, cookies, waffles, fruit tarts, and other regional specialties and their description—coupled with personal ratings. Asking about the origins of these specialties may turn up all sorts of rich lore. *Antwerpse Handjes,* for example, a crumb cookie in the shape of a hand, brings to light the extraordinary information that Antwerp means "the place of hand throwing"; in the Middle Ages inhabitants punished thieves here by cutting off their right hand, which was thrown into the Scheldt River. Cheese tarts from Mons, Nivelles, and Waterloo are known as *tartes au fromage. Coquelet a la Tournaisienne* is a chicken specialty of Tournai. Dinant specialties are cheese tarts *(flamiches)* and elaborately molded chewy gingerbread figures *(couques de Dinant).* In Brussels you can add *cramique* (a sweet raisin bread), *craquelin* (a light, spongelike bread without raisins), and Brussels waffles to the list, in addition to shortcake, *speculaas* (a rich spice butter cookie), rice tarts and almond bread, specialties also found in other towns. Bruges has spiced biscuits called *noeuds* (knots) and *kletskoppen.* Waffles *(gaufres)* are a Belgian treat, served with sugar, whipped cream, and/or fruit; those of Liege are thick and sprinkled with caramelized sugar. Lier has custards, creamy and rich. Hard candies called *babelutes* are seacoast specials. Belgian pralines shouldn't be confused with our caramel-walnut confections; here *pralines* is the generic term for scrumptious chocolate bon-bons. *Pain a la Grecque* is a light, sweet rusk which babies adore. *Boterletters* are butter cookies in alphabet shapes (children have fun eating their names).

Many of these cakes and cookies can be sent by parcel post to America, and they are the sort of treat a child will take pleasure in sharing with classmates at school.

The Belgians cook and eat well; but where can you get snacks and food quickly and inexpensively in **Brussels**? At the *Frite* Stands, the *friteurs,* or *frituurs* in most of Brussels' (and Belgium's) city squares, where you get a huge paper cornucopia filled with hot fried potatoes, golden brown, crisp to the bite, hot and luscious inside, to be dipped into an array of mayonnaise- and ketchup-based sauces. The *pomme frite a la Belgique* is cut in thin strips and served at *friteries* with *moules* (mussels) or with beef *(boeuf)* or steak tartare *(filet americain).* **Au Vieux Saint-Martin** (38 place du Grand Sablon) is for those who like steak tartare (most children don't, however), and **Chez Leon** (18 rue des Bouchers) close to the Grote Markt, is for those who prefer their frites with mussels. At **Maison du Boeuf,** the restaurant in the Brussels Hilton, the specialty is frites with boeuf for the boeuf buffs. The best frites are those served from **Antoine's,** a van stand open afternoons up to 3 a.m., in Place Jourdan, dispensing deep-fried, julienned Bintje potatoes in paper spillets—no more calories, I'm told, than 3 apples, and nutritionally excellent. (Try to convince the children that the frites are just as good, if not better, without all those sauces!) The **Grand Cafe** in Grand' Place is hard to resist. Also, there is the enchanting **Le Chalet Rose** (49 Ave. du Bois de la Cambre)—best if you can eat outside. Your teenagers will find you very with-it if you take them to **Drugstore Louise** (Galerie Louise 52–53). Teenagers and older children will like the **Atomium** (Heysel), a holdover from the '58 World's Fair and a magnified version of a Lego construction; great view and fun, even though the restaurant and cafe are no great shakes. **Uncle Joe's** (12 rue Jourdan, Porte Louise) is good for steak and hamburgers. **Le Manhattan 2** (Woluwe Shopping Center; Tel: 719165) specializes in spareribs, lobsters, take-out meals. On the outskirts of Brussels, have a meal in a 15th-century windmill, **Moulin de Lindekemale** (av. J.F. Debecker 6; Tel: (02) 700957); closed Mon. and Aug., a special spot with good food. If you feel like splurging, one of Brussels' best restaurants is the **Chalet de la Foret** on a little island in a lake near the Bois de la Cambre. In the same vicinity are: **Fond Roy, Vert Chasseur,** and **Foret de Soignes et Ferme St. Hubert,** to mention only a few. Formerly one of my favorite places to stay with children, **Robinson** (Bois de la Cambre; Tel: (02) 743013) has been reported closed as a guest inn but remains open as a restaurant to boat across the lake to. Do try this chalet—it's very special!

Restaurant in **Antwerp** open at all hours for sandwiches? **De Rolmops** (Statiestraat 13) and **Panache** (Statiestraat 17), which provides full-course meals as well. Quick snack tearooms and goodies shops are **Thijs** (De Keyserlei 26) and **Schoenaers** (Belgielei 101).

In **Bruges** the place to have tea, coffee, snacks, or a light lunch is

Ban den Berge, (Markt 26). Also, **Deleu's Patisserie** in Grand' Place is delightful.

Several free booklets on Belgian cuisine and other ethnic restaurants are available from the BTO in New York.

BABY FOOD A wide variety of American and foreign brands is available. Pharmacies and the food dept. of department stores stock them. Supermarkets often have Baby Corners.

DIAPERS AND LAUNDRY The word for diaper is *lange,* and a disposable diaper is a *lange en papier;* both are stocked in pharmacies, department stores, and baby specialty stores. A **diaper service** that supplies diapers and makes daily pickups and deliveries in Brussels: **Baby Service.** Elsewhere in Belgium, you should have no trouble at all getting diapers laundered either at your hotel or at a commercial laundry.

EMERGENCIES MADE EASY ***Pharmacies*** are listed in the telephone book under *Pharmacies* or *Apotheek* (or ask the concierge at your hotel). Pharmacies rotate evening and Sun. duties; those open for emergency calls day or night are listed in the daily papers. Otherwise, they are usually open from early morning until 8 p.m., daily except Sun. In **Antwerp,** try **Central Pharmacy** (Meir 97).

Doctors are listed in the telephone directory in Flemish under *Doctors in Geneesekunde* and in French under *Docteurs en Medecine*. For advice and information about English-speaking doctors particularly recommended for overseas visitors call: In **Antwerp:** American Consulate (Frankrijklei 101; Esso Bldg., 1st floor; Tel: 321800); British Consulate (Frankrijklei 105; Tel: 328829). In **Brussels:** American Embassy (blvd. du Regent 27; Tel: 5133830 Canadian Embassy (rue de Loxum 6; Tel: 513 79 46); British Consulate (rue Joseph II 42; Tel: 217 9000).

In case of an emergency, accident, ambulance, fire, police, etc., you have only to call 900—operative throughout Belgium.

If your 2-year-old munches Daddy's deodorant stick, the **Anti-Poison Center** in **Brussels** (Tel: 345 4545) has analyzed and classified most toxic products, will find the antidote, and give you advice you may need before the doctor arrives. Keep this number and the area code of Brussels (02) on hand and call it from any other country. You'll get expert advice fast.

For teenagers and students who have problems about money or health, contact the **S.O.S. Jeunes** (rue de la Blanchisserie 27; Tel: (02) 217 15 15 days; 24-hr. service number is (02) 736 36 36).

MAGIC FAMILY HELPERS **Baby zitters** (as they are sometimes spelled and pronounced) can be obtained in **Antwerp** from **Babysit Aid** (Tel: (031) 496833); **Babysit Centrale** (Tel: (031) 389595); and **Baby Dienst** (Cardinal Mercier Lann 10; Tel: (031) 391166).

In **Brussels, Babysit Service** (rue des Cygnes 20; Tel: (02) 648 8426 or 649 8714) is excellent. Hotel and family pensions along the seaside are particularly good about arranging babysitting. Baby parking, for children from 8 mos.–3 yrs is available for a maximum of four hours at a time from 7:30 a.m.–6 p.m. at **Halte-Garderie** (rue des Charpentiers 2, Brussels). At Brussels National Airport, the Nursery is open from 7 a.m.–10 p.m. for children up to 12 years. In **Ghent,** children 18 mos.–6 yrs. can be looked after for a small fee in one of the municipal children's playing gardens, such as the one in the center of town (Onderstraat 10) open, like the others, Mon.–Fri., except during festivals, 8:30 a.m.–11:30 a.m.; 2 p.m.–6 p.m.

For older children, children's companions and babysitters as well can be summoned from the **University Employment Bureau** in Brussels; Tel: (02) 649 34 43 between 9 a.m. and noon. Commercial organizations and student groups which do babysitting in Brussels and elsewhere are listed in the Yellow Pages of the telephone books. Rates for these services escalate after midnight, and babysitters require being taken home by car or provided with late-night taxi-fare. The **Maison des Jeunes de Forest** (Place St. Denis) runs workshops, plus debates and films for teenagers and children, 6–12. Call (02) 377 25 50 for details. Contact **The American Women's Club of Brussels** (1 Ave. des Erables) and **The British and Commonwealth Women's Clubhouse** (rue de l'Association 20). Both these active groups have a "pool" of babysitters. The **American Protestant Church of Brussels** (19 Kattenberg) welcomes newcomers and residents to Brussels every Thurs. in July and Aug. at special coffee hours from 10 a.m.–12 a.m. and plans special activities for resident and visiting children. Different movies for parents and children shown at the same time on Saturdays only? This plan, complete with escorts for the children, is operative at the **Ambassador Disney-Cine** (rue August Orte 7), and at the **Saturday Cinema, Twin Cinema** (Passage 44).

Schools and kindergartens in **Brussels: The Brussels American School** (John F. Kennedylaan, 1960 Steerebeek), only for children whose parents are connected with the U.S. military, the diplomatic corps or NATO; **The British School** (Steenwueg op Leuven 15 B, 1980 Tervuren). Both schools take children from preschool age (as young as 2½) up to college entrance exams. Call the **International School** (Kattenberg 19; Tel: (02) 720958); or **Catholic Education Secretariat** (rue de l'Industrie 1; Tel: 122344) for details of all schools and institutes under their control.

Personalized Services: A good bet for tutors and children's companions, who can also act as guides, is the **Brussels**-based student placement bureau, **Office de Placement Estudiantin** (av. Paul Heger 22; Tel: (02) 6472385). Ask for an English-speaking student. This office may also find you a suitable *au pair* girl. Friendly and enthusiastic residents of Brussels will show you and your family around for free and for fun. Between 10:30 a.m.–11:30 a.m., or between 6 p.m.–7 p.m., go to the **Meet Brussels and Sleep Well-Auberge du Marais** (rue de la Blanchisserie 27) and get a list of names and telephone numbers of these English speaking Bruxellois/Brusselaren. These hospitable citizens are not professional historians, but they are splendid instant friends, companions, and guides. If you are suffering from momentary culture shock, miss your friends, or just need someone to talk with, call **Help Line Pats** in Brussels (Tel: (02) 648 40 14), which has English-speaking volunteers who will try to help solve your problems. If you need a multilingual secretary on an hourly basis or fully equipped office for a day or longer, or just want a mail drop or answering service, contact **Your Office in Brussels** (33 rue du Congres, 1000 Brussels; Tel: (02) 2185005). In **Antwerp** excellent guide service at **Korte Beeldekensstraat** (Tel: (031) 363520) and from the City Tourist Office.

▶ **Note:** If you need a carnival costume, every town has a rental agency for special occasions (Ceremonie Kledij, Location de Vetements de Ceremonie). Check the telephone directory for the agency nearest to you.

HOLIDAYS FOR CHILDREN ON THEIR OWN Many foreign touring families make arrangements for their children to stay by the day, week, month or even longer periods at ***children's hotels*** or pensions, or, as they are often rather misleadingly called, children's boarding houses. This last term seems rather depressing for these small, homey inns that combine the functions and pleasures of school, home, and holiday resort. Most of these offer optional French or swimming lessons or, if you are so inclined, the Belgian school syllabus from kindergarten up to the equivalent of our Junior High School! The food is good, the children seem to get along happily. All are equipped to take English-speaking children. Facilities may vary considerably, but all are efficiently controlled by the Belgian Ministry of Public Health with regard to comfort and hygienic conditions. Here is a list winnowed from a much larger harvest—all are along Belgium's busy and popular seacoast, a perfect playground for children:

De Haan (Tel. Area Code (059): **Chat Botte** (Driftweg 195; Tel: 23 32 07); **Duinen en Velden** (Sparrenboslaan 3; Tel: 23 32 79); **Hirondelles** (Duinenpad 7; Tel: 23 34 37); **Jong en Blij** (Tollenslaan 3; Tel 23 35 19); **Merlijn** (Tenierslaan 12; Tel: 23 31 43); **St. Cecile** (Duinenpad 10; Tel: 23 36 44). **Wenduine** (Tel. Area Code (050): **Les Lutins** (Goedeluchtstraat 12; Tel: 41 19 22; **Spermalie** (Kerkstraat 72; Tel: 41 26 02); **SVV Morgenrood** (Park Leopold II, 1; Tel: 41 24 39). **Koksijde** (Tel. Area Code (058): Recommendations are **Bambino, Les Dauphins, De Pelikaan.** Write for more information about these to the City Tourist Offices: Stationsstraat 27, 8420 **De Haan;** Town Hall, 8460 **Koksijde;** Town Hall, 8410 **Wenduine.**

Similar facilities are at: **Knokke,** the vacation retreat rapidly being developed as the Riviera of the Belgian coast; **Middelkerke** (where the beach is still to be discovered by vacationers); **De Panne** (delightful); **Nieuport,** and *Oostende/Ostende/***Ostend.** Addresses and conditions change so fast it's better to get information from the local information bureau 3–4 months in advance.

CASTLES AND OTHER HAPPY FAMILY ACCOMMODATIONS In the alphabet of accommodations, B&B (for bed-and-breakfast) comes before Castles. B&B accommodations are proliferating. I have no personal experience with these in Belgium, so let the BTO advise you. The best castle accommodation I can suggest is in the immediate vicinity of **Brussels: Domein van Huizingen,** an 18th-century moated manor house appealing to children; sits prettily in a magnificent parkland with shaded walks, waterfalls, boating lake, swimming pool, browsing deer, tennis courts, miniature golf, children's playgrounds, a small zoo, and facilities for football and basketball (all open to the general public).

Between Antwerp and Boom on the road to Brussels, the **G.B. Motor Hotel** at **Aartselaar** has babysitters, pleasant garden, heated swimming pool.

On the outskirts of **Antwerp, Riverenhof** (Turnhoutsebaan 244) is a handsome castle; adequate accommodations; 15 rooms, six baths; tennis court; grounds are lovely.

Among other provinces offering castle accommodation, **Namur's Chateau de Namur** (ave. de L'Ermitage 1) is wonderful for travelers without children, but of rather limited value for families—a drawback that applies, in my opinion, to most guest-castles in Belgium. In **Herbeumont-sur-Semois Prieure de Conques,** a venerable abbey with modernized interior and lovely surrounding park, is heavenly, but prices are also sky-high for most families. In **Oostkamp,** though, **Chateau des Brides** is a fine stopover for the night. Owner-hosts Baron and Baroness Peers de Niewburgh provide ten luxuriously furnished period rooms with private bath—but no meals except breakfast. The Belgian National Tourist Office will send you a list of other castles accepting guests.

Farming holidays have become so popular that you have to make reservations *months* ahead. For information about these accommodations in West Flanders, contact **V.Z.W. Poldervakantie,** Polderweg 8, 8480 Veume. For information about the Ardenne-Meuse-Hainaut area, try **Agritourisme,** Avenue de la Bouillon 29, 6600 Libramont.

An apartment in Brussels? For a few days, a week, or longer **Brugmann Sun House** (40 av. Brugmann; Tel: (02) 443957) provides daily upkeep, linen. For villa rentals, get in touch with **Housing Europe** (Tel: (02) 647 79 46); **New Homes** (Tel: (02) 343 98 22); **Find A Home** (Tel: (02) 687 84 14/ (02) 687 8156); or **Immo V** (272 Dreve Richelle, Waterloo). The *Bulletin* (see Information) has up-to-date listings of private and agency offerings.

CAMPING AND CARAVANING For detailed maps and information, write to **Royal Camping and Caravanning de Belgique** (rue de Namur 51, Brussels) or to the **Touring Club Royal de Belgique,** Camping Section (rue de la Loi 44, Brussels), or ask the Belgian Tourist Office in New York.

ATTRACTIONS FOR CHILDREN IN BRUSSELS Belgium's foremost amusement park, **Walibi** (open all year (Tel: (010) 41 44 66), has action galore for younger children and teenagers. **Huizingen** (Tel: (02) 356 38 03) is an 18th century moated manor-turned-restaurant, whose grounds have been turned into a lovely pleasure park, with boat rides, miniature golf, swimming, waterfalls and wandering deer. Just north of Huizingen is **Beersel,** a romantic 14th-century feudal castle, with towered brick walls, a moat, dungeons, torture chamber, and a drawbridge. On certain fine summer evenings, Shakespearean and folk plays are presented in the courtyard. You could go there during the day for lunch at its adjoining restaurant, the **Auberge du Chevalier,** furnished in medieval style; south of the city, it's located on a little byroad that probably will be hard to find unless you have precise directions. Open daily. For horse-lovers, there's a Fri. morning market until 2 p.m. at **Place de la Duchesse.** The medieval castle of **Gasbeek,** open daily except Fri. and Mon., has four-language sound and light performances, concerts, flower paintings and matching flower arrangements. It is no strain at all to get to it in under 20 minutes from Brussels. Well worth going to. Idyllic park as well. **Boat trips?** Yes, indeed. During the summer only, climb aboard at the Pont de Flandre for trips along the maritime canal.

The **Flea Market** (Marche aux Puces) in the Place du Jeu de Balle, daily from 8 a.m. to noon. Sun. mornings in rue des Radis. Sat. and Sun. mornings are the best. Be sure not to confuse the Flea Market with the much costlier open-air **Antique and Book Market** that goes on all day on Sun. at the Place du Grand Sablon; a wondrous collection of violins, belaying pins, bearskins, swords, armor, cradles, books, knick-knacks, and mountains of junk to mine for treasure. Bargain and haggle wildly. Consider everything fair and square if the price is knocked down by ⅓ or at least ¼. Children are astoundingly skillful at bargaining as a rule. Presented with a little spending money, and left to his own devices (keep a watchful eye), the average child will have a glorious time acquiring some prized goody. **Market Place** (Grand' Place), the city's most important square, is surrounded by impressive 17th century guild-houses and encompasses an ornate gilt-encrusted Town Hall, floodlit at night. The square is the site of a fruit and vegetable market in the early morning, a flower and plant market later in the day, and on Sun., a fore-noon Bird Market. Daily guided tours leave from here in horse-drawn carriages for a 25-minute clip-clop around town.

At the corner of rue de L'Etuve and rue du Chene, is the famous

Manneken Pis; at the Maison du Roi (in the Grand' Place) are the 398 costumes that have been presented to him. Museum hours are irregular in Brussels. Ask the CTO, or call the Museum directly to ascertain days and times. **The Children's Museum** (rue Tenbosch 32; Tel: (02) 640 0107), for children 4–12, is designed to stimulate their curiosity with games, workshops, and exhibits. They get to use microscopes and radio transmitters, drive a tram, print, cook, garden, photograph, and much more. The **Planetarium** (Ave. de Bouchout 10; Tel: (02) 478 90 03) provides a starry display of the heavens every Tues., Wed., Thur. all summer long. In July and Aug., there are lectures and an audio-visual show in English, every Thurs. at 10:30 a.m. Call for schedule of other events. The **Royal Art and History Museum** (Cinquantaine Park 10; Tel: (02) 733 96 10) has a collection of old toys, a museum for the blind, car and bicycle exhibits. **Costume and Lace Museum** (Rue de la Violette 6; Tel: (02) 512 7709). **The Museum of the Spoken Word** (Bibliotheque Royale Albert I; Tel: (02) 513 6180) has recordings of famous voices. **The Gallery of Old Masters** (Rue de la Regence 3; Tel: (02) 513 9630). Junior naturalists will enjoy the **Exotarium** (Manhattan Centre, Place Rogier, Tel: (02) 218 62 00), with exhibits of fish, reptiles, insects. The **Railway Museum** in the North Station is worth seeing if you're in the neighborhood. **Porte de Hal** is a museum of arms and armor. Next to the Royal Conservatory of Music is the **Musical Instrument Museum** (Tel: (02) 513 2554). Musicians consider this the richest of its kind in the world. If you're interested in trolley-car relics, go to the **Tram Museum** (Chaussee de Ninove, Schepdaal; Tel: (02) 521-0007).

Children like playing hop-skip-jump on the red and white marble squares up **av. de la Toison-d'or** between rue des Chevaliers and Porte de Namur.

Children's puppet theaters include the **Coeurs de Bois** (Tel: (02) 735 03) in Park Josaphat in **Schaerbeek** every Wed. and Sat.; the **Ratinet** (44 Ave. Defre; Tel: (02) 375 15 63) in suburban **Uccle** on Weds. and Suns.; **Place de la Monnaie** (Tel: (02) 512 91 64); **Parc de Bruxelles** (Tel: (02) 512 9164); **Le Perruchet** (Ave. de la Foret 50, Ixelles; Tel: (02) 673 8730); **Brialmonttheater** (rue Brialmont 11; Tel: (02) 217 24 21); and **Theatre des Jeunes de la Ville de Bruxelles** (rue du Marais 57; Tel: (02) 217 5754).

Royal Park with its Chinese Pavilion and Japanese Tower is in **Laeken,** a northern suburb of Brussels. Also, the **Bois de la Cambre,** a great big park reachable in 20 minutes by tram. (The lake has canoes for hire.) Adjoining it is the **Forest of Soignes,** a forest mostly of beech trees, with restaurants, and stretching out to Waterloo.

In **Hekelgem** there are a number of cafes, more or less grouped together, that exhibit sand paintings or sand carpets, where the works of the great masters and medieval tapestries are recognizably copied in colored sand with astounding expertise. It somehow is more intriguing to children—some, not all. Admission is free if you have refreshments in any of these cafes. **Waterloo,** like most famous battlefields, is pretty dull and is one attraction you can skip unless your offspring demand to be taken there. If you do go, the medieval fortress of **Lalaing,** nearby, offers exhibits of flowers, arts, and crafts.

During the summer, you can ride streetcar #28 to the end of the line, disembark, and board a little car train that picks up passengers at 9 p.m. and takes them for a two-mile ride along back roads and byways past an illuminated historic chateau, a windmill, farmhouses, chapel, and watermill with an accompanying commentary in French and Flemish and a musical sound track. A restful and inexpensive adventure.

ATTRACTIONS FOR CHILDREN IN OTHER CITIES In **Antwerp,** on Dec. 21, parents and teachers are held at bay in the street until they bribe their children with presents to let them in out of the cold. This ritualistic folklore performance at the **Cathedral** at Groenplaats should be seen and enjoyed by children. The largest church in Belgium, it has a 47-bell carillon and 42 other beautiful chiming bells. Other things to do and see include visits to: The **Plantijn-Moretus Museum.** If the children are interested in seeing the most complete antique and engraving plant in the world, this is considered the finest museum of 16th-century printing to be seen anywhere.

The National Zoo, **Zoological Garden** (Koningin Astridplein 26), is open daily, 8:30 a.m. to sunset. A good aquarium, reptile house, planetarium, and delphinarium (shows at 11:30 a.m. and 3:30 p.m.).

Tour of the harbor by motorboat or in the restaurant-steamer *Flandria* (Tel: (031) 337422); cruise up the River Scheldt on excursions of varying length—whatever suits your fancy—or all the way to Vlissingen in Holland; embarcation from the landing stage at Steen castle, on the river, down the road a piece from the **Vleeschuis** (butcherhouse), which houses an interesting collection of arms and ship's models. **Steen,** by the way, is a turret fortress-castle converted from a dungeon prison to a maritime museum (1 Steenplein). The **Printing Museum** (Plantin Moretus, 22 Vrijdagmarkt) is recommended for bibliophiles. If the children are feeling sportive and want to do any waterskiing or boating on the Scheldt, the Albert Canal or other waterways, call the CTO for all the information.

Punch and Judy show at Van Campen (Lange Nieuwstraat 7) and a puppet theater (Repenstraat 1–3), under the auspices of the **Museum of Folklore**–both surefire entertainment. Check with the CTO for details; also ask if there's a performance scheduled at the **Provincial Open-Air Theatre** at Riverenhof (Turnhoutsebaan 244; Tel: (031) 352564).

Rubens' House (Rubensstraat 9), the perfectly restored house and studio of Peter Paul Rubens is in dazzling contradiction to the stereotyped image of the artist's garret. A memorable example of the sumptuous style to which a famous and successful man was accustomed in the 17th century. The **Permament Diamond Exhibition** in the Provincial Institute for Safety (Jezusstraat 28–30), has diamond processing exhibits and collections of gems and jewels. The **Butchers' Guild House** (Vleehuis, Vleehouwersstraat 30–40) shelters an interesting collection of archaeological and historical artifacts, and musical instruments. The **Royal Museum of Fine Arts** (Leopold de Weelplaats 1–9) has the world's finest collection of Rubens, plus a splendid collection of Flemish primitives. The **Museum of Folk Art** is appealing. **Ridder Smidt van Gelder Museum** has a handsome garden, but its porcelain collections have a paucity of charm for most children. The little **Mayer van den Bergh Museum** (Lange Gesthuissstraat 19), with gold carvings, lace items, tapestries and paintings, is interesting.

Downtown Antwerp features the **Hof van Leysen,** with a remarkable garden for the visually handicapped, with plants to feel and smell. In the suburb of **Deurne** there is **Rivierenhof,** a 320-acre recreational park with boating, rose gardens, playgrounds, and the **Sterckshof Provincial Museum of Arts and Crafts. Middleheim Park** is more placid. The nature reserve and arboretum at **Heide-Kalmthout** (2 Hevuvel) is good for picnics.

For junior archaeologists, **Arlon** is a trove of **Roman ruins** with an important archaeology museum, the **Luxembourg.** For the military minded, the **Nuts Museum** in **Bastogne** commemorates the siege of American troops who, as Gen. MacAuliffe said, replied ''Nuts'' to the proposal to surrender. At **Beloeil, Chateau de Ligne** has a moat and a beautiful park with ponds and gardens. **Binche:** The time to be in town is on Carnival Sunday and Carnival Tuesday for a revelation concerning the universality of the mask and its profound resonances, magical and religious, from liturgical mysteries and sacred theater to the holiday pleasures of feast and frolic. See the **International Museum of the Carnival and of the Mask** (rue de l'Eglise, 7130 Binche), which offers a two-hour guided tour and information. More information is available at the CTO (rue St. Paul 21). In **Bokrijk,** the ***open-air museum*** has 1400 acres of rivers, ponds, woodlands, a deer park, tennis, minigolf and fishing, in addition to the reconstructed medieval village, which features peasant crafts, windmills, beehives, sheep, horses, a water mill, and much more. Afterward, have a meal at **Kasteel Bokrijk** (Bokrijklaan 8), a pleasant castle-restaurant.

In the alphabet of children's attractions, **Bruges** come before Brussels, the capital. I've stayed in Brussels and in Bruges—as a child and as a grownup, and my preference is Bruges. Stay there overlooking the lovely Lac d'Amour (the Lake of Love), and make an excursion (1 hr.) to Brussels, rather than the other way around. The market square, **Grote Markt** (Grand' Place) in the center of town has a belfry containing a master carillon of 49 bells that chime the hours; concerts given by carillonneurs take place from mid-June–mid-Sept., on Mon., Wed., Fri., and Sat. from 9 p.m.–10 p.m.; Sun. all year, and Wed. and Sat. in winter, from 11:45 a.m.–12:30 p.m. Boats for **canal rides** can be hired at: **Venetie Van Het Noorden** (Huidenvettersplaats 13); **Claays** (Rozenhoedkaai 9); **Podevyn** (St. Katelijnestraat 4); the most popular is directly behind the Town Hall. The standard trip takes 40 minutes by day or night. The night trip is best when the town is illuminated from June 1–Sept. **Begijnhof** (the Beguinage) consists of many little houses bordering on cobbled streets that surround a wooded meadow. A quiet retreat founded in the 13th century as a community where women might go voluntarily to sequester themselves without taking religious vows; now lived in by nuns who will be delighted to show you a typical old house and garden; in the meadow expect to see a little grove of artists and easels. **Horse-carriage rides** stop here on their 40-minute circuit, from the Markt. You can't be in Bruges for half an hour without seeing women making lace, but if you want to visit the **Lace School** (Timmermanstraat), where girls 6 and over are taught lace making by Catholic sisters, you'll have to get permission from the City Tourist Office. **St. John's Hospital** and the **Memling Museum,** is a very special attraction with six stunning pictures painted by Hans Memling and a completely furnished 12th-century pharmacy in which prescriptions are still being filled. The **Groeninge Museum** houses some of the great masterpieces of Flemish art, paintings children like for their color and detail. **The Gruuthuse Museum** offers an excellent display of 15th-century life.

Ten mins. SE of town by #2 bus is the **Children's Farm of the Seven Little Towers** (41 Canadaring, Assebroek), a real, working 14th-century farm with a variety of animals. It is best visited in spring or summer. **Boudewijn Park** (A. de Baeckestraat 12, St. Michiels) is an amusement/recreation park with a mini-train, go-karts, ponies, rowboats, and swimming and ice-skating. It's open April–Oct., with a single charge for all rides. **Stockmanshoeve** (Doornstraat 16, Sijsele/Damme) is a 100-acre nature reserve with a children's farm, zoo, fishing ponds, a playground and museums. Open Easter–Oct. **The Klein Strand Recreation Park** (Zandstraat 29, Jabbeke) has water skiing demonstrations and a water circus from July to the end of Aug. For details call (050) 81 14 40. **Aviflora Toeristisch Centrum** in Ingelmuster is a lovely ornamental flower and water garden with a variety of exotic animals and a children's playground. Open year round. Other pleasant parks are: **Koningin Astridpark,** with a playing garden; **Tillgembos** (St. Michiels); **Municipal Park Beisbroek;** and the botanical garden at **Tudor Municipal Park** (Zeeweg). Ask the CTO or Parks Service (Tel: (050) 31 33 97/31 98 93) for details. Bruges is an ideal base for excursions to the Belgian seaside.

In **Dinant,** try the chair-lift ride to the Monfort Tower, and cable car up to the Citadel to see the fort-cum-museum, or the chair-lift ride to the Mont-Fat grotto inhabited by early cavemen.

In **Ghent,** let the children stand on **St. Michael's Bridge** and gaze at the loveliness of the floodlit town (another view is presented after an elevator ride to the top of the **belfry,** where you will share your 280′

loft with a great gilded dragon). There's a nice **museum** of folklore (Kraanlei 65), a **Botanical Garden,** and the **Gravenkasteel** (Castle of the Counts), a massive bastion with a chilling collection of torture instruments. There is a fine puppet theater **(Poppenteater Magic)** performing on weekends. Call (091) 26 42 18 for details. The **Flea Market** (Beverhoutplein) swings into action every Fri. from 8 a.m.–noon, and every Sat. from 8 a.m.–noon. The **Flower Market** (Kouter) blooms daily from 7 a.m.–1 p.m. For **boat trips** on the Leie River check with the Tourist Office (Belfortstraat 9; Tel: 253641) An animal and bird market takes place every Sunday at the **Oude Beestemarkt.** For **boat trips** on the Leie River check with the Tourist Office (Belfortstraat 9; Tel: 253641). See *The Adoration of the Mystic Lamb,* a 20-panel painting, in the **Cathedral of St. Bavo.** Not far from Ghent, the **Chateau de Laarne** has over 1000 pieces of gold and silver plate inside and a sound and light performance outside (summer only).

Han-Sur-Lesse has some of the best grottoes in the area. Go prepared for a subterranean world that can get slodgy and chilly. The **Subterranean World Museum** and the **Safari Park** are good bets, for which there are specially priced combination tickets for children 6–15. A narrow-gauge train takes you to a wonderland of stalagmites and stalactites formed in limestone by the Lesse river. The trip concludes with a fun boatride. Then you board a tram to the Safari Park, which has a wonderful variety of animals. Get tickets from the **Bureau de la Societe des Grottes,** or call Safari Park information at (084) 37 72 13. **Hofstade** is the site of **Planckendaal,** a sanctuary for the breeding of endangered species, and a natural habitat for animals of the area. Nearby is **Hofstade-Rijksdomein,** a recreation park with safe swimming, sailing, canoeing, and other activities.

The town castle dominating **La Roche-en-Ardenne** offers sound and light pageants in English during the summer and some of the prettiest country in Europe, with orchards, trout streams, woods, and undulating roads. **Lichtaart** has **Bobbejaanland,** a 75-acre amusement park with a Western theme, parachuting, cafes, theaters, and a rollercoaster. In **Liege,** there is the **Palace of the Prince Bishops** and the **Arms and Weaponry Museum. Lier** is an historic town, 14 minutes from Antwerp by train, with an intriguing centenary clock, astronomic studio and observatory housed in **Zimmer Tower. Mechelen** (Malines), a town known for its bell-ringing school, has a *Stadsmuseum* with a section devoted to carillons; **St. Rombout's Cathedral** has carillon concerts during summer. **Namur:** The cable car from Pied-du-Chateau square to the Citadel is fun, and boat trips are offered on the Meuse to Dinant. Also, there is an archaeological museum in the Citadel; the **Convent of the Sisters of Our Lady** houses treasures of gold; the **Museum of Ancient Namur Arts,** in an 18th-century chateau, has engravings and paintings by Felicien Rops. I'd also suggest an excursion to **Oostduinkerke,** with a wide beach of fine smooth sand and dunes. Here, fishermen go

shrimping on horseback, winter and summer; the one place in Belgium where you'll see this strange method of fishing; for days and hours when this can be seen, contact the Oostduinkerke tourist office. On the *Sat. before the first Sun. in July,* there is a *shrimp-fishing competition,* not only for the fishermen on horseback, but for children as well. Children equipped with nets wade about with great excitement trying to capture as many shrimp as possible. All sorts of festivities take place—band concerts, a giant parade glorifying the fish and shrimp, and in the evening splendid ballets and folk songs. **Remouchamps** has the "world's longest subterranean boat trip." **Rochefort:** of more interest than its caves is its **animal park** (European bison, wild boar, auroch).

FUN TRIPS Belgium has many **castles** with magnificent formal gardens, some with outdoor swimming pools in which you and your children can swim, all of which have opened their private apartments and family treasures to the public. Many are floodlit during the summer. From May–Sept., special events attract traveling families. The **Belgian National Tourist Office** outlines itineraries that link the castles together with other attractions along the way; you can pick up this booklet in Belgium, but it's better to request a copy before you leave.

Hippotour (12 rue de Moulin, 1331 Rosieres; Tel: 6532487) will trot out details of its equestrian excursions for intermediate and advanced juniors and their parents. Sightseeing included.

The **Flandria Interprovincial Steamboat Services, Ltd.** (Tourist Building, Steen Square; Tel: 33–74–22/33–49–27) tours Antwerp's harbor every half hour and also plies the Schelde River to Ostend. All departures from the Steen. If you want to barge through Belgium on a 12-passenger floating luxury hotel that drifts through canals from Bruges to Ghent to Antwerp, try the excellent tours offered by **Floating through Europe,** 271 Madison Ave., New York, NY 10016. Recommended for parents with children over 12. The narrow-gauge steam engine railway at **Rebecq,** 20 miles SW of Brussels, is enchanting. Also at Rebecq are boat trips on the Senne, nature trails, water mills, an arts and crafts museum (Moulin d'Arenberg) and a beer brewery. **Sint Truiden** has an Astronomical Compensation Clock which puts on a show every hour on the hour. **Tongeren:** Belgium's oldest town's leading attractions are the **Provincial Gallo-Roman Museum** and the **Basilica of Our Lady.**

West Flanders comprises the following fabulous seaside resorts. You can find their CTOs at the following locations: *Blankenberge:* Leopold III-plein; *Bredene:* Town Hall; Tel: (059) 70 59 78; *De Haan:* Stationsstraat 27; Tel: (059) 23 34 47; *De Panne:* Town Hall; Tel: (058) 11 13 02/ 04; *Knokke-Heist:* Information Office; Tel: (050) 60 15 15/16 16; *Koksijde:* Town Hall; Tel: (058) 51 10 62; *Middelkerke:* J. Casselaan 4; Tel: (059) 30 03 68; *Nieuwpoort:* Town Hall; Tel: (058) 23 56 94; Oostduinkerke: Town Hall; Tel: (058) 51 11 89; *Oostende/Ostende/Ostend:* Wapenplein; Tel: (059) 70 11 99/ 60 17; *Wen-*

duine: Town Hall; Tel: (050) 41 50 01; *Zeebrugge:* Markt 7 (Brugge/Bruges); Tel: (050) 33 07 11.

At *Zillebeke/Ieper,* there is the **Bellewaerde Safari Park** and the **Deweer Outspanningcentrum** (Moorsledestraat 6) amusement park.

FUN AND GAMES Belgium is a fine place for swimming and land-yachting. For ***beaches*** and fun in the sun, head for the North Sea coastal resorts, less than two hours from Brussels via the superexpressway. These resorts are exceedingly lively, with many special events. Even if, like me, you think a wonderful beach is one where you are alone, remember that children almost always prefer the gaiety of popular resorts; here you'll have to thread your way through the crowds to the sea, but the swimming is wonderful and safe for the children; you can rent bathing suits, and undress in a little house on wheels. There are donkeys to ride, and beach scooters—four-wheel jobs that children can pedal up and down the beach—and land yachts *(chars-a-voile)* that you can rent. See Fun Trips for a list of seaside resorts.

There are ***yacht clubs*** in Antwerp, Brussels, Ghent, Liege, Namur, and Ostend. The **Brussels Yacht Club,** the **Royal Yacht Club** (Chaussee de Vilvoordel), and the **Antwerp Waterski Club** will give you details about waterskiing and rental of equipment. To find out how to paddle your own canoe, contact the **Brussels Kayak Club** (blvd. d'Ypres 66). **Confederation des Pecheurs a La Ligne** (33 rue de Wynants, Brussels) will tell you the best spots for line fishermen; licenses obtainable at any post office. For information about riding and horseracing, contact **Federation des Sports Equestres** (av. Hamoir 38, Brussels). ***Tennis*** and ***archery*** are commonplace. An ordinary bow is an *arc.* An *arbalete* is a crossbow; crossbowmanship, outmoded in the 16th century with the introduction of firearms and a rarity elsewhere, can still be seen practiced in Bruges, Brussels, Ghent, and Tournai as an everyday sport. The **Societe Royale St. Hubert** (av. de l'Armee 25, Brussels) will give you all the gen about shooting and hunting.

Great sport for children in canal criss-crossed cities like Bruges is sailing ***toy boats*** on a string (some even practice this from hotel windows two stories up); inexpensive boats can be bought in toyshops.

Children interested in ***racing pigeons*** will find many fellow enthusiasts. If they know nothing about training racing pigeons, ask at your hotel or the local tourist office for an English-speaking pigeon-fancier to educate them in the finer details and the super squabs that qualify.

Bicycles with and without motors—you'll be grateful for motors in those Ardennes hills—are easily rentable. The tourist office will help arrange this.

Hang gliding courses are run by **Fulmer Ultralight Diffusion,** 285 A Rue des Palais, 1030 Brussels.

For detailed information write the following about ***flying*** (Aero Club Royal de Belgique, Rue Montoyer 1, 1040 Brussels); ***golf*** (Royal Golf

Club de Belgique, Chateau de Ravenstein, 1980 Tervueren); ***rock climbing*** (The Belgian Alpine Club, Square Ambiorix 37, 1040 Brussels).

SHOPPING WITH AND FOR CHILDREN Shops are open weekdays and Sat. from 9:15 a.m.–6 p.m. Late shopping night is Fri., when the stores are open until 8 p.m.

For children's underwear, sand-pails, and everyday necessities, there are excellent chain stores—**Nopri, Priba, Sarma, Delhaize "Le Lion," Unic, Super Priba,** and **Sarma Lux.** The merchandise is the sturdy, attractive-utility variety. Branches everywhere. Department stores with a food department carrying yummy picnic foods, and good children's clothes and equipment (like car seats), are slightly more expensive and have many attractive buys; with branches everywhere, there are **A l'Innovation, Au Bon Marche, Aux Galeries Anspach.** There are also supermarkets. Ask for the nearest *supermarkt* or *super marche*.

For camp and sport articles, department stores usually carry a few basics, but the specialized sporting goods and camping equipment shops outside of main tourist targets are excellent. In Charleroi, there's **Au Feu de Camp** (blvd. Tirou 113), **Le Campeur** (av. des Allies 43), and **Martin et Fils** (rue Dampremy 39). In Dinant, **Caoutchouc** (rue Grande 107) and **Dinasport** (same address). In Hasselt, **Camping Sport** and **de Kampeerder,** both at Galerie Albert. In Knokken, **Camping and Sport** (Kustlaan 730). In Kortrijk, **Tigris-Sport** (Rijselstraat 4). In Leuven, **Butage** (Bondgenotenlaan 45). In Mons, **Sport Camping** (rue de la Chaussee 17). In Namur, **Camping** (rue de Fer 23–25), **Dermina** (rue de l'Ange 56), **Sports** (rue des Croissants 4). In Ostend, **Deweert** (Leopoldsplain 1).

For chocolates, **Godiva** is the best known and has branches everywhere. For teenage clothing, make a bee-line for **Butch Ji** and its many branches.

In **Antwerp:** English books at **Mommens** (St. Pieterstraat 4–6). Lace? **Au Point de Chantilly** (Schoenmarket 21). Infant clothes at **Premaman** (Meir 25). Nearby is **Princess** (Meir 51–55); children's and junior wear. Toys at **Poppengasthuis** (St. Jacobsmarkt 34). Shoppers without time, hie yourself to Huidevetterstraat, where you'll find, all on one street, children's wear at **Karine** (#17); children's and junior wear up to age 14 at **Ysabel** (#34); toys at **Christiaensen** (#12); and both clothes and toys at **Taymans** (#39–41). You can locate those hand-shaped cookies at **Locus** (Schoenmarket 14), a delicious-smelling pastry shop and afternoon-tea place. For camping and sports goods, **Van Schelle Sport** (Meir 71); **Braine Sport** (Frankrijklei 41) and **Trigano** next door (Frankrijklei 43); and **De Kampeerder** (Leopoldstraat 21).

In **Brussels:** English bookshop (blvd. A. Max 71–75). Excellent toy stores: **Christiaensen** (rue Marche-aux-Herbes 36); **Palais du Jouet** (av. Louise 130); **Serneels** (av. de la Toison d'Or 28), which also stocks nursery furniture. The best place to get toys and children's clothes and furniture is that exceptional children's store, **Dujardin** (av. Louise 8–10). For *articles de sport* or *sport artikelen* (no language problems here!) try **Van Schelle Sport** (Galerie du Roi 1–3); **Harker's Sport** (rue de Namur 51); **Jadorex** (av. de la Toison d'Or 15); and **van Kalk** (rue du Midi 46).

In **Bruges, Premaman** (Simon Stevinplaats 19) is the baby and maternity clothes shop. For lace collars for party dresses, the **Little Lace Shop** (Markt 11 and Wijngaarstraat 32) is a good choice because they will mend a collar for you in case it is ever scorched or torn. Sweet toys at both **Cinderella** (Philipstockstraat 27) and at **Devilder** (Philipstockstraat 24B). Also at **Germeys** (Mariastraat 24). Noeuds can be found at **Bayens** (Wollestraat 8 and Depla 26). Sporting goods? Try **Machiels** (Steenstraat 86), **Henneman** (Noordzandstraat 75) or **Wimme-Catrysee** (Academiestraat 12). Divine chocolates at **Corne de la Toison d'Or** (De Keyserlei 78) and at **Godiva** (De Keyserlei 31).

BELGIAN FRIENDS AND PEN PALS To meet Belgian families, make arrangements through the **Institut Belge d'Information et de Documentation** (rue Montoyer 3, Brussels). Better write in advance, however.

CALENDAR OF EVENTS Check with the local tourist bureau on the dates for these as they are subject to change. In **Feb.–Mar.** (depending upon the date upon which Ash Wed. falls), four days before Ash Wed., Malmedy offers an exciting, three-day colorful ***carnival*** that is highly recommended. One day later, on Shrove Sun., Alost and Eupen both offer a similarly outstanding carnival. On Sun., Mon., and Shrove Tues. itself Binche begins its spectacular ***Carnival of the Gilles*** (the latter being the leaders of the Carnival, who wear white ostrich-plumed hats 5′ high and lead the crowd in a dancing Grand Parade, throw oranges at the crowd, and are full of fun and frolic). Spectators not in masquerade costume or disguised will be pelted painlessly with balloonlike skin bags that pop; riotous, wonderful. Wear a costume or old clothes. Fireworks and general frenzy.

In **Mar.,** on the second Sun. in Lent, the ***Cat Festival*** at Ypres goes on for three days of processions, plays, folklore dances, fair, and festivities complete with folklore giant. Highlight is the tossing from the belltower of lots of small toy cats to spectators. Those catching a cat win prizes. (This ceremony has its origins in the conversion from pagan to Christian beliefs and the renunciation of sacred pagan cats.) On the fourth Sun. of Lent (Laetare Sunday), Fosse and Stavelot provide carnivals similar to that of Binche. Fosse has its Chinels and Stavelot its Blanc Moussis as the kings of the carnival. Costumed crowds, marvelous parades, floats, dancing in the streets, fun and games. On the same day Namur begins its own celebration with its giants, the oldest in Belgium, who parade around the town.

In **May,** on the Mon. after May 2, Bruges features the ***Holy Blood Procession,*** commemorating the arrival of the Relic of the Holy Blood in 1150. Floats, processions, pageantry. The Procession is an annual event, but the related ***Passion Play*** (Sanguis Christi) is performed only once every 35 years in summer. In **May–June,** on Trinity Sun. (8 weeks after Easter) Mons hosts St. George's Battle with the dragon—called ***Lumecon.*** Procession and marvelous dragon with a ribboned tail that sweeps over the heads of the crowd. Comic battle between St. George and the Dragon-Lumecon. Fun and frolic.

In early **July,** Ostend and Coxyde provide ***Festivals of Blessing the Sea.*** On the first Sun. in July, Oosterduinkerke has the Shrimp-Catching Competition for Children in connection with the colorful high and happy jinks of the ***Shrimp Festival.*** July 21, ***Belgian Independence Day,*** brings celebrations everywhere—parades, processions of fantastic animals and characters, floats, flowers, and fireworks. Processions are often referred to as *Ommegangs* or *Tours.*

In **Aug.,** at Namur, there is the ***Summer Carnival of the Giants.*** On the fourth Sun., at Ath, the Wedding of the Giants transpires—a frolicking fair and festival with parades; exciting battle between David and Goliath; amusement fair; procession of folklore giants; a *must* for the young in heart! In mid-Aug, the ***International Jazz Middelheim Festival*** is held in De Brandt Park in Antwerp. In **Sept.,** on the first Sun., Ghent offers a ***Flower Pageant*** with procession of giants. On Sept. 2, there is a ***Community, Horse and Cattle Fair*** at Louvain.

In **Dec.,** on the first Thurs., Arlon's ***Lovers' Fair*** takes place—featuring the Hellechsman, a marriage-making giant represented as a carnival figure 18′ tall who sings, talks, and dances. Parade and festivity. On the 6th, ***St. Nicholas' Day,*** throughout Belgium, a children's preview of Christmas festivities. Illuminations and, toward Christmas, reenactment of manger scenes; choral groups; traditional Christmas festivals generally observed.

There are hundreds of ***folklore events,*** many in summer, that shouldn't be missed. For a complete list free for the asking, contact the Belgian National Tourist Office. There are also scores of annual ***flower festivals*** (the one at Lochristi, near Ghent, is the most lavish).

LANGUAGE AND PHRASEBOOK The inhabitants in the half of the country adjoining Holland speak Flemish, a Dutch dialect, and those in the southern half speak Walloon, a derivative of medieval French. Brussels is officially bilingual. English is widely spoken. A Dutch-speaking Fleming of the north would prefer you to speak English to him rather than French, just as a Walloon of the south would prefer you to speak English to him rather than Flemish.

Hello (Good morning)	*Goeden morgen.*	*Hooden morgan*
My name is—	*Mijn naam is*	*Main narm iss*
I am an American	*Ik ben Amerikaan*	*Ickh ben Amerikam*
I can't speak French	*Ik spreek geen Frans*	*Ickh sprake hayn France*
I can't speak Flemish	*Ik spreek geen Vlaams*	*Ickh sprake hayn Flarms*
Please	*Ais-t-u blieft*	*Alst eu bleeft*
Thank you very much	*Dank U vriendelyk*	*Dankeu freendleg*
Yes	*Ja.*	*Yah*
No	*Neen*	*Nayn*
I am having a wonderful time.	*Ik vermaak my zeer*	*Ickh Furmark mayrzair*
I am—years old.	*Ik ben jaar oud*	*Ickh ben—yahr out.*
1	*een*	*ayn*
2	*twee*	*twee*
3	*drie*	*dree*
4	*vier*	*veer*
5	*vijf*	*vife*
6	*zes*	*zess*
7	*zeven*	*zayven*
8	*acht*	*akh-t*
9	*negen*	*nay-gen*
10	*tien*	*teen*
11	*elf*	*elluf*
12	*twaalf*	*twalf*
13	*dertien*	*dair-teen*
14	*veertien*	*vair-teen*
15	*vyftien*	*vife-teen*
Goodbye	*Tot Ziens*	*Tote zeens*

DENMARK

Denmark is going all-out to become a family vacation resort. The accent is on family vacations, with many accommodations, creative workshops and activity holidays—art, batik, bicycling, botany, ceramics, music, painting, weaving—to choose from. Children will have a splendid time because the Danes haven't skimped on playrooms, playgrounds or attractions for children of all ages.

Denmark is divided into three parts—Sealand (where Copenhagen is), Funen (the smallest), and Jutland (the largest)—made up of 500 lushly green islands with towns that charm and a rural countryside that touches you with a kind of magic.

No family traveling to Denmark should dream of missing Funen or Jutland, both ideally seen by car. Funen, the birthplace of Hans Christian Andersen, still retains its fairytale quality. Jutland's west coast is 250 miles of almost solid beach, dunes, and sand. You'll see Viking funeral mounds, remains of prehistoric dwellings and sacrificial sites all over Jutland.

Copenhagen, set around the enchantment of the Tivoli pleasure park, is a city with many attractions, green copper spires, the King's Palace and palace guardsmen, glittering fountains, and ships at curbside canals.

INFORMATION ABOUT DENMARK Before you go, write the **Danish Tourist Board** (DTB) at 75 Rockefeller Plaza, New York, NY 10019, or contact its offices in Toronto or Los Angeles. The DTB can supply detailed information on activity holidays, trains, buses, ferries, car or bicycle rental agencies, and with a complete list of hundreds of city tourist offices, plus a map of Denmark. In Denmark, the DTB is at H.C. Andersens Boulevard 22, DK–1553 Copenhagen V.

Other major tourist information offices are at: **Gilleleje** (Gilleleje Hovedgade 6 B); **Helsingor** (Havnepladsen 3); **Hillerod** (Torvet 1); **Koge** (Vestergade 1); **Roskilde** (Fondens Bro 3). Regional offices: **Birkerod** (Stationsvej 36); **Fredensborg** (Slotsgade 6); **Frederikssund** (Ostergade 3); **Frederiksvaerk** (Norregade 19); **Hundested** (Norregade 22); **Horsholm** (Usserod Kongevej 31); **Lyngby** (Lyngby Torv 5); **Tisvilde** (Tisvildevej 28, Vejby).

Dantourist (Hulgade 21, DK-5700 Svendborg; Tel: (45) 9 21 07 41) is a wellspring of information about activity and hobby holidays, farmhouse holidays, rentals, transportation. Ask the DTB for the Dantourist *Holiday in Denmark* booklet.

For information about driver's licenses and all things related to car travel, contact the Federation of Danish Motorists at Bledgamsvej 124, Copenhagen. For breakdown and road service in the Jutland Peninsula, contact the Call Center (Tel: (06) 13 33 99); for service in the islands of Sealand or Lolland, the Call Center can be reached at (01) 13 33 99. For a fee, FALCK ((01) 14 22 22) will come to your rescue, day or night. See also Emergencies Made Easy.

Telephones? All Danish telephones are fully automatic. If you need help telephoning, dial 0030. For information, dial 0034.

Information about special facilities for the handicapped—wheelchair rental, hotel and cottage accommodations with easy access, camping possibilities—is obtainable from the **National Association of the Disabled,** Hans Knudsens Plads 1, DK–2100 Copenhagen.

The English-language *Scandinavian Times* will give you up-to-the-minute news about entertainments and attractions.

HEALTH, WATER, AND FOOD Health standards are enviably high. The water is safe to drink everywhere.

Danish food specialties that children will enjoy are *Helstegt svinekam,* roast neck of pork; *kalvestag,* roast veal; *Havarti* cheese, samsoe and Danbo cheeses, *skinke met spejlaeg,* ham and fried egg on brown bread; *kylling* (chicken) or a roastbeef (roastbeef!) sandwich; *Lever postej* (liver pate) sandwich; and other open-faced sandwiches, *smorrebrod* (*smor* is butter; *brod* is bread); miniature meatballs called *frikadeller; Fransk bof,* or beef filet, rare and topped with lemon, butter and parsley; roast pork with apples and prunes; *hakkebof,* hamburgers capped with sauteed onions; *bof med log,* steak and onions; tiny shrimp, salmon smoked or fresh—if they like fish; a variety of berries crowned with *flodeskum* (whipped cream); *Wienerbrod* (Vienna bread, which translates out in English as Danish pastry!); and *rodgrod med flode,* a mixture of red and black currants and raspberries, thickened with sago flour and served with cream and sugar. If your children like hot cereal, the porridges are delectable. The Danish variation of what we know as Apple Betty or Brown Betty is called *Bondepige med slor* (Peasant Girl with Veil) and is made with apples and rye-bread crumbs, sprinkled with grated chocolate, and covered with clouds of whipped cream. Judged very OK by children also are *Kraemmerhuse med flodeskum,* cookie cornucopias filled with whipped cream garnished with jam or fruit. Fresh orange juice is, as it is practically everywhere else in Europe, hard to come by outside of the major hotels. Nor do the Danes go in much for green salads, vegetables, or egg dishes. Dairy products are superb. The only trouble with the milk is that it is so rich and good that children often take a day or so to get used to it. Karoline, a red-cheeked cow with a flower in its mouth is the beguiling symbol for the healthy cows that supply the milk for the superb Danish dairy products.

In **Copenhagen** the young crowd delight in **Bernstorff Cafe** (Bernstorffsgade 7), which is one of over 600 restaurants throughout Denmark serving a *Danmenu,* a two-course lunch or dinner, often of local specialties, served at a reasonable fixed price which includes VAT, service charge and tips. The Danmenu is simple, well prepared, and always fresh and wholesome. The DTB will give you a free booklet with addresses and telephone numbers of all restaurants serving the Danmenu. **Oscar** (Radhuspladsen 55) has a variety of some 200 open-faced sandwiches. **The Royal Hotel** (Hammerichsgade 1, Copenhagen V) has an excellent luncheon. **Burger King** and **McDonald's** are at Radhuspladsen and Vesterbrogade 2. **Arkade Konditoriet** (City Arcade, 32–34 Ostergade) is heaven for pastries.

Country inns *(Kroer)* make ideal and charming stops for meals; here are a few highlights: **Aeroskobing: Kobinghus** is a 17th-century cafe with wonderful goodies. **Ans** (on the Aarhus-Viborg road): **Kongensbro Kro,** with a charming interior; at the Gudenaa River; good place for lunch plus an afternoon of canoeing and fishing. At **Ebeltoft,** a fairytale town, there are two sweet inns: **Hos Juliane** (on the main street with a romantic courtyard) and **Mellem Jyder** (one of the oldest houses, restored in 1660, with a little garden, just behind the town hall). North of **Grindsted, Filskov Kro** has swimming pool; small private airport nearby; fine place for lunch and swim. At **Hald Lakes** (south of Viborg), with national parklands of hill and moor, is **Nils Bugges Kro. Holte** (12 miles from Copenhagen): **Sollerd Kro,** in a forest-embraced, romantic little town. **Hvidsten** (north of Randers): the historic **Hvidsten Kro.** At **Kvaerndrup** (south of Odense) in Egeskov Park (attractive garden and stable, courtyard cafeteria), you'll find the apricot-colored, 400-year-old moated **Egeskov Manor House** and lovely park grounds. **Mariager** (town of roses): the **Apothekergaarden,** once an 18th-century pharmacy, is now a many-chambered restaurant that makes a delicious lunch stop on the way north. **Moesgaard** (south of Aarhus): **Moesgaard Skovmolle** is a lovely thatchroof inn across from an old windmill. **Odense:** treat yourself at **Den Gamle Kro** (The Old Inn) and the **Sortebro Kro** (part of the open-air museum). **Ribe:** the 17th-century **Weis' Stue** is ideal. **Ronnede** (between Koge and Vordingborg on the No. 2 road): **Ronnede Kro.** In **Skanderborg** near the Silkeborg lake district, and north of Horsens Fjord, right in the heart of town, **Munkekroen,** after lunch try sailing or fishing at Snaptun Faergegard, Snaptun, on Horses Fjord. **Sonderho** (island of Fano): **Sonderho Kro** has a view of the centuries-old skippers' cottages in town. **Springforbi** (north of Copenhagen): **Strandmollekroen** is near the entrance to the Deer Park; fine beaches. In **Svaneke** (Bornholm, with cherry trees and nightingales, white-sand beaches, strange rock formations, fields of sun-warmed heather and conical-roof round churches), stop for light refreshment at **Braendegaardshaven;** happy little amusement park here too. **Svogerslev,** (between Roskile and Holbaek): the 18th-century, thatched-roof **Svogerslev Kro.**

BABY FOOD Wide assortment of American and foreign brands obtainable at delicatessens, supermarkets, and grocery stores. Plumrose has an excellent line of baby foods, including strained fruits, vegetables, puddings; also a wide variety of Heinz.

Gastronomic dictionary to baby food:

Bl. grontsagsmos, mixed vegetables; *Bl. grontsager med lever,* mixed vegetables with liver; *Bl. grontsager med skinke,* mixed vegetables with ham; *Bl. grontsager med kalveko,* mixed vegetables with veal; *Gronaer temos,* green peas; *Gulerodsmos,* carrots; *Gulerodsmos med troskerogn,* carrots with fish roe; *Spinatoms,* spinach; *Spinatmos med fisk,* spinach with fish; *Kalvekod med ris,* Veal with rice; *Kalvekod med grontsager,* veal with vegetables; *Oksekod med grontsager,* beef with vegetables; *Honsekod med ris,* chicken with rice; *Honsekod med bonner,* chicken with green beans; *Grontsager med lever,* vegetables with liver; *Grontsager med Bacon,* vegetables with bacon; *Abrikosmos,* apricots; *Aeblemos,* applesauce; *Solbaermos,* blackberries (watch the stains!); *Jordbaermos,* strawberries.

DIAPERS AND LAUNDRY The word for diaper is *ble* (pronounced blee) and the word for disposable diapers is *papir ble* (pronounced pap-peer blee). Both are available in baby specialty shops and department stores; disposable diapers also at almost any large pharmacy. No trouble about getting diapers laundered at your hotel or at a commercial laundry. Copenhagen and Aarhus also have regular diaper services that pick up and deliver. Your hotel hall porter can make arrangements.

BABY EQUIPMENT FOR HIRE Strollers and carriages can be rented for the day. Inquire at the local tourist office.

EMERGENCIES MADE EASY ***Pharmacies*** handling medicines and prescriptions are known as *Apoteker,* open ordinarily from 9 a.m.–5:30 p.m. In Denmark, only medicines prescribed by Danish or other Scandinavian doctors can be dispensed. Also, many preparations that can be bought without a prescription elsewhere in Europe are only sold on a doctor's prescription in Denmark. In the Copenhagen area, 24-hour pharmacies are: **Sonderbro Apotek** (158 Amagerbrogade); **Steno Apotek** (Vesterbrogade 6 C); **Glostrup Apotek** (Hovedvejen 101). In Lyngby: **Svane Apotek** (Lyngby Hovedgade 27).

Doctors: In Copenhagen, emergency service can be called day or night by dialing 00 41. If you cannot get a doctor in an emergency, dial

000 (alarm signal also for fire, police, ambulance, sea or air accident.) Emergency alarm calls from public telephones are free (no coins necessary). For doctors and dentists recommended by the American community, contact the **American Embassy** (Dag Hammarskjolds Alle 24, 2100 Copenhagen 0). An emergency dentist is on duty between 8 p.m. and 10 p.m. during weekdays and from 10 a.m.–noon on weekends and holidays at Oslo Plads 14. Fees of both doctors and dentists, expected to be paid in cash, are reasonable.

Emergency wards on 24-hour service in Copenhagen are: **Kommunehospitalet** (Oster Farimagsgade 5); **Rigshospitalet** (Blegdamsvej 9); **Sundby Hospital** (Italiensvej 1); **Frederiksberg Hospital** (Nordre Fasanvej 57); **Bispebjerg Hospital** (Bispebjerg Bakke 23).

MAGIC FAMILY HELPERS In **Copenhagen,** multilingual babysitters and children's companions are available from **Minerva** (Akrogen 20, DK–2600 Glostrup; Tel: (02) 45 90 45). Arrangements for late-afternoon or night-time sitting should be made before 5 p.m. If you would like an *au pair* girl as a traveling companion during your stay, I would recommend advertising, *months* in advance, in either of these Copenhagen daily papers: *Berlingske Tidende* (34 Pilestraede, DK–1147 Copenhagen K) or *Politiken* (Radhuspladsen, DK–1585 Copenhagen V). Outside Copenhagen, ask the local Turisbureauet or advertise (for Jutland) in the *Jyllands-Posten* (DK–8260 Viby/Jutland); for Funen in the *Fyens Stiftstidende* (Jernbanegade 1, DK–5000 Odense C). ***Nursery?*** The **Rodovre Centrum,** (about 8 miles west of Copenhagen off main highway #1) is a huge shopping center complex heated in winter, open in summer; doctor, dentist, restaurant, banks; up-to-date nursery playroom with a kind and competent staff. ***Supervised children's playgrounds*** are found in most large towns. In **Copenhagen** (tell the supervisor that your child is English-speaking, and when you expect to return): **Christianshavns Vold** (Amager Boulevard, S); **Enghaven** (near Enghave Pl., V); **Faelledparken** (Blegdamsvej/Norre Alle, O); **Valbyparken** (Rosegarden; Hammelstrupvej, SV), a traffic playground where children can learn how to drive and the rules of the road in mini-cars, suitable for over-5's; **Ostre Anlaeg** (Solvtorvet, K., Osterport Station, O). The hotsy-totsiest attractions in town are the saunas at the **Sheraton, Royal,** and **Scandinavia** hotels.

Authorized guide service can be arranged through travel agencies or in Copenhagen by telephoning (02) 63 01 79 daily 9 a.m.–noon, and 3:30 p.m.–5 p.m., May–Sept. For English-speaking driver guides for sightseeing by taxi in the Copenhagen area, call (01) 35 35 35.

Air taxis make daily trips to the islands of Anholt, Laeso and Samso. Contact **Copenhagen Air Taxi** (Kobenhavns Lufthavn Roskilde) or **Beeline Flight Academy** (Lufthavensvej 34, Roskilde).

HOLIDAYS FOR CHILDREN ON THEIR OWN No children's hotels or pensions in Denmark that I know of.

CHILDREN'S CAMPS The **Solhojgard Riding Camp,** a country estate in Hjortdal with seven acres of enclosed parkland near the beach and a 40-acre woods with good bridle paths, offers weekly accommodation, an excursion to Farup Sommerland, and a choice of 20 Icelandic ponies to "children 8–21" from mid-June to early Aug. Parents can also participate with their children from late May–mid-Sept., and weekend arrangements are possible. Ask the DTB for details.

CASTLES AND OTHER HAPPY FAMILY ACCOMMODATIONS Many castles and manor houses to see and visit, but no castles to stay in that I know of. Reserve your kronen instead for staying in a *Kro;* these small, charming country inns are located in villages outside Copenhagen, on the "South Sea" islands, Funen, and especially on the Jutland peninsula. The following Kroer are particularly convenient for families: **Morkenborg Kro and Motel** (Stillebaek, Veflinge), in the **Funen** countryside, with lawn, lake, forest, children's playground, and ponies to ride; **Falsled Kro** (Assenvej 513, DK 5642 Millinge), at **Faaborg,** near the lakeside gardens and island fortress of Egeskov Castle; **Steensgard Herregardspension** (DK 5642 Millinge), a half-timbered manor house with horses, tennis and fishing; **Hotel Kommandorgarden** (Melby, Havneby), on the island of Romo, has its own private schooner for excursions and fishing, indoor and outdoor pool, sauna, bowling; **Filskov Kro** (Amtsvejen 34, Filskov, Grindsted); **Hovborg Kro** (north of Holsted, Tel: (05) 39 60 33); **Hotel Aulum Kro** (Jernbanegade 1, Aulum); **Kongensbro Kro** (in Ans, Tel: (06) 87 01 77); **Hotel Rebild Park** (Skorping, Tel: (08) 39 14); **Morup Molle Kro** (Morup Mollevej 71, Bedsted); **Sallingsun Faergekro** (Sallingsundvej 104, Nykobing); **Tranekaer Gjaestgivergard** (Slotsgade 74, Tranekaer). North of Copenhagen in **Sealand,** down the street from the royal palace in Fredensborg, is **Hotel Store Kro** (Slotsgade 6), an especially luxurious inn which the Danish royal family uses as a guesthouse and where Europe's royals are put up during Danish royal weddings. Near enough to Copenhagen to drive out for lunch or dinner is the **Sollerod Kro** (Sollerodvej 35) with a garden cafe and each room with a different country-life motif, and a castle next door. Check with the DTB for information about the Inn Cheque discount system for families staying in Kroer.

What about a holiday on a ***Danish farm?*** Thanks to cooperation between farms and local tourist offices in East Jutland and Funen, standards have been worked out for comfort and prices (full board or bed-and-breakfast plus lunch *or* dinner). You'll have good food, a good bed, good fun, and for families with children, it's possible to stay on a farm where there are children of the same age. At least one person on the farm will speak English. You may have to share the bathroom with the family or with other guests, but some farms do have private baths for guests. Minimum stay is one week. Tourist offices will send you details—about areas, accommodations, local attractions, distance to the nearest beach—if you write them your requirements: how many you are, the age of your children, how many rooms you'll need, how long you'll stay, if you want full board or just breakfast and one other meal, whether you're interested in swimming, fishing, sightseeing. **Horsens Tourist Office** (25 Kongensgade, 8700 Horsens, mid-Jutland); accommodations here are at the fjord or around Horsens; 26 miles from Aarhus, 47 miles from the Silkeborg Lake district; 30 miles from Legoland. **Kolding Tourist Office** (18 Helligkorsgade, 6000 Kolding, Southern Jutland); accommodations at the fjord of Kolding; 34 miles from the 1000-year-old town of Ribe; 11 miles from historic Christiansfeld; 25 miles from Legoland. **Viborg Tourist Office** (Nytorv 5, 8800 Viborg, Central Jutland); about 25 miles from the nearest beaches, but you'll be in the heartland of the Dollerup Hills and the Hald Lake district with lots of canoeing and fishing.

Farmhouse holidays can be booked at **Dantourist** (see Information), through a travel agent, or by contacting the Turistbureauet in the abovementioned and following towns: Turistbureauet, H.P. Hanssengade 5, DK–6200 *Aabenraa;* Turistbureauet, Osteraagade 8, DK-9000 *Aalborg;* Turistbureauet, Markedsgade, Postbox 33, DK-8500 *Grena;* Turistbureauet, Vestergade 1, DK–*Koge;* Turisbureauet, Hovedgaden 4, DK–*Ronde;* Turistbureauet Osterbro 7, DK–*Skive;* Turistbureauet, Radhustorvet 7, DK–6400 *Sonderborg;* Turistbureauet, Det gamle Radhus, Store Torv, Postbox 210, DK–*Thisted;* Turistbureauet, Torvet 5, DK–6800 *Varde*.

Inexpensive, self-catering cottages and apartments are also available in the abovementioned areas, as well as in Brande, Christiansfeld, Hjorring, Skorping, and Slagelse. Accommodations are leased on a weekly Saturday to Saturday basis and one has to supply one's own towels and bed linen. These holidays are listed as "Carefree Country Holidays, Self-Catering," and can also be booked through the same center as the Farm Holidays.

You can also rent a "Holiday Home" in Denmark. These are accommodations for four to six persons, with living room, modern kitchen, shower, fireplace, sauna, three twin-bedded bedrooms. These are available on a weekly basis at reasonable prices. Bookings can be made with Dantourist.

Combining meals at an inn with your farm vacation on a demipension plan might be a good idea for active families who enjoy motoring.

There are about 118 ***youth hostels*** at 10–15-mile distances. Accommodations are usually dormitories, but small rooms for four persons are normally reserved for families with children 4–15. You can get a booklet listing the hotels, opening and closing dates, number of rooms and showers, and distance from the nearest beach from **Herbergs-Ringen** (Youth Hostels Association; Vesterbrogade, 1620 Copenhagen V). ▶ **Note:** If hotel rooms aren't available, accommodation in someone's house can be arranged in most towns through the local tourist offices; rooms have been inspected and approved. In Copenhagen, the **Accommodation Bureau** (Kiosk P, Central Railway Station) will help you to find hotel accommodations or put you up in a private house; open to midnight every day, May 1–Sept. 15; shorter hours off season.

For budgeteers, *Budgetcheck,* a voucher program for low-cost accommodations, is in effect at about five dozen small hotels, at which room rates, not always including private bath, but with breakfast included, are about ⅓ less than the *Kro Check* voucher program for inn reservations. The *Dancheck* voucher program is valid for major hotels, and *Danish Hotel Checks* is a voucher system operative at Denmark's finest hotels. Information on all programs is available from the DTB.

CAMPING AND CARAVANING Over 500 supervised and approved camping sites are listed in an official guide obtainable from local tourist offices, booksellers, at the frontier, or at a campsite; full information, locations (with maps), facilities, and best routes.

Headquarters for Danish camping information is **Friluftsradet/Det Danske** Lejrpladsudvalg, Skjolosgade, 10, DK–2100 Copenhagen O.

The **Motor Touring Club** of Denmark (FDM) owns a number of sites accessible only to FDM members or members of affiliated clubs.

In Jutland, eight-day riding-camping holidays are possible, with days spent trekking, nights spent in five different scenically located camps with heated sleeping and dining tents. Shower and lavatory facilities are said to be excellent. Meals included for a reasonable fee which is halved for children under 12. Details from the Hobro Turistbureauet. The **Baunehoj Riding School** (Faellesejevej 21, DK–4700 Naestved) in Sealand, offers a week of riding, instruction, excursions and tent accommodations with full board. Dantourist also offers riding holidays.

Canoeing and Kayaking Camping Cruises: During the season from May to Oct., thousands set out for the streams of Gudena, Karup A, Morup Molle A and Skjern A or the Sealand stream of Susaen. For Karup canoeing vacations of one–four days, contact the **Skive Tourist Office.** For Morup Molle A, apply to **Krik Marine,** Agger Havn, DK–7770, Vestervig. For Skjern A, apply to **Vester Molle,** DK–7323 Give, Jutland. For Susaen apply to **Susa Kanoudlejning,** Slusehuset, Astien, DK–4700 Naestved, Sealand. Dantourist (see Information) offers two ready-made canoe camping holidays—one in the south and one in the north. Both trips include hire of canoe for seven days, all camping and canoeing equipment, and transport of the canoe. Each canoe takes a maximum of three people.

ATTRACTIONS FOR CHILDREN IN COPENHAGEN From May to the end of Aug., Copenhagen offers opera, ballet, open-air theater—many performances light and entertaining for older children.

The **Tivoli Gardens:** This is the heart of Copenhagen, 20-acre garden with shade trees fountains, flowers; a lake with little putt-putt boats for children to captain; a children's supervised playground, open 10 a.m.–6 p.m.; amusement park section, gay as a bag of jelly beans; merry-go-rounds; giant roller coaster; the **Tivoli Boy's Guard,** a junior edition of the King's Royal Guard, march merrily through the park to the music of their band; pony rides; 23 restaurants, among which there are special ones for children (*Valkonen, Gyngen, Konditoriet,* and *Bistroen*); **acrobats** and **jugglers;** a theater for the **marionettes** so dear to the heart of Hans Christian Andersen; theater with a curtain like a peacock's tail that unfolds early in the evening upon a delightful **pantomime play,** and later upon one of the world's most gracefully precise **ballet** companies; choice of music for every taste to be heard in a strikingly handsome **concert hall** or from curlicued little bandstand gazebos, or from the **discotheque.** Breathtaking **fireworks** (Wed., Sat., Sun. and holiday evenings). Open May 1 to mid-Sept., from 10 a.m.–midnight.

The **Zoo** (Main entrance: 32 Roskildevej) and **Zoological Gardens:** May 1–Aug. 15, open from 9 a.m.–6 p.m. All the rest of the year from 9 a.m.–4 p.m. Admission trifling. The gardens are situated on top of a hill *(Frederiksberg Bakke),* close to **Frederiksberg Castle** *(Frederiksberg Slot),* and bounded by two public parks *(Sondermarken* and *Frederiksberg Have,* a delightful attraction on its own with canals for rowboats, a wading pool, a pond for ducks and for toy sailboats). **Play Zoo** (animals to pet and to ride); **tower** from which you get a fine view of the town, its environs, and even the shores of Sweden on a clear day. Try to see the animals being fed; (feeding times are thoughtfully posted beside the main entrance and at various other places). There is a restaurant; refreshment stands, and a "family garden" for your own picnic. Copenhagen Zoo is noted for its cleanliness and the fine condition of its animals. Delightful! In the **Circusbuilding** (Axeltorv, in front of Tivoli), **Benneweis,** Europe's biggest and oldest circus opens mid-Apr.–end-Sept.; a one-ring affair, with the quality of purity; beautiful animals. Tickets: Booking Office (8 Jernbanegade, 1608 Copenhagen V; Tel: (01) 14 21 92); advance tickets by writing; up to one week in advance only by telephone. The **Aquarium** in **Charlottenlund** at Strandvejen is just a few miles north, and reachable by S-train or #1 or #27 bus.

The **Arms and Armor Museum** *(Tojhusmuseet, 3 Tohusgade):* A paradise for boys and girls; one of the outstanding collections of weapons, uniforms, armor, and battle flags in the world; open May–Sept., afternoons; longer hours Sun. Admission free.

National Museum *(12 Frederiksholms Kanal):* Viking camps, ships;

folklore exhibits; collections and exhibits of prehistoric, medieval, mid-18th-century Denmark.

Christiansborg Palace *(Christiansborg Slot):* The children may want to take a look at the **Royal Reception Rooms** for a tiny admission charge—open daily except Mon. 10 a.m.–4 p.m. from June–mid-Sept. and from mid-Sept.–May, Thurs., Fri., Sat., and Sun. only. But while you're on Castle Island *(Slotsholmen),* point out to the children that this is where, some 700 years ago, Copenhagen had its beginnings in a fortress-castle that was built for one of the best pirate-fighters there ever was—Bishop Absalon. (There's a statue of him in armor right across the way in the fruit and vegetable market at *Hojbro Pl.*) If it hadn't been for this fierce genius, who rode, fought, swam, and thought better than anyone else around at the time, Denmark would probably have been wiped out by the Wendish pirates. So take a look at the **ruins under Christiansborg** where his old castle-fortress was. Open daily 10–4. Also in one of the wings of the palace there's a **theatrical museum** (actually a court theater) all gilt and red plush, that used to be a king's plaything back in the 18th century. It doesn't sound like much, but it's the sort of thing that appealed to me as a child and still does. Only Sun. and Wed. from 2–4 p.m. Stroll through the **garden of the Royal Library** (very pretty garden) and walk around the Ministry buildings to the **Stock Exchange** *(Borsen),* which has a tower of dragons doing headstands with their tails twisted together. From here, wander over to **Knippelsbro Bridge** for a fine view of the inner harbor (all sorts of interesting craft, including island schooners, to watch).

The **Radhuspladsen,** (City Hall Square) is where a lot of action is. Most city tours start from here. Let the children climb up the **City Hall Tower** for a view of the town. Just to the right as you enter City Hall, you'll see **Jens Olsen's World Clock,** a handsome affair.

Canal and Harbor Tours and Motorboats: Brief motorboat rides through the city's canals are always fun, but the trip you shouldn't miss is the harbor trip to the park and seaside promenade at *Langelinie,* where Andersen's *Little Mermaid* sits on a rock at the water's edge. Boats leave for this trip from Kongens Nytorv at Nyhavn and Gammel *Strand* (the fish, vegetable and flower market, near *Hojbro Pl.*) at the Canal that encircles the Castle Island. The market is fun to see, as all markets are. Tours leave daily, every ½ hour from 10 a.m. For information, Tel: (01) 13 31 05.

At **Amalienborg Palace** (Amalienborg Slot) daily at noon *when the Queen is in residence* (mostly during the winter months; the swallowtail flag is flown from the roof of the east wing when she's there); the **Changing of the Guard** is held in the Palace Square; complete with Palace Guardsmen in crimson coats and black bearskin helmets, and in grand style, performing with a band the wonders of precision marching and the presenting of arms; do get there early so that you can get a good place to watch from. The Guard starts from Rosenborg Castle on Gothersgade at about 11:30 a.m. In the spring and fall, the guard can be seen at Fredensborg Castle in North Sealand. After the ceremony, there is a band concert.

The **Museum of Applied Arts and Crafts** (Kunstindustrimuseet) is open daily from 1 p.m.–4 p.m., Sept.–May, admission free. All sorts of arts and crafts from the Middle Ages to the present.

Rosenborg Palace, a Renaissance castle, with towers and turrets capped with copper green with age, is set in a garden and castle park. The palace serves as a museum for the treasures of Danish monarchs; the magnificent glitter of the **Danish Crown Jewels** is the main attraction. You can't miss them, they're on display in the center of the ground-floor hall. Open June–Oct., 11 a.m.–3 p.m. daily; shorter hours off season. If your child is interested in astronomy, then, of course, you must go to the **Round Tower** (62 *Rundetarn; Kobmagergade*), a 17th century observatory open Apr.–Oct., 10 a.m.–5 p.m. Nov.–Mar., 11 a.m.–4 p.m.; Sun. all year, noon–4 p.m., and 7 p.m.–10 p.m. The **Historical Astronomical** collection is open Sun. from noon–4 p.m. For the astronomy-minded, this is a treat, and the **Observatory of Tycho Brahe,** the renowned Danish astronomer, should certainly be put on the Must See list.

If your child loves the sea and ships, Copenhagen is a paradise. Go to the **Naval Museum** (Orlogsmuseet) (open daily except Mon., June–Aug., 11 a.m.–4 p.m.; Sept.–May 1 p.m.–4 p.m.) and to the canal street of **Nyhavn** during the day. You can watch sailors being tattooed and see all sorts of small craft, two-masted schooners, and other boats engaged in inland shipping. At night, this area is rowdy with sailors' bars and general riproaring whoopee and not the sort of place you take children to.

The **Tobaksmuseet** (Amagertorv 9) has a collection of pipes from all over the world. **Bing & Grondahl** display their porcelain at Vesterbrogade 149. Miniature model theaters from many lands at **Dukketeatermuseet, Priors Papierteater** (Kobmageragde 52). Danish railroad models, equipment, trains at **Jernbanemuseet** (Solvgade 40). **Legetojsmuseet** (Teglgardstraede 13) has toys from the mid-19th century to mid-20th century; closed Mon. and Tues.

The **Zoological Museum** (15 Universitetsparken) has working models, sound effects, dioramas, a museum of natural history that is fun; open daily 10 a.m.–5 p.m., May–Oct.; afternoons only off season. The **Music Historical Museum** (Musikhistorisk; 30 Abenra) open daily 1–4 p.m. *except* Mon. and Thurs., gives visitors the sound of various musical instruments throughout the ages; press a button and you hear flutes, harpsichords, drums, a lur, cithara, helicon, lute, anything. Children adore this. Sensational!

The **Geologisk Museum** (Oster Voldgade 7) has a fine geological display. The **Medical-Historical Museum** (Bredgade 62) has collections showing the development of medicine and dentistry. Open June–

Sept., 11 a.m.–3 p.m. except Sat. and Sun. The **Kobenhavns Bymuseum**—the City Museum—(59 Vesterbrogade); exhibits history of Copenhagen; memorabilia of Kierkegaard.

The Danish Tourist Board sponsors many imaginative ***guided tours.***

One father told me that he took his 10-year-old son to the **Carlsberg** (140 Ny Carlsbergvej Elephant Gate, Mon.–Fri., 9 a.m., 11 a.m., and 2:30 p.m.) and the **Tuborg** (54 Strandvej, Hellerup, Mon.–Fri. between 8:30 a.m. and 2:30 p.m.) breweries and that this was "a grand success." Free samples of beer add to parents' pleasure. The **Industrial Art Tour** (1 p.m. Tues. from City Hall Sq.) visits silver and porcelain workshops.

Copenhagen's parks are lovely: the **Botanisk Have** (botanical gardens; 128 Gothersgade); the **Frederiksberg Have,** with a playground (not supervised) and duck pond, wading pool, canals for rowboats, pond for sailing model boats; plus all the parks with supervised playgrounds (see "Magic Family Helpers").

The DTB can tell you about possibilities for summer **pleasure-boating** on lakes, trips on Fureso, Lyngby So, and Bagsvaerd So, or boating at Peblingeso and at Christianshavn Torv and lakes in that vicinity. There are splendid three to four hour cruises aboard Denmark's oldest schooner, the *Isefjord,* built in 1894, now sailing daily from Copenhagen's Admiral Hotel (Toldbodgade 24). Children are half price, and lunch or dinner is available on board. **Bakken** is an amusement park in greater Copenhagen's northern region in the center of the royal deer park. There's an open-air stage with top-notch performers—a fire-eating Pierrot, fortune tellers, jugglers—fun rides, and good restaurants. Bakken is reachable by #160 or #176 bus, or the S-train to Klampenborg Station.

Children's holiday parties with entertainment are given at Tivoli every Tues., from the end of June until the beginning of Aug. Horse-drawn carriages can clip-clop you around the city daily, May–Oct. (Tel: (01) 12 22 96).

Just outside Copenhagen is the **Frilandsmuseet** (Kongevejen 100), an 85-acre open-air museum of Danish country life, with beautiful landscapes, farmhouses, costumed folk dancers, demonstrations of sheep-shearing, weaving, folk arts, and crafts. The museum is reachable by S-train to Sorgenfri, or by #84 and #384 bus from Norreport.

ATTRACTIONS FOR CHILDREN ELSEWHERE **Aalborg,** (northern Jutland), has a **zoo** and a **park** open mid-Apr.–Sept. with special children's performances on Wed. from late June–mid-Aug. Also the **Moesgard Museum of Prehistory,** with pre-Viking archaeological finds; the **Fire Brigade Museum** has five dozen fire engines of varying ages on view; the **Tivoli Friheden** has Denmark's oldest merry-go-round. Take the ferry to Egjolm Island and drive under the Limfjorden to Norresundby to see the largest Scandinavian **burial site.** **Aarhus,** a Jutland port with heavenly scenery and excellent beaches, has a fascinating Old Town **open-air museum** (Den Gamle By), a collection of Danish townhouses. Everything is furnished according to historical periods from the 16th century on; pharmacies and workshops of jewelers and shoemakers are captivating. The Burgomaster's House and the Alborg House (exhibits ceramics and old stoves) are particularly nice. Several houses feature special collections. All the old handcrafts are here; **theater** in late June and early Aug.; **opera** in early Aug.; in summer, there are weekly ***concerts*** (using an 18th-century organ of the sort played by Bach) in **Aarhus Cathedral,** an immense and splendid church. **Aero** is the perfect island that makes children walk around on tiptoe full of happy joy. The trip takes about 1¼ hours from Svendborg by ferry to **Aeroskobing,** capital of this gem, or in 50 minutes by car ferry from Faaborg in Funen. The best place to stay is the 32-room **Aerohus,** with an orchard garden and courtyard cafe. There's a little **museum** whose three main exhibits are Danish **postage stamps, pipes,** and marvelous **model ships** and ships in bottles. Half-timbered houses are so low here that the children can pat the roofs affectionately. At the museum called **Hammerichs Hus** (corner of Gyden and Brogade), rooms furnished with the ***arts and crafts*** of South Jutland and the neighboring islands will delight you and the children. Have a swim on the beach. There are other villages on the island, and you can go to at least two of them: **Marstal, model-ship museum;** and the little fishing town of **Soby-Bregninge,** where the children can explore its **lighthouse. Amager Island** (where Kastrup Airport is) has a sweet little town, **Dragor,** well worth seeing—**Dragor Museum** in the oldest house of the village (at the harbor) displays ***furniture, costumes,*** and the ***history of fishing and shipping.***

At **Billund** (12 miles west of Vejle in Jutland) is **Legoland,** a family pleasure park, a 30-minute flight from Copenhagen. Lego, a Danish toy-manufacturing firm, has created **Miniland,** which has miniatures of the world's best-known towns and landscapes, as well as Legorado, a Wild West town, Titania's Palace, a fantastic doll's house, a traffic school, a minitrain. There is a children's 200-seat theater with puppets, marionettes, films, music, ballet, and plays; a marvelous antique collection of 300 dolls displayed in doll-sized interiors from the 16th–19th centuries. The Exhibition Hall has large panoramas illustrating Hans Christian Andersen's best known fairytales and also shows changing exhibits of models built from Lego Toys. I love the Lego people for providing this happy park, a place where parents can relax. Those thoughtful people have also provided restaurants, a first-aid station and rooms for washing and dressing babies. Open May 1–Sept. 30.

Bornholm (only 70 miles in circumference) is a sunny island far out in the Baltic, 45 minutes by air from Copenhagen, seven hours by sea, remote despite ten boat and five air connections daily in summer. The island possesses **four round churches** (at Osterlars, Olsker, Nyker, and Nylars), unique in Europe, that serve the purpose of church and fortress. Houses with red-tile roofs have color-washed walls. Moors of flowering broom and heather, cliffs to the north—on which **Hammerhus Castle** perches near **Allinge-Sandvig,** the island's main resort (open-air pool between the cliffs and a fine natural beach) has many halftimbered houses, a sweet small folk museum (Tommehuset); a summer 70-minute boat trip to the lovely island of Christianso (Ertholmene). In the south, there is the historical town of **Svaneke,** plus **Dueodde,** the 30-mile beach at the island's southern tip which has the finest sand in Denmark. **Ronne** is the largest town, with many half-timbered buildings, an interesting museum, aerial sightseeing, and a theater said to be the oldest in use in Denmark. For more tourist information, check with the Bornholm Tourist Office, Havnen, DK–3700 Ronne. Cherry trees bloom in early summer; in late summer and early autumn the heather blooms.

Christiansfeld abounds in gingerbread shops and historic charm. Djurs Sommerland (Randersvej 17, Nimtofte), between Randers and Grena in Djursland, is a recreation park with canoes, rowboats, mini-trains, go-carts, crazy bikes, minigolf, bowling, trampolines, archery, and more, in a wild west setting. Open mid-May–Aug. **Ebeltoft** is another fairy-tale town with a 100-year-old wooden man-o'-war left over from the battle of Helgoland on display at the **Fregatten Jylland Museum.** Also a **craftsman's house** (13 Adelgade) from the 17th century with an interesting garden. Visit **Elsinore** in North Sealand to see **Kronborg Castle,** the setting of Shakespeare's *Hamlet.* Denmark's **Technical Museum** is nearby in **Helsingor,** as is moated **Frederiksborg Castle** in **Hillerod,** which houses Denmark's **National Historical Museum.** From Elsinore, you can take the old-fashioned steam train to the fishing village of **Gilleleje** on the Kattegat, or board a ferry to Helsingborg in Sweden (leaving every 15 minutes.) **Fano** is a heath-covered island, ten miles long and three miles wide, right outside of Esbjerg harbor on the western coast of Jutland; ferries leave Esbjerg every 20 minutes. The island can be explored by bus, car, or bicycle; splendid beaches; at the 300-year-old village of **Sonderho,** folk costumes are worn with unaffected grace and charm on festival days. At **Nordby,** the **Fan Museum** is housed in a remarkable old Fano house with 200-year-old interior. Whatever you do, don't miss the Viking plays at **Frederikssund** in July, as part of the **Viking Festival;** the rollicking old sagas are performed with lots of derring-do and action, and are marvelously entertaining, with 200 citizens of Frederikssund taking part. A bus from Copenhagen's City Hall takes you there. After the performance, you can revel in a Viking Banquet with Viking entertainment. For older children and parents this is great fun.

At **Givskud** (southern Jutland) is the 20-acre **Lion Park** (Loveparken) open May–Sept. where you can take a safari in your car (or a zebra-striped jeep provided by the park) through a wooded park where giraffes lope, elephants amble, and lions loll in the sun. **Gjern** in Jutland has an automobile museum. At **Glud** (Jutland, between Horsens and Vejle Fjords), you can visit the open-air **Glud Museum,** that tells an outstandingly good historical narrative about the life of the farmer in bygone days. At **Havnstrup** is the Jutland **Mini-Zoo.** At **Herning** (Jutland), the open-air museum has special displays of the textile industry and several fully furnished old farm houses complete with costumed figures that look very real. At **Humlebaek,** the **Louisiana** modern art exhibition in a large park is open 10 a.m.–7 p.m. in summer; 10 a.m.–5 p.m. in winter; all contemporary art forms on display; a do-it-yourself-selfexpression section for children to paint, sculpt, make mobiles, and collages; a lovely park to explore. At **Jelling,** the home of ancient Danish kings, you'll see a runic inscription of the unification and Christianization of Denmark.

Kvaerndrup (South Funen, near Ringe): **Egeskov Castle,** a Renaissance island fortress, rising sheer from the water, has summertime concerts in its Great Hall, and is my favorite castle in Denmark, surrounded by a 35-acre park of Baroque topiary gardens with lifelike trimmed animals and birds, an amazing maze, a rose garden, farmhouse garden, herb garden, and Renaissance parterre garden. Also, there's a museum with veteran cars, planes, motorcycles, and a horse carriage museum. Reachable by bus from Kvaerndrup or Nyborg. Information from Nyborg Tourist Office (Torvet 9).

In the south of Jutland, I think you'll enjoy the little village of **Mogeltonder** outside of Tonder. The town of **Nyborg** (East Funen) is built around its **Castle** in a countryside abounding in moated manor houses, old water mills, and bordered by beaches. From **Nykobing,** in northwestern Jutland, your children might want to go birdwatching in the flats by the Limfjord. Near **Nysted** (Lolland Island), you'll find **Alholm Castle** housing veteran cars from all over the world. Near beach and the **Knuthenborg Safari Park,** Denmark's largest. Twenty miles off the express route to the Continent, this is a worthwhile detour. The **Danish Bluebell** line tracks around the park in summer for railway enthusiasts; a **traffic school** with old cars too!

Odense (Funen), where Andersen was born, houses the **Hans Christian Andersen Museum** (43 Hans Jensensstraede) where you can see, among other things, his traveling equipment—a bag, walking stick, umbrella—and his favorite saying in his own handwriting: "To travel is to live!" The **open-air museum** (Fynske Lansby) has a charming reconstructed village. From mid-July–mid-Aug., the **Hans Christian Andersen Festival** is held here at which his fairy tales are beautifully performed. Also see the **zoo;** the **statue of Hans Christian Andersen** in the city park and the house where Andersen lived as a child (5 Munkemollestraede). **St. Knud's Cathedral,** built by Canute the Holy, a nephew of Canute the Great, who bade the tide turn back just to prove to his flattering courtiers that it wouldn't, is in nice contrast to all the little thatched-roofed houses. The golden altar piece is absolutely lovely. **Fyns Tivoli** (304 South Blvd., near the zoo) is a bright, attractive fun-fair, open April–Sept., 2–11 p.m. From May–mid-Sept., one of the nicest things you can do is to ***cruise along the Odense River.*** Departures daily from Munke Mose to the zoo, Fyns Tivoli, and Fruens Boge (The Funen Village). For details, Tel: (09) 13 83 43 or get in touch with the Odense Tourist Information Office (in the Town Hall; Tel: (09) 12 75 20). There's a good open air **swimming pool** at Elsesmindevej, and four indoor pools. Other attractions include: **Horses and ponies for hire** at **Dalum Rideskole** (Dalumgards Alle) or at **Fyns Rideklub** (Tarupgardsvej 3); rowing at **Rowing Club** (Kanalvej 10); sailing at **Sailing Club** (Ostre Kanalvej 10); **Golf Club** (Hestehaven 201); and there is the **Squash Center** (Nyborgvej 341 B).

Nature-lovers' excursions from Odense include the **Terrarium** in Vissenbjerg, about 12 miles distant, with the largest collection of snakes, toads, and crocodiles in Scandinavia, along with colorful botanical exhibits; the **Funen Aquarium** in Rold (Roldvej 53), with 27 separate aquaria among which is said to be the largest aquarium in Europe; the **Frydenlund Birdpark** (Skovvej 50, Naarup) is a pleasant flowery park with 80 aviaries; open Easter–Nov.

The Tourist Office can arrange transportation for you to neighboring places of interest; do make the 12-mile excursion to **Kerteminde** to see the **Ladby Viking Ship;** dates back to about A.D. 850 its chieftain was buried aboard and even though his grave has been plundered, the ship gives a splendid idea of the size, construction, and appearance of these ancient craft; closed Mon.

In **Randers** *(East Jutland)* or in **Ribe** *(South Jutland)* you can see storks nesting on the chimney tops, and lovingly preserved medieval houses, courtyards, and lanes. The storks arrive in the early part of May for nesting; the strong-flying males arrive several days before females. In the latter part of Aug., they take off for South Africa, where they arrive around mid-Nov. and leave again in Mar. They have no call, but clap their bills at you instead. At **Rebild National Park** (18 miles south of Aalborg) the **Danish-American Emigration Museum,** Lincoln's Log Cabin, donated by Danish-Americans, may be of patriotic interest. Our Independence is celebrated here on July 4th; fireworks at night in Aalborg. **Ribe:** a 1000-year-old town; splendid cathedral, monastery, and antiquarian collection; a ruined castle on a hill; half-timbered houses; several excellent modern handicraft shops; also see Randers. At **Ringkjobing** (western coast of Jutland) junior ornithologists will want to make an excursion to see the bird life in **Stadil Fjord.**

Roskilde is 30 minutes by train from Copenhagen, and even though its medieval cathedral with all the royal tombs won't be of riveting interest to the children, the Viking ship museum is fascinating; with five Viking ships from 1000 AD; explanatory film in English; this is *wonderful*—a must. Open daily; hours vary. Also, at nearby **Lejre** is a historical-archaeological research center and open-air museum. At **Rye** (near Silkeborg in Jutland) is **Om Kloster,** a 12th-century Cistercian monastery with a herb garden of medicinal plants and a collection of skulls and skeletons—children are usually fascinated with this.

Silkeborg (in the lake district of Central Jutland) is famous for its **Hovedgaard Museum** which houses the mummified 2000-year-old Tollund Man. There's a great 1½-hour ***excursion*** on a 100-year-old paddle steamer, **Hjejlen** (The Heron), through the chain lakes, daily, mid-May–mid-Sept. You can also go canoeing, take steamers and motorboats, but the paddleboat is more fun. A moated castle I am particularly fond of for its extraordinary simplicity and compactness is **Spottrup Castle** not far from **Skive** (northwest Jutland). Nearby at **Hjerl Hede** is an open-air museum in which an iron-age house, stone-age settlement and village come to animated life during July; on view, however, Apr. 1–Oct. 30. The **Viking camp** at **Trelleborg** (near Slagelse) is also worth a look. This is what remains of the Viking stronghold some 1000 years ago when Viking forays were planned as large-scale military operations. **Troense,** on Tassinge Island (reachable from Svendborg) has the **Sofartmuseet,** a maritime museum with a huge collection of model boats, sailing ships. In **Ulstrupp** is a castle occupied by dolphins; frequent performances mid-Apr.–Sept. 30.

FUN TRIPS Take the hydrofoil or the new hovercraft service from Copenhagen and zip across to Sweden's third largest city—Malmo. Once there, take the 45-minute canal boatride which embraces the Old Town of the city.

Danish waters are good for summer sailing and boating. Ask the DTB for a list of rental firms, or check out information on the spot at the local Turistbureauet at Aalborg, Arhus, Gilleleje, Holbaek, Ronne, Sonderborg, Stege and Svendborg.

Bicycle tours? There are dozens of tours planned for from four to nine days. You and your family can start on whatever day you wish and set off on your own individual family tour. Hotel or youth hostel accommodation, full board or half board, rental of bicycle with carrier bags, route descriptions, maps, tickets for ferry crossings if any and a few admission fees to local attractions are all included in the price. The DTB and Dantourist can help you with arrangements.

Take an overnight ferry to Bornholm (see "Attractions"); cabins available. Odense to Svendborg (only 27 miles), and then by ferry to Aero. On the way, a little way out of Ringe, off the main road, please stop to see the prettiest castle in Funen—**Egeskov Castle.**

A city sightseeing tour by helicopter, known as the Red Tour, or for longer tours, the Blue Tour along the Danish Riviera, or the Green Tour over the castles of North Sealand, can be arranged by SAS, or by a travel agent.

FUN AND GAMES ***Swimming?*** Most towns have excellent open-air pools. The indoor swimming pool is a feature of many hotels and motels, but in Denmark you are never far from a white sand beach, cliffs with curving crescents of sandy foreshore, and rocky coasts beloved by snorkelers and scuba divers.

In Copenhagen, there are nine public open-air swimming pools, open mid-May–end Sept. Try **Bavneho Friluftsbad** (Tel: (01)214900). There are 20 indoor public swimming pools, clean and attractive as they can be.

Some of the best beaches in Sealand are: **Julebaek, Hornbaek, Dronningmolle, Gilleleje, Rageleje, Tisvildelege,** and **Liseleje**—all between Elsinore and Hundested. Farther west, all of the **Odsherred** beaches, from Rorvig to Sjaellands Odde, by Hove and the Ordrup Naes. Farther south, fine beaches at **Korsor** and **Karrebaeksminde.** In Funen, good beaches around **Strib** and **Fyns Hoved,** good swimming near **Marstal** and **Aeroskobing** on **Aero,** and **Langeland.** In **Bornholm** the 30-mile beach along the south coast is a major attraction and nowhere is it better than along the dunes of Dueodde. Avoid the small, sandy bays of the cliff coast from Gudhjem to Hammerknuden and Vang: currents and undertow. **Allinge-Sandvig** has a beach and an open-air pool.

There are indoor and outdoor ***tennis courts*** everywhere, and guest cards are issued. In **Copenhagen,** get in touch with **Dansk Lawn-Tennis Forbund** for details on where to rent rackets and at which clubs you can become a member. There are ***golf courses*** at **Eremitagen** and **Rungsted** near Copenhagen. Rungsted is the top choice. There are good courses in **Aalborg, Aarhus, Esbjergve Kolding, Herning, Randers, Ebeltoft, Silkeborg,** and on **Fano.** Guests are welcome everywhere and greens fees are reasonable. In **Copenhagen,** there's also badminton and cricket. ***Cycle racing*** on the **Ordrup Track,** Charlottenlund, usually Mon. or Tues. from the beginning of May–mid-Sept., weekdays 7–10 p.m. Ask your local tourist office about automobile racing. June–Aug., you can play ***squash*** at the **Kobenhavns Squashklub.**

There are ***riding schools*** in all major towns where a horse can be hired with an escort. In **Copenhagen,** get in touch with the **Sportsrideklubben.** You can hire horses to ride in the **Deer Park** (Dyrehaven), much the prettiest riding paths. Horses for hire also at **Barthahus** about 25 minutes by car from Copenhagen. If you just like to look at horses, there are trotting races on Sun. and some Wed. at the Amager and Charlottenlund tracks in Copenhagen, and at Aalborg, Aarhus, Bornholm, Nykobing, Odense, and Skive. There's ***horse racing*** at Copenhagen's **Klampenborg Race Course,** and at **Aalborg, Aarhus, Odense,** and **Skive.** The local tourist offices can give you schedules.

Fishing and hunting. Fishing in lakes and streams is commonplace. You have to get a license from the landowner, but your hotel porter or the local tourist office will help you with advice and information. For sea fishing, non-Scandinavians must apply for fishing licenses from the Fishery Control, stating passport number and nationality and sending along an international reply-coupon. In **Copenhagen,** for information, get in touch with **Fiskeriinspektoren.** Elsewhere, the local tourist offices will guide you through all the formalities, which sound worse than they are. In Copenhagen, for information about fishing in general, check things out with the **Lystfiskeriforeningen.** There is forest, field, and shore shooting, but rights are privately owned and prior arrangement and game license must be obtained. The DTB can supply details. And, ah, yes, clay pigeon shooting at the **Storkobenhavns Jagtforening** shooting ranges at **Amager.**

Skating rinks in **Copenhagen** are open Oct.–end of Mar.

Young toxophilists will be happy to hear that every Sun. morning, 10 a.m.–noon, May–Oct. there's ***archery*** at **Valby Idraetspark,** Ellebjergvej.

The children can ***fence*** at **Salle d'Armes Mahaut** (24 H.C. Andersens Boulevard, Copenhagen V). The children should wear leotards, but be sure to telephone to find out if quilted fencing jackets are supplied or whether you should make do with a heavy polo shirt.

Bicycles, regular or tandems, which cost 50% more, plus special rear seats for the tots, can be hired in **Copenhagen** at **Jet Cycles** (Istedgade 71); at **Kobenhavns Cyklebars** (Gothersgade 159). At railway stations in the suburbs, and for rentals in North Sealand, call (01) 14 17 01.

SHOPPING WITH AND FOR CHILDREN Shopping hours 9 a.m.–5:30 p.m., Mon.–Thurs.; Fri., stores stay open until 7 p.m.; early closing on Sat. at 1 p.m. In **Copenhagen,** the Stroget, the main shopping street, is a Pedestrian's Promised Land—all traffic is banned except for early-morning deliveries, and the variety and display of its shops is appealing.

Moms, watch out for MOMS, a value-added-tax on all goods you buy in Denmark which can be refunded in certain cases when goods are sent directly to your home address. Ask when you buy and, if the store is going to send your purchases back to the U.S. for you, note the store's name and address and keep the receipt until the goods are delivered.

There are outstanding ***toy*** buys in Denmark, Danish-designed and Danish-manufactured superbly well. **Kay Bojesen's** wooden monkeys are internationally recognized as the high monkey-monks of the toy world. His other animals and people are also remarkably pleasing. Sturdy, strong and original toys available at his toyshop in Copenhagen. **Lego** plastic building blocks are also a Danish concern (and we owe them a hearty round of thanks for Legoland in Billund). The Danes are also responsible for the **Jolly Jumper,** a chair on springs that you attach to a door or whatever else is handy; baby bounces up and down—great exercise and great fun; you can find them in the children's departments of major department stores and in children's specialty shops. Another Danish specialty is the basket you can tote a baby about in. A good basketware shop is **R. Wengler** (7 Amagertorv). The best toys can be found at **Kay**

Bojesen (47 Bredgade) at **BR-Legeto** (Bremerholm 4), and **Ronberg-Legeto** (Store Kongensgade 60).

The Danes also excel in the manufacture of children's ***furniture.*** For furniture and home accessories, the best can be found at **Den Permanente** (8 Vesterbrogade) which also carries dolls in Danish national costumes, some beautiful and special children's clothes, and year-round displays of wonderful Christmas decorations (their mark-up is horrific in the U.S.). The porcelain figurines at **Bing and Grondahl** (Amagertorv 4) may be collectibles for your child.

Handsome children's clothes are at **Magasin du Nord** (13 Kongens Nytorv), a fine department store to just wander through, which also stocks dolls in national costumes.

Great hand-knitted Icelandic and Danish sweaters at the huge **Sweater Market** (15 Frederiksberggade).

In **Aalborg, Aarhus,** and **Odense,** the place to go for handicrafts and regional articles is **Handarbejdets Fremme.**

DANISH FRIENDS AND PEN PALS To meet the Danes, all you have to do is go *in person* as soon as possible after your arrival to the **Tourist Offices**—in Copenhagen, Aalborg, Aarhus, Esbjerg, Fredericia, Herning, Horsens, Kolding, Odense, Silkeborg, Skanderborg, Skive, Slagelse, and Vejle, where the program is operative—to make arrangements. Visits are usually fixed for 8 p.m. (after dinner). *No visits are arranged on weekends, Christmas, Easter, or Whitsun.*

For a fee of $30, **Friends Overseas** (68–04 Dartmouth Street, Forest Hills, NY 11375) will arrange three contacts between Americans and residents of Copenhagen to make whatever arrangements they wish about meals together, an evening of conversation, sightseeing or other activities. For example, Emily writes: "All summer I will be working at a news agency as a journalist. It's now almost five years since I left the States after a year at a New England College. I miss the country and would appreciate the opportunity to brush up on my English. I am 25 and would like to meet people of both sexes my age and older." (See also Norwegian Friends and Pen Pals).

CALENDAR OF EVENTS Particulars of fairs and exhibits, horse, dog, and flower shows, automobile racing, sports events, and other events can be had from the Danish National Tourist Office. Here are a few highlights, but be certain to check dates, as they are subject to change:

Shrove Monday, which falls in Feb. or Mar., at Amager, children are costumed in fancy-dress cavalcade and there is tilting at a barrel. In **Mar.** too, at Givskund, the Lion Park opens (through Dec.). On the 11th, in Copenhagen, the ***King's Birthday*** is celebrated; children gather at Amalienborg Square to watch guards parade and listen to the band concert. On the 28th, the ***Queen's Birthday,*** the celebrations are repeated. In mid-**Apr.,** in Copenhagen, the ***Benneweis Circus*** (through Sept.) opens and, out at the Deer Park the ***Bakken Fun Fair*** opens (until end-Aug.).

On **May** 1, in Copenhagen, ***Tivoli*** opens; early May brings ***folk dancing*** to Viborg; May 31, ***Fire Festival*** at the Deer Park in Klampenborg. From May–mid-June, at Hillorod, Andersen's "Big Claus and Little Claus" is performed by children. And at Billund (until end-Sept.), ***Legoland*** is open.

In early **June,** Odense has the ***Nordic riders meeting*** and Aalborg the ***Hjallerup Fair.*** In Copenhagen, June 15 is ***Valdemar's Day,*** with parades to celebrate the 13th-century Danish victory in Estonia. June 23, throughout Denmark, there are ***Midsummer Eve*** (Sankt Hans Aften) celebrations; bonfires lit all along coasts; witches burned in effigy; fireworks; folk dancing. In late June to early July, at Frederikssund, the glorious ***Viking plays*** open, with pageantry, exciting battle scenes—not to be missed! From mid-June to the end of the month there are ***cattle fairs*** at Roskilde, Odense, Maribo, Aalborg, Aabenra, and Herning. In late June or early July there are ***tilting tournaments*** (medieval fencing on horseback, where riders duel with lances) at Aabenra, Tonder, Ribe, and Grasten.

Beginning in **July** (and running into Aug.), Odense has the ***Hans Christian Andersen Festival;*** well-known fairytales are performed in Danish and English. Danes celebrate our own ***July 4*** at Rebild National-Aaark near Aalborg. Around July 5–8, Nordby has ***Fanniker Days;*** civic festival; pageants, general fun and frolic. In mid-month, Sonderborg has ***Ringridfest,*** the biggest and best-known of all tilting tournaments, with 400 riders dueling on horseback; great excitement. On July 18, Sonderho holds ***Sonderho Day;*** traditional festival including a wedding procession in national costumes.

Aug. 15, in Copenhagen, is ***Tivoli's birthday;*** the Tivoli Boy Guards celebrate from early morning; magnificent fireworks at night. Mid-month in Logumkloster is the time of the ***Kloster Maerken,*** a wonderful fair. On the 30th, at the Deer Park, the ***Bakken Fun Fair*** closes with a festival. In early **Sept.,** Aarhus has ***Festival Week,*** with opera, ballet, and concerts, and Egeskov has the ***Egeskov Fair,*** with election of the King of the Beggars. In mid-month, in Copenhagen, the ***closing of Tivoli*** winds up with a torchlight parade. In **Nov.,** if you're in Copenhagen on ***Thanksgiving Day,*** an annual dinner is given by the American Club and the American Women's Club.

From **Dec.** 16–25, throughout Denmark, there are ***Christmas celebrations*** and ***Christmas Eve festivals.*** On the 31st, fireworks and ***New Year's Eve festivals.***

LANGUAGE AND PHRASEBOOK Pronunciation offers far fewer pitfalls, it seems to me, than French or German. Copenhagen is pronounced Copen-*hay*-gen, and Odense, *Oh*-den-suh. *J* is pronounced as a *Y,* so the town of Jelling becomes Yelling. The letter *ø* is pronounced like *u* in fur; *Aa* (or a) is pronounced like *aw,* and *ae* like *ay.* Boy is *dreng* (boys, drenge); girl is *pige* (girls, *piger*—rhymes with meager); a child is *barn* and children are *børn* (rhymes with learn).

Hello	*God Dag*	*go th—day*
My name is__	*Mit navn er*	*Meet noun air*
I am an American	*Jeg er Amerikaner*	*Yeye air Amairykay-naw*
I can't speak Danish	*Jeg kan ikke tale dansk*	*Yeye can eeker tail dansk*
Please	*Vaer saa venlig*	*Vayr saw venlee*
Thank you	*Tak*	*Tak*
Yes	*Ja*	*Ya*
No	*Nej*	*Nigh*
I am having a wonderful time.	*Jeg morer mig dejligt.*	*Yeye more er my dial-it.*
I am__years old.	*Jeg er__aar gamen*	*Yeye air__or gamel.*
1	*en*	*een*
2	*to*	*toe*
3	*tre*	*tray*
4	*fire*	*fee-rah*
5	*fem*	*fem*
6	*seks*	*secks*
7	*syv*	*sue*
8	*otte*	*oh-tuh*
9	*ni*	*nee*
10	*ti*	*tee*
11	*elve*	*el-vuh*
12	*tolv*	*tahlv*
13	*tretten*	*trett-un*
14	*fjorten*	*fyawr-tun*
15	*femten*	*fem-tun*
Goodbye	*farvel*	*fahr-vel*

ENGLAND AND WALES

England is a superb country for children and families. London provides an extraordinary range of entertainments and facilities for children of all ages. Childcare, education and delights for children are a national pride. For children old enough to appreciate the healthy outdoor life, for nature-loving families, for families with special interests, for families on a budget, England and Wales are paradises.

"Children are happy as the grass is green," Dylan Thomas said about Wales. The Saxons were responsible for the word "Welsh," which means foreigners; the Welsh refer to their people as *Cymry* (pronounced Kuhmry), which means Friends, and they are just that for families with children.

No wonder London and Britain are the leading destinations of American travelers to Europe. They offer vacations that will enrich your life and give you wonderful value for your money.

INFORMATION ABOUT GREAT BRITAIN For information, your main source of supply is the **British Tourist Authority** (40 West 57th St., New York, NY 10019; Tel: (212) 581–4700). BTA has branches in Chicago, Dallas, Los Angeles, Toronto, and Vancouver.

Abroad, the **Wales Tourist Board** (Brunel House, 2 Fitzalan Rd., Cardiff CF2 1VY) has a branch office in London at 23 Madox St., W.1.

There is a network of over 700 Tourist Information Centers (TIC) throughout Britain where you'll find polite, accommodating people to help and advise. A list of TICs is available from BTA.

In London, there is also the **City of London Information Centre** (by St. Paul's Cathedral; Tel: 606–3030). In British usage, the city (lower case) means all of London; the City (upper case) means banks, medieval churches, other historic sites bordered by Smithfield Market to Liverpool Street Station at the north, The Temple to the Tower at the south. The **London Tourist Board** (26 Grosvenor Gardens, London S.W.1) provides information, theater and tour tickets, and a same-night accommodation booking service if you appear in person. Branch information offices at *Victoria Station* (for information about London and England;

open 8 a.m.–10:30 p.m.); *Heathrow Central Station; Heathrow Airport;* Harrods (4th floor) and Selfridges (ground floor), open during store hours. Telephone information at (01) 730–0791, Mon.–Fri. 9 a.m.–5:30 p.m. Address letters of inquiry to 26 Grosvenor Gardens S.W.1 W0DU, London.

A service operating round-the-clock: **Owner Drivers Radio Taxi Service Ltd.** (144 Shirland Rd., W.9; Tel: 286–4848). **British Rail Travel Centres** are based at mainline stations and will answer questions on services covered from that station. Look in the telephone directory under *British Rail* for numbers and areas. *British Rail Travel Centre* in Lower Regent St., near Piccadilly Circus, is where you go in person to have any and all questions answered concerning *British Rail Services* and *Sealink Channel sailings. London Transport Headquarters* (55 The Broadway, London S.W.1; Tel: (01) 222–1234) operates a 24-hour telephone service, but rely on the information offices at the subway (Underground) stations at Euston, Heathrow Central, King's Cross, Oxford Circus, Piccadilly Circus, Victoria, and St. James's Park for free maps, general tourist information, and sorting out travel problems. For ***sightseeing highlights,*** call 246–8041; for what's going on for children in London, call 246–8007; for London's weather, 246–8091. For ***bedtime stories,*** different each night from 6 p.m., call 246–8000; and, best of all, *Kidsline* (Studio D, Floral Hall, Covent Garden, London W.C.2: Tel: 222–8070) with information covering all children's facilities in the city. Call from 9 a.m.–4 p.m. during British school vacation time; 4 p.m.–6 p.m., Mon.–Fri. when schools are in session.

Transportation

Trains You can buy a BritRail pass in the U.S. before you go. A seven-day pass costs $147 in first class, or $107 in second, less than the cost of one round trip between London and Glasgow. For information about these and many other good BritRail offers, as well as useful free booklets, contact BritRail at 630 Third Ave., Sixth Floor, New York, NY 10017, or at one of their offices in Chicago, Los Angeles, Toronto or Vancouver.

For information about the *Venice Simplon-Orient-Express,* departing London in the grandest style and going on to Paris, Milan and Venice, or for reservations aboard this sumptuous beauty, get in touch with *Orient-Express* (Suite 2847, One World Trade Center, New York, NY 10048) or in London (Orient-Express, Sea Containers House, 20 Upper Ground, London S.E.1). Children 3–12 travel at half fare; children 13–16 receive a 25% reduction. No children under 16 accepted unaccompanied. This journey is a 24-hour, 926-mile experience in comfort, luxury and style. You are advised to book well ahead for it.

Godfrey Davis Europcar is Britain's largest car rental company with over 250 locations throughout the country, of which over 70 are located on major BritRail Inter-City stations and 18 at UK airports; except for prebooked requests for cars to meet trains, Rail Drive offices are closed on Sun.

London Transport offers "Go As You Please" money-saving tourist tickets valid for three, four, or seven days for unlimited travel on the Underground, trains and buses.

If you want to rent any type of car, camper, mini-bus, self-drive or chauffeur-driven, or even a boat, contact *Car Hire Centre International, Ltd.* (23 Swallow St. Piccadilly, London W.1), who are in touch with over 400 rental stations throughout Britain. It's a free public service which also handles hotel reservations and educational tours.

You can hail a taxi in London or you can telephone for a cab (look in the Yellow Pages of your telephone directory under Taxis) or through a radio service (Tel: 286–6010 or 286–4848).

British Airways (65–81 Regent St., London W.1) have many other branch offices, all with the same telephone.

British Caledonian Airways (Piccadilly Circus, 215 Piccadilly, London W.1 Tel: for information (0293) 51 8888/27890; for reservations (01) 668–4222) offers trained escorts to care for children traveling alone on BritCal flights; the cost for personal, individual escorts is 50% of the regular fare; special attentions for children 6–12 is also offered by an escort staff and cabin crew. Friendly "Aunties" are on hand, at no extra charge, on BritCal's scheduled services and at their base at Gatwick Airport, and at the Central London Air Terminal inside Victoria Station from which the Gatwick rail link operates. They also operate a Gatwick-Heathrow helicopter transfer service.

Telephones: If you have trouble using the telephone, dial 100 for assistance. New blue pay telephones offer direct dialing to the U.S.

You should get a copy of *What's On in London* or for other events like street fairs and demonstrations, *Time Out.* BTA's free guides, *London Week* and *Quick Guide to London* are concise and easy to read.

There is a half-price ticket booth for theater tickets on Leicester Square. The Barbican Centre is the home of the Royal Shakespeare Company and the London Symphony Orchestra, and tickets for these and other key events, such as performances of the Royal Opera and Royal Ballet, can be obtained before leaving for London by contacting Edwards and Edwards (226 West 47th St., New York, NY 10036; Tel: (212) 944–0290 (in NY state) or (800) 223–6108 (nationwide).

Booking seats for London's theater and other West End attractions can be arranged by the *British Tour and Theater Center, Inc.,* (The Berkeley Building, 19 West 44th St., Suite 718, New York, NY 10036) who also book sightseeing tours by chauffeur-driven cars or motorcoach. *Keith Prowse and Company, Ltd.* (234 West 44th St., New York, NY 10036; Tel: (212) 398–1430) not only book seats for the London theater, but also can get you seats on the center court at Wimbledon.

In London, *Keith Prowse Supersports* (24 Store St., London W.C.1; Tel: (01) 631–4920), the official tour promoter appointed by the All England Lawn Tennis Club, offers the Wimbledon package. *Topline Events* (Top Line House, Archway Corner, London N.19) arranges Wimbledon outings with the best available tickets.

The BTA also has *Young Visitors to Britain* (a guide for students) and information sheets for families with young children, both exceptionally helpful.

The *British Travel Bookshop* (40 West 57th St., New York, NY 10019) will send you on request a list of books about Britain that are instructive, lively, entertaining, a veritable feast for the eye and the imagination. For a glorious selection of illustrated children's books, art books, special interest books while in England, let me recommend *Heywood Hill Ltd.* (10 Curzon St., London, W.1). British magazines and other periodicals can be ordered from *British Publications Inc.* (11–03 46th Ave., Long Island City, NY 11101).

As for *Special Interest Holidays,* a BTA catalog of more than 2500 choices can tell you where to pursue your hobby or undertake a new one. You can review Shakespeare at Cambridge; learn lace-making, ironwork, lithography, Gaelic; paint and sketch in the English countryside, and 2494 other things.

HEALTH, WATER, AND FOOD No problems here at all. Health standards are excellent. Water is drinkable everywhere. Pasteurized milk is always available.

Children find British food scrumptious. For breakfast, porridge and thick cream, scones (biscuits) or toast with marmalade or heather honey or other good English jam, milk or cocoa, bacon, eggs, sausages, fruit or kippers (smoked herring), if you feel like it. For lunch, roast beef and Yorkshire pudding, toad-in-the hole (sausages in batter), bangers and mash (sausages and mashed potatoes), and a fruit flan or fruit tart or a raspberry or gooseberry "fool" (cream added to strained fruit) or trifle (layers of cake, jam, and fruit topped with custard) for dessert. Tea at four, accompanied by sandwiches, shortbread, fruitcake, pound cake, scones or crumpets, and thin, thin slices of bread and butter. Tea may turn into "high tea" for younger children with the addition of boiled eggs and fruit poured over with Devonshire (thick, clotted) cream, in which case supper will merely be cocoa and thin slices of bread and butter, an apple, or biscuits (cookies). Avoid spaghetti (generally rubbery).

Kedgeree, a rice and fish dish, is excellent. So is Welsh rarebit (sometimes wrongly spelled rabbit)—melted or toasted cheese poured over toast or crackers. For snacks, there is always fizzy ginger beer, or lemon and barley water, or different sorts of bottled fruit drinks. The ices, or ice cream, are generally of the frozen-custard kind, but the British excel at making jams, jellies, marmalades, jelly desserts, fruitcakes, pound cakes, and biscuits (cookies and crackers) of every variety.

Their desserts—steamed chocolate puddings, fig puddings, Christmas plum puddings and other steamed puddings—are heavy and rich enough for every child to enjoy; pie crusts and pastries are generally exceptionally light and flaky.

Welsh food specialties are lamb, lobsters, mussels, fish, breakfast rolls called Baps and Laver Bread—spinach-like cooked seaweed, a health food obviously bursting with vitamins and minerals, generally served with bacon. If you like soul food, collards and vegetable tops, this is in the same category.

In **London,** eating out with children is easy, as you'll find a wide variety of food in all price ranges. If you ask, some restaurants will provide small cutlery and little glasses or cups, and will heat up baby food or a bottle. Special children's menus and portions are available at some restaurants; others are willing to serve your child half an adult portion–but ask in advance about this, as a few places have been known to insist on charging full-portion price.

Besides the **Top of the Tower,** and the **London Zoo** eateries (see "Attractions for Children in London"), the **Dell** in Hyde Park is notable for views and convenience. If you're anywhere near Piccadilly, pick the dilliest place of all, **Fortnum & Mason's Fountain** (see "Shopping"), with counter and table service; ambiance and service have a nice old-fashioned grace and charm; excellent food; cake wagon with salads and special open-faced sandwiches, drinks for Mom and Pop. Morning coffee and afternoon tea with delectable cakes, cookies, and pastries are served in the store's main restaurant. You can find sustenance at any big department store. At **Harrods** (Knightsbridge, S.W.1), the restaurant provides high chairs. Special children's dishes at **D. H. Evans** (Oxford St., W.1).

Tea-time, usually between 3:30 and 5:30 p.m., is a civilized and soothing ritual, with small sandwiches, not scones, clotted cream and jam, cakes, and eclairs. Some top tearooms are: **Richoux** (86 Brompton Rd., London S.W.3); the **Ritz Hotel** (Picadilly Circus, London, W.1); the **Waldorf Hotel** (Aldwych, London W.C.2); the Thames Foyer in the **Savoy Hotel** (Savoy Hill, London W.C.2); **Brown's Hotel** (Dover St., London W.1).

At cocktail time, a little later, at the Causerie at **Claridge's,** the center table is mounded high with eye-appealing hors d'oeuvres. At the Savoy Grill, everyone is attentive; your waiter will bring small portions, purees, and diced meats for the little ones; and your children will be impressed by the long white aprons the waiters wear and by the silver and elegance.

For fast foods, there's the **Great American Disaster** (335 Fulham Rd., S.W.10); **Burger King** (108 New Oxford St., W.C.1); **Huckleberry's** (108 Queensway, W.2); **Hamburger Heaven** (159 Old Brompton Road, S.W.5); **McDonald's** (everywhere! Just ask any Londoner). For Pizza: **Pizza Express** (10 Dean St., W.1); **Pizza on the Park** (11 Knightsbridge, Hyde Park Corner, S.W. 1); **Pizza Hut** (149 Earl's Court

Road, S.W.5, and many other locations). **Geale's Fish Restaurant** (2–4 Farmer St., W.8) is renowned for its fish and chips as is **Seashell Fish Bar** (35 Lisson Grove, N.W.1). **Staveley's** (642 King's Road, S.W.6) and **The Hungry Fisherman** (24 Thurloe St., S.W.7) are also recommended. For wonderful creperies, try: **Asterix** (329 King's Road, S.W.10) or **The Creperie** (56a South Molton St., W.1). For the best ice creams and sherberts in London, go to **Marine Ices** (8 Havertstock Hill, N.W.3).

Other recommendations are: the **Tate Gallery Restaurant** (Tel: 834–6754), reservations necessary, only open for lunch, with children's portions for under 11's; **Tutton's** (11 Russell St., W.C.2); **Le Routier** (Camden Lock off Commerical Place, Chalk Farm Road, N.W.1), reservations necessary, but children's portions available; **Parsons** (301 Fulham Rd., S.W.1) for milkshakes and spaghetti or **SPQR** (87 Dean St., Soho) for Italian food; reservations are necessary. **Richoux** (86 Brompton Rd. S.W.3) has an Edwardian tearoom atmosphere, hot dishes, and snacks. For Chinese food, **Chuen Cheng Ku** (17 Wardour St., W.1), or ask the **Dumpling Inn** (Gerrard St.) to give you a banquet.

Motorway Service Station Restaurants have special meals for children.

For families whose children get hungry at odd hours of the night, **Dial-a-Meal** (Tel: 581–2266/3888), will rush amazingly good food to your threshold within one hour. The Carlton Tower Hotel (Cadogan Pl., s.w.1); late at night, coffee and sandwiches only. **Maze Coffee Shop,** Royal Garden Hotel (Kensington High St., W.8). **The Pelican,** Londonderry House Hotel (Park Lane, W.1). **Ribblesdale Restaurant,** Cavendish Hotel (Jermyn St., S.W.1). At the airport, hot meals are served in the **Grill and Griddle** restaurants in Terminals one, two, and three, 24 hours a day.

Health foods? **The Nuthouse** (26 Kingly St., W.1) is vegetarian and chockful at lunchtime; **Food for Thought** (31 Neal St., W.C.2) is fine; **Heal's** (Tottenham Court Rd.); **Peter Robinson** (Oxford St. and Neal St., W.C.2); **Cranks** (8 Marshall St., W.1).

Picnicking? Going to Glyndebourne for the opera? Taking the children to the beach? Feeling Edwardian and extravagant? **Fortnum and Mason's** will do up a beautiful picnic hamper for you if given advance notice. Not for budgeteers! Picnicking on a budget can mean simply ordering a box-lunch from your hotel. Or you can make a production of locating English farmhouse cheese, Cheshire and Cheddar at **Paxton and Whitfield** (93 Jermyn St., S.W.1); brown bread and farm butter at **Groom and Sainthill, Ltd.** (3 Halkin Arcade, S.W.1); meat pies at **Martines** (45 Kensington Church St., W.8); take-away cooked things from **The Midnight Shop** (223 Brompton Rd., S.W.3); delicious apples, pears, and dawn-fresh fruit from **L. Booth,** a greengrocer (3 St. Andrews Hill, E.C.4); pastries and cakes from **Shell's Bakery** (26 and 59 New King's Rd., S.W.6).

If you would like to celebrate your child's birthday with a cake just like the one young princes and princesses blow out the candles on, **Floris** (39 Brewer St., W.1 Tel: 437–5155) is noted for its royal birthday cakes!

Elsewhere in Great Britain, the **Trust Houses** are extremely good when touring with the children. A growing number of them have butteries, the British version of the coffee shop or informal restaurant, devoted to children's gourmet fare, at fair prices; many butteries stay open all day and evening, so that early or late lunches or suppers are no problem. Also, all Trust House places have high chairs and supplies of Heinz baby food, and couldn't be more obliging about warming bottles, heating jars, sterilizing spoons at 10 a.m., 2 p.m., 6 p.m., and midnight; most will serve half-portions at half-prices on request.

Special! **Pubs** are great places for lunching if you are touring with children. Although children aren't allowed in the bar, there are often gardens and tables outside that are ideal for them. Pub food is usually home-cooked and good value, and a special is the **Ploughman's Lunch** (fresh hunks of crusty bread, butter, farmhouse cheese such as Cheddar). A list in *Pubs That Welcome Children* (David and Charles) is useful. Egon Ronay's *Just A Bite* (Penguin) and AA's *Eat Out* are other good guides. There are also ***pubs in London with gardens that welcome children.*** You'll find a list of these in Vanessa Miles' *A Capital Guide for Kids* (Allison & Busby), and of those listed **Old Rose** (22 Medway St., S.W.1) and **Arab Boy** (289 Upper Richmond St., S.W.15) are two I can vouch for. Medieval banquets are served in candlelit splendor in the old halls of many castles and manor houses. Presented with the heraldic pageantry of bygone days, with minstrels' traditional music, entertainments, and costumed attendants, these really are pretty fascinating. Honeyed wine, or mead (more potent than you think!) is served in pewter goblets. You spear the delicacies before you with a dagger. Beginning at 8 p.m., these are great fun and beautifully educational for older children; not recommended for the younger ones, however. Among the places you'll find these banquets are: **Ruthin Castle** (N. Wales), **Seaton Delaval Hall** (Northumberland), **Caldicot Castle** (Gwent), **Warwick Castle** and **Bull Hotel** (Lincolnshire). **Chilham Castle** (near Canterbury, Kent), with the oldest heronry in England, has a falconry display during the meal. For details, consult the BTA's *Banquets* and *Specialized Entertainments* information sheet.

Elizabethan banquets are lavish year round at London's **Elizabethan Rooms** (190 Queen's Gate, S.W.1; Tel: 584–6616); also at **Ludley Castle** in Durham (Tel: 3267). **Grimsdyke** (Grimsdyke Hotel and Restaurant, Old Redding, Harrow Weald, Middlesex), where W. S. Gilbert, of Gilbert & Sullivan fame, once lived, holds dinners that include a Gilbert and Sullivan musical entertainment. Tra la! Not far from town. In **Wales,** evenings with traditional food and entertainment are laid on in style at **Plas Glansevin** (Llangadog, Dyfed) and at **Plas Maenan** (Llawrst, Gwynedd). Contact BTA for details of tour companies that arrange excursions to banquets which saves the problem of working out your own transport.

BABY FOOD There is a large assortment available at major chemist shops not only in England, but in Wales. Cow & Gate baby and junior foods in jars, Heinz's in tins, are reassuringly prevalent.

Robinson's and *Boots' Own Brand* produce dehydrated foods which you just mix with water to cook up such fare as chicken casserole, veggies and liver, and many desserts as well. *Farley's* rusks and *Ovaltine* rusks are widely available for the teething and the chewing. Baby-milk formulae are put out by Cow & Gate, SMA, Ostermilk, Milumil; also soya-based varieties. *Delrosa* Vitamin C orange or rosehips drinks are recommended, as is *Ribena* blackcurrant syrup.

The chain of **Boots the Chemists** (branches all over Britain) has a wide variety of baby food and baby supplies. **John Bell and Croyden** (50 Wigmore St., W.1; Tel: 935–5555) is another haven in London for mothers looking for baby food. Both stock sterilizing equipment; the latter also stocks Playtex baby nursers.

DIAPERS AND LAUNDRY Diapers called nappies in Britain, are available in chemist shops. The all-in-one disposable nappy makes traveling a lot easier, and you can find many brands in sizes to fit newborns to toddlers. Widely available, brand names to feel safe with are Robinson's Cosifits, Snugglers, Pampers, Peaudouce, Boots' Own Brand. There are also disposables that fit in plastic pants, such as Tufty Tails, Paddipads and Boots' Own Brand.

Diaper services? **Babycare Nappy Service,** (3 Hythe Rd., N.W.10; Tel: 969–6456), serving within a 30-mile radius of London, offers daily except Sun. delivery and collection of diapers. **Mothercare Disposable Nappy Service** (Cherry Tree Rd., Watford, Hertfordshire) will deliver disposables to your door or hotel; they deliver all over the country. Order at least three weeks in advance for the initial delivery. Fast laundries? **Whitsters of Chelsea** (7 Elystan St., S.W.3) collects and delivers. ***Coin-operated launderettes*** are everywhere; just ask. **Collins Cleaners** (88 Jermyn St., S.W.1; Tel: 839–5172) will clean clothes the same day if they are delivered before 11:30 a.m. Cautionary note: some dry cleaners have the barbaric custom of snipping off all metal buttons, and returning the cleaned article to you with the buttons in an envelope. Request, beforehand, that if buttons have to be removed, they be resewn before article is returned.

BABY EQUIPMENT FOR HIRE The **Hire Service Shops, Ltd.** chain (31 London Rd., Reigate, Surrey; branches throughout S.E. England) rents a full range of baby goods. **Hire Equipment** (14 Queenstown Road, S.W.8; Tel: 622–3444) is another good rental outlet. Baby scales can be hired at **John Bell and Croyden** (see "Baby Food") or **Guardian Baby Scales** (45 Holloway Rd., N.7; Tel: 607–6105).

EMERGENCIES MADE EASY London ***Pharmacies?*** Or ***chemists,*** as they are often called? Police stations keep a list of local emergency pharmacies/chemists. **Bliss** (50–56 Willesden Lane, N.W.6) is open 24 hours daily. **Underwoods** (75 Queensway, W.2) is open weekdays 9 a.m.–10 p.m., and Sun. 10 a.m.–10 p.m.; with a branch at 205 Brompton Rd. open weekdays 9 a.m.–7 p.m. and Sun. 10 a.m.–6 p.m.. **Boots** (Piccadilly Circus, W.1) is open Mon.–Fri., 8:30 a.m.–8 p.m., Sat. 9 a.m.–8 p.m.

Hospitals and doctors are excellent. Despite the National Health Service plan, nonresidents are expected to pay for medical services. Emergency medical treatment is summoned in London by dialing **999.** In other towns, dial O for the operator. For doctors recommended by the American community contact the **American Embassy** (24 Grosvenor Sq., W.1; Tel: 499–9000). A Consulate General is also at the **Cunard Bld.,** Pierhead (Tel: 236–8501) in **Liverpool.** In London, the **Hospital for Sick Children** is at Great Ormond St., W.1; Tel: 405–9200. Central hospitals with 24-hour emergency (casualty) depts. are: **Middlesex** (Mortimer St., W.1; Tel: 636–8833); **St. Mary's Hospital** (Praed St., W.2); **Westminster Children's Hospital** (Vincent Square, S.W.1) **Charing Cross Hospital** (Fulham Palace Road, W.6).

St. George's (Tooting Grove, S.W.17; Tel: 672–1255) emergency dental unit is open 24 hours but requires an appointment. A toothache or broken brace can be attended to during the day at the **Royal Dental Hospital of London** (32 Leicester Sq., W.C.2; Tel: 930–8831); **Eastman Dental Hospital** (256 Grays Inn Rd., W.C.1). But, if the problem is achingly awful or has to be fixed at once, call **REDS** Radio Emergency Dental Service: Tel: (01) 834–8345). **Moorfields Eye Hospital** (High Holborn, W.C.1; Tel: 836–6611; and at City Rd., E.C.1; Tel: 253–3411) is open day and night for emergency eye problems.

If you need a nurse, try **BUPA Nursing Service Ltd.** (36 Dover St., W.1).

Stranded? Broke? The **American Aid Society** (24 Grosvenor Sq., W.1; Tel: 499–9000), a charitable organization, will do its best to help.

Teledata (Tel: (01) 200–0200) provides 24-hour information on where to obtain emergency help such as locksmiths, car breakdown services, plumbers, electricians.

From 9 a.m.–5:30 p.m. Mon.–Fri., **Capital Radio's Helpline** (Tel: (01) 388–7575) offers immediate response, will answer all questions or put you in touch with someone who can, about legal, financial, social and personal problems.

In London, open 24-hours, **Chequepoint** (236 Earl's Court Road, S.W.5) will cash checks if you can produce a bank credit card.

MAGIC FAMILY HELPERS—BABYSITTERS The English nanny is famous for her concern and devotion to her charges and for her pride in "her" family, and facilities for child care are superb.

In **London,** an agency that will provide competent and reliable people to take children shopping and sightseeing, to sit with or travel with children, to meet children at trains, to take full charge of children while their parents are elsewhere, to deliver a child, let's say from Copenhagen to London, in short, to do everything from the simplest to the most complex duties, is **Universal Aunts** (250 King's Rd., London S.W.3; Tel: (01) 351–5767); cable Uniaunts, London S.W.3 to save time and money). They'll also help plan holidays (hear, hear!); provide maids for the day; provide secretarial services, secure travel tickets, mend your clothes, or anything, as they say, except lend money, give legal advice or arrange a marriage. They are open Mon.–Fri., 9:30 a.m.–4 p.m.

If you need tickets, a set of Crown Derby, a private helicopter, someone to pack, a good-natured companion for yourself or the children, or don't know what to do when the bathtub overflows try **Solve Your Problem, Ltd.** (25A Kensington Church St., W.8; Tel: (01) 937–0906).

Babysitters are simple to locate. Besides Universal Aunts, there are several good sources: **Babysitters Unlimited** (313 Brompton Rd., S.W.3; Tel: (01) 584–1046) with a hire fee every time you hire a sitter or an annual subscription; **Babyminders** (67A Marylebone High St., W.1; Tel: 935–3515), with a fee when you register; **Childminders** (67A Marylebone High St., W.1; Tel: 935–9763) with similar arrangements.

Part-time, full-time child-minding, baby-sitting help can also be obtained from **Knightsbridge Nannies** (5 Beauchamp Place, S.W.3; Tel: 584–9323). **Problem Limited** (44 Lupus St., S.W.1; Tel: 828–8181) can help with baby-sitting and other problems. **Nannies Unlimited** (313 Brompton Rd., London S.W.3; Tel: (01) 589–8482) sends excellent nannies, and **Nannies** (16 Stratford Rd., London W.8; Tel: (01) 937–3299) is topnotch for short- or long-term nannies. So is **Occasional and Permanent Nannies** (15 Beauchamp Pl., London S.W.3; Tel: (01) 589–3368) which also has a **Nannie Advice Bureau,** *a free telephone service for those wanting instant advice on a baby/child problem!*

The **Search Agency** (25 King's Rd., London S.W.3; Tel: (01) 730–8122) is another recommendation for Norland-trained nannies, as well as well-trained domestic staffers of many nationalities.

Help finding **au pairs** is available from **The Federation of Personnel Services of Great Britain Ltd.** (120 Baker St., W.1; Tel: 487–5250).

Elsewhere in the British Isles babysitters are also easy to find; at most hotels the Hall Porter, or your hosts at a castle or farmhouse, can inform you.

Some special agencies: **Consultus** (17 London Rd., Tonbridge, Kent) and **Country Cousins Ltd. and Emergency Mothers** (6 Springfield Rd., Horsham, Sussex; Tel: Horsham 5188 and 61960) supply helpers capable of taking over the household for a couple of weeks in the absence of one or both parents. They also escort children (even to the Continent); take on a score of other helpful chores (such as shepherding a child to the dentist or shopping).

Day Nurseries where tots can play with other tots and be looked after full or part-time during the day, fed and everything? In **London,** there's **The House on the Hill** (Unitarian Hall, Hoop Lane, N.W.11), whose principal takes on children aged 2–6 during the week from 8:45 a.m.–3 p.m.; closed mid-July–mid-Aug. and seven days at Christmas and Easter. The **Walton Day Nursery** (239 Knightsbridge, S.W.7; Tel: 584–9847), is a happy service—a nursery staffed by trained teachers who will look after visiting 2-to-5-year-olds for a half-day or a whole day.

Playgroups for 3–5 year olds usually have 2½-hour sessions daily Mon.–Fri. For information and details about the nearest playgroup to you, contact the **Pre-School Playgroup Association** (314–316 Vauxhaull Bridge Rd., S.W.1) if you are in Inner London; and the PPA (Tel: 828–2417) for Greater London, or the suburban area.

The sections on ''Instruction'' and ''Attractions for Children'' also contain suggestions of places where your children may be safely left.

MAGIC FAMILY HELPERS—INSTRUCTION Unless otherwise noted, the following are all in **London: Edward Sturges** (106 Pavilion Rd., S.W.1; Tel: 235–4234) has daily gymnastic classes for children from 3½ on; great fun for the little and limber. There are Baby Bounce classes for under-5s who can climb, jump, leap and bounce on pint-sized equipment and trampolines at the **Britannia Leisure Centre** (40 Hyde Rd., N.1). **Eternit Wharf Recreation Centre** (Stevenage Rd., Fulham, S.W.6) holds ''roly-poly'' gym sessions on Thurs. at 2:30 p.m. for 5s and under. Gymnastics for 4-year-olds and up at **Ferndale Sports Centre** (Nursery Rd., S.W.9). **Jubilee Hall Recreational Centre** (Central Market Square, Covent Garden, W.C. 2) holds acrobatic sessions for 4–5-year-olds at 10 a.m. every Sat.

Ballet, singing, rhythmic movement, dance? **The Pineapple Dance Centre** (7 Langley St., Covent Garden, W.C.2) has Sat. lunch-time sessions for 5-year-olds and up. **Battersea Arts Centre** (Old Town Hall, Lavender Hill, S.W.11) has ballet classes for 3s and up on Sat. at 10:30 a.m. The **Rudolph Steiner House** (35 Park Rd., N.W.1) has sessions for 3–5-year olds during the school year only. Baby and beginner classes in dancing for children 2½ and up at **Biddy Pinchard Studio** (20 Raleigh Gardens, Brixton Hill, S.W.2). If you're staying in London any length of time, you'll be glad to hear that the **Ballet Rambert School** (Mercury Theatre, 2 Ladbroke Rd., W.11), considered one of London's most famous dance companies, will take children from the age of 4 for lessons on a 12-week term basis.

Pottery, printmaking, painting courses of a week's length are offered at the **Camden Arts Centre** (Artwright Rd., N.W. 3) for 7 and up during the summer. The **Camden Institute** (Holmes Rd., N.W.5) offers a Sat. morning program for all the family so that parents and children can work together in relaxed and informal workshops. **Battersea Arts Centre** (Old Town Hall, Lavender Hill, S.W.11) is a superb center for children of all ages, with workshops, puppet shows, ballet classes, and much more. Children's pottery classes are given by the **Chelsea Pottery** (13 Radnor Walk, S.W.3; Tel: 352–1366) on Sat.

Also see "Attractions for Children in London" for museum workshops and "Sports" for other lessons.

Understanding, intelligent, remarkable educational tutors able to imbue girls with a love of learning are **Misses Dixon and Wolfe** (25 Victoria St., S.W.1, Tel: 222–7117), who accepted my daughter at short notice with an accommodating ease that was stunning to anyone who has ever coped with the school systems operative on our own Eastern Seaboard. My daughter has never been happier or done as well academically, thanks to these magic helpers. **Gabbitas-Thring Educational Trust** (6–8 Sackville St., W.1) will give advice on private schools, tutors and tutoring; well-known and well-recommended.

Special Interests? Where you can pursue your hobby or involve yourself in an new one is a matter of serious consideration in Britain; 2500 choices offered in the BTA publication *Special Interest Holidays* (see Information); for private tutors, **Truman & Knightley Associates** (78 Notting Hill Gate, W.11; Tel: 727–1242) are recommended also as consultants. Schools receptive to young Americans based in London for a year or so, conveniently located, and approved by the Department of Education? For boys 7–13, try **Sussex House Preparatory School** (68 Cadogan Sq., S.W.1; Tel: 584–1741). Coeducational up to 8 and for girls up to 12 is **Norland Place School** (162 Holland Park Ave., W.11; Tel: 603–9103).

MAGIC FAMILY HELPERS—CHILDREN'S TOURS All of the following originate from **London:**

Junior Jaunts (4A William St., S.W.1) has children clamoring for second helpings of imaginative outings for small groups, between the ages of 5–15, escorted by a responsible and knowledgeable guide.

Undergraduate Tours (6 S. Molton St., W.1; Tel: 629–5267) sponsors the Juniors London tour. This is by car and costs vary according to time and car size. Guides are young and cheery, and may be Oxford or Cambridge students. Service is door to door; many special interest tours to choose from; tours for unaccompanied children as well as individuals of any age. **Take-A-Guide Ltd.** (85 Lower Sloane St., S.W.1; Tel: (01) 730–9144) is the well-known, well-established personalized guide service that will whisk young ones 5 on up on a Junior London tour including Madame Tussaud's, Pollock's Toy Museum and the Science Museum. They will go anywhere with you or the children and have many attractions for families; 24-hour answering service; heavenly tours and itineraries to combine with your own ideas, starting whenever you like, setting your own pace; a truly super service. In the U.S., contact TAG before you go (63 East 79th St., New York, NY 10021). **Grosvenor Guide Service** (13a Harriet Walk, S.W.1) is also good.

Children can be safely entrusted to **Visitors Welcome** (17 Radley Mews, W.8; Tel: 937–9755) who will arrange escorts for children anywhere, and provide babysitters. A member of the staff will take the children into her own home for the night or even longer! Parents can be accompanied on shopping forays, and a birthday or Christmas dinner can be expertly packed for the entire family to enjoy.

Guides that don't have special children's tours but who are recommended for families are: **Autoguide** (Tel: 235–0806); experienced driverguides will take you around London or out to Windsor, Stratford-upon-Avon, Oxford and so on; old inns for lunch; and stately home tours. Prices are average.

For those who can't afford luxury, **London Transport** (55 Broadway, S.W.1.; Tel: 222–1234) offers an inexpensive two-hour circular tour of London landmarks covering some 20 miles, that start off every hour on the hour from 9 a.m.–8 p.m. in summer, 10 a.m.–4 p.m. in winter, from Piccadilly Circus, Marble Arch (Speakers' Corner) or Grosvenor Gardens, Victoria. There is no guide on board, but you are provided with a map that shows you the route. You don't have to book in advance. Just show up at the departure point on time; half-price for children; or use a Red Rover ticket, available at London Transport Inquiry Offices at underground stations, for an excursion around London from the top deck of one of London's heavenly stoplight-red double-decker buses that children love.

Walking tours of London for the family are an interesting thought, and certainly non-pedestrian in themes and subjects, such as Lawyers' London, Jack the Ripper's London, Dickensian London, Ghosts of London, Riverside London, to name but a few of your choices. Walks generally last about 1½ hours, and you don't have to book ahead, but can just show up at the appointed hour at the appropriate meeting place. For details of walks, contact **Discovering London** (Tel: Brentwood 21 37 04); **Hidden London Tours** (Tel: 600–8244); **London Walks** (Tel: 882–2763); **The Londoner** (Tel: 883–2656). BTA can tell you about or give you information sheets on daily programs. The back page of the London *Times* also gives daily details of scheduled walks.

MAGIC FAMILY HELPERS—PERSONALIZED SERVICES Here are tips on a miscellany of services available in the British Isles. Unless otherwise stated, the addresses are in London.

Performers for ***childrens' parties,*** magicians, ventriloquists, or a Punch and Judy performance can be hired from **Arnold Stoker's Entertainment Agency** (32 King's Rd., Wimbledon, S.W.19; Tel: 542–1967). **Der** (8 Eccleston St., S.W.1; Tel: 730–3277), a television rental company, has a party-pack that includes TV-video rental, two cartoon films, plus party plates and cups for an all inclusive fee.

For party clowns for children 5–7, try **Rhubarb** the totally silent clown (10 Shelburne Rd., London N.7); **Barney,** a slapstick clown (24 Sanderstead Ave., London N.W.2); **Click** "an amazing woman who involves children in plays" (Field House, Meysey Hampton, Cirencester, Gloucestershire); **Peri Aston,** actress and mime artist (37 Gunmore Rd., London S.W.20). **Norman Myers** (80 Bridge Lane, N.W.11; Tel: 458–5055), will enable you to be a guest at your own child's party. They provide balloons, party favors; Punch and Judy show; magician; movies; and can do all the catering. The **Children's Party Agency** (32 Edge St., W.8; Tel: 727–8476) can also cater, organize, and provide the entertainment for children's parties. **Catering for Kids** (275 Dover House Rd., S.W.15) is also splendid. Another good bet is **Smartie Artie** (4 New Greens Ave., St. Albans) for a child's party in or near London.

You can get a list of puppeteers to perform for your child's party from **The Puppet Trust** (Battersea Arts Centre, Lavender Hill, S.W.11).

Party playthings, decorations, favors? Wonderful places to know about are: **Lewis Davenport** (51 Great Russell St., W.1); The **Kensington Carnival Company** (123 Ifield Rd., S.W.10); **Theatre Zoo** (21 Earlham St., W.C.2); **Knutz** (1 Russell St., W.C.2); **Partymad** (67 Gloucester Ave., N.W.1).

You can take your child into almost any ***hairdresser*** and ask them to give your child's hair a wash or a trim. THE hairdresser for children is at **Harrods,** where there is a jolly little section next to the infants wear on the first floor for boys up to 10, girls up to 14. In the country, hairdressers are always obliging about "doing" children. Cautionary note: With teenage boys, let them go to Harrods or **Vidal Sassoon** (44 Sloane St., S.W.1. and 56 Brook St., W.1), or **Ivan's** (20 Jermyn St., W.1), or **G.F. Trumper** (9 Curzon St., W.1), places their father can also go with confidence. Avoid the Unisex, Mod, In-Cult places with tight-panted young men.

The children will be glad to know that there is a **Doll's Hospital,** (16 Dawes Rd., S.W.6; Tel: 385–2081) where dolls and soft toys can be made good as new. If the new car or train suffered some catastrophic fate, **Beatties** (see "Shopping") is the place for repairs or replacements.

The **Wigmore Studios** (38 Wigmore St., W.1) rents studios by the hour.

If you decide you want to take movies of the children you can rent a camera at **Pelling and Cross, Ltd.** (104 Baker St., W.1; Tel: 487–5411), or at **Samuelson Film Service, Ltd.,** (303 Cricklewood Broadway, N.W.2; Tel: 452–8090). Like to have the children photographed? Try **Whitecross Studio, Ltd.** (3 Jubilee Pl., S.W.3; Tel: 352–3649) which is superb with children. **Patrick Lichfield** (20 Aubrey Walk, W.8; Tel: 727–4468) does the noble job expected on flattering family portraits.

Interested in your ancestral origins? Want your children to know all about their English heritage? If you know the name of a grandfather to look up in the birth, marriage, or death registers, **General Register Office,** St. Catherine's House (10 Kingsway, W.C.2) is open to those calling in person, Mon.–Fri., 8:30 a.m.–4:30 p.m. The **Society of Genealogists** (37 Harrington Gardens, S.W.7) have a library to which nonmembers have access to pore through birth, marriage, and death registers in England and, less widely ranging, in Scotland and Wales; a small search fee is charged. Research is also done here. An interesting building houses this library. If you would like someone else to do the research, write to the Secretary, c/o the **Association of Genealogists** (''Oakdene,'' 64 Oakleigh Park N., London N20 9AS) enclosing five International Reply Coupons, and they will send you a list of experienced researchers. Also, the BTA has a helpful free leaflet called *Tracing Your Ancestors.* For a custom-tailored tour that could lead you to long-lost relatives, contact **Family Heritage Holidays** (105 Himley Green, Linslade, Leighton Buzzard, Bedfordshire).

For a list of ***toy lending libraries*** in London and surrounding areas, contact the **Toy Libraries Association** (Wyllyots Manor, Darkes Ln., Potters Bar, Hertfordshire).

Children's Libraries: To find out about the facilities of children's libraries nearest you, call the **Library Association** (Tel: (01) 636–7543).

Lost Property Office (15 Penton St., N.1) is where to go if you've left something in a London taxi. **London Transport Lost Property Department** (200 Baker St., N.W.1) is where to go if you have left something on the underground or bus.

For information about ***free legal help,*** telephone **Law Centres Federation** ((01) 387–8570).

London's West End department stores are particularly thoughtful in their provisions for family shoppers. **Heal's** (196 Tottenham Court Rd., W.1) has strollers available at the front entrance for use in the store. **Fortnum & Mason** (181 Piccadilly, W.1) has a first-aid room. Facilities for nursing mothers and diaper-changing are provided at **Harrods, Selfridges, John Lewis** (Oxford St.).

The **National Children's Bureau** (8 Wakley St., London E.C.1) is an independent voluntary organization concerned with children's needs and the evaluation and improvement of services and practices in childcare. Under its aegis is the **Voluntary Council for Handicapped Children** which provides a comprehensive service for all categories of handicap, and provides help both to parents and professionals, as well as an informational fact sheet, *Help Starts Here.*

Single parents can call upon **The National Council for One-Parent Families** (255 Kentish Town Rd., London N.W.5). Parents concerned with the development of gifted children can call upon **The National Association for Gifted Children** (1 South Audley St., London W.1).

HOLIDAYS FOR CHILDREN ON THEIR OWN Children's holiday homes-away-from-home, infant care, and farm holiday for babies, toddlers, and under-12s are a British specialty. **Park School** (Bicclescombe, Ilfracombe, Devon) arranges holidays for children from overseas as paying guests with English families who have children of their own. Selected families offer a warm welcome; visits to places of interest; picnics and other outings; and the children's individual interests are always taken into consideration. Families are located in the heart of England and West Country areas where children can find wonderful opportunities for outdoor life, swimming, boating, sailing, riding; all travel arrangements are undertaken. For older children, as well as the under-12s, this service seems to work out exceptionally well, as the greatest care is taken to ensure the most happy relationship possible between the visiting child and his hosts. Unaccompanied children 5 years and up are accepted for minimum stays of two weeks.

There are residential nurseries for children age 2 weeks to 7 years at **Norland Nursery Training College** (Denford Park, Hungerford, Berkshire), whose graduates become "Nannies" to top families all over the world; each child, while in residence, is looked after by an individual nurse. Day care facilities are also possible, from 8:30 a.m.–5:30 p.m., including lunch, for less than one half the full boarding price. By prearrangement, Norland can also accommodate physically or mentally handicapped children.

Langley Children's Holidays, for boys and girls 6–14, in the Cotswold Hills of Gloucestershire during August offer a varied program of games, rambles, swimming, athletics, riding, ice skating, excursions and indoor activities. The **Langley Romford Center,** based in Essex, is open during the late May–early June Spring Bank holiday week, and for three weeks from the end of July to mid–Aug. Children go by train to East Anglian seaside resorts and also to Cambridge, Ely, London and other places when the weather militates against seaside outings. For inquiries and reservations about both holiday centers, contact *Langley Children's Holidays* ("Doonside," 22 Manor Rd., Romford, Essex RM1 2RA). **Barton Children's Holidays** (Spyway, Langton Matravers, Swanage, Dorset) offers a variety of holidays for a large age range. For boys and girls 5–12 at their **Swanage Center;** riding holidays for girls 10–16, and tennis coaching holidays for boys and girls 10–16 at their **Dicker Center** in East Sussex; canoeing and sailing for boys and girls 9–16 at the Dicker Center; soccer and cricket coaching holidays also at their Dicker Center for boys 9–16; holidays at their **Barton Center** in Hampshire for sportsminded girls and boys 13–18, with swimming, squash, sailing, canoeing, riding, football, contests, competitions, disco; and many, many more. **Casterbridge Hall** (Bowden Rd., Templecombe, Somerset), located in Thomas Hardy country, is a manor house accommodating 30 boys and girls 13–18, with a summer program of one to six weeks. Recreational excursions are many and varied. This program seems exceptionally good to me, the ambiance attractive and pleasant, and the rates reasonable.

CHILDREN'S CAMPS ***Pony trekking and riding holidays*** for families and/or unaccompanied children are immensely popular as a means of discovering countryside accessible only on horseback—such as the hilly, moorland areas of Scotland and Wales or the valleys in the north and southwest of England.

Riding holidays, available year round, place more emphasis on instruction (courses in stable management, dressage, show jumping) and, in general, operate as riding camps for accompanied or unaccompanied children aged 10 on up who have had some riding experience. Expect to be taken to hunter trials, gymkhanas, horse shows and sometimes to participate in them. Contact the **British Horse Society** (British Equestrian Centre, Kenilworth, Warwickshire).

Trekking is quite different, and undertaken almost entirely at a walking pace owing to the nature of the country—beautiful wild country and old drove roads not suitable for faster paces—and therefore can be enjoyed by complete novices. Only the most elementary instruction is given in most cases. Treks start out at approximately 10 a.m. and return to the base at approximately 4 p.m. with picnic lunches mid-day. Very few centers go in for post treks, overnight trips lasting four to five days or more; post trekking centers are not recommended for learners, in my opinion.

In the estimable opinion of the **Ponies of Britain Club** (Ascot Racecourse, Ascot, Berkshire) trekking for children 12 years or under is also a mistake—"they get bored and tired." Younger children, they say, are much better off at a riding holiday center with others of their age group, and with other activities. Generally true, I feel, but there are exceptions. If your children only like galloping, or jumping, for them the riding centers are best unquestionably. But a 12-year-old, who has never even sat on a pony, can go out trekking in safety and in confidence, provided he goes only to the reputable establishments approved by the Ponies of Britain Club. First check that they take 12-year-olds and under.

What do you need in the way of clothing for trekking? Corduroy slacks, or cavalry twill trousers or well-fitting jodhpurs which give you a firmer grip, are more comfortable and less likely to rub than blue jeans. Waterproof over trousers, such as golfers wear in Britain, are good for wet days and aren't expensive at Lillywhite's (see "Shopping"). Aertex cotton underwear is ideal. Nylon should *never* be worn. Riding boots are useless for trekking, which includes a little walking; jodhpur boots are the best choice. Bring along rubber boots for stable work or walking in the fields and shoes for indoors. A good raincoat (essential) can be obtained at Harry Hall (see "Shopping"). Plastic raincoats or anything that flaps will scare horses out of their wits and also tear easily, so forget them! Other essentials: a couple of sweaters for cooler weather and to carry along even on warm days; velvet hunting cap (becoming and efficient), a scarf to protect the back of the neck from sunburn; insect repellent (a *must!*), something for sunburn.

For riding holidays, it is essential to have well-fitting jodhpurs or riding breeches, jodhpur boots or riding boots with a proper riding jacket, a velvet hunting cap. Otherwise, much the same supplies are necessary. For trekking and riding holidays, you should also have a small, light knapsack for carrying your picnic lunch, a pocket knife, and some cord (handy for attaching things to the saddle or tying the knapsack around your waist so that it doesn't bump against you as you ride).

The blue-ribbon, silver-loving-cup-prize winner in riding instruction-cum-accommodation for children 14 and older is, of course, **Porlock Vale Equestrian Centre** (Porlock, Somerset, Tel: Porlock 862338), the equestrian Eton of England. Well-justified snob appeal attaches to this one. **Abbots Lea School of Riding** (Northfield House, Court Farm Rd., Willesbridge, Bristol, Avon) takes 7–17 year olds, and is reasonably priced. **Harroway House** (Penton Mewsey, Andover, Hampshire; Tel: Weyhill 2295) is also highly recommended. Unaccompanied children from 8 accepted. Also in Hampshire, **Knight Bridge Riding School** (Sway, Lymington) accepts 10–18 year olds and, like all the above-mentioned establishments, receives the hard-won approval of the British Horse Society.

Pony trekking over meadowland, wooded slopes, rocky granite heights, and vast spaces of open hill in the lakeland of Wales at the **Rhayader Pony Trekking Association** (Nanserth House, Rhayader, Powys). Unaccompanied children over 11 and accompanied children over 7 accepted. Accommodation in hotels, guesthouses, farms, and private houses; May–Sept. Pony trekking amid mountains, forests, streams, and waterfalls also offered by **Llanwrtyd Wells Pony Trekking Association** (Tir Ithel, Llanwrtyd Wells, Powys).

For descriptive lists and pamphlets (including holidays in Austria and Iceland, post trekking over natural country for five to ten days, staying in inns and farmhouses) consult the Ponies of Britain Club whose information is more personalized than that provided by the BTA. Many relevant and interesting books, magazines, and pamphlets are published by this splendid organization.

The sports favored by the Royal Family are riding and ***sailing.*** Able to communicate part of the ecstasy of sailing small boats is Group-Captain Searl, who first sailed a boat alone at the age of 7, and who skippers what seems to me the best sailing school for young people—and their parents—in Britain. Recommended by the Royal Yachting Assoc., the **Emsworth Sailing School** (59 Bath Rd., Emsworth, Hampshire; Tel: Emsworth 3743) is unique. "Our aim," he says, "is to get you sailing *by yourself* in the shortest possible time, because all too many sailing schools put you through a perfectly satisfactory course, but at the end of it the pupil has never sailed without an instructor close at hand." A high standard of helmsmanship is usually reached; supervised solo sailing normally starts on about the fourth day. To encourage a competitive spirit, young sailors have knot and splice and other competitions, and the course ends with racing. You don't do anything but sail, so I suggest this only for youngsters who really want to learn how to handle a boat with confidence and expertise. Special courses for juniors, 9–17, during Easter and summer vacations.

Other schools which conduct Junior Courses (accommodation extra) recommended by Group Captain Searl are: **Newton Ferrers Sailing School, Ltd.** (Westerly, Yealm Rd., Newton Ferrers); minimum age for unaccompanied children, 10 years. **Bosham Sea School, Ltd.** (Bosham, near Chichester, West Sussex; Tel: Chichester 572112); children from 9 up. Information about other sailing schools is yours for the asking from BTA.

Adventure and activity holidays for small groups of children in age groups 9–12, 12–14 and older are arranged at several centers in Yorkshire by **Northern Field and Activity Centres** (Larpool Hall, Whitby, North Yorkshire). Birdwatching, geology and geography are among the courses offered at the **Preston Montford Field Centre** (Montford Bridge, near Shrewsbury, Shropshire). For children 9 years and up during the summer. **Mill on the Brue Activity Holidays** (Gants Mill, Bruton, Somerset) offers weekend and weekly holidays for children in rural surroundings where children can participate in collecting brown eggs, milking cows and feeding calves; with excursions, crafts and sports aplenty.

P.G.L. Adventure Ltd. (180 Station St., Ross-on-Wye, Herefordshire) runs sailing, canoeing, and pony-trekking holidays for children 7–12, 12–17, for one or two weeks; longer holidays add visits to Holland and France. Their *Holidays for Young People* 6–18, and their *Family Adventure* catalogs of activity program to suit all ages and activity preferences include computer and robotics courses, a week barging about the Netherlands, grass-skiing, multi-activity programs for low tariffs.

A traditional English summer of sports, games, and excursions is organized by **Barton Children's Holidays** (Spyway, Langton Maltravers, Swanage, Dorset) at several centers, some by the sea, and some inland in southern England. Holidays are arranged for age groups 5–12, 9–16, 10–17, and activities include canoeing, swimming, treasure hunting, tennis, squash, volleyball, cricket. The **Youth Hostels Assoc.** (Adventure Holidays, Trevelyan House, St. Albans, Hertfordshire; Tel: St. Albans 55215) offers ages 11–15 holidays for special interests—bird-watching, fossil hunting, riding, photography, fishing, sailing—with accommodation in youth hostels. In Wales, over 50 hostels provide bed and breakfast for outdoor enthusiasts from age 5—yes, 5!—in all sorts of establishments (former schools, farm and church buildings, cottages, even an old mill at Cynwyd), all clean and pleasant. Also in Wales, the **Penlan Centre** (St. Clears, Dyfed) runs activity holidays for 8–15 year olds encompassing hill walking, fishing, riding, and Canadian canoeing (canoes, not kayaks). Camp periods during July and Aug.

Tennis? Coaching for all levels, including special courses for juniors, is provided by the **Beaconsfield School of Lawn Tennis** (The Oval, Beaconsfield, Buckinghamshire). Accommodation is in local hotels; unaccompanied children can also be housed with local families.

Computers? **Beaumont Summer Camps** (100 New King's Rd., London S.W.6) has just the setup for 10–17 year olds to familiarize themselves with all aspects of computing. Beaumont also provides a residential adventure camp in the lovely Lake District.

Special interests in sports or the decorative arts? **Millfield Village of Education** (Millfield Street, Somerset) has 300 courses for 8–16 year olds including archery, badminton, golf, painting, pottery, shooting, and more.

Situated in Snowdonia National Park on the west coast of Wales is **Celmi** (Concealed Place), there is a camp operated by David Hedley Charlton (Llangegryn, Near Tywyn, Gwynedd, Wales) for ages 14–19. Campers are encouraged to experience ''adventure with imagination, freedom with responsibility,'' and face the challenge of creative activities such as drama, film, photography, pottery, kiln building; or the opportunities for mountain walking, windsurfing, riding, trekking, rafting, rock climbing; or time to meditate, contemplate, get in touch with their feelings and thoughts. **John Pughe** (Pant Farm, Glyn Ceiriog, Llangollen, Clwyd, Wales) runs pony-trekking holidays for unaccompanied children 8–18, to families, and to adults, with year-round accommodations at his old Welsh farmhouse. Campers are encouraged to participate with animal care and farm chores, and trekkers can explore moorland, mountain, valley and pine forest trails.

Enjoy Britain, Ltd. (146 Gloucester Rd., London S.W.7) offers activity holidays at interesting centers for 8s on up.

Bicycling holidays for ages 11–15 in various parts of England and Wales are arranged by the **Cyclists' Touring Club** (see ''Fun and Games'').

Music? **Rural Music Schools Association** (Little Benslow Hills, Ibberson Way, Benslow Lane, Hitchin, Hertfordshire) adds the grace note of weekend courses to its one week courses on an arpeggio of interests—voice, chamber music, and wind, string, and percussion instruments—for the music-minded, ages 14 and up. **Wavendon All Music Plan** (The Stables, Wavendon, Milton Keynes) offers summertime music camp programs for 8–17 year olds, as well as courses in jazz and classical music for over 14s. ***Theater?*** **Young Theatre Association** (9 Fitzroy Sq., London W.1) runs summer courses; ages 14–19; includes full board and festival excursions.

A two-week schooner voyage, covering 700–1000 miles, for ages 16–24; Mar.–early Dec.; contact the Secretary General, **The STA Schooners** (2A The Hard, Portsmouth, Hampshire). Courses in snorkeling (for ages 12 and up) and scuba diving (for ages 15 up) are efficiently and safely supervised by **Fort Bovis Underwater Centre** (Plymouth, Devon).

Outward Bound Trust (12 Upper Belgrave St., London S.W.1) stresses physical challenge, adventure, comradeship for rugged outdoorsy types, the physically handicapped, and the sight- or hearing-impaired at its many facilities. Concentrations include seamanship skills, mountaineering, and speleology. Campers as young as 10 are accepted for week-long courses, while 12–, 14–, and 21–day holidays are offered to young people over 13. My own feeling is that the courses, expeditions, and voyages offered are wildly strenuous and sometimes grueling, more a matter of endurance than fun, and operated by stern organizers; but many parents tell me I'm just an over-cautious softie to think that way. **Acorn Camps** (National Trust, Old Grape House, Cliveden, Taplow, Maidenhead, Berkshire) offers almost unbelievably small weekly fees, although for information you'll have to send $1.25 to cover postage and handling. For conservation-minded, youth-hosteling types 18 and over, who like to rough it, Acorn Camps are based on various National Trust properties throughout Britain. Campers are expected to pitch in with the unskilled-labor tasks that benefit the National Trust's historic castles, houses, and other properties. Or ask the **British Gliding Association** (Kimberley House, Vaughan Way, Leicester) about the summer courses (accommodations provided) run by many gliding clubs for teenagers.

CHILDREN'S NONRESIDENTIAL DAY CAMPS IN THE LONDON AREA For 5–15 year olds, **Beaumont Summer Camps** (100 New King's Rd., London, S.W.6) has a fun-packed trio of activity centers with some 30 sports and crafts—archery, canoeing, computer training, fencing, painting, swimming, pony trekking, windsurfing, tennis and two dozen more alternate choices. Transport to and from will be arranged; fees for lunch, activities; excursions are reasonable. **Harrow Summer Camp** (16 Broadley St., London N.W.8) operates both a day and residential camp for boys and girls 5–15 at its site on the grounds of Harrow School, one of Britain's greatest public (private) schools, 12 miles NW of London. For day campers, there's a fleet of minibuses providing door-to-door transportation as well as a service that will meet unaccompanied campers at, and return them to Heathrow Airport. Campers may spend an optional 12 hours a week at the Harrow-Dolphin Computer Camp. Rates for day and residential campers are a fine value.

CASTLES AND OTHER HAPPY FAMILY ACCOMMODATIONS The BTA provides excellent information on accommodations custom-tailored for every purse, preference, and purpose, and Britain is unequaled in the field of special facilities for families traveling with children. There is even a hotel in that wonderful West Country that caters *only* to families with children of all ages. **Radfords Country Hotel** (Lower Dawlish Water, Dawlish, South Devon, EX7 0ON), a ten-minute drive from the M5 motorway, through a tunnel of beech trees, is within an hour's drive from Barnstaple, Bath, Bristol, Dartmouth, Exeter, Plymouth, Torbay, Totnes, plus scores of other attractions and comforts. A 16th-century thatched house in six acres of wooded valley with lawns and gardens, Radfords has commodious bedrooms, double rooms and family suites with private bathrooms; children's supervisors, facilities, and activities, even babysitters on duty in the evening. There are separate adult activities and entertainment, too. The atmosphere is relaxed and informal; the safety standards are high. In association with local tourist boards, Radfords has its own Guest Information Centre to cue you in to the best in Devon and Dartmoor. Owner-hosts, Terry and Janet Crump, offer friendly, helpful family service and high standards for reasonable rates. Not chic, not for snobs or the unsociable, but a terrific find for fun-loving, relaxed families.

From the British Travel Bookshop or from Heywood Hill Ltd. (see Information) you can get a wealth of information in excellent, general and specific hotel and restaurant guides for England, Scotland, and Wales. **Trusthouse Forte Hotels** offer a select choice of over 200 hotels that offer Bumper Funbags and Babycare Kits for children and babies; children under 5 are accommodated free of charge, and those under 14 sharing a twin room with two adults or a single with one are charged a tiny token fee; special menus are offered for children, and children under 14 may choose from the adult menu at half-price. Weekend bargains also offered. Reservations may be made in England at the **Trusthouse Forte Hotel Centre** (Paramount House, 71–75 Uxbridge Rd., Ealing, London) or in the U.S. (810 Seventh Ave., New York, NY 10019). *Do not confuse these hotels with the National Trust or Landmark Trust.* Trusthouse Forte is a hotel chain that maintains a high standard of service—for the affluent. **Holiday Inn** hotels offer programs approved by the BTA, bargain activity weekends in some British and Continental locations with special attractions for children and their parents. Reservations can be made through the **London Reservations Centre** (10–12 New College Parade, Fincley Rd., London N.W.3).

A BTA publication, *Stay on a Farm* lists fascinating possibilities from a flower farm in the Scilly Isles to a horse farm in Surrey; almost all of these offer reductions for children. To get the most of this experience, it would be preferable to spend a week or at least a few days. Of inestimable value from BTA is *Stay at an Inn,* which offers over 750 delightful solutions to where to stay. With characteristic reserve, the BTA says that "visitors miss a great part of the charm of Britain unless they spend a night in at least one inn. Most of them have historic interest and are architecturally beautiful." **Note:** Because of their architecture—narrow, wedge-shaped stone stairs, heavy doors, tilting wooden floors, stone floors—British innkeepers are often worried to have children younger than 12 on the premises for fear of accidents (and subsequent litigation), and, therefore, do not welcome small children, so always check in advance.

The National Trust (42 Queen Anne's Gate, London SW1H 9AS) owns historic houses open to the public, tracts of land, and coveted cottages that you can rent in the Lake District and in fishing villages along the golden beaches of Cornwall. You have to book at least six months in advance for these cottages and other properties. For a list of these Cornish gems and prices, send an International Reply Coupon to the National Trust, Lanhydrock Park, Bodmin, Cornwall.

The best-kept secret bargain accommodations in Britain? The **Landmark Trust** (Shottesbrooke, near Maidenhead, Berkshire) has historic houses—astounding structures called Follies—you actually can rent and live in (some exist only as "sights"). These highly individualistic accommodations require booking well in advance. Ask the BTA how much you should send for a two-month sea mail or ten-day airmail delivery of the Landmark Trust handbook from which to choose your rental. Select several places suitable to you and then telephone the booking agent (Littlewick Green (0628) 82 3431) to find out which one is possible. Once you have selected, you send a deposit and then send the rest three months before the rental begins. On receipt of the final payment, the Landmark Trust will send directions for your house and the name of the caretaker. You can book by mail, but I am a great believer in telephoning. Very few Landmark properties are accessible by train, and a rental car is really a must. **Heart of England Cottages,** a varied group of houses in all price ranges, available by the week without maid service, is run by Peter Anstell (Buckland Manor Estate, Broadway, Worcestershire, WR12 7LY). Write directly for information.

Modest-priced accommodations and fascinating courses lasting a weekend to a week, in archaeology, canals and railways, ornithology, natural history, wildflowers and traditional crafts, at **Losehill Hall** (Castleton, Sheffield, North Yorkshire) a national park study center; about 400 such offerings are also included in BTA's *Special Interest Holidays*.

From Tewkesbury up a 40 mile stretch of the Avon river to moor overnight in Stratford and at various points along the river for free, **UK Waterways Holidays** (Rickmansworth) can offer you a narrowboat, or barge, for reasonable rates. See also "Fun Trips" for other waterborne accommodations.

For discerning travelers whose standards are high, a new dimension in accommodation is offered—that of meeting people in their own ***castles and manor houses,*** and of enjoying their gracious way of life, cuisine, and culture. Your hosts' local knowledge of places and people will enable you to discover aspects of Britain which few visitors are privileged to enjoy. Over 100 absolutely ravishing castles, mellow manor houses, battlemented and castellated houses, elegant, romantic, cosy—are open to you on an exclusive basis, courtesy of an organization that has graded them: A (stately homes and castles in extensive parkland); B (country mansions and castles); C (charming country houses and cottages). An illustrated brochure and all details are available from *Country Homes and Castles* (Rand Tours, 138 A Piccadilly, London W1V 9SH).

Bed and Breakfast in South and South-West England and *Bed and Breakfast in Wales, Northern England and Scotland* are available by writing directly to Herald Advisory Services (Herald House, 23A Brighton Rd., South Croydon, Surrey); dependable and informative for touring notes and descriptions of inexpensive stopovers.

If you would like to ***rent a house*** or a flat in London or the country, get in touch with **James and Jacobs** (94 Jermyn St., S.W.1Y 6JL; Tel: 930–0261); Minimum rental period of three months. For shorter stays, consult **Taylings** (14 High St., Godalming, Surrey; Tel: Godalming 28525) who have attractive rental properties all over Britain. Useful guides also are BTA's publications, *Apartments in London* (to rent, or to let, as the British say); *Holiday Homes,* which details places to rent outside of London.

Seaside Resort Hotels: Thousands of smallish hotels and guesthouses advertise (in the travel sections of newspapers and in numerous British vacation guides) laundry facilities for diapers, children's playrooms, babysitters, children's playgrounds, children's meals, cots, cribs, and low prices. They do have these facilities—but that's about all they have to recommend them, I suspect. This is not to say you should avoid hotels whose advertisements stress family facilities, just be wary of hotels where *nobody* else but families go.

For ***home-swapping*** opportunities in England, plus London agencies that can help you rent a villa on the Continent, see Chapter 7; also BTA's information sheet on Home Exchange Agencies.

▶ **Note:** In **London,** to save yourself fruitless telephone calls trying to find accommodation at short notice, try **Hotac,** the hotel accommodation service (Globegate House, Pound Lane, London N.W.10; Tel: 451–2311). They are speedy and efficient, charge nothing if you book from abroad or from London. Be on the lookout for weekend or mid-week hotel rate reductions; during the off-season, hotel chains often offer beautiful bargains.

Unless otherwise indicated no reduced accommodation rates apply to a child occupying a room by himself. There is great variance, however, in children's hotel rates so find out beforehand if, and under what conditions, reduced rates apply to children.

If your child isn't used to a Potty-Po, watch out, they tip. They should be held under hot water to warm them if they are porcelain.

In **London,** in the hotel category, word has got around about the admirable **Eden House** (III Old Church St., Chelsea, S.W.3; Tel: 352–3403; *not to be confused with the neighboring Hotel Eden*), which is breakfast-only; other meals only by special arrangement; snacks and breakfast-in-bed available; over a dozen restaurants are in the vicinity; babysitting can be arranged; hotel car available for economical sightseeing; laundry and dry cleaning can be done in four to five hours if necessary; you can leave luggage here free if you intend to return. Kindly, attentive service. Seemingly inconvenient, everything somehow can be arranged for you; it would be hopeless with a baby or toddler, I think, but with older children things work out very well.

Hotel Lexham (32–38 Lexham Gardens, W.8; Tel: (01) 373–6471) offers babysitting service, provides cots, and happily proffers children's portions at its restaurant. **Henry VIII** (19–21 Leinster Gardens, W.2; Tel: 262–0117) has restaurant, with children's portions available on request; babysitter can be arranged; swimming pool.

In a particularly nice area is the **Diplomat** (2 Chesham St., S.W.1; Tel: 235–1544), a conversion of Georgian houses; the staircase and the dome window let into the roof retained, but the bedrooms are modernized and each has private bath or shower; scrumptious breakfast served in bed; no other meals. If you would like something large, contemporary, expensive but not ruinously so, that opens right into Kensington Gardens so that the babes can be trundled out to play by your Nanny, there's the **Royal Garden** (Kensington High St., W.8; Tel: 937–8000). The **Kensington Close** (Wright's Lane, W.8; 937–8170), warmly welcomes children with cots ready to be set up, a babysitting service, a baby-care kit; heated indoor swimming pool, squash courts; restaurant service, special children's menus. **Grosvenor House** (Park Lane, W.1 Tel: (01) 499–6363), a deluxe name hotel with higher prices, also has a heated pool.

At **Dolphin Square** (Westminster St., S.W.1; Tel: (01) 834–9134 you can get a two- or three-room apartment with kitchenette; indoor heated swimming pool, plus a shopping arcade with butcher, baker, grocery, chemist, dry cleaners, hairdresser, stationery and magazine shop; a moderately priced restaurant is open until midnight except Sundays; private gardens; sauna; rentable cots or extra beds; "laundrette"; and a quiet but central location backing onto the Thames. Similar, but without the swimming pool, is **St. James Court** (Buckingham Gate, S.W.1; Tel: 834–2360); service suites of one or two double rooms, each with bath, living room-dining area; and with or without kitchen; full meal and maid service; coffee shop; kiosk snack-bar; restaurant that serves children's portions on request. **Rentasuite Ltd.** (17 Sloane Gardens, Sloane Sq., S.W.1; Tel: 730–4847) has suites for two to four people, each with bath, kitchen, and telephone. Suites for three or four people consist of a double and a single bedroom, a living room and dinette. Other good, solid hotels are the **Basil Street** (Basil St., Knightsbridge, S.W.3 Tel: (01) 581–3311) which prides itself on personal service; and has an air of old-fashioned elegance. **Wilbraham** (Wilbraham Pl., S.W.1 Tel: (01) 730–8296); **Ebury Court** (26 Ebury St., S.W.1 Tel: (01) 730–8147) with low rates; **Hendon Hall** (Ashley Lane, Hendon, N.W.4; Tel: (01) 203–3341); **Brown's Hotel** (Albermarle St. and Dover St., W.1; Tel: 493–6020). Near to Piccadilly, Bond St., Burlington Arcade and, as it's been said, to many people's hearts. Traditional and tranquil; impeccable service; it's probably best not to bring the children here unless, like the service, they can be counted upon to be beautiful and unobtrusive.

White's Hotel (Lancaster Gate, W.2; Tel: (01) 262–2711) overlooks Kensington Gardens.

In the ***apartment*** category, **Fairlawn Apartments** (booking office at 109 Elgin Crescent, W.11; Tel: 229–5006) has one to four-room apartments with bathroom and furnished kitchen; all bed linen and towels; iron and ironing board; TV; maid service. Cribs, strollers, and high chairs available; babysitting can be arranged. Rates depend on the season and the number of occupants; babies in their own crib or carrycot are free of charge.

Durley House Ltd. (115 Sloane St., London S.W.1; Tel: (01) 235–5537/8) is a block of 11 service flats (twin bedroom, or a twin bedroom and single bedroom, sitting/dining room, bathroom and kitchen) overlooking the private gardens of Cadogan Place; maid service; private metered telephone lines; entry telephones so that you can admit guests; porter, resident housekeeper; provisions for English or Continental breakfast, three-course lunch, cold pretheater suppers or snacks; bookings accepted for no less than three weeks as a rule; moderate rates, averaging about a third of what the rates are for a suite at the discreet, quiet **#11 Cadogan Gardens** (Sloane Square, London S.W.3; Tel: (01) 730–3426). Old-fashioned decor in #11, and strictly a personal recommendation sort of place without a brochure, unpretentious, kindly and accommodating; ready to hunt up another service flat for you if they are fully booked. **Athenaeum Apartments,** adjoining the Athenaeum Hotel in Mayfair, are at least 50% more expensive, with 30 apartments available and use of hotel facilities and services; bookable in the U.S. through **Rank Hotels,** 444 Madison Ave., New York, NY 10022; Tel: (212) 421–2353 (in NY State); (800) 223–5560 (nationwide). **Keith Cardale Groves** (43 N. Audley St., Grosvenor Square, London W.1; Tel: (01) 629–6604) can be contacted for a furnished flat. For those who don't want to pay Grand Hotel prices, I've heard of a pleasant, central luxury pension called **Number Sixteen** (16 Sumner Place, London S.W.7; Tel: (01) 589–5232). **Searcy's,** a well-known catering firm, offers single and double rooms with private bath, opening onto an attractive roof-garden in a quiet mews in central Knightsbridge; Continental breakfast available on request; some doubles with sitting room; small, but attractively furnished; moderate tariff; for information contact the manager during business hours at Searcy's Roof Garden Rooms (30 Pavilion Rd., Knightsbridge, London S.W.1; Tel: (01) 584–3344).

Sleeping in turreted chambers and enjoying the pleasures of British ***country life*** are such great travel extras for children and yourselves that I'd like to mention just a few of the enticing possibilities. Near **London: Gravetye Manor** (near East Grinstead, West Sussex; Tel: Sharpthorne 81–05–67) is an Elizabethan manor in hill and forest countryside; ten beautifully furnished rooms named for trees; excellent food. "Smugglers' Lane" and "Smugglers' Cave" nearby; lovely gardens; wonderful grounds, including a lake; games room with TV and Ping-Pong; golf; and fishing. In East Sussex, **The White Hart** (Lewes; Tel: Lewes 4676) is eight miles north of Brighton and ten minutes by car from Glyndebourne Opera House. **Great Fosters** (Egham, Surrey; Tel: Egham 33822), a 16th-century hunting lodge, in the heart of polo and racing country; celebrated for its gardens (armies of gardeners have kept up the topiary work for 400 years) and its residents (which have included Queen Elizabeth I, James I, and Ann Boleyn). Its 40 guest rooms, attended by three times that many servants, feature canopied beds; a vast dining hall and drawing rooms with oak beams, huge fireplaces, and acres of carved paneling, open onto a velvety reach of lawn, brilliant flowers, the dark-green geometry of shrubbery; charming sunken rose garden; large swimming pool; tennis; and medieval banquets!

Eastwell Manor (Eastwell Park, Ashford, Kent; Tel: Ashford (0233) 35751) about 1½ hour drive from London, a 30 minute drive from Dover and Folkestone, 20 bedrooms all luxurious; surrounded by 3000 acres of parkland; fine cellar and restaurant; walled rose and herb gardens and immense lawns; riding can be arranged locally; tennis courts are available; near Canterbury and quiet Kent villages; great for rich grandparents traveling with teenage grandchildren appreciative of the finer things in life.

In **Buckinghamshire,** the **Compleat Angler Hotel** (Marlow; Tel: 4444) is where Izaak Walton wrote his eponymous book; once an inn, now converted into a luxurious riverside hotel; ten miles from Windsor Castle. By far the grandest and most prestigious are accommodations offered by the Duke and Duchess of Bedford at **Woburn Abbey** with its $15 million art collection, zoo, and the constant round of entertainments on its 3000-acre woodland park; thousands of visitors avail themselves of its Safari Service just to see the grounds; general fanfare advertising it as *the* stately home to visit (see "Attractions For Children") but the rich cream pleasures of staying here and dining with the Duke and Duchess are not to be had under the three-figure bracket. To inquire about this highly sought-for privilege, address the Duke's

Comptroller (Woburn Abbey, Bletchley; Bedfordshire well in advance. Tel: Woburn 666).

Cotswolds and Shakespeare country: At **Weston Manor** (Weston-on-the-Green, Oxfordshire; Tel: Bletchington 50621), do try to get one of the bedrooms with a four-poster bed and canopy. Open-air swimming pool; facilities for riding, hunting, fishing, and golf within easy distance; squash court, putting green, croquet, TV, secret chamber in the chimney where Prince Rupert hid from Oliver Cromwell. Also a cottage, named for Prince Rupert, with four additional twin-bedded rooms that can be let separately or as a whole. **Whatley Hall** (Banbury; Tel: 3451) is within 20 miles of Stratford-upon-Avon and Sulgrave Manor (home of George Washington's ancestors); has secret stairways and passages in its old part; a modernized bedroom wing extension; lovely gardens. **The Lygon Arms** (Broadway; Tel: 2255), with mellow Cotswold stone houses all around, has 16th-century charm, a peaceful garden, golf, tennis; lowest telephone surcharge rates no matter where you call, and is 15 miles from Stratford-upon-Avon; Broadway is engaging and pleasing. The surrounding area is hunting country. **Malvern View Hotel** (Cleeve Hill, Cheltenham, Gloucester; Tel: Bishops Cleeve 2017) is very attractive; with excellent food; only seven bedrooms. **The Manor House** (Castle Combe; Tel: Castle Combe 782206), surrounded by lawns and wooded glades, has a stream with stepping stones; lovely gardens; trout fishing. Castle Combe, with pale gold 15-century houses, and heralded as England's prettiest townlet, was a favorite haunt of Shakespeare.

Devon and Cornwall: Sited in 60 acres of wooded parkland, **Portledge Hotel** (Fairy Cross, near Bideford; Tel: Horns Cross 262) is a 17th-century manor with parts of the house dating back to the 13th century. Extremely comfortable. Fresh fruit and vegetables from own gardens and greenhouses; very good food indeed. Very good service. Private bathing beach, perfect for children over 5 (under 5s not accepted) outdoor heated swimming pool; tennis court; croquet; golf, riding, fishing, sailing, and boating within easy distance. Rates very reasonable. **The Manor House Hotel** (Moretonhampstead; Tel: 355) is a huge gray stone manor house overlooking its own 18-hole golf course (with its own professional); two tennis courts, two trout streams, a squash court, games room with billiards and Ping-Pong, pinewoods, moorland, and buttercuppy pleasures for the children. **Tregenna Castle** (St. Ives; Tel: Penzance 79–52–54) is set in 100 acres of grounds; 81 rooms; this 18th-century turreted castle offers exceptional service, food, and amenities. Wonderful beach, swimming pool, riding, tennis, golf, badminton, squash. Resort hotel life rather than that of a private country house. **Budock Vean** (Budock Vean, near Falmouth; Tel: Mawnan Smith 250288) is a large converted country house with a swimming pool, tennis, golf, fishing, its own mooring, and boats available for exploring rocky coves; a games room. Lovely lawns. But, alas, no children under

5 accepted. **East Anglia:** The 18-room **Seckford Hall** (Woodbridge; Tel: Woodbridge 5678) with Tudor architecture, diamond-paned windows, strangely high chimneys; some of the greatest four-poster beds I've ever seen. Beautiful gardens; walled-in vegetable gardens, seven greenhouses, and fruit trees happily contribute to the cuisine. Sailing, fishing, a lake bobbing with ducks and 34 acres to explore, plus a nearby village where houses have golden thatch and chimney-stacks of stone. **The lake district: Langdale Chase Hotel** (Windermere; Tel: Ambleside 2201), a large manor house overlooking Windermere Lake, standing in acres of wooded grounds; spacious, comfortable accommodations, some with balconies; private boat pier; putting green; nearby golf course; well-equipped games room; tennis; croquet; and swimming; car and chauffeur available for tours; launch and rowing boats can be hired for excursions around the lake. **The Swan** (Grasmere; Tel: Grasmere 551) is another of my favorites. In a class by itself, having won just about every prize possible for its cuisine, is the **Sharrow Bay Hotel** (Penrith, Cumbria; Tel: Pooley Bridge (08536) 301/483), open early Mar.–early Dec. with 12 bedrooms in the main building, four in the lodge, four in the cottage, seven at Bank House; all the rooms individually furnished and named after characters in the works of Hugh Walpole; the menu is the richest, creamiest and most varied you're likely to find anywhere. Only for prosperous, pleasure-loving, non-dieting families with appreciative teenagers.

Isle of Wight. In the **Farringford Hotel** (Freshwater; Tel: Freshwater 752500), a country manor which used to be the home of Tennyson, every care is taken to retain associations with the poet. The main house has 38 rooms, but sweet little cottages in a wooded glade close by have been specially designed for families, each with two bedrooms, bath, and telephone. Beautiful gardens, lawns, wooded parkland, and farmland comprising 235 acres; fresh produce from the kitchen garden; the beach is one-half mile away and wonderful for children; playroom and games in the main house. Tennis court; croquet, putting green; Ping-Pong; two golf courses, 9-hole and 18-hole; own stables. You can hire a bicycle, canoe, boat, or pony; go sailing, fishing, on a picnic with basket packed by the management; on a tour of the island by car, or on an excursion by steamer. Reserve well in advance for a cottage.

North Yorkshire: The **Worsley Arms** at Hovingham (Tel: Hovingham 234) is a Georgian coaching inn set in heavenly countryside; children are most welcome; good food, service, value.

Wales: Wales has hundreds of charming, reasonably priced inns, guesthouses, and country hotels. The following are outstanding:

Aberdovey: **Trefeddian** (Tel: Aberdovey 213) welcomes families; own swimming pool; lovely gardens; delicious food; the beach, fishing, pony trekking all nearby. Isle of Anglesey: At Amlwch, the **Dinorben Arms** (Tel: Amlwch 830358) is a fine old Georgian house; at Beaumaris, **Ye Olde Bull's Head** (Tel: Beaumaris 81–03–29) was the original posting house of the area. Beddgelert: **Tanronen** (Tel: Beddgelert 3471). Brecon: **Castle of Brecon** (Tel: Brecon 2551) is exceptional; a country house has been built around the original castle wall; beautiful surroundings; trout fishing. Builth Wells: **Pencerrig Country House** (Tel: 55–32–66); lovely lawns and flower gardens; riding, swimming, games room, Ping-Pong. Caernarfon: **Prince of Wales,** (Tel: Caernarfon 3367). Cardigan: **Angel** (Tel: Cardigan 612561). Carmarthen: **Boar's Head,** Tel: Carmarthen 6043, an old coaching inn. Chirk: **Hand** (Tel: Chirk 772479), a 16th-century coaching house. Dolgellau (Dolgelley): The **Golden Lion Royal** (Tel: Dolgellau 422579). Also, **Bontddu Hall** (Tel: Bontddu 661) at Bontddu; large Victorian country house converted into an extremely comfortable hotel; bonny views of the mountains; putting green; games room closed in winter; most pleasant. Harlech: **St. David's** (Tel: Harlech 366). Lake Vyrnwy: **Lake Vyrnwy Hotel** (via Oswestry, Shropshire; Tel: Llanwddyn 244) is a country house overlooking the lake; fishing; shooting; swimming; tennis; nursery for children's supper. Llandudno: **Gogarth Abbey** (Tel: 76212), the original home of the Liddell family where Lewis Carroll wrote part of *Alice in Wonderland;* is a marvelous base for attractions in Llandudno: swimming pool, games room, badminton. Llangollen: **Chain Bridge** (Tel: Llangollen 86–02–15). Llanrhaeadr: **Bryn Morfydd Hotel** (Tel: Llanynys 280); swimming, tennis, magnificent views of mountains and valleys; excellent home-grown food. Llanwrda: Glanrannell Park, **Crugybar** (Tel: Talley 230), a country house overlooking a lake parqueted with water lilies; fishing, riding, extensive gounds. Llechryd: **Castell Malgwyn** (Tel: Llechryd 382), an 18th-century manor house on 50 acres. Maenan: **Maenan Abbey** (Tel: Dolgarrog 247), a country house hotel built in the 1800s on the site of the old abbey; trout and salmon fishing; 300 acres of woods and moorland; very comfortable. Newbridge-on-Wye: **New Inn** (Tel: Newbridge-on-Wye 211) a 16th-century inn. Pembroke: **Old King's Arms** (Tel: Pembroke 3611) Near Pembroke, at Lamphey, is the **Court** (Tel: Lamphey 67–22–73) a country hotel set in its own grounds with swimming pool, riding stables; baby-listening service; children's menu available. Penrhyndeudraeth: In a class by itself is the **Portmeirion** (Tel: 77–02–28), probably the most expensive hotel complex in Wales. At the sea's edge, set in Italianate gardens and subtropical woodlands on its own private peninsula, its amenities include swimming pool; shops. A number of oldish Italianate buildings have been dismantled and reassembled here; all very chichi and resorty; advertised as "a uniquely gay ensemble" for the "fastidious," to me it's Victorian Miami Beach hysterical-historical style, pretentious, a conceptual elaboration of the Leaning Tower of Pizza or the Garden of Eatin' without the humor. No children under 9. Ruthin: **Ruthin Castle** (Tel: 2664), is a 13th-century fortress converted into a luxury hotel with most of the old walls, battlements, and dungeons remaining to be explored; riding; putting green; fishing; badminton; billiards, Ping-Pong; craftsmen workshops. Be sure to be here for a medieval banquet in the candlelit great hall with medieval dishes served to the accompaniment of harp music and with costumed ladies to cosset you. Three Cocks: **Three Cocks** (Tel: Glasbury 215) a marvelously ancient hostelry with excellent food. Tintern: **Royal George** (Tel: Tintern 205) a nice 17th-century inn; a good base for touring the Wye Valley. The **Beaufort** (Tel: Tintern 202) close by, is a good alternate. Tremadog: **Madoc** (Tel: Portmadog 2021).

In **Wessex,** closer to Exeter than Bristol, is the **Castle Hotel** (Taunton, Somerset; (Tel: Taunton (0823) 72671) once part of a Norman fortress, with attractive gardens, a luxurious, elegant, comfortable hotel with 45 heavenly bedrooms; splendid cellar and food; just the place if you have an urge to splurge in the history-laden countryside of Bath, Exmoor, Wells Cathedral.

Interested in cottage rentals?

The **National Trust** (22 Alan Rd., Llandeilo, Dyffed) has rental cottages in South Wales, but you have to write six months in advance to have a chance!

Country Farm Holidays (11 the Place, Ham Lane, Powick, Worcestershire; Tel. Worcester (0905) 83–08–99) has cottages small and large (accommodating 16!). Some offer free fishing and riding. The Wales Tourist Board's publication *Where To Stay in Wales* lists hundreds of possible cottages to rent, farms with guest houses or guest rooms, hotels and inns.

CAMPING AND CARAVANING Camping sites have been compiled in a booklet, *Britain: Caravan and Camping Sites* available from BTA in Britain; sites are neatly chartered on easy-to-read maps. The **Camping Club of Great Britain and Ireland** (11 Lower Grosvenor Pl., London S.W.1; Tel: 828–1012) lists over 2000 campsites; use of exclusive sites to members; temporary membership for foreign visitors available; this helpful organization also gives advice about all aspects of camping and caravaning. For Wales, additional information is available from the national parks information offices: **Snowdonia National Park** (Penarlag, Dolgellau, Merionethshire for postal inquiries; office at The Bridge in Dolgellau; Tel: 341); **Pembrokeshire Coast National Park** (Guildhall, Tenby; Tel: 2402); **Brecon Beacons National Park** (6 Glamorgan St., Brecon; Tel: 2763). Local tourist offices can tell you about site availability and, during the summer months, can help with bookings: **Lake District** (Tel: Windermere 5555); **Cornwall** (Tel: Truro 74057); **Devon** (Tel: Exeter 79088); **Southern England** (Tel: Eastleigh 616027); **Derbyshire** (Tel: Bakewell 4341).

Caravaning? See Chapter 7 for general information. The **Motor Caravanners' Club** (52 Wolseley Road, London N.8; Tel: (01) 340–5865) publishes *The Motor Caravanner* that can help you through the intricacies of insurance, and documents necessary for touring on the

Continent and in Britain, and alert you to special events. The **Royal Automobile Club** (85 Pall Mall, London S.W.1; Tel: (01) 839–7050) issues booklets about sites in Britain and the Continent, and approves only those sites that meet their high standards. The **Automobile Assoc.** (Head Office, Fanum House, Basing View, Basingstoke, Hampshire RG21 2EA; Tel: Basingstoke 20–123). Offices at Fanum House, Leicester Sq., London W.C.2; Teddington, Middlesex; Halesowen, W. Midlands; Cheadle, Cheshire; Bristol, can supply you with legal and technical advice. But to get help from these organizations you must belong to an affiliated motoring association. A *Camping and Caravaning in Britain* guide available from bookshops or the British Travel Bookshop in New York.

Camping gear and tents (see "Shopping") and motor caravans can all be easily hired; sources are listed in BTA's Caravan and Camping Sites. It is advisable to make arrangements in advance about hiring a motor caravan. **H. F. Edwards (Self-Drive) Ltd.** (11–13 Adam and Eve Mews, London W.8; Tel: (01) 937–0802) is a recommendation, as is **Apex Leisure Hire** (64–65 Albert Embankment, London S.E.1; Tel: (01) 735–5956), **Car Hire Centre Ltd.** (23 Swallow St., Piccadilly, W.1. Tel: (01) 734–7661) and many others. Prices vary according to size, length of time you use it, and time of year.

ATTRACTIONS FOR CHILDREN IN LONDON In London, most of the sightseeing attractions are as much fun for parents as they are for children. The following list is just a starter; other suggestions, with full details of admission fees, hours, and how to get there can be had from the BTA.

The Changing of the Guard. Recommended background reading: A. A. Milne's *When We Were Very Young,* "Buckingham Palace." There are two daily ceremonies: The grander and longer one (with less spectacular uniforms but with a super-compensatory military band) is the one-half-hour Changing of the Queen's Guard at Buckingham Palace; daily at 11:30 a.m., but you should arrive at 11 a.m. to get a good viewing place from the top steps of the Queen Victoria Memorial; no ceremony in bad weather, and it's wise to check with BTA before going, as *occasionally* the guard is changed only on alternate days.

Less celebrated is the Changing of the Queen's Life Guard at the Horse Guards, Whitehall (approached through the Admiralty Arch to the Mall); the Life Guards, magnificently uniformed—white-plumed, breastplates gleaming—and mounted on black horses, change places with the scarlet-plumed Royal Horse Guards daily at 11 a.m. (10 a.m. on Sun.); the forecourt is tiny, so arrive early for a good view; the ceremony takes about 20 minutes.

For younger children, I recommend you combine the two ceremonies, because a 15-minute to one-half-hour wait at the Memorial, then another one-half-hour of the ceremony itself can be a bit overlong; however, this means you'll arrive late at the Memorial, when the good viewing places will have been preempted.

The Royal Family's horses and ponies, gilded royal carriages, the Coronation Coach, and the finest collection of antique coaches in the world can be seen at the **Royal Mews** (Buckingham Palace Rd., S.W.) every Wed. and Thurs., 2 p.m.–4 p.m. throughout the year; closed during Royal Ascot Week; may also be closed at other times if there is a Royal Event.

You will want the children to see **Big Ben** (Ben is the bell, not the clock), **Westminster Abbey** (plus the museum in the crypt with the wax figures of historic and royal personages), and **St. Paul's Cathedral** (with its whispering gallery); read up beforehand; don't attempt to look at all the memorials and statues; try to go after 11:30 a.m., when most of the bus crowds will (hopefully) have left.

The **Tower of London** (Tower Hill, E.C.3) was started by William the Conqueror back in 1078. Here you'll find the Yeoman Warders and the "Yeomen of the Guard," with the nickname "Beefeaters" because they were given such a large ration of beef. Tower Green is the site of the scaffold where many famous people came to a sudden end. Ravens bounce about upon the grass; their wings are clipped, as it is said that when they leave the Tower the British Empire will come to an end. The Tower is open Mon.–Sat. 9:30 a.m.–5 p.m. Closed in Feb.; open in summer Sun. 2–5 p.m.; weekdays are slightly less crowded; you can see the Crown Jewels in the **Jewel House,** which fascinate most children (at least for those first few rapturous moments). The central keep, the **White Tower,** houses marvelous armor, arms, and torture and execution instruments.

Madame Tussaud's (Marylebone Rd., N.W.1) is open seven days a week, 10 a.m.–6 p.m. (5:30 p.m. Oct.–Mar.). The oldest, largest, and best wax exhibition in the world. Nextdoor **Planetarium** (performances every hour on the hour), open 11 a.m.–4:30 p.m. daily.

A continuous performance in town for children is the **London Zoo,** 35 acres housing a varied collection of animals. Plus the Aquarium, plus the endearing carryings-on of small nocturnal mammals in the Moonlight World. Pay a visit to the Snowdon Aviary towering 150′ above the Regent's Canal and providing an unusual view from a walkway cantilevered 40′ from the cliff face. *Elephant bathtime* is at 11:30 a.m. *Summer feeding times:* sea lions at noon and 3:30 p.m. except Fri.; penguins at 2:30 p.m.; pelicans at 2:45 p.m.; lions and tigers at 3 p.m. except Wed.; birds of prey at 3:15 p.m. except Thurs.; reptiles 2:30 p.m. Fri. only.

Lunch, children's portions (with small cutlery and baby food available), and snacks are served yearround at the **Regent Cafe** and **Regent Restaurant** (where parents can have a drink); baby bottles may be heated at the **First Aid station.** In summer there's also the **Pavilion** cafe (where parents can have drinks), and the **Mappin Terrace, Garden,** and **Penguin Pool cafes** (where they can't). The **Zoo Shop** has books, souvenirs, and guides.

A young zoologists club, **XYZ Club** (London Zoo, Regent's Park, N.W.1) for ages 9–18, entitles members to free tickets to London or Whipsnade zoos, magazines, films, talks, special events; a letter of application and $5 sent three months in advance of your trip will pay for overseas postage for magazines, membership, and free entry (children like this VIP prestige).

The **British Waterways Board** (Delamere Terrace, W.2; Tel: 268–6101) runs a Zoo Waterbus service from Little Venice daily from Easter through the first week in Oct.

For little angels, **The Little Angel Marionette Theatre** (14 Dagmar Passage, Cross St., N.1; box off. Tel: 226–1787) has performances for the very young on Sat. mornings, and for slightly older ones in the afternoons on Sat. and Sun. and weekdays during school holidays. The little theater is said to be, after Covent Garden, the most beautiful in London; melodramas, pantomimes, mystery plays, folk tales; advisable to book in advance, as these super shows are absolutely marvelous. **The Unicorn Theatre Club** (Arts Theatre, 6 Great Newport St., W.C.2; Tel: 240–2076, box off. Tel: 836–3334) is a theater club for ages 4–12. For a small membership fee, your child can join in on their weekend and holiday workshops and courses; also weekend performances. First class! **Polka Children's Theatre** (240 The Broadway, Wimbledon, London S.W.19; Tel: (01) 543–4888) stages excellent shows for children and also has holiday and weekend workshops and courses. There is a permanent exhibition of toys and puppets, and a cafe serving child-appeal food. A wholly imaginative and worthwhile venture. **Lyric Theatre** (King St., Hammersmith, London W.6; Tel: (01) 741–02311) has Sat. a.m. entertainments including clowns, short plays, puppets for various children's age groups. **Riverside Studios** (Crisp Road, Hammersmith, London W.6; Tel: (01) 748–3354), with selfservice snack bar and bookshop, features weekend entertainments. **Nomad Puppets** (8 Kingly St., London W.1; Tel: (01) 437–5396) gives two performances on weekends for an audience of no more than 30 children; you can leave your child if you like. Plays and puppet show suitable for children of all ages, including 5s and under, are staged by **Roundhouse** (Chalk Farm Rd., London N.W.1; Tel: (01) 267–2541). **Upstream Children's Theatre** (St. Andrew's Church, Short St., London S.E.1; Tel: (01) 633–9819) explores the magic of theater through improvisations, games, performances, workshops. Sessions take place on Sat., 10 a.m.–noon, and 1 p.m.–3 p.m. for children 4 on up. Give the children tea-money when they go to the matinee performances at grownup theaters where tea and biscuits are served at your seat. The **British Theatre Museum** has a fascinating collection for theater-minded offspring.

For movie-mad minors, the **Institute of Contemporary Arts** (ICA,

Nash House, The Mall, London S.W.1; Tel: (01) 930–3647) has a cinema club with regular weekend shows. Look out also for seasons of children's films at the **National Film Theatre** (8 South Bank St., London S.E.1; Tel: (01) 928–3232), and at the **Rio Centre** (107 Kingsland High St., London E.8; Tel: (01) 254–6677) screening special children's shows during the school holidays. **Barbican Centre for Arts** (London E.C.2) also has exhibits, informal lunchtime and early evening performances; restaurant; and library (Information: Tel: (01) 638–4141).

Ernest Read Concerts for Children (9 Cotsford Ave., New Malden, Surrey: Tel: 942–0318) tune up Sat. mornings at the Royal Festival Hall in London for children 8–11. **Youth and Music** (Tel: (01) 379–6722) offer cut-price tickets for ballet, opera, concerts for 14–25-year-olds; contact this organization well in advance for bookings. They also run a series of four "cushion concerts" during June and July at the Royal Academy of Arts in Piccadilly, combining a look at the summer art exhibition and a concert afterward for 14s and over. Throughout the year, **Purcell Room** (South Bank, London S.E.1; Tel: (01) 928–3191) offers special miniconcerts for children on some, not all, Sun. afternoons when 5-year-olds and up are entertained by music and story-telling. For dates and program details, telephone direct. Once a month, **Morley College** (61 Westminster Bridge Rd., London S.E.1; Tel: (01) 928–8501) offers an opportunity for the entire family to listen to or join in all kinds of music—opera, jazz, steel bands—in relaxed and informal sessions.

▶ **Note:** The *circus* comes to town at Christmastime, Easter, and other holidays.

London Dungeon (28–34 Tooley St., London S.E.1; Tel: (01) 403–0606), open daily 10 a.m.–6 p.m. (summer), 10 a.m.–4:30 p.m. (winter) is a horror show of life in the Middle Ages with weird sound effects and lighting to spook the audience.

Instruction and materials for making your own brass rubbings is supplied at the **London Brass Rubbing Centre** (St. James's Church Hall, Piccadilly, London W.1), open Mon.–Sat. 10 a.m.–6 p.m.; Sun. 12:30 p.m.–6 p.m. Another center, open May–Oct. in **All Hallows Church** by the Tower of London (Byward St., London E.C.3) has guided tours of its *Undercroft Museum* with a model of Roman London, Roman and Saxon exhibits up to 18th century. You can also make a brass rubbing at *Westminster Abbey* (Parliament Square, London S.W.1) weekdays 9:30 a.m.–5 p.m. For information, Tel: (01) 222–2085.

If you would like to attend church, and/or like church music and choirsong, hear the boys' choir at **St. Paul's Cathedral** (Ludgate Hill, London E.C.4) when Evensong takes place every weekday at 5 p.m. in summer, 4 p.m. in winter, 3:15 p.m. on Sun., year-round. You can hear the choir at **Westminster Abbey** (Parliament Square, London S.W.1) at morning services on the second and fourth Sun. each month. Evensong Sat. and Sun. at 3 p.m., weekdays at 5 p.m. **Brompton Oratory**

(Brompton Rd., London S.W.7) is well-known for its choral recitals, music (the organ has 4000 pipes). For times of masses and special music, Tel: (01) 589–4811. All memorable and beautiful moments.

Museums? There's one for every taste, every inclination. Most have special facilities for children, plus films, lectures, and exhibits of children's interests; I've indicated those which run informal children's workshops.

Pollock's Toy Museum and **Toy Theatres,** (1 Scala St., W.1); dolls, games magic lanterns, foreign and antique toys, lovely toy theaters with sets and characters; also shop (see "Shopping"); open Mon.–Sat. 10 a.m.–5 p.m. **The Museum of London** (London Wall, E.C.2; Tel: (01) 600–3699), open Tues.–Sat., 10 a.m.–6 p.m., Sun. 2 p.m.–6 p.m. Devoted to history of London, with a continuous sound-and-light show of the Great Fire which swept London in 1666 (five min.) on the podium level; Victorian shops; ancient armor; special activities during school holidays; quiz sheets for your whiz kids available. The **Geffrye Museum** (Kingsland Rd., E.2), open Tues.–Sat. 10 a.m.–5 p.m., Sun. 2 p.m.–5 p.m., and bank holiday Mon. 10 a.m.–5 p.m. has a children's room open on Sat. and during school holidays (7-to-10-year-olds in the mornings, over 11s in the afternoons) in which all sorts of activities go on. Series of period-furnished rooms from the 17th century to the present; also street with shopfronts.

Scientifically inclined? Head for the **Science Museum** (Exhibition Rd., S.W.7); a floor of life-size locomotives and cars; a floor of planes and a floor of ships. Here is a paradise of equipment that can be worked, illuminated models demonstrating chemical processes, engines that can be set in motion by pressing a button; fabulous fun for everyone. Open Mon.–Sat., 10 a.m.–6 p.m., Sun. 2:30 p.m.–6 p.m. Next door (around the corner at Cromwell Rd.), the **Natural History Museum** has life-size models of prehistoric animals; drawers of beetles which can be pulled out for inspection; galleries of stuffed animals; exhibitions on ecology and human biology; a Children's Centre open Sat. and Christmas holidays, and a Family Centre open Easter and summer holidays, with special exhibits to examine in detail; much to draw and crayon. Interested in seeing just about everything man has ever made? There are bizarre oddities; fascinating rooms furnished in chronological style throughout the ages; a turn of a handle will activate many gadgets from Javanese shadow puppets to music boxes. All to be enjoyed at the wonderland of the **Victoria and Albert Museum** (Cromwell Rd., S.W.7); open Mon.–Thurs., and Sat. 10 a.m.–5:50 p.m.; Sun. 2:30 p.m.–5:50 p.m.

If you are planning to see the *Cutty Sark,* you'll want to go to the **National Maritime Museum** at the same place; marvelous exhibits of Britain's maritime history; model ships; battles; instruments; charts, uniforms (including Nelson's worn at Trafalgar); open Tues.–Sat. 10 a.m.–6 p.m. (5 p.m. in winter); Sun. 2 p.m.–5:30 p.m. (5 p.m. in winter). At the same time, you may also want to look upon the **Greenwich Ob-**

servatory (same hours as above), where time is Mean; many navigational and astronomical instruments; **Caird Planetarium** with performances weekdays except Wed. at 3 p.m. in summer, and other seasonal programs; ask the BTA for details.

The **Geological Museum** (Exhibition Rd., S.W.7), open weekdays 10 a.m.–6 p.m., Sun. 2:30 p.m.–6 p.m. has seasonal children's film program talks and tours at varying hours; programs can be had for the asking. Beautiful collections of semiprecious stones, minerals, gems; connected by a gallery with the Science Museum. **Horniman Museum** (London Rd., Forest Hill, S.E.23 Tel: (01) 699–2339), open Mon.–Sat., 10:30 a.m.–6 p.m., Sun., 2–6 p.m., has a Children's Centre which furnishes a variety of activities and programs. Telephone for details. Musical instruments; aquarium; exhibits relating to natural history, evolution, and the history of time; Magic and Religion section.

Bethnal Green Museum (Cambridge Heath Rd., E.2), open Mon.–Thurs. and Sat. 10 a.m.–6 p.m., Sun. 2:30–6 p.m., houses dolls, dolls' houses and clothes, and toys that have appealed to children throughout the ages; also costumes, textiles, silver, and other applied arts. A Saturday Club; special holiday workshops and activities. A charmer! **National Postal Museum** (King Edward Bld., King Edward St., E.C.1) has 19th-century British and foreign stamps, and other items of enveloping interest to young philatelists. Open Mon.–Thurs., 10 a.m.–4:30 p.m.; Fri. 10 a.m.–4 p.m. The **Imperial War Museum** (Lambeth Rd., S.E.1), open Mon.–Sat. 10 a.m.–5:50 p.m.; Sun. 2 p.m.–5:50 p.m. Film shows on weekends and during school hols. Records World Wars I and II and other British and Commonwealth operations since 1914. Weapons, uniforms, decorations, models, aircraft. **Wellington Museum** (Apsley House, Hyde Park Corner, W.1) is the Duke of Wellington's London home with personal relics, important paintings, uniforms. He defeated Napoleon at the Battle of Waterloo, as most American children *don't* know! Open Tues.–Thurs. and Sat. 10 a.m.–6 p.m.; Sun. 2:30 p.m.–6 p.m. **Gunnersbury Park Museum** (Acton, W.3; Tel: (01) 992–1612) is primarily a local history museum, but it has a charming toy collection as well. Open Mar.–Oct., Mon.–Fri. 1 p.m.–5 p.m.; Sat. and Sun. 2 p.m.–6 p.m. Nov.–Feb. closes at 4 p.m.

The **British Museum** (Great Russell St., London W.C.1) is abloom in Bloomsbury with the Elgin Marbles, the Magna Carta, the Rosetta Stone and other worldwide treasures; extraordinary jewelry clocks, and prints; glorious medieval manuscripts. Buy a guide and map before you start out. You should also get the brochure of Lectures/Films/Gallery Talks available at the main desk or through the Education Service located in the museum building. Quiz sheets for 7–11-year-olds are available; so is an inexpensive cafe that can be crowded and noisy. Open 10 a.m.–5 p.m. daily; Sun. 2:30 p.m.–6 p.m.

The **Public Record Office** (Chancery Lane, W.C.2) open Mon.–Fri., 1 p.m.–4 p.m. has five of Shakespeare's autographs, showing that you don't have to be able to spell in order to write; also the Domesday Book, a record of 11th-century life.

Sir John Soane's Museum (13 Lincoln's Inn Field, W.C.2), open Tues.–Sat., 10 a.m.–5 p.m. is an early 19th-century private house with a fine collection of paintings (Hogarth's *The Rake's Progress* is here); architectural drawings, and many surprises; archaeological treasures; library. Teenagers will love this place. Teenagers also will be taken by **Leighton House** (12 Holland Park Rd., London S.W.14), open weekdays 11 a.m.–5 p.m., the romantic home of a Victorian painter, Lord Leighton, with a blue-tiled Arab Hall in the foyer, pre-Raphaelite paintings, a garden in an area that suddenly seems "out in the country," only a few blocks from Kensington High St.

If you *really* are a tennis fan, you might want to know that there is a **Wimbledon Lawn Tennis Museum** (The All England Club, Church Rd., London S.W.19) that tells you all about the history of the game with displays of old-time balls, rackets, nets, outfits. Open Tues.–Sat., 11 a.m.–5 p.m.; Sun. 2 p.m.–5 p.m.

The **Tate Gallery** (Milbank, S.W.1) open Mon.–Sat., 10 a.m.–6 p.m., Sun.; 2–6 p.m. has special activities for children during the school holidays (including tours) and quiz sheets for different age groups. Strollers available on loan for tiny tots. Take your children over 8 to see the Turners, Constables, Blakes, the Victorian and Edwardian paintings; the modern sculpture and painting collections; the Reynoldses, Gainsboroughs; George Stubbs' horse pictures, a Lichtenstein comic strip panel; the Mondrians were the pictures a 10-year-old "liked best." **The National Gallery** (Trafalgar Sq., W.C.2,) open Mon.–Sat., 10 a.m.–6 p.m., Sun., 2–6 p.m., has children's lectures and some public lectures that are suited to children; all major European schools of paintings; among London's top-ten sights. Pick your favorite period and country and see that—attempting anything more is totally exhausting. Most children love the English section. The **Wallace Collection** (Hertford House, Manchester Sq., London W.1) is a great town house of the 18th century at its cultured best; superb armor—open daily 10 a.m.–5 p.m.; Sun. 2 p.m.–5 p.m.

The **London Transport Museum** (39 Wellington St., Covent Garden, London W.C.2; Tel: (01) 379–6344) displays a wooden milk van, locomotives, subway cars, trolleys and trams. Good for a brisk through and then to hop aboard the vintage bus that runs from the museum.

London's *parks* are filled with surprises for children and parents alike. In summer, many have free shows for children (puppets, Punch and Judy, folk dancing, magicians, clowns, ballet), usually at 11 a.m. and 3 p.m.; some have tennis and soccer instruction for over 15s. For details, see the free booklet *What's On,* published by and available from Department for Recreation and the Arts (Information Office, Greater London Council, Room #3, South Block, Country Hall, London S.W.1; Tel: (01) 633–1707). Available also from public libraries. The booklet details what's on in GLC parks from April–Nov. In Battersea Park (S.W.11), Holland Park (W.14) and Parliament Hill (N.W.5) are **One O'Clock Clubs** and playparks. One O'Clock Clubs (1–4 p.m. weekdays only) are for under-5s; paints, seesaws, story sessions; mothers have to stay in the area of the club. Over 5s can use the playparks (adventure area where dens, camps, treehouses, and rope railways are constructed), each staffed with experienced play leaders; parents are usually kept out of the area.

London Parks Lovely **Regent's Park** N.W.1 has prolific bird life on the islands in its lake; boating, sailing, playground; stylistically designed gardens; and, of course, the magnificent London Zoo (good to ride to via the Zoo Waterbus or Jason's Boat Trip). I also recommend making the trip to Whipsnade Park, some 30 miles out of town, which breeds many rare species supplied to the London Zoo and has a lot else to recommend it (see Dunstable, and see also Chester, the site of another gem of a zoo in a lovely setting).

Hyde Park, W.1 with soapbox orators on Sun. afternoons in its northeast corner, has a bridle path called Rotten Row; self-service, glass-walled restaurant with terraces overlooking the lake is a fine place for children's meals. At the Serpentine, a pleasant artificial lake, your child can rent a rowboat, paddle in the pool, or play in the sandpit. If you want to ride in style on Rotten Row, you can get riding gear from Moss Brothers (see "Shopping") and hie yourself to the **Bathurst Riding Stables** (63 Bathurst Mews, London W.2; Tel: (01) 723–2813) where you and your child can ride every day except Mon. At **Kensington Gardens** W.2 and W.8 (adjoining Hyde Park) you'll find the statue of Peter Pan; Kensington Palace is where Queen Victoria lived as a child and you can see her nursery with displays of her toys, clothes and original furniture; and the Round Pond on which children gather daily to sail model boats; kite-flying can be watched here; the children's playground deserves marks for the safety of its equipment; lovely gardens and friendly gardeners. **Kew Gardens (Royal Botanic Gardens)** is famous for its hothouse, the largest in the world, and for its **Japanese pagoda,** open 10 a.m.–5 p.m.; gardens cover nearly 300 fresh-scented acres; **Kew Palace** contains some of the royal nursery memorabilia; palace open 11 a.m.–5:30 p.m. daily; Sun. 2 p.m.–5:30 p.m. April–Sept. **Kew Gardens** are in Surrey, as is **Richmond Park,** ten square miles of woodland and open space with herbs of red and fallow deer; also ponds, where you can feed ducks and other water birds near the Sheen and Richmond Gates, and sail model boats. **St. James's Park** S.W.1 (running along the Mall) has a duck pond, pelicans, flamingoes, other interesting water birds. At 4 p.m. in summer, the pelicans waddle onto the lawn near the old Birdkeeper's lodge on Duck Island to receive their ration of fish. St. James's is unique, charming; the flower beds are considered the finest in town. **Green Park** (across the way from St. James's Park) is heavily wooded, the trees leafily luxuriant. Lovely, lush, dark, grassy lawns.

The **Crystal Palace National Recreation Centre** (Norwood, S.E.19, Tel: 7780131), has topnotch facilities for swimming and diving, tennis, squash, badminton; cricket and soccer games, basketball, track; and heaven knows what else going on to watch; in winter, an artificial ski slope; boating lake in the southwest corner with islands inhabited by great white plaster dinosaurs and other prehistoric animals; children's zoo Easter–Sept.; playing fields; and just about everything for the sports enthusiast. Membership costs a trifle and can be instantly arranged.

Hampstead Heath is 1000 acres of green about a ½-hour from the center of London; swimming in natural lakes and pool; plenty of space; fish, ride, stroll around, or listen to a band; fly a kite or sail a model boat on Whitestone Pond; pool and playpark at Parliament Hill. Fairs are held here on bank holidays.

Greenwich Park (S.E.10). When you go to see *Cutty Sark,* there may be time for the children to enjoy this green village (which is what the park's name means in Saxon). By the Queen's House at Park Row Gate is a large playground with a boating pond.

Battersea Pleasure Gardens and Fun-Fair (Battersea Park, S.W.11) is by the Thames and has a paddling pool, children's zoo (April–Sept.); summertime shows and special events.

Alexandra Park, N.22, at the foot of Alexandra Palace, has a Ski Centre (Tel: (01) 888–2284), open Oct.–April; children's play area, boating lakes, paddling pool; holiday specials. Ask BTA for details of current events, or check directly (Tel: (01) 444–7696). **Chelsea Physic Garden** (Royal Hospital Rd. Walk, London S.W.3; Tel: (01) 352–5646), by the Chelsea embankment on the Thames, is a four-acre walled garden, with every rare plant, medicinal and culinary herb labeled; rock garden, woodland garden; for the serious botanist and those interested in medicinal and other properties of plants, but open recently to the public; every Wed. and Sun. from 2–5 p.m., also on Mon. bank holidays from 11 a.m.–5 p.m. Pleasant residential environs. **Holland Park,** W.8, has an adventure playground for over-7s, an adjoining One O'clock Club for under 5s; peacocks to feed, attractive gardens; a cafe near the Orangery at Holland House open from Easter–Nov. Easy to get to from Kensington High St. **Wimbledon Common,** S.W.19, has 1000 acres of woods and heath; deer; lakes; a museum sheltered inside a windmill that explains the workings of a windmill, open Sat. and Sun. 2 p.m.–5 p.m. **Syon Park,** Brentford, Middlesex—far away, I used to think, until I took the Underground to Gunnersbury, then the #237 or #267 bus to Brent Lea Gate (or take the Underground to Hammersmith and then the #267 bus to Brent Lea Gate)—and worth the effort to get to this home county just for the tropical greenhouse gardens a-flutter with butterflies from all over the world; insect exhibit behind glass; lovely parkland and gardens stretching to the Thames; an aviary and aquarium, but watching the butterflies flutter by is an astonishment. Gardens and conservatory open daily 10 a.m.–6 p.m.

For details about military band concerts and other entertainment in Hyde Park, Regent's Park, Greenwich Park, Kensington Gardens, Richmond Park, St. James's Park (the Royal Parks), call (01) 212–3434; and for information on what's doing in London's other parks, read the *Parks Diary,* available free from Greater London Council Parks Information Service (Tel: (01) 633–1707) which gives full details of all events and entertainment April–Nov. (See Information.)

Romantic ***boats*** to see afloat: The *Cutty Sark,* in drydock (near Greenwich Pier, S.E.10); last of the famous tea-clippers; boardable daily Mon.–Sat. 11 a.m.–6 p.m. (5 p.m. in winter); Sun. 2:30 p.m.–6 p.m. (5 p.m. in winter). A collection of ships' figureheads with the naive charm of merry-go-round figures is an extra attraction. *Gipsy Moth IV,* Sir Francis Chichester's boat in which he sailed alone around the world is nearby. *H.M.S. Belfast,* a Royal Navy cruiser with plenty to see aboard, is moored near Tower Bridge, open daily 11 a.m.–5:50 p.m. (4:30 p.m. in winter). The **Historic Ships Collection** (St. Katherine's Dock, London E.1) is a time-warp wharf of boardable historic British trade vessels. Come aboard daily 10 a.m.–6 p.m. (5 p.m. in winter).

Tower Bridge Walkway offers spectacular views with photographs for orientation. Exhibits detail the bridge's history and explain its operation. Open daily 10 a.m.–6:30 p.m. (April–Oct.); Mon.–Sat. 10 a.m.–4:45 p.m. (Nov.–Feb.). March? Daily, 10 a.m.–4:45 p.m. Another nifty (but not for the thrifty) panoramic viewing center is **The Top of the Tower** (66 Cleveland St., London W.1; Tel: (01) 636–3000) a revolving restaurant or so; open seven days a week for lunch and dinner. Pricey French cuisine; very touristy; reservations necessary.

London ***markets?*** **Petticoat Lane** (Middlesex St., and its neighborhood) on a Sun. morning has just about every curio you can imagine plus every conceivable sort of second-hand merchandise. **Caledonian Market** (Tower Bridge Rd.) open Fri., only from about 5 a.m. to around lunch-time. Silver, antiques, curios, fascinating junk and junky junk. There usually is a street artist working, maybe an organ-grinder with a monkey, an exuberant pitchman selling mechanical mice or friction cars. Let the children find their own bargains. **Portobello Rd.** (Notting Hill Gate, W.11) for antiques is open Sat., 8 a.m.–5:30 p.m.; toys and general bric-a-brac of interest to children.

Don't go to the Sun.-morning **animal street market** at Club Row in the East End. Children want to "rescue" every animal in sight and take it home with them. If you want a pet, go to Harrod's (see "Shopping").

From dusk until midnight, the **Admiralty Arch, Banqueting House, Whitehall, Houses of Parliament, Clock Tower, Victoria Tower, Marble Arch, National Gallery, Somerset House, Trafalgar Square's fountains, Nelson's Column, Wellington Arch, Westminster Bridge** are floodlit throughout the year.

Snares and Delusions: The **Charles Dickens House** (48 Doughty

St., W.C.1), **Dr. Johnson's House** (17 Gough Sq., Fleet St., E.C.4), **Keats House and Museum** (Wentworth Pl., Keats Grove, Hampstead, N.W.3) I feel are a waste of time. The **Old Curiosity Shop** is an antique and gift shop with no association with Dickens's novel. The quotation from *The Tempest* on the **Shakespeare Memorial** in the Poets' Corner in Westminster Abbey is incorrect. Take along a copy of the play and let your child pick out the errors—a lesson to him not to believe everything he reads even when it is carved in stone.

By boat: Excursions upriver to Kew Gardens, Richmond Park, and Hampton Court, or downriver to the Tower, and Greenwich; refreshments on board; boats leave from Westminster Pier, Charing Cross Pier, and the Tower of London. During April–Oct. pleasure launches leave Westminster Pier on a round-trip sightseeing cruise every 45 minutes, from 11:30 a.m.–5 p.m., for a one-hour trip. For further details, telephone (01) 839–4859. For more information on Kew and Richmond Park trips, call (01) 930–2074/2026. London Transport Board's Information service about riverboats (Tel: (01) 730–4812), Mon.–Fri., is on the ready to supply details.

Specials: The narrow boat *Jason,* one of the original brightly painted canal boats, cruises daily (April–Oct.) on the Regent's Canal from Little Venice past Regent's Park for 1½ hours; children must be accompanied if under 14. You can also hire the *Jason* all for yourself and family. Call Jason's Trip, **Little Venice Ltd.** (Argonaut Gallery, opposite 60 Blomfield Rd., W.9; Tel: 286–3428). You may find the *Jenny Wren,* a sister narrow boat which runs from Camden Town to Little Venice, more convenient for boarding and disembarking: daily trips (in reverse order); April–Oct. Trip lasts about one hour. Call **Jenny Wren Reception Centre & Bookings** (Commercial Pl., Chalk Farm Rd., N.W.1; Tel: (01) 485–4433). The *Porta Bella Packet* (Ladbroke Grove and Kensal Rd., London W.10; Tel: (01) 960–5456) takes you up through Paddington to Little Venice and Browning Island (where the poet lived), stops at the Zoo, then sails beneath Lord Snowdon's Aviary and on to the Cumberland Basin and back again, a four-hour roundtrip; stop at the Zoo and pack a sufficient picnic. When you make inquiries about special cruises, be sure to ask how long they are; a three-hour one-way excursion may be fine for adults, but little children will probably become restless.

You can combine train and river trips on daily excursions from London to Dunstable, Hampton Court, Windsor and Eton, Kingston, Oxford; fares are astonishingly reasonable; operative end-May–end-Sept.; the BTA has details. The BTA will also fill you in on the many day excursions from London, often at special rail or bus rates, to Brighton, Stratford-upon-Avon, Canterbury, Oxford, Stonehenge, Isle of Wight, and many others.

ATTRACTIONS FOR CHILDREN IN ENGLAND Children in Britain have opportunities to see more puppets, marionettes, and animals than anywhere else in the world. Besides permanent puppet and marionette theaters, the **Midland Arts Centre** in Birmingham, the **Harlequin Theatre** at Rhos-on-sea, and the **Caricature Theatre of Wales,** there are mobile companies. **Clifford Heap's Miniature Theatre** with perfect marionettes no more than 4″ high; **Hogarth Marionettes** who use over 100 marionettes in their production of *Aucassin and Nicolette;* Violet Philpott's **Cap and Bells Company;** the **Polka Children's Theatre** who combine puppets and live actors; the **Prospice Puppet Theatre,** among whose unusual productions Noye's *Fludde,* set to Benjamin Britten's music, is wonderful; the **DaSilva Puppet Company** who do swinging versions of old favorites; the **Barry Smith Theatre of Puppets** whose repertory ranges from 19th-century extravaganzas to Regency Gothic melodramas; and **Harry Corbett's** TV-famed puppets are all outstanding companies with programs both for children and teenagers. They can be seen in dozens of towns and many beach resorts (where there are also Punch and Judy performances). The local TICs will have details of programs.

Here are a few highlights: **Southern England:** Beach resorts, safe bathing at Bognor Regis, Pevensey Castle; half-timbered houses in Chilham; **Dover Castle.** World's smallest railway to ride on from Hythe to Dymchurch as far as Dungeness lighthouse. Union Mill, Cranbrook, a working windmill. Chislehurst Caves. **Arundel Castle.** Maritime Museum at Beaulieu, **Beaulieu Abbey** with its National Motor museum. **Canterbury Cathedral.** The Norman Cathedral at Chichester and the open-air museum at nearby Singleton, with medieval buildings. **Winchester Cathedral** and **Salisbury Cathedral.** Old Sarum, a fascinating jumble of Roman, Saxon, and Norman ruins, more interesting to children than Stonehenge. The towns of Lewes, Rochester; Nelson's flag *Victory* at Portsmouth; and Lymington, from both of which ferries run to the Isle of Wight; an Iron Age fort and Bronze Age tumuli on the hills and downs near Wareham in Dorset. **East Anglia** is the flat, Arcadian country reproduced in Turner and Constable paintings. Quiet villages, winding canals, with seaside resorts, fishing ports. The interlocked lakes and streams of the **Norfolk Broads** beckon sailing enthusiasts. Windmills; **Cambridge University;** the medieval town of Norwich; the cathedrals in Ely, Peterborough, Norwich, the town of Dedham and the pretty villages of Lavenham and Woodbridge. Dedham, is alive with the **Vale of Dedham Heavy Horse Centre;** special events. In the **West Country,** the Roman remains and charming Georgian architecture at Bath; the medieval village of Dunster; Glastonbury (a town of ancient myths and legends); Salisbury and Wells with their cathedrals; Shaftesbury (disguised as "Shaston" in Hardy novels); the Blaise Castle House Museum at Harbury, Bristol Zoo and Brunel's vast iron ship, the *S.S. Great Britain;* Stourhead, a stately home, with its landscaped garden; spectacular Corfe Castle where King Edward was murdered in A.D. 978; the holiday resort of Bournemouth; Cadbury Castle, arguably the model for

Camelot; Winchester, England's ancient capital, with a Norman cathedral and castle; Sherborne's vaulted abbey, castle where Sir Walter Raleigh lived; mystical **Stonehenge;** and as a curiosity, Cheddar Gorge and Wookey Hole with strangely shaped, colorful caves; walks along the Dorset coastline; Market Day at Hereford.

Devon and Cornwall are King Arthur's country—Devon with wild ponies on the vast stretch of heather and course grass of Dartmoor; the south coast with red cliffs and gorse-capped headlands, creeks, sandy coves, smugglers' hideouts, and delicious "cream teas." The medieval town of Exeter which has a fascinating Maritime Museum. Ilfracombe, whose beaches are reached by tunnels in the rocks. Salcombe clings to the hillside with a good sandy beach below. Exmouth's lovely beach and harbor or small-boat sailing. A river trip up the Dart from Dartmouth up the wooded estuary to Totnes or by a stream train on the Dart Valley Railway from the Buckfastleigh to Totnes. Rock shrimping at Shaldon. Devonshire cream and lobsters straight from the sea. Plymouth, where the *Mayflower* set sail, and Sir Francis Drake chased away the pirate galleons of the Spanish Armada. Compton Castle near Torquay. The Fair at Widecombe-in-the-Moor. Clovelly with its winding cobbled streets, donkey carts and sweet little houses. **Cornwall,** bounded on three sides by the sea, has a rugged coast, eyed with smugglers' caves, dotted with fishing villages, and guarded by the **Eddystone Light.** The fishing villages of St. Ives, Botallack, Porthleven, Zennor, with prehistoric tombs called quoits. Surfing at St. Ives and St. Agnes. Looe, the center for shark fishing (20 miles out to sea, so children still can safely wade!), is a lovely little town; so is Fowey. Pony trekking on the wild expanse of Bodmin Moor. **Lanhydrock,** near Bodmin, is a splendid historic house with extensive kitchen quarters on view for a peep at downstairs life; also beautiful gardens and woods. Penzance; and nearby **St. Michaels's Mount,** the English version of Mont-St.-Michel, should also be seen. Also **Tintagel Castle** and shell-collectors' beach at Porthcurno. St. Anthony-in-Roseland with panoramic views of Falmouth and St. Mawes. The fishing village at Mullion Cove. **Restormel Castle** and **Caerhays Castle** at St. Austell Bay. The Maze at Glendurgan Gardens, four miles southwest of Falmouth.

East and West Midlands, including Shakespeare Country. The town of Stratford-upon-Avon, Shakespeare's birthplace, is surrounded by lovely countryside—thatched-roof cottages, **Warwick Castle,** red-brick Tudor mansions and half-timbered houses. Robin Hood's **Sherwood Forest,** Nottingham with its dungeoned castle; Shrewsbury with its black-and-white houses; The cathedral city of Hereford and the parklands of Herefordshire. Sheepfarmers and the red-coated (called pink-coated) hunting set around Belvoir (pronounced Beaver). Chipping Campden and Cirencester with their beautiful old houses. The Cotswold region where walls, roofs, chimneys, even the walls that make Tic-tac-toe lines around the fields are built of honey-colored limestone. Norman and Saxon churches, Painswick and Ludlow. **Hidcote Manor** in Gloucestershire with gardens that are luxuriant, part maze, part jungle—both peaceful and adventurous. Villages with charming names like Moreton-in-Marsh and Stow-on-the-Wold. Stokesay Castle, moated and fortified. **Oxford University, Tewkesbury Abbey.** The **Lake District** enchanted Wordsworth, Tennyson, Scott, Keats, Shelley, Coleridge, and De Quincey. Quaint towns, rolling hills, lakes. **Windermere Lake.** See the towns Penrith, Troutbeck, Ambleside, Grasmere, and Keswick; and Beatrix Potter's Hill Top Farm, the setting for at least half of her tiny books about Peter Rabbit and his kinfolk. In **Northern England, Chatsworth** (near Bakewell) and nearby **Haddon Hall** and **Hardwick Hall** (near Chesterfield) are three of the most beautiful country houses in England. The castles of Raby and Richmond. York's beautiful Minster (cathedral), with blue glass from Chartres, and its cobbled streets. County Durham and Northumberland are rich in old customs, pageants.

Other things to see: **Beaconsfield: Bekonscot Model Village and Railway** (Warwick Rd.), scale-model village open year round (railway is in operation); on the recommendation of Denys Parsons combine with a trip to West Wycombe Park. **Beamish North of England Open Air Museum** in Stanley, near Durham and Chester-le-Street, open all year daily 10 a.m.–5 p.m. (6 p.m. April–Sept.), is a 200-acre site with restored and furnished cottages, market-town shops, a railway station, farm, a coal mine (colliery). Train and tram rides, a lot of walking is involved, so take a stroller if you have tinies along. Lumley Castle Hotel at Chester-le-Street is a good place to stay nearby.

Beaulieu is where you'll find the **National Motor Museum** installed at Palace House in Hampshire; open daily 10 a.m.–5 p.m.; an exceptionally fine collection amassed by Lord Montagu who pronounces Beaulieu as Bewley. If you're in the neighborhood of **Beer,** near Seaton, Devon, check out the **Modelrama** model railways and garden exhibit, gardens, Children's Corner, refreshments, minirailway to ride on. Open Mon.–Fri. 10 a.m.–5:30 p.m., Sat. 10 a.m.–1 p.m., holidays, summer, Sun. For more information, call Seaton 21542. **Bickleigh** (see Tivertan). **Bicton Park:** (East Budleigh, near Sidmouth, Devon; Tel: Colaton Raleigh (0395) 68465) on Route A376 Newton Poppleford-Budleigh Salterton Rd. provides a full family-fun day, April 1–Oct. 31, 10 a.m.–6 p.m. with special events and permanent attractions of 50 acres of gardens, greenhouses; **Bicton Woodland Railway** (steam and diesel); picnicking; countryside museum with local craftspeople at work; Hall of Transport; Sir Walter Raleigh exhibition; pleasant Orangery restaurant, also self-service restaurant; through the winter, gardens only are on view, 11 a.m.–4 p.m. Nearby is **Otterton Mill Centre,** a working flour mill cum art gallery with crafts demonstrations and crafts and bakery products for sale. During summer on Sun., a market takes place along the riverside and meadow. The Centre is open 11 a.m.–5:30 p.m. daily in summer; 2 p.m.–5:30 p.m. daily in winter. For information, call

Colaton Raleigh 68521/68031. (See also Newton Poppleford.) **Biggleswade:** The **Shuttleworth Collection** (Old Warden Aerodrome) is a collection of historic planes, cars, carriages, bicycles, and motorcycles; open daily 10 a.m.–5 p.m.; events and demonstrations include a Military Air Pageant, parachute competition, aerobatic displays, and all manner of other events in the sky (remember to take dark glasses). Admission according to events. The BTA can clue you in. Bleak **Boscastle** in Cornwall, has a chilling Museum of Witches. Open daily, 10 a.m. until dusk.

Bourton-on-the-Water: a lovely old village 85 miles NW of London, near Chipping Campden and Stratford-upon-Avon is the site of vibrant, colorful **Birdland Zoological Gardens,** four captivating acres with 1200 birds from 20 countries; fascinating penguin group with underwater viewing; tropical house, wildlife art gallery; seashell exhibit; free-flying macaws and other species; gardens, walks. Open daily Mar.–Nov., 10 a.m.–6 p.m.; Dec.–Feb., 10:30 a.m.–4 p.m. In Bourton-on-the-Water, the **Brookside Hotel** has a restaurant with good trout and homemade pastries; the **Old New Inn** is also recommended. The **Windrush Trout Farm** is another attraction.

Bovington: SW England, has a **Tank Museum. Bridgnorth:** has the outstanding Midland Motor Museum with one of the best collections of sports cars—over 80 of them, plus racing motorcycles—on view in Europe.

Brighton, with its rollicking beach and crunchy sticky candy called Brighton Rock, is one hour out of Victoria Station. If you're curious about a Mandarin's or a Maharaja's Palace, you'll find them both combined in the **Royal Pavilion,** the former seaside palace of George IV. A wilder conglomeration of oriental fantasy would be hard to conceive of, but let's say that it looks just the way children thought it would look. Open all year daily 10 a.m.–5 p.m. (6:30 p.m. July–Sept.). Brighton is the British version of Atlantic City—along the **Amusement Pier** there are lots of carnival stalls and games. There are seven miles of beaches, a new marina; a 19th-century train ride called **Volks Railway** along the sea; entertainment extravaganzas at Brighton Centre; an Engineerium exhibiting locomotives, ships and other technological achievements; 3000 acres of parkland for strolling and picnicking; **The Lanes,** the old part of town, is an antique center with many pubs and cafes. Near Palace Pier is the **Aquarium** and **Dolphinarium** open all year with five or more shows daily. In contrast, the town of Brighton is attractive, with its Palladian-style hotels and buildings, squares and parks and flowers, and winding back streets chock-a-block with antique shops. **Bury St. Edmunds:** The **John Gershom-Parkington Memorial Collection** of clocks and watches; Wed. and Sat. market days in this historic town. **Chard:** Visit **Hornsbury Mill,** a Somerset riverside corn mill with working water wheel; quality craft shop, with restaurant offering morning snacks, lunches, evening meals Tues.–Sat. Open Mon.–Sat. 10:30 a.m.–6 p.m.;

Sun. 2 p.m.–7 p.m. (6 p.m. in winter). See also **Cricket St. Thomas.**

Charmouth's fossils, collected on its Dorset beach, are displayed at **Barney's** on The Street (Tel: Charmouth 60336), an enviable one-man collection; country life exhibition, play area, open Easter–Sept., 10 a.m.–5 p.m. **Chessington: Chessington Zoo** and the added allure of summer fun fair, a pet animal corner, miniature railway, and circus performances; for details, Tel: Epsom 27227. **Chester**, an old Roman encampment and medieval town, with medieval Rows, two-story arcaded shops, and cathedral. Fine collection of Roman antiquities at **Grosvenor Museum,** and the **Chester Zoo,** which alone is worth making the 18 mile trip from Liverpool to see, as not only are the pleasant gardens of England to be seen here in all seasons, but the animal habitats are also lush with flowers that add a welcome fragrance to the indoor enclosures and brightness to the outdoor ''zoo without bars'' moated-enclosures.

Chichester: Charming cathedral town, 55 miles from London, with popular year-round Festival Theatre; lively pedestrian shopping district centered around Market Cross. Seaside village of **Bosham** a few miles west, with yacht harbor and sailing school; at **Singleton,** six miles N on A–286, is the Weald and Downland Open–Air Museum, with restored rural buildings open daily in summer, daily except Mon. in spring and fall, Sun. only in winter. Interesting Roman remains and restorations at nearby **Duncton** and **Fishbourne;** historic **Petworth House,** with major paintings and 700-acre deer park, 13 miles NE of Chichester on Route A–285. For **Chichester Festival Theatre** information, write to Box Office, Festival Theatre, Oaklands Park, Chichester, West Sussex PO19 4 AP; (Tel: Chichester 781–312). **Chipping Sodbury:** 18th-century Dodington House has a carriage museum and Adventureland play area for children. Open daily Easter–Sept. 11 a.m.–5:30 p.m. **Christchurch: Tucktonia** is the largest model landscape in Europe, with boating, minigolf, lots more fun and games to tuck into. **Cirencester** has a great collection of Roman art and artifacts at the **Corinium Museum. Colchester,** the first Roman colony in Britain, has a castle with one of the finest castle museums in the country. **Cricket St. Thomas,** on A30 between Chard and Crewkerne in Somerset, near the borders of Devon and Dorset, combines a large historic estate (manor house and gardens) with a wild-life sanctuary for deer, flamingoes, et al; freeflying hummingbirds in its fine aviary; an adventure playground and playland; farm and countryside museum; pets corner and horse center; meadowland picnic area; self-service restaurant open daily during the summer; wildlife (llamas, lions, elephants, etc.) park; garden and farm food produce shop; dairy farm with automatic carousel milking machine; tiny church with Sun. services; butterfly-breeding unit; open daily 10 a.m.–dusk, winters; until 6 p.m. summers; For further details, telephone Winsham (046–030) 396. Go, and, if the sun is out, you'll all be chirping with pleasure! **Crich,** near Matlock, features the **National Tramway Museum**

with a unique collection of historic trams; some to ride on. Open Easter–Sept., Mon.–Thurs., 10 a.m.–4:30 p.m., April–Oct., Sat., Sun., and Bank Holidays, 10:30 a.m.–5:30 p.m. **Dart Country Park** (Holne Park, Ashburton, South Devon; Tel: Ashburton 52511). You may not have come to England so that the kids could swing on rope-strung tires across a woodland stream, but the children will have a good time here doing just that in the Woodland Adventure Playground; swimming, pony riding, fly fishing, nature trails, picnic meadow beside the Dart River, a campsite with tennis court and swimming pool; woodland and riverside, meadow and lake settings for a pleasurable outing.

Dartmoor National Park: Park HQ at Parke, Haytor Rd., Bovey Tracey, TQ13 9JQ; (Tel: Bovey Tracey 832–093) can provide you with detailed information about the area and the accommodations and attractions in the West Country, Plymouth and Devon areas nearby as well. *Dartmoor Wild Life Park* (Sparkwell, near Plymouth, Devon; Tel: Cornwood (075–537) 209), open every day of the year from 10 a.m. to dusk, with timber wolf pack, donkey rides for children, hawk lawn, ornamental peafowl and colored bunnies, nine miles from Plymouth and reachable from there by bus is nothing compared with the stone rows, kists (burial chambers), cairns, and enclosed hut groups of the extraordinary trove of Bronze Age sites, densest collection of prehistoric remains in Western Europe, to be found here as evidence of the Beaker People (1400–900 B.C.), with the best example of these at *Grimspound*. Your children may not immediately agree with this fiat, but I hope they will in years to come. At *Yelverton,* on the W side of the park, the *St. Tudy Paperweight Collection* is an unusual museum, open a week before Easter through Oct., 10 a.m.–5 p.m., closed Sun. Some paperweights are on sale; restaurant, picnic area close by (7 miles from Plymouth). Full or one-half-day riding, trekking over Dartmoor for both beginners and experienced riders offered by *Shilstone Rocks Stud* (Widecombe-in-the-Moor; Tel: Widecombe 281). (See also Exeter, Plymouth, Tavistock, in the area). Oops! I almost forgot to mention **Castle Drogo,** four miles NE of Chagford overlooking the Teign Valley in all its grim splendor. Great to go there for a look around and a game of croquet on its circular lawn (you rent the mallets and balls from the Administrator, (Tel: Chagford (06473) 3306) and a day's notice is required). On site restaurant for lunches, teas, is recommended, and there's one of those nice National Trust shops to thin your wallet. The castle is open Apr. through Oct., daily 11 a.m.–6 p.m. (last admission at 5:30 p.m.). In the NE section of DNP, there's brown trout, sea trout and salmon fishing. The *Anglers Rest* (Fingle Bridge, Drewsteignton; Tel: Drewsteignton 287) can arrange for permits.

Didcot has a remarkable Railway Museum, with special days when these puffers are "in steam." Let the BTA tell you when. **Dunstable:** Zoo buffs interested in seeing musk oxen, Manchurian cranes, tiny Mongolian wild horses (Przewalski's horses), African white rhinos,

Chilean flamingos, cheetahs, pygmy hippos, muntjacs (deer the size of small dogs that bark), mustachioed Chinese deer, take the train to Dunstable, some 30 miles from London, or drive out there and then ride the "Whipsnade and Umfalozi Railway" or, if you have strong legs, walk around the 500-acre Whipsnade Park which combines a sophisticated collection of wild animals, considered one of the world's best, with the rural vistas of Bedfordshire that serve a remarkable breeding program of Whipsnade. You can picnic here, 600′ up on the edge of the Chiltern Hills where a 600′-long lion, gleaming white against the green turf, has been carved on the slopes of the chalk hills. Ponies and camels to ride, a Children's Zoo, meals in the Cloisters Cafe, a dolphinarium with summertime displays all make for a happy day's outing. Open daily at 10 a.m. **Durham:** Anthony West, a brilliant writer, points out that Durham Cathedral, begun by Benedictine masons in the 11th century, gave him the enormous excitement of understanding the point of departure from Romanesque to Gothic architecture; interesting, if you know enough about architecture to be able to point out to your children what the diagonal vaulting of Romanesque barrel vaults means in the history of architecture. Climb to the top of the tower for a view of the city. Part of Durham University, the **Gulbenkian Museum of Oriental Art** contains one of Europe's best and most beautiful collections of Chinese, Japanese, Indian, Tibetan art, plus Egyptian and Mesopotamian antiquities, open Mon.–Fri., 9:30 a.m.–1 p.m.; 2:15 p.m.–5 p.m.; Sat. 9:30 a.m.–noon, 2:15 p.m.–5 p.m.; Sun. 2:15 p.m.–5 p.m. (See also Beamish). In **Exeter,** visit the **Maritime Museum** (a 6-minute jog downhill from the Cathedral), with a *fabulous* display of the world's working boats, ferry transport. Open daily except Dec. 25 and 26 from 10 a.m.–5 p.m., Oct.–May; until 6 p.m., June–Sept. **Powderham Castle** (Kenton; Tel: Starcross (0626) (890–243) with lavish interior and lovely deer and wild bird park, has a tea room, picnic area, special events and times of admission you should check in advance. **Folkestone** has Port Lympne animal park with a herd of those adorable Przewalski Mongolian ponies. **Frinton-on-Sea** is a quiet holiday beach resort with a very good golf course. About two miles E of **Guiting Power,** between Cheltenham and Bourton-on-the-Water, is the **Cotswold Farm Park,** also known as a Rare Breeds Survival Center, an extraordinary collection of rare and ancient breeds of British farm animals, such as Manx Loghtan rams with four to six horns, red-wooled sheep and the strangest looking pigs, cows, goats, poultry, sheep you ever saw in the pastoral surrounds of the Cotswold Hills; a nature trail, drive-in picnic area; children's corner where animals can be stroked; summertime wildflowers attract red admiral and small blue butterflies; limestone rocks laden with fossilized seashells; ancient burial mounds or barrows; study center with audiovisual presentations; gift shop and cafe; seasonal activities such as sheep shearing and harvesting; occasional bus service direct from Cheltenham; you can take the train to Moreton-in-Marsh, hire a car for remaining 13 miles, or drive

N five miles from Bourton-on-the-Water. (See Bourton-on-the-Water). **Hampton Court** Palace and Grounds, ten miles from London, quickly reached by train from Waterloo Station, is Henry VIII's former stomping ground on the banks of the Thames; an enormous red-brick building of 1000 rooms, 3000 pieces of armor, plus the State Apartments; meticulously designed gardens. What really will impress the children here, apart from the statistics of the number of rooms and so forth, is the maze, a labyrinth of clipped box hedge, thick as a castle wall. Children love getting "lost" and found again. Gardens open all year; maze open April–Sept. State rooms open all year. There are many restaurants near Hampton Court for lunch or dinner. Ideal is **Tiltyard Restaurant** (Hampton Court, East Molesey; Tel: 977–1474); closed in winter; traditional English food. At Hampton Court Way, the **Jolly Boatman** (Tel: 979–1010); at 6 Bridge Rd., **The Ferryboat Inn** (Tel: 977–6486); on Hampton Court Rd., the **Queen's Arms Hotel** (Tel: 977–3998) and the **Greyhound Hotel** (Tel: 977–8121) with a children's menu; at Hampton Court, the **Mitre Hotel** (Tel: 979–2264). Let the children choose which restaurant they'd like to eat at.

Hastings, with its old and new towns, beaches, amusements. In Sussex, you will find the great brick castle of **Herstmonceaux** with crenellated towers, moat, arched gateway and portcullis, now the official residence of the Astronomer Royal; not far away, **Bodiam Castle** with its moat thick with water lilies, its machioated gatehouse fitted with three portcullises. **Ironbridge:** The **Ironbridge Gorge Museum,** near Telford in Shropshire, depicts the life and times of a 19th-century industrial village with cottages, a printing shop, the **Coalport China Works Museum,** audiovisual presentations; strenuous, as the six square mile site encompasses the **Coalbrookdale Iron Works** and museum with a working model of a blast furnace; a museum shop; **Blists Hill,** part of the mining village, with candlemaker, cobbler, sawmill; and yummy butcher shop, a pub, serving refreshments. Site open daily 10 a.m.–6 p.m.; a family ticket admits two adults and up to five children. **Kessingland** (near Lowestoft): **Suffolk Wildlife and Country Park. Keswick** in Cumberland is the place where lead pencils were invented, and there actually is a **Pencil Museum** across the street from the Cumberland Pencil Company. **Kettering: Wicksteed Park,** a children's recreational park, amusement fair, miniature railway, boating, sailboat pond, games of all kinds. **Kingsbridge** in SW Devon, with ferry service, coastal and estuary cruises (see Fun Trips), has a mini-minirailway and the nostalgic home-farm-**Victoriana Cookworthy Museum** (108 Fore St.; Tel: Kingsbridge (0548) 3215), open Easter–mid-Oct., Mon.–Sat., 10 a.m.–5 p.m., with country crafts demonstrated on the second and fourth Fri. in July and Aug.

Lancaster: A **Museum of Childhood** at the Judge's Lodgings (Church St.); The remarkable **Barry Elder Doll Collection** is housed here, with 500 lifelike and even life-size dolls of all materials. Open

April–Oct., Mon.–Fri. and Sat. afternoons from May–Sept.

Leeds: well-preserved, Gothic ruins, of 12th-century Cistercian monastery, **Kirkstall Abbey;** across from **Abbey House** museum, an open-air exhibit of three cobbled streets lined with 18th- and 19th-century shops and cottages; folk galleries to illustrate the life in these times, with collections of period dolls, dolls' houses, toys and costumes up to the 1930s. Open Apr.–Sept., 10 a.m.–6 p.m.; Sun. 2 p.m.–6 p.m.; Oct.–Mar. closing at 5 p.m. About 2½ miles from the **Industrial Museum of Leeds;** machines, films; open Apr.–Oct., Tues.–Sat., 10 a.m.–6 p.m.; Sun. 2 p.m.–6 p.m.; Nov.–Mar. closing at 5 p.m. All part of a nine-mile trail of museums and picnic spots from city center to the 18th-century village of Rodley. Easily negotiated by car or taxi; buses involve too much walking, I think. A walk from the train station to the Leeds TIO (Calverley St.; Tel: (0532) 46–24–53), for details, is definitely advisable, however. An 80 minute train ride from London's King Cross Station for this day trip. In **Lincoln,** the cathedral houses one of the four original copies of the Magna Carta. **Longleat House** (near Westminster), 90-room ancestral home of the Marquess of Bath with Safari Park, a miniature railroad.

Maidenhead: Courage Shire Horse Centre, open Mar.–Oct., is where you can see those incredible equine heavies; wagon rides; children's playground; a geegee whiz of a place. The **Dog Museum,** housed in **Leeds Castle,** a mighty medieval redoubt centered in a perfect lake in Kent (not to be confused with Leeds in Yorkshire) surrounded by acres of rolling parkland and gardens, is about six miles SE of **Maidstone,** 36 miles S of London; admission to the castle grounds and admission to the castle itself and museum required. Thurs. excursions to the castle (all too briefly) aboard the Venice-Simplon-Orient Express. (See Fun Trips). **Morwellham:** near Tavistock, West Devon (Tel: Tavistock (0822) 832–766) offers a full day exploring the living past in the Tamar Valley where costumed workers, recreate the boom years of a copper port in the 1860s; ride the riverside tramway underground into a copper mine with a sound-and-light show; hayrides; 19th-century farm, quays, raised railways; audiovisual shows; Tavistock Canal; children's playground; working waterwheels; picnic areas; crafts' workshops; tea rooms open Apr.–Oct., but Morwellham, a Dartington Hall Trust enterprise, is open all year, seven days a week (closed Christmas Day), 10 a.m.–6 p.m., or until dusk Nov.–Mar. with a blend of attractions at an all-inclusive inexpensive admission. Go early to get the most from this heavenly-Devonly attraction.

Newcastle-upon-Tyne remarkable for the **National Bagpipe Museum** (The Black Gate, Castle Garth), open Wed.–Fri., noon–4 p.m.; Sat. 10 a.m.–1 p.m., is easy to reach from London by train. Near Hadrian's Wall. Visit the **Museum of Antiquities** within the gates of Newcastle University; see the reconstructed wall section at Vindolanda and its small and memorable museum; and visit the fort at Housesteads, two miles away. Birdoswald to the west is the most easily accessible part of the wall; you can get out of your car and touch it, although you do need a car to see the wall and the wall country in comfort. A museum in Carlisle in **Tullie House,** near Carlisle Castle, displays treasures from the western part of the wall. **Dalston Hall,** a Best Western converted castle/hotel is nearby. **Lumley Castle Hotel** at Chester-le-Street, on the eastern part of the wall, south of Newcastle-upon-Tyne, another converted castle, is another excellent base. The booklet and ordnance Survey map, both entitled *Hadrian's Wall* are available in the U.S. from the British Travel Bookshop (see Information) and from various sites along the wall. **New Forest** (near Southampton): Wild ponies roam through this natural forest wildlife reserve; you may see fox, badger, deer, rabbit—a lovely setting. The **National Horseracing Museum** is in **Newmarket,** 63 miles NE of London; open May–mid-Dec., Tues.–Sat., 10 a.m.–5 p.m., Sun. 2 p.m.–5 p.m. In **Newton,** not far from Hadrian's Wall, in Northumberland, near Corbridge, is the **National Tractor and Farm Museum,** open daily 10 a.m.–5 p.m.

If you're in the area of **Bicton Park** (see Bicton Park), a fine-weather experience worth a detour is **Newton Poppleford,** a village near Sidmouth in Devon, that serves a sensational cream tea at the **Southern Cross Guest House.** The **International Donkey Protection Trust and Sanctuary** (Slade House Farm, Salcombe Regis, Sidmouth; Tel: Sidmouth 6391), welcomes visitors to this donkeys' paradise and runs an indoor riding center to help handicapped children enjoy petting and riding donkeys. In Sidmouth, there's a **Vintage Toy and Train Museum** (Field's, Market Place), displaying over 50 years of metal toys, on view Easter–Oct. **Northampton:** At the Old Blue Coat School, Bridge St., you'll find a **Leather Museum,** open 10 a.m.–1 p.m., 2 p.m.–5:30 p.m., Mon.–Sat.; no admission; mouse skins to sharkskins, an Egyptian loincloth of gazelle skin, gloves so thin they can be stored in a walnut-shell. The Roman Wall within **Northumberland National Park:** milestones and remains of Roman camps built along the frontier wall engineered by Emperor Hadrian. The wall is best seen from the road which climbs from the Once Brewed Youth Hostel up to its edge (where there is a car park). **Okehampton,** on the northern edge of Dartmoor National Park, has the impressive ruins of a 13th-century Norman castle. The **Museum of Dartmoor Life** (3 West St.), housed in an old mill near the White Hart Hotel, offers a DNP Information Centre. Also visit the **Courtyard Arts and Crafts Centre** (1 St. James St.). Behind the Craft Centre is a miniature model Victorian fairground plus an extraordinary miniature Disneyland (both with lots of stuff in motion) in **The Small World of Arthur New.**

At **Oxford,** 61 minutes by train from London, some of the glories are **Christ Church College;** the **Bodleian Library, New College** (new in 1379) with its chapel, **Magdelen** (pronounced Maudlen) **College, Balliol College; University Church of St. Mary the Virgin;** the **Ash-**

molean Museum, and more, more, more. Let the Tourist Information Office on St. Aldate's St. near Carfax, the main intersection, take you on a two-hour guided tour at 10:45 a.m. or 2:15 p.m. **Paignton** is a Regency-style resort on Devon's Riviera, featuring a 75-acre zoo with one of the largest collections of animals in England and a Jungle Express to take you around the lakes and back to a restaurant. Open daily from 10 a.m. in the surrounds of Botanical Gardens; children's playground. **Parke,** Bovey Tracy is a National Trust and Dartmoor National Park Interpretation Center, with a **Rare Breeds Farm,** pets corner, children's play area, picnic site; light refreshments and cream teas served in farm buildings. Parkland open year round; Rare Breeds Farm on view from Easter–Oct., 11 a.m.–6 p.m. Bring your Wellington boots so you can enjoy the walks throughout this 200-acre estate, while you look at the many domestic animals.

Penshurst (seven miles from the spa of Tonbridge in Sussex): **Penshurst Place** in itself has enough to attract visitors: the original 14th-century romantic great house of Viscount de L'Isle, with admirable portraits and furniture; magnificent yet intimate gardens perfect for strolling; arms and armor, historic swords; teas with fresh cream and home produce served daily in the Old Kitchen. But also a **Toy Museum.** Attractions include a gingerbread house filled with gingerbread men; an Edwardian wedding procession of dolls; a toy toyshop; a fort; games; rocking horses; a Noah's ark formed from colored straw made about 1810 by French prisoners of the Napoleonic wars. Open daily except Mon., 1 p.m.–5:30 p.m., April –Oct. **Plymouth:** Check with the Tourist Information Centre (Civic Centre Bldg., Royal Parade; Tel: Plymouth 264–849) for guides, local and Dartmoor information, and accommodation bookings. They have a good regional ***guide service*** (15 Culme Rd., Mannamead; Tel: Plymouth 660–582). At least eight historic houses in town and nearby. The **Millbrook Steamboat Co.** operates 1-hr. river cruises from Apr.–Oct. Call Plymouth (0752) 822–202 (24-hr. service) for information about longer trips. Close by at **Yealympton,** are the **Kitley Caves,** two of which have illuminated cave passages with information panels and the usual interesting rock formations; also at Yealympton, the **Devon Shire Horse Farm Centre** Dunstone, Yealympton; Tel: Plymouth 880–268), where you can see Shire horses, blacksmith shop, local craft shop, antique farm machinery, and livestock your children can pet. Daily parades at 11:30 a.m., 2:30 p.m., 4:15 p.m. Restaurant for lunches and those good Devonshire cream teas. Small all-inclusive (except for food) admission. (See also South Carver.) **Portsmouth:** The *H.M.S. Victory,* the *Mary Rose,* and the most treasured time capsule of naval life in Tudor England is on display. Check with the BTA about this extraordinary and dramatic 1982 salvage operation. **Rottingdean:** The Grange Art Gallery and **Toy Museum. Sharpitor:** 1½ miles SW of Salcombe in Devon in the site of **Overbecks Museum and Garden.** The elegant Edwardian house contains collections of model boats, shells, moths, butterflies, birds (stuffed), birds' eggs, dolls, toys, shipwrights' tools, late 18th-century photographs of the area and its people; and a secret room for children; open Apr.–Oct., daily 11 a.m.–1 p.m.; 2 p.m.–6 p.m. The garden, where picnicking is allowed, is superb, filled with perfumed and scented shrubs and open every day during daylight hours. Tel: Salcombe (054 884)2893 to ask if a tour with the head gardener is possible. There's a nice ship; ferry service from Salcombe to South Sands (¾ mile distant) May to end of Sept. every 30 minutes weather permitting. **Sidmouth:** See **Bicton Park, Newton Poppleford.** The gardens of **Sissinghurst** in Kent, about an hour by car or train from London, are sheer delight and justly celebrated; unappreciative children can be mollified by the scones with cream and Kentish honey available on the castle grounds; other, simple fare obtainable.

South Carver, a 20-minutes car-ride S of Plymouth, is where you can board the **Edaville Railroad,** a narrow-gauge railway; also the **Museum of New England Heritage,** with a splendid collection of railroad memorabilia, antique toy trains, vintage fire engines and automobiles, in which I promise you won't feel bogged down. Open spring through fall, and holidays. Check times with the BTA. In **Stapleford** (Leicestershire), Stapleford Park has miniature passenger-carrying railroad and steamships; interesting house. **Stoke-on-Trent:** The **City Museum and Art Gallery** (Broad St., Hanley), open Mon.–Sat., 10:30 a.m.–5 p.m.; Wed. until 8:30 p.m., has a recreation of Victorian life and is a magnet for Staffordshire and Wedgwood collectors. The **Gladstone Pottery Museum** (Uttoxeter Rd., Longton) is a working museum of the pottery industry. Museum open all year on weekdays, 10:30 a.m.–5:30 p.m. (closed Mon., Oct.–Mar.); Sun., 2 p.m.–6 p.m. The **Chatterley Whitfield Mining Museum** in nearby **Tunstall,** open Tues.–Fri., 9:30 a.m.–4:30 p.m.; Sat., Sun. and public holiday Mondays, 10 a.m.–5 p.m., is a coal mine in use from 1860–1976. Groups of 12, plus guide, are outfitted and led into a cage, 700 feet down to the coal face; 10-year-olds are the youngest allowed on the tour. In Somerset, in a town called **Street,** there's a **Shoe Museum** on High St., open Easter–Oct., Mon.–Sat., 10 a.m.–4:45 p.m.

Stratford-upon Avon: The accoutrements of everyday Elizabethan life are to be seen in Shakespeare's birthplace on Henley St. The Birthplace Trust also administers **Anne Hathaway's Cottage, Mary Arden's House, New Place Museum** (site of Shakespeare's last home) and **Hall's Croft** (childhood home of Shakespeare's wife); an admission ticket for all can be bought at the trust's headquarters in the **Shakespeare Center** adjacent to his birthplace. All sites open daily 9 a.m.–6 p.m., Sun. 2 p.m.–6 p.m. Apr.–Oct.; Nov. 1–Mar. 31 9 a.m.–12:45 p.m.; Sun. 2 p.m.–4 p.m. **Guide Friday** (32 Henley St.; Tel: Stratford 294–466) operates half-day bus tours to all properties. Visit the Holy Trinity church by the river, where Shakespeare is buried, on your own. The **Royal Shakespeare Theatre** with Thurs. and Sat. matinees in summer, does have seats you can reserve by telephone using your American Express card. (Tel: Stratford 29–71–29.) You can make brass rubbings at the **Brass Rubbing Centre** (Avonbank Gardens); visit the **Motor Museum** (Shakespeare St.); have a light lunch at **Opposition** (Sheep St.) for inexpensive fare. If you travel by train from London to Coventry, you can rent a car there to drive to Stratford. Check with the BTA, or TIC, for nearby excursion possibilities. **Sudbury,** in Derbyshire, is noted for its 17th-century **Sudbury Hall** with fantastic plasterwork and interior carving; also its **Museum of Childhood,** open Apr.–Oct., Wed.–Sun., and Mon. bank holidays also, 1 p.m.–5:30 p.m. **Thursford,** near Fakenham, is where you'll find the exceptional Thursford collection of *mechanical musical organs,* including a Wurlitzer theater organ on which concerts are to be heard Tues. evenings from mid-June–Sept. The collection is open Easter–Oct., daily, 2 p.m.–5:30 p.m.

Tiverton: Castle with medieval gatehouse, curtain walls, and *international clock collection;* open daily 2:30 p.m.–5:30 p.m., except Fri. and Sat., Apr.–end Sept. (Tel: Bickleigh (08845) 363). About four miles from town is **Bickleigh Mill Craft Centre and Farm** (Tel: Bickleigh (08845) 419); old world village with craftsmen's workshops, mill workings, traditional farm; rainbow trout fish farm; **Millstones Restaurant** with home-cooked food and Devonshire cream teas plus a large craft, farm, and gift shop. Up the road is **Bickleigh Castle** (Tel: Bickleigh (08845) 363) with spy and escape gadgets in its collection; an armory; a collection of toys; moated gardens, tower, shop, tearoom. The **Grand Western Horseboat Co.** (The Wharf, Canal Hill, Tiverton; Tel: Tiverton (0884) 253–345) has an 11-mile towpath for its horse-drawn 2½-hour canal-boat trips (bar, teashop, and lavatory aboard) that start and finish at **Tiverton Canal Basin** where there is a booking office in the summer open 10 a.m.–5 p.m. weekdays, noon–5 p.m. Sats., 11 a.m.–6 p.m. Sun. Telephone for schedule. You can also hire rowboats here.

Torbay is the area, **Torquay** is its cliff-backed, beachside, sea-fronting resort town, with the **Paignton Zoo** close by. Illuminated *Kents Cavern* is a 40-minute, circular, one-half-mile walking tour with a guide; the **Model Village,** closed only on Christmas Day and open 9 a.m.–5 p.m., mid-Oct.–Easter, and 9 a.m.–10 p.m. with illuminations Easter–mid.-Oct., is an elaborate miniature landscape with town, village, railway, waterfalls; **Aqualand's** displays of tropical marine fish; **Torbay Aircraft Museum** with a display also of **Devonshire Period Costumes.** The **Imperial** and **Grand** are the top hotels with swimming pools, saunas, golf, riding, tennis, boating.

Totnes in Devon is a mecca for those interested in contemporary and avant-garde culture, dairy farming and its produce, gardening, tasteful restoration of domestic medieval architecture, rural renaissance, all of which thrive together at **Dartington Hall; Garden Centre;** farm foods and handcrafted articles. **Dartington Glass** factory at Torrington, North Devon (Tel: Torrington (08052) 3797) with a large choice of glass to buy at its factory shop. **Cider Press Center** (Tel: Totnes 864–171) on the road from Totnes to Buckfastleigh, open Mon.–Sat., 9:30 a.m.–5:30 p.m. You can also see raw wool transformed to tweed at the **Dartington Hall Tweed Mill** and shop around the corner. **Cranks Vegetarian** restaurant nearby serves health-food fare at moderate prices; garden patio. The **Dart Valley Railway** has vintage steam trains making a 14-mile round trip, spring and summer (see Fun Trips for details), and you can ramble or ride just north on the hills of **Dartmoor National Park.** Information about concert and plays at Dartington Hall from the **Dartington Arts Society** (Totnes, Devon TQ9 6EJ; Tel: Totnes 863–073). Information about the summer school of music from the **Dartington Summer School of Music** (48 Ridgeway, London S.W.19) which includes music, dance, theater. The village of Totnes is an antique-lovers delight; the **Devonshire Collection of Period Costume** (10a High St.) is charmingly displayed in a Tudor merchant house, open Mon.–Fri., 11 a.m.–5 p.m., closed Sat., open Sun., 2 p.m.–5 p.m. The **Totnes Motor Museum,** situated on Steamer Quay, near the old bridge over the Dart river, is signposted from the town center, with everything from a child's pedal car to a Grand Prix car; vintage, sports, racing cars and **Wheels,** an irresistible model car shop. Call Totnes (0803) 862–777 for Oct.–Easter hours; otherwise, museum and shop open every day, Easter–Oct., 10 a.m.–5 p.m.

Turton Tower, Blackburn local history museum. **Ugbrooke,** the ancestral home of the Lords Clifford of Chudleigh, believe it or not, features "Uggie," a *talking robot* who presides over an extensive exhibition of model whatnots in this castle-style Adam house. Lakeside walks, picnic area, children's Adventure Playground; permits for trout fishing available; *"nostalgia" museum* of '30s and '40s; Wyvern Cafe located in the former stables. Cafe and grounds open 12:30 p.m.–5:30 p.m., house open 2 p.m.–5 p.m., May–end Sept. Bank holidays and Sun. the rest of the year. Found off the A380 Exeter-Torbay road in Devonshire. (Tel: Chudleigh (0626) 852–179.) In **West Wycombe,** the **Hell Fire Caves** in West Wycombe Park; a lake and Hellenic-style temples in the park, plus a Palladian house. The caves are man-made chalk with an underground River Styx; sound and light performances reinforced with life-size figures in period costumes. **Wimbledon,** reached in 35 minutes from London via the Underground and a taxi to the main complex, has such crowds that people faint in the standing-room section and queue for hours to get tickets, to use the restrooms, or to make a telephone call. **Windermere,** with its lovely lake, is the setting for the **Steamboat Museum;** rides on the lake on a steam launch. Open Easter–Oct., weekdays 10 a.m.–5 p.m.; Sun. 2 p.m.–5 p.m.

Windsor Castle, 21 miles from London, is the largest inhabited castle in the world. Paintings (Leonardo da Vinci and Van Dyck) and other treasures in the State Apartments. The children may skim by as they make their way to Queen Mary's Dolls' House. (Open mid-Mar.–

late Oct. weekdays 10:30 a.m.–5 p.m. (closes 3 p.m. other months), also mid-May–Oct. Sun. 1:30 p.m.–5 p.m. The castle is closed for court visits at certain times, so check with BTA before setting out). The castle grounds are open from 10 a.m.–sunset daily. **Windsor Safari Park** (daily 10 a.m.–dusk) is in Windsor Forest, not Windsor Park. Go by car (no convertibles or soft-tops allowed for the Jungle Ride) or Safari bus, which just isn't as much fun at all. You'll see baboons, lions, tigers, rhinos, cheetahs, and the elephant-zebra-giraffe contingent roaming freely. Aviary, monkeys, killer whale on view. Pet corner with baby animals; children's play areas (with equipment); dolphin show. You can picnic in this 100-acre park; there is also a restaurant.

At **Woburn, Woburn Abbey** has nearly everything: art treasures in state apartments, park with rare animals and birds, a lake for fishing and boating, forest and meadowland for picnicking, children's playground, antique market, special weekend events in summer, a truly beautiful deer park, a storybook garden, a restaurant (Tel: Woburn 662). You can tour the 3000-acre park on an open truck or chair-lift. The 1300-acre Woburn Wild Animal Kingdom features lions, giraffes, and herds of bison and white rhinos. The Pets' Corner has baby animals and pony or coach-and-four rides. The Abbey itself, a magnificent 18th-century house with gilded ceilings and a $15-million art collection (paintings by Rembrandt, Murillo, Gainsborough, Reynolds among others), is, on the whole, less interesting to children than are the animals. You can spend the night at Woburn (see "Castles and Other Happy Family Accommodations"), but nearby hotels are much cheaper. Open Feb.–Nov. daily from 10 a.m. (Park); 11 a.m. (Abbey) in summer; noon–1 p.m. (Abbey) in winter.

Yeovilton's Fleet Air Arm Museum and Concorde Exhibition, just off the A303 route near Ilchester, Somerset, is the largest collection of historic military aircraft massed together that you'll probably find in Europe. Flying displays as well. Children's play area; ship and aircraft models. Open daily 10 a.m.–5:30 p.m. or dusk in colder months. (Tel: Ilchester (0935) 840–565). **York Castle Museum** in **York** is a superb folk museum with cobbled streets and authentic shops. The **Railway Museum** contains historic locomotives, royal coaches, railway memorabilia. **Zennor,** D.H. Lawrence country in Cornwall, six miles from Penzance, has a privately owned, reverently created **Folk Museum;** ancient burial mounds, "quoits," have a more somber appeal.

ATTRACTIONS FOR CHILDREN ON THE CHANNEL ISLANDS These—Jersey, Guernsey, Alderney, Sark, and Herm—are islands of flowers, about 2 weeks ahead of London in temperature; all are inexpensive; Jersey and Guernsey are incredibly beautiful and seem very French (France is only 15 miles away). **Jersey,** my favorite, blooms with an August festival, the Battle of the Flowers, when flowers are everywhere. St. Helier (the capital) is only a few minutes away from sandy beaches; at low tide you can walk along a causeway to offshore **Elizabeth Castle,** a 16th-century fortress, but don't get moored out there by losing track of time and tide! Beaches have golden sand, and the best is at **St. Brelade's Bay; Bonne Nuit Bay** and **Bouley Bay** are also fine. Gorey is a colorful harbor village at the foot of glorious **Mont Orgeuil Castle**—what a castle, particularly at night when it is illuminated! Hotel space is limited, so book ahead; babysitters are easily come by. *Crowded* in summer, but the BTA can provide lists of accommodation, as can the local tourist boards; take advantage of package deals offered by travel agencies; go, if possible, out-of-season for peaceful pleasure. The Wildlife Preservation Trust, sometimes known as the Durrell Zoo, breeds animals in danger of extinction. If you like some endearing creature, you can make him your own by contributing an annual sum to his board; your wardship is acknowledged on the cage, and you are notified should your foster pet have youngsters or acquire a mate.

Guernsey, smaller and quieter, is a picturesque family island with country-house–like hotels and a cluster of beautiful bays—**L'Ancress** (north side), **Cobo** and **Vazon** (west coast) are perfect for young children; **Marlin Huer, Saints,** and **Petit Port** bays (all in St. Martin's) have nice clean sand. You need a car here because nothing is very accessible. The wind blows all the time, and you are furnished with a wind guide which tells you where to go to get away from it (or where to seek it out on hot days). The capital, St. Peter Port, has the grand **Castle Cornet** housing militia and maritime museums; cobbled streets, and produce markets. There's a **Guernsey Folk Museum,** the **Guernsey Museum and Art Gallery** in Candie Gardens, the **German Occupation Museum,** and the **Guernsey Tomato Museum;** also a zoo and fishing boats for hire. Seafood specialties at the quay-side restaurants; the **Steak and Stilton** (23 The Quay) is restful with its tables each in its own compartment. Less expensive than Guernsey's prestige hotel, **The Old Government House** (which isn't all that expensive) are **L'Atlantique Hotel** on the west coast at Perelle Bay, with swimming pool and cottage, or the **Hotel Hougue du Pommier** in Castel, with swimming pool and golf course. At low tide you can walk out from the northern arm of Rocquaine Bay along a causeway to explore the monastic ruins of **Lihou Island.** There's a sweet little 17th-century shell-studded church (rococoquille style) called **Les Vauxbelets** and the home of **Victor Hugo** (his Parisian home is much more interesting). The August Battle of the Flowers is not as spectacular as Jersey's. If the wind doesn't bother you—it makes me nervous—this is a romantic little island.

No car traffic on **Sark,** but you can rent a bike from **Jackson's** (Rue Lucas, opposite Midland Bank) or hire a horse carriage. Stay at **Stock's Hotel; Dixcart Hotel,** open Apr.–Oct., same price, but with three meals instead of two included. No cars either on tiny **Herm** (just walk about). Herm has a fabulous shell-sand beach. Sark's best beach is **Grande Greve,** and the island is a haven for birds and butterflies.

Herm has one hotel, the **White House Hotel,** on the western shore, and masses of stone circles and giant cromlechs where the Neolithic settlers buried their dead some 4000 years ago. To get here from Guernsey, take **Trident Launches;** from Sark, via the Sark-Guernsey ferry.

At **Alderney** (8 miles from Normandy), **Braye Bay** and **Longy Bay** are ideal for young children; few hotels, few guesthouses; prices are reasonable; daily air shuttle via **Aurigney Air Services** plane from Guernsey. A steam locomotive carries passengers from Brave Harbour to a quarry; there are conducted tours of the many Victorian fortresses around the headlands and promontories. St. Anne is the island's only town. Stay at the 18th-century **Georgian House Hotel.** With all meals, the rates are extremely reasonable.

Jersey and Guernsey are served by various British airlines, and Aurigney Airlines operate interisland services. There are regular car ferry services operated by Sealink from Weymouth and Portsmouth to Jersey and Guernsey (a 5–6½ hour trip). Sark is a nine-mile hydrofoil trip, and Herm a three-mile launch trip. Travel agencies can arrange package deals including transport and accommodation.

ATTRACTIONS FOR CHILDREN ON THE ISLE OF MAN Set in the Irish Sea about 60 miles off the Lancashire coast is the mountainous Isle of Man, a former Viking kingdom and presently a country with its own parliament (the Tynwald, the oldest in the world), laws, language, and cats with no tails. It had quadrilateral castles, among them **Castle Rushen** (the grandest) and **Peel.** You can pony trek, bird watch at seabird sanctuaries, trout fish, scuba dive, or just loll around like the barrel-fat fleecy sheep and look at the ravens and falcons. **Douglas,** the capital, has a beach that would be famous if it were anywhere else. **Ramsey** is a nice family place on the northeast (and warmest) coast, with a beach, boating lake; palm trees here prove the mild climate. **Laxey** has the world's biggest water wheel. There is a variety of unusual transport. A mountain railway goes to Snaefell (2000′, the highest point on the island); horsedrawn trams trot along the promenade at Douglas, and there are steam trains between Douglas and Port Erin, and electric trains from Douglas to Ramsey. At Port St. Mary you're only about a mile away from the **Manx Village Folk Museum** at Cregneash, showing how the islanders lived in bygone centuries. At Ballaugh, the wildlife park features Manx Loaghtan sheep that have four (!) horns. See the **Manx Grand Prix** motorcycle races in Sept.; **Sheep Dog Trials** in July; Viking festival and boat race at Peel in Aug. You can get here by air from London and many provincial airports; an all-year-round car ferry service from Liverpool and summer services from Fleetwood, Ardroseen; a Sealink service from Heysham (near Lancaster).

ATTRACTIONS FOR CHILDREN IN THE SCILLY ISLES Not comparable in beauty to Jersey or Guernsey, but blessed with a mild climate;

the Isles of Scilly are some 28 miles off Land's End, Cornwall; of more than 100 islands, only five are inhabited. Holidaying here is to swim, fish, see the seals and the seabird colonies on Annet, picnic on the uninhabited islands, and to enjoy sunshine, the sea, and a sense of peace. It's worth crossing the Atlantic to go to the beaches. Most visitors stay on **St. Mary's,** the largest island, and explore the others by boat from Hugh Town harbor. Above Hugh Town are the massive walls of the old Elizabethan Garrison. An excellent **Island Museum** (in Hugh Town) gives the history of the Scillies from the Bronze age to the modern treasure hunt for the bullion of the *Association,* a ship wrecked off the coast in the 18th century. **Tresco,** the second-largest island, is noted for daffodils in the spring, peace, and quiet (no cars here); collection of wooden figureheads from some 2000 ships that splintered on the outlying rocks; the water is brilliantly blue and clear. Between its two harbors, Old and New Grimsby, are the pine forests of the Middle Downs with brakes of gorse and masses of wild flowers; south of here the island is almost divided in half by the large freshwater lake, Great Pool, with **Tresco Abbey** and its subtropical gardens. The other three inhabited islands are **Bryher, St. Agnes,** and **St. Martin's,** all very small with only limited accommodation. British Airways helicopters (20 min.) and passenger ferries (2¾ hrs; no Sun. service) run between Penzance and St. Mary's. Cars may be transported (Mon.–Fri.) but are not welcome, and indeed not necessary. During peak holiday months, it's advisable to book accommodation in advance. Information available from BTA and TIC (Town Hall, St. Mary's, Isles of Scilly: Tel: Scillonia 22536).

ATTRACTIONS FOR CHILDREN ON THE ISLE OF WIGHT The Isle of Wight is a diamond-shaped chunk separated from the south coast by the narrow seaway known as the Solent. Very sunny, it has majestic cliffs, gorges or chines filled with luxuriant jungley vedge, and colorful towns climbing terraced hillsides. **Arreton Manor,** a 17th-century house shelters an **Echoes of Childhood Museum,** with a toy and doll collection; also a folk museum. Open Easter–Oct., weekdays, 10 a.m.–6 p.m.; Sun. 2 p.m.–6 p.m. Winter months, Sat. only, 10:30 a.m.–4:30 p.m. Cowes is the top yachting port in Britain, renowned for the Cowes Week regatta in Aug. (when a carnival is also held). **Newport,** the island's capital, has a market and interesting old buildings; about a mile away is magnificent **Carisbrooke Castle. Osborne House** was Queen Victoria's favorite residence; she and Albert designed it. **Osborn-Smith's Wax Museum** at **Brading;** a quickie for a rainy day. **Ryde** has five miles of sandy beach, a canoe lake, and is fine for children; carnival in Sept. **Sandown** is also good for families, with cliff-sheltered sandy beach. **Ventnor,** built on the terraced cliffside, has a sandy beach below and good walks along the Undercliff, also a canoe lake and paddling pool; a merry folk dance festival in May. **Yafford Mill,** near Newport, is a restored working mill, with a farm museum, children's playground, picnic area. **Yarmouth** has a yachting harbor. Ferries to the island run daily from Southampton to Cowes; they take about one hour. Regular hovercraft service from Southampton to Cowes and from Southsea to Ryde; crossing time 20 minutes or seven minutes, depending on your transport, and great, good fun.

ATTRACTIONS FOR CHILDREN IN WALES The ancient Celtic reverence for music and poetry crops up everywhere in eisteddfodau—festivals of music and folk dancing—in almost every hamlet, with the International Eisteddfod taking place in Llangollen (see "Calendar of Events"). Wales also has three national parks (see "Camping and Caravaning"); quiet bays on Anglesey Isle and the Lleyn Peninsula; sandy bays and cliffs on the Gower Peninsula; and the get-away-from-it-all coast of West Wales, looking across at romantic Caldy Island where Cistercian monks still fish, sow, and distill perfume. Seaside resorts offer donkeys in the sand and the traditional pleasures of seaside holidays in Britain (promenades, amusement piers, concerts, pavilions, festivities).

The *sheepdog trials* here are certainly something to see. For information about forthcoming events, contact the *South Wales Sheepdog Trials Association* (Tel: Glamorgan (0685)74620); *North Welsh Sheepdog Trials Association* (Tel: Gwynedd (049) 269–662); *International Sheepdog Society* (Tel: Bedford, England (0234) 52672). The *Great Little Trains of Wales,* 14 in all, are lovingly preserved steam engines. With the sea town of Aberystwyth or Porthmadog as a base, you can see this area of Wales as no driver can. (See Fun Trips.)

Aberavon, summer fair. **Abercrave:** In the Tawes Valley are **Cathedral Caves,** the largest and longest public caves in Britain. **Abergavenny:** Pony-trekking center in the nearby Black Mountain area; the **Queen's Head** pub in idyllic Llanthony Valley has a stableful of ponies and a few bedrooms for trekkers; the former prior's house of lovely Llanthony Abbey has been restored to make a small guesthouse in this rugged, unspoiled area. In town, Tues. Market Day for food, flowers, handknit baby clothes; Fri. and Sat. sheep and pony sales; 12th-century castle ruins enfold pleasant folklore museum. Stay at the **Angel Hotel,** a restored 17th-century coaching inn. **Abergele,** seaside resort; livestock market on Mon. **Aberystwyth,** and the hill country reached by narrow-gauge railway up the Rheidol Valley to Devil's Bridge. **Angelsey Isle** has **Beaumaris Castle** and, at **Benllech,** a four-mile beach with a children's playground and a riding school; **Museum of Childhood** at Menai Bridge; **Bala** has a picture-pretty lake where you can sail, fish, and swim. **Bangor,** near the cathedral, has a **Bible Garden** with plants arranged in the chronological order of their appearance in the Bible; about two miles east of town is **Penrhyn Castle,** with old trains and 1000 dolls in its museum (open Apr.–Oct.). **Barry** seaside resort, amusement park; nearby is the **Welsh Hawking Centre** with 200 birds of prey flown every hour. Have a look! Summer fair. **Betws-y**

Coed is a beauty spot with waterfalls and **Pont y Pair** (the Bridge of the Cauldron) in the village. The **Park Hill Hotel,** Victorian-cozy, has an indoor heated pool and spa; the **Henilys Hotel,** overlooking the river Conway, is even kinder to your wallet. Visit the **Penmacho Woolen Mill,** about a mile away, with mill shop open daily Apr.–Oct., and Penmacho village's **Eagles** restaurant. **Blaenau: Ffestiniog-Llechwedd Slate Caverns** with entrance and travel-through aboard a little railway; also **Gloddfa Ganol Mountain Centre** where you can examine a slate mine, view quarrymen's cottages, explore craft shops; children's playground. **Brecon: Brecknock Museum, Welsh Craft Centre,** gateway to **Brecon Beacons National Park** in the highlands of South Wales; **Mountain Centre,** five miles Southwest is the place to go for additional information; food kiosk. You can take a cruiser or rowboat out for an hour or day on the refreshingly rural Brecon Canal, parallel to the Abergavenny-Brecon road. **Caerleon, Roman Museum** and excavations in progress. **Caernarvon** has a castle gray and grim, an armory museum in its Eagle Tower, and a market in the castle square every Sat. **Caerphilly:** The main attraction is a great, gray 13th-century castle.

In **Cardiff,** the **Caricature Theatre of Wales** (which goes on tour) performs *Pilgrim's Progress* and Welsh legends with almost life-size rod puppets; the **National Museum of Wales;** tattoo on the castle grounds in Aug.; also peacocks and peafowl on the Cardiff Castle lawns; nearby, housed in St. Fagan's Castle, **Welsh Folk Museum** with an open-air annex and craft demonstrations; weekdays 10 a.m.–5 p.m.; Sun. 2:30 p.m.–5 p.m. A bit farther is **Caerphilly Castle,** equipped with the most elaborate defense system of any fortress in Britain; a tower leans more than 9′ from the perpendicular owing to an attempt to destroy it with gunpowder in the Middle Ages. **Castell Coch** (6 miles out), on a wooded slope, looking across Wales, is a compact little gem with three-turreted round towers; was a baronial residence; very much an enchanted sort of castle.

At **Cenarth** and **Cilgerran** you can see men fishing for salmon from coracles (round tublike boats made of reeds and wicker, ancient in design, vehicles of the sun gods in the days of the Druids). **Chepstow** has the marvelous ruin of **Chepstow Castle,** built on a spur pricking into the River Wye; **Tintern Abbey** is nearby; and **Raglan Castle** (8 miles from Monmouth) is a moated ruin. **Chirk:** Splendid castle, inhabited since the 14th century (see Llangollen). Beautiful **Colwyn Bay** has a lot to offer children; among the attractions of its beach and amusement pier are a miniature railway, donkey rides, Punch and Judy, paddling pool. Its park has a playground (trampolines, bowling, tennis, boat pond). From the entrance to the amusement pier, a bus goes up to the **Welsh Mountain Zoo** high on a wooded hillside, where you can picnic or eat at the Tree Tops Safari Restaurant; afternoon daily display of free-flying falcons; also a pet animal corner; sealion display. **Conwy-amend,** an ancient walled town, has **Conwy Castle,** one of the magnificent fortresses built by Edward I; 15′ curtain walls; eight round towers; another Welsh monument children will love. **Corwen,** a market town with a Fair Day every third Tues. of each month. **Criccieth,** a large coastal village, has a hilltop castle. **Denbigh** has **Denbigh Castle** (another Edward I magnificence) with a museum commemorating the birthplace of Sir H. M. Stanley (Mr. Livingstone, I presume?).

At **Harlech, Harlech Castle** is as stirring as "Men of Harlech" (the song inspired by its defense during the Wars of the Roses); originally the sea lapped at its watergate; now the sea is a mile away. **Hay-on-Wye** is a browse of second-hand book stalls. **Laugharne** is where Dylan Thomas lived briefly at **The Boathouse.** You can visit a small museum and see where he is buried in the churchyard of St. Martin's.

Llanberis has the **North Wales Quarrying Museum** in Gilfach Ddu, open Mar. 15–Oct. 15, daily 9:30 a.m.–6:30 p.m. Take the **Snowdon Mountain Railway,** the only rack-and-pinion mountain-track railway in Britain, to the summit of Mt. Snowdon (Mar.–Nov.), a seven-mile, two-hour round trip; runs only in good weather if there's sufficient demand; take warm sweaters. **Llandudno,** an up-to-date and immensely popular resort, has wonderfully safe beaches, amusements and recreations galore; **Doll Museum;** model railway. **Gogarth Abbey** is the original home of the Liddell family, where Lewis Carroll wrote part of *Alice in Wonderland*; summer pleasure steamers take you to Anglesey, Liverpool, or the Isle of Man; the **Great Orme** aerial lift provides thrills and great views. **Bodysgallen Hall,** a 17th-century manor with 19 guest rooms set in its own parkland, is a fine place to stay; and the Welsh tea with scones is an expansive, not expensive, treat; not far from the 13th-century castles of Conwy and Caernarfon. **Llanarch, St. Asaph Zoo. Llanfairfechan,** a sailing resort, has a model boat pond and Aber waterfall. **Llangeller** in Dyfed is the site of the **Museum of the Woollen Industry,** open Apr.–Oct., Mon.–Sat., 10 a.m.–5 p.m.

Llangadog's Plas Glansevin Hotel features *Hwyrnos* evenings with folk singing and clog dancing; inexpensive merry times; only six bedrooms in this hostelry.

Llangollen, site of the Eistedfodd in July, has canal boat rides, also a **Canal Museum; Llangollen Weavers** are making tweeds and tapestries in a former corn mill on the banks of the River Dee. Stay at Glynceiriog's **Golden Pheasant Hotel** (Tel: (69172) 281) nearby, with golf, fishing, shooting, riding all possible if arranged in advance in this hostelry nearby, close to Chirk (see Chirk). **Llanrwst** has peacocks on the lawn of **Gwydir Castle.**

Machynlleth (Powys): **Centre for Alternative Technology,** an open-air living museum devoted to the discovery, development, and implementation of sources of energy, land use and food, about a mile north of town. **Martin's Haven** is the embarcation point in **Pembrokeshire National Park** for the ferry to **Skomer Island** where a guide from the

West Wales Naturalists' Trust will escort you over trails to view nesting birds and gray seals.

Newcastle Emlyn is notable for a working water mill that produces stoneground flour (more interesting than I first thought when I hadn't seen it!) In **Newport,** visit **Tredgar House** with country park encompassing a children's farm, bird garden, aquarium.

Pembroke, a splendid castle. **Porthcawl,** summer fair. **Porthoer**'s clean white sands have a whistling sound when walked on. At **Porthmadog** take the narrow-gauge **Ffestiniog Railway** (Tel: (0766) 2384), the world's oldest passenger-carrying steam locomotive. **Prestatyn,** seaside resort. **Rhyl** has a children's paradise sea front. At **Rhos-on-Sea,** a coastal resort near Colwyn Bay, the little **Harlequin Theatre,** with 130 seats and over 600 marionettes, presents a July–Sept. repertory. **Ruthin,** West Denbighshire, North Wales, is an appealing town with many fine old buildings. **Ruthin Castle,** located on the Corwen Road, set in 30 acres of wooded parkland and meadows, is a moderately-priced hotel presenting medieval banquets; a high old time for all except young children. **Swansea,** a Victorian seaside resort, summer idyll of young Dylan Thomas, **Oystermouth** and the village of **Mumbles,** all within a five-mile radius, easy to visit aboard an open-air, double-decker "Skyrider" bus, with a marvelous hilltop castle in Oystermouth, Punch and Judy shows during the summer at Southend along the sea-front at Mumbles could also be your family's idyll. The best hotel in Mumbles is the **Ashleigh Mermaid. Welsh Cottage Craft Shop,** on Oystermouth Square and **Treasure** on Newton Road are recommended. For more details and information, consult the Mumbles Tourist Office, Oystermouth Square, Tel: (07920) 81302. Fishing from Mumbles Pier, where there is also a disco; exploring; visiting the lighthouse are among the pleasures to sample. **Tenby,** a lovely walled seaside town. At **Towyn** you can board a 100-year-old steam train for a trip along the **Talyllyn Railway** to Abergynolwyn. If you're anywhere near the hamlet of **Trapp,** go just to see the ruins of Carreg Cennen, a 13th-century castle cresting a hill. **Wrexham: Erdigg** is a 17th- to 18th-century house to illustrate the problems and labor of housekeeping endured by mistress of the house and her servants. Museum shop. Open Sat.–Thurs., noon–5:30 p.m.

FUN TRIPS You can gypsy through Wales with a horse-drawn caravan—fully equipped with Dunlopillo mattresses, bottled gas for cooking and lighting, pots, pans, kitchen utensils and, of course, Dobbin between the shafts. How you secure him between the shafts isn't hard to learn given directions as clearly and specifically as you will be by the grooms or manager of the hiring firm; if harnessing or unharnessing should present any problems, just head for the nearest farm or riding stable, where helping hands will be readily available. You're given instructions about the care, watering, and feeding of your horse, which will be placid, docile, and tolerant of strangers. You can roam at will on empty mountain roads, visiting castles, Roman forts, Celtic monasteries, or just ambling off the nearest beach. Children usually adore this for a day or so, until the novelty wears off, at which point you will know whether you want to carry on or circle back to the caravan company's home base. For full details, write to **Welsh Horse Drawn Holidays** (Rhyd-Y-Bont Farm, Talgarth, Powys; Tel: Talgarth 71–13–46).

Cruising Britain's inland waterways by the traditional canal narrow boats gaily decorated with "roses and castles" paintings, Turk's Head knots, and pony tails is another world of locks and weirs, tunnels, and canal bridges. Accommodation aboard is comfortable, and you can skipper your own boat (no previous experience necessary; free trial run and instruction provided all novice skippers) or hire someone to do it for you. You can hire canal craft by the day, weekend, or week. What child wouldn't be intrigued with an adventure like this? British boat hire rates are very reasonable. **Inland Waterway Holiday Cruises** (Preston Brook, Runcorn, Cheshire WA7 3AL; Tel: Aston 376) offers cruises on 12-berth traditional narrow boats with all meals provided. Trips include Llangollen, Oxford, Warwick, Lincoln. For a wee bit of heaven in Devon, Apr.–Oct., **Dart Pleasure Craft** (Tel: Dartmouth (08043) 3144) run day and evening cruises from **Dartmouth, Totnes** and **Kingswear.** For information about the Kingsbridge-Salcombe *ferry service* and short estuary and coastal cruises, call the **River Maid Motor Launches** in Kingsbridge (Tel: Kingsbridge (0548) 3607/3525).

To hire a houseboat, a luxury motor cruiser, or a yacht contact BTA who will provide you with details of hire companies. **Blake's Holidays Ltd.** (Wroxham, Norwich, Norfolk NR12 8DH; Tel: Wroxham 2911, for holidays on the Broads; Wroxham 3224 for other waterways) acts as agents for companies operating boats on a large number of waterways. **The Inland Waterways Association** (114 Regent's Park Rd., London N.W.1.; Tel: 586–2556) publish a range of informative books. The **Britsh Waterways Board** (Melbury House, Melbury Terrace, London N.W.1; Tel: (01) 262–6711) is also a source of excellent information. **Boat Enquiries Ltd.** (43 Botley Rd., Oxford, OX2 OPT; Tel: Oxford 727288).

Norfolk and Suffolk Broads (rivers that widen in places into broads) is one of the few stretches of the inland waterways with sailing yachts for hire; also many riverside bungalows for rent. **The Shropshire Union Canal** is considered the most beautiful in England and Wales; Chester, an archaeologist's special, is on the main line. Ulster's lakeland in Northern Ireland is one of the largest navigable areas in Europe; the **Erne Waterway** will earn your family's affection with its wildlife, uninhabited islands, water-skiing, swimming, and getting away from it all. For some of the loveliest waterways in Europe, see Scotland.

In Wales, you can hire a two to six berth modern motor cruiser and navigate the **Brecon-Abergavenny Canal** which abounds with fish and wildlife. Salmon and trout fishing on the nearby River Usk, and pony-trekking for those who want to go into the hills is available close by. Reserve a boat early from **Red Line Boats** (Goytre Wharf, Llanover, Abergavenny, Gwent; Tel: Nantyderry 88–05–22).

In London, even if you have no intention of buying a boat, a visit to **Boat Showrooms of London Ltd.** (286 Kensington High St., W.14; Tel: (01) 602–0123) is an adventure; a wide range from dinghies to high-speed cruisers; boat kits; marine equipment; sailing clothes. A place where royalty and heads of state come for their nautical needs is a good place for the children to develop their instincts for the better things in life! Representing British yachting and power boating is **The Royal Yachting Assoc.** (Victoria Way, Woking, Surrey; Tel: Woking 5022); Prince Philip is president. If you want books on sailing, go to **Captain O. M. Watts** (49 Albemarle St., W.1; Tel: 493–4633). For sea charts, **J. D. Potter** (145 Minories, E.C.3; Tel: 481–1369). Shorter boat trips from London are covered in "Attractions for Children in London."

Floating Through Europe (271 Madison Ave., New York, NY 10016; Tel: (212) 685–5600) can set you aboard a luxury hotel barge for 3-day mini-cruises and 7-day cruises on the Thames and the Avon rivers for relaxed, gracious, civilized cruises with enjoyable shore excursions if you can afford the money and time for luxurious dawdling.

A trip on the **Bluebell Line** is for railway enthusiasts. It runs from "nowhere to nowhere," or specifically, 4½ miles from Sheffield Park to Horsted Keynes, East Sussex, and back again. It operates occasionally during fall and winter, and daily during the summer. From stationmaster to fireman, it is staffed entirely by amateur train enthusiasts who travel from all parts of England just for the fun of running this little railway, whose rolling stock consists of 16 vintage steam engines and a wooden set of turn-of-the-century carriages. The Bluebell Line got its name because, prior to World War I, the trains used to run so slowly that people said you could get out along the line, gather an armful of bluebells, and catch the train again. From the Victoria or London Bridge Station in London, you go to Haywards Heath and catch a bus. Be sure to check with BTA or call the station (Tel: Newick (082572) 2370) for further details. The 5-mile excursion leaves every Sun.; Sat., March–Nov.; Wed. in Oct.; daily June–Sept. The **West Somerset Railway** operates year round and has a 20-mile run, plus a luncheon train connecting with the resort of **Minehead.** In NE England, you have the **Middleton Railway, North Yorkshire Moors Railway,** with descriptive guides for hikers who would like to get off to explore the scenic **North Yorkshire Moors National Park.** In NW England, the **Lakeside and Haverthwaite Railway** connects with Lake Windermere steamboats, and combined tickets are available for this (Ulverstan, Cumbria) treat of steaming through mountains and across lakes as well; operating daily May 2–Oct. 3; and Sun. in Oct. A free guide to steam lines can be obtained from the **Association of Railway Preservation Societies,** Sheringham Station, Norfolk, England. Enclose international coupons or postage and a self-addressed envelope (large). *Light Railways, Transport, and Industrial Preservation,* published annually by Avon-Anglia Publications (Annesley House, 21 Southside, Weston-super-Mare, Avon, England) is a comprehensive booklet about steam railways and the Industrial Revolution.

Wales has **Ffestiniog Railway,** the pioneer of narrow-gauge railways—which runs from Porthmadog for 13⅓ miles, giving you an unparalleled view of Snowdonia's mountain scenery; operates weekends most of the year; daily Mar. 27–Oct. 31. For schedules, check the station (Tel: Porthmadog, Gwynedd (0766) 2384). **Brecon Mountain Railway,** Pant Station, Merthyr Tydfil, Mid Glamorgan operates weekends Sept. 18–Oct. 31, and in early Dec. runs daily May 23–Sept. 13 and Dec. 26–Jan. 2 for a 2-mile climb into the **Brecon Beacons National Park.** Details of timetables and unlimited travel tickets for all the Welsh lines are obtainable from **Talyllyn Railway** (Wharf Station, Tywyn, Gwynedd; Tel: (0654) 710472). Connections to all these stations can be made by car, bus and British Rail for these nine lines and five more that the Wales Tourist Board or BTA can tell you more about.

BTA can fill you in on Hovercraft and ferry services to the Continent or to islands off the British mainland. If you don't feel like springing for the price of the 25-hour Venice-Simplon-Orient Express on its London-Paris-Milan-Venice glide, you can sample the luxury and loveliness of the English segment of its sumptuously refurbished historic coaches for about ⅕ the price on summertime Thurs. for a 90-minute ride, including a day excursion to **Leeds Castle** (see Maidstone) and Folkestone; on Fri. for a 96-minute ride, including a day excursion to **Hever Castle** and Folkestone; both trips combined with lengthy bus rides; on Sat. for a 3-hour-50-minute ride, including a day excursion to the stately home of **Beaulieu** with only a short bus ride, for about ¼ the price. Details and reservations from any of the Orient Express offices or agents. (See Information, Transportation, Trains.)

FUN AND GAMES Riding, tennis, sailing, fishing, golf are all sports that the English excel at and for which facilities are excellent. There are over 100 golf courses in Wales (the Wales Tourist Board will provide a directory) where visitors are welcomed and green fees and short-term membership subscriptions are no handicap to even the slimmest wallet. Except for golf, children can be seen enjoying these sports everywhere. Croquet, badminton, bowling, archery, climbing, and canoeing also figure prominently. The **Sports Council** 70 Brompton Rd., London S.W.3; Tel: (01) 581–1212), which has several regional offices, gives out information and organizes courses at six national sports centers in Britain. Courses are mainly "on" in summer and are for 15-year-olds and up. BTA's *Activity Holidays* book provides encyclopedic details about air, land, and water sports in Britain for the able-bodied and activity-minded.

Spectator sports are, of course, cricket, rugby, soccer, the tennis matches at Wimbledon, and ***racing.*** **Royal Ascot** week in June is when the Queen and other Royal Family members drive along the stands; the most glamorous race meet anywhere, six races a day, every one a stakes race, and all bringing out the cream of the horses in training in England and France. You dress for Ascot, as we all know—men in formal dress, with gray or black top hats; the ladies looking Eastery in June; and children in their best day clothes, not party dresses. Moss Bros., like St. George to the rescue, can outfit Father (necessary if you're in the Royal Enclosure). A badge to the Royal Enclosure for the day is easily arranged at the American Embassy. If you can afford it, take the children if they are over 8. They might as well be exposed to social ritual at its sportiest best. Many other races; the five classics are the **Derby** and the **Oaks at Epsom** (end of May or beginning of June); the **Two Thousand Guineas** and the **Thousand Guineas** at Newmarket (end of Apr.); and the St. Leger at Doncaster (early Sept.). The **Grand National** at Aintree, Liverpool (late Mar. or early Apr.) is the world's greatest steeplechase. The fashionable day at Epsom is Ladies Day (the Oaks) held two days after the Derby. The **Moet** and **Chandon Silver Magnum** (end of Aug.) is a race for amateur jockeys over the Derby course. The polo matches at Cowdray Park, Sussex, are fun to go to for children; check the schedule with the **Hurlingham Polo Assoc.** (137 Victoria St., London S.W.1; Tel: 842–5407) or with the BTA. On summer Sun. at 3 p.m. there are also exciting matches at the **Polo Club** near Richmond, easily reached from London. For other horse and boat races see Calendar of Events.

You can ***pony trek*** in **Wales** for an hour, a day, or a week, ambling through the valleys and forests by lakes and waterfalls or galloping along golden sands; for information, consult the BTA. In **Northern Ireland,** the countryside is full of donkeys for the children to ride. In **southern England,** donkeys are not so easy to come by.

There are dry ski slopes for summer skiing at **Crystal Palace National Sports Centre** (Norwood, London S.E.9) and at **Alexandra Palace** (Wood Green, London N. 22).

Children can go ***swimming*** in the pool at the **Crystal Palace** where there are facilities for every sport and diversion or at the open-air **Oasis** (32 Endell St., High Holborn, W.C. 2) or at **Swiss Cottage** (Winchester Rd., N.W.3); at the **Elephant and Castle Leisure Centre** (Elephant and Castle, London S.E.1; Tel: (01) 582–5505) and **White City Pool** (Bloemfontein Road, White City, London W.12), the pools have a shelved bottom, just like a beach, plus tropical plants and a wave machine. Other recommended pools with paddling or learner pools are: **Chelsea Baths** (Chelsea Manor Road, London S.W.3); **Clapham Baths** (Clapham Manor St., London S.W.4); **Essex Road Baths** (Greenman St., off Essex Road, London N.1); **Kensington Baths** (Walmer Road, London W.1); **Pickett's Lock Leisure Centre** (Pickett's Lock Lane, Edmonton, London

N.9); **Queen Mother Sports Centre** (Vauxhall Bridge Road, London S.W.1). Skating at **Queen's Ice Skating Club** (Queensway, W.2; Tel: (01) 229–0172). Ice skating also, with rental skates for children, at the **Sobell Sports Centre** (Hornsey Road, London N.7); **Streatham Ice Rink** (386 Streatham High Road, London S.W.16).

They can go ***roller skating*** at **Alexandra Palace** (see above), where there is also a boating lake and a playground. Roller skating rinks also at the **Electric Ballroom** (184 Camden High St., London, N.W.1); **Finsbury Leisure Centre** (Norman St., London E.C.1); **Jubilee Hall Recreation Centre** (Central Market Square, Covent Garden, London, W.C.2); **Pickett's Lock Leisure Centre** (see above); **Starlight Roller Disco** (208 Shepherd's Bush Road, London W.6); **Tottenham Sports Centre** (703 High Road, London N.17). Roller skates can be rented.

The BTA can give you the names of ***bicycle rental*** establishments everywhere, as well as comprehensive information about bicycling in Britain. **The Cyclists' Touring Club** (69 Meadrow, Godalming, Surrey; Tel: Godalming 7217) will provide itineraries (for members only) for cycling in England, Scotland, Wales, and Northern Ireland, as will the **British Cycling Federation** (3 Moor Lanes, Lancaster), also for members only, and who will also give you a 25-mile route for you to circuit in the London area (if you get tired halfway, you can put the bicycle on the train at Richmond).

Mountaineering. Summer season sees the greatest number of climbers in action in the Snowdonia area of **Wales,** where the rock-scaling centers are Llanberis, Capel Curig, and Beddgelert; climbs of all grades of difficulty. Nant Ffrancon is better suited to the beginner and moderate climber, the Llanberis to the expert, (and I do mean expert!—climbs here are much harder than what is normally found with alpenstock and crampons in the Alps). In South Wales, the climbing areas on igneous rock and limestone are in Powys (Breconshire) and Dyfed (Pembrokeshire). For what the Welsh refer to as walking, and for what I consider huffing-puffing mountain climbing, there's the Cader Idris, the Snowdon Horseshoe, the Brecon Beacons, and the Black Mountains. Guides, instructors, and mountaineering courses are all available. You might as well know that I think rocky mountain climbing is utter madness; your best sources of information are obviously not me but (1) **Plas y Brenin** (Capel Curig, near Betws-y-Coed, Gwynedd; Tel: Capel Curig 280; or see Sports Council above); mountain activities, mountaineering, mountain leadership certificate; mountain rescue and survival; rock, snow, and ice climbing; skiing; canoeing; fly fishing. (2) **Outward Bound Trust** (Avon House, 360 Oxford St., London W.1; Tel: (01) 491–1355) who run courses in the Lake District and Wales; The **British Mountaineering Council** (Crawford House, Precinct Centre, Manchester University, Boot St., East Manchester) can provide information about this rugged sport, as can **Plas Y Deri National Outdoor Pursuits Centre for Wales**

(Caernarfon, Gwynedd; Tel: Port Dinorwic 67-09-64).

Speleologists, spelunkers, or cavers should go to Wales for the important archaeological caves in the Gower Peninsula, the extensive systems of the Swansea Valley, the many caves associated with underground rivers in South Breconshire. Cave rescue is organized by the **South Wales Caving Club** (Powell St., Penwyllt, Swansea Valley, Glamorgan); who can also be contacted by the Glamorgan Police; said to be the best-equipped in Britain with guides for visiting parties, plans and maps of all cave systems in Wales, reading rooms, kitchen, workshop, bunk facilities. Consult the **National Caving Association** (c/o Geography Dept., The University, Box 363, Birmingham 15) for advice and suggestions. **Whernside Cave and Fell Centre** (Dent, Sedburgh, Cumbria; Tel: Dent 213) specializes in courses on caving and speleology, and accepts 14s on up. **Dartmoor Expedition Centre** (Rowden, Widecombe-in-the-Moor, Newton Abbot, Devon; Tel: Widecombe 249) includes caving among the activities it offers in their courses for young people.

If you're interested in ***gliding,*** the information about gliding clubs is available from the **British Gliding Association** (Kimberley House, 47 Vaughan Way, Leicester; Tel: Leicester 53-10-51) who can also tell you about the possibilities of passenger flights, weekend courses, and holiday instruction. Some gliders are launched by winch, **South Wales Gliding Club, Swansea Gliding Club;** others are auto or plane-towed at **West Wales Gliding Assoc.** (Withybush Airfield, Havefordwest) where there are three runways for launching and instruction for beginners, 16 or older. You are not allowed to glide unless you are 16 or older!

To ***paddle your own canoe,*** contact the **British Canoe Union** (Flexel House, 45–47 High St., Addlestone, Weybridge, Surrey). It's more complicated than you might think, as canoers have to obtain permissions from the landowners through whose land rivers run, can't paddle on rivers used for salmon and trout fishing except out of the fishing season (although white water canoeing—horrors, not for children!—can be done year round on the Teifi River); and there are wisely many restrictions about sea canoeing and canoe surfing which can be done at Rhossili Bay, Gower; Port Ceiriad, and at Newgale. For canoeing courses or vacations, get in touch with the **Youth Hostels Assoc.** (see above).

Waterskiing in **Wales** is wonderful; Water Ski Clubs at Anglesey, Llangorse, Penarth, Penmaenmawr, Porthcawl, Rhyl, Swansea, and other centers. ***Scuba diving and snorkeling*** is popular from Gower along the southcoast of Wales, westward through Pembrokeshire and Cardigan Bay to the Lleyn Peninsula and Anglesey in the north. Visibility in rock pools and lakes is good, but the water is f-r-r-r-e-e-e-z-i-n-g. Contact the **British Sub-Aqua Club** (16 Upper Woburn Place, London W.C.1; Tel: (01) 387–9302) for information about training under expert tuition at their numerous branches; many organize outdoor and weekend dives, welcome visitors, have their own compressors, and offer facilities for replenishing cylinders. **Fort Bovisand Underwater Centre** (Plymouth, Devon; Tel: Plymouth 42570/45641) offers courses for 12s up in snorkeling, and scuba-diving for 15s up.

Probably the most popular holiday pastime in Wales is ***fishing and angling;*** you first have to obtain a River Authority rod license to fish; and a permit to fish in the chosen section of river, lake, or stream is also necessary. Ask the Wales Tourist Board or the nearest fisherman in a Welsh coracle to be your oracle. If you can get a ride for your children or yourself in a coracle, do. You'll feel like baby Moses! ***Special:*** If you're a sports-minded family, **Eurosports Village** (Shotley Gate, Ipswich, Suffolk; Tel: (047) 334–683) is a sports center with superb facilities, indoor and outdoor, that proffers a generous cornucopia of sports courses for beginners, intermediates and experts.

Believe me, the foregoing is mere surface skim. If you really would like in-depth information about other possibilities, seize upon the BTA's *Activity Holidays* booklet for other ideas and addresses to contact.

SHOPPING WITH AND FOR CHILDREN In London, to lead off with bedwear that makes bedmaking child's play—the **Slumberdown Altogether**—the all-in-one replacement for the whole of top bedding as we know it. It is a big, soft, downfilled quilt that makes blankets, top-sheet, and bedspreads obsolete. Available at Harrods and Heal's (see below).

New Style toys, usually made of wood, are manufactured with a sound regard for their safety, quality, and play value, and are just what children love; they are available from the better toyshops and children's dept. of major department stores. Prices of these well-designed, carefully made products are inevitably higher than for mass-produced, gimmicky items; but in relation to what I judged these items would cost in the U.S., prices are moderate. The best source of information is the **Design Centre** (28 Haymarket, S.W.1; Tel: 839–8000), a permanent display of the best design of consumer goods where you may consult the Design Index for an illustrated record of British merchandise; excellent reference books; a well-spring of all information; open daily, and Wed. and Thurs., until 9 p.m. My list of toys for babies and preschoolers would include most of the excellent toys made by **Kiddiecraft** whose set of plastic stacking beakers can provide years of constructive entertainment for building towers and bathtime floating and pouring toys. **Britains** fabricates scale models of tractors, farm equipment, farm buildings and animals, a plastic-fantastic assembly that is reasonably priced and available from good toyshops. Safe and cuddly stuffed animals are made by **Alresford Crafts Ltd.** Besides teddy bears, their range includes ducks, hedgehogs, badgers and other birdies and beasties that are equally irresistible. They also produce enchanting dolls. Construct-it-yourself model kits of period buildings and shops are made by **Innovate.** Each kit contains all you need except the glue, and the line includes an antique shop, country cottages, and all the buildings you're likely to find in an English town that you can tuck into your suitcase and take home with you. Teddy bears, clowns, and other nursery favorites linked by hoops form endearing mobiles made by **Elphick Designs.** The **London Game,** a family game based on the Underground System, is another winner. A set of **Peter Rabbit china** made by Wedgwood—soup or porridge bowl, cereal bowl, mug, plate, and egg cup—can be shipped home for you. Doulton makes a similar set with the **Bunnykins** characters.

In London, toyshops Old and New Style: **James Galt** (30 Great Marlborough St., W.1), makers of educational equipment for schools, who branched out happily into the toy world, specialize in ''Sensible'' (i.e., suitable, durable, safe) toys refreshingly original in design—as are their ingenious playroom accessories. Purists, they do not stock mechanical, electric, or battery-operated toys. Established since 1848, their products are paradoxically, very much New Style. They have made a special study of the needs of a child confined to bed and have solved that problem (and what a problem it is) with scores of beguiling solutions. **Children's World** (229 Kensington High St., London W.8) is the largest children's bookshop in Europe, with a superb collection of children's toys. Kensington High St. is a mecca for toy shops and along the road you'll find **Early Learning Centre** at #225, packed full of ''sensible'' and ''educational'' toys for younger children, plus toys that can be ''tried out,'' such as a wooden work bench complete with wooden nails to bang in and hammer (hours of fun for a little boy and quick-the-ear-plugs! for parents); also, thank heavens, a good selection of books. At #237, the adorable **Tree House** with an ace selection of toys for all ages. **Paddington and Friends** (22 Crawford Place, London W.1) is devoted to lovers of Paddington Bear—and who isn't?—with cuddly Paddingtons, outfits for Paddingtons, quilt covers, notebooks, all sorts of other things bearing his image, and imaging this enchanting bear. **Tiger Tiger** (219 King's Road, London S.W.3), **Zebra Crossing** (1 Salsibury Pavement, Dawes Road, London S.W.6), **Rainbow** (66 Fortune Green Road, London N.W.6) are among other targets for toy lovers. **Habitat** (next door to Heal's, 196 Tottenham Ct. Rd., W.1; also at 203 King's Rd., London S.W.3 and provincial branches) is a very trendy New Style shop, with dishy dolls and toys with style and humor. **Heal's,** the outstanding contemporary furniture store, has a toy dept. with a mixed bag of New and Old Style toys.

The traditional Old Style toystore is **Hamley's** (200 Regent St., W.1) with eight floors of toys, games, magic tricks, sporting equipment, puppets; walking, talking, and dancing dolls; Lego, Matchbox, Corgi toys; huge model railway and model train section; books; make-your-own balloons; stuffed animals; hobbies and crafts; musical toys; jigsaw puzzles; all price ranges.

Pollock's Toy Museum (1 Scala St., W.1) (see also party playthings, Magic Family Helpers) displays and sells model toy theaters; some are of wood with a molded plastic procenium and most of the assembly is done for you; others are printed in color on precut cardboard, ready for assembly with glue. Theaters come with wire slides for moving the characters, plus a play; additional plays, scenery, footlights are available. The shop stocks the sort of toy one thinks of as "old-fashioned," many interesting imported toys, many inexpensive little wonders. **Kay Desmonde's** shop (17 Kensington Church Walk, W.8) has over 1500 antique dolls and doll houses (some expensive). **The Dolls' House Toys** (29 The Market, Covent Garden, London W.C.2), with a branch at 116 Lisson Grove, London W.1, is devoted to antique and handcrafted dolls' houses and furniture, with accessories including tiny tea sets, plates and food to place on them, and every other reproduction in miniature you or your child can imagine.

Other special interests for older children? For authentic models of fine craftsmanship in the train, boat, and car line, try **Beatties** (112 High Holborn, W.C.1); fine scale models of marine and locomotive engines. **Steam Age** (19 Abington Rd., London W.8) is marvelous for toy trains and accessories. Scale model railway equipment in 000, TT, and 00 gauges can be found also at **W&H Models** (14 New Cavendish St., W.1), a firm established for some two centuries. For 00 gauge railways, the specialists are **Hambling's** (29 Cecil Court, Charing Cross, W.C.2).

For magical tricks and apparatus, or books about magic and sleight-of-hand, there's **Davenport, Lewis and Co.** (51 Great Russell St., W.C.1).

Miniature pistols that work (two ″) are at **Peter Dale,** 12 Royal Opera Arcade, Pall Mall, S.W.1); girls like these more than boys; the shop is filled with arms and armor, which make it wonderful to visit. Military models and toy soldiers at **Hummel** (16 Burlington Arcade, W.1), with bric-a-brac and bits and pieces of china that young girls like. The Burlington Arcade is lots of fun just to walk through.

Sticky tape, heelball, and rolls of paper up to 60″ wide for brass rubbings at **Phillips & Page** (50 Kensington Church St., W.8). Budding numismatists and philatelists can head for the **London Stamp Exchange** (5 Buckingham St., London W.C.2), or the world-famous **Stanley Gibbons** (391 Strand, London W.C.2) for coins and stamps.

English children's books are exceptionally well written and illustrated; entertain without a self-conscious limit of vocabulary. Apart from the aforementioned **Children's World** highlighting Kensington High St. with its quantity and variety of children's books, London's most unusual children's bookshop is probably the **Bookboat** (Cutty Sark Gardens, Greenwich, London S.E.10), a boat afloat on the Thames and awash with juvenile trade books. Closed on Thurs.! I liked the collection of children's books at **The Owl and the Pussy Cat** (11 Flask Walk, Hampstead, London N.W.3) with toys as well. **Foyle's** (119 Charing Cross Rd.) is the largest bookshop in the world (4 million volumes in 32 different depts.). Any child interested in horses can be put out to pasture in **The Horseman's Bookshop** (1 Lower Grosvenor Pl., S.W.1);

modern and antiquarian books and manuscripts; veterinary books. Booksellers **W. H. Smith** (branches all over London) and **John Menzies** (a dozen or so outlets) stock books for children along with newspapers, foreign-language magazines, stationery, guidebooks galore; many mother's-interest magazines; magazines for children.

Department stores? Renowned for its hampers ranging from munchies to truffled foie gras, **Fortnum & Mason** (181 Piccadilly, W.1) has a restful soda fountain; restaurant; downstairs food dept.; sweets on the mezzanine. Super-rich toys incline to scale-model vintage cars; koala bears with exceptionally soft fur; luxurious dolls; prams; cuddly animals. It's best for chiffon-lined lacy woolies for sensitive-skinned infants, lacy white lawn dresses for the 6-to-18-month-old, and the classic velvet shorts with ruffled white shirt special-occasion outfit for the 2-to-6-year-old boy. Don't miss the monumental clock with 4′ high figures of Mr. Fortnum and Mr. Mason, who bow to each other every hour on the hour; after the clock has chimed the hour, a little carillon plays a series of 18th-century songs. A delight!

Harrods (Knightsbridge) has a Way In shop on the top floor for teenagers which is exciting—teen-age cosmetics, people making jewelry, a disc jockey, a soda and snack bar, and satisfactory contemporary clothing. Vast range of children's wear for every age and size; good shoe store; fine baby equipment; good toy depart. The pet shop is worth a visit—cuddlesome puppies and rabbits. **Selfridge's** (Oxford St.) has a good toy dept.; good, moderately priced children's clothes. Teenagers will be happy in the Miss Selfridge annex. **Liberty's** (Regent St., W.1) has distinctive cotton prints and silk fabrics for making your daughter's dresses; also a small children's section where ready-to-wear clothes in Liberty prints can be bought.

Trendy clothes for the up-to-the-minute look, sturdy, bright, easy-to-care-for, generally heralding what will be the envy of U.S. classmates in the months to come, are another London specialty for children. Stock changes so frequently that I can only tell you where to go with no promises or assurances about what you'll find. Prepare to make the rounds because the collections are individual. Don't get discouraged if the first stop or two is a disaster. I'd try at least four of these boutiques so that you won't miss out on the really good things not all of them have at the same time. **Colts** (5 Hampstead High St., N.W.3), for boys 4–16; casual clothes. **Fenwicks** (63 New Bond St., W.1), for boys and girls 2–10. **Laura Ashley** (9 Harriet St., London S.W.1), with all those lovely country prints is perfect for children and teenagers-through-twenties. **Humla** (235 Camden High Street, London N.W.1) has a playpen, a special area for children to play with games and puzzles; books, toys and lollipop-bright handmade knitwear. **Anthea Proud** (61 South End Road, London N.W.3) has pride of place for Liberty-print dresses in cotton and Viyella, casual kinds of clothes, too. **Mother's Ruin** (126 Holland Park Ave., London W.11) has lovely party clothes; shoes, toys, books; and may indeed wreck your budget. **Pollyanna** (660 Fulham Rd., London S.W.6), for boys and girls 2–8. **Small Wonder** (75 Heath St., N.W.3 and 296 King's Rd., London S.W.3), boys and girls from 6 months–7 or 8 years. For children's kilts and other Scottish specialties, **Scott Adie** (14A Clifford St., Bond St., W.1), or **The Scotch House** (2 Brompton Rd., S.W.1). For custom-tailored or ready-made children's clothes, for tweed coats with velvet collars, excellent jodhpurs and riding breeches and velvet riding caps, **Rowe's Ltd.** (120 New Bond St.). For handmade heavenlies for the baby, **The White House** (51 New Bond St.). Sloane mothers use **Mothercare, Marks & Spencer** (458 Oxford St., W.1, main branch) and **C&A** for underwear, wool sweaters, all inexpensive at these chains. For shoes, **Peter Jones** and **Kickers** (183a Brompton Rd., S.W.3) for tough, long-wearing boys' shoes. Generally, for ''best'' clothes, smocked dresses, tweed jackets, Sloane mothers frequent these stores: **Rowe, The White House, Harrods;** also **Chelsea Design Co.** (65 Sydney St., S.W.3); **Harvey Nichols** (Knightsbridge, S.W.1); **Meenys** (241 King's Rd., S.W.3); **Mome** (27 Harrington Rd., S.W.7); **Anthea Moore-Ede** (16 Victoria Grove, W.8); **Please Mum** (69 New Bond St., W.1 and 22 Sloane St., S.W.1); **Simple Garments** (39 Sloane St., S.W.1).

You can rent festive or sports clothes from **Moss Brothers** (Bedford St., Covent Garden, W.C.2; Tel: 240–4567) for every member of the family; excellent materials; everything cleaned after every lending, naturally. Have no qualms about renting; the list of customers reads like Burke's Peerage. You can rent binoculars, impeccable riding clothes, and a complete range of skiing gear for children and parents. Or you can go to **Lillywhites** (Piccadilly Circus, W.1; Tel: 930–3181), where you will find sportswear for every occasion for men, women, and children, but only children's riding gear. For children's and teenage raincoats, **Aquascutum** (100 Regent St.). For remarkably good-looking and inexpensive children's navy-blue raincoats, particularly nice for little boys, money-saving **Marks and Spencer's** (Oxford St., plus branches) is the place to go; Shetland sweaters are also a good buy here. At **Harry Hall** (Regent St., W.1), you can find lightweight short raincoats (ask for mackintoshes) ideal for riding or pony trekking. **Pindisports** (14–18 Holborn, E.C.1; Tel: 242–3278) will supply a complete skiing outfit consisting of ski trousers, ski jacket (anorak), mittens, goggles, and two pairs of ski socks. All you need then are sweaters, boots, and skis.

For ***camping gear and tents,*** try: **Black's of Greenock** (53 Rathbone Pl., London W.1), who are tent makers, also supply skiing and mountaineering equipment. The **Hire Shop** (865 Fulham Rd., S.W.6 and other branches; Tel: 736–1769) will provide a catalog of camping and motor-repair equipment and hundreds of other things for hire, including beds, blankets, prams, and cots. **Laurence Corner** (62 Hampstead Rd., N.W.1; Tel: 387–6134) have a huge stock of reasonably priced tents, government surplus clothing, camping equipment.

Crafty advice on ***British craftsmanship?*** The **British Crafts Council** (8 Waterloo Pl., S.W.1; Tel: 839–6309) is government-sponsored, nonprofit—to buy here is often cheaper than anywhere else because there is less mark-up. The Council's primary function is to introduce the public to unknown or new furniture, pottery, weaving, glass, silver, Batik, treen. If you want a handcrafted item, the Council can tell you who will make it best for you.

Vintage cars? To check current market prices of veterans, saunter into **Vintage Autos** (20 Brook Mews N., Lancaster Gate, W.2).

For anything you would like to get or have to have that seems to transcend your ability to find try **Obtainables Agency** (Panton House, 25 Haymarket, S.W.1; Tel: 839–5363); or call on **Universal Aunts** (see Magic Family Helpers). **Anything Left-Handed Ltd.** (68 Beak St., London W.1) in Soho has everything for left-handed people, from scissors to golf clubs.

Elsewhere in England, the New Style toyshops are proliferating, to the delight of parents and children. In **Bath, Tridias** (6 Bennett St.) has the best variety of toys in all price ranges that I've seen anywhere. Many of their own designs have been specially made up for them; these include two pretty doll's houses and an excellent fort. London branch; catalog on request. In **Canterbury,** try **John for Toys** (20 Sun St.); in **Chester,** James Galt (see London) has opened **Galt Toys** (25 Bridge St. Row). In **Leeds, Offspring** (Butterfly St., Leeds 10) is the best toyshop in the north of England. In **Reading, James France (Toys) Ltd.** (7 Gun St.) is decidedly special; Mr. and Mrs. France personally design or select all the toys they sell; also a good selection of children's books. Every town has a toyshop and every city a department store with a toy department. Most of the historic houses owned by the National Trust have a shop on the premises, often with locally made whatnots, and always stocked are items to entertain the children, including a card game relating to architectural styles and periods of furniture that children have great fun with while acquiring an astonishing expertise.

In Wales, for fishing tackle and camping equipment: in **Aberaeron, A.S. Thomas & Sons** (Compton House; Tel: Aberaeron 210); in **Aberystwyth, North Cardinganshire Farmers Ltd.** for camping equipment (Chalybeate St.; Tel: 2766) or **The Sports Shop** (31 Pier St.; Tel: 7033); in **Bala, W. E. Pugh** (74 High St.; Tel: 248) for shooting and fishing gear, guns; rifles, ammo, all sports goods; in **Caernarvon, Howards** (72 Pool St.; Tel: 2671), specializing in fishing tackle; in **Cardiff, Arthur Bale & Sons** (3 Frederick St.; Tel: 29929), fishing tackle and sporting gun specialists, can supply fishing licenses for the Ely, Wye, and Usk rivers; in **Colwyn Bay, W. E. Pugh** (52 Sea View Rd; Tel: 30651); In **Dolgellau, Fishing Tackle Shop** (Lombard St.; Tel: 388) has sports, hobby, and music supplies; in **Haverfordwest, County**

Shooting Supplies (Old Bridge; Tel: 3740) for fishing tackle too; in **Llanberis, Joe Brown Shop** (Tel: 327) has walking, climbing, mountaineering equipment; in **Llandysul, J. E. Davies & Son** (The Arcade); in **Tenby, Morris Brothers** (High and St. Julians Sts.; Tel: 2105) distribute local fishing licences. Fascinating to children and a great activity for a rainy day are craft shops and workshops with craftsmen nimble-fingering nice things into being. The Wales Tourist Board's *Crafts Guide* lists places which welcome visitors. Woolen mills, such as **Trefiw Woollen Mills** (Trefiw, Gwynedd) and **Brynkir Mill** (Golan, North Wales) produce woolen skirt lengths, jackets, small purses, and are interesting to visit and buy stuff from. **Porthmadog** has an active pottery works, as does practically every other town in Wales, and most children fancy having a bowl or a mug after they have seen how they are made. The **Model Farm Folk Collection and Craft Centre** (Wolvesnewton, near Chepstow, Gwent) is a museum with craftsmen to watch at work.

Regional handiwork, including basketware, pottery, fabric, perfume made by the Cistercian monks, and jewelry, can be found at **Celtic Crafts Ltd.** with branches at Nannerch (near Mold), Llangollen, Capel Curig, Chester and Ruthin. **Craftcentre Cymru** has branches at Bala, Barmouth, Caernarfon, Colwyn Bay, Conwy, Criccieth, Llandudno, Llangurig, and Porthmadog.

ENGLISH FRIENDS AND PEN PALS The BTA has a pamphlet, *Meet the British,* listing organizations whose activities and services, to a greater or lesser degree, offer opportunities to overseas visitors to meet British people; some can also provide accommodations. A sampling: **Junior Tourism** (2 Castle St., Aylesbury, Buckinghamshire; Tel: Aylesbury 31661) arranges hospitality in private families for young people aged 11 up. **Holiday Parents Ltd.** (P.O. Box #7, Petersfield, Hampshire; Tel: Petersfield 3484) arranges home stay and paying guest accommodation in southern England for 10s up. **English Families Agency** (The Old Vicarage, Higham, Colchester, Essex; Tel: Higham 248) does the same for 8s up. Activities such as sailing, tennis and excursions to places of interest are also arranged. **International Friendship League** (Pen Friend Service, Saltash, Cornwall) organizes pen-friends worldwide. Send four International Reply Coupons and a self-addressed envelope together with details of age, interests, the sort of person you'd like to correspond with, and any other pertinent information to activate this exchange. Invitations to tea, free and paid; invitations to paid lunches and dinners are listed in a BTA information sheet *Meet the British, Lunches and Teas.* Some of these include musical entertainment, demonstrations of local crafts and traditions, tours of historic houses, dinners with private families; some on your own, some with small groups.

There are many British publications for school children combining stories, things to do, tricks, puzzles, games and comics. Most of these also feature a Pen Friends Corner. Many newspapers and women's magazines in Britain have special children's pages that publish letters from children asking for pen friends and that also publish photographs and letters submitted by young readers.

CALENDAR OF EVENTS As the dates of annual events are subject to change, and as space prevents me from listing the scores of art, musical, and theatrical events, my list should be regarded simply as a rough guide; a complete schedule of events may be had from the BTA. Do check particularly on the agricultural shows, fairs, carnivals, festivals—they have many attractions of interest to children.

Until about **mid-Jan.** in London, there are usually ***circuses and traditional Christmas pantomimes*** (a delight for all ages), plus special children's shows that can be seen as well in provincial theaters. The ***International Boat Show*** is held at Earl's Court. Haxey (Humberside) has the ***Haxey Hood Game,*** an old custom, which is a sort of football game taking place Jan. 6. In **Feb.**, in London, ***Cruft's Dog Show*** is held at Earl's Court. On Shrove Tuesday, Olney (Buckinghamshire) has a ***pancake race*** and all the village of Alnwick (Northumberland) play a primitive type of ***football.***

Events in **Mar.** and **Apr.** are often determined by the day on which Easter is celebrated. The ***Oxford and Cambridge Boat Race*** takes place on the Thames from Putney to Mortlake. There is a three-day ***National Hunt*** (steeplechasing and hurdles) race meeting at Cheltenham in mid-Mar. Easter Mon. is celebrated in London with the ***Harness Horse Parade*** (Regents Park), and there is an ***Easter Parade*** on Easter Sun. at Battersea Park. The ***Grand National,*** the world's most grueling steeplechase, is held at Aintree. Also in Apr., ***Shakespeare Theater Season*** at Stratford-upon-Avon starts and lasts until Jan.; three-day ***horse trials*** at Badminton (Avon).

May events begin on May 1 with a ***6 a.m. service*** at Magdalen College Tower, Oxford; ***maypole dancing*** at Ickwell (Bedfordshire), Padstow (Cornwall), with a hobby horse dancing through the streets. Helston (Cornwall) holds the ***Helston Furry Dance. Arts festivals*** in Bath and Malvern. ***Glyndebourne opera season*** begins and lasts until Aug. ***Chichester Festival Theatre Season*** opens and runs until Sept. In London, the ***Chelsea Flower Show*** is held in the Royal Hospital Grounds. At Spalding (Lincolnshire), there's a ***Flower Parade*** with a procession of flower-decked floats. ***Royal Windsor Horse Show*** in Home Park.

At the end of May and beginning of **June,** at Epsom, the ***Derby,*** the greatest of all horse races, and the ***Oaks*** and other important flat races are run. The ***Bath Festival*** continues. June brings to Regents Park (London) the ***Open Air Theatre*** which runs to Aug. ***Lawn tennis championships*** at Wimbledon which run into July. ***International TT Motorcycle races*** at Douglas (Isle of Man). On the second Sat., the Queen celebrates her official birthday with the ***Trooping the Colour ceremony*** at Horse Guards Parade in London. ***Royal Bath and West Show*** at Shepton Mallet (Somerset); ***South of England Show*** at Ardingly (West Sussex); ***Royal Norfolk Show*** at Norwich. ***Henley Royal Regatta*** (Oxfordshire) is held. ***Flat Racing*** at the Royal Ascot Meeting is a festive, glamorous, crowded occasion.

In **July,** throughout the country, there are flower shows, horse shows and, in certain areas, sheep dog trials. In Llangollen (Clwyd, Wales) there is the ***International Musical Eisteddfod,*** with music, poetry (in Welsh) and traditional dancing. ***Cowes Week*** is celebrated on the Isle of Wight in July/Aug. The Royal Yacht Squadron, the most exclusive yachting club in the world, joins with others to make this the most notable regatta of the year. ***Royal National Agricultural Show*** at Stoneleigh (Warwickshire), ***Great Yorkshire Show*** (Harrogate); ***Royal Welsh Show*** at Builth Wells (Powys, Wales), ***Royal International Horse Show*** at Wembley in London. ***Royal Tournament*** is held at Earl's Court and consists of displays by the armed forces. At Cheltenham, a ***music festival. International Air Tattoo*** takes place at Newbury (Berkshire). ***British Grand Prix*** motor racing at Silverstone (Northamptonshire). ***Horse racing*** at Goodwood (near Chichester, West Sussex). July 5 is ***Tynwald Day,*** a parliamentary ceremony on the Isle of Man. ***Swan Upping,*** an old custom involving swans on the Thames, takes place between Henley and London. At the end of July and beginning of Aug., the ***International Folklore Festival*** takes place at Sidmouth (Devon). The ***Royal National Eisteddfod*** of Wales takes place with its venue varying from year to year.

In **Aug.** in Cardiff, the ***Cardiff Searchlight Tattoo*** is held at Cardiff Castle and is spectacular. The ***Welsh and English National Sheepdog Trials*** are held during this month in varying venues. At Cleveland, the ***Billingham International Folklore Fesitval; Three Choirs Festival*** at Gloucester, Hereford or Worcester alternately. In the Channel Islands, the famous ***Battle of the Flowers*** is celebrated in Jersey. In Dartmouth (Devon) the ***Port of Dartmouth Royal Regatta.*** Throughout the country, the first Mon. in Aug. is a ***Bank Holiday,*** a traditional time for ***fun fairs*** at London's Hampstead Heath, and other special events.

In **Sept.,** at Widecombe-in-the-Moor (Devon), the wonderful ***Widecombe Fair.*** At Doncaster (South Yorkshire), the ***St. Leger,*** last of the five classic English horse races. Burghley (Lincolnshire) has ***Horse Trials.*** Abbots Bromley (Staffordshire) has its ***Horn Dance*** where men dance through the parish carrying a set of antlers which weighs about 25 pounds (old custom). At Southampton, the ***International Boat Show.*** Blackpool has special illuminations.

In **Oct.,** in London, there's the ***Horse of the Year Show*** at Wembley. In Notting, the annual ***Goose Fair. Horse racing*** at Newmarket. ***Music Festival*** at Swansea (South Glamorgan, Wales). ***Sale of wild Exmoor ponies*** at Bampton on the last Thurs.

In **Nov.,** in London, the pageantry attendant on the ***Lord Mayor's***

Show when the new Lord Mayor of London drives through in his coach with a parade that's a blast in the City of London. For the ***State Opening of Parliament,*** the Queen drives in a state coach to the Houses of Parliament to open the new session. The London to Brighton ***Veteran Car Run*** (old crocks and vintage cars) starts from Hyde Park. Nov. 5 is ***Guy Fawkes Day,*** which is celebrated throughout the nation but is best at Lewes and Rye; bonfires, fireworks; straw effigies of Guy Fawkes, who tried to blow up Parliament, are burned; children make little figures of him and trundle them through the streets of towns and villages. The Sat. following Guy Fawkes Day, Rye has a ***Fawkes Pageant*** and Beaulieu has a ***Fireworks Fair!***

In **Dec.**, London offers the ***Royal Smithfield Show,*** the ***Agricultural Machinery Exhibition*** at Earl's Court, the ***National Cat Club Show*** (Olympia), ***Olympia International Show Jumping Championships.*** Birmingham is host to the ***National Exhibition of Cage and Aviary Birds,*** and the ***Ladies' Kennel Association Championship Dog Show.*** There is a tremendous choice of children's entertainment during the school holidays—circuses, pantomimes, puppets, theater, special events—holiday workshops and special events swing into action at most museums. Other than church-going, I know of no other festivities on Christmas Day, so that's the time to join with a British family for Christmas Dinner. Hotels have seasonal menus and often offer Christmas ''packages,'' which can include special entertainment suitable for all the family. Carol services are thrilling to hear in all cathedrals, but the famed ***Festival of the Nine Lessons and Carols*** at King's College Chapel in Cambridge is by ticket-only-admission, so you're just as well off gathering around the television set to see and hear it. ***Boxing Day*** on Dec. 26 is traditionally a day for football and soccer matches, horse races, fox hunts and invitational open-house parties.

LANGUAGE AND PHRASEBOOK George Bernard Shaw once said that England and America are two countries separated by the same language. This may be exaggerated, but be prepared for several varieties of English—the Queen's English, Cockney, Lancashire and various other dialects and accents—and be prepared for different usages of familiar words.

Anthea Bickerton, a small publisher in Somerset, has brought out an English/American, American/English dictionary that runs to about 300 words and expressions. The most frequently misunderstood words on our part include knickers (the English call them plus-fours); jelly roll (swiss roll); and bill (banknote). The most difficult Americanism to adjust to, according to Miss Bickerton, is backyard—she thinks it is slightly offensive when American guests comment on her own; always say garden instead.

Garters are suspenders, suspenders are British braces, our wire braces for teeth are plates in Britain. Undershirts are vests, vests are waistcoats; you go to the ironmonger's instead of to a hardware store where a flashlight is a torch; brogues in Britain refer to walking shoes not accents. Balhousie is pronounced Boozy; Beauchamps is Beech-um; Beaulieu is Bewley; Borrowstouness is Bones; Cliveden is Cleevdun; Featherstonehaugh is Fanshaw; Godmanchester is Gumsister; Leominster is Lemster; Ulgham is Uffam and homely in Britain means home-loving and not ugly or plain. My fantasied revenge is to have a British friend tell me he would like to visit Niagara Falls. I would look at him blankly. Then, "Ah," I would say, with happy comprehension, "you mean Niffles!"

The Welsh have their own language, but about all I can tell you is that J, K, Q, V, X, and Z are missing from it; W is pronounced like *oo* in hoot, except in a word such as gwyn (white) when it's pronounced the way it looks; *cw* is pronounced like *coo, y* like the *u* in fun, *f* like *v,* double *ff* like *f,* double *dd* like the *th* in this, and double *ll* is pronounced with great difficulty! Common words are: llan (church), llyn (lake), myndd (mountain), pwll (pool), bryn (hill), ynys (island), traeth (beach), caer (castle or fort), afon (river), bach (small), mawr (large), cader (seat), bwlch (pass), coed (wood), cwm (valley). You don't have to worry—everyone speaks English. The children might, though, like to learn good morning (sounds like borrow—dah) and good night (sounds like norse-dah).

If you're going to Wales, Cornwall, Scotland, or Ireland, your children will get more out of the trip if you bone up on Celtic language and mythology. Professor Lancelot Hogben's *The Mother Tongue* shows the family likeness with Indo-European words; this sort of thing, like codes, fascinates children.

FINLAND

More and more families are going to Finland; child-entertainment and childcare facilities are the lodestar. While the country may seem expensive for tourists interested only in night-clubbing and dinners at 8, it isn't expensive for families because what you'll save in childcare facilities can pay for your nights on the town.

The Midnight Sun and the Polar Night turn night into day and day into night. For general travel with children in Finland, I strongly recommend June, July, and Aug. when night is day. Most American children over 10 consider the sauna simply fantastic. Another Finnish custom is hand-shaking. You and the children are expected to shake hands at every meeting. Another is punctuality.

Finland is peace, rugged grandeur, sparkling air, cleanliness and simplicity, good food, friendliness, fabulous fishing, swimming, and camping. And a fine place for the young, vigorous and sports-loving.

INFORMATION ABOUT FINLAND Get in touch with the **Finland National Tourist Office** (FNTO) (75 Rockefeller Plaza, New York, NY 10019; Tel: (212) 582–2802).

In **Helsinki,** the master organization for all of Finland is the *Finnish Tourist Board* (Kluuvikatu 8, Helsinki; Tel: (90) 65–01–55). The **Helsinki City Tourist Office** (Pohjoisesplanadi 19; Tel: (90) 16–93–757) will help you with everything involving your stay in the city. Available from the CTO or your hotel are *Helsinki This Week, Helsinki Today,* and *Helsinki Guide*.

City Tourist Offices (CTO) are *outstandingly* helpful, cooperative, and intelligent about anything involving children's activities. I guarantee that local offices will go all out for you if you have children along. (The word for "tourist office" is *Matkailutoimisto*—look for the green-and-white sign.)

In Helsinki, Savonlinna, Turku, Hameenlinna, and some other cities, CTOs provide numbers to call for useful information.

Ask at bookstores stocking books in English for the wonderful *Moomintrolls* series by Tove Jansson, translated into English; *Santa Claus,* by Mauri Kunnas about Finland's Lapland's Santa Claus.

The **Helsinki Tourist Card,** a bargain, offers its possessors discounts and free admissions at more than 100 museums, exhibitions, sightseeing tours and restaurants, as well as entitling the holder to unlimited travel on the subway, municipal public buses and trams. Valid for three days, it's available to Americans and Canadians who have but to ask for it at the **Helsinki Tourist Association** (Lonnrotinkatu 7, 00120 Helsinki 12), and pay the modest, money-saving fee.

HEALTH, WATER, AND FOOD Health standards are high. The water is safe to drink everywhere.

Food specialties that most children enjoy are *voileipapoyta,* or smorgasbord—a vast array of hot and cold meat, fish, vegetables, cheese, and egg tidbits; *piirakka,* meat- and rice-filled egg pancakes; pancakes with lingonberry sauce; *lihapullia,* meatballs; and fishcakes. Milk, butter, potatoes, meat, fish, and rye bread are mainstays of the Finnish diet, plus all sorts of berries—strawberries, raspberries, lingonberries, cranberries, Arctic brambleberries, blackberries, black and red currants, huckleberries, and cloudberries (a kind of pearly pinky-yellow raspberry). On leading restaurant and hotel menus you'll also find many French, Swedish, and Russian specialties as well as salads, vegetables, and desserts that are American standbys.

Elk steak or reindeer steak, marrow bones, *kulebiaka,* salmon or pike-perch folded in pastry, or grilled Baltic herring may also appeal to older children.

Breakfasts are whopping—milk, porridge, sausage, cheese, boiled eggs, bread, butter, and jam. Cafeterias—called *Baari*—serve cakes, pastries, ice cream, and hot and cold snacks; the many snack-bars serve hamburgers and sausages—called *Grilli, Grilli-Kioski,* so the food problem for younger children is solved quite simply and inexpensively. Almost all restaurants and hotels serve children's portions at reduced prices or have special children's dishes. Highchairs for toddlers are usually available.

At **Hango,** the **Hotel Regatta** is good for children's meals; **Tant Brun ja Gredelin,** at **Bulevardi,** is a good summer cafeteria; the **House of the Four Winds,** a summer cafeteria at the seaside. In **Helsinki,** take the children to **Fazer's** (Kluuvikatu 3, not the one at Keskuskatu 6), the Finnish version of Vienna's Demel coffee and pastry tea place with good ice cream. **Restaurant Kreisi** has a Count of Monte Cristo prison cell room for the entertainment of children, also children's menus and diversions. **Kasvisravintola** (Korkeavuorenkatu 3C) is a vegetarian restaurant with a good bakery and natural food shop next door. **Happy Days** (Pohjoiseplanadi 2) is a recommended self-service snack-bar/cafeteria. For hamburgers? **Carrols** (Keskuskatu 3); **Clock** (Etelaesplanadi 24). **Sesto** (Annankatu 18) is a good supermarket; **Valintatalo,** an alternative, is an inexpensive chain with shops all over Helsinki. For specialty foods, biscuits, munchies, try **Stockman** department stores' food section (Alekanterinkatu 52). In **Imatra,** the **Valtionhotelli** adores children and serves Sun. lunch *free* to children under 4. In **Iisalmi,** the cafes in two department stores are recommended, **Pelikaani** cafe (Pohjolankatu 6) and **Rosso Restaurant** (Savonkatu 18). In **Jyvaskyla,** take the children to **Mummin Pullapuoti** (Asemakatu 7) or **Topikatti** upstairs in the same building. The **Alfa department store cafe** is useful (Kauppakatu 35). Finnish mothers recommend the **Laajavuori Hotel,** Kissanviikset (Puistokatu 3), and both of **Ruth's Cafes** (Yliopistonkatu 40 and Seminaarikatu 19). In **Joensuu, Karjalan Talon Ravintola** (Ilosaari) features local specialties; **Maijerin Baari** (Kanavaranta) has inexpensive children's lunches; **Kahvila Helenna** (Siltakatu 16) is a good coffee shop where you can sample the local pastries; **Porssiravintola** (Rantakatu 4) is a pleasant, quiet restaurant; and **Teatteriravintola** (Kaupungintalo) is also recommended. Buy and sample those famous Karelian pies in the market!

In **Kuopia,** teashops and snackbars seem to be centered mostly around the market place. In the main market hall, try **Neliherkku** cafe; also **Pikku-Pietari** (Haapaniemenkatu 24–26). **Mytka-Kahvio** (Piispankatu 9) features regional specialties and also displays local handcrafts for sale; local pottery, recommended pastries are to be found at the cafeteria **Savipaja Savisammo** (Sairaalankatu 10). In **Kuusamo,** stuffed animals decorate Karhunpesa, where children can snack and have fun while parents can have a refreshing beer. In **Mikkeli, Jaatelobaari** (Porrassalmenkatu 19) is a convenient ice cream and snack bar. **Teatteriholvi** (Savilahdenkatu 11) is a pleasant restaurant for family dining. In **Naantali, Kaivohuone restaurant** and **Tavastin Kilta restaurant-cafe** are recommendations. In **Oulu,** the **Steakhouse restaurant** (Pakkahuoneenkatu 16) serves local specialties; **Kaarlenholvi** (Aleksanterinkatu 19) has divine desserts. Where to take the children to eat and/or snack in **Rauma**? The **Water Tower restaurant/cafe; Raumankrouvi restaurant** (Valtakatu 3); **Keskusaukio snackbar** or any of the market square snackeries.

In **Savonlinna, Evas-Baari** (Olavinkatu 53), the **cafe in the Harbor Park,** and **Punaapila** (Tulliportinkatu 2); **Carlos** (Olavinkatu 19); **Wanha Weijari** (Olavinkatu 53). Local specialties are served in **Majakka** (Passengerharbor); also at the **Spa Restaurant Casino; Hotel Tott,** and **Hotel Seurahuone.** In **Tampere,** one of the best places to have lunch is **Sorsanpuiston Grilli** (Sorsapuisto 1), which also serves children's portions. For really delicious food, take bus #18 to **Rustholli restaurant** (Rusthollintie 1). In **Turku,** among other restaurants and hotels offering special menus for children are: **Gallia** (Humalistonkatu 2), **Jarrita** (Martinkatul), **Myllarin Matti** (Eerikinkatu 16), **Pinella** (Porthaninpuisto), **Pippurimylly** (Stalarminkatu 2), **Pizzeria Dennis** (Linnsnksyu 17), **Pizzeria Napoli** (Puutarhakatu 20), and **Taurus** (Yliopistonaktu 29B). The **Pata-Akka** chain and the **Aschan cafe** chain are also good bets. For snacks and munchies, pop into **Hesburger** (Kristiinankatu 9),

Ice Cream Dennis (Forum, Linnankatu 9), **Lehtinen** (Kauppiaskatu 9), **Aschan** (Eerikinkatu 15), **Fazzeria** (I adore that name—Hameenkatu 8), and **Le Pirate** summer cafe (Boren Puisto). **Kasvisravintola Verso** (Linnankatu) is a vegetarian restaurant nestled in an historical house, good for lunch.

BABY FOOD The word for baby food is *Vuavan Ravinto,* pronounced vow-an ra-vin-toe. You'll find baby food in the food depts. of department stores, in food shops and in supermarkets. *Valio* manufactures a special liquid milk formula *(aidinmaidonvastike)* called *Tutteli.* There are two brands of powdered milk: Chymos's *Bona* and Jalostaja's *Piltti,* both stocked in almost every grocery store. Regular milk is safe and good.

As for baby foods, Piltti and Bona dominate the market with a variety of excellent baby meats and fruit purees. For baby *cereals,* the operative English word is "gruel."

DIAPERS AND LAUNDRY A diaper is *vaippa,* pronounced vie-uh-puh, and disposables are *vaippa kertakaytto.* Disposables come in a variety of brands: Piccolo, Veitikka, Vauvi, Lenina. Get them from department stores, drugstores, and Kemikalio shops where cosmetics are sold as opposed to pharmacies where medicines are dispensed. Also at supermarkets and baby specialty shops such as **Instrumentarium** in Helsinki (Mikonkatu 6) where everything for the under-2 child is sold, and where you can buy washable diapers, stocked also in **Lahti** at **Aino Virtanen & Kumpp.**

Disposables are so widely in use that no diaper services are operating. If you use cloth diapers, ask your concierge where you can have them laundered.

EMERGENCIES MADE EASY Good hospitals, good medical facilities, good doctors. ***Pharmacies*** are recognizable by the sign *Apteekki,* and there is always one on night-duty in major towns. In every town there is a ***health center*** *(Terveyskeskus)* with full medical service; also an ***emergency clinic*** with 24-hour service ready to cater to visitors. Your hotel can direct you to the best and nearest service. A *Kemikalio* or *Kemikaali* is a drugstore type operation useful for baby soaps, suntan lotions, and that sort of thing, but not for prescription drugs. There are three all-night pharmacies in **Helsinki: Yliopiston Apteekki** (Mannerheimintie 5; Tel: (90) 17–90–92), **Yliopiston Apteekki** (Mannerheimintie 96; Tel: (90) 41–57–78), and **Hakaniemen Uusi Apteekki** (Siltasaarenkatu 18; Tel: (90) 75–37–496). All pharmacies display a notice in their windows that gives the address of the nearest pharmacy on night duty.

In Helsinki, the ***Children's Hospital*** is called the **Children's Castle** (Lastenlinnantie 2; Tel: (90) 41–82–11) with topnotch facilities. The

Aurora Hospital (Nordenskiolinkatu 20; Tel: (90) 4701) is also highly recommended. First aid from the **Toolo Hospital** (Toolonkatu 40; Tel: (90) 40261), noted for great efficiency. On 24-hour emergency duty, the **Helsinki University Central Hospital;** Tel: (90) 4711. For ***doctors,*** get in touch with the **American Embassy** (Itainen Kaivopuisto 14A; Tel: (90) 17–19–31).

For summoning the Helsinki fire brigade, ***ambulance,*** doctor, the gas works, the electricity people, or the transport board (!), just say Oh! Oh! Oh! and dial 000.

MAGIC FAMILY HELPERS *Babysitters?* You can readily hire babysitters and children's companions in Finland through the Labor Exchange or student employment bureaus set up in all towns; the local city tourist information office can alert you or arrange for them through your hotels. Special agencies that can help include: the **Helsingin N.N.K.Y.** (Young Women's Christian Society); in **Helsinki,** Tel: (90) 44–52–28). In **Turku, Turun Sairaanhoito-Oppilaitos** (Nurses' Training School); Tel: (921) 36–65–17.

Free city playground day care services. In **Helsinki,** the Children's Day Care Office operates 36 park-playgrounds that provide a safe and stimulating environment for children of all ages. Located throughout the city, the playgrounds—some open year-round, some only in summer—offer programs for both the smallest children and for the older ones. Activities at each playground are supervised by two to six games leaders employed by the city. Playgrounds are usually open from 8:30 a.m.–6 p.m., Mon.–Fri. Signs posted at the playgrounds give details about times and the programs for the week. There is no admission, and all ages are welcome. Children under 4 must be accompanied by a parent or other person responsible for them. In addition to the city's own playground staffs, there are also private "Park Aunts" (often multilingual students) who receive a fee from parents for looking after their children. The city day-care authorities also supervise these services to ensure that quality care is provided. During the summer months, children are given a free meal at the playgrounds each day. The day-long supervised program for children in the Family Park, in the city center of **Jyvaskyla** (Oikokatu 7) is outstanding. The playground near Sibelius Park at Sibeliuksenkatu in **Hamenlinna** is a charmer. Some playgrounds like the one in Imatrankoski park in **Imatra,** have a children's paddling/wading pool. In **Iisalmi,** the Luuniemi park and wooded area, and the Paloisvirta park and playground are exceptionally attractive. **Joensuu** has three fine park playgrounds: Kalastajankatu 1, Pohjiskatu 9, and Linnunlahti. There are excellent playgrounds in **Lahti, Mikkeli, Naantali, Oulu, Rauma.** Extra nurseries and facilities are laid on in **Savonlinna** during festival time. At **Tampere,** there are old cars, a ship, a streetcar and a train engine in the park playgrounds, also paddling pools. **Turku's** parks are described in Attractions for Children.

Valkeakoski has a children's traffic park, plus storks, peacocks, and swans in Apianniemi Park, and a grand total of 13 playgrounds. ***Kindergartens*** that accept English-speaking children? In **Hamenlinna, The Finnish-American Society Kindergarten** (Koulukatu 13; Tel: (917) 63386) and the Finnish-speaking kindergarten **Muksula** (Etelakatu 3; Tel: (917) 26531) are open only during the summer. **Joensuu** has the **Finnish-American Society's** kindergarten (Lansikatu 15, Louhelan Ala-Aste; Tel: (973) 27621). **Kokkola** has an English kindergarten (Konepajankatu 3; Tel: (968) 15990); during the Kaustinen Folk Musical Festival here every July, there are additional nursery daycare services. Ask the CTO for details. In **Kuopio,** the CTO can tell you about the English-speaking children's playschool. **Oulu** has good kindergarten facilities (Tel: (981) 15330). In **Turku,** call the **Finnish-American Society's** kindergarten (Ratapihankatu 44; Tel: (921) 30–82–51) or the English Club's **Wendy House** (Tel: (921) 33–16–86).

Instruction? In **Konvola,** southeast Finland, 85 miles from Helsinki, **Oy Varpa Looms Ltd.** conducts courses for beginners and advanced weavers who want to learn Finnish techniques; during July and Aug. at the **Varpapuu Weaving School.** Another interesting possibility for a teenager and accompanying adult is a weaving course at the **Toika Loom Company** in **Toijala,** about 100 miles north of Helsinki. Further information and applications are available from the **Hanslin Travel Service,** 1290 Avenue of the Americas, New York, NY 10104; (Tel: (212) 489–0888).

Personalized services: Guides and secretaries, people to help you with odd jobs, companions for your children? In **Helsinki,** try the A–1 **Temporary Help Service** (Topeliuksenkatu 15C; Tel: (90) 44–01–51). For guide service in Helsinki, call (90) 60–19–66. ***Maids, houseworkers, au pair girls?*** Get in touch with the Employment Office (Haapaniemenkatu 4; Tel: (90) 7021).

▶ **Note:** *Disposable sheets,* about the same texture and quality as those used in doctors' offices, are available at many camping site kiosks. Elsewhere, ask the CTO in which store you can buy. They're ideal for use in rental cottages where sheets aren't provided.

HOLIDAYS FOR CHILDREN ON THEIR OWN To the best of my knowledge, no children's holiday homes or hotels, and no special provisions, exist for children too young for camp.

CHILDREN'S CAMPS Camps are locally run, little English is spoken, and unless your children have a smattering of Finnish, these camps aren't generally suitable for non-Finnish campers. In **Naantali** a **Young People's Music Camp** operates during June; for details, check the CTO. In **Savonlinna,** a three-week international music camp for ages 12–20 is held during the summer festival; the **Lutheran Parish** has a camp by the nearby lake; and there are several scout camps; contact the CTO about all of these. For scout camps elsewhere, contact the **Guides and Scouts of Finland** (Italahdenkatu 13, 00210 Helsinki 21; Tel: (90) 69–22–421); for participation in their program, you'll need an international letter of recommendation. The local Lutheran parishes operate a variety of summer camps, including camps for all family members. For information contact the local Lutheran parish offices of the areas of interest to you; the CTOs can provide lists of addresses and telephone numbers for you. In **Tampere,** the **Tampere Riding Club** runs a summer riding camp at the Iso-Taulaniemi House (Teisko, Tel: (931) 83752), with a branch at **Teiskotalli** (Maisansalo: Tel: (931) 84141). For information about riding camps elsewhere, contact the **Finnish Equestrian Federation** (Topeliuksenkatu 41A, 00250 Helsinki 25; Tel: (90) 47–37–318). Late entry, too late to check into thoroughly, is the **Jamsa Riding Centre,** 36 miles outside of Jyvaskyla, in central lakeland Finland, with children's five- to six-day pony and riding camps, riding and trekking. Information from **Central Finland, Vacation Finland Association,** Vapaudenkatu 38, 40100 Jyvaskyla 10; Tel: (941) 29–40–83. (See also Fun and Games).

CASTLES AND OTHER HAPPY FAMILY ACCOMMODATIONS No castles to live in. Finland's specialty is the sparkling fresh air retreat. To lead off with the most interesting possibility, you can ***rent an island*** on one of Finland's 60,000 lakes, or a cottage on an island in the sea near the mainland.

An average island is about 90 acres of woodland, usually no more than a mile from the mainland. Your cottage, built in the last few years, has a living room with picture window, bedroom, kitchenette, and usually a sauna. Be sure you have your own sauna for invigorating and relaxing steambaths. In the 5-star category, cottages have electricity and "every modern convenience;" in the 4-star category, electricity is provided, but if you want hot water, you'll have to heat it yourself; no indoor john; in the 3-star range, there's generally electricity; and in the 1-and-2-star category, you "camp out" in your cottage with open fireplace, gas stove, outdoor privy, and water from the well. For a week this isn't deprivation. It may even be fun! Cottages are furnished in simple, modern Finnish style. Kitchen utensils are provided, as are electric or gas stoves. You may rent sheets and towels. Most cottages have an open fireplace for heat; logs are included in the price of the cottage. Your drinking water may be piped in or may come from a well. Usually the island owner lives on the opposite corner of the island and you can buy milk, butter, home-made bread, vegetables, and fresh cream from him. For other provisions you have to go to the mainland. Rent a motorboat if you like—a rowboat generally comes with the property—or make arrangements for the regular island cruiser to pick you up when you wish to go to town. A fishing permit is easy to obtain for your entire stay. Rentals are very reasonable; the price is for the cottage and not for the number of people occupying it. Some people prefer to take along an *au pair* girl to lend a hand. If this interests you, get in touch with **Alands Resor Ab,** Post Office Box 62, Norra Esplanadgatan 1, 22101 Mariehamn; Tel: (928) 12 140. Similar holiday cottages located in all other regions of Finland in the 1–5 star range are handled by **Lomarengas-The Holiday Chain,** Museokatu 3, 00100 Helsinki 10; Tel: (90) 44–13–46.

You can also find lots of ***farmhouse accommodation;*** rates include two full meals a day with two "coffee meals" of home-made pastry and bread; 50%–75% reductions for children. The majority of the farms are almost all close to lake, river or sea. In the cheapest range, as a paying guest you'll have to make do with gas or oil lamps, portable heater, chemical john, cold water or no running water (you have to lug water in buckets from a well), no shower, but always a sauna. In the 2-star category, you have gas light and heating or oil heating, hot and cold water, flush john, sauna. Farmhouse accommodations that rate 3-stars have electricity, wood stoves for heating or electric heaters, hot and cold running water, flush john, shower, sauna. In the 4-star category you get electricity, central heating, hot and cold running water, flush john, your own separate shower, sauna, and a private beach location. The majority of farms taking paying guests are in central and east Finland. You can get a brochure *Farm Holidays in Finland,* further information, and make bookings from **Suomen 4H-liito,** Bulevardi 28, 00120 Helsinki 12; Tel: (90) 64–51–33.

If you'd rather not live with a family, you can rent a ***farm-based cottage,*** fully furnished including blankets but not towels or sheets which you are expected to rent or provide, and in many cases (the only ones to consider) with a boat and sauna. Here I'd definitely take along a university student to make the sauna, act as interpreter, and generally lend a hand. You have your choice of being a full-board guest while living in your own cottage, with all your meals provided either at the farm family's table or brought to your doorstep, renting a farm-based self-catering cottage, or renting an apartment with electric stove and refrigerator if you prefer to cater for yourselves. ***Self-catering apartment*** prices in a farmhouse or outbuilding are cheaper and may be more suitable for you if you're on a special diet or have a child who is allergic to or won't eat certain foods. But I'd take the full-board Finnish farm vacation. Weekly rates include full board and twice-weekly sauna for farm cottage rental. For the brochure *Finn Vacations,* information, details, bookings, contact **Lomarengas-The Holiday Chain,** Museokatu 3, 00100 Helsinki 10; Tel: (90) 44–13–46; also Suomen 4H-liito (see above). Whatever star-category cottage you may choose, you can count on the cottage being scrupulously clean.

Another thought is one of approximately 200 ***holiday villages.*** In Lapland, you'll find just a cluster of comfortable and cozy log cabins minus running water (climatic conditions make piped water a rarity in the area); elsewhere you'll find a dozen two- to four- or four- to five-bed-cabins by lake or sea, each cabin with its own boat and private beachground. Cottages usually comprise a bed-sitting room, a kitchen with gas or electric hotplate, refrigerator, cutlery, crockery, kitchen utensils. Towels and bed linen are usually, but not always, included. Generally, there is running water and a flush john in the cottage, and optional use of the village sauna. Cottages in the top price luxury bracket come with all modern conveniences, additional rooms and space, a restaurant and hotel on site, and a communal TV. Holiday villages are usually near a village where there are shops. In wilderness locations, a mobile camper shop or a mobile boat-borne shop will stop by twice a week. Cottages are usually rented by the week from Sat.–Sat. The top-class holiday villages are open all year; bookings for the peak season, mid-May–Sept. should be made six months ahead. Many villages arrange boat and fishing expeditions, children's games, outdoor fish and sausage cookouts with beach campfires, guided walks and rambles in the surroundings; some provide facilities for minigolf, tennis, volleyball, canoeing, windsurfing, sailing, waterskiing; wintertime ski instruction, guided cross-country ski tours, skating, ice fishing, ski rental. Guided bus and other tours are arranged, including boat cruises around the archipelago. Information and bookings from Lomarengas—The Holiday Chain cover all Finland except the Aland Islands and can send you their *Finn Vacations* brochure. **Lomaliiton-Matkapalvelu** (Toinen Linja 15, 00530 Helsinki 53; Tel: (90) 76–58–77) covers all Finland and offers the most luxurious and highest priced holiday village cottages with the most extensive and varied recreational possibilities.

Mud baths? Well, there are over 100 boarding houses in Finland and 15 on the Aland Islands that arrange keep-fit programs with mud baths, massage, keep-fit exercises, health baths, physical therapy, nature treatments. Some are simple, some are expensive. Almost all have lakeside boats, beaches, and fishing facilities. Prices vary; most are reasonable. The FNTO can tell you more.

▶ **Note:** The Finncheque system offering reductions and set rates for different accommodation price categories includes a low rate that is the same for ALL hotels in ALL price categories in the system for a child 4–14 sleeping in an extra bed in his/her parents' room. Children are free if they do not occupy a separate bed.

Hotel discounts are also available if you are a *Scandinavian Bonus Pass holder,* which entitles you to 15%–50% room reductions at all Arctia Hotels and Kantaravintolet Hotels in Finland as well as other hotels in Denmark, Norway, and Sweden. Children under 15 are accommodated free of charge in their parents' room. The FNTO and FTB can tell you all about this.

Many ***Finnish Youth Hostels,*** with no upper age limit for admission, function as motels, inns, summer hotels. I can't recommend a wiser choice for bargain-minded families than some of these converted farmhouses, manor houses, schools, student residences, most open only during the summer. Facilities in the 4-star category will have you starry-eyed. (See Camping).

The **Hotel Booking Service** located in the Railway Station tunnel in **Helsinki** (Tel: (90) 17–11–33), open 9 a.m.–6 p.m. and until 9 p.m. mid-May–mid-Sept. when it is also open Sat. 9 a.m.–7 p.m. They can always find accommodations for you and yours.

Ahtari: The **Mesikammen Hotel,** with corridors hewn from the natural rock of its setting, is an interesting stopover. In **Haikko:** the handsome 300-guest **Haikko Manor** with Health Spa, is an international deluxe establishment that looks like an updated pillared Southern mansion; lawns are bordered with swales of trees that taper down to a point with a boathouse. You can rent rowboats or outboarders; fish; waterski; swim in the indoor or outdoor pool; have a sauna; amble over 25 acres. During the summer, the steamship *Runneberg* operates the Helsinki-Haikko-Porvoo run, pleasant and convenient. In winter, a snow-scooter, a slalom slope, ski lift, and a jingling sleigh. (The medieval town of nearby Porvoo is a sweet little spot to explore.) At **Hameenlinna,** the ugly, concrete **Hotel Aulanko,** in a national park, has a viewing-tower for surveying masses of lake and pond water birds. Boat rides in summer; sleigh rides and ski school in winter; riding courses; waterskiing; fishing; golf; tennis; bicycles for rent; every July a special fairytale theater at the fake-but-fun castle ruins; a fulltime babysitting service; children's special Sun. smorgasbord; a splendid family retreat.

The luxurious choice in **Helsinki** is the trimly modern **Fisherman's Cottage** (Kalastajatorppa, 20 min. from the center of town) in the woods, overlooking the sea; renowned restaurant; nice indoor pool; tennis courts; the best golf course in Finland is nearby; restful terraces, radio, TV; up-to-date bathrooms. An outstanding budget summer hotel is the **Academica** (Hietanienmenkatu 14; Tel: (90) 44–01–71). At **Hyvinkaa,** the **Rantasipihotelli Hyvinkaa** has accommodation for 400 guests; babysitting service; children's playroom; indoor pool with saunas; tennis. In winter, ski lift, slalom slopes, toboggan slope for children, skating and curling rink nearby; the trails are lit in the evening; all very romantic and beautiful.

Iisalmi: The **Hotel Koljonvirta** (Savonkatu 18; Tel: (977) 23511) can arrange babysitting. **Imatra: Valtionhotelli,** offering Sun. lunch free to under-4s, has a pleasant pool for the entire family. In **Joensuu** the **Kimmel Hotel** (Itaranta 1; Tel: (973) 34521) has indoor pool with saunas; children's lunches; babysitting service.

Jyvaskyla is the focus of the **Central Finland Holiday Association** (Vapaudaudenkatu 38; Tel: (941) 10866), which fields all inquiries about local farm accommodation. If you want modern comforts, head for the **Hotel Cumulus** (Vainonkatu 5; Tel: (941) 21–51–11), first-class, with luxury sauna and indoor pool. About three miles from the town center, however, there's the recreation center of Laajavuori with winter ski lift to the slalom slope; summer chair lift to the observation tower;

skating rink; beach; swimming pool; and children's shallow pool. The **Laajavuori Rantasipi Hotel,** not as snazzy as the Cumulus, has a playroom for children, and can arrange babysitting. The **Vehkakyla** is a good holiday village at **Kasiniemi;** beach; boats; fishing; licensed restaurant; each cottage with sauna, telephone, radio, shower, boat, refrigerator, hot and cold water, electric heater, in a perfectly beautiful birch forest. Another good bet is **Loma-Koli** Holiday Village at **Koli** (Tel: 67–22–41), with cottages, fishing tackle, boats, and windsurfing equipment for rent; licensed restaurant; volleyball; playground; and a good beach.

In **Kuopio,** the **Rauhalahti Kuopio** (Tel: (971) 31–17–00) is a pleasant manor house hotel about four miles south of the center of town.

In **Kuusamo,** in the wilderness bordering Lapland, you've got a choice of the quiet little **Ukkoherra Motel,** the **Hotel Kuusamo** with bungalows, and the **Rantasipi Rukahovi Hotel** with indoor pool and a winter ski school.

North of Turku is the **Kustavi** archipelago—no pines on the islands, just rowans and birches and lots of little rocky islets and bays. The water is as clear as any coral island's—you can see pike following your bait way off the stern of the boat. Right by the sea is the **Merimotelli** (Kustavi, Kiparluoto), a motel with swimming pool, sauna, licensed restaurant; boats and fishing tackle for hire. Next door is a **Holiday Village** with four-bed self-service cottages with gas stove, kitchen, utensils, sauna, and each comes with a private beach. No luxury, more like an Adirondacks camping cabin.

Lahti offers the **Lahden Seurahuone** (Aleksanterinkatu 14; Tel: (918) 25161) in the heart of town with good food, two saunas and two swimming pools, about 120 rooms, and its own casino. Also, about six miles west, the **Messila Holiday Center** (Tel: 53–16–66), a manor house with a good restaurant, saunas, glass-enclosed indoor swimming pool, riding stables, a summer toboggan slope about 5000′ long; merry-go-round, minigolf, rollerskating, handicraft workshops; and in winter, southern Finland's largest downhill center, with easy slopes also for beginners. A *great* family retreat. The **Mukkula Tourist Center** has a huge park and a sandy beach. The **Motorest Musta Kissa** is Justa Missa in my opinion. In **Mikkeli,** there's the **Visulahti Tourist Center** (for information, contact Mikkelin Matkailu Oy, Hallituskatu 3A, 50100 Mikkeli 10; Tel: (955) 13938). The **Holiday Village** has cottages with kitchen, livingroom, bedroom, shower and fireplace. In the area, a restaurant, cafe, shop, and sauna enclosure on the beach; plus minigolf, children's playground, boats, tennis courts, sandy beach, a camping-site, and the nearby Wax Museum. I don't know how you feel, but I can take just so much Finnish modern. The only place I know of with antique charm is at **Muhniemi,** northeast of Helsinki and near nothing else one is likely to hear about (there is a private airfield, if that helps). It's called **Wredy Manor** (Tel: Anjalankoski 75117), its furnishings might be called Scandinavian Victorian—all very light and delicate with a formality resembling state settings for *The Cherry Orchard*. It offers a sauna and a TV room; all bedrooms with bathroom or washbasin (hot and cold water); a restaurant in a separate building. Peaceful and refreshing; the scenery is beautiful.

In **Naantali,** your best choice is the modern **Kultainen Aurinko Motel** or **Naantalin Terveysklpyla,** both with pool and sauna. **Kuparivuori Hill** has a beach, campsite, and cottages for four. Naantali's wooden houses and narrow streets, its church and harbor all very charming. During the summer, rooms at the **Apartementos Hotel** overlooking the yacht harbor are an attractive possibility. At **Overnasgarden,** the **Holiday Village** rents out four-bed cottages with electric heater, kitchen (with utensils), electric light, refrigerator, and hot water; bathing beach at your door, saunas, fishing, boats for hire. Book through the **Alands Turistforening** (Norra Esplanadgatan 1, Mariehamm).

The holiday village **Kultakiven Lomakyla** at **Punkharju** is one of the best camping sites, with riding, fishing, saunas, licensed restaurant, a good beach, waterskiing equipment and fishing tackle for rent, tennis court, and salmon pond. Cottages with four to six beds, each with sauna, electricity, shower, and electric heater. Book through **Lomarengas** (see above). At **Rovaniemi,** right on the arctic circle, there's the ultra-modern **Ounasvaara** (Ounasvaara; Tel: 3771), overlooking the Ouna River with an excellent restaurant, luxury sauna and babysitting services. A white concrete monstrosity in **Savonlinna** called the **Spa Hotel** and Restaurant Casino has the redeeming virtue of large parks with tennis courts, pool, summer and winter fishing and skiing. Or see the CTO to book a room in a manor, farmhouse, private home, or to rent an apartment; for cottage rentals, contact **Savonlinna Tourist Service.**

In **Tampere,** the **Uimahallitalo** (Pirkankatu 10; Tel: 29460) has a swimming pool, the Iso-Taulaniemi farm has a stable full of horses, and the hotel on the lake at nearby Aitolahti offers a floating cafe, a sauna, a restaurant. But my choice would be the **Domus** (Pellervonkatu 9), a summer budget hotel with pool or the **Rosendahl Hotel** (Pynikintie 13), with a babysitting service and a playroom for children. See the Kultainen Aurinko listed under Naantali, a suburb. **Turku?** (See the **Kultainen Aurinko** listed under **Naantali,** a suburb.) Hotels with swimming pools: **Hamburger Bors** (Kauppiaskatu 6), **Marina Palace** (Linnankatu 32), **Rantasipi Ruissalo** (Ruissalo), **Rantasipi Turku** (Pispalantie 7). The **Turku** is a tour-group hostelry. The **Marina** is superb, expensively luxurious; located on the west bank of the Aura River. The seaside **Ruissalo** makes up in location what it lacks in aesthetics.

CAMPING AND CARAVANING With 60,000 lakes, there's hardly a campsite among the almost 400 available that doesn't offer swimming, waterskiing, fishing, motorboats and rowboats for hire, riding, keep-fit trails. (Camping elsewhere than on camping sites without the landowners permission is forbidden.) The majority of the camping sites are under the aegis of the **Finnish Travel Association's Camping Department** (Mikonkatu 25, 00100 Helsinki 10; Tel: (90) 17–08–68), with its annual listing of sites. FTA camps rated on a star system from one to three always include children's playgrounds and swimming beaches in the two to three star category. Family camping cards, sold on the sites, serve as Finnish camping identity cards, are valid for the entire camping season, and cost less than a package of marshmallows. Check for details on cottages.

Finnish Hostels have no upper age limit. There are about 150 of them which also function as inns and which are extremely convenient; an excellent bargain for motoring families. You can choose among farmhouses, manor houses, camping centers, student residences, schools. Self-service kitchens are available and coffee and refreshments can be bought at most hostels, where you can almost always hire bicycles or boats. Most of the hostels are open only for the summer, but about 50 of them are open all year-round. Hostels are classified in four different star classifications, and those which belong to the 4-star category have a happy constellation of facilities. Further information from the **Finnish Youth Hostel Association,** Yrjonkatu 38B 15, 00100 Helsinki 10, Tel: (90) 694–0377.

ATTRACTIONS FOR CHILDREN IN HELSINKI **Linnanmaki Amusement Park** (open Apr. 30–Sept. 4, 5 p.m.–10 p.m. daily except Mon. Sat. open 2 p.m., Sun., 1 p.m.; open June 28–Aug. 12, 3 p.m.–10 p.m. except Mon., in May open only on weekends. Tel: (90) 75–03–91); peacock circus theater, merry-go-rounds, Viking-swing, safari-ride monorail, switch-back railway, restaurants, and the steepest roller-coaster in Europe (!). **Korkeasaari Island Zoo** is a 10-minute ferry ride from North Harbor; departures hourly from May 1–Oct. 15; restaurant snacks and ice cream. To the island fortress of **Suomenlinna,** the ferry leaves frequently for the 15-minute ride from South Harbor (Etelasatama). Pleasant restaurant, **Walhalla,** set in the ramparts of the 18th-century fortress that served as a harbor defense. Nice seaside walks and a **Naval Museum** to explore as well as rock-climbing possibilities.

Seurasaari Open-Air Museum on Seurasaari Island. Open May 1–Sept. 30. You can go by bus. Farm and manor buildings from all over Finland; open-air theater featuring folk-dancing exhibits; outdoor restaurant. The **market** in the harbor square directly in front of the Presidential Palace, open 7 a.m.–2 p.m. and from 3:30 p.m.–8 p.m., Mon.–Fri. from mid-May–mid-Sept. is fun, with local food, flowers, and handicrafts sold in little canopied stands; look for the pottery whistles in the shape of birds. Music and other free and lively entertainment. From the pier here you can get the two-hour **water bus** sightseeing trip around the city; check the CTO for schedule.

Picnicking is pleasant in the **Botanical Gardens** (Kaupunginputarha), **Elaintarhan Park** (admission free), or on any of the islands known as **Saaristo** (Skargard). You leave Helsinki by motorboat, spend the day sunbathing, swimming, and picnicking, and return late in the afternoon. Check the CTO for details. Usually there are local fishermen around from whom you can hire a boat to row or outboard to other islands nearby. The **University Botanical Garden** (Unioninkatu 44) is pleasant also. All the ***parks*** are fun to walk in and all have playgrounds—Topelius, Sibelius with minigolf, Hesperia, Toolo bay and its park, Mustikkamaa National Park and Kaivopuisto Park. The **Children's Traffic Park** (Nordenskioldinkatu) is predriver's training for children and lots of fun in minicars; marvelous for boys 7–8 on up. Model train enthusiasts will love the **Railway Museum** at the Railway Station. The **National Museum** (Mannerheimintie 34) has charming dolls' houses, costumes, toys. For animal lovers, the **University Zoological Museum** (P. Rautatiekatu 13). There are many art, technical historical, scientific, and special-interest museums in Helsinki, a list of which is available in a special Museum Booklet free for the asking from the FNTO, the FTB or the CTO. The **Museum of Arabia** houses collections of the Finnish Arabia porcelain factory; Paavo Nurmi's gilded spiked running shoe lies in the **Sport Museum** at the Olympic Stadium. See the fire engines at the **Automobile Museum** in Espoo (Pakankyla Manor; Tel: (90) 855–7178). **Heritoniemi Museum** (Linnanrakentajantie 14; Tel: (90) 78–98–74), open Sun. and by appointment, combines a manor house, a peasant farmhouse and a windmill; the **Missionary Museum** (Tahtitorninkatu 16; Tel: (90) 17–73–05/63–63–23) contains a missionary's study and his African and Chinese collection of artifacts, usually only open Sept.–May. The **Burgher's House** (Kristianinkatu 12) is the oldest surviving wooden house in the city decorated in the mid-19th century style, with an exhibition depicting its renovation. Museums devoted to watches, paper, paleontology, veterinary equipment, philately, telecommunications, a WWII submarine, photography, architecture, applied arts, theater, numismatics and more are detailed in the above mentioned Museum Booklet. Further information from the **Helsinki CTO** (Pohjoiesplanadi 19; Tel: (90) 169–3757/17–40–88). Telephone 058 to find out daily events in the city.

Tapiola, the Utopian garden city, has a sapphire-blue lake plumed with fountains and a great supervised playground serving the Heikintori shopping center; fine indoor swimming pool. Information: **Espoo City Tourist Office:** Tel: (90) 46–76–52).

You can swim the year through in Helsinki at nine ***indoor pools:*** Helsinginkatu (Tel: 765–255); Kontula (Tel: 301–133); Pirkkola Sports Center (Tel: 745–022); Yrjonkatu (Tel: 647–801); SVUL (Tel: 47–37–375); Tikkurila (Tel: 83–93–281); Leppavaara (Tel: 515–087); Lauttasari (Tel: 671–841); and Tapiola (Tel: 460–560). There are also two ***outdoor pools:*** Uimastadion (Tel: 40–29–383) and Kumpula (Tel: 794–154). The Swimming Stadium has an irresistibly high diving platform, a tower, a real parent-scarer!

ATTRACTIONS FOR CHILDREN ELSEWHERE Ahtari: Visit the **Ahtari Wildlife Park,** a nature and wildlife preserve. Nearby, there's a traditional Finnish farm, the **Domestic Animal Park.** The **Mekkoranta Holiday Village** has a children's playground and sandy beach. The **Mesikammen Hotel,** where you might like to stay, has corridors blasted out of the rocky terrain that children like to run their hands along. **Hango:** Natural wonders called **Giants' Kettles** (geysers) are to be seen in the Park mountains and the mountains near the Chapel Harbor. (Other people may think of them as hills or fells.) Looking around with the telescope on top of the **Water Tower** is fun, as is the summer excitement in the Easter Harbor during Regatta-week. **Hyvinkaa,** close to Helsinki, is where you'll find the oldest preserved **steam locomotive** in Finland, circa 1868, the **Emperor's Train,** and a **Railway Museum. Iisalmi:** Weekend visitors to the local **museum** get served hot pancakes. Another touch of local color: the log-built **windmill** with sails that look like giant bamboo rakes. In **Imatra,** a tiny town with a giant timber industry, you should see the **rapids** *(Koski)* after the boys' band has welcomed you to the state-owned Valtionhotelli, a pleasant hostelry near an **open-air theater.**

In **Joensuu,** at the **Town Theater,** Kaupungintalo (City Hall), children stage an annual performance in summer. The **North Karelia Museum,** Ilosaari, Karjalan Talo, is worth a wander-around; interesting icons. It's conveniently located in the Karelian House restaurant. Also the **Art Museum** (Kirkkokatu 23) and local handcrafts to see and buy (Rantakatu 2). In winter the skiing action is at **Parnavaara, Ylamylly,** where the slalom slopes are illuminated at night; ski lift; fine children's toboggan slope. Ski school at Loma-Koli. The **Sports Hall** recreation center (Koskikatu 12); indoor pool at Ilosaaren Uimala (Ilosaari). And at the **ski lodge** at nearby Onttola, there is a riding stable. **Jyvaskyla: Boat tours** on Lake Paijanne from mid-June–end-Aug.; two hours; check with the CTO, the Harbor Kiosk (Tel: (941) 18885). Every Sun. from early June to the end of Aug. You can have a three-hr. cruise around the lake with lunch aboard a steamer. Or take a 2½-mile water-bus trip to **Savutuvan Apaja,** a reconstructed and restored Finnish homestead of olden times, complete with buildings typical of those in Central Finland and crafts demonstrations. Ask the CTO for details and, if you're interested, about the rental of boats or windsurfing boards. **Skating rinks** in winter on the Harja and Hippos sports grounds. In summer, the **beaches** to go to are Tuomiojarvi, Kohniojarvi, Vuorilampi in the Laajavuori recreation area (which operates as a skiing resort in winter). American films frequently shown at local movie houses on Sun. afternoons. **Kokkola:** See the **K.H. Renlund Historical Nautical Museum** with its collection of model boats. The **Alvar Aalto Museum** is here too, with many of this master architect's designs and mock-ups; changing exhibits. **Kalvola,** about 40 miles south of Tampere, is the site of the Iittala glass works where you can watch the work of glass-blowers and view a large art glass collection, artfully designed. **Kuopio:** Hie yourself to the **Puijo Observation Tower** on **Puijo Heights** for the ecologist's dream vista of lakes and forests. **Horse-carriages** are assembled at the **Vossikka Villa** in the market square. The **Vainolanniemi Sport Park** is worth a look. Pony riding for children is available at the Rauhalahti campsite. The **Valkeisenlampi**—a lake and fountain in the center of town—is an attractive spot in summer. In winter: skiing, Puijo slalom, ski-lifts, crosscountry skiing, and the **Ski Hotel Lahkovuori** in the suburb of Nilsia. **Kuusamo:** The highlight is ***shooting the rapids*** at Juuma, which also has a sandy beach for swimming and a sauna. The mile walk in **Oulanka National Park** to the Kiutakonka rapids is not too strenuous for young children; do let them pick berries along the way—so simple a thing seems infinitely romantic to children in the remembering. Great fishing in the area. In winter, Kuusamo is a wonderland for children: **Children's "ski garten"** where children can learn to ski while playing; a pony lift to the beginners' slopes, a **"Snow Town"** children's and young people's center. In the evenings, apres ski activities include children's films and a disco for sophisticated preteens and young teenagers. **Lahti:** A **Fairyland Amusement Park** may or may not be open in Peikkometsantie. Check. Modern Lahti is a visual arts center in summer, with a year-round puppet theater for children. If you're not hustling to take the lovely three-hour hydrofoil trip to Jyvaskyla, try to see **Messila Manor,** five miles from city center, with pony riding, carousel, minigolf, roller skating rink, a 5000′ toboggan slope; handicrafts workshops including doll, jewelry, and pottery makers. You can also hire boats, bicycles, windsurfing boards. In winter, you can ski, ride in a horsedrawn sleigh, or fish through a hole in the ice on Lake Vesijarvi.

The **Museum** at **Lappeenranta** has spectacular costumes and jewelry. **Mikkeli,** site of the **Visulahti Tourist Center** (see Castles and Other Happy Family Accommodations), 140 miles northeast of Helsinki, reachable by rail or bus, features a Holiday Village, fun, frolic, and the **Wax Museum,** new in 1983. Open from noon–8 p.m.; 11 a.m.–9 p.m. May through the end of Aug. Movie-price admission, half-price for children, but even if marked up, the quality is memorable. **Oulu** has a children's **traffic town** (Hollihaka) and a **zoological museum** (Kasarmitie 8).

Rovaniemi, the capital city of Lapland, has good hotels, motels, youth hostel, camping sites, and a score of restaurants including the **Waskooli-discoteeki** (Korkalonkatu 27); a radio taxi service (Tel: (991) 12222); air taxis, **Rovalento Oy** (Tel: (991) 60655) and **Rovaniemen Lentopalvelu** (Tel: (991) 10125/ 10122); also Hertz, Avis, Inter-Rent, and Europcar car rentals. Also minigolf, riding, tennis, boat rides on the Kemijoki, indoor and outdoor swimming pools (Nuortenkatu 11). The **Lapland Provincial Museum** with an extensive Lapland collection and the **ornithological-geological museum** down the street, are both a treat; gold-panning center for tourists along the tributaries of the Ivalojoki and Lemmenjoki rivers. (The main organizer in **Helsinki** for all this is the **Finnish Travel Association Travel Agency,** but the helpful CTO in Rovaniemi can also help and will arrange transportation for you to cross the arctic circle where you will receive an Arctic Circle Crossing Certificate. The CTO will also guide you to the Ounasvaara ski trails and slopes, to wilderness areas where you can sail dinghies in the summer and go on reindeer safaris in winter (see Fun Trips). **Rovaniemi CTO** (Aallonkatu 2C, SF 962000; Rovaniemi 20; Tel: (991) 16270) is open in summer from 8 a.m.–7 p.m., and in winter during regular office hours.

Savonlinna has **Olavinlinna Castle;** opera festival at the end of July; year-round guided tours; from mid-May–mid-Aug., open 8:30 a.m.–6 p.m. During the summer, open-air concerts and folk-dancing at **Harbour Park,** where there is a children's playground. **Tallisaari Park,** an island by the castle, has a pool where you can fish for salmon; an island spa hotel in the center of town called Casino Island lies in the middle of a wild forest park; stuffed birds in the **University Museum;** children's Sun. matinees at the Olavi (Olavinkatu 51) and the Killa movie houses (Punkaharjuntie 3); all other entertainments involve boating in one form or another. If the children want to swim, take them to the open-air Heikinpohja swimming pool (Heikinpohjantie 18) or the Casino Island Hotel pool. **Saviniemi** has an indoor municipal pool (Uimahallinkatu 2).

Tampere offers an **aquarium,** with an open-air seal pool; a **planetarium;** the **Nasinneula Observation Tower** with a revolving belvedere restaurant at the **Sarkanniemi Leisure and Recreation Park,** open mid-May–Aug. 21, from noon–8 p.m.; and from 11 a.m.–9 p.m. June 25–July 31. A **Children's Zoo,** duck pond, Puppet Theater; slides, ponies to ride, and a super playground; a separate **amusement park;** the **Sara Hildren Art Museum,** with a collection of modern and contemporary art. On to the **Tampere Summer Theater** at **Pyynikki,** which has a revolving stadium; you sit in an outdoor auditorium and around you go while the scenes change behind your back; children's plays included in the repertory toward the end of Aug. Hatenpaa Manor has opened as the **Tampere Municipal Museum;** inside, it's 19th-century-oriental-Renaissance, with a wild staircase (don't let the children slide down those banisters!) leading up to an arcaded balcony. From industry exhibits in the basement to top-floor modern art, you must have a look at this. Other attractions in town: a children's traffic park and wading pool; wading pool at Hameenpuisto Park too; school museum; a **Technical Museum** (Itsenaisyydenkatu 21) all worth brisking through. About six miles east of Tampere, another old manor house, Haihara, set in a grove of linden trees, has opened as a **Doll Museum;** and **Costume Museum;** open daily noon–4 p.m.; in winter, Sun. only. The dolls are from 60 countries. **Puppet shows** on Sun., in the building next door, Javanese shadow puppets and beautifully articulated stick puppets, innocent-faced Lapp puppets, and a large cast of other puppet characters are manipulated through lively performances. Haihara is definitely not ho-hum. Toys also are displayed. Costume exhibits are a history of the world's fashions. In Tampere proper, go to **Kallenautio,** an old coaching tavern. The CTO is bound to suggest you visit the homes of artist Akseli Gallen Kallela (at Ruovesi) and of Emil Wikstrom (at Visavuori), but I would put these last. From Tampere, take the *S.S. Tarjanne* on the "Poet's Way" route via the Murole Canal through Ruovesi to Virrat, or take the white boats of the Silver Line to cruise from Tampere to Kangasala, Valkeakoski, Visavuori, Aulanko, Hameenlinna and on. Do go to **Valkeakoski** to see the **open-air museum** of farm houses and craft demonstrations; motorboat cruises, waterbus trips, and waterskiing can be arranged at the Apianlahti campsite (Tel: (937) 42441). For maps and tourist information, contact the **Tampere City Tourist and Congress Service,** Aleksis Kiven Katu 14B; Tel: (931) 26652.

At **Turku,** Finland's oldest city, you'll find **Turku (Abo) Castle** (8 Linnankatu), sheltering an armory; historical museum; dank prisons; toy museum; and all sorts of other collections. Open 11 a.m.–3 p.m.; from May–Sept., 10 a.m.–6 p.m. The nearby cathedral is worth a look; then you might have a restful cafe interlude at the charming Market Square (open 7 a.m.–2 p.m. weekdays). Visit the **Sibelius Museum** near the Cathedral. You can hear all your Sibelius favorites while you admire a collection of musical instruments from many countries, as well as memorabilia of Sibelius himself. The **Handicrafts Museum** on Luostarinmaki Hill is unique; these hilltop houses escaped the early 19th-century fire which destroyed almost the entire town and now house workmen's tools which are demonstrated during the summer and on Handicrafts' Days (in Aug.); open 11 a.m.–3 p.m., and from May–Sept., 10 a.m.–6 p.m. About 40 craftsmen's homes to see, including a lithographer's workshop and that of a fellow who used to make chewing tobacco. A museum shop sells wonderful old-fashioned candy. The **Pharmacy Museum** (Lantinen Rankatu 13). Clamber up **Puolala Hill,** and the children may be too tired to walk through the **Art Gallery** with the second largest art collection in Finland. **Kupittaa Park** has a children's traffic park; ponds afloat with ducks; and St. Henry's springs, legendary site of the first Christian baptism in Finland; also the Finnish version of baseball, and a brutally fast and furious game in the ice hockey stadium, also a special area for rambling, and a playground for children of all ages. **Samppalinna Park** has a swimming stadium, a 19th-century windmill, plus an overlook of the city from its hill. Other museums include: **Biological Museum** (Neitsytopoluku). **Suomi Terrarium** (Yliopistonkatu 20; Tel: 22873); giant collection of snakes, spiders, lizards, scorpions, frogs, and tortoises. **Zoological Museum** at the university; **Planetarium** at the School of Navigation; and the **Waino Aaltonen Museum,** where his works are on display. By the harbor, the **Sigyn**

Museum Ship is open during the summer, and you can climb aboard this 19th-century windjammer. Also by St. Martin's Bridge, waterbus connections to Naantali (June–Sept.) daily at noon; connections to the Vepsa recreation grounds, and other happy excursions including sightseeing trips on the River Aurajoki, a boat connection to Ruissalo on the trip between Turku and Naantali. You might also like to tour the president's summer residence at Kultaranta to watch the children's drawing competitions (summer only) on the sidewalks and in parks, or investigate Tuula Pesonen's **riding school** at Hirvensalo. About five miles out is **Vanhalinna** in Lieto, an ancient fortress dating back to A.D. 300, now housing an archaeological museum. About six miles out and only a 15-minute bus trip (frequent bus service from the Market Place) is the lovely island of **Ruissalo,** where you can walk in the Botanical Garden; the campsite here is most popular, with rowboats, waterskiing, saunas, riding, golf, and a restaurant; connected with it is **Saaronniemi** beach and recreation grounds, with excellent playgrounds on the beach, and fine outdoor and swimming facilities. About eight miles out is the **Vepsa** recreation grounds; these primitive, unspoiled islands have saunas and rowboats, and cottages for hire by the day. Across the harbor from Turku are the **Aland** islands with the idyllic town of Mariehamn; here the four-masted barque *Pommern* is moored as a museum ship; children will also like the bird park and Lilla Holman beach. Aland has old churches with frescoes, ruins of ancient castles, little fishing villages for the locals, and Holiday Villages for foreigners like us. In summer, it may be warm enough to dive into the Samppalina municipal outdoor swimming pool.

For further information, check with the CTO (Kasityolaiskatu 3, SF-20100 Turku 10; Tel: (921) 33–63–66), open 8:30 a.m.–4 p.m.; June–Aug., 8:30 a.m.–6 p.m.; Sat. 8:30 a.m.–1 p.m.; Sun. noon–1 p.m. Information kiosk at the Market Place, Tel: (921) 15262, open 8:30 a.m.–8 p.m.; Sat. 8:30 a.m.–6 p.m.; Sun., 8:30 a.m.–3 p.m. Information kiosk at the Harbor in the Silja Terminal, open 8:30 a.m.–12:30 p.m. and 6 p.m.–9:30 p.m.

FUN TRIPS For hunting and fishing trips, special interest trips, charter flights, special sightseeing, go to **Ageba** in **Helsinki,** main office: Pohjoisranta 4; branches at Olympialaituri, Etelasatama; Tel: (90) 66–91–93; branch at Helsinki Airport; Tel: (90) 82–24–48; this travel agency deals in unusual and individual travel requirements.

You might take the train from Helsinki to modern, industrial **Lahti,** about a 75-minute ride, then take the three-hour trip by **hydrofoil** (carrying about 100 passengers) to Jyvaskyla, from which you can fly back to Helsinki. In summer, Lahti is a visual arts center, often with art exhibitions sufficiently far out to interest children and teenagers. Winters, you can stay at Messila Manor, ski, ride about in a horsedrawn sleigh, or fish through a hole in the ice on Lake Vesijarvi. From Helsinki, you can take the overnight train to **Savonlinna,** with its Swedish castle-fortress, St. Olaf, or Olavinlinna, and take a trip by speedy water coach or slower woodburning steamer to Punkaharju, a six-mile-long ridge dividing Lakes Puruvesi and Pihlajavesi. You could take the boat also to **Lappeenranta** and **Imatra** with its magnificent falls and whirlpools called Devils' Churns, which is fairly descriptive. Imatra is the gateway to Russia and to Europe's largest lake-touring area. In **Lappeenranta,** have lunch aboard the *Princess Armada,* a restaurant that occupies an old ship in the bay. Scoot around the archipelago and Saimaa Channel on board the *M/V Vainamoinen.* Have a look at the provincial Karelian Kotitalo museum in **Imatra.** From **Naantali** there are several daily ferryboats (via Mariehamn) to Kapellskar, Sweden.

From **Savonlinna,** the list of boat excursions organized by **Savonlinna Tourist Service** (Olavinkatu 35; Tel: (957) 13492) and the CTO is as long as a canoe paddle. Guided sightseeing tours around town (one-hour boat ride); a three-times-a-day city tour from the harbor via *M/S Salmetar* June–Aug.; a three-hour ride to **Rauhanlinna,** an old wooden manor in Lehtiniemi village, and **Putkinotko** outdoor museum (which takes up a day by the time you have eaten and returned, fine for 12-year-olds, but young ones will be plumb tuckered after a day like this). You can also canoe in a group on the Saimaa; or take a boat as far as Mikkeli via Lappeenranta—a trip which describes a baseless triangle—along the way you'll see **Sulkava Linnavuori,** an old fortress, at which the boat may or may not stop. Other possibilities are day and night trips daily by ancient steamer *S/S Saaristo* to the islands of Saimaa with fishing, sauna, swimming, fishing, picnicking. You can spend the night on board or at island farms (more fun). From **Tampere,** modern **Silverline** ships and lakesteamers cruise a "Poet's Way" through a labyrinth of lakes. From **Joensuu** or **Koli** on **Lake Pielinen,** you can take the Sat. boat to **Nurmes,** spend the night at the Bomba House, Scandinavia's largest wooden structure, visit the Karelia villages and return.

If you head for Lapland approximately between mid-June and mid-July you'll arrive at a time when a mystical blue-gray dusk will brighten the skies all night long.

If you head for Lapland in winter, all bundled up in thermal underwear, fur hats, fur gloves, fur boots, I'd skip the reindeer sleigh rides at Ounastunturi (Muonio to Enontekio by sleigh through the snowy wilderness) because 1½ days in a sleigh is too long. Instead, I highly recommend the **reindeer driving school** at Pohtimolampi Sports Center (see Fun and Games). Or you can go skiing and tobogganing at **Ounasvaara Hill** (Ounasvaaran Hiihtoseura; Tel: 12966); ski jump, ski lift, slalom slopes, and great toboggan run. From Pohtimolampi you also can take a couple of hours excursion by motorsleigh around the arctic countryside—my idea of a morning well spent because that snow is unforgettable; children love this. This wintertime Lapland excursion is only, I think, for over-10s, although you see a lot of younger children on the slopes, particularly at the **Saariselka Hiking Centre,** Finland's most popular cross-country skiing center, with nine slalom slopes, three ski lifts. Hotel, motel, youth hostel accommodations, plus children's playrooms, ski schools and nearby pony riding at **Tankavaara,** which also has the attraction of a museum dedicated to gold, attract many families to the area which is easy to reach: **Ivalo Airport** is only 18 miles away. For details about accommodations, tours, and other arrangements, contact **Lapland Travel Ltd.** (Pohjanpuistikko 2, 96200 Rovaniemi 20; Tel: (991) 16052).

The **Finnish Travel Association Travel Agency** (Mikonkatu 25, SF 00100 Helsinki 10; Tel: (90) 17–08–68) makes motoring and exploring Finland on your own a whole lot simpler. Ask about package deals with reduced car rental rates. You can also drive across the Russian border to **Leningrad** or **Moscow;** fly across the border, make the 8½-hour train trip from Helsinki to Leningrad. Finnair has first-class hotel accommodation packages. *Be sure you get your Russian visas in the U.S.* because it's a hassle and time-consuming to make arrangements in Helsinki. Allow two months for the visa to come through. A sea-going children's supervised nursery and play area makes the trip aboard Finnjet's car ferry from Lubeck to Helsinki a dream for families with young children, with cinema, swimming pool, gym, sauna, solarium for additional family pleasure. Daily cruises from **Helsinki** and **Turku** aboard delightful Silja Line cruise ships to **Stockholm** offer reductions for families, and children under 12 in the care of parents or guardian get to travel free! The Silja Line also goes via Mariehamn. The Viking Line has a separate swimming pool for children, children's playroom, and a Milk-Shake Disco for the younger set.

Renovated traditional lake steamboats, restored to their turn-of-the-century glamour operate from **Kuopio** daily, except Mon., and make a variety of luncheon sailings, dance cruises, weekend cruises and other trips including **Lake Kallavesi, Vehmersalmi** straits, and the **Suvavesi channel** to Levalahti. Romantic, wonderful, memorable. The Blue Saimaa Cruise, during June and Aug., leaves **Lappeenranta** on a two-day overnight cruise to **Puumata** and **Savonlinna,** with an optional sightseeing tour which includes **Olavinlinna Castle.** You spend the night on board.

FUN AND GAMES The hunting season is in the fall. The best skiing is in Lapland or nearby during Mar. and Apr. The best fishing, June–Sept. Spectator sports include winter skiing and ski-jumping championships, reindeer-drawn sleigh races, summer log rolling, yachting regattas. The swimming facilities are extraordinary, pools everywhere and beaches seldom out of reach until you go north and inland to Lapland! Children swim and ski at remarkably early ages. There are beach swimming schools at Jyvaskyla that make a big splash in summer.

For young skiers and all the family, there are ***ski schools.*** About five miles from **Lahti,** you'll find the ski school at the manor house hotel **Messila** (Tel: (918) 53–16–66). **Hotel Ellivuori** (Tel: (923) 41400), near **Tampere** has a ski school and also illuminated night trails, slalom slopes, and ski lifts. **Loma-Koli Vacation Center** near **Joensuu** features a six-mile slalom slope and good winter ski school (Koli; Tel: (973) 67–22–41). About four miles from the center of **Jyvaskyla, Laajavuori sports resort** has slalom slopes, four ski lifts, ski school. The ski lift station (Tel: (941) 25–10–87) or the CTO (Tel: (941) 29–40–82) can give you all details. **Kuopio's** ski schools? Ask the CTO (Tel: (971) 12–14–11/11–41–01) for details about the **Ski Hotel Lahkvuori** in the suburb of Nilsia and the *Puijo slalom*. **Kuusamo** not only offers a ski school, but a wonderfully well-conceived wonderland in winter for children (see Kuusamo). **Lapland?** (See Fun Trips). At **Sotkamo,** the **Vuokatti Sport Institute** offers courses to please even the littlest on skis, I'm told, but I haven't been there, so check the CTO.

Riding courses? Many.

The **Finnish Equestrian Federation** (Topeliuksenkatu 14A, 00250 Helsinki 25; Tel: (90) 473–7318) offers riding schools and riding lessons. Some of the best facilities for children can be found about 15 miles outside of **Hameenlinna** at the **Kuurila Ponystable** (Tel: 5612). The CTO at Hameenlinna can tell you more (Tel: (917) 20–23–88) and furnish further details about the stirrups and stables at **Hotel Aulanko.** The **Jamsa Riding Centre** about 36 miles outside of Jyvaskyla offers a choice of riding holidays lasting from two to seven days. Riding camps and children's pony camps last five to six days. Information and details from **Central Finland, Vacation Finland Association,** Vapaudenkatu 38, 40100 Jyvaskyla 10; Tel: (941) 29–40–83. In **Joensuu, Linnunlahti** stable (Tel: (973) 25605) or **Onttola** stables (Tel: (973) 80260). Except for July, year-round riding in **Jyvaskyla** at the **Killerjarvi Equestrian Centre** (Tel: (941) 25–10–15). The **Kokkolan Ratsastajat** (Tel: (968) 15332) is your source for bit-and-bridle advice in **Kokkola.** The CTO in **Kuopio** (Tel: (971) 12–14–11) has all the gen on prices and schedules in the neighborhood. There's a riding school at **Messila Manor** in **Lahti** (see Happy Family Accommodations, also Lahti). The **Aimarautio** stable (Tel: (981) 22–10–30) in **Oulu** is a recommendation. **Savonlinna**? The **Vuohimaki** riding stables, check with the CTO (Tel: (957) 13492/3.) The **Tampere Riding Club** manages a winter riding school at **Lusankatu** (Tel: (931) 51276); at **Teiskotalli,** Maisansalo (Tel: (931) 84141; at **Teisko** (Tel: (931) 83752); also riding camps for all ages and riding skills. In **Turku,** the **Hirvensalo riding school** (at Hirvensalo; Tel: (921) 58–01–10). In **Valkeakoski,** the **Kuurila Pony Stable** (at Kuurila (Tel: 5612).

Instruction in ***driving reindeer*** is offered during the winter at the **Pohtimolampi Sports Center** (about 25 miles from Rovaniemi). You sleigh around with reindeer power. Unless advance notice is received at the Rovaniemi CTO, don't expect to find the reindeer lined up like Hertz-Rent-a-Cars. They have to be rounded up for you. Reindeer round-ups are arranged weekly in Lapland from Oct.–Jan. You'll get the best antler and sleigh information from **Paliskuntain Yhdistys** (Koskikatu 33A, 96100 Rovaniemi 10; Tel: (991) 22057). The **Finnish Central Sports Federation** (SVUL) is the main national sports organization in Finland, with 45 affiliated cycling, skiing, rowing, canoeing, skating, yachting, orienteering, recreational sports associations and more than 3000 associated sports clubs and institutes. For any sports information, call SVUL, Topeliuksenkatu 41A; SF 00250 Helsinki 25; Tel: (90) 47371.

SHOPPING WITH AND FOR CHILDREN Shop design and the design of the products inside is amazing. Department stores generally have restaurants and coffee shops.

The quality of children's clothes and toys is splendid. **Vuokko** and **Marimekko** fabrics are outstanding. Birchbark slippers don't last worth a penni, mark my words. Gnome-like, fantasy **Fauni** trolls or **Muumi** dolls, handwoven materials, fabrics, candles, pottery, ceramics, and the ryijy rugs. Regional and Lapp costumes are singularly becoming, durable and attractive (remove the apron and the artsy-craftsy, costume-party look disappears). The Finns are mad about candles and lanterns; **Desico** makes beautiful candles, so does **Aarikka.** Famous designer **Timo Sarpaneva** has also designed candles. For boys, one of the best buys is a camping knife called a *puukko.* Winter wear and ski wear is generally functional and warm but not particularly snappy looking. Children's snowsuits, however, are superb. Knitwear is interesting because of the odd shades of wool that it comes in. All in all, regional and Lapp costumes, ryijy rugs, and toys are the best bargains, I think. **Helsinki's Stockmann's** (Aleksanterinkatu 52) is the leading department store. Among other things I recommend here are reindeer slippers made in Lapland, children's hand-woven sweaters, skirts, and socks; pewter buttons; good selection of toys and children's clothes. Anything you buy can be shipped directly back to you by the export service on the fifth floor—the ''Vientipalvelu''—and they'll do it all for you with 14% discount. Wheee! The immense **Academic Bookstore** (Akateeminen Kirjakauppa, Kekuskatu 1) is a separate store, but shares the first floor of Stockmann's premises; many English books, children's books. A bibliophile's paradise. Another excellent department store for clothes and toys is **Sokos Oy** (Mannerheimintie 9); souvenirs; fine bookshop.

Other department stores of interest: **Pukeva** (Kaisaniemenkatu 5); **Aleksi** 13 (Aleksanterinkatu 13); **Kaivopiha** shopping center (Vanha Ylioppilastalo). For children's clothes (and dresses for mama); **Marimekko** and **Pihastudio** (Pohjoisesplanadi 31); the **Marimekko fabric outlet** is at Hakaniemi Hall (second floor, Hameentie). For children's clothes and dresses, try also **Leenanpuoti** (Keskuskatu 4); **Jukkala** (Mikonkatu 8) **Aapiskukko** (Iso Roobertinkatu 19). Infants' and toddlers' clothes are wonderful at **Bunukka** (Kasarminkatu 44); also pretty children's clothes at **Tsuppu** (City Kaytava, second floor); **Jassu puti-**

ikki (Korkeavuo-renkatu 6); **Muorinpuoti** (Ympyratalo, Hakaniemi). Attractive knit-wear, mittens, sweaters, skirts and scarves at **Neovius Oy** (Olavinkatu 1). For cloth diapers and everything for the 2-year-old and younger, try **Instrumentarium** (Mikonkatu 6). You will find Instrumentarium's products in most department stores all over the country. For children's toys which are exceptionally well made, solid, and good, try **Aarikka** (Pohjoisesplanadi 27). Toys also at **Alba** (Fabianinkatu 17) and **Julesverne** (Olavinkatu 2). One of many toys I liked were blocks of wood that come in a cotton sack. For other toys: **Kaleva Koru** (Unioninkatu 25); reindeer slippers, *pukkos* (sheath knives) from Lapland; ornaments inspired by the national epic, the *Kalevala*. **Invaliidien Tuotteiden Myyntikeskus** (INVA, Mannerheimintie 44), well made and designed craft items toys and accessories for children. For handicrafts, go to **Helsky** (Annankatu 16), **Kotikasityo Oy Tellorvo** (Lonnrotinkatu 26). Exhibition of **Finnish industrial design and handicrafts** (Kasarminkatu 19); **Vokki Oy** (Merikannontie 3) has exclusive designs and gifts.

Helsinki: Handwoven textiles and gifts at the **Lena Rewell Shop** (Etelaesplanadi 22). Wooly blankets here that are useful, the sort used for chaises lounges. **Kotiteollisuuden Keskusliitto** (Temppelikatu 15A) has Finnish handicrafts, carvings, knitwear, pottery; handwoven material for making little girls' dresses. For souvenirs, **Hakaniemi Market Hall** (2.floor, Siltasaarenkatu). **Arabia** Oy (P.Esplanadi 25), has sturdy children's stoneware breakfast sets. For children's furniture of contemporary design, lamps, and decorations for children's rooms, the **Alvar Aalto** designs can be seen at **Artek** (Keskuskatu 3). Finnish folksong records at **Musiikki Fazer** (Aleksanterinkatu 11). **Lehitomisto-Pressbyran** (Pohjoisesplanadi 33) has a good selection of overseas newspapers and magazines. Maps and picture books of travel interest are found at **Yliopistokirjakauppa** (Aleksanterinkatu 15).

Jyvaskyla: Baby and children's clothes: **AB-Pukimo** (Kauppakatu 41), also at **Marimekko** (Kauppakatu 39). A complex including two restaurants and a coffee shop, **Tammivuori Design** (Kauppakatu 25). Children's clothes and toys: **Alfa** (Kauppakatu 37) and **Sokos** (Kauppakatu 24). Local handicrafts: **Perinnepuoti** (Kauppakatu 19).

Rovaniemi: Toys: **Lapin Kansan Lelukauppa** (Koskikatu 19). Toys and handicraft materials: **Lelu-ja Askartelupaja** (Rovakatu 16). Lapp handicrafts: **Matkamuisto Noitarumpu** (Maakuntakatu 29); **Nili** (Koskikatu 20); **Matkamuisto Mi-Sa-Ko** (Rovakatu 25); **Lapin Lahja** (Harrikatu 3); **Lauri-Tuotteet Oy** (Pohjolankatu 25). Children's clothes: **Nuorisopukimo Seita-Asu** (Rovakatu 20); **Nuorisopukimo loive-Asu,** teenage clothes for girls mostly (Koskikatu 10). Vuokko dresses: **Mekkomeeri** (Kansankatu 14).

Savonlinna: Toys: **Savonlinnan Lelukauppa** (Olavinkatu 51). Department stores **Ita-Savo** (Olavinkatu 54) and **Keski-Saimaa** (Olavinkatu 57) have children's clothing sections; in the toy depts., Lapp trolls, dolls in national costume, wooden toys designed by Jussila. National costumes as well as a special children's dept. at **Kinnunen's** (Olavinkatu 52). Children's clothes: **Muksu Special Shop** (Olavinkatu 38); **Lasten pukineliike Karki Oy** (Olavinkatu 50); **Lastenliike Rape** (Tulliportinkatu 11). Bookstores: **Savonlinna Kirjakauppa** (Olavinkatu 57); **Edit Strengin Kirjakauppa** (Olavinkatu 34); **Paaskykirja** (Karjalantie 8).

Tampere: Toys and handicrafts made by the blind: **Sokeain Yhdistyksen Myymala** (Aleksis Kivenkatu 30). Children's clothes: **Ruusupuku** (Hameenkatu 30); **Mikkomaija** (Hameenpuisto 25); **Lastenkamari** (Nasilinnankatu 24); **Tuulantei** (Hallituskatu 13). Children's clothes and toys also at the department stores: **Stockmann** (Hameenkatu 4); **Sokos** (Hameenkatu 21); **Centrum** (Hameenkatu 11). **Vuokko-dresses** for teenagers at **Muoditar** (Aleksis Kivenkatu 13, Kauppakatu 12). **Marimekko** (Nasilinnankatu 32) for teenagers and mamas.

Kasityokeskus: Handicrafts and gifts: **Pohjan Piika** (Hameenkatu 14); **Pentik** (Yliopistonkatu 25); **Aarikka** (Yliopistonkatu, 27B); **Kankurit** (Sirkkalankatu 22 + Cafe); **Kasityokeskus** (Kauppiask. 11). Local handicrafts, national costumes, craft supplies to make your own at **Sylvi Salonen** (Kauppiaskatu 10, Yliopistonkatu. 22).

Turku: Toy shops: **Casagrande R** (Linnankatu 9–11), **Elise Tmi** (Hameenkatu 7), **Neulatyyny** (Yliopistonkatu 7), and the department stores. Special children's shops: **Autere** (Kristiinakatu 9 and Eerikinkatu 9), **Baby** (Brahenkatu 7), **Fiilis-asu** (Maariankatu 1), **Maitohammas,** (Eerikinkatu 12), **Mammakeskus Oy** (Forum, Kauppiaskatu 4–6) **Marimekko** (Forum), **Pirpana** (Yliopistonkatu 24) **Tiia Oy** (Kauppiaskatu 10, Brahenkatu 5, Hameenkatu 8). Department stores: **Stockmann** (Yliopistonkatu 22), **Centrum** (Eerikinkatu 19), **Kestila** (Yliopistonkatu 26, Eerikinkatu 12), **Wiklund** (Eerikinkatu 11).

Valkeakoski: Toy shop: **Kosken Muovi-Ja Kumi** (Saaksmaentie 9). Local toys on sale also at the market, open on Tues. and Fri., 7 a.m.–2 p.m. Children clothes: **Tenavapuoti** (Valtatie 11).

FINNISH FRIENDS AND PEN PALS In **Tampere,** contact the English School (Amurinkatu 21B; Tel: (931) 28775) or the English conversational groups at the Workers' Evening Institute (Tel: (931) 54043). In **Turku,** get in touch with the International Youth Service (Kristiinankatu 5; Tel: (921) 24536).

As for ***pen pals,*** the most important thing to know is that Santa Claus, or Father Christmas, who will answer all letters, lives in Korvatunturi (99999 Korvatunturi).

In **Helsinki,** pen pals for the young may be contacted through the junior magazine *Suosikki* (Eerinkinkatu 3B, 0100 Helsinki 10), or the *Helsingen Sanomat* newspaper *Nuorten Horisontti* (P.O. Box 240,00100 Helsinki 10); in **Naantali,** through the newspaper *Uutis-Valjakko* (Kauppiaskatu 21B); in **Kuusamo,** through the newspaper *Koillissanomat* (Kitkantie 31); in **Savonlinna,** through the newspaper *Ita-Savo* (Kaartilantie 10).

CALENDAR OF EVENTS A complete schedule of events and details about festivals can be had, free for the asking, from the Finnish National Tourist Association.

In **Mar.** the ***International Winter Games*** are held in Kuopio. In mid-Mar. in Hameenlinna, the ***International Skiing*** competitions take place.

In **Apr.** the ***Ski-jumping Championships*** are held in Kuusamo. Beginning in the afternoon of Apr. 30, a carnival-like atmosphere invades Helsinki and the nation as a whole. Students crown the statue of Havis Amanda in the capital with a white student's hat at midnight. On ***May Day,*** singing and general wearing of white student's caps abound in Helsinki, and singing and other festivities take place elsewhere.

June until Sept. sees a parade of dance, opera, and various kinds of ***music festivals*** nationally, but the notable ones are held at Kuopio, Jyvaskyla, Savonlinna, Turku, Tampere, Helsinki, Kokkola, Vaasa, and Pori. Children will like the performances at the ***Peacock Theater*** at Linnanmaki Amusement Park in Helsinki which features puppets, acrobats, Indian fakirs; a program that ends at the end of Aug. with a youth concert and a children's party enjoyable for the whole family. In June, on the Fri. closest to June 23, the ***Midsummer Festival*** occurs nationally, celebrating the longest day of the year with dancing and singing around bonfires. Around these "kokko" fires there are plays and recitals, and national costumes are worn. Birch boughs are everywhere.

On **July** 26–27, Naantali celebrates the ***Sleepyhead Carnival,*** and on the 27th in Hango one is awakened on ***Lay-a-bed Day*** at the crack of dawn by a charivari parade through the city ending at the Casino summer restaurant with dancing and general entertainment. In **Sept.** in Hango there is a special party just for children. The second Sun. in Sept. marks ***Turku Day*** in Turku, and the second weekend marks ***Handicrafts Day.*** In **Oct.** Turku offers a ***Youth Art Happening Festival.***

LANGUAGE AND PHRASEBOOK Please take at least two Finnish phrasebooks with you. Each member of the family should have one. You can buy them at bookstores in Finland, but American ones are often simpler. Except for the endearing Motellis, Hotellis, Baaris, and Grillis, few Finnish words sound like English or have English derivatives. The language looks impossible, but it isn't really as hard as it looks. Each letter is pronounced. *Å* with a circle over it is pronounced like the *aw* in *law; ä* with two dots over it like the *a* in *hat; ö* with two dots over it like the *ur* in *fur*. *Ei* like *ei* as in sleigh. *Y* like the French *u* or like trying to say *ee* with your lips puckered up for whistling. The accent is almost always on the first syllable. A boy is a *poika* (Plural, poikia). A girl is a *tyttö* (Plural tyttöjä). A child is *lapsi*, children *lapsia*.

Hello	*Terve*	*Tair-vay*
Good morning	*Hyvaa Paivaa*	*Hee-vair Pay-vair*
I am an American	*Olen amerikka-lainen*	*Ohlen ah-mairika-lienin*
My name is____	*Nimeni on____*	*Neemaany on____*
I am__years old	*Olen__vuotta vanha*	*Ohlen__vwatta vanhuh*
Please	*Olkaa Hyva*	*Ohlkuh Huevair*
Thank you	*Kiitos*	*Keytoes*
I cannot speak Finnish	*En osaa puhua suomea*	*En ohsar pooh-who-uh swoymay-uh*
Yes	*Kylla*	*Kuehla*
No	*Ei*	*Ayee*
I am having a wonderful time	*Minulla on hauskaa*	*Minuella on housecar*
1	*yksi*	*ueksey*
2	*kaksi*	*cocksey*
3	*kolme*	*cole-may*
4	*nelja*	*nail-ya*
5	*viisi*	*veesy*
6	*kuusi*	*koosey*
7	*seitseman*	*sate-see-man*
8	*kahdeksan*	*car-dayk-san*
9	*yhdeksan*	*ueh-dayk-san*
10	*kymmenen*	*kuemennen*
11	*yksitoista*	*ueksey-toy-eesta*
12	*kaksitoista*	*cocksey-toy-eesta*
13	*kolmetoista*	*colemay-toy-eesta*
14	*neljatoista*	*nailya-toy-eesta*
15	*viisitoista*	*veesy-toy-eesta*
Goodbye	*Nakemiin*	*Nack-a-mean*

FRANCE

Alors, la belle France! This is the land where cotton candy is called ''Daddy's beard'' *(barbe a Papa),* where your child can solo temporarily in a chateau hotel exclusively for infants to 10-year-olds (at the Cote d'Amour); where you can see the world's most famous paintings one day, the animals painted by prehistoric cavemen the next; where your child can earn a snowflake for achievement at a nursery ski school while you, if you're a beginner, can learn to ski by playing leapfrog. You will find that the French believe in order and in doing well what they specifically arrange to do; that they delight in the grace and pungency of conversation and language. Children often seem to intuit or understand better than their parents, however, that the French respond graciously to intelligence and less well, if at all, to undifferentiated benevolence or instant first-name familiarity; kindness is particular and not diffused in France, something to be won from others and from yourself. If you bear this important point in mind, France's charm, culture, practicality and sophistication will be lavished upon you and your children, from Amiens to the Cote d'Azur. You can float leisurely through France on a barge, fly over the countryside in a balloon, or zip from Paris to your destination in the world's fastest train. The French have been an inspiration to me, and I hope they will be for you also. Remember that it was the French who coined the now universal phrase: *Bon voyage!*

In summer, you'll find Brittany a perfect playground for children; superb beaches; peaceful without being dull; often inexpensive. And Brittany is a land of legends, strewn with vestiges of pagans and Christian cults; for Feb.'s or Aug.'s religious processions, called *Grands Pardons,* there are special *Pardons* even for horses. Many neolithic menhirs and dolmens, with the most remarkable plantations of them around Carnac. Normandy has innumerable bustling seaside resorts and family beaches, many also inexpensive. In the Pyrenees-Basque country—with spectacular scenery and remarkably colorful villages—there are folk festivals with whiz-bang pelota, bullfights, and good riding. (But prepare your children beforehand for the fact that Basque men wear black berets—as this sometimes seems very funny to small children.) Also, let me recommend the believe-it-or-not Languedoc-Roussillon, where everything seems somewhat strange and remarkable to children.

"Allons, enfants," should get you in the mood for the days of glory for all families traveling to France.

INFORMATION ABOUT FRANCE The splendid **French Government Tourist Office**—FGTO—(610 5th Ave. New York 10020) has branch offices in Chicago (645 N. Michigan Ave, Suite #430, Chicago, IL 60611); Dallas (World Trade Center, Suite #103, P.O. Box 58610, 2050 Stemmons Freeway, Dallas, TX 75258); Los Angeles (9401 Wilshire Blvd., Beverly Hills, CA 90212); San Francisco (℅ Air France, 360 Post St., San Francisco, CA 94108); in Montreal (1840 Sherbrooke St. West, Montreal); and Toronto (372 Bay St., Suite #610, Toronto, Ontario. They will supply you with information about hotels, inns, restaurants, transportation, the location of museums of interest, sightseeing, tours, and much other useful information for free. To find out more about art, museums, schools, travel-study vacations for children and teenagers, contact the **French Cultural Counselor** (972 Fifth Ave., New York, NY 10021) or its offices in Los Angeles, San Francisco, New Orleans, and Houston. Also, the CIDJ (*Centre de Documentation pour la Jeunesse,* 101 quai Branly, Paris XV) can supply you with extremely useful information about clubs, workshops, vacation possibilities as the guest of a French family combining language-study and sports or arts and crafts, open to young visitors. There are also **Syndicats d'Initiative** in all cities from which information can be obtained. In Paris, your questions will be fielded by the **Commissariat General au Tourisme** (127 av. Champs-Elysees). The **Office de Tourisme de Paris** and its hostesses can get information for you on anything concerning Paris and its surroundings; buy guides here and get masses of free brochures, maps, and event notices. It also offers a good reservation service for hotels in Paris and in France. The **Paris-Accueil** or the Paris Welcome office, handles bed-and-breakfast accommodations and solves problems the OTP may find too specialized or personal for them to solve. Brand-new is a *French Summer international bilingual telephone network* providing information on touristic attractions and accommodations throughout France. From 7 a.m.–10 p.m., the number to call is (01) 249–3333.

Other Paris Welcome Information Offices with English-speaking hostesses are at: **Air Terminal des Invalides,** open weekdays 9 a.m.–noon, Sun. and holidays 10:30 a.m.–1:30 p.m. and 3:30 p.m.–7:30 p.m.; **Gare du Nord** (18 rue Dunkerque), weekdays 8:30 a.m.–8:30 p.m.; **Gare St.-Lazare** (rue St.-Lazare), weekdays 9 a.m.–9 p.m.; **Gare de Lyon** (20 blvd. Diderot), weekdays 6:30 a.m.–12:30 p.m.; and **Gare de l'Est** (pl. Strasbourg), weekdays 6:30 a.m.–12:30 p.m. and 5:30–11:30 p.m.; **Gare d'Austerlitz** (55 Quai d'Austerlitz).

Welcome Information Offices that also change your money and arrange for hotel bookings within a 100-mile radius are at: **Aix-les-Bains, Besancon, Cannes, Dijon, Evian-les-Bains, Grenoble, Lyons,**

Marseilles, Nice, Le Puy, Reims, Rouen, Strasbourg, Toulouse, Tours, and **Vichy.**

For special information about regions I suggest the following, all in Paris: **Maison d'Auvergne Bourbonnais et Velay** (53 av. Franklin-Roosevelt, VIII); **Maison des Basques de Paris** (10 rue Duban, XVI); **Maison de Bretagne** (3 rue Depart, XIV); **Maison du Dauphine** (85 rue Cherche-Midi, VI); **Maison de la Lozere** (1 bis rue Hautefeuille, VI); **Maison du Mont-Dore** (63 blvd. Malesherbes, VIII); **Maison de Nice** (30 blvd. Capucines, IX); **Maison de Pyrenees** (24 rue 4-Septembre, II); **Maison du Rouergue** (3 rue Chaussee-d'Antin, XI); and **Maison de Savoie** (117 av. Champs-Elysees VIII).

Just because you're not a student doesn't mean you can't get terrific tips and help from student travel organizations; try any of these, in Paris: OTU, **Office du Tourisme Universitaire** (137 blvd. St.-Michel, V); GSTS, **German Student Travel Service** (11 rue Carmes, V); SSTS, **Scandinavian Student Travel Service** (125 av. Champs-Elysees VIII); DIS, **Danmarks Internationale Studenterkomite** (142 av. Champs-Elysees, VIII); USIT, **Irish Student Travel Service** (24 rue Dames, XVII); and CIEE, **Council on International Educational Exchange** (49 rue Pierre-Charron, VIII).

In Paris, you can read the Paris *Herald Tribune*. The English *Daily Mail* lists all events, as do *Une Semaine de Paris* and *Paris Weekly Information,* all broader in scope than *Allo Paris.* Several weekly guides to amusements appear on the newsstands each Wed.; *Pariscope* is one of the best and *L'Officiel des Spectacles* is another. Even livelier is *Passion,* an English-language publication, irreverent as New York's *Village Voice.* A bi-monthly brochure listing national and municipal museums and their special exhibits is obtainable at most large museums. Your best bet for buying guides and periodicals in English is one of Paris' English-French bookshops: **W.H. Smith and Son** (248 rue de Rivoli, I); **Brentano's** (37 ave. de l'Opera, II). **Michelin Salon d'Accueil** (46 ave. de Breteuil, VII) has a welcoming array of fine publications and maps. The green *Michelin* guides for Paris and the provinces are terrific for sightseers. They even illustrate the sort of trees you may be seeing and may find difficult to identify. Hachette-Vendome's *Chateaux of France* is a luxurious essay on all the chateaux, with splendid photographs.

If you are interested in crafts and craftsmanship, enjoy creating things with your hands, check out the *Compagnons,* a guild of French artisans, with expositions that are knockouts, workshops you can visit sometimes, and a special museum of their work (see Tours). Contact **l'Association Ouvriere des Compagnons du Devoir du Tour de France** (82 rue de l'Hotel de Ville, Paris IV); **Federation Compagnonnique des Metiers du Batiment** (161 rue Jean-Jaures, 75019 Paris); **l'Union Compagnonnique des Devoirs Unis** (7 rue Claude-Guy, 94220 Ivry-sur-Seine).

Tickets for music festivals in Avignon, Besancon, Lyons, Orange,

Paris, Prades, Strasbourg, Vaisons-la-Romaine and elsewhere, as well as *tickets for theater festivals* and sports events are available from **American Express** (11 rue Scribe, 75009 Paris) and **Thomas Cook and Son** (2 place de la Madeleine, 75008 Paris). Other agencies, such as **France Voyages, Agence Gallia, Location Theatres, Paris Excursions** and **Theatres, Wagons-Lits,** all located in Paris and listed in the telephone directory, are other recommended sources.

▶ **Note:** *Public Bathrooms:* The charge is usually three francs or less, extra for soap and towels. Find them in department stores, cafes, restaurants, Metro stations, bus and railway stations, but remember to carry coins for them! The attendant expects a tip of three francs. *Movies and plays:* For showing you to your seat, ushers expect a tip of three francs at the cinema, five francs at the theater. *Telephones:* To take the sting out of the ring, the money-saving services of Teleplan are operative in the Comfort Hotels International, Holiday and Hilton chains. The old-fashioned pay telephones of Paris require tokens called *jetons* which you can buy at post offices and cafes with telephones. You deposit the tokens and push the knob on the front of the telephone when someone answers. Newer telephones accept coins and can be be used for long-distance calls.

Paris is divided into numbered arrondissements: I is the center, with shops, the Louvre, and the Tuileries; II includes the Bourse and the Opera Comique; VII is heaven on the left bank. The green *Michelin* guide illustrates the areas for you with graphic clarity.

HEALTH, WATER, AND FOOD Health standards are excellent. Tap water is safe to drink. The French drink bottled water because of its different taste, its carbonation, or for special mineral properties. Children enjoy trying different kinds. A few of the best known brands are *Perrier,* (one of the bubbliest), *Evian* (noncarbonated), *Vittel,* and *Vichy.*

Most milk is pasteurized, but in rural areas exercise the same care that you would at home about unpasteurized milk.

As for French food, volumes have been written about its wonders. Superb though the French *haute cuisine* is, fast-food bistro fare is nutritious and well-prepared, particularly the grilled sandwiches, which have many variations; most common are the *croque-monsieur* (grilled ham and cheese) and the *croque-madame* (the same plus a fried egg on top). You certainly should familiarize yourself and your children with French cooking terms and French restaurants so that you won't deprive yourselves of something perfectly delicious because you didn't know what it was. There are local and regional specialties, and you can't go wrong if you order the *specialties de la maison* (the house specialties).

An extremely helpful list of Parisian restaurants (from deluxe to perfectly adequate ones with a modest price range) is available from the FGTO in New York. Truck drivers *(routiers),* like all Frenchmen, have palates of exquisite perception, but since they don't have money to spend on France's multi-starred and tocqued wonders, their gastronomical guidebook is practical to have while touring; get it from **Les Routiers** (7 rue de l'Isly). The **Buffets de Gare** (station restaurants) usually prepare regional specialties at moderate prices; but don't expect to dine divinely; generally noisy, crowded, brightly lit. Restaurants marked **Restaurants de Tourisme** offer a specially priced tourist menu. If you choose a la carte and order the tourist menu for the children, waiters will treat you with respect. The red *Guide Michelin* tells you in detail about hotels and restaurants everywhere in France; *Le Bottin Gourmand,* by Jean Didier, in French with no English translation that I've come across, lists over 400 Parisian restaurants by district and classifies them by price. The French version of Gault Millau's *Guide de Paris,* cut and edited into an English version called *The Best of Paris,* tells you about shops and hotels as well. I heartily recommend your reading *The Best of Paris* by Henri Gault and Christian Millau.

Paris: the great restaurants—such as **Taillevent, L'Archestrate, La Tour d'Argent, Maxim's**—are expensive and, unless you have pots of money, a wild extravagance for taking children to for lunch; dinner is out of the question (children wreck the ambience for other diners). Teenagers in turtlenecks usually won't be accepted. Ties must be worn. Older teenagers can accompany parents to restaurants of elegance, but they must be dressed well!

Older children and teenagers, often awed by the prices of food at top restaurants, are often impressed or gratified that you're willing to spend all that money to educate their palates, but fine food does not have to be extravagantly pricey in Paris. Many small restaurants offer regional cuisine for a lot less money than most two to three star establishments. The choice is vast in this land of some 38,000 restaurants and around 180,000 cafes and brasseries, but here are just a few suggestions for starters. **La Petite Chaise** (36 rue de Grenelle) said to be the oldest restaurant in Paris, and serving since 1680, is a favorite lunch place for graduate students and personnel from nearby publishing houses; open also for dinner.

For main course and dessert souffles, **Le Souffle** (36 rue du Mont-Thabor), near the Place Vendome; **L'Amanguier** (51 rue du Theatre) near the Eiffel Tower and at 110 rue de Richelieu between the Opera and the Bourse. **Le Roi du Pot-au-Feu** (34 rue Vignon) in the 9th arrondissement is a small bistro where you can enjoy a real pot-au-feu. If you're in the 2nd arr., try **Gerard** (4 rue du Mail) not only for pot-au-feu, but also for other typical bistro offerings and an unusually good flaky-pastry apple tart.

The **Eiffel Tower,** happily renovated in 1983, has a fast-food bar and a fresh sherbet stall on its first platform; a cafe near the entrance to **Le Parisien,** a pleasant bistro with simple a la carte platters; a more elaborate restaurant, **La Belle France,** with a fixed-price menu offering a most affordable children's version; and yet another restaurant, expensive but not necessarily better, with direct express elevator service from the base of the tower, completed in 1984 (if you prefer elevated prices for less of the view than you can see up until 11 p.m. in the panoramic elevators). On the second platform, with souvenir and photo shops, there's the **Belle Epoque** snackbar to nourish exhausted shoppers.

Exhausted shoppers always need nourishing. Sit on top of *tout* Paris at **La Samaritaine** department store and eat ice cream and cake while enjoying the view from the tenth floor terrace (closed Oct.–Mar.) of their shop #2. Have tea if you will in any of these four connecting stores, but I'd steer clear of the cafeteria. On the other hand, the main store of **Galeries Lafayette** on Haussman Blvd. offers a cafeteria (open 10:30 a.m.–6 p.m.) where you'll find a delicious buffet with good meat and tempting desserts; also a grill open from 11 a.m.–3 p.m. A few doors away, at the main store of **Au Printemps,** you can have lunch in the charming Square du Printemps. There's an agreeable tearoom-restaurant on the fourth floor of **Aux Trois Quartiers** (17 blvd. de la Madeleine, I) where everything is restfully tasteful and elegant. **Fanny Tea** (20 place Dauphine, I), what the children call "a Granny special," closed Mon.; **Le Flore en l'Ile** (4 quai d'Orleans), open daily 11 a.m.–1:45 a.m.; **Laduree** (16 rue Royale, VIII), where formality and courtesy reigns, closed Sun.; **Muscade** (36 rue de Montpensier, I) under the arcades at the Palais-Royal Gardens, garden terrace open May–end Sept.; **Pandora** (24 Passage Choiseul, II) charming, old-fashioned, closed weekends; **A Priori-The** (35-37 galerie Vivienne, II), closed Sun.; **Saint-Louis** (81 rue Saint-Louis-en-l'Ile, IV) open daily until 8 p.m., on weekends until 11 p.m.; **W.H. Smith** (248 rue de Rivoli, I), open 10:15 a.m.–6 p.m., closed Sun.; The **Tea Caddy** (14 rue Saint-Julien-le-Pauvre, V), open noon–7 p.m. daily, Sun. 2 p.m.–7 p.m.; **Verlet** (256 rue Saint-Honore, I), open noon–6:30 p.m., closed weekends.

The *drugstores* stock gifts, gadgets, video-cassettes, luggage, perfume, books, almost anything you can think of, including a variety of food and thirst quenchers, and are open from 9 a.m.–2 a.m. **Drugstore Saint-Germain** (149 Blvd. Saint-Germain, VI) opens at 8 a.m. and has a pharmacy that's open late; many comic books in French; everything new in the way of *nouveautes,* good sandwiches, ice cream with whipped cream. **Drugstore des Champs-Elysees** (133 Champs-Elysees, VIII) has good, solid food as well as floats, excellent sundaes; plus a theater-booking outlet and a take-out deli. **Drugstore Matignon** (1 ave. Matignon, VIII) has a snack bar and a real restaurant, **Le Drugstorien,** above; in between, on the mezzanine, is a bar offering daily specials, a mixed grill, salads and desserts. **Drugstore Opera** (6 blvd. des Capucines) with cafeteria and terrace for your eating pleasure, also has an entrance on rue Halevy with a pastry shop, liquor store, and six restaurants (including a pizzeria), with the next least expensive being **La Corbeille** and the most expensive **Aux Provinciales.** Drugstores qualify not only as shopping and eating places, but as *attractions*. Just visit the Champs-Elysees, the

Matignon, or the Opera and you'll see what I mean!

For *classic cuisine in a country inn* that takes credit cards and is idyllic and not all that expensive for Sun. lunch, head for the delightful **Restaurant Le Relais Conde** (42 ave. du Marechal Joffre, 60500 Chantilly). Reserve ahead as there are only nine tables beneath the vaulted, beamed ceiling. Closed Mon. and Tues., Jan. 15–Feb. 5, July 15–31.

For budget-priced *picnic* items, try the **Codex** or **Felix Potin** market chains, with branches leafing up all over Paris. Two of the largest low-cost *supermarches* are located in the **Monprix** store next to Galeries Lafyette on the Right Bank, and in the basement of **Bon Marche,** the largest department store on the Left Bank.

Special: For a birthday celebration for your child, a chocolate cake with candles, fruit juice or other soft drinks for him or her and guests, reserve a place two weeks in advance during the summertime at **La Ferme du Golf** (Bois de Boulogne, Jardin d'Acclimation, porte des Sablons, XVI), which can accommodate 40 children Weds., Sat., or Sun. afternoons in a large room where ducks, sheep, goats, hens and chickens roam about freely. Visit this spot anyway, have a snack, and afterwards enjoy all the attractions of the **Jardin d'Acclimation.**

Places where you don't have to make reservations ahead may be crowded but, with children along, nipping into a cafe, brasserie, tearoom/quick lunch place, or even a Paris-style drugstore that features a little bit of almost everything, is usually eminently satisfactory. Some good choices are open daily until midnight (or later) unless noted. **Cafe de la Paix** (12 blvd. des Capucines, IX), a national landmark. Good food, fast service; classic English tea and old-fashioned lemonade served between 3 p.m. and 6 p.m. **Les Deux Magots** (70 blvd. Saint-Germain, VI) terrace cafe pleasant for breakfast. **Brasserie Lipp** (151 blvd. Saint-Germain, VI) quiet in the morning, but progressively livelier later when reservations are not taken, so go early to put your name on the list. **Mollard** (115 rue Saint-Lazare, VIII) elaborate decor is charming. **Cafe de la Mosquee** (39 rue Geoffroy-Saint-Hilaire, V), on the patio with fountains or in the lounge at the close of a guided tour about the mosque and steam bath, is a charmer for mint tea, Turkish coffee, pastries; closes at 10 p.m. **L'Innocent** (12–14 rue Berger, I) in Les Halles territory, still offers charm beside the Fountain of the Holy Innocents, and in the summer, beneath umbrellas away from the pedestrian hordes, open noon–1 a.m. **Ma Bourgogne** (19 Place des Vosges, IV) is one of my favorite places, a charmer, familiar to devotees of Inspector Maigret. **La Closerie des Lilas** (171 blvd. du Montparnasse, VI), open noon–1 a.m., with awnings, enclosed terrace, garden, and copies of *Paris Match* provided for diners, is splendid for a summer's Sunday lunch, or lunch anytime; I don't recommend any meal but lunch or an early afternoon snack. *For inexpensive quick brunches and lunches; leisurely teas with biscuits, pastries, cakes, tarts; attractive ambience:* **Angelina** (226 rue de Rivoli, I) open daily; **Boulangerie Saint-Philippe** (73 ave. Franklin-

Roosevelt, VIII), open 7:30 a.m., closed Sat.; **Christian Constant** (20 rue du Bac, VII), open 8 a.m.–8 p.m. daily; **Ciboulette-Terrasse** (141 rue Saint-Martin, IV), across from the Centre Pompidou, closed weekends; **La Croissanterie** (Forum des Halles, fourth level, I) and on the third level, **Tartes et Galettes; Dattes et Noix** (4 rue du Parc-Royal), next to the Carnavalet Museum, (teenagers adore the place) open daily 11 a.m.–midnight. If you're off to the races at the Longchamp course in the Bois de Boulogne, there's no way you can miss the two-toque restaurant of **La Grande Cascade,** that fabled pavilion where, of course, you're not going to take the children for lunch, but where, of course, you'll take them for the chic-est ice cream or lemonade of their lives after the races, in the spring, on a sunny day, on that be-flowered terrace. Sun. tea at 4:30 is another tradition you might like to enjoy indoors in that lovely rococo salon. For other Sun. suggestions, see Day-trips outside Paris, Poissy, Saint-Germain-en-Laye, Versailles.

BABY FOOD You'll find this in grocery stores, supermarkets, pharmacies. The pharmacies are the safest bet because they almost always carry baby food. Baby food is *aliments bebe*. Junior foods are *aliments junior*. Bledina makes both kinds. The jars come in 100- (3 mos. up), 130- (5 mos. up) and 200-gram (8 mos. up) Junior size. Bledina also makes bottled juices: *carottes-oranges* (carrots and orange), *jus de legumes* (vegetable juice—carrots, tomatoes, celery, beets, lemon juice); *pommes-ananas* (apple, pineapple, orange, and apricot); *pruneaux-raisins* (prunes and grape juice), *raisins-framboises* (grape, raspberry, cherry juice). Before 5 months this should be given in two, three, four demitasse spoonfuls mixed with one-half-cup water; after 5 months in diluted form; great straight for older children.

Bledina 100-gram baby foods come in these varieties: *Artichauts,* artichokes; *carottes,* carrots; *epinards,* spinach; *haricots verts,* string beans; *jambon-carottes,* ham and carrots; *boeuf,* beef; *veau,* veal; *abricots-pommes,* apricots and apples; *coings-pommes,* quince and apple; *oranges-bananes,* orange-banana; *pommes-bananes,* apple-banana; *pommes-framboises,* apple-raspberry.

In the 130-gram jars, you get: *Legumes assortis,* mixed vegetables; *puree de legumes,* mixed vegetable puree; *legumes-boeuf-foie de veau,* vegetables-beef-calves' liver; *legumes-cervelle,* vegetables and calves brains; *legumes verts-agneau,* green vegetables and lamb; *legumes-viande,* vegetables and meat; *poulet-semoule,* chicken and semolina; *legumes au filet de sole,* vegetables and fillet of sole.

In the Junior foods: *Carottes-riz de Provence,* carrots and rice with tomato sauce; *boeuf-jardiniere,* beef and vegetables; *jambon-boeuf-legumes,* ham, beef, and vegetables; *jardiniere au jambon,* vegetables and ham; *timbale a la viande aux oeufs,* meat with eggs; *poulet au riz,* chicken and rice: *colin mousseline,* a potato mixture: *dessert aux abricots,* apricot pudding; *peches au jus de fruits,* peaches and fruit juice.

Then there is the line of Guigoz Baby Foods: six bottled fruit juices; three dozen kinds of baby and junior foods in 100-, 150-, and 200-gram jars; powdered milks are *Lait Partiellement Ecreme en Poudre Sucre* (blue tin, with cream and sugar added, for babies from birth-4 mos.) *Lait en Poudre Sucre Complet* (pinky-orange tin, regular powdered milk, sugar added, for babies from 4 mos. on); *Guigolac Partiel* (green band, for babies from birth-4 mos. who need extra nourishment); *Guigolac Complet* (red band, slightly less rich mixture for babies up to 4 mos. in need of extra nourishment). Guigoz makes *Cereales Biberon* (bottle cereals) in five varieties which you mix with the bottle up to 3 months, and five *Cereales Bouillie* enriched with honey *(au miel)* that you mix with boiling water for babies from 4 months on; *Cereales Enrichie* with protein added to dilute in the bottle; *Cereales Lactee* to thicken in boiling water for children from 4 months on; *Cereales Printaniere* to add to soup or to thicken by boiling water for children from 4 months on.

Gallia makes *Lait Partiellement Ecreme en Poudre Sucre* and *Galliazyme Aliment Lacte Pour Nourissons* (milk food for extra nourishment)—for the newborn. Also *Galliasec Lait en Poudre Sucre* for older babies; this is known as Gallia Orange because it comes in orange box (*not* because orange juice is added). Farigallia cereals *(Farine Instantee)* dissolve instantly in the bottle, for newborn up to 4 months. For the 4-month-old set, Farigallia *fruits* and *legumes* are cereal-fruit, cereal-vegetable mixtures that can be fed in bottles. Farigallia cereals to be fed by the spoon are marked *2e Age;* of these, there is yellow-boxed cereal, cereal (milk added) in a blue box called *Farigallia Lactee,* and red-boxed cereal for Junior eaters. Gallia puts out a line of Baby-Gallia foods in 75-gram and 100-gram jars; Baby-Gallia 130-gram jars of vegetables, vegetables and meat (more vegetables), meat and vegetables (more meat), and fish and vegetables; Junior vegetables, and meat and vegetables, come in 185-gram jars.

Some Heinz and Gerber baby foods and English baby foods around, but in no great variety or quantity. *Lait Gloria,* condensed milk without cream or sugar (non sucre, non ecreme), is sold in grocery stores everywhere. Biscuits, cookies, rusks, and other baby cereals are obtainable in supermarkets, groceries, and pharmacies.

▶ **Note:** In **Paris,** for baby food, clothes, everything for little babies, try **Hygiene de la Femme et de L'Enfant** (155 av. Victor-Hugo, VI); In **Nice,** try **Pharmacie de France** (13 blvd. Gambetta) for baby food and milk supplies; English spoken; personnel most helpful.

Bebe-Confort, a baby-equipment manufacturer, has an incredible gadget—*Chauffe-Biberon Auto-Chauffant* (bottle warmer self-heating unit)—that works without wires, batteries, or gas. Except for having to buy a lot of little heating pots to take along, this bottle warmer is a fabulous gadget; equally good for heating coffee or soup; available at **Au Printemps** (see Shopping) or most stores stocking the Bebe-Confort line.

A baby bottle is a *biberon;* check to see if yours are the same size as the Bebe-Confort ones.

DIAPERS AND LAUNDRY The word for diaper is *couche* (pronounced coosh). Disposable diapers are *couches cellulose;* they come precut or in a roll which you cut yourself. Disposables, called *couches-nuit,* are nighttime diapers, heavier than daytime ones. Most pharmacies have Mono-Couches Polive, (the cut-your-own type) or packages of 20 Couches-Nuit Polive. And, of course, Chux, Luvs, Pampers or their absorbent feel-alikes, look alikes.

Vima (cut-it-yourself), Vima, Orlys, and Lilia are other disposable brands that you can find in pharmacies, but more easily at a department store such as Au Printemps (also has splendid cloth diapers). In **Paris,** both cloth and disposables are at these everything-for-the-under-2 shops: **Premaman** (branches everywhere) and **Prenatal** (branches at 4 rue Havre, IX; 39 rue Rivoli, IV; 67 rue Sevres, VII; 3 av. General-Leclerc, XIV). The **American Diaper Service** (109 rue Tahere, St.-Cloud) in the suburbs of Paris will deliver 600 disposable diapers at one time. They don't speak English. **Bebelange** (14 rue Maine, XIV) delivers sterilized cloth diapers. Service is two times a week; 24-hour answering service. You can also arrange for the service at any of the Prenatal baby stores.

▶ **Note:** The French have an extraordinary range of plastic waterproof baby pants. Those with pockets for disposable diapers are called *porte-couches;* I'd recommend those made by Bebe-Confort, called *Culotte Miracle.* Waterproof training pants are called *couches-culottes.* Bebe-Confort's *plasticouche a doublure Rhovyl* (plastic pants with Rhovyl lining) keep a baby's bottom dry and free from rashes; plain and fancy styles; some have adjustable belts *(couches avec ceinture reglable).*

BABY EQUIPMENT FOR HIRE In **Paris, Bebelange** (see Diapers) will rent a baby scale. **Mag-Bel** (111 blvd. Magenta, X) will lend you free a clean second-hand stroller or baby carriage if you are staying a week or less, can produce a note from your hotel or Embassy saying that you are a good risk, and leave a (returnable) deposit. Carriages and strollers can be hired from Etablissements Rambaud (58 rue Pompe, XV) Simpler and better, I think, are the **"Maisons de Troc"** where you can pick up used—but in good-as-new condition—*outgrown children's clothes, baby carriages* (landaus), *strollers* (poussettes), *car seats* (sieges d'auto), *carrycots* (lits pliants), *toys, games, books, bicycles, skis, ice-skates.* At these exchanges you can buy everything at 50% discount or even less. Highly recommended are: **Baby Troc** (16 rue de Magdebourg, XVI) for children 6 mos.–7 years, clothes and equipment; closed Mon. a.m. **Maman Troc** (6 bis—the same as #6A—rue Fourcroy, XVII) for boys and girls from infancy to 16; clothes and equipment; closed Sat. **La Marelle** (21–23 galerie Vivienne, II) for boys and girls up to 14, specializing in sports clothes and equipment as well as strollers, bicycles, prams, playpens (parcs) closed Mon. and Sat. a.m. **Tante Amelie** (2 rue Pierre-Haret, IX) which specializes in party clothes for girls, infants to 18 years; baby beds, strollers, prams, playpens etc.; and antique christening dresses, some extremely costly but fine value; closed Mon. and Sat.

EMERGENCIES MADE EASY Excellent hospitals, English-speaking doctors, medical facilities, and drugstores (pharmacies) that specialize in medicines and prescriptions rather than merchandise competitive with the local supermarket.

Pharmacies open at night? About five dozen of them—your concierge or the Commissariat de Police in your arrondissement will provide the name of the one nearest you, as well as those open Sun. and holidays. A pharmacy open 24 hours: **Pharmacie Les Champs** at 84 Champs–Elysees, VIII, Tel: (01) 562–02–41. English-speaking personnel, American brands (high-priced though they may be), to be found at: **British and American Pharmacy** (1 rue Auber); **Pharmacie Grignon** (2 rue Duphot); **Pharmacie du Rond Point** (49 bis av. Franklin-Roosevelt); **Pharmacie des Champs-Elysees** (62 av. Champs-Elysees); **Pharmacie Caron** (24 rue de la Paix); **Roberts & Co.** (5 rue Paix); **Pharmacie Anglo-American** (37 av. Marceau); and, of course, at **Le Drugstore** des Champs-Elysees at 133 Champs-Elysees, VIII; Tel: (01) 723–5434.

A prescription from your doctor at home will have to be rewritten by a French doctor unless, in Paris, you go to the **American Hospital** (63 blvd. Victor-Hugo, Neuilly; Tel: (01) 747–5300) for advice about American medicines and their substitutes. The outpatient dept. is open daily except Sat. afternoon and Sun. from 9 a.m.–noon and from 2:30 p.m.–5 p.m. American staff; French specialists available on appointment; dental clinic by appointment also. The **British Hospital** (48 rue de Villiers, Levallois; Tel: (01) 757–2410) is also useful to know about.

The best thing to do in an emergency is to call the **Police-Secours.** In Paris, just dial 17. By radio-telephone, SAMU (Service Aide Medicale d'Urgence) will be alerted and will send an ambulance to take you to the nearest hospital.

If the situation is not desperate, just hysterical, in Paris, you can call any time, day or night, emergency doctors to rush to your side: **S.O.S. Medecins** (Tel: (01) 337–7777); **S.O.S. 92** (Tel: (01) 603–7755) has few doctors affiliated with its organization, but can supply emergency doctors and nurses, also; **AUMP** (Association pour les Urgences Medicales de Paris et de la Region Parisienne) (Tel: (01) 828–4004) performs the same services. Each member organization of this trio has medically equipped vehicles prepared to administer whatever aid you need.

S.O.S. Infirmieres operates an Emergency Clinic (Tel: (01) 278–2441). To summon an ambulance, call **Ambulances de la Ville de Paris** (Tel: (01) 887–2750). Helicopter and air-ambulance services, under the aegis of the Police and Fire Department, operate as a public service for SAMU. In Paris, just dial 18 (17 is for an ambulance). **S.O.S. Dentistes** (Tel: (01) 337–5100) provide emergency service for aching teeth and other dental problems. There are hospitals that specialize in the care and treatment of the following:

For your child's *severe burns,* call **Trousseau Hospital** (Tel: (01) 346–1390; for adults, call **Saint-Antoine Hospital** (Tel: (01) 344–3333), **Cochin Hospital** (Tel: (01) 329–2121), or **Foch Hospital** (01) 772–9191). If your child's finger gets mashed by a slammed door, or for other *severe injuries to fingers and hands,* call **Boucicaut Hospital** (Tel: (01) 554–9292). **Hospital Marmottan** (Tel: (01)574–0004) and **Hospital Sainte-Anne** (Tel: (01) 581–1120) specialize in *drug-related problems.* If your child eats your cortisone cream or other cases of incipient *poisoning,* the toxicological department of **Fernand-Widal Hospital** ((01) 205–2441) is the best set up to deal with it. If you need a *trained nurse* or a *companion with nursing experience,* call **La Bouee** (114 Champs-Elysees, VIII; Tel: (01) 359–7460) during business hours; closed Sat. (See also Babysitters, Magic Family Helpers). If Annie's ankle goes on the blink, or Tommy's slipped disc makes walking difficult, *crutches* (bequilles), *wheelchairs* (fauteuils roulants) etc. can be rented or bought at **Le Material Para-Medical** (1 rue Danton, VI; Tel: (01)326–7500).

For doctors recommended by the American community, call the **American Embassy** (2 av. Gabriel; Tel: (01) 296–1202/261–8075). Or the American Consular offices in **Bordeaux** (22 Cours du Marechal Foch, 33080; Tel: Bordeaux 56/52–65–95); in **Lyons** (7 Quai General Sarrail, 6954 Lyons; Tel: Lyons 824–68–49); in **Marseilles** (9 rue Armeny 13006; Tel: Marseilles 54–92–00); in **Strasbourg** (15 ave. d'Alsace, 67082 Strasbourg; Tel: Strasbourg (88) 35–31–04/05/06)

▶ **Note:** *French medication is often given by the rectal rather than the oral route; suppositories often more favored than pills; before the doctor writes his prescription, alert him to your children's preference.*

MAGIC FAMILY HELPERS—BABYSITTERS AND CHILDREN'S COMPANIONS In spite of the Government's war on "Franglais" (see Language), babysitter is as firmly established in the French vocabulary as le Drugstore, le weekend, le cowboy. Air France will cable ahead to any of its 138 offices to alert a babysitter to meet a passenger on arrival. The Paris Welcome Information Office (7 rue Balzac) has telex connections with all the other Welcome Information Offices and can cable ahead for a babysitter to meet you on arrival or at your hotel.

Babysitters in **Paris:** English-speaking babysitters and children's companions if not available at one of the organizations listed below will be available at another; charges often go up after midnight; for some you must pay carfare (for a cab if the Metro has closed). **Institut Catholique** (21 rue d'Assas), call the day before. Students for the day or the night. **Kid Service** (17 rue Moliere); **Luderic** (11 rue Petrarque, XVI); **Nurse Service** (33 rue Fortuny, XVII); **Maison Service** (10 rue Mesnil, XVI) which has trained nurses and nurses aides (minimum 4 hrs.), as well as laundresses, cooks, maids, housekeepers; **Baby Club** (15 rue Saussier-Leroy, XVII); **Baby Sitting** (18 rue Tronchet, VIII); **Gard d'Enfants** 3 rue de Duras, VIII).

Sitters for older children and student companions for older children? Contact the **American College in Paris** (31 ave. Bosquet, VII) or the **Medical Students Association** (105 blvd. de l'Hopital, XIII). If you like your babysitter/child's companion, you may be able to arrange for him/her to travel with you. However, for an *au pair* girl as a traveling companion and mother's helper, you are required to provide room and board, weekly "pocket money," and some time off. Of the number of organizations who can help you find a young helper, the most efficient by reputation is **Accueil Familial des Jeunes Etrangers** (23 rue du Cherche-Midi, VI) who can supply you with girls of all nationalities, as can **Alliance Francaise** (34 rue de Fleurus, VI), only open 1:30 p.m.–6 p.m.; and **L'Arche** (7 rue de Bargue, XV). **Relations Internationales** (100 rue Saint-Lazare, IX) specializes in young American, Australian, and English girls; **Inter Sejours** (4 rue de Parme, IX) in English girls; **Mission Catholique Hollandaise** (39 rue du Doctor Heulim, XVII) in Dutch girls; **Foyer Porta** (14 rue Pierre-Demours, XVII) in German girls; **Entreaide Allemande** (42 ave. George V, VIII) Austrian and German girls. All agencies closed Sat. and all would appreciate your inquiries a month or two in advance. For a domestic, practical nurse, dressmaker, chauffeur, children's companion, someone to help do anything from packing to cooking, just call **Madame Service** (76 rue Lemercier).

Department store babysitting services? At **Au Printemps** (see Shopping), I was told that the hostesses in the Welcome Room (main floor, new building) would look after babies and little children. **Si Tu Veux** (68 galerie Vivienne, II; Tel: (01) 260–5997) a luxurious shop for boys and girls' clothing up to 8 years, toys, games, furniture for children, books, has a free supervised playroom (garderie d'enfants) where you can park your beloved for one half-hour while you whisk off to that heavenly shopping area of the galerie Vivienne. Closed Mon.

At **De Gaulle** and **Orly** Airports call on the Airport Hostess (on duty 24 hrs.) at the Welcome Sevice to find out about the nursery (supervised), play area for older children, shower room, and clothes-pressing service.

Outside of Paris, ask your hotel concierge.

In **Nice,** call **Azur Baby-Sitter** (Residence Negresco; Tel: 88–83–09) for babysitters or **Euro Nurses Express** (29 rue Pastorelli; Tel: 80–10–30) for nurses and children's companions. In **Lyon,** call **Azur Baby-Sitter** (18 rue Waldeck-Rousseau; Tel: 24–87–62).

MAGIC FAMILY HELPERS—CHILDREN'S COUNTRY CLUB In **Vichy,** the queen of spas and the monarch of watering places, **Le Parc du Soleil** is, in essence, a glorious country club (daytime facilities only) for unaccompanied youngsters from 4–14; staffed with supervisor for every seven children in the 4–7 group, and supervisor for every 12 children in the 8–14 group. English-speaking interpreter on hand at all times, but—and this seems very sensible to me—foreign children are encouraged to learn French by practice with other children. The daily cost (1:30 p.m.–sunset, fully supervised) is a trifle. Children can have tennis, swimming lessons; teenagers have access to the Allier River, with boats, canoes; stable, mini-golf, and basketball. Also driving lessons in mini-cars (tested by a real uniformed policeman); lovely gardens; swimming pool. On rainy days, indoor activities. Children's bar and cafe; special events (plays, costume parties, folk dancing, magician, and a sand-castle building championship). Open daily from June 1 to back-to-school time. Grownups are welcome. If you don't come with your child, do provide pocket money for refreshments!

MAGIC FAMILY HELPERS—NURSERIES Throughout France you will find *Pouponnieres,* nurseries that care for children under the age of 3, day and night, sometimes on a daily basis, sometimes for prolonged stays. There are two kinds: One is for children who are underweight, delicate, or in need of particular care. These, under rigid state supervision, are like baby sanitariums; many are large and institutional, located by the sea or the Alps, but some are modern and charming chalets where motherly care is considered as important as medical surveillance. Besides these *Pouponnieres a caractere sanitaire,* there are *Pouponnieres a caractere social.*

Of the Pouponnieres for healthy children, some are simply child-care centers, but some serve as orphanages or adoption centers, or for the convenience of unwed or working mothers. As nurseries operating as a child-care convenience are often small, working mothers and traveling families have become tolerant of having their babies and toddlers looked after in the company of less fortunate children; all the children are medically healthy (otherwise they would be in the *Pouponnieres for les enfants debiles*). Almost all are inexpensive. The atmosphere is orderly, brisk, hospital-like, and toddlers are accorded rational, polite treatment in the somewhat detached manner of most hospital nurses. This care seemed to me lacking in warmth, but French mothers are more concerned with cleanliness, orderly supervision, and fair prices. The small, privately run Pouponnieres are friendlier, but it is often difficult to find accommodation in these. Naturally, you have to make advance arrangements in all these types. English is rarely spoken, but this will not bother infants or toddlers.

MAGIC FAMILY HELPER—KINDERGARTENS The French call them *ecoles maternelles* (motherly schools) or *jardinieres*. For information about registering your child at a public school kindergarten in **Paris,** get in touch with the **Rectorat** (Service E. 10, 37 rue Jacob VI). Elsewhere, consult the **Service des Ecoles** at the Mairie (Town Hall) wherever you happen to be.

English-speaking kindergartens? Among the English-speaking and bilingual schools are: The best for short-term visitors, the **UN Nursery school** (14 rue Louis-David, XVI); children from 3–6. **Ecole Active Bilingue** (39 av. Bourdonnais, VII), branches at 6 av. Van Dyck, VIII; 141 av. Suffren, VII. The **Pershing Hall School** (68 rue d'Auteuil, XVI). **American School of Paris** (41 rue Pasteur, St.-Cloud 92), in the suburbs. The **English School of Paris** (38 quai Ecluse, 78 Croissy-sur-Seine) has an excellent kindergarten. **Marymount International School** (72 blvd. Saussaye, Neuilly) a day and boarding school, from kindergarten through high-school.

French private kindergartens and schools, for girls, all Catholic, all with kindergartens: **Cours d'Hulst** (21 rue Varenne, VII), from age 3–22. **Institut Science Ste.-Therese** (1 rue Boinod, XVIII). **Cours Victor-Hugo** (8 rue St.-Germain-Godard, VII). Ages 4–20. For boys only, all Catholic, all with kindergartens: **College Stanislas** (22 rue Notre-Dame-des-Champs, VI). Ages 3–18. **Ecole St.-Louis-de-Gonzague** (12 rue Franklin, VII). Ages 5–18. **Ecole Secondaire St.-Jean-de-Passy** (72 rue Raynouard, XVI). Ages 4–19.

There are a few non-Catholic (referred to as nonconfessional), coeducational private French schools: **L'Ecole en Marche** 9103 av. Ternes, XVII). Ages 3–6. **Ecole Alsacienne** (109 rue Notre-Dame-des-Champs, VIII). Ages 4–19. This school specializes in languages.

In **Cannes,** I've heard good things about the **International Riviera School** (rue Grant-Milne, 06400).

MAGIC FAMILY HELPERS—INSTRUCTION For children's artistic activities no city provides a greater variety than **Paris.**

ADAC (L'Association pour le Developpement de l'Animation Culturelle) has over 200 *ateliers* or workshops to introduce children as well as grownups to the joys of theater, painting, drama, marionettes, dance, music, bookbinding (relieure), photography, cooking, pottery, manual arts, sports, mosaic-work, handcrafts, judo, chess, magic, gymnastics, architecture and more, more, more as well as just simple supervised playtime. For a modest annual membership fee, you can join ADAC which will give you access to all the ateliers on a list that will be sent to you if you telephone or just stop by for it at ADAC headquarters at 27 quai de la Tournelle, Paris V; Tel: (01) 326–1354. (Closed Sat.) Fees, dates, times differ for all the ateliers. (Courses starred offered on an hourly, one-half-day basis): **Association Culturelle Maine-Montparnasse** (8 rue du Commandant-Rene-Mouchotte, XIV); **Atelier Anne Felix** (26 rue Pradier, XIX); ***Atelier des Enfants** (Centre Georges-Pompidou, III); **Atelier Noor-Zade-Brenner** (130 rue de Vaugirard, XV); ***Les Bleus-Blancs** (18 rue Sibuet, XII); **Caree Silvia Montfort** (Centre d'Action Culturelle de Paris) at 106 rue Brancion, XV; **Centre de Loisirs et de Jeux Organises** (CLEJO) at 26 rue Charles-Fourier, XIII; ***Ecole Industrielle et Commerciale Saint-Nicolas** (92 rue de Vaugirard, VI); **Interclub 17** (47 rue de Saussure, XVII); ***Les Loges de la Cuisine** (8 rue de Nevers, VI); **Musee des Arts Decoratifs** (107 rue de Rivoli, I); ***Musee des Monuments Francais** (Palais de Chaillot, aile de Paris, place du Trocadero, XVI); **Musee de l'Affice** (18 rue de Paradis, X); ***Orange Bleue-Bargue Bleue** (48 rue Bargue, XV).

There are many others. New ateliers spring up as others relocate or close. Get the current ADAC list, and if you can specify your needs, the ADAC can advise you even better.

▶ **Note:** There are workshops whose fees are extremely low to which you are entitled to go once you have paid your modest membership to ADAC and whose sessions are open to all ages on a short-term as well as a monthly basis; also more expensive, more formal courses are available.

Dance and music lessons for children? There is a huge choice of classes in ballet, rhythmic movement, tap (claquettes), ethnic dance offered for children from classical to modern, African and gymnastic. For information, consult the **Federation Francaise de la Danse** (12 rue Saint-Germain-l'Auxerrois, I) and **Federation Internationale de Danse a Claquettes** (177 faubourg Poissonniere, IX), an organization that also knows everything about dance and tap-dancing. Many of the courses and lessons available are on a monthly or three-monthly basis. But you and your children can enjoy an hour's instruction at **Claquettes Sylvia Dorame** (Salle Pleyel, 252 faubourg Saint-Honore, VIII) or **Centre de Danse de Paris,** at the same address. Your teenagers might like to check out **Centre de Danse du Marais** (41 rue du Temple, IV) with an American Tex-Mex restaurant called The Studio, with Tues., Thurs., Fri. performances by various groups.

The American Center for Students and Artists (261 blvd. Raspail, XIV) devotes Weds. for children's classes in dance, art, photography, magic, guitar, mime, yoga, but is mostly concerned with fun, instruction and entertainment for your teenagers and older students. **Janine Solane** (1 bis rue Grande-Chaumiere, VI) for children as young as 3 on up, teachers who speak English; operates during the school year. **Ballet** classes at your hotel or house? Telephone 35–981–02 for both children's and adult instruction. Tout Paris knows about **Baraduc** (55 bis rue Ponthieu, VIII), for ballroom dancing and the lastest in pop rock; superb for children from about 10 on.

Also highly recommended are: **Academie de Guitare** (42 rue Descartes, V) **Les Musigrains** (11 rue Saint-Louis-en-l'Ile, IV); and **Jeunesses Musicales de France** (1 ave. Delcasse, VIII). **CNAM** (Centre Nationale d'Animation Musicale; 55 rue de Varenne, VII) can tell you the best places both for children and adults to learn how to play any musical instrument, and all about music schools and conservatories for music and dance in Paris and the rest of France. For short-term visitors this is also good to know about as you can visit classes often.

If your son is 8–14, a choirboy in your church or thinking of becoming one, he can hear or join groups of boy sopranos by getting in touch with: **Manecanterie des Petits Chanteurs de Saint-Laurent** (20 rue du Terrage, X); **Groupe Choral de Saint-Germain-des-Pres** (5 rue de l'Abbaye, VI); **Federation des Petits Chanteurs** (1 rue Garanciere, VI).

Classes, courses and demonstrations of classic French cuisine, pastry, summer cooking, regional cooking, candy making, nouvelle cuisine, party cooking? Ongoing, in French, with English translations, classes at **Ecole de Cuisine La Varenna** (34 rue Saint-Dominique, VII) have super demonstrations by local chefs of their specialties. Reserve ahead for these, and also for afternoon demonstrations at **Le Cordon Bleu** (24 rue de Champ-de-Mars, VII) **Marie-Blanche de Broglie Cooking School** (18 ave. de la Motte Picquet, VII) presided over by Princess Marie-Blanche de Broglie, also offers weekend and week-long demonstration and participation classes at its Normandy chateau. Other cooking classes in France are offered that include lodging and meals, and often regional tours in Bordeaux, Burgundy, Loire, Normandy, Perigord, Provence, Quercy. The FGTO can fill you in on all the delicious details.

Photography, electronics, modeling, astronomy, and other arts and professions? **Club des Jeunes Techniciens** (292 rue St.-Martin, III), sponsored by the National Conservatory of Arts and Professions, offers library and workshops for young people from 15 up. Open Thurs., Sat.

French lessons for children? By far the best and most conveniently arranged instruction is at **Alliance Francaise** (101 blvd. Raspail VI).

Recommended schools, chosen for their surrounding parklands, facilities, and for their high standards of education and administration are:

Ecole des Roches (Verneuil-sur-Avre, Cleres 76, Normandy) a boarding school for Catholic and Protestant boys from 8–18. The French equivalent of St. Paul's or Pomfret. Swimming pool, woodworking, ironwork, languages, photography, boxing, fencing, riding; good sports equipment and food; good vibrations all around. **Ecole Secondaire Suger** (Sente de l'Abbe-Suger, Vaucresson 92) is a girls' private boarding school; coeducational kindergarten; ages up to 18; goes in for the cultural and artistic activities. A bit bleak, it seems to me. **Chateau de l'Andelle** (St.-Denis-le-Thiboult, Ry 76, near Rouen) takes boys 11–18 as boarders in a chateau; hikes, riding, swimming, botany club, and the credo of a healthy mind in a healthy body (which always signals to me that there aren't many luxuries around). **Institution France-Afrique** (Dormans 51, Marne) charming grounds and buildings. Designed to educate children of France's overseas consular staff, it takes both boys and girls with about the same quota of token black students most of our boarding schools are required to take. The facilities for all sports are excellent. **Ecole du Montcel** (Jouy-en-Josas 78) in a vast park in the Valley of la Bievre, is a boarding school for boys 9–19. With religious instruction but not a church school, run on the lines of an English school with an accent on physical education, the honor system, and the right attitude. Summer course, combining classes with sports and relaxation. **Ecole Pascal** (33 blvd. Lannes, XVI) is both a day and boarding school for boys from 9–18 offering excellent language courses; extras such as judo, fencing, piano. The annex at Morzine (Haute-Savoie) takes boys and girls from kindergarten to third grade. During school vacations, it becomes a ski resort for children of all ages; a modern chalet in a pine-forested setting; accommodates 48 children; for information get in touch with the Ecole Pascal, Sejours de Vacances (Route du Telepherique d'Avoriaz, Morzine 74).

Ski schools and beach clubs for children: Every winter and summer ski resort has its ski school for children 4–12, at which children learn how to ski by organized play in groups that meet in the morning for classes. Lunch is either brought or provided at the site. There are usually afternoon classes as well. Classes may be conducted in French, or may be polylingual. Fees are modest.

In July and Aug. beach resorts usually have beach clubs for children. Clubs are organized by families experienced in making summer fun for children, and equipment includes jungle gyms, trampolines, swings, slides, with the family-organizers arranging games, volleyball, supervised swimming competitions. Activities begin around 10 a.m. with a break for lunch, then they resume in the afternoon until about 5 p.m. Children are grouped according to their ages, and the age range is generally 4–12. Clubs are conducted in French, but children speaking other languages adapt quickly. Fees by the week or month are modest, and there are reductions if more than one child in a family is enrolled. Concierges at pensions and hotels can make arrangements for you, as can the local syndicat d'initiative, or tourist office. On the **Cote d'Amour** which stretches along the southern coast of Brittany, from Saint-Nazaire to the rocky coast of Le Croisic, beaches are among the best and most varied in Europe, and beach clubs line the water from **Le Pouliguen** to **Pornichet,** with **La Baule** as a paradise for children among many smaller paradisiacal resorts in Brittany.

MAGIC FAMILY HELPERS—CHILDREN'S TOURS AND TRANSPORT

You can get satisfactory interpreter guides from the **Bureau Officiel de Placement des Guides et Interpretes** (50 rue de Malte, XI; Tel: (01) 355–4405) open 8:30 a.m.–11 a.m. Closed weekends.

In **Paris,** the pleasing and pleasantly cooperative **Inside France** (15 rue l'Arcade, VIII; Tel: 265–6116), comprised of car-borne French students, will pick up children or the whole family and show them the sights in and around Paris. Reasonable fees that vary according to what you want to see and for how long. Equally good for excursions to Versailles, Fontainebleau, Chartres, or Normandy. Chauffeur-driven cars with English-speaking chauffeurs who can be entrusted to drive your children hither and yon are available from **Massey** (37 rue des Acacias, XVII); **Wladimir Reine Executive Car-Carey** (2 passage Dombasle, XV). If you have a car and just need a chauffeur to take your child here and there, contact **Chauffeurs Services** (132 rue d'Assas, VI). If you would like your child met at the airport, taken to the station, met at the airport and entertained until you arrive, or any of the emergencies coped with that involve children boarding or getting off planes when you can't be there yourself, contact **La Marelle** (70 blvd. de Port-Royal, V). Their ''Enfant Vole'' service is terrific and reasonably priced.

Museum tours for children, with French commentary, dealing mostly with the applied arts, are organized by the **Musees des Arts Decoratifs** (Pavillon de Marsan 107, rue de Rivoli) for ages 5–8, 8–12, interesting even if one doesn't speak French; parents can't accompany their children; tours last about an hour, start every Wed., Oct. to May, at 2:30 p.m. The **Caisse Nationale des Monuments Historiques** (62 rue St. Antoine, IV) has history–of–art and walking tours for children 10–14; they may be accompanied by parents; you can also pick up maps and information.

Architectural and art tours for teenagers are sponsored by **L'Art Pour Tous** (24 ave. Duquesne, VII); **Service de Museologie et d'Action Culturelle** (9 quai Anatole-France, VII) has a program of tours for children and grown-ups and can sign you on if you give them a fortnight's notice. **Promenades et Conferences de Paris** (62 rue Jean-Jacques Rousseau, I) organizes visits for children 10 and older to visit workshops of glassblowers, bakeries, artificial flowermakers and many, many more places of interest, with groups of young enthusiasts setting off frequently. **Anne Ferrand** (Tel: (01) 270–71–62), *on dit,* arranges children's tours of special interest.

MAGIC FAMILY HELPERS—PERSONALIZED SERVICES A magician who eats fire, saws his wife in two, and puts on a two-hour performance for a reasonable fee can be hired from **Mystag** (31 rue des Prairies, XX; Tel: 3668026). You can hire a poet from the **Club des Poetes** (30 ru de Bourgogne, VII; Tel: (01) 705–0603) to read or recite whatever you'd like to hear. If the children don't speak French, they may become hysterical with laughter or be fascinated, depending on the way the poet appears to them, so be warned. However, this can be a moving experience. For a children's ***birthday party*** or a celebration involving children, clowns, films, marionettists, magicians, guitarists, musicians, whatever you'd like, can be organized for you by that great magic family helper **Luderic** (20 rue Petrarque, XVI; Tel: (01)553–9393) which seems to me much easier than calling separate entertainers and organizing it all on your own. Closed Sat. For a catalogue of party favors, games, toys, decorations, records, wigs, paper costumes, paper lanterns, confetti, masks, paper hats, more than 10,000 party-time accessories listed and illustrated in *Guide du Spectacle et des Fetes,* free for the asking, call or write **L'Amicale-Comptoir des Articles de Fetes** (32 rue des Vignoles, XX; Tel: (01) 370–2100). You can mail-order everything or go in person to collect items for a fabulous *fete accomplie!* Closed Mon. Another shop, more expensive, for party favors, invitations, decorations, hats etc. is **La Boutique Verte** (83 rue du Ranelagh, XVI; Tel: (01) 527–3527), also closed Mon. Ice cream and sherbets packed in dry ice from **La Sorbetiere** (12 rue Gustave-Courbet, XII; Tel: (01) 553–5959) and a cake that tastes home-made, cupcakes or other goodies from **Le Moule a Gateaux** (lll rue Mouffetard, V; Tel: (01) 331–8047) or other of its branches (closed Mon., but open Sun. a.m.) where you can also buy ice cream and sherbets, and, voila, a party in Paris!

Doll's hospital, cosmetic treatment for teddy bears and other toys? Visit **La Clinique des Poupees** (22 rue Gerbert, XV); in case the toy is beyond repair, there is a consoling selection of new toys. Rag dolls that have fallen into the bath, a teddy who has lost an ear or an eye or been left out in the rain can be rejuvenated and fixed up good-as-new at **Bobin-Madroux** (27, rue de la Vanne, 92120 Monrouge; Tel: (01) 657–6400) in the outskirts of Paris. Closed Sat. **A La Poupee Merveilleuse** (9 rue du Temple, IX; Tel: (01)272–6346) repairs antique and new dolls, and is a fun place to visit as it also sells all sorts of party favors, masks, decorations. **Aux Poupees d'Atours** (18 rue des Feuillantines, V; Tel: (01)329–3126) not only sells dolls' clothes, but will make clothes-to-order for antique or modern dolls; also this is a place where you can find enchanting folk and fairy-tale costumes for children to buy: princesses and pierrots for ages 2–10, ready-made, or your darling's dream costume made to order.

To ***rent clothes:*** Paris is particularly good when it comes to artistic costumes and dresses from the latest Paris collections. Boys' and men's riding and evening clothes from **Jean-Jacques** (36 rue de Buci, VI; Tel: (01) 354–2556), pleasant, courteous service; reasonable prices. For *fancy-dress costumes* for carnivals, parties, and masquerades, go to **Sommier** (3 passage Brady, X; Tel: (01) 208–2701); costumes for children are next door at #4. Another fine choice is **Les Costumes de Paris** (21 bis rue Victor-Masse, IX; Tel: (01) 878–4102) but you have to reserve eight days ahead and plonk down a deposit equal to the value of the costume. *Wigs and historical costumes* also from **S.E.P. Vachet** (17 rue Rodier, IX; Tel: (01) 878–7085) and **Pontet** (24 rue Cadet, IX; Tel: (01) 824–4804). For costumes to buy, **Aux Poupees d'Atours** (18 rue des Feuillantines, V; Tel: (01) 329–3126). If you've been invited unexpectedly to some grand dinner dance or reception and no one has the proper clothes to wear, Mummy and teenage daughters can rent something wonderful at **Eugenie Boiserie** (32 rue Vignon, IX; Tel: (01) 742–4371) which is closed Mon. and requires a deposit; or at **Troc de Truc** (37 rue du Colisee, VIII; Tel: (01) 562–0800) open 2 p.m.–7:30 p.m. The men of the family can find what they need at **Beral** (2 rue Caulaincourt, XVIII; Tel: (01)387–7237) or at **Au Cor de Chasse** (40 rue de Buci, VI; Tel: (01) 326–5189) or **Jean-Jacques** (Previously mentioned).

Skis and ski boots for the entire family can be rented at **Drugsport au Bivouac** (226 rue La Fayette, X; Tel: (01) 607–1258); skis, ski boots, ski suits and everything you need for camping can be rented at **Dethy** (20 place des Vosges, IV; Tel: (01) 272–2067) **Locations** (rentals) in a wonderful location! If you need to rent a car to go off camping in, hie yourself to **Car Away** (60 rue de Caen, 92400 Courbevoie; Tel: (01) 334–1581) or **Dreamcar** (6 ave. du Bas-Meudon, 92130 Issy-les-Moulineaux; Tel: (01) 736–0175). (To rent a *balloon, bicycle* or *sailboat,* see Fun Trips; to rent *a swimming pool at night,* see Fun and Games). *Helicopter rental?* See Information, Transportation.

If you would like someone to take ***telephone messages for you while you are away,*** call **Abonnes Absents** (Tel: (01) 742–3940), on call 24 hour. If you want a ***telephone wake-up call,*** call (01) 463–7111. To relay a cable in English, see Information, Telephones.

If you need something Xeroxed, or a secretary, conference room, telex machine, your answer is **Ibos** (15 ave. Victor-Hugo, XVI; Tel: (01) 502–1800).

If your child is grumpy without his video game or you'd like to ***rent a toy*** or a ***movie projector,*** head for the nearest *ludothèque,* the best of which is **Ludotheque du Luxembourg** (15 rue du Regard, VI; Tel: (01) 544–6756), open Tues. and Thurs. from 4 p.m.–6:30 p.m., Wed. from 10:30 a.m.–6:30 p.m., Fri., 3:30 p.m.–7 p.m., Sat., 2 p.m.–5 p.m. More than 1500 games and toys are available for rent for little more than a token annual fee and tiny rental fees. Well worth paying the membership fee even if you rent only a single game, and certainly if you'd like to rent a movie projector. You can rent golden oldies, silent, sound or today's video-cassettes at **Cinematheque Goulard** (47 rue d'Amsterdam, VIII; Tel: (01) 874–2408); **Cinematheque de Paris** (68 blvd. Malesherbes, VIII; Tel: (01) 522–2236); **Franfilmdis** (70 rue de Ponthieu, VIII; Tel: (01) 572–4461). To rent or buy camera, video equipment, sound equipment, your best bet is **Ghilbert** (62 rue Chardon-Lagache, XVI; Tel: (01) 288–3646) and **Shop-Photo Montparnasse** (33 rue du Commandant-Mouchotte, XIV; Tel: (01) 320–1535).

If you don't want to waste time getting your child's hair or your own shampooed, cut, blown dry, or it's rainy and you don't want to go out, call **S.O.S. Coiffure** (Tel: (01) 874–33–16 or (01) 280–48–01 nights and holidays) who will come to you day, night, holidays. If you feel frazzled, they will also do good make-ups. **At Home** (Tel: (01) 208–2828) will also come to your place and do shampoos, blow-drys and manicures, at any hour, day or night. A great time-saver, and just about the same price as going off to **Carita** (11 faubourg Saint-Honoré, VIII; Tel: (01) 265–79–00) who does fantastic things for men's, women's and children's hair, as well as make-up, massages, pedicures and manicures.

Messenger services? Errands? Of course, there are people to *faire les courses* for you and your family, to run errands, to pick up and deliver packages. Listed in the telephone directory under *Coursiers,* and better chosen in your area as they are cheaper and faster that way; most are closed on Sat. **Courses Service** (16–18 rue Abel, XII; Tel: (01) 344–6735) is open Sat. a.m. however. For Mon.–Fri. service, contact **Allo-Courses** (8 rue Blanches, IX; Tel: (01) 281–4444); **Inter-Courses** (147 rue Lamarck, XVIII; Tel: (01) 627–6058); **Liaison-Courses** (178 rue Legendre, XVII; Tel: (01) 229–2233).

Open until 1 a.m. or 2 a.m. for almost anything you need or crave: a suitcase, magazine, toy, baby bottle, perfume, liquor, tobacco, pharmaceuticals, food to eat or take out, other night owls? The **Drugstores** at 133 Champs-Elysees, VIII; 1 ave. Matignon, VIII; 6 blvd. des Capucines, IX; 149 blvd. Saint-Germain, VI. (See Food).

MAGIC FAMILY HELPERS—YOUR HOTEL CONCIERGE Never underestimate the power of a concierge. Provided they like you and approve of your style, provided that you graciously give them a monetary offering on your arrival at the hotel to take care of routine matters, and give them extra for any special services, a concierge can and will do almost anything for you that otherwise would be seemingly impossible—reservations and seats, for instance, on trains, planes or at restaurants and theaters that are said to be booked solid, or resolve almost any emergency situation requiring efficiency and resourcefulness.

HOLIDAYS FOR CHILDREN ON THEIR OWN A children's hotel for guests 5–13, a home away from home, an international vacation resort for boys and girls, and a study center, **Chateau de Bellevue** (49940 Le Bourg-d'Ire, Maine-et-Loire; Tel: Segre (41) 92–51–42) is a chateau hotel about 32 miles W of Angers, a few miles away from the little village of Segre just off the main Paris-La Baule route. Open in late Mar. through mid-Apr. for the spring vacation, and from June–early Sept., stays can be arranged for two to three weeks, with or without courses in French, English, mathematics (at all levels of expertise). If so desired, children can be escorted to Le Bourg-d'Ire from Paris. Summer excursions are optional and cost a bit extra, but I'd recommend you let your child sign up for all of them; the added expense is well worth it. Riding, swimming, and other sports are the major activities. A doctor is always on call if needed. Rooms are pleasantly furnished; the food is good. During the school year, the directors, M. and Mme. Collet, may be reached at 45380 La Chapelle-Saint-Mesmin, Loiret, 21 route d'Orleans; Tel: Orleans (38) 88–21–16, the address of the school-time headquarters of Chateau de Bellevue, which also accommodates 40 boys and girls 5–13. Both branches are qualified as *Homes d'Enfants. Homes d'Enfants,* under the aegis of the **Association Nationale des Homes d'Enfants de**

France (Boite Postale 30, 66120 Font-Romeu; Tel: (68) 30–08–61), fulfills state requirements of health, safety, cleanliness, supervision that should be nerve-soothing to most parents; *homes d'enfants* are private homes away from home, combining family atmosphere, school courses and holiday activities for children no younger than 3 and no older than 14, with age groups accommodated generally 3–10, 4–10, 6–12. Many are open all year; all are co-ed. Some are large, grand, and luxurious as is the abovementioned Chateau de Bellevue, others are like chalets and, obviously, some are more charming and attractive than others. In the **Paris** area, there's **La Source** (95300 Pontoise, Val-d'Oise; 40 rue des Patis; Tel: (163) 031–03–56), for a dozen boys and girls 4–10; open all year, lessons on site or in town for older children; pleasant grounds for outdoor play. **La Pelouse** (Montgeron 91230, Seine-et-Oise; 140 ave. de la Republique; Tel: 903–50–80) scrupulously clean, is near the forest of Senart, with riding, tennis, swimming; language lessons; accommodation for 45 children 5–16. In the suburb of Yvelines, **Chante-Clair** (Chanteloup-les-Vignes, 78570 Andresy; 41 rue de l'Hautil; Tel: 974–65–03) accommodates 21 children 3–10. Also in Yvelines, and really close to Paris, **La Maison de la Foret** (Saint-Germain-en-Laye 78100; 138 ave. Foch; Tel: (01)451–14–26) takes an international group of 45 children 5–12. Near **Maux,** in the Seine-et-Marne area, **La Grimpette** (Monthyon 77122; Tel: 436–21–46) houses 18 children 6–14; coaches children who are behind in their classes or who have to make-up work, who are dyslexic or who have other reading disabilities. Teaching is bilingual; languages; special courses; lessons can also be done in local schools; swimming and riding in summer. In **Megeve,** the Haute Savoie, **Home Montjoie** (Tel: Megeve 21 01 56) takes 30 boys and girls 3–11; well-equipped, small, charming establishment; swimming, ice-skating, riding, hiking, and excursions in summer, marvelous skiing in winter, with a ski school; children can be met in Paris; open Christmas, Easter, July–mid Sept. Also in Megeve, about 20 miles from Chamonix is **La Colombiere** (Tel: Megeve 21–10–96) with excellent facilities including heated pool, craft workshop, gym, riding, skiing, and lessons if required by its 40 guests, 6–12. Nearby, **Le Petit Poucet** (Tel: Megeve 21–20–44) offers skating, skiing, swimming for its co-ed sledders aged 3–13; open during the Christmas vacation only! In the zip code area of **Morzine** 74110, also in the High Savoy peaks, are at least five *homes d'enfants:* **Le Roitelet, Le Petit Prince, Les Alouettes, Les Avettes,** and **Les Fauvettes.** Special flights from Paris weekly during vacation periods; children can also be met at Geneva airport. Open Christmas, Easter, and June–end Oct. In **Villard-de-Lans,** in the Isere region, **Les Boules de Neige** (Tel: Villard-de Lans 95–13–51) for children 6–12; **Les Capucines** (Tel: Villard-de-Lans 95–10–90) for children 3–10; **Les Lutins** (Tel: Villard-de-Lans 95–15–37) for filles and garcons 6–14; **Le Nid Alpin et Super-Nid** (Tel: Villard-de-Lans 95–10–11) accommodating 53 fledglings 4–14 are among 9 excellent facilities. In the Eastern Pyrenees, **Azurea** (Font-Romeu 66120; Tel: Font-Romeu 30–08–69) is a fabulous recreation center for children 4–14. Another **Le Petit Poucet** (Val-d'Isere 73150, Savoie) for 22 Tom Thumbs and Thumbelinas aged 3–12. *By the seaside,* **Les Caplains** (Tourlaville 50110, Manche; Sur La Rade; Tel: (33) 53–370–3) takes 16 boys and girls 4–13 year round for bilingual classes in English and German; children can be met in Paris. **La Poussiniere** (Cabourg 14390; Tel: (93)76–72–92) accommodates 40 children 3–10 in Calvados country. **Les Marmousets** (62155 Merlimont-Plage; Tel: (21)94–72–53) right on the Avenue de la Plage, about two miles from **Touquet,** is open all year. The local **Syndicat d'Initiative** can give you information, as can the **Association Nationale des Homes d'Enfants de France,** or you can write directly to these establishments for illustrated brochures.

Special: **La Marelle** (70 blvd. de Port-Royal, Paris V; Tel: (01) 707–50–20) is an organization which, for a moderate enrollment fee, arranges for children from 4–17 to be the guests of French families for weekends or during the school vacation, and to take part in a French family's life-style, often with children their own age.

CHILDREN'S CAMPS The French, ever practical, don't build special plants for camps, but use the facilities of schools, chalets, pensions, hotels during Christmas, Easter, and summer vacations. Children are generally grouped according to age. Instruction in languages, art, and sports are usually part of the program. Whether these are optional or not, the atmosphere at these *Vacances* and *Sejours* is no more restrictive than that of an American camp, with adequate free time for diversions, and many excursions. Some are now making strong bids for American guests, and at these the roster will be chiefly English-speaking. Many U.S. families, however, are sending their children to primarily French-speaking vacation centers. For children who just aren't "good at languages," an American-majority camp is recommended.

It will cost you much more to send your 12-and-older offspring to Europe as a member of an American group who will live in France for one to six weeks, with an American camp roster, and a staff of French- and European-born bilingual counselors than it will to send them to a French camp. Expensiveness is not always a measure of superior quality—and in this instance my opinion is that you should carefully consider what you want for your children before laying out the extra money. The advantages of sending your child to a French camp with French-speaking children and staff are numerous; they will learn French, gain insight into themselves from seeing themselves through foreign eyes and, comparing foreign culture and customs with their own, they will begin to see for themselves what it is they really like and want, and have confidence in themselves and honesty in their own relationships. They will not be deprived of all English. Directions will be given in English at first. They will be absolutely safe and well-instructed in all sports. After a week of frustration, impatience, even agony at being reduced to speaking no better than a year-old baby, after some loneliness and lack of self-reinforcement, then, as a reward, will come the exquisite joy of communication and rapport, a new self-pride, and a new self-image. On the other hand, children in American-filled camps or travel-study groups pick up some French and acquire the names of new foods, persons, places and a superficial sophistication. They talk knowingly of European trifles but, in my opinion, with few exceptions they come back knowing very little of Europe or themselves. If you want your child to have the richer inner rewards then I think you should unquestionably choose a French camp.

OCCAJ—Organisation Centrale des Camps et Activites de Jeunesse (9 rue de Vienne, 75008 Paris; Tel: (01) 294–21–21) open Mon.–Fri. 9 a.m.–6 p.m., is a central organization for camps under government aegis; branches and associated groups in many French cities can also inform you about the many camps. Prices are a terrific value for what you get, but summertime crowds may give you the feeling of traveling second or third class. I do recommend OCCAJ camps and vacation villages for inexpensive enjoyment of winter and spring-time skiing, riding, sailing, tennis. At **Trebeurden,** near the Tresmeur beach on the North Coast, children 6–10 can have the pleasures both of the ''Poney-Club'' de Tregastel (Poney is Franglais for pony) and of seaside fun. This is an Easter offering, as is the ''Poney Club'' at **Saint-Fargeau,** where the children, 6–12, live in a chateau, not far from **Auxerre,** in the Yonne region. At **Autrans** (Isere), the OCCAJ vacation village is open for children 6–12, during both Christmas and Easter vacations for winter sports and creative workshops. There's an equestrian farm, **Saint-Jean-la-Vetre** (Loire) open during Easter for ten-day holidays for 13–15-year-olds, and for 6–17-year-olds during Christmas and Easter for seven-to-ten-day sejours at **Chamberet** (Correze) about 22 miles from **Uzerche;** not only riding, but also nature study, creative workshops, sports, and much more. Sailing for the 14–17-year group over Easter at Trebeurden, and at **Bendor** island, near the port of Bandol, in the Mediterranean. Riding and tennis for 13–15s in **Provence,** over Easter; Christmastime and Easter skiing at Autrans, in the Olympic village for all levels of expertise, also tennis and judo; skiing also for 15–17s at **Tende** in the Alpes-Maritimes; and in the southern Alps, for 13–17s, at **La Foux d'Allos;** at **Mont de Lans** (Isere) for 14–17s; at **Mouthe** (Jura) for 15–17s, at **Fond de France** (Isere) for 8–13s, and at **La Toussuire** (Savoie) for 8–12s; at **Arvieux** (Hautes-Alpes) for 6–14s; at **La Chapelle d'Abondance** (Haute Savoie) for 6–13s. Skiing in the High Alps at **St. Michel de Chaillol** for 6–12s at Christmastime, February and Easter; also at **Le Sappey** (Isere) on the Massif of Chartreuse about nine miles from Grenoble, where the slopes are for beginners and tiny ones; for 6–12s at Uriage/Chamrousse (Isere) over Christmas and Easter for 6–12s. If your 6–12s vaguely know how to ski, they'll have more fun at St. Michel de Chaillol where, of course, they can also be entertained with workshops, costume parties, games.

The family vacation centers are OK, but not to be compared with the joys of **Le Club Mediterranee,** but they're bargains, and there's always a lot to be said for that. **Association Jeunesse et Avenir** (35, rue Saint-Georges, Paris IX; Tel: (01) 526–52–62) organizes vacations during the winter for the young, 6–20, and in summer, for those 6–16. For over 17s, **STAJ (Service Technique pour les Activites de Jeunesse)** located at 27 rue du Chateau-d'Eau, Paris X; Tel: (01) 208–56–63) does the same thing, with special mountaineering, caving, workshop courses, sports and crafts of all kinds. Both these organizations are closed Sat.

Young naturalists and volcanophiles of all ages eager to see volcanic sites can go on organized weekend trips to the Auvergne, to summer camps near volcanic sites in Italy. All you or they have to do is to contact **L'Association des Jeunes Naturalistes Francais Volcans** (47 rue de Saussure, Paris XVII; Tel: (01) 227–68–81)

The **CCCS,** or Le Centre de Cooperation Culturelle et Sociale (26 rue Notre-Dame-des-Victoires, Paris II; Tel: (01) 261–53–84), is a national educational association concerned with international exchanges of friendship and goodwill, with provincial delegations in Strasbourg, Bordeaux, Bourges, and Rennes; it has several centers also in America (see French Cultural counselor in "Information"). Contact them at least six months in advance. The CCCS vacation programs, blessed by the French Ministry of Education, the Commissariat General au Tourisme, and the State-Secretariat concerned with Youth and Sports, are an excellent value. Campers are primarily French-speaking, but English and German parents are now discovering these too. Instructor for every eight to ten children; expert instruction in sports; the types of children, variety of activities, and locales of these camps are pleasingly varied. Younger campers and girls in houses; tent accommodations, if necessary, are reserved for older boys—and I'll use the abbreviation TOB (Tents Older Boys) to designate these.

Camps for children 6–12 (all are open in July and Aug. unless otherwise noted): For 6–9-year-olds a vacation center in **Anglet** near Biarritz; housing in a large park-encircled villa; excursions into the Basque country and beach areas. A similar setup nearby but closer to the beach for the 10–12-year-olds; more space for football and other games; TOB; this one not operative in Aug. Other swimmingly successful sites: For 6–12s, **St.-Jacut-de-la-Mer** on the Emerald Coast of Brittany; right on the sea, with many beaches, canoeing, lots of excursions around the Breton countryside; TOB. No tents and not such an accent on canoeing at **Plestin-les-Greves** and **Plouha,** both also on the coast of Brittany. Open only in Aug., **Locmariaquer** in the Quiberon region; TOB. Other camps: In green and wooded mountains at **Meaudre** (Isere); a comfortable pension to live in; swimming pool; all mountain activities; excursions. A similar center at **Autrans.** A much more beautiful choice is **Notre-Dame-de-Bellecombe** enchantingly situated in an alpine village overlooking the Val d'Arly; excursions around Chamonix; heavenly Lake Annecy. Between Thonon and Chatel, in the **Valley of Abundance**, young vacationers take over during July and Aug.; forests and flowered alpine meadows. Another chalet at **Sallanches;** lake bathing; excursions around Chamonix; TOB. Twin enclaves at **Morzine** (for the 6–9s) and at **Essert-la-Pierre** (for the 10–12s); alpine meadows and forests; swimming pool; lodging in a chalet at Morzine; open only in July. At Essert-la-Pierre, two neighboring chalets to live in; swimming pool at Morzine to use; excursions to the Lake Geneva and the Valley of Abundance, and other lakes and valleys. Other centers at **Vars, St.-Lary** (in the Pyrenees), in the Valley of the Rhone, or at **St. Vaury.**

CCCS seems to plan exactly the sort of entertainment each age group prefers. For 13–14s, activities satisfy the need for autonomy, initiative, and working with a group. At **Buis-les-Baronnes** excursions cover the ancient and the medieval; swimming pool; camping out; 13–14s also explore the Valley of Abundance, staying at a chalet called Les Ecureuils overlooking a waterfall. For this age group too the CCCS offers opportunities for living with English families—in **Maidstone, Wembley,** and **Botley** for example—with sports and excursions. CCCS also offers (to those with a working knowledge of German) a stay in the Tyrolean village of **Brandenburg** (Austria) in a mountain chalet; excursions; swimming. Similar programs in Germany. Also in the Italian village of **Massa** in a magnificent setting of pine forests on the edge of the Tyrrhenian sea; activities based on exploring the artistic and natural richness of the countryside; well seasoned with swimming and other sports.

The possibilities for *15–18-year-olds* proffered by CCCS are imaginative and extended variations of the themes offered to younger age groups. Living in tents on the edge of the bay of **Mont-St.-Michel** and learning to sail. Mountaineering courses at **Villeneuve.** Sailing and riding at **Logonna/Menez-Hom** in Brittany at Brest. Cruising on the Rhine. Language-study trips in Germany, England, and Ireland. A vacation in **Massa** and **Venice** or **Rome.**

In winter, there are ***skiing*** vacations for the *6–13-year-olds* at **Meadre** (Isere), at **La Chapelle-en-Vercors,** at **Aulon,** and at **Thun** (Switzerland), Christmas–Feb., for beginning and intermediate skiers. For *13–15-year-olds,* skiing for beginners and intermediate talents at Autran; for intermediate and good skiers at Morzine and at Avoriaz; all with skating too. For the *15-to-18 group,* intermediate and good skiers can head for Morzine or **Clavieres** (Italy); beginning and intermediate skiers can go to **Reuti** (Switzerland).

FUAJ, The **Federation Unie des Auberges de Jeunesse** (6 rue Mesnil, 75116, Paris; Tel: (01) 261–84–03)—the French youth hostelling association—offers cultural, sporting, and do-what-you-like holidays to card-carrying children over 14. The **Touring Club de France-Jeunesse** (14 ave. de la Grande Armee, Paris XVI; Tel: (01) 380–68–

58) has a modest membership fee that entitles you to an incredible array of activities, mostly outdoor, for the young, 6–16-years, during the school year, with over 220 vacation possibilities organized in France and Europe for all members of the family. The TCdFJ runs many camps either with specialized activities such as sailing or skiing, or multi-sport and entertainment centers. A small membership fee enrolls your child as a prospective camper, and then it's up to you to select the camp best-suited to his or her requirements and your budget. Great values here; as with the parent organization, the **Touring Club de France,** same address and telephone. If you are interested in the possibility of a camp in a certain area, or a specific type of camp, or the possibility of your child living with a French family or with a group of young people lodged in a chateau, combining language courses and sports, contact the **CIDJ** (Centre de Documentation pour la Jeunesse, 101 quai Branly, Paris XV; Tel: (01) 566–40–20) and the offices of local **Syndicats Initiatives,** a list of which you can get from the FGTO. For more about the CIDJ, see Information.

Students Abroad, Inc. (179 North Fulton Ave., Mt. Vernon, NY 10550; Tel: (914) 699–8335; or in the south at 2378 Northeast 28th St., Lighthouse Point, FL 33064; Tel: (305) 941–3889) offers programs that include study, arts, and sports during July and Aug. for high school students. Some programs include travel and family stay; others are essentially campout trips, traveling by van, sleeping in sleeping bags, hiking, skiing, etc. They offer summer ski and tennis camps in **Val d'Isere/Tignes;** also many other suggestions for similar programs in Austria, Italy, and Switzerland combined with French segments. Longtime experience with teenagers; well-traveled, professional, mature group leaders.

*For **pony and horse-loving children 6–18,*** France offers an exceptionally interesting variety of *vacances a cheval* organized by members of the **Association Nationale pour le Tourisme Equestre et l'Equitation de Loisirs** (15 rue de Bruxelles, 75009 Paris; Tel: (01) 281–42–82). On request, ANTE will send you a catalogue.

Poney Club de Saligny (36 Grande-Rue Saligny 89100 Sens; Tel: (86) 65–75–13) in **Burgundy** is for ages 7–18. **Societe Hippique de Saint-Malo** (38 rue du Chapitre, 35400 Saint-Malo; Tel: (99)81–20–34) offers youngsters 11–16 riding holidays in **Brittany. Le Cavalier d'Herault** (Villeneuvette 34800 Clermont-l'Herault; Tel: (67) 96–04–83) in the **south of France,** reachable by train from Montpellier or Beziers, is for kids 12 up. In various sections of **Ile-de-France,** in the **Paris** area, there's the **Centre Equestre** (77116 Recloses; Tel: (Recloses 424–21–10), daily riding, longer holidays for children 12 up. **Poney Club de la Biberonne** (24 rue des Trois Villes, Thieux, 77230 Dammartin-en-Goele; Tel: Thieux 026–06–39) also in the Seine-et-Marne area, is for ages 6–12. **Poney Club d'Evry** (Ferme de Trousseau Grand-Bourg 91130 Ris Orangis; Tel: Grand-Bourg 079–38–13) has riding activities for ages 6–18. In the Val-d'Oise area, also in Ile-de-France, riding activities are offered to 9–18-year-olds at **Centre Equestre du Moulin de Giez,** Viarmes, 95270 Luzarches; Tel: Viarmes 470–40–99); and for over 13s at **Gens Europeene Equestre** (95560 Montsoult Maffliers; Tel: Monsoult 473–9030 (day) and 473–9083 (eve.). **La Joyette Poney Club de Compiegne,** RN 31, route de Soissons, 60200 Compiegne; Tel: Compiegne 441–63–63) in the Oise region of **Picardy;** in the Somme area of **Picardy, Foyer Rural de Ribemont Mericourt** (Ribemont-sur-Ancre 80113; Tel: (22) 42–60–20; office at 101 ave. de l'Hippodrome, 8000 Amiens; Tel: (22) 92–02–23) offers children 8–13 daily riding. There's the **Centre Hippique de Mougins** (Chemin de Font, Curault, 06250 Mougins; Tel: (93) 45–75–81) for children 6–10 and children 10 up for weekends.

Special: *For boys only,* in the Rhone Alpes in the area of Isere, **Club Vercours** (38250 Villard-de-Lans; Tel: (76) 95–13–07; office in Paris at 32 rue Eugene-Flachat, XVII; Tel: (01) 380–63–40) organizes riding holidays for boys 11–15 with instruction and trekking during July and Aug. Also daily riding, tennis, bicycle touring, speleology, archery, ice skating, swimming, football, mountaineering, camping; riding excursions through the Ardeche also, with bicycle touring, mountaineering, and speleology, for *boys and girls 14–17.*

CASTLES AND OTHER HAPPY FAMILY ACCOMMODATIONS *Vive la France* for coming up with the nonprofit **Federation Nationale des Logis de France** (26 rue d'Artois, Paris VIII; Tel: 225–38–18), dedicated to maintaining high standards at reasonable prices; they have hand-picked almost 3000 hostelries, ranging from provincial chateaux to ultramodern motels that have agreed to provide good service, adequate plumbing, parking space, telephone, room service, central heating or electric radiators, good laundry service, and delicious food (including regional specialties) for reasonable all-inclusive daily rates. Send for their full list or a free abridged edition from the FGTO in New York. Also free from FGTO is *Relais de Campagne,* a list (with tiny photos) of manor houses, abbeys, and inns singled out for their table, restful country ambience, decor and comfort, quality of service, charm, scenery, and cachet; invaluable for motorists. They will also send you free price lists of hotels and inns. A more comprehensive guide to *Relais et Chateaux,* with illustrations in color is available from David B. Mitchell & Co. 200 Madison Ave., New York, NY 10016; Tel: (212) 696–1323.

The **Association des Chateaux-Hotels de France** has gone a long way to adapt chateaux and stately homes to modern standards of comfort while preserving their historic character. Offerings run to the elegant, fairytale, dreamlike; accommodations are attractive to sumptuous, and prices spiral accordingly.

Chateaux-Accueil is an association of private chateaux-owners, some of whom rent space for conventions, weddings, coming-out parties, receptions in their salons; and all of whom will be delighted to have you and your family stay with them in the chateau itself in *chambres d'hotes,* or in outbuildings or guest-houses or apartments on the estate (adjoining or close to the chateau) and also with free access to the chateau gardens and parklike surrounds. (These accommodations are referred to as *sejours en maisons individuelles ou appartement.)* General information, an illustrated booklet, a list, information about these chateaux for your possible sejours in *chambres d'hotes* can be had by contacting Madame La Vicomtesse de Bonneval, La Presidente de l'Association Chateaux-Accueil, Chateau de Thaumiers, Thaumiers, 18210 Charenton-du-Cher. General information, illustrated booklet, a list and information about stays in individual guest-houses, outbuildings or apartments can be obtained from Madame Illich, La Secretaire Generale de l'Association "Chateaux-Accueil," Chateau de Memillon, Saint-Maur-sur-le-Loire, 28800 Bonneval.

During the summer, you might like to stay in a maison individuelle for three to four persons at **Chateau de la Roche Pichemer** (Saint-Ouen-des-Vallon, 53150 Montsurs) in the **Maine-Loire Valley** area, with tennis and fishing in the chateau park, a forest, golf nearby; a historic monument, there is, alas only one chambre d'hote available. English spoken. Right in the *Chateaux de la Loire touring area,* near Azay-le-Rideau, Saumur, Usse, Langeais, you can stay in the 17th-18th-century **Manoir de Montour** (Beaumont-en-Veron, 37420 Avoine; Tel: (47) 58–43–76), a former cocoonery with mulberry trees still there; a swimming pool, tennis, nearby riding, skating, fishing, golf. There are two individual houses for two to four, also two *chambres d'hote* for reasonable rates and a charming atmosphere; open all year. A divinely beautiful castle-chateau with turrets, and a chapel by a lake in the middle of a forest, **Chateau de la Verriere** (Oizon 18700 Aubigny-sur-Neve) has an apartment and three double rooms, with tennis, swimming, canoeing, riding, nature walks in the chateau forest; open June–mid-Oct;, also an inn, **La Maison d'Helene,** open from 11 a.m.–6 p.m. in the chateau park, fine for lunch; closed Tues. You can stay in five *chambres d'hotes* or in two suites accommodating three to four persons chez Madame La Vicomtesse de Bonneval at **Chateau de Thaumiers** (see above for address) with its turrets, vineyards; nearby swimming pool, tennis, riding.

Formal, elegant, impressive, with manicured lawns and topiary trees, with two apartments for one to three persons, **Chateau de la Bourbansais** (3570 Pleuueneuc; Tel: (99) 45–20–42) is an extremely impressive manor-house in **Brittany,** the former residence of members of the Brittany parliament; tennis, hunting, fishing; English spoken; expensive. Far cozier and more charming, to my way of thinking, would be a stay in any of seven *chambres d'hote* at **Chateau de Recagnac** (24440 Beaumont), a 14th-15th-century country house with a tour near the **Valley of the Dordogne,** in the midst of the Bessede forest in **Perigord.** Not only is your breakfast included, but you can order your meals here as you will for a reasonable surcharge. Open all year except Nov. and Feb. Tennis, a swimming pool, riding nearby. Very special, not on any list, and only by writing months ahead, and asking for prices and the possibility of accommodations, *chambre d'hote* or in an individual guest-house, would it be possible for you to stay at **Chateau de Boisset les Prevanches** (27120 Pacy-sur-Eure) in **Normandy,** about an hour's drive from Giverny. Your host, Comte Hugues de Bonardi, is a world traveler, a writer, a gourmet, and knows the countryside and its people as few others do. Don't telephone; write. It would be a good idea to suggest ahead in your letter what you would like to spend; think on the affluent side, and perhaps you will find yourself in an enchanting surrounding in an enchanting part of France in the company of an extraordinary host.

There are also independent Chateaux-Hotels and inns with atmospheric charm located in the countryside. A list of these is available from **Chateaux-Hotels Independants et Hostelleries d'Atmosphere** (c/o Hostellerie du Chateau de Pray, Boite Postale 146, 37401 Amboise-Cedex). If you relish country-quiet and the luxe life in the heart of touristic regions in which you and your family can be surrounded with forested parks from which you can, if you like, venture forth to see the sights, then **Les Grandes Etapes Francaises** (140 rue de Bellevile, 75020 Paris) is your source of information for the following rich-cream group of deluxe homes away from home, not all as expensive as you might imagine, and one, **Le Mas d'Artigny,** with private swimming pools hedged around outside a dozen or so rooms; plus cottages, as well as more customary accommodations. **Chateau d'Esclimont** (28700 Saint-Symphorien-le-Chateau), **Chateau d'Artigny** (37250 Montbazon), **Domaine de Beauvois** (37230 Luynes), **Le Prieure, Chenehutte-les-Tuffeaux** (49350 Gennes), **Le Mas d'Artigny** (06570 Saint-Paul-de-Vence), **Le Vieux Castillon,** Castillon du Gard (30210 Remoulins), and **Chateau d'Isenbourg** (68250 Rouffach).

To rent an apartment in Paris or a house on the French Riviera or in Brittany—fully furnished, with or without maid service, and within easy walking distance of the beach (a 3–6-year-old's definition of "easy" walking distance is ⅛–¼ of a mile, and I'm ashamed to say it's mine too)—just write to the FGTO in New York, or, better yet, to **France Hebergement** (18 ave. Carnot, 75107 Paris), including dates of stay and number of people. Stays of 3 days to 3 months can be arranged for approximately $10–$25 a person per night. *Bed-and-breakfast accommodations* can also be arranged, and these I do know are not only economical, but also, inevitably, an adventure. There's always something about a B&B stay that children remember, something that delights them, strikes them as pleasurable, odd, hysterically funny, surprising, or something dreadful that is even more fun to joke about that grown-ups rarely understand. French friends tell me that inexpensive studios to 5-room duplexes can be rented through **Flatotel International** (43 rue St. Charles, 75015 Paris). Prices per day they quoted, with a week-minimum, certainly sounded very good to me, particularly a duplex that could sleep 7 (!) for the price of less than what another friend had just paid for a double at Disneyworld. It's possibly cheaper to rent a villa than stay in a hotel, but look into the maid, linen, and marketing situation before you leap. Independent real-estate operators in America advertise that they specialize in short-term leases of furnished flats and villas along the Cote d'Azur. I recommend that you deal only with the agents recommended by the French government; it is more concerned about the happiness of your stay than a real-estate firm. The advantage of a good agent is that he will go beyond villa rental to help you with renting cars or boats or bicycles and tell you where the tennis courts are. Don't be snobbish about good, solid, middle-class "family resorts." In a place where practically all the summer families are European or English, you'll find far fewer tourist traps and gyppo outfits. Chic resorts are always nearby, and you can make use of their facilities. In a familial resort everyone knows if you are a summer resident to be befriended or a transient tripper who won't miss that extra surcharge.

It really isn't any harder to rent a villa than to buy a train ticket or rent a car. Everything down to the last egg whisk you need comes with the house except linens (French vacationers rent these from the local laundry; reserve in advance by letter). Refrigerators almost always come with villas, but check on this. Prices vary according to location and season.

From June to Sept., summer rentals abound, and the **Syndicat d'Initiative,** an organization not only for touristic information, but serving also as a local chamber of commerce, of every village and town, always has a list of properties, from single rooms to houses sleeping at least four, to rent, a list they will send you on request if an international reply coupon accompanies your inquiry. The FGTO can supply you with the addresses of any Syndicat d'Initiative anywhere. If, for instance, you are interested in thatched cottages or timber farmhouses near with five or six bedrooms in **Veules-les-Roses,** a summer beach resort on the N coast of Normandy, Dieppe, write to the **Syndicat d'Initiative** (rue Victor-Hugo, 76980 Veules-les-Roses), enclosing an international reply coupon. Rentals are reasonable, at least 25% lower in June or Sept. when many summer visitors haven't arrived or have left; other months, 50% less. This rent-scale formula holds more or less, throughout France.

You'll find the FGTO in New York very helpful about villas for rent or sale in the **Languedoc-Roussillon** region—the "New Riviera" the government has been refashioning along a 100-mile stretch of almost uninterrupted Mediterranean beach. Local agencies deal in seaside bungalows. You might want to take advantage of the low rates before these resorts really get developed.

For really unusual self-catering vacations contact **Gites de France** (35 rue Godot-de-Mauroy, Paris 90). A gite is a private, self-contained unit, usually part of an individual's home, or sometimes, a separate lodging on an individual's private property—a gatehouse, let's say, on a country estate. Owners of a country gite voluntarily apply for accreditation through the **Federation National des Gites Ruraux de France,** which subsequently rates the gite as standard, comfortable or deluxe. A standard gite passes basic requirements for sanitation and cleanliness and is equipped with at least a shower, lavatory and wash basin, but no kitchen facilities. A comfortable gite has, in addition, kitchen equipment and more attractive furnishings. A deluxe gite has superior kitchen equipment, snazzier antiques or modern decor, and a courtyard garden. Prices for deluxe gites are astonishingly inexpensive; your deluxe gite might comprise one-two bedrooms, bathroom, kitchen-dining area and garden, and the price you might pay for it for a two-week stay could be the same as the price for one day at deluxe hotel. You have to send for a guide at least four months in advance, or ask the FGTO to get one for you. Then, after studying the guide, indicate your preference as well as stating how many there are of you looking for accommodation, and request a contract. You have to prepay the whole amount of your rent in advance in American dollars. An agency such as Eurocar can arrange for rural car rentals. Most gite owners don't speak English. But if these conditions don't faze you, a gite is a terrific bargain. *French Farm and Village Holiday Guide* is available from Bradt Enterprises, 95 Harvey Street, Cambridge, MA 02140. Or you can obtain full details about 3000 gites and chambres d'hote (rooms available within someone else's house) from the **Federation Nationale des Gites Ruraux** (35 rue Godot-de-Mauroy, Paris 75009; Tel: (01) 742–25–43).

OCCAJ (Association de Vacances Familiales, 9 rue de Vienne, 75008 Paris: Tel: (01) 294–21–21) has set up 24 inexpensive family vacation villages on sites remarkable for scenic beauty at which all sports and activities have been provided, along with entertainment centers, babysitting and entertainment facilities for children 3 months–10, 12, or 13 years and discotheques and youth centers for teenagers. These packaged deals are cheap, comfortable, convenient, and come in summer and winter choices. Catalogue of *Vacances Familiales* on request (See also Children's Camps).

▶ **Note:** If you are considering renting a furnished house, villa, or an apartment, and have three or four children, you will be told that finding anything for a *famille nombreuse* is extremely difficult—a tactful way of saying that everyone is wary about the wear and tear three or four children might inflict on the furniture and walls. Everyone knows that American children have the run of the house (unlike French children who stay in their own rooms and come into the living room only when invited). When writing to real-estate agents or placing an ad in the local papers, it's advisable to be vague and specify simply a large house or apartment.

All reservations for chateaux and hotels should be confirmed in writing if you are traveling with young children. The hotels I have listed are all delighted to have children. I have never had any problems traveling with my children anywhere in France, but I am told that chateaux, relais, and some hotels can be arbitrary and difficult about accepting children if prior reservations have not been made. So book ahead, reply prepaid, whenever possible.

▶ **Important:** Please avail yourself of a red *Michelin* guide, which will update you far better than I can about hotels in Paris and France which take credit cards, and which ones they take. Many hotels you'd think would take credit cards, don't, and vice versa.

Hotels in **Paris:** Be prepared for giant differences in the decor and comforts of a hotel costing only a little less than another. Be prepared in inexpensive hotels for dark, depressing rooms facing a court; reject these at once and demand a bright room facing the street. You never know in Paris what the reduced rates for children are going to be or whether smaller hotels are even going to accept children unless you have made all arrangements in advance. You have to ask to be sure if there will be a direct-dial telephone, a radio, a TV, if such are your pleasures. As a single parent, you might delight as well in elevators like fragile gilded cages, enormous bathtubs, marble-topped furniture as found at the **Hotel Montalembert** (3 rue Montalembert, VII). A sunny room with French windows opening onto a sliver of a balcony looking down on the rue Bac, good restaurant downstairs; small, and beloved by *Time* correspondents and me, for its convenience, comfort, and simplicity, children's beds in the same room as yours. A classic, four-star hotel, and a hop and a skip from the Pont Royal, the Tuileries, the Louvre. Many people think it's very expensive for what you get, or don't get—and I agree with their logic—I like it mostly for its ambience and location. But if you are married, try **Le Marais** area instead which is great fun for families. (See below).

Small hotels with charm? **L'Hotel** (13 rue des Beaux Arts, VI) has 25 rooms and a few suites accommodating up to five persons, Venetian marble bathrooms, free beds for children in the same room as yours, air-conditioning, fresh flowers everywhere, elegant decor, fountain and talking parrot in the dining room, which is gardenlike even in gray weather; a four-star joy for you as well as your fortunate girl or boy. Reserve several months in advance. As you also should do for the **Esmeralda** (4 rue St. Julien-le-Pauvre, V). Ask for one of its three rooms with beamed ceiling and private bath. Other of the 19 rooms may be dim, dingy, dark, tiny, or with a view of Notre Dame or the little park of St.-Julien-le-Pauvre; there is a sauna, and the tiny, cheap rooms are really cheap. No credit cards. Note the rooms you like in this two-star jolie-laide. **Hotel l'Abbaye Saint-Germain** (10 rue Cassette, VI) has main floor rooms that look out onto an arbored courtyard with a flower garden; marble baths in this enchanting 18th-century convent renovated and transformed with charming rooms, greenery, charm and calm; no credit cards; no dining room but many restaurants nearby. A three-star hotel, as in **Hotel Saints-Peres** (65 rue des Saints-Peres VI), surrounded with art galleries, restaurants of all kinds and that pleasant, easy, do-as-you-please Saint-Germain ambience. **Angleterre** (44 rue Jacob, VI) is a classic small hotel with 31 rooms, a patio garden where you can have breakfast in the summer, TV on request and for an extra tiny sum; four high-ceilinged suites; great bathrooms, and some wonderfully large rooms. No credit cards for this three-star hotel, and you'd better reserve at least a month in advance. The 30-room authentic 18th-century town-house, **Hotel de l'Universite** (22 rue de l'Universite, VII) is a three-star darling, with beautifully, sumptuously, interesting period furniture; bathrooms sybaritically marble and modern; some rooms with beamed ceiling. Guests have the privilege of temporary membership in the exclusive Bottle Club in the vaulted cellars. Bring a teenager here to encourage his or her appreciation of the finer things of life. This is no place for children under 14, but you deserve this luxury. Reserve well ahead. Just down the street is the **Lenox** (9 rue de l'Universite, VII); with 34 rooms, mostly small but crisp and contemporary. Opt for the duplexes on the top floor with beamed ceiling and flower-filled balconies. A bar, but no restaurant. Light meals, however are served to you in your room until midnight. There is TV, but you'll have to pay extra plus 30% of the tariff of this three-star hostelry for a child sleeping in your room in a cot.

The Family Hotel (35 rue Cambon, I) however, is just what it says it is. Old-fashioned, peaceful, and with soothing two-star prices for its 25 rooms in an exceptionally convenient location. Reserve at least a month ahead. **Hotel Les Trois Couronnes** (30 rue de l'Arc de Triomphe, XVII), a converted *hotel particulier,* or town house, in a wonderful area, has rooms fitted with TV and minibars, Art Nouveau and Art Deco furnishings; new in '83, with 20 rooms. No dining room, but several restaurants *"juste a cote,"* and a pleasant breakfast room; courtesy is a watchword for this three-star charmer, splendid for a single parent and a teenage child.

Good solution for families? Suites of 2 connecting rooms, bath, and kitchenette (utensils on request) at the **Pacific Hotel** (11 rue Fondary, XV); 66 rooms; only 49 with private bath or shower, so book ahead. Small old-fashioned rooms, French doors, balconied windows, telephone. Rooms with double bed plus single bed for children can be arranged. A two-star hostelry. Furnished more grandly, with antiques and either campy or quaint decorative accessories, **Hotel Residence Plaza Mirabeau** (10 av. Emile-Zola, XV) right by the Seine and the heart of Paris; patio-garden; English spoken; every room has private bath and completely equipped kitchenette. Terms are daily or by the month (cheaper). A three-star hotel. An *hotel particulier* of the Sun King's vintage, renovated in '83, is the **Residence Dullin** (Place Charles Dullin, VI). At the foot of the great landmark of *Sacre-Coeur,* with 75 studios and apartments with kitchenettes, and direct-dial telephones, typing services for business-minded Mummies and Daddies, and rates for two bedrooms with bath *en suite* that can accommodate five people rather inexpensively. There are, thank heavens, ***small hotels on the Right Bank where you can use credit cards;*** some of these are luxury establishments. **Regent's Garden** (6 rue Pierre Demours, XVII), is a four-star, a townhouse of 41 rooms, right there by the Arc de Triomphe, the Etoile, and the Champs-Elysees; yet, with its astonishing garden filled with fountains, statues, flowers, it's like being in the country and living in a house with high ceilings, large marble fireplaces, chandeliers, plasterwork, interesting furniture; no dining room, but room service for light meals and sandwiches; concierge service for booking theaters, attending to your needs and desires; and, of course, breakfast. Color TV; tiny fee for children's cot in your immense room. **Residence du Bois** (18 rue Chalgrin, XVI) is another Second Empire mansion, with 20 rooms; remarkably comfortable, perfect service; no restaurant, but light meals can be served in winter before a roaring fire, in summer by the garden, or in your room; a four-star member of the Relais-Chateaux group. **La Tremoille** (14 rue de la Tremoille, VIII) another four-star, fine, classic hotel, right by the Theatre des Champs-Elysees. No dining room, but you can sign for your meals at the nearby Relais-Plaza or Regence. Everything sparkly, elegant, air-conditioned; huge bathrooms, be-flowered balconies; great service. You'll find a mix of old world and modern comforts at the **Inter-Continental Paris** (3 rue Castiglione, I) with 500 rooms equipped with individual hairdryers and scales; air-conditioned, in-house movies, color TV, minibars in every room, 24-hour room service and a charming courtyard with tables, fountain-pool, where you can enjoy buffet lunches and candlelit dinners; disco; suites with enormous bathrooms equipped with saunas and jacuzzi; overlooking the Tuileries; a four-star indulgence. In the same four-star palatial class is the **Hotel-Residence Saint-James et Albany** (202 rue de Rivoli, I) admirably located within walking distance of the Tuileries, the Louvre, etc., this hotel offers studios, two-room units, duplexes, apartments of various sizes, all furnished in contemporary style, with kitchenettes, color TV; a restaurant, a brasserie, a ground-floor grocery-caterer-gourmet delicatessen; health club with sauna; breakfast available from room service; courtyard and garden. For reservations and information, you can call in the U.S. (800) 223–7733 or in NY (212) 697–6230.

Special: **Le Marais,** around the place des Vosges, a favorite area of mine, has now been "discovered," and is a wonderfully relaxed area for families, with easy access by Metro to the areas considered more formal, elegant and certainly more expensive. I think it's a great area for families, and easy on the purse strings. **Hotel Place des Vosges** (12 rue Birague, IV) has no restaurant, but serves breakfast, and there are inexpensive French, Italian, even Chinese restaurants all around. Higher floor rooms are preferable; each of the 16 rooms has a private, modern bath; European credit cards or Diners Club are accepted; but please reserve way ahead for this two-star, narrow-but-nice (4 rooms to a floor) hostelry. If you can afford four-star prices and like big, modern hotels, let me recommend the Japanese special, **Nikko de Paris** (61 quai de Grenelle, XV), which is very exercise-oriented, with body-building classes, squash courts, and the usual. Restaurants serving agreeable French cuisine, a Japanese restaurant, and a Japanese pastry shop are here. Some rooms front the Seine, air-conditioning, color TV; credit cards accepted. The **Sofitel Paris** (8–12 rue Louis-Armand, XV) also has a swimming pool with a summertime sliding roof, sauna, solarium, gym, winter garden, air-conditioning, color TV, exterior elevators in plexiglass sheathes, five-language translation services for international business-minded parents, good restaurants, piano-bar, and takes credit cards. Both of these charge nothing for children under 12 sleeping in a cot in their parents' room, and unless you're planning on taking the Metro or the bus or bicycling, this may compensate for the taxi fares to other interesting sections of Paris.

Possibly Special: From Nov.–Mar., you can live aboard the hotel barges *Escargot* and *Litote,* moored on the Seine at the centrally located Quai Anatole, VII. Reservations can also be made through **Continental Waterways** (11 Beacon St., Boston, MA 02108). Rates are wonderfully inexpensive, because we all know that the weather is cold, rainy, damp, foggy, windy during these months. Accommodations, however, are said to be snug and cozy. The only time I don't mind gray weather is when I'm on the water, and teenagers might think this is a lark. Just a thought. I haven't been aboard to check these out.

Country retreats near Paris? **Hostellerie de Varennes** (Varennes-Jarcy), has five cheap, clean, simply furnished rooms; lovely dining terrace. Riding, flying, golf, skeet shooting nearby. Closed in Mar. **Chateau de Chaumontel** (Chaumontel, near Luzarches, Val-d'-Oise), a hunting castle of the Princes of Conde, is towered, turreted, moated. Secluded, rustic, romantic; an easy change of pace. The neighborhood is famous for its hunting grounds, the castle park charming to wander in; you can fish, ride, play golf, swim in a nearby pool. **Moulin de Jarcy** sits atop stone arches 12 miles southeast of Paris; only six rooms. The mill at **Ivry-la-Bataille** has an enchanting garden; you dine (on trout) facing the Eure River. Lovely **Moulin des Ruats,** on the outskirts of Avallon is a spectacular gorge, has superb food.

At **Amboise, Le Choiseul** (49 quai Ch.-Guinot;) is so superbly furnished with antiques that I'd be terrified to let my child's hand go for fear he'd send bric-a-brac crashing to the parquet floor; the atmosphere is far too formal for most families, but might be pleasant with teenagers. Parkland for walks; remains of a 15th-century convent; ancient Roman cellars. Restaurant with panoramic view. **Antibes: Hotel du Cap Eden Roc,** with terraces overlooking the Mediterranean, pine forest, private beach, heated salt-water pool, four tennis courts, is the classic, traditional, grand luxe resort hotel; teenagers and younger children can have a spree at **La Siesta,** an amusement center/casino nearby, with go-karting, trampolines, water sports, jazz and pizzazz. In **Ascain,** near beach resorts such as St.-Jean-de-Luz, with tennis, golf, fishing, shooting, is **Etchola;** moderate rates.

Baix: the 17th-century **Hostellerie la Cardinale et sa Residence**

was once the manor of Cardinal Richelieu; charming bedrooms. On the banks of the Loire at **Beaugency,** the delightful old **Abbaye de Beaugency** offers 27 comfortable, good-size rooms, 12 with bath; garden dining room with excellent food; a good way station for chateau touring; fishing and swimming (nice sandy beach); open all year; moderate rates. Beaugency is a small wine town where Joan of Arc defeated the English, and its castle is illuminated at night. **Biarritz:** the luxurious **Hotel du Palais** was once the summer palace of Napoleon III; private beach, heated sea-water outdoor pool with cabanas, four golf courses, tennis courts, squash, jai-alai; nearby riding and fishing; sauna; poolside restaurant as well as palatial classic restaurant; all very Belle Epoque in style, and just the place if you want to be ritzy in Biarritz. Credit cards happily accepted. **Bonnatrait-Sciez:** The 13th-century castle **Chateau de Coudree** on Lake Leman is a gem; a lovely forest; private beach; heated pool; tennis; fishing; golf; boating; and riding nearby. You'll like the Gobelin tapestries, painted ceilings of the chapel, the flanking turreted round towers, and the great *donjon* keep. Its 15 fresh and cozy rooms win family approval. Children welcomed with open arms! **Bourget-du-Lac,** across Lake Bourget from Aix-les-Bains, offers **Ombremont** on the lake, with lovely views; swimming pool; tennis; golf; fishing. Just outside of **Brignoles, Abbaye de la Celle** is an 11th-century abbot's lodge restored and furnished with taste; 15th-century dining room; 20th-century swimming pool; 20 very pleasant rooms; garden; lovely park; terrace restaurant; **Cabourg,** a pleasant old-fashioned beach resort with casino and the Grand Hotel frequented by Marcel Proust, one-half-hour drive SW of Deauville, with lush gardens and attractive Normandy villas. At **Cagnes-le-haut, Le Dagnard** is a 14-room hideaway. At **Camaret** in Brittany, the summer **OCCAJ Vacation Village** specializes in sailing; baby and children's clubs; swimming lessons for children 8–13; fishing; workshops; recreation room; tennis, mini-golf, beach sports; bungalows, or rooms in a main building. At **Carteret,** on the southern coast of the Cotentin peninsula, some 210 miles west of Paris, you'll find a charming beach with water so shallow it almost retires from sight. Carteret's twin, the town of **Barneville,** has a long sand beach of its own. Both towns, quiet and unassuming, are inexpensive delights with a relaxed family atmosphere. The **OCCAJ Vacation Center** at **Cayres,** surrounded by lakes, mountain gorges, breathtaking scenery, offers rustic little bungalows with kitchenette; cafeteria. Bowling, group games (ugh!), recreation room, paddling pool and sand for toddlers; a maze; but no supervised babysitting or nursery. In the village below, you can rent boats, horses, ponies. Fishing and canoeing on Lake Bouchet; salmon in the Allier; blackberries *(myrtilles)* and mushrooms to gather. Nearby is divinely beautiful Le Puy for sightseeing, riding, tennis, movies, car rental, and a swimming pool. At **Chaise-Dieu, OCCAJ Vacation Village** (also in the Auvergne) offers similar entertainment, lake sports; a well-equipped playground; a baby club and a children's club.

Chalais: Chateau de Mavaleix between Limoges and Perigueux, is the color of rich country cream, with swimming pool, tennis, riding, fishing, hunting. **Cheronnac's Chateau de Cheronnac** is a pink-stone house with a blue-slate roof with red chimneys, surrounded by trees and lawns; offering 14 tastefully decorated rooms. An elegant *petit chateau* has been transformed into this small, chic hotel for sophisticated family travelers. **Cordes: Au Grand-Ecuyer,** a 14th-century house with 18 rooms; delightful dining room with stone walls and beamed ceiling; summer terrace; open all year; very attractive and comfortable, beautifully furnished.

Corsica: At **Porticciolo, Hotel Le Caribou** has a large pool; above it, the terrace with canopied swings is a favorite children's rendezvous. In **Calvi,** the **Grand Hotel de Calvi** (Tel: 5), overlooking the bay.

Dinard: an **OCCAJ Vacation Village** offers a beach, a countryside arbored with roses, the attractions of Mont-St.-Michel, St.-Malo, and Dinan, plus an olympic-size pool with heated seawater; swimming and beach sports supervised; fishing, golf, tennis, sailing; a baby and a children's club. **Eze:** the **Chateau de la Chevre d'Or** clings to the ramparts of this ancient town. In **Fleurville** for lovers of wine, horses, and Burgundian pleasures, **Chateau de Fleurville** is a low-slung, pink-stone 18th-century country house set in a beautiful flowered estate. Horses to ride; tour of Roman churches and local vineyards. In **Fouesnant** in Brittany, **Le Manoir du Stang,** a 17th-century Breton manor with antique furnishings and modern comforts, is extremely attractive and comfortable. Close to the beach; excursions with fisherman arranged; woods for picnicking; tennis and golf. **Honfleur: La Ferme St-Simeon,** an old Norman house, is a perfect base for Deauville (5 miles); golf course nearby; beautiful garden; **La Baule:** the **Hermitage,** not architecturally very elegant, is a fine hotel, catering to children; its own beach club and park with a playground.

La Caze: Chateau de la Caze, a dramatic 15th-century castle overlooking the Tarn River gorge; only 14 rooms, most with canopied beds and regal bathrooms; six lovely suites have been set up in an ancient farm building in the garden, boat trips; swimming in the Tarn. This medieval chateau comes complete with the ghosts of eight French maidens, great fireplaces, gleaming cobblestone halls, and a moat you can fish in; it will exist in your imagination long after you have stayed here. The first chateau in France to be transformed into a hotel to which early paying guests came by boat! Moderate rates.

Prices at **OCCAJ Vacation Village** at **La Faucille** in the Jura Mountains, for skiing, with babysitters and counselors for older children only during school vacations, and not many extras, are low. **OCCAJ Vacation Village** at **Lanau** has cottages of wood and stone, with terraces and garden furniture; group games; playground; sailing lessons for teenagers; fishing; heated swimming pool—and mountain lakes and gorges for exploring.

At **Le Rozier, Grand Hotel du Rozier et de la Muse,** with 40 rooms and a magnificent terrace view of the forested Tarn Gorge. **Le Touquet,** 140 miles north of Paris, is an elegantly old-fashioned beach resort hidden away in a pine forest behind lofty dunes. The modern **Novotel Thalamar** has an indoor swimming pool. At **Lodeve,** the 25-room relais situated in large park grounds, **Residence les Violettes,** is always open; attractive airy ambience with canopied four-poster beds. **Luynes: Domaine de Beauvois** is a *Grande Etape Francaise,* with prices to match; an L-shape chateau in a wooded park with its own private fish pond; 35 rooms. Canoeing, tennis, olympic-size heated pool, hunting, riding.

Megeve: Hotel Mont Blanc in the Haute Savoie, with all winter sports available and swimming in the outdoor heated pool in the summer; mountaineering, riding, tennis, hiking nearby; in the center of town, but surrounded by its own parkland; sauna, hairdresser; credit cards mercifully accepted. **Mercues:** the 12th-century (with 18th-century additions) **Chateau de Mercues** is a towered and turreted fortress castle crowning a 400′ rocky escarpment overlooking the Lot River Valley. Beautiful grounds, woods, terraces; heated pool; stables; boating on the river; four dozen handsome bedrooms and six suites. Food is yummy, and in a region specializing in truffles, expect to have these delicacies as a garnish or encased in pastry for at least one meal. The children will be entranced. One of the most comfortable and attractive guest chateaux in France. Open all year.

At **Meribel-les-Allues** (near Moutiers), **Hotel du Grand Coeur** is idyllic for small children, who like to sit in the canopied swing by the pool. Chalet-style buildings, all with terraces and balconies. **Meyrargues: Chateau de Meyrargues,** once the proudest bastion of Provence, has been transformed into a small, beautifully decorated castle. Only nine rooms, most with bath. At **Meyrueis, Chateau d'Ayres,** a 12th-century castle with a few 15th-century touchups and recent interior modernization. Lovely park, swimming pool, fishing and hunting; own heliport. Delicious food served in the dining hall or packed in a picnic basket to take on forays to the Tarn Gorge or the Dargilan Grottoes. Only about 20 rooms so telephone or wire proprietor, in advance.

At **Montbazon, Chateau d'Artigny** (See *Les Grandes Etapes Francaises*) is a huge palace with handsome rooms, a courtyard chapel that is a reproduction of the one at Versailles, heated pool, tennis, fishing, riding, golf, boating; grounds for scenic walks; 57 elegant rooms. This used to be particularly good for children because entertainment directors gave them lessons in riding, fishing, and swimming; do please check this out because since my last visit things may have changed. Also here, **Domaine de la Tortiniere** overlooks the meandering Indre River; a comfortable creamy-white and blue turreted manor built a century ago by the Count de Rigny; 20 airy, spacious rooms; a garden dining terrace (don't miss the orange souflee) and plenty of space for children to romp. Tennis, golf, swimming within five miles. **Monte Carlo:** The **Hotel de**

Paris is Monaco's ode to opulence, a Belle Epoque fantasy at right angles to the Casino; extravagant, rococo; heated sea-water pool, saunas; the rider of the bronze horse in the lobby is Louis XIV and the horse's knee is shiny from being rubbed for good luck, which guests here already obviously have. The pleasant **Chateau de Colliers** in **Muides-sur-Loire;** 18 rooms, four with private bath; good food; boating, fishing, tennis, swimming, fine sand beach, and forests for the children to explore. Off the tourist route, and rated only in the plain-but-comfortable class; but getting here is easy and you have the satisfaction of living and dining well in chateau country for what everyone else is spending for rooms alone! **Nieuil: Chateau de Nieuil** is a classic countryside chateau with blue roof, dormers, turrets, white-stone facade, formal gardens, wooded park, private lake and all. A dozen gracefully furnished rooms. Swimming pool and tennis nearby. **Nice:** Rooftop swimming pool at the modern, 200-room **Hotel Frantel;** reasonable rates. The **Meridien** has a heated pool; the **Negresco,** a national historical landmark, has minibars in the rooms, and is much the grandest of the hotels around, right on the beach, ten minutes from the airport, and takes credit cards in case you overspend.

At the **OCCAJ Vacation Village** in **Orcieres-Merlette** (about 23 m. from Gap), set up to receive babies from one month on, you get nightskiing, a covered heated swimming pool, a magnificent view of the Drac valley; supervised youth club, kindergarten, and nursery; art workshops for children 6–12; photography and craft studios for grownups and teenagers; discotheque; solarium; bar; children from 6–12 eat in a special dining room. Skis and boots can be rented. In **Paimpol** in Brittany, **Le Relais Brenner** on a little slope overlooking a bay, with its own beach and dock, specializes in grilled oysters and lobsters freshly caught along the rocky coast; tennis. At **Pelvoux** (near Briancon) you live in chalets in the **OCCAJ Vacation Village;** nursery and ski camp counselors for children; no pool. A good base for "doing the Cro-Magnon area" is **Perigord,** at the **Hotel Royale-Vezere;** roof garden; swimming pool; ask for a room overlooking the river.

Ostellerie du Vieux Perouges in the heart of medieval **Perouges** is just about as quaint a little place as you could hope to find, all stone and vines and half-timbered walls. Tiptop food and tapestry too! Perouges, a tapestry-making town, is absolutely charming. Between Carcassonne and Narbonne, at **Peyriac-Minervois, Chateau de Violet;** open year-round; ten rooms. Heated pool nearby. In Brittany, at **Pleven-Plancoet, Manoir de Vaumadeuc** has nine rooms and suites; a simple 15th-century manor with ivied walls, big beamed ceilings, beautifully preserved and decorated rooms. Moroccan pigeon stew is a specialty, so is lobster au gratin; and you'll be in very gratin (top) society staying here. Plenty of partridge shooting in the area. Also in Brittany is the **Auberge Tal Moor** at **Port de Kerdruc en Nevez,** a small, simple hotel with excellent food.

Horseback hunting of wild boar and stag with your chateau host? **Chateau de Mimont, Pougues-les-Eaux.** Open all year, this opulent, resplendent chateau is not for small children, as each room is luxuriously, exquisitely furnished in different period—Regency, Louis XIV, Louis V, Empire, Directoire, with Louis XIV parquet floors; a staircase of pink marble; chandeliers illuminate the dining room—get the picture? A chauffeured car is at your disposal; the atmosphere is one of a private house; 10 lovely chambers. Pool, riding, fishing, but the hunting from horseback with owner-proprietor takes place only Nov.–Mar. Children can ride along if they are good riders, at least 12, and capable of following directions. Expensive, yes, but how pleasant to be blessed with such sense of privilege!

At **Prangey, Hostellerie du Chateau de Prangey,** part castle with moat, part 18th-century house with high-ceilinged rooms and fireplaces; 19 rooms; very good food. Nearby lake, fishing, and hunting. The garden was designed by Le Notre, who landscaped Versailles. Check winter closing. **Chateau de Roumegouse** is one of the prettiest little chateaux in France, its walls pale gold, towered and turreted; once the shelter of pilgrims making their way to and from Rome on foot, the Roumieux, from whom it takes its name. Located in an area of canyons, grottoes, and prehistoric caves, about three miles from Rocamadour; 12 captivating rooms with period furnishings; a beautiful terrace; a fine stopover. Nearby pool and riding stables. At **St.-Nabord,** in an attractive wooded grove on the banks of the Moselle, **Hostellerie Claire-Fontaine** is expensive, but food, service, and rooms furnished in period style are all outstanding; heated pool; discotheque for teenagers; best time is the last Sun. in July, when a carnival is held in the old town of Remiremont with attractive floats, parades, dancing in the streets. At **St. Palais-sur-Mer** is the friendly **Le Corduan** hotel with beach club and garden. In **St.-Pantaleon** (just outside Autun), **OCCAJ Vacation Village** has facilities similar to those at Choise-Dieu give or take a little; no baby club but a children's club; swimming; sailing school; waterskiing. At **St.-Paul-de-Vence, Le Mas des Serres** offers riding, tennis, fishing; ivied walls; red-tiled roof; a lovely stop; only seven rooms; regional cuisine; but "more better" as a child said happily, is **Le Mas d'Artigny,** with regular hotel rooms, a dozen or so rooms with *private swimming pools* (!!!) and *cottages!* In **Vence,** four miles away, the 25-room **Hotel Diana** (ave. Poilus); no restaurant, but balconied rooms where you can sit and have a well-served breakfast, and balconied rooms *with kitchenettes* at extremely reasonable rates! What a convenience *that* is, and what a money-saver, especially with a *super-marche* down the street, as well as many restaurants in the neighborhood. Rooms are comfortable, modern, bathrooms fine and, at these low rates, wonder of wonders, credit cards are accepted!

About five miles west of **Saumur** is **Le Prieure** (Chenehutte-les-Tuffeaux); a 15th-century manor house, accommodation in the mansion or in pleasant and gaily decorated cottages. Beautiful 65-acre park, heated pool, mini-golf, sandy beach and fishing on the Loire, delicious food, a breath-taking view, a delight.

At **Stainville,** on the Paris-Strasbourg road, **Chateau Choiseul,** a courtly 13th-century castle, the former country house of the Dukes of Choiseul-Stainville; 11 large, high-ceilinged, attractively furnished rooms with fireplaces; especially good food. Don't confuse this with *Residence* Le Choiseul at Amboise! Chateau Choiseul is sturdier and more comfortable for families, I'm sure you'll agree! At **Talloires, L'Abbaye de Talloires,** an 11th-century Benedictine abbey transformed into a comfortable hotel on the edge of Lake Annecy; 65 rooms; pleasant open-air restaurant with delectable specialties. At **Tence** in the upper Loire, the **OCCAJ Vacation Village** has riding, fishing, swimming, a playground, a baby and children's club, many excursion possibilities; cheap, but accommodations looked more suitable for the parking of cars than people. Near **Tourtour, La Bastide de Tourtour,** a restful spot, surrounded by a park; heated swimming and paddling pool; luxurious rooms. Riding in July and Aug. at Tourtour (15 miles). **Tremolat** (Dordogne), **Le Vieux Logis et ses Logis des Champs** *is* an old house with ancient furniture and ivied brick walls; stream with stepping stones.

If converted fortress-stronghold castles appeal to you, your best bet is **Chateau de Trigance,** a dramatic medieval affair set on a wild hillside; inaccessible except for a long, winding roadway and then stairs (carved out of the rock which forms the ramparts) debouch onto a peaceful terrace leading into a vaulted dining room. Unalloyed delight for children, scholars, and romantics in the Var region; only 4 rooms. At these prices, one is willing to forego luxury—bedrooms are small and sparsely decorated. **Trouville,** with a more relaxed family atmosphere than its neighbor **Deauville,** across a river inlet, has a year-round population of fisherfolk and reasonable family hotels. On the 4th Sun. in August, you can enjoy the Grand Prix, the horse race of the year at Deauville where hotels cost twice what they do at Trouville! **Valencay** has a tiny treasure for connoisseurs: Called by some the last good small hotel in France, and located near all the famous chateaux in the Loire Valley, the **Hotel d'Espagne** (8 rue du Chateau) is so-called because the King of Spain and his family were interned there during Napoleon's day; Talleyrand's chateau up on a bluff; a park with peacocks, flamingoes, dromedaries, deer; a museum Napoleonic buffs will be mad about. Intimate and peaceful, it has only 25 rooms, which look out onto a flower-filled courtyard; room service, bathrooms, creature comforts all exceptional. Superlative hot croissants for breakfast; Michelin-starred restaurant; savor-and-sigh wines. **Chateau de Castel Novel, Varetz,** near Brive-la-Gaillarde, is casual, comfortable, warmly hospitable. Its 13th-century towers once sheltered the lords of Aubusson, as well as novelist Colette. With 16 snug rooms, a delight. **Vence** (see St.-Paul-de-Vence).

CLUB MEDITERRANEE (See Ch. 7.) All of the Club Meds have ample activities, from golf to riding to archery to yoga. In the Vosges mountains by Alsace, in **Vittel,** set in a forested estate of more than 1000 acres, is a luxurious Club Med vacation village, with housing in a reconstructed "station balneaire," or spa hotel; a Baby Club for babies 4 months and older; a Mini Club, and a Kid's Club; nurses and counselors to keep your children occupied and happy. As a combination vacation village and optional health spa, welcoming also babies, toddlers, children, teenagers, Vittel offers great variety and value plus the option for active nature-loving families with teenagers of a week's hiking, picnicking, mountainclimbing with stays in hotels and farmhouses in the Alsace-Lorraine area, with a maximum of five to six hours hiking daily. (Club Mediterranee, Vittel, France 88000.) In another reconstructed health spa in Limousin, in a fascinating area of the Perigord and Dordogne region, is **Pompadour** with a Pony Club for children 8–12 and a Kid's Club where they can enjoy sports instruction; riding available for children 12 and older; and a Mini Club for the 4–8 set. Accommodation in cottages. A week's bicycle and camping tour of the area in a group no larger than a dozen is an option parents with teenagers might want to avail themselves of, but you also might prefer to tour on your own in a car to visit prehistoric Cro-Magnon cave paintings at Thot; the town of Quercy and the extraordinary medieval village of Rocamadour; a fortress and troglodyte cave settlement; several chateaux (all covered in the bicycle-camping expedition, which also includes a canoe trip on a river in the Vezere Valley). (Club Mediterranee, Domaine de la Noaille, France 19230; Tel: (55) 73–31–33.) On the Cote d'Azur, at **Les Restanques,** there's a *case* village, with a Kid's Club, for those who don't mind roughing it as far as accommodations go. (Club Mediteranee, Les Restanques, Saint-Pons-Les-Mures, France 83360.) The three Club Med villages on Corsica have far greater appeal to me, however. A Mini Club and a Kid's Club operative at Club Mediterranee, Cargese, France 20130.) On up to the north, another village is at **Sant'Ambrogio,** also with bungalow lodging, but no special counselors for children (who are welcome as guests from age 6 on). Waterskiing, but fewer and less attractive facilities than those at Cargese and **Santa Giulia** on the southeast coast, where there is a Mini Club and a Kid's Club, and you can stay in Polynesian-style huts or cottages. Many young families come here. (Club Mediterranee, Santa-Giulia, Porto-Vecchio, France 20210.) There are also optional week-long tours of the island for small groups by car or backpacking. If you prefer mountain scenery, choose from **Chamonix, Tignes val Claret, Monetier,** each with a Mini Club and a Kid's Club.

In winter, it's *les enfants au ski* to Club Med's *villages de neige,* with Kids' Clubs operative at each during the French school holidays and Mini Clubs open all season at **Les Arcs** in Savoy and **Avoriaz** in the high Savoy (Haute Savoie); ski schools at both for children from 6 years up; at **Chamonix,** also in the Haute Savoie, ski school for children from age 5 up; at **Serre-Chevalier** in Monetier, which has Mini and Kid's Clubs operative only during school vacations, ski school for children from age 6 up. **Tignes-Val Claret** (Savoie) has a Mini Club, but only for children 6–8; unlike the other winter Club Med retreats, *Tignes Val-Claret accepts children no younger than 6*. For kids in the Kid's Club bracket (8–12), cadets (12–14), and juniors (14–18), there are woodworking and painting workshops, marionettes, classes in macrame and printing, music, dancing, cinema and more, with each age group kept to its own interests. From age 10, if their skiing level warrants, children ski with the grown-ups.

CAMPING AND CARAVANING Useful addresses are **Auto-Camping and Caravaning Club de France** (37 rue d'Hauteville, 75010 Paris; Tel: (01) 246–33–27); **Automobile Club de France** (8 place de la Concorde, VIII; Tel: (01)266–43–00) issues camping licenses; all you want to know about camping/driving is here. The **Touring Club de France** (6–8 rue Firmin Gillot, Service Camping, 75737 Paris Cedex 15; Tel: (01) 532–22–15) is also generous with information. They have a *Camping Canoe-Camping Section* at the same address. If you have a van, minibus, or caravan, check with **Camping Club de France Caravane Club** (218 blvd. Saint-Germain, 75007 Paris; Tel: (01) 548–30–03). The **Camping Club International de France, Centre de Documentation au Service des Campeurs** (22 ave. Victoria, 75001 Paris; Tel: (01) 236–12–40) supplies free information for foreign campers, and its location may be the most convenient for you. **Federation Francaise de Camping et de Caravaning** (78 rue de Rivoli, 75004 Paris; Tel: (01) 272–84–08) publishes the French camping-grounds guide. You can rent *camping-cars* from **Car-Away** (60 rue de Caen, 92400 Coubevoie; Tel: (01) 334–15–81) that will accommodate three to six people; insurance and all the necessaries can be arranged for you.

Camping sites: Consult **Castel et Camping Caravaning** (169 ave. Victor-Hugo, XVI; Tel: (01)727–07–38); closed on Sat.; rents camping gear and supplies information about the 40 four-star camp sites in the parkland of chateaux. You can camp right in Paris in the heart of the Bois de Boulogne between Puteaux and Suresnes bridges, Paris XVI; Tel: (01) 506–14–98 (closed Jan.) Also in Champigny, at Quai de Polangis; Tel: (01) 288–38–24 (closed Feb.).

Bicycle rental and touring: The SNCF rents bicycles at about 140 railway stations for low rates. Within 20 miles of Paris' Chatelet-Les Halles Metro station, five railway stations rent bicycles on weekends and holidays at $1.25 an hour or $5 a day, wonderful for idyllic picnicking outings. Call RER Velo (Tel: (01) 346–1414). Check with **Paris-Velo** (2 rue de Fer a Moulin, 75005 Paris; Tel: (01) 337–59–22) or **Bicyclub de France** (8 place de la Porte-Champerret, 75017 Paris; Tel: (01) 766–

55–92), an organization which can arrange trips in Aquitaine, Brittany, Burgundy, and weekends in Normandy. In **Brittany,** bicycles can be rented from **Association de Ker Dreuz** (22290 Treguidel; Tel: (96) 48–04–79); **Cyclorandonneurs de Cornouaille-Prat-Len** (route de Concarneau, 29000 Quimper); **Entente Cyclotourisme de Goele** (Le Kerbroch, 22500 Paimpol). In **Languedoc-Roussillon,** rentals can be arranged at tourist offices at Port Barcares, Port Leucate, La Grande Motte. **La Federation Francaise de Cyclotourisme** (6 rue Jean-Marie-Jego, 75013 Paris; Tel: (01) 580–30–21) can arrange bicycle itineraries for all the provinces for you.

See also *Maps* in this section.

Camping du Tremblay (on the fringes of town at quai de Polangis, Champigny-sur-Marne); at **Creteil** (Camp des Cicognes in Ile de Brise-Pain), along the Marne, about 11 miles southeast; St.-Maurice (La Grade Terrace, 46 rue du Marechal-Leclerc), about a mile from the Pont de Charenton and about six miles from the center of Paris. Other suggestions are in **Val-d'Oise, Seine-St.-Denis, Essonne.** For a difference, go to **Corsica,** where the whole island is your campground. With eight branches, **Au Vieux Campeur,** offers clothes and equipment for camping and all active sports and activities for reasonable prices. Each branch specializes in gear for different sports: the main branch (48 rue des Ecoles, V: Tel: (01) 329–12–32) deals with speleology, mountaineering, hiking; #50 rue des Ecoles, next door, has everything for riding, tennis, jogging, sailing, scuba-diving; #1–3 rue de Latran offers everything for camping, downhill skiing, and cross-country; the #75 rue Saint-Jacques branch has rain gear and specializes in motorcycle and bicycling tourism; #3 rue du Sommerard stocks boots for trekking and hiking; #2 rue de Latran and #10 rue Jean-de-Beauvais has a stronghold of maps, books, guides, and compasses; also, their catalogues make them a sort of Gallic L. L. Bean. For Orvis counterparts, what you need for fishing, the best place in Paris is **Wyers et Brehier** (30 quai de Louvre, I: Tel: (01) 233–99–71) with casting rods, rods for deep-sea fishing, spear guns, everything.

In the telephone book, under *Camping,* listings go on for several pages about tents *(tentes),* camping clothes *(vetements),* camping equipment *(materiel, accessoires)* and everything for camping *(Tout pour le Camping),* including pneumatic igloo tents—at **Igloo Tente Pneumatique** (94 Rte. Nationale 10 Coignieres, Yvelines, Versailles); skiing, boating *(nautisme),* and mountaineering gear (operative word—*Montagne*). You can get a free catalog from **La Hutte** (19 rue Racine, Paris V), one of many branches of a large chain of camping equipment stores. To rent camping gear (usually easier than lugging it along), the operative phrase is *service location.* Second-hand gear is called *materiel d'occasion.* If these services aren't listed in tourist literature or telephone directories, see "Shopping," also Castel et Camping Caravaning above.

ATTRACTIONS FOR CHILDREN IN PARIS In Aug., about two million Parisians depart. On July 31, down come the rattling shutters over many small shop fronts, restaurants, cafes, pharmacies, and other service institutions, and up they rattle again on Sept 1. Major theaters close, and although there is no opera, ballet, or dance, Festival Estival, organ concerts, and brass bands are around. Many hotels offer reduced room rates during the August lull, and many have more lower-priced rooms available; at least 300 restaurants remain open, and getting tables in them or outside is simpler than usual; shops are less crowded, salespeople more obliging. Many museums are closed Tues., holidays, other days; smaller museums often have irregular hours and a flighty way of closing without notice for staff holidays or repairs; do confirm times and hours with the Paris tourist office, or your concierge or the museum itself. Almost all museums charge $1–$2 or more admission during the week, but many, if open, are free of charge on Sun., or have reduced admission fees. Most museums and other attractions are open 10 a.m.–5 p.m., but some also close between noon and 2 p.m. for a two-hour lunch break. Please double check, because many Paris museums are just too glorious to miss. Pause a moment, to get a sense of the history and heartbeat of Paris, at the **Place de la Concorde.** Open daily 9:30 a.m.–11 p.m. the Eiffel Tower has been refurbished. The Palais de Chaillot, across the Pont d'Iena from the Eiffel Tower, houses the **Musee de l'Homme** (see reference in list of museums following) and the **Musee de la Marine** and offers an even more impressive view of Paris—more of a child's eye view, let's say—than the towering Eiffel. And you can have lunch there, too.

You can climb to the top of the **Arc de Triomphe** (284 steps) or you can take the elevator. The memorial ceremony for the unknown soldier takes place daily at 6:30 p.m.; the museum has memorabilia of Napoleon and WW I. The colossal arch is reached by an underground passage from the Champs-Elysees or from the Avenue de la Grande-Armee. A little funicular (rue Steinkerque) takes you to the top of Montmartre where the front terrace of the **Basilica Sacre-Coeur** also offers a beautiful panorama. For a fascinating view, go up to the top of one of the large department stores, **Galeries Lafayette** or **La Samaritaine;** you can eat at either (see Food). If the sky is the limit, *helicopter flights* of eight minutes to La Defense and/or Versailles are offered by both **Heli France** (Tel: (01) 557–53–67) and **Heliport de Paris** (Tel: 901) 554–12–55), both located at 4 ave. de la Porte de Sevres, XV. Heli France also offers tours over the Loire chateaux. Heliport offers a 20 minutes flight over *tout Paris*. Have a whirl; rates are about the same as a good meal, depending where you eat it, and infinitely more memorable as a family experience. Police helicopters land on top of the **Maine-Montparnasse Tower** (33 ave. du Maine, XV), but you can take the elevator up to the 56th floor, two floors below their landing stage, and walk up two additional flights for a joli panorama. The tower is open daily 10 a.m.–10 p.m., and from 9:30 a.m.–11:15 p.m. in summer. Small admission. A lot less tiring than climbing the 238 steps of **La Colonne de Juillet** (place de la Bastille, IV), open every day except Tues., from 10 a.m.–4 p.m. (*Unlike* the Arc de Trimophe, there's no *ascenseur* to zip you to the top).

Notre-Dame and the **Ste.-Chapelle:** Walk along both banks of the Seine to see Notre-Dame from both sides and all angles of Ile de la Cite. You get to the top of the west facade via a spiral staircase in a turret at the side of the north tower. The chimeras and gargoyles on top delight children as much as the spectacular view. Wonderful free organ concerts every Sun. at 5:45 p.m. Outside the cathedral, a 270-foot tour through a crypt shows the real foundations of Paris and a section of a 4th-century church. At the opposite end of the island is the **Palais de Justice.** Rather cramped in the courtyard is the Ste.-Chapelle, built to hold pieces of the True Cross and the Crown of Thorns brought home from the Crusades. The exterior isn't much, but the interior is sheer magic; one of the largest and finest walls of stained glass that has survived from early Gothic times. Do try to come when you can hear the religious music. See also the **Conciergerie,** where so many victims of the Reign of Terror were held prisoner; the cells of Marie Antoinette and Robespierre; also a little reliquary museum connected mostly with Marie Antoinette. Closed Tues. Tel: (01) 354–30–06.

For romantics and children, there's nothing quite like the **fiacres,** the horse-drawn carriages stationed at the Rond-Point av. Champs Elysees, at the Madeleine, Opera, Tuileries, Bois de Boulogne, Eiffel Tower. No official fare; establish the cost in advance with the driver.

Boat trips on the Seine. You can take 1¼ hour rides in very comfortable and pleasant **Bateaux-Mouches** (Embarcation: Pont de l'Alma, rive droite (Right Bank), VIII; Tel: (01) 225 9610); restaurants, snack bars, orchestras, even TV aboard. Tourist menus served on the 12:30 p.m. and 1:20 p.m. voyages; gourmet dinners on the 8:30 p.m. voyages. Frequent departures from the Right Bank wharf between Pont des Invalides and Pont de l'Alma, every day and evening from Apr. 1–Nov. Maps are available on board so that you can spot the landmarks as you glide by. If the children are old enough, the night trips are memorable because Paris is illuminated. **Bateaux Parisiens** (Embarcation: Port de la Bourdonnais, VII; Tel: (01) 551–33–08) has hour rides, leaving every one-half hour from 10 a.m.–5 p.m. Oct.–Apr.; 9:30 a.m.–10:30 p.m. Apr.–Oct. Evening cruises at 7:30 p.m. every evening in summer, only on Sat. eve. in winter. **Vedettes du Pont-Neuf** (Embarcation, Pont-Neuf at Square Vert-Galant, I; Tel: (01) 633–98–38) also has one-hour rides, departing 10:30 a.m., 11:15 a.m., noon, and then every half-hour from 1:30 p.m.–6 p.m.; every eve. from May–mid-Oct. cruises to see the night lights at 9 p.m. and 9:30 p.m. The prices are all about the same. The *Bateaux-Mouches* are the best for most children, I think, as their size lets you walk around on deck or below, and they're livelier, and there's food and music. But don't scorn trips on the other craft which have a magic also of their own.

At the **Louvre** (Tel: (01) 260–39–26), closed Tues. and holidays, open from 9:45 a.m.–6:30 p.m., entrance at Ponte Denon, Cour du Carrousel, let the children look at the postcards first; ask them to pick out 10 they like best. Let them dawdle. You'll get a batch of pictures that will indicate the sort of pictures they really like. Certain galleries are open Fri. evening and some are illuminated. Explanatory walkie-talkies available; prints for sale in the Chalcographie section (some of them the greatest buys in Paris); nice outdoor terrace for a snack. The cafeteria or *salon de the* where you can have coffee or tea, snacks and munchies, is between the Mollien Wing and the Salle Mollien, where the 18th-century French paintings end and the 19th-century French paintings begin. (Important to know if you're not up to going to **Angelina** (226 rue de Rivoli) or any other place within easy walking distance in the 1st arrondissement.) To get to the nearest of several restrooms, just ask the guard for the W.C. or the toilettes, because they're not all that simple to find. To find out about membership benefits write **Societe des Amis du Louvre** (107 rue de Rivoli, I); Tel: (01) 260–70–64). When you come out of the Louvre, look through the arch of Carrousel, and ahead to the Arc de Triomphe—it is said that the day of Napoleon's death, the sun set in this arch.

Museums? The wealth and variety of museums (there must be at least 100) is positively stunning, but it's hard to know which are most interesting. Here are some you might like to see; all are closed Tues. or as noted. ALWAYS check, however!

Musee Municipal d'Art Moderne (11 ave. du President Wilson, XVI); paintings, sculpture, and decorative arts from the Post-Impressionists to the present; comprehensive excellence; many major works. Children's section. There's the **Musee Muncipal d'Art Moderne/ Musee d'Art Moderne de la Ville de Paris** for modern art; **Centre National d'Art et de Culture Georges Pompidou** (rue Rambuteau, corner of rue Saint-Merri, with an entrance also at 120 rue Saint-Martin, III) is something else again, a national museum of modern art housed in a wild-looking building, high tech or very yeccchhh depending on how you look at it, and generally called **Le Beauborg** or just simply **Centre Pompidou.** Teenagers have fun here and there's much that's really great to see. Also children's *ateliers;* for information about these, see Magic Family Helpers. The plaza outside is a continuous entertainment and hang-out for teenagers and students. A life-saver when hungry, **La Ciboulette** (141 rue Saint-Martin) with a gourmet restaurant upstairs, a good, but not all that inexpensive restaurant downstairs, and in summer a wonderful terrace facing Centre Pompidou where you can have lemonade, sandwiches, pastries, tea, coffee, wine, and snacks. Mounted on the wall of #8 rue Bernard, adjacent to the Beaubourg or Pompidou Center is the **Defenseur du Temps,** an animated clock 13′ high. Every hour, a clockwork man defends himself with sword and shield against a crab (symbolizing the sea), a dragon (symbolizing the land), a rooster (symbolizing the sky). At noon, 6 p.m. and 10 p.m., the brass clockwork man defends himself against all three attackers (The clock has given the area its name *Quartier d'Horloge*). Close by is the **Las Vegas Museum** (23 rue Beaubourg, III), open daily, even Sun., 11 a.m.–7 p.m., Wed. until 10 p.m.; a collection of slot machines and wonderful coin devices children adore, including an automatic chicken that lays a rainbow-colored egg when you insert a coin into its machine, a mechanical elephant that dispenses bon-bons, and a slot-machine at the entrance that lets you gamble for the reduction of your admission fee. **Musee du Jeu de Paume** (Jardin des Tuileries, pl. Concorde, I), French painting of the late 19th century—Monet, Manet, Cezanne, etc.—the best available presentation of Impressionist painting; a must. **Musee Jacquemart-Andre** (158 blvd. Haussmann, VIII); furniture, decorative arts, Brussels and Gobelin tapestries, all installed as if this were still a private house; some great frescoes by Tiepolo, Donatello bronzes, works of Della Robbia, Ucello, and Carpaccio, three Rembrandts; also paintings from the French school, Fragonard and others. **Musee de l'Orangerie** (pl. Concorde, VIII), small museum reserved for temporary exhibits which are always worth seeing. **Petit Palais** (ave. Alexandre III, VIII), one of the richest museums in France—more Courbets than you can see anywhere else, furniture, tapestries, objets d'art; never crowded; fascinating. **Musee des Arts Decoratifs** (107 rue de Rivoli, I) open from 1 p.m.–7 p.m. Sat. and Sun.; weekdays, 11 a.m.–6 p.m. closed Mon. and Tues., often has exhibits of children's interest; special room for children to create watercolors or play with modeling clay during certain exhibits; special guided tours for children aged 5–12 every Wed. at 2:30 p.m. For children's *ateliers,* see Magic Family Helpers. Closed Mon. and Tues. and during lunch hour, noon–2 p.m. **Musee des Gobelins** (42 av. Gobelins, XIII), on the second floor of the Manufacture des Gobelins. Beautiful rugs and tapestries that date back to the 17th century; you can watch people working on designs of today as well. Worth checking up on (open afternoons, Wed., Thurs., Fri. 2:30 p.m., 3:15 p.m., 3:45 p.m. Telephone to check times (Tel: (01) 570–12–60). **Musee Nissim de Camondo** (63 rue Monceau, VIII), a rich collection of 18th-century art and furniture presented as if it were all still contained in a private house. Closed Mon. and Tues. Brisk through. **Musee Carnavalet** (23 rue de Sevigne, III); history of Paris; furniture, carvings, sculpture, paintings, all packed into the former house of Mme. de Sevigny. Closed Mon. **Musee Cernuschi** (7 ave. Velasquez, VIII); Chinese and Japanese art, great bronzes, terra cotta funerary statues; small, selective collection attractively installed in what was once a private house. For older children. Closed Mon. Entrance at 111 blvd. Malesherbes.

Musee de Cluny (6 place Paul-Painleve, V); enchanting; a lovely garden; a room of Roman baths that is huge, airy and will hopefully be sun-filled for you and yours; the most beautiful medieval art in the world; the art of Paris from Roman through Gothic periods; absolutely wonderful. A beautiful Gothic chapel and the famous tapestry of the lady with the unicorn, and the Seigneurial life. Incomparable collections. A must! **Musee Cognacq-Jay** (25 blvd. des Capucines, II), little treasury of 18th-century paintings, drawings, furniture. Closed Mon. **Musee de la Mode et du Costume** (Palais Galliera, 10 ave. Pierre I[er]-de-Serbie, X) costumes and accessories from the mid-18th century to today's haute couture. Closed Mon.

Musee du Jouet (2 enclos de l'Abbaye, Poissy) open daily but closed during lunch hour from noon–2 p.m. An excursion on its own just getting there, but never mind the 20-minute train ride from Gare St.-Lazare. This is a fabulous collection covering the 19th-century and about 25 years of the 20th. Antique dolls, dolls' houses, extraordinary model grocery and other shops, toys; three floors accommodate the collection; sit in the Abbey close along the banks of the Seine. **Musee de la Musique Mecanique** (13 rue Brantome, quartier de l'Horloge, III) is open from 11 a.m.–7 p.m., with some extraordinary musical instruments.

If you're in the hair-dressing trade, write ahead for permission to visit the **Musee de la Coiffure** (44 rue du Marechal-Foch, 95620 Parmain; Tel: (01) 473–04–60) or call the Conservateur, but not on Sun., Mon. or holidays when it's closed.

Doctors may want to take their children to see the **Musee de l'Histoire de la Medecine** (12 rue de l'Ecole-de-Medecine, VI). Medical objects and instruments of the 17th-to-19th-century to shudder at. If you go, please explain to children that doctors and surgeons used these horrors long ago, and *do not use them now! Not* to be confused with the **Musee du Pain** (25 bis rue Victor-Hugo, Charenton-le-Pont) which is a delicious little museum open to the public 2 p.m.–5 p.m. Tues. and Thurs. only and devoted to bread-making and the baker's trade; a charmer. **Musee Guimet** (6 pl. d'Iena, XVI), extraordinarily fine Asiatic art, the most beautiful Khmer heads outside of Cambodia, an extension of the Louvre's Asiatic Arts dept. and just as remarkable as you would expect. **Musee du Vieux Montmartre** (17 rue St.-Vincent, XVIII). Here, among wax figures, 18th-century porcelains, and everything concerning Montmartre's history, you'll find the famous posters of Toulouse Lautrec. **Musee Rodin** (Hotel Biron, 77 rue de Varenne, VII), one of my favorite of all spots in Paris; Jean Cocteau lived here; many of Rodin's works inside, many more set about ravishing gardens. **Musee Gustave Moreau** (14 rue Rochefoucauld, IX); the works of this Academic painter, now being rediscovered as a painter of fantasies; special; teenagers will dig Moreau, whose work seems contemporary. Closed Mon. and Tues. **Musee Jean-Jacques Henner** (43 av. Villiers, XVII); an Alsatian painter whom Degas nastily called ''Leonard de Vingt Sous'' (a pun on Leonardo da Vinci), but whom Rodin appreciated. An artist you might like to discover with your teenagers; open afternoons, closed Mon. **Musee Delacroix** (6 rue de Furstenberg, VI), the studio of artist Delacroix with changing annual exhibitions which may and may not be of interest, but the little square is a visual delight in Saint-Germain-des-Pres. **Maison de Balzac** (Musee Balzac, 47 rue Raynouard, XVI); dear little 18th-century pavilion in a charming garden; another entrance from rue Berton, a street you must see as it is the last trace of country-in-town in Paris. A discovery as much fun as a Balzac story. **Bibliotheque Nationale** (58 rue de Richelieu, II); 400,000 medals, cameos, Greek and Roman antiquities, all to be found in the **Cabinet des Medailles** a museum in itself; a superb, SUPERB collection of illuminated medieval manuscripts. Closed Sun. and for two weeks in the spring around Eastertime. Check!

Please go to the heart of 17th-century Paris, the **Place des Vosges,** a square of lime or plane trees cut like candelabra, bordered with orangey houses, arcaded walkways off the street. Victor Hugo's house is #6; interesting to see his pyrography work, his design of the Chateau of Vianden with a spider web in the foreground, the touching portrait by Chatillon of the author and his son. Closed Mon. and hols.

The **Hotel de Soubise** (60 rue des Francs-Bourgeois) houses the National Archives **(Musee de l'Histoire de France-Archives Nationales).** A letter dictated by Joan of Arc is on display. Open daily from 2 p.m.–5 p.m., except Tues., of course. If you want to see early inventions and some 8000 devices, machines, apparati with working models of some of their capabilities have a look at the **Musee National des Techniques** (270 rue Saint-Martin, III), open noon–5:45 p.m. Closed Sun. **Musee de Neuilly** (12 rue du Centre, Neuilly) is open 2:30 p.m.–4:30 p.m., but get there, please, by 2:45 p.m. so you can see the automata in action at 3 p.m. which is the whole point of going to this collection of five dozen automata of the 19th century. If you aren't familiar with these animated mechanisms, all the more reason to see them. **Musee National des Arts et Traditions Populaires** (6 route de Mahatma-Gandhi, XVI); marvelous laboratory of anthropology of France and countries with a French heritage; documents and recordings of oral folk literature and music, folk art (including tools, toys, and costumes). **Musee de l'Homme** (Palais de Chaillot, pl du Trocadero XVI), a restaurant-bar with a great river view; anthropological exhibits; film, record, photograph, library. The **Naval Museum** (Musee de la Marine) is in the same palace, with fabulous models, paintings, exhibits, audiovisual rooms, films, old sailing charts, everything that's marvelous and maritime. The **Musee des Monuments Francais** is here also, with models, reproductions, murals, paintings, audiovisual exhibits; infinitely more interesting than you might think it would be. Scientifically-minded? At the **Palais de la Decouverte** (av. Franklin-Roosevelt, VIII) is the **Planetarium;** also large halls concerned with all sciences; over 100 experiments are presented daily in which visitors can participate; many lectures, films, and cultural activities for teenagers and students. Scientific films at the Planetarium—3 p.m. and 4 p.m.—get there early. Closed Mon. **Musee de l'Ecole Superieure des Mines** (60 blvd. St.-

Michel, VI), mineralogy, geology; meteorites; paleontology. Closed Sun., Mon. all of June, but check!

Musee Postal (34 blvd. de Vaugirard, XV), history of mail; earliest stamps and mailboxes; how stamps are made; special cancelations for sale. Even if you aren't a philatelist, this is pretty engaging. **Musee de l'Affiche** (18 rue de Paradis, X), open noon–6 p.m.; closed Mon. and Tues., has Wed. and Sat. painting workshops for children 6–14; call for information. The museum itself holds an astonishing collection of 50,000 posters. **Musee National de Ceramiques** (Grand Rue, Sevres). Across the bridge from the Pont de Sevres Metro station, this prestigious collection is installed in an old priory; here you can see service plates from which Madame du Barry and Catherine the Great and Napoleon ate, Sevres porcelain, and Limoges. **Musee des Transports** (60 ave. Sainte-Marie, Saint-Mande) on weekends and holidays, Apr.–Oct. 2:30 p.m.–6 p.m., in the suburbs, you can see public transport vehicles from horse-drawn trams to contemporary models all in working order. Miniature models and old trains too! **Musee de l'Air et de l'Espace,** located at Le Bourget Airport, is a heavenly array of "montgolfieres," the first balloons of the 18th-century, and everything airborne since that time. Open until 6 p.m. May–Oct.; closed Tues. and from noon–2 p.m. when it reopens on weekends and holidays. **Les Caves de la Tour Eiffel, Musee du Vin** (14–18 rue des Eaux, Passy) (with an entrance also at Square Charles-Dickens, XVI) are the only wine caves in Paris, hollowed into the limestone across the Seine from La Tour itself; tunnels displaying wine-making implements, bottles of wine, a few of which you can sample; also an audiovisual presentation. **Musee des Antiquites Nationales** (place du General-de-Gaulle, Saint-Germain-en-Laye) is an easy ride on the R.R. express Metro, and quite something to make an effort to visit for its Gallo-Roman, Merovingian, paleolithic and neolithic collections; chapel, gardens, allees, terraces, rond-point rose garden and the Grande Terrasse designed by Le Notre all right there to walk about in or have a picnic in. **Musee Marmottan** (2 rue Louis-Boilly, XVI) has a superb collection of paintings by Claude Monet and other Impressionists. A dazzle of medieval illuminated manuscripts are to be found among stately rooms filled with furniture, tapestries, and objets d'art from the Middle Ages to the 19th century. Closed Mon., but open on all public holidays. **Musee de la Monnaie** (11 quai Conti, VI); money, medals, coins from antiquity on, many of them works of art. Money-minting workshops open on Tues. and Thurs. afternoons; rest open daily except weekends and holidays. **Musee de l'Armee** (Hotel des Invalides, pl. Invalides, VII); the best art illustrating military history, including scale models of artillery; French regimental regalia; fabulous arms and armor including those worn by the kings of France. **Musee de la Chasse et de la Nature** (60 rue des Archives, III) in a superb building (Hotel Guenegaud); trophies and hunting tableaux paintings by Chardin, Rubens and others; hurray for this museum in the Marais, hurray, hurray! **Musee**

Grevin (10 blvd. Montmartre, IX) waxworks exhibit; a mixture of popular surrealism, Hollywood-type historical tableaux, fantasy, and strange lighting make this fun (possibly even educational) for children; open afternoons, Sat. and Sun. too. There's a branch of the Musee Grevin at the **Forum des Halles** (107 rue Pierre-Lescot, I) the largest pedestrian area in Europe, it's said. The *Forum des Halles* is a super attraction for all members of the family, an underground innovative complex with restaurants, snack shops, stores, and theaters. There's a ***public cultural center*** nearby on rue Lescot, with an electronic board listing Parisian cultural events and much practical information; an art pavilion, poetry center, conservatory of music and dance, young people's library *(bibiliotheque),* ateliers for skills from weaving to computers, and more to come by the time you get there!

Parks and public gardens are children's paradises.

The **Menageries du Museum d'Histoire Naturelle** (3 quai St.-Bernard, V) combine the attractions of the **Jardin des Plantes** (entrances at rue Buffon, rue Censier, and Place Valhubert) encompassing the Natural History Museum (if you're keen about fossils and dinosaur skeletons, but worthwhile just to see the mural history of monkeys by, of all people, Dufy! Also fine minerals), the Botanical Gardens, a marvelous labyrinth children like to get lost in, a Vivarium for lizards and other cold-blooded creatures; an ape house; a snake house; and animals who live in semifreedom. Then, on your way out at the western end, you find on your right a little corner of Morocco (Mosque, cafe, souk, and steam bath); if you take off your shoes, you can walk through the Mosque. The cafe is special. (See Food.) The 2000-acre **Bois de Boulogne** has seven lakes and ponds; the Shakespeare Theater; Auteuil and Longchamp racetracks; two little 18th-century palaces; rose gardens and water lilies of the Parc de Bagatelle and springtime displays of iris, tulips, and daffodils that are exquisite; cafes, restaurants; and the Jardin d'Acclimation (porte des Sablons, XVI) with a miniature train to the porte Maillot; playgrounds, Punch and Judy fun-house mirrors, camel and pony rides, Enchanted River, go-karting pistes, ''zoo'' and much more; restaurants, cafes (at the **Pavillon des Oiseaux** there are special children's plates at reasonable prices). Tables under the trees in summer at **Pre Catalan** look divine, but the prices are certainly not in the average family budget for lunch with the children, so don't make the ghastly mistake of assuming they will be. Admission a pittance, children under 4 free. This one is a must, but bring money for all attractions! The 2300-acre **Bois de Vincennes** (53 av. St.-Maurice at Porte Doree) with racetrack, three lakes, incorporates a menagerie swelled to the category of a zoo; outcroppings of many heights and shapes of artifical rock for children to climb on; many tree-shaded cafes; Punch and Judy. Also the Chateau de Vincennes (the keep is a historical museum). A wonderful sound and light performance here in summer. Also, the enchantment of the **Parc Floral de Paris** with *summer* and *winter* gardens; Sun. afternoons from Apr.–Oct., there are musicians, clowns, jugglers and acrobats performing indoors or out, according to the weather; and a collection of sculpture set about the covered walks and pavilions. The **Exotarium de Paris,** a tropical Aquarium filled with a variety of corals (beautiful) and reptiles (fascinatingly shuddery), open daily 9:30 a.m.–6:30 p.m. Facing Lake Daumesnil is the **Musee des Arts Africains et Oceaniens** (293 ave. Daumesnil, XII) with a fantasy of primitive art as beloved by Picasso as by children, plus a real zinger of a tropical aquarium in the basement; open daily except Tues. from 9:45 a.m.–noon, and from 1:30 p.m.–5:15 p.m. Very tame by comparison is the **Aquarium du Trocadero** (ave. Albert-de-Mun, I), swimming with French lake and river fish in cool caverns in the Trocadero gardens by the Palais de Chaillot; open daily 10 a.m.–5:30 p.m., until 6:30 p.m., May–Sept.

The **Zoo d'Ermenonville** or **Zoo Jean-Richard** (Tel: (04) 454–00–28), at the edge of the beech forest of Ermenonville, 25 miles NE of Paris, is open daily from May–Sept., 10 a.m.–6 p.m. and every Sun. in Mar., Apr., Oct. and early Nov. from 1:30 p.m.–5 p.m.; closed mid-Nov.–Feb. But please check these times and dates which may be subject to change; performing sea-lions and dolphins; **La Mer de Sable** (Tel: (04) 454–00–28), open daily, *except Fri.,* from Apr.–Sept. 30, 11 a.m.–6:30 p.m., an around-the-world theme park with camel rides, an African safari, a Moroccan market, a Normandy farm in miniature, an entertaining labyrinth, and a miniature train leaving from a village of mechanical toys to take you all around. The park itself is lovely with its gardens and network of streams for children to wade in when no one's looking. I think this is plenty for a day's outing, but there are those who press on a few miles NW, just N of Senlis, to **La Vallee des Peaux Rouges** (Tel: (04) 454–11–00) at Fleurines, so tiny it's not even on the map, to this amusement park, a French version of the Wild West, with a corral and a saloon (soft and hard drinks), stagecoach, and ponies to ride.

A vivarium? A crash of rhinoceroses? A troop of baboons? **Chateau de Thoiry** (Yvelines) is a vast park; picnic area; restaurant; gas station; photo and souvenir shop; free parking lot for 3000 cars; free kennels for any pets you might have brought; a beautiful pond set aside for rare water birds; all manner of animals; baby animals; children's pet corner. Then, of course, the 16th-century chateau itself; a treasury of priceless furniture, tapestries, a library. Summer concerts, some with children's musical fare (such as Peter and the Wolf, Carnival of Animals).

The **Parc de Saint-Vrain** (Tel: (01) 492–10–80 and (01) 456–10–80) offers safaris by car and boat in an African game reserve 28 miles from Paris. There's a zoo, an amusement park, and a prehistoric museum, I don't know about this safari attraction; but it can't compare with Thoiry. A special bus gets you there, leaving from 23 ter blvd. de la

Bastille, IV. For schedules, telephone (01) 456–00–07.

Punch and Judy, Guignol, Marionettes, call the performances what you will, you can see them at **Guignol des Batignolles** (Square des Batignolles, XVII); **Marionettes du Champs-de-Mars; Theatre d'Animation de Vincennes** (37 rue de Montreuil) and, also in the Vincennes area, at **Theatre Astral** (ave. de la Pyramide, XII) on Wed., Sat. and Sun. afternoons); **Theatre de la Plaine** (13 rue du General Guillaumat, XV). Your concierge or the OTP can give you the times and schedules of these and the following, if you really want to know, although they just happen, it seems to me, with no real way of planning. **Jardins des Champs-Elysees** VIII, has the oldest marionette theater in Paris; Theatre du Vrai Guignolet, for Punch and Judy, with almost continuous performances. Mar.–Sept.; ponies to ride; horse-drawn carriages; goat carts; donkey carts. **Jardin du Luxembourg** (blvd. St.-Michel VI) has a Theatre des Marionettes daily; performances out of season too; model sailboat pond (you can rent a boat); playground; tennis and croquet; cafe; merry-go-round; donkeys to ride. **Jardin des Tuileries** (place de la Concorde) has a big model boat sailing pond; Punch and Judy; playground with some red, yellow, and blue monstrosities in the shape of giraffes and the like, along with barrels and things to climb through and on, of contemporary design. One of the loveliest parks is **Buttes-Chaumont** XIX in the northern sector of Paris, with a lake, a waterfall, a little island with a small temple from which you get a magnificent view of Paris, a marionette theater, horses to ride, a playground, and several restaurants. Great merry-go-round, rocks to climb on, Punch and Judy. **Parc Monceau** (blvd. Courcelles, XVII) has a river, a grotto, ruins to explore, a playground and a sand pit, tiny carousel, charming seasonal flower gardens, statuary, and a snack stand selling crisp, fresh waffles. **Parc Montsouris** (blvd. Jourdan, XIV), has a reproduction of the Beylical Palace in Tunisia; an English garden; a waterfall; an observatory; swings, seesaws; Punch and Judy; a lake; restaurant-cafe; very special surprises.

On weekend afternoons, all the ***sidewalk performers***—weightlifters, sword-swallowers, fire-eaters, quick sketch artists—can be found around the *Montmartre area,* around the *blvd. Clichy* and near *pl. Pigalle,* so if you are in the area, allow time for taking in these sights. Don't linger too long because this area is transformed into a steamy sex-market at night.

Fireworks, dancing in the streets, and good times on Bastille Day (July 14), at Pont-Neuf, Carigliano Bridge, Sacre-Coeur Basilica, Parc Montsouris, Parc des Buttes-Chaumont. Wild and wonderful. Beautiful fireworks, lots of noise. Of all the bridges, be sure to let the children linger on **Pont Alexandre III** with its golden winged horses.

On most weekend and holiday evenings Paris is floodlit, there are tours, but you could do your own in a fiacre or just walking, which is always a joy in Paris. The following are ***floodlit:*** Hotel de Ville, Arc de Triomphe, pl. de la Concorde, the Madeleine, Notre-Dame, the Ste.-Chapelle, the Sacre-Coeur, the Tour St.-Jacques, the Pantheon, the Colonne and the pl. Vendome, the Opera, the Conciergerie, the Colonne de Juillet, the pl. de la Nation and de la Republique, St.-Germain-l'Auxerois, the Fountains of the pl. St.-Michel, the Palais de Chaillot; the fountains of the Rond-Point des Champs-Elysees. Mid-Mar.–Oct., at the **Invalides,** there are nightly ***sound and light*** pageants in English. Tape-recorded English commentary is available at the Pantheon, Ste.-Chapelle, and the Arc de Triomphe.

Children's choirs? At St.-Severin, La Trinite, St.-Etienne, you can hear children's choirs. **Les Petits Chanteurs au Croix des Bois** (The Little Singers of the Wooden Cross), the French counterpart of the Vienna Boys Choir, give concerts all over France, and in Paris at the Salle Pleyel, (252 Faubourg-St.-Honore), and at the Palais de Chaillot, (Place du Trocadero), and a Midnight Mass at St.-Eustache. The Paris *Herald Tribune* will usually list these under their entertainment section, but it's wisest to check with **Jeunesses Musicales de France** (1 ave. Delcasse, VIII; Tel: (01) 887–19–54); **Centre Nationale d'Animation Musicale** (55 rue de Varenne, VII; Tel: (01) 222–93–60); **Federation Francaise des Petits Chanteurs** (1 rue Garanciere, VI; Tel: (01) 329–56–70) all of which can provide helpful information for music-lovers of all ages. ***Religious music?*** Best heard at the Dominican Church (222 Faubourg St.-Honore); the Oratoire; Ste.-Chapelle; St.-Eustache; St.-Francois-Xavier; St.-Louis-des-Invalides (Hotel des Invalides); St.-Merri (78 rue St.-Martin); St.-Phillipe-du-Roule (pl. Chassaigne-Goyon); St.-Roch; St.-Sulpice; Temple d'Auteuil, Saint-Severin, Saint-Julien-le-Pauvre, Saint-Germain-des-Pres, and at all Pontifical and other High Masses. High Mass, with organ and choir; time is given in the papers; telephone numbers of churches provided in a free booklet from the OTP. Free concerts every Sun. at Notre Dame, 5:45 p.m.; on Sat. at 9:30 p.m. at St. Severin. Beautiful, memorable.

Children's plays. There are several children's theaters where performances are given from Oct.–June on Thurs. and Sun. afternoons. Prices are little for charmingly presented versions of Cinderella, Snow White and the Seven Dwarfs, and the Three Little Pigs in French. They may sound unfamiliar, but the action is easily followed. Check with the OTP or *Pariscope* for details about what's playing at **Theatre du Petit Monde** (Studio Bertrand, 29 rue du General Bertrand, VII, Tel: (01) 700–23–77) or call yourself, before going to the 3 p.m. Wed. or Sun. matinee. ***Circuses?*** Yes, but not in summer, unless a traveling circus stops somewhere on the outskirts of Paris. Do go. You'll be surprised by the color and talent. **Cirque d'Hiver,** (110 rue Amelot; XI; Tel: (01) 700–12–25) open from Oct. 1 until the box-office falls off. Closed Fri. Absolutely great, splendid animal acts and very talented performers. Reachable by the *Metro* Filles-du-Calvaire.

To market, to market: The Flea Market, **Marche aux Puces** (Porte de Clignancourt XVIII) open all day Sat., Sun., Mon., has an absurd collection of stuff for sale that children enjoy. If your child is a horse- or dog-fancier, then there is a point in going to see dogs for sale or horses, donkeys, and mules at 106 rue Brancion—The **Bird Market** is different. It is held Sun. at pl. Louis-Lepine on the Ile de la Cite near the Cathedral of Notre-Dame; amusing to watch. **Flower markets** at the Conciergerie, IV, also the aux Fleurs de l'Ile de la Cite (everyday except Sun.); on the eastern side of the Madeleine; at the pl. de la Republique; at the pl. des Ternes. The **stamp market** (av. Gabriel and av. Marigny), is open Thurs., Sat., Sun., and holidays. Not a flea market but a cooperative display by antique dealers, complete with carpeting and crystal chandeliers, where you can find anything from signed commodes and poudreuses to entertaining trinkets at **La Cour aux Antiquaires,** (54 Faubourg St.-Honore); no bargains, but an interesting array to check over before you go hunting at the Marche aux Puces—an eye-sharpening experience. Children might be interested in small apprentice pieces and antique toys that are generally on view. The **clothes market (Marche de la Friperie,** Carreau du Temple, IV) open all week, except Mon.; 8 a.m.–7:30 p.m., and open Sun., 8 a.m.–1 p.m. is where your jeunes filles will flip out over the frippery, flappery, retro, thrift shop gear for men, women, children; plus accessories. If you're in Paris during Mar., Apr., May, you can't and mustn't miss the **Foire Nationale a la Ferraille a la Brocante** (The Junk, Scrap-Iron Fair); the **Foire aux Jambons** (the Ham Fair); **Foire au Pain d'Epice** (Gingerbread Fair) which is open two months from the eve of Palm Sunday; **Foire des Poetes** (Poets' Fair). All are popular, with hundreds of indoor and outdoor stands selling regional food, second-hand whatnots, trinkets, snacks; entertainment and general merry-making. ***Covered markets:*** Near Gare du Nord, Gare de l'Est, **Marche Saint-Quentin** (corner of blvd. de Magenta and rue de Chabrol, X) and **Marche de Passy** (corner of rue Bois-le-Vent and rue Duban, XVI) are both attractive with an array of top-quality merchandise and produce. ***Open-air markets and food shops:*** **rue Mouffetard,** V (#134 has its 4 storeys painted with hunting murals), a classic and popular street, but **Rue Cler, VII,** near rue Saint-Dominique and the Champ-de-Mars, is classier with a broad pedestrian street for easier browsing; **rue Poncelet** beginning at ave. des Ternes, XVII, where foie gras, home-made sausages and pastries are highlights; **rue des Belles-Feuilles** (beginning at ave. Victor-Hugo, XVI). From 7 a.m.–1:30 p.m. ***fresh produce markets*** around **place d'Iena** and **ave. du President Wilson, XVI;** Wed. and Sat.; around **place Breteuil, VII;** Thurs. and Sat.; between rue du Cherche-Midi and rue de Rennes, **blvd. Raspail, VI;** Tues. and Fri.; for sites and times of others, ask the OTP. ***Roller skating?*** If you didn't bring any *patins a roulettes* with you, you can pick up second-hand ones at the **Maisons de Troc** mentioned (See Baby Equipment for Hire). Call first to see if they have any before you go. You can roller-skate at the **Tuileries;** at the end of the **Luxembourg** gardens, **Champs-Elysees** gardens, **Trocadero** gardens at the Palais de Chaillot; at **Champ-de-Mars;** in the **Bois de Vincennes,** in **Parc Montsouris,** in the **Jardin d'Acclimation,** in the **Buttes-Chaumont** park, all previously mentioned. Children can swim, ride, ice skate at rinks where skates can be rented; play tennis; see Fun and Games.

▶ **Note:** To obtain information on Paris entertainment programs by telephone, just call (01) 720–88–98.

Now then, three things I *don't* recommend: The **Sewers of Paris** *(Les Egouts).* **The Catacombs.** An underground vault heaped with bones, skulls, and skeletons. **Le Cimetiere des Chiens,** a cemetery for cats, dogs, birds, and pets of all kinds. Rin-Tin-Tin is buried there, to be sure, but this graveyard is of interest chiefly to grownup pet-lovers, not to children.

ATTRACTIONS FOR CHILDREN ELSEWHERE Wherever you go, every town, every village, there's always a *place,* a square, a park, for children; always a miniature train, a merry-go-round, miniature golf, a playground, something attractive for children not only to see, but to do. Remember that Sundays are family days, and you can take your child with you anywhere, and everyone will be accommodating. Overlooked, astonishing little museums crop up all over France. They may be listed in guidebooks but generally too inadequately to suggest their treasures. Outside of Paris, museums are generally open from 10 a.m.–noon, and 2–5 p.m.; closed Mon.; but hours are frequently irregular and small museums may close without notice for repairs, so check before you go.

On the **Ile d'Aix** (off the coast of La Rochelle), where Napoleon surrendered to the English, is the **Napoleonic Museum,** with drawings, paintings, weapons, furniture, miniatures, and many of the Emperor's possessions and artifacts. **Aix-en-Provence:** A town of distinction and tranquillity, with the usual quota of museums, all excellent; the **Cezanne Museum** includes a cathedral; the Cours Mirabeau; a magnificent music festival in summer but no other special attractions for children. **Albi:** A lovely town 50 miles NE of Toulouse, 55 miles N of Carcassonne ideal to visit if you're on a Canal du Midi barge cruise, with a really splendid immense fortified cathedral of rose-colored stone; the **Toulouse Lautrec Museum** (Palais de la Berbie) is the world's most important collection of his work, open daily except Tues. in winter. Go to the covered market on rue Emile Grand for picnic supplies. The 20-room **Reserve,** 1½ mi. out of town, with swimming pool, tennis, and lawns along the Tarn river is four-star bliss; the **Hotel Chiffre,** in the new part of town, has remarkably reasonable rates for a three-starrer. In the old part of town **Hotel du Viel Albi** (25 rue Toulouse-Lautrec), a restaurant, not a hotel, offers terrific value for its lunch and dinner. Music festivals in summer. Grand Prix racing in Sept. In July and Aug., nightly illuminations of the cathedral with musical accompaniment. From here, make the 15-mile excursion to the medieval fortress village of **Cordes,** no cars allowed inside (parking lot provided outside). Its *Grande-Rue* is lined with 13th-and 14th-century houses—now artists' and craftsmen's studios; traditional crafts; summer music festival and medieval celebrations. Sugar sculptures in the dining room of **Maison du Grand Ecuyer,** a three-star, antique-filled hotel with 18 rooms, will enchant your offspring, and the prices for all this culinary artistry are not exorbitant. **Alpe d'Huez** has swimming pools (heated); high altitude skiing; discotheques; chair lifts to Pic Blanc for experts' skiing on Sarenne Glacier. **Annecy:** In summer, one of the loveliest resorts at the foot of Mont Blanc; arcaded streets, weeping willows and pink roses over winding canals; yummy pastry shops; castle in the old section; modern amenities in the new section; boats on Lake Annecy, including a three-hour steamer trip; fishing; swimming; waterskiing; exploring the countryside. A bus excursion to Chamonix via Megeve is 3½ hours up the mountain and three hours back. At **Antibes,** a charming old port town on the Riviera, the **Musee Grimaldi,** with Picassos; town market. **Arles:** Many Roman ruins, including an amphitheater still used for bullfights and other events. Many Picasso drawings in **Musee Reattu** in a medieval priory. Have supper at **Da Guido** and listen to gypsy music. **Avignon:** children should see the remains of the **Bridge of St.-Benezet,** the bridge of *Sur le Pont d'Avignon* where everyone danced, according to the nursery rhyme. A Festival of Light and Sound outside the **Palace of the Popes** is more enjoyable for children than the guided tour of its interior. From here you can arrange a boat trip of any length along the Rhone. **Avoriaz,** a ***ski resort,*** allows no traffic; you must leave your car at the parking space outside the entrance and then proceed by sleigh, drawn by horse, Lapland reindeer, or sleddogs. Or come up by funicular from Morzine. The **Children's Village,** a large chalet with eating, rest and play areas for little ones to enjoy while learning how to ski is run by two retired ski champions. Older children can participate in classes ranging from beginners through racing; open daily 9 a.m.–5 p.m.; daily fee includes lifts, instruction, food. Also two-hour ski classes with reduced prices for the kiddies. Two ski schools have classes and can guide you through the **Portes du Soleil,** encompassing a dozen or so resorts on both sides of the Franco-Swiss border. **Residence Snow,** across from the Children's Village, has family accommodations including bunk beds and regular beds. Efficiency apartments at the **Residence Les Portes du Soleil;** more sumptuous accommodation at the **Hotel Les Dromonts;** or you might want to rent an apartment. Details from the FGTO or from the Syndicat d'Initiative (74110 Avoriaz, Morzine, Haute-Savoie). The mountain transport facilities were laid out by super-star Jean-Claude Killy. International swingers love this resort; and for the sophisticated, well-off family it should be very pleasant. Club Mediterranee has a *village de neige* here, also. **Balleroy,** in Calvados country in Normandy, not far from the **Relais Chateau d'Audrieu** (Tel: (31) 80–21–52), for a big-spending family, and not far also from **Chateau de Fontaine-Henry,** a classically beautiful Norman chateau to visit, is a chateau that is the home in France of Malcolm S. Forbes, American magazine publisher, art connoisseur and ballooning enthusiast, with a **ballooning museum** on the premises (open 9 a.m.–noon, 2 p.m.–6 p.m., closed Wed.).

Bayonne—where bayonets come from—has bullfights. **Biarritz** is not a place I'd take children except to see the aquarium in the **Musee de la Mer. Benodet** in Brittany has excellent uncrowded beaches, brisk and cool; boats constantly sailing in and out of the bays; terrific excitement during the summer regattas; very pleasant. **Bidart:** clifftop village; special. **Belle-Ile-en-Mer.** See Quiberon. **Bourges:** A museum city, quite wonderful to wander about in. The **Cathedrale St. Etienne** is incredibly beautiful, Gothic; golden candelabra seem to drop out of the ceiling; its gardens were designed by Le Notre. At **Cagnes-sur-Mer, Renoir's villa,** filled with his paintings and sculpture. In tiny Cagnes-le-Haut, on a 400′ rock promontory, the Chateau has everything from Chagalls to ancient olive presses. In the hills is the **Fernand Leger Museum. Cahors:** Medieval town, interesting and charming. See its impressive **Cathedral de St.-Etienne** and the **Pont Valentre,** a six-arched, fortified medieval bridge over the Lot River, with three towers with parapets. **Carcassone:** An incredibly lovely walled medieval town, capital of the Dept. of Aude; the first sight of this towered town, backed by the Pyrenees, will captivate your children. Other towns and other scenes pale when you see Carcassonne. An ancient little **museum** is filled with surrealist pictures by Miro, Ernst, Tanguy, Masson.

Carnac: remarkable dolmens, menhirs, and other neolithic remains; many boat trips possible from the special places around the Gulf of Morbihan and beyond; rent a villa unless you're able to spring for a stay at the two-star **Chateau de Locguenole** nearby in Hennebout. **Chamonix:** the doyen of ***ski resorts,*** with mountains on all four sides; for ski buffs, always a challenge, varied terrain. It has joli panoramas and some very attractive package all-inclusive deals. Vast skiing fields at Grands Montets. Your children will sense the awe and majesty of Mont Blanc. Chamonix has a style all its own—no steep-roofed chalets; it could be a Mediterranean town. Skiing never stops completely. In summer come the mountaineers. The cable car rides will thrill or terrify you; children who like roller coasters will adore them. A teleferique goes to the top of Mont Blanc; a cog railway to the great **Mer de Glace** (bring warm sweaters); a cable car for a three-hour ride into Italy for lunch; sightseeing planes too. Also Olympic pool, ice rink, golf, tennis, and huge sauna.

Chantilly, 28 miles from Paris, a chateau surrounded by a park designed by Le Notre and a beautiful forest. Best for children are its stables that have become a living museum of the horse—**Musee Vivant du Cheval**—open daily except Tues., from 10:30 a.m.–5 p.m., with ***equestrian presentations*** at noon, 3 p.m., 5 p.m. between Apr. 1 and

Oct. 31, and at 2:30 p.m. and 4 p.m. the rest of the year; exhibitions. (For further information about these equine exhibitions, telephone (04) 457–13–13). You could combine this with the races, nearby and exciting, feeding the carp that swim in the moat of the chateau, a picnic in the forest. Inside the chateau, the **Musee Conde** contains over 300 miniatures. Many works by Poussin, Fouquet, Watteau, in this extremely important little collection. Guided tours of the apartments are given in French, but if you telephone ahead (04) 457–03–62), an English-speaking guide will be provided; open daily 10:30 a.m.–6 p.m. between April 1–Sept. 30, and from 10:30 a.m.–5 p.m. the rest of the year. **Chartres:** The cathedral. **Collonges-la-Rouge:** Houses are built of deep red sandstone with red roofs or blue and turreted roofs of schist. **Colmar:** A storybook village—white houses with chocolate wooden framework and high gabled roofs. Canals overhung with willow trees—floodlit at night. The conventional sights—**Musee d'Unterlinden,** with its rose-colored sandstone cloister arches, and inside a collection of folk art and the marvelous, nightmarish masterpiece of the Issenheim Altarpiece; the old **Custom House;** the restaurant in the **Maison des Tetes,** where the *tetes* turn out to be grinning wooden gargoyles—are all appealing to children. **Concarneau:** A walled town; those hand-dyed nets and sails, bright little sardine and tuna boats, and fishermen in red denim, wooden sabots, and stocking caps that have provided so much subject material for so many paintings. Arrangements can be made to explore the **Ville Close,** a walled village in the middle of the harbor, or for a fishing trip. During Aug., the Festival of the Blue Fishing Nets livens up the area with folkloric events. The **Musee de la Peche** is a delight with exhibits about fishing from all over the world, with emphasis, naturally on Breton fishing; also model ships and a small **Aquarium** with the names of the fish in Breton as well as French. The **Grand Hotel** is the best place to stay unless you don't mind bathrooms curtained off from the room, which you'll find in the **Hotel Moderne** unless it's recently been renovated; one-star restaurant at the Grand; fine meals at **Chez Armand,** and you can have the ultimate fish soup at **Le Galion** in the Ville Close. Nearby, at **Pont-Aven,** is the **Moulin Rosmadec,** romantic old mill overlooking a millrace, lovely place to eat and fine food, but pricey, and you have to reserve at least a day in advance in season. (Tel: Pont-Aven 06–00–22); they don't take credit cards. **Conques:** The adorable **Church of Ste.-Foy,** with marvelous golden reliquary in its treasury, is extraordinarily special. **Cordes:** See Albi.

Cote d'Azur: The hill towns of the Riviera (such as cliff-clinging Eze, Cap Ferrat with a little zoo, or Villefranche slanting steeply to the quays) and any one of the three roads along the seaboard (but preferably in the mountains) are all pretty breathtaking, but scenery is of no real appeal to children under 14. Teenagers like the tandem pedi-cars rentable at St. Tropez along the rue Poste; and nearby Tahiti Beach is one of the best in the south; but it's far too jet-setty for the young. Le Lavandou is about the best choice for families with under-18 teenagers. However, this sundrenched part of the world is probably one of the best lessons in art appreciation you could possibly give your children, because these are the scenes and colors repeated over and over again in the work of Cezanne, Matisse, and Van Gogh. But, though the Riviera is very pretty and fun if you have a boat, *except for Nice,* in my opinion there isn't anything that the children could do here that they wouldn't have more fun doing in other places. The 60 miles of better beach area is between Hyeres and St. Raphael.

The **Cote Vermeille** is a 110-mile stretch of beach that owes its name to the red-porphyry rocks that slope into the Mediterranean. It is far more relaxed as a seaside resort area for children than the Cote d'Azur. Cap d'Agde, is the site of a *huge* tennis camp. The new resort of **La Grande-Motte** near Montpellier is preferable, I think, to the new resort **Port-Camargue.** I prefer **Collioure** for family stays. Leucate-Barcares forms a natural lido along a five-mile isthmus between sandy beach and navigable lagoon linked with canals. One of the main attractions is the liner *Lydia,* permanently anchored in the sand and turned into a shop of pleasures with its own swimming pool. When the children are in bed, you may enjoy the nightclubs aboard, too! Among the ***festivals*** in the neighborhood are the Pablo Casals Music Festival at Prade in July; water-jousting in Aug. in the harbor of Sete; the Muleteers' Festival and other folkloric events during Aug. at Amelie-les-Bains. The area, developed as a yachting center (many sailing schools in full swing) also has tennis and riding. The immediate surroundings of Cap d'Agde and Gruissan Plage are interesting and picturesque. The Cap is a peninsula formed from the lava of two extinct volcanoes; various 12th-century buildings at Agde; a trading post built by the Greeks and later used by the Romans. Gruissan is surmounted by the ruins of a medieval castle. Narbonne Plage, at **Narbonne,** naturally, is 30 miles south of **Carcassonne.** Tiny ports filled with boats with colored sails—Cerbere, Banyuls, **Collioure,** with its anchovy fishermen and its **Templars' Castle;** then Argeles-sur-Mer, with its groves of umbrella pines and its fine sand beach, followed up the curving coast by a succession of other fine sand beaches. There are six-passenger open buses, which look like bathtubs on wheels that will transport you into the Pyrenees. Inland, to the west, the large and lively town of **Perpignan** has a great castle, the fortifications of its citadel and a cathedral. For those who like the new and contemporary with the possibility of exploring the old and the charming in the neighborhood, the Cote Vermeille should be of interest. July and Aug. are festival time for all the resorts.

Courchevel, in the Trois Vallees area, the largest ski resort in France, has many intermediate runs, many blue (easy) and green (very easy) runs; good ice skating as well, hotels right alongside the ski runs, so you don't have to cope with hauling skis and long walks to lifts; modern, relaxed, informal, lively and comprising four stations, each with its cluster of hotels, shops, restaurants. Nearby **Meribel** has small apartments and chalets for rent, as does **Mottaret,** but on a larger scale. For ***skiing*** at all levels—forget charm, atmosphere—Courchevel is the place for families who just want to concentrate on *skiing,* beginner, intermediate, and expert. **Deauville,** in the peak July and Aug. season, attracts the Beautiful People, who stay at the **Normandy,** the **Royal** (courtyard filled with flowers and apple trees), the Golf hotels, or on their boats. Life centers about the casino which overlooks the famous flowered beach with flower beds and tented changing rooms, the **Bar du Soleil** where everyone people-watches, and a Pompeian swimming pool that older children like. Notices about the casino, races, and other amusements are often posted on the church door. A feeling of Saratoga-Palm Beach-Newport, with a dash of Hollywood—and Atlantic City. Bumper-to-bumper traffic to and from Paris on weekends. It offers Mont Canisy, the original village; not-very-good golf course; boardwalk, beach, and icy sea (where fishermen wade in waist deep with long-handled nets to scoop up the delicious tiny Channel shrimp). **Le Notre,** a branch of the French patisserie house is here. Prices are sky high at Deauville during the season. Out of season, it's not cheap, but reasonable. **Dinan,** S along the Rance River from Dinard and reachable by excursion boat from St. Malo in summer, is a center for woven material; whether you stay at the **Hotel d'Avaugour** or not, treat yourself to a meal there—the food is superb! In **Dinard,** in Brittany, very popular with the English, everyone seems smiling, helpful, friendly. A river port with three beautiful sandy cliff-enclosed bays, a great round swimming pool overlooking the beach, trees growing almost to the water's edge, you'll find very safe swimming and vast, clean, golden beaches, plus a casino, sound and light performances during the summer season. The **Grand** is a large, comfortable hotel. A seaside walk on the *Promenade du Clair du Lune* is memorable.

Flaine: A new ***ski resort,*** comprises Marcel Breuer-designed stark, white cube-shape buildings grouped around a central plaza of which the focus is a skating rink, whose music is audible only to the skaters. Plenty of nightclubs and restaurants; a day-nursery for young children; an abundance of pistes for all skiers; a ski school. In addition to three hotels, there are furnished flats for rent, ranging from two-room studios sleeping two to four persons to four-room flats sleeping eight to ten. **Fontainebleau:** On the way, dawdle in the **Forest of Fontainebleau** and have a meal in the village of Barbizon in a two-star restaurant to give you strength for Fontainebleau whose horseshoe stairway is probably one of the best known details of French architecture. The paintings of Hercules and murals of the story of Alexander may ring a bell with the children if they happen to be pointed out in the general munificence.

A sweet grotto in the **Jardin des Pins,** a fine piece of fantasy with human figures emerging in sculpture from the arches, is worth hunting out. This will be a strain on the children's good nature, but the lasting impression will be worth it. **Fontaine-de-Vaucluse** hasn't a fountain but a very pretty spring at the foot of a sheer cliff where you can have a picnic by the side of a ruined chateau and a house where Petrarch lived. The spring turns into a foaming torrent during the spring and winter, but whenever you go it really is very pleasant. Restaurants nearby. **Fougeres,** a walled town in Brittany with a many-towered, massive castle, a lovely old quarter by the river, a pretty public garden.

Giverny, 50 miles from Paris, in Normandy, is where Claude Monet lived, painted, gardened; open 10 a.m.–noon, 2 p.m.–6 p.m., daily except Mon. Summer concerts here, some with young people's choirs. The all butter-yellow dining room in the restored house is a sunny surprise for children who also like the lily ponds and wandering about the exquisite gardens. About an hour's drive from Paris, but the train is easier.

In **Grenoble,** queen of the French Alps, a **Stendhal Museum** on the site of his birthplace, far more interesting than most author-dedicated museums. On the heights of the town, in the convent of Ste.-Marie-d'en-Haut, the **Dauphiny Museum** has a fascinating collection of regional lore. **Guerande:** See La Baule. **Honfleur:** Historic seaport of the Seine (you can hire a boat and follow the Seine from Paris to here) with old harbor, cobbled streets; wooden church of Ste. Catherine; the local speciality of chocolate mousse; half-timber and stone houses; ***artists' colony*** which cradled the Impressionist school. Many amateur artists still sitting about with sketch pads and easels, none of whom seem to mind being asked questions in English by small children. **La Baule** is one of France's top resorts, a children's paradise, with a five-mile crescent of beach on the Atlantic, deep-eaved villas and hotels, dozens of tennis courts, waterskiing, heated swimming pools, a casino, an 18-hole golf course. **Grand Hotel de l'Hermitage** is the most elegant and lavish in town. The **Castel Marie-Louise,** a member of the Relais et Chateaux Hotel Association, open all year, is smaller, cozier, has a one-star restaurant, is just down the street; many smaller hotels and pensions. Also pleasant rooms and apartments to rent by the week or the month; agencies which handle these are: **Gam** (2 ave. de la Plage) and **Utoring** (103 blvd. de l'Ocean). **Manuel's,** by the harbor, in downtown La Baule, serving homemade ice cream and sherbets, crepes and Breton waffles filled with sugar or fruits.

Dozens of play-group clubs for children 4–12 line the beach, well-equipped with swings, slides, jungle gyms, see-saws. The families who run them are delighted to have your children. Your concierge or the **Syndicat d'Initiative** can make the arrangements if you don't speak French. Don't worry about your children. There's a tennis club of La Baule, the **Poney Club de la Cote d'Amour** (Tel: La Baule 61–31–62) where children 4–12 can take riding lessons, mini-golf nearby, bicycle rental at **Locacycle** (223 ave. de Lattre-de-Tassigny). You can picnic in the **Foret d'Escoubiac** or toward **Le Croisic,** a fishing port, with sandy coves for picnicking, a sheltered beach, and all the joys of the simple life. There's an aquarium, and in-between, **Batz-sur-Mer,** with inexpensive outdoor restaurants, and **Le Pouliguen,** the next town from La Baule, with summertime concerts in its Church of Saint- Nicholas; wonderfully inexpensive pensions, such as the **Hotel Beau-Rivage** and a delicious seafood restaurant, **Voile d'Or. Pornichet,** on the other side of La Baule, like Le Pouliguen, also has beach clubs for children. Half-day bicycling excursions can be made to **Guerande,** about four miles from La Baule, a preserved medieval walled village, with Thurs. organ concerts in the summer in the **Collegiale de Guerande;** a museum in the towers at the Main Gate has a nice collection of Breton odds and ends, and a history of the *marais salants,* the local salt marshes, and the *paludiers,* the people who cultivate them. You can also visit the nearby 14th-century **Chateau de Careil,** with its regional museum, a charmer, and a swimming pool you and campers on the property may swim in. **La Cote Sauvage:** See Quiberon. **La Plagne** is an all-recreation resort, no roads, no cars. Outdoor swimming, theater, concerts, and the **France** (a shipshape hotel operated by the French Line); **Lascaux,** site of the famous prehistoric grotto rock-paintings from the Aurignacian period of the Stone Age, painted by Cro-Magnon man, was closed in 1963 when the paintings began to deteriorate. But **Lascaux II,** about 150 yards from the original site, is an authentic copy of its paintings, completed in 1983; open for public view. **Le Cabellou,** a lovely forest-backed little bay, quiet; smooth, sand beaches, definitely a family resort; even tiny **Hotel de la Bonne Auberge** on the beach offers a playroom for children, enclosed garden, and a warm welcome for families. **Les Andelys,** in the Seine Valley 20 miles SE of Rouen, is where you can explore, as Flaubert once did, the ruins of Richard the Lion-Hearted's **Chateau Gaillard** on its height above the river. **Les Arcs** (Savoie) comprises three villages of ski instruction, outstanding for their creative approach at all levels. **Club Mediterranee** has a *village de neige* here. For details, the FGTO or Maison des Arcs (Arcs 1800, 73700 Bourg St. Maurice, Savoie). **Les Baux** is a charming village two hours W of Marseilles, known for its great De Baumaniere restaurant and its Christmas santons.

Les Eyzies: Prehistoric sites and caves around this village are fascinating, and there is a wonderful **museum of prehistoric relics** (far more interesting than they sound) housed in a castle. This Dordogne region is considered a treasure trove of prehistory by scientists, but the cave paintings are also one of the world's great and unusual sights. Try to see the 70 caves and rock shelters before they are closed owing to damage or defacement—here and at **Le Moustier, Font-de-Gaume** (the animal paintings are as remarkable and endearing to children as to archaeologists), **Les Combarelles, Rouffignac, Abri Cap Blanc, La Greze; Cabrerets** (the **Pech-Merle** cave plus Cougnac cave), in the neighboring department of Lot; the prehistoric caves at **Mas d'Azil** and **Niaux** in the department of Ariege in the Midi-Pyrenees area, and the **Gargas** grottoes in the Hautes Pyrenees; prehistoric grottoes also way to the NE near Macon, at **Aze** where there's a museum, and a sloth of bears hibernating there in wintertime. For more information about these sites, contact **Association Nationale des Exploitants de Cavernes Amenagees pour le Tourisme** c/o the FGTO. Better yet, if you're really interested in seeing these extraordinary caverns and prehistoric shelters, individual visits as well as small group tours for the dedicated student and avocational archaeologist are arranged by David Abrams, Past Times, Archaeological Tours, 800 Larch Lane, Sacramento, CA 95825; Tel: (016) 485–8140. (See also Lascaux, Niaux.)

Le Touquet, about 20 miles from Boulogne, is relaxed, with pine forests and bracing sea air; a sumptuous casino; tennis; two fine golf courses; excellent riding stables; enormous unheated swimming pool on the beach; the English come here, but few Americans. The old rich and their families come for the quiet, fine food, pheasant shooting. Teenagers and children often prefer the excitement and gaiety of Deauville. Life in Le Touquet is far more casual. **Le Val Andre** in Brittany, a little ***sailing resort*** with a yacht-filled harbor, casino, every diversion, great beach, and many private villas. **Limoges,** where that china comes from; but the factory and the museum of porcelain bore almost all children literally or figuratively to tears.

Loire chateaux: The hub of the chateau country is the city of Tours, with other bases being Orleans, Blois, and Angers, from which buses set out for chateau-viewing trips daily and nightly; from Easter through Oct., the **Son et Lumiere** programs, only in French, although English texts are available. A minimum of three days is recommended, so if you don't want to skip the chateaux, you have, as I see it, the following choices: (1) Stay in Tours, take the children with you on the motorcoach daytime runs, and, if they are not up to the nocturnal bus ramblings and spectacles, get in a babysitter to watch them while you go off and see the past come alive. (2) Stay in a chateau-hotel and avail yourself of babysitting facilities day and night, leaving you free to roam around while the children roam the gardens and woods of the chateau during the day, reliably supervised. To be certain of getting an English-speaking babysitter or children's companion, get in touch with the local Syndicat d'Initiative. The Loire Valley, even early in the year, is so jammed with traffic that you should either plan to visit early in the spring or late fall, or leave sufficient time to tour via bicycle or car on the smaller, less known roads which may be narrow, but are hard-surfaced. Take Route #760 from Loches to Valencay. Going from Loches to Montresor, you'll see a charming chateau called **Chartreuse de Liguet** where chartreuse is still made. Henry II of England built this chateau and it's worth a stop. Farther along the same road, overlooking a lake, is the 12th-century Courorie, also a producer of chartreuse, and parchment for church scribes. At **Amboise,** please don't skip **Clos Luce,** linked to Amboise by a subterranean passage, a gothic castle-museum, filled with models constructed from the plans of Leonardo da Vinci, as well as memorabilia of this extraordinary genius who lived and died here in the 16th century. The chateau at **Valencay** has a park filled with deer, dromedaries, peacocks, flamingoes and a small museum devoted to Tallyrand. Don't expect your children to be as impressed with the beauty of **Chenonceaux,** for example, as you are. Children generally will be more interested in such curiosities as dungeons, or the spiraling staircase at **Chambord,** where the people walking up can't see the people walking down. Handsome historic chateaux are being restored and opened to the public constantly. **Bouges,** an elegant 50-room affair is one of the more recent to be added to the list. In addition to the stacks of information you get from the FGTO, be sure to pick up the detailed Michelin's *Chateaux de la Loire*. The *Chateaux de France,* an Hachette/Vendome publication, incorporates everything you want to know about chateaux, not only in the Loire, but throughout Paris. The annual calendar of the sound and light shows, or son-et-lumiere spectacles, varies as to times, dates, programs. The term "sound and light" is also deceptive, because many of these pageants involve hundreds of costumed actors, horsemen, fountains playing, ballets, fireworks, as well as the lights, music and commentary which, naturally, is delivered in French with only occasional English versions. Admissions for children according to their age groups can be reductions for children 5–12 at Valencay, reductions for children between 10 and 12 at Amboise, reductions for children between 5 and 15 at Beaugency, for children less than 12 at Blois, for children up to 16 at Chambord, for children between 7 and 15 at Chenonceaux, for children under 12 at Nibelle, or even no reductions at some chateaux. So check before you go. The FGTO can supply you with relevant information. **Amboise, Lassay, Le Lude, Nibelle, Nohant, Sologne-Chaon, Valencay** always can be counted on to produce splendid shows, and **Les-Espresses-le-Puy-du-Fou** on Fri. and Sat., June–Aug., is usually truly fabulous. At **Blois,** you can count on an English commentary following the French version. When in **Tours,** you can check about the Loire castle extravaganzas with the **Office de Tourisme** et Accueil de France (place Marechal Le Clerc; Tel: (47) 05–58–08).

Lourdes: Annual pilgrimages are at their peak in Aug. At **Luchon,** an elegant all-year resort with great skiing in winter, a cog railway will take you 6000′ up to Superbagneres; see Lake Oo, with a spectacular waterfall. Near **Lyons/Lyon,** a **Firemen's Museum** at La Duchere; seven miles north, **Musee Francais de l'Automobile** set inside and about the Chateau de Rochetaillee-sur Saone; automobiles, bicycles, motorcycles housed grandly amid pink marble columns, parquet floors, ivied walls. Great fun for fathers and sons! **Lyons,** once the capital of Gaul, is under three hours from Paris by TGV (the high-speed express train) and is dominated by the Fourviere hill, with the **Fourviere Gallo-Roman Museum,** a vast concrete-and-glass structure with an interior ramp (like the Guggenheim in NY) hollowed into its side, open 9 a.m.–noon, 2 p.m.–6 p.m. daily except Mon. **Vieux Lyon,** the old Lyons quarter, just below **Notre Dame de Fourviere,** is a network of medieval churches, cobblestone alleyways, 15th- and 16th-century houses(!) an area of craftsmen, small shops, pleasant cafes. The town is flowed through by the Rhone and Saone, so that **Presqu'ile** (''almost an island'') thrusts into the city center, with a lovely square, **Place Bellecour,** where you can get information and guidebooks from the **Accueil de France** visitor's bureau (Tel: (78) 42–25–75); also a cozy two-star family hotel, the **Bayard** (Tel: (78) 837–39–64) is here, only a brisk from the Bonaparte bridge that leads you to Fourviere. The **Musee des Beaux-Arts** has exceptional sculpture by Despiau, Rodin, Daumirer and Avignon primitives. Let's hope your life will be as smooth as the Lyons silk exhibits in the **Musee Historique des Tissus** (rue de la Charite); also Coptic textiles which children like for the designs; Middle Eastern, Oriental, Italian, Spanish fabrics. A 30 minute drive to the NE, will bring you to the fortified medieval village of **Perouges,** a recommended excursion. (See Perouges). Beajolais vineyards, **Pilat** and **Vercors** regional parks, Haute Savoie lake district, ski resorts are all within two to three hours by car or through air links.

Malmaison, the country house where Napoleon and Josephine lived, just outside Paris is simple, charming, rustic; all sorts of interesting exhibits, such as Josephine's jewels and lavish clothes, Napoleon's coronation robes, camp furniture, notebooks, many personal belongings. The surrounding park is lovely. **Marseilles:** You can skip Marseilles as far as the children are concerned, and don't let anyone tell you the marshes of Camargue are any Wild-West Wonderland. During festival times, there are wonderful horse processions, but on ordinary days I've never seen many horses or riders around. An outstanding **bird sanctuary,** but take along plenty of insect repellent because there are more mosquitoes than birds. The **Musee du Vieux Marseille** is near City Hall. However, if you're near here in Dec. to early Jan., don't miss the **Santon Fair.** Santons are pottery figures designed for Christmas creches or manger scenes. Many are given local costumes of Provence; the art of making santons is handed down from father to son; quite special. Arles has an exhibit of figurines made by master santon craftsmen. **Megeve** is a chic, ***high fashion resort*** with skating, swimming pools, discotheques, nightclubs, casino and the Mont d'Arbois hotel. Swingers, serious skiers, and families all seem perfectly accommodated. Several children's hotels (Maisons d'Enfants) are open all year, but more fun during the winter, when young guests can board and take skiing lessons with children of their own age. **Minerve:** An **Archaeological Museum** with special emphasis on the history of wine. In the principality of **Monaco,** in an elegant villa set in an exquisite summer rose garden, is the **National Museum,** and the de Galea collection of dolls and automatons dating from the 18th and 19th centuries, perhaps the most important trove of its kind in the world—an unexpected and fascinating highlight on Ave. Princess Grace across from the Centenary Hall. Open daily from 10 a.m.–12:15 p.m. and from 2:30–6:30 p.m. Admission is about $2, half-price for children 5–15 (under 5 free). Enchantment for a pittance! An excellent Oceanographic Museum. Also a zoo, the royal palace, the cathedral, all up on **Le Rocher** the promontory of old Monaco, with a maze of pastel-painted houses set about lanes with restaurants that place their tables out in the streets; a short drive east to Italian border or west to the French Riviera. The eroded stones of **Montpellier-le-Vieux** cause it to take on the appearance of an other-worldly town; its area is an object lesson of what rainwater infiltration and river erosion can do, and the contrast of natural wonders and medieval towns makes the province of Languedoc-Roussillon a favorite of mine.

Mont-St.-Michel A prime target during June–Sept., it is considered one of the wonders of the world. Sitting in the middle of the Bay of Mont-St. Michel and connected by a causeway with the mainland, it is a rock about a mile in circumference on which is built a great monastery with 13th-century fortifications encompassing a medieval village of around 300 inhabitants, and maybe a few less shops and eating places. The streets are all cobbled and lead you up into the **Abbey** and up its stairway to a gallery 400′ above the sea. If you can afford it, stay at **Mere Poulard,** spend the night, which entails moving your car from the parking lot where it will be covered with water when the tide rolls in (specific times signposted everywhere), up on to the causeway where it can overnight safely. A great deal of walking on cobblestones and stair-climbing is involved in this expedition; wear your comfiest shoes. Less expensive rooms are available at the **Mouton Blanc** and the **Vieille Auberge.**

Morgat is a well-sheltered, lively swimming and ***beach resort*** beloved by the English. **Morzine** has sleigh riding in pine forests, swimming pool, ice shows, seven cabarets; services of Avoroiaz reachable by funicular. **Mougins,** a tiny, enchanting village, has a pink church on its hilltop, a splashing fountain in its tree-shaded square, and super *sorbets* sold by the scoop from an old-fashioned ice-cream wagon stationed in front of **Le Relais de Mougins. L'Amandier,** a 1-star restaurant built into an old millhouse is among 16 *cordon bleu* dining sanctuaries of this gastronomic enclave. Nearby this minuscule village where Picasso once lived is a woodland swamp where many water-loving birds can be seen and heard. **Mulhouse: National Automobile Museum** (192 ave. de Colmar) with 500 Maseratis, Bugattis, Ferraris, Lotuses and others on display in two vast carpeted (and heated-in-the-winter-time) halls; open 11 a.m.–6 p.m., except Tues., Christmas, New Year's. Restaurant, special access also for the handicapped to see these historic treasures collected by the brothers Schlumf and preserved now by the French government. **Nantes,** ancient capital of Brittany. A look at its medieval **Josselin castle** with its towers and turrets reflected in the **Canal de Nantes a Brest** (on which you can take boat rides) is instant enchantment and there's a fine **Breton Museum** inside, with displays of regional costumes and furniture. The **Musee Dobree** comprises three buildings housing armor and weaponry, wonderful pre-historic collection in the modern building, traveling exhibits. **Musee de Salorges** is a fascinating maritime museum; **Musee des Beaux Arts** has a masterpiece by Ingres you can let your children search out; the **Cathedral** is splendid, light and white inside, with some of the tallest naves in France; **Ile Feydeau,** the main street, has some lovely old houses; the **Jardin des Plantes** is a dream of a botanical garden; boat rides on the scenic Erdre river take you to **Suce sur Erdre,** as enchanting an image as Josselin castle, and an imperative excursion if you have time. **Relais du Chateau** is for gourmandising, and next door to the **Hotel Duchesse Anne,** old, comfortable, traditional hotel with no restaurant, but convenient to the Josselin Chateau and the Cathedral. **Aux Deux Musees** is a self-service cafe. **Le Coq Hardi** is the Sun. noon dining place for the bourgeoisie Nantaise. **Hotel Jacques Borel** (Ile Beaulieu), not convenient without a car, is a modern chain hotel with a good grillroom and good food. **Niaux:** An Outward-Bound sort of struggling adventure is necessary to see these prehistoric drawings and paintings, and only if you join an archaeological guided tour. See **Les Eyzies. Nice:** The great, white **Hotel Negresco** (37 Promenade des Anglais), and its restaurant, **Chantecler,** are expensive but worth every penny. Closed Nov. Beaches are rocky, but there are good museums: **Natural History, Archaeological,** and **Terra Amata Pre-History,** and the **Marine** as well as those up on the hill at Nice-Cimiez. New in town is the **Musee International d'Art Naif Anatole Jakovsky,** housed in the elegant Chateau Sainte-Helene, with a collection of naive/primitive painting from the 18th century to the present; open daily except Mon., 10 a.m.–noon, 2 p.m.–5 p.m., 6 p.m. June–Sept. 30. The Flower Festival *(Fete des Fleurs)* and Carnival are the times to be here. At **Nice-Cimiez,** the **Matisse Museum,** with hundreds of his works including furniture and memorabilia. Check opening hours as they vary. Also the **Marc Chagall Museum,** with many of his works on Biblical subjects. **Nimes:** Roman ruins a-plenty; **Maison Carree,** a Roman temple used as a museum for all sorts of Roman antiquities, is special (don't try to see everything at once); the monumental Roman amphitheater is still in use for bullfights and outdoor attractions. **Orange:** Roman ruins. **Pau** with its English colony, and much to see including a **castle-museum** (with the cradle of Henry IV made from a single turtle shell, and excellent tapestries). **Perouges,** is all Gothic houses and original cobblestones (wear sneakers); tiny medieval restoration enclave 25 miles NE of Lyons. **Hostellerie Vieux Perouges** is the restaurant, with an adjacent manor house to stay in (Tel: (78) 61–00–88)—neither for budgeteers. Guild museum, demonstration of old crafts; ruins nearby that haven't been fixed up; vineyards in this Beaujolais area all around. **Perigueux:** Exceptionally good prehistoric collections are in the **Perigord Museum. Perpignan** has lovely sidewalk cafes; the sardana is often danced evenings. **Perros-Guirec,** fashionable and popular; sheltered bays, many offshore islands; development going on at a great clip. Many villas, all the amenities of a top resort. Extraordinary landscape of seaside and pink granite boulders. **Poissy** is the site of the **Musee du Jouet** (see Museums, Paris); an 11th-century church, a 20th-century villa built by Le Corbusier, with **L'Esturgeon restaurant** (6 Cours 14-Juillet; Tel: (03) 965–00–04), right across from the train station, an ideal place for lunch on its summer porch along the banks of the Seine. The restaurant is closed Tues. and the month of Aug. **Puy-de-Dome** rests on volcano, the site of a Gallic shrine replaced by a **Roman temple of Mercury** where Pascal established the weight of air in the 17th century, and where Caesar centuries before ultimately captured Vercingetorix. **Puy-en-Velay** is extraordinary, with a chapel, cathedral, and enormous statue of Notre-Dame-de-France perched on top of a narrow volcanic hill (a drumlin) rising from a valley of orchards and poplars, vineyards and cattle. **Quiberon** is a town on a peninsula of the same name jutting from the Brittany coast, 310 miles SW of Paris, wonderful family resort with lovely wide beaches, striped tents and pedalos to rent; no great architecture, no splendid restaurants, but immensely appealing with its rocky coastline, great for walks and picnics and a visit to the **Point du Congruel,** a nature sanctuary. Further along the coast road is **Port Haliguen,** a dream and a delight with its fishing port as well as a *''port de plaisance''* a pleasure port, where there's a ***sailing-school.*** An attractive modern restaurant here with an interesting but not over-ambitious menu is **Relais des Iles.** The Sofitel **Thalassa Hotel,** with a marvelous view, outside Quiberon, overly modern though it may be, is comfortable, the staff pleasant, and a good choice for a first visit. The **Thalassotherapy Institute** is here. Restaurants? Nothing special, but you won't do badly at **Hotel des Druides,** simple and good, and **Restaurant des Pecheurs,** with good, local food, but crowded at lunch time. **Le Goursen** is splendid for gourmets. At the top of the Quiberon peninsula, do visit **Pub Naval,** a garishly painted galleon of uncertain provenance, serving as a seashell museum and bar-cafe. The **Fort de Penthievre** is nearby. **Port Maria,** the port of the peninsula, is charming, with sardine boats unloading their catch, and many boat excursions: **Belle-Ile-en-Mer,** the **Gulf of Morbihan,** up the local coast **(La Cote Sauvage)** and to local islands, **Houat** and **Hoedic.**

Belle-Ile is a 35-minute boat-ride from Quiberon to the main port of **Le Palais,** with a harbor winding back into the hills, small houses with soft, bright colors; **La Citadelle,** its superb military architecture housing an interesting museum of Belle-Ile's history. The best hotel in Le Palais is the **Hotel de Bretagne.** Steeper tariffs, but worth every franc, is **Castel Clara** at **Port de Goulphar,** near the **Grand Phare,** or lighthouse. There's also the **Hotel du Cardinal,** modern, at **Sauzon,** a tiny town at the head of a tidal estuary. An excellent ***ferry/bus tour*** of Belle-Ile is available and worth taking, although it skips the wondrous Citadel at Le Palais. Mrs. Katherine Blodgett Winter of Boston, the mother of Matthew, Anthony, and Andrew reports: ''The **Aerodrome de Belle-Ile-en-Mer,** at Bangor, right in the middle of the island, runs sightseeing tours, can take you back to Quiberon, and also has a truly splendid bi-plane. Built in 1938, it was used for training French pilots in England during World War II, and was rebuilt in 1958. As it is hand-started, call (phone 52–83–09) to make sure that two pilots are available. Aerobatics possible. Missing a ride in this plane was one of the few disappointments of my trip.''

The island of **Houat,** a simple island with wide, sandy beaches and tiny houses, is a 60-minute boat ride from Quiberon by ferry. Take sandwiches, or have a simple meal there at the **Hotel des Iles. Hoedic** is a 105 minute trip. Strange, elemental, so flat it's called the ''ile au flottage'' because it does seem to float like a lily pad, the island is even simpler than Houat, with stone or whitewashed houses, a tiny church, a graveyard, a signal station.

Quimper is famous for its potteries, cathedral. The **Breton Museum** in the cathedral grounds is fascinating, with costume and ceramic rooms, a marvelous pottery room with plates painted with animals children like, and always something unexpected, such as the bronze Lares in the room where you enter the museum. The **Fine Arts Museum** is so-so, given over in part to traveling exhibits. Children prefer it at **market** time (Wed. and Sat. mornings), when everyone turns out in costume—or at least enough people do to make it interesting. Men in black velvet hats with streamers (you know Breton sailor hats!), women in starched white lace collars and coifs. All very gay and bustling with colored tents and excitement. You can buy dolls in local costume, straw slippers lined with rabbit fur, velvet Juliet caps with embroidery, and the local pottery, which you can see being made on the spot. In June, don't miss the Pardon of the Birds, a pilgrimage without religious significance. Bretons in native costumes display and sell real and toy birds at the end of **Carnouet forest.** Singing, dancing, music, and picnicking.

At **Rennes,** the **Beaux-Arts Museum** and the **Musee de Bretagne,** with audiovisual material covering Brittany's history and life, and excellent publications, are both housed in the same building. Lovely old quarter with half-timbered houses and a fine public garden, the **Jardin Thabor,** with mini-zoo, waterfalls, rose-garden; and a nice cathedral. Not a major stop, but if you do stay there a night, the **Hotel du Guesclin,** right by the train station, is comfy and old-fashioned, preferable to the plastic **Frantel. Ribeauville,** north of Colmar, has two of its four storks' nests regularly occupied; fun on the first Sun. in Sept., when there's a Fiddlers' Fete! **Riquewihr** seems to wall in the Middle Ages; to the north is the highly dramatic restored castle of Haut-Koenigsbourg, perched upon a forested hill. **Rocamadour,** built incredibly in tiers up a practically vertical cliff, will bring cries of delight. Ancient streets with medieval gates, interminable flights of steps, ancient sanctuaries with relics collected by pilgrims of the Middle Ages; in the department of Lot, in the valley of the Alzou; extraordinarily appealing to those who like to explore the strange and special.

Rouen's Flaubert Museum (Hôtel-Dieu, 51 rue de Lecat) is devoted both to Flaubert and the history of medicine; open Tues.–Sat., 10 a.m.–noon, 2 p.m.–6 p.m. Another Flaubert museum at **Croisset,** 4 miles out of town. A 75 minute train ride from Gare St.-Lazare in Paris, or a 70 mile drive NW of Paris, Rouen also has a **Corneille Museum** for the literary, an over-modern and plastic hotel-member of the Frantel chain with a delightful and helpful staff who dote on children; a restoration of old Rouen's Gothic grandeur and Renaissance monuments; cathedrals, churches, the churchyard behind St. Ouen where Joan of Arc was condemned; a **Museum of Fine Art;** a **Museum of Antiquities,** Gallo-Roman and Renaissance; the **Museé Le Secq des Tournelles,** devoted to iron-work and fascinating street signs. There's also a Joan of Arc waxwork museum in the market square, which schoolchildren frequent. **Sables-d'Or-les-Pins** in Brittany is what its name implies, golden sands and pines; a new resort with ***riding school, golf, large tennis club, casino,*** entertainments galore, and modern hotels. The **Hotel de Diane** here has a large private garden, sand to play in for children and swings, and gives special attention to children's meals. Prices moderate. At **St.-Augustin,** about 21 miles from St. Amand, is a **Chateau and game preserve,** open July 1–Sept. 30.

St.-Briac (west of Dinard), has a small fishing port, good golf course, tennis, sailing, and several good beaches. **St.-Brieuc:** Old Breton capital of the Cotes d'Armor or the Cotes du Nord; beach at **Les Rosaires;** it's a shopping center with a busy small airport; many inexpensive restaurants. So-so. **St.-Cast** in Brittany has a beach a mile long, with many *moniteurs* to help you entertain the children. A busy, bright resort, with hotels debouching onto the sands. Off to the west is a nearly always deserted bay that you have to cross a farmyard to get to; a fine spot for a picnic with rocks and beach and little tidal pools. **St.-Egreve: Museum of the French Revolution.** At **St.-Enogat** the waves break against the cliff beneath the bedroom balcony at the little hotel **Port-Riou-Plage;** very reasonable rates, all comforts, and a chef who will go out of his way to make special meals for children. **St.-Germain-en-Laye:** about 13 miles NW of Paris, and about a 25-minute train ride. Well known for its chateau, which houses the **Musee National des Antiquites Francaises,** France's major museum for some of the finest French pre-Christian art, from the caveman to the Merovingians (see Museums, Paris). **Louis IX's chapel** is lovely; terrace overlooks the Seine. **Pavillon Henri IV** (21 rue Thiers) at the edge of the park, will give you an excellent meal; expensive; **Ermitage des Loges** (11 av. Loges) is also expensive but has a swimming pool. Minus luxury, views, and pool, but inexpensive, **Le Trouvere** (53 rue Paris). At **St. Lunaire** (adjoining Dinard) in Brittany; small, quiet, charming; beautiful beaches; sailing, tennis, mini-golf. Thanks to steady patronage by English families, splendid little hotels like **The Richmond,** with swings in the garden, excellent food. The seaside resort and fishing port of **St.-Jean-de-Luz,** with its striped bathing tents and pleasant beach, is a good family beach resort.

St. Malo is *special,* with a fabulous history, forts, ships, coastal walks, beaches (but watch out for those wild tides that are remarkably strong and high!). The ramparts are marvelous for walks or a Sun. afternoon promenade when the entire town seems to walk there. The **Mole des Noires** has a wonderful view of the town. The **Chateau** houses the **St. Malo Museum** with historical collections; also the Wax Museum in its Quic-en-Groigne Tower. The **St. Malo Art Museum** is worth seeing and housed in a deconsecrated chapel. At low tide, **Fort National,** marvelous, is accessible, as is the **Grande Be,** with Chateaubriand's tomb looking out to sea, a perfect escape from summertime tourist hordes, and in Sept., lots of ripe blackberries there for the picking. You can walk, rather than wade, when the tide is completely out, to the **Petit Be** and climb up the rocks to the ruined **Vauban fort** on the summit. The **Central** is a very comfortable hotel with a good restaurant. **La Duchesse Anne** is a one-star restaurant; **A l'Abordage** (pl. de la Poissonnerie) has, as you would expect, great seafood; the **Gargantua** is kids' heaven with grilled meats, baked potatoes, fried potatoes *(frites),* piped-in music. For ***picnic supplies,*** several shops along rue Porcon de la Barbinais sell roasted chickens and salads as well as breads, pastries; **Aux Armes de France** has really good pastries. ***Excursions and side-trips*** from St. Malo include: a must to St.-Servan nearby where the medieval **Tour Solidor** is wrapped around the **Musee International de Long-Cours Cap-Hornier,** an international museum of Cape Horn vessels that's fabulous for boat-lovers with everything from astrolabes to paintings and 19th-century photographs. There are ***harbor trips*** by boat. Hydrofoil trips are possible to the Channel Islands.

Ste.-Marie-de-la-Mer: Gathering of gypsies from all over the world in honor of patron saint Sarah. Processions of *gardiens* (the French cowboys of Camargue). ***Folk dances,*** brilliantly gay old costumes, ***horse***

races, bullfights. One of the great French festivals. The inland Breton town of **St.-Michel-de-Braspars** is a little-known gem, and if you are near it, go there! In **St.-Paul-de-Vence, Auberge Colombe d'Or** is a remarkable **restaurant-museum,** fine food, and finer paintings by all the men of the School-of-Paris; the **Matisse Chapelle du Rosaire,** murals depicting the Road to Calvary in this contemporary chapel entirely decorated by Matisse. And the **Fondation Maeght,** an extraordinary gallery, includes the work of Braque, Kandinsky, Calder, Tal Coat, Ubac, and Van Veldes. **St.-Quay-Portrieux** in Brittany has several bays; a delightful old town with a swimming and a paddling pool. The British flock to its furnished villas and hotels; **Hotel Gerbot d'Avoine** is said to be excellent for families with young children. The harbor is packed with small craft and sailboats. **Sarlat:** House walls of yellow stone, special and charming as the Land of Oz. **Senlis,** at the far edge of the Chantilly forest; a cathedral and charm. The **Musee de la Venerie,** a hunting museum housed in the 18th-century Priory of St. Maurice is next door to the **Chateau Royal** where, in alternate odd-numbered years like '85, '87, a sound- and light-spectacular "Royal Hunts of Senlis" is held on weekends at 9 p.m. from May–Sept. Concerts on Sat. and Sun. at 4 p.m., Apr.–June, and during Oct., Nov., are held in the **Franz Liszt Auditorium** in a 12th-century church. Lots of Gallo-Roman remains in this sylvan retreat, only 28 miles N of Paris, surrounded by beech forests. Stay here at **Pavillon St.-Hubert,** near Lys-Chantilly, a country inn with inexpensive sleeping accommodations, but pricy food in its cozy dining room. **Sevres,** famous for its porcelain manufacture and its **Musee de Ceramique** (thousands of exhibits from the prehistoric to contemporary, including much of the local Sevres). **Strasbourg,** a leading commercial river port, part modern city, part old town known as *La Petite France* with covered bridges, winding streets, canals, half-timbered houses, and a cathedral spire second only in height to the one at Rouen. Inside the **Cathedral** is an astronomical clock with mechanical religious figures, the Four Ages of Man, and a chariot, that all go into action at noon–12:30 p.m., when tickets are sold for the event for about the price of a stamp, and the best visibility is at the back of the standing-only space and goes to those who get there early. From mid-Apr.–end-Sept., there are son-et-lumiere spectacles in the cathedral. Nearby is the **Musee de l'Oeuvre Notre-Dame,** a treasure house of Alsation art; the **Chateau de Rohan,** riverside, houses a complex of art and archaeology museums; **Musee Historique,** a few steps away, has collections of weaponry and military uniforms; **Musee Alsacien,** across the Ill river is a regional museum with roomsful of costumes, dolls, toys, agricultural implements, pottery, furniture reconstructed as they were in bygone times—the rooms, not the things within them. Children enjoy the ***one-hour sightseeing rides*** on the train of little carriages that leave from the S side of the cathedral every half-hour from late Mar.–Oct. 31. ***Boat***

rides on the Ill river, under low bridges, between swans swimming near the Palais de l'Europe, through a lock, operate almost hourly during the summer, several times daily Oct.–May from in front of the Chateau des Rohan, two blocks from the Cathedral; ***Rhine cruises*** from 3–11 hours operate during the summer. More information from the **Office de Tourisme de Strasbourg,** Palais des Congres, Ave. Schutzenberger, 67000 Strasbourg, Bas-Rhin. The **Musee des Beaux Arts** has fine paintings. Ask younger children to find the painting of a bunch of flowers with a snail (school of Jean Breughel) so they can feel independent; they'll like the picture even though the snail looks more like a baby seal. Every Sat., Sun., and holiday from May–early Oct. and on some weekdays during July and Aug., you can make a three-mile run on the **Abreschviller** logging railway hauled by *fin-de-siecle* puffing steam engine; picturesque and pleasant short trips. Ask the tourist office to check this for you. You'll catch the train at 3 rue Premiere Armee.

Talloires on Lake Annecy is an enchantment. **L'Auberge du Pere Bise,** with eight rooms, eight suites, is *the* place to stay, because of the reputation of its restaurant; unless food means all that much, try the nice **Hermitage** instead.

Near **Tarbes,** there are the **grottoes of Medous** to explore, stalactites and stalagmites crystallized into unusual formations. **Tarn Canyons:** The Tarn River has cut through the limestone plateau until its valley has turned into a canyon about 2000′ deep. You can rent flatboats to negotiate all of the 33-mile long canyon, or just part way through some of the more spectaclar sections where you can safely but thrillingly shoot the rapids. The steep cliffs rising from the river are honeycombed with caves. The caves at **Roquefort-sur-Soulzon** are filled with ewe cheeses ripening into Roquefort, another rather curious sight; subterranean caves. At **Aven Armand,** electricity and colored screens turn the grottoes into an extraordinary spectacle that appeals to most children. The **Dargilan grottoes,** close by, easily and quickly accessible, are one of the few scenic wonders that children really enjoy. In **Tours,** don't miss the **Musee du Compagnonnage** (6 rue Nationale) housed in a 13th-century abbey, in the old part of town by the banks of the Loire; open daily except Tues. and the day after major holidays; craftsmen's masterpieces in wood, stone, glass, iron, chocolate, and macaroni absolutely dazzling in their creativity and skill. Tours, of course, is where most people headquarter while they tour the Loire Valley and the chateaux. The **Museum of Fine Arts,** housed in the 17th-century Archbishop's Palace, is well worth a detour to Tours. **Tregastel** and **Trebeurden** are small resorts in Brittany. **Troyes: Modern Art Museum,** new in '82, with giants of all the art movements from 1850–1950 represented, is 100 miles southeast of Paris, housed in the old Episcopal Palace; open 11 a.m.–6 p.m. daily except Tues. In **Uzes** is **Le Museon di Rodo,** with old automobiles, paintings, and scale models of cycles and trains. **Vaison-la-Romaine:** Roman ruins. **Val Thorens** is the world's highest ski resort in the French

Alps. Its Jumbo ski-lift travels from its 6900′ station to the tops of Mont Caron's 9600′ summit in three minutes and 40 seconds to the tune of piped-in music. Crass vulgarization of skiing and nature, I think.

Vannes, a delight with marvelous old quarter, medieval ramparts surrounded by formal gardens; charming old Breton buildings and squares; **Chateau Gaillard Museum** of prehistoric art and Breton archaeology; the **Oyster Museum** may disclose unknown pearls of information. **La Marebaudiere** is a smallish, comfortable hotel, with a restaurant across the street, **La Maree Bleue.** Many other choices. **Versailles:** The palace and gardens designed by Le Notre for Louis XIV are the world's most sumptuous, and most exhausting for children to trek through. You take them there because you feel it's something they should see, and so they should. The interior is immense and you can see it only by a guided tour. The dazzling **Galerie des Glaces** (Hall of Mirrors) moves most children to awe, often giggles. If you tell the children you want to see it all and would be grateful if they'd come with you, things will go better. It's not going to be any fun for them until they get out in the garden to the **Bassin de Neptune** (one of the most magnificent of the fountain basins) and the **Allee d'Eau** (a long walkway with 22 small fountains surrounded by bronze sculptures of children). There is a snack bar adjoining this glittering chateau; also in town **Les Trois Marches** (3 rue Colbert; Tel: (03) 950–13–21), a pricey restaurant within a restored 18th-century town house. A few minutes from the center of town is the 500-acre **Arboretum de Chevreloup.** A nominal fee buys a serene stroll among infinite varieties of rare and ornamental trees, or a place just to sit down and listen to the rossingnols.

Vichy, with the **Parc du Soleil** for children's entertainment also has ***fireworks*** at night along the Allier River, ***boat trips, horse show*** and ***music festival*** in June, bullfighting, horse-racing and special fireworks displays during July and Aug., and ballet and music festivals in summer. A pleasant place for parents too. **Villard-de-Lans:** family resort with many activities; most fun for winter sports; Hurray for **Vitre** a wonderful place to walk around and poke about, with ramparts and a Breton castle that makes you feel good just to look at it; inside, a museum of castle and town, with its owners' collections of stuffed birds, a cheerful hedgehog and frog skeletons as aide-memoires of life in Brittany.

FUN AND GAMES The French approach to sports seems to be one of looking great at whatever you're doing. The casual chic that shows up on sailing boats is extraordinary. Everyone appears in beautifully cut ensembles for tennis, skiing, riding, shooting. You don't slop around with sports in France. You show off your body, your clothes, your competence. If you can't do something well, the point seems to be that you must at least look great doing it.

But you can't do anything unless you have the right equipment for doing it. **Au Vieux Campeur** has equipment, some clothes, and accessories for mountaineering, hiking, speleology, tennis, jogging, riding, diving, sailing, skiing, bicycle touring, camping. **Wyers et Brehier** have rods, flies, spear-guns. (See Camping.) If your child wants darts, arrows, or a boomerang, you can find them at **Paris-Sport** (43 blvd. Voltaire, XI). And if it's a frisbee they're desperate for, you can find them at the **Association Francaise de Frisbee** (6 rue Maryse-Bastie, 93120 La Courneuve) in the Paris area.

Riding is a top French sport. How to find out everything you want to know is all in *Tourisme Equestre en France,* a useful booklet published by the **Association National pour le Tourisme Equestre et l'Equitation de Loisirs** (15 rue de Bruxelles, 75009, Paris).

In **Paris,** and the environs of the Ile-de-France, your best sources of information and opportunities for riding are: **Federation Equestre Francaise** (164 rue du Faubourg-Saint-Honore, 75008 Paris); open 9 a.m.–noon, 2 p.m.–6 p.m.; closed Sat., Sun., hols; can put you in touch with amateur riding clubs and provide information. **Societe Equestre de l'Etrier** (Maneges, Steeple-Chase, Grounds: route de Madrid-aux-Lacs, Bois de Boulogne, 75016 Paris) can tell you about their facilities. **Touring-Club de France** operates a riding center (Route de Neuilly, Bois de Boulogne, XVI). Closed Sun. afternoon and Thurs. a.m. **Societe d'Equitation de Paris** (Route de Neuilly a la Muette, porte de Neuilly, XVI) operates a "Poney Club" for children 6–11. If you just want to hack around and can reserve four to five days in advance, get in touch with **Manege de Neuilly** (19 bis, rue d'Orleans, Neuilly-sur-Seine) open every day except Sun. afternoon. **Cercle Bayard** (22 ave. des Reservoirs, Joinville-le-Pont) open daily except Tues., 7 a.m.–10 p.m. operates a "Poney Club" for children 5–11 at its branch at ave. du Polygone, Bois de Vincennes. For the male members of the family, there's the **Club des Gentlemen-Riders** (140 rue du Faubourg Saint-Honore, 75008 Paris); open 10 a.m.–noon, 2 p.m.–6 p.m., Sat. 10 a.m.–noon.

The "Poney-Clubs" in Paris and throughout France, those under the aegis of the **Association Nationale pour le Tourisme Equestre et l'Equitation de Loisirs,** ANTE for short, organize trips for children, day excursions, jumping lessons, excursions on a lead-rein, promenades in the park or in the country, and provide excellent value. The **Poney-Club de France** (15 rue Mesnil, 75116 Paris; Tel: (01) 553–59–29) is the source of all information about dozens of these riding stables. In **Paris,** the **Poney-Club de la Cartoucherie** (Bois de Vincennes, XII) has a large arena, an area for jumping instruction, and can arrange for weekend excursions to Fontainebleau or Orleans forests and environs. **Poney-Club de Brimborion** (19 ave. de la Division-Leclerc, 92310 Sevres) is another recommendation. Specially recommended for children 4–16 elsewhere in France are in **Brittany, Poney-Club St.-Yann**

(Ecuries de Penfrat, 29118 Gouesnach-Benodet); **Poney-Club de Rennes** (Ferme de Fenicat, 35170 Bruz); **Shamrock Poney-Club** (la Planche Fagline, 35740 Pace); in **Burgundy, Poney-Club des Meures** (Ourouer, Aux Amognes 58130 Guerigny); **Poney-Club de Trangy** (Trangy, 58000 Nevers); in **Limousin, Poney-Club de Lesches** (23210 Marsac); in the **Loire Valley, Poney-Club de Villeneuve** (41120 Sambin); in **Normandy, Centre Regional d'Equitation sur Poney, Poney-Club de Caen** (14112 Beuveille); in **Picardy, Poney-Club du Riez** (Occoches, 80600 Doullens); in **Savoy-Dauphine, Poney-Club Cavalcade** (Chateau de Neuvecelle, 74500 Evian).

Polo players have the use of a polo field and seven tennis courts if they join **Polo de Paris** (Pelouse de Bagatelle, Bois de Boulogne, 75016 Paris) open daily from Apr. to Nov., from 8 a.m.–9 p.m. with the polo season in full swing from May–Oct. (See also Children's Camps and Riding Holidays.) Racing—horse and car—are major spectator sports. Do take the children to the races in Paris.

Skating: Children can *roller-skate* with French children at the Luxembourg gardens, Square de l'Observatoire, in the Parc Monceau, the Champs-Elysees gardens, at the Palais de Chaillot, at the Tuileries gardens. *Ice-skating rinks* are generally closed from May–mid-Sept., but **Gaite-Montparnasse** (16 rue Vercingetorix) is open all year *except Aug.*, with skates to rent, evening classes except on Sun. **Centre Olympique de Courbevoie** (place Charles-de-Gaulle, 92400 Courbevoie) has sections for children from age 4 to glide about, plus pool, bowling and a bar for exhausted parents. For all information about skating, ice hockey, speed-skating, pirouetting on ice etc., contact the **Federation Francaise des Sports de Glace** (42 rue du Louvre, I).

Fencing: All information from the **Federation Francaise d' Escrime** (13 rue de Londres, IX; Tel: (01) 874–36–54).

Tennis: Outdoor and covered courts throughout the country. For size, the **Club Pierre Barthes** at Cap d'Agde in the south of France has no rival, with 62 outdoor and six indoor courts. In Paris, get in touch with **Federation Francaise de Tennis** (2 ave. Gordon-Bennett, XVI) or the **Ligue d'Ile-de-France** (74 rue de Rome, VIII). ***Badminton:*** Badminton in French, and the **Federation Francaise de Badmington** (49 rue du Tocqueville, XVII; Tel: (01) 622–42–36) will give you a list of clubs and all their fixtures. Unlike tennis, ***squash*** is a game even a beginner can play, and a game children adore, because they can just smack the ball and it goes ricocheting, or at least caroming, with every shot; fast, active, great and fun even without a partner, just practicing; at the **Stadium** (66 ave. d'Ivry, XIII). **Squash Front-de-Seine** in the basement of the Nikko Hotel (21 rue Gaston-de-Gaillavet, XV) has ten courts. **Squash Montparnasse** (Tour Maine-Montparnasse 37 ave. du Maine, XV) has free lessons for children 5–16. **Cercle Interallie** (33 faubourg Saint-Honore, VIII) is a private club. Try the **Squash-Club de Saint-Cloud**

(338 Bureaux-de-la-Colline, 92213 Saint-Cloud). For a list of squash clubs in the Paris area and more information, contact **Comite Francais du Squash** (74 ter, rue Lauriston, XVI). Tel: (01) 554–26–43, mornings).

Bowling: Your source of information is the **Federation Francaise des Sports de Quilles** (17 rue Guerin, 94220 Charenton-le-Pont). Try the **Bowling Club of Paris** (Jardin d'Acclimation, Bois de Boulogne, XVI), **Bowling Etoile-Foch** (8 ave. Foch), the **Front-de-Seine, Bowling Montparnasse** (Montparnasse Park Hotel, 27 rue du Commandant Rene Mouchotte, XIV), **Mouffetard** (73 rue Mouffetard, V), and **Le Stadium,** with its squash courts.

Go Karting: Driving around a track in a bodyless car on a seat constructed on the chassis. You can go quite fast and it is wonderful fun for people big enough to reach the brake and accelerator pedals—long-legged 12s on up love this. A track on the outskirts of Paris at **Palais du CNIT** (Rond Point de la Defense); at Villacoublay (in back of the airfield near the Jouy-en-Josas woods), two tracks, for beginners and pros, for whom there are competitions. Ask the Welcome Information Office, every major city usually has at least one track in the area.

Bicycling in France is a family affair, and it's easy to rent a bicycle—the French call them a *velo*—almost anywhere in France for a day, week, or month. Get information from **La Federation Francaise de Cyclotourisme** (8 rue Jean-Marie-Jego, 75013 Paris) and **Le Bicyclub de France** (8 place de la Porte Champerret, 75017 Paris). The French National Railroads (SNCF) rents bicycles in about 150 railroad stations. (See Transportation.) In **Brittany,** you can rent bicycles from the **Association der Ker Dreuz** (22290 Treguidel); **Cyclorandonneurs de Cornouaille-Prat-Len** (route de Concarneau, 29000 Quimper); **Entente Cyclotourisme de Goele** (Le Kerbroch, 22500 Paimpol). In the **Languedoc-Roussillon** area, at the tourist offices in **La Grande-Motte, Port-Barcares, Port-Leucate.** In **Paris,** the recommended source for bicycle rentals is **Paris-Velo** (2 rue du Fer a Moulin, V). **Cyclobus** (24 ave. de la Liberte, Bois de Vincennes) bicycles fitted with infants' seats too; **Cyclobus** in the Bois de Boulogne at ave. Charles de Gaulle in the parking lot of the Hospital Ambroise-Pare, has the same set-up, and the rental costs are a bargain. In the Saint-Cloud Park, **Velocipederie de la Grande Gerbe** (Parc de Saint-Cloud, 92210 Saint-Cloud) has tricycles, tandem bikes, three-seater bikes, four-seaters, and bikes with carriage attachments. **La Maison du Velo** (8 rue de Belzunce, X; Tel: (01) 281–24–72) is British-owned, which means that English is spoken, which is a help when you want to organize either a day's outing or a longer biking trip; books, maps, guides also on hand for the bicycling enthusiast. ***Motorized bicycles,*** called *mobylettes,* or *velomoteurs,* can be rented from **Autotheque** (80 rue Montmartre, II).

Skiing: The Alps have always been a magnet, but many resorts are developing like mad. **Tignes** (a typical example—lifts start at the doorsteps of high-rise apartments and studio-apartments; 75 lifts and cable cars handle 50,000 skiers an hour), **Avoriaz, Flaine, La Plagne, Les Arcs, La Daille, Le Corbier, Superdevoluy,** and **Les Menuires** have banded together so you can buy tickets good in them all. They cater to families; many of the hotels have creches and babysitters; good restaurants; underground shopping centers; horse-drawn sleds and all the fun of winter. **Courchevel,** the largest ski resort area, is strongest on convenience. **Les Arcs** is the ultimate in the creative ski scene. **Les Deux Alpes** is a good family resort for winter and summer skiing. **Megeve** has charms and pleasures. (See individual listings.) For details, contact the FGTO. For interesting bargain ski packages, get in touch with *Air France*. Information about **Avoriaz, Les Arcs, Chamonix, Courchevel, Flaine, Megeve, Les Menuires, La Plagne, Tignes, Val d'Isere, Les Deux Alpes, La Clusaz, Val Thorens,** France's most prestigious resorts, specially equipped for international ski buffs, is available from **France Ski International** (2 place de la Porte-Maillot, 75017 Paris). **Association des Maires des Stations Francaises de Sports d'Hiver** (61 blvd. Haussmann, 75008 Paris) and **Federation Francaise de Ski** (34 rue Eugene-Flachat, 75017 Paris) are wonderful sources of information. If the *snow bulletins* obtainable from the speaking clock in Paris (Tel: (01) 266–64–28) tempt you, and you want to rent equipment, go to **Drugsport au Bivouac** (226 rue La Fayette, 75010 Paris); for teenagers and grownups also **Dethy** (20 place des Vosges, 75004 Paris).

Fishing requires permits generally; get in touch with the **Conseil Superieur de la Peche** (10 rue Peclet, 75010 Paris, Tel: (01) 842–10–00).

Hunting and shooting: You can rent everything for the *grande chasse* from **Jeannot** (9 rue Louise-Michel, 92300 Levallois-Perret) in the Parisian suburbs. Information from the **Office National de la Chasse** (88 bis ave. de Wagram, 75017 Paris) about hunting in general, also from **Federation Internationale de Tir Aux Armes Sportives de Chasse St.-Hubert Club de France** (21 rue de Clichy, 75009 Paris), open daily 9 a.m.–noon, 2 p.m.–6 p.m.

For ***mountain-climbing,*** the **Club Alpin Francais** (7 rue la Boetie, 75008 Paris) can give you details. Group expeditions are arranged by **Federation Francaise de la Montagne** (20 bis rue la Boetie, 75008 Paris). ***Old-fashioned trains:*** Write to **Federation des Amis des Chemins de Fer Secondaires** (134 rue de Rennes, 75006 Paris), for information about all the narrow-gauge steam trains in France, when you can see them in action, when you can ride them, where you can meet with other train buffs.

Swimming is great in France, and beaches are a great institution, highly organized for children with beach clubs you join for a small fee. The *moniteurs* or *organisateurs* in charge are university students or physical culture teachers, extremely competent and generally idolized by boys and girls; they give the children calisthenics once or twice a day; swimming lessons; organized games; rope climbing; races; volley-ball, and things like that. For wading, sand-castling, digging for shrimp at low tide; tennis, golf, sailing, windsurfing, riding, the French side of the English Channel coast offers resorts as unassuming and charming as **Carteret** and **Barneville,** relaxed and modest as **Trouville,** old-fashioned and elegant as **Cabourg** and **Le Touquet,** sophisticated as **Deauville.**

Beach swimming seems best to me at Brittany's **La Baule,** with its C-shaped beach, no rocks, no pebbles, just sand. Down the Atlantic coast, you'll come to **d'Arcachon,** another divine family beach resort. Farther down, Biarritz is dangerous and huge-waved, not for little children. **St.-Jean-de-Luz, Bandol, Hyeres,** and **Le Lavandou** are good family beach spots.

Swimming pools in France? The French are sedulously careful about the purity of their pool water. Crowds, changing rooms, showers and attentiveness of personnel are the criteria, not the water which is, to the best of my knowledge, pure everywhere, although occasionally it may be overly chlorinated. You can nip over to the **Nikko de Paris** or the **Sofitel de Paris** (see Hotels). Admission for non-guests at both these hotels is less than a movie ticket. Also in the same area is **Tour Montparnasse** (rue de l'Arrivee, XV) with its year-round pool. Out of city center: **Piscine Municipale d'Issy-les-Moulineaux** (70 blvd. Gallieni, 92130 Issy-les-Moulineaux) where a Baby Club is operative on Sat. with trained medical assistance to supervise swimming and instruction for babies 6 months up to 5-year-olds; **Piscine de Saint-Germain-en-Laye** (Route de l'Octogone, 78100 Saint-Germain-en-Laye) is another sparkling whopper. For information about other municipal pools, **Direction Regionale de la Jeunesse et des Sports** (6–8 rue Eugene-Oudine, XIII). The **Hippodrome d'Auteuil** (Routes des Lacs, porte de Passy, XVI) has a *garderie* for children; there's also a nice pool at the **Stadium** (66 ave. d'Ivry, XIII). The **Deligny** (25 Quai Anatole France, VII) open daily 8 a.m.–8 p.m. from the end of Apr.–end-Sept., is a giant barge on the Seine, a floating island almost, with a pool. During summer it's wildly crowded; best time is lunch when everyone hangs out at the bar-restaurant. Instruction here in waterskiing and sailing; you may also find a contingent in topless bikinis. Infinitely preferable in summer, I think, is the **Piscine Keller** (14 rue de l'Ingenieur Keller, XV) closed on Mon. or the **Piscine de l'Etoile** (32 rue de Tilsitt, XVII), you can rent the entire, very small pool at night for a reasonable fee if you want to celebrate your child's birthday with a swimming party. **Piscine Blomet** (17 rue Blomet, XV), **Roger-Le-Gall** (34 blvd. Carnot, XII), under the aegis of the **Club des Nageurs de Paris,** is well-run. I'd skip the **Molitor** (2 ave. de la Porte-Molitor, XVI) which was crowded and had unconcerned personnel when I went. The **Piscine Valeyre** (22–24 rue de Rochehouart, IX) is ideal for children, who outnumber the adults swimming about ten to one. The **Pontoise** (19 rue de Pontoise, V), the **Pailleron** (30 rue Edouard-Pailleron, XIX), **Piscine Georges-Vallery** (148 ave.

Gambetta, XX), **Oberkamf** (160 rue Oberkamf, XI), **Chateau-des-Rentiers** (184 Chateau-des-Rentiers, XIII), **Ledru-Rollin** (10 ave. Ledru-Rollin, XII), and **Georges-Rigal** (115 blvd. de Charonne, XI) are a-splash with children. **Emile-Anthoine** (9 rue Jean-Rey, XV) and **Jean-Taris** (16 rue Thouin, V) both have access for the handicapped; both are modern, but the latter is mostly used by students going to and from the cafes on the Place de la Contrescarpe. **Piscine du Stade-Francais** (165 rue Vieux-Pont-de-Sevres, Boulogne-Billancourt, 92100 Hauts-de-Seine) is wonderful for children and teenagers, with lessons for beginners; part of a recreation center.

Except for the pools at hotels, the Stadium, Tour Montparnasse, Deligny, Etoile, Keller, Oberkamf, all the above-mentioned pools are municipal pools and *all are closed Mon. a.m.;* they are used during part of the day by schools and sport associations, but are also available to the public at various hours during weekdays, and all day Sat. and Sun. During summer vacation, they are open to the public daily, but do check out the hours and times with the **Bureau des Sports** (17 blvd. Morland, IV) who can give you a more complete list with full details. For information about suburban pools, consult the above-mentioned **Direction Regionale de la Jeunesse et des Sports.**

▶ **Note:** Don't take any child to a pool in Paris if he can't swim reasonably well without a support. A regular life-jacket is all right, but *in a crowded pool a ring support is disaster*. For a list of swimming clubs in Paris and its environs and clubs specializing in the instruction of babies and young children, get in touch with the **Federation Francaise de Natation** (Comite de l'Ile-de-France, 148 ave. Gambetta, XX). They can also tell you all about ***snorkeling, scuba-diving, spear-gunning,*** categorized as *sports sous-marins*. For information about ***waterskiing*** and the scores of clubs involved with this sport, contact **Federation Francaise de Ski Nautique** (9 blvd. Pereire, XVII).

Boating: The **Touring Club de France** (6–8 rue Firmin-Gillot, 75737 Paris Cedex XV) has a houseboat moored at the **Port de Plaisance de Paris** at Pont de la Concorde, VII; open daily except Mon. from 10 a.m.–11 p.m., with a bar-restaurant and all the information a boatsman would want to know about the waterways of France, services, mail, telephone, etc. The Touring Club also has a special **Canoe-Camping** section in its main office that can give you all the information about canoe lessons and cruises. The **Centre Nautique des Glenans, School Concarneau Club** (opposite 1 quai Louis-Bleriot, XVI) is the source for ***sailing and yachting schools,*** many in Brittany. There also is a **Yacht Club de France** (6 rue Galilee, XVI) open daily, except Sun. and hols., 9:30 a.m.–12:30 p.m., 2:30 p.m.–6:30 p.m. Sat. 9 a.m.–noon, to which foreign members can be admitted. And a **Federation Francaise de Canoe-Kayak** (87 quai de la Marne, 94340 Joinville-le-Pont) that can tell you about clubs, rentals, itineraries.

Other sports: There's a **Federation Francaise des Sports au**

Trampoline (4 rue de Capri, XII) for those who bounce and turn somersaults in the air. Ask the Paris Hostesses to fill you in about the free school for young ***archers*** at the **Stade Pierre-de-Coubertin,** and in the **Bois de Vincennes.** If other kinds of bulls' eyes are of interest, the ***bullfights*** at Frejus in a Roman amphitheater, and at Nimes, weekly in Aug., are fine for children, since the object is not to kill the bull but to snatch a ribbon from his horns.

FUN TRIPS The ultimate in windborne fantasies for well-to-do travelers is the **Great French Balloon Adventure,** available annually from May–Oct. Discover Burgundy in a three-passenger-plus-pilot-carrying wicker gondola (unsteerable, but guidable); a "chase team" follows your every move in a van below; an adventure that is a marvel of safety and efficiency; under the aegis of the **Bombard Society** (6727 Curran St., McLean, VA 22102). Combined with gourmet food, deluxe accommodations, sampling rare wines of the region, plus the perfectionism of the organization and its pilots, this week is like no other; it's worth every dollar spent a hundred times over.

Eight ***balloon-and-barge adventures*** during July and Aug. are also possible, staying aboard the new luxury 24-passenger barge *l'Escargot,* making daily flights as she cruises through the parklike terrain of the Burgundy Canal between Montbard and Pouilly-en-Auxois; other seven-day programs are luxurious and memorable, and a tad more expensive. Bookings for a seven-day *Ballooning in Burgundy* program, staying at the **Chateau de Cezy,** with excursions, are offered for less than the Bombard Society's by **Horizon** (215 N. 75th St., Belleville, IL 62223). Quality and expertise aren't necessarily cheap, but I think the Bombard Society wins out every time.

Balloon ascensions of 60 minutes are also possible if you barge through Burgundy on either of two deluxe hotel barges, *Bateau Ivre* or *Le Sancerre*. The *Sancerre* is great because you can cruise on her for a weekend rather than a week. These inspired Quiztour offerings can be booked through Air France or your local travel agent. Floating Through Europe (covered later) also combines ballooning with cruising on its *Linquenda* "Barging Through Burgundy" trips and has expanded its program to include three-day cruises. But if you just want a safe balloon trip with an experienced pilot at reasonable rates, your best bet is the **Centre Aerostatique de Bourgogne** (Residence du Lac, Les Hetres, 21200 Beaune). From May–end-Oct. you can float above vineyards and castles. Children travel for one half-fare at rates that seem reasonable to me. **Les Montgolfieres de France** (55 quai Bourbon, 75004 Paris) can tell you where else you can enjoy similar promenades; in the neighborhood of Paris, flights can be arranged by **Club d'Intervention Aerostatique** (Librairie Roux-Devillas, 12 rue Bonaparte, 75006 Paris).

Floating Through Europe specializes in travel by deluxe hotel barges throughout France's canals and waterways, doing so with such flair and organization that what a few years ago might have been a fun trip has now become a legitimate mode of transportation. Refer back to the Transportation section if the prospect of a 3-, 7-, 14-, or 21-day barge journey (interspersed with walking, bicycle, and motor excursions) sounds enticing. Teenagers only on scheduled trips; if you have juniors or younger children, FTE also arranges chartered trips. Cautionary advice: Barges are s-l-o-w. Bring books, writing materials, needlepoint, sketchbook, portable games; mosquito-gnat-fly repellents, as on all boat trips, are strongly recommended, as is an aerosol can of Rhulispray or other analgesic-anesthetic. Ballooning-and-barging is a delightful combination, so do, if possible, bear that in mind.

If you prefer do-it-yourself sailing, motor-cruising, or hiring a craft with captain or crew on boats with living accommodations, contact the **Syndicat National des Loueurs de Bateaux de Plaisance** (SNLBP) (Port de la Bourdonnais, 75007 Paris). Boat rental agencies where English is spoken—they may write you about crude boats when they mean crewed, or about births when they mean berths—are generally reliable, knowledgeable, honest, although what they forget to tell you, assuming that you obviously know, is that canal locks only function by day from 6:30 a.m.–7:30 a.m. to 5:30 p.m.–7:30 p.m. depending on the season, and don't function at all on Christmas, Easter, May 1, July 14, or Nov. 11. So plan your itineraries accordingly!

If you're interested in ***yachting***—North Sea, English Channel, Atlantic, Mediterranean—by all means apply for membership in the **Yacht Club de France** and/or the **Touring Club de France,** previously mentioned. The Touring Club de France has representatives in London and New York and the FGTO will put you in touch with either. That marvelous TCF can also supply you with a list of agencies where small craft are available for hire in many coastal resorts on the Channel, Brittany and Atlantic and Mediterranean coasts. Superior agencies generally belong to the TCF, or at least to the SNLBP and are so marked. The **Federation Francaise de Voile** (55 ave. Kleber, 75016 Paris) can also provide useful information, as can Paris' **Federation Francaise Motonautique,** knowledgeable about all the clubs for power craft and motor cruisers.

Passenger cruisers ply the Seine, Rhone, Saone, Rhine for one to three hour trips, but as any boat-trip freak can tell you, they aren't half the fun that ***inter-island and coastal ferries*** are in the **St.-Malo** and **Quiberon** area of Brittany and, in particular, ferry sailings out of the **Gulf of Morbihan,** which can offer adventure and the ultimate in serendipity. From Charente, there are some pleasant daily interisland cruises from **La Rochelle** to the superb **Ile de Re** beaches, also cruises from **Rochefort** to **Sainte** and **Cognac.** The **Grands Bateaux d'Aquitaine** (5 place de la Comedie, 3300 Bordeaux) offers cruises up the Gironde to arrive pierside in Bordeaux. The wine region can often become a whine region for younger children, but GBA's floating restaurant **Alienor** offers on-board haute-cuisine; children and teenagers appear somewhat unbored, but these trips are obviously more for parents.

Quiztour (19 rue d'Athenes, 75009 Paris) is one of many French tourist associations that offers a Midi-Pyrenees trip of leisurely travel in *roulottes gitanes* (gypsy caravans) accommodating four, *conestogas/grands chars du Far-West baches* (Little-House-on-the-Prairie-style covered wagons) accommodating 12, or *breaks/petits chars du Far-West baches/non baches* (smaller versions, with or without tarpaulin coverings) accommodating six. You can cook and sleep in all. *Caleches* (four-wheeled carriages with folding hoods) or two-wheeled versions, properly known as *cabriolets,* itineraries include overnights and meals in inns or post-houses. I'd opt for two two-passenger caleches rather than one for four people so you can change driving partners *and* have the safeguard of two horses and two separate vehicles. The offices of ANTE, are located in Limousin, Midi-Pyrenees, Provence, Rhone-Alps. In the Lot Valley in the Midi-Pyrenees, the **Attelage La Taillade** (46700 Duravel) rents roulottes, caleches, and bicycles for you to bring along; from Mar.–early Nov.; trips can be arranged by the day, weekend, or week. In the Vaucluse area of **Provence, Attelage Les Authentiques Roulottes Gitanes de Joel Moyne** (Domaine de Saint-Sauveur, 84320 Entraigues-sur-Sorgue) rents authentic gypsy caravans, conestogas, and breaks. In the Ain region of the **Rhone-Alps, Attelage Cheval Bugey** (01250 Ceyzeriat) offers roulottes and caleches; day or weekly camping programs, or a week or longer circuit staying as paying guests at farmhouses and manors with stables. In the Rhone section of the Rhone Alps, **Attelage Caleches Sainte-Catherine** (SICA Tourisme des Monts du Lyonnais, M. Chambe, Hameau de Accole, 69116 Sainte-Catherine-S/Riverie) rents caleches by the half-day or day. ANTE can provide you with more information and details.

Besides Quiztour, you might want to check out the following travel organizations: **Cheval et Loisirs en Limousin** (La Ferme d'Eymenoux, 19250 Meynac), **Cheval-Voyages** (8 rue de Milan, 75009 Paris), **Tours-Coche** (1 rue Lobin, 37000 Tours), and **Lozere Voyages** (10 blvd. du Soubeyran, 48000 Mende).

For adventures combining ***caving and pre-historic art,*** see **Les Eyzies.** A list of suggested itineraries for ***bicycle tours*** can be obtained on request from the FGTO, and locally in France from the Syndicats d'Initiative. **Country Cycling Tours** (167 West 83rd St., New York, NY 10024), offer a variety of two-week bicycle tours in the Loire and Dordogne Valleys.

SHOPPING WITH AND FOR CHILDREN In **Paris,** nursery comforters, sheets, pillows, baby things, christening dresses, baby shoes, toys, children's clothes and accessories are all so ravishing that you're bound to want to have another baby, instantly become a doting grandmama, toss your financial cap over the moon, or just allow all your fine financial resolves to be swept aside in the intoxication of a shopping spree. Then, in all likelihood, you may be tempted to buy things for your older children, yourself, your husband, for Christmas, for birthdays, rationalizing it all. Before you are overcome with this mania, be practical about the **Value Added Tax** and plan ahead about store hours. Contact the FGTO for specifics. TVA is VAT tansposed in French. If you are not sufficiently affluent to have TVA matter very much, you can still splurge on inexpensive French smocks, tasteful educational toys, buttons, chic baby clothes, birthday party favors, French comic books, wonderful fabrics for making children's dresses, and an infinity of other goodies.

Store Hours: Most *Department stores* are open Mon.–Sat., from 9 a.m.–6:30 p.m.; usually two nights the store is open until 9. p.m. or later; many department stores are closed Mon. mornings. *Boutiques* are open Tues.–Sat. generally; some are closed only Mon. morning. Boutiques may close daily at noon and re-open at 2 p.m. *Small shops* almost always close at noon, re-open at 2 p.m. *Hairdressers* close Mon. *Food* shops are open Tues.–Sun. (until noon), from 7 a.m.–1:30 p.m., and from 4:30 p.m.–8 p.m. *Bakeries* open earlier in the afternoon, usually around 2 p.m. The *Parisian Drugstores,* combining restaurant, pharmacy, department stores are open from 9 a.m.–2 a.m. daily.

Shopping Centers: In Paris, a three-mile pedestrian area, the **Forum des Halles** (1–7 rue Pierre-Lescot, I) is centered with a four-level underground shopping center, eclectically devoted to cinemas, theaters, disco, waxworks museum, banks, services, information, fashion and accessories in clothes as well as home furnishings, plus restaurants (see Food). The Forum is a magnet for the young who flock here to shop, eat, rendezvous, listen to concerts, attend craft workshops; attractions to be enjoyed by all age ranges. At the **Montparnasse Shopping Center** (between the rue de l'Arrivee and the rue du Depart, XIV) besides children's fashions boutiques, toy shops, shops of all kinds, including a branch of department store **Galeries Lafayette** (Tour Montparnasse, 22 rue du Depart), you'll also find restaurants, hairdressers and a municipal swimming pool. The **Palais des Congres de Paris Boutiques** (2 place de la Porte-Maillot, VII) is a good bad-weather shopping center, because it's all under the roof of the Convention Building; you'll find children's fashion boutiques, toy shops, a Japanese department store, crafts; also hairdressers, restaurants.

Department Stores in Paris: **Galeries Lafayette** (40 blvd. Haussmann, IX) boasts a stained-glass cupola that's a historical monument; haute couture boutiques, terrace bar, travel service; food, bicycle and decorating services, toy and camping department, vast kitchen and home-furnishings departments. Trendy fashions on display that teenage girls and young mamas may find affordable in the *Club 20 ou 30 ans.* (See also Food.) **Au Printemps** (64 blvd. Haussmann, IX; branches: **Au Printemps-Nation,** 21 cours de Vincennes, XII and **Au Printemps Italie,** Centre Galaxie, place d'Italie, XIII) has multilingual hostesses to guide you about the store, a welcome room for tourist and shopping information on the ground floor, marvelous clothes for children, luxury and elegance in all departments and a great Toy Floor. The *Nation* branch has a huge Food Department and, like the main branch, is *open until 9 p.m. on Fri.* The *Italie* branch stays open until 9 p.m. on Tues. (See also Food.) **La Samaritaine Pont-Neuf** (19 rue de la Monnaie, I) is the only department store with an entire floor devoted to animals; wonderful place for useful and durable smocks, aprons, old-fashioned cotton nightgowns, old-fashioned fabrics; tea-terrace, open in summer, closed Oct.–Mar.; if you're looking for something for your child that you enjoyed as a child, you're most likely to find it here. Open until 10 p.m. Wed., until 7 p.m. Sat. (See also Food.) **Aux Trois Quartiers** (17 blvd. de la Madeleine, I). The atmosphere is old-world British, and aristocratic country French, with an emphasis on cashmere and tweeds, attractive underwear; the entire second floor is just for children—clothes, toys, nursery furniture. An ambiance of calm, quiet, courtesy prevails. Tea room (See also Food.) **Au Bon Marche** (100 rue de Sevres, VII), its ground floor given over to food specialties of France and far-away places, is a family department store with, would you believe, considerable space devoted to *Aux Trois Hibous,* where children can read in a supervised playroom and also be given instruction in weaving, enamel work, modeling, music, and basketmaking! Of the popular, inexpensive chain stores—**Inno, Monoprix, Prisunic, Euromarche,** and **Carrefour** located in every quarter of Paris—it's impossible to say which is best, because that all depends on the location and the buyers for the shops. You'll find in all of them astonishingly well-designed practical things like schoolbags, picnic equipment, children's underwear and overalls in the 4–6, 6–12 range at prices competitive with Woolworth's and Lamston's.

Bebe-Confort products are most impressive for their range and quality. A coordinated set of baby equipment (with tubular chrome or white lacquered frames) is light, portable, versatile; in conventional colors; also in a most effective dark-blue-and-white check and in a black-and-white-and-yellow pattern that couldn't be crisper. A canvas bed on a wheeled frame, with canopied top, doubles as a carrycot; the frame folds into something no more inconvenient to carry than a schoolbag, and the bedding can be stowed in a special traveling case. A graceful carriage also folds into nothing; Bapip, a multipurpose stroller that serves as shopping cart or car seat, operated with only one hand; a recliner-chair with adjustable awning doubles as a bed; a charming portable upholstered basket in which a baby can lie. Given the quality, style, and practicality, prices seemed marvelously reasonable. Their baby cosmetics are made with herbs and plant extracts, guaranteed nonirritating, hyperallergenic, and presented with all the lavishness of luxury cosmetics; attractively packaged at modest prices. All the products mentioned are made by **Bebe-Confort** (11 rue d'Avron, 93-Villemomble) and are available in department stores.

A company called **Baby Op** has a baby shoe that zips in two so you can slip it on with no strain and secure it so that the baby can't kick it off; made for babies 7–14 months; at Au Printemps.

Pret-a-porter boutiques for babies and children have been opened by all the other big names in grownup ready-to-wear—**Dorothy Bis, Cacharel, St. Clair, Gudule, Bistrot du Tricot, Daniel Hechter.** Paco Rabanne has made raincoats for children. Cacharel and St. Clair are bringing out children's shirts in current colors and fabrics. Cardin and Ungaro have fairly inexpensive children's clothes, although Prisunic knocks them off before first lines are even out. **Baby Dior** (28 ave. Montaigne, VIII) takes the little ones from the cradle and clothes them with delicious sumptuousness up to the age of 4; slightly less lavish, next door, under the archway, is the **Junior Boutique** for brothers and sisters up to 12. **Miss Dior** (11 bis, rue Francois I, VIII). **La Chatelaine** (170 ave. Victor-Hugo, XVI) has layettes of the utmost elegance and happily sturdy children's smocks for toddlers and the 4–6x group, for whom clothes are classic, tasteful, beautifully made so that they will last and remain wearable for your children's children. Made-to-order clothes, irresistible party clothes, christening robes. **Bonpoint** (67 rue de l'Universite VII; 64 ave. Raymond-Poincare, XVI; 184 rue de Courcelles, XVII) Beautifully wearable, luxurious infant wear; wedding wear; romantic, sweet, classic clothes. Nursery furniture environments at **Bonpoint annex** (7 rue de Solferino, VII). Accessories, nursery linens, pillows, wallpaper, material, cribs, bassinets. Children's shoes of all kinds at Bonpoint (86 rue de l'Universite, VII) across the street from its main clothing boutique. **Alphabet** (77 rue du Cherche-Midi, VI) has christening dresses for babies and divine underwear for their mummies; jacquard pullovers for children, pajamas, shorts; table linens, curtains, hand-painted and hand-embroidered and handknit everythings imaginable. **A Cote** (Agnes B, 13 rue du Jour, I) specializes in handmade ready-to-wear skirts, jeans, sweaters, T-shirts, everything for baby girls up to the age of 14. **Benetton** (59 rue de Rennes, VI; Galerie du Claridge, 74 Champs-Elysees, VIII; 82 ave. Victor-Hugo, XVI) Shirts, sweaters, shorts, jeans, overalls in all the colors imaginable for boys and girls, 2–16, and their thin mums. Louis Feraud designs clothes for the 4–16 group; available at Au Printemps. For children's clothes that are beautifully styled and cut, classic and ageless, **Caddie** (112 av. Victor-Hugo, XVI) has imported English baby things, ready-to-wear or altered so that they look custom made; charming but more expensive than they are in England, naturally. **Helene Vanner** (402 rue St.-Honore, XVI) makes handmade things for little boys whose mothers want them to look like princelings in the old tradition; prices are comparable to those of a top man's tailor; her pret-a-porter boutique, hand-picked with charm and taste, is less expensive.

Claude Demachy (42 rue de Grenelle, VII) Classic clothes for baby; layettes, sweaters, knit slippers, knitted bonnets, pram sets; classic clothes for girls and boys up to 12. *Dresses with matching bloomers!* Overalls, pinafores, bib-fronted shorts for little boys, coordinated shirts and tops for twin brother-sister outfits in cotton, wool, flannel. Clothes may be reminiscent of things you wore as a child, but they have an indefinable style that makes them just as becoming and practical as ever; machine-washable woolens; sweaters. **Sophie Dess** (67 ave. de Suffren, VII) clothes for up-to-10s that are enchanting. Smocked dresses, apron-coveralls like Alice in Wonderland's, summer and winter dresses and shorts, classic clothes, including layettes. **Francoise Ezanno** (4 bis rue du Cherche-Midi, VI). For children up to 10, adorable bathing suits, seersucker and flannel culottes, unbelted dresses, skirts, shorts, jeans, rompers, playsuits. **Petit Dom'** (18 ave. Franklin-Roosevelt, VIII). For princes and princesses up to the age of 8; baby clothes, culottes, smocked dresses, velvet-collared coats, velvet and flannel shorts and skirts that button to shirts and blouses. **Le Petit Faune** (33 rue Jacob, VI) for children up to 12, christening dresses, machine-washable knit sweaters in wonderful colors, dressing gowns, party clothes, clothes to wear for young members of weddings, and a remarkable idea: clothes for tout-petits, all cut and ready-to-be-stitched in exclusive fabrics at extremely reasonable prices for instant heirlooms! **Vert-Pouce** (66 rue de la Tour, XVI) for the tout-petits, from birth to about 4, dresses and bibbed-shorts, rompers, exquisite trousseaux for babies; darling crib cushions, and bed dressings; naive paintings decorate chairs, tables, wardrobes that are charming. **Marie Dominique** (9 ave. Victor-Hugo, XVI) for infants and children up to 10; you'll find darling bathing suits, rompers, dresses, shorts, pajamas, nightgowns, dressing gowns made with exceptionally attractive materials; summer things, party clothes, winter wear. **Daniel Hechter** (50 Champs-Elysees, VIII; 12 faubourg Saint-Honore, VIII). Designer-label clothes for the tout-petits as well as children up to 16. **Nahala** (8 rue des Saussaies, VIII). Baby trousseaux embroidered by hand, incredible lace confections, taffeta and velvet party dresses for girls up to 16; clothes for boys up to 8; with prices you will not believe unless you come from a Forbes 400 family or think nothing of paying up to $1000 or even more for your daughter's evening dresses or *costumes de fete*. **Manby** (9 ave. Victor-Hugo, XVI) has sensible back-to-school apparel for boys and girls and teenagers 4–18; classic ensembles, time-honored that "work," endure; also clothes for mama that are impeccably designed to "work" and endure. **Pomme d'Amour** (31 rue Hamelin, XVI). Everything handmade for the tout-petits and children up to about 10 in Viyella, Liberty silks and cottons; smocked dresses, chemises, mini-caftans or dresses cut like a choirboy's robe, dressing gowns. Then, surprise, a young Brooks Bros.-type of department for young boys up to about 14.

La Puce Habillee (25 rue de Penthievre, VIII). Summer and winter apparel for children up to about 8 in cotton, wool, pique, flannel; bibbed-shorts, culottes, sweaters and cardigan; Breton sailor hats, adorable party slippers for girls in leather and in silk; smocked dresses; winter and summer shorts and jeans; overalls short and long. Reasonable prices, except for a few handmade things. **Le Petite Gaminerie** (28 and 32 rue du Four, VI). Clothes for children 2–6 at #28, and for juniors 8–15 at #32. Cacharel skirts, raincoats, everything very trendy, distinctive; amusing, dashing, flamboyant, striking for the most part; also some wince-makers. At #30, nursery furniture and baby things. **Les Bonnes Fees** (57 ave. Mozart, XVI) orchestrates big-and-litttle sisters matching outfits, coordinated brother and sister clothes from birth to 14. T-shirts, jeans, shirts, blouses, dresses for an attractive lookalike look; infant layettes as well. **Camomille** (Viviane Guire, 250 rue de Rivoli, I; 5 rue Brea, VI; 10 rue Bois-le-Vent, XVI). A soothing tisane here of classic well-cut clothes for girls and boys from birth to 16; mix-and-match, blazers; custom-made clothes for christenings, parties, weddings; the well-bred look, conservative preppy style, country look, the British look, and the Brooks Bros. look. For the trendy-preppy look, rather than the conservative-preppy look, the wearers of which the French slangily call Mickeys, there's **Vroom** (62 rue de Rennes, VI).

Special Bargains in Children's Clothes and Accessories, Infants-Teenagers: **Jacadi** has about four dozen stores throughout France and, at last count, ten in Paris, where you pay 40%–50% off designer-label prices for delicious clothes for small children and babies, and wonderfully wearable and attractive clothes for boys and girls up to 16. A Parisian branch of Jacadi (38 place du Marche-Saint Honore, I) happens to have a tiny children's hairdressing salon as well. Closed Mon. a.m. **Cacharel Stock** (114 rue d'Alesia, XIV). A huge and cheerful outlet for the feminine contingent, toddlers to 20s at 35%–50% discounts with attractive changing rooms to try on sweaters, summer and winter skirts, overalls, beach-wear, shorts, shirts, T-shirts, blouses, smocks, caftans, pinafores, dresses in a wide variety of styles, colors, sizes. At **Baby-soldes** (161 rue de Grenelle, VII; 72 ave. Victor-Hugo, XVI; 2 rue Guichard, XVI) terrific knock-downs on clothes that have had their designer labels removed for infants to 14-year-old girls. Attractive and delightful clothes also at **Les Soldes Enfantines** (159 rue de Rennes, VI; 17 rue Tronchet, VIII; 5 place de la Republique, XI; 9 rue de Passy, XVI) for ages 3–16 with about 20% off unmarked designer clothes; sportswear, rainwear, beachwear, ski wear; headgear, skirts, jeans, sweatsuits, coats. Out-of-season clothes on sale for infants–16-year olds at **La Soldetiere** (76 rue de la Pompe, XVI). **Les Trouvailles** (55 rue de la Convention,

XV) has mostly classic and conservative children's clothes, ski wear, coats, dresses, suits, sweaters at 50% discounts. **Stock Austerlitz** (16 blvd. de l'Hopital, XIII) offers Daniel Hechter designs at 30%–50% off; coats, trousers, shorts, slacks, jeans, flannel, velvet, wool, cotton skirts and trousers, caftans, dressing gowns, shirts, blazers, jackets, sportswear.

Fantastic Bargains: Children's slightly worn clothes in perfect condition from all the designer collections, along with baby equipment, toys, games at **Maman Troc** (6 bis rue Fourcroy, XVII) closed Sat; **Baby Troc** (16 rue de Magdebourg, XVI), closed Mon. a.m., specializing in sport clothes and special activity clothes for children up to 14; also bicycles, play pens, carriages, strollers and infants wear, just like new at **La Marelle** (21–23 galerie Vivienne, II), closed Mon. and Sat. a.m. Antique clothes of good quality and style and vintage clothes for children and girls up to 18; maternity clothes; children's furniture and baby equipment one-half-price at **Tante Amelie** (2 rue Pierre-Haret, IX)

Children's Shoes, Girls' Shoes: **Cendrine** (3 rue Vavin, VI) are specialists in children's shoes for problem feet; recommended by foot specialists and pediatricians. **Breacuir** (21 rue Brea, VI) closed Mon. afternoons, is the specialist for orthopedic shoes, corrective shoes; shoes with ankle braces; medically fitted shoes. Conservative, classic, party, fanciful, flowered, enchanting slippers and shoes for your children at **Pascal** (55 ave. de la Bourdonnais, VII) that sells only infant and children's footgear designed by *Froment-Leroyer.* Shoes of many kinds including mini-versions of grown-up styles at **Sidonie Larizzi** (28 rue de La Tremoille, VIII) with no bargains in sight. Shoes, party and bedroom slippers; boots, sneakers, sandals, beachwear and sportswear at **Arbell** (102 faubourg Saint-Denis, X), **Aux Enfants du Parc** (103 blvd. Malesherbes, VIII) **Bessy** (7 rue Vavin, VI), **Bonpoint** (already mentioned), **Camille** (50 rue Vital, XVI); and, of course, at department stores. **Amina** (29 rue du Dragon) had marvelous lowheeled, slightly-wedged, ballet-type slippers in red, white, blue, yellow and black **rubber** for girls and women, bargain-priced, and an incredibly good idea for boating, country wear, rainwear, mud and slush and ordinary wear, because you can't tell without close inspection that they are made of rubber. I hope this will become a standard item and is not a passing fad.

SPECIAL!!!! Nursery and children's furniture that grows with your child, imaginative designs; easily cleaned, washable rugs for children's rooms; toys, games, books, records for children; fancy-dress costume rental for three days; craft workshops for boys and girls up to eight every Wed. from 2 p.m.–4 p.m.; 30-minute free **garderie d'enfants** daily, any time except Mon. when the store is closed; small collection of slightly used or shopworn books and toys at bargain prices; an information center listing ideas, opportunities, events, information, sales, services of import and interest to parents and children—all this at **Si Tu Veux** (68 galerie Vivienne, II).

Toys: **Au Nain Bleu** (408 rue St.-Honore, VIII), large, comprehensive; doll-house furniture; dolls and stuffed animals with enchanting clothes (also can be made to order); unusual and charming toys of every description; some electric trains. **Le Train Bleu** (2 av. Mozart, XVI), dolls, toys, games, stuffed animals, records, books. **Le Chaperon Bleu** (14 bis av. Hoche, VIII), and **Le Chaperon Rouge** (15 av. Mozart, XVI), superb continental toys, games, scientific toys, and entertainments. **La Source des Inventions** (60 blvd. Strasbourg, X), working models, scientific games, and toys. **Baby Train** (9 rue du Petit-Pont, V), marvelous miniature trains and precision working models of planes and boats; remote control models; will handle repairs. **Clarel** (25 rue de la Roquette, XI), specializing in H.O. and N. electric trains that are exact reproductions of every type of French rolling stock. **Hobby Train** (23 rue de Rivoli, IV) Everything for the model train buff. Closed Mon.

Scaramouche (14 rue Andre-del-Sartre, XVIII) has dolls' houses with every imaginable accessory exquisitely fashioned, marvelous beyond belief; new, antique and reproductions. Closed Mon. **Le Cerf Volant** (43 blvd. Saint-Marcel) has every imaginable type of kite, even montgolfieres or hot-air balloons; also marionettes, wooden toys, and fireworks (forbidden to import into the U.S.); an array also of little nonsenses, imaginative and tasteful. Closed Mon. **Le Jardin des Enfants** (20 ave. Felix-Faure), with wares requiring little money for such pleasure; original and imaginative stock of small goodies as well as good, solid, substantial wooden toys, including outdoor games such as croquet sets, bowls; children's furniture. Closed Mon. **Le Monde en Marche** (34 rue Dauphine, VI) A treasure trove of Christmas creches, dolls' house furniture, wooden toys, marionettes, music boxes at reasonable prices. Closed Mon. **Jouets Extraordinaires** (70 rue d'Auteuil, XVI) specializes in puzzles for every age from everywhere. Closed Mon. a.m. **La Maison du Jouet** (41 blvd. de Reuilly, XII). Model lead soldiers to paint; model boats, cars, planes, covered wagons in plastic to assemble. Closed Mon. **Rouge et Noir** (26 rue Vavin, VI) has every sort of game and puzzle and intellectual diversion for chess players, kaleidoscope watchers, card players, scrabble buffs, puzzle-lovers; for the solitary or sociable, 8 up. Closed Mon. **Magictoys** (Centre Beaugrenelle, 16 rue Lincis, XV) The largest store in Paris for games, toys, stuffed animals, models, dolls, puzzles, miniatures, educational games, tricycles, roller skates, rocking horses, inflatable swimming pools; international assemblage, open daily, Mon.–Sat. from 10 a.m.–8 p.m. I prefer the more select open sesame of **Ali Baba** (29 ave. de Tourville, VII). Dolls, miniatures, lead soldiers, stuffed animals, trains, models, electronic games. Closed Mon. except during Nov. and Dec. **Maria Kristina** (59 rue de Boulainvillers, XVI). Toys, doll carriages, stuffed animals, wooden toys, marionettes, Scandinavian Christmas decorations, wooden trains, everything for babies and children up to 8. Closed Mon. **Multicubes** (110 rue Cambronne, XV). Nursery furniture, wall decorations, marionettes, educational games, dolls' houses, good wooden toys. Closed Mon. a.m. **L'Automobiliste** (42 rue du Bac). For the budding motor-car fancier, this is it; mechanical toys, some stuffed toys, robots, but the main attraction is the cars, and a great reason for staying opposite at the Montalembert Hotel if your son dreams of vintage cars or Le Mans. Closed Mon. **Anna Joliet** (9 rue de Beaujolais (in the Palais Royale), I) specializes in music boxes from the elementary to collectors' treasures. Closed Mon.

Antique Toys: **Pain d'Epices** (29 passage Jouffroy, IX). All the toys of bygone years *reproduced;* I've been recommending throughout this book. Also, on the first floor above the ground floor, presents for babies, baby clothes for the newborn up to age 4, nursery accessories, baby toys and china. Closed Mon. a.m.

For authentic antique toys, 100 years old or more, **Monsieur Renard** (6 rue de l'Echaude, VI), closed Mon. a.m. Less expensive are the dolls in the collection of **Sophie du Bac** (109 rue du Bac, VII) with all their clothes, furniture, accessories; antique dolls superbly restored also. **Polichinelle** (20 rue Andre-del-Sarte, XVIII) specializes in 19th-century porcelain-headed dolls, dolls with wax heads and arms, bisque-headed, papier-mache headed. Next door, **Scaramouche** has some antique dolls' houses and accessories. **Robert Capia** (24–26 galerie Vero-Dodat, I) specializes in antiques dolls and all their trousseaux and accessories. **Charles Marchal** (46 rue de Miromesnil, VIII) has, among other extraordinary antique weaponry, a large collection of lead soldiers. Closed Sat. **Deyrolle** (46 rue du Bac, VII) extensive minerals, crystals, semiprecious stones, shells, butterflies, stuffed birds, insects and snakes and animals mounted, stuffed, or massed in decorative arrangements; seashells seemed very high to me; inexpensive for ostrich eggs and stuffed birds.

For children's **books** in English and French, magazines, guidebooks, I'd suggest **W. H. Smith and Co.** (248 rue de Rivoli, I)—it also has a tearoom!—(see Food) or **Brentano's** (37 ave. de L'Opera, II). **Albion** (13 rue Charles-V, IV) is an Anglo-American bookshop with a large French student clientele eager to learn English. Besides serious reading, shelves of science-fiction, detective stories, and mysteries. **Nouveau Quartier Latin** (78 blvd. Saint-Michel, VI) has an enormous collection of paperbacks; art books—paintings, architecture, photography, music, illustrated travel books. And then, of course, the celebrated **Shakespeare and Company** (37 rue de la Bacherie, V) open daily from noon to midnight for the delectation of parents romantic about Hemingway and the '20s, as well as literary-minded teenagers.

I was enchanted by the *Images d'Epinal, Contes de Fees, Imageries Pellerins,* and other fairytales and stories in this series presented in the form of paneled drawings reproduced from original 19th-century plates; beautiful books, the size of a tabloid; that will give you and your children pleasure for years. The **Asterix** books—a take-off on Vercingetorix, chief of the Gauls—are clever and funny; they come in English translations; a slight knowledge of history and a smidgin of Latin will add to your enjoyment; teenagers are mad about them. *Babar* in French or English is an old favorite you will enjoy seeing in a new edition. Any of the children's books printed by **Hachette** in French can be relied upon to be excellent.

Aux Quatres Vents (77 av. Ternes, XVII) stocks 3000 books for the 7-to-15-year-old reader. **Garnier-Arnoul** (39 rue Seine, VI) specializes in children's literature about marionettes, circus, and mime. **Education Nouvelle** (10 rue Littre, VI), a rallying point for all teachers of the young; interesting material in French, some in English. Better yet is **l'Abecedaire** (68 rue Crozatier, XII), closed Mon., open Sun. a.m., with child-psychology reference material, books, records of interest for both teachers and children up to 15, in French, of course. Children's supervised atelier on Wed.; educational games; charming books in French, beautifully illustrated. **Chantelivre** (13 rue de Sevres, VI) has picture books, pocket paperbacks, art books, fairytales, non-fiction, fiction for children; plus a corner where children can read and draw; also pedagogical and psychological references for parents and teachers; educational games. **Scarabee** (3 rue de la Montagne-Sainte-Genevieve, V) is where you'll find marvelous French records, songs and dance music, nursery rhymes as well as children's books and all those psychological and pedagogical texts for parents and teachers. **Pierre Sieur** (3 rue de l'Universite, VII) closed Mon. is an enchantment with wonderful children's books; beautifully illustrated stories, poems and, set about, all sorts of fascinating objects, antique games, interesting diversions. And not a pedagogical or psychological childstudy reference to be seen!

Huge, windowless, white shoebox-style ***shopping centers*** have been set up amid acres of parking space on city outskirts elsewhere in Europe, but France's hyper-size supermarkets for discounted everything are remarkable. The 18-acre **Venissieux Carrefour,** at a crossroads on the outskirts of Lyons, does 40% of its business 6–10 p.m. On Fri. evenings when workers from neighboring factories begin to pile in, it takes on the quality of a giant fairground. You can find anything from wallpaper to potatoes; laundromat; tour bookings; cut-rate gas; while-you-wait shoe repair; tanks of live fish, where your choice will be killed for you to take home. Off-the-peg suits, dresses, and coats are altered while you wait. On Fri. or Sat. on the outskirts of Marseilles, all the lines of cars you see are headed to the biggest of France's 24 Carrefours and the largest hyper-market in Europe. At **Cap 3000** (near the Nice airport) you can buy clothes and food; snack bar; swimming pool.

DRUGSTORES in Paris deserve to be capitalized. I've mentioned them in Magic Family Helpers and in Food sections. Drustores will give you free samples of perfume (echantillons) if you ask for them and express an interest in buying perfume. Children adore these and they make great presents if you have the will power not to use them yourself.

FRENCH FRIENDS AND PEN PALS If you would like to get together with a French family sharing your interests with children the same age approximately as yours, get in touch well ahead of your visit (or while you're there) with **Meet the French** (18–20, place de la Madeleine, 75008 Paris). The **American Club of Paris** (49 rue Pierre-Charron, 75008 Paris) and the **American Women's Group in Paris** at the same address can also be helpful in this regard, as can the **Club France-Amerique** (9 ave. Franklin Roosevelt, 75008 Paris), open daily 11 a.m. to midnight, and delighted to receive American visitors as members. The **Cercle du Bois de Boulogne** (Tir aux Pigeons, Pelouse de Madrid), open daily 9 a.m.–noon, 2 p.m.–6 p.m., with its pleasant restaurant and a playground for children is a casual way of getting together with compatible people and their same-aged children.

Serving as business hostesses for time-pressed executives, helpful in planning appointments and visits of a business nature, able to serve as secretaries and interpreters in 32 different languages, the **Hotesses de France** (7 rue Michel-Ange, 75016 Paris) as well as the **Centre Feminin d'Etude et d'Information** (6 cite Martignac, 75007 Paris) and the **Conseil International des Femmes** (13 rue Caumartin, 75009 Paris) should also be able to organize contacts and pen-friends, and put you in touch with individuals or groups of interest to you and yours.

CALENDAR OF EVENTS Here I can list only a few of the hundreds of fairs, exhibitions, sound and light programs, festivals, and sports events each year. Carnivals are usually mobbed, with much "shoutmost shoviality," so it's best for children to see them from a balcony, not ground level. Dates of annual events are subject to change, so for these and other attractions, be sure to check with the FGTO, and request their brochure *France in a Holiday Mood* available free from FGTO offices in the U.S.

Throughout **Jan.,** Monte Carlo features international ***motor racing.*** Jan. 5, the ***Festival of the Guiding Star*** is held at Pertuis (near Aix-en-Provence); Jan. 6 all France celebrates the ***Procession of the Three Wise Men,*** with drums, fireworks, galettes des rois (flat cakes containing favors). From **Feb.–Mar.** is ***carnival*** time in Nice; also, there are winter festivals and ***skiing championships*** in the Savoy Alps. In Lourdes, Feb. 11–18, a festival commemorates ***St. Bernadette's vision.*** On Shrove Tues., Aix-en-Provence (beginning the previous Thurs.) and Chalon-sur-Saone hold ***Mardi Gras.***

Beginning mid-March, nightly ***sound and light*** pageants (9 and 11 p.m.) are held through Oct. at the Invalides, Paris. Other events in Mar.: ***horse races*** at Pau; ***bullfights*** at Nimes and Arles where the bull is not killed. Around Easter, there are ceremonies throughout France; Sat., a week before Easter, Parisians flock to the ***Gingerbread Fair*** at the Pelouse de Reuilly. In **Apr.,** Biarritz has a ***Basque folklore festival*** with sword dancing. From Apr.–May, Arles hosts the ***Festival of the Gardiens*** (French cowboys), with Spanish-style bullfighting (the bull is killed). **May** 1 marks the beginning of the summer festival season; ***sound and light*** spectaculars are presented at chateaux and palaces through Oct. ***Bullfights*** resume at Nimes (through June). ***Joan of Arc*** festivals are held at Orleans and in Rouen, Paris, and Donremy (mid-May). Other events in May: fabulously colorful ***gypsy gathering*** at Stes.-Maries-de-la-Mer; processions of Gardiens (the French cowboys of the Camargue); the ***"Bravado,"*** celebration of 17th-century victory over Spain with mock battles (St. Tropez). At Whitsuntide, Alsatian villages celebrate ***spring festivals;*** Whitmonday, there's a frolicsome ***folk festival*** at Wissembourg. Apt and Biarritz also mount festive Whitsuntide activities.

In **June,** ***horse racing*** begins at Chantilly, Auteuil, and Longchamp (Paris); also, ***auto racing*** at Reims (the "12 hours of Reims"). In mid-June, the world-famous ***Grand Prix*** auto race is run at Le Mans. ***Sound and light*** festivals are held in the Loire Valley, June–Oct. Other events in June: ***Pardon of the Birds,*** a nonreligious pilgrimage honoring birds at Quimperle; June 24, festivals and bonfires for ***St. John's day*** (St.-Jean-de-Luz); last Sun. in June, at Tarascon, ***folklore festival*** commemorating the fire-breathing dragon (Tarasque). **July** 14, ***Bastille Day,*** is the French national holiday; especially in Paris, the fireworks are superb and the street celebrations riotous; the Versailles fountains are illuminated. During Paris' ***Festival du Marais,*** the quarter's mansions and churches become theaters and concert halls. July brings ***bullfighting*** to Bayonne and Mont-de-Marsan. At Quimperle, thousands of dancers and bagpipe and tuba players participate in the ***Festival of Old Cornwall,*** one of the finest folklore events in Brittany. Also in July: Martigues fishermen hold ***jousting tournament*** with lances on horseback; tuna fishermen compete at St.-Jean-de-Luz; and folklore enthusiasts flock to Nice for an ***international festival.*** Early in July, ***Ste. Odile*** is honored throughout Alsace.

Early in **Aug.,** Bayonne celebrates Basque and Pyrenean ***folk festivals,*** with music, bullfights, and great gaiety. Sporting events, pelota championships, and folklore festivals are held throughout the Basque area during Aug., especially at Pau, Tardets-Souhulus, St.-Jean-Pied-de-Port, Dax, and Bayonne. ***Horse racing*** and ***polo*** begin at Deauville; also, ***skin-diving*** competitions at Antibes. Other events in Aug.: at Biarritz, a ***sea festival*** with fireworks and illumination of rocks and beaches; sea festivals at Dinard; ***the Festival of the Golden Gorse*** at Pont-Aven, featuring local costumes and music; the ***Festival of the Blue Nets*** at Concarneau, with colorful costumes, dancing, and wrestling exhibitions. Ceremonies honoring the ***Virgin Mary*** are conducted at Lourdes. On Aug. 15, Chamonix hosts a ***festival of Alpine guides.***

On **Sept.** 1 the ***Medrano Circus*** (Cirque Medrano) opens in Paris (to Apr. 30). Early in Sept., Ribeauville presents the fun-filled "Pfiffertag," a fiddlers' festival. Also in Sept., there's ***bullfighting*** in Bayonne and an ***international folklore festival*** at Amelie-les-Bains. **Oct.** in Paris marks the opening of the ***Winter Circus*** (Cirque d'Hiver) and the ***Children's Theater*** season (to June), also you can see ***horse racing*** and the ***automobile show.***

Dec. 6 is ***St. Nicholas' Day,*** when presents are given throughout northern France. From Dec.-early Jan., at Marseilles and Arles, master craftsmen exhibit their ***santons.*** At Vence everyone wears regional costumes. In Menton life-size santons are paraded to Place St. Michel. Lourdes holds a ***festival*** in Dec. On Dec. 24, shepherds at Arles, Les Baux, Aix-en-Provence, and elsewhere bring lambs as an offering to the church; ***Christmas Eve*** services are held throughout France. On Dec. 25 all France celebrates ***Christmas*** (Noel).

LANGUAGE AND PHRASEBOOK: English is spoken in all the big hotels, shops, and restaurants. But few cab drivers or people off the beaten track speak English. Take along a phrasebook. (If a salesperson suggests a brassiere for the baby, she means a little shirt. A bra in France is called a *soutien-gorge.*) A child speaking to an adult always should add *Madame* or *Monsieur* after *Bonjour* or *Bonsoir.* We have no exact equivalents of many French sounds, but if you ask a Frenchman to pronounce the words as they should be, your children will probably be able to reproduce the accent and tone without much trouble. On the other hand, *le hot dog* is a standard menu item, le ''Poney Club'' is a favorite recreation, and *le jogging* is fast becoming a national sport. The French Government has seen fit to combat ''Franglais,'' banning such terms as *le jet* (now *l'avion a reaction*), *le discount, le weekend, le cowboy* from official publications, although these and 100 other terms are in common usage. As long as you make an effort to be polite, smile and do your best to communicate, the French will do their best to understand your French, no matter how fractured or anglicized. A *Larousse* pocket dictionary is a great help, but *Harrap's Two-volume English-French French-English* dictionary is the greatest. *The First Thousand Words in French,* a picture book for children filled with handy words and phrases, an index, many useful words incapable of illustration, is published in England by Usborne Publishing Co., Ltd., available in the U.S. from the **Manhattan Laboratory Museum** (314 West 54th St., New York, NY 10019).

I am an American		
(boy)	*Je suis Americain*	*zhuh swee za-may-ree-can*
(girl)	*Je suis Americaine*	*zhuh swee za-may-ree-ken*
My name is —	*Je m'appelle*	*zhuh mapell (rhymes with lapel)*

I am —— years old	*J'ai——ans*	*zhay——awnh*
Please	*S'il-vous-plait*	*seel voo play*
Thank you	*Merci*	*mair see*
I can't speak French	*Je ne parle pas francais*	*zhern parl pah frawn-say*
Yes	*Oui*	*wee*
No	*Non*	*nawh*
I am having a wonderful time	*Je m'amuse beaucoup*	*zhuh mamuze bow koo*
1	*un*	*uhn*
2	*deux*	*der*
3	*trois*	*trwah*
4	*quatre*	*catra*
5	*cinq*	*sank*
6	*six*	*seese (rhymes with geese)*
7	*sept*	*set*
8	*huit*	*weet*
9	*neuf*	*nuff*
10	*dix*	*deese (rhymes with geese)*
11	*onze*	*awnz*
12	*douze*	*dooze*
13	*treize*	*trays*
14	*quatorze*	*cattawz*
15	*quinze*	*cans*
Goodbye	*Au revoir*	*Oh-vwar*

GERMANY

The Federal Republic of Germany is often known as the Fatherland. The attitude toward children has—so far—not been permissive. Children, for instance, seldom appear in restaurants or other public places at night. Children must certainly not trespass on other people's property. There is a 10 p.m. curfew in bars and discotheques for teenagers under 18. Children under 6 travel free on streetcars and buses; 6–14s pay half-fare. Children are expected to yield seats to older persons and not to occupy seats reserved for the handicapped. Nevertheless, during Fasching (carnival time) there are lavish Kinderballe in the afternoon when children can use noisemakers and even cap pistols with abandon, and on festival occasions like the Munich Oktoberfest, children shriek with joy.

Facilities for children are super. Public swimming pools are scrupulously clean and attractive. Your children will have a grand time in the beautiful parks, fantasy fun fairs, fairy-tale parklets (with characters automated and wired for sound), and in the safari parks featuring African wildlife. The zoos in Frankfurt, Hamburg, Hanover, Munich, Stuttgart and West Berlin are notable for their landscaping and the optical illusion that they are, for the most part, free, open, and cageless. By zoo authorities they are regarded as among the world's greatest. Your children will find Germany particularly special because it is the home of the Pied Piper of Hameln (in whose memory there are still children's pageants), home also of the Grimm brothers and of most of our Christmas customs.

INFORMATION ABOUT GERMANY The **German National Tourist Office** (GNTO), with branches in Chicago, San Francisco, Montreal, and New York (747 Third Ave., New York, NY 10017; Tel: (212) 308–3300), can give you information about castles and other accommodations.

In Germany, the main information center is in **Frankfurt** (Deutsche Zentrale fur Tourismus, Beethovenstr. 69; Tel: (0611) 740–531); U.S. Tourist Information Bureau (Grobe Gallus Str. 1–7; Tel: (0611) 291–056); and Tourist Information Office (Tel: (0611) 331–108). In **Berlin** Europa Center; Tel: (030) 212–324 or (030) 782–3031); in **Munich** (2

Bahnholfsplatz; Tel: (089) 239–1256; and at the Airport Arrival Building, Tel: 239–1266 and 907–256. Also an information counter at Tegel Airport (Tel: (030) 41–01–31–45), in **Hamburg** (Bieberhaus; Tel: 241–234). There are regional tourist offices *(Fremdenverkehrsverbande)* in other major cities and a tourist information booth *(Verkehrsamt)* in every town, which can give you detailed maps and bushels of brochures. Information about East Germany, known as *der Deutschen Demokratischen Republik,* or German Democratic Republic, can be obtained from the **Reiseburo der DDR** (Postfach 77, 1026 Berlin, Deutschen Demokratischen Republik), an information office situated in Alexanderplatz in East Berlin (see East Berlin). Information about East Berlin, Potsdam, Leipzig, Weimar, Eiserach, Karl Marx Stadt, Dresden, Meissen, Neubrandenburg, and other places of interest ought to be available from your travel agent. If not, contact **Koch Overseas Company, Inc.,** 206–208 E. 86th St., New York, NY 10028; Tel: (212) 535–8600. Or try the East German Consulate (Consulate der DDR), 1717 Massachusetts Ave., NW, Washington, DC 20036; Tel: (202) 232–3134.

Information about the Rhine from Cologne/Bonn to Koblenz, and the myriad attractions to the west in the Eifel/Artal area: **Fremdenverkehrsverband Rheinland** Postfach 1420, D–5400 Koblenz; Tel: (0261) 35025; **Landesverkehrsverband Rheinland,** Bad Godesbuerg, Rheinallee 69, Postfach 200861, D–5300 Bonn 2; Tel: (02221) 36–29–21/22 (N.B. *Postfach* means Postoffice Box.)

If you would like to know more about the *state of the arts* in Germany, as they were or as they are, check with **Goethe House** (1014 Fifth Ave., New York, NY 10028; Tel: (212) 744–8310).

The German-American Information Center (410 Park Ave., New York, NY 10022; Tel: (212) 888–9840) proclaims itself the Window of Germany, dispensing information about politics and current events. They do extend the courtesy of providing telephone numbers and addresses from current telephone directories, but not the yellow pages.

For information about **Armed Forces Recreation Centers** which may and may not have special programs for your older children and day care centers for your younger ones, as well as information relating to U.S. military land, sea, and air bases, get in touch with the Public Affairs Office, Headquarters, U.S. Army Europe in Heidelberg (Tel: (6221) 57–66–47 or 57–63–59). (See Armed Forces Benefits.) Their affiliated Community Relations Office (Tel: (6221) 57–72–35 or 57–82–95) can give civilian families information about American women's clubs in Frankfurt, Garmisch, and other centers near military bases.

I strongly recommend that you layer your and your children's clothing to accommodate cool mornings, hot afternoons, cool evenings. Remember also that weather conditions in the Alps change rapidly, so always bring along raingear even on the sunniest of days.

Always carry extra washcloths and soap in a container because many small hotels, pensions, inns do not provide them.

Telephones? Owing to the surcharge system, overseas calls placed from hotels are exorbitantly expensive. When you see a number such as (0611) area code 7572–1, the hyphen indicates there is a switchboard. However, you just ask for or dial 75721. Telephones in Munich, Frankfurt, and other major German cities accept coins. Deposit coins before you dial; money remaining is displayed, and an arrow lights up when it's time to add more. International calls can be made from booths displaying a green sign, *Ausland*.

For pennies you can buy pocket-size pamphlets detailing the *Wochenbummel* (weekly happenings) in all major towns. Many, like the *Munich Weekly (Munchner Woche),* have good English translations and coverage of everything from museums to children's theater, as does the *Official Monthly Program* available from the City Tourist Office (Fremdenverkehrsamt). The *Munich Times* is an English language newspaper, published weekly, available at most leading hotels and bookstores, useful for "what's on" references. Because of our American military communities, many major cities have special American telephone information numbers and American military **Information Operators** (e.g., in Munich, (089) 622–992).

HEALTH, WATER, AND FOOD Health standards are excellent. Water and milk are excellent throughout the country, although when you're in untrammeled areas, check the milk for pasteurization. If your children are sensitive to changes in water, bottled varieties are available (such as Fachinger or Apollinaris).

Food? It's the absolute wurst—*Bierwurst, Fleischwurst, Bockwurst, Schinkenwurst, Kalbsbratwurst;* pork sausages *(Bratwurstl)* seem to be the favorite with children. From Frankfurt came—you guessed it—the frankfurter. Plenty of roast pork chops, local trout *(Forelle),* or boiled and smoked Rhine salmon *(Rheinsalm)* and Westphalian ham. *Knodel* are heavy dumplings; *Spatzle* are a lighter variety. Sauerkraut is plentiful. Children who don't like vegetables will be happy to hear that Germans don't like them much either. Vegetables all seem to go into soup and seldom make separate appearances except in major hotels and tourist centers. Plenty of fruit is available, however. Apples are *Apfel,* and oranges are *Apfelsinen*.

The best doughnuts are *Berliner Pfannkuchen*. Austrian hazlenut cake is *Linzertorte; Gugelhupf* is a light coffee cake; potato pancakes are *Pickert*. There is a variety of cookies: *Printen* (honey cookies), *Kuchle* (flavored with essence of roses and batter-fried), and *Mandelspekulatius* and *Muzenmandln* (crisp, almond-shaped doughnuts). From Nurnberg come *Lebkuchen,* or gingerbread cookies. *Schwarzwalder Kirschtorte* is Black Forest cherry tart, a whipped-cream cake covered with thick chocolate and thicker cherry sauce that children love. The most charming and decorative specialty is marzipan—an almond and sugar confection that appears in colorful molds of fruits, vegetables, flowers, and little pink pigs with ribbons around their necks.

You can pick up snacks in supermarkets, great delicatessens *(Feinkostgeschafte),* the food depts. of department stores, and open-air markets. In *Molkerei* (dairy shops) you can have a glass of milk and a sandwich. Pastry shops *(Konditorei)* feature pastry and candy treats, ice cream, cakes *(Kuchen),* cookies *(Platzchen),* butter tea cookies *(Teegeback),* meringue kisses *(Baisers),* and light sandwiches. Cookies, delicious breads, and pastries can be taken home from the *Backerei* (bakery). For picnics, liverwurst *(Kalbsleberwurst)* and *Mettwurst* are for spreading and eating cold; they don't keep without refrigeration. Nor do *Bierschinken* and *Mortadella*—wursts you slice and eat cold. *Gottinger, salami,* and *Cervelat* keep unrefrigerated for a long time, even in the glove compartment of your car. If you want to sample a slice or two of all those wursts at the butcher shop *(Metzgerei),* ask for *Aufschnitt* (cold cuts). Cheeses are ideal for picnics or train snacks. If children prefer soft cheese, ask for *Huttenkase* (like our small-curd cottage cheese but expensive) and *Quark* (a deliciously creamy cottage cheese). You can find diet, health, organic, nature food items at a *Reformhaus;* also *Schneekoppe-Erdnusscreme,* a particularly sumptuous brand of peanut butter (generally a rarity in Europe).

To avoid confusion, *Schinken* (ham) has nothing to do with *Palatschinken* (a kind of pancake dessert). Another bit of useful nomenclature is *Tagesuppe* (the equivalent of *soup du jour*). Nutritious but light is consomme with marrow *(Kraftbruhe mit Mark)* or noodles *(Nudeln).*

Restaurant chains, for quick snacks more substantial than Konditorei fare, are Burger King, McDonald's, **Wienerwald, Wimpy,** and **Movenpick;** this last one is far and away the best, with "real" food; and special balloons and whatnots for children, and highchairs! Hearty but not pricey fare can always be had at a **Ratskeller,** a large cellarlike restaurant usually located beneath the town hall (Rathaus). You and your teenagers will enjoy dinner of full-course meals at **La Cave** (Maximilianstr. 25), the best food I ate in **Munich.** Expensive. In the Marienplatz, you can eat at the **Ratskeller;** open to midnight. If you go to the 7th floor (not the downstairs cafe) of the **Peterhof** in time for a late breakfast (around 10:15 a.m.) and secure a window seat, you will have a fine view when the New Town Hall's Glockenspiel goes into delightful action at 11. Nice also for afternoon tea, although enjoying flaky apple strudel at a small table facing the square is more pleasant on sunny days at the **Cafe am Dom.** Branches of the reliable **Wienerwald** restaurant chain (Residenzs. 3, Frauenstr. 4, plus 48 other convenient sites) are open seven days a week. The open-air **Viktualienmarkt,** where fresh foods and flowers are for sale, south of the old town hall in the Marienplatz, is a charmer (see Munich) but for the best carryout picnic foods and food displays, to eat at leisure or at buffet bars, and where just being there is an experience, take the children to **Dallmayr** (14–15 Dienerstrasse, near the Marienplatz), closed Sun. and after 1 p.m. Sat., or to **Kafer** (1 Schumannstrasse), closed Sun. and after 2 p.m. Sat.

BABY FOOD **Hipp** baby food, can be found in all *Apotheken,* helpfully labeled—for example, *Von 3. Lebensmonat* (from the 3rd mo.). Garden vegetables, summer vegetables, mixed fruit, carrots, bananas, peas, apricots, peaches, pineapple, raspberries, spinach, carrots and rice, chicken, egg noodles, veal, liver, beef, ham, turkey, potato puree, applesauce, both baby and junior textures, are the most commonly found. *Heidelbeere* (bilberry, a sort of whortleberry) is rather like a currant crossed with a cranberry. For other translations and information about Hipp baby food, refer to Austria.

Cereals and milk powders are widely available, as are **Alete** Vitamin C fruit drinks for children. English brands (mostly confined to cereals and milk formulas), plus a fairly wide distribution of **Gerber** baby foods, scattered supplies of Swiss and Italian baby foods, are in many pharmacies, supermarkets, and department stores, as are rusks and crackers.

Fresh nonfat or skimmed milk is not always obtainable. Skimmed milk, however, can be bought in powdered form *(Pulver aus entrahmter Milch)* in supermarkets and health food shops *(Reformhauser);* the most popular brand is **Gloria.** VITAL!!! Pasteurized milk is date-stamped for day of production. *Markenmilch,* also pasteurized, has 0.2% more fat than ordinary *Milch* (3.5%); also date-stamped. *Vorzugsmilch* is not pasteurized or homogenized, just filtered and cooled. This may be 99% safe but *with children don't take chances!!!* On the other hand, DON'T BUY *sterilmilch,* treated to stay fresh for as long as two months without refrigeration; it has lost most nutritional value and ALL vitamins. *H-Milch,* homogenized, is treated to stay fresh four to five weeks without refrigeration and *retains all vitamins,* but it tastes different from fresh milk, vaguely like *Kaffeesahne* (unwhippable cream containing 12–18% fat). Cream is *Rahm,* whipping cream is *Sahne* and whipped cream is *Schlagrahm* (containing 31–33% fat). Buttermilk is *Buttermilch.*

DIAPERS AND DIAPER SERVICES A diaper is a *Windel,* pronounced vin-dle (rhymes with spindle), and the plural is *Windeln.* Disposables are *Papier Windeln. Schwedenwindeln* are disposables bought by the yard in perforated triangle shape which can be easily separated one from the other. Sold in packs of two to three dozen; least expensive are **Page, Wohli,** and **Zewa;** most expensive, **Molny** and **Moltex.** Diaper liners *(Windelein lagen),* like disposable diapers, can be bought at all pharmacies. Zewa, Camelia, and Babyli are all recommended brands—Zewa the cheapest, Babyli the most expensive. All-in-one plastic-covered diapers, Luvs, Chux, Pampers, or reasonable facsimiles thereof are readily available in all major cities.

For diaper services *(Windeldienst),* which supply and pick up diapers, check the classified telephone directory. There are many Washerettes *(Waschsalon)* where you can do your own machine load for pennies, and plenty of laundries *(Waschereien)* with quick service to take care of diaper and laundry at reasonable prices.

BABY EQUIPMENT FOR HIRE Scales can be rented at any pharmacy, but I had no luck finding any other equipment for rent. Ask the city tourist information office *(Verkehrsamt)*.

EMERGENCIES MADE EASY Medical care and hospitals are excellent. Two types of ***drugstores:*** the *Apotheke* sells only pharmaceuticals and supplies prescriptions; the *Drogerie* sells standard drugs, notions, and cosmetics. *Apotheken* usually close nights and weekends, but a few always stay open for emergencies; each has a sign on the door listing the nearest one open; your doctor or concierge can also tell you this. Usually someone at every large Apotheke speaks English. In **Munich,** the **Schutzen** pharmacy (Schutzenstr. 5; Tel: 557–661), opposite the main train station, is one of many recommended. **Internationale Apotheke** (Neuhauserstr. 8) carries a large stock of foreign medical preparations and can order for you those not in stock.

The newspaper and your weekly city guide list the ***doctors*** *(Artze)* ***and dentists*** *(Zahnartze)* on weekend or night duty; your concierge can also help you locate them.

For recommended English-speaking doctors and dentists, contact our **Embassy** in **Bonn** (Delchmannsaue, 5300 Bonn 2; Tel: (0228) 339–3390); the **American Consular Mission** in **Berlin** Clayallee 170, D-1000 Berlin 33; Tel: (030) 832–4087); or the **American Consulates General:** Cecillienalle 5, 4000 **Dusseldorf** 30; Tel: (0211) 490–081; Siesmayerstrasse 21, 6000 **Frankfurt;** Tel: (0611) 74–00–71; Alsterufer 27/28, 2000 **Hamburg** 36; Tel: (040) 44–10–61; Koniginstrasse 5, 8000 **Munich** 22; Tel: (089) 2–30–11; Urbanstrasse 7, 7000 **Stuttgart;** Tel: (0711) 21–02–21. In the German Democratic Republic, our **Embassy** is at 108 Berlin, Neustadtische Kirchstrasse 4–5; Tel: 220–2741.

Known as a *Kinderschwester,* a trained ***nurse*** will take care of an infant or a sick child with scrupulous attention if you, dear Mumsie or Dadzo, are sick. Check the telephone directory or the consular services well in advance. In **Munich,** try **Pius Maria Heim** (Mauerkirchnerstr. 79; Tel: 58–25–31. If a practical nurse will do, inquire for a *Krankenschwester*.

If you have a true crisis, call on the nearest American military installation; hospitals and/or installations are located in over a dozen German cities.

MAGIC FAMILY HELPERS The concierge at your hotel can usually get a ***babysitter*** for you, given a day's notice. The U.S. Consulate or Embassy can put you in touch with women's clubs or American-German friendship organizations who can suggest possibilities; or you can call upon the local church or labor office *(Arbeitsamt)*. When you book reservations in a castle, advance requests for babysitters are usually honored. The American Women's Club of **Frankfurt** maintains a *nursery* for children 6 mos.–9 yrs. at the Military Base, near the Abrams Bldg., open daily except Sun. 7 a.m.–11 p.m. Meals are available, and there is a small membership fee. The Armed Forces Recreation Center in **Garmisch** has a **Kinder Kastle Child Care Center** for children under 5, as well as a daily Just for Kids *summer program* for children 5–12 which includes two Kids Night Out evenings each week; imaginative and well-supervised (see Garmisch-Partenkirchen). Other Armed Forces Recreation Centers may have childcare facilities worth investigating. For a long-term stay, an ad in the local paper will bring instant results. Many university student services are opening up babysitting agencies, such as **Munich's Student Quick Service** (Studentenservis, Martiusstrasse 5; Tel: 39–50–51), which will send English-speaking students to help keep your *kleine puppchen* company, take him to marionette shows, play in the park, or swim. All odd jobs (even that of guide) cheerfully performed. You may also call on the **International Opera Assoc.** (Tel: 266–601) for young singers and actresses who do part-time babysitting; very good they are too. Most major cities have an office for international youth labor, students, *au pair* girls, and the like. In **Munich,** for instance, high standards obtained at the **Verein fur Internationale Jugendarbeit** (Friedrich Loystrasse 16; Tel: 30–16–77).

In **Munich,** the **Karstadt department store** (Neuhauserstr.) operates a small babysitting service, **Kinder Babysit,** for the convenience of shoppers; nothing elaborate, but helpful; playroom is in a building next to the store; plenty of playthings for children age 4–8. Department stores in other cities are likely to follow.

There are public, private, church-affiliated, English-Language ***kindergartens,*** French kindergartens, U.S. Armed Forces-sponsored kindergartens, and kindergartens in elementary and grade school (where classes may be in English or German). All seven varieties can be found in **Munich.** Elsewhere, there may be less of a choice, but there will be at least one kindergarten near you. Almost all require a health certificate and a contract for a stated number of months' tuition for which you are liable even if you withdraw your child earlier. Getting a child into a kindergarten isn't easy. Every major city has its **Stadtverwaltung-Schulreferat** (state school administration referral board) who will give you advice. Children 3–6 are eligible for any public kindergarten if there is space. Private kindergartens cost more; the age-range is 3–6, sometimes 4–7; except for a vacation in Aug., these usually operate year round. In West **Berlin,** there are over *25 supervised playgrounds* where preschoolers can have a bash; also kindergarten and babysitting (see Berlin).

In **Munich** there's an English-language kindergarten, the **En-**

glischer Kindergarten (Milbertshofenerplatz 8; Tel: 35–78–95). The **Munich American High School** (Cincinnatistr. 61A; Tel: 622–983–54) and the **Munich American Elementary School** (Lincolnstr. 62; Tel: 622–983–56) accept children of nonmilitary families if space is available; both are sponsored by the U.S. Armed Forces; the latter has a kindergarten for over-5s, plus bus service from most parts of Munich. The **Munich International School** (Schloss Buchhof, 8136 Percha uber Starnberg; Tel: (08151) 89161) offers schooling from prekindergarten through grade 11; teaching in English; prekindergarten and kindergarten candidates accepted from 4⅔–6 years; bus service from most parts of the city; contact Headmaster John Long. The **Rudolf-Steiner-Schule** (Leopoldstr. 17; Tel: 348–142) with a 4th-grade elementary school and a 9th-grade secondary school, also runs a kindergarten for children 3–6; classes in German. The **French School** (Oettingenstr. 15; Tel: 294–161) with a 5th-grade elementary school and a 5th-grade lycee, runs a kindergarten for children 3–6; classes in French.

You can hire a ***private guide*** from the tourist office of whatever town you're in. Arrangements for a university student guide are less organized, take longer, cost one-half as much (sometimes only ⅓ as much) and, with luck, can be twice the pleasure.

HOLIDAYS FOR CHILDREN ON THEIR OWN There are three types of children's hotels. (1) ***Kinderheim***—summer and winter holiday hotels. *Kinderheim Schlichter* (8166 Fischausen–Neuhaus am Schliersee; Tel: (08026) 6446) would be in this category. Accommodating 45–60 children from 4–14, it offers swimming, boating on the lake, special picnics and parties during summer; winter sports, skiing and skating. Hearty, appetizing meals; lovely surroundings. There are many, many others in this category, some in the mountains, some by the sea. (2) ***Kinderkurheim, Kindererholungsheim,*** or ***Kindersanatorium***—children's hotels that cater mostly for children 4–14 who are delicate or in need of convalescent care, with special emphasis upon diet, exercise, health checkups and controlled sunshine, vitamins, sunlamp treatments, and sleep. The health regime is enlivened with dancing, music, arts and crafts, and relaxed playtime. There are small family-type places that accommodate 15 children, medium-size ones, and large sanitariums that accommodate 350 children. (3) ***Baby hotels*** accept small guests from the age of 6 weeks to a year. Some will even accept oldsters of 2! Board, lodging, loving care by competent, motherly proxy parents (many of whom are registered nurses or pediatricians). These can be found in Wiesbaden, Karlsruhe, Mannheim, Frankfurt, Bad Godesberg, Hamburg, and many other locales. Your baby can be cared for by the day, week, or month. For further information, write the GNTO nearest you, or in Frankfurt.

CHILDREN'S CAMPS The **Ponyhof** is a popular establishment, and there are about a dozen of them. They combine camping, overnight pony treks, riding lessons, living quarters in inn-like buildings; modest prices. Parents can be accommodated as well. Ask the GNTO for their recommendations of Pony Holidays. Girls and boys 8–13 can take part in a two-week sailing course at the Chiemsee, from early June to mid-Sept. The Chiemsee is a beautiful lake close to Munich. For further information write to the **Chiemsee-Yachtschule** (Harrasserstrasse 71, D–8210 Prien) Nearby, boys and girls 5–13 can also holiday with children their same age from all over the world at **Internationales Kinderheim** (Fliederweg, D–8210).

In Nuremberg's sports grounds, six-day holiday courses for boys 12–16 are available between early July and late Aug. with football stars and world gymnastic champions, a corporate program organized in association with *Deutsches Reiseburo (DER).* For information, write to the **DER** (Postfach 2671, 6000 Frankfurt 1) or contact them in person at Eschersheimer Landstrasse 25–27, Frankfurt 1). In **Garmisch,** the Armed Forces Recreation Center has a super day camp program for children 5–12. (See Garmisch.)

CASTLES AND OTHER HAPPY FAMILY ACCOMMODATIONS In the alphabet of things, ***Bed and Breakfast*** homes come before castles and provide inexpensive, personalized hospitality for foreign visitors. This type of accommodation is a longtime tradition in Germany. The GNTO will provide details. *Burgen* (castles)—some 20,000 of them—are found perched on *Berge* (mountains), some in ruins, some operating as dazzling super-museums, some housing restaurants, many converted to hotels (about 50 belong to the "Gast-im-Schloss" castle hotel assoc. which issues a free overnight to guests who have spent nine nights in member hotels during the year; ask for the form at your 1st castle!) with modern plumbing, central heating, and other solid comforts; many are run by descendants of their original royal owners. They offer a high degree of personal service and excellent regional food specialties; comforts scale from the cozy to the luxurious. Prices, in most cases, are moderate. Castles dot the landscape from Westphalia (where they are moated and floated around by swans) to Alpine Bavaria (where they command breathtaking views from turret windows and towering keeps). Palaces, royal hunting lodges, and romantic manor houses also come under the heading of castle hotels. One 18th-century pleasure palace, **Monrepos** (see below), comes complete with a Fairy Tale Garden, a Grimm Brothers' fairy story flower park with talking toadstools. The GNTO will send you *Gast Im Schloss* (D3526 Trendelburg, Germany) an illustrated booklet with details about their member hotels and restaurants in German castles, stately mansions, and historic hostelries. My favorites among these and others (plus a few other choices for families) are:

Altwiedermus (NE of Frankfurt): Castle-Restaurant-Cafe **Ronneburg** (Tel: (06048) 7130), a 13th-century castle with antiques liberally allotted to every room; museum; outlook tower; attractive gardens and restaurant. **Anholt** (almost on the Dutch border): **Parkhotel Wasser-**

burg (Tel: (02874) 20446) is a moated castle with extensive park; light, airy interior with contemporary furnishings strangely reminiscent of those aboard ship; Schweiz game preserve only a mile away; swimming and fishing nearby; golf course; deer park; an ancient tower dating back to the 12th-century; museum. **Attendorn** (about 50 miles NE of Cologne): **Burghotel Schnellenberg** (Tel: (02722) 4081), closed Dec. 26–mid-Jan., is an authentic 13th-century beautifully restored castle crowning a forested hill above famous stalactite caverns; formidable on the outside, but inside, a comfortable, historic treasure trove; meals in the original Knights' Hall; old chapel; museum; skittle alley; hunting, fishing, riding, tennis, swimming. **Baden-Baden:** Brenner's Park Hotel (An der Lichenaler Allee 7570) a luxurious resort-spa hostelry; gardens on the Oos River, indoor pool, sauna, solarium, fitness studio and seven-day treatments at its own Beauty Farm; golf, tennis, riding, horse racing, fishing, hunting, skeet shooting, skating, skiing, hiking all nearby. **Badenweiler: Hotel Romerbad** (7847 Badenweiler), located at the intersection of Germany, France, and Switzerland, is one of Germany's last dream hotels; tennis courts, indoor/outdoor swimming pools, fitness center, children's playroom, sauna; riding and golf nearby; luxurious, elegant. Near **Bayreuth: Hotel Jagdschloss Thiergarten** (8581 Post Wolfsbach; Tel: (09209) 711); a tiny 18th-century hunting castle, comfortable; fine food; quiet isolation; woods; during the Bayreuth festival its nine rooms are prized beyond pearls.

Berlin: The **Schlosshotel Gehrhus** (Brahmsstr. 4–10, Tel: (030) 826–2081), surrounded by three acres of parkland, is only five minutes from the Kurfurstendamm. Formerly a palatial residence, it has a fine restaurant, art gallery, all comforts. A standout. The **Schweizerhof** in town offers special family rates and the adventure of sightseeing in a horse-drawn mail coach. **Boppard: Hotel Klostergut Jakobsberg,** a former monastery lofted above the Rhine, is far better than it sounds; indoor pool, tennis, Ping-Pong, bowling, clay-pigeon shooting, wildlife park, heliport, garden chess on an enlarged "board" with oversize pieces. **Brodenbach** (on the Trier-Koblenz route in Rhineland-Pfalz): **Burg-Hotel Ehrenburg** (Tel: (02605) 2432) *Ehren* means honor, and all honor is due this marvelously preserved 12th-century knights' castle, the property of Count Kanitz of Nassau. The 15-guestroom hotel, built in '67 in the ruins of the stables, is a happy mix of old and new. **Celle:** In the vicinity of Bremen, Hamburg, Walsrode, **Furstenhof Celle,** a 17th-century baroque country mansion the color of raspberry sherbet, offers indoor swimming, sauna, solarium, bowling, a beer pub, bar, discotheque—all dynamite for teenagers.

Cologne: Hotel Mondial (Bechergasse 10; Tel: (0221) 219671), facing the Cathedral, overlooking the Rhine, is a contemporary, reasonably priced hotel that offers Bambino suites—a twin-bedded room with private bath and connecting child's bedroom. The nice manager will do everything possible to help families. **Dorsten** (see Lembeck).

Eltville/Erbach-im-Rheingau (W of Wiesbaden): **Schloss Reinhartshausen** (Tel: (06123) 4081), a 12th-century palace of the Knights of Erbach; its proprietor is Prince von Preussen; famous vineyards; homemade, yummy confectionery. **Essen** (see Kettwig).

Frankfurt/Neu-Isenburg: Hotel Gravenbruch Kempinski (D–6078 Frankfurt/Neu-Isenburg) is a deluxe hotel overlooking its own private lake, 15 minutes by car to Frankfurt's city center; heated indoor/outdoor swimming pools, tennis, hiking, sauna; golf and riding nearby, limousine and taxi service, dancing, disco, snacks and informal meals served in a 15th-century hunting lodge. **Friedrichsruhe** (Baden-Wurttemberg): **Wald und Schlosshotel Friedrichsruhe** (Tel. (07941) 7078), an 18th-century rustic stone manor and annex, accommodates 100 in its historic rooms where once Count Friedrich of Hohenlohe disported himself and his guests. Private fishpond; playground; sauna and heated swimming pool indoor and outdoor; nearby golf course; magnificent forest park setting with deer. **Garmisch-Partenkirchen:** Reasonable rates at the **Partenkirchner Hof,** with indoor pool, sauna, gym; old-fashioned atmosphere and furnishings. **Hamburg: Atlantic Hotel Kempinski** (An der Alster 72–79, 2000 Hamburg 1) outstanding, beautiful, and luxurious; with indoor pool, sauna, solarium, 24-hour room service; **Hotel Vier Jahreszeiten** (Neueur Jungfernstieg 9–14, 2000 Hamburg 36) distinguished, elegant; on the banks of the Alster Lake in downtown Hamburg; with its own pastry and confectioner's shops; golf, riding, tennis, sailing nearby. **Hammelburg** (35 m N of Wurzburg): Hotel-restaurant **Schloss Saaleck** (Tel: (09732) 2020); 11th-century home-away-from-home for the Prince-Abbots of Fulda, served as a monastery for a number of years and has a massive watchtower on top of a vineyard and tree-covered hill. Folkloristic restaurant. **Hassmersheim-Hochhausen** (E of Heidelberg on the Neckar River): **Gastehaus Schloss Hochhausen** (Tel: (06261) 3142), a baroque manor with excellent cuisine. **Hofgeismar** (some 30 m N of Kassel): **Burghotel Sababurg** (Tel: (05678) 1052/55); space for only a dozen lucky guests; a deer park; a virgin forest nature preserve; pretty gardens; allegedly the setting for the "Sleeping Beauty"; sauna; stables; carriage trips. **Hinderzarten (Black Forest): Parkhotel Adler** (Adlerplatz, D–7824 Hinterzarten) is a traditional deluxe hotel in a four-acre private park with children's playground, jogging trails, deer park, open-air restaurant, glass-enclosed swimming pool, fitness center, bowling, riding, fishing, indoor/outdoor tennis courts; golf and watersports nearby, and all winter sports. **Hohenstein** (W of Frankfurt): The tiny Hessen-state-sponsored **castle inn and Waffenschmiede restaurant** (Tel: (06120) 3357); situated 660′ above the valley of the Aar River; nine studio-style guest rooms, each with private balcony, all very spacious and sunny. It shares this rocky pinnacle with a magnificent 800-year-old castle ruin, Hohenstein, about which your children should be ecstatic; playground too. Have a meal here at least, if you possibly can. It's absolutely wonderful.

Jagsthausen: (Schoental) (about 45 m N of Stuttgart): **Burg Jagsthausen and Guesthouse of Gotzenburg** (Tel: (07943) 2222); a medieval castle surrounded by meadows and forests; room for about 20 guests; comfortable sunny rooms; ninepins; fishing, rifle shooting; the castle has been renovated extensively except for the wing housing the museum—containing the iron-hand of Gotz von Berlichingen, who was born here and who gives the castle its claim to fame. Berlichingen is the medieval version of Robin Hood and Captain Hook combined, a hero of the oppressed with an artificial iron fist and forearm. This marvel of medieval engineering is on display in the museum and is unforgettable. Every July and Aug. an annual Gotz festival takes place in the courtyard with Goethe's play being the principal attraction. **Kettwig** (S of Essen, well away from the smokestacks of the industrial Ruhr); **Schloss Hugenpoet** (Tel: (02054) 6054), a massive, fortressed manor rising from a lagoon-like moat complete with swans; goosedown beds, a decor that gives the impression of being Victorian (but isn't); fine food, including a famous Nesselrode pie—this was the family seat of the barons of Nesselrode; tennis courts; nearby swimming; pleasant gardens. **Kronberg im Taunus** (just N of Frankfurt): **Schloss Hotel Kronberg** (Tel: (06173) 7011), is a Victorian folly on the grand scale filled with paintings by Fragonard, Titian, and Reynolds; architecturally eclectic—combining a frieze of half-timbered work with a scalloped Dutch gable, an English *portecochere* adapted from the Arc de Triomphe, an Italian campanile, dormer windows, English chimneys—this is a sumptuous 19th-century manor built by Empress Friedrich III (daughter of Queen Victoria) set in an attractive park. Handsome treasures, paintings, and tapestries, suits of armor, paneled dining room and restaurant with excellent food, all modern comforts and every operational detail ticking with the perfection of a German music box, brisk 18-hole golf course; swimming pool.

Lauenstein/Oberfranken (about 100 m NE of Nurnberg): 1000-year-old **Burg Lauenstein** (Tel: (09263) 256) encloses within defensive walls bridges, towers, medieval torture chambers and, happily, a restaurant plus accommodations for 50 guests. Surrounded by vast forests of fir, perched on a pinnacle overlooking the Franconian valley; a picture-book castle. Romantic, beautiful, memorable. **Lembeck** (some miles N of Recklinghausen): **Schlosshotel Lembeck** (Tel: (02369) 7213) is a late–17th-century lake palace with beautiful interior decoration; only 14 guests; owned by the Counts von Merveldt; this gem has its own museum, a large park, riding stables; water lilies on the lake give it a dreamy Monet-like quality. **Lindau (Lake Constance): Hotel Bad Schachen** (8990 Lindau) is right on the lake and offers indoor/outdoor heated pools, sailing, windsurfing, waterskiing, tennis; golf and riding nearby. **Lohmar** (see Wahlscheid). **Ludwigsburg** (just N of Stuttgart); the ivied, arcaded halls of **Schlossgaststatte Monrepos** (Tel: (07141) 30101); 70-bed, 18th-century pleasure palace of Duke Carl Eugen von Wurttemberg; furnished in early–19th-century style in a comfortable nondazzling way. A lake at its doorstep gives you the feeling of being on a dreamy paradise island in another world, an 8-year-old commented. From a cupola, with a wrought-iron grilled walkway around it, one can be king of all one surveys; fine restaurant; heated swimming pool; radio if not TV in the rooms. What makes all this so marvelous is that 2½ miles away, along a tree-shaded allee, is an elaborate 18th-century baroque Italianate palace, the residence of the kings and dukes of Wurttemberg, blessed with acres of flowers that bloom in nearly every season; doesn't require garden-club expertise to appreciate—children find the gardens, the changing perspectives and optical illusions baroquely created, as interesting as any flower enthusiast. The best part, however, for children, is the Fairy Tale Garden; legends and recorded voices at the displays may be all in German, but any child will recognize Sleeping Beauty awaiting her prince, Hansel and Gretel and the wicked witch, Cinderella charming pigeons from their perch, a giant guarding dungeon treasure. Aviary; flamingos; frog and parrot fountains that spurt when you step on a "magic" stepping-stone. Staying here is like having a special Grimm Brothers Land at one's feet. If little feet get tired at this big fete, scattered about are giant toadstools (musical chairs, wired to fill the air with music). **Ludwigsstadt** (see Lauenstein).

Munich: The **Residence Hotel** (Artur-Kutschur-Platz 4, 8000 Munich 40) features large rooms, sitting rooms, and adjoining children's rooms, all with refrigerators and balconies; an indoor swimming pool; neither advertised nor publicized, this is a comfortable base for families. **Neckar** (see Obrigheim). **Neckarzimmern** (E of Heidelberg): The small **Burghotel-Restaurant Hornberg** (Tel: (06261) 2758) towering above the Neckar River valley, a 1000-year-old structure with giant keep; museum; engravings, paintings, wrought iron, and tin; homemade wines and international cuisine, with feasts of spit-roasted meat outdoors on the terraces (the views make children feel like kings); private vineyard; riding; tennis; swimming; mini-golf; motorboating nearby; comfortable and well-furnished guest rooms.

Oberwesel (about 30 m W of Wiesbaden): The 8-guest **Burg-Hotel** and restaurant **Auf Schonburg** (Tel: (06744) 8198); a 1000-year-old knights' castle high above the Rhine, romantic and comfortable; a Princesses' room with a spinning wheel and frilly-canopied bed; riding; nearby heated pool. **Obrigheim** (E of Heidelberg on the Neckar River): Hotel-Pension **Schloss Neuburg** (Tel: (06261) 7330), a pleasant hill castle. **Olsberg/Gevelinhausen: Hotel Schloss Gevelinghausen** is the place to go for family fun and entertainment in a handsome setting of a former manor estate; close by to the ***Freizeit-Zentr. Fort Fun,*** with riding, riding instruction, summer skiing, many attractions including giant water chutes, outings in covered wagons, "Western City" model mine and mining museum open to visitors, plus its own swimming pool, sauna, solarium, and tennis courts. **Petershagen** (about 60 m S of Bremen):

Schloss Petershagen (Tel: (05702) 346) on the Weser River is the exquisite little (room for only 12 guests) former residence of the Prince-Bishops of Minden; tranquil and comfortable period-furnished rooms (do reserve one overlooking the river); delicious food; lovely terraces, tennis; flower-filled gardens; its own beach for fishing and watersports. **Riedenburg:** (about 75 m N of Munich): **Burghotel Schloss Eggersburg,** (Tel: (09442) 1498), open Easter–mid-Oct.; from the Riedenburg train station you can be picked up by hotel car. On a forested peak; 12 spacious rooms; suites; furnishings are mostly period; fishing, riding, swimming, badminton, Ping-Pong, summer music and art festivals; playground; And, joy of joys, a wildlife park with animals to feed. **Rieneck** (some 60 m E of Frankfurt): **Gastehaus Gut Durnhof** (Tel: (09354) 641); an updated feudal manor in the meadowlands and woods of the Sinn valley; its 40 modern rooms come with balconies, few private bathrooms (and these with showers but not baths); the bath is down the hall; however these drawbacks can be overlooked because the children have ponies, donkeys, and horses; playgrounds; mini-golf; fishing nearby. **Rothenburg ob der Tauber** (about 100 m E of Heidelberg): **Hotel Goldener Hirsch** (Tel: (09861) 2051) book ahead to get rooms in the Spitalturm (gate tower); a particularly nice hotel (friendly to families) in this lovely medieval town.

Stuttgart: Schlosshotel Solitude (Tel: (0711) 69–10–91), a Rococo palace on top of a forested hill, that was a reveling place (a Lustschloss) for nobility in the 19th century; glittering chandeliers; painted ceilings; walls covered with tapestries and frescoes. Formal, ornate as the cakes for weddings which are held here, I would recommend one night to test the reaction of your children. It confers a certain sense of oneupmanship to which children are not insensitive! **Trechtingshausen** (on the left bank of the Rhine, about 25 m W of Wiesbaden): **Schlosshotel Burg Reichenstein** (Tel: (06721) 6101), a glorious ivy-covered 13th-century stronghold with a drawbridge and iron portcullis (still in alarmingly good working order) guarding a museum of arms and weapons. A lawn for relaxing where knights once jousted for the hands of fair maidens; observation tower; own vineyard; stables; the proprietor will arrange excursions; closed Dec. 1–Feb. 1. Medieval and marvelous. **Tremsbuttel** (near Hamburg): An exceptionally lovely 17th-century hunting lodge built by the princes of Schleswig-Holstein, **Schloss Tremsbuttel** (Tel: (04532) 6544) is a deluxe turreted hotel in a 10-acre park; tennis, mini-golf; gourmet food; 20 comfortable rooms.

Trendelburg (some 25 m N of Kassel): **Burghotel Trendelburg** (Tel: (05675) 1021/22); one of Germany's best-preserved castles (built in the 13th century). The hill it surmounts rises like a volcanic island from a green level sea of farmland; its steep gradient compels the coach houses, stables, church, and village houses to huddle on a lower level around its walls. Keep with a flag waving on top, three lesser walled towers, and a tall dormer-windowed great house built in a later century around the original knights' chapel. Ravens fly down from the slate-shingled tower for crumbs when the tourists who have come for tea depart. Children can fish in the shallow river, gather violets in the woods, swim at the castle's heated pool down the road apiece fronting the guesthouse (where other people may stay but not you or me who prefer the castle comforts of time-mellowed furniture, goosedown quilts, and pillows that make for fine small-fry pillow fights). Children may founder themselves on homemade pastries and chocolates at their bedsides, courtesy of the *Burg-Geist* (castle ghost). They will enjoy the homemade bread, country butter, local venison, trout, sausage, and steak. The village church has ancient frescoes; the halls are antlered and chandeliered; there is a habitable tower room with a fireplace; horse-drawn coach rides Wed. for a small charge; meals can be enjoyed on the terrace above the waterless moat; all rooms have great country charm; the staff will help you find suitable babysitters and explain the history of the fascinating family treasures, including a rare Japanese Ninja suit of armor, a porcelain stove, and interesting tapestries. Oh, to be in Trendelburg again!

Wahlscheid (SE of Cologne): **Schloss Auel** (Tel: (02206) 2041/2/3) ancestral home of the Marquis de la Valette, is an 18th-century baronial establishment where Napoleon (as legendary a noctivigant as George Washington) once slept in the little 4-poster canopied bed (which now has a telephone beside it). Beautifully furnished; 26 rooms, only 15 with bath; a few suites; tennis courts; a heated pool; fishing; riding stable; skittle alley, baroque chapel popular for weddings at which child-spectators gather. **Waldeck am Edersee** (not far from Kassel): **Burghotel Schloss Waldeck** (Tel: (05623) 5324), for 30 guests, ancestral seat of the Counts of Waldeck is situated on a craggy hill by the shore of Lake Eder, with a private beach, fishing, and 1000 years of history. A splendid medieval Knights' Hall; homemade confectionary including marzipan; an adventurous-to-climb keep; fabulous forest and lake views; the dungeons are horrid enough for any child's satisfaction; good fishing (pike and perch); open Mar. 1–Oct. 30. **Wassenberg** (almost on the Dutch border, W of Cologne): The Hotel-Restaurant **Burg Wassenberg** (Tel: (02432) 4044), a 9th-century castle surrounded by parkland on the Burgberg; a dozen rooms, some with balconies; swimming pool, fishing, a game preserve, riding, tennis, playground, large gardens. **Wasserburg** (Lake Constance): Hotel-Pension **Schloss Wasserburg,** an old-fashioned hideaway (Tel: (08382) 5692), bathing beach, the landing stage for vessels plying Lake Constance at its doorstep. **Weitenburg** (some 60 m SW of Stuttgart on the Neckar River): Hotel-Restaurant **Schloss Weitenburg** (Tel: (07457) 8051), a combination of medieval castle, baronial mansion, Gothic chapel, with swimming pool; horse-drawn carriages; porcelain stoves; *objets d'art;* antique furniture; horses to ride; and all comforts in its 25 rooms. Flowers spill from window boxes overlooking the courtyard—lovely, romantic, more like a French chateau than a fortress. **Xanten-Winnenthal: Hotel Burg Winnenthal** is the oldest moated castle in the Lower Rhine area; four miles away from the old Roman city of Xanten and within the castle walls are a modern farm, pleasant hotel, and restaurant; tennis, riding stables nearby. **Zell** (on the Mosel river): **Hotel Schloss Zell** (Tel: (06542) 4084) perfectly preserved 16th-century electoral palace, originally the 13th-century residence of the princes of Trier; own vineyard; Devonian fossil collection for young geologists; tennis, swimming pool. Closed Dec. 20–Jan. 20.

CAMPING AND CARAVANING Camping enthusiasts have a choice of some 1000 well-equipped camp grounds. Send for the schedule of **Deutscher Camping-Club** (Mandlstr. 28, 8000 Munchen 40; Tel: (089) 33–40–21) and the campgrounds list, "Camping Federal Republic of Germany," from the GNTO. If your teenagers want to go hiking, there are more than 700 youth hostels, some sited in modern buildings, some in old castles; for information, write to **Deutsches Jugendherbergswerk** (Bulowstr. 26, 4930 Detmold 1; Tel: (05231) 22772) In Munich, from the end of July through Aug., a giant tent is available that sleeps 400; open all night from 5 p.m.–9 a.m. For a small fee you get an air mattress, blankets, and hot tea in the morning. Canteen, lavatories, showers, and an information bureau are all laid on as well at this **Sleeping Tent/Youth Camp am Kapuzinerholzl** (Franz-Schrank-Strasse; 8 Munchen 19). One of the more attractive camping sites is the German-Luxem-Luxembourg Park, with crags to climb, castle ruins with swans drifting in the moat, children's zoo, rocky streams ribboning the forested hills of the Eifel and the Ardennes. It's in an area bracketing the Our River and the lower part of the Sure River, complete with all the facilities of recreation ground and holiday resort.

ATTRACTIONS FOR CHILDREN IN MUNICH (Munchen): As most visitors get to hear sooner or later, the name means at the monk's place, and the city's symbol is the Munchner Kindl, a child in a black or yellow monk's robe, holding a beer stein or a prayerbook. Attractions children would enjoy (most open at 9 or 10 a.m. and close at 5 or 6 p.m.) are:

The **Deutsches Museum** largest scientific museum in the world; you'd have to walk at least ten miles to see all the exhibits; complete alchemist's laboratory; marvelous planetarium; exhibits showing the development of watches, cars, bicycles, and trains; press a button and things start whirring, clicking, humming, moving. The lightning exhibit is noisy and thrilling. You can watch glass being blown. The Man and Space show includes replicas of *Sputnik* and *Explorer*. Do get the illustrated guide in English (at the bookshop by the main entrance) *in advance* of your visit. Otherwise, you won't know where to go first or what demonstrations to see when. Open daily; restaurant on the ground floor.

The **out-of-town raft ride**—with an oom-pahing, jolly Bavarian brass band—starts from **Wolfratshausen** on the Isar River, about 18 miles south of Munich, stops at **Pupplinger Au** and then at the **Bruckenfischer Restaurant** at Schaeftlarn so that all aboard can fortify themselves before the bargelike raft takes off again for the "rapids," a drop of 60′ in 180 yards, perfectly safe but exciting for children; the ride ends at Muhltal, where you turn around and come back again; about four hours round trip. You can swim along the way; this is a delight from start to finish. The tourist office can give you detailed instructions (Fremdenverkehrsamt in the main train station at the Bayerstrasse exit; Tel: (089) 239–12–56/7/8/9/, 239–12–60; or at the Airport Arrival Hall; Tel: (089) 90–72–56, (089) 239–12–66. Or, if you feel qualified as a VIP, to the main administrative office, Rindermarkt 5, D–8000 Munchen 2; Tel: (089) 23911).

The **Valentin Museum** (Isartor Building) of practical jokes; but there's no use going unless you speak German or have someone along to translate. Closed Mon. The **Glockenspiel** at the New Town Hall (Rathaus) in the Marienplatz goes into action every day at 11 a.m.; dancing barrel-makers, a knight unhorsing another knight; a crowing rooster; exceptionally good. The large **English gardens,** with a Chinese pagoda at which you can buy light refreshments; ride in a kayak or canoe; hire a horse-drawn carriage for sightseeing; Monopteros, a Greek-style temple on a hilltop which is a meeting place for teenagers; heavenly old-fashioned carousel. You can rent a bicycle right at the entrance (Koniginstrasse and Veterinarstrasse) when M. Buss's bicycle rental is open, 9 a.m.–8 p.m. in good weather only. Closed in winter. The **Marionette Theater** (Marionetten Theater; Blumenstr. 29A) has puppet shows (e.g., *Little Red Riding Hood, Hansel and Gretel*) on Wed., Sat., and Sun. afternoons. The **Munchner Marchen Buhne** (Leopoldstr. 17; Tel: 394–081) performs fairy tales at 3 p.m. Cartoons and Disney films are shown weekends in many movie theaters; check the newspaper for time and program. Hand puppets and puppet shows can be seen at the **Munchner Puppentheater** (Lenbachplatz 8; Tel: 591–414) at 2 and 3:30 p.m.; classical productions Sat. at 8 p.m. Young opera buffs should try to get opera tickets—Munich's **Opera House** is famous. Junior music-lovers can also join the **City Music Library** (Stadtische Musikbibliothek; Salvatorplatz 1; Tel: 222–704) for listening and reading rooms, a studio for taping, and you can borrow records! Book enthusiasts should contact the **International Youth Library** (Kaulbachstr. 11A; Tel: 285–261) or the children's section of **America House** (Giselastr. 10; Tel: 345–583).

There's ice skating year round at the **Olympia Tower** (Eissportstadiom Oberwiesenfeld) daily except Fri. You can rent children's skates, but you need a passport for identification and as a deposit! In winter, an outdoor rink is also in operation. Have a snack at the revolving **Olympia Tower;** speedy elevators lift you 546′ to the restaurant, 10 a.m.–midnight (fun, but expensive for a meal; have a snack a la carte), and observation platforms—one especially protected for children (with a roofed-over, less expensive snack bar). Panoramic views are splendid. Olympia Park is a giant recreational center with huge studio for sport and culture, and free open-air pop concerts in Theatron by the lake during the summer. Have supper and watch the Schuhplattler performances at the **Platzl Restaurant** (8 Munzstr.; Tel: 293–101), site of hi-jinks and noisy merriment. The xylophone, zither, and yodeling performances have charm. The rest seemed to me like a noisy, tasteless tourist trap, but the place was mobbed and everyone else seemed to enjoy it. Supposedly "typically Bavarian." You may disagree, but I think it's the pits.

One of many riding academies is **Universitats-Reitschule** (Koniginstr. 34; Tel: 398–803); for others, check the telephone directory under *Reitschule* and *Reitclub*. There are many swimming pools, exceptionally nicely laid out, landscaped, with restaurant facilities, sandboxes, Ping-Pong tables (few, if any lifeguards in attendance). An indoor pool open all year which offers swimming lessons is **Norbad** (Schleissheimer Str. 142). Charming summertime outdoor pool is **Maria Einsiedel** (Zentrallandstr. 28); also **Georgenschwaige** (Belgradstr. 195). For others near you, check the telephone book under *Schwimmbad*.

For views of the city, the children may adore climbing the spiral staircase to the head of Bavaria, Bavaria's patron (Theresienhohe) above the Theresienwiese. Or panting up the stairs of **St. Peter's Church** (Rindermarkt) known as Der Alte Peter, with an extraordinarily beautiful interior. In the Marienplatz, the two domed-towered **Church of Our Lady** (Frauenkirche) has an elevator. You might want to go to the wonderful **Hellabrunn Zoo,** with its special children's section, the *Kinder-Tierpark*. At 2 p.m. the chimps and monkeys put on a special show.

Why not nibble on breads, sweets, *weisswurst* (a white sausage whose casing you must peel back before you attempt to eat it), at the **Viktualienmarkt,** a cobblestoned square behind the Marienplatz and St. Peter's Church? This is where the Munchners go to browse, snack and chitchat in the midst of an attractive open-air food market. Or visit Dallmayr's. (See Food.) Or just flake out with flaky apple strudel at the **Cafe am Dom** in the Marienplatz and have another coffee and try a *Schmalznudel,* the Bavarian equivalent of a doughnut.

On a sunny day, you might bestir yourself to picnic by the Isar, the river which divides Munich into east and west, and is lined on either side with pleasant grounds where you can settle yourself with all those goodies you have bought from **Dallmayr** or **Kafer**. Children like to sit on the paved river bank and dangle their feet in the icy water which flows down from the mountains. Temple sculptures from the Greek island of Aegina, and the marble sensuality of the un-figleafed Barberini Faun may give your daughters a lifetime interest in classical Hellenic culture as nothing but the **Glyptothek** can (at Konigsplatz), and if you're interested in Greek, Roman, Etruscan antiquities, the **Antikensammlung** nearby, with smaller statuary, ancient jewelery and vases is a ravishing arcaeological delight.

Only two minutes away is the **Jager Museum** which you can't miss because of the pranksters snorting behind a bronze statue of a wild boar at the entrance which agreeably echoes their noises and makes them its own. The new Jager Museum is the most important hunting museum in all Europe, filled with hunting horns, relevant art dating back to prehistoric times; all exhibits presented with style, flair and latest museum techniques. Children *adore* this museum with its wild life tableaux that, alas, may freak you out if you are a save-our-wild-lifer.

More museums? The **Old (Alte) Pinakothek** (27 Barer Str.) open daily except Mon., also open Tues. and Thurs. evenings. One of the world's great museums. The altarpiece panels, the Durers, Cranachs, Grunewalds, Altdorfers, the Italians are ravishing, children linger before them. One curiosity is Bernhard Strige's picture of Conrad Rehlingen's eight children—each, if you look closely, with his or her age inscribed above the head. The children may also be interested in the Murillo ragamuffins. The **New Pinakothek** (across the way at 29 Barer Str.) has Gauguins, Van Goghs, Cezannes, Monets, paintings by Degas—German Romantics, French Impressionists—your child is bound to find a "favorite" painting. The **Bavarian National Museum** (Prinzregentenstr. 3) exhibits more than 8000 creches from Bavaria, the Tyrol, and Italy; arts and handicrafts dating back to the 4th century. The **Municipal Museum** (Stadtmuseum; St. Jakobs-Platz 1), has toys, dolls, doll houses, musical instruments, puppets, costumes, life in period rooms, cottages and an artist's studio, many special demonstrations; particularly interesting for children. The Treasury (Schatzkammer) of the **Residenz Museum** (Max-Joseph-Platz 3), has crown jewels and a great coin collection. **Nymphenburg Palace** comprises the Pagodenburg (a Chinese pavilion teahouse), Badenburg (luxurious bathhouse), Amalienburg (hunting lodge incorporating the classiest kennels in the world), and Marstall. If you brisk through this gilded, glittering complex, stopping only if you see something really riveting, you'll have a much better feel of the whole thing than if you go on a guided tour; restaurant; a glorious expanse of lawn, flowers, topiary; foundations, trees, and lakes. The sleighs, carriages, and coaches in the Marstall (with King Ludwig's state coach, and his favorite horse—stuffed) are certainly worth seeing. If you can totter through them, there's even a Botanical Garden and the Nymphenburg Porcelain Factory.

The **Circus Krone** (Marsstr. 43; Tel: 558–166) from Christmas to Easter has almost daily performances, afternoons and evenings, of a one-ring, old-fashioned circus, with wonderful acts, a MUST. The last week in Sept. and for the following two weeks is ***Oktoberfest,*** a gigantic fun fair, carnival, and popular fair. If you possibly can, do try to include this in your stay. Centering around Theresienwiese, are costumed processions, magnificent horse-spanned brewery wagons, folkloristic dance ensembles, exhibits of marksmanship (including cross-bowmanship), 12-cannon salutes, roller coasters, carousels, shooting galleries, ox roast, and an all-out effort of Munich's breweries to make this an enormously happy brass-band occasion for families. *Caution:* the brewery horses can be mean and bad-tempered, so keep the children well out of their way. ***Fasching,*** or Carnival time, (Jan. 6 until Shrove Tues.) means costumed balls, including *Kinderballe* for the children. You can buy wigs and masks at department stores—**Beck am Rathaus** has the widest possible variety—or rent costumes in all sizes at **Dr. Breuer Verleih,** (Hohenzollernstr. 11); **Kostumhaus Heiler** (Corneliusstr. 7), or **Kostumhaus Cinyburg** (Lindwurmstr. 16). The **Christkindl Markt,** a lovely little fair with creches and toys, is held during the weeks before Christmas in the Marienplatz, when the center of the city becomes an enchantment of cherubim and angels.

▶ **Note:** Tickets for the circus, for puppet shows, for concerts, opera and the theater may be easy for you to pick up if you are in the neighborhood. I think it's easier to call the **Abendzeitung** (Sendlingerstrasse 79; Tel: (2377) 223). **Max Hieber** (Kaufingerstrasse 23; Tel: 224–281) can also help you. Do please go to the City Tourist Office where you can pick up for free or at minimal charges large, detailed city maps in English; a copy of the *Official Monthly Program,* published on the 27th of last month for this month, which details museum hours, special exhibitions, theater, opera, concert events. The friendly *Fremdenverkehrsamt* can provide you with English-speaking guides for hire, a 24-hour ticket for unlimited travel on the bus, streetcar, U–Bahn (underground subway) and S–Bahn (above-ground, or S for Surface train); information about hotels, pensions. And Munich posters, great for wall decor and presents if you can secure a cardboard tube to mail them home.

Recommended ***excursions:*** To the three castles of mad King Ludwig II: **Neuschwanstein,** reached from Hohenschwangau near Fussen by horse-drawn carriage. **Linderhof** is 9 miles west of Oberammergau. For **Schloss Herrenchiemsee,** on an island in Lake Chiemsee and modeled after Versailles, you take the train to Stock—a 1st-class ticket entitling you to a run in King Ludwig's open touring car (!), and board the boat to the island. (See also Fun Trips.) Excursions may also be made to Landshut, Marchenwald at Grafath, the Starnberger See, Berchtesgaden, Oberammergau, or Garmisch-Partenkirchen.

ATTRACTIONS FOR CHILDREN IN BERLIN Almost ⅓ of this city consists of woods, parkland, or open water. Children like looking for golden orioles in the parks (Tiergarten and English Garden are among the most popular), and in the Grunewald, Tegel, and Spandau forests (where Berliners like to show off with their well-trained dogs); in winter, never stroll without taking along seed or bread for the birds.

Havel and Tegeler See lake chain: Top attraction for watersport enthusiasts; divine also for duffers like me who can enjoy a spree on the Spree River, a tributary of Lake Havel which goes snaking through the city. In the **Tiergarten,** at **Cafe am Neuen See,** Lichtensteinallee, and at the beautiful **Freizeitpark** in the northern section of town, you can rent rowboats *(Ruderboote)* and pedalo boats *(Tretboote).* At **Schildhorn,** a wee peninsula beckoning from the green forest of **Grunewald** into **Lake Havel,** you can rent water bicycles, rowboats and other craft at **Bootsvermietung Schildhorn.** At **Schlachtensee,** an inland lake in the southern section of town, south of Krumme Lake on the eastern border of the Grunewald, you can rent rowboats and other craft at **Bootsverleih Hensel am Schlachtensee** (Marinesteig 6A, 1000 Berlin 38). At **Gross Glienicker See,** a lake in the **Kladow** area, on the western shores of Lake Havel in the southern part of town, you can rent boats along the lakeside promenade at the bathing entrance booth (Strandbaude). You can cruise from **Wannsee** on the southern shore of Lake Hevel up to **Tegelen See** and **Heiligen See** bifurcating the northern shore. Between Apr. and Sept., a fleet of excursion boats are in operation, including *Moby Dick,* a whale of a boat (complete with scales, tail, and jaws). For information about cruises and excursions in the *Unter* (southern) and *Ober* (northern) parts of Lake Havel, and for excursion sprees along the Spree River, check with **Stern und Kreisschiffahrt,** a company whose pleasant boats have cafeterias aboard; also try **Reedereiverband der Westberliner Personenschiffahrt.**

If you want to rent waterskis; charter a sailboat, motor-cruiser, or canoe, or get advice or information about anything in Berlin, head for the **Verkehrsamt,** the **City Tourist Office,** located at the Tauentzienstrasse entrance of **Europa Center,** a five-acre site of shops with a restaurant, heated swimming pool, sauna, massage rooms and an unspeakably complicated glass-enclosed water-siphon-pendulum-operated mechanism of technological art known as the *Flow-of-Time-Clock,* best seen in action at 1 p.m. and 1 a.m. Children 6 and older may be interested in the **Multivisions-Theater** on the floor above ground level. With continuous 90-minute performances from 9 a.m.–9 p.m., this is a veritable marathon for eye and ear, open Mar.–May. The *telescope lane* on the rooftop for star-watchers is another bonus here. Serious *sternwarte,* however, will prefer the **Zeiss Planetarium** (Munsterdamm 90) on Mt. Insulaner with its lovely park surrounds.

Some children may be just as fascinated by the *pavement artists* who usually get shooed off the **Kurfurstendamm,** where double-decker buses proliferate but hurdy-gurdies are down to a handful. In Berlin's back streets, *street vendors* shout their wares (from eels to perfume). The U–Bahn (Untergrund Bahn), the city's subway system, is a model of cleanliness, efficiency, and eye-popping color. Public transportation is great, and the Tourist Office can tell you how to make the best use of it to get to such outstanding attractions as **Schloss Pfaueninsel** (Peacock Island Castle) a nature preserve with pavanning peacocks and many other birds, swans, ducks, oaks, weeping willows. That wonderful **Wannsee** area (Europe's largest inland white sand beach) offers a huge **children's playground,** ***Kinderspielplatz*** close by a huge *outdoor swimming pool.* **Strandbad Wannsee,** one of the city's inviting two dozen. The **Egyptian Museum** (Schloss Strasse 70) opposite **Charlottenburg Palace** in the Eastern Stuler building, with treasures from all dynasties of ancient Egypt, includes the original head of Queen Nefertiti. Across the street in the Western Stuler building, is the **Museum of Antiquities** (Schloss Strasse 1) with spectacular displays on the lower floors of the *Roman Hildescheim Treasure* of silver, gold, gems, jewelry; and Greek ceramics, marbles, bronzes in the upper galleries. The East Wing of the Palace, Knobelsdorff building, houses a **Museum of Applied Arts,** with collections from the early Middle Ages to art nouveau and Bauhaus, and offers concerts by candlelight in yet another gallery in the evening. In the West Wing of the Palace, in the Langhans building, there are artifacts from the Stone, Bronze, and Iron Ages up to the 11th century housed in the **Museum for Pre- and Early History.** Sensational collections all, and all beautifully arranged. In the park around the Palace, there's the **Schinkel Pavilion** with paintings and furniture of the early 19th century; a *Belvedere* teahouse with an extensive collection of Berlin porcelain; and a royal mausoleum. I'd be inclined to take the children to see the museums in Charlottenburg Palace, if I were pressed for time, rather than go to the **Zoo** (Haupteingang Hardenbergplatz) with 8044 animals representing 1638 species, the *world's largest animal collection,* including somersaulting pandas and the entrancingly tiny Przewalski horses to covet, a **Children's Zoo** and the nearby **Aquarium** (Budapester Strasse 32). And even though the **Botanical Garden** in the borough of Steglitz (Konigin-Luise-Strasse 6–8 and Unter den Eichen 5–10) displays flora of five continents in 16 showcase greenhouses, with a **Botanical Museum** adjacent, I'd skip that in favor of the complex of museums **(Museum fur Volkerkunde)** in **Berlin-Dahlem** (Lans Strasse 8) with absolutely riveting anthropological collections: Fabulous, great, extraordinary! Telephone 83–20–31 to find out about events, exhibits, and performances of special interest to children scheduled to coincide with your visit, or ask the City Tourist Office about these *children's specials* at the Museum fur Volkerkunde.

If you're lucky, or operate on advance precision planning, your visit will coincide with a ***children's film festival*** or ***folk festival,*** such as the Oktoberfest in Sept./Oct., the Weihnachtsmarkt in Dec., or other events in June, July, and Aug. The **Domane Dahlem** (Konigin-Luise-Strasse 49) is an interesting open-air museum of life on a 19th-century estate for the gentry and farmhands; the **Museumsdorf Duppel** at Clauerstrasse, also an open-air museum, is a reconstruction of a 13th-century village, which will take you to Berlin's beginnings on this original excavation site. Other museums to save for less sunny days are: the **Transport Museum** *(Verkehrsmuseum fur Verkehr und Technik)* (An der Urania 15); a **Museum for Postal Service and Telecommunication** permanently installed at the same address; the **Deutches Rundfunkmuseum** (Hammerskjoldplatz 1) a must see, not to be confused with the **Funkturm** (490′ radio-TV tower) with an elevator to the top and an up-high restaurant; and the **Berlin Museum** (Linden Strasse 14), with the city's historical memorabilia, including toys. There are fine art galleries, collections of contemporary art, a criminal science museum open only for persons over 16, a library relating to costumes and art history; also a **Musical Instruments Museum** (Bundesallee 1–12), the **Brohan Collection** (Max-Eyth-Strasse 27) of paintings and objects from art nouveau to art deco, and always some special exhibit on view at the **U-Bahn Wittenbergplatz** (Trebinner Strasse 9).

The **Tiergarten,** with its marked nature trails and boating lake, is a heavenly park for a family outing, but better yet, I think, is the **Grunewald,** lakeside by **Schildhorn.** Or continue on the Havelchaussee to the Karlsberg, where the **Grunewald Tower** is situated. The Tower restaurant offers splendid home cooking and Berlin specialties, plus warming hot toddies if the day is chilly. Be on the safe side and telephone the **Grunewaldturm** restaurant for reservations (Tel: 304–1203). Another treat of an eating place is the **Grillchen** (Knesebeckstrasse 49) an adjunct of the **Grille** (Kurfurstendamm 202 (in the passage way). The Grillchen is open from 7 a.m.–1 a.m. **Heckers Deele** (Grolmannstrasse 35), open 9 a.m.–midnight is attractively rustic. In the basement beneath, there's a coachmen's pub where you can sit in niches between saddles and harnesses, but beware the discotheque noise which makes dinner conversation difficult. For reservations, Tel: 8890/1, 882–20–26.

What to do if you have infants? A day kindergarten, operative Mon.–Fri., 9 a.m.–6 p.m., **Frau Klos** (Stuttgarten Platz 19) is enthusiastically recommended. Babysitting arrangements can be made here also. The City Tourist Office also commends Frau Klos as outstanding, and may also be able to offer other recommendations.

What to do if you have very active children under 5? The Board of Education, Youth and Sport, **Senatsverwaltung fur Schulwesen, Jugend und Sport** (Tel: 260–42–588) has three dozen **Spielplatze** around town where expert counselors supervise little ones who can hammer, make mud pies and all the noise they want, and tear wildly about from excitement to excitement—and have a glorious time. The City Tourist Office and the SSJS can give you all the welcome details.

What to do if you and your older children crave exercise besides museum walking/jogging? Head for the **Freizeitpark** in the borough of Tagel (Campestrasse 11, An Der Malche), where from mid-Apr. to the end of Oct. you can rent single bicycles *(Tourenrad)* or tandem bikes at the **Fahrradverleih;** rent pedal boats at the **Bootsverleih;** or play volleyball and tennis. (And if you tire before the kids do, you can also rent a canvas chair for postage-stamp money.) Ask the City Tourist Office or check the park (Tel: 433–60–66) for other activities available. Go to **Krumme Lanke,** another lake recreation area (and it is *lanke,* not lake) at Fischerhuttenstrasse (Tel: 834–42–01) and rent a bicycle at that **Fahrrad Verleih.** No tandems here, however. You can also rent bikes to wheel through the forest paths of Grunewald at the S–Bahnhof (the surface train railway station) at Grunewald, Schmetterlingsplatz (Tel: 811–58–29). Or rent a bicycle at **Fahrad-Buro Berlin** (Crellestrasse 6; Tel: 1784–55–62) to explore Berlin's 485 miles of bicycle paths and hiking trails.

Check the City Tourist Office about the locations of all the *indoor and outdoor swimming pools.* The **Ponyhof Wittenau** (Wittenauer Strasse 80, Tel: 402–85–35)—and please call here in advance to reserve a mount—is a riding stable-school for younger children with just ponies available. **Ponyhof** (Buckower Chaussee 82), however, has ponies, small hacking horses *(Kleinpferde)* and hunters *(grosse Pferde),* and you can get there by S–Bahn. Or take the U–Bahn out to Olympia-Stadion, climb the clocktower *(Glockensturm)* for the view (open Apr.–end Oct.).

What to do if you're foot-weary and your young children want to be entertained? If you're anywhere near the **Cafe Schalotte** (Behaimstrasse 22, Berlin 10), take your children there and let them play games in the **Spielort** while you relax in comfort. Another Spielort at Freie Volksbuhne (Kassenhalle, Schaperstrasse 24, 31), and **Kammerspiele** (game arcade) at Alt-Moabit 99 (21). **Klecks** (Berlin 44) is a children's theater with puppet performances. There's also **Figurentheater** (Berlin 30), **Rote Grutze** (61), **Birne** (31), **Tribune** (10), and **Grips-Theater** (21) for the cream of the children's theater crop. Check in the official tourist guide, inquire at the City Tourist Office, or ask your concierge to call for you for more specific information. Tickets for all performances should be ordered directly from the theaters or theater ticket agencies. Your concierge can do this for you.

The best shopping in Berlin is for antiques from sleazy, flea-market junk at the **Karree** (Kurfurstendamm 207) to objets d'art in hundreds of antique shops. At **Nollendorfplatz,** a former elevated station of the old S–Bahn, antiques are displayed in 16 old subway cars circa the '20s, with the "Nolle" pub car offering edibles and drinkables. Open daily, except Tues., from 11 a.m.–7:30 p.m. The least expensive flea market, at the **Reichpietschufer** (between Potsdamer Strasse and Hafenplatz), operates on weekends only, rain or shine, from 8:30 a.m.–3 p.m.

Dancing parties are held for children throughout the year by the **Keller Dancing School.**

A wide range of ***sightseeing tours*** of West and East Berlin is offered by **Berliner Baren** (Tel: 883–60–02) from the corner of Rankestrasse and Kurfurstendamm, near the Gedachtniskirche; by **Berolina** (Tel: 881–68–75) from the corner of Meinekestrasse and Kurfurstendamm; and by **Severin and Kuhn** (Tel: 883–10–15).

East Berlin? If the wall, that dark magnet, attracts you, just be sure you have your passports with you before you go. A glimpse of East Berlin will assure you this is no *kinderparadies*. Although Bahnhof Friedrichstrasse, accessible to U–Bahn and S–Bahn, may appear to be the simplest entry checkpoint, Checkpoint Charlie is less crowded and quicker. Bring an umbrella if it's raining, because the passageway is not sheltered. If you don't have a car, take the U–Bahn to Kochstrasse, a block away from Checkpoint Charlie, or the #29 Bus from the Kurfurstendamm. Don't bring books, newspapers, magazines unless you're prepared to have them taken from you and ''read'' while you wait. You will be asked to make a currency declaration and are required to buy 25 East German marks (approx. $11) that you must spend because you cannot legally take East German marks back with you to West Berlin. When you go back to West Berlin, you must return through the same checkpoint by which you entered, and you'll be asked to account for every penny of the East German marks you spent with itemized receipts—as you also will with every penny of cash or traveler's checks disbursed. Any surplus East German marks you return with will be deposited in a ''bank'' that gives you a receipt which can be redeemed on a later visit. *When in East Berlin, do not exchange any of your hard currency for East German money* because the East German police, Volkspolizei (Vopos for short), will get you. Also, *you cannot photograph checkpoints, soldiers, trains, subways, policemen, or the Wall.*

All this is worth the effort for **Museum Island**—a complex of museums reached by walking up Friedrichstrasse, crossing Unter den Linden, and then via a bridge across part of the Spree River. You'll first see **Bode Museum,** housing Egyptian, early Christian, and Byzantine art, architectural sculpture, Dutch masters' paintings, and sculpture from the Middle Ages to the present. The **Altes Museum** has a rich collection of prints and drawings; the **Pergamon Museum** with an enormous Hellenic temple called the **Pergamon Altar,** the **Ishtar Gate** dating back to the time of Nebuchadnezzar, and a fabulous collection of classical art (the pictorial representations on the frieze tiles, like those of the Parthenon, are *sensational!*); the **National Gallery** with 19th- and 20th-century art, mostly German, Nolde, Kokoschka, but also some Rodin sculptures, still lifes by Degas and Cezanne. You *can* take pictures in the museums and outside. If you have visited the **Reichstag** in West Berlin (with a history of Germany from the West's view, with an English language tape), you'll be interested in going to the **Zeughaus** in East Berlin to see the East German view of Germany's history. Possibly you will also want to visit the **Checkpoint Charlie Museum,** open 9 a.m.–8 p.m., which gives a history of the building and descriptions of all the ingenious successful and unsuccessful escape attempts.

The **Painting Gallery** (Arnimallee 23–27) is ravishing, with works of Cranach, Durer, Botticelli, Raphael, Titian, Holbein, Van Dyck, Vermeer, Rubens, and Rembrandt. If you're an archivist at heart, the **Kupferstichkabinett** has old master drawings from the 14th–18th centuries, prints, illustrated books from the 15th–20th centuries, illuminated manuscripts, artists' sketch books from the 16th–18th centuries, and a map collection. In another section is the **Museum of German Ethnology** *(Museum fur Deutsche Volkskunde* in galleries #6–#8) where you'll find cult objects, tools, furniture, textiles, costumes, and jewelry from 17th-century Germany to the present, and often special exhibits for children.

You can usually get tickets for evening performances at the rebuilt **Staatsoper** for the price you'd pay anywhere else for a sack of popcorn, so it's worth going if only to have a look; hear Grand Opera where it originated. Just don't go expecting *Der Rosenkavalier, Carmen,* or *Aida.*

The center of modern East Berlin is **Alexanderplatz** with a *TV tower* you can ascend in an elevator to an observation platform halfway up. At the base of the tower is the only **East Berlin tourist office** that dispenses information in English. East Berlin shops and restaurants will gladly take your West German Deutsche marks at the official rate. The biggest bargain in East Berlin is food at restaurants and writing paper sold at the **Centrum,** the big department store in Alexanderplatz.

I am told that the **Reiseburo der DDR** (German Democratic Republic Travel Bureau) (Postfach 77, if you're writing, or) Alexanderplatz, 1026 Berlin; Tel: 2150) can arrange for you to hire a private chauffeur-driven car, guide/interpreter, or car hire without chauffeur (''Rent a Car-GDR''); and can secure theater tickets for you. You can call them from West Berlin before you go to East Berlin. You might also be interested in touring Dresden, Leipzig, Meissen, Eisenach, Potsdam, Neubrandenburg, and other places in the GDR; the Reiseburo der DDR in Alexanderplatz can provide information.

Parks: *Marchen* means fairytale; *wald,* wood; *garten,* garden or park. *Tier* means animal. *Tiere aller Art* means all kinds of animals. *Safari* means you can drive or be driven through wild game *(Wild)* parks. *Ponyreiten* and *Kamelreiten* means you can ride on ponies and camels. A *Kinderzoo* is where your child can pet and feed animals. *Kinderspielplatz* means a children's playground, and anything with the word *Spiel* in it means fun. *Kinderkarussell* is a merry-go-round. *Freizeit* indicates general recreation—ballgames, swimming, riding. A detailed list of these, in German, is available from the **Deutscher Fremdenverkehrsverband** (DFV), 6000 Frankfurt/Main, Untermainanlage 6. If you're in the vicinity, check out the following. In northern Germany: **Lower Saxony** *(Niedersachser),* **Serengeti-Grosswild-Reservat** (3035 Hodenhagen/Walsrode), **Rasti-Land** (3216 Salzemmendorf), **Freizeitpark** (Tuttheide 309 Verden, Schleswig-Holstein), and **Lego-Land** (243 Neustadt-Sierksdorf). In the western areas of **Hesse: Schlitzerlander Tierfreiheit-Safaripark Schloss Richthof** (6407 Schlitz-Unterschwarz), **Safariland** (6081 Wallerstatten), and **Taunus-Wunderland*** (6229 Schlangenbad-Wambach). In **North Rhine-Westphalia** (Nordrhein-Westfalen): **Senne–Grosswild-Safari-park*** (4815 Stukenbrock),

Lowenfreigehege* (5135 Selfkant/Niederrhein), **Phantasialand** (5040 Bruhl), **Marchenwald*** (5071 Altenberg), **Marchenpark Gogarten** (5291 Kluppelberg), **Marchengarten Auf dem Homerich** (5223 Numbrecht), **Marchenwald** (5290 Wipperfurth) **Natur-und Tierpark Schwalmtal** (4057 Bruggen), **Freizeit-Zentr. Fort Fun** (5781 Gevelinghausen), **Liliputstadt Minidom*** (4035 Breitscheit), **Potts-Park*** (495 Minden) (see text). In the **Rhineland-Palatinate** (Rheinland-Pfalz): **Tier-und Marchenpark*** (5438 Westerburg), **Ferienpark Mosel*** (5592 Klotten), and **Hunsruck-Freizeitpark*** (5449 Sauerbrunner). In the **Saar: Gulliver-Welt** (66 Saarbrucken). In the *southwest province of* **Baden-Wurttenberg: Safari-Tierpark Hudelmeier*** (7061 Gmeinweiler) and **Europa-Park** (7631 Rust bei Ettenheim). In **Bavaria** (Bayern): **Vogel-Pony-Marchenpark Steigerwald*** (8602 Geiselwind) and **Freizeitpark Thurn** (8551 Heroldsbach).

ATTRACTIONS FOR CHILDREN ELSEWHERE Near **Augsburg** at **Haumstetten** is a city rebuilt on a miniscale with active minitrains and ships, all at a special amusement park. **Berchtesgaden:** From here you can take a bus and an inside-the-mountain elevator to see Hitler's **Eagle's Nest.** Have an hour's tour of the *Salzbergwerk (Salt Mine).* You're given a protective cloak, hood and pants to ward off the chill and the dripping brine, and off you go on a miniature tram into the tunnel of a solid salt mountain; you are transferred to a little chute you slide down toboggan-style; and after this you are rowed around a briny lake within the mountain. Another excursion (15 min. by electric railway) is to the **Konigssee,** motor launch ½- or 1-hour trips). The scenery is spectacular, but for children the ride's the thing. There's an ice grotto at Schellenberg. If you're family-conscious, you can trace your lineage, pick out your family coat of arms at the **German Heraldic Museum.**

The **Black Forest** is a region neither black nor one solid forest, as I imagined it as a child. Its mountains and hills are covered by dark pine forests, giving the area its name. For years the area has conducted a thriving cuckoo-clock and carved-wooden-toy business; and the region abounds with mountain villages where everyone wears traditional folk costumes—**Glottertal** and the **Gutach Valley** north of **Freiburg** is particularly famous—but most of the cuckoo clocks are made in factories in **Triberg Schwenningen** and **Villingen** rather than by hand in some forest cottage. **Bonn:** This may be the capital of the Federal Republic, but there's not much here of interest to children. Between **Bruhl** and **Euskirchen,** near Cologne (Koln), all signs point to **Phantasialand,** open Apr. to Nov. 1. Monorail system, water flume ride, rides in tubby boats, and a zippy "Bobbahn" like a rollercoaster in an Alpine setting; a horse-drawn tram and hurdy gurdy men in "Old Berlin"; a Turkish

*Particularly attractive of its kind.

village with a cafe; other places to eat; a gondola trip through the "Arabian Nights"; a Chinatown; Viking boats to ride in; dolphins and seals; the Wild West and the Wild Far East. Wear sneakers if you go. **Bremen** is not a city of primary interest to children, except as the locale for the ***Bremen Town musicians,*** animals all, to which there are two enchanting monuments. Be sure to have the children read the story first. The **Market Square** is exceptionally lovely; a little zoo in **Burger Park.** The time to be here is at the end of Oct. for the glorious Freimarkt fair with merry-go-rounds. **Braubach** (the GNTO in Frankfurt can give you directions) is a good place to stop for a meal at **Marksburg,** the only intact knight's castle on the Rhine, with a splendid **weaponry museum. Cologne:** Cathedral and treasures plus **Kolner Tivoli** in the north of the city, with rodeo, roller coasters *undsoweiter* open Apr.–Oct. The **Verkehrsamt,** opposite the Cathedral, is the place to go for all tourist information. Take the elevator down from the new city hall nearby to see the **Praetorium,** the Roman palace; also the **Roman-German Museum.** Summertime organ recitals at 8 p.m. Tues. (free) in the Cathedral; rotating restaurant at 544′ in the TV tower; boat trips on the Rhine from Hohenzollerbrucke and the Deutzenbrucke (longer trips booked through the **Koln-Dusseldorfer Rhine Navigation Co.**). Hotel Ludwig arranges inexpensive family accommodations. Inexpensive, hearty buffet at Alt Koln restaurant next to the Excelsior. Ask the GNTO about the carnival celebrations. All museums closed on Mon. **Lake Constance** (Bodensee) offers glorious opportunities for every form of ***watersport and boating*** either on the do-it-yourself or the excursion level. There's a car ferry, steamers, and white paddle-wheelers to ride where you will. **Mainau** is a tropical garden island with pavanning peacocks and a castle. Many enticing entertainments in the town of Konstanz are tailormade for light-hearted vacationers. **Konstanz** is on the Swiss side of the lake, a German enclave frequented by many Swiss who cross the frontier for the night life at the gambling casino. Across the lake on the German side are many quieter, smaller resorts such as **Nonnenhorn** and **Meersburg,** where you may prefer to stay.

There's **Dusseldorf,** luxurious, lively and special. Its main street, *Konigsallee,* a canal bordered on either side by a tree-lined promenade and a boulevard lined with princely shops and sidewalk cafes, graced by superb parks at both ends, makes you feel good just to look at it. Groups of boys turn cartwheels in the streets—it's an old Dusseldorf-custom—and you're expected to give them a little *trinkgeld,* sodapop money. Visiting children generally want to whirl into instant competition. Whisk the *Liebchen* off to the nearest sidewalk cafe for a snack *(Mandelspekulatius* or almond cookies are a Rhenish specialty) and then head for the **Verkehrsverein** (Konrad-Adenauer-Platz 12; Tel: (0211) 35–05–05), opposite the main railway station, for information about what's going on—always something—or, if you aren't surfeited with fortified medieval towns, inquire about **Schloss Benrath,** a castle in a flower-filled park. From the west bank of the Rhine at Oberkassel, you can take off for the medieval river-toll town of **Zons,** moated, walled, watch-towered, windmill, an **open-air theater** where there are fairy tale performances during July and Aug. for children. Just a few miles northeast of Dusseldorf in **Breitschied** is **Minidom Park** with miniature models of castles, churches, monuments, farms, bridges and ports. Mini-people love mini-worlds and this is a great one. You might make the trip to **Neanderthal** game parks and museum of geology, with exhibits about Neanderthal man, whose bones were discovered in this valley.

Frankfurt-am-Main, a commercial city that most tourists use as a starting point for touring the fabled Rhineland and southern Germany, is a pleasant enough jumping-off point, and it does have a few children's attractions. It is the birthplace of Goethe and hot dogs; it also has a **Zoo.** Judged as one of the world's greatest amusement parks, here you can see penguins waddling on real ice in the "Exotarium," hummingbirds in the aviary, otters sliding playfully down a chute, and young monkeys and other animals beautifully cared for and entertained. The **Opel Zoo,** in the suburb of Konigstein, is a children's zoo with a small collection of animals children can feed and pet. The children will enjoy going to the **Romer** (Town Hall) looking at the scale model of medieval Frankfurt, changing into felt slippers and looking at the **Kaisersaal,** where the Holy Roman Emperors used to stage their coronation banquets. The felt slippers not only keep the floor from being scratched, but also serve to polish it. (This is a common floor-polishing European custom.) There's a ***merry-go-round*** with swinging chairs near the Cathedral. In **Goethe's house** (25 Grosser Hirschgraben), a giant-sized *astronomical clock* with a bear on a chain whose disappearance signals rewinding time. The **Senckenberg Museum** is the largest natural history museum in West Germany. The city center park, the **Palmengarten** contains tropical plants, palms, Alpine gardens, playgrounds, a miniature train, mini-golf, mini-cars, row boats, ducks, swans, peacocks, and band concerts. The **Stadel Museum,** closed Mon., contains wonderful Dutch primitives, 16th-century German masterpieces, and paintings and drawings that children generally like. After all the sights, I recommend a visit to the **Cafe Kranzler** (7–8 Hauptwache) to loaf lazily while the waiter brings on the yummy pastries and the iced chocolate. For **Wimpy Bar** hamburger buffs, there's one at Biebergasse. Also **McDonald's, Burger King,** and **Movenpick;** but **Lum's** (Goethestrasse 1) with hamburgers, steaks, shakes, and salads, has appeared on the scene to rival them all. From Frankfurt, you might consider taking a short excursion to **Bad Homburg** in the *Taunus Hills;* or nearby **Saalburg,** with its Roman museum and remains of a Roman fortress; or **Marburg.** The **Frankfurter Verkehrsverein** (Tel: (0611) 25–27–37) can give you all the details about these and other easily accessible attractions. In-depth information from: GNTO, Beethovenstrasse 69, 6000 Frankfurt/Main. For a pleasant Saturday morning, wend your way to **Sachsenhausen,** a suburb on the left bank of the Main, with the city's largest flea market open Sat. a.m. and lots of tree-bordered courtyards as settings for restaurants, with open-air tables in the summer, where you can sample Apfelwoi, the local vinegary cider, and simple, good local food.

Freiburg: Lovely old town, run through by mountain streams; arcaded streets; famous Gothic spire on its cathedral; a park with a summer stage built over its lake, the *Waldsee,* prettily floodlit in summer. The children might want to take the ***cable car*** to the top of the *Schauinsland Mountain.* **Titisee** and **Schluchsee** are nearby popular lake resorts with plenty of opportunities for bathing, boating, or fishing. In winter, both are skiing resorts. **Garmisch-Partenkirchen** is a leading winter resort and sports center. Trains leave hourly during the daylight from Garmisch for the 65-minute ride to the top of the **Zugspitze,** the highest mountain in Germany, and I recommend this only for the older children of hardier mothers than I. First, you get on the cogwheel train to Grainau; from here you grind upward and through a three-mile tunnel for 100 minutes, going 11 miles higher to **Schneefernerhaus,** the one oasis of the whole trip, a cozy, warm hotel. From here, you are supposed enthusiastically to climb aboard an aerial cableway, and be lifted another 1000′ to an even more spectacular view, but not without climbing three flights of stairs to a viewing terrace. From *Schneefernerhaus* you also can walk through a tunnel to the Austrian side of the mountain, and after presenting credentials to mountain frontier guards, descend by aerial cableway to **Obermoos,** a village from which you can walk for an hour or take a 10-minute bus ride to a train that gets you back to Garmisch. You can take a buttercup-yellow stagecoach from Garmisch to **Grainau,** complete with horn-blowing postilion; great fun. Or there is a ten-minute ride in a bus-size cable car to **Kreuzeckhaus,** very exciting. Or you can take the cog railway only as far as **Eibsee** (around 3000 feet). From Eibsee to the summit of the Zugspitze a cableway lifts you 10,000 feet in nine minutes. You can take a ski lift in the summer to near **Wamburg,** Germany's highest town, or to **Partnach Klamm,** a spectacular mountain gorge. Visit **Garmisch's Olympic Ice Arena** and the **Alpspitz Wellenbad,** with its choice of seven indoor swimming pools, including a "wave" pool that provides surf-swimming every 45 minutes. Now then, for the best news of all: The **Armed Forces Recreation Center** (Center Golfpl. 8100 Garmisch) has daily summertime full or half-day programs and evening programs on Tues. and Fri. nights for children 5–12 which, depending on the weather, include everything from swimming to arts and crafts to nature walks in Alpine meadows to movie festivals. Supervised lunches on excursions; pick-up and return to your hotel by a special Fun Bus. Call **AFRC's Kinder Kastle Child Care Center,** Tel: (08821) 2535. Younger children can be cared for by the day or by the hour with advance notice. Reserve in advance for the summertime **Just for Kids** and **Kids Night Out** programs supervised by a super staff. **Geiselwind** in Bavaria, on the Wurzburg-Nurnberg

Autobahn, is where you'll find the **Vogel-Pony-Marchenpark Steigerwald** with 5000 varied birds, a bird safari, a compound of monkeys and apes, adventure playground, pony and camel riding, a wild west fantasy, fairy-tale wood, tropical fauna and flora, and many other attractions.

Goslar: This 1000-year-old jewel is a National Monument. You walk or drive through the city gate smack back into 16th-century architecture and atmosphere. If you are interested in seeing the important sights, stop off at the tourist bureau *(Verkehrsburo)* close by the **Hotel Der Achtermann** (wonderful garden and dining room, where you should have a meal) for folders outlining all the buildings and narrowest of streets plus the millwheel (near *Hoher Weg*). Ask for a guide or an interpreter to take you to one of the local breeders of those famous Harz canaries, which are trained to sing by listening to the recorded songs of nightingales. There are canary-singing contests on Midsummer's Day (June 23) as a rule in **St. Andreasberg** and **Hohegeiss,** towns to the south, which are ski resorts in winter. Guess who judges the best male songsters? Not a human judge, but a female canary who unerringly singles out the most brilliant songster of the lot. Near **Grafath** (about 25 m from Munich), **Marchenwald,** the enchanted fairy-tale forest for children; open Easter–Nov., 9 a.m.–6 p.m.; three acres of fun and games, including a miniature train on a 500′ track; large playground; electric cars; a boat ride through the parkgrounds; tunnels; fun-house; a regular-size train to be explored; fairy-tale figures housed in cottages and cowboys and a Pony Express and a rocket station and . . and . . and . . . !

Hamburg, West Germany's largest city and major seaport and a primary target for playboys of the western world, also has appealing attractions for children. **Hagenbeck's Animal Park** is fun. A rabbit village; enormous dinosaurs sculptured in stone lurking behind the trees; a Japanese garden, all animals displayed in their natural surroundings; and tropical wildlife. But the big daddy of all free, open, cageless zoos in the world is the **Stellingen Gardens,** just out-of-town and so ingeniously landscaped that you think many of the animals are so free as to be almost on top of you. Let the children stay up past their bedtime to see the ***Waterlight Concert*** *(Wasserlichtkonzert)* in the **Planten un Blomen** pleasure park. Fountains, jets, and sprays are played and colored to synchronize with music; more unusual and equally as exciting as fireworks (which are also featured here); daytime playground where children may be watched over by trained nurses while parents explore other pleasures. Twin lakes in the center of Hamburg, the Inner and the Outer Alster, are a terminal for **water buses.** Countless canals arched with trees, some 2000 bridges, and boat trips are many, varied, and fun. From the quay of Jungfernstieg, close beside the Alster Pavilion (with delicious pastries in its *Konditorei*—) built out over the water, sea buses take off every ten minutes for excursions that take about 35 minutes each way through the city. Every day from the St. Pauli wharves, every half hour or so, daylight cruises around the harbor last about two hours; also excursion steamer to **Blankenese,** hourly departures on Sun. and several services on weekdays by the **Hamburg-Blankenese-Este Line.** Blankenese, some ten miles downstream on the Elbe, is a former fishing village and now a very pleasant residential suburb with lots of good places for lunch and supper. Transportation by the U–Bahn (subway) which runs mostly above land and water as an "elevated" is cheap and scenic. Two out of six museums of special interest to children: the **Museum of the History of Hamburg** (24 Holstenwall; Tel: (040) 34912/32360), fascinating old ship models; and the **Hamburg Postal Museum** (1 Stephansplatz). The small **aviation museum** at the airport has live performances of model planes and an interesting film. For moderately priced food, you can count on the Movenpick restaurant chain to provide a handful of convenient restaurants in the **Hanse Viertel.** Many Wimpy bars and McDonald's in this town where the hamburger originated. From Hamburg, it's just a short car or train ride to **Timmendorfer Strand,** a beach on the Baltic (brrr!) with nice little thatched-roofed houses offering bed-and-breakfast accommodations if you don't want to stay at the Golf and Sport Hotel with its golf courses, tennis courts, and own beach area, or the Maritim See Hotel on the beach. By train, car ferry, or plane, you might want to zip over to **Kampen** on the island of **Sylt** (Sylt is to Germany what Southampton is to New Yorkers, plus a touch of Fire Island, one of those elitist, trendy, smart seaside resorts). A 50- minute or less airtaxi ride from Hamburg, and you're there among Friesian-style houses with thatched roofs and long eaves, and a bird sanctuary on the eastern side where avocets breed. Fashionable Kampen is where everyone saunters in to **Gogartchen** for afternoon tea or coffee; smart little nightclubs. **Westerland,** the capital of Sylt, has a casino, concert hall, and a *Kurhaus* specializing in thalassotherapy. Besides Kampen and Westland beaches, there are Wenninstedt, List, Rantum, and Hornum, each beach with enormous wicker baskets to curl up in like kittens, and each beach with a regular section and an effkaka section (FKK for *Frei Korper Kultur*—Free Body Culture, i.e. nude). Skipping over the unattractive sections, I find Hamburg a most attractive city with its ancient almshouses near St. Michael's Church, colonnaded houses, race course, golf course, yacht clubs and boats, and even more special when seasoned with a dash of Sylt!

Hameln (Hamelin): the town of the Pied Piper, known in Germany as the town of the Ratcatcher *(Der Rattenfanger).* From Sept., every Sun. noon, the drama is restaged in 30 lively, funny, lovely minutes. The piper, dressed in a very pied costume of green and red, purple and yellow, with two long pheasant feathers stuck in his hat, strikes out for the Weser River, tootling his flute, with an army of town children dressed as rats dancing their rat dance behind him. Unlike the real rats, the children escape drowning, but the piper goes through the motions of asking the burgomaster and his councilors for his fee and being refused; so the piper flutes away another mob of children, this time dressed as children, presumably to some mountain cavern from which they never return. On weekdays, in the Station Restaurant, there are **marionette performances** at 10:30 a.m., 12:30 p.m., and 5 p.m. Children love these! While your children are drinking all this in, you can be drinking in the half-timbered Renaissance architecture. **Hannover** not a city of primary interest to children, although it does have beautiful parks, two **zoos** and swimming and boating on the Maschsee, the city lake. There's **Heidelberg,** dominated by its rose-red castle (reached by cable railway), illuminated during summer; also fireworks, concerts, and drama festivals. One of the castle buildings houses the gee-whizz sight of the biggest barrel in the world, with a platform built over it on which you can dance in festival times. There's a great museum for geological, archaeological, and zoological potential Ph.D. candidates to look at. **Kassel: Wilhelmshohe Park,** with castle ruins, a bath house with tropical plants, fountains, flowers; children will want to walk through it. At Rimberg, on the Frankfurt-Kassel autobahn, **Baron Dornberg's** leisure park has a super playground equipped with games; cable car to the Kinderspieldorf (children's play village) with towers for climbing, footbridges, forts, tents, trampoline, mini-railway, whirligig, and children's zoo. **Koblenz:** where the Rhine and the Moselee join, is a wine hamlet; fabulous **water ballet** and **light-opera** on a floating stage. **Kommern:** Open-air museum with old farmhouses, mill, a mini Rhineland Williamsburg. Information about opening times from nearby Verkehrsamt in Mechernick/Eifel, near Euskirchen and Bonn. **Kulmbach,** in northern Bavaria, is the site of a castle containing the only museum in the world of tin soldiers, over 300,000 of them set up in authentic detailed battlefield tableaux. At **Landshut** every three years (usually in late June, early July) Germany's greatest historical pageant takes place—a fortnight's commemoration of the 1475 marriage of Jadwiga, the King of Poland's daughter, and Duke George of Bavaria; 1200 men, women, and children costumed and armored, relive the most sumptuous event in the annals of the German court; court ball; bridal pageant with pipers, fifers, and drummers; torch-bearing pageboys; trumpeters, jesters, falconers; knights in armor; the bridal coach drawn by six white horses; jousting, tilting, and horsemanship; crossbowmen and magicians; fair; feast; general merry-making. You need at least three days to take part in all the frolic. Check with the GTNO about the date of the next celebration.

Lubeck: If you are drawn by the cultural attractions of this Queen of the Hanse and the Baltic, the children's counterpoise for all those medieval guild-halls, sculpture, and Gothic architecture is a goodly supply of rich Lubeck marzipan. **Ludwigsburg:** see Fairy Tale gardens of Monrepos (see Castles). **Mainz: Cathedral** and **Gutenberg museum. Marburg:** a costume village—children wear red, married couples green, and senior citizens violet and black—is a jewel, with *Fachwerk* (half-timbered) houses and the earliest Gothic church in Germany, **St. Eliz-**

abeth's (its golden reliquary should be seen). **Minden,** on the Cologne-Hanover Autobahn is the site of **Potts-Park**—lots of fun—with aerodrome, full-scale model trains, go-karts; miniscooters, trains, boats; pony riding, merry-go-rounds, playgrounds, intergalactic pinball; mini-golf, games, sports; and funfair attractions that are in action Easter–Oct. **Mittenwald,** memorable mountain village close to the Austrian border, with murals on the housefronts, with a world-famous violinists' school and violin makers demonstrating their craft. **Moselkern:** On the Munstermaifeld-Wierschem highway, for a restaurant that's something else, stop at **Burg Eltz** (5401 Gemeinde Wierschem, Kreis Mayen), 23 miles southwest of **Koblenz;** located in a beautifully preserved 12th-15th century castle; open Good Friday–Sept. 30th. For more information, ask the GNTO, Frankfurt. **Neckarmuhlbach:** The castle falconry at **Burg Guttenberg** offers daily flights of eagles and vultures 11 a.m. and 3 p.m.; museum and tavern with 15th-century entertainment and ''knightly meals.'' **Nurnberg** is the toy capital of Germany, and its ***Christ Kindl Markt*** in Dec. is a wonderland of gingerbread and gold-leaf angels for toy-lovers. Along with the Cranachs, Holbeins, Durers, and other matchless art treasures in the **Germanic National Museum** (1 *Kornmarkt*), splendid toys and doll houses. Mirroring the life and times of women and children, with scarcely a man around, is the extraordinary **Doll Museum,** with many of Europe's oldest dolls. Museums, medieval buildings, churches, concerts, festivals galore. At noon, the mechanical clock of the **Frauenkirche** (Hauptmarkt square) goes into action with drumming and bulging figures paying homage to Emperor Charles IV. The immense **Imperial Palace,** the Burg, as it's called, is a must. Boys will like the **Verkehrsmuseum** (6 Lessingstr.) a traffic museum with mail coaches, old locomotives, a gorgeous royal train, model trains in action, and a stamp collection. Also a pleasant zoo. **Oberammergau:** Every year that ends in a zero the whole town, or half of its citizens, at any rate, stage the world's most famous passion play. If you go there out of season, you can buy animals and figures for Christmas trees or mangers and watch such animals and figures being carved by teenage boys at a woodcarving school, **Schnitzerschule,** near the outskirts. **Starnberg:** The Starnberger See, a sweet lake southwest of Munich, has swimming, boating, and many outdoor cafes. **Steinau** is a tiny village in Hesse's Kinzig Valley where Wilhelm and Jakob Grimm spent their boyhood; castle; cobbled streets; half-timbered houses; remarkable marionette theater in the former *Marstall* (stables) called the *Holzkoppe* (Woodenheads) presents performances of familiar stories on Sat. and Sun.

Stuttgart: A mercantile hub, but nonetheless an attractive garden city with attractions for children: **Hohenpark Killesberg,** a pleasure park, can be toured by a miniature railway. The **TV tower** has a restaurant about 560′ up, and an observation tower. Perversely, children like the elevator ride better than the view. The zoologically major **Wilhelma Park Zoo** has trained chimpanzees. Stuttgart, home of Daimler and Mercedes-

Benz, naturally has an **Automobile Museum** (Mercedesstr.). At **Sindelfinger,** close by, you can tour the MB factory in glass-topped minbus in tours touted as ''family affairs with films, food, rooms to freshen up in.'' At the three-mile-long sandy beach of **Travenmunde** (neighboring resorts on the Baltic) you can enjoy good swimming, rent a basket chair that looks like a little wicker house, and admire swans in the park that borders the beach, and maybe play in playgrounds (pony rides) or a penny arcade. **Grossenbrode,** the chief Scandinavian ferry port, is nearby. At **Tuddern** (near Aachen), from your car or a park bus, you can see as many, if not more lions than you do in South Africa's Kruger Park; 40 lions; and you have the feel of Africa, the sense of Africa at the Tuddern Lion Park (5 135 Selfkant/Niederrhein, near the Dutch border). At **Wallerstadten** (about 5 m from Darmstadt) there is a Kinderparadies, a playground fun-fair combined with a lion park; another enclosure houses elephants to zebras, kangaroos, and camels. **Safari Park,** Frank und Delzer KG (6081 Wallerstadten). **Ulm** has an unusual **Bread Museum;** its Protestant Cathedral has the world's tallest church spire (528′), begun in 1377 and completed 1890—an inspirational curiosity! **Wuppertal** has a whopper of a **Clock Museum.**

FUN TRIPS ***Rhine excursions:*** The Rhineland of castles, vineyards, storied cities, and cathedrals; a land of great appeal to poets, musicians, folklorists, and travelers of 20 centuries. From Cologne to Mainz, the track may be beaten but it remains pretty wonderful, no matter what. From early Apr.–mid-Oct. the *Europa, Deutschland, Nederland, Austria, Italia, Helvetia,* the sleek *France,* and the *Britannia* operated by the **Rhine Passenger Service** (Rheindampfschiffahrt), make the run from Rotterdam to Basel three times a month; five days upstream (north to south) in summer, with overnight stops at Dusseldorf, Boppard, Mannheim, and Strasbourg and intermediate stops at Cologne, Bonn, Koblenz, Wiesbaden, Mainz and Mannheim. Four days downstream, summer and autumn. After a minimum of two nights aboard, you can get off at any stop. Each ship has air conditioning, swimming pool, 80 cabins with running water and with/without private shower and/or john. Large, windowed dining rooms; the fare includes three meals plus two snacks daily. Over Christmas and New Year's, these cruises are wildly popular and sold out weeks in advance, so do book ahead.

Cologne-Bonn-Koblenz-Bingen-Mainz by Rhine Excussion Steamers: also operated by the Rhine Passenger Service also known as the *KD Rhine Line* or under the full title of **Koln-Dusseldorfer Rheindampfschiffahrt.** Of the 100-odd-mile trip (much too long for children), I'd take the part from Koblenz to Bingen, the highlight scenically, with castles and forts, vineyards and villages in such quantity that even children are pretty fascinated for at least an hour. You can make a full-day excursion, an overnight round trip or intermediate voyages. The trip takes from eight to ten hours downstream (south to north) from Mainz to Cologne, and from 14 to 16 hours upstream. Take an express steamer whenever possible and do, *do* make advance reservations for a rest cabin or an overnight cabin. All the steamers, ordinary and express varieties, have restaurant facilities.

Moselle excursions: You could make a similar trip from Koblenz along the Moselle to Cochem and continue by train to Trier with its impressive Roman ruins and cathedral. The Moselle, with vineyards and medieval castles, is especially beautiful, lovely to idle along in a small steamer or in a tiny train called the *Kleinbahn*. Either way, make a midway stopover. Otherwise this trip can be tedious for children. The KD Rhine Line also has two-day, two-night cruises on the Moselle along the scenic stretch between Koblenz and Trier, from late July–mid-Aug., as well as day trips for a look at all those picturesque castles, fortresses, and vineyards. There's also a seven-day cruise between Holland and Switzerland that combines cruising on the Rhine and the Moselle.

▶ **Note:** Arrangements can be made for your car to be forwarded on by train or by chauffeur to the point of debarkation on Rhine or Moselle excursions. The ideal way to cover either river is a combination—one way by steamer, one way by car or by train. At almost every Rhine River stop there is a ferry service to take you across to the other side. For more information about car transport and the Rhine passenger steamer service contact KD Rhine Line, 15 Frankenwerft, 5000 Koln; Tel: (0221) 20880. Also, for information and reservation, contact the Rhine Cruise Agency, 170 Hamilton Avenue, White Plains, NY 10601; Tel: (914) 948–3600, or their office at 323 Geary St., San Francisco, CA 94102; Tel: (415) 392–8817. Contact the German Federal Railroad or, while in Germany, the Central Tourist Information office in Frankfurt-am-Main.

The ***Romantic Road*** begins in **Wurzburg**—or ends there, depending on your itinerary—and takes in a series of medieval towns—Rothenburg, Dinkelsbuhl, Nordlingen, Augsburg, Landsberg, Schwangau and Fussen. In the Fussen-Schwangau area, around the lake called Forggensee, you'll find *the* castle, **Neuschwanstein** (New Swan Rock; the one always pictured in travel posters), that grand and giddy folly of mad King Ludwig II, as well as a **Hohenschwangau** (High Swan District), with the swan motif worked into the decorations and furnishings with fantastic abandon as an expression of Ludwig's frenzied idolatry of Wagner. Wagner brings Parsifal on stage just after he has wounded a swan, and Parsifal's son Lohengrin, called the Knight of the Swan in German legends, makes his stage entrance in a swan-drawn boat. Anyway, both these swan castles, are extravagantly whimsical. The Romantic Road, with all its lovely scenery, its picturesque medieval towns, fabulous castles, cathedrals, and romance, is certainly educational for children but nowhere near the treat for them that it may be for you. **Bamburg,** a medieval town miraculously spared from bombs and war damage; with extravagant baroquecoco touches is every child's dream of a fairytale town; off the beaten track; heaven! ***Raft rides.*** An entrancing excursion along the Salzach River (near the Austrian border), starts at **Tittmoning,** where you board a bargelike vessel known as *Plaeteen,* and off you go on a ten-mile trip with a brass band aboard, to a remarkable medieval town called **Burghausen,** which has a cliff-perched castle comprising six successive courts, each reached by a drawbridge, and in all about ¾ miles long. Midway, you stop at **Raiten-Haslach** for refreshments. If you can't make this ride, there is a similar band-raft trip from Wolfratshausen (see Munich).

Hameln is the down-river terminus of the ***Weser excursion steamers,*** which make an 11-hour downstream trip from **Hannoversch-Munden** to **Hameln** and stops on the slower upstream run, for an overnight stay at either **Karlshafen** or **Hoxter,** (like all riverside villages along the way much like the illustrations in Grimm's Fairy Tales). That 11-hour downstream trip is way too long for children, but the upstream trip for a couple of hours just as far as **Karlshafen** is fun. Not, of course, to be compared with the Rhine trip. Contact the local tourist office or **Oberweser-Dampfschiffahrt GmbH,** Postfach 499, An der Munsterbrucke, 3250 Hameln 1. There's a boat service along the Fulda River, connecting with Hannoversch-Munden's boat service to Hameln.

Heidelberg-Heilbronn-Stuttgart is a ten-hour boat ride through the castle-studded vineyards of the lovely Neckar Valley. Meltingly beautiful, but too long for most children.

Ask the **Cologne** tourist office (am Dom) about the four-mile, Wiehl-Numbrecht run in a nine-passenger stagecoach; coachman-owner Friedhelm Stoecker had the coach built from an 1871 model.

FUN AND GAMES Germany has more than 130 ***deer parks*** with special species of deer, stags, and does to be seen in areas near Hamburg, Dusseldorf, Frankfurt, Cologne, the Hartz and Eifel mountains, the Black Forest. Germany's ***zoos*** are world-famous (see Introduction). As mentioned before, there are many wonderful ***safari parks*** and many charming ***"fairy tale forests"*** that usually include ducks, swans, peacocks, and playgrounds. Along with castles, do try to include at least one in each of these categories if you have time in your itinerary. The City Tourist Offices can tell you how to get to the best and nearest to you. I've mentioned some, but space does not permit me to mention all or include all the details I'd like to. Germany offers topnotch ***skiing*** facilities at over 300 winter resorts, mostly centered in the Black Forest, Lake Constance, and the Bavarian Alps (the most important). The skiing on the glacier high on the Zugspitze above the twin resort towns of **Garmisch-Partenkirchen** begins in fall, runs into summer, with four active mountains in winter. Details from **Verkehrsamt der Kurverwaltung,** Bahnhofstrasse 34, D–8100 Garmisch-Partenkirchen. Also indoor tennis, swimming, year-round skating on three ice rinks, hockey, tobogganing, spring and summer watersports, all plentiful and well organized. Near Bayreuth, you can go skiing in summer at **Bischofsgrun** in artificial snow, but the artificial snow is made from powdered glass. The only safe-for-children artificial snow (made of koalin clay waste) covers the slopes of the White Sandhills at **Hirschau,** southeast of Nurnberg. A good ski resort for a child has horse-drawn sleighs, wild deer to feed, a skating rink, an indoor swimming pool, toboggans, folklore plays and performances of the rowdy Schuhplattl dance, carnival costumes, a ski kindergarten (children his own age, gentle nursery slopes), a ski school. Many resorts fill most of these requirements with additional attractions for parents. However, ski kindergartens, where you can leave your child for the major part of the day, are a rarity. There's one tucked away in tiny **Lenggries** (near the Austrian border) and two only in the Allgau, in minuscule **Steibis-Aach** and in **Pfronten.** But there are ski schools at almost all resorts where your child can be supervised. Costs are extremely moderate.

Sports: There are international and local racing events involving motorcycles, cars, and bicycles as well as rowboats, canoes, and gliders, speedboats and fast-paced horses and human beings; boxing matches, horse shows, watersports, soccer, tennis and golf tournaments, many sailing regattas to watch. If you get a license and permits, you can go hunting for all kinds of game and fishing for trout, salmon, carp. You can rent a canoe, foldboat or a sailboat; go hiking, mountain climbing; ride; play tennis; swim, or play mini-golf almost everywhere. For instance, Berlin has 359 tennis courts, 353 gyms, 32 toboggan runs, 15 indoor pools, 13 outdoor pools, 16 roller skating rinks, 12 riding academies, and 875 sports clubs! If your family is fond of anything outdoorsy, just ask for the encyclopedic lists from the GNTO.

Public outdoor swimming pools are open from May–Sept. Indoor pools, open daily, require your wearing a swimming cap, obtainable at the site as are hot and cold showers. Check the exact opening times in the official weekly and monthly guides available from City Tourist Offices.

At **Leutkirch** in the mountainous Allgau south of Munich, a skydiving academy charges about $2000 to learn how to jump or dive; but it costs nothing to watch! There are eight gliding clubs, and often the possibility of going along for the glide. The **Deutscher Aero-Club** (Postfach 71–01–03 Lyonerstrasse 16, 6000 Frankfurt/M.–Niederrad; Tel: (0611) 66–67–31) will supply information! You can ***rent a bicycle*** (Fahrrad-Verleih) at almost every town, and most S–Bahn stations, where rental costs are about ¼ the regular rate. Taking the train from the large city where you may be staying and hopping off at small outlying towns to rent a bicycle for a tour can be wonderful fun!

▶ **Note:** A rather wonderful program for mothers and their children (aged 3–6), in playing together for fun, exercise, and laughter is sponsored by the **City of Munich Sportamt** at Dantestadion (Dantestr. 14 and Dietramszeller Str. 9, Thalkirchen). The Tourist Office will give you details; costs little.

A trio of sports equipment stores in **Munich—Sport Scheck** (Sendinger Str. 85), **Sport Munzinger** (Marienplatz), and **Sporthaus Schuster** (Rosenstr. 5–6)—offers special children's ski outings during Christmas and Easter vacations, a supervised 5-day holiday for children 7–13; similar courses for adults any time of the year. Ski rentals for adults, but not for children. Sport Scheck also runs a ***riding*** school at **Unterfohring** (Munchner Str. 15, Tel: 486019); a ***sailing*** school (**Attersee Yachtschule** in Austria); arranges for reservations and rentals for outdoor ***tennis courts*** (Tel: 224028); operates a baby Mount Everest at its all-weather location north of Munich in conjunction with a ***mountain-climbing*** course; offers private classes in limbering up for you and the children (Tel: 211661). Sport Munzinger operates an excellent ***sailing*** school on Lake Ammersee, the **Munchner Segelschule Schondorf** (Tel: 08192); an exciting family vacation. They also rent equipment and arrange for reservations at Munich's ***tennis courts.***

SHOPPING WITH AND FOR CHILDREN

▶ **Note:** Before you even flex a muscle to send a parcel home, STOP! Let the store do it for you. Whatever extra any parcel-sending service costs, it's worth it to spare yourself endless form-filling, time-consuming aggravations. German-speaking citizens throw up their hands in horror at the thought of sending parcels on their own; and if you don't speak German . . . !!

In **Berlin:** Toy store? **Eickelberg** (7 Joachimstaler Strasse) (33 Kufurstendamm) and **KaDeWe** (Tauentzienstr.). The Marklin trains are enthralling, and all the toys are highly recommended. If you are rich as Croesus, you might want to buy a hurdy-gurdy—or for much less, hire one from **Drehorgelverleih** (Pohl u. Weber Schellingstrasse 8, 1000 Berlin 30).

A unique solution for redecorating is photographic wallpaper, developed by the firm of **Kleopatra Werkstaetten** (Lutzowstrasse 102; Tel: 2612565). Scenic shots of places you have visited or pictures of your children and yourselves can easily be adapted; also mountain, pastoral, sea or city scenes.

In **Frankfurt,** children can have the special treat of picking out one (and just one takes willpower) toy from any of these sensational toy shops: **Spielzeug-Onkel** (26 Goethestr.); **Behle** (28 Kaiserstr.); **Haus der Kinder** (18 Neue Mainzerstr.); **Spielzeugschachtel** (11 Kaiserstr.). Or, if you can extricate yourself from all those dolls, trains, and mechanical wonders, do a little shopping around for Loden coats or dirndls, leather shorts or other Bavarian specialties. In **Hamburg,** there's a toy store in **Children's Paradise** (Kinderparadies, 7 Neuer Wall). One floor devoted to toy trains alone. Another dandy toy shop is **Spielzeug Rasch** (Gerhart

Hauptmann Platz 1). In **Karlshafen,** beautiful books for children, art and flower books for yourself, ancient books and maps, **Antiquariat und Buchhandlung Bernard Schafer** (Conradistr. 2).

In **Munich, Einkaufs-Zentrum** (am Stachus), a four-level underground shopping complex with three neighboring department stores, 40 boutiques, and 33 escalators. The department stores, which have just about everything (including good food dept. in the basement) are **Karstadt, Kaufhof** and **Hertie.** To simplify bedmaking, you might want to invest in an *Oberbett,* a soft, thick cover filled with feathers or down, which replaces the bottom sheet and mattress cover. The downy quilt which goes over this, often with a sheet buttoned over it, is a *Steppdecke* (replaces top sheet and blankets); pillow to match is a *Kopfkissen.* Marvelously durable and long-lasting, but not inexpensive, they can be found at any good bedding store, such as **Betten-Ried** or **Betten-Lang.**

For English and American books, by far the best selection is at the **Anglia English Bookshop** (Schellingstr. 3, Tel: 28–36–42). ***Children's clothing?*** For sport outfits, **Sport Scheck** (Sendlinger Str. 85) is dazzling. **Sporthaus Schuster** (6 Rosenstr.), with all sports equipment, has great bathing suits and underwater gear. For blue jeans, **Amerika-Mode** (Von-der-Tann-Str. 6) and the Empire State Clothing (Hertogspitalstrasse 24). Loden coats can be bought for about one half the U.S. price at **Loden Frey** (Maffeistr. 7–9) where coats and dirndls, sweaters, Tyrolean hats and suede knickers and other togs are mostly for adults and teenagers. For dirndls, Loden coats, Bavarian jackets and other *Trachtenkleidung* (costume clothes), try **Ludwig Beck** (Marienplatz) or **Die Mode Maria Maier** (Ledererstr. 4), mostly for juniors and teenagers. **Uschi's** (Briennerstr. 10) has beautiful high-fashion clothes for children. **Bei Danielle** (Dachauer Str. 7) has nice knitted things for *puppchen* and older brothers and sisters. Other possibilities are **Les Petits** (Schrammstr. 3); **Schlichting** (Sonnenstr. 25); and **Haus des Kindes** (Rosenstr. 4). The challis dirndls for little girls are wonderfully practical; get extra silver buttons for blouse and dress, simple to get in Munich and a pain in the neck to try to find elsewhere! **Rabel** (Dienerstr. 16) has such buttons. ***Children's shoes?*** Both **Schlichting** and **Les Petits** (my favorite). For suede boots for children, try **Schuh-Klein** (Marienplatz 28/29). **Bally** has shoes, boots, all sorts of footwear; branches where narrow-width footwear can also be found (Neuhauserstr. 53, Theatinerstr. 36)—a few doors away from Charles Jourdan's elegant and expensive bootery for mamas and rich-cream teenagers! For bargain hunters, a thrift shop with ski clothes, ice skates, ski clothes, and many amazing buys, **Freie Selbsthilfe** (Theresienstr. 66). You can have custom-made lederhosen for your sons; try **Fritz Hackenschuh** (Sendlingerstr. 56).

Toys? **Nurnberg's** mechanical toys are among the world's finest, steam engines and Marklin trains are superb. In **Munich, Obletter Spielwaren** is a fantastic toyland; **Spielwaren Schmidt** (Neuhauserstr. 20) has a fine stock. **Egon Wiedling** (Theatinerstr. 13) offers the town's best selection of military miniatures and ship models. For wooden and one-of-a-kind handcrafted toys, handicraft, art supplies (lovely paint sets), try **Kunst und Spiel** (Leopoldstr. 48). If Hummel figurines are your fancy, **Haertle** (Neuhauserstr.) has them, as does **Kuchenreuther** (Sonnenstr.). As for woodcarvings, Oberammergau angels and creche carvings can be found at **Dehm's** (Bayerstr.) or **Holzkunst Bauer** (Karlsplatz). For Bavarian handcrafts, decorations for Christmas trees, and candles, try **Bayerisches Kunstgewerbe** (7 Pacellistr.). In **Nurnberg** itself, **Kunstgewerbe Wiesler and Mahler** (Karolinerstr. 27), where you can also get Christmas candles and all sorts of Bavarian folk art items.

GERMAN FRIENDS AND PEN PALS For a penfriend, contact **International Youth Exchange and Correspondence Service,** Internationaler Jugendaustausch-und Besucherdienst der Bundesrepublik Deutschland (IJAB), Kennedy-Alee 91–103, 5300 Bonn 2, Federal Republic of Germany. In **Munich, Federation of German-American Clubs,** the **Columbus-Gesellschaft,** the **German-American Men's Club** have activities. The **Deutsch-Englische Gesellschaft** (in Munich) has varied programs fostering German-British understanding. Amerika Haus has many clubhouses. Jointly sponsored by the U.S. and German governments, **America Houses** are primarily concerned with introducing Germans to American culture (lectures, films, and a conspicuous absence of TV reruns such as "Hogan's Heroes"), and are, therefore, excellent places for Americans to meet Germans. You'll find them in Berlin, Cologne, Frankfurt, Freiburg, Hanover, Heidelberg, Munich, Nurenberg, Regensburg, Saarbrucken, Stuttgart, Tubingen. **German-American Associations and Clubs** are also congenial gathering places to meet Germans and their families. So, if you're in **Bremen,** you might want to visit the **Karl-Schurz-Gesellschaft** (Bahnhofplatz 29) or the **ICC International Community Center** (President-Kennedy-Platz 1); in **Darmstadt,** the **John F. Kennedy Haus** (Kasinostrasse 3); in **Frankfurt,** the **Steuben-Schurz-Gesellschaft** (Barockhausstrasse 18); in **Hamburg,** Atlantik-Brucke (Sanderskoppel 5), or **Amerika-Gesellschaft** (Tesdorpfstrasse 1); in **Karlsruhe, the Verband der Deutsch-Amerikanischen Clubs** (Oberfeldstrasse 26); in **Kassel Amt fur Kulturpflege** (Schlosschen Bellevue); in **Kiel, John F. Kennedy Haus** (Holstenbrucke 2); in **Mainz,** the **Meet the Americans Association** (Sudring 133).

You could also contact, in **Munich,** the **Community Services** (Tel: 62–29–92), a volunteer service of the American military community, for information on many clubs and groups. The **Munich International School** and the **Munich American Kindergarten** (see Magic Family Helpers) are other sources for meeting children and parents. The **Dip 'n' Divers Square Dance Group,** open to square dancing fans of all nationalities, meets Tues. evening at the AYA building (Harthauser Str.

48, in Harlachin; Tel: 690–47–41), might be good for teenagers. The **Verein fur Internationale Judgendarbeit** sponsors a club where young people can get together; for information contact Mrs. Berg (Landwehrstr. 81; Tel: 53–10–04).

In **Berlin,** the Tourist Office can be helpful in arranging meetings with congenial people of similar interests.

CALENDAR OF EVENTS Scads of music festivals, sports events, and local attractions have been omitted from this list. For more detailed information, consult the GNTO.

Dec. until Christmas, throughout Germany, there is ***Carol Singing*** by star-carrying children; magnificent trees, many lit by traditional candles. The ***Christmas Fair*** features gingerbread and marzipan, toys, puppet and marionette shows, and creches of all kinds. Christmas trees are everywhere. In Germany, Christmas is special, and probably the nicest places to be would be in Munich, Nurnberg, Mittenwald, Garmisch, or any small village in the Black Forest or Bavaria. Families in Munich often clear out an entire room to put up an historical creche with wooden figures, handed down from generation to generation, and they open their houses to visitors. (If you are interested in seeing the creches in different houses, ask the Munich Tourist Office for information.)

LANGUAGE AND PHRASEBOOK In tourist centers, hotels, important shops, and well-known restaurants, English is spoken and understood. Not so in the hinterland. I strongly recommend that you take along a phrasebook. Don't expect most Germans to recognize the English versions of their place names. Munich is Munchen. Cologne is Koln, Lake Constance is Bodensee, Nuremberg is Nurnberg, Bavaria is Bayern, Brunswick is Braunschweig *und so weiter*. There are many words in German that are spelled and mean the same as English words (since German and English share a common Indo-European origin) and many loan-words, so you'll pounce with relief upon: Park, Pony, Separate, Absolute, Hotel, Restaurant, Butter, Halt, and Gas, to mention just a few. According to the *Dictionary of English and American Expressions* (Deutscher Taschenbuch Verlag), German has 3000 American words and phrases in circulation! There are many more words that are spelled differently but which have much the same pronunciation as their English equivalents, such as Fisch, Haus, Komfort, romantik, wunder, beste, Glas, Tee, and Kaffee. (In German, all nouns are capitalized.)

Hello	*Guten Tag*	*goo-ten-tahk*
My name is	*Ich heisse*	*ickh highsuh*
I am an American	*Ich bin ein Amerikaner*	*ickh bin ine amay-ree-karner*

I can't speak German	*Ich spreche kein Deutsch*	*ickh shprecker kine doytch*
Please	*Bitte*	*bit-tuh*
Thank you very much	*Danke sehr*	*donk-uh zare*
Yes	*Ja*	*yah*
No	*Nein*	*nine*
I'm having a wonderful time	*Ich finde es wunderschon*	*Ickh finn-der ess woon-dershern*
I am____years old	*Ich bin____ Jahre alt*	*ickh bin____yarr-uh alt*
1	*eins*	*eyentz*
2	*zwei*	*tzveye*
3	*drei*	*dry*
4	*veir*	*fear*
5	*funf*	*fewnf*
6	*sechs*	*zecks*
7	*sieben*	*zeeben*
8	*acht*	*ahkht*
9	*neun*	*noyn*
10	*zehn*	*tsayn*
11	*elf*	*elf*
12	*zwolf*	*tzverlf*
13	*dreizehn*	*dry-tsayn*
14	*vierzehn*	*fear-tsayn*
15	*funfzehn*	*fewnf-tsayne*
Goodbye	*Auf Wieder-sehn*	*owf vee dair-zayn*

GREECE

Greece, its islands, its beaches and transparent water, its wildflowers, white-as-sugar villages, its pinewoods are a joy; its crags, cliffs, gorse and fennel, and archaeological treasures can be golden and glorious. Delphi Sounion, Olympia, Mystra, and Meteora are musts! It is a wonderful country to discover and make your own. Your dollar will go a long way, and your children reign as ruling monarchs with the friendly Greeks.

Don't, whatever you do, judge Greece by the conditions that prevail in Athens, where invading herds of bewildered tourists can be sourly patronized. In the islands and in the country, the Greeks are all smiles, eager to prove that the word for stranger and guest is synonymous in their lexicon.

The glories of Greece are much better seen if you avoid guides with their boring recitatifs, tours, and cruise ships (with one exception). Of course, outside of tourist hotels and shops, the language barrier can be frustrating, so arm yourself with a phrasebook. Greek is simple to pronounce phonetically and it is an inordinate thrill to read aloud your first Greek word (mine was on a jam label). Be prepared to do some hiking and climbing up hills to temples and monasteries for the exceptional and offbeat pleasures they offer. Exploring Greece in summertime can be extremely hot and thirsty going; sunglasses and canteens of icewater for each family member are blessings you should not be without! Closing times for museums and archaeological sites are as early as 2 p.m. Jellyfish can be a nuisance in many swimming areas. But Greece is unique, her wonders are legendary, and I'm an ardent Hellenophile!

I recommend traveling with children over 8 for your first sojourn in Greece, even though I am informed by mothers with young babies that they had no problems.

INFORMATION ABOUT GREECE Greece lags behind in promoting tourism, but you can get good information from the tourist offices *if* you persist and insist on details. The **Greek National Tourist Office** (645 Fifth Ave., Olympic Towers, NY, NY 10022; Tel: (212) 421–5777) supplies brochures, maps, and information about special happenings. Other

GNTO offices in the U.S. and Canada are at the National Bank of Greece Building, 168 North Michigan Ave., 4th Floor, Chicago, IL 60601 (Tel: (312) 782–1084); 611 West Sixth St., Suite 1998, Los Angeles, CA 90017 (Tel: (213) 626–6696); Esso Plaza, 2 Place Ville Marie, Suite 67, Montreal, Quebec H3B 2 C9 (Tel: (514) 871–1535).

Fascinating, relevant, and delightfully easy reading are any or all of the illustrated booklets obtainable for $1.75 each from the American School of Classical Studies at Athens, % Institute for Advanced Study, Princeton, NJ 08540; Tel: (609) 734–8386. (You can order now and be billed later.) They are also available in the Agora Museum's shop, Stoa of Attalos, Athens. Another treasure is Lawrence Durrell's *The Greek Islands* (Viking Press and Penguin), his personal guide, weaving together history, description, myth, architecture, archaeology, flora, fauna, festivals, everything. Lovely photographs which are as true and timeless as the text. In Greece, tourist information bureaus, abbreviated to E.O.T. (Greek National Tourist Organization) have their head office in Athens at 2 Amerikis St. (Tel: (01) 322–3111/2/3/4/5/6/7/8/9); at the Information Desk, National Bank of Greece, Syntagma (Constitution) Square, 2 Karageorgi Servias St. (Tel: (01) 322–2545); East Main Terminal, Ellinikon Airport (Tel: (01) 979–9500); and at Piraeus (Directorate of Tourism of Eastern Mainland and the islands), 105 Vassillissis Sofias St. (Tel: (01) 412–9492, 412–1400). Regional offices are in Cephalonia, Corfu, Cos, Crete, Ioannina, Kavala, Larissa, Patras, Rhodes, Thessaloniki, Volos, and duly noted as you read on! In Athens, the English-speaking Tourist Police run a 24-hr. service (Tel: 01–171).

Familiarize your children with the gods, heroes, and heroines of ancient Greece. From Ares to Zeus, their identities and tales are fascinating and relevant.

Your hotel will provide you with a copy of *The Week in Athens* and the monthly *Athenian*. If you have a car or are renting one (Hellascar Rent-A-Car, 7 Stadiou St.; Tel: 323–3487), sources of information are the **Automobile & Touring Club of Greece** (ELPA 2–4 Messogian St., Athens; Tel: (01) 779–1615).

American Travel (Patriarchou Ioakim 11, Athens; Tel: (01) 733–863) run by Jane Hill, a young American married to Johnny Georgiades, specializes in travel arrangements for individuals and families. Jane and Johnny, strong on interesting and off-beat excursions, are extremely helpful. Another wonderfully imaginative and helpful travel bureau is **Horizon Tours** (14 Nikis St., Athens; Tel: (01) 323–3144).

Some telephone numbers, as you can see, have six digits, and some seven, in a transitional stage of six digit numbers changing over to seven digit numbers. Which brings us to the subject of telephones. Recorded instructions in English, French, and German for making international calls can be had by dialing 169. Recorded messages are available in Greek for the correct time (141), weather (148), news (115), theaters (181), pharmacies open 24 hours in Athens (107), pharmacies open 24 hours in the suburbs (102). Always call ahead to museums to check when and if they are open that day and when they close; to bus stations to confirm arrival and departure times; to hotels to find out if you can use their swimming pool; to restaurants to make reservations. Opening times, closing times, departure and arrival times are rather quirky in Greece. Just as quirky, it seems to me, is the regulation that the main Post Offices at Syntagma Square and at 100 Aeolou St. (where the stamp collectors in the family can subscribe to the Philatelic Service) will not handle any package weighing over a kilo (2.2 lbs.). Parcels to be mailed abroad weighing over one kilo may be mailed *from the following Post Offices only:* 29 Koumoundourou St., 4 Stadiou St. in the Stoa (shopping center) at the Tamion Bldg., Psychic, Ambelokipi. *Parcels should be left unwrapped until after inspection.* Bring wrapping paper, string, sealing tape, and scissors with you. Post offices are usually open Mon. through Fri. from 7:30 a.m.–7:30 p.m. The main offices at Aeolou St. (Tel: (01) 321–6023) and Syntagma Square (Tel: (01) 323–7573) remain open until 8:30 p.m., until 10 p.m. during the tourist season.

You may find yourself buying a lot of books that you want to mail home before you leave. If you are interested in traditional Greek handicrafts, **EOMMEX,** National Handicraft Organization at 23–25 Lekka St., 6th floor, open mornings only, has an excellent range of books and information (Tel: (01) 324–1211). For guides and art books with English texts, plus books and paperbacks on all subjects in English, visit the **Compendium** bookshop, 33 Nikis St., in the Plaka (Tel: (01) 322–6931). For books and periodicals about Greece in Greek and English, go to the **Hellenic American Union Library,** 22 Massalias St., 7th floor (Tel: (01) 360–7305), open 9 a.m.–1 p.m. and 6 p.m.–9 p.m. except Sat. afternoons and Sun. The libraries of the **American School of Classical Studies** are Grennadius at 61 Souidias St. (Tel: (01) 721–0536) and the Blegan at 54 Souidias St. (Tel: (01) 723–6313). **Eleftheroudakis** has three bookshops: at Athens Towers, Bldg. A, for office supplies, paper goods, some books; at their Music Centre, same address, for records, cassettes, recordings of Greek folk-songs, some reworked and arranged with electronic instruments by "Vangelis," Greek composer of the sound track from the film "Chariots of Fire"; the **International Book Centre,** Syntagma at 4 Nikis St., is where you'll find titles for every reading interest and need.

Car rental rates are significantly higher in Greece than in the rest of Europe. Besides Avis, Hertz (which doesn't permit rentals to be taken to the islands) and Budget, try Hellascars which do permit a rental in Corfu with a drop-off in Athens.

▶ **Note:** Showing the palm of your hand in a gesture of goodbye is not done in Greece (this used to be a cursing gesture—horrors!), so tell your children just to smile and say goodbye on partings. If they must wave, tell them to wave with the back of their palms outward and to waggle their fingers inward. Just smiles are best!

You'll be lucky if you can hail a free taxi in the street. Generally, you can only pick them up at hotels, or call for them, or have someone in a cafe, shop, taverna, pizzaria or ouzerie call one for you. The number for the taxi station at Syntagma Square is (01) 323–7942; in Piraeus (01) 417–8138; and there are about a dozen other stations in Athens and the suburbs. The city buses, buses to the provinces, and subways are the most inexpensive transport.

HEALTH, WATER, AND FOOD Health conditions are excellent. You may see black, buzzing rock bees, which usually won't sting you. Insect repellent wards them off. Jellyfish come and go, but the water is so clear along most beaches that you can see them when they do float about calm waters, so they aren't much of a problem either. Sea urchins, which look like little marine porcupines, are a problem if you step on one in a rocky seaside pool or offshore in some places—very ouch, indeed—but wearing rubber bathing shoes or sneakers when wading, swimming, or walking on the beach, or wearing flippers when snorkeling, diminishes the risk of this hazard. No problems about water—except the lack of access to it on archaeological sites and hillsides, which makes canteen-carrying on any jaunt strongly advisable. Milk is homogenized and pasteurized, and a great deal of it is treated so that it lasts for weeks without refrigeration, mostly a European import or franchise called **Longlife,** plain and chocolate-flavored. Condensed milk, **Nouncu,** a brand with a picture of a lactating female on the tin, is also widely available. Ice cream comes in many brands, flavors, textures. **Delta** and other commercial brands of yogurt come plain and with fruit, but for the really great, truly wholesome and delicious yogurt, ask for *yiaourti sakoulas*. Every village foodstore has it. No food more healthy for you or the children. Today, Greek salads, either owing to the quality of the olive oil in the dressing, or the atmosphere in which they are consumed, are still incredibly delicious. In general, you'll always eat well at any quayside, seaside *psarotaverna* (fish taverna), where you can enjoy the owner's morning catch, and other tavernas specializing in traditional country fare with main courses usually grilled meat, grilled fish, or a sturdy casserole at deliciously affordable prices. There are, of course, hundreds of more formal, more elegant, more conventional restaurants. For pages of suggestions, consult the monthly *Athenian* or the GNTO's Travel Agent's Manual. In Greece, since it's customary to dine at 8 p.m. or later and take a long time eating, tavernas, fish tavernas, and *psistarias* (where you can inspect your lamb, chicken, or pork turning barbecue-style on a spit) are unalloyed pleasures for most children. In Athens, for quick lunches, the souvlaki stands, densely packed between Syntagma Square and the Agora, are unbeatable. **O Thanasis** on Mitropoleo toward Monastiraki, with waiters rushing to seat you, is a great choice for a good, filling meal under $5. In smaller towns, you can usually find a *zacharoplasteio* for a quick tea or coffee and pastry.

Plenty of tasty roast and grilled lamb; there's no better way to eat lamb than kabob fashion. Skewered lamb *(souvlakia)* is often sold by sidewalk vendors. You can buy excellent sesame-seed pretzels, *torropita,* or cheese-filled turnovers, and pastries from local bakery shops. Most teenagers like the appetizers, *mezedakia* or *meze,* served at tavernas—olives, cheese, sausage. The best part of taverna eating is that the cook invites you to have a look into the kitchen. You can order as you would a Chinese meal, each person trying something different and sharing. The custom is to eat an appetizer and main course at one restaurant, then "walk off" the food and end up somewhere else for coffee and dessert. This is fun. *Baklava* (nut pastry in honey syrup), *kadaifi* (a nut, honey, and shredded wheat concoction), and *galaktobouriko* (a custard-filled pastry) are popular. Honey sometimes tastes like kerosene; honey from Delphi is preferable to honey from Parnassus. Fruits—watermelon *(karpouzi),* figs, pomegranates, strawberries *(fraoules),* grapes *(stafilia)*—are superb. In the fish department, the Greeks excel—smelts *(marides)* couldn't be tastier—but stay away from shrimp unless you have had your gamma globulin shots. Other foods that appeal to children: *melitzanossalata* (eggplant salad, served as an appetizer); feta cheese (a soft white cheese made of sheep's milk); *avgolemono* (egg and lemon soup); *moussaka* (minced meat, potatoes, vegetables, cream sauce); *fassolada* (hot bean soup); *youvarlakia* (mincemeat with rice and egg sauce); *astakos ladolemono* (lobster with oil and lemon); *dolmas* (rice and meat wrapped in grape leaves). Octopus *(oktapodi)* and squid *(kalamarakia)* are for sophisticated palates. *Tarama* (carp roe) and *taramosalata* (tarama mixed with oil and lemon) are salty—an acquired taste, nutritious and filling.

Milkshakes are famous at **Syntagma Coffee House** (just off the square on Apolonis St.). The confectionary shops—**Floca** (9 Eleftheriou Venizelou St., **Zonar's** (Venizelous and Voukourestiou St.), or **Floca's Self-Service** (16 Emanouel Benaki St.; branch in Corfu)—offer cakes, sandwiches, ice cream, and other munchies. Rather than the bustling activity of Syntagma Square, the hub of Athens, Kolonaki Square, in the residential area, is a more serene enclave in which to sit at one of several outdoor cafes, of which **Lykovrysi** is a happy choice. **Hellenikon** (Kolonaki Sq.) has scrumptious pastry, candy, ice cream. In the Plaka, **Xynos** (in a courtyard) with frescoed walls, and the roof garden of **Taverna Bacchus** are pleasant and inexpensive, but I'd skip most of the tourist joints in this area as the singing and entertainment starts too late for children to enjoy.

A must for children is the **Stagecoach Restaurant** (Loukianou 6, Kolonaki) open daily from 11:30 a.m. and Sun. evening; all sorts of wild-west gimmicks (hitching posts, saddles, etc.); steaks, fried chicken, clam chowder, and apple pie. Another children's favorite is the Hilton's ground floor Byzantine cafe for milkshakes and hamburgers. Way up on Lycabettus Hill, **Vladimir's** (Aristodimou 12) backs onto a little pine grove where children can romp while you wait to be served. **Dionyssos,** nearby, also recommended for a panoramic view and moderately expensive menu. **Ta Nissia,** downstairs at the Athens Hilton, Tel: (01) 720–201, with a wide assortment of Greek and international dishes, is a luxury class version of an island tavern; open daily from 12:30 p.m.–3 p.m. and, beginning at 7 p.m. old and new Greek songs sung by tableside-wandering troubadors to charm you and your children. Also luxury class is the **Cafe Pergola,** a garden, coffee-shop-style delight for snacks and meals at the Hotel Athenaeum Intercontinental, overlooking the pool and landscaped waterfalls; Tel: (01) 922–6950. **The Eighteen,** 20 Tsakalof St., Kolonaki, Tel: (01) 362–1928, open daily except Sun., from noon–5 p.m. and 8 p.m.–2 a.m. is small, simple, inexpensive and charming. Across from the Astir Beach at the Yachting Marina in **Vouliagmeni,** head for **Moorings,** open daily for lunch and dinner, Tel: (01) 896–1113; for Sun. lunch, **Toscana,** Thisseos 16, also in Vouliagmeni, Tel: (01) 896–2497, moderately priced and attractive with terraces and much greenery; only open for dinner, 7:30 p.m.–1 a.m. the rest of the week. In **Kifissia, Symposium,** Platia Neas Politias, Tel: (01) 801–6707, open daily from noon to midnight, moderately priced, is simply super for lunch or supper. In **Glyfada, Psaropoulos,** 2 Kalamou St., Tel: (01) 894–5677, open noon–3:30 p.m., 8 p.m.–midnight, with medium to high prices, is a venerable seafood restaurant, open daily, the year round.

In **Patras,** the **Sweet Palace,** at Diakou, Tel: (061) 225–484, a coffee and pastry shop, also has a restaurant and a lovely summer roof garden with a spectacular view. In **Thessaloniki,** tourists are always told to go to **Krikelas,** Vassillissis Olgas, and to **Olympos Naoussa,** Vassillissis Konstantinous 5, which is only open for lunch and usually jampacked. A better choice might be **Remvi,** Nea Krini, Tel: (031) 411–233, with a beautiful garden, pricey, but definitely not a dicey choice, as you can eat indoors or out beneath the mazarine Macedonian sky, and the food and service are special.

In **Piraeus,** all the seafood restaurants in the tiny port, Microlimano, are recommended for good meals. And don't miss **Vasilena** (72 Aetolikou; Tel: (01) 461–2457) where you can enjoy 18 Greek eating treats for under $5. Open daily from 7 p.m.–11:30 p.m., closed Sun.

Near Peania on the old Lavrion Road toward **Sounion,** is a great taverna, **Kanakis;** Michael Kanakis does all the cooking, grows all his own produce, even prepares his own wine grapes (by hand, not by foot!), and loves children.

In **Corfu,** it's **Akteon,** at the edge of the plateia, Tel: (0661) 37894, for palatable moussaka, souvlakia; cozy, crowded; will also provide juicy roast chickens and anything else you'd like to take along on a picnic. If you want to treat yourself to the best, luxuriate at the **Corfu Palace Hotel.** The taverna at **Danilia,** the replica of an old Corfiot village, is where you can collapse after you have done the museum and shopped. In **Rhodes,** at the wonderful fish restaurant on the beach as you turn off the coastal road toward the Golden Beach Hotel, the children can gather shells while you down martinis. Beside it is a small playground. The **Casa Castellana** (33 Aristotelous St.) in the old town, has a lovely garden where you can eat, also a medieval-style dining room. **The Farm House,** nearby the Grand Hotel, has a terrace where you can eat in summer, overlooking the sea, great for cooling drinks and simple, delicious, inexpensive fare.

▶ **Note:** In Athens, at wonderful **Vassilopoulos** on Stadiou St., you can get all-American groceries such as breakfast cereals, cake mixes, frozen fish and meat, Carnation milk and other baby food, imported cheeses. Other good supermarkets in the Kolonaki area.

BABY FOOD In pharmacies, supermarkets, and delicatessens, there is a good variety of baby food and a good selection of powdered milk. Most outlets stock Gerber's or Beechnut. European brands are Cow & Gate, Nutricia, Nam Bebelac, Guigoze, Nestle, Milupa; the Greek Yiottis brand offers powdered milk and dried cereals, mostly corn and wheat.

In Athens, **Bakakos Pharmacy** (Omonia Sq.) features a downstairs drug dept. and an upstairs corner of baby supplies and food (Milupa, Bebelac skimmed milk powder, Nutricia, Nido and other mixtures by Nestles, Similac with minerals and the American formula S-26, Cow & Gate, Materna); also a good selection of plastic bottles—hard to find elsewhere—rubber pants, training pants, disposable diapers, rubber nipples, and pacifiers, pre-moistened towels, Wet Ones.

Caution: Outside of Athens, Rhodes, Heraklion in Crete, Thessaloniki, and other tourist areas, it is unlikely that you will find a widely varied selection of baby foods or powdered milks. The phrase you need to know is "Where is the baby food?" *(Poo eenay ee poe-dick-ess trofess?)*—there the baby supplies will usually also be.

DIAPERS AND LAUNDRY The word for cloth diaper is *panes*. Disposables are *chartines panes*. Available in pharmacies and supermarkets, you can find Pampers, Luvs, Chux, or products much like them. Fimulin are the only cloth diapers recommended.

No diaper laundries that I know of, but at the invaluable phrase *"Bore-race nah pleen-uhs aff-TUH"* ("Can you wash these things?") any maid will accommodate you.

EMERGENCIES MADE EASY The splendid **Tourist Police** in all major cities can find you a doctor, accommodations, help with what you need. In Athens, they are at 7 Syngrou Ave., Tel: (01) 923–9224. Their hotline number in Athens is 100 for all emergencies. The **Poison Control** number in Athens is (01) 779–3777. Certain pharmacies are open 24 hours in Athens and the suburbs. If you understand Greek, you can dial 107 for their names and addresses in Athens; 102 for the suburban ones, or ask the concierge to do this for you and translate your requirements to be delivered. Good pharmacies in Athens are **Bakakos** (21 Omonia Sq.; Tel: (01) 523–2631); **Damvergis** (6 Panepistimiou St.; Tel: (01) 363–9006), with a fine prescription department, baby supplies, and food; **Marinopoulos** (23 Kaneri St., Kolonaki; Tel: (01) 361–3051).

If you should require the services of a trained nurse for your child, call the **English Speaking Nurses Society of Greece** headquartered in Athens, Tel: (01) 652–3192 for advice and recommendations. The 24-hour emergency hospital call number in Athens is 166.

The Children's Hospital is **"Aghia Sophia"** (Thevon and Mikras Asias Sts., Goudi; Tel: 771–659), but your best bet is simply to visit or call the **American Embassy** (91 Vassillissis Sophias Blvd.; Tel: (01) 721–2951; *American Consulate General* (59 Vasileos Constantinou St.; Tel: (031) 266–121).

MAGIC FAMILY HELPERS There aren't many ***babysitting agencies,*** but in Athens, I am told you can make arrangements with **Polina,** in Halandri, Tel: (01) 681–3017; **White Rabbit** (Mesogion 316 in Aghia Paraskevia; Tel: (01) 652–7002). The women at the **American Club,** reachable through the Kastri Hotel, Kifissia, Tel: (01) 801–3971, may have other suggestions and recommendations, and might be able to give you their positive or negative comments about noteworthy kindergartens in the Athens area which have been especially recommended: **The American Community Schools of Athens, Inc.** (preschool, elementary, middle school and high school) (Aghias Parskevis 129, Ano Neon Halandri; Tel: (01) 659–3200); **Campion Schools,** which has separate infant and junior schools in Psychico, and a combined junior and infant school in Ano Glyfada in the southern suburbs with boarding facilities. Write for further information to The Headmaster, Campion School, P.O. Box 9, Psychico, Athens, Greece; or for general information about the senior school, call (01) 813–3883, 813–3013 or after hours, (01) 682–2250. For information about the Junior School, Psychico, ring (01) 672–4004; Infant School, Psychico, ring (01) 6272–3248. For inquiries about transportation, call (01) 813–5952 for the Psychico area; for Glyfada, ring (01) 991–8673. Both these schools are recommended for children of families resident in the area. For part-time or temporary infant and child care are: the German-speaking kindergarten, **Ulli Beck** (Karditsis 41, Kato Halandri; Tel: (01) 671–7968); **Playland** (Agia Ioannou 90, Agia Paraskevi; Tel: (01) 659–6716; **Athens Baby Center** open 24 hours a day, where baby care is provided by the hour, day, or night (Tritis Septemvrious 87, Victorias Square; Tel: (01) 883–2347); **ABC** (Taygetous 27, Psychiko; Tel: (01) 672–5640); **ABC** (Kapodistrious 35, Philothei) Tel: (01) 681–2232); **Bizzykidz** (Vassilecs Georgiou 39, Glyfada; Tel: (01) 894–7926).

The American Community Schools of Athens, Inc. (see above), have special programs for after-school activities, field trips, languages at the main Halandri campus, and at a smaller elementary school, **Kif-**

issia (Athanasiou Diakou and Kokkinaki Streets, Kifissia; Tel: (01) 808–0475). Both schools have full U.S. accreditation. Then there is the **Tasis Hellenic International School.** For more information, contact Director of Admissions, Tasis Hellenic International School, P.O. Box 25, Xenias and Artemidos Streets, Kifissia, Athens, Greece. **St. Lawrence College,** the British International School, expanded both its junior and senior schools in 1982, and opened a large kindergarten and infant school at Alexander Beach Complex, **Patras.** The headmaster, Mr. R.J.O. Meyer, O.B.E. (Order of the British Empire), will accept applications or inquiries at any times of day except Christmas and Easter (50 Agiou Dimitrious, Paleo Psychicho, Athens, Greece; Tel: (01) 671–2748).

Other instruction? The YWCA (Xen) at 11 Amerikis (Tel: (01) 362–4291) gives pottery, cooking, art lessons for families, also special courses in local dancing. The Union of Licensed Guides (9A Apollonos St., Tel: (01) 322–9705) will guide families and individuals around archaeological sites in Athens and suburbs; instant expertise, if you can cope with minutiae you really don't need to know. I'd recommend calling the American School of Classical Studies at Athens, (01) 723–6313, and hiring one of their archaeological students who annually summer and dig around the Agora to accompany you on weekends when they are free. They can tell your children how to tell which culture and which century the potshards came from, and what went on and goes on in the Agora, all the things children really do want to know and are interested in.

If your child is celebrating a birthday in Athens, you can order pastries, munchies or a wonderful cake from **Fresh Gateaux de Luxe,** Anagnostopoulo St. 15–17, near Kolonaki Sq.; Tel: (01) 364–1025. You can call any of the night spots in Athens; they all keep names on file of performers who dance, sing, juggle, do magic and conjuring tricks, play the guitar.

If you want a mail drop, telephone message service, material Xeroxed or typed, a multilingual secretary who can type letters for you, get in touch with **Executive Services, Ltd.,** Athens Tower B; Tel: (01) 778–3698 or 770–1062; Telex 214227 exse GR. Mail handling, secretarial and typing services, translations also are offered by **International Business Services,** 29 Michalakoppolou, behind the Hilton; Tel: (01) 721–0774 or 724–5541.

CHILDREN'S CAMPS Apollos age 5–12 and Dianas age 5–7 can live for wonderfully low rates for a week or more at **Kinderland Hellas** in a pine forest about 30 miles from Athens and less than a mile from Kalamos village, facing the Euboean Gulf. This German-Greek-English-organized camp has a well-equipped playground, and many indoor (chess, Ping-Pong, movies, shadow plays) and outdoor games (swimming, volleyball, bicycling, gymnastics, watersports). Children live in 8-bed tents (floored with mosaic tiles, electrically lit, insulated, and comfortable), with one counselor for every seven children; modern lavatory facilities (showers, but no tubs); infirmary and resident doctor; good cooking; library; even a small zoo and aviary! Run on European lines rather than the superorganized American pattern, it offers campfires, dances at night, music, frequent excursions to local spots of interest, and a generally happy atmosphere. Many children of the U.S. military and foreign diplomats come here, and American kids find it a joy. For details, write Director (5 Pendelis St., Athens; Tel: (01) 323–5659).

Mr. Meyer, headmaster of St. Lawrence College (see above) runs a summer camp at Alexander Beach complex in Patras from late June on. Augustus Van Seggelen of the **Seahorse Rent-A-Yacht and Sailing School** (see Fun Trips) will also lodge children from 12 up to 14 days while teaching them how to sail.

▶ **Note: The American Farm School** (Box 140, Thessaloniki) is a busy, beautiful, exciting enterprise, directed by Bruce Lansdale, which deserves your support and mine—BUT it is a school for Greek boys, not a vacation retreat for Americans.

CASTLES AND OTHER HAPPY FAMILY ACCOMMODATIONS During the summer, in Athens, it is imperative to stay at a "nice place"; otherwise you'll be quivering with repressed or expressed indignation at the steamy heat, pullulating tourist density, and racketing motorscooters, car engines, and human voices. The best possible place to stay, ingratiatingly cool, plush, and ideal for the big-budgeted family is the **Athens Hilton,** 46 Vassilissis Sofias Ave.; Tel: (01) 722–0201–9. There is, unfortunately, nothing for children at the lovely Grande Bretagne. The St. George's site is steeper than the Hilton's but the prices less so. The Hilton has a pool as does the **Athenaeum Intercontinental,** the **Caravel** and the **Royal Olympic.** But what about the **St. George Lycabettus** (2 Kleomenous St.; Tel: (01) 729–0711)? It's ¾ way up the lovely Lycabettus Hill, with a funicular to the top where St. George's Church is (you can also drive, of course) and, in the Kolonaki residential area, is a delightful retreat with a *wonderful* rooftop pool and an atmosphere of comfort, style, serenity. The funicular ride up does mean a ten-minute walk—and, if you're not careful, slide—down to the nearby restaurants, cafes, and the hotel. Wear rubber-soled shoes or crepe-soled sneakers! For families who relish peace in lovely environs above the hub and summer hubbub of Athens, St. George to the rescue! Also in the Kolonaki area, the **Athenian Inn** is about four times less expensive than the *luxe* hotels, and is said to be charming.

Among *apartment hotels*—terrific if you have an infant or toddlers along—recommended as tops are the **Delice** (3 Vassileos Alexandrou; Tel: (01) 723–8211) just behind the Hilton, which charges reasonable rates for twin-bedded room-living-room with rollaway bed, breakfast nook, kitchen and bathroom; air conditioning here and at the **Embassy** (15 Timoleonthes Vassou; Tel: (01) 642–1152) near the American Embassy.

About 10 miles out, the **Astir** bungalows on **Glyfada Beach** are deluxe and offer snack bars, mini-golf, changing cabins, green lawns in a village-like complex, restaurants, swimming pool, and many other Americans with families. The majority are one-room cottages, but there are also two- and three-room villas and some larger units. These are less pricey than those at the **Astir Palace** compound in **Vougliagmeni** 15 miles from Athens, where there is a marina, beach, indoor and outdoor swimming pools, tennis, central hotel, boating clubhouse with restaurant. Some bookings are made a year ahead as they are for the beachside bungalows of the Hotel Xenia, situated on the beautiful headland of **Lagonissi** about 35 miles from Athens. Do reserve in advance if you can.

For families like ones I know who rented summertime villas on the island of Spetsae to get away from it all, and who are now grizzling about the invasion of tourists and trippers, you can rent a Greek island in the Aegean and enjoy all of its hilly, wooded, wild-flower sprinkled 60 acres in blissful exclusivity, living in a traditional Greek homestead that has been modernized; dining on produce from the island's own farm, waited on hand and foot, except when you need to steady yourself on a windsurfer or a boat (all free of charge except for fuel costs). You can explore *your* island as well as the nearby islands of Euboea (Evia), Skiathos, Skopelos, Alonissos with all their enchanting ports and villages. The name of the island? **Argironisos,** ''Silver Island,'' off the northeast tip of Euboea. Services of baby-sitting staff and boatmen free of charge to take you fishing or waterskiing are included. Do I need to tell you there are also donkeys for the children to ride? Your nearest GNTO can send you further information, brochure, and an official form to make reservations via Vouliagmeni, Greece or Nelspruit, South Africa.

As a change of pace, what about the good old days with accommodations priced the way they used to be? Visual charm and economy combined? Believe it or not, they do exist, clean, simple and wonderfully affordable in GNTO's first phase of developing fortress towers, church cloisters, merchants' houses, frescoed mansions, village houses, restored or conserved and converted into guesthouses that offer traditional architecture and the atmosphere of hand-carved furniture, woven rugs, local handicrafts plus private shower and lavatory. Some with kitchens for self-catering, some without where there is, however, a modest fee for breakfast included in the tab that astonishingly comes to little more than youth hostel rates or the price of daily tent-rental. So far, there are less than ten of these **Paradosiakos Ikismos.** Information about these can be had from the Xenia Hotel at Portaria Village, Tel: (0421) 25922, (0421) 39158. Santorini is the most spectacular of all the Greek islands, quite unlike the rest of the Cyclades in the Aegean, and has a funicular up the cliffs to Thira; an archaeological site, a museum and the influx of cruise boats which stop for a day only. For information on

PIs here, write Paradosiakos Ikismos Oias, Oia, Santorini, Greece. Another gem is the **Kapetanakos Tower** in Areopoli. Great if you are touring along the eastern coast of the Messiniakos Gulf separating those first two fingers of the Peloponnesus to the south of Sparta, Mistra, and Kalamata. Telephone ahead (0733–51233).

WINDMILLS, VILLAS, APARTMENTS TO RENT From comfortable to luxurious, from prices quoted by villa rental agencies in the U.S. ($275 weekly to $3000 and up with reductions on rentals of a month or longer) to the same prices often quoted locally for monthly *rates,* there's a vast selection of housing in all the island groups in the Ionian and the Aegean, and from the southern Peloponnese to Athens, Attica and on up to northern Macedonia. I strongly recommend getting an overview or else specific, reliable advice from someone who's been there before you rent. And don't trust all that you read. I've read about Hydra described as the jolliest place imaginable, when actually it's closer to my way of thinking of being just a mass of bars and beachless rocks; and Santorini, which I think is wonderful, has been described woefully. So have a look before you rent.

If you'd like to rent a windmill in Crete, Rhodes, or Patmos, rent one only if its blades are firmly anchored and stationary while you have tenancy, and check out the locale thoroughly. I'd suggest subscribing to *The Athenian,* Greece's most informative English language monthly (39 Kosmas Balanou, Mets, P.O. Box 3317, Athens, Greece). *The Athens News,* the English language daily paper (23–25 Lekka St., Athens, Greece; Tel: (01) 322–4253 or 323–6324) (calling from the U.S. the code is (01331)) carries many local summer rentals. Placing a few ads there might be profitable. Two U.S. agencies which have won a seal of approval from the GNTO, and from whom you can obtain information and brochures about rentals in Greece are: **ITP Worldwide Luxury Villa Holiday,** 318 Royal Palm Way, Palm Beach, FL 33480; Tel: (800) 327–4505 or (305) 833–6943; **Interchange Vacations,** 213 E. 38th St., New York, NY; Tel: (212) 685–4340. The best agencies recommended by the GNTO in Athens are: **Argel Travel** 65 Vassilissis Sophias Ave.; Tel: (01) 721–2766; **Olympic Villas Holidays** 4 Fillelinon St.; Tel: (01) 323–8512 or 323–7313. For **Corfu** selections, the agency with GNTO's accolade is **Corfu Villas Ltd.** 43 Cheval Place, Knightsbridge, London, W.7, England; Tel: (1) 581–0851; international access code (01144). **Special:** For a royal-style vacation, Sir Richard and Lady Musgrave have opened their cliff-top villa and private beach with swimming bay and diving board on the island of Syros in the Cyclades. Sir Richard, a superstar baronet, who supervises every detail, promises Cordon Bleu meals and attentive service. A week's delicious pleasures (visits to tavernas, excursions, all drinks, meals, laundry, absolutely *everything*) offers no reductions for children, but babies are free. The Musgraves like children. They have six grown children of their own. From Apr. 1–Oct. 30, write to Sir Richard Musgrave, "Fili tou Amenou," Komito, Syros, Greece; Nov. 1–May 31, at Riverstown, Tara, County Meath, Ireland; or contact Mr. Hanns Ebensten (705 Washington St., New York, NY 10014; Tel: (212) 691–7429). Mr. Ebensten, by the way, is a man to get in touch with for exotic, fun, offbeat vacations, but this is the only villa for which he is an agent.

CLUB MEDITERRANEE There are five vacation villages, each offering one- to three-day excursions and eight-day car-plane-boat tours for an additional charge. Each village, with beach, sea and mountain views, offers all inclusive rates for instruction and equipment for sports such as windsurfing, waterskiing, snorkeling, sailing, boat trips, evening dances, nightclub, concerts. All are open approximately from mid-May to early Oct. **Gregolimano,** on the northern tip of Euboea (Evia), Greece's largest Aegean island, just off the coast of central Greece, is the largest and most luxurious of these villages, with an air-conditioned hotel and bungalows, a Mini-Club for children 4–8, a Kid's Club for over 8s. **Kos,** located on the Dodecanese island off the southwest Turkish coast for which it is named, is near a pretty little valley village, Kefalos, and has a hotel with balconied rooms, myriad bungalows right on the beach facing the ruins of the basilica of Aghios Stefanos; Mini Club and Kid's Club. **Aighion** is a village of Polynesian huts set in an olive grove fronting the Corinthian Gulf. Children from the age of 6 are welcomed, but no special clubs or counselors for them. On the island of Corfu, another "case" village at **Ipsos,** also in an olive grove, where physical fitness is emphasized; children 12 and older, only, are accepted. No special counselors for children. Also on Corfu, lush and green, on a hillside slopping down to the Ionian, is **Helios,** with an air-conditioned hotel, where children 8 and older are welcomed, but for whom no special counselors are provided. Small group tours to Crete, to other islands, to the highlights of southern Greece from any of the Club Med vacation villages may also be of interest to parents with teenagers.

CAMPING AND CARAVANING Organized camping grounds with white sand beaches, showers, kitchens, restaurants, food shops, some with two double-bedroom chalets, facilities for fishing, sailing, tennis, first-aid stations are run by the GNTO and the Hellenic Touring Club, with 90% of the sites by the seashore, with their amenities listed by number, thank heavens, not indecipherable symbols, in a booklet, *Camping Sites and Facilities in Greece,* available from GNTO offices. All campsites must meet with GNTO standards, and of some four score and more clean, well-equipped campsites, the GNTO has 11 beachside beauties with a full range of services including, at most sites, pedal boats and canoes for hire. All but two of these are in Macedonia and in the Chalkidiki area of northern Greece, plus **Voula,** which I don't recommend because you're surrounded by a forest of highrise apartments on a grid of level sites; and **Ayia,** in the suburbs of Patras, the busiest car ferry terminal in Greece, in a secluded wooded site along the rocky Peloponnese coast. Be prepared for transistor radios, singing and dancing in some sites. Beautifully landscaped **Aghia Trias,** close to Thessaloniki, with beach, 17 chalets each with two double-bedded rooms; **Olympus,** beneath the massive range with four-bed huts fronting the Aegean; Pretty, pleasing, peaceful **Paliouri,** lovely site; **Asprovalta** with a safer beach recommended especially for young children; **Kavala** with beachside campsite near a medieval castle, ancient theater, and horse-drawn carriages; **Alexandropoulos,** seaside. Camping in Greece is allowed only in organized camping grounds. As yet, there are no shops specializing in camping equipment rentals.

The only hostel in Athens recognized by the International Youth Hostel Organization is the **Athens Youth Hostel** at 57 Kypselis St., which requires International Student I.D., and reservations should be made in advance. The Plaka hostels are the pits; avoid them.

Bring all camping equipment with you. Outside of Athens, where the best camping store is **Parnassas** (87 Hermou St.), equipment is hard to find and wildly expensive. You'll need blankets for cool nights, and insect repellent (the mosquitoes can be quite aggressive).

ATTRACTIONS FOR CHILDREN IN ATHENS Brace yourself before you arrive. Athens is not the ''Midsummer's Night's Dream'' as Shakespeare romanticized it. Yes, the Parthenon is even more fabulous than you anticipated, the museums are fascinating—*but* Athens as a town is bound to be a disappointment unless you seek out its pleasures. The outskirts are tatty; the central square, Syntagma (Constitution) ordinary; in summer it all seems like a hot, crowded, trafficky madhouse; shopkeepers appear a gross lot; the old city area, Plaka, tourist-picturesque (but irresistible as its souvlakia and rollicking tavernas). So before disillusion sets in, take a happy cablecar ride up Lycabettus Hill (entrance at Ploutarchou and Aristippou streets in Kolonaki), walk about with (or bring along an extra pair of) comfortable no-slip shoes, take a breath, cool off at the St. George or at one of the cafes or restaurants, gaze at the Parthenon; or skip a museum if you have to, to go to Mt. Hymettus's **Kaissariani,** the 11th-century monastery on the lower slopes, and the cool shelter of cypress and Aleppo pines. The Byzantine church has 17th- and 18th-century frescoes, and this is truly an exceptionally lovely spot for picnicking. The golden gorse and thistles with which Hymettus is covered—fragrant also with rosemary, thyme, wild sage— is prickly, so don't let the children run around bare-legged. The **National Garden** (Ethnikos Kipos), near the old Royal Palace, has a lake, ducks to feed, a small zoo.

Try **Piraeus,** the harbor area—wonderful for children. Just opposite the Neon Phaliron subway or Metro station is a Children's Paradise (I Pediki Hara), a play area right by the sea with modern equipment; colorful swings for parents to collapse in. In the summer, Lunaparks dot the coastline from Piraeus to Glyfada, which has a really nice Lunapark 12 miles distant off King George Ave. opposite the Hotel Galaxy which features all forms of rides and games, Ferris wheels. Getting in a taxi or bus and simply riding along the shore, you'll come upon many of these cheap and fun-filled outdoor entertainments. Also in Piraeus is the **Veakio Theater** which generally holds a series of ballet, acrobatic, and other performances through Aug. Tickets for these outdoor performances may be purchased at the Palace Cinema theater, between Stadiou and Panepistimious St. in the arcade. For further information, Tel: (01) 322–8275. On summer evenings, rather than follow the tourist route through the Plaka for bouzouki and folk dancing, why not watch in comfort Greek folk dances from all over Greece performed at the **Dora Stratou Dance Theater** at the Philopappou open-air theater behind the Acropolis? Information and tickets from 4 Stadiou St.; Tel: (01) 322–1459 or 324–4395, eves. (01) 921–4650. Other good places for Greek folk dancing and music area nightspots such as **Neraida** (Paleo Phaliro); **Fantassia** (Glyfada); and **Philopappou.** Also check the programs at the **Herodes Atticus** theater, a fabulous ancient 5000-seat Roman structure featuring ballet, classical drama, opera, concerts, modern dance; similar programs at the **Lykavittos** open-air theater on top of Lycabettus. Tickets and information available at the Athens Festival Box Office, 4 Stadiou St., and 1 Voukourestiou (in the arcade). Tel: (01) 322–3111, ext. 240 or (01) 322–1459. Information here also about performances of classical Greek drama at **Epidauros** (Epidavros) in the ancient open-air theater with its extraordinary acoustics.

On Sun. mornings, head for the colorful pageantry of the Changing of the Guard outside the Parliament building at 11 a.m. Outside the barracks, next to the **Presidential Palace,** Herodou Attikou St., white-skirted evzones, with tasseled caps and pomponned slippers members of the troop, are amiably disposed to posing for pictures holding your child's hand.

On to the **Acropolis,** site of the most outstanding and well-known ancient Greek ruins, the Parthenon and Temple of Wingless Victory. Spectacular sound and light except on full or gibbous moon nights (ask your concierge to check the time for English-language performance) Apr. 1–mid-Oct.; seating is on the Pnyx hill, either chairs or cushions; take sweaters and a fan as evening temperatures are changeable. One of the best performances I've seen anywhere, romantic and beautiful. Although the Acropolis itself is a vast open-air museum, it also has a museum exhibiting the famous frieze and finds discovered on the hill, among which is a unique collection of statues of women known as "Korai with the archaic smile." Also the **Agora** (marketplace), **Stoa** (shopping center), **Arch of Hadrian,** and **Temple of Hephaestus** are all pretty breathtakingly memorable. The reconstructed **Stoa of Attalos,** with deep colonnaded porches, is a splendid museum with superb publications on sale. Wonderful scale models of buildings, miniature sculpture, comic masks, pottery including ancient spouted pottery baby-feeders; coins; pottery lamps shaped like feet and animal heads; jewelry. A great museum. Bathroom facilities are excellent and usually welcome before you trudge up or after you have trudged down the Panathenaic way. Don't miss the large statues of giants and tritons (half men, half fish) at the **Roman Odeon.** The Agora and the Acropolis and both museums oughtn't to be attempted in a single visit. The problem with collapsing in the Plaka (the old town) in a cafe afterward is that the Plaka is also interesting to walk around, and mostly an exclusively pedestrian precinct. Wear sneakers for this fabulous excursion!

Spirited Greek shadow plays, reminiscent of Indonesian shadow puppets, are performed nightly at **Karagiozis Theater** in the Plaka at Fanari Diogeni (Lyssikratous Sq.; Tel: 322–4845); fun to watch and transcend the language barrier. English-language movies are shown regularly at 16 theaters in Athens and its suburbs.

Museums. There are small entrance fees for museums, but an international student ID card will get you a 50% discount. Museum floors are marble, so wear your space shoes or crepe-soled ones; be prepared for bad acoustics, bad lighting, and perhaps crowds. On summer weekdays, museums are usually open 8 or 9 a.m. to 2 or 3 p.m. Sun. and bank holiday hours are generally 10 a.m.–2 p.m. Winter hours vary considerably. Ask the GNTO for their mimeographed booklet on museums (which they generally only issue to travel agents and archaeological students), invaluable for checking hours of admission.

Attention all camera carriers—and this applies to kiddies with Kodaks just as it does to their parents with Leicas—a fee is charged for photographing in all museums (some allow a portable camera but others insist you check even those at the door; amateur fees can run from perhaps $2.50 for still shots to $35 for movies; professionals pay about double); home movies nick you at least $20; professional fees can run to hundreds of dollars!

National Archaeological Museum (1 Tossitsa St.) is *the* great target. The Mycenean collection is world-renowned and the archaeological exhibits fabulous; extensive numismatic collection, but the real golden treasury is the magnificent array of classical Greek art. Closed Mon. The **Benaki Museum** (Vassilissis Sofias Ave. and Koumbari St.) offers a mixed bag of popular art (costumes, embroidery, furniture, and household objects); wonderful ancient jewelry; Byzantine icons; prehistoric and classical Greek art; Coptic and Chinese art. The popular art is housed in the "Kozani Mansion House," which is a unique exhibit in itself. Interesting and special restaurant and nice museum shop. The **Byzantine Museum** (22 Vassilissis Sophias Ave. Tel: (01) 721–1027) encloses a cypressed courtyard centered with a handsome fountain. Children will delight in the left wing with icons of popular art in vivid comic-book colors; allegorical paintings that are nice and violent (saints about to ax the devil, a shipwrecked sailor, hellfire and brimstone and paradise); exquisite icons painted by a Cretan artist (particularly one of St. George). The two-story central building has frescoes, sculpture, beautiful Byzantine icons; jeweled and illuminated gospels. Fabulous—shouldn't be missed.

The **Folklore Museum,** 17 Kidathineon St. Plaka, Tel: (01) 321–3018, is a glorious array of popular painting, costumes, stamps, jewelry, Bible covers, lavish ecclesiastical vestments, Greek embroidery and needlework, gorgeous Byzantine artifacts and crucifixes. Lots of fun to explore this fine treasury. Closed Tues. The **National Painting Gallery and Alexandros Soutsos Museum** (opposite the Hilton) is closed Tues. The little **Museum of Keramikos** (148 Hermou St.) on a pretty parklike archaeological site, a cemetery of ancient Athens, owes its name to the pottery workshop nearby (fun to visit) and contains funerary stelae and pottery, not of *riveting* interest to the young, but has some nice small pieces of glass and jewelry. The **Historical and Ethnological Museum** (Stadiou St. in the Palaia Vouli, former Parliament House) has lots of paintings of battle scenes, an armor collection, flags, historical manuscripts—exhausting if you insist on seeing it all. Closed Mon. Boys might prefer the **War Museum** (Vassilissis Sophias Ave. and Rizari St., Tel: (01) 715–035), which has a magnificent collection of armor, weapons, uniforms, helmets from the 5th century B.C. (!!!) to the present. **Maritime Museum** (Freatis, Akti Themistokleous, Piraeus) is a must for ship-model buffs; models date from the ancient period to the present. Also paintings of historical naval battles, uniforms, and a hodgepodge of nautical memorabilia.

Quick trips from Athens: Kaessariani and its monastery, already mentioned, a MUST! A picnic at the 11th-century monastery at **Dafne** (6 miles); superb mosaics; swinging wine festival in summer. **Eleusis** (15 miles), famous for the Eleusinian Mysteries of ancient times, has the ruins of the temple of Demeter. **Tatoi** (on the slopes of Mt. Parnes) is densely wooded; royal summer palace and royal family graves; magnificent landscape; model farm. **Kifisia** (10 miles inland), a popular summer resort, is cool and wooded; have lunch at **Blue Pine Farms** and ride horse-drawn carriages. Children also enjoy all the rides at an amusement park here. You can take the train from Monasteraki Square to get here in about 15–20 minutes.

Within an hour's drive along the **Apollo Coast,** you can flake out at any of the seaside resorts: **Paleo Phaleron** (6 miles; the least attractive; noisy with jets), **Aghios Kosmas** (near the airport; has everything but is far too crowded for my taste), **Glyfada** (12 miles; the most elegant; golf course; popular beach; loads of up-to-date tourist amenities, including a large amusement Luna park). **Voula** and **Kavouri** (17 miles; good marina and water-ski schools). The 50-mile drive to **Cape Sounion** is beautiful either along the coast or inland through attractive villages; heavenly beach; plenty of hotels; the 5th-century temple of Poseidon atop the promontory is magical at sunset. Also within an hour's drive (through lovely scenery with many villages to explore) are the glorious, pine-shaded, uncrowded beaches of **Aghios Andreas, Rafina, Lutsa,** and **Porto-Rafti** on the east coast of Attica. But watch for jellyfish.

ATTRACTIONS FOR CHILDREN ELSEWHERE **Corinth** has an interesting excavated ancient section but the main thrill is to steam through the **Corinth Canal** with its steep cliffs, or to cross the bridge that spans it. Well worth the 1½ hour bus ride for the medically minded, is the museum, at this former shrine of Aesculapius, with terracotta models of legs, arms, hands, ears, feet as thank-offerings by suffering ancients who were cured at this site. There's a great view of the Peloponnesus, an old fortress and a Turkish mosque to be seen if you have the energy to climb the Acrocorinth. At **Delphi** (on the way—a 3-hour bus ride) stop at the tiny village of Arakhova for the extraordinarily engrossing rug weaving), the museum is fascinating but the major attraction is the eerily wild, enormous **stadium**—really awe-inspiring—relax and let the children explore it on their own. **Epidaurus,** about a 150-mile, 3½-hour car or bus ride from Athens via Corinth, comprises Palea (Old) and Nea (New) Epidaurus, a small Aegean port village 12 miles from the 2300-year-old, 14,000 seat, 55-tier amphitheater where it's a fabulous treat to be during the Festival, mid-June to early Sept., watching the old hair-raising melodramas Euripides, Aeschylus, Sophocles, and Aristophanes used to toss off that today still have the audience gasping, cheering, whistling or laughing. Tickets can be bought in Athens at the Festival box office, or at Epidaurus two hours in advance of Sat. and Sun. performances which begin at 9 p.m. Young children may get bored stiff with Greek drama performed in Greek, but they love to come to the theater site during the day when they can picnic in the pinewoods, or beneath grape arbors and groves of orange, lemon and peach trees and fragrant herbs and flowers; they, as well as you, will have fun checking out the acoustics of the amphitheater. A match struck on stage can be heard way up to the top seats, as can a whisper from center stage. There's a museum nearby (closed Tues.) containing remarkable medical artifacts relating to Aesculapius, god of healing, whose sanctuary this was; also a temple dedicated to Aesculapius and an enchanting archaeological site, reachable in 20 min. by bus or taxi if you are staying in Palea Epidaurus (at the **Paola,** on the beach; the modern **Maik,** the **Plaza, Poseidon);** better yet, stay at the **Xenia** with bungalows, right at the theater and archaeological site. **Epirus,** the most mountainous region of Greece, its NW corner, south of Albania, is off the tourist track, well worth exploring, particularly for Ioannina and Metsovo in the central Zagoria area. Spectacular view of Vikos, a mountain gorge, from the village of Monodentri, a ten minute walk from Ioannina. In West Zagoria, at the mouth of the Vikos gorge, traditional settlements of Mikro and Mega Papingo, about 50 miles NW of Ioannina, a site so fabulously beautiful even the children are interested. **Epirotica,** annual art festival during summer. **Ioannina,** with many horse-carriages for transport and picturesque as all get-out, with a marked oriental character, is renowned for its silver and **handicrafts;** splendid municipal museum of arts and crafts housed in a mosque; streets of working silversmiths and craftsmen; visitable Byzantine monasteries on lake islands; stalactite cave at nearby Perama is colorful and well lit. In central Greece, an 8-hour bus ride, 45-minute plane trip from Athens, Ioannina is a lovely place, with puppet shows and a playground in the square next to which ferries embark for lake islands ideal for picnicking. (See Epirus.)

Mani (Peloponnesus) has three spectacular **stalactite caves** along the bay of Diros that you can explore by boat. **Meteora** is great, fabulous, a *must,* and has to be seen to be believed. Topping extraordinary rock formations are 24 **monasteries** built in the middle ages, and until 1952 access to them was by a netting hoist or jointed ladders which could be pulled up in case of marauders. Children are fascinated and think nothing of the climb. Five monasteries are still in use and can be visited; the Monastery of the Metamorfossis has converted a wing into a comfortable guest house; the Monastery of Varlaam has a 10-bed guest house. **Metsovo,** in the mountains, known for its home-spun material, gold embroidery, and woodwork, has an attractive exhibit of popular art and handicrafts in the Tossizza mansion; beautiful ikons in Aghia Paraskevi, its principal church; good trout fishing, winter skiing. **Mistra,** a Byzantine city now in silent ruins, is fascinating for a leisurely afternoon picnic. **Mt. Olympus** (Thessaly) is one of the foremost mountaineering centers of the country; you can experience the thrill of ascending the throne by climbing to an alpine refuge. **Mycenae,** with its massive lion gate, palace, hillside tomb with its beehive-shaped central chamber is another must-see; and about five miles south toward **Argos** is the sanctuary of Hera called the Argive Heraion from when Agamemnon set forth to fight the Trojans.

Lovely **Nauplion**/Nafplion/Nauplia is dominated by the Venetian fortress of **Palamidi,** a 999-step inadvisable climb (or short drive by car); the Venetian castle **Pasqualigo** on the island of **Bourtzi** at the harbor entrance is floodlit at night. The **Xenia Palace** and the **Xenia Hotel** are the best places to stay. The **Peloponnesian Folklore Museum** (1 Vass. Alexandrou) is dazzling, open daily, except Tues., and on Sun. and holidays from 10 a.m.–2 p.m. The **Archaeological Museum,** in Syntagma Square, with the same hours—and check these hours, please, before you go—is filled with Neolithic and Mycenaean treasures, including a boar's tusk helmet and a full suit of Mycenaean armor. Possibly the loveliest town in the entire Peloponnesus. **Olympia,** site of the Olympic Games, sprawls out in a serene site, with the **Museum of the Olympic Games** (outstanding philatelic collection) and **Archaeological Museum** (houses the Hermes of Praxiteles and most of the important finds from the ruins). **Parga,** with a Venetian fortress dominating a bay blue as butterflies' wings, is a resort area, and has a magnificent sandy beach. **Patras** is spectacular during carnival—glorious fireworks, streets filled with chariots and costumed, dancing citizens. **Salonika** (or Thessaloniki) has old Turkish-style buildings, marvelous **Archaeological Museum,** Byzantine monuments, and mosaic-filled churches; nearby **beaches** at Aghia Triada and the Mikron Emvolon beach at Aretsou are recommended. This city—childhood playground of Alexander the Great (take the excursion to **Pella,** believed to be his birthplace)—is a modern business center, but the unspoilt countryside of Chalkidiki is noteworthy. Access to the nearby mountain monastery of **Mt. Athos** is strictly taboo "to all children, all female animals; every woman." **Tiryns,** birthplace of Hercules, heavily fortified since prehistoric times, is a most impressive site.

ATTRACTIONS FOR CHILDREN—GREEK ISLANDS No one should visit Greece without taking an island cruise. Apr.–Oct., there are arrangements to suit every vacation span, taste, and wallet—local steamers from island to island at very thrifty prices; cruises from one-day to seven-days. The *Athens News* lists the daily sailings; the weekly schedule is usually available at the GNTO in the National Bank of Greece in Syntagma Square. Cruising saves time over flying since the ship does most of its sailing while you sleep, and you are spared the hassle of packing and unpacking.

Many cruise ships have pools and other amenities for *adults,* but to my mind ONLY the *Stella Solaris* truly caters to children. She is owned by the **Sun Line Co., Inc.** (2 Karageorgi Servias St., Athens; Tel (01) 322–8883), with offices in the U.S. 1 Rockefeller Plaza, Suite 315, NY, NY 10020; Tel: (212) 397–6400; Watts (800) 223–5760, which also dispatches the *Stella Oceanis* and *Stella Maris,* but *only* the *Stella Solaris* has a supervised playroom and programmed entertainment for children; also swimming pool; sauna; gym; movie theater; discotheque; library; doctor and nurses; closed-circuit TV in public rooms and inside staterooms; possibility for arranging babysitting aboard. She sails to Delos, Mykonos, Santorin, Crete, Rhodes and Turkey.

For a general idea of what each island has to offer, be sure to ask for GNTO's handy chart listing the islands, how to get to them, and amenities offered (including yacht facilities)—a most concise and helpful list! **Crete, Corfu,** and **Rhodes** are the most developed of the islands, **Hydra, Mykonos,** and **Spetsai**—are easily reached resorts from Athens with complete up-to-date amenities and a good selection of accommodations (in hotels, bungalows, and private homes).

Attractive and with an adoring following are **Aegina, Cephalonia, Chios** with its distinctive and charmingly decorated houses, **Ios** (many European university students and nude beaches), **Kos, Naxos** (Lord Byron's choice as the most lovely of the Cyclades with its mountains, remote villages with inhabitants who still wear the Cretan costumes of their ancestors), **Paros, Patmos, Poros, Samos, Santorin, Sifnos, Skopelos.** Relatively "untouristy" for the moment are: **Andros, Cythera,**

Folegandros, Kalimnos, Kea, Kithnos, Lesbos, Mylos, Serifos, Syros with its April abundance of wildflowers; **Tinos** with its sacred icon, beautiful villages and dovecotes which are like a mix of dolls' houses and modern art; **Zante.** Really off the beaten track, with simple accommodations and less frequent transportation are: **Alonissos, Amorgos, Antiparos, Astipalaia, Ikaria, Kassos, Kastelorizo** (off the southern coast of Turkey in the Antalyan Gulf, with a perfect horseshoe harbor, and where you may be the only tourists that week), **Karpathos, Samothrace,** and **Thassos** with its summertime drama festival, where you can stay at the Makyrammos Bungalows (Tel: Thassos 22101).

Crete, second-largest island in the Mediterranean, is home of the kri-kri, a chamois Homer referred to as a proud, untamed animal which lives where man cannot go; but if you like, you too can go mountain climbing in any of Crete's three mountain ranges. The **Creta Travel Bureau** (August 25th St., Heraklion; Tel: 282–521) organizes tours. At Heraklion (birthplace of El Greco and author Kazantzakis) look in at the small, appealing **Archaeological Museum,** one of the most important in the world, unique for its Cretan antiquities, and buy the excellent English guidebook. Children delight in the figurines, the baby-bath-shape sarcophagi, the pottery swings that are relics of a culture that held the swing sacred as it made the rider feel like a winged bird; birds, bulls, snakes, and fish had special cults and worshippers, whose ritual jewelry and pottery are particularly charming. Closed Mon. afternoon. **The Historical Museum** has good regional artifacts and handicrafts, plus interesting examples of the Byzantine, Venetian, and Turkish periods. See the **Palace of Minos at Knossos,** a fascinatingly reconstructed Minoan site. The **Plateau of Lassithi** is a wonderful world of 6000 windmills, and grain is still threshed in summer with wooden-yoked oxen. The **Caves of Dicte** at Psychro, where Zeus is said to have been born, should be open for your visit. Few of the island's 3400 caves are accessible to the public. **Anogia** is an embroidery and weaving center with looms in every home; dances in local costumes performed regularly. **Rethimnon,** with its Venetian-Turkish remains, its minarets, its park, little museum, and harbor, is a delight. You can combine a rigorous six-hour trek through the **Gorge of Samaria** (through the White Mountains) with a visit to Sfakia. **Chainia,** the ancient capital, with its orange orchards is pleasant, but a visit to the Minoan palace at **Malia** and then swimming, shopping, and eating at **Aghios Nikolaos** (with beaches, harbor islets—the lighthouse is on one, chamois goats are raised on the other—and volcanic lake) is even more agreeable. From Aghios Nikolaos, a one-hour bus trip from Heraklion, you can take an excursion to the salt-lake of **Elounda,** a six-mile cab ride where there is a beach hotel resort with cottages, via the harbor town of **Schisma** (with hotel and restaurant), from whence you take a 20-minute motorboat ride to the island of **Spinalonga,** which has a Venetian fortress. Many Minoan palaces, settlements, and towns are still being excavated; one of the most interesting is at **Zakro,** where you can relax at the nearby palm-fringed beach of

Vai. From Heraklion archaeological fans should head for the Minoan city of **Phaistos** which is sheer majestic grandeur and the Minoan villas at Hagia Triada. *Tip:* In Heraklion, right by the Astoria Hotel, is **Adam-Rent-A-Scooter.**

Corfu is a joyful resting place—no great sights or archaeological sites, just a place to enjoy for its charm and beauty. It has splendid **beaches** (especially on the west coast) but by far the best is **Glyfada,** with excellent snorkeling and surfing; rowboats for hire. Paradise! The monastery in **Paleokastritsa** houses a spine-tingling array of dinosaur bones; lovely blue coves and grottoes here beside the slopes where Ulysses is said to have landed; savory local lobster and roast lamb. Amble about the old town of **Corfu;** a museum in the Royal Palace has (besides the usual pottery) notable Japanese and Chinese art; fine 18-hole golf course with elaborate clubhouse, swimming pool, and restaurant. You can travel by canvas-tented caique used as a water taxi to **Dassia** where the swimming is lovely and the Albanian coast beckons.

Rhodes (Island of Roses) was an escape resort for Caesar and Cicero, and Hippocrates sent his affluent patients to be cured by its mineral waters. It was a fortress stronghold of the Knights of the Order of St. John, and the ruins of the Trojan War towns of **Lindos, Ialysos,** and **Kamiros** are still well preserved; its medieval walls are very grand indeed; it should be savored at leisure, not hustled in a one-day cruise stop. The **Aquarium** in the town of Rhodes is particularly nice, wonderfully laid out to make you feel as though you're right underwater with the fish. Son et Lumiere of the fall of Rhodes takes place most nights at the **Palace of the Grand Master,** an elaborate reconstruction of a medieval residence, in the mosaic-floored formal gardens; concerts and plays are presented in the palace courtyard. Ancient Greek tragedy is staged in a restored 700-seat amphitheater on Mount Smith. The new open-air theater created around a vast courtyard within the heart of the medieval quarter of Rhodes presents a nightly program of folklore ballet with happy music. A very special museum housed in the old **Knights' Hospital** has a room of creamy-, pink-, and fawn-colored marble statues (sea-smoothed Aphrodite is remarkable) and an outside courtyard (with mosaics, fountains, and an old Venetian marble lion). Hidden away in the backroom of the tiny **Turkish Library** (end of Orpheos St.) are some illuminated manuscripts of Arabic calligraphy. Rhodes also has an 18-hole golf course, with minigolf, tennis, a private harbor and beach, restaurant, and a children's playground.

A pleasant ten-mile excursion through pinewoods is **Philerimos,** with hilltop ruins of a small Byzantine church, a monastery, a temple; a short walk away is the famous Doric Fountain on the site of ancient Ialysos, a lovely place to picnic. The one-half-hour drive to the **Valley of the Butterflies** (Petaloudes) brings you to a breathtaking valley dotted with little benches hewn out of old trees, rickety bridges across shallow streams poured into by waterfalls (in July and Aug. best before 10 a.m. or in the early evening); at the sound of a whistle or a clap of the hands, thousands of small brown butterflies with red-marked wings fly into the air, then disappear again into the trees. On the way to **Petaloudes,** stop along the coastal road at **Krimasti** village, to see children and men carving olive wood into figurines and bowls, and at the **Nassos** ceramic factory that turns out all that lovely Rhodes pottery; behind the shops are kilns, potters, and small boys hand-painting designs. The fortress town of **Lindos** is beautiful, with its temple to Athena, crusader-built castle and church; artists' colony; a donkey ride up to save you a one-half-hour walk, but the divine beach below is alone worth the trip—with its luminescent water, ideal for wading, swimming, and underwater fishing.

Aegina, readily accessible from Athens, has wonderfully carved mountains, rolling valleys, great sweeps of pine, vineyards, orchards; good roads; swimming and fishing a beautiful temple to Aphaea; a few ruins to explore; several hotels with detached bungalows, among them the Hydra Beach Hotel, which has a beach and a supervised children's playground, a swimming pool, and the usual complement of tourist amenities including open-air cinema. **Alonissos,** undeveloped and ideal for underwater fishing has wonderfully cheap guest houses in Patitiri. **Chios,** a charmer, still has low prices. **Delos** (reached by caique from Mykonos) is the supposed birthplace of Apollo; extensive ruins and small museum; great mosaics; children will like collecting potshards on the hillsides and chasing lizards; a few hours, with a swim, is an adequate visit. **Hydra** (a quick trip from Athens) is a yachting center and haven for artists and far-out types. **Kos** is rich in Hellenic, Byzantine, medieval, and Turkish remains; the birthplace of Hippocrates and the sanctuary of Aesculapius (god of medicine); beaches for bathing and fishing; nice small museum; Roman villa with admirable mosaics; life is exquisitely leisurely. On **Lesbos,** whose capital town of Mytilene is dominated by a giant fortress castle, the life of the island centers around the harbor; worth a visit is the studio of popular painter Theophilos; artists and intellectuals find their way to Methyma, an attractive town.

Mykonos, arid, craggy, set about with white houses and fig trees, and having lively waterfront esplanade, is all too popular; nude beaches; a handful of white-sailed windmills around the town. **Paros** where the Parian marble comes from, has a sleazy bayside, a Venetian fortress, the Church of One Hundred Doors, an exaggerated miscount, but with splendid icons within, a good archaeological museum; Naoussa is the place to stay here. Attractive beaches.

Patmos is where you can see sponges alive in the sea and dried for sale. The treasury of the fortified monastery of St. John is rich and beautiful. Taxi up to it, and ride down on a donkey. Many windmills, and a beach where sea-polished stones look like striped toffee. Accessible by boat or ferry. **Poros,** with sandy coves and pine-covered slopes, is pretty, an ideal spot for fishing and a good base for excursions into the Peloponnese. **Samos** has magnificent sandy beaches. White sand, no jellyfish. Low prices. Samian wine with which Anthony toasted Cleopatra. Its temple of Hera is overgrown with weeds, but in Vathi, the capital, a lovely little port town, the museum is excellent and behind it, a zoo with deer, an aviary, plashing fountains, a coin-operated horse for children to ride. You can fly here in 30 minutes from Athens, and can then make a three-hour ferry excursion to Ephesus, for which arrangements must be made for visas and messing about with passports at least a day in advance. The volcanic, crescent-shape island of **Santorin** (Thira), a major target of most cruises, is thought to be the lost continent of Atlantis Plato described; its steep cliffs, topped with the gleaming white town of Thira (which possesses possibly more churches than barrel-vaulted houses), are traversed by a zigzag path of 587 steps one negotiates on the back of a donkey (a bit scary to most children as the donkeys seemingly want to brush you off against the protective walls). Also a funicular; it might be fun to stay a few days to see the excavations of a **Minoan city** at **Akrotiri** which have produced interesting pottery and enormous storage vessels painted with abstract octopus patterns. Accommodations here are inexpensive.

Skiathos is attracting increasing numbers of tourists who delight in **Koukounaries beach,** the finest in the area, with the Sklathos Palace Hotel. On **Skopelos,** accommodation is mostly in village guest houses; wonderful green and purple plums here. **Skiros,** where poet Rupert Brooke is buried, is famous for its wild ponies, its handicrafts, attractive beaches and underwater fishing. **Spetsai** is more social a retreat, with good **beaches** such as Costa and Aghioi Anargyroi, Aghia Marina and Sogheria. **Thasos,** lying off the coast of Thrace in the north, celebrates a Festival of Ancient Theater during July and Aug. Green, cool; beautiful beaches. Old villages. Many young people. Leave your car in Thessaloniki and rent one on the island to avoid the hassle of a crowded car-ferry service.

FUN TRIPS A spectacular 45-minute ride aboard the **Kalavrita Railway** from Dhiakofto (about 10 miles east of Patras) wends its way through deep gorges, tunnels, and precipitous cliffs to Zakhlorous. From here, hop on a donkey to visit the monastery on the hill above the village, or take the train to overnight in another monastery at Kalavrita. Regular service three or four times a day; *very* cheap.

From Piraeus, ferry boats and steamers (old-fashioned, casual, scruffy, very cheap) chug regularly to scores of ports and islands. Speedy and inexpensive day trips can be made to islands on a hovercraft from the **Zeas Marina** (Tel: (01) 452–7107). **Olympic Airways** (96 Syngrou Ave., Tel: (01) 923–2323) helicopter and air taxi service is reasonably priced; the summer hydrofoil to the Saronic islands is delightful. Car ferries whisk you to Italy from Piraeus (to Venice and Ancona) and Patras (to Ancona and Brindisi—these have children's playrooms!).

The best family holiday fun in Greece is ***sailing.*** *Greece for the*

Yachtsman, published by the GNTO, gives information about weather, navigation, regulations, port facilities, charter contracts, suggested cruises, and helpful telephone numbers. Further information from the **Royal Yacht Club of Greece** (Mikrolimanon, Piraeus, Tel: 479730).

With the incomparable beauty of the Greek seas and islands, with fishing and skin-diving equipment (provided on many yachts or for hire on the islands), with antiquities on almost every island, and with fabulous seafood and plenty of wine, ***cruising*** in Greece can be the experience of a lifetime. Approximately 2000 private yachts of every type and size are available for chartering through agencies in Athens and Piraeus. Prices run from reasonable to sky's-the-limit; if you split the cost with friends, a yacht with crew need not run you any more than would a moderate-priced hotel. All you need to navigate are the British Admiralty charts and the Greek Hydrographic Service charts, appropriate pilot-guides, and Captain H.M. Denham's Sea-Guides to the Eastern Mediterranean and the Aegean. Two good yacht brokers are **Valef Yachts** (Akti Themistokleous 22, Piraeus; Tel: (01) 452–9571, evenings (01) 452–9486; cable Wilefa Piraeus; Telex 212000 Val Greece) and **B. Koutsoukellis** 6 Ermou St., Athens; Tel: 322–7011; cable Kellistour; Telex 215315 Yach Greece). Both can send excellent brochures; offerings range from an air-conditioned 64-footer (accommodating 8–10; saloon and bar; two bathrooms; water-ski boat; a crew of four including cook) to 177′ motor yachts; sailing yacht with auxiliary engines, accommodating eight with a couple of crew members; caiques (cheapest). American Travel (see Information) offers *The Odyssey* (50′, crew of two, sleeps eight in three cabins). The GNTO can provide further information and list of yacht brokers and consultants affiliated with the Hellenic Yacht Owners Association. Augustus van Seggelen of **Seahorse Rent-A-Yacht** (see Fun and Games) charters bare boats or skippered cruisers, open sloops, catamarans, ocean cruisers, motor sailers, and motor yachts; reasonable prices; *one of the best deals going in the Athens area* are his skippered day trips for four people to an uninhabited island of caves and beaches. Besides renting quality yachts designed by Sparkman and Stephens of New York, luxurious ketches and sloops, motor-sailers, Greek caiques, von Seggelen arranges bareboat and *flotilla charters* along the Turkish coast from Kusadasi and Marmaris, booked through the Glyfada office. Other flotilla charters are available. For sailing enthusiasts, flotilla sailing allows for freedom and independence, as well as security and convivial gatherings at landfall. At Porto Carras, in Chalkidiki, southeast of Thessaloniki, **Hellas Charters** (24 Dodecanisou St., Thessaloniki; Tel: (031) 540–373, 538–648) operates a flotilla of about a dozen vessels which each sleep four to six, each boat also equipped with a radio to keep in touch with the pilot boat. Handling luxury crew-operated yachts in the U.S. is the wonderful agency, **World Yacht Enterprises** (14 West 55th St., NY, NY 10019; Tel: (212) 246–4811). For a family of four a 43′ ketch would run the same as a moderate hotel, but you could also splurge on a larger boat. This extremely reliable organization is highly recommended. *Special!* Christopher Bowles and his Swedish wife, Kerstin, who have two children of their own, specialize in arranging luxury yacht charters in the Aegean and the southern coast of Turkey aboard their own yacht, *Viking Girl* (a 57′ motor-sailing vessel) and other choices, larger and smaller. They provide snorkeling, windsurfing, speargun, waterskiing gear for their passengers—usually no more than six—and cruises aboard the *Viking Girl* with Chris as captain and Kerstin as gourmet cook are enthusiastically recommended as personal, individualized, tremendous fun, and fascinating. Write for itineraries (you can also chart your own) and information to **World Holidays Afloat,** 16 High St., Woodstock, Oxfordshire, England; Tel; (0993) 811–183.

Rides in small boats are available at almost every beach for a pittance. Every island has motor launch services that will run you around the island, take you fishing, snorkeling, scuba-diving, waterskiing; these are fun as the children can often reach overboard to capture a live sponge.

FUN AND GAMES ***Scuba diving*** is wonderful and, with no currents or tides to fight, few sharks and no barracudas, Greek waters are among the safest in the world away from jellyfish areas, which vary from year to year. Diving cruises are available out of Athens to Salamis, Aegina, and Poros; very reasonable for certified divers (having completed a 3rd-class course); amateurs must pay extra for an English-speaking Dive Master. On one-day cruises a picnic lunch is served aboard; departures 9:30 a.m. Sat., Sun., Mon., Tues.; diving and snorkeling equipment is provided; you can also collect sea sponges and shells. On three-day cruises accommodation (either Cabin Class or Lounge Class) is aboard the dive boat. Contact **Argo Diving Cruises** (11 Niki St., Athens; Tel: (01) 322–4321). You have to provide your own equipment plus diving certification and statement from doctors stating fitness for diving.

Greek seas abound in fish, and anglers will find Greek fishermen very helpful in pinpointing happy ***fishing*** grounds. The Saronikos Gulf is especially popular; almost every coastal village hires out fishing boats and motorboats for very little; tackle and bait can be bought from harbor shops or in open-air markets along the sea front. Good trout areas in northern and central Greece. For further information: **The Amateur Anglers and Maritime Sports Club** (Aki Moutsopoulou, Zea Harbor, Piraeus: Tel: (01) 451–5731). Spear-gun fishermen can enjoy this sport safely along the shores of Mt. Athos, the Sporades, Lesbos, Limnos, the southern Peloponnesus, Kefalinia, and elsewhere. The use of portable oxygen apparatus is allowed only along the coast of the Calkidiki Peninsula and the Ionian islands. The **Greek Confederation of Spear Gun Fishermen** (Aghios Kosmas; Tel: (01) 981–7166) organizes instruction seminars in July and Aug. with four-hour lessons daily for a week. The private school **Kartelia** (3 Karageorgi Servias St. in Kastela,

Tel: (01) 412–2047) offers six-to-eight day courses. Rhodes also has a spear-gun-fishing school.

Sailing instruction: Championship yachtsman Augustus van Seggelen, an extraordinarily attractive Netherlander who has made Athens his home, runs the wonderful school, **Seahorse Rent-a-Yacht** (Marina 4, Glyfada; Tel: (01) 894–8503) with instruction in 20-foot, unsinkable self-bailing open sloops. Courses (each a minimum of 10 hours) are: Basic (introduction to boat and rigging, basic skills from setting sails to running and coming about, and man-overboard maneuvers); Intermediate (heavy-waters techniques, capsizing, reefing, spinnaker); and Advanced (spinnaker, disabled boat, navigation, maintenance, introduction to large yachts). Course prices are based on a boat accommodating four students plus instructor, so a family of four (or four friends) can share the cost. Augustus also rents yachts (see Fun Trips).

Waterskiing in the Athens area is particularly good at Lake Ireon at Vouliagmeni; near Loutraki, where the **Automobile Touring Club of Greece,** ELPA, provides visitors with all essentials. Lake Ioannina and the island of Salamis are also popular. Waterskiing schools are prevalent.

Children's ***swimming lessons?*** Head for the nearest **Naval Club;** instructors always on hand; no problem about tides, currents, rough water; water crystal clear almost everywhere. In Athens, the Hilton Hotel's pool is where the young folk like to make a splash. Guests swim for free, non-guests have to pay cash. Call before setting out: (01) 722–0201. For locations of other pools which are members also of the **Swimming Federation of Greece** (2 Nicodemou St., Athens), call (01) 323–8025.

In Athens, every Wed. and Sat. ***horse races*** start at the **Phaleron Race Course** at 2:30 p.m. You can ***ride*** at the **Hellenic Riding Club,** 19 Paradissou St. in Amaroussion; Tel: (01) 682–6128; 681–2506); for others, ask the **Athens Horse Riding Club** (Gerakas; Tel: (01) 661–1088). ***Donkey rides*** through village streets and on island roads are available everywhere out of Greece's main towns. Don't worry if this sounds vague. Once you're there, you'll see how easy it is. Just see a man with a donkey, point to your child, and the next thing you know, your child is hoisted up and led off for less than you would pay for a subway ride back home.

In most towns you can rent ***bicycles;*** ask your concierge. The phonetic pronunciation of "Is there a bicycle renting shop?" *(Epahi katastima ennikeassios podilaton?)*—Ay-pah-he cah-tahs-teem-uh ay-nee-kee-ahss-yos po-dee-lah-tone—seems to produce results without any great strain. For ***tennis,*** the **Athens Tennis Club** (2 Vassilissis Olgas; Tel: (01) 923–2872) charges either an enrollment fee or by the day. At **Agios Kosmas** sportsgrounds (which also has go-karting and everything else) you can rent a racket and balls for less than 25¢! Use of courts at **Voula** and **Vouliameni** is cheap. ***Golfers*** can rent clubs, buy balls, and pay nominal greens fees at the excellent **Glyfada** 18-hole course. (Rhodes and Corfu have the only two other 18-hole courses, both super.) Minigolf at the **Kalamaki Club** (Akti Possidonos); instructor available afternoons.

Details on small game ***shooting*** (season Sept.–Feb.) from the **Confederation of Hunting** (2 Korai St., Athens; Tel: (01) 323–1212). A glorious two-week wild-boar shooting festival takes place in Jan. at the River Evros delta (Derei-Dadias area). ***Mountain climbing?*** You'll find huts with 16–100 beds on all the mountains, both on the mainland and the islands; details from the **Mountaineering Club** (7 Karagieorgi Servias St., Athens; Tel: (01) 323–4555).

Greece has some 7000 ***caves,*** some just dark holes and others glittering stalactite fairylands that you can negotiate by foot or rowboat. Of the latter, only eight are set up for ordinary tourists: **Koutouki cave** about 17 miles out of Athens toward Messogia; **Perama cave** at Epirus near Lake Ioannina; three adjoining caves in the gulf of **Diros; Lake Melissani cave** at Kefalinia; the cave on **Antiparos** islet near the island of Paros. Spelunkers can consult the **Hellenic Speleological Society** (11 Mantzarou St., Athens; Tel: (01) 361–7824).

In winter, you can ***ski,*** and the GNTO can tell you all about it. (But who wants to go to Greece when it's snowing?)

SHOPPING WITH AND FOR CHILDREN Wonderful! A treasure trove of bargains! Greece abounds in attractive regional handicrafts: Gold charms, jewelry; woven bags (ideal as bookbags); fun furs and embroidered clothing; needlepoint pillows; leather and bead belts; fishermen's sweaters; costumed dolls; rugs, handwoven, and *flokatis,* made of lambswool, thick and shaggy, sold by weight; carved metal and wood figurines and chess sets; pottery. The inexpensive worry beads come in endless variations and colors. Sponges, potshards, and beautiful shells and beach stones ranging from Santorin's smooth, polished black lava ones and hunks of pumice to unusual mottled and marbleized island stones are available for free or a few pennies.

Shopping hours from May to Oct. are 8:45 a.m.–1:45 p.m.; 4:15 p.m.–7:45 p.m. In winter, 8 a.m.–1:30 p.m., 5–8 p.m. Food shops, barber shops, and hairdressers close Wed. afternoon; all other shops close Sat. afternoon.

In **Athens,** the **flea market** (Monasteraki) can be found in full swing on Sun. at the end of the first part of Hermou St. around Omonia Sq.

For ***handicrafts,*** Athinas St. is filled with shops selling traditional crafts, and the area is fun for children and collectors. **National Organization of Hellenic Handicrafts** (9 Mitropoleos St.) in Athens, and with branches and showrooms in Alexandroupolis, Corfu, Chanea, Ionnina, Patras, Rhodes, Thessaloniki and elsewhere. Also in Athens, the **Hellenic Artisan Trades Cooperative** (56 Amalias Ave.); **The YWCA,** (11 Amerikis St., with branches in Kifissia and Thessaloniki; Corfu, Rethymnon in Crete, Pireaus, Rhodes, Sima, Thira on Santorin and elsewhere); **Ethniki Pronia Institute,** 6 Ipatias St., Athens. For flokati rugs and wares (original colors of white, gray and brown are preferable to the dyed products which fade), the best shops for service, quality and reasonable prices in Athens are: **Vlaha Flokatis** (19 and 27 Mitropoleos St.); **Don Sebastian's home workshop** (5 Ipiridou St., a block from Syntagma Square); in Glyfada, **Nicolakopoulos Flokatis** (3 Xanthou St.). Toys can be found at **El Greco** (Solonos St.). **A. Pallis** (8 Hermou St.), has art supplies, coloring books, and American comic books with Greek dialogue which are fun.

The fun shopping, the real bargains, though, are at the points of origin of local handicrafts. Out of Athens, prices drop, and you can bargain a bit.

On **Rhodes, Phoebus** (36B Orfeos St.) will ship home for you marvelous brass chess sets in the Minoan fashion (bulls for pawns, crenellated oakleaf thrones for rooks, handsome kings and queens), furs, shirts, and souvenirs; ask for Nick Koufos.

In **Mykonos,** you can buy fishermen's sweaters in every quayside boutique. Needlepoint rugs in folkloric patterns, beautiful for children's rooms, are best bought at **Epiros, Florina, Skyros.** The woolen things in **Metsovo** are charming and unique.

▶ **Note:** Newsstand kiosks also sell worry beads, pencils, paper pads, combs, shoelaces, suntan lotion, toothpaste, candy, chewing gum, etc. There are many of these tiny dispensaries, and they're very handy and agreeable.

GREEK FRIENDS AND PEN PALS Write in advance to the GNTO in Athens.

CALENDAR OF EVENTS I can include here only the largest celebrations, so please check with the GNTO for local events during your visit and also to verify the dates given below:

Jan. 1 is ***St. Basil's day,*** when gifts are exchanged throughout Greece. On Jan. 6, crosses are immersed in sea, river, or fountain for the ***Blessing of The Waters*** ceremony throughout Greece; grandest festivities are at Pireaus. On Jan. 8, women in Komotini Xanthi, Kilkis, and Serea go to the cafes while their husbands attend to housework and the children.

From mid-**Feb.**–early **Mar.,** ***Carnival*** is celebrated throughout Greece with masked dances, processions, dancing in the streets, and fireworks; lively crowds in Athens, Patras, Myrsini, Naoussa, and Rethymnon (Crete), but fun too on smaller islands (Skyros, Corfu, Zakynthos, etc.). On Shrove Monday, Greeks flock to the country for picnics of delicacies (especially seafood such as lobster and oyster) and kite-flying. Also in Mar., Thebes celebrates a ***Mock Peasant Wedding*** (with costumes, wine drinking, and dancing in the streets) and the ***Feast of the Annunciation*** is celebrated throughout Greece, but especially on Tinos.

Apr. 10–12, Kalimnos island has ***folk dancing*** and other festivities to celebrate the sailing of the sponge divers. On ***Good Friday*** there's an impressive procession to the Cathedral in Athens, and another (candle-lit) winds up Lycabettus Hill; waterfront processions also on Hydra and Corfu. On ***Holy Saturday*** outdoor midnight Resurrection services are held throughout Greece, followed by rejoicing and fireworks. Throughout Greece ***Easter Sunday*** is celebrated outdoors, with lambs roasted on a spit and folk dancing in costume; especially famous are the festivities in Livadia (visitors are offered wine and Easter eggs), Kalamata (includes a dart-throwing competition), Tripoli, Vityna, Dimitsana, Ioannina, Hydros, and Andros. In late Apr., Arahova and on Lemnos and Kos islands celebrate ***St. George's day*** with horse races, feasting, and dancing. Megara has a ***fair*** with folk dancing.

On **May** 1–2 ***orange festivals*** with singing and dancing competitions are held in the orchards near Chania, Crete. In Athens' suburbs, ***flower festivals*** on May 1 include a parade of decorated chariots. ***Folk dancing*** can be seen in early May at local celebrations in Trikeri and Cephalonia, and on May 21 (St. Constantine and St. Helen day) throughout Greece. May 21 is most spectacular in Langhada and Aghia Eleni when ***firewalkers*** enter into trances at the beating of a drum and then dance barefoot on live coals. On May 22 Tripoli celebrates the ***Feast of St. Paul*** and on May 26 Crete celebrates its ***1821 revolution*** at Sfakia.

On **June** 21, there are ***regattas*** and at Volos, a re-enactment of the sailing of the Argonauts. On June 24, throughout Greece, wreaths are burned in ***bonfires,*** and children jumping over their wreaths have their wishes come true. In June and **July** there are ***naval fetes*** in Athens, Piraeus, Kalamaki, and on Salamis. The ***Epidaurus festival*** takes place June–Aug.; the ***Athens festival*** July–Sept.

In **Aug.**–Sept., festivals in Philippi Dodoni, Ioannina, Paros, Zante, Kos, and on Thasos, and ***ancient dramas*** Eleusis are performed by the State Theatre of Northern Greece. Also in Aug., the ***Lukas Festival of Art and Literature*** includes lectures, poetry reading, mandolin serenades, handicrafts displays, pantomimes, and folk dancing from all over the world. Aug. 15 (Assumption) is an important religious holiday with ***festivals and fairs*** in many areas, celebrated with great pageantry on the island of Tinos, and a ***Mock Peasant Wedding*** in Gardiki. Aug. 23 (St. Agatha), Aitolikon has two days of festivities with folk dancing. Aug. 29, Serres' ***religious festival*** includes local costumes and dances.

During the 2nd week in **Sept.,** Heraklion celebrates the ***Grape Festival*** with exhibits, dancing, music. The ***Pilgrimage to the Monastery*** in Chania (Crete) takes place **Oct.** 6–7. In late Oct., the ***Dimitria Festival*** of music, dance, and drama takes place in Thessaloniki. On Oct. 20, Pylos celebrates the naval battle of Navarine with folk dancing and other events. On **Oct.** 28, a national holiday commemorating Greece's entry into WW II, large cities (especially Athens and Thessaloniki) have ***military parades.***

On **Dec.** 24, children go from house to house caroling and playing triangles. Dec. 25, Christmas celebrations. Dec. 31, on Chinos island, local seamen parade with ship's models and sing folksongs. The New Year is welcomed with an exchange of gifts, singing, games of chance.

LANGUAGE AND PHRASEBOOK Outside of hotels, tourist shops, and major restaurants, you certainly can't count on everyone speaking and understanding English, so phrasebooks and dictionaries are a great help. It is remarkably easy to learn the alphabet and the phonetic pronunciation of key words. Children like learning Greek as it seems no more difficult to them than figuring out runic code messages in Tolkien's *The Hobbit*.

Hello (how do you do)	*Pooze ees thay*
I am an American	*Ee may Amerikanos (boy)*
	Ee may Amerikana (girl)
My name is	*Oh no mah zo may*
I am____years old	*Ee may____ay tone*
Please	*Para kahlo*
Thank you	*Eff hahr eestoe*
I can't speak Greek	*Den mee lao ayleeneeka*
Yes	*Nay*
No	*On he*
I am having a wonderful time	*Ta pare now or ray ah*
1	*ay nuh*
2	*dee oh*
3	*tree oh*
4	*tess erruh*
5	*pen tay*
6	*ex he*
7	*ep tuh*
8	*ok toe*
9	*enn nay uh*
10	*decks*
Goodbye	*Add dee oh*

ICELAND

Iceland, with a large population of young people, geologically a land-child among the older countries of the world, is filled with natural wonders that delight a child's eye: purple mountains; white glaciers; active volcanoes you can safely watch, vast lava fields frequented by American astronauts to familiarize themselves with moonlike terrain; unpolluted skies, perpetually golden in summer nights, shimmering with Northern Lights in fall and winter; rivers and lakes abounding in trout and salmon; rushing waterfalls and geysers; and a stunning variety of birds—including rare little auks, and clown-faced puffins.

Everyone is addressed, according to ancient Norse custom, by his or her first name (even in the telephone directory listings are alphabetized by first name). A woman is allowed to keep her maiden name after marriage, and every Icelander is known as the son or daughter of his or her father, i.e. Agusta, the daughter of Bjorn, or Agusta Bjornsdottir; Helgi, the son of Arna, or Helgi Arnason. The nation is known for fascinating chronicles and sagas written in the 12th and 13th centuries; an extraordinary collection of illuminated histories, transcribed narrations (sagas), transcribed spoken poetry (eddas) of breathtaking strength and forthrightness describing their life, their land, their battles, and their boats, those great ''sailing swans'' whose bows chiseled the sea into spray-storms. English translations of *Njal's Saga, King Harald's Saga, Laxdaela Saga, Volsunga Saga,* and *Eirik the Red* are highly recommended reading for teenagers.

No reason to worry about the cold—summers average out at 50° or 60°; encircling the island, the Gulf Stream warms the air; natural hot springs supply home and greenhouse heating. May–Oct. is the best time to visit, but Nov.–Mar. is acceptable if you don't mind having only five to eight hours of daylight. Iceland has no unemployment, no poverty, and no pollution!

INFORMATION ABOUT ICELAND Write or call Iceland National Tourist Board (75 Rockefeller Plaza, New York, NY 10019; Tel: (212) 582–2802) for brochures. For information about transportation, contact Icelandair (630 Fifth Ave., New York, NY 10111; Tel: (212) 572–9440).

Once in **Reykjavik,** for all questions and help with individualized flights, call Icelandair (Tel: 26011) or Eagle Air (Tel: 29577). The **Iceland National Tourist Board** (Laugavegi 3, Reykjavik Tel: 27488) knows exactly what children love to do. In **Akureyri,** the tourist board is at Radhustorg 3; Tel: 25000. ***Telephone information:*** in Reykjavik, time: 04; weather: 17000; Bible selections: 10000; all in Icelandic.

Recommended especially as travel agents is the Iceland Tourist Bureau (Reykjanesbraut 3, Reykjavik; Tel: 25855). The Iceland National Tourist *Board* is the government information agency; the Iceland Tourist *Bureau* will help you book travel arrangements and are knowledgeable about special interest tours such as photography, geology, nature and wildlife, locations of Viking ruins, pony trekking, bird-watching. They are also the people to consult about farmhouse vacations (see Accommodation). In Akureyri, a good agency is **Ferdamidstodin Travel** (Geislagotu 10, Akureyri; Tel: (96) 24970). The city telephone code of Reykjavik is 1; for Akureyri (96), for the Westman Islands (98). The **Iceland Automobile Club** (FIB) is located at Noatun 17, Reykjavik; Tel: 29999.

▶ **Note:** Bring a bathing suit whether you're traveling in summer or winter, because swimming is a national Icelandic pastime; indoor and outdoor pools are plentiful. The weather is as temperamental sometimes as a 2-year-old. Brilliant sunshine, clouds, rain and sun again can all occur within an hour on a summer day. Sunglasses, an extra sweater and a fold-up travel umbrella are musts. Driving on gravel roads in the country can be dusty going and glasses are useful to protect your eyes from dust as well as sun-glare. In spite of these seeming negatives, Iceland's food, and fresh, crystalline air are both wondrously invigorating and revitalizing.

Tipping, although not expected, is appreciated, particularly by waiters.

HEALTH, WATER, AND FOOD Iceland's health standards are tops. The cold water, piped from icy reservoirs, is pure and delicious. The hot water, tapped from underground springs, is sulfurous (anything silver washed in it will turn black). To use hot water for drinking or for mixing with powdered-milk baby formulas, you have to heat cold water.

The food is a yummy blend of American and Scandinavian specialties. Eggs are eggs; bacon is bacon; ham, *skinka;* orange juice, *appelsinusafi;* tomato juice, *tomatsafi;* grapefruit juice, *grapeadinsafi;* fresh milk, *mjolk;* cheese, *ostur;* a roll, *runstykki;* butter, *smjor;* marmalade, *marmelad;* jam, *sulta;* toast, *ristad braud;* wheat thins with butter, *hrokkbraud m/smjor*. What we call Danish pastry, the Icelanders call Icelandic pastry, or *Vinarbraud,* which they home-bake. All of the above are on the breakfast menu for hungry children, plus a specialty, *skyr* (pronounced skeer), the national dish. Made under rigidly sanitary conditions from pasteurized skim milk, low in fats, highly nutritious. An ideal baby food, and a good substitute for cottage cheese. Served with sugar. You can sample 40 varieties of Icelandic cheeses at Ostabudin in Reykjavik (Snorrabraut 54; Bitruhals 2).

Apart from Coca-Cola and *ostborgari* and *hamborgari* (cheeseburgers and hamburgers, not quite as good as they are at home), children will enjoy *wienerschnitzel* (veal); hot chocolate; cold cuts of all varieties; lamb and pork chops; omelets; tiny pink shrimp *(raekjur);* salmon (*lax,* pronounced lox); roast beef *(uxasteik);* roast lamb *(lambasteik);* chicken salad *(haensnasalat);* and open-faced sandwiches, *samloka m/skinku og osti* (with ham and cheese). Rye bread is *rugbraud,* white bread *franskbraud,* whole wheat bread *heilhveitibraud.* Pancakes with whipped cream and jam are the national afternoon snack. Candy is *saelgati,* or *gott* (sweet) for short. Cakes and icings tend to be overly sweet, as do napoleons and French pastries, but the doughnuts are great. *Skarnsa,* a sort of thick pancake, is good with cheese for instant picnic sandwiches. Beware of the lollipops: they temporarily stain children's teeth and tongues.

The buffet luncheon cold table at many hotels and restaurants features fish, including dried halibut *(riklingur)* and dried haddock *(hardfiskur);* also, smoked lamb *(hangikjot);* and delicacies such as shark meat *(haskarl);* sheep heads *(blodmor* and *svid*) ground and processed.

In Reykjavik, if the excellent salads of vegetables, fish, or lobster and shrimp—always with mayonnaise—aren't sufficiently filling to ward off hunger pangs until supper, try the inexpensive cafes: **Hressingarskalinn** (Austurstraeti 20), popular also for morning and afternoon tea and coffee; **Askur** (Sudurlandsbraut 14; Tel: 38550), a snack bar and grill that also delivers; **Mjolkurbar** (Laugavegur 162), a self-service milk bar. For tea and cold snacks, the **Mokka-Espresso** (Skolavordoustigur 3A), patronized by Icelandic painters, exhibits their works; for grills and more elaborate meals, **Le Gourmet** (Hafnarstraeti 19). Another fine place for coffee is **Nordic House.** In a town of excellent bakeries, a long-time favorite is **Arnabakari** (Falkagata 18). **Torfan,** a restaurant housed in a 19th-century residence (Amtmannsstigur 1) is a delight for lunch or dinner, as is **Hornid (Haffnarstaeti** 15), another cozy restaurant located in one of Reykjavik's oldest houses. Down by the quayside in old Reykjavik is **Naust,** a treat for children with its old sailing ship decor (6–8 Vesturgata). More casual and less pricey is **Kaffivaghinn** on the fish wharf (Grandagardi 10). **Lakjarbrekka** (Bankastraeti 2; Tel: 14430) is a refreshing a place to eat. Soothing decor. Delicious pastries on the breakfast menu served from 8:30 a.m.–11 a.m. From 11:30 a.m., a varied menu with moderate prices offered in this tastefully restored 150-year-old house which once belonged to a Dane by the name of Bernhoft, whose family were the only bakers in Reykjavik for two generations. For a picnic lunch, supermarket cold meats, fruit, cheese, *skyr,* and milk—supplemented with bakery goodies—will provide a healthy feast.

BABY FOOD Pablum, Heinz, and Gerber products are obtainable at supermarkets (see Silli and Valdi under Shopping). **SMA** and **Litamin** are obtainable at any large *apotek* (pharmacy); **Reykjavikur Apotek** (Austurstraeti 16; Tel: 11760) is especially recommended.

DIAPERS AND LAUNDRY A cloth diaper is *bleija* (pronounced blaya); the word for disposable diapers is pronounced pappish blayur. Both kinds are available in Reykjavik, with cloth and gauze diapers sold in baby specialty shops and at **Vidir** (Austurstraeti 17). Softdown and Finess disposables can be bought at most pharmacies. Mami Ble-Buks, imported from Denmark and sold at baby specialty shops, are wetproof outerpants into which disposable diapers can be inserted. No diaper service, but your hotel's reception desk will arrange for diapers to be laundered and returned the same day.

BABY EQUIPMENT FOR HIRE No organized service. Inquire at your hotel's reception desk.

EMERGENCIES MADE EASY Medicines and prescriptions are available at any *apotek;* for locations, ask your hotel reception desk. For an emergency prescription or pharmacy *(apotek),* dial 18888 in Reykjavik. **Reykjavik City Hospital** (Borgarspitali; Tel: 81200) is excellent. For an emergency doctor on weekdays, call 11510, nights and weekends, 21230. An American-trained pediatrician, **Dr. Bjorn Gudbrandsson** (Braedraborgarstigur 26; Tel: 19995); at home (Graenuhlid 6; Tel: 33995). English-speaking doctors are easy to find in Reykjavik and Akureyri. Outside of Reykjavik, dentists are scarce. An orthodonist, **Thordur E. Magnusson** (Domus Medica, Egilsgata 3; Tel: 14723). The **American Embassy** (Laufasvegur 21; Tel: 29100) can further inform you about English-speaking doctors.

MAGIC FAMILY HELPERS Babysitters are greatly in demand. There is no organized agency, so ask your hotel reception desk. Try schoolgirls on summer vacation; they're competent and mature.

Reykjavik's ***playgrounds*** *(leikvollur)* are supervised by adults; a 5- or 6-year-old will be safely entertained for an hour or so. For location, ask your hotel.

HAPPY FAMILY ACCOMMODATIONS In **Reykjavik,** most expensive and elegant is the **Hotel Saga;** 8th-floor restaurant overlooking the bay, mountains, and city; barbershop, hairdresser; sauna; bank; souvenir shop; florist; travel bureau; and the USIS library. Situated at the airport—and fortunately soundproofed—is the **Hotel Loftleidir** (Tel: 22322); abundant modern conveniences include telephone, radio, TV, and temperature control in each of its 219 guestroom-and-bath combinations;

hairdresser, barber; travel office; gift shop; sauna, masseur; indoor swimming pool (an excellent place to meet young Icelanders) plus a tub pool with sulfurous water to relax in. Erling Aspelund, the resident director, deserves medals for his wisdom; his reception desk can solve any problem from locating babysitters to delivering hot milk to your room at 2 a.m. **Hotel Gardur** (Hringbraut; Tel: 15656, 15918), on the campus of the University of Iceland, offers bright, clean, simple, modern suites with living room, kitchen, bedroom, bath, and balcony. Use of playground and child-care is available, as well as self-service restaurant and coffee shop with reasonably priced open-faced sandwiches, pastries. Close to downtown Reykjavik and with the University Bookstore housed in the same building, this might be a fine base for a budget-minded family. Rooms with running water, but no private bath, also available.

Around the country, modern boarding schools, scenically sited and within easy reach of many of Iceland's spectacular natural wonders, are converted to EDDA hotels during the summer, many with restaurants and swimming pool. Single rooms that can be doubles only if you bring your own sleeping bag, all with h/c water and ample bathroom facilities on every floor. Good bases for the budget-minded touring family, but about five times as expensive as Iceland's eight **Youth Hostels,** which offer singles and doubles with bath, breakfast, and no stay limitations; *only if you have a Youth Hostel card,* for about $6, in Reykjavik, Akureyri, Seydisfjordur, Hofn, Vestmannaeyjar, Berunes, Leirubakki, and Fljotsdalur. For information about hostelling, consult Icelandic Youth Hostel Association (Laufasvegur 41, Reykjavik; Tel: 24950). In a spotlessly clean 4-storeyed building in Reykjavik, the Salvation Army Guest House (Kirkjustraeti 2; Tel: 13203) also offers inexpensive rooms and lunch room in the city center.

In **Akureyri,** capital of North Iceland, population about 13,000, the **Hotel Kea** is first class, with restaurant, a self-service cafe, and the option of dancing every Sat. night in the ballroom or every night in the H–100 Disco down the street (Hafnarstraeti 96; Tel: 22000). Sleeping-baggers and self-caterers head for the **Dalakofinn Guest House** (Lyngholt 20; Tel: 23035). In **Husavik,** where hot water from the Hveravellir springs heats most houses, there's a new, modern, comfortable hotel for birdwatchers and those drawn to natural phenomena, **Hotel Husavik.** The church and the hotel are the fishing town's most unusual buildings (Tel: (96) 41220).

Pensions and guesthouses—prices about $25 for a single room, $35 for a double—are to be found throughout the country. One of the most interesting is hosted by Pall Helgason, the official guide of the Westman Islands, one of the brave few who stayed on the main island when Helgafell erupted in 1973. His self-catering guesthouse (Tel: (98) 1515) is an excellent base for your stay in Vestmannaeyjar. The Iceland Tourist Bureau in Reykjavik can tell you about others. If you are driving, farmhouse accommodations—about $45 for a double, half-price for children, including full board—are ideal since there are no minimum-stay requirements, and you can drive from one to another. Your English-speaking host or hostess can probably also arrange for you to ride on the farm's horses, and you are guaranteed three good meals plus afternoon coffee and cake and a chance to get to know more about your hosts and their unique country. Some traveling families return to Iceland just to vacation at one of these attractive farms with their hospitable and accommodating hosts. These stays can be booked through the Iceland Tourist Bureau (see Information).

CAMPING AND CARAVANING The interior of Iceland is uninhabited, seldom traveled. You shouldn't venture into these parts without a guide, but camping is becoming increasingly popular in Iceland, whether you travel by car, bus, air or on foot. Outside towns and villages, tents may be pitched anywhere except on cultivated ground or fenced-in areas. In the vicinity of farms, permission should be obtained from the owner, and this is usually readily granted. "Tjaldstaedi bonnud" is a sign meaning that camping is prohibited, but you'll see many more signs marked "Tjaldstaedi" which means camping (permitted). With no pollution in Iceland, water in almost any stream or lake is perfectly safe to drink. Campers must bring their own paraffin or gas stoves for cooking and heating, as no firewood or other fuel is to be found in Iceland. It is prohibited by law to tear up and burn the scant shrub found in some areas. Camping equipment can be rented in Reykjavik only. Advance reservations are advisable for tents, sleeping bags, air mattresses, rucksacks, gas cookers, tables—all available from **Tjaldleigan Rent-A-Tent** (Hringbraut v/Umferdarmidstodina, opposite B.S.I. coach station/bus terminal); Tel: 13072). There are many campsites with varying amenities for which no advance reservations are possible, and no camping licenses required. INTG can supply you with all available details. Check also with the Icelandic Youth Hostel Association (see Happy Family Accommodations). The best equipped camping grounds are in Reykjavik, Husafell, Isafjurdur, Varmahid, Akureyri, Myvatn, Eglisstadir, Laugarvatn, Thingvellir, Jokulsargljufur and Skaftafell.

ATTRACTIONS FOR CHILDREN Reykjavik: You can walk from the center of town to Sudurgada, where you'll find the **National Museum** (Hringbraut), near the University; open daily, 1:30 p.m. to 4 p.m. Church antiquities; good cross section of Icelandic history and culture. In the oldest part of town, near the harbor, the **Parliament** building is just off Austurvollur Square. The harbor, the shops on Austurstraeti and Hafnarstraeti, and the **Icelandic Handicrafts Centre** (see Shopping), where you can watch traditional weaving and spinning, all make a full morning.

You might also want to take in **Natturugripasafnid,** the Museum of Natural History, at Hlemmtorg, entrance on Hverfisgata; open Tues., Thurs., Sat., and Sun., 1:30 p.m. to 4:30 p.m. Also **Landsbokasafnid,** the National Library and Archives (Hverfisgotu 17), open Mon.–Fri., 9 a.m.–7 p.m., Sat. 9 a.m.–noon; the **Kjarvalsstadir,** the Municipal Art Gallery, with changing exhibits open daily 4 p.m. to 10 p.m., closed Mon.; the **Nordic House** (Hringbraut) with an Exhibition Hall for Scandinavian graphic and decorative arts, open daily 2 p.m.–10 p.m.; offers frequent entertainment events; a pleasant cafeteria open daily 9 a.m.–7 p.m., on Sun., noon–7 p.m. There are several painting and sculpture galleries in Reykjavik, but the watercolors and oils of Asgrimur Jonssen of Iceland's landscapes, fairytales and folklore, trolls and other supernatural beings, with changing exhibitions every few months are most interesting, I think, and are shown in **Asgrimssafn,** a gallery in his house (Bergstadastraeti 74), open daily except Sat. from 1:30 p.m.–4 p.m. A walk around the lake, where there are always ducks to feed, in the **Botanical Gardens** in the center of town, is always pleasant and possible daily from 10 a.m.–10 p.m. At **Hallgrimskirkya,** the church tower is open daily except Mon. 10 a.m.–noon, and afternoons from 2 p.m.–4 p.m., Sun. afternoons only, so that your children can scamper up the steeple or, mercifully, prefer the elevator up to admire the view. From early July to Aug. 31, a performance in English, "Light Nights," of traditional Icelandic folksongs, folktales and saga readings is performed every Thurs., Fri., Sat. and Sun. at 9 p.m. by the lake (Frikirkjuvegur 11). Movies from all over the world, with Icelandic subtitles, are shown at eight movie houses (*bio*). For teenagers, weekends swing at the discotheques: **Fellahellir** (Nordur fell 17–19); **Arsel** (Rofabaer); **Villi Trillti** (Skulugata). These are for the 16-year-old and younger crowd; they serve no liquor; all are well run. Indoor and outdoor swimming is year round; pools are pleasantly heated with natural hot-spring water. Open weekdays from 7:20 a.m.–8:30 p.m., Sat. from 7:20 a.m.–5:30 p.m., and Sun. from 8 a.m.–5:30 p.m. and after 6:30 p.m. Bathing suits and towels can be hired; entrance fee about 20¢. For indoor swimming, don't overlook the **Hotel Loftleidir.** Of the outdoor pools, **Sundlaug Reykjavikur** in Sundlaugavegur is best; handsome setting; shallow pool for teeny-tinies; open all year. At **Sundlaug Vesturbaejar,** in Hofsvallagata, smaller pool and three hot pools; dandy.

Most children will enjoy a visit to the **Krysuvik hot springs and geysers** or the **Hellisgerdi lava park,** just off the main highway leading to Keflavik. In **Keflavik,** a small museum, **Vatnsnes,** with exhibits and craftsmanship from the past, is well worth a visit. A leisurely day's car trip could also include a ramble around the lighthouse at **Reykjanes** and the fishing village of **Grindavik.** Take bus #10 from Hlemmur to the **Arbaer Folk Museum;** open daily except Mon., 1–6 p.m., June 1–Sept. 14. Arbaer also has a collection of furnished **old-style houses,** with church, smithy, farmhouse, laborer's house, and poet's dwelling, all collected from different parts of the country and reconstructed; Sept.

15–May 31, only the church and farmhouse are open, 1–4 p.m. Best time to visit is Sat., when you can see folk dancing and wrestling (*glima*), barring rain. Light refreshments are available.

Go to **Akranes,** one-hour by boat across the bay; departures daily at 10 a.m., 1 p.m., 4 p.m., 7 p.m.; we loved the $4.50 round trip; the beach, the picnic, and the immaculate town you can walk around in ½ hour; the *Akraborg,* a tug-sized cargo ship, leaves Reykjavik harbor three times a day. At the Hotel Akranes (Tel: 932–020), rates are reasonable; babysitter available. Ask for directions to the 9-hole golf course, the bathing beach, or to the **Bjarnalaug,** a children's indoor pool—admission a pittance—where you can rent bathing suits. There is an excellent toy shop with wares from Scandinavia and England; a jewelry and souvenir shop owned by Helgi **Juliusson** (Sudurgotu 67); for a low price you can pick up a fleecy lambskin rug; next door, a camping and picnicking outfitter; numerous children's clothiers too, including exceptionally nice handknit mittens (about 60¢). Also a little folk museum, **Byggdasafn;** and for toddlers, the Akranes playschool-kindergarten. A **bus tour** leaves Reykjavik 9 a.m., returns 7 p.m., and goes to **Geysir** (the Great Geysir may perform spectacularly), **Gullfoss** (beautiful, cascading waterfall), **Thingvellir** (site of the world's first national legislative body, the Althing, in a pastoral setting; popular fishing, boating, and lakeside picnicking spot; nice hotel), and **Hveragerdi** (a hot-springs-heated township whose greenhouses grow tropical fruits and flowers; one houses a mynah bird that says "hello"; at the local hotel you can snack on pancakes and doughnuts or, for a modest fee, rent a double room for a child to nap in; overnight stays recommended for students only; stalagmite and stalactite caves at nearby Raufarholshellir). Instead of returning to Reykjavik, you may stay over in **Laugarvatn** and revel in the cheerful resort atmosphere of two comfortable summer hotels, indoor swimming pool, swimming lake, boating, sauna, trout fishing, and shaggy Icelandic ponies to ride. **Skogar,** near the black sand desert of Myrdall Sandlur, features a folkloric museum with cow-bone skates, horsehair clothing, and other fascinations.

From Reykjavik you can arrange for ***air tours*** with Eagle Air's Arnarflug (Kelflavik Airport; Tel: 29677) offering a 1½–2-hour view of glaciers; the Surtur volcano on the island of **Surtsey,** which emerged from the sea in 1963; and **Mt. Hekla** (with an intermittent, red-hot lava flow so awesome that medieval Europeans regarded it as the chimney of Hell); a fine view of the bird-breeding cliffs of the **Westman Islands,** with courting gannets, fulmars, razorbills, and puffins. An 8:30 a.m. flight returns by 8 p.m., 2-hour sight-seeing drive or four-hour boat trip on Sat., extra. Overnight accommodations at **Hotel Hamar Heimaey** are pleasant. Swimming pool at Heimaey, the main island. Icelandair has five daily flights to the Westman Islands a 25-minute flight which allows you to stay for a few hours or longer. **Akureyri** has hot springs, steaming geysers, boiling sulfur pits, natural underground swimming pool, and trees, in an almost treeless nation—beautifully memorable even to children unimpressed with scenic wonders. ***Skiing*** in winter; summers you can take an excursion to the Lake Myvatn area, where children can ride ponies. Enjoy a couple of days of family ***pony trekking*** at prices even students can afford. **Hotel Kea,** comfortable, up-to-the-minute Scandinavian in decor, offers swimming and sauna. The town features golf, shops, botanical garden, museums, a duck pond in a pleasant garden, two bios, and a hospital. Check with the Akureyri Tourist Bureau for details. June–Aug., a flight to **Grimsey Island** with its peak-roofed, turf-covered farmhouses athwart the Arctic Circle—is a special for lucky half-fare under-12s and teenagers. Midnight sun cruises on the weekends to Grimsey on the ferry *Drangur* (Skipagata 13, Akureyri; Tel: 24088).

Are you rich, adventurous, an original? What about a flight, with as many half-fares as you can afford, to **Greenland?** It's two hours from Reykjavik to the airfield at Kulusuk Island, where you'll find a radar station and the Eskimo village of **Kap Dan.** Wear gloves, sweater, and leg covering, headscarf for mothers and daughters. In the village you will see kayaks custom-tailored by wives for their husbands, and *umiaks,* large boats used by women; hear old songs and poems chanted to the beat of a drum; watch, if you're lucky enough, a head-banging contest in which Eskimos butt each other like goats; and buy beautiful little figures *(tupilaks)* carved from whalebone. For longer visits, ask the Iceland Tourist Bureau or Icelandair.

SHOPPING WITH AND FOR CHILDREN A *dunsaeng* (downsack) weighing about 2.2 lbs. can be bought for about $60 and airlifted home or compressed into a shopping bag. A *dunsaeng* saves storage space, solves bedmaking problems, and is comfortable summer and winter; invest in two, and making a bed becomes as easy as slipping on two pillowcases.

In **Reykjavik,** for handknitted sweaters, mittens, TV socks, hats, scarves, all in natural wool colors and traditional patterns, try **Icelandic Handcrafts Centre** (Laufasvegur 2), with a cozy, old-fashioned atmosphere; also Hafnarstraeti 3, a newer building, with spinning and weaving demonstrations during summer, 2–4 p.m., Mon.–Fri. Sweaters knit from unspun woolen threads *(lopi)* have an unusual finish, are thick, warm, and lightweight, and snow and rain repellent. Such exported woolen wear sells in America at three times the price. Also other woolen goods; miniature churns; spinning wheels; woolly lambs and shaggy horses; oil lamps; miniature Viking ships; dolls; jewelry; fur slippers; lava-based ceramic souvenirs, many printed with signs *(galdur)* mentioned in the sagas and Edda-songs—ask to see the snowflake-like design known as *Aegishjalmur* (the Helmet of Terror); in days of old it was said that if you placed this sign between your eyebrows with your right ring finger, using blood drawn from your own body, you would thereafter go fearlessly against your enemies.

The same items, plus fur-covered books; sealskin wallets; taxidermic specimens of museum quality; magnificent sea urchin shells from Gulf Stream waters; dried flower arrangements mounted under glass, and stamps are all available at **Rammagerdin** (Hafnarstraeti 5). For baby ***clothes,*** try **Endur Og Hendur** (Adalstraeti 9) and **Glitbra** (Laugavegur 7). Teenage hip fashions at **Karnabaer** (Austurstraeti 22, Laugavegun 20, Laugavegur 66). **Vidir** offers toys. Also selling ***toys*** is **Tomstundahusid** (Laugavegi 164), plus branches, known as *Tomstundabudin,* throughout town. For sports equipment, try **Godaborg** (Freyjugotu 1). For wonderful books in English, books about Iceland, it's Snaebjorn Jonsson & Company, **The English Bookshop** (Hafnarstraeti 4 and 9); **The University Bookstore** (Hringbraut) for magazines and newspapers. **Eymundsson Bookshop** (Austurstraeti 18).

ICELANDIC FRIENDS AND PEN PALS No organized service. If you address a letter giving details about yourself and requesting a compatible correspondent to any of Reykjavik's three leading newspapers, *Visir, Morgunbladid,* or *Timinn,* letters bearing Icelandic postmarks should soon be winging your way. Be sure to specify if you could also correspond in German or Danish. The 7–14-year-old set would do best to request pen pals through the children's magazine, *Barnabladid Aeskan,* in Reykjavik. At 16, most Icelandic youth speak and understand basic English and are familiar with the latest rock stars.

CALENDAR OF EVENTS Check with the National Iceland Tourist Board for additional information. Jan. 1 to Dec. 31, chess competitions every Tues. and Thurs. in Reykjavik.

Twelfth Night, **Jan. 6,** is celebrated nationally, but the greatest festivities are at *Mosfellsveit,* with costume parades of legendary characters, particularly *Jolasveinar,* troll-like creatures.

In **Feb.** "Thorri," a month-long feast, on the Mon. before Shrove Tues., children celebrate the national holiday ***Bolludagur.*** Especially in Akureyri, children get colored sticks to thump grownups (or barrels) in exchange for *bollur* (cream buns). Parades, costumes. Ash Wed., in Akureyri, children tie little bags of ash of backs on unwary adults. Children put on masks, collect money for charity. In **Mar.,** "Saeluvika Skagfirdinga," a country festival featuring art, music, theater. Third Thurs. in **Apr.,** is the national celebration of ***first day of summer.*** Carnival queen, dancing and merrymaking in the streets, celebrated mainly by and for children with processions and entertainment. At the end of **May,** see the annual ***Whitsun Pony Race*** in Reykjavik.

June 17, ***National Day.*** Processions, amusements, dancing in streets and parks. Children's singing groups perform. First weekend in **Aug.,** on Heimaey Island, at Herjolfsdalur, a tent city is set up for 2–3 days.

Amusements, sports, athletic contests, dancing, feasting—SPECIAL!

In **Sept.,** sheep and horse round-ups by farmers everywhere in the country. **Oct. 9,** ***Leif Ericson Day,*** commemorates the discovery of North America, about 1000 A.D., by Leif Ericson; ceremony at his statue in Reykjavik. **Dec.** 24, Christmas Eve, presents are exchanged. On Dec. 31 there are midnight ***bonfires and fireworks;*** special fireworks in Reykjavik.

LANGUAGE AND PHRASEBOOK Icelandic is pronounced in a straightforward way. Accents indicate stress. A capital *D* with a line through it or a little *d* with a tiny Thor's hammer flying like a flag from its stem has the same sound as *th* in "that"; an *I* with a bulge in the middle is pronounced like the *th* in "thin." *A* and *E* snuggled together (*Æ*) is pronounced like "eye," and *Ö* is pronounced like the *O* in "work." Two *n*'s are pronounced like a *T*.

Hello	*Hello*	*Hello*
I am an American	*Eg er ameriskur (boy)*	*Yayg air amureeskur*
	Eg er amerisk (girl)	*Yayg air amureesk*
My name is	*Nafn mitt er*	*Noff'n mitt air*
	or	
	Eg heiti	*Yayg haytee*
I am ____ years old	*Eg er ____ gamall (boy)*	*Yayg air ____ gamull*
	Eg er ____ gomul (girl)	*Yag air ____ germull*
Please	*Gjordu svo vel*	*Gerda shvaw well*
Thank you	*Takk fyrir*	*Tack fear ear*
I can't speak Icelandic	*Eg tala ekki islenzku*	*Yayg tala akey eezlenzskoo*
Yes	*Ja*	*Yow (rhymes with how)*
No	*Nei*	*Nay*
I am having a wonderful time	*Eg skemmti mer dasamlega*	*Yayg skemmtea mair dow-some layga*
	or	
	Her er dasamlegt ad vera	*Hair air downsome-lekt owth verra*
1	*einn*	*ate*
2	*tveir*	*tuhveer*
3	*thrir*	*threer*
4	*fjorir*	*feeyourear* like *f'yorear*
5	*fimm*	*fimm*

6	*sex*	*sex*
7	*sjo*	*zhur, pronounced just like "je" in French as in "Je suis"*
8	*atta*	*arta*
9	*niu*	*knee-oo*
10	*tiu*	*tee-oo*
11	*ellefu*	*ettlerver (two l's are pronounced like two t's)*
12	*tolf*	*toe-lf*
13	*threttan*	*threttawn*
14	*fjortan*	*fyortawn*
15	*fimmtan*	*fimmtawn*
Goodbye	*saelir (to a boy)*	*sighleer*
(formal)	*saelar (to a girl)*	*sighlar*
(informal)	*bless*	*bless*

IRELAND

Ireland is the least populated country in Europe; a place to relax, to spend a family vacation fishing, riding, swimming, sailing, golfing, shooting, or hunting. Over 800 lakes and rivers provide salmon, trout, bream, and pike. The unspoiled countryside will stir children—Connemara ponies and donkeys to ride; plenty of horse-drawn carriages and carts; 3000 miles of coastline and 200 beaches; boats; country fairs. Comfortable accommodations, comparatively low prices, and the friendly, welcoming hospitality of the Irish makes Ireland a country-cozy haven for families.

It rains in Ireland, but in a soft, gentle way so that no one pays much attention. Overshoes and waterproof jackets for the children take care of the problem nicely. After 11 a.m., days are usually sunny, the air sparklingly fresh. Accommodations in hotels, castles, and inns are up-to-date in all comforts. Hunt balls are formal and elaborate. Everything else—the thatched cottages, the fishing villages, the stores, the architecture, the pubs, the clothes, the towns—has a country feeling of solidity, frill-less functionalism, and wholesomeness with all the old-fashioned virtues implicit. Incurably individualistic, the Irish bless all their planes and name them after Irish saints; decorate their coinage with pictures of animals, birds, and fish; possess a lulling blarneying tact and humor; and believe in the little creatures that inhabit springs, wells, and the imagination.

INFORMATION ABOUT IRELAND Brochures and data should be requested from the Irish Tourist Board (590 5th Ave., New York, NY 10036; Tel: (212) 869–5500); plus branches in Chicago, San Francisco, Toronto.

In **Dublin,** get in touch with the Irish Tourist Information Office (TIO) (14 Upper O'Connell St.; Tel: (01) 747–733). Regional Offices in **Cork** (Grand Parade; Tel: (021) 23251); **Galway** (Aras Failte, Ireland-West House; Tel: (091) 63081); **Limerick** (The Granary, Michael St.; Tel: (061) 47522); **Mullinger** (Dublin Rd.; Tel: (044) 8761); **Sligo** (Temple St.; Tel: (071) 6120); **Waterford** (41 The Quay; Tel: (051) 75788).

In Dublin, all questions about Irish folklore are answered by the

Irish Folklore Department, University College Belfield; Tel: (01) 693–244 (in the Dublin suburbs). Pick up a copy of *This Week in Dublin* at your hotel or at the Tourist Office; lists local attractions, movies and special events, many regional attractions.

If you intend to see many historic houses and castles, you can save on entry fees by buying the "Passport to Ireland's Heritage and Culture" from your travel agent or from the Irish Tourist Offices. Discount vouchers are included for admission fees in this well-documented and illustrated booklet. ***Bicycles can be rented*** at over 100 locations throughout Ireland, and details are available from any TIO. You can book in advance by writing to **TI-Irish Raleigh Ltd.,** Broomhill Road, Tallaght, Co. Dublin; Tel: (01) 52–18–88.

Riding holidays can be arranged for the handicapped (see Children's Camps). A list of activities and facilities for disabled persons is available from the ITB and TIOs throughout Ireland. Wheelchairs are available on loan from the **Irish Wheelchair Association,** Blackheath Drive, Dublin. Advance notice requested. There is no rental fee, but donations are gratefully received!

Although English is spoken everywhere, public lavatories are often labeled in Gaelic: *Fir* (for men); *Mna* (for ladies). "Confusing, when ya suppose Mna is just Man spelled wrong," as a 7-year-old boy once mumbled in embarrassment. ***Telephones?*** Ireland is a member of the Teleplan service, so the standard surcharge you pay when telephoning from your hotel room (in addition to the official cost of the telephone call) is not going to bankrupt you.

Cut crystal, uncut crystal, glass blowing, leather, pottery, crochet and Carrickmacross lace, hand-woven fabrics in gossamer weights and thick wooliness, woven cotton and linen, silver work, hand-tied fishing flies are some of the craft products and craft-based industries that may interest you and your children. An excellent guide to these crafts, including where you can watch them in operation and buy the finished products, is available from the ITB and ITOs. (See Shopping.)

Literary interests? Irish writers William Butler Yeats, Jonathan Swift, Edmund Burke, William Congreve, John Millington Synge, James Stephens, Sean O'Casey, George Bernard Shaw, James Joyce, Brendan Behan, Samuel Beckett, Oliver Goldsmith, Oscar Wilde, Richard Brinsley Sheridan—if you would like to follow the footsteps of your favorites, visit their places of birth or favorite haunts, make this a family, school, library project, and ask your travel agent to help you work out an itinerary; ask the ITB for recommendations of special literary study vacations. The ITB can send you an information sheet about *legends, superstitions, traditional music, customs and traditions, fairs, the making of St. Brigid's crosses, the celebration of Shrove Tuesday,* and *the fairies*, a tiny sample of aspects of ***Irish folklore*** about which you can find out a great deal more from the **Department of Irish Folklore,** University College, Belfield, Dublin. *Ireland's Heritage*, a booklet containing photographs and descriptions of a selection of houses, castles, gardens, national monuments, nature parks and visitor attractions is an easily affordable guide available from the ITB.

HEALTH, WATER, FOOD Health standards are generally good. The water is safe in cities, but in the country exercise care about milk. Make sure it is pasteurized. Pasteurized milk is rich and delicious. (For extra-thick creamy milk, ask for Jersey milk.)

If you like American farm-style food, you'll like Irish food. Farm-fresh eggs, crunchy bacon, juicy steaks, lamb chops, excellent roast beef and baby lamb.

Soda fountains, called milk bars, are scattered throughout the large towns. A peculiarity of small country inns is that lunch is the big meal rather than dinner, which is usually a comparatively light meal. "High tea," a substantial snack of scones, cake, sliced ham, boiled eggs or whatever, is usually served between 5 p.m. and 7 p.m.

Special!! You can banquet medievally at **Bunratty Castle** all year round and **Knappogue Castle** (May–Sept.), both in County Clare. **Dunguaire Castle** (County Galway) has similar banquets May–Oct. but the emphasis is more literary—old songs, country airs played sweetly on harps, flutes, and medieval stringed instruments. Bookings for medieval castle banquets can be made through the ITB or by **Brian Moore International Tours,** 89 Main St., Medway, MA 02053; Tel: 800–343–6472, and 800–982–2299 from Massachusetts. Free for the asking is the Irish Tourist Board publication called *Tourist Menu,* listing restaurants in all counties that provide good food, service, and value for fixed-price menus. For a bagatelle you can buy another annual ITB publication, *Dining in Ireland,* listing recommended restaurants in all price categories, with information about specialties, awards of excellence and credit card acceptance.

BABY FOOD Heinz, Cow & Gate, Farley's baby and junior foods and cereals widely available in chemist's shops, grocery stores, supermarkets.

DIAPERS AND LAUNDRY Chemists and supermarkets sell disposable diapers, Pampers and Johnson's brands, and less expensive brands. Cloth diapers are stocked by children's departments of all major department stores.

No diaper service that I know of, but many launderettes and washerettes, such as Dublin's conveniently located **Com-Op Centre** (46 Baggot St. Upper) and **The Speedy Laundromat** (19 Aungier St.). The yellow pages lists others.

BABY EQUIPMENT FOR HIRE For cot and mattress rental, contact Mrs. D. Nolan (13 Woodbira Park, Blackrock; Tel: (01) 691–803) in suburban Dublin.

EMERGENCIES MADE EASY Chemists are open during normal business hours, and on Sun. between 11 a.m. and 1 p.m. Check yellow pages for late-night pharmacies. There are always doctors on duty in hospitals.

Medical facilities are excellent. Dublin's children's hospitals: **Children's Hospital** (Temple St.; Tel: (01) 748–763); **Children's Hospital** (Crumlin; Tel: (01) 503–111); the **National Children's Hospital** (87–89 Harcourt St.; Tel: (01) 752–355). For ***doctors and dentists*** recommended by the American and Canadian communities, call the Dublin-based **American Embassy** (42 Elgin Rd., Ballsbridge; Tel: (01) 688–777) or the **Canadian Embassy** (65 St. Stephens Green; Tel: (01) 851–246).

MAGIC FAMILY HELPERS ***Babysitters?*** In Dublin, **Childminders** (22 Kildare St.; Tel (01) 767–981). Any hotel, farmhouse, castle, guesthouse, town or country house you stay in will have colleens delighted to look after your children. Your main problem will be keeping the nursemaid from spoiling the children! For children's companions and *au pair* arrangements, consult the school managers of the **Dublin School of English** (11 Westmoreland St., Dublin) and/or the **Language Centre of Ireland** (9–11 Grafton St., Dublin).

In Dublin, care, play, and meals for your little ones is provided at the **Ballsbridge Nursery and Montessori School,** 2 Pembroke Park, Ballsbridge, Dublin; Tel: (01) 68–02–44. From mid-June to mid-July, **Pine Forest Children's Art and Craft Centre** (Glencullen, Kilternan, Co. Dublin) will organize private bus service from many Dublin southside suburbs to their two-week courses in pottery, painting, batik, sculpture etc. for boys and girls 5–12, and senior group 13–16; courses for both groups run simultaneously at the center and are informable, enjoyable, instructive in an ambiance of forests, streams and mountains. For personal guide service, try the **Federation of Irish Guiding Interests** (30 Firhouse Ave., Templeogue, Dublin) or **Irish Guide Services** (38–40 Parliament St., Dublin).

▶ **Note:** Interested in your ancestry? Dublin's **Thomas Mullins, Heraldic House** (36 Upper O'Connell St.; Tel: (01) 741–133) maintains an extensive Heraldic Reference Library with records for most family names of European origin, and will reproduce coats of arms on practically anything from a wall decoration to a doorknocker. **Heraldic Artists, Ltd.** (3 Nassau St., Dublin; Tel: (01) 76–23–91) stocks interesting maps, family history books, crests, and coats of arms appropriate to Irish surnames; Family crests and genealogical and heraldry books are also to be found at **Historic Families** (8 Fleet St., Dublin; Tel: (01) 77–70–34). For roots-conscious families of Irish descent, the **Irish Heritage program** will help untangle your ancestral threads. For details, contact **Aer Lingus** (122 East 42nd St., New York, NY 10168). **Hibernian Researchers** (Windsor House, 22 Windsor Rd., Rathmines, Dublin) employs a group of fulltime professional genealogists to undertake searches. If your ancestors were Presbyterian, the **Presbyterian Historical Society** (Church House, Fisherwick Place, Belfast) may be able to help. If your forebears came from the north of Ireland, contact the **Public Record Office of Northern Ireland** (66 Balmoral Avenue, Belfast BT 9 6 NY), also the Hon. Secretary of the **Ulster Historical Foundation** (same address).

HOLIDAYS FOR CHILDREN ON THEIR OWN No special holiday homes or hotels for unaccompanied children that I know of for children under 9. Many home-stay opportunities combined with sport and special interest courses available for older teenagers (see Children's Camps). A comprehensive student accommodation booking service including home-stay in selected and approved family homes is available from **Dublin Tourism,** Education/Group Travel Section, 14 Upper O'Connell St., Dublin.

CHILDREN'S CAMPS Irish camps provide a rich mix of sports, cultural activities and learning experiences, excellently supervised and planned for ages 8–18. For boys and girls 9–18, **Clongowes Summer Camp,** by 100 parkland acres, offers indoor and outdoor tennis, track, golf, football, swimming, squash, badminton, volleyball, and basketball; disco, movies, cultural activities; riding and canoeing are nearby and optional; accommodation in dormitory cubicles; camp is open in July. For further details, contact Mr. Vincent Murray, Clongowes Wood College, Naas, County Kildare. Also for boys and girls 9–18, **Irish International Camp** offers lovely rural surroundings; excellent living quarters; good food; individual daily programs provided for each camper; tennis, riding, swimming, basketball, volleyball; modern gym. Personal supervision by owner-director and his wife. Campers come from all over Europe and America; camp open from late June through July. For information and reservations, contact Tom and Delma Fitzsimons, Rockmahon, Newtownpark Ave., Blackrock, County Dublin. For boys only, 9–18, there are adventure holidays—two-week periods during July and Aug.—of living in tents, learning to sail on Lough Gill, canoeing on lake and rivers, mountain-climbing, fishing in the locale of the Dartry mountains in County Sligo. For information and reservations, contact The Director, Hill House, Loughanelteen, Sligo, County Sligo. For boys and girls, 8–16, **Camp Rockwell** (Rockwell College, Cashel, County Tipperary) set in surroundings of lawn, lake, and forest, provides golf, tennis, basketball, volleyball, football; private lake for boating, canoeing, swimming; indoor heated pool; games rooms, theater, cookouts, parties, dancing. Camp open from early July to mid-Aug. For boys and girls 12–18, at Easter, and for those 12–17, from June-mid-Aug., the **Little Killary Adventure Centre** (Salruck, Renvyle, Connemara, County Galway) offers canoeing, rowing, fishing, sailing, windsurfing, walking and climbing; accommodation in four-bunk rooms in converted farm building. Courses also possible in watersports during July only.

Special interest holidays: For coed intelligentsia, aged 13–17, **Explore Ireland** (48 Elm Rd., Donnycarney, Dublin) based in Greystones, provides, during July, an Irish studies course. Accommodation is arranged with culturally sympatico and carefully selected Irish families. The **Irish Way,** a vacation study program for students 13–18, operates early July–mid-Aug. and blends a stay in an Irish home, field trips, attendance at Irish *ceilis* (dances) and films, student-produced dramatic playlets, other recreation and sports with a curriculum of Irish studies. Some scholarships are available. Early application is strongly recommended as enrollment is limited. Contact The Irish Way, Irish American Cultural Institute, 683 Osceola Ave., St. Paul, MN, 55105). For young sailing enthusiasts, Elizabeth Dineen provides accommodation with neighboring families, and sailing tuition in her own fleet of sailing dinghies moored at Malahide. For further details, write to **Dineen's Sailing Centre,** 51 St. Brendan's Ave., Dublin. From Easter to Sept. ***ponycraft courses*** with riding and instruction about stabling (seven horsey hours daily) are laid on by the **Errislannan Connemara Pony Stud** (Errislannan Manor, Clifden, Connemara, County Galway). Accommodation is in the **Ardilaun Guesthouse** (Ballinaboy, Clifden) whose proprietors provide transport, pack lunches, and other meals. Errislannan is a member of the Association of Irish Riding Establishments. During May to Sept. week-long courses of riding instruction, stable management, grooming and feeding ponies are provided by the **Ravensdale Pony Camp** (Ravensdale Riding Stables, Claregalway, County Galway). Equestrian enthusiasts, 10 and older, board in nearby farmhouses. Information and reservations from Miss Grainne Ward.

Riding in Ireland is wonderful; it should come as no surprise that children 4+ can pony trek and that unaccompanied children 7–18 are welcome to board at equestrian centers. Recommended riding schools with special facilities to accommodate unaccompanied children follow. **Carribeg Riding Stables** (Carrigbeg, Bagenalstown, County Carlow); open all year (closed Sun.). **Millbrook Riding Centre** (Millbrook, Ballinasloe, County Galway); open all year. **Melody's Riding Stables and Pony Trekking Centre** (Ballymacarberry, near Clonmel, County Waterford); open mid-Apr.–Oct. 1. **Lisderg Riding Centre** (Lisderg House, Belmont, near Birt, County Offaly); open all year. **Ashton Equestrian Centre** (Ashton Manor, Castleknock, County Dublin); open all year. **Rockmount Riding Centre Ltd.** (Rockmount House, Claregalway, County Galway); open all year (closed Sun.); member of the Association of Irish Riding Establishments. **Westfield Riding School** (Kilcarty, Dunsany, County Meath); open all year. **Slaney View Riding School** (Brownswood, Enniscorthy, County Wexford); member of the Association of Irish Riding Establishments. Another member of the AIRE,

Horetown House Riding Centre (Horetown House, Foulksmills, County Wexford) is open all year. AIRE-member **Glendara** (Granard, County Longford) open all year; caters to "nervous riders." **Collins Riding School** (Meelehera Farmhouse, Meelehera, Kanturk, County Cork); open Apr. to Oct. (closed Mon.). **Thornfield Riding School** (Rathcline, Lanesborough, County Longford); open all year (closed Sun.); AIRE member. **Malahide Riding School** (Ivy Grange, Broomfield, Malahide, County Dublin); open all year; AIRE member. AIRE-member **Calliaghstown Riding Centre** (Calliaghstown, Rathcoole, County Dublin); open all year. **Sligo Equitation Co., Ltd.** (Carrowmore, Sligo); open all year, with an indoor riding school; trekking/riding outdoors. **Church View Riding Stables** (Church View House, Kilglass, Strokestown, County Roscommon); open June 1–Sept. 30 (closed Sun.). Many other family residential riding courses/trekking opportunities listed in the ITB's *Guide for the Equestrian Visitor to Ireland.*

Good news for the handicapped: There are more than 20 centers catering to children and young adults with a variety of physical and mental disabilities, all under the aegis of the **Riding for the Disabled Association** (28 Castlepark Rd., Sandycove, County Dublin).

CASTLES AND OTHER HAPPY FAMILY ACCOMMODATIONS Starting from the top, there are castles, elegant 18th-century country houses, and guesthouses on castle estates for rent, all staffed with cooks, housemaids, and gardeners and ghillies so that you don't get the willies fishing alone or unaided. Tempting listings and details from **At Home Abroad, Inc.** (405 East 56th St., New York, NY). Other offers of elegant, exclusive castle, country-house, cottage rentals (with optional driver guides) to dream over from **At Home In Ireland** (42, Castle St., Dalkey, Dublin).

Any of over 70 TIOs can make reservations for you, and your travel agent can make them in advance. You can make reservations, too, for approved accommodations that include hotels, guesthouses, farm houses, self-catering cottages, barges, horse-drawn caravans, and more (providing your request is received four weeks prior to your arrival) at the **Central Reservation Service** (Bord Failte, Baggot Street Bridge, Dublin).

There are also *castle hotels* with special charm and *country-manor* hotels. You'll find these listed in *Discover Ireland Hotels and Guesthouses,* an ITB publication you can buy for less than the price of a hamburger. Also included in this booklet (which I *urge* you to get) are grand hotels, family-run hotels, inns, and lodges. In *Discover Ireland Irish Homes,* another ITB publication and an invaluable guide for motorists, you'll find dozens of bed-and-breakfast accommodations in all 26 counties. Almost all offer babyminding facilities, gardens; nearby golf, fishing, riding, swimming; and many other extras.

Self-catering accommodations: **Rent an Irish Cottage Ltd.** (Shannon Free Airport, Shannon, County Clare) has constructed idealized versions of old-fashioned Irish cottages, with all conveniences, open-hearth fireplace, and accommodations for six to eight people. Cottages clustered like little villages crop up in counties Clare, Galway, Donegal, Limerick, Tipperary. **The Shannon Development Company** (590 Fifth Ave., New York, NY 10036) can also send you information about over 100 cottage rentals mostly situated within 50 miles of Shannon Airport. The ITB can supply three booklets listing descriptions of houses to rent with names and addresses of owners or agents. These booklets cover counties Cork, Kerry, Clare, Limerick, North Tipperary, Galway, and Mayo. See Camping for caravan accommodation information. *Holiday cruising:* You've got it all in Ireland at reasonable rates. The River Shannon, the Erne, the Grand Canal, Shannon Harbor, widening into island-dotted lakes with water as clear as any coral, and the River Barrow offer a 250-mile network in all, with lovely loughs and plenty of locks that many parents and most children love to see. *For Shannon River cruising:* **River Shannon Carrick Craft** (P.O. Box 14, Reading RG 3 6 TA, England); **Emerald Star Line Ltd.** (St. James's Gate, Dublin); **Flagline Ltd.** (Shancurragh, Athlone, County Westmeath); **SGS (Marine) Ltd.** (Ballykeeran, Athlone, County Westmeath); **Athlone Cruisers Ltd.** (Shancurragh, Athlone, County Westmeath); **Silverline Cruisers** (Banagher, County Offaly); **Shannon Castle Line** (Dolphin Works, Ringsend, Dublin); **Atlantis Marine Ltd.** (Bob Parks Marine Centre, Killaloe, County Clare); **Derg Line Cruisers** (The Country Club, Killaloe, County Clare). *For Erne River cruising:* **Book-a-Boat Ltd.** (Drumully, Emyvale, County Monaghan or Belturbet, County Cavan during the spring and summer months). *For Grand Canal cruising:* **Celtic Canal Cruisers Ltd.** (Tullamore, County Offaly). These companies offer luxury cabin cruisers for self-drive hire with two to eight berths; all come with refrigerators, gas cooking facilities. Some have central heating, hot water, showers. Dinghy, charts, binoculars and safety equipment are included; radios, portable television sets, angling dinghies, sailing dinghies, bicycles, fishing tackle and cars to meet you at docks and moorings can be hired; groceries and supplies can be ordered in advance to await your arrival. Free instruction is provided in boat-handling. No license is required. I recommend sending for the *Shell Guide to the Shannon* and *Guide to the River Barrow*. Both publications contain navigation charts, information on the fishing, wildlife, and sites and sights of interest along the River Shannon, the Grand Canal and the Barrow. Obtainable from **Eason & Co. Ltd.** (40 Lower O'Connell St., Dublin). Self-catering or all-inclusive skippered cruises of one to two weeks on the River Shannon for four to ten persons are offered on converted river barges during May–Sept. by **Weaver Boats Ltd.,** Carrick-on-Shannon, County Leitrim. I've never tried these, but they sound pleasant and fun, and a happy thought for two families to contemplate sharing.

Castle Hotels and Special Hotels: **Adare,** County Limerick: **Dunraven Arms Hotel,** on the banks of the River Maigue, is first class, but nearby **Woodlands House** at Knockanes is an attractive modern house on 65 acres of land, offering a pony for children, fresh farm produce, home baking; 16 bedrooms, 12 with private shower; warm welcome for families at this farm-based guest-house; prices little more than standard B&B accommodation. **Ballina,** County Mayo: **Belleek Castle.** Beautifully restored baronial castle, set in a forest; 16 rooms, all with private bath; fireplaces; sailing, fishing, riding, golf, shooting; archaeological relics and abundant fossil sites nearby; many local fishing festivals. Close by is **Mount Falcon Castle,** in 100 acres of parkland, a manor house noted for its homecooking; pony trekking arranged, fishing, angling, beaches, tennis court. **Ballinascarthy,** County Cork: **Ardnavaha House Hotel** is a Georgian house in 40 acres of lawns, woods, meadows, with nine horses for riding and trekking; swimming pool, sauna, tennis court; indoor and outdoor games; children's playground; a few miles from safe, unspoiled beaches; golf course nearby; Grade A; 36 bedrooms each with private bath, balcony, telephone. **Bantry,** County Cork: Parents with taste will opt for the **Sea View Hotel** a charming country house in parkland setting, with delicious food, fine wine cellar, and most bedrooms en suite. In the same B+ rating category, but more expensive, is the utterly charmless **Westlodge Hotel** with surrounding parking lot, BUT it does have indoor heated swimming pool, squash courts, tennis court, children's play area, pitch and putt, sports complex; junior menus. **Birr,** County Offaly: The **County Arms Hotel** welcomes families to its converted Georgian house set in its own broad lawns with squash courts and sauna on the premises; nearby facilities for riding, golf, fishing, tennis, mountaineering; six miles from the River Shannon; 18 bedrooms with connecting bathrooms and facilities to boil water for tea. **Ballynahinch,** County Galway: **Ballynahinch Castle Hotel** (Tel: Clifden 135/Ballinafad 4). Located at the foot of a mountain, overlooking the Owenmore River; 20 rooms, all with private bath; **Bunratty,** County Clare: **Fitzpatrick's Shannon Shamrock Hotel,** a modern ranch-style hotel, is located on the grounds of Bunratty Castle, five miles from the Shannon Airport, with indoor heated swimming pool, sauna, free hotel bus to and from airport. Radio and TV in all of the 110 rooms. **Carrickmacross,** County Monaghan: The **Nuremore Hotel** has its own private golf course; 100 acres of woodland setting; indoor heated swimming pool; squash court; sauna; private lake fishing. **Cashel,** County Galway: **Cashel House Hotel** is a delightful country house with award-winning gardens and 50 acres by the sea to relax in and walk about. Fresh-from-the-garden produce and freshly caught fish enhance the table. Garden suites among nine available suites in this luxurious hideaway. Reservations and information: Tel: (800) 233–6764 nationwide; (212) 758–4375 in NY City; (800) 522–5568 in NY State. **Cashel,** County Tipperary: If you are a horse-loving family and want to hunt in the best packs for pony trek, **Cashel Palace Hotel,** formerly an 18th-century archbishop's palace, will arrange it; also fishing; 20 rooms; fine wine cellar; traditional music played in the bar. The real Rock of Cashel is nearby, crowned with a cluster of impressive medieval monuments including towers, turrets, a 12th-century cross and 13th-century cathedral. In **Castledermot,** County Kildare, you'll find **Kilkea Castle,** the oldest inhabited castle of Ireland, a 12th-century Norman masterpiece, with 55 rooms, all with private bath; outdoor heated swimming pool; fine food; golf, riding, fishing, hunting, shooting. The castle stands in an estate of 110 acres ribboned-through by the trout-filled river Greese, and has its own stables. In **Clifden,** County Galway: The **Abbeyglen Hotel** (Tel: Clifden 33) is a Grade A country hotel with a heated swimming pool, tennis and the Connemara Golf Links nearby. In **Clonmel,** County Tipperary: Family suites are available at the **Hotel Minella,** a stately home with 32 bedrooms; great sweeps of flower-bedded lawn, the River Suir flowing through the spacious grounds; fishing, pony-riding, supervised pony treks; good food. **Cong,** County Mayo: **Ashford Castle,** set on the edge of Lough Corrib, has been cited as "the most outstanding hotel in Britain and Ireland"; 77 large, sunny bedrooms, all with private bath; very good food, almost all of it home-grown or locally produced; its own fishery, salmon-smoking plant, orchards, vegetable gardens; 300 acres of grounds planted with trees that secure a continuing effect of color at all seasons; maze for children to play hide-and-seek in; tennis courts; river and forest walks; seaplane slipway; lake beach; caves to explore; archaeological remains; a chapel; Japanese garden. For a fishing holiday, I can't think of a lovelier spot; also 9-hole golf course; boating and shooting. **Connemara** (see Leenane). In **Courtmacsherry,** near Bandon, County Cork: **Courtmacsherry Hotel,** in 10 acres of woodland and garden, is a country charmer, with riding, angling, tennis, golf available and 16 attractive bedrooms. In **Dingle,** County Kerry: **Hotel Sceilig,** at the entrance to Dingle harbor, makes up for what it lacks in esthetic appeal with an outdoor seawater swimming pool, tennis court, children's outdoor play area, indoor games rooms, video films; safe, sandy beaches in the area; local riding.

Dublin City: The **Berkeley Court,** the **Burlington,** and **Jury's** are modern, deluxe establishments with swimming pools. (See Killiney) In **Dundalk,** County Louth: **Fairways Hotel** is next to the golf course, also with an 18-hole pitch-and-putt; indoor heated swimming pool, saunas, solarium, gym, badminton, squash; hairdresser. The nearby **Ballymascanlon House Hotel** is a modernized historic house, with three dozen rooms, all with bath, set in a 130-acre demesne between Dublin and Belfast; with squash courts, indoor heated swimming pool, sauna, solarium, children's playground; fishing; riding; lovely garden. **Galway:** In town, **Galway Great Southern Hotel** has a health center and an indoor heated swimming pool. On the outskirts of town, the **Galway Ryan Hotel** has teenage disco dancing, video films, play and games room for children and grownups, musical entertainment. The **Corrib Great Southern** is also on the outskirts of town, and has an indoor heated swimming pool and sauna baths. **Glin,** County Limerick: **Glin Castle** is owned by the knight of Glin. The Georgian-Gothic castle is noted for its "flying staircase," furniture and paintings; lovely castle gardens, walls, grounds on the banks of the River Shannon. In **Innishannon,** County Cork: **Innishannon Hotel** is a peaceful riverside retreat; early 18th-century house with 13 bedrooms all with private bath/shower; nine acres of grounds; fishing. **Kanturk,** County Cork: **Assolas Country House** a 17th-century gem, with beautiful grounds, prize-winning gardens, fishing waters, tennis, croquet, boating, excellent food. Special. **Kilkenny,** County Kilkenny: The largest hotel is **Rose Hill,** within walking distance of the city's attractions, a manor house with a health center; a choice of ballads, bands, or disco on weekends. **Killarney,** County Kerry: **Cahernane Hotel,** former residence of the Earls of Pembroke, old-world; 35 rooms; surrounded by parkland and pastureland; tennis court, pitch and putt, croquet lawn, fishing. The **Killarney Great Southern** is a grand Victorian hotel with 180 bedrooms; indoor heated swimming pool, saunas, tennis courts, children's playground in parkland surrounds; two championship golf courses nearby, fishing and rising available. **Killiney,** County Dublin: **Fitzpatrick's Castle,** a Victorian sand-castlelike building, is country-quiet, with indoor heated pool, squash, tennis courts, sauna, solarium; hairdresser; golf, riding, fishing facilities nearby, and a hotel bus service. The only castle accommodations in the Dublin area, with 50 bedrooms, all with private bath, telephone, radio, TV, and video. **Kingscourt,** County Cavan: **Cabra Castle,** a great, gray castle next to the Dun-a-Ri Forest Park, has two dozen rooms, all with bath; 9-hole golf course, fishing, pony trekking, shooting. **Leenane,** Connemara, County Galway: The **Leenane** overlooking Killary Bay, a center for fishing, is an attractive built-onto house with hill and garden setting; swimming pool, tennis, boats, sauna and self-catering cottages in the heart of Connemara. **Midleton,** County Cork: **Kilcrone House** is a taste of country life close to the **Ballinamona bird sanctuary,** and the **Fota Island wildlife park;** golf and the freedom to ride horses to the nearby beach; the owners and proprietors welcome children and have swings and other entertainments for them. In **Mulrany,** County Mayo: The 19th-century, **Great Western,** perched on a hillside above Clew Bay, provides 71-bedrooms and family rooms, games room, swimming pool, tennis court; pony trekking available on the hotel grounds. **Newmarket-on-Fergus,** County Clare: **Dromoland Castle** is a Gothic-style gray stone castle built in the early 19th century, surrounded by velvety green lawns with a velvety green golf course; boating, tennis, and bicycling available all on the estate. With turrets, towers, and ramparts, the castle is splendid and handsome. The castle has its own bridle paths and the County Clare hounds meet here occasionally. Ducks in the lakes on the 500-acre grounds; salmon and trout fishing; watersports; sailing. The 67 rooms, all with private bath, have a comfortable blend of period and contemporary furnishings. Turret rooms are gloriously spacious. The more conventionally sized rooms, facing the small lake, are charmers. The new rooms built into a former courtyard have less appeal. Located just eight miles from Shannon Airport. **Oughterard,** County Galway: **Currarveagh House,** a 19th-century country house beside Lough Corrib in 150 acres of woodland, has its own boats, ghillies, trout fishing; food that Gault et Millau recommend for its classic simplicity. **Parknasilla,** County Kerry: **The Great Southern** is warmed by the Gulf Stream on the shore of Kenmare Bay; a grand 19th-century hotel, with heated indoor pool, riding, golf, tennis, saunas, fishing, sailing, waterskiing, pony trekking on the 250-acre property. **Rathmullan,** County Donegal: **Fort Royal Hotel** a pretty houselike hotel with a family atmosphere, excellent service, on the edge of Lough Swilly, with private sandy beach, golf course, tennis court, squash court, sailing, its own stable of Connemara ponies, and its own boats on nearby loughs for lake-fishing; open from Easter to Sept. **Roscommon,** County Roscommon: **The Abbey Hotel** is a comfortably converted abbey with suites in the Irish midlands. **Roscrea,** County Tipperary: The **Racket Hall Hotel,** with a charming packet of 10 rooms sheltered with ivied walls, is a dear country house to overnight in. **Rosses Point Road,** County Sligo: **Ballincar House** is a converted country house in the heart of Yeats country; all 20 bedrooms are spacious; good food; tennis court, squash complex, sauna, and solarium. Nearby golf, riding, beaches. **Rosslare,** County Wexford: **Kelly's Strand Hotel** is a large edifice with indoor/outdoor tennis, indoor swimming pool, sauna, solarium, squash; bicycles, crazy golf; hairdresser; children's playroom, and giant outdoor chess and checkers (or draughts, as they are known in local parlance). **Skibbereen,** County Cork: **Liss Ard House** is a historic Georgian mansion; exclusive, luxurious, on a 70-acre estate with pony trekking, jumping and hunter trials, tennis court, croquet lawn, fishing, rowing, nature walks and its own stable. In **Tomhaggard,** County Wexford: **Bargy Castle** is a 12th-century Norman castle; 14 rooms, all with bath; beaches, fishing, waterskiing, riding, tennis, golf; four-poster beds, secret passages, and opportunities for digging through recently uncovered ruins. Unheralded, unsung, but a secret hideaway, so secret that it's generally unlisted! In **Tralee,** County Kerry: **Ballyseede Castle** stands in a secluded wooded estate with nearby sandy beaches; deep sea fishing in the Bay of Tralee can be arranged, along with golfing, riding; quiet and pleasant.

CAMPING AND CARAVANING Camping equipment rental firms, camping cars (caravans), and camping sites are listed in the ITB publication *Discover Ireland Caravan and Camping Parks,* obtainable in the U.S. or in Ireland from any of the TIOs. There are camping sites in the majority of the counties, and many of these have a children's playroom, food shops, tennis, and minigolf (pitch-and-putt) on the premises, along with laundry facilities, children's paddling pools, and other recreational activities at the site or nearby. **The Association for Adventure Sports**

(AFAS), located at the **Tiglin Adventure Center** near Ashford, County Wicklow organizes seven-day canoe/kayak tours, adventure holidays with accommodation under canvas while mountain camping, windsurfing, mountain walking, rock climbing, orienteering, walking. **Connemara Adventure Holidays** (Atlantic Coast Hotel, Clifden, County Galway) combines hotel stays with camping and such activities as deepsea and freshwater fishing, pony trekking, mountain climbing, swimming, and excursions with five-day accommodation in tents. **An Oige** (the Irish Youth Hostels Association) provides dormitory accommodations and facilities for cooking your own meals in over 50 sites. An official handbook and further information available from the **Irish Youth Hostel Association** (An Oige), 39 Mountjoy Square, Dublin.

Horse-drawn caravans: For unhurried traveling (8–10 miles a day on an average). Mood, personality, temperament, and weather are all factors to take into consideration, but facilities for horse-drawn caravaning are inarguably more extensive in Ireland than in any other country. Each caravan is a rubber-tired covered wagon with four berths/bunks/ mattressed sleeping shelves, and comes equipped with a hot plate, gas lights, linens, kitchen utensils, and light housekeeping equipment. Many operators have service stations where you can bathe or shower and have the horse groomed. Evening stopovers may be local farms or pubs. Well-planned routes are available from the following operators: **County Cork:** *Blarney Romany Caravans,* Blarney, County Cork; *Ocean Breeze Horse Caravans,* Kilbrittain, County Cork; **County Kerry:** *Slattery's Travel Agency,* Tralee, County Kerry; **County Limerick:** *Shannon Horse Caravans,* Adare, County Limerick; **County Mayo:** *Connemara Horse Caravans,* Westport House Country Estate, Westport, County Mayo; **County Wicklow:** *Dieter Clissmann Horse Drawn Caravan Holidays,* Carrigmore, Glenealy, County Wicklow. The high season is mid-June to the end of Aug. Advance bookings can also be made through the Central Reservation Board, Dublin.

ATTRACTIONS FOR CHILDREN IN DUBLIN Within a 20-mile radius, there are good facilities for swimming, tennis, golf, fox-hunting, boating, yachting, and fishing. The TIO will be glad to supply all details. **Phoenix Park and Zoo,** the largest (1700 acres) enclosed park in Europe, with elephant, pony, and pony-cart rides; an amusement section for children; beautiful lakes with Ireland's largest collection of exotic water birds; ball grounds and race course. Lakeside coffee shop, restaurant-cafeterias; The **Dublin Zoo** is noted for lion breeding, only two miles from the city center. **St. Patrick's Cathedral;** choral services (weekdays at 10 a.m. and 5:45 p.m. are lovely. **Trinity College Library;** fine manuscripts and books, the prize being the illuminated 8th-century *Book of Kells,* whose richness of decoration is considered unparalleled. However, the book is under glass and therefore doesn't look as impressive as it might. But do take the children to see it. The college itself is absolutely beautiful. Dublin's libraries and their collections of rare books and manuscripts are a star attraction the ITB will gladly detail for you. The **Douglas Hyde Gallery** (Tel: (01) 77–29–41) is a center with changing exhibits that might beguile, suit your style. **Guinness's Brewery** (James St.), the largest brewery in Europe offers an informative museum program at St. James' Gate; only children 12 and over allowed, as the program is climaxed with a free sample of Guinness! **Dublin Castle** houses a unique **Heraldic Museum** where you can trace your armorial bearings. Also a throne room and state apartments. The **National Botanic Gardens,** 50 acres in the Glasnevin suburb; conservatories open daily from 9 a.m. in summer, 10 a.m. in winter, 2 p.m. on Sun. (although the rest of the garden is open on Sun. at 11 a.m.). Varied seasonal color.

You should take in a ***Greyhound Race*** at Harold's Cross Park or Shelbourne Park; or watch a ***Hurling Match*** at Croke Park—hurling is a fast and furious game somewhat like hockey, excitedly played with a ball that can be struck on the ground or in the air. The **Tourist Trail** is a specially selected sign-posted walking tour through the center of Dublin; many landmarks of historic and cultural interest; three hours is the average walking time. Ask for the Tourist Trail booklet from **Dublin TIO Leinster House** (Kildare St.), now housing Parliament, was used as a model by the architect L'Enfant in designing the White House in Washington. The **National Museum** (Kildare St.) has dazzling neolithic and early Christian gold objects, including the famous Tara Brooch. Other museums: The **Hugh Lane Municipal Art Gallery** (Parnell Sq.), Impressionists to the present; the **Royal Irish Academy Library** (Dawson St.), beautifully illuminated ancient manuscripts; the **Civic Museum** (South William St.), material relating to the history of Dublin. **The Museum of Childhood** (The Palms, 20 Palmerston Park, Rathmines) houses a collection of dolls, dolls' houses, miniature furniture, rocking horses; a charmer. To see what coats of arms are really about, head for the **Heraldic Museum** in Dublin Castle. The **National Maritime Museum** is in Haigh Terrace in nearby **Dun Laoghaire** (pronounced Dun Leery). The **James Joyce Museum** is in James Joyce Tower, in nearby **Sandy Cove;** the 18th-century Martello Tower, where Joyce lived, is mentioned in the beginning of *Ulysses*.

Depending on the performances, the children might enjoy an Irish play at the **Abbey Theatre** (Middle Abbey St.). You can get tickets at service desks of Dublin's major hotels, or at the box office of the Abbey Theater, open 10:30 a.m.–8 p.m., Mon.–Sat.; tickets can be charged to a Visa credit card. Special **Irish concerts** take place on weekdays at lunchtime during July and Aug. in St. Stephen's Green, and band concerts take place regularly in some of Dublin's parks. Details and schedules from the ITB.

Depending on the program, you might also be interested in attending a performance at the **Gate Theatre,** with its 18th-century auditorium; the **Gaiety,** where pantomime, ballet, musical comedy, drama are presented across the Liffey; the **Olympia,** with ballet, pantomime, drama; or the **Lambert Mews Theatre** (Clifden Lane, Monkstown) with puppet performances. The new **National Concert Hall** (Earlsfort Terrace) is felicitously varied in its offerings.

Beginning in May, there are **horse shows and gymkhanas** in Dublin, County Cork, County Tipperary and scores of other places, but the grandest show of all is the ***Dublin Horse Show*** in Aug., with over 2000 horses, international jumping competitions, auction sales of horses and ponies, and special riding and jumping competitions for children. Horse Show Week transforms Dublin so completely that the city streets become anterooms to the show ring as horsemen make Dublin their own. Reservations should be made far in advance; accommodation is practically impossible; hotel rates are at their highest.

Powerscourt Estate and Gardens, 16 miles south of the city in Co. **Wicklaw;** comprises 40 acres; open Easter–Oct. Sights include a 400′ waterfall; wishing well; Italianate gardens; lake; deer park; Japanese garden; bring a picnic or eat at the cafe. Nine miles north of Dublin is **Malahide** at the mouth of the Broad Meadow estuary. Nice sandy stretches for swimming; **Malahide Castle** where the James Boswell papers were discovered hidden in a croquet box in the attic is open to the public. The castle turret rooms are dear; the furniture is interesting, and part of the National Portrait Collection is on view. Make an excursion to **Rathfarnham** to the **Marley Craft Centre** if you're interested in weaving, pottery, glass-blowing, crystal cutting, and other crafts; adjoining shop; open Mon.–Fri., 10 a.m.–5 p.m.

ATTRACTIONS FOR CHILDREN ELSEWHERE Look for antiquities, art, and architecture. Along the west coast you can see circular fortifications dating from the Bronze Age. The carved high stone crosses dotting the countryside are typical of Irish medieval sculpture (the **Cross of Muiredach** at Monasterboice is considered the finest example). Pre-Christian dolmens, Druid circles, and Celtic crosses are plentiful in Galway.

The **ruins** of monasteries, abbeys, and churches—and the restoration and preservation of them as national monuments—make for beautiful and mystical places (the less restoration, the more mystical) if you are lucky enough to come upon them when there are few or no other visitors. They can become places your children can claim as their own. A random mix of such special places might be: **Clonmacnois,** County Offaly; **Gallarus Oratory** and **Ardfert Cathedral,** County Kerry; **Glendalough,** County Wicklow; **Jerpoint Abbey,** County Kilkenny; **Mellifont Abbey** and **Monasterboice,** County Louth; **Rock of Cashel, Holycross Abbey,** and **Hoare Abbey,** County Tipperary; **Askeaton Friary** and **Adare Abbey,** County Limerick; **Cong Abbey, Rosserk Friary,** and **Ballintubber Abbey,** County Mayo; **Clonfert Cathedral,** County Galway; **Creevelea Friary,** County Leitrim; **Inishmurray Is-**

land and **Sligo Abbey,** County Sligo; **Killeshin Church,** County Laois; **Boyle Abbey,** County Roscommon; **Ennis Abbey** and **Quin Abbey,** County Clare.

County Clare offers pleasant beaches; good coastal fishing along Milltown Malbay; good trout fishing at Corofin and Ennistymon; the towering limestone cliffs of Moher, where the Spanish Armada was wrecked in the 16th century. The cliffs of Moher, which rise 700′ from the sea, abound in myths, legends, birdlife, geology, and history that you can learn about at the **Cliffs of Moher Visitor Centre,** near Liscannor. The lunarlike Karst limestone formations of the **Burren** area, with its Arctic, Alpine, and Mediterranean wildflowers are explained with push-button audiovisual presentations at the **Burren Display Centre** in **Kilfenora** where you'll also find the **Poulnabrone Dolmen,** a Stone Age structure, and **St. Fachnan's Cathedral.** You can inspect the **Aillwee Cave,** two miles southeast of **Ballyvaughan,** part of the underworld of the Burren (clean, well-lit, no bats). All open in Mar.–Oct. **Bunratty and Quin:** At **Bunratty Castle and Folk Park,** on a Clare County day, you can see yesteryear; open-air museum with village shops, farm cottages, agricultural displays, demonstrations, and more. Open daily 9:30 a.m.–5 p.m. (until 8 p.m. in summer), with access to the restored 15th-century castle where you can enjoy medieval banquets with singing and festivities staged at 5:45 p.m. and 9 p.m. every night; morning and afternoon teas throughout the year in a romantic castle setting. In **Quin,** you can visit **Knappogue Castle,** tastefully restored, offering tempting morning and afternoon teas May–Sept.; medieval banquets with accompanying historical pageant at 5:45 p.m. and 9 p.m. every night from Apr.–Oct. Nearby, about six miles southeast of **Ennis** is the **Craggaunowen Castle** with medieval art objects inside, and outside, on the grounds of this restored 16th-century tower house, a Bronze Age "crannog," or lake dwelling, has been reconstructed, also a ring fort of the early Christian period, also a replica of the 6th-century vessel used by St. Brendan, the Navigator, on his voyages. On another site, visit the Franciscan cloisters of Quin Abbey. All stimuli for the imagination. In **Corbally, Kilkee,** the **Coosheen Folk Museum** is County Clare-voyant. Handspinning, weaving, embroidery, jewelry-making, and other crafts can be visited Mon.–Fri., 10 a.m.–4 p.m. at **Ballycaseymore House** in **Shannon.**

County Cork: Crosshaven, Youghal, and Glengariff are popular ***seaside resorts,*** the latter still a gem despite its holiday amenities. Since everyone is going to ask the children if they kissed the Blarney Stone, you might as well head for **Blarney Castle,** and go through the rigmarole of letting a guide hold your lambkins by the ankles while they lean over backward and kiss that stone. (The commercialism is far less tiresome than that at Killarney.) Idyllic ***picnicking and boating*** terrain for family excursions around St. Finbarr's Hollow, where the River Lee begins its course, and also in the village of Bantry and the 20-mile sweep of Bantry Bay. **Bantry House,** an 18th-century showpiece on the outskirts of Bantry, is worth a stop; refreshments and craft shop. **Castle Gardens** in **Timoleague Village, Bandon,** with ruins of Barrymore Castle, has a children's playground and picnicking sites. The star-shaped **Charles Fort** is two miles southeast of **Kinsale** and is the best-preserved 17th-century fort in Ireland. The **Regional Museum** in Kinsale is an amuse 'em. The **Gougane Bara Forest Park** with the ruins of an ancient monastery, is two miles off the Macroom/Bantry Road at the Pass of Keimaneigh. **Fota Island,** nine miles from Cork, is only open from Easter through Oct., but has a lovely arboretum and wildlife park. The **Cork Public Museum** in Fitzgerald Park has archaeological and natural history collections. If you're interested in crafts, have a look at the **Craft Yard** in **Aheria;** open Mon.–Sun., 9:30 a.m.–5:30 p.m. Also the **Kilworth Craft Centre** in **Kilworth;** open Mon.–Fri., 10 a.m.–5 p.m. The **West Cork Regional Museum** in **Clonakilty,** the **Cobh Museum** in **Scotschurch, Cobh,** the museum in the clock tower in **Youghal's** Main St., the **MacSweeney Museum** in **Kilmurray, Lissarda,** are all fun to brisk through. In **County Donegal,** heart of Yeats' territory, at **Glencolumbkille,** site of an early Christian monastery with dolmenlike decorated grave slabs, there's an open-air folk village, all cottage furnishings are authentic. **Doe Castle** is a beauty and the remains of a circular fort called **Grianan of Aileach** are also interesting if you're in the neighborhood. The **Donegal Museum,** housed in the Franciscan Friary, **Rossnowlagh,** has a mixed bag of archaeological, numismatic, folkloric, military and historic exhibits.

In **County Galway,** Salthill is a popular ***seaside resort.*** Don't forget the **Aran Islands,** reachable by steamer and air from Galway City. (The slow steamers make for a long daytrip, so I'd recommend their use for older children only.) Your children will come across these rugged, rocky islands of Inishmore, Inishmann, and Inisheer again when they read John M. Synge's *Riders to the Sea.* Men struggle here against nature to earn a living that is startlingly simple. Good swimming here, and a number of early Christian buildings and relics; three simple but adequate guesthouses if you feel like staying longer. The TIO (Eyre Sq., Galway; Tel: (091) 63081) has more details. Have a look at the **Museum Arainn** in **Kilronan, Inishmore,** and the **Museum nan Oilean** in **Inishmann.** On the Clifden-Wesport road, search out the village of **Moyard** for the pleasure of lunching at the **Doon** restaurant, open noon–3 p.m. daily for lunch only; closed Weds., Oct.–Easter.

Connemara with its mists, stone walls, is wild, bleak country with a radiant light and seemingly unchanging customs and way of life. See the *harp-maker* and *bodhran-maker* at work in the **Roundstone Craft Centre,** Mon.–Fri., 10 a.m.–5 p.m. The **Connemara National Park** is a lovely nature preserve. Visit **Dunguaire Castle,** a small 15th-century tower house at **Kinvara,** for a medieval banquet followed by historic skits and music, twice nightly at 5:45 p.m. and 9 p.m., mid-May to the end of Sept. If the poetry of William Butler Yeats entrances you, don't miss **Thoor Ballylee,** about 22 miles S of Galway, six miles E of Gort; the four-story Norman keep which was his summer house; Yeats' memorabilia; open Easter–mid-Oct.; teas served. You can enjoy boating and bird-watching at **Portumna Forest Park.** The history of Galway is encompassed in its **City Museum** next to the Spanish Arch. **Lynch's Castle** and **St. Nicholas' Church** are the major tourist attractions. **Aughnanure Castle,** on the Drimneen river, is about two miles SE of **Oughterard,** and has a grim four-story tower-house; open mid-June–Sept. 30.

If you are in Dublin for the Aug. Horse Show, do try to go to **Dingle** in **County Kerry** for the annual races and country carnival. Tinkers, and peddlars herald the **Puck Fair** at **Killorglin;** streets are crowded with gypsies, acrobats, processions, bands, people in costumes, thousands gathering for the jovial merrymaking. This festival, a survival of a major Celtic festival, is followed by the Single Agricultural Show. The steep hillsides of Mount Brandon are dotted with white beehive-shape huts built by Christian hermits. It is said that everyone in this remote and primitive area has heard the mermaids singing and seen a sea monster at least once. Legend has it that 18 ships of the Armada entered Dingle Bay and never left, the Spanish crews having settled and intermarried with the Irish. Across the bay, underwater excavations of ships wrecked here in the 16th century are carried on each summer; any fisherman will row you out in his coracle. **Valentia Island, Ballingskellings, Waterville, Castlecove, Parknasilla** (good fishing, shooting, and golf), and lovely **Tahilla** village are all beauty spots with adequate accommodations from which you can sally forth to search out your own private beach paradise. From **Portmagee** you can hire a motorboat to visit **Skellings Rocks,** breeding place of sea birds, with a lighthouse and monastery ruins to explore. And onshore, across the way, the 2000-year-old **Staigue Fort,** surrounded by bank and ditch, is on private property; you'll have to pay a fee if you trespass. About five miles north of Dingle near **Kilmalkedar** is the early Christian **Gallarus Oratory,** a small structure in the shape of an upturned boat, probably built between the 8th and 12th centuries on the site of an earlier monastery. The stones were handfitted, wedged so tightly together that they still remain leakproof in pelting rain. An unprepossessing national monument, but somehow, this primitive pyramid is mystical and magical. These spots are all more entrancing for children than overcommercialized **Killarney,** where jaunting cars and pony-driven carts are a specialty; most of the principal tours are pretty exhausting for children, though the region is undeniably lovely. **Muckross House and Gardens,** about 3½ miles from Killarney on the Kenmare Rd., in the heart of the Killarney Lake District, is the **Kerry Folklife and Folklore Center,** with weavers, basketmakers, blacksmiths, potters all plying their crafts in a lush garden setting with a craft shop and refreshments available. By arrangement, you can clip-clop around the surrounding **Killarney National Park** in a jaunting car or you can bicycle on trails.

Co. Kildare: In **Robertson,** 26 miles from Dublin, 18th-century candlelight banquets are combined with a barge trip on the Grand Canal and a visit to the Falconry of Ireland located on the grounds of the Old Grand Canal Hotel with an eclectic museum of canal transport, radios, bottles, holy wells, and other curiosities of the region. A great excursion and diversion in good weather. For information and details, check with the manager of the Old Grand Canal Hotel, Robertstown. The **Irish Horse Museum** at the National Stud in **Tully,** about a mile S of Kildare town, is a quest for equestrians; across the road is a **Japanese Garden.** Do go to **King John's Castle** in **Limerick, County Limerick,** on selected summer evenings when traditional music is played. **Westport House,** a Georgian mansion overlooking Clew Bay, with art center, zoo park, souvenir, antique, craft shops, a mile from **Westport** town in **County Mayo** is a must in the area. In **County Meath,** near enough to Dublin just to zip out there are burial mounds along the Boyne River at **Newgrange, Dowth,** and **Knowth** where the ancient kings of Ireland were buried. The mound at Newgrange contains a passage tomb from the Stone Age. Only four miles from Drogheda, you'll find another passage tomb with decorated stones at Dowth, also dating from the Stone Age, around 3000 B.C. If you're headed for the **Knock Shrine, Claremorris, County Mayo,** take in the **Knock Folk Museum** on the site, with its collections of folklife, archaeology, history, religion. The **Monaghan County Museum** in the courthouse, **Monaghan,** highlights exhibits of lace, crafts, local history, folklife, archaeology; was awarded the Council of Europe Museum Prize; a true gem among small museums.

County Offaly offers **Clonmacnois,** the remains of a 6th-century monastery, with churches, Celtic crosses, round towers, and gravestones rising by the Shannon River. **Birr Castle Demesne,** with its gardens, waterfalls, rivers, lake, astronomical artifacts and box hedges is open all year; it's close to the **Portumna Forest Park** and **Clonfert Cathedral** in neighboring Co. Galway. If you're interested in the uncommon in **County Roscommon,** head for the **Strokestown Craft Centre** in **Strokestown,** where pottery, musical instruments, glass, and copper are crafted; open Mon.–Fri., 10 a.m.–5 p.m. The **Sligo County Museum,** Stephen St., **Sligo** has collections of rare books, manuscripts, history, archaeology, folklife, and paintings. **Cahir Castle, County Tipperary,** on a rocky island in the Suir River, is the largest castle built in Ireland in the 15th and 16th centuries. Recently restored, with the only working portcullis in Ireland, it features an audiovisual presentation on Ireland's architectural heritage in the Great Hall.

Toomevara offers a folk museum of 19th-century rural exhibits.

County Waterford, with rugged cliffs and seaside villages (some secluded; others, like Tramore, offering resort facilities and a fun-fair to delight the children), also abounds in ponies and jaunting cars for hire.

In **Athlone,** the Castle houses a museum of archaeology and folklore **(County Westmeath). Lough Key Forest Park** in **County Roscommon** and the **John F. Kennedy Park** in **County Wexford** have restaurants open May–Sept.

Dun a Ri Forest Park and **Killykeen Forest Park** (County Cavan); **Gougane Barra Forest Park** (County Cork); **Ards Forest Park** (County Donegal); **Connemara National Park** and **Portumna Forest Park** (County Galway); **Derrynane National Historic Park** and **Killarney National Park** (County Kerry); **Rossmore Forest Park** (County Monaghan); **Avon Forest Park** (County Wicklow)—these parks are all open year round. Good for picnics, outings, walks.

FUN TRIPS *Crystal factories:* An otherwise impeccably well-spoken grandmama was heard to observe with witty vulgarity that the **Waterford Glass Factory** was a ''pain in the glass'': advance reservations required, no children under 12 allowed; closed from the end of July to late Aug.; no shop on the premises, so forget Waterford in County Waterford if these conditions don't appeal. **Galway Crystal Ltd.** in **Merlin Park,** County Galway, has a shop open all year, but the factory is closed July 26–Aug. 13; welcomes all visitors, five days a week, 9 a.m.–5 p.m.; no guided tours Fri. afternoons; guided tours Apr.–Sept. **Cavan Crystal Ireland Ltd.,** situated on the Dublin Rd. just outside of **Cavan** town in Cavan County, has guided tours Mon.–Fri.; factory shop open all year; factory closed first two weeks in Aug. **Dublin Crystal Ltd, Blackrock,** County Dublin, has escorted tours Mon.–Fri., 9 a.m.–1 p.m. and 2 p.m.–5:30 p.m.; factory shop open all year.

Enjoy a 40-minute cruise aboard the motor-vessels *Lady Nicola* or *Lady Sarah* in Lough Key Forest; offered by **Shannon Cruises Ltd.,** Cootehall, Boyle, County Roscommon. Or sail aboard *The Jolly Mariner* from Athlone to Lough Ree, a day trip with lots of time to spare. Information from **Aloma Cruises,** 5 Retreat Heights, Athlone, County Westmeath. You can ***rent your own sloop*** for day sailing or coastal cruising at the **Dun Laoghaire Sailing School,** 115 Lower George's St., Dun Laoghaire, County Dublin. *Family yachts* and *cruiser/racers,* with or without skipper, can be hired for the day or longer from **Andrew Stott Yacht Charters,** Rossbrin Cove, Schull, County Cork. Family yachts, sleeping from five to nine, with or without skipper, are available from **Irish Atlantic Yacht Charters,** Ballylickey, Bantry, County Cork. ***Harbor cruises, bird-watching cruises, Fastnet Rock cruises, private training cruises*** are also possible.

Rides on a ***narrow-gauge railway, steam engines, tractions engines,*** and other mechanical wonders of yesteryear? The collection of the late Col. Charles Kidd draws many visitors annually to the little village of **Stradbally.** On the first weekend in Aug., a three-day steam and traction engine rally provides steering competitions for visitors. Parents and children have a fine time with this. Year round, the museum exhibits models dating from the 1850s on. The TIO has more details.

FUN AND GAMES The ITB can send you free, precisely detailed and informative print sheets about bird watching, bicycling, canoeing, caving, fishing, golf, hang-gliding, hill-walking and rock-climbing, horse racing, hunting, orienteering, sailing, sailing schools and tuition, various watersports, traditional music. Contact the following places for additional courses, holidays, and outings: **Dublin School of English** (11 Westmoreland St., Dublin), **Adventure Holidays-St. Paul's Summer School** (St. Paul's College, Sybil Hill, Raheny, Dublin), **Andrews Travel Consultants** (10 Meadow Vale, Blackrock, County Dublin), and **Horetown House** (Foulksmills, County Wexford).

The **Rathmichael Historical Society** (c/o Joan Delany, Falls Rd., Shankill, County Dublin) offers courses in archaeology. An 18th-century banquet-cum-barge trip with entertainment is offered by the **Old Grand Canal Hotel** in Robertson, County Kildare, from Apr.–Oct. Check out the Traditional Music information sheet offered by the ITB. And if you're in Tralee, County Kerry, **Siamsa,** Ireland's National Folk Theater presents traditional mime, song and dance Mon. and Thurs. from mid-June–mid-Sept., as well as Tues. and Fri. in July and Aug. Classes in folk music, instrumental playing, Irish *ceili* and step-dancing are available year round from the **Congress of Irish Musicians** (Comhaltas Ceoloiri Eireann). The **Irish Cultural Institute** offers a year-round program on various traditional instruments and dances. Contact Comhaltas Ceoltoiri Eireann, Culturlann na hEireann, Belgrave Square, Monkstown, County Dublin) for more programs and entertainment.

Courses in archaeology, history, natural history, are offered by the **Corrib Conservation Centre** (Rosscahill, County Galway). Courses are arranged for adults, but teenaged students can be included. Painting and other arts and crafts courses: **An Grinian** (Termonfeckin, County Louth) has weekend and weekly courses. The **Irish School of Landscape Painting** has centers in Dublin and Clifden, Connemara, for winter, summer, and weekend courses; information and reservations from **The Blue Door Studio,** Prince of Wales Terrace, Dublin). **The Burren Holiday Painting Centre,** O'Neill's Guesthouse, Lisdoonvarna, County Clare.

Ask the ITB for information about other courses in creative writing, drama, and other specialized interests which are often combined with home stay accommodation and enticing extras. Many possibilities are listed in the *Discover Young Ireland* booklet, described as "A guide to learning and leisure opportunities for the teens and twenties."

Garnett's and Keegan's Ltd. (31 Parliament St., Dublin; Tel: (01) 77–74–72) tackle-makers, gunmakers, and sporting estate agents, will advise you ably about buying or renting any equipment you need (their fishing rods, flies, and firearms are superb). Ask the TIO for its data sheet on game fishing. Permits and rod licenses are inexpensive and easily obtained. Although there are good facilities for salmon, trout, and sea fishing near Dublin, and, broadly speaking, good ***fishing*** facilities in every county, **Lough Corrib** probably offers the best all-round free fishing—salmon, trout, pike, perch. A region of magnificent scenery, lakes with brilliantly clear water, mountains, moorland, and a coastline indented with rocky coves and sandy beaches, Lough Corrib provides endless opportunities for picknicking and boating (plenty of boats and boatmen, called "ghillies," to take you out). "Dapping," a method of fishing with live insects, originated here. The mayfly, an insect with big net-veined wings like those of a dragonfly, gives rise to the uniquely Irish sport of blow-line dabbing. Good fishing spots in Connemara are the **Ballynahinch River** and lakes. **Clifden,** a lovely little town, offers good sea fishing; a number of sandy beaches a mile from town provide excellent safe swimming. At **Cleggan,** seven miles northwest, the mailboat will take you to the island of **Inishbofin,** a trip I certainly recommend.

Hunting? Horse and hound are an integral part of Irish country life, whether you are following staghounds, foxhounds, or harriers. Ireland offers the cheapest hunting in Europe. Big contingents of children on ponies are a regular feature of most hunts, and if your youngsters have had sufficient riding experience to take jumping in their stride, they will never have more fun hunting than they will here. The season is Nov.–Mar. Topnotch horses can be rented in all hunting districts. Arrangements can be made with riding stables or the Secretary of the Hunt. Details can be supplied by the local TIOs, and the ITB publication *A Guide for the Equestrian Visitor to Ireland*.

Your child need not be an expert horseman to sample the joys of cantering along woodland paths. ***Pony trekking*** instruction is given to children and beginners. Many hotels and guesthouses have ponies available for clients on hourly, half-day, or full-day bases. You can also book mounts for yourselves as a family at a daily hiring charge, including a picnic basket, and follow a go-as-you-please itinerary, guided by the groom's knowledge of the neighborhood. Dozens of riding schools in every county. Mr. Jeremy Castle (Glebe House, Aglish, Roscrea, County Tipperary) offers a week's full-board accommodation at Glebe House including two full days hunting with the Ormond Hunt. **Travel Ireland Ltd.** (76 Grand Parade, Cork) offers two hours riding tuition a day, five days a week. Also five hours sailing or windsurfing tuition a day.

Racing? Meets in Galway, Killarney, Tramore, Limerick, Punchestown, Phoenix Park, the Curragh, and just about everywhere else. The Classic, the Great Race, of course, is the **Grand National** run at Fairyhouse, County Meath, on Easter Mon. Steeple-chasing and hurdling mostly during the winter months. Flat racing Apr.–Oct. The All-Ireland

Polo Club in Phoenix Park, Dublin is one of the oldest polo clubs in existence. Matches take place on Wed. evenings, and weekend afternoons from May–mid-Sept. Free admission!

Horse-loving families might find the following Dublin addresses useful: **The Racing Board** (9 Merrion Sq.; Tel: (01) 76–11–71); **Royal Dublin Society** (Ballsbridge; Tel: (01) 680–645) for information about the **Dublin Horse Show; Show Jumping Association of Ireland** (58 Upper Leeson St.; Tel: (01) 60–58–32).

Golf is a leading sport. **Portmarnock,** outside Dublin, is one of the greatest courses in the world. Over 250 courses dotted around the country, some of the best at Lahinch, Waterville, Rosslare, Connermara, Carlow, Killarney; Royal Dublin, Rosses Point, County Sligo. Golf lessons are given by pros at almost all Irish courses. Reasonable fees. Try the **Leopardstown Golf Centre** (Leopardstown, Foxrock, County Dublin), the **Clare Manor Driving Range** (Clare Manor Hotel, Malahide Rd., Dublin), and the **Spawell Driving Range** (Tallaght, County Dublin). Send for the ITB information sheet. ***Pitch-and-Putt,*** not to be confused with minigolf, has courses everywhere; a list is available on request from **The Pitch and Putt Union of Ireland** (rear 32 Shandon Gardens, Philsboro, Dublin), the only official union of its kind in the world!

Beaches: Ireland has a number of resort beaches with merry-making amenities, most of them with hotels or guesthouses where children are specially catered to and always welcomed, but families in search of virtually untrodden sand and ravishing bays should try **Kerry, Sligo,** and **Donegal;** all offer blissful private paradises. At dusk, when the lobster boats come in, there is bound to be an inshore fisherman ready to give the children a line to catch a silvery mackerel.

Swimming pools in Dublin? The open-air, sea-water-filled pool (at Clontarf) gives swimming lessons for children. The **Burlington Hotel,** Leeson St., has a very pleasant indoor heated pool. (See Castles and Other Happy Family Accommodations for more suggestions!)

Adventure? The **Creeslough Adventure Center** (County Donegal located in the highlands of Donegal, offers qualified instruction in canoeing, snorkeling, surfing and other watersports on rivers, lakes, sea. Information and reservations from the **Union of Students in Ireland** (USIT), (7 Anglesea St., Dublin) a travel company that also offers bicycle, sailing, and walking holidays.

Surfing or Waterskiing? If you're interested, send for the ITB information sheets. If you're *serious,* write to the **Irish Water Ski Association** (7 Upper Beamont Dr., Ballintemple, Cork) and to Brian V. Britton, Chairman, **Irish Surfing Association** (266 Sutton Park, Sutton, Dublin 13). Clubs and clubmembers will be delighted to welcome you. ***Board sailing?*** **Dun Laoghaire Sailing School** (115 Lower George's St., Dun Laoghaire, County Dublin) welcomes students 12 and over. Also try **Fingall Sailing School** (Malahide, County Dublin). For information about other courses, clubs, details, send for the ITB information sheet. ***Canoeing/kayaking?*** The **Association for Adventure Sports** operate canoeing courses at **Tiglin Adventure Centre** (Ashford, County Wicklow) and **Creeslough Adventure Centre** (County Donegal). Also **Sand House Hotel** (Rossnowlagh, County Donegal) and **Riversdale Sailing Centre** (Riversdale Farmhouse, Ballinamore, County Leitrim). Send for the ITB's information sheet which will give you the details and guidelines.

Sailing? There are many schools and centers for pupils 8–65 who can swim. Recommended are: **Baltimore Sailing School** (The Pier, Baltimore, County Cork), **Dun Laoghaire Sailing School** (115 Lower George's St., Dun Laoghaire, County Dublin), **Fingall Sailing School** (Malahide, County Dublin), **Galway Sailing Center** (8 Father Griffin Rd., Galway), **International Sailing Centre** (Cobh, County Cork), **St. Brendan's School of Navigation** (St. Brendan's, Derrymore West, Tralee, County Kerry), **Slieve Foy Sailing School** (Omeath, County Louth), and **Skerries School of Sailing** (18 Harbour Rd., Skerries, County Dublin).

Bicycles are easily rented in all major towns. A specially designed bicycle called the Tourer is available from over 60 **Rent-a-Bike** dealers throughout the country—list of dealers available from the TIO.

SHOPPING WITH AND FOR CHILDREN Shopping hours: Weekdays 9:30 a.m.–5:30 p.m. Stock up on children's sweaters, tweeds, lace collars, and linen sheets (which also make great curtains for children's rooms). The *Craft Hunters Pocket Guide* is an illustrated booklet listing local crafts and where you can buy them (available from the ITB and TIOs). In **Dublin,** The **Powerscourt Town House Center** (South William Street) an 18th-century complex comprises dozens of shops beneath a glass-roofed courtyard where you can buy a variety of handcrafts. **The Craftsmans Guild** is a cooperative store there. Another place for indigenous quality handcrafts is the **Kilkenny Shop** (Nassau St.) with a large selection of Irish goodies at high but not unreasonable prices.

For clothes and toys: **Switzer & Co., Ltd.** (Grafton St.), department store with a good selection of Irish dolls. **Brown Thomas and Co., Ltd.** (Grafton St. and Duke St.) lives up to its slogan as "The loveliest store in Ireland." Complete selection of tweeds, linens, Carrickmacross lace, wonderful collars for little girls' velveteen dresses; sweaters made in the Isle of Aran are outstanding; tourist information bureau on the ground floor. **Arnott's** (Henry St.) and **Clory's** (O'Connell St.) are two other department stores with children's clothes and toys. Excellent values for baby clothes and toys for infants up to 4 at the **Baby Shop** (14 Chatham St.).

Hand-knit wearables and tweeds: **Irish Cottage Industries** (44 Dawson St.). ***Riding clothes for parents and children:*** **Callaghan's** at Brown Thomas and Co., Ltd., has a well-stocked Pony Club dept.; has everything for children and their ponies.

Good bookshops: **Eblana Bookshop** (46 Grafton St.); **Paperback Centre** (20 Suffolk St.); **Hodges Figgis and Co., Ltd.** (56 Dawson St.); **Eason and Son Ltd.** (40 Lower O'Connel St.). Irish ***Records and musical instruments*** at **Walton's** (2 North Frederick St.).

Everything from rosary beads made of bog oak and Connemara marble to chocolates at **Shannon Airport.** Mail order catalog available.

In **Spiddal,** County Galway, the leading shop for hand-made Irish goodies, including tweeds, sweaters, sheepskin rugs, linens is **Mairtin Standum** (Tel: (091) 83150). Open daily plus Sun. Free illustrated catalog if you enclose postage.

IRISH FRIENDS AND PEN PALS The TIO's "Meet the Irish" program provides a great way to get together, even just for a cup of tea.

If you write to the TIO of your choice or to "Meet the Irish" (Bord Failte, Baggot St. Bridge, Dublin), and give your name, address, profession, interests, age group, dates of visit, and places where you would like to have introductions, everything will be arranged for you. Applications must be received at least a month in advance of your arrival.

CALENDAR OF EVENTS For particulars, ask the TIO for a copy of Calendar of Events. Sports events, referred to as sporting fixtures, are as widespread and popular as shamrocks on St. Patrick's Day.

Apart from the hunting and horseracing covered earlier, Ireland features: car racing (year round); football, rugby, hockey, badminton (spring, autumn, winter); fishing competitions **(Mar.–Sept.);** golf tournaments **(Apr.–Sept.);** tennis, swimming, sailing, and boating competitions, with many junior events **(June–Aug.);** annual yacht regatta at Dun Laoghaire; bagpipe and hornblowing competitions. Greyhound racing goes on year round at some 2000 meetings at 18 licensed courses. Fencing championships may interest the children **(Jan.–June),** since there are many school and junior participants. Gaelic games—Gaelic football looks to me like a combination of basketball, soccer, and volleyball; hurling, a variety of hockey at the speed of light; handball, played in a three-wall court between single opponents or pairs—are played year round; hurling and Gaelic football are particularly exciting.

On **Mar.** 17th, of course, ***St. Patrick's Day*** is celebrated with parades, dogshows, football, horseracing, folk dancing, motor races; Gaelic games, dances, and parties. In **Apr.,** the ***Irish Grand National*** is run at **Fairyhouse.** Limerick hosts the ***Festival of Limericks.*** In **May** Dublin offers the ***Royal Dublin Society Spring Show and Industries Fair.***

June brings forth the ***Irish Sweeps Derby*** at Curragh; In **July,** throughout Ireland, don't miss the ***county fairs agricultural and dog shows, and horse shows.*** In the latter part of the month, Galway City's ***Race Week*** takes place—six days of racing and general festivities. In

Aug., Kilkenny offers the Annual ***Fleadh Ceoil na hEireann,*** Ireland's annual gathering of traditional musicians—dancers, fiddlers, flautists, whistlers, pipers, ballad singers—the most colorful event reflecting Ireland's folk life and music. Aug. finds Dublin astir with the ***Royal Dublin Society Horse Show*** (first Tues.–Sat.). At Killorglin, near Dingle, the ***Annual Puck Fair*** is held. At the end of Aug., Waterford hosts the ***International Competitive Festival of Light Opera.***

Sept. brings the Dublin ***Theater Festival*** and, at Tralee, the ***Kerry Festival*** (Rose of Tralee contest, horse racing, other sporting events).

In **Oct.,** ***An tOireachtas*** highlights a national cultural festival with music, drama, sporting and chess competitions, Gaelic games held in Carraroe, County Galway. At Wexford, the ***Festival of Music and the Arts*** offers concerts, film programs, operas, recitals and sporting events. ***Harvest Festival*** at Listowel. In **Dec.** most of the major towns provide ***pantomime performances*** for the traditional holiday delight of children. On the 26th Dublin holds its annual ***Dog Show.***

ITALY

Italians delight in children. You often see four generations going off on an excursion, but the children are the ones who get the most attention. Fathers are particularly proud of their children, often take them along with them on business calls, and on any pretext produce pictures and engage in long discussions about their and your offspring. Italy is one country where you really should take your children with you on almost every occasion except nightclubbing! You might expect that Italy—where the stay-at-home mother and the extended family diminishes the need for babysitting and child-care facilities—might be difficult for mothers with young children. Not at all. Italy has astonishingly good children's hotels, nurseries, babysitting agencies. Parks come equipped with marionettes, boat ponds, donkeys to ride, and other joys for children. If there aren't high chairs at a small restaurant, waiters rush to get cushions and telephone books. Shopkeepers delight in giving children candy. Nothing is ever too much trouble if you have the *bambini* with you. Children will love Italy!

Cautionary note: Italy contains the world's largest accumulation of art and archaeology, and museums are everywhere. It's hopeless to try to see them all. A child will get more out of a brisk through three museums than he will from a thorough exploration of one. Remember that childrens' attention span is shorter than yours! Enjoy the delight of walking in the pedestrian malls of the old cities—free of the rush and noise of traffic.

INFORMATION ABOUT ITALY Before you leave America get in touch with **ENIT,** the Italian Government Travel Office (Ente Nazionale Italiano per Il Turismo (630 5th Ave., New York, NY 10020; Tel: (212) 254–4822); or branches in Chicago, San Francisco, or Montreal.

In Rome, the main office is ENIT (2/6 Via Marghera; Tel: (06) 491–646) there are branches in all tourist centers and almost every town—called **EPT** (Ente Provinciale Turismo), or regional tourist information offices—plus many city information offices. Local ***tourist boards*** (Azienda Autonoma Soggiorno) operate in all places of tourist interest. Contact ENIT for a complete list.

CIT (Compagnia Italiana Turismo), the highly efficient official Italian travel agency that offers information and excellent facilities for tours and excursions, will act as your travel agent's Italian representative should you so desire. They have over 60 offices in Italy.

The **Italian Cultural Institute** (Istituto Italiano di Cultura) in New York (686 Park Ave.; Tel: (212) 879–4242), 1 Charlton Ct., Apt. 102, San Francisco, CA 94123; Tel: (415) 927–4177, and in Montreal (1200 Docteur Penfield St.; Tel: (514) 849–3473) sponsors lectures, concerts, exhibitions, and cultural exchanges. See them for the *museum pass, free of charge,* available to teachers and students of art.

Rome's *Daily American,* available all over Italy, will give you an idea about what's going on. Information of interest to travelers is contained in a weekly magazine *This Week in Rome* (with Milan and Naples supplements), usually presented to you free of charge by your hotel or pensione.

Italy is divided into 20 regions, and if you are accustomed to alphabetized information, this may drive you batty because you may find yourself searching through informational material which is alphabetized only in *regional* classifications, which means that you hunt up hotels in Bologna not under B, but in the section dealing with Emilia-Romagna. Each region has its capital, and this list of regions and their capitals may simplify matters, and give the children yet another educational memory game to unravel their Italian travel.

Abruzzo—L'Aquila
Aosta Valley—Aosta
Apulia—Bari
Basilicata—Potenza
Calabria—Catanzaro
Campania—Naples (Napoli)
Emilia-Romagna—Bologna
Friuli-Venetia Julia—Trieste
Latium—Rome (Roma)
Liguria—Genoa (Genova)
Lombardy—Milan (Milano)
The Marches—Ancona
Molise—Campobasso
Piedmont—Turin (Torino)
Sardinia—Cagliari
Sicily—Palermo
Trento-Alto Adige—Trento
Tuscany—Florence (Firenze)
Umbria—Perugia
Venetia—Venice (Venezia)

Each region is divided again, into provinces. For a clearer picture—for you and your children—you'll can find helpful maps in the ENIT booklet (available in the U.S.) called *Italy, an ideal holiday for all the family.* You'll also find the *only* complete list of provincial and local tourist boards inside *(Enti Provinciali per il Turismo* and *Aziende Autonome di Soggiorno, Cura e Turismo).*

HEALTH, WATER, AND FOOD With the exception of southern Italy and certain polluted waters such as the Bay of Naples (avoid seafood; gamma globulin shots a wise precaution), health standards are good. Water? Perfectly safe in all the better hotels and restaurants. Stick to bottled water, such as *San Pellegrino, Crodo,* and *Recoaro* (carbonated), *Fiuggi* (nonfizzy), and *San Gemini* (preferred for children by Italian parents), in rural areas.

In all large cities, milk is pasteurized, as is the milk used to make ice cream. Avoid milk in rural areas.

Italian ice cream, by the way, is delicious; Motta, Giolitti, and Ciampini are the best brands and the only kind you should buy from street vendors. *Gelato* (Italian ice cream) comes in flavors from anisette to zabaglione, and is at its most delicious when you buy it at a neighborhood *gelateria.* Small cones are sold at espresso bars; a *coppa speciale* is the Italian version of a sundae, a gaudy fantasy of various flavors, candied fruits, silver sugar beads, sprinkles, whipped cream; a *granita* is something liquid frozen then ground up and usually served with whipped cream unless you say *"senza panna"* (without cream).

As for the food, it is not redolent with garlic and floating in olive oil, as the popular misconception would have it. Italian food is wonderful, and among the many specialties that children will enjoy are any of the dozens of variations of pasta, in every shape and size. *Fettucine,* thin ribbons; *farfalle,* little bows; *conchiglie,* shells; *cannelloni,* stuffed with meat and baked in a sauce; *manicotti,* stuffed with cheese and baked in a sauce; macaroni with butter and parmesan cheese; *cappelletti* (little hats) stuffed with various mixtures; *calzone,* stuffed with meat, cheese, and eggs and baked until it puffs up; *capellini,* very thin noodles, usually found in soup; *lasagne; linguini strascinati,* narrow noodles in egg sauce; *mafalde,* curlicue noodles; *maccheroni,* macaroni, the generic description for all types of pasta; *tagliatelle verdi,* flat green noodles, colored by being cooked with spinach or some other green vegetable; *ravioli;* and *pizza.* However, our American version of *pizza* is often so different from the original that it's confusing, especially when it comes to *pizza di ricotta,* a sort of Italian cheesecake, and *pizza figliata,* a desert made with honey and nuts. This should give you some idea of all the oodles of noodles. In northern Italy, rice replaces *pasta* as a staple food, and *polenta,* a stiff cornmeal porridge, is a local favorite that some children may like better than *gnocchi* (cornmeal dumplings). *Risotto* is rice simmered in broth plus a variety of additions. *Risi e bisi,* a name children like to pronounce "reesy beesy," is rice and peas, often with ham added. Northern Italians cook with butter, while olive oil, garlic, mozzarella, and tomatoes used with a generous hand are associated chiefly with southern districts. Plenty of vegetables of every variety and excellent salads. *Minestrone,* a thick, vegetable soup, is particularly good, so is *zuppa di patate* (potato soup). *Zuppa inglese* is not a soup, but a rum-soaked cake.

Chicken, veal, and ham are usually better choices than *bistecca* (beefsteak) or *rosbif* (roast beef), although *turnedo,* a tender fillet of beef, is delicious. Italian fish, lobsters, crabs, and shrimp are excellent—the lobsters are the clawless or crayfish kind.

Ricotta is much like cottage cheese; *formaggio di crema* is cream cheese; *mozzarella* is the mild, soft cheese that gets rubbery when melted; and there are certainly many others.

Italians excel in making candy of all kinds and in packaging it with artistic and gastronomic good taste. Individual pieces of nougat *(Torrone)* wrapped in edible paper are packed in sweet little boxes with charming animal pictures. From Perugia, Italy's candy-making city, comes an assortment of chocolate with different flavors that surpasses any I've eaten anywhere.

Macaroons *(amaretti)* are celestial fare, and so is sponge cake. *Panettone,* a Milanese Christmas specialty rather like coffee cake, is one of our family favorites. *Monte Bianco* is a delight of meringue, whipped cream, and pureed chestnuts. Nut cakes, pastries, fritters, and cookies are regional specialties. Except as ornaments, forget *biscotti frascati,* biscuits from Frascati, which are made into pleasing figures of mermaids, camels, horses, angels, and fanciful shapes (the cookie shapes are about 10 x 6 inches for an angel); but their preservative makes them too tough and dry to be eaten with any pleasure.

Breakfast in Italy consists of rolls, jam, fruit, coffee or tea, but cereal, ham, eggs, and orange juice can be produced in a trice. Save money by breakfasting in a bar-cafe. The main meal is lunch, served between 12:30 and 2:30. Dinner is served between 8–11. Meal times are a bit earlier in the north, a bit later in the south. Children are always welcomed at restaurants. It's a good idea to order *mezzo* (½) portions of pasta dishes for the children because the helpings are enormous.

You'll not only save money but you'll enjoy regional fare at its best if you eat at trattorias rather than restaurants. A *trattoria* is informal, kitchen-style, or farmhouse-style, and crowds are a fairly reliable index of its quality: the more jam-packed, the better the food. You can eat inexpensively at restaurants if you ask for the *menu turistico.* Remember also that sitting down at a table in a cafe to have your coffee and ice cream will cost almost twice as much as sitting or standing at the bar.

Contorni on the menu refers to vegetables, and you usually won't get any unless you order them specifically. Most dishes are served ungarnished. When white beans are offered as a side dish, you are expected to drizzle olive oil on them. Spinach generally arrives cold and is served with oil and lemon. If you want it hot, ask for *al burro.* Italian menus are supposed to specify when something is frozen *(surgelati)* or canned *(conservati).* Many restaurants have a bread and cover charge *(coperta)* as well as a service charge of 15% added to the bill. Even so, you're expected to add a few hundred lire *in cash* for the waiter. In Rome, you don't save money by eating lunch rather than dinner at expensive restaurants. Lunch and dinner menu prices are the same.

Many castles have been converted into inspired restaurants such as the Hostaria dell'Orso in Rome, elegant and expensive, not for children, but an extravagant treat for teenagers. Below are others more appropriate for children.

Alessandria: Castello di Melazzo, you can eat veal and chicken in the halls where Edward II of England hid in fear and trembling back in the 14th century after his deposition. Surrounded by a parklike estate, this 14th-century castle-fortress also has a few rooms for overnighting. **Bergamo: Castello di Clanezzo,** more like a manor than a fortress, has a courtyard fountain (from which trout are "fished" for your lunch) and French food (including *fondue Bourgignonne* that will be specially made for children with a great deal less wine than usual). Near **Bolzano: Castel Schloss Hochnaturns,** a 13th-century castle in **Naturno,** about 15 miles away on the Bolzano-Malles-Venosta railway line close by a tiny church, St. Procolo, with 8th- and 9th-century frescos.

Florence: Florentines claim that **Vivoli** (7 Vie delle Stinche) near Santa Croce, is the best *gelateria* in Italy, if not in the world, with 20 creamy flavors of homemade *gelato*. The outdoor cafes around the Piazza della Repubblica are almost all recommended for delicious ice cream and pastries. As for "bongo bongo," enjoy these chocolate and vanilla custard puffs here, or at most restaurants or trattorias which also serve fresh fruit and a wedge of *pecorino,* a mild local cheese for dessert, or prunes, strawberries or other fresh berries soaked in Chianti (for teenagers only!). You can eat, or buy to eat later, spit-roasted chickens, ducks, quail, lamb, beef at *rosticerias*. **Giannino** (37 Borgo San Lorenzo) in nearby San Lorenzo, is a rosticeria with self-service and takeout counters, plus dining rooms that serve everything yummy from pizza to roast baby lamb. Hearty Tuscan peasant dishes, with such rustic and sturdy fare as *crostini* for the antipasto (toasted bread spread with a paste of chicken livers); *prosciutto dolce,* the Parma variety, or *prosciutto,* the Tuscan version which is saltier and tougher; soups made with vegetables and bread; *pappa al pomidoro,* a dish of tomatoes, bread, olive oil, seasoned with onions and basil; cookies called *bruti ma buoni* (ugly but good) or dry biscotti you're meant to dunk in wine after meals—red is suggested as better than white, and OK even for children 7 on up—are served at restaurants and trattorias. *Trattorias,* being informal, casual, are highly recommended. **Antico Fattore** (1 Via Lambertesca); **Buca del Orafo** (28 Via del Girolani) near the Ponte Vecchio jewelry market, are more pleasant than noisy jampacked **Coco Lezzone** (Via del Parioncino) which looks like an ugly take-out deli, but is popular and, as crowds are a criterion of popularity and quality of food served, enjoy its heartening fare. **Osteria del Cinghale Bianco** (43 Borgo Sant' Jacopo) is more agreeable with its farmhouse-style decor for leisurely eating. **Cantinetta Antinori** (Palazzo Antinori, 3 Piazza Antinori) just inside the walls of Palazzo Antinori, is lacily surrounded with wrought iron, and serves traditional Tuscan fare with many of the ingredients produced on the Antinori estate. Simple stews, such as *spezzatino,* made with beef or veal are recommended, almost anywhere, and *bistecca alla fiorentina* is justly celebrated as all steak-lovers will know at first bite. **Buca Lapi** (1 Via del Trebbio) is a small steakhouse that's suitably informal for family dining. **Ottorino** (6 Via Sant-Elisabetta) is another recommended restaurant for family meals. **Gradara** (about 10 m N of Pesaro): **Castello di Gradara,** in the immediate vicinity of the Rocca Maltestiana, with great summer doings—archery tournaments, historical processions, art exhibits. Check with the local tourist office to see what's happening. Also check **La Casaccia,** nearby, and the **Mastin Vecchio di Adriano** on Via Dante Alighieri. What's cooking in the castle is great *tagliatelli* and roast fish. **Ischia: Castello Aragonese** has a Spanish-style restaurant, **El Castillo de Aragona** reached by a stairway carved in the rock; private beach with motorboats and waterskiing; spaghetti with clams, stuffed peppers, noodles and beans, flavored with more oregano than children will enjoy. **L'Aquila: Castello di Balsorano** has a great weapons room, a torture chamber worthy of a Borgia, two dining rooms, a tavern with a large spit for roasting whole lambs, and a delicately seasoned, delicious cuisine. Interesting mountainous country.

Marostica (near Vicenza): Superb food at **Castello Superiore di Marostia;** in the square in front of you a famous chess game with live people dressed as chess pieces takes place annually. The scenic road up Pausolino hill to the castle is lovely. **Montecchio Maggiore** (about 8 m from Vicenza); Romeo and Juliet's castle *(Castello di Giuletta e Romeo)* has been transformed into a typical medieval tavern known as the **Castle of the Bella Guardia;** the view and food are divine. **Monte Oliveto Maggiore:** About 15 miles from Siena, **La Torre,** in a crenellated tower reached by a drawbridge; surroundings look like a garden park on the moon—lots of flowers and greenery planted around deep clay pits; the roast lamb and *tagliatelle* are sure-fire hits with most children.

Naples' restaurants are special because they feature musicians playing and singing Neapolitan songs. On the hillside of Posillipo, **D'Angelo** and **Le Arcate** on Via Falcone, and **Belvedere** on Via Angelini are all fun. On the sea front at Santa Lucia, **Zi Teresa, Transatlantico** are best. On the sea front at Posillipo, try **Da Giuseppone.** All around **Piacenza** there are castle-restaurants. **Castello di Rivalta** in Rivalta Trebbia (about 15 m from Piacenza) is one of the best-preserved castles in the province, walled and surrounded by a park, sheltering a rustic house transformed into a restaurant. **La Taverna del Falconiere,** serving cannelloni, has been transformed from the old falconry. Near **Parma,** at Torrechiara, is **Taverna del Castello,** a remarkable restaurant in an enchanting 15th-century village in the shadow of the village castle; ravioli-like *tortelli* filled with greens, guinea hen cooked in a paper bag, chicken *cacciatore,* chocolate and almond tarts, all sorts of pastries.

Piossasco: About 12 miles from Turin, Castello di Piossaco has a castle restaurant **Nove Merli** serving regional dishes in an area rich in castle-dotted hills.

In **Rome,** you can get jelly doughnuts for what seem to me outrageous prices at **Doney's;** a beautiful view of the Bernini fountains from **Tre Scalini;** marvelous batter-dipped spaghetti, spaghetti *carbonara.* Children will like **George's** (near the Excelsior) for *fettucine;* the *cannelloni* at **La Biblioteca del Valle; Ranieri** (via Maria d' Fiori 26) with a superb *Monte Bianco* for dessert; **Casina Valadier** on the Pincian Hill with a terrace view of Rome; the **Caffe Greco** (86 Via Condotti); **La Maiella** (Piazza S. Apollinare) for seafood; and you haven't lived till you've tried Spaghetti alla Cowboy at **Vecchia America** (Piazzale Marconi). For snacks, **Pasticceria Euclide** (Via Filippo Civinini 119); **Piccadilly** (Via Barberini 2), **Alemagna** (Via del Corso 181), but *the greatest snack discovery of all,* off the tourist track, is **Vanni** (Via Col di Lana 10) with yummy sandwiches, ice creams, cakes, breads, cheeses, and fruit, and take-out and delivery service. The ultimate ice cream parlor is **Giolitti's** (40 Via Uffici del Vicario), closed Mon. Next to the **Tre Scalini** in the Piazza Navona, is the *gelateria annex,* also named **Tre Scalini** (closed Wed.) where you can relax at an outdoor table with the house specialty, a frozen truffle (a hunk of bittersweet chocolate ice cream). The fig ice cream, the marron glace, and the Coppa Olympia, a singular composition of sherbets, ice cream, whipped cream and wafers, are also to swoon over. **Babington's Tea Room** (23 Piazza di Spagna) next to the Spanish steps, is for pancakes, waffles, hamburgers, homemade cakes and pies. **Rosati's** (4 Piazza del Popolo), an indoor-outdoor cafe, is for ice creams, cakes, coffee. **Fassi's** (Coro d'Italia) at Piazza Fiume, is an enormous indoor-outdoor cafe, with a garden that is a summertime dream of palm trees and columns, which is another place for ice cream, snacks, cappucino. Anywhere, when you see **Tira Misu** (make-me-happy) on the dessert list, order it—a moist, coffee-flavored cake made with *mascarpone,* a cream cheese, Italian brand, *Fragoletti* (crumbs) is a dessert served, I know at **El Toula,** but other restaurants have copied it, and, as a first-time experience, expect children to laugh—a shortbread-like cookie round is presented to each diner by the waiter who then gives this cookie a whack with a large spoon, thus producing *fragoletti* (crumbs). In the Vatican, next to the sacristy in St. Peter's Basilica an unmarked door leads to a pleasant little bar (anything from milk to scotch); a restaurant below ground level in front of the picture gallery has a tree-shaded terrace looking toward St. Peter's. In Trastevere, go after dark to festive Piazza dei Mercanti, to **Da Meo Patacca,** #30 (the huge menu makes a fine poster); extravagant decorations (armor to olive presses); a bit touristy, but FUN and moderate in price.

Salerno: Torre dei Normanni, a restaurant in the Norman tower of Maiori, which dominates the landscape of gardens, terraces, groves of lemon and orange trees; adjoining beach; wonderful stop en route to Calabria. **Sardinia** has food specialties that may distress children—stewed thrushes and blackbirds—or delight them: bread baked in many shapes and sizes; *fregula* and *succu,* tiny balls of saffron-colored pasta; wild asparagus and artichokes; spit-roasted lamb scented with myrtle *(agnello allo spiedo); tiazolas* and *sa fresa* cheeses, both mild; excellent fresh fruit. Baby octopus and lobster turns up in cold *insalata di crustacei.* Spit-roasted suckling pig is another specialty. At the **Hotel Sporting** in **Porto Rotondo,** if you like lobster, you'll delight in their grilled langoustines. *Sabada,* sweet cheese pastry covered with honey; crisp, sugar-topped *tilicasas;* macaroons stuffed with almond cream are desserts served at the splendid Hotel Sporting and **Hotel Cala di Volpe** and at Porto Rotondo's **San Pellegrino,** at their best, but you'll probably sample them elsewhere on the island. **Siena:** the 16th-century **Fortezza Medicea** has converted its cellars into a restaurant offering all those yummy Sienese goodies for the sweet-toothed—*panforte, ricciarelli,* and *cavalucci.* **Tavoleto** (about 20 m inland from Pesaro): The medieval **Castello di Tavoleto** houses a restaurant specializing in poultry and game roasted on a spit; near Urbino. In **Tivoli,** the enchanting **Sibilla** (Via della Sibilla 50) overlooks a gorge and has two tiny ruined temples in its terrace garden.

Venice: Caffe Florian in St. Mark's Square, with its outside tables, constant band music, and little inside rooms, for snacks and simple fare is just the place to relax and people-and-pigeon-watch in the unfailing joy of the piazza. At the Lido, the **Quattro Fontane Hotel** offers a riveting display of *antipasti* to visiting gourmets and features a Sunday brunch at which children, requested to be dressed in their bathing suits, are seated in a special corner of the dining room, and served oodles of noodles and fettucine to eat with their fingers, with tomato sauce, of course. After the bambini have stuffed, spilled and made as revolting a mess as possible, the chef obligingly hoses them clean. For families who love food, children, the sound of laughter, and the sense of the ridiculous, this is an irresistible Sunday attraction, and a tradition with the Quattro Fontane for years. But do confirm these details before you go!

Money-Saving Tips: In sit-down and stand-up-at-the-counter cafes, the rate for drinks, cones and snacks may be twice as much when you consume them sitting down as when you do standing up. And for picnic fare, most groceries make sandwiches out of anything they sell, and if they don't sell bread, they will put cheese, sausage or meat between the slices of bread or halves of roll that you bring in. Children usually make out better on this deal than their elders.

BABY FOOD Baby food *(nutrimento* or *alimento per bambini)* is available in pharmacies, specialty food shops, supermarkets (Jolly, CIM, Romana chains), and department stores (UPIM, SMA, Stands chains).

Several brands (including Gerber's) of strained fruit, vegetables, and meat are usually stocked. The best-known Italian brands are **Plasmon** and **Nipiol,** put out by Buitoni. Nipiol *frutta puree* (strained fruit), *verdure puree,* (strained vegetables) and *carne puree* (strained meat) are excellent. Sometimes, instead of *puree,* the term *concentrato* or *homogenizati* is used.

Wherever you find baby food, you'll likely also find diapers, feeding equipment, and playthings; among the many excellent Chicco products are a *biberon isotermico* (vacuum bottle), bottles, pants, and toys. In Rome, the Romana branch at Vilaggio Olimpico has a large stock of baby goodies (many American imports).

DIAPERS AND DIAPER SERVICES Cloth diapers *(pannolini)* and paper diapers *(pannolini di carta, pannolini igenico,* or *assorbenti per babini)* are available in department stores or shops specializing in children's accessories. Brands to look for are Chicco, Kleenex, and Baby Scott. Imported precut diaper pads and do-it-yourself rolls (Linas, Polin, and other brands) are found with feminine hygiene items. Pampers, Luvs, and their equivalents are available, but they're not easily found.

Baby Service (Via L. Manicinelli 49; Tel: 837–000) picks up and delivers diapers; also rentals. Diaper laundering can be done by arrangement with your hotel or pensione. In **Rome, La Cicogna** or **Baby Parking** (see Babysitters) will launder diapers.

EMERGENCIES MADE EASY ***Pharmacies*** stock Swiss, German, American, English, and Italian medicines. If you are at a loss to choose among them, you can count on a staff member of a *farmacia* to recommend the best. If you bring a child with a skinned knee into a *farmacia,* cotton wool, antiseptic, and melting tenderness instantly appear and someone generally produces a piece of candy or a Coca-Cola.

Italian ***doctors*** seem to be particularly good with children and the doctors of Rome have a reputation not only for great skill but also for infinite kindness. Settle your bill at the time of treatment. Tell your doctor you've had your tetanus shots or he'll give you serum (which can cause a reaction). For recommendations of ***English-speaking doctors and dentists,*** call the **American Embassy** in **Rome** (Via V. Veneto 119/A; Tel: (06) 4674); an English-speaking pediatrician of note is Dr. Eva Landsberg-Lewin (13 Largo Giovanni Chiarini; Tel: (06) 571–896). **U.S. Consulates** in **Florence** (38 Lungarno Amerigo Vespucci; Tel: (055) 298–276; **Genoa** (Banca d'America e d'Italia Bldg., Piazza Portello 6; Tel: (010) 282–2741); **Milan** (Piazza della Repubblica 32; Tel: (02) 652–841); **Naples** (Piazza della Repubblica 80122; Tel: (081) 660–966); **Palermo** (corner of Via Marchese di Villabianca and Via Vaccarini; Tel: (091) 291–532/5); **Trieste** (Via Roma 9; Tel: (040) 687–28/9). Or in **Rome,** Embassy of Canada (Via G. B. de Rossi 27; Tel: (06) 855–

341) or in **Milan,** Canadian Consulate General (Via V. Pisan 19; Tel: (02) 657–0451.

Private clinics *(clinica),* though more luxurious than public hospitals *(ospedale),* don't have ***emergency rooms*** *(pronto soccorsi).* Central *pronto soccorsi* in Rome are **Polyclinico** (Viale Polyclinico) and **S. Spirito** (Lungotevere in Sassia).

In **Rome,** ***pharmacies*** open 24 hours are: **Carlo Erba** (145 Via del Corso; Tel: (06) 679–0866); **Garinei** (31 Piazza San Silvestro; Tel: (06) 679–3198); **George Baker and Co.** (92 Via E. Orlando; Tel: (06) 460–408); **Farmacia Internazionale** (49 Piazza Barberini; Tel: (06) 462–996), which has a good supply of baby products; **Farmacia Lepetit Internazionale** (417 Via del Corso; Tel: (06) 679–1347). **Anti Poison Center** (06) 490–663. ***Baby hospitals:*** several, but I'd opt for the **Salvator Mundi International Hospital** (Viale delle Mura Gianicolensi 67; Tel: (06) 58604) as the best with English-speaking staff. **Medical Service at home** (nights); Tel: (06) 475–6741; **First Aid, ambulance;** Tel: (06) 5100.

In **Florence,** pharmacies open 24 hours: **All'Insegna di San Giovanni di Dio** (Borgognissanti 4OR; Tel: (055) 210–877) and **Santa Maria Nuova** (Piazza Santa Maria Nuova IR; Tel: (055) 216–021) and **Codeca** (Via Ginori 50; Tel: (055) 270–849). ***Hospitals*** include **Ospedale di San Giovanni di Dio** (Borgognissanti 20; Tel: (055) 278–751) and **Anna Meyer Pediatric Hospital** (Via Luca Giordano 13; Tel:(055) 277–41).

In **Milan,** ***pharmacies*** take turns at 24-hour duty. Your hotel can tell you which is open. The **Clinica Pediatrica** (Via Commenda 9; Tel: 544541) cares for infants and children up to 4. The **Ospedale dei Bambini** (32 Via Castelevetro; Tel: (02) 318–2286) treats children 12 and under (including infants).

▶ **Note:** The tales you hear about bicycle and motor-scooter thieves on Italian streets, and thievery from outdoor cafes, are often exaggerated, but do take the precaution of carrying traveler's checks instead of cash, and keeping a list of these numbers on file at home with your lawyer, banker, secretary or trusted friend, as well as a list with you in quadruplicate, with copies stashed or carried separately. Carry handbags on the wall side of the sidewalk to foil street-side snatchers, or wear them as you should your cameras, strapped bandolier-fashion across your chest. Take all precautions possible about the family passports. If you think you are going to need them, and can't leave them in the hotel vault, let Father, if possible, carry them in a money belt.

MAGIC FAMILY HELPERS A babysitter is a British and American custom imported only recently to Italy, where maids and relatives have traditionally assumed these duties, and listings of professional guardian angels are to be found only in big-city telephone directories in the yellow pages *(Pagine Gialle)* under "B" for Baby Sitters. Elsewhere, your hotel concierge, your hotel maid, or the grapevine can usually produce an unlisted babysitter for you with a few hour's notice. If she is non-English speaking, get someone reliable to interpret any instructions for you. Don't worry about the children being able to communicate their needs and wants or the babysitter having trouble understanding them. They will and she will. I have yet to experience or hear to the contrary. A list of professional agencies follows, but first, let me assure you that the institution of baby and childcare *outside* the home is well-organized and widespread in Italy. In every village or town there's almost always an *Asilo,* an *Asilo Infantile,* an *Asilo Nido,* a *Materna,* a *Scuola Materna,* a *Nido per Bambini,* a *Casa dei Bambini.* Just look in the yellow pages under the heading of *Nidi d'Infanzia.* (Anything called an *Asilo* without a special name, or a *Scuola Materna* or an *Asilo* with a religious appellation [Asilo Infantile "Divina Provvidenza" or Materna Santa Rosa] is likely to be a Catholic day-nursery or kindergarten connected with the Church and/or operated under the aegis of the state for the benefit of children of working mothers; usually closed in Aug. These I don't feel are suitable for recommendation generally to travelers as they just aren't set up to take foreign children.) Still, it's good to know that wherever there's a church, some child-care facility will be available. Many are free, some charge small fees; they take children in the morning, afternoon, all day; you bring a lunchbox or pay for standard fare; the age range encompasses the newborn to about 5.

Privately owned and operated ***day nurseries and day-play-care centers*** are subject to government inspection. You can "park" your baby, toddler, or 5–10-yr.-old at these places, called (most likely) Baby Club, Baby Parking, Mini Club or designated as a *Nido* (nest). When these day-play-care centers assume kindergarten status, as we understand the term, or employ the Froebel or Montessori or some other pedagogical method, they are listed in the yellow pages under S for *Scuole ed Istituti di Insegnamento Privato,* with the subhead *Scuole Materne.* Unless designated *"Prima e Seconda Elementare,"* the equivalent of first and second grade, *Scuole Materne* are primarily for the newborn, infants, and toddlers. Some *Nidi* take children from a few months to ages 10–12, combining nursery-kindergarten-play center.

Kindergartens, in Italy, also known as *Kinderheime,* may serve as kindergartens as we know them; but generally they are private villas, small or hotel-size establishments where babies, toddlers, and children can stay overnight for days, weeks, or even months. Distinctions among these terms tend to be flexible: always get details. Some offer interesting courses.

But, thank heavens, a **babysitter** is a baby sitter, and a joy forever, and here is a list of organizations where you can find all these excellent, highly recommended services where English is spoken. (Be sure to preface all telephone calls, however, with *"Parle Inglese?"* and wait until the signora comes on the line. In **Rome: La Nutrice** (Via Merulani 268); **Signora E. Parisi** (34 Via Ricci Curbastro); who also operates **Al**

Circulo Dei Bambini, with tender loving care provided by the hour, day, night, plus all meals for the newborn to 10-yr.-olds at the same address. In **Bologna: Baby Sitters** (10 Via Battisti); **C.A.D.I.A.I. Cooperativa** (Via Zacconi 14) is an agency with nurses, governesses, and companions qualified also to care for the handicapped and the aged. In **Milan: Baby's Club** (5 Via Cusani) will send sitters to you; also operates as a pleasant baby "parking" center. **Centro Italiano Baby Sitters** (Piazza Risorgimento 3); **Centro Italiano Baby Sitters** (16 Via Lattuada).

The following are baby "parking," day-play-care centers for part-time or fulltime childcare accommodating English-speaking children. In **Rome:** Al Circolo Dei Bambini (see Babysitting, above); **Baby Parking** (Via San Frisca 16); **Mini Club** (Via Niccolo' Tomaseo 2); in the Monteverde area; **Nursery-School of Rome** (Corso Francia 235); **Baby Garden Nuovo** Salario (Via Montaione 38); **Casa Dei Bambini Montessori Alla Camilluccia** (Via Pistelli 16, Piazza Igea); **Casa Dei Bambini Emy** (Viale Vigna Pia 2); **Casa Dei Bambini** *La Maisonette* (Viale Monte Oppio 7), a nursery school of special assistance to children with learning disabilities or psychological problems or medical problems, and a happy playground located in the Parco Colle Oppio. **Casa Dei Bambini "La Rondinella"** (Via Antistio 12, Cinecitta); **Casa Dei Bambini M. Luisa** (Via Tenuta S. Agata 8; where Via Trionfale intersects with Piazza Sacchetti); **Casa Dei Bambini Teresita** (Via della Storta 808); **Greenwood Garden** (Via Sinisi 5; by Via Due Ponti); **Garden Bimbo** (Via Santuario Reg. Apostoli 8; S. Paolo-EUR C. Colombo), an *Italian-style* kindergarten; **Asilo Nido "Pippi,"** another Italian-style kindergarten located at Via E. Bianchi 13 at the intersection of Via del Serafico); **Asilo Nido di Aldo Crollalanza** (Via Giorgio Baglivi 12); **Nido Club** (Via S. Quintino 18; S. Giovanni); **Club Dei Bambini** (Via Luciani 19). If you're holidaying by the sea just outside of Rome, at **Ostia,** you have a choice of the **Froebel Garden** (73 Via Olivieri), **Casa del Bimbo "Diamante"** (76 Via Dei Velieri), **Casa Dei Bambini Peter Pan** (199 Via Azzorre), and others.

▶ **Note:** A *Casa* prefix generally signifies baby and toddler boarding, but the Casi I have mentioned are combined with *Nidi* and *Scuole Materne* where children are accepted on a part-time basis.

Special! Montessori's **Parco Dei Bambini** (Via della Bufalotta, 1052) which offers part-time and fulltime care for children of elementary school age, is open all year, offers summer vacations by the sea and also gives you a chance to attend and participate in a full range of sports and applied arts activities *with* your children. Transport to and from the school and park grounds involves Bus N. 237 and a special Pullman service.

Bologna: Part-time/fulltime care for babies and toddlers at **Baby Club** (42 Via Indipendenza); **Kinder Nest** (13 Via C. da Pistoia); and others. Nursery school boarding for children aged 2–6 at **Kinder Haus** (Via Cino da Pistoia 7). **Florence: Paida** (Via delle Gore 43) and **Mary**

Poppins (Via Masaccio 18). **Baby's Club** "A Montalto" (Via Del Salviatino 6); **Asilo Il Girotondo** (Viale Volta 52); **Casa Dei Bambini** (22 Via R. da Mandello); **Jo Jo** (Via Antonio dei Pollaiuolo); **Nursery School Savonarola** (13 Via Ficino); **Little Academy** (163½ Via Bolognese); **Little Academy** (176 Via Masaccio); and **Full Time School** (112 Via Galliano). In the beautiful hills of suburban **Fiesole, Kindergarten Fiesole** (Via Vecchia Fiesolana 64) operates an attractive daycare center, preschool-elementary school with a summer program, swimming, language courses, dietician-supervised meals, and schoolbus transport.

Genoa: Il Giardinetto (Corso Magenta 7; funicolare Santa Anna); **Club Dei Piccoli** (Via Domenico Chiodo 68); **Istituto Villa Gioia** (Via Zoagli 29, 16147 Genova Sturla Al Mare); and **Nido Dei Bimbi** (2 Via P. Salvago). In nearby **Nervi,** a seaside suburb, **Lo Scarabocchio** (Villino Gilla, Salvatore Morelli 6) Tel: (010) 32–36–40) has a resident child psychologist, a resident pediatrician, and English-language conversation for the benefit of Italian students. In the same Genoa-Nervi locale, **Kinderheim San Ilario** (Via San Ilario 92, 16167 Nervi San Ilario, Genova) is open June–Sept. for 40 children aged 3–10 to enjoy a variety of games, sports and swimming. **Messina: Materna "Oio Baby Park"** (25 Via Ignatianum) and **British College** (Via C. Battisti 62). I know nothing about the **Disneyland School** (97 Viale Italia) or **Materna M. Mouse** (Tel: (090) 77–39–04), but I have heard that **Club Dei Bimbi Park Palace** (Via Ducezio) has a helpful center for the little ones. **Milan: Il Girotondo** (27 Via Crocefisso) is an Asilo Nido that answers every need. Also try **Baby Park** (Via Carlo Ravizza 53/a); **Le Noccioline Kinderheim** (Viale Cirene 5); **Nidiata Gioiosa** (Viale Monte Rosa 80); **Baby College Nursery** (Via Claudiano 7, Zona Fiera); **Primi Giochi** (Vimodrome, Via XV Martiri 2/30, Res. Mediolanun); and **Baby Parking, Il Clubino** (Viale Coni Zugna, 1). 7:30 a.m.–7 p.m. SPECIAL! For part-time or fulltime care for tinies to tens by the hour, day, overnight, holidays, weekends, (and babysitting at your place, by special arrangement) your best bet is deceptively named **Baby's Club** (Via Cusani 5). Others are **Il Club dei Piccoli** (Via Pisacane 5), with garden supervised by highly qualified personnel; **La Cuccia Baby Parking** (Corso Garibaldi 72/3); **Primi Passi** (Viale Marche 37); and **La Culla** (Via Martiri Oscuri 17). Also, **Il Galileo** (Via Cosimo del Fante 7). In **Naples:** You've got the **Nido Asilo Froebel** (Piazza Vanvitelli 10; Vomero); **Nido Azzurro** (Via Parco Margherita 2); **Nido Del Passerotto** (Viale Augusta 9; Fuorigrotta); **Fantasia** (203 Via Posillipo); **Il Poggio** (180 Via Fontana); **La Fatina** (223 Via San Francesco); and **Rudyard Kipling** (76 Via Pigna). For the last quartet I have no details.

In **Sardinia,** in **Cagliari,** the best nursery school facilities, I'm told, are at **Euroschool** (Via Rossini 62/78). **The Anglo-American Centre** (46 Via Mameli) could advise you better than I can about local facilities elsewhere on the island (see also Schools).

In **Sicily,** in **Agricento, S.S. per Aragona Asilo La Coccinella** (42 Via Imera); and in **Marsala, La Girandola** (12 Via Sanita).

All major Italian ski resorts offer ski schools and ***snow nurseries*** for children during the winter season.

In **Rome,** the top ***schools*** are **St. Stephen's** on the Aventine Hill (American, co-ed, day and boarding, grades 9–12); **St. George's** (English, co-ed, day, kindergarten–high school); **Marymount International School** (instruction in English, for girls kindergarten–high school and for boys through grade 3); **Overseas School** (American, co-ed, kindergarten–high school, mostly day but boarding for older students); **Notre Dame International School** (American, boys, grade 4–high school, boarding for grades 7–12); **New School** (English, ages 7–18); **International School of Rome** (kindergarten–8th grade); **Monti Parioli** (British, kindergarten–grade 4). **Scuola Montessori Bilingue,** for French-speaking youngsters, is a nursery school and elementary school with a seaside summer program. In **Florence, Petite Ecole Francaise** (49 Via Serragli) is an excellent elementary school. For older children, there's the **American Academy of Florence** (32 Via di Vacciano, Ponte a Ema, Bagno a Ripoli) in the suburbs of Florence. In **Milan,** the British community school is **The Sir James Henderson School,** kindergarten through high school or "A" level. With excellent classes at the elementary levels are the **American School of Milan** in the Opera district, and the **International School of Milan** in Via Montichiari. In **Sardinia,** in **Cagliari,** there's **St. George School, Euroschool, Big Ben Academy, British Government School;** the European School in **Olbia;** in **Sassari,** the British School. Educational courses and programs at the **Anglo American Centre** in Cagliari; at the **English Centre** in Sassari.

Personalized Services: The **Alberghi Diurni** (daytime hotels) found in all reasonably sized cities, near the main railroad station and also sometimes in the center of town have every facility from hairdresser to showers to dry cleaners to sitting rooms to help you carry on in a tidy, refreshed fashion. Open 6 a.m. to midnight.

Interpreters and secretaries are available in **Rome** from the **S.T.O.C.** (Via Laurentina 203; Tel (06) 540–3741) and **Palazzo dei Congressi** (at EUR; Piazza Kennedy; Tel: (06) 596–5268). For special cultural interests, a super private guide service is run by **Anna Lelli** (Via Lorenzo Magalotti 2). Less costly and less personal are the authorized guides available from **E.P.T.** (Via Parigi 5, Tel: (06) 463–748) or **Sindacato Nazionale** (Rampa Mignanelli 12; Tel: (06) 678–9842). The **American Women's Association of Rome** (Cavalieri Hilton Hotel) (7 Via Nazionale; Tel: (06) 475–5268) is also helpful with advice, information, and family tours.

You and your daughters can relax in one of Europe's most glamorous hairdresser's establishments: **Olivier** (Via del Babuino 76; Tel: (06) 678–0470).

HOLIDAYS FOR CHILDREN ON THEIR OWN In **Rome,** see Kindergartens. For children 5–12 years, **Casa Montessori dei Bambini Scuola Materna** (Via Luigi Bodio 2; Tel: (06) 327–0828) is a boarding-school for the very young. From 8:30 a.m.–noon, classes are given for English-speaking children; trimesters begin in early Oct., mid-Dec., mid-Feb. From mid-June to Sept. the school moves to seaside Fregene (Via Riccione 59/61, Fregene 00050). Children may stay at the school during vacation periods. Montessori method, in which each child is encouraged to develop at his own level, surrounded by a loving family atmosphere. Elementary reading, writing, scientific experiments are taught here to toddlers. For normal children, but a few children with low IQs or motor difficulties may be incorporated from time to time. In the summer, sports, painting, ceramics.

Centro Turistico Studentesco Giovanile (Via Nazionale 66, Rome) Italian Youth Tourist Center—organizes hundreds of trips weekly utilizing youth hostels, campgrounds, and vacation centers. Splendid organization and a great help for arranging inexpensive and pleasant vacations with preteens and teenagers.

Elsewhere in Italy, **AKI** (Associazione Kinderheim Italiani) is the guiding light behind Italy's hotels-for-children-only project, with over 30 state-controlled establishments. All provide excellent medical care, and some furnish tutoring and school-work; their general atmosphere is like a children's houseparty, a home away from home with attentive supervision. The **Val d'Aosta,** a mountain paradise, has four Kinderheime situated between Aosta and Courmayeur, 20 miles distant. **Aosta,** called the Rome of the Alps because of its ancient Roman ruins, is an iron and steel center. **Courmayeur,** one of the oldest mountain resorts in Italy, nestles at the foot of Mont Blanc surrounded with glittering mountain splendor and the world's largest cable car. There are **Kinderheim "Le Marmotte"** (11010 Pre Saint Didier, Frazione Pallesieux, Aosta) that offers various sports as does **Kinderheim "Villa Malina"** (Casella Postale 10, 11013 Courmayeur, Aosta) and **Kinderheim "Chez Nous"** (Frazione Villa 4, 11020 Challant Saint Victor, Aosta). For information, write Direzione ad Aosta, Viale M. Grivola, 14).

Courmayeur, Cervinia, and **La Thuile** are the most attractive skiing resorts and vacation spots in the area. From Milan, Alitalia can arrange Alpine downhill and apres-ski packages. (Also see Accommodations.) You might like to check out **Istituto Alpino Kinderheim** (11025 Gressoney St. Jean, Aosta) a Swiss-type chalet open summer and winter for 85 children from 3–13. Alpine excursions with a variety of games and sports.

Bolzano: In the southern Tyrol, **Kinderheim "Villa Sole"** (39059 Soprabolzano-Renon) is in the Dolomites with sports and games.

Brescia: Kinderheim "I Folletti" (Via Plaza 4, 25056 Ponte di Legna, Brescia; Tel: (0364). Accommodating about four dozen boys and girls, 4–11, in 4–6-bedded rooms. A sunny mountain spot; a private train for weekly excursions; mountainclimbing trips and stays in Alpine huts, under the eye of an Alpine guide; minigolf, skiing, skating, tennis, other games, diversion, recreation. Excellent ski school during Christmas and Easter vacations, mid-June to the last Sun. in Sept. Children can also ski at nearby Passo del Tonale.

In **Cortina d'Ampezzo,** there's one of the plushest and best European children's hotels—**La Meridiana** (Zuel di Cortina d'Ampezzo, Belluno; Tel: (0437) 2700)—with superb facilities and supervision for 50 children. Unusual modern architecture; nicely landscaped, rimmed with rugged mountains; a fresh, cool, sunny *ambience;* spacious, immaculate, exceptionally pleasant rooms with two or three beds. Main playroom dazzlingly modern and well-equipped; well-stocked library; piano, and TV. Outdoor activities include skiing (with expert instruction), skating, and other winter sports; picnics, hikes, tennis, and games in summer. English-speaking boys and girls from 4–15 are welcomed for short or long periods. Schooling provided if desired; special diets can be followed; house pediatrician. Rooms with private bath can be reserved for parents. Signora Silvestra Pavoni is the gifted director, and is assisted by a competent, kind, attentive staff. The food is wholesome, fresh, and delicious. Also in the area of the Dolomites, in Italy's South Tyrol, north of the Venetian Plain, are three kinderheime near **Trento. Kinderheim "Dolomiti"** (via V. Monti 47, 38079 Tione di Trento) with painting and photography, sports, and a pretty garden. For **Kinderheim "Guardaval"** (38039 Vigo di Fassa, Trento) write Signora Nunzia Facchini, Via Vignazza 18, 21050 Besano, Varese); game rooms, bobsled runs, a skating rink, film shows, delightful excursions and trips in the area. For **Kinderheim "Casa Degli Scoiattoli"** (38010 Coredo-Sfruz, Trento) write Signora Zueneli Tosi Maria Letizia (Via degli Alfani 57, 50121, Firenze) with diverse recreations and sports. In the foothills of Lombardy, about 75 miles NW of Milan, in **Sondrio,** there's **Kinderheim "Biencaneve"** (Via Italia, 223031 Aprica, Sondrio) that offers outdoor games and sports. **Kinderheim "Vanossi"** (23024 Madesimo, Sondrio), an old-fashioned chalet, with 1001 things to do in the summer, mini-cars, various sports, games, and excursions.

Near **Genoa:** Try **Kinderheim "Temossi"** (Via Comunale, 16041 Temossi de Bertigaro, Genova) and write for information to Bo Romana, oppure Camporese Vincenzo, Via Como 5, 16030 Cavi di Lavagna, Genova). Gymnastics, nature walks, painting classes, ballgames, and other sports and recreation. Near **La Spezia,** at the head of the gulf of the Riviera Levante in the Val di Vara in the Ligurian Alps, is **Kinderheim "Il Bosco"** (Passo di Cento Croci, 19028 Varese Ligure, La Spezia). For information, get in touch with Maria Avancini (Via del Brennero 4, Pisa). **"Il Bosco,"** as its name implies, is surrounded by green and shady trees; riding stable, archery, various games and activities, including treasure hunts! Near **Perugia**—rich with centuries of great art and great chocolate-making—and **Assisi** is **Kinderheim "L'Aquilone"** (06024 Gubbio, Fraz. Ghigiano, Perugia); for information, contact Pandolfo Michele, via Mar Nero 7, 20152 Milano). Facilities and entertainment are excellent: photography laboratory, workshops for woodwork, ceramics, nature studies, journalism, riding, fishing, tennis, theatrical performances by the children, excursions.

Near **Turin** is **Kinderheim "Villa Dei Bimbi"** (Via Modane 7, 10052 Bardonecchia, Torino). Situated in a lovely garden with game room, skiing, and other recreational facilities. Near **Varese,** there's the Alpine Village organized by the Touring Club Italiano (*Villagio Alpino del TCI in Valganna,* 21039 Boarezzo, Varese). For information, write Touring Club Italiano, Corso Italia 10, 20122, Milano). Surrounded with a vast, wooded parkland and panoramic views, this children's camping village has all sorts of games, activities, sports, arts and crafts. In the **Vicenza** area, **Casa-Albergo Per Bambini "Villa Serena"** (Via Bettinadi, 36010 Canove di Roana, Vicenza). For information, get in touch with Guido Fanton, Via F. De Sanctis 14, Vicenza). Surrounded by an immense pine-wooded park, Villa Serena includes ball games, skiing, rollerskating, iceskating, and tennis. Vicenza, 20 miles W of **Padua,** is the birthplace of the architect Andrea Palladio, whose *palazzi* can be seen in the neighborhood.

In **Fregene,** run in connection with the Casa Montessori in Rome, and highly recommended, is **Baby Sea Montessori** (see above Kindergartens.) In **Forli,** there is **Kinderheim "Villa Il Germoglio"** (Via Orsa Minore, 47030 San Mauro Mare). For information, contact Croce Azzurra di San Giorgio, Via B. d'Este 4, 20100 Milano). By the sea, open June for children 4–6; July–Aug., for children 6–12. Sports, games, recreation, excursions. In **Imperia,** by the sea, there's **Kinderheim "Villa Magnolia"** (via Romana 125, 18012 Bordighera). For information, write Silvestrini-Maizzani, Via Decembrio 25, 20137 Milano); swimming, tennis, Ping-Pong, a variety of games, sports, and recreational facilities. Also in this palmy hillside resort area, a British favorite is **Kinderheim "Piccolo Nido"** (Via Romana 51, Villa Roseto, 18012 Bordighera, Imperia). In **Livorno, La Nuova Corallina** (57020 Marina di Bibbona); when the hotel is closed, write to Maria Gilardi (Via Lunigiana 45, Milano) who caters almost entirely to Italian children but welcomes children of other nationalities; accommodates 45 children from 3–12. Slides, seesaws, swings, Ping-Pong, basketball, and swimming instruction. One staff member for every 5 children; family atmosphere; simple, pleasant surroundings, and inexpensive rates. Also in Leghorn is **Kinderheim "La Caletta"** (Via di Caletta 13, 57013 Castiglioncello, Livorno). For information, get in touch with Signora Antonia Mantegazza, Via Magenta 3, 22100 Como). By the sea, this kinderheim accommodates 18 children from 4–12. In **Massa Carrara, Kinderheim "Montessori"** (Via F. Micheli 35, 54036 Marina di Carrarra, Massa Carrara) has swimming, gymnastics, sports, games, excursions. And **Kinderheim**

"Giada" (Via Lungofrigido Ponente 9, 54037 Marina di Massa, Massa Carrara) offers games, sports, swimming, skating, riding, tennis. In **Novara, "Il Nido di Villa Mater"** (Via Troubetzkoy 174, 28058 Verbania-Suna, Novara). In **Ravenna, Kinderheim "Villa Irma"** (Viale Raffaello 8, 48016 Cervia-Milano Marittima, Ravenna) is set in serene pinewoods near the sea; recreation, sports, camping activities. "Villa Irma" also has facilities for a camp for girls up to the age of 18. For information, contact Professor Giovanni and Irma Cominelli-Barth (Via S. Sebastiano 31/A, 20100 Bergamo). In **Rovigo, Kinderheim "Villa Serena Marina"** (Via Torino 39, 4510 Rosolina Mare, Rovigo) is located right on the beach; swimming, ball games, recreational facilities. For further information, get in touch with Giuliana Fanton Zanguio, Via Carpagnon 11, 36100 Vicenza. In **Udine,** there's **Kinderheim "Adriatico"** (Lungomare Trieste 140, 33054 Lignanò Sabbiadora, Udine), on the sea-front, in a garden surrounded with pines; heated swimming pool, Ping-Pong, a playground with slide, seesaws, trampoline, etc. For further information, contact Gustavo Zamparutti, Via R. Battistig 28, 33100 Udine). **Kinderheim Vanossi** (Madesimo) has rooms in an old-fashioned wooden chalet; 1001 things to do in the summer—mini-car driving, private lake steamer, and, for the older children, overnight trips to an Alpine refuge; skiing lessons and skating on a private rink in winter. **Turin: Guardaval** (Vigo) is a small mountain chalet, with balconies and terraces, surrounded by a large, parklike garden. Ball games, Ping-Pong, tennis, golf, and winter sports. Expert ski instruction. Open June 28–Sept. 2, and during Christmas vacation.

CHILDREN'S CAMPS American-directed **Camp Farfa,** at **Farfa** in the Sabine Hills, is co-ed for ages 7–14; swimming, crafts, sports, stargazing, music, games are offered in a family atmosphere. Small but pleasant. Details from Mrs. K. S. Harris, International School of Rome (111 V. della Storta). At **La Spezia, Campeggio Estivo** (Marinella di Sarzanna), for 13–18-year-olds. Accommodations for about 100 in tents and 8-bed bungalows in a pine forest with private beach and boats; supervision for all watersports. Basketball, football, volleyball, Ping-Pong, TV, excursions. Very healthy and athletic environment. Group travel can be arranged. Open late-July–early-Sept.

See also "Children's Camps" in the chapter on France for Italian camping possibilities in Massa, offered by the French CCCS for 12–14s, and the Massa camp plus excursions to Venice and Rome offered for the 15–18s.

CASTLES AND OTHER HAPPY FAMILY ACCOMMODATIONS Many villas, castles, castellos, and a palazzo or two will bridge the abyss between the present and the past. ENIT will fill you in on this, as well as send you a list of modestly priced pensions. The villa pension has been an Italian tradition; genteel living on-the-cheap in walk-up accommodations is possible still, but now more villas are offering a sampling of Medici high life.

To ***rent a summer cottage or villa,*** write to the EPT in the area, or consult **Agriturist** (Radnor House, 405 Regent St., London W.1). Try also **Villas Italia** (Corse Victor Emanuele 101, Rome) or **Continental Villas** (38 Sloane St., S.W.1; Tel: (01) 2459181) (see Ch. 7).

For a villa in **Rome,** try the Thurs. and Sun. *Rome Daily American*. Via Appia Antica is best for swimming pools. Most beautiful areas are Via Giulia, Via dei Coronari, Piazza Navona, the Forum, Piazza Farnese. EUR and **Casal Palocco** (two planned communities) and the compounds along **Via Cassia** are for those who like stateside conveniences. Old Rome ***apartments*** are often in a 15th–18th-century palace with high ceilings, sculptured marble fireplaces, courtyards filled with statues and fountains (generally beautiful but broken). Apartments centrally located near Via Vaneto are usually well-maintained, elegant, and modern. In new developments on the outskirts, many apartment buildings come with tennis courts and swimming pools. **Vigna Clara** and **Due Pini** are two popular developments for Americans. EUR and **Casal Palocco** (two planned communities) and the compounds along **Via Cassia** are for those who like stateside conveniences.

Snares, hazards, pitfalls! It's helpful to work with English villa-renting companies since landlords and real estate agents often charge Americans more than anyone else, a practice so common it even has a name—*prezzo Americano* or American price. Americans are accustomed to paying a great deal for a villa. The English aren't! There are hidden snags about leases and locations. The required 3-month deposit for long leases is hard for an American to get back—so hard, that many renters wisely live out 2 of the 3 months and let the 3rd month absorb the damage claims which landlords will undoubtedly make. If you have children, for heaven's sake make out an inventory carefully and get the landlord to sign it. Haggle about the rent. Then, check your location. If you're up on a high hill, water pressure may be low (the tap will trickle and the john will be slow to flush). If you're near a beautiful church, fine, until the bells start clanging at 6 a.m. Restaurants give off cooking smells, a clatter of dishes, and loud conversation. Piazza Navona, the Spanish Steps, and Piazza Santa Maria, hangouts of students and peripatetic youth, do not provide music to sleep by.

Amalfi: An old monastery has been converted into the **Cappuccini Hotel** (see Positano). **Belgirate:** Facing Lake Maggiore is **Villa Carlotta,** with 68 well-furnished rooms, private beach, tennis courts, swimming pool, a remarkably good fine restaurant (lake perch baked in paper! wild boar!) and gardens to run off all those delicious calories. **Bellaggio:** See Como. **Bressanone** (Brixen): The **Hotel Elefante** (4 Via Rio Bianco; Tel: (472 22288) in this well-preserved medieval southern Tyrolean town is named for an elephant in the 16th century that was a royal gift to Emperor Ferdinand of Austria, and which stopped here, en route from Genoa to Vienna. There's a refurbished fresco of this tusker, and elephants are embroidered on bedroom pillowcases; authentic antiquity of decor is wonderfully combined with direct-dial telephones, instant hot-water in modern bathrooms, home-made and mostly home-grown food, an annex with a swimming-pool shaped like a large comma on a tree-shaded lawn—where you and yours can stretch out comatose with pleasure. Bed-and-breakfast, as well as full-board rates for extraordinarily good food (Italian, German, South Tyrolean specialties) are surprisingly inexpensive for this exceptional hotel.

Calabria: Amantea and **Praia a Mare** both have first-rate hotels. **Tropea** has family cottages, swimming pools, tennis courts, and playgrounds on a series of terraces facing the sea. **Camogli** (near Genoa): Hotel **Cenobio dei Dogi,** comfortable for families; interestingly furnished; lovely gardens. **Cernobbio: Villa d'Este,** built in the 16th century as a private palace for Cardinal Tolomeo Gallio, occupied later by Princess Torlonia, the dowager empress of Russia, and the Princess of Wales, has beautiful gardens, statuary, indoor and outdoor pool, children's pool, boating, tennis, an 18-hole golf course, watersports, skiing with a parachute. Paradise for a big splurge. To make reservations, contact Leading Hotels of the World, Hotel Representatives, Inc., 770 Lexington Ave., New York, NY 10021. If you live in Alaska, Canada, Hawaii, or New York, telephone *collect* (212) 751–8915. Elsewhere in the U.S., Puerto Rico, and the American Virgin Islands, Tel: (800) 223–1230. (See also Attractions of Interest, Como.) **Cervinia:** At the foot of the Matterhorn, where skiing is possible all year long, the **Plein Soleil Residence,** one-half mile from the center of town, offers accommodations with 2/3, 4/5 or 5 beds, all apartments with kitchenettes; no restaurant but at half the price of the neighboring **Cielo Alto Hotel** which has sauna, disco, restaurant and swimming pool for neophyte skiers and the experienced ones who ski to Zermatt in Switzerland and back to Cervinia the same day.

Coca dei Marini: About 20 miles from Salerno, the **Convent di Santa Rosa** is an old monastery with original furnishings; nearby cove of Conca ideal for all watersports.

Como: (See Cernobbio, also Attractions of Interest to Children in Como.) Overlooking the lake at **Bellagio,** a 30-minute drive NE of the Villa d'Este in Cernobbio, five minutes aboard a car ferry, and you're in Bellagio; another deluxe dream, the magnificent, wonderfully comfortable **Grand Hotel Villa Serbelloni,** with a heated swimming pool, private beach, tennis, gardens, and an outdoor dining terrace with a view as stunning as the food. Grand, but so intimate, you feel as though this could be your own heavenly palace. Ideally, you should divide your time between the Villa d'Este and the Grand Hotel Villa Serbelloni for the best in acCOMOdations. About five miles west of Bellagio is **Tre-**

mezzo, and its **Grand Hotel Tremezzo,** about half the price, with turn-of-the-century charm, private beach, swimming pool, tennis and flowery park setting. Less expensive accommodations with charm? In the center of Como, with lake views, is the pleasant, old-fashioned **Hotel Metropole Suisse au Lac,** on Piazza Cavour. On Bellagio's promenade, small, modest, but prettily done-up, is the **Hotel Florence,** with a good restaurant and terrace. **Courmayeur:** In this skiing resort, dominated by Mont Blanc, and the world's largest cable car, the **Royal Hotel,** with regal prices, offers swimming pool, sauna, gymnasium adjacent to the ski facilities of Val Veny.

Elba: If luxury appeals, the most expensive and finest hostelry is the **Hotel l'Hermitage** at Biodola bay; enormous pool, outstanding beach, garden park, tennis. **Hotel del Golfo** on a secluded promontory at Procchio also has pool, tennis, and great food. Marciana Mariana is considered the family community where fishing and yachting are popular. Market day on Fri. in Portoferraio, Sat. in Porto Azzurro, Sun. in Marciana Mariana are special occasions. Underwater swimming is superb; go-karting at Piombino. **Florence:** Excellent hotels with swimming pools are **Villa Medici** (Via il Prato); **Minerva** (Piazza Santa Maria Novella 16); **Kraft** (Via Solfarino); and the delightful **Villa Belvedere** (Via B. Castelli 3, in the hills near the Piazza Michelangelo) if you have a car. **Villa Villoresi** (Colonnata di Sesto Fiorentino), an authentic Renaissance villa; swimming pool. **Villa Park San Domenico** (Via della Piazzola 55) is a noble 14th-century villa that hasn't been stripped of its *objets d'art;* parklike setting in the center of town; all 19 rooms luxuriously furnished. Other nice choices: **Villa Carlotta** (Via Michele de Lando 3); **Villa La Massa** in **Candeli.** And **Villa San Michele** (Via Doccia 4) in **Fiesole,** a 15th-century monastery whose elegant facade and loggia are credited to Michelangelo; view of Florence; air conditioning, heating, heated pool and snack bar in the upper garden. During May and June, Villa San Michele's concierge will arrange garden tours for you of other Florentine villas run Tues., Thurs. and Sat. from 2:30 p.m.–5:30 p.m. Whoppingly but worthily expensive; closes in winter.

Residences (furnished apartments/flats)? Try **Palazzo Benci** (Lungarno alle Grazie 28; Tel: (055) 293–151); **Palazzo Ricasoli** (Via delle Mantellate 2; Tel: (055) 495–001); **Villa La Bugia** (Via Santa Margherita a Montici 4; Tel (055) 807–7121); **Porta al Prato** (Via Ponte alle Mosse 14; Tel: (055) 476–071), **La Mantellate** (Via delle Mantellate 2; Tel: (055) 410–876); **Mini Residence** (Via Caccini 20; Tel: (055) 410–876); **Firenze Nova Apartments** (Via Panciatichi 51; Tel (055) 477–851). Furnished and unfurnished apartments at **Mobilare ed Immobilare Mirella** (Via Galilei 200; Tel: (055) 463–3030).

Gignese: In the hills above Stresa, overlooking Lake Maggiore, midway up Monte Mottarone, the family-run *pensione* **Hotel Golf Panorama,** has comfortable balconied rooms, delicious home-grown fruits, vegetable and game which the owner-chef hunts for. The rate for double room and full board is remarkably inexpensive. **Isola dei Pescatori:** With only a dozen rooms, the **Hotel Verbano** is charming and cozy, simply furnished, and with good homemade pasta and fish dishes. The price for double room and all meals on this Borromean island will not have you borrowing from the bank even if you have quadruplets with you. **Lake Maggiore and the Borromeo Islands** (See Belgirate, Gignese, Isola dei Pescatori, Pallanza, Stresa). **La Thuile:** In **Val d'Aosta,** seven miles from Courmayeur, and linked to slopes on the French side of a fan-shaped mountain range, the **Planibel Hotel Residence** situated at the hub of slopes and ski facilities, has a swimming pool, solarium; apartments with two to six beds, balcony, kitchenette, dining room. **Orvieto: La Badia** (Tel: (0763) 90359), in the province of Terni, among the rolling hills of Umbria, midway between Rome and Florence, in the midst of its own vineyards, 2½ miles from the art-filled city of Orvieto, is a renovated 12th-century Romanesque-Lombardesque abbey and church with important frescoes, tennis courts, swimming pool, garden, surrounding vineyards, a vaulted kitchen converted into a grill-room, and first class accommodations that couldn't be goodier. **Pallanza:** Across from Stresa, on Lake Maggiore, the Grand Hotel Majestic is set in a lakeside park with private beach and dock, with tennis, an indoor pool. Large and splendid, but with moderate prices. **Piancavallo:** In this ski location with a snow-making system 62 miles from Venice, you might want to unbuckle your boots at the comfortable **Editour Apartments,** accommodating 2/3, 3/4, 5/6 guests; kitchenettes but no restaurant. A money-saver.

The pleasures of **Positano** simply must not be missed: the town itself, tiered like a wedding cake with cliff-hanging 18th-century houses, and a constellation of charming hotels, each with garden, grape arbor and a view of the sea, mountains and cliffs that is inspirational. Treat yourself to a stay in the sumptuous **Hotel San Pietro,** mined out of the cliffside in bougainvillea-covered tiers, with an elevator that descends to the sea, grape arbors over every balcony and a rose garden planted on the roof of the dining room. Small children will delight in the shallow pool on a sunny terrace; an elevator gently lowers you to a bathing platform with deliciously cool water lapping at its edges for swimming. The food is a sybaritic delight. Children will founder themselves, and so will you, on a tart non-alcoholic drink called "elephant milk," made of almond milk, a specialty of the house. This is one of those special, blissful dream hotels, but expensive if you eat all your meals there. Nearby, **La Sirenuse,** a 19th-century villa, rated first class, has a swimming pool. Rated second class but regal with its golden mosaic dome is the 18th-century **Palazzo Murat; L'Ancora,** a former private villa; and the inexpensive and charming **Vittoria.** Just down the coast in **Ravello,** a village filled with Moorish architecture, overlooking the Gulf of Salerno, is the **Hotel Palumbo,** a 12th-century Sasso palace with 16th-century frescoes, lots of English antiques, scrumptious food, and a guest list of writers, film stars, poets and playwrights partial to this gem of a hotel, rated first class. Other hotels are the **Caruso Belvedere; Villa Rufolo; Parsifal Ex Convento,** a former convent with cloister; **Villa Amore** in the Santa Chiara area. **Riva: Hotel du Lac et du Paro,** set in a park that is large and lovely, has its own beach, two swimming pools, tennis courts, gymnasium, three restaurants, hairdresser, and little villas accommodating up to five persons at affordable prices at this modern, luxury establishment on Lake Garda.

In **Rome,** family hotel **Ambasciatori Palace** (Via Veneto 70) is pleasant, with family suites, refrigerators in every room, wonderful service; the concierge can arrange for everything imaginable; ask to see the little aviary in the terrace restaurant. One of the best pensions is **Home in Rome** (Via Corsica 4) in a quiet section, about ten minutes from the center, with an English-speaking person on duty 24-hours a day; telephones in all rooms; suites for families; a pool in summer. Budgeteers might try **Bellavista Milton** (via di Porta Pinciana 16A); functional rooms; nice roof garden. Special for the ambiance of classic Rome, small, friendly, kind to the pursestrings is **Albergo del Sole** (Piazza del Pantheon 63); English-speaking babysitters available. There are about 20 ''residences'' (furnished apartments/flats) in Rome with minimum stays usually about five days, so don't let anyone tell you that ''Home in Rome'' is your *only* choice. **Parioli House** (Viale Parioli 39) is in a pleasant garden ex-urb, I'd call it, rather than suburb. Others? **Palazzo del Velabro** (Via del Velabro 16); **Casalbergo Residence Duse** (Via Eleanora Duse 5); **Palace Hotel** (Via Archimede 69) and, great if you have the wherewithal, the **Residence Cavalieri Hilton** (Via Cadlolo). Others listed under ''Latium, Rome'' in that handy ENIT publication *Italy, an ideal holiday for all the family* listing camping grounds, tourist villages, holiday homes, bungalows (*not* where you might expect to find such a list!)

Roman friends suggest the first-class **Forum Hotel** across the street from the Forum, but for a better location, directly across from the Hassler (at ½ the price) is the small **Scalimata di Spagna** (7 Trinita dei Monti), considered the best of the inexpensive accommodations a hop away from the Spanish Steps. Even less expensive is the **Sicilia,** a good *pensione,* just off the Via Veneto and a block from the Excelsior.

A valuable money-saving suggestion for a Roman Holiday is booking your hotel through the *United Service Organization* (USO), an organization that can book hotel space anywhere in Rome at a substantial discount if you have ever served in the U.S. Armed Forces or are a service man or woman.

▶ **Note:** Italian hotels often impose a 3-day limit on summer stays, but will consider longer stays if application is made by mail well in advance. Carry this correspondence with you!

In the luxury group of hotels, the **Hassler Villa Medici** (Piazza Trinita dei Monti), with the Borghese Gardens in back, is convenient for families. The **Quirinale** (7 Via Nazionale) is a quiet garden oasis in the heart of Rome, and by means of an inside corridor, connects directly with the Opera House. Extremely pleasant garden restaurant. The **Cavalieri Hilton International** (Via Cadlolo 101), overlooking Rome from the top of Monte Mario, has a great view, a swimming pool, two tennis courts, jogging paths and putting greens; an informal trattoria and a formal rooftop dining spot, **La Pergola,** with nightly dancing. In a 3-acre park outside of Rome is **Villa Valle Giulia,** with high ceilings and marble staircases, frescoed walls, spacious rooms.

Sansicario: Opposite to the ski facilities of this resort on the western slope of the Piedmontese Alps are the **Fraiteve** and **Monti Della Luna** Residences, recently constructed complexes of apartments with 2/3, 4/5, 6/7 (!) beds; kitchenettes, but no restaurant, a moneysaver. In **Sardinia** at Porto Cervo, you can stay at the elegant **Cala di Volpe** (where, if you are enormously rich, you can take over a penthouse with private roof-top pool) with Olympic-size pool; 18-hole golf course; and mooring for your yacht. Close to Porto Cervo on the NE coast is **Romazzino,** and the **Hotel Romazzino,** with 30% reductions for children 12 and younger, offers saltwater pool, poolside barbecue, boat rentals, windsurfing, tennis, 18-hole golf course nearby, sunny terraces, flower gardens. The most expensive house rentals are on this same Costa Smeralda. ENIT can supply you with a list of agents. **Aquarius Travels** (24 Via Nazionale, Palau; Tel: (789) 709–676) specializes in rentals in the Porto Rafael area N of the Costa Smeralda, with ferry service to La Maddalena and from there, ferry service to Corsica, Porto Rafael is as modest as a fishing village, with a flowering of English gardens, a good base for families. Elsewhere, there are many moderate-to-cheap accommodations. At Alghero is **Villa Las Tronas,** one of the better hotels; once belonged to the Italian royal family; boasts fine sea frontage. At Cagliari, the tourist village of **Santa Margherita di Pula** accommodates 1600 guests and expects to expand to twice that many; facilities include five swimming pools, two mini-golf courses, and a huge park. At Santa Lussurgiu, the government has built a **tourist hotel** with swimming pool and playground; picnic ground among waterfalls and fountains. In **Sicily,** at **Palerma,** the **Villa Igiea** is sumptuous, overlooks Roman ruins, has a garden of palms, pines, flowers. At Taormina, the **San Domenico Palace Hotel** is deluxe, converted from a monastery with great flair and style. In **Siena,** the **Park Hotel** is a 16th-century villa on the Marciano Hill; panoramic view of city and surroundings; set in a park; delicious cuisine. **Villa Scacciapensieri,** set on a Chianti hillside, has swimming pool, tennis, lovely gardens, produce from its own farm, refrigerators in rooms; open mid-Mar.–early Nov. **Sirmione:** The **Villa Cortine Palace,** its park safeguarded with gates in the old quarter of this popular spa resort, is a luxurious retreat with tennis courts, a swimming pool. About half the price, plus two meals, is the modern, luxuriously furnished **Hotel Continental** with its own pier on Lake Garda, swimming pool, gardens, and terraces leading off all the pretty rooms. At **Stresa** on Lake Maggiore, facing the Borromean Islands, a good base with contemporary comforts in an Old World setting is the **Regina Palace** with tennis courts and swimming pool, and balcony views of the Lombardy mountains, and the lights of Isola Bella shining up from the water. **Trento: Castel Madruzzo** (about 13 m from Trento) is a beautifully restored medieval manor with waterskiing on the lake, mountain sports, and the lovely Cavedine Valley to roam around. You can picnic, ride and hunt in the park. Heavenly. About eight miles from Trento is the magnificent **Castel Pergine,** an oasis of country quiet and beauty with a handsome Room of Weapons; dining room called the Room of Justice with splendid meals; gastronomical specialties of snails—children like the taste but not the idea. Watersports at nearby Lake Cristofaro. A charmer! Another beauty is **Castel Toblino** (about 15 m from Trento), a marvelous 15th-century castle; lovely courtyard; its frescoes and merlons will have you feeling like Medici princes. Great trout fishing in Lake Toblino and the Lake Santa Massenta nearby; mountain excursions; and a specialty called *canederli,* large *gnocchi* made with bread, flour, milk, eggs, sausage, ham and eaten in a broth of its own or with sauerkraut, of all things. Superb. **Tremezzo:** See Como. **Treviso:** About eight miles out is **Villa Condulmer** (Mogliano Veneto), a 17th-century building in the remains of a monastery, converted to a luxurious hotel and restaurant with the yummiest *tortellini* in cream sauce, a dessert called *zucotto,* and a magnificent park, lake, garden, and golf course. Watch the children in the lance-crossbow-dagger-filled corridors! **Turin: Villa Sassi** (Via Traforo del Pino 47), a historic villa. **Venice:** Small, elegant, so unobtrusively a hotel that it seems still to be the private palace it was, is 15th-century **Palazzo Gritti;** sumptuous furniture, divine food, impeccable service. Matchless. Very expensive. **Hotel Bisanzio** (Calle della Pieta), spotless, well-located, and well-staffed; pension a favorite of large families owing to its flexibility in making up suites. The deluxe **Cipriani Hotel** (10 Giudecca, 30100 Venice), set on a 3-acre site on Giudecca Isle in the center of a Venetian lagoon across from Piazza San Marco and the Doge's Palace, whisks you in 4–5 min. by free hotel express motor launch to the Piazza San Marco (the regular service *vaporetto,* with all its stops, takes about 40 min.); has its own private yacht harbor, Olympic-size heated swimming pool; offers, besides peace and luxury, a cooking course demonstration, including market tours, trips to vineyards, banquets, run spring and fall. For about one-fourth the price, there's the **Hotel Marconi & Milano** (708–824 Marconi, 729 San Polo) with 30 rooms, 11 baths, a modestly priced and delightful open-air restaurant bordering the Grand Canal, right by the fabled Rialto Bridge. Children also like the **Lido,** a chic little island about 15 minutes by motorboat from Venice, where a good many small hotels are highly satisfactory as family headquarters; swimming is safe (you have to wade out almost ½ mile before the water gets deep); go-kart tracks; waterskiing; sailboats for rent; and a marvelous playground make the Lido a delight for all-aged children. High season as far as rates are concerned is July–

mid-Sept.; but during May and early June, late Sept. and Oct., when the Lido and Venice are at their loveliest, they are also less crowded.

▶ **Note:** Youth hostels are often housed in castles throughout Europe, but Italy has two extraordinary hostels in castles that also house sensationally good restaurants. **Castello di Lerici** (about six m from La Spezia). The watersports are splendid; also mini-golf, excursions to Portovenere and Cinqueterra. **Castello degli Alberi Montagnana** (about 25 m from Padua), a 14th-century, most impressive castle; restaurant specializing in prosciutto. If your teenagers want to spend time in Rome on their own, check out *convent accommodations* and *religious residences*. Savvy guides for students—*Let's Go* is exemplary—usually list these incredibly inexpensive, immaculate facilities with/without meals available to teenagers and students of all ages, all religious faiths, who report they "had a good time," "felt safe and secure"; found the nuns and uniformed *religieuses* "sweet," "adorable," caring"; a guesthouse in this category close to the Vatican is: **Casa Delle Diaconesse Germanische di Kalserwerth,** Via Alessandro Farnese 18, Rome; Tel: (06) 35–25–61. For further information about rooms in seminaries or convents, contact the office of **Perigrinatio Sedem** (Pilgrimage to the See of St. Peter), Piazza Pio 12, office number 3. Tel: (06) 698–4896/698–5038. Call only during business hours, 9 a.m.–5 p.m. weekdays. The office is across the street from St. Peter's Square.

If the idea of a furnished apartment, a floor in someone's *palazzo,* a paying guest arrangement appeals to you, ask the local tourist office when you are *there,* so you can see for yourself what is available, either for now or for when you return as you are sure to.

CLUB MEDITERRANEE **Kamarina** is the largest Club Med resort village on the Mediterranean. A 1½-hour drive from Catania and in the presence of Mt. Etna, Kamarina boasts of what must be one of the largest swimming pools anywhere, a hotel complex and a delightful village. A Mini Club and a Kid's Club and a "big top" where the children put on a circus performance of their own every week; tennis, sailing, and windsurfing, to archery, photography laboratory, and concerts. Even a computer center where beginners can learn languages or play galactic games. Idyllic for families who can also make half day excursions to Ragusa, Agricento, Syracuse, or longer trips to Taormina, Etna, Palermo. (Club Mediterranee Kamarina, 97100 Ragusa, Sicily, Italy.) (See also Ch. 7.) In the north of Sicily, **Cefalu,** on Cefalu Bay, a "case" village, where only over-12-yr.-olds are accepted (no special counselors for them) in a Garden of Eden setting of flowers and Polynesian huts. Swimming pool, scuba diving, and the usual Club Med activities. (Club Mediterranee, 90015 Cefalu, Palermo, Sicily, Italy.) **Otranto,** on the Adriatic, is a Club Med village with a Kid's Club for children 8 and older. Accommodation in bungalows. Tennis, golf, sailing, scuba diving, picnics, boat trips, archery, football, and 30 horses to ride (small extra charge for riding). Also nightclub, dancing, concerts, hairdresser, applied arts workshops, excursions. (Club Mediterranee, 73028 Otranto, Lecde, Italy.) **Palinuro** in Calabria accepts children from 8 on without special counselors for them in a ''case'' village where the major activity is scuba diving with specialized instruction for beginners. There's a lot more, too, including pony trekking at a small extra charge. Excursions possible to Capri, Pompeii, Paestum, Vesuvius. (Club Mediterranee, 84064 Palinuro, Salerno, Italy.) In Tuscany, another ''case'' village, **Donoratico** has an immense beach, Polynesian huts, Mini Club, Kid's Club, and special restaurant for the kiddies. Bountiful activities, sports tournaments, pony trekking and riding at a small extra charge, nightclub, dancing, concerts, and much more. Considered one of the best family ''case'' villages. (Club Mediterranee, 57024 Donoratico, Livorno, Italy.) In Sardinia, on the NE coast, another ''case'' village sheltered by umbrella pines, **Caprera,** with special facilities for families: A Mini Club, Kid's Club, a special playhouse, and restaurant for the offspring of families who can enjoy all the sports and workshops associated with Club Mediterranee (07024 La Maddalena, Caprera, Sassari, Italy). In northern Sardinia, **Santa Teresa** is a new resort village, attractively laid out on terraces around a natural bay. A Mini Club, a Kid's Club, three swimming pools, tennis, picnics, sailing, windsurfing, trips in caiques, applied arts workshops, a special restaurant-bar on the beach, nightclub, dancing, concerts, excursions, and special emphasis here on scuba diving. (Club Mediterranee, Santa Teresa, Santa Teresa di Gallura, Sardinia, Italy.)

During the winter, there's a Club Mediterranee snow village at **Sestrieres,** in the Piedmont mountains, with both Mini Club and Kid's Club operative during the Italian school holidays; also a ski school operative all season for children 6 years and up.

CAMPING AND CARAVANING Over 500 official camping sites are in operation; details can be obtained in *Parchi di Campeggio* a publication of the Touring Club Italiano (Corso Italia 10, Milano). An abridged list with a useful map can be had from **Federazione Italiana del Campeggio,** from ENIT, or from **Centro Nazionale Campeggiatori Stranieri** (Via Mameli 2, Firenze), the center for all Italian camping information.

Camping sites around **Rome** and vicinity: **Roma Camping** (Via Aurelia); **Camping La Pineta di Roma** (Via Cristoforo Colombo; Tel: 605–0063); open in summer. Outside **Florence,** in Fiesole, **Camping Panoramico** is large, wooded, with excellent facilities. About 6 miles from **Venice** on the airport road, just past the turnoff for Mestre, is small, attractive splendid swimming pool. Information about caravan rental, free legal assistance in the event of accidents, free maps, and other services from the Automobile Club d'Italia (membership fee), **Servizio Turismo** (Via Marsala 8; Rome), or at any ACI office on the Italian border or in the provinces. Good camping equipment in Rome available at **Salinas** (Piazza S. Sonnino 42). The address for the national organization of youth hostels is **Associazione Italiana Alberghi Gioventu,** 3 Lungo tevere Cadorna, Rome: Tel: (06) 396–0009. A deposit of about half the price for the daily rate is requested. You are also advised to buy your youth hostel membership card in the U.S. where it costs less than it does in Italy.

By far the best guide is *Italy, An Ideal Holiday for All the Family,* a listing with maps, readable symbols, and regional descriptions of the locations of camping grounds, bungalows, holiday homes and tourist villages (vacation settlements with a variety of recreational facilities such as bowling, mini-golf, riding, scuba diving, waterskiing, sailing, tennis, childrens' playgrounds and swimming pool). Published by ENIT, this *excellent* guide is obtainable from the Italian Government Travel Office in New York, Chicago and San Francisco. Many camping grounds provide bungalows, resident doctors, swimming pools, riding stables, sports equipment, and facilities that are admirable at bargain-basement prices. Friends of mine, on a bicycling trip with their children, told me I was being snobby about the tourist villages and that they were delighted to use "Logonova-Spina" along the Comacchio Lido near Ferrara in Emilia-Romagna as a base before they bicycled on to Padua and Venice where they reported that the camping grounds with bungalows had many recreational facilities. You must reserve well ahead for these attractive facilities because they are extremely popular and solidly booked during the summer. The ENIT booklet provides addresses and telephone numbers of all these convenient spots.

ATTRACTIONS FOR CHILDREN IN ROME There's no point in trying to take in all the sights and beauties, because there's too much to see, but there's no reason to miss out on the highlights either. Most attractions are closed Mon., open 9 a.m.–4-or-5 p.m. daily plus 9 a.m.–1 p.m. Sun. and holidays; but check with ENIT before you go.

Here's ancient and early Rome in a form that won't overwhelm children: Your children probably already know about Romulus and Remus and the she-wolf symbol of ancient Rome which still stands for Italy. Keeping alive this 3000-year-old tradition, a live ***she-wolf*** is kept in a cage beside the steps up the **Capitoline Hill;** the caged eagle on the hill is symbolic of the Roman empire. At the foot of Palatine Hill is the **Forum Romanum,** which used to be the center of ancient Rome; impressive sound and light spectacles June–Aug. Then the **Colosseum,** where the gladiatorial contests were held. Have a look at the **Pantheon,** probably the best-preserved building of ancient Rome, and the **Baths of Diocletian** (now called the Museo della Terma) near the railroad station. The earlier **Baths of Caracalla** with opera and open air ballet from June–Aug.; this is the best way I know to introduce children to opera; the atmosphere is informal and there are many children in the audience. Snacks are available; performances are lighthearted and spectacular; and if the children feel tired, just let them stretch out and go to sleep.

Also take a look at: **Castel Sant-Angelo,** the tomb of the Emperor Hadrian, housing a museum of weapons and warlike gear from the Stone Age to the present. The **Forums** of Trajan, Julius Caesar, Augustus, and Nerva, extending across from the Victor Emmanuel Monument, along and on either side of the Via dei Fori Imperiali. The **Etruscan Museum** at Villa Giulia (9 Piazzale Villa Giulia); excellent collection of Etruscan art. **Capitolino Museum** (Piazza del Campidoglio) and, across the court, **Palazzo dei Conservatori;** in both, all sorts of interesting coins, ancient household objects, statues (including the famous bronze she-wolf), parts of old boats, paintings, and many mosaics. **Museo della Civilta Romana** (Piazza Agnelli) has fascinating exhibits of the history of Rome. The **Museum of Popular Arts and Traditions** (Piazza Marconi) has folk art, costumes, and crafts, including: strange Sicilian charms; a Neapolitan presepio of everyday life detailed down to a chamberpot beneath a bed; playing cards smaller than a child's fingernail; primitive Sardinian paintings.

Monte Testaccio is a mound about 100 feet high that once was the dumping ground for earthenware jars of grain imported from Spain and Africa; you are welcome to take whatever bits and pieces you can find; great fun for most children. **Pyramid of Caius Cestius,** about as high as **Monte Testaccio,** towers above the fortressed wall of the **Porta San Paolo** and above the **Protestant Cemetery** (where you can find the tombs of Keats and Shelley).

The **Catacombs,** underground passages and rooms where early Christians gathered to worship, for protection and refuge, and to bury their dead, extend around Rome in a wide circle, the majority concentrated between Via Salaria and Via Nomentana on one side, and Via Latina, Via Appia, and Via Ostiensis on the other. The paintings that decorate many of them are symbolic of the doctrines and hopes of Christianity, and most represent scenes with which children are familiar—Noah in the Ark, Daniel in the Lions' Den, Jonah swallowed by the whale. Contrary to what one might expect, the Catacombs are not depressing or frightening. The Catacombs of San Sebastiano are the best known and the least interesting. I'd recommend instead the Catacombs of Domitilla (22A Via delle Sette Chiese, branching off Via Appia), of St. Priscilla (430 Via Salaria), or of Sts. Marcellino and Pietro, all with many frescoes; or the Jewish Catacombs (19A Via Appia).

Take a ***ride in a horse-drawn carriage*.** Although they have meters, haggle beforehand about the cost, which usually involves the number of people, the distance, and the length of time. If you speak as little Italian as the driver speaks English, don't let the arrangements become unduly exasperating. There's no use having a lovely drive spoiled.

Puppets*.** The word puppet comes from the Italian *pupa,* meaning doll, and our Mr. Punch derives from the Italian *Punchinello.* The crocodile in Punch shows is an early Italian invention. Italian puppet shows are interesting from a historical viewpoint, and children find them delightful. A marvelous marionette theater is **Il Torchio** (Via Morosini 16; Tel: 582–049); also **Teatro delle Marionetti degli Accettella** (285 Via Conca D'oro; Tel: (06) 810–1887). The Borghese Gardens has a marionette theater on the Pincio. In late fall and winter, a **circus** is headquartered on the Viale Tiziano. ***Parks. The **Borghese Gardens** is the largest. At the Galoppatoria you can hire horses; nearby, a children's moviehouse; bicycle and tricycle rental; ponies, donkeys to ride and donkey carts to drive. At Giardino di Lago, ducks, and swans can be fed; boats for hire; zoo, plus a Zoo Museum (18 Via Alrovandi). In the Pincio section, a merry-go-round. **Luneur** (Luna) **Park** (Via delle 3 Fontane, EUR) is an amusement fun fair and happy playground with lake and boat rentals. Opposite the park is a miniature-car traffic school for children, and a cafe with nearby playground. **Villa Sciarra** (not too far from Monte Testaccio) is a little park; donkey carts; merry-go-round; exquisite flowerbeds; wandering peacocks (they scream, as all peacocks do, which can frighten an unprepared child). Ponies at the **Villa Glori** in the Parioli section. Cannons fired at noon in **Gianicolo Park.** Merry-go-round, ponies, train on large track, bicycle rentals at **Parco Nemorense** (Piazza Crati); small amusement park at beautiful **Colle Oppio** near the Colosseum; rollerskating and bicycle track at **Villa Ada** near Piazza Istria.

The demesne of the **Supreme Military Order of Malta** has a palace in downtown Rome (68 Via Condotti) where you can wander into the courtyard to see the goldfish pool and gargoyle fountain.

Vatican City is another independent domain, where the Pope is absolute monarch. Dominating the City is **St. Peter's,** the largest church in Christendom, beautified by Bramante, Raphael, Bernini, and Michelangelo, among many other artists. When you take the children to St. Peter's and perhaps also look at the Treasury (with jewels, crowns, gem-covered crosses, ecclesiastical robes, and caskets), don't try to cover the Vatican in the same trip. You don't need special papers to go to the *Vatican Museums,* but to enter *Vatican City* proper or to visit the *Apostolic Palaces,* you have to apply to the **Segreteria della Commissione Pontificia per la Citta Vaticano, Vatican City** (Tel: (06) 6982). You might be pleasingly astonished by the *Vatican gardens,* but the children will be far more interested in the *mosaic factory* where workmen tweezer around 28,000 shades of colored glass chips and geometrical glass pieces into copies of celebrated masterpieces. You can walk up to the dome of St. Peter's for a small fee, and for double the amount, take the elevator for a spectacular view of the Vatican gardens and all of Rome. Entrance to the stairs and elevator is to the left of the interior entrance to St. Peter's.

As for the ***Vatican Museums,*** open daily except Sun., the real nucleus is the **Museo Pio-Clementino,** divided into 11 depts. You'll find the famous *Laocoon* and the *Apollo Belvedere* in the Belvedere Court, and far more interesting, if less famous, statues, mosaics and other treasures in this unbelievably rich collection. How can this be exciting rather than exhausting for children? My suggestion is to get an illustrated guidebook well in advance of your visit. Let the children look through it so they'll have some idea of what to expect. Since many of the statues refer to mythological figures and events, you might help the children familiarize themselves with Apollo, Zeus, Venus, and so on. Then, when you visit the museum, just walk through and let your children see what they want to for themselves. With a little advance preparation, it will be a memorable excursion. In the same way, familiarize your children with the Michelangelo ceiling frescoes, and the Botticelli, Ghirlandaio, and Pinturicchio frescoes in the **Sistine Chapel** and with the paintings in the adjoining **Raphael Stanze** and the **Pinacoteca.** Permission to visit the **Necropolis beneath the Vatican** with an English-speaking group can be had by writing to the director of **Ufficio degli Scavi,** Vatican City, Italy, who advises you when you arrive in Italy to call (06) 698–5318 to confirm arrangements. The **Tomb of St. Peter** is here; also sarcophagi and mosaics as rare and strange as Christ in a sun-chariot; and impressive Street of the Dead.

The **Vatican Post Office** sorts and sends out mail the same day, and is the most efficient mail service in Italy. Its stamps are also popular with collectors the world over, so be sure to buy some when you're there.

Via Giulia, a long straight street parallel to but one street away from the Tiber—from the back of the Palazzo Farnese to the piazza at which Corso Vittorio Emanuele II reaches the river—is an eminently strollable street, lined with churches, palaces, antique and arts-and-crafts shops where, at Christmastime, Romans take their children to see creches displayed in shop windows. In summer, there are occasional concerts of Baroque and Renaissance music; a good place for a city picnic, or pause for a soothing cappuccino, cold drink or ice cream at any fountain-facing outdoor cafe for a moment of pleasant reflection.

There's no point in making a special trip to look at the ***fountains of Rome.*** You'll just come upon them as you walk around. Walk over to the Piazza Navona, sit down at one of the sidewalk cafes, and while the children are enjoying their ice cream they will also be enjoying the **Fontana dei Fiume** (Fountain of Rivers). Walking along the Corso, turn off at the Via delle Muratte and there's the **Fontana di Trevi.** Another of Bernini's fountains is the **Fountain of the Triton** (Piazza Barberini), or the **Barcaccia** (''Old Boat''), made by his father, at the base of the Spanish Steps. Have tea and cookies or orangeade at Babington's, Rampoldi, or the Caffe Greco in the vicinity. Many other fountains to see and to discover for yourselves.

Churches of special interest for children are: **St. John Lateran** (Piazza di Porta San Giovanni), topped by 16 statues of Christ, the Apostles, and saints; on St. John's Day (June 24), the piazza is packed as people fire off skyrockets and Roman candles at the statues—a solid hit brings good luck. **St. Maria in Aracoeli** (Capitoline Hill), during the Christmas season until Jan. 6, usually between 3–4 p.m. daily, children from 5–10 come here to recite carefully studied poems in honor of the Christ Child. **St. Maria in Cosmedin** (Piazza della Bocca della Verita); under the portico is an ancient marble face whose mouth is supposed to snap shut when the hand of a fibber is put into it. **San Paolo Fuori le Mura** (St. Paul's Outside the Walls, about a mile outside Porta Paola) has a dazzling and shimmering interior which appeals to children. The chapel of **St. Maria della Concezione** (Via Veneto 27) is decorated with the bones of 4000 Capuchin friars. **S.S. Cosma e Daniano** has a spectacular creche. **San Luigi de Francesi** (Largo San Luigi de Francesi) has some great Caravaggio paintings.

To fill time at the Piazza de Cinquecento train station, see the lower-level **aquarium.**

When the President is in residence (usually not in Aug.), the **Changing of the Guard** takes place every day at 4 p.m. at the Palazzo Regio del Quirinale; marching and music. **Villa Farnesina** (Via Lungara 230) has frescoes by Raphael and his pupils; among them the stories of Psyche and Galatea. It's said that Michelangelo stopped by to see Raphael's work and, when the custodian wasn't looking, drew a charcoal head on the wall at the north end; the sketch is clearly visible, an exception to the rule of not drawing on walls! Take the children some evening to **Trastevere,** "Romanest" section of Rome. Teenagers will like the **Piper Club** (Via Tagliamento 9). ***Movies*** in English at four theaters: Archimede, Rubino, Pasquino, and the Film Studio. ***Excursions:*** One pleasant one is the 20-mile drive to **Tivoli.** Picnic by the ruins of **Hadrian's Villa,** and try to see the gardens and fountains of **Villa d'Este,** especially at night, when the fountains are illuminated. Archaeological treasures are still being unearthed here; there are five large swimming pools (filled with bacteriologically pure water with a high sulfur content); dressing rooms; fountains, shrines, temples, medieval towers, reconstructions, ruins, gardens, a medieval quarter, craftsmen at work, a sauna center, health treatments central to the mineral-rich thermal springs at Terme Acque Albule, and a great waterfall across the Ponte Gregoriano. Take your pick; don't try to see and do it all in a day! Another nice excursion is to have lunch and a swim at one of two elegant hotels: **Helio Cabala** at **Marino** or the **Villa Fiorio** near **Frascati.** Italian families relax at the **Castelli,** the hill towns along the Via Appia by Lake Albano and Lake Nemi in the Alban Hills. Under the cliffs where the town of Nemi (about 18 miles from Rome) is perched, stood the sacred grove of Diana of the wood and the tree with the Golden Bough, (whence the title of the world classic by Sir James G. Frazer). The area is an archaeological and folkloric trove, the site of the Pope's summer residence at Castel Gandolfo, mud baths at Albano, vineyards, patrician villas, good restaurants with local specialties including luscious strawberries from

Nemi and "porchetta" (roast pig). Information from Azienda Autonoma di Soggiorno e Turismo, Via Olivella 2, Albano Laziale), about 12 miles from Rome. At **Monte Mario** close to Rome, see the planetarium and swim at the nearby Hilton Hotel.

ATTRACTIONS FOR CHILDREN IN FLORENCE This splendid, beautiful, greatest of all indoor and outdoor museums of Renaissance art is filled with attractions, but it is not a town that most children would add to their list of favorites if sightseeing is overdone. My advice would be to take the children to: The **Uffizi Palace,** one of the richest galleries in the world; children will greatly enjoy the evening concerts. The **Bargello Museum,** a castle-fortress housing the National Museum. The **Fine Arts Academy's** museum gallery (60 Via Ricasoli, adjacent to the Academy) to see Michelangelo's original David and many of his unfinished sculptures. The **Stibbert Museum** (26 Via Stibbert), once a private villa, set in a charming park, to see 16th-century mounted knights, fully equipped, plus European and Oriental armor and costumes. And children really do appreciate the **Piazza della Signoria** and the statues in the **Loggia dei Lanzi.**

Then call it a day as far as formal sightseeing goes; call in a babysitter or companion, and while you go off to see the rest of Florence, let the children go off in responsible hands to watch the craftsmen in **San Croce Square** (they can see mosaic, silver, leather, and ceramic beaten, pounded, and tooled, and molded into wonderful colors and shapes). Or give them some loot to spend at the **straw market** (Mercato Nuova); if you rub the nose of the bronze boar here, it is believed you will return to Florence. Or give them money for a carriage ride (carriages are usually stationed at all main squares) to visit lovely **Viale dei Colli.** Take a bus across the Arno and into a treelined boulevard to **Cascine Park,** with lots of benches, bicycles, picnics, ice cream and food vendors, men playing cards on folding tables. There's a playground with slides and swings near the grandstand of the hippodrome where they have flatracing and harness racing in the spring and fall, and other special events. Let the children discover the bronze doors of the **Baptistery** or **Giotto's Bell Tower** on their own; let them point out buildings and statues to you rather than the other way around. Then, at night, listen to outdoor orchestras in the Piazza della Repubblica.

Drive to **Fiesole,** explore the **Etruscan ruins** nearby, or just drive in the surrounding landscape crowded with hilltop fortresses and walled towns.

Day hotels can be found at 5 Via dei Pecori; Piazza Stazione; Via Porta Rossa 23; Via Sassetti 5; Via Cavour 19.

The tourist offices for printed material and information (**Azienda Autonoma di Turismo,** Via Tornabuoni, 15; **Ente Provinciale per il Turismo,** Via A. Manzoni, 16) are understaffed and crowded. Tip your concierge, enlist his help, and you'll find life simpler. A booklet, *Flor-*

ence, Information for Tourists, available from ENIT, lists the telephone numbers of 20 taxi stands and two radio taxis (210–321 and 296–230), foot-saving information; also the bus numbers and where the buses go. (Bus tickets have to be bought at "bars" [coffee shops] and tobacconists and then cancelled in the ticket machine on the bus.) This same booklet lists all the museums, galleries, gardens, and their opening and closing hours; churches, palaces, libraries, clubs, theaters, restaurants and "trattorie" in town and in the countryside; pizzerias. Mary McCarthy's *Stones of Florence* is still the best reference book I know and, except for telephone numbers and services, hotels, restaurants and shops, Florence remains unchanging in its spellbinding appeal of art and architecture with so much to see that space doesn't let me go on and on and on into the Arno and beyond.

ATTRACTIONS FOR CHILDREN IN VENICE Built on 117 little islands bound together by 400 arched bridges that span 160 canals, Venice is a dreamlike city.

However, Venice is indeed sinking, an inch or so annually. Affiliated with the UN, Venice Committee of the International Fund for Monuments, Inc. (15 Gramercy Park, New York; Tel: 982–9864) is doing a noble job helping to rescue Venice.

Most attractions are open 10 a.m.–noon, and 2 p.m.–5:30 p.m., but check with the tourist office before you go. However, gazing upon lacelike palaces and the dazzling interiors of churches unfortunately exhausts a child long before his parents would like to believe. For many families, the ideal solution is to stay at the Lido (see Castles) where the children can saturate themselves with beach activities under the watchful eye of a babysitter while you go off to see the sights. The things I would recommend you see and do with your children are: The **Basilica of St. Mark's,** with the Pala d'Oro (gold altar screen), Treasury, and giant blackamoors on the clock tower which gong the hour; vendors sell corn here for pigeon-feeding. At Christmas and Whitsuntide, the Three Wise Men, a trumpet-playing angel, and the Virgin also appear on the clock tower. A **gondola ride** along the 2½-mile Canal Grande.

Palazzo Ducale (Dodge's Palace) where you can cross the Bridge of Sighs to the Palace of the Prisons. The **Ca d'Oro, Rialto Bridge, Accademia di Belle Arti, Palazzo Rezzonico** (18th-century pharmacy created on its top museum floor), and the 15th-century Gothic church of **St. Maria Gloriosa dei Frari** and **San Rocco** are sights any child over 6 should see and enjoy.

Walking in Venice is also fun, the streets so narrow you have to walk in single file, along quays clustered with peppermint-stripe mooring poles for the gondolas, along colonnaded galleries of the Piazza San Marco.

A visit to **Salviati's** shop and ***glass-making*** establishment (78 San Marco; 195 Dorsoduro), filled with Venetian glass, everything rather rich, solemn, and hushed as it is at Tiffany's or Cartier's; rather nerve-wracking as you feel apprehensive about the children accidentally breaking something. But endure this anxiety and quickly move to the back room and ask if you may watch glass being made. Children will be enchanted if they can "help" make a glass leaf. Highly recommended. If you don't go to Burano, you can see ***lace*** being made at **Jesurum and Co.** behind St. Mark's.

The old guild-halls are famous for their paintings, fun to get to, fun to see: **School of San Rocco** (Campo San Rocco), is the most important, with major works of Tintoretto; **School of the Carmine** (Santa Margherita), famous paintings by Tiepolo. If you have time, the **Dalmation School of Sts. Giorgio e Trifone** (Castello, Calle dei Furlani 3259); and the **School of San Giovanni Evangelista** (Calle della Lacca 2454), with paintings of Tintoretto.

Your own ***motorboat*** is fun; with or without chauffeur; one boat-hire firm is **Ernesto Cercati** (Ponti delle Guglie, Cannaregio 331; Tel: (041) 715–787). Of special interest to children are ***excursions*** to Murano, Burano, and Torcello by boat; *Carnet de Venezia,* a pamphlet available from the tourist office or your hotel, has a timetable; boats leave frequently from the Fondamenta Nuove: **Murano** (about 10 min. away) is comprised of five islands connected by bridges; it is the ancient **glass-blowing** center; you are welcome to walk into any of the factories and showrooms on the Fondamenta dei Vetrai to watch glass being made. **Museo Vetrario** (glass museum); three churches, of which **San Pietro Martire** has the most outstanding paintings. **Burano** (about 30 min. away) is the center of Venetian **lace** industry; the men fish, the women make lace; you're welcome to watch both skilled operations. The hour's ride across the lagoon to **Torcello** is beautiful; the island is picturesque and peaceful, and nobody does anything much here except relax, glide down a reed-lined canal in a barge, inspect the mosaics of 11th-century **Church of St. Fosca** and 7th-century Duomo (favorite chair of Attila, King of the Huns, is inside); or eat at **Locanda Cipriani,** the country branch of Harry's Bar (the headwaiter can make arrangements for a launch and dinner).

Day hotels are San Marco-Ascensione and St. Lucia Station, which has far fewer facilities.

ATTRACTIONS FOR CHILDREN ELSEWHERE With children along, you will have to place more emphasis on pleasure rather than on dutiful sightseeing. If you have time, by all means go to Pisa to see the Leaning Tower, to medieval Lucca and Gubbio, to Padua, Ravenna with Byzantine glories, to Ravello to the Italian lakes: Como, Maggiore, Garda (see below). All of Italy might well be an attraction for children, but below I've listed places that seem to me to be superlatively entertaining, educational, and enjoyable for parents as well as children.

Afragola (10 mi. W of Naples): shabby, spontaneous village, packed with color; renowned for its strawberries and miniature donkeys used by itinerant peddlers. **Amalfi-Positano,** both accessible by ferry and hydrofoil from Capri or by a 2½-hour drive south of Naples, the star attraction of the Sorrento-Salerno drive, are white-on-white whitewashed towns, rising like wedding cakes up into the cliffs. **Arezzo:** If you can't be in Siena for the *Palio,* do try to come here on the first Sun. in June or Sept., for the marvelous **Tournament of the Saracens,** a pageant in its medieval square with knights in armor competing. **Bari:** At nearby Roca Priora is a **safari park. Bolzano** (Bozen) in South Tyrol, a bilingual (Italian and German) enclave, has three funiculars to take you from city center into the Alps in minutes; arcaded streets; many coffeehouse-restaurant-guesthouses; pleasant promenades along the Talvera River and from the upper terminals of the funiculars; 13th-century **Maretsch Castle** with frescoed rooms and a restaurant, closed Sun.; **Runkelstein** (Roncolo) **Castle,** another beautifully preserved 13th-century castle, has even better frescoes of medieval feudal and court life—guided tours only, Tues.–Sat., 10 a.m.–noon, 3 p.m.–6 p.m., also with a restaurant, well worth a brief but rugged climb for its castle-studded Alpine panorama, frescoes and food (even if, like me, you loathe guided tours). Don't miss an excursion to **Bressanone** (Brixen) a 60-minute drive north; and, if you have time, to **Kaltern** with a **Wine and Castle Museum** housed in **Ringbert Castle.** Both have lovely churches, but the Cathedral at Bressanone with its frescoed-vaulted cloister is outstanding. The train ride from Bolzano (Bozen) to Bressanone (Brixen) is infinitely more scenic than the bus ride, and children prefer trains to buses. No airport, but an express train connection from Milan (3 hrs.) Information about hotels, garden restaurants, walking tours and other information from **Azienda Soggiorno Bolzano** (39100 Bolzano, Piazza Walther 28) and **Ufficio Provinciale per il Turismo** (39100 Bolzano, Piazza Walther 22).

Calabria: the toe of Italy, beautiful as Sicily, but with no luxurious centers. Children can pick oranges, walk through pine forests, or go spear fishing. Recently excavated **Sibari** is being developed as a major archaeological site. From Tropea onward, the lushness of tropical fruit and flowers becomes richer and lovelier. Tropea has streets that end in balconies above the sea and a great castle overhead on a rock. Scilla, opposite the whirlpool of Charybdis, and Bagnara are centers of ***swordfish hunting*** from Apr.–July. Reggio has plantations of the rarest orange of all, grown only here, the bergamot; the oil is used in making perfume. At **Villagio Mancuso,** a sort of chalet village with Tyrolean-like wooden houses, you can see black squirrels, wild goats, and a flash across the alpine flora that may be a wolf. Nicastro and Tricola are notable for traditional costumes and ***handicrafts***—lace, embroidery, pottery—but Castrovillari and Spezzano Albanese may be more interesting to stay in. The people here are tall, often fair-haired and blue-eyed descendants of Albanians who fled from the Turks in the 15th century.

Check with the local tourist offices for dates of feast days. **Capri:** In summer, far less appealing and wholesome than Coney Island unless you detach yourselves from the swarms of day trippers. Off season, however, it's as attractive as it always was and children are delighted with the ride from Naples; take the boat ride around the island into the **Blue Grotto,** visiting *all* the grottoes, Verde (Green), Bianca (White), Meravigliosa (Marvelous, with stalactites and stalagmites) and others; the 12-minute chairlift from Piazza della Vittoria up Mt. Solaro, Capri's highest point; the Gardens of Augustus; the excavations of Emperor Tiberius's Villa Jovis. You can take a four-hour rowboat trip around the island which seems interminable. The 1½-hour trip by motorboat from the Marina Grande is plenty. The **Azienda Autonoma di Cura Soggiorno e Turismo** (local tourist office) at Piazetta Ignazio Cerio 11 in Capri or at Banchina del Porto at the Marina Grande or at Via G. Orlandi, 19A in Anacapri, can give you two handfuls of walking itineraries to the lighthouse, windmill, Carthusian monastery, Villa Romana at Damecuta, the Marina Piccola, ideal for picnicking and swimming. Public bus and taxis are available. Hydrofoil and ferry service to Amalfi and Positano. The funicular trip from the port to the village; the chair lift to Anacapri to visit the **Church of San Michele** and Axel Munthe's villa; and swimming in the lovely quiet bathing places. In **Collodi** see the **Vilaggio di Pinocchio. Como,** cupped in a valley alongside its cool lake (Europe's deepest, a 16-mile-long aquatic playground for water-skiers, crisscrossed with hydrofoils and romantic ferries plying among dozens of lakeside villages with vine-covered lakeside restaurants) is an experience in a life as smooth as the silk for *haute couture* woven and printed here, particularly if you stay in the fabled Villa d'Este hotel (for accommodations, see Cernobbio), the grandest of grand hostelries, home to royalty and celebrities, with a reproduction Roman aqueduct in the garden and a swimming pool that floats into the lake nearby a boat anchorage. Brass band concerts in the town square. If your teenage daughter is your princess, or vice versa, this is where to take her. **Cortina d'Ampezzo:** Leading summer and winter resort; year-round skiing; cable cars, chair lifts, bobsleds; tennis, golf; glass-enclosed swimming pools; bowling alleys; saunas; speed skating; horse-riding trails; wonderful Cortina observatory; plus glorious scenery and superb facilities at ski schools and children's hotels.

Elba: Although definitely "in," this beautiful little island, about 8 miles off the west coast of Italy, has the fascinating atmosphere of being forgotten, left out of the world. The cobbled streets, walls, and piazzas create the glow of the medieval past, but accommodations are attractive and comfortable. **Portoferraio** with its lovely bay is the island's capital, enclosed by an amphitheater of mountains; the beaches are long, spacious, uncrowded, and the waters off them a treasure trove for scuba divers and snorkelers, with particularly good hunting grounds off Sant' Andrea. Advice on good skin-diving locations is obtainable from the **Teseo**

Tesei Club in **Portoferraio.** The most popular beach is at **Marina di Campo,** near the tiny airport, where you can go out in pedal boats or windsurfers, fish and sail; other wonderfully empty beaches are reachable only by boat. The foothills are fine for walking, riding, picnicking, exploring or collecting the gemstones and minerals that you can find on the lower slopes of Monte Capanne near the villages of Sant' Ilario and San Piero, or on the East coast near the Punta Calmita. You could stay in **Poggio,** a hill village, or at **Villa Ottone,** in Ottone, with tennis, its own beach and a swimming pool; or at the more expensive cottages in the pine woods at **Hotel Hermitage** in **La Biodola,** with tennis, two swimming pools and all watersports; or in **Portoferraio,** Marina di Campo, San Martino. April–Oct. is the season, and after Oct. almost all accommodations close down. You can rent a car from Avis, rent boats, or go on the boat excursions leaving from **Porto Azzurro** to the nature-reserve island of **Monte Cristo,** or **Pianosa,** a small flat island covered with Roman remains, or the other Tuscan islands of **Gorgona, Capraia,** and **Marciana.** For more information on arrival, consult the **Elba Tourist Office** (Ente per la Valorizzazione dell' Isola Elba, 26 Calata Italia, Portoferraio). You can get to Elba by the Livorno ferry in three hours; by car ferry, June–Sept. in 60 min. from Piombino, departures daily almost-every-hour; also by hydrofoil in 30 min. trips six times daily from Piombino. Information about sea service to Elba from **Toremar Line** (Piazzale Premuda 13–14, 57025 Piombino). Air service twice a day out of Pisa via **Transavio** (43 Via Zanella, 20133 Milan). **Lake Garda:** (See Italian Lakes and the Borronean Island.) **Genoa,** birthplace of Columbus, has its share of palaces, museums, churches, piazzas, and many mysterious *caruggi* (byways that were the arteries of the medieval city), arched pathways, and little open lanes that debouch near the Campetto Square, Via Luccoli, and Banchi Square; except for the tiny squares, each with its church or medieval house, this labyrinth feels as if it were underground; this is a strange part of the city that de Maupassant, Mark Twain, and Longfellow wrote about. The ancient *casaccie,* workmens' brotherhoods, still appear in processions headed by marvelous statues and religious tableaux while guildsmen appear hooded, their costumes elaborately embroidered in gold. A **naval museum** at the Doria mansion at Pegli includes ship models, prints, battle tableaux and armor, globes, atlases, and books. The gardens of **Piazza delle Vittoria** are fun for children as they have pictures made by flowers and lawn. The art gallery of the **Palazzo Bianco** is pretty overwhelming for children; they will probably prefer the gallery of the **Palazzo Rosso** (wonderful carved creche) figures, coins, and many fascinating gilded wood statues).

Italian Lakes and the Borromean Islands: With Milan as a central point, the lakes cover a region filled with reminders of the Etruscans, Gauls, Romans, and Longobards. The major lakes of northern Italy—Como, Garda, Lugano and Maggiore—are each surrounded by smaller lakes between the central Alps and the Po Valley. Extremely popular in July and Aug., the least crowded months when the countryside is at its most lovely, are April–June, and Sept.–Oct. An autostrada links the lakes, and you get around by car ferry, hydrofoil, canopied fishing boats, lake steamer, cruise boats, motor-launches, privately rented motorboats, rowboats equipped for fishing, or sailboats. Visit **Nesse** and its stone stairways or magical **Bellagio.** Lake Como is gentle, majestic, languorous, animated. **Lake Garda** is dramatically beautiful. The **Gardone Riviera,** the principal resort area, comprising fashionable **Gardone, Salo, Gargnano,** peaceful with promenades, Old World elegance and luxury, are less interesting stopovers than **Riva,** with its medieval fortress to defend the shores from pirates, and **Sirmione,** on a peninsula, a spa resort known for its sulfur mud baths, with a 13th-century moated castle, an ancient village and its own brand of Sirmionese cookies which you can buy, freshly baked, at **Al Cigni,** a cafe in the center of the old town. At **Bar Losa,** a lakeside villa cafe, a delicious specialty is fresh fruit ice cream served with freshly whipped heavy cream. Catullus' villa is here; a Sun. morning flea market. Where to stay? See Accommodations for Sirmione and Riva. From either place, you can make excursions to **Cassone,** with its windmill, bridge, chapel; **Torbole,** where Goethe dreamed of Iphigenia; or up the tunneled mountain road to **Lake Ledro** and Alpine meadows; and down to the cliffside village of **Limone,** garlanded not only with lemons but oranges.

Lake Maggiore has a funicular that transports you from bowers of roses at the base of Monte Rosa to its summit where you can throw snowballs even in July and Aug.; a ravishingly pretty, animal park with parrots squawking. All this in **Stresa,** facing the Borromean Islands. Where to stay? See Accommodations for **Stresa;** also **Belgirate, Gignese, Pallanza, Isola dei Pescatori.** I think Stresa is the best base. At **Villa Pallavacini,** a ***garden paradise*** and ***animal park,*** the kiddies may tire of greenhouses filled with wild orchids, but they are sure to love the baby kangaroos, the llamas, deer, yaks, zebras, and the eclectic assortment of other beasties and birdies, including talkative parrots (open Mar.–Nov.) Ride the funicular up **Mt. Mottarone** and discover the incredible seven-lake panorama from the top, with **Lake Orta** right below on the other side (its namesake town, with a 16th-century townhall, single main street is an esthetic treat from which you can canoe across to **Isola San Giulio,** tiny island with ancient houses, a basilica founded by dragon-slaying St. Julius and the arbored **Ristorante San Giulio**). Drive midway up Mottarone to **Gignese,** where there's an **Alpine Garden** and an **umbrella and parasol museum** Mary Poppins would love. Take the ferry from Stresa's main wharf to the three Borromean Islands: **Isola Bella** with a sumptuous, wildly elaborate 17th-century palace, 16th- to 18th-century paintings, and grandeur which includes coachrooms displaying equine finery; formal gardens that are a Baroque fantasy; **Isola Madre** with lush, tropical vedge and orchid-swatched gardens in its parkland setting for a princely palace; **Isola dei Pescatori** (fishermens' island), which has changed little in 500 years, with an adorable village of red and yellow houses, fishing nets hung to dry on fruit trees, cobblestoned alleys. A sweet pension here (see Accommodations) if you feel like staying. If you want to "excurze," as my children used to say, you might be lucky and strike it right for the annual ***dogshow*** at **Baveno,** on the coast to your left, facing the islands, from Stresa; or take in **Belgirate,** to the right along the coast; or boat across to **Pallanza** with its magnificent magnolias, spa facilities and the 50-acre bonny **Botanical Gardens of the Villa Taranto** (with waterfalls, fountains and shaded benches) created by a Scot who bequeathed them to Italy; and then feed the seabirds along Pallanza's waterfront while waiting briefly for the boatride back. Don't miss the bus tour to **Monte Rosa,** 90 minutes and 40 miles up in the Alps to the funicular at **Macugnaga,** then 13 minutes up to the summit to a mountain-top inn for pastries and cappucinos and snowball throwing in the sunshine. (Don't even consider making this trip by private car; buses negotiate the mountain roads better.) Drive instead to **Cannero Riviera** where the 14th-century **Cannero Castles of the Malpaga** rise in ruins on two islets, and villages and churches to hike to if you're feeling energetic; and if you're still game, onto **Cannobio,** beloved by campers and ride three miles from the Italo-Swiss frontier. **Lerici** for its harborside restaurants, old castle, Saturday market, and boatride to **Portovernere** (castle, Byron's Grotto, cliff-hanging church); **Tellaro** (3 mi.) is a lovely fishing village not far from the marble quarrying at Colonnata. **Milan:** The **cathedral** is awesome, the largest Gothic building in Italy; superb **Brera Gallery** (Via Brera 28); other splendid museums include the **Sforzesco Castle Museum** with Michelangelo's *Pieta Rondanini,* old musical instruments, and glorious gold and silver work; **Leonardo da Vinci National Museum of Science and Technology** (Via San Vittore 21). Don't let the tiny ones climb to the top of the Duomo as there aren't many railings!

Naples: The **Aquarium** (Villa Comunale) is a don't miss for children. The **Zoo** (Via Domiziana) is fun too. **Edenlandia** (Mostra d'Oltremare, Viale Kennedy) is a marvelous, noisy fun-fair amusement park; good restaurant. Via San Biagio is one of the noisiest streets, festooned with laundry, overrun with *scugnizzi*—the children who surround you clamoring to sell things or take you places. The **National Museum** (Piazza Museo), a great archaeological museum which children enjoy. **G. Filangieri** (Via Duomo), civic museum with terrific armor. Good armor, also at **Capodimonte Museum** (Palazzo Reale di Capodimonte). For older children, a visit to **San Carlo Opera House** (Via Vittorio Emanuele III) is a treat. For a spectacular view, eat at the Ambassador Hotel or, better, take the Funicolare (cableway) from Via Roma to **Vomero,** a hilltop monastery and museum. ***Excursions*** are many. Organized tours to **Campi Flegrei** to the temple of Apollo, Lake Averno, the tomb of Virgil, craters, geysers, and bubbling mud pools *(fuma-*

roles), the cave of the Cumaean sibyl, ruins, grottoes, and assorted temples are acceptably educational for children—not thrilling, but interesting. You're more or less expected to take the Circumvesuviana railway to Herculaneum and bus to the chairlift up to **Vesuvius,** the only active European volcano. Children will then understand just how that lava and volcanic ash *(lapilli)* did what it did to Pompeii—a subject of surprising interest to children. Do read up on **Pompeii** (an hour's ride away by narrow-gauge electric train) and Herculaneum before you go, so that you can be selective. These fascinate children over 6 for only about 1½ hours. Children's interest is riveted by the cast of a dog writhing in the final death agony in the Pompeii museum, which best illustrates the tragedy for them. Children will also be interested to watch cameos being made at the factory of **G. Apa** (Torre del Greco, down the road from Pompeii).

Ortisei: Many easy runs for the novice and child skier; Olympic skating rink; a community of wood-carvers whose work is absolutely beautiful; in winter you are met at the funicular station with one-horse sleighs, jingling with bells; weird pinnacles and rock formations here look rather like our badlands. Don't miss the **ancient Greek ruins** at **Paestum;** extraordinary museum with recently excavated treasures. **Perugia:** Beautiful historical and art treasures; an Italian Disneyland, called **La Citta della Domenica** (3 mi. away at Spanolia, open only on Sun.) which children may beg you to drive 100 miles from Rome to go to!

Pontedassio, near Imperia, on the western tip of Italy's Ligurian boot-cuff, is worth searching out for a visit, with permission required—to be requested from the Agnesi family in residence—to explore their privately owned **Museo Storico Degli Spaghetti,** which traces the history of *pasta* in all its varieties from the discovery of its Chinese origins by Marco Polo. **Ravenna:** Dante's birthplace; mosaics not to be missed at the **Basilica of San Vitale.**

Sardinia has much to offer besides its golden and pink sand beaches, its emerald water, sailing, swimming, tennis, expensive and elitist accommodations. The **Costa Smeralda** (Emerald Coast), was so named by the Aga Khan IV who, with friends, acquired some 35 miles of unspoiled coastline now developed into fabulously beautiful resort. **Porto Cervo,** a wealthy residential section, has a tennis club; indoor-outdoor pool; a splendid shopping center. This is a favorite vacation spot for royalty (who put up at the Hotel Pitrizza where children are *not* welcomed). Stay instead at the **Cala di Volpe.** For the throwaway chic of a secluded Eden, there is nothing quite like the Costa Smeralda. Yet despite the tourist and Beautiful People targets, the island is largely undiscovered. Towns are clean, people charming and hospitable; domestic help cheap; beaches the best, to my way of thinking, in the Mediterranean. Possessed of all the warmth and geniality of Italy, Sardinia is minus slums, noise, dirt. Outside the Aga Khantrolled rim, you will find hidden coves, untenanted beaches, a vast territory that is like an open-air museum of history and folklore. Roman ruins at **Nora** and **Tharros.** In Neolithic times, people built conical fortifications, walls and tunnels called *nuraghi,* which can be seen everywhere on hilltops. The people wear colorful costumes, and traditional handicrafts have preserved their authenticity. You can see masked dancers at Sassari on Ascension and Assumption Day. **Nuoro,** a leisurely town built in a graceful but haphazard fashion on the lower slopes of the sugarloaf mountain of Ortobene, is supremely Sardinian. The view from the top of Ortobene, across a valley of granite plateaux and peaks and the whiteness of sun striking rock surfaces, counterfeits glaciers and snowfields. These mountains are the last refuge of Europe's wildest animals, including the moufflon and a species of pygmy wild boar. **Orgosolo** remains possibly the most archaic community of Italy; you can see figures from pre-history—old men in stocking caps and shepherds carrying the triple-reed pipes depicted in the Nuragic bronzes to be seen in town museums. Hidden behind the facades of normal houses, there are still *fughiles,* ancient stone habitations. Bandits and semibandits *(dogaus)* still hide in the hills. The spiritual capital, Orgosolo's special contribution to the arts is the poetical funeral lament, living epic poetry still written and recited by professional mourners. You also hear beautiful, sad, and strange songs called *sos poetas* and the brightly discordant bells of goat flocks. Singers and poets come down from the mountains to take part in contests of improvised verse during the Aug. *festa* and other feast days; subjects include everything—even space travel, or commentaries on the new tourism. **Alghero** is a popular resort for the British and Germans, offering big-town diversions as well as donkey carts in the streets; many *nuraghi* to explore; back of the port, a large and beautiful public garden with flowers; a Lido; camping in a pine woods; a **Grotto of Neptune** (connecting stalactite caves reached by a long, steep stairway from the sea or by boat, IF you want to spend time which, to me, can be better spent elsewhere.) Sardinia is an astonishing world for children: The rusty red of the ferrous earth, shepherds in velveteen costumes, cavalcades of gypsy horsemen—they'll be dazed by the prehistoric bronzes in Cagliari's **Archaeological Museum;** fed on honey made from almond blossoms and *candelaus* (bittersweet pastry shells filled with orange-flavored almond paste); relaxed to a state of pleasurable inertness.

At 6665′, **Sestriere** offers *skiing* until early Apr.; aerial tramways, chairlifts; spacious, wide-open slopes; ski schools for children, plus lessons in other winter sports; easy rental of all equipment. In summer, the skating rink becomes bowling ground; skeet shooting and tennis; chairlifts continue to operate for sightseeing. The outdoor heated pool is open year round. Snow nurseries for the teeny-tinies in winter.

Sicily: Let me recommend this particularly during winter, spring, and autumn for unhurried family vacations. Little English is spoken, so that first-time travelers might be best off in lovely **Taormina;** natural fireworks go off almost every night from Etna's almost always active volcano—nothing to worry about, there's always ample advance warning of an eruption. **Agricento** (a treasure trove of Greek archaeology and architecture) and **Syracuse** are targets for enchanting scenery, a climate so balmy that you can swim in Jan. and Feb. (and ski the same day on Etna), a luxuriance of flowers, shrubs, beautiful beaches, snow-capped mountains. Those whimsically decorated Sicilian donkey carts are still very much in evidence. One of the small attractions that appeals to children is the caves in Syracuse, one in particular called the **Ear of Dionysius** where the acoustics make paper tearing sound like a launching on Cape Canaveral, or a match being struck like the sound of a cannon. In **Gela,** a jewel of a **museum** with technically perfect and richly imaginative installations to house coins, pottery, architectural fragments of the great Greek city it once was. The mosaics of **Monreale,** the great **cathedral,** are among the world's greatest. Scarcely less beautiful and stunning in impact are those in the fabulous **imperial villa** near Piazza Armerina up in the hills beyond Noto, a baroque town carved out of honey-colored stone where the tyrant Dionysius held sway; the setting for an annual festival of classical plays in its magnificent **Greek theater** each spring. Especially in **Palermo** in the old part of town—at **Argento** (Via del Pappagallo 10), **Cuticchio** (Via Orologio 14), Mancuso (Via del Medico 6), and **Sclafani** (Via Busara al Capo 58)—there are wonderful **puppet theaters** with bewitching performances; the tourist office will give you the hours. I wish I had been taken to Sicily as a child because I feel this would have given me a giant headstart on all those mythological references that crop up in literature, for here Daedalus touched down after his flight from Crete, Pluto captured Proserpine, the one-eyed Cyclops hurled rocks after Ulysses. Here villages are still steeped in folklore (folk songs and dances in costume on feast days), and temples and castles are as much a part of the countryside as pinewoods and lemon groves. There are puppet festivals in Palermo in Nov. There is also an engaging **puppet museum** housed in the Palazzo Fatta (Museo delle Marionette di Palermo). Do visit the abandoned **church of St. John of the Hermits** (San Giovanni degli Eremiti). Kumquats, cactus, lovely domes and garden. The **Pitre Museum** has puppets, vividly painted carts, ceramics, glass inlay, embroidery, and costumes representative of the singularly attractive native art. There is a Greek island quality about Sicily and Palermo, with its dazzling Palazzo dei Normanni, and its worldly speed and noise is a strong contrast to quiet, isolated mountain villages, and a vivacious Club Med at Kamarina. The **Aeolian Islands** north of Sicily, offer marvelous swimming, underwater sightseeing (enjoyable for children 5 and older), super scenery, archaeological explorations, active volcanoes, grottoes, boat trips. These are still off the beaten tourist track. Near Palermo is the beautiful, unspoiled island of **Ustica,** with fortress, lovely blue grotto, fishermen's houses decorated with paintings, local transport by donkey.

Siena: One of Italy's loveliest towns, at its spectacular medieval best every July 2 and Aug. 16, when the **Palio,** the wild horse race around the Square, takes place. Parades, officials dressed in medieval costume—no child over 6 will ever forget it. Climb the Town Hall tower to see the enormous bells that ring out the hours. **Tarquinia** is an excursion from Rome I love with the older children; walled, largely medieval; a shabby town, filled with corridor-like streets that open out into charming piazzas; its 15th-century palace, **Palazzo Vitelleschi,** houses excellent regional antiquities. On the outskirts, the fun is finding the 25 underground **Etruscan tombs,** containing wall paintings, in plowed fields and meadows of wild flowers and clambering down from the 20th century into the 6th–2nd century B.C. See the *Tomba della Caccia e Pesca* (wonderful scenes of hunting and fishing); *Tomba dei Leopardi* (leopards); *Tomba dei Tori* (bulls), and *Tomba degli Auguri* (prophetic auguries). Directions from the city tourist bureau. **Turin:** The **Carlo Biscaretti di Ruffia Motor Car Museum** and excursions to the **castle museums** in the Aosta valley (Fenis and Issogne are best). See **Urbino,** for its rose-red charm, treasure-filled **Palazzo Ducale,** 14th-century **Albornoz fortress,** house where Raphael was born.

FUN TRIPS The Italian Automobile Club (ACI) and AGIP motel chains, located all along Italy's highways, are constantly expanding. ENIT can supply a complete list of these handy and excellent stopovers.

Car ferries: Reductions for foreign cars are offered by the Sardinian Tourist Board on the crossing to Sardinia except during July, Aug., and Sept.; to Sicily on a round-trip ticket *if* you are planning to stay for at least six days and leave on the same ship on which you arrived. A cabin is well worthwhile if you are making any trip with children that lasts more than a couple of hours. You can go to Capri from Naples by ***boat*** or by ***hydrofoil***—the latter, faster and more fun, leaves from Mergellina. By ***hovercraft,*** leaving from Rotonda Diaz on Via Caracciolo in Naples, the Capri trip takes 20 minutes. Ischia enjoys steam, hydrofoil, hovercraft transport from Naples. The Naples-Sorrento run is by steamer in 70 minutes, hydrofoil in one-half-hour. Steamer service from Piombino to Portoferraio (Elba) is a cheap 50-minute crossing, about twice as much via hydrofoil provided by **Tosco Sarda di Navigazione** (Via Manganaro, Portoferraio, Elba). Daily steamer services except Sun. from Livorno to Sardinia by *Tirrenia* for whom the Italian Line are general agents. Steamers ply the lakes of Garda, Como, and Maggiore.

In **Como,** take a Lucia, a canopied fishing boat, to an island or across to the opposite shore to a vine-covered restaurant or a restaurant shaded with olive branches. Motorboats and launches are also available for private rental. For information, contact Navigazione Sul Lago di Como, Piazza Volta 44, Como. In **Rome,** weather conditions permitting, no special projects interfering, Nov.–Mar., the **Goodyear Europa Airship** makes 10–16 30–60-minute flights daily over the hilltop towns from its home base at Capena Airport about 20 miles N of Rome (about a 45 min. drive from the city center because of the horrendous traffic). If you would like your children or yourselves to be among its six lucky passengers write in advance to the Director of the Goodyear Italiana Public Relations Office, SpA (not a typo—that's the proper abbreviation for "Incorporated" I am assured) Casella Postale 10768, 00100 Roma; Tel: (06) 592–6548. Take the old-fashioned, bell-ringing streetcar #30 from the beginning of the line at the Piazza del Risorgimento, between St. Peter's and the entrance to the Vatican Museums, cross the Tiber and weave your way around the heart and treasures of Rome, including the Villa Giulia with its Etruscan treasures, the Borghese Gardens, National Gallery of Modern Art, the Borghese Gallery with all those Titians and Bernini's best works, the Zoo with its great aviary, the Colosseum, the Roman Forum, the Palatine Hill, the Baths of Caracalla, the flea market of Porta Portese (open Sun. until noon), and into Trastevere, a one-hour trip. The #30 with a red slash through the number makes a shorter run just to the Borghese Gardens. The longer trip is the greatest 15¢ sightseeing ride I know. Bus passes can be bought in tobacconists' shops. Otherwise, get on the bus by the rear door and pay your fare. The Roman subway, the *Metropolitana,* is fun, too. The **Italian Lake District:** The wildest car ride, with 70 tunnels, is the *Gardesana Occidentale,* around Lake Garda, a nightmare in the dark, but a day-light in the sun. For information about lake steamers, hydrofoil service, car ferry at Garda: **Navigazione sul Lago di Garda** (2 Piazza Matteotti, Desenzano sul Garda) will give you all details. For information about motorlaunches and rowboats equipped for fishing, contact **Virgilio Bertoldi,** Piazza Castello 11, Sirmione. For information about steamer, hydrofoil service, car ferry and motorboats and launches for rent at Lake Como, contact **Navagazione Sul Lago di Como,** Piazza Volta 44, Como. At Lake Maggiore, for information about cruise boats, some with bar and restaurant, which offer lake tours, and all the gen about car ferries and the boat service to the Borromean Island and other highlights, contact **Biglietteria di Stresa,** Piazza Marconi, 28049 Stresa.

Take the hydrofoil from Capri to Positano or Amalfi and do make that legendary Amalfi-Positano drive, one of the exceptions to the rule that children don't enjoy scenery. From 5 on, I guarantee they will enjoy and remember this ride.

In **Venice,** canal steamers are a few dollars from stop to stop (for details about the day trip from Venice to Padua to enjoy the constructions of Andrea Palladio, see Venia); gondolas rent by the hour or from the railway station to the Piazza San Marco. By *private* motor launch, the trip from airport to hotel costs a bundle if you go alone, and scales down for a group; by *public* motor launch, the price is less, so check which type you are stepping aboard.

For boat, hydrofoil, hovercraft trips, there seems to be no hard and fast rule about fares for children; reduced rates usually obtain, but sometimes only if you book in advance. On trains, children 4–10 pay half-fare, under-4s travel free; if a family of four or more travels together adults get 40%–50% off and children under 14 pay half-fare—you must produce passports to prove you're a family.

All kinds of craft, sail and motor, even yachts, can be rented at **Moncada Yachts** (32 Via Visconti di Modrone Uberto) in Milan.

FUN AND GAMES For skiing, my choices would include: **Cortina d'Ampezzo, Bressanone, Sestriere, Ceruinia, Courmayeur. Selva** (with a lot of modern chaletstyle hotels with swimming pools) and **St. Christina** are also excellent skiing possibilities for the children, with plenty of ski schools. **Pinzola** and **Madonna di Campiglio** feature abundant snow, sunshine, fragrant pine woods, and a hospitable atmosphere for children. **Claviere** and **Limone Piemonte** have good slopes for children and beginners. Ski rentals everywhere; nursery and ski schools for children.

The Touring Club of Italy will give you information about ***mountaineering***. The **Club Alpino Italiano** (Via Ugo Foscolo 3, Milan) owns about 600 alpine huts and publishes information about equipment, routes, and fees for each one.

The Italian coastline, with many natural harbors, is ideal for ***yachting***. Write to **Federazione Italiana Vela** (Porticciolo Duca degli Abruzzi, Genoa) or **Federazione Italiana Motonautica,** Via Cappuccio 19, Milan, for information. For details about lake sailing, get in touch with **Ufficio Navigazione Interna,** Ministero dei Trasporti e Aviazione Civile (Piazza della Croce Rossa I, Rome). Waterskiing is terrifically popular; and motorboats and water skis can be hired at almost any seaside and lake resorts.

Swimming? Great! All major towns have indoor and outdoor swimming pools, but the best are those belonging to the hotels. Beaches are found along the Italian Riviera. If you keep on going all the way around to Trieste, you have about 2500 miles of almost uninterrupted resorts, and I fling in the beach towel right now at attempting to recommend 50 beaches against 500 other beaches. Match your itinerary with the information available from ENIT. In **Rome,** the best municipal pools are **Piscine delle Rose** at EUR. **Fregene** (24 mi.) has delightful swimming in its pools (not the beach).

A word of caution about swimming where the beach and sea bottom are pebbly. Sneakers, espadrilles, or some sort of bathing slippers must be worn; and you have to watch out for jellyfish and prickly black sea urchins (the white ones are harmless). If you do get "stung" by a sea urchin, don't try to tweeze out the black splinterlike pricker. Squeeze lime juice or ammonia on the spot and the prickly spine will dissolve. If you try to tweeze it out, it will break and be quite painful for several days. Don't be alarmed and put off swimming. There are more sea urchins and jellyfish in the Caribbean than in the Mediterranean, but no one ever tells you about them either.

Hunting in the Alpine and Apennine area, in Calabria, Sardinia, Sicily. Seasons vary; query **Federazione Italiana della Caccia** (Viale Tiziano 70, Rome).

Seasonal game includes an extraordinary list of bird-life—from turtle doves and skylarks to plovers and lapwings—all considered delicious appetizers and entrees. As a devoted member of the Audubon Society, may I direct your attention to masses of clay-pigeon shooting fields available all over Italy? In Rome, **Campo di Tiro Tor Sapienza** (Via della Martora); **Camp di Tiro Lazio** (Via Eugenio Vaina 21); **Skeet-shooting Club** (Via Tiberina). Many shooting ranges around Rome (Latina, Rieti, Viterbo, Froinone).

Fishing A license issued by provincial authorities is necessary to fish in fresh water, and you must belong to **Federazione Italiana della Pesca Sportiva** (Viale Tiziano 70, Rome) from whom all information can be obtained.

Hiring or buying fishing equipment is simple everywhere. FIPS can provide you with lists of suppliers. Fishing for sport in the Italian seas is free—swordfish, tuna, and dogfish are the main catch. The coast abounds in mullet, bass, crabs, lobsters, moray eels, and sea urchins. For information about the Latium coast, get in touch with the **Sezione Provinciale della FIPS** (Via Cassiodoro 19, Rome).

Golf? About 3 dozen golf courses in Italy; many clubs with swimming pools; for further information, **Federazione Italiana Golf** (Viale Tiziano 70, Rome; Tel: 3140). ***Tennis*** lessons in Rome at **Circolo Parioli** (Via di Ponte Salario). ***Bowling?*** **Bowling Brunswick** (Lungotevere dell'Acqua Acetosa); **Bowling Roma** (Viale Margherita 181).

In **Rome,** the best ***riding schools*** are Circolo Ippico de Tebro (Via Tiberina 198); **Circolo Privato Scuola d'Angelo** (Via Flaminia 871); **Societa Ippica Romana** (Via Monti della Farnesina); **Campo di Gara Pony Club Roma** (Via dei Campi Sportivi 43).

Great fun for the older children is ***go-karting,*** driving around a track in an open-chassied car. Exciting, but safe. A good small track in Rome at **Luna Park** (EUR); in Florence **Pista del Sole** (Via del Termine).

Kids 14 and older don't need a license to rent Vespas and Ciaous; for Hondas you must be 18 and licensed; contact **Agenzia Noleggio Moto-Scooter** (Via Magenta 57; Tel: 474242), **Viminal** (Via Torino 39; Tel: 4705210, or **Scootalong** (Via Cavour.).

Spectator sports? Car races at the Autodromo di Roma, dog races at the Cinodromo a Ponte Marconi; horse races at the Ippodromo delle Capannelle; trotting races at the Ippodromo di Tor di Valle; bicycle races at Velodromo Olimpico (EUR); check with your concierge for dates and times.

SHOPPING WITH AND FOR CHILDREN Shopping hours in Rome and throughout much of Italy are from 9 a.m.–1 p.m. and from 4 p.m.–8 p.m. during summer. In winter, afternoon opening and closing hours are ½ hour earlier. Owing to the forging of art works, be careful before investing in art objects as heirlooms for the children. New streamlined Italian designs may be safer bets. In Milan, center of new Italian design, the **Fly Casa** (Galleria de Cristoforia 7) is one of a galaxy of superb furniture boutiques where you may find furniture ideal for a children's or family playroom. Italian clothes for children are also colorful and innovative. Paolo and Giorgio Zingone are the oustanding designers; contact the Commercial Offices of the Italian Embassy and the offices abroad of the Italian Institute for Foreign Trade, or the **Camera Nazionale della Moda Italiana** (Italian Fashion Chamber; Via Lombardia 44, Rome) or just ask at children's clothing stores. Italian toys are superb, imaginative, charming, innovative, a particularly good buy.

In **Rome,** for children's ***toys:*** **Lenci** (Via Bissolati 33), expensive but marvelous dolls; **Sonnino** (Via Due Macelli 23); **Guffanti** (Via Due Macelli 59D); **Ve-Bi Giocattoli** (Via Parigi 9, Via di S. Maria in Via 57, and Viale Europa 97); **Biffignandi Jumbo** (122 Via Trionfale; 92 Via Ottaviano; 124 is less expensive, less overwhelming. **De Sanctis** (Via Veneto 94) has the best model soldiers; made by Luciano Antonini (Via Lago di Lesina 15; Tel: (06) 838–0894), from whom you can order models not carried by the store. **Presepio Musanti** (Via Liberiana 22) is good for creche figures. For ***English books:*** Lion Book Shop (Via del Babuino 181); **Economy Book Center** (Piazza di Spagna 27). For ***children's clothes:*** **Zingone** (Via della Maddalena 27), a department store with reasonable prices. **La Cigogna** (Viale Regina Margherita 131; Via Frattina 139). **Leri** (Via del Corso 344; Via Salaria 34). **Capriccio dei Bambini** (Via Piave 25). **Massarenti** (Via Condotti 60), where clothes are handmade, exclusive and expensive. **Eleganza Infantile** (Via Nationale 236), lovely baby clothes. **La Casa del Bambino** (Via della Maddalena 27) has nice children's gloves.

In **Florence,** ***children's clothing*** shops: **Baby's Confezioni** (Piazza Stazione 63R); **La Moda dei Ragazzi** (Borgo S. Lorenzo 36). Charming straw slippers can be found at the **Straw Market** (Mercato Nuova); they aren't very durable, so get several pairs; very reasonable, but haggling is expected (you should settle at around half the asking price). For ***baby equipment and supplies:*** **Prenatal** (Via Brunelleschi 22R).

In **Genoa,** all kinds of ***fireworks*** at the **Garbarino Fireworks Factory** in Cogorno, in the suburbs (San Salvatore). In **Livorno,** don't miss the ***flea market*** in the center of town.

In **Venice,** for ***children's clothes:*** **Maricla** (San Marco 2401). For baby things: **Paradiso del Bebe** (San Marco, Spadaria 678), **Style Baby** (San Marco, Ponte Rialto). For young children: **Bambi** (San Marco,

1066). **Al Girotondo** (6/c Gran Viale at the Lido), specially nice bathing suits. For ***toys:*** **Sabbadin** (San Marco, 47/5); **Linetti** (31 Gran Viale, Lido); **Molin** (5899 Cannaregio). In **Livorno,** ***clothes for babies:*** **Petit Enfant** (36 Via Magenta); **Babyland** (Via Grande 18). ***Clothes for children*** up to 14 at **Casa del Bambino** (Via Maggi 12); **Peter Pan** (Via Ricasoli 9); **Mondo Piccino** (Via Marradi 205); **Anni Verdi** (Piazza Grande 25); **Paradiso dei Bambini** (Corso Amadeo 11). ***Toys*** at **Catanorchi** (Via Toscana 13); **Di Ciuccio** (Piazza D. Chiesa 7); **Emporio Formichini** (Via Grande 69 and 148); **Baldi Fiorella** (Via della Cornocina 8); **Giudici** (Via Maggi 76); and also at the U.P.I.M. chains (Via Grande 46 and Via Marradi 91). In **Messina,** a walk along Viale San Martino turned up the following ***children's clothing*** shops: **Rotino** (#154), also toys; an excellent choice at Arcidiacono Salvatore (#162); **Marchese Dr. Felice** (#108), the best of all, it seemed to me. ***Toys*** at: **Bambi** (#219). I liked the selection at **Peter Pan** (Via XXVII Luglio 21); APE's inexpensive things (Corso Garibaldi 77); **Miuccio** (Via Palermo 166). In **Milan,** many boutiques for children's clothes, many toy stores, but ***children's shoe stores*** seem particularly remarkable. **Spataro** (Via San Pietro all' Orto 17), makes shoes to order for children. **Gusella** (Via Victor Hugo 3 plus branches) is an excellent shoe-store chain for little ones up to teenagers; **Medolla** (Via Torino 23) is also outstanding.

In **Naples,** ***clothes for children*** at **Siola** (Via Chiaia 113/15) and **Peter Pan** (Via Filangieri 25 also Via Diaz 48). ***Toys*** at **Leonetti** (Via Toledo 350/1).

In **Sardinia,** in Sassari, toys at **Tuttogiochi Depaolini** (Via Cagliari 11). In Cagliari, at **Bolla** (Via Manno 53), **Carosello** (Via Dante 83 A); **Peter Pan** (Via Pessina 8); **Zorro** (Via Sonnino 206); **Dessi Dr. Peppino** (Corso Vittor. Emanuele 2). For handmade rugs, laces, and other native ***handicrafts,*** money is better spent at the workshops and factories where these are made rather than in stores.

In **Sicily,** in Agricento, children's clothes, toys and specialties on Via Atenea at Americo, Bordenca, and Scalia.

Flea markets, with outdoor arrays of second-hand goods and antiques are compelling attractions held on certain days in cities and towns throughout Italy. Some of the best are:

Arezzo: (Tuscany) Antique Fair (Piazza Grande) first Sat. and Sun. each month, all day; **Bologna's** La Piazzola (Piazza 8 Agosto) Fri. and Sat. 7 a.m. until twilight; **Ferrara,** also in the prov. of Emilia-Romagna, at Piazza Travaglio every Mon.; **Florence:** at Piazza Ciompi daily except Sun.; **Genoa:** at Piazetta Lavagna, off Via Luccoli, Mon.–Fri.; **Gubbio** (Perugia): at Via Baldassini, second Sun. of each month; **Livorno (Leghorn):** at Piazza XX Settembre, daily, 9 a.m.–7:30 p.m.; **Messina:** at the intersection of Via La Farina and Viale Europa, every morning; **Milan's** ''Sinigallia Market,'' Via Calatafimi, every Sat, 8 a.m.–7 p.m.; ''Oh Bei! Oh Bei! Market (Piazza Sant'Ambrogio, last

Sun. in Nov. and Dec. 6, 7, 8; **Naples:** at Corso Malta, Mon. and Fri.; at **Corso** Novara on no regularly scheduled dates; **Palermo's** Flea Market at Piazza Domenico Peranni, daily 9 a.m.–sundown; Sun. and hols. 9 a.m.–1 p.m.; **Rome:** at Porta Portese every Sun., 8 a.m.–2 p.m.; at Via Sanno daily except Sun., from early morning until sundown; **Turin's** "Il Balon" in Porta Palazzo (Piazza della Repubblica) every Sat., all day. **Viaregio:** in the Piazetta near the dock every Thurs. morning.

ITALIAN FRIENDS AND PEN PALS There is no official hospitality program, but if you would like to meet an English-speaking Italian family, your best bet would be to write to the local EPT (see Information). The **American Consulate** in the appropriate location might also be able to offer advice.

CALENDAR OF EVENTS **Jan.** 6 (Epiphany), Piana degli Albanesi displays the most beautiful costumes in Sicily; Revine Lago and Rivisondoli feature the ***Living Crib,*** with costumed participants, illuminations, and music; Rome holds ***Befana*** (12th Night). In Jan. and Feb. in Dolomite and Alpine areas there are ***skiing championships*** and winter sports; ***horse racing*** in Cortina d'Ampezzo. Jan.–May in Florence, Milan, Naples, Palermo, Parma, Piacenta, Rome, and Trieste is ***opera and concert*** season. Early **Feb.** brings to Catania the ***Festival of St. Agatha.*** At Putignano the ***Annual Carnival*** gets under way with floats and parades. From Feb.–Mar. in Agricento, the ***Almond Blossom Festival,*** a folklore and costume event, is staged in the Valley of the Temples. In Feb. or Mar. at Padua is the ***Univ. Students' Festival,*** a parade of allegorical floats. Late Feb. or early Mar. is ***Mardi Gras;*** carnivals with parades, allegorical floats, masked contests, and sports events are celebrated at Ascoli Piceno, Viareggio, Cagliari, Tempio Pausana (all in Sardinia); and Bologna. Oristano features ***Sa Sartiglia,*** a medieval jousting tournament with masked knights on horseback.

Mar. 19 at the Trionfale (near Vatican Rome) and in Florence is the ***Feast of St. Joseph.*** Festivities open Mar. 25 at the Piazza SS. Annunziata in Florence with the ***Fair of the Annunciation;*** waffles are the specialty. On **Apr.** 2, every two years in Sassari there's a ***handicraft exhibition.*** On the same day Cagliari celebrates the ***Festa a Mare di San Francesco di Paola.*** Holy Thurs. in Caltanisetta (Sicily) features a marvelous ***procession;*** on Good Fri. there are processions in Grassina, L'Aquila, Savona, and Trapani. On Sat., Easter Eve, in Florence, the ***Scoppio del Carro***—explosion of the Chariot—commemorating the victorious return from the First Crusade. In Rome, the papal blessing is given during Holy Week. The traditional ***Byzantine celebration*** of Easter takes place at Piano degli Albanesi. Apr. also features an ***International Trade Fair*** in Milan; an ***International Horse Show*** and an ***International Tennis Tournament*** in Rome; the ***Feast of St. Catherine*** (Siena); and a ***regatta and Festa*** in Venice. Assisi celebrates ***Calendimaggio;***

medieval costumes, song and dance competitions; late Apr.–early May.

The first Sun. in **May** brings to Florence ***Il Gioco del Calcio,*** a medieval football match played in 16th-century costume in the Piazza della Signoria; marvelous pageantry. May 1–4 in Cagliari is the ***Feast of San Efisio.*** On May 3, fireworks at Nora. May 6, in Naples, the ***Miracle of San Genaro;*** religious procession; sports events. Ascension Day in Florence is celebrated with the ***Festival of the Cricket,*** in Cascine Park; crickets sold in tiny cages. Florence also boasts a ***Flower Festival.*** The most famous festivity in Cagliari takes place in early May; at the ***"Sagra di Sant'Efisio,"*** about 3000 people in magnificent costumes take part in a lavish procession; a three-day festival culminating with exciting ***horse race.*** At Gubbio, there's an ancient ***festival of Ceres;*** at its conclusion the city's youth race through town with the *ceri* (heavy wooden sacred figures) in their arms. Also in Gubbio, the ***Palio of the Crossbowman,*** a medieval crossbow contest. There's a ***Horse Show*** and ***Polo Tournament*** in Rome. Late May in Potenza features a ***Parade of the Turks;*** fireworks, costumes, music in honor of St. Gerardo. In Sassari in late May, a ***song and dance festival;*** splendid cavalcade. From May–mid-June Florence has a ***music festival.***

In **June,** the ***Festival of the Republic*** is celebrated in Rome; grand military parade along the Via dei Fori Imperiali. In Pisa, there are three events; a ***medieval pageant*** (the Bridge Game); ***river illuminations*** for San Ranieri; and a ***regatta*** and rowing contest the following day; medieval costumes. In Pavia, a ***River Festival*** and the ***Palio of the Geese.*** In Terni, ***fireworks*** explode at a waterfall and lake. Arezzo, the ***Joust of the Saracens.*** June 21 throughout Italy various processions and parades celebrate ***Corpus Christi. St. John's*** Day is celebrated June 24; great fireworks in Rome in the Piazza Laterano, and bonfires, fireworks, folklore events, and lake regattas in Isola Comacina. Florence holds a gala ***medieval football match.*** From June–Aug. in Frascati, ***sound and light*** spectacles at Villa Torlonia; Rome has them in the Forum, plus ***open-air opera*** at the Baths of Caracalla and ***open-air concerts*** in the Maxentius. Tivoli features ***sound and light*** spectacles at Hadrian's Villa. In Trieste, sound and light festivals (to Sept.) at Miramare Castle.

In **July,** the ***opera*** season opens at Caracalla. July 1/3 in Siena is ***Palio***—exciting folklore event; thrilling procession and horse race. Other July events: in Cortina d'Ampezzo, ***International Ice Hockey*** and other sporting events; in Nervi, ***International Ballet Festival;*** in Palermo, Sicily, the ***Feast of Santa Roalia U Festinu,*** a five-day festival; Medieval and archery festivals in Ravenna and in Rome, a ***Festival at Trastevere,*** with outdoor concerts and fireworks. On the third Sun. in Venice is the ***Feast of the Redeemer;*** lighted gondolas, music, fireworks, and all-night procession. July–Aug., Naples has a ***Summer Music Festival;*** Verona holds ***open-air opera*** in the Verona Arena. **Aug.** events include: the ***Joust of the Quintana,*** in Ascoli Piceno, a race with caparisoned horses, tournament, torchlight procession, over 700 townspeople in medieval costume; at Gubbio, the ***International Palio of the Crossbow;*** at Positano, the ***Landing of the Saracens;*** at Montepulciano, ***Brucello,*** a traditional religious and folkore event in the Piazza Grande; and in Venice, ***illuminations and floating concerts.*** On Aug. 14, Sassari, a ***Candlelight Procession;*** Aug. 15/17, Siena repeats its July 2 ***Palio;*** and on Aug. 29, at Nuoro, Sardinia, there's a ***Procession of the Feast of the Redemption.***

Sept. 3, in Viterbo, the Procession of the Car of Santa Rosa; 90 men carry more than 1000 torches and light a 90′ tower. Venice, a ***Grand Canal Regatta;*** Arezzo, the ***Joust of the Saracens*** in the Piazza Vasari; Naples, ***Piedigrotta Festival,*** with music, fireworks, illuminated boats, floats, and parades; Monza, ***International Motorcycle Race;*** Naples, ***Festivities of San Genaro;*** Sansepolcro, the ***Palio of the Crossbowmen*** features competition with Gubbio's bowmen; Marostica, a ***Chess Game*** with people in period costumes. In early **Oct.,** Assisi holds the ***Festival of St. Francis; Christopher Columbus celebrations*** in Genoa; Rovigo has a ***Traditional Fair*** and sports events. **Dec.** in Rome features ***Children's Pilgrimages*** to the Church of the Aracoeli; recitation of Christmas poems in the chapel. Revine Lago holds a ***Sacred Christmas Pageant;*** entire population joins in. Sorrento exhibits its ***Creches.*** Dec.–Mar. is ***opera*** season in Florence, Milan, and Rome.

LANGUAGE AND PHRASEBOOK English is understood in the principal tourist centers and in practically all shops. It's surprising how far you can carry on without any Italian at all, but I would certainly take a phrasebook and dictionary. In southern Italy, sign language is routine; children love watching the way Italians use their hands to express every known emotion, and are adept at picking up these mannerisms. Be sure to tell the children that water taps are marked C (caldo) for *hot,* not for *cold,* as most children suppose; F (freddo) is the cold-water tap. Coffee shops are known as "bars," so if you're advised to get a bus ticket there, you can safely take the children with you.

Hello (Good morning or Good evening)	*Buon giorno* *Buona sera*	*bwawn johrnoh* *bwawnah sehrah*
I am an American	*Sono americano (boy)*	*So-no amaireecahno*
	Sono americana (girl)	*So-no amaireecahnah*
My name is ——	*Mi chiamo*	*Me kee-yarmoh*
I am——years old	*Ho——anni ——*	*Hoe—anny ——*
Please	*Per piacere*	*Pear pyah-cheh-reh*
Thank you	*Grazie*	*Grah-tsyeh*
I can't speak Italian	*Non parlo italiano*	*Nohn parloh eetalyanoh*

Yes	*Si*	*See*
No	*No*	*No*
I am having a wonderful time	*Mi diverto molto*	*Me dee-vair-toe mohltoh*
1	*uno*	*oonoh*
2	*due*	*doo-ay*
3	*tre*	*tray*
4	*quattro*	*kwah-troh*
5	*cinque*	*cheen-kway*
6	*sei*	*say*
7	*sette*	*settay*
8	*otto*	*awtoh*
9	*nove*	*nohvay*
10	*diece*	*dee-aychee*
11	*undici*	*oon-dee-chee*
12	*dodici*	*doh-dee-chee*
13	*tredici*	*tray-deechee*
14	*quattordici*	*kwah-tohr-deechee*
15	*quindici*	*kween-deechee*
Goodbye	*Arrivederla*	*Ah-reeva-dair-lah*

LUXEMBOURG

Luxembourg's picturesque towns are dotted with 120 castles. You can drive all over Luxembourg in a couple of days. The southern half, Bon Pays (the Good Country), has broad, fertile valleys; the northern half, Esleck, is hilly and rocky and includes part of the Forest of Ardennes. The eastern border is covered with wine caverns. This Grand Duchy, fragrant with history and the scent of good food, seems friendlier and more fun than it was on my first visit.

INFORMATION ABOUT LUXEMBOURG For advance information, telephone or write the **Luxembourg National Tourist Office,** 801 Second Avenue, New York, NY 10017; Tel: (212) 370–9850.

In **Luxembourg City,** contact Director, **National Tourist Office** (77, rue d'Anvers; Tel: 487–999) for general information plus details on campsites and sports. Or call the **Syndicat d' Initiative** (pl. d'Armes; Tel: 22809), which has local offices in other towns. For information about fairs and festivals, contact **Foires Internationales de Luxembourg** (Boite Postale 110 Luxembourg).

HEALTH, WATER, FOOD *Health standards* and the quality of drinking water are excellent.

Food specialties that children will enjoy include fresh trout, Ardennes ham, jellied suckling pig, calves' liver, partridge, pheasant, crawfish, steak with Bearnaise sauce, seasonal fruit (particularly yellow autumn apples), cheese, butter, and the assorted cakes, pastries, ice cream, and chocolates available at one *confiserie-tea room* after another. Oct. and Nov. specials are marzipan mice and pigs, and chocolate molds of birds, angels, and St. Nicholas. Carnival season features fried pastry dough bowknots called *Les Pensees Brouillees* (mixed-up thoughts).

In the capital, for superlative sweets and pastries try **Namur** (32 and 66, av. de la Liberte), the city's finest, and **Confiserie Albert-Conter** (64 Grand' Rue). Also recommended are: the **Oberweis Tearoom** (19 Grand' Rue); **Confiserie Weidacher** (17 av. de la Gare); serving ice cream topped with paper parasols and cakes molded in bird and animal shapes; and **Scheer** (1 Place de la Gare), with another branch in the old part of town.

BABY FOOD Swiss, French, German, Belgian, and American brands are available at supermarkets, pharmacies, *drogueries,* and *traitteurs* (food specialty shops). **AZ** (av. de la Porte Neuve) is a good source of supply.

DIAPERS AND LAUNDRY Disposable paper diapers are obtainable at most *drogueries* and children's specialty shops. Ask for *langes a papier*. The department store **Monopol** (branches at av. de la Gare, av. de la Liberte, and 33 Grand' Rue) has plastic outerpants in which to insert disposable diapers, and cloth diapers, or *langes*. No diaper service is available. Laundry arrangements can usually be made at your hotel.

BABY EQUIPMENT FOR HIRE None. Canvas carriers and strollers and convertible canvas cot prams are generally stocked at **Beffort Bandermann** (corner of Mamergaas and rue du Marche aux Herbes) and at **Willy Capus** (av. de la Liberte).

EMERGENCIES MADE EASY Your concierge can direct you to the nearest ***pharmacy*** and tell you which will be open all night. In an emergency, English-speaking ***physicians and dentists*** can be reached through the **U.S. Embassy** (22 blvd. Emmanuel Servais; Tel: 40123). A good ***children's hospital*** is the state clinic (Clinique Pediatrique de l'Etat, c/o Centre Hospitalier; rue Barble; Tel: 44111). Also recommended is the **Clinique St. Therese** (36 rue Zithe; Tel: 488–121).

MAGIC FAMILY HELPERS Given two days notice, the National Tourist Office or the Syndicats d'Initiative will do their best to round up a babysitter or children's companion. Otherwise, ask the concierge.

CASTLES AND OTHER HAPPY FAMILY ACCOMMODATIONS The inn-hotel-restaurant-pension guide issued by the tourist office does point out with symbols (all but indecipherable) hotels with children's playgrounds, gardens, swimming pools, and easy-access bedrooms. In **Turtange,** a highly recommended Youth Hostel is housed in **Hollenfels Castle.** Apart from the **Hotel Heintz** in **Vianden,** located in a former Trinitarian monastery, with a nearby chairlift to a terraced forest-type chalet, I have no personal recommendations for this edition.

ATTRACTIONS FOR CHILDREN **Luxembourg City** was once one of Europe's great fortresses. Now illuminated May–Oct., the fortifications are interspersed with parks and paths that make the city interesting for children to walk through—particularly the lower, older part, with casemates, networks of underground passages, and medieval shelters for placing cannons and quartering troops. **Le Fort des Trois Glands** (3 Acorns Fort) was named for its three acorn-like towers. You can enter the Casemates at the pl. de la Constitution, but for a more dramatic approach take the Corniche Promenade which ends at the Bock rock and enter beneath the fortified gate. The ***Changing of the Guard*** takes place at the Grand-Ducal Palace. Archaeology? Mineralogy? History? Folklore? Zoology? Art? Try the **State Museum** (Marche aux Poissons). Open 10 a.m.–noon; 2 p.m.–6 p.m. Closed Mon. Children will enjoy the little **Senningen Zoo** (near the airport).

Bettembourg features the **Parc Merveilleaux;** lake for canoeing or pedal boating; slides, swings, and whirligigs; children's racing cars and airport; car train for park transportation; delightful zoo and aviary; miniature farm; Luna park fun fair; restaurant; marionette theater; and scenes from "Hansel and Gretel" and other stories as backdrops for plays and play-acting. **Clervaux** has midget golf links, camping grounds with playground and playrooms, and a marvelous feudal castle, illuminated at night, housing an exhibit of miniature Luxembourg castles; also "Family of Man" photography by Edward Steichen, and Battle of the Bulge exhibits. **Dalheim** has interesting archaeological excavations in progress. **Diekirch** boasts remarkable Roman mosaics, mini-golf, and seasonal attractions. In **Echternach,** on Whit Tues., thousands of pilgrims, from morning well on into the afternoon, dance in procession to the shrine of St. Willibrord, patron of the physically handicapped. In olden days the handicapped took part in the procession, but now the parade is composed of the hale and hearty. Each village has its own band, which plays the German folksong, "Adam Had Seven Sons." If you miss Whit Tues., other attractions are the parish church, the Benedictine Abbey, and varied attractions at the recreation center, with pedal boats. **Ettelbruck** has a regional museum devoted to the Battle of the Bulge and General Patton.

In **Hamm,** my son saw the Military Cemetery where Gen. Patton is buried and came away understanding for the first time the losses sustained in the Battle of the Bulge. **Hosingen** has a natural wildlife preserve featuring deer and wild boar. **Larochette,** in the wooded, hilly region—the "little Switzerland of Luxembourg"—has a playground, a pony farm, mini-golf, and illuminated castle ruins. Ruminate in **Rumelange** at the **Mine Museum,** open daily 2 p.m.–6 p.m. Easter–Oct. (second weekends only of each month Oct.–Easter). **Vianden,** a medieval city with forests, ramparts, and stone houses nestled around a ruined fortress-castle illuminated at night, offers boating, mini-golf, and a chairlift. This child's delight swings over houses, forests, and a small game preserve. Municipal heated swimming pool nearby. Other features include: the **Victor Hugo House museum;** a folklore museum; and Europe's most powerful hydroelectric pumping center, smack inside Mount Nicholas. In **Walferdange,** don't miss the **Paradis des Enfants,** a delightful pleasure-ground open daily, May–Oct., from 2 p.m. **Wiltz,** a place of Catholic pilgrimage, has a feudal castle, church, and mini-golf.

FUN AND GAMES In **Luxembourg City,** you can rent a bicycle from **Francis I** (16 rue Beaumont). Also in **Reisdorf** at the confluence of the rivers Ous, Ernz, Sure. You can rent a horse either at the **Cercle Hippique Fetschenhaff** at Luxembourg-Fetchenhaff (Tel: 43–42–04) or the **Riding School Lallemand** (Sanem; Tel: 591–402). Blue jeans and sneakers are acceptable riding gear.

Riding tours: Inquire about the Tour of Luxembourg, the Tour of the Valley of the Seven Castles, and more from the **Secretariat de la Federation Luxembourgeoise des Sports Equestres** (90, route de Thionville, Luxembourg). Close to the French and Belgian border at the foot of the Tetelbierg, with Roman fortifications, at **Rodange,** there's an old-fashioned train to ride to **Fonds de Gras** with a family ticket reduction.

Near **Useldange, Cercle Luxembourgeois de Vol a Voile** (Tel: 8–56–82) operates a ***glider-flying*** center and school and ''air-baptisms'' are offered to guests every weekend and holiday, May–Oct.

SHOPPING WITH AND FOR CHILDREN A flea market in **Luxembourg City** every second and fourth Sat. of the month. Toys here are imports—a mixture of the well-constructed, mechanically ingenious, and the schlocky. Shopping hours vary. Some shops are open only from 8 a.m.–noon; 2 p.m.–6 p.m., Mon–Sat.; most closed Mon. a.m.

For toys: **Sternberg** (corner of rue du Fosse and rue du Cure; **Toyland** (11 av. de l'Arsenal); **Lassner** (46 pl. Gillaume, near the Palace); and **P. Mamer** (rue du Fosse). For infants' and children's clothes: **Aach Sender** (52 av. de la Gare); **Monopol** (see Diapers and Laundry); **Pre-Maman** (52 Grand' Rue); **Chez Bambi** (16 rue du Marche aux Herbes); **Palais d'Enfants** (1 pl. de Paris). For bicycles and sports equipment; **Joseph Schmitz/Parrard** (28 rue du Cure). **Arnold Kontz** (16 av. de la Gare) has mostly bicycles. Entertaining apothecary items: **Droguerie Goedert** (8 av. de la Liberte).

LUXEMBOURGER FRIENDS AND PEN PALS Write in advance to the **American-Luxembourg Society** (11A blvd. Prince Henri), the National Tourist Office, or the American Embassy.

CALENDAR OF EVENTS On Easter Mon. in Luxembourg City is reenacted the medieval ***Emaischen,*** a pottery fair and market, in costume. From May–Sept. every Sun. in various towns ***Kermesse festivals*** (village fairs) are celebrated. On Whitmon., in **Wiltz,** the ***Fete des Genets*** (the Gorse or Broom Festival) with Folklore Procession is rather like

Halloween. Whit Tues. in **Echternach** —a dancing procession in honor of St. Willibrord.

June 23 is celebrated in Luxembourg City as ***Luxembourg National Day.*** Official observance of the birthday of H.R.H. the Grand Duke Jean; military parades; sound and light spectacles; marvelous fireworks; and St. John fires (firewheels rolled down hills). During **July** and **Aug.,** Luxembourg City sponsors a rose and ***flower parade, sports events,*** and a ***sound and light*** show. Beginning on the last but one Sun. in Aug., the two-week long ***Schobermesse Amusement Fair,*** complete with folk pageantry and archery competition. In **Vianden,** second Sun. in Oct., visit the Nut market.

LANGUAGE AND PHRASEBOOK Official languages are: French, German, and Letzeburgesch or Luxembourgeois (a potpourri of French, German, and Flemish with English and Spanish seasoning). Most Luxembourgers have little trouble speaking English.

Hello (Good morning or Good evening)	*Bon jour* *Bon soir*	*Born zhoor* *Born swar*
I am an American	*Ech sin en Amerikaner*	*Ersh zinn urn A-may-ri-kan-er*
My name is____	*Mein numm ass____*	*Mine noom (oo as in foot) uss____*
I am____years old	*Ech sin____ joer aal*	*Ersh zin____your Al (rhymes with pal)*
Please	*Van ech glift*	*Van ersh gleeft*
Thank you	*Merci*	*Mair-see*
I can't speak Letzeburgesch	*Ech schwetzen noet Letzeburgesch*	*Ersh shwett-zen nert Lert-zer-boor-yush*
Yes	*Jo*	*Yo*
No	*Neen*	*Neen*
I am having a wonderful time	*Ech amuse' eren mech gutt*	*Ersh ah-moo-say-err-ren mesh goot (oo as in foot)*
1	*eent*	*aint*
2	*zwee*	*tsvay*
3	*drei*	*dry*
4	*fe'er*	*fay-err*
5	*foennef*	*fernurf*
6	*sechs*	*zecks*
7	*siewen*	*zeeven*
8	*acht*	*ahct*
9	*neng*	*ning*

10	*zeng*	*tseng*
11	*eelef*	*ay-leff*
12	*zwiellef*	*tsvelleff*
13	*dreizeng*	*dry-tseng*
14	*fe' erzeng*	*fay-err-tseng*
15	*fofzeng*	*fawf-tseng*
Goodbye	*Au revoir*	*Oh-vwar*

NETHERLANDS

This is a wonderful country for children, with delights for the young of all ages. The Dutch love children and feel specially warm toward Americans. They even indulge our illusions: the story about the boy averting a flood by sticking his finger in a hole in a dike has no basis in fact, but since so many of us like to believe the legend (extracted from Mary Mapes Dodge's *Hans Brinker and the Silver Skates*), not so long ago the Dutch amiably erected a statue of our boy at Spaarndam.

Lace caps, wooden shoes, men bowling cheeses along cobbled streets, tree-mirroring canals, windmills, are all at hand as well as a rich and diversified cultural heritage. But it's the unexpected joys, the things that are done for you and things that you and your children can do that make the Netherlands the delight of first-time and seasoned family travelers. Child-care facilities are *super. There are 100 babysitting agencies,* hotels just for children, hundreds of playgrounds with a stunning range of equipment. Puppet shows and barrel organs are taken pretty much for granted by Dutch children (who run and perform in two circuses of their own). Even the museums are furnished with many children's attractions.

You'll relish Holland's compactness—nothing is ever too far away to get to! Along the coast are inexpensive family resorts where, despite gloomy predictions about the weather, you can tan yourself to the color of licorice. Vlissingen is a ship-watcher's paradise; Friesland is a bird-lover's mecca (the tourist office can fill you in on where to see some 300 varieties of birds), and for the romantic who love stories of lost Atlantises, there is a lake over a washed-away Sailand village (Beulaker) where, legend goes, if you take a boat out at midnight when the moon is full, you can hear the bells ringing from a submarine church tower.

Add a lion park, a fairy-tale world in a wood, horse-drawn trains, dolphins doing tricks, a miniature city, and you can see why Holland should be the rising star on your travel horizon. Your children are missing the time of their lives if they don't visit the Netherlands.

INFORMATION ABOUT THE NETHERLANDS A bounty of outstanding booklets is yours for the asking from the **Netherlands National Tourist Office** (NNTO) (437 Madison Ave., New York, NY 10022; Tel: (212) 223–8141), its San Francisco branch at 681 Market St., Room 941, San Francisco, CA 94105, and its Canadian branches at 327 Bay Street, Toronto, Ontario M5G 1Z3, and in Vancouver. The Netherlands National Tourist Office is headquartered in The Hague (Bezuidenhoutseweg 2, 2594 AV Den Haag; mailing address is Postbus 90415, 2509 LK, Den Haag). The same address is your contact for the head office of the Holland Hostess team (English-speaking girls of outstanding character and intelligence who will arrange for shopping aid, tours and guides).

The Netherlands are divided into 11 provinces, each with its source or sources of tourist information: **Vereniging Voor Vreemdelingenverkeer,** abbreviated as VVV, pronounced Vay Vay Vay, and identified by blue signs with triple white Vs, each office a treasure trove of information, advice, help. For a small fee, the VVV Accommodation Service will make a hotel reservation for you; also secure theater and concert tickets for you; locate babysitters and children's companions; your problem is their problem, and they will help you resolve it happily.

Amsterdam is in the province of **North Holland; The Hague** and **Rotterdam** are in the province of **South Holland.**

In **Amsterdam** the **Amsterdam Hostesses** are headquartered at Rokin 9–15. The main office of the VVV is at Rokin 5. A VVV office can also be found at Stationsplein 10. Elsewhere in the province of North Holland, you will find VVV offices in **Haarlem, Hilversum** and **Texel** (in the West Frisian Islands).

VVV The Hague/Scheveningen is at Groot Hertoginnelaan 41.

VVV Rotterdam (Stadhuisplein 19); **VVV Delft** (Markt 85) is the head office of the province; offices also in **Dordrecht** and **Leiden.**

VVV Drenthe (Postbus 95, Assen) is provincial headquarters for that province, with **Assen** as its country seat. The provincial **VVV Friesland** is located in **Leeuwarden** (Stationsplein 1). Provincial **VVV Gelderland** (Apeldoornsweg 53, Arnhem) is the main source of information for this lively province; other offices in **Apeldoorn; Nijmegen, Gelders Rivierengebied, Noord-and-Midden-Veluwe, Zutphen. VVV Groningen** (Grote Markt 23, Groningen) can fill you in on many details of interest to families; so can **VVV Noord-Limburg** (Keulsepoort, Venlo), and **Limburg's** provincial VVV at Den Halder Castle, Valkenburg. In **North Brabant,** try **VVV Hertogenbosch** (Markt 77, Den Bosch); offices also in **Eindhoven, Tilburg** and **Breda,** the provincial HQ (Willemstraat 17). The provincial office for **Overijssel** is at Grote Kerkplein 14, Zwolle. Other offices in **Almelo** and **Raalte.** The provincial and regional information offices at **Utrecht** are centered in the city of **Utrecht** (Vredenburg 90), offices also in **Amersfoort**

and **Zeist.** For the province of **Zeeland,** consult **Zeeuwse VVV** (P.O. Box 123, Middelburg).

For anything to do with ***cars and motoring,*** consult the **Royal Dutch Touring Club** (ANWB) at Wassenaarseweg 220, The Hague. ANWB regional offices are in Amsterdam (Museumplein 5), Apeldoorn, Arnhem, Breda, Eindhoven, Enschede, Groningen, Haarlem, Hilversum Leiden, Maastricht, Rotterdam, Utrecht. All highways are patrolled from 7 a.m.–11 p.m. by qualified mechanics in tulip-yellow pickup trucks. If you need help, call the operator from the nearest roadside telephone. Offices at The Hague or Amsterdam will send help at any time of day or night. In the Netherlands, children 4–12 may only ride in the front seat of your car if they are wearing a hip-type safety belt, or if they are in an approved safety seat.

There are no cruising taxis in Amsterdam. You have to go to a cab stand (at all railway stations or at the major squares) to fetch a cab. Or, ring **Taxi Centraale** in Amsterdam: 77–77–77. The **Schiphol Lijn subway,** operating from the airport, will whisk you to Minervaplein in Amsterdam, and to the Centraal Station in The Hague. KLM personnel at the airport can help you find the right train or bus, if you want to save on taxi fare for the 20–30-minute ride from the airport into Amsterdam. On arrival, however, I'm all for taxis. **Schiphol Airport** is a pleasant airport, and has a nice nursery (see Ch. 5).

From Apr.–Sept., you can pick up NLM City Hoppers (Fokker Friendship planes, small and comfortable) to fly to Groningen, Eindhoven, Enschede, Maastricht. **The Netherlands Railways** (Nederlandse Spoorwegen) have an excellent information bureau at the Central Station in Amsterdam; Tel: (020) 23–83–83. Open 8 a.m.–10 p.m. Mon.–Fri.; Sat., Sun. and festive days, from 9 a.m.–6 p.m.

Amsterdam and Rotterdam have a **Metro** (subway). All bus and tram companies have synchronized their rates and offer something called a National Strip Ticket that you must buy in advance from railway stations, some VVV's and postoffices, for reduced fares. You can buy "day tickets," which entitle you to as many rides as you like during a day, at the Municipal Transportation System (GVB) booth in front of the Centraal Station in Amsterdam, or from the driver of a bus or tram.

Telephones? The system is fully automatic. In public booths, just take the telephone off the hook and insert a gulden/guilder/florin. Dial 088 for directory assistance. For long-distance calls from your hotel, service charges can be whopping. Some hotels, including all Golden Tulip Hotels, have included Teleplan (see Ch. 12). If your hotel isn't a subscriber to this service-charge reduction system, and you're energetic and thrifty, the nearest post-office is best for long-distance calls.

This Week in Amsterdam, and similar publications, list special attractions. In Amsterdam, **The Information Center for Foreigners** (Beginhof 35; Tel: (02) 22–23–10) will tell you about religion and culture.

For young, backpacking parents there is **MAI** (Mauritsweg 58, Rotterdam) the Social Advice, Youth Tourism and Information Bureau run by the Union Association for Young People. They help to find rooms and boarding houses, mothers' helpers, supply addresses of eating places, clubs, courses, and advise on travel. Other offices in **Amsterdam** (J. W. Brouwersplein 9, for housing). Information for the budget-conscious can be found in a free newspaper called *Together,* obtainable at the VVV.

In **Rotterdam,** for the 15–25 set, there's **JAC,** Young People's Advice Center (Gravendijkwal 60).

Information about flowers and bulbs, blossom time, floral pageants and shows can only be had in advance of your trip by writing or telephoning for special brochure to the NNTO.

For a Dutch treat, and a living cultural reality, avail yourself of the *Holland Culture Card Information Kit* which, for a token fee, also entitles you to a courtesy membership in the **Arti et Amicitiae Club** (Rokin 112, Amsterdam). Privileges include free admission to more than 170 museums, castles, churches and cathedrals, special reservations at theaters, special rates for first class rail travel, and much more. For information about the Holland Culture Card, contact the NNTO.

HEALTH, WATER, AND FOOD Health standards and the quality of drinking water are tiptop. Bottled water is also available.

Dutch cuisine is a hearty mix of regional, French, and international specialties. Some of the genuine Dutch dishes—*jachtschotel* (hunter's pie) and *bruine bonen met appelmoes* (brown beans with apple sauce); *hutspot* (a delicious hodgepodge); *huzarensla,* a meat and vegetable salad; *erwtensoep* (pea soup made with milk, potatoes, leeks, celery, and meat); *spekpannekoeken* (bacon pancakes, the size of dinner plates)—are so hearty that the usual wallopingly generous serving is enough to keep even a teenager feeling well fed from one meal to the next. Some hotels, and many cafes and restaurants, feature *Kindermenus,* with half-sized portions at half-prices for your *Kinderen*. The Dutch have developed a firm, plump, succulent strawberry called a *Tamella*—a special treat. Dairy products state-controlled in quality. The classic Gouda and Edam cheeses are mild enough for most children. For breakfast if you would like the children to have orange juice, ask for *sinaasappelsap*. *Pannekoeken* (pancakes) are the specialty of many traditional pancake restaurants. Children are usually fond of a favorite national snack, the *uitsmijter* (pronounced out-shmayter), a ham or roast beef sandwich topped with a fried egg.

Caramel candy *(haagse hopjes)* are yummy. *Zoute dropjes*—salty licorice drops the Dutch chew constantly—are not recommended for children. Most children won't like them, and, if they do, you'll find them thirst-making. Droste and Van Houten chocolates and cocoa are famed, and chocolates wrapped to look like Delft plates are great for presents. So are milk-chocolate wooden shoes. During Nov., in the pre–St. Nicholas season, Droste turns out chocolate initials, a delicious custom, and molded marzipan sugar hearts, and molded fondant which is even too sweet for most children. The Dutch excel at baking; the *speculaas* (spicy cinnamon) and *taai-taai* (aniseed flavored, tough, chewy, honey ginger) cookies are also molded, decorated with slivered almonds or colored sprinkles, and make fetching Christmas tree ornaments. In Friesland, the specialties are *dumkes,* a kind of seeded cookie; *suikerbrood,* a coffee-cake bread with sugar and cinnamon baked into the dough; and *drabbelkoeken,* a sweet cookie that looks like vermicelli. You will find chocolate eclairs, *room hoorntjes* (crispy cornucopias filled with whipped cream flavored with too much brandy or rum for toddlers), letters made from pastry, *moorkopjes* (blackamoor heads), and other specialties at any of the hundreds of **Jamin** bakery chain stores. Be sure to try the *poffertjes,* small sugary fritters.

The Dutch are fond of Indonesian food (introduced during their colonial history). *Rijsttafel* (rice table) comprises dozens of dishes that bear some resemblance to Cantonese cuisine; the experience of all those platters and side dishes to nibble at, and occasionally turbaned waiters, makes Indonesian restaurant-going a must. Hollandaise sauce? Yes, it originated in Holland.

Where can you find inexpensive three-course meals? At over 600 restaurants displaying the Tourist Menu sign of a flower-hatted fork with a tine-slung camera. The VVV will send you the complete list. During the week, one restaurant, the **Wip Inn** in Naaldwijk asks you to pay what you think the meal is worth. **Orange Julius** semi-self-service restaurants (featuring a drink made of orange juice) are thriving; a fine, inexpensive place for a quick lunch. For snacks, there are *broodjeswinkels* (sandwich shops) in every large town, offering a delicious and generously filled soft roll; the *broodje* (rhyming with oh, gee!) fillings of meat, egg, cheese are wholesome, inexpensive. The VVV can also supply you with a list of restaurants featuring Holland Home Cooking, of which there are over 100 first class restaurants bearing an emblem of a soup tureen, and the words *Neerlands Dis.* Expensive, but delicious and nutritious.

I am dumbfounded by the quantity and quality of **Amsterdam's** reasonably priced restaurants. (Service is usually included in the bill; if so, you need not tip a penny more.) Here are some restaurants I think you and your children will enjoy (almost all are closed Sun.): **Bols Taverne Creperie** (Rosengracht 106) has light crepes, with over 40 tasty fillings; wine and cider served in jugs; all the Bols' liqueurs; gallery upstairs is decorated in the Dutch *Hindelopen* style. For *broodjeswinkels,* the **Broodje van Kootje** chain has outlets throughout the city. **V. D. Berg's Sate Bar** (Van Woustr. 44). **Hans en Grietje** (Spiegelgracht 27).

Het Stuivertje (Hazenstr. 58; phone for reservations 231–349), dinner only; closed Tues. **Travellers Grill** (Gelderslanderplein 2) serves family brunch Sat. and Sun, with reduction for children. **Prins** (Ceintuurbaan 350) has sandwiches and wonderful ice cream. **De Prinsenkelder** (Prinsengracht 438) has blue-tiled walls, delightful atmosphere. **Cafe Americain,** in the American Hotel on Leidesplein, is a 100-year-old cafe open for morning coffee until after the theater, and inexpensive daily specials. The **Pancake Bakery** (191 Prinsengracht) has every known variety of *pannekoeken*.

The **Molen De Dikkert** (Amsterdamseweg 104B, Amstelveen; Tel: (020) 411–378) is a 300-year-old windmill in the suburbs; super food; children's menu. Delicious game in season—hare, venison, pheasant. Soups in winter are a meal in themselves. Terrace in summer. Included in the price is a free pick-up in a Rolls Royce on Tues., Thurs., and Sat. at your convenience. On World Animals' Day (Oct. 5) the manager plays host outside to cows, horses, cats, dogs, and tame mice who feast by tables decorated with carrot-labra (carrots in silver holders). Interesting too is the **Kras-Havenrestaurant** on top of the Havengebouw (Harbor Building, De Ruyterkade 7) overlooking the harbor; very good food; handsome ship model in its lobby. Youngsters should enjoy the palmy pleasures of the **Hotel Krasnapolsky's** garden restaurant (children may keep their menus, printed on balloon-bright postcard portraits of stuffed animal figures). **Het Begijntje** (The Little Nun, Begijnensteeg 6)—with leaded glass windows, candlelit dinners, is a romantic place to treat appreciative children. **Adrian** (Regulierswarsstr. 21) is an elegant treat for teenagers.

De Gravenmolen (Lijnbaanssteeg 5–7; Tel: (020) 223–641) is magically appealing; a pair of centuries-old houses; everywhere the cachet of its host-proprietor (purple is his favorite color and desserts are decorated with candied violets); comfortable barrel-backed chairs; tapestries and ceramics are all family-made. Of great gastronomic merit, but not astronomic prices. Order dessert souffle in advance (otherwise, there will be a 45-min. wait). Best for older children because there is no special children's menu; *petite-carte* for lunch is inexpensive. For snacks, **'t Gravenhoekje** (Lijnbaanssteeg 1) or **In de Oude Goliath** (Kalverstr. 92). For *rijsttafel* feasts, there's **Bali** (Leidsestr. 89) or **Djawa** (Korte Leidsedwarsstr. 18).

The **Five Flies** (Spuistr. 294) is a 17th-century building, all brick and mahogany, Delft tiles, copper, brass, pewter; charming decor. The attraction for children is the Five Flies Fantasy dessert, ice cream with a flaming sparkler stuck on top. Other money-savers are **Honed's Bakhuisje** (Kerkstr. 39) for hearty meals; **Markus-Petit Restaurant** (Oudezijds Voorburgwal 250) for French specialties. Between Heemstede and the North Sea is **Kraantje Lek** (Duirlustweg 22, Overveen), one of the oldest restaurants in Holland; great pancakes; a favorite with children.

BABY FOOD You'll find baby food in the food dept. of major department store **Bijenkorf** and its branches, in grocery stores and supermarkets, and in the nearest pharmacy *(Apotheek).* Baby and junior varieties of **Heinz, Nestle, Birdseye,** and **Findus** brands exist in ample quantities, but the excellent **Nutricia's Olvarit** foods (fruit juices, milks, and cereals) are most widely distributed. The baby-food *(babyvoeding)* list includes:
Rose-hip syrup, *Rozenbottelsiroop;* Strawberry and rose-hip syrup, *Frambozen-Rozebottel-Bessen-Siroop;* apricot and honey fruit drink, *Abrikozen met honing;* Orange-banana fruit drink, *Sinaasappel-banaan;* Fruits: apricot-apple puree, *Abrikozenappel;* Mixed fruit, *Gemengd fruit;* Strawberry–rose-hip puree, *Frambozen-rozenbottel-bessen;* Orange-banana puree, *Sinaasappel-banaan;* Applesauce, *Appelmoes;* Vegetables, *Groenten;* Carrots, *worteltjes;* Spinach, *Spinazie;* Chicory, *Andijvie;* String beans, *Sperzieboontjes;* Green peas, *Doperwtjes;* Brown beans and applesauce, *Bruine bonen met appelmoes;* Carrots and potatoes, *Worteltjes met aardappelen;* Tomatoes and rice, *Tomaten met rijst;* Brown beans with carrots, *Bruine bonen met worteltjes;* Spinach with potatoes, *Spinazie met aardappelen;* Chicory with potatoes, *Andijvie met aardappelen;* Main course meals, *Maaltijdjes;* Macaroni with ham and tomato, *Macaroni met ham en tomaten;* Stringbeans with potatoes and veal, *Sperziebonen met aardappelen en kalfsvlees;* Carrots with potatoes and meat, *Worteltjes met aardappelen en vlees;* Chicory with potatoes and beef, *Andijve met aardappelen en rundvlees;* Peas, carrots, rice and meat, *Erwtjes, worteltjes, rijst en vlees;* Liver with mixed green vegetables, *Lever met gemengde groenten;* Chicken with baby peas and rice, *Kip met doperwtjes en rijst;* Lamb with spinach and potatoes, *Lamsvlees met spinazie en aardappelen;* Veal with green vegetables and potatoes, *Kalfsvlees met groenten en aardappelen;* Brown beans with applesauce and beef, *Bruine bonen met appelmoes en rundvlees;* Spinach with egg and potatoes, *Spinazie met ei en aardappelen.*

Plain meat, to be mixed with vegetables, comes in a small round tin labeled *Vlees* and is a homogenized beef puree. Junior foods *(Kleutervoeding)* add cheese *(kaas),* haddock *(kabeljauw),* bacon, scrambled egg *(roerei),* vanilla pudding with apple, pineapple and bananas *(Vanillevla met appel, annanas en banaan)* to combinations of the foods already mentioned.

Nutricia also puts out **Nutrix** (cream of rice); **Bebirix** (complete unto itself with milk, honey, vitamins, minerals, and a blend of 3 grains); and **Bambix,** for toddlers (a whole grain cereal blend). Holland rusks are famous, and the variety has to be seen to be believed in the food dept. of Bijenkorf.

DIAPERS AND LAUNDRY A diaper is a *luier* (rhyming with liar). Disposables are *weggooibare luiers;* made of celstof. **Hygi, Celstoft, Molny,**

and **Celwa** brands are most common. Teddy liners and Baby Slipje, waterproof britches with pockets for holding the diaper, are sold in department stores or at the drugstores *(drogisterij)* which will deliver disposables to you in any quantity or on regular order.

Diaper services pick up and deliver two or three times weekly; you supply your own diapers; they also wash baby clothes for very reasonable prices. In **Amsterdam: Simpson Babywas** (Lynsbaangracht 55; Tel: (020) 220–304) picks up three times a week.

In **Arnhem, N.V. Wasserij Spaan-Coenders** (Shaapsdrift 85; Tel: (085) 23306). **The Hague: Eerste Nederlandse Luiercentrale** (Ledeganckplein 54; Tel: (070) 989–567); twice a week pick-up but no service for a week or less. **Nijmegen: Babywascentrale Brilliant** (In de Betouwstr. 29; Tel: 33340) take a maximum 25 lbs. weekly; three times a week pickup. **Rotterdam** has **Stoomwasserij N. Nijman N.V.** (Stadhouderslaan 1–9, Schiedam; Tel: (010) 69134). Servicing Rotterdam, Schiedam, and Vlaardingen, they pick up twice a week. Also in Schiedam, is **Baby Service** (Tel: 269134). In **Utrecht: De Utrechtse Babywascentrale De Ster** (N.V., Zonstr. 102; Tel: (030) 15639) picks up three times a week and, for a pittance will rent you a diaper pail and laundry bag.

Dry cleaning? I had incredibly good luck with **Chemische Reiniging W. De Moor** (Willemstr. 57) in Amsterdam. Clothes sent in the morning with notes to stitch seams, mend, tighten buttons, clean, and press were returned looking like new by supper time.

Wasserettes are laundromats, usually open 8 a.m.–10 p.m. weekdays, until 4 p.m. Sat. In **Amsterdam** you'll find them near the Harbor Building and the Centraal Station (Haarlemmerdijk 157; Rosengracht 34 near the Westerkerk, the West Church; at Doelenstr. 12; Herenstr. 24) and other locations.

BABY EQUIPMENT FOR HIRE Ask the VVV.

EMERGENCIES MADE EASY Holland is extremely health-minded and healthy. There are about 300 hospitals, and it is very easy to obtain a topnotch doctor at any time of the day or night, Sun. and holidays included. Dental and medical fees are about half of what they are in America.

Drogisterij handle nonprescription medications. An *Apotheek* is a pharmacy; when closed, the names of the nearest one open and the all-nighters are posted on the door; your concierge can call for you and arrange deliveries. Recommended pharmacies in **Amsterdam: Damapotheek** (Damstr. 2), also known as Pharmacie Internationale; English spoken. Also recommended: **Majoor** (Gravenstr. 20); **Duffels** (Javastr. 80). Ask your hotel concierge to recommend an English-speaking doctor or call the Embassy, or call the Municipal Health Service, in Amsterdam, (020) 555–5555.

Amsterdam: U.S. Consulate General (Museumplein 19; Tel: 790–321); **The Hague: U.S. Embassy** (Lange Voorhout 102; Tel: (070) 624–911); **Rotterdam: U.S. Consulate General** (Vlasmarkt 1; Tel: (010) 117–560). Middle-of-the-night or weekend medical and dental problems can be set right by calling the central medical service **Centrale Dokterdienst.** In Amsterdam, the number is (020) 642–111. For dentists in Amsterdam, call 79–18–21. For police, call 22–22–22. For the fire department, call 21–21–21.

MAGIC FAMILY HELPERS ***Babysitters:*** There are 100 babysitting agencies in this country that is smaller than Rhode Island. You can be met at the airport, dock, or station by a children's companion through the local VVV or KLM if you notify them in advance. Some services are under the auspices of the UVV, an organization of Dutch women dedicated to high standards in child care and domestic work; the VVV will put you in touch with them. Just a few addresses and telephone numbers to start you off:

North Holland: In **Amsterdam, Babysit Oppas Centrale** (Tel: (020) 23–17–08).

South Holland: In **The Hague, Hotel-Babysitcentrale** (Westduinsweg 1033; Tel: (070) 542–065). **Kriterion** (Noordeinde 21; Tel: (070) 469–443). **Rotterdam: Oppas Centrale** (Rotterdamse Rijweg 142; Tel: (010) 12–08–69).

For mother's helpers and *au pair* girls, the MAI (see Information) is an excellent place to find not only helping hands while you are in the Netherlands, but helping hands willing to travel with you or work for you back home!

Members of the Dutch Amateur Guides' Assoc.—BBTBBA—(Statenlaan 51, The Hague), most of whom are students, act as guides in their free time; no payment necessary; particularly nice for children. The VVV Holland Hostesses will also act as guides (see Information). **The Guidor Guide Service** (P.O. Box 3387, 1001 AD Amsterdam) handles inquiries of travelers requiring qualified guides for any region of the Netherlands.

Department stores with babysitting services? In **Amsterdam, C&A** (Damrak) has a simply super one in the basement, free of charge to customers 9 a.m.–6 p.m. weekdays except Mon. mornings. **Eindhoven**'s **Piazza Center** has a nursery for tots and moppets if their parents take a four-lesson cooking course of two-hour lessons. **Bijenkorf's** branch here has a creche in the basement.

The **Schiphol Airport** nursery offers a playpen and playroom for your children while you are in transit, plus a room in which to change, and feed, and spruce them up. Make arrangements in advance with the VVV or KLM for a babysitter to meet you or be there at your departure time if you would like the children to be supervised while you take time off.

Play centers where children can be left for the morning or the afternoon at little cost? Ask the VVV.

Instruction? A boy's and girl's school is their castle if they are lucky enough to be going to the **International School** housed in Beverweerd Castle near Utrecht; founded on Quaker ideals; courses for English-speaking students from 12–17; student body never exceeds 140 and all board on campus; staff of 50; 31-hour-a-week academic program plus sports, handicrafts, wood-working, dressmaking, pottery and painting, choral groups. Relaxed atmosphere; older children have private rooms; the rest pillow down in four to six-bed rooms; each dormitory has its own kitchen and recreation room. Meals are served in the castle dining hall. Special recreation hall for music, billiards, and snacks is run by students. American graduates are eligible for a college preparatory diploma; Commonwealth students can get their A-level requirements. For details, write Headmaster, **International School** (Beverweerd, Werkhoven, Province of Utrecht, Netherlands; Tel: 341).

Personalized services? For a child's birthday party you can hire jugglers, singers, dancers, musicians, magicians, quickly and inexpensively at **High Noon,** Amsterdam, **Nederlands Theaterbureau,** The Hague; **Theaterbureau Frijters,** Tilburg; **Theaterbureau Maassen,** Zwolle. For reading families, **Overseas Book Club** (New Herengracht 31) will airmail U.S. books to you anywhere in Europe.

To track down your family history or know more about your Dutch ancestors, help, cooperation, and an incredible research library are to be found in The Hague at the **Central Bureau of Geneaology** (Prins Willem Alexanderhof 22, 2502 AT Den Haag). Your coat of arms can be copied or designed by an heraldic expert and artist.

HOLIDAYS FOR CHILDREN ON THEIR OWN In **Amsterdam,** is millionaire Georgius van der Vlugt's hotel for children, **The Children's Hotel** (Johan Huizingalaan 126; Tel: (020) 153–355), with pool, sandpit, and supervised playroom. Space for 150 children 3 months–6 years, but mainly geared to the 2–6 set. This *nonprofit* hotel provides a hot lunch, excellent overnight care, and swimming lessons. Price for infants is higher because of the special care necessary (one nurse to every four babies). The ratio for the 2–6 group is one nurse for every 12. Qualified medical care is available.

Also in Amsterdam, The **Hans Brinker Stutel** (Kerkstr. 136; Tel: (020) 220–687), beds 225 student travelers from 15–30 in one, two, three, and four-bed rooms with hot and cold running water, six dormitories for six to eight persons; laundry room; breakfast; centrally located. I know a family who lodged their teenagers here and stayed elsewhere with their younger children, meeting for lunch and family sightseeing in the afternoon.

At **Noordwijk aan Zee, Hans Brinker Huis** (Erasmusweg 3) offers 30 children up to 12 loving care by the day or week in an internationally-famous gabled brick hotel, a five-minute walk from the beach; trained, experienced staff doctor. Wide range of recreational facilities, indoor and out; highly recommended. My first choice in South Holland.

Other children's hotels that are fully qualified by the **Netherlands Camping Council** (NKR; Utrechtseweg 223, 3818 EE Amersfoort), include several particularly recommended, delightful, and inexpensive:

At **Elst,** the **Water Eaton** children's farm (Tel: (08819) 1389), accommodates about 65 *jongens* (boys) and *meisjes* (girls) aged 3–10 during spring and summer vacations. Pony riding, swimming, bicycling, nearby pool and playground, sandbox and wading pool for little ones; cows, ponies and small animals. Ping-Pong and other indoor games. The tiny ones sleep in the main house; bungalows for older boys and girls. In **Dronten,** in a forest, a creative youth camp, "Kreatief Jeugdkamp," for 40 boys and girls from 8 up, open mid-July–Aug. 21. For information, contact Stichting Kreative Recreatie, Sluis 3, 1398 AR Muiden.

In South Holland, at **"Brielse Zeilschool"** (Postbus 269, Delft) takes 32 boys and girls from 12–16 during July and Aug. for instruction in sailing. At **Mook, Bosmanege** (Papenbergseweg 23; Tel: (08896) 1590) a coed junior pony-camp-hotel for 15 equestrian-minded 9–14-year-olds during Easter, summer, fall, and winter vacations. Swimming, hiking, mini-cars are other attractions.

Write to the NNTO or the provincial VVV for prospectuses.

CHILDREN'S CAMPS Many. Some with generalized interest, many specializing in pony riding, trekking, or sailing. By all means, rent a bicycle and let your child take it to camp. To begin with, those of generalized interest:

In **Drenthe,** province of caves, dolmens, and menhirs, **De Hertenhoeve** (Bossehasteeg 2) is a summer camp for 100 boys and girls, 6–12, from late June–early Sept. Overnight tenting (tents with wooden floors), nearby swimming pool, wading pool, recreation room. In **Doornspijk, Hopsi Topsi Land** (Tel: (05255) 1757), is open from June 1 for the summer. Before then, contact Montessori-qualified directress Mevrouw Rie Versteegvan Zon (Het Laagt 40, Amsterdam-N; Tel: (020) 362–884). Co-ed, ages 7–11; lovely and pleasant; open-air pool. Accommodations for 55 in wooden-floor tents. Large community hall and weekly party. Variety of games and sports. Moderate rates.

On the island of **Texel,** at **Den Hoorn,** is **Zeemansduin,** open Mar. 25–Oct. 21, for children and students, ardent birdwatchers, and the young who like to sleep in sleeping bags, and live in a woodsy, tent camp life. Call (02226) 292 for information.

At **Wieringen, Lutjestrand,** and **Amstelmeer,** a clutch of camps, called "De Bellen," are under the direction of J. Pottinga (Middelhof 35, Heiloo). At the **Sailing Camp De Boekaniers** for beginners, 16 boys and girls from 10–17 sleep ashore in cabins in the woods. For ten of their more experienced counterparts, aged 12–17, the **Sailing Camp De Vikings** has a day program. For a dozen seaworthy 12–17-year-olds sailing school **De Centauren** is open on weekends from Apr.–Oct. as well as vacation periods.

Write directly for prospectuses or, to cut down on correspondence, to the local VVV office of the place concerned.

Riding and pony camps: The Netherlands offers children riding opportunities undreamed of at prices that make the greatest horse sense possible. There are some 50 horse and pony centers with horses of all breeds and nationalities. What do they offer? Overnight trips and a bed in a cozy farmhouse, pension, hotel, tents, a beached schooner, or stable bunk; weekend treks; pony trekking and youth hosteling.

Riding and living in a horse-drawn covered wagon is the attraction at **Paardesportcentrum De Kempen** (Eerssel). Cowboy weekends are the specialty at **Ponyfarm De Vrijbuiters** (Epen). Trekking through the countryside in horse-drawn covered wagons is offered by **Manege De Distelhoeve** (Helvoirt). There are special pony trips for handicapped children at **Ponyruimte Zandewierde** (Hoog Keppel).

No experience is necessary at many pony clubs—you can have lessons or practice riding in a paddock. The **Ponysafari Hans de Koning** (Venlo) offers a Whitsun safari for youngsters 8–80 for five days, a *Kinder-Safari* for children 8–15. Weekend camping is offered at **Ponykamp Edda Huzid** (Voorthuizen). For pony camping for children from 6–12, for young teens up to 20-year-olds, both the **Netherlands Riding Information Center** *(De Nederlandse Ruitersport Vereniging)* and the **Netherlands Pony Club** are at Waalsdorperlaan 29A, Wassenaar (Tel: (070) 245–484); call or write for information. It's helpful to give ages and riding experience of the children, the type of pony or horse they are interested in, the time you have, and whether you are interested in straw pallets or downy mattresses. Yes, yes, you equestrian-minded parents, you too can join in the unbridled fun—many clubs accept grownups on weekends.

Sailing school camps? Friesland—with miles of lakes, good following winds, easy berths, connecting waterways, harbors, and easy tack from rustic peace to lively watersports center—offers schools that teach you sailing in a convivial atmosphere of fellow enthusiasts of all ages. They house you in rustic lodges, farmhouses, or youth hostels—a great possibility to consider for the whole family, for teenagers on their own, or for children as young as 9. All schools cope with beginners as well as advanced water lovers. Write to the provincial VVV for details.

CASTLES AND OTHER HAPPY FAMILY ACCOMMODATIONS Hotels and baronial mansions have wonderful attractions for children, though there aren't many really castle-looking houses to stay in. Often hotels come with miniature fun-fairs, playgrounds, zoos, and pet animal farms; babysitters provided, but do call in advance if possible during the summer season.

The local VVV will open up lots of options for ***bungalows*** and tell you where to eat out at prices to suit all budgets; groceries are delivered; you can order vegetables prepared for cooking; or have a young girl to do all chores at a price that can make a first-time traveler wince with guilt. The bungalows I've seen, particularly the six-bed ones, are set apart with plenty of privacy. You can go off to the islands of Terschelling or Ameland, with their famous nature reserves and bird sanctuaries, wide beaches, dunes, sandbanks, ferry and train transport to the mainland; snuggle into a bungalow on the mainland with its own jetty and ponies; go to Drenthe to a site with a pool, ponies, fishing, playground. Or charming Apeldoorn. Hundreds of other choices. If you like to live in jeans and communes, you can in a camping house—facilities, but bring a sleeping bag. A free booklet from the VVV, gives all the details. For renting furnished or partly furnished ***apartments,*** see these Amsterdam agencies: **International Housing Service** (Prinsengracht 989); **Amsterdam Rent-house International** (Amsteldijk 162); **Holland-Verlof Service** (Koninginneweg 198).

Where to stay in **Amsterdam?** With children? Many choices: the **Amsterdam Sonesta,** incorporating a number of restored 17th-century houses has a dozen suites with kitchenettes, 24-hour room service. Expensive. The **Hotel Pulitzer** incorporates a score of 17th-century houses, linked by enclosed walkways around a series of courtyards, combining antique charm and modern comforts, including refrigerators in all rooms, pleasant canalside coffee shop and small restaurant. The big front rooms of the century-old **Hotel Krasnapolsky** (Dam 9; Tel: 63163), in the heart of the city overlooking Dam Square and the plaza beyond with pigeons and puppet shows, the cathedral carillon chiming in counterpoint with a tinkling street organ. The staff is uniformly patient and friendly with children. Chief virtues, however, are: (1) the kitchenette-equipped spacious front rooms with plenty of space for stowing luggage; (2) rollaway beds for children sharing a room with parents or brothers or sisters; (3) family suites, two or three connecting rooms sharing a bath; (4) baby cribs and baby baths available; (5) babysitters easily engaged at the desk. Even the restaurant has special baby chairs; charming old-fashioned garden dining room; the chef *likes* to make birthday cakes. **Beetsterzwaage:** Hotel-cafe-restaurant **Lauswolt** (van Harinxmaweg 10; Tel: (05126) 1245), a country house set in 2600 acres, with Lauswolt Golf Club and a tennis court; French cuisine. **Boekelo:** The first-class hotel-cafe-restaurant **Crest Hotel** (Oude Deldenerweg 203; Tel: (05428)1444), dandy playground amusement section; mini-golf, tennis; nearby riding stable; great expanse of forest; painting equipment provided; salt-water pool. Expensive, however. Near **Gulpen** (at Wittem):

Hotel-restaurant **Castle Wittem** (Wittemerallee 3) is a 15th-century castle with moat; pleasant cafe-terrace; wooded park and flowers; good food and service; 18 very pleasant rooms.

Haarlem: Hotel Vienerwald (Grote Markt); or the more expensive **Lion d'Or** (Kruisweg 34). **The Hague:** The **Kurhaus** and the **Europa,** by far the most luxurious. **Koudekerke: Zeeduin** (Dishoek 22), a residential apartment hotel, has a garden, mini-golf, children's playroom. **Leuvenum** (NW of Arnhem): Hotel-cafe-restaurant **'T Roode Koper** (Jhr. Sandbergweg 82–84, post Elspeet), a lovely country seat in 296 acres of private woods and heath with pet animal farm, riding, tennis.

Oosterbeek: Hotel-cafe-restaurant **De Bilderbeg** (Utrechtseweg 261; Tel: 3060), with a 345-acre estate; indoor swimming pool, mini-golf, riding stables nearby; all sorts of entertainments for families in Aug.; every modern convenience. Beautiful woods. **Oranjewoud:** Hotel-cafe-restaurant **Tjaarda** (Kon. Julianaweg 98) in a forest; deer park, tennis, fun-fair playground. **Rotterdam: The Central** (12 Kruiskade) is a four-star hostelry with indoor and outdoor play areas for children.

Zeist: Hotel-cafe-restaurant **'T Kerckebosch** (Arnhemse Bovenweg 31), country house with antiques and a large wooded park; riding stables. **Zoutelande:** The **Hotel Distel** (1 Westkapelseweg) is the winner here with indoor and outdoor swimming pools, garden and playground, dining terrace. At **Zutphen,** a lordly house in mid-city is hotel-restaurant **'S-Gravenhof** (Kuiperstr. 11); French cooking. The walls of the entrance are covered with seashells.

For information about youth hostels affiliated with the **Stichting Nederlandse Jeugdherberg Centrale,** get in touch with the NJHC at Prof. Tulpplein 4, 1018 GX, Amsterdam. Some of the youth hostels are housed in castles and other interesting locales, and in some you can cook your own meals.

CAMPING AND CARAVANING You camp at specific campsites—you don't just drive your trailer or pitch your tent on any old field—The Netherlands are *organized* for camping. You can camp with the illusion of solitude, but with laundromats, cafes, modern plumbing, and electricity, provision stores nearby. Or you can camp in a recreation park:

Camping Duinrell (Wassenaar 1), for example, a magnificent wooded estate of over 250 acres close to the beach where one can take solitary walks, yet have all the attractions of the recreation center. Bungalows for hire. Excursions to nearby Rotterdam and The Hague. A laundromat and mini-taxis.

Near **Maastricht,** bird and monkey park, **Eurofauna** (Gulperberg, Panoramaweg 1, Gulpen), offers all camping comforts, plus mini-boats, mini-golf, monkey house, aviary, model train, artificial bobsled run, electric scooter track, attractive restaurant, a pleasant rustic cafe, a fun-fair section, with easy excursions to the Belgian Ardennes, Echternacht in Luxembourg, or Monschau and Keulen in Germany. Near **Eindhoven** at Westerhoven in North Brabant, you'll find the **Eurostrand** (Eurodreef 2) an enormous playground-recreation center with tent and trailer campsites, camping shop, large lake (sailing, rowing, water-bicycling); mini-cars, mini-golf, mini-railway, trampolines, gardens, bowling, woods, sports fields, restaurant with sunbathing terraces. West of Breda, **Hoeven** (Oude Antwerpse Postbaan 81b) which offers water-bicycling, trampolines, rowboats, tennis, mini-golf, an exceptionally good heated children's pool, pool for parents, and an amusement playground. If you like lake swimming, recreation park **De Beekse Bergen** at **Hilvarenbeek** near Tilburg is a far better bet. At **Enkhuizen,** recreation park **Enkhuizer Zand** (Wierdijk/Oosterdijk; Tel: (02280) 7289) has heated swimming pool, mini-golf, waterskiing, boating on the IJsselmeer. If you like horses, try **De Goudsberg** (Hessenweg 32A Lunteren), with a summer bungalow colony, tent sites and trailer, plus mini-golf, trampolines, an amusement section and good pony- and horse-riding facilities. **Het Land van Bartje** (Buinerweg 8, Ees) have at their disposal ponies, pony-carts, trampolines, a pedal railway, a sulky riding track, mini-scooters, bowling, an amusement funland, a pleasant bathing beach, and a pool with artificial waves.

You can rent all-in-one-unit campers, tents, and sleeping bags throughout the Netherlands. The VVV will send you booklets about campsites. The ANWB (see Information) has a marvelous booklet, *Kampeerplaatsen,* in Dutch, but still relatively comprehensible, providing all the details, with symbols that are legible (and explained in English) of hundreds of campsites that are good for the abundance of attractions and the special interests they cater for, including sites suitable for the handicapped (Gehandicapten), for windsurfers, sailors, riders, swimmers, game players. A superbly organized book, cross-referenced, camps listed by province and by locale, many with cabins, some with sauna, many with restaurants. *Wat gaat dat kosten?* Very little!

ATTRACTIONS FOR CHILDREN IN AMSTERDAM Most attractions are open 9 or 10 a.m.–5 p.m., plus Sun. and holidays 1–4 p.m. The first must is a *rondvaart,* a round-trip ***canal-boat tour*** of the city and harbor. As the canals flow in concentric circles radiating from Centraal Station, it is in this area that most boats (most of them with glass roofs) leave at 30-minute intervals: from the Damrakbridge, Prins Hendrikkade, Stadhouderskade, Nassaukade, and Amstel; 1½-hour ride. The canals (*Gracht* means canal) carry illustrious names such as *Keizersgracht* (Emperor's Canal), *Prinsengracht* (Princes' Canal), *Heerengracht* (Gentlemen's Canal)—and the *Singel* (Moat). Gliding under some of Amsterdam's 600 bridges, children will be interested in the narrow canal houses and the pulleys jutting out (for hauling up furniture too broad to be carried up the narrow, steep stairways). Special illuminations in summer makes an after-dark trip even more memorable. You pass historic towers, among them the Tower of Tears (marking the departure point of Henry Hudson's 1609 voyage to the New World) and the Munttoren (a former money-mint). The boat firm, **P. Kooij** (Tel: (020) 233–810) makes a three-hour trip, leaving from the intersection at Spui and Rokin.

A visit to a ***diamond-cutting workshop,*** just so you won't regret not going and thinking you missed something. Very pleasant people, however, at **Holshuijsen Stoeltie** (Wagenstr. 13–17). Everyone is extremely knowledgeable about every facet of the diamond business; the Star of Africa, the Koh-I-Noor, and Cullinan II were all cut by Amsterdam's master craftsmen; a ring given away to every 100,000th visitor. The **Rijksmuseum** (Stadhouderkade 42), tiny admission fee, children accompanying an adult free of charge; a self-service restaurant (good to know, since you may end up spending a day here). Children won't be as interested in the Rembrandts as you are, but they'll like the Vermeers, Jan Steens, and Frans Hals. Steen's *Feast of St. Nicholas* shows the good little girl getting presents, the bad little boy getting the birch in his shoe (but his grandmother gives him a consoling present hidden away in the bedstead). Children will like his *Merry Family* and their extravagance (if they want to know why the rug is on the table, that's how rugs were once used) and Brueghel's lovely flower painting. It may interest them that Rembrandt's *The Night Watch* is a misnomer for a setting originally simply a shaded street—oxidation of the paint created the nocturnal effect. Of several doll houses, the best is housed in a bureau, a nine-room marvel filled with exquisite miniature things.

Madame Tussaud's Waxworks (Kalverstraat 156), open every day from 10 a.m. is not to be compared with London's, but it's worth a visit. A Rembrandt tableau is prefaced by an amusing kiosk of all the things that have been given his name—soap, sardines, cigarettes, cigars, etc. You'll see Queen Wilhelmina, Mata Hari, Erasmus, Castro, Van Gogh, Madame Tussaud (in bottle-green silk with a carpetbag), contemporary celebrities. The **Begijnhof,** entered through a small arched doorway in the Spui, is a quiet square surrounding narrow gabled houses and a church—an early 18th-century religious retreat; the oldest house (#34) built in 1478. It's the sort of secret garden place children love, and so will you. The **Stedelijk Museum** (Potterstr. 13, Museumplein) has a large cafeteria (soft drinks and hard); Pollock to Rauschenberg to Warhol to Klee. Also furniture, mobiles, and sculpture. The Van Gogh Museum—properly **The Rijksmuseum Vincent Van Gogh**—(Museumplein) houses drawings and documents plus work of his contemporaries. **Historical Museum** in the former convent of St. Lucia off Kalverstraat has varied exhibitions.

The **Tropenmuseum** (Tropical Museum; Linnaeusstr. 2) contains folk art, costumes, paintings, and artifacts of the Pacific, Indonesia, Africa, and Southeast Asia, and a rich schedule of music and performances. Many do-it-yourself exhibits to delight children plus a *creative workshop* and playground for children. The **Amsterdam Historical**

Museum (Kalverstr. 92), a courtyard and convent, arcades, and farmhouse-restaurant complex in de Oude Goliath, entered by a hard-to-find 16th-century portaled door. Various exhibits; a peaceful spot, a surprise. The **Jewish Historical Museum,** housed in the Waagebouw (Weighing House), a cylindrical turreted building in the center of Nieuwmarkt Square, with many ceremonial religious objects; Amsterdam historical collections on lower floors. Handsome weather vanes! The **Anne Frank House** (Prinsengracht 263) was the hiding place of teenager Anne Frank until discovered by the Gestapo and sent to her death. The Anne Frank Foundation has made the house an international meeting place for young people. Next door is the Anne Frank Student House, a youth hostel. In the 17th century, after the Reformation, Catholics conducted semiclandestine services in the attics of their houses, hence, **Our Lord in the Attic Museum** (Ons' Lieve Heer op Solder) or the Amstelkring Museum (Oude Zigds Voorburgwal 40). A miniature cathedral is hidden within three 17th-century canal houses whose furniture has also been preserved. Note the wooden foot-warmers—they're the little boxes with holes in them which secreted braziers. There's a priest's bedroom with an enclosed bed, paintings, and art objects. **Rembrandt's House** (Jodenbreestr. 4–6). More interesting if you know something about Rembrandt's life. Etchings, etching press, water colors, memorabilia of the artist.

Maritime Museum (Kattenburgerplein 1) offers delights for the nautically minded. The **Theatermuseum** Herengracht 168); the **Biblical Antiquities Museum** (Herengracht 366); the **Allard Pierson Archaeological Museum;** the **Geological Institute** (Nieuwe Prinsengracht 130); the **Medical-Pharmaceutical Museum** (Koestr. 10–12); the **Wine Museum** (same building as the Medical Pharmaceutical Museum); the **Zoological Museum** (Plantage Middenlaan 53); **Foundation von Loon** (672 Keizersgracht) a 17th-century furnished canal house, and **Museum Willet Holthuysen** (605 Herengracht) a 17th-century furnished canal house in patrician style; the **Netherlands Institute for Industry and Technology** (224 Rozengracht) with varying exhibitions of the technical professions; the **Aviodome National Aeronautics and Space Travel Museum** (Schiphol Airport) where you can test your skill as a pilot in a link trainer, complete with radioed instructions from ground control, and inspect models and replicas of planes of all eras; the **Money Box Museum** (20 Raadhuisstraat) are all possibilities for specialized interests. The cream of specialized museums, however, is the **Historical Museum of the Dutch Bakers' and Confectioners' Society** (Banketbakkermuseum, Wibaustr. 220–222) combined with a school in which a six-year course is given in confectionery (and a few ordinary subjects like arithmetic and languages). The school is upstairs; the museum, with antique cooking utensils and an 18th-century confectioner's shop, is downstairs. Open Wed., 2–4 p.m.; and also by appointment. When we went there, there were some 300 enthusiastic students (the youngest 12;

one girl and the rest boys) wearing floppy white chef's hats, learning decoration and history of regional cookies, cakes, and candies—my children were fascinated. Similar schools exist, I'm told, in The Hague, Rotterdam, and Leeuwarden.

Pleasure flights from Amsterdam's Schiphol Airport are offered by **Moorman Air** (Tel: 159–098) and by **KLM North Sea Helicopters** (Tel: 492–455).

Amsterdam's Marionettentheater (Brouwersgracht 51) has performances with explanations in English. Puppet shows also at the **Poppentheater Diridas** (Hobbemakade 68) on Sat. and Sun. afternoons, Sun. mornings. Check for performance times. The **Kleine Komedie** (Amstel 56–58) has plays for both adults and children. Check schedules.

Carillon concerts at the Oude Kerk, Wester Kerk, Munttoren and Zuider Kerk, all beautiful, all guaranteed to be memorable if you are in the neighborhood (ask the VVV for dates and times). On Wed. and Sat. afternoons, a free ***puppet show*** sets up its stage in Dam Square. Punch and Judy and other players give Dutch-language performances continuously.

The **Artis Zoo, Aquarium, Pet Animal Farm** (Plantage Kerklaan 40) where a child can play with the animals, and feed ducks and geese, is especially attractive; many rare animals (pygmy hippopotamuses, wombats, flying phalangers, and onagers); also a house for nocturnal animals (flying squirrels, owls, and bats). Aquarium stocked with over 700 varieties of fish from all over the world. Flamingos, cranes, all sorts of birds; miniature trains; wild animals—presented as naturally as possible. Plantage Restaurant 1½ blocks away at #37. Open 8:30 a.m.–dark. Children also have happy times at the **Amsterdam Woods Recreation Area** (Amsterdamse Bos) where there are pony and riding facilities, wading pools, and an amusement area. On Sat. noon–6 p.m. and Sun. 10 a.m.–6 p.m., old-fashioned trams leave Haarlemmermeerstation (Amstelveenseweg 264) every 20 minutes for **Vondel Park,** close to the Museumplein; has 120 neatly laid-out acres with ponds and flowerbeds, pleasant for a picnic, even nicer if your visit coincides with lilting band music, the scheduled performances of which are usually listed in the morning paper.

Look for the charming *draaiorgels,* large, tinkling and chiming barrel organs on wheels that can be seen at various places in town. Your hotel will tell you where you'll be likely to find the nearest one. An odd little statue, known wryly as *Het Amsterdamse Lieverdje* (the Amsterdam loveable), the city mascot, is on Spui Square. A holy terror who delights in practical jokes.

The ***markets*** of Amsterdam: The **Holland Art and Craft Centre** (Nieuwendijk 16) shelters Dutch crafts and craftsmen. You can watch wooden shoes being whittled, diamonds cut, glass blown, pottery painted, cheese made, silversmiths, coppersmiths and pewter craftsmen at work. A 30-minute audiovisual documentary of the Netherlands past and present is presented here, year-round, small admission. **Flowers** are sold along the Singel daily except Sun. On Mon. a **bird** and racing pigeon market at Amstelveld (sometimes on Sat. as well, check to see). A **flea market**—with second-hand everything, junk and some good things sold from pushcarts and off the sidewalks—at Waterlooplein every day but Sun. On Albert Cuypstrasse (corner of Ferdinand Bolstr.) everything from flowers, fish, and filigree is sold every day but Sun.; colorful and attractive. **Books** are sold daily at the Oudemanhuispoort. On Wed. and Sat. afternoons, rain or shine, the **stamp** market takes place at the Nieuwezijds Voorburgwaal across the way from the Telegraaf Building.

At the **House of Cutty Sark** (Spuistr. 304), open noon–8 p.m., closed Sun., ask Papa to pick up a kilo of 2000-year-old ice straight from a glacier in Greenland. The cost is negligible, and as you put the ice into water, it crackles and makes funny noises as the compressed air of the ages is released—fascinates children just as an idea. Me too.

I should mention, so that it won't come as the surprise to you that it did, and still does, to me, that ladies-of-the-night are illuminated with red neon in groundfloor showcases in many narrow streets and all along the Oude Zijds Voorburgwal. Respectable families live above them, grocery stores and libraries flank them. I don't quite know how you would explain this to the children. Unlike other countries where prostitution is carried on in special quarters, the hookers of Holland are accepted as a fact of life and integrated into the respectable life of the city. Regularly examined by the Health Dept. and the police, there they are, looking rather like commercialized Christmas decorations. The children probably won't notice them. If they do, I hope this will serve as a cautionary note to preserve your calm and cool assessment of the situation.

Many easy and entertaining excursions are possible from Amsterdam: Aalsmeer, Alkmaar, Bergen, Haarlem, Hemestede, Hilversum, Hoorn, Muiden, Zaandvoort, and other places in North Holland, depending on your interests.

ATTRACTIONS FOR CHILDREN IN ROTTERDAM Probably the best way to get an overall idea of this bustling port is the harbor tour offered by **Spido sightseeing boats.** They leave from the Willemsplein daily every 30–45 minutes. Evening trips and special excursions are also possible. Riding a spiral lift up to the **Euromast** (Parkhaven 20) for a 570′ view of the harbor is fun; two good restaurants in the crow's nest; a ship's wheel for junior navigators; the bridge is interesting with its modern navigational instruments. Rotterdam's subway is a town-planner's dream, as is the **Lijnbaan**—a pedestrian shopping mall brightened with birds, flowers, cafes, and statues (let the children admire the aviary while you shop). Near the Euromast a **funicular** carries you (legs dangling) for a 1½-mile ride over the city. Children love it. **Rhoon Castle,** a manor house south of Rotterdam, is a charmer, with sound and light performances at night in Sept. and Oct.

The **Museum Boymans-Van Beunigen** (Mathenesserlaan 18); paintings from Van Eyck and Bosch to Van Gogh. The **Prins Hendrik Maritime Museum** (Jacobplein 8), with ship models and nautical exhibits. The **Blijdorp Zoo and Botanical Garden** (van Aerssenlaan 49) conceived harmoniously as a unity, it's lovely; cafe, restaurant, fun-fair, lake, aquarium, aviary. Worth going to just to see the Przewalski pony, the world's smallest horse, no larger than a Labrador dog. These tiny horses originated in North America, where they are now extinct, and migrated in herds to Mongolia. Another interesting nautical experience is the museum ship "De Buffel" at Leuvehaven.

Seventeenth-century **Delfshaven,** with twisting canals, steep, gabled houses, winding streets, is where our Pilgrim Fathers started the first leg of their voyage to America. Visit the **Zakkendragershuis** (Sack Carriers' house) where copies of old Dutch pewter are made and sold; also the Old Church with exhibits pertaining to the Pilgrims. Rotterdam has two snuff and spice-grinding **windmills,** De Ster (The Star) and De Lelie (The Lily) both on the east side of Kralingen, the recreation lake; plus the Four Winds (at Hilligersberg) and The Sandy Road (in the south). The VVV will tell you how to get to see them. The historical museum, **De Dubbelde Palmbloom** (Voorhaven 12), houses the history of the town, toys and crafts, and has a pleasant coffee shop high in its rafters.

Pony-riding, motorboating, canoeing, miniscooters, carousel, and more at **Plaswijckpark Recreation Area** (C.N.A. Looslaan 23). Ask the VVV when the special "Windmill Days" are—when the windmills of Blokweer, Nederwaard, and Overwaard are operating at *Kinderdijk.*

ATTRACTIONS FOR CHILDREN IN THE HAGUE This is the center of government. The name means "the hedge," referring to the time when the city was ringed with a hedge. See **The Hague's Municipal Museum** (Stadhouderslaan 41), with Mondrians, contemporary art, exhibits of old arts and crafts, musical instruments, and town history. Stamp collectors may want to see the **Dutch Postal Museum** (Zeestr. 82). The **Royal Numismatic** collection (Zeestr. 71B) has cameos, intagli, and Dutch coins from the Middle Ages to the present. The **Costume Museum** (Lange Vijverberg 14) exhibits 200 years of costumes. The **Panorama-Mesdag** (Zeestr. 65B) is an enormous painting that shows what Scheveningen looked like in the 1880s. The **Peace Palace** is open May–Oct. Or you could trek through the enormous complex of the **Binnenhof,** the seat of the Administration, stately, elegant, magnificent, but exhausting to children except for the prison and torture chamber—the **Gevangenpoort** (Buitenhof 33), which contains instruments of torture used mostly during the Reformation. The **Mauritshuis** (Plein 29), a 17th-century Dutch Renaissance palace, contains one of the most impressive small collections of paintings in Europe in an elegant yet intimate ambience. Outside, the city's ornamental lake sparkles in the sun, fountains play, ducks paddle around the moat of Knight's Hall. The exciting museum for education, **Museum voor het Onderwijs** (Hemsterhuisstr.) aims exhibits on history, sciences, ethnology at schoolchildren. Ask the VVV for address and times to see the very special **puppet museum** run by puppeteer Felicia van Deth in her home; puppet shows weekend afternoons.

The miniature city of **Madurodam,** in a modern setting halfway between The Hague and Scheveningen, is a delight—a typical Dutch city reduced to exactly 1/25th of its dimensions, with sailing ships in canals, two miles of railway running past farms, factories, bridges, medieval streets, modern architecture, brass bands that play, a carnival in full swing, windmills, castles, shops, fountains. Visit early in the morning or at twilight to avoid crowds, but do allow plenty of time.

Scheveningen, where you can swim, has a playground at the foot of the pier with super amusements. Mini-golf and pony-riding on the beach, as well as fireworks on many evenings. The old section of town, a fishing village, is fun too—old-world charm, plus a lighthouse. The **Scheveningen Museum** (92 Neptunsstraat), open Mon.–Sat. from 10 a.m.–5 p.m., small admission, tells of the seafaring life in room settings and photographs with voluble fishermen who serve as volunteer guides an additional entertainment. The **Marine Biology Museum** (Dr. Lelykade 39) has sea aquaria and fine displays of corals and seashells. At Leidschendam and hard to find is the **National Automobile Museum** (Veursestraatweg 280), quite something indeed for aficionados and young mechanics; the oldest car is an 1894 Benz; repair shop; masses of engines and technical models; fabulous exhibits in open-air settings.

Spend another afternoon in The Hague's **Zuiderpark;** open-air pool (May–Oct.); deer camp; rose garden; flower park; trick fountains and ponds; roller-skating rink; playground; and a pet animal farm. **Duivenvoorde Castle,** about eight miles N of The Hague, spans an 800-year history, and is a lovely setting for its candlelight concerts. Check with the VVV for details.

ATTRACTIONS FOR CHILDREN ELSEWHERE A specialty of the Netherlands are ***recreation parks*** for the entire family.

These true pleasure gardens—with all the advantages and beauties of nature (woods, boat ponds, flowers), plus amusement park facilities, cafes and restaurants, extras such as lions or performing dolphins or living fairy tales, and often with supervised child-care and camping facilities—are wonderlands not to be missed. Wear comfortable clothes and shoes, and let the children set the pace.

Zoos: Throughout the Netherlands you will find *Kinderboerderijen* (children's pet animal farms), with donkeys, piglets, marmots, birds, deer, and other animals, all of which may be fed, many of which may be patted and cuddled. Bring cookies or bread as all-purpose animal and bird food! You'll also find *Speeltuinen*—miniature fun-fairs—which may be elaborate (with carousels, boating lakes, miniature trains, and pools) or simple (pony rides, trampolines, and swings). Many cafe-restaurants have some form of these attractions for children. A zoo, called *Dierenpark* (animal park) or *Dierkunde,* combines animals to pet, fun-fair playgrounds, and sometimes (not always) recreational parks with swimming pools and boating. At Harderwijk, Hellendoorn, Rhenen, Stein, and Zandvoort, you'll find ***dolphinaria*** where these intelligent marine clowns leap through hoops and bounce balls on their heads for an hour.

Children's circuses, in which the performers are children, are unusual; but here there are two: **Il Grigio** (c/o The Rector, Kerkstr. 19, Haaren); the performers, aged 7–16, may be seen at the Haaren Sporthal (Kerkstr. 15) daily during July in the afternoon; **Elle Boog** (pronounced and often referred to as The Elbow Circus; c/o Pro Juventuete, Egelantierstr. 167–171, Amsterdam). The performers, aged 6–14, may be seen in July and Aug. in Amsterdam, Amstelveen, Arnhem, Hilversum, and Rotterdam. Performances are irregular, so check directly or with the VVV. These circuses are beautifully done and should be included in your itinerary if you possibly can manage to do so!

Flowers are a specialty, with flower auctions all year round in at least 20 towns. The largest in the world, however, is at Aalsmeer.

In spring (the last Sat. in Apr.), a Lenten floral parade (the Bloemencorso) proceeds on its spectacular way from Haarlem to Bennebroek, Hilegom, Lisse, and Sassenheim, with huge floats all made of flowers which you can see the preceding Fri. in the Lisse bulb auction halls. Among the many processions, in Aug. (on the 1st Sat.), one goes from Rifnsburg to Leyden and back, with the floats on view Fri. evening and Sat. morning in the auction hall. In Sept., one goes from Aalsmeer to Amsterdam on the first Sat., with floats on view in the Central Auction Halls the day before the procession. Many flower processions in Sept. too. From June–Oct., there is an International Rose Show in **Westbroek Park** at the Hague. From the end of Mar.–May, if you are lucky enough to be here, there is a unique open-air flower show in a 66-acre flower garden at **Keukenhof.**

Windmills: To understand them and the centuries-old war that the Dutch have waged against the sea, you can do no better than read the out-of-print but still findable *Of Dikes and Windmills,* written and illustrated (beautifully) by Peter Spier (Doubleday and Co.) Some 1300 windmills still work hard conveying rainwater through canals into the sea to keep low-lying regions habitable. The custodian of the national heritage of mills is the **Society De Hollandsche Molen** (Reguliersgracht 9, Amsterdam). There are Windmill Days (Sat. in July and Aug.) when, if conditions are suitable, the 19 mills of the Kinderdijk are in operation and open (1:30 p.m.–5:30 p.m.) to visitors. Why is the Kinderdijk (The Children's Dike) called this? In the 15th century, during the terrible St. Elizabeth Flood, a baby in a cradle, steadied by a cat that leapt from side to side to keep the cradle from overturning, was safely washed ashore here. Information: **South Holland** VVV, Groot Hertoginnelaan 41, The Hague.

Costumes: Costumes indicating age, marital status, village solidarity are worn for traditional reasons and not for the benefit of sightseers. Costumes from the past, accurate to the last button, can best be seen at the **Open-Air Museum** in **Arnhem,** or at the **Zuider Zee Museum** in **Enkhuizen.** The best places to see costumes worn are Marken, Volendam, or Huizen (all near Amsterdam), Bunschoten-Spakenburg and Alkmaar, a bit farther on; Scheveningen and Katwijk (near The Hague), Kampen, Staphorst, Urk, Doornspijk, Oldebroek, Nunspeet, Walcheren, Hindeloopen, and Schagen are worth a day's trip if you are interested in costumes.

Wooden shoes (1 shoe-klomp; 2 shoes-klompen) are sold almost anywhere. Not as comfortable as slipper-socks, they are not madly uncomfortable either. They are extremely practical for wear in the mud, rain, slush, or snow because (1) they keep feet warm and dry; and (2) they are easy to slip on and off. You wear them with heavy woolen socks. Therefore, get them large enough so they don't fit tightly around the heel. There are about 40 skilled klompen makers (the other klompen are machine-made in factories). A wooden shoe workshop in Amsterdam is **De Klompenboer** (N.Z. Voorburgwal 20th 1012 RZ Amsterdam). You can also see wooden shoes being made close to Amsterdam: **Ratterman & Son** (Noordammerlaan 3, Bovenkerk); **A.P. Hoogendoorn** (van Cleefkade 14, Aalsmeer, next to the Central Auction Halls); and **Van Al** (Parkeerterrein, Broek in Waterland). The VVV can give you directions.

Here is a roundup of places I think your children will like most. (Note: Most museums and other attractions are open 10 a.m.–5 p.m. weekdays, plus Sun. 1–5 p.m. Be sure to check dates, as many recreation parks and other attractions are open only spring through fall.): **Aalsmeer** (12 m SW of Amsterdam) at Legmeerdilje: **Flower auctions** daily except Sun. and holidays, but Tues. and Sat. are best. Best time to go is 8 to 9 a.m. After 9:30, the most spectacular flowers have been whisked away. The **Minicorso,** a miniature reproduction of the Aalsmeer Flower Festival displayed inside a glass house, is well worth seeing. Hothouses; flower parade first Sat. in Sept.; wooden shoemaking; one-hour round-trip boat ride across Westeinder Lake, through narrow waterways and canals lined with interesting houses can be arranged. **Alkmaar:** On Fri. is the **market for cheeses** the size of cannon balls; late Apr. or May–Sept.; 9:30 a.m.–noon (but the earlier you get there, the better). As cheeses are auctioned, bidders clap each others' hands and shout the prices; porters wear white suits and lollipop-bright lacquered straw hats signifying the companies they belong to. It's well worth the 30-minute train ride on the Kaasexpres (Cheese Express), 24-mile car ride, or slow boat ride (check the VVV for schedule). The clock in the tower above the Waggebouw (Weighing House) by the market has mechanical figures that appear to joust every hour while the trumpeter blows his clarion call. You might ask at VVV about buses for **Alkmaarse Hout** (the Alkmaar woods), with small but charming recreation center with aviaries, llamas, deer to feed, and a flower clock. Six miles from Almaar is the **Alkmaardermeer,** a lake from which you can make excursions to Volendam and Purmerend.

At **Alphen aan de Rijn** (where the Rhine flows down to the sea carrying so much waste that the Dutch refer to it as a "scenic sewer"), **Avifauna** is a magnificent tropical bird park and recreation center (with round-trip excursions by boat on the Braassemermeer); illuminated at night. There is a cafe-restaurant (pleasant wicker-furnished restaurant upstairs, a self-service cafe on the ground floor); children's nontippable canoes, ponies, rowboats, trampolines, dodgem cars, play equipment; a giant pool; flowers, fountains, and flamingos; an amusement hall; a toddler's carousel cloudland with mite-size attractions; animals to pet and feed. You can sail here by rivers, lakes, and canals on seagull-white **cruisers;** departures daily from The Hague (Goudriaankade, Rijswijkse Bridge); from Leyden (Wilhelmina Bridge); or Beestenmarkt; Tel: (071) 23633; and on Sun., from the harbor around 1:30 p.m.; from Amsterdam. **Ameland:** To get away from it all; good riding; for ardent nature lovers. **Amersfoort:** engaging 13th-century town with a zoo; two playgrounds; special toddlers' corner; pony wagons and a miniature train; enormous collection of Australian parakeets; a pleasant drive where pheasants, fox, and deer are part of the scenery. Year-round Fri. a.m. flower market in **Het Havik** harbor area. **Flehite Museum** (Westsingel 50) is nice, too. **Apeldoorn:** The **Malkenschoten Recreation Park** (Arnhemseweg 355) has a children's pet animal farm for family fun. **The Koningen Julianatoren Recreation Center** (Amersfoortsweweg 35) offers motor and water scooters, fairy tale grotto, a spook house, a scenic railway, and more. **Appelscha:** A recreation park, **Duinenzathe** (Boerestreek 9), has a spook house and a good vintage car display. **Arnhem: Burgers' Zoo** (Scheimseweg 85) is not as much of an attraction as **Burgers' Safaripark** (Deelenseweg, down the road apiece) for safe-safariing; lions are in one section; in another preserve (through which you can also drive), giraffes, zebras, wild boar, eland, secretary birds, marabout scavenging storks, flamingos. The 60-acre landscape resembles the savannas and bushveldt of Africa; but unlike Africa, you see game here every minute: a *great* experience! Netherlands **Open-Air Museum** (Schelmseweg 89), 82 acres displaying windmills; farms complete in every detail including *uilegaten* or owl holes, in the eaves of the barns; wagon wheels on barn roofs for storks to nest in; villages, with traditional houses; living folklore exhibits; early handicrafts; a paper mill; all aspects of town and country life are represented with meticulous authenticity; spend at least half a day here—this condensed version of traditional Holland is so special it merits an outstanding recommendation. **Arnhem Museum** (Utrechtseweg 87) has exhibits of decorative arts. **Assen:** Fens and heathland; stone burial mounds and Roman ruins known as *Hunebedden* (Giants' Beds). **Provincial Museum of Drenthe** (Brink 5) incorporates 18th-century rooms and extraordinary ancient objects preserved in the local peat bogs. A five-acre children's traffic park, **De Gouverneurstuin;** junior policeman books road offenders, who take their driving seriously; also miniature trains, pony wagons, auto scooters, mini-golf, and a cafe.

Barneveld looks like an open-air museum, except that none of its people have vanished. On any Thurs. in July and the first Thurs. in Aug., everyone dresses in costumes to conduct a **farmer's market** circa 1850; children in costume display traditional dances; afternoon auction of antiques and curios at prices lower than in the shops; great fun. By all means eat the town's chicken and egg specials at **Kippen En Eirestaurant** (Hoevelakenseweg 1); playground attached. **Bennebroek** (not far from Amsterdam): **Linnaeushof Recreation Park** (Rijksstraatweg 4), encircled with tall green woods, embracing a lake with water-scootering and water-bicycling, blooms beautifully with roses, tulips, and dahlias in spring and winter; miniature flower exhibits; miniature car-racing track (to get in the mood, drivers receive helmets); a bell-ringing, choochooing Western-express train; pony rides; an Indian village; indoor and open-air cafe; mini-golf; special section for toddlers; a pet animal farm; demonstrations every half hour of wooden shoe-making. **Berg en Dal:** The **African Open-Air Museum** (Postweg 6) village, music, zoo; a famous collection of masks, fetishes, and art work in rustic surroundings. Also, there is the **Tivoli Recreation Park** (Oude Kleefsebaan 116). **Biddinghuizen,** in the province of Gelderland, is the site of the **Flevohof Recreation Center** (Spijkweg 30) featuring a children's village, cowboy saloon, Indian village, agricultural displays, TV studio for young people, children's pet animal farms, and pony riding. **Born,** in Limburg, has a zoo and bird park in its castle grounds, and a farm where children can get aquainted with furry and feathered friends. **Breda:** Set in beautiful woods, **Breda Castle** is now the Royal Dutch Military Academy. Playground and riding horses at the **Cafe de Zeven Heuveltjes** (Galderseweg 27). **Ethnological museum** (Kasteelplein); **ecclesiastical museum** (Grote Markt). A 16-lane bowling alley (Nassausingel 28) with a restaurant. **Brielle:** A walled and fortified town; fascinating. Head for the VVV (Asylstr. 2) for a guided tour around town and to the **Tromp Museum,** a 14th-century jail housing interesting artifacts of the town's history. By all means have a meal at **De Nymph** (Voorstr. 45). **Broek:** Once famous as the cleanest town in Europe, this old town in Northern Holland has a dairy you can visit. **Bunschoten:** Costume village; best on Mon. (traditional washday) when you see costumes on the line to dry as well as worn.

Callantsoog: The largest dune lake in Europe; a colony of spoonbills interrupted from time to time by visiting flocks of campers; peace, quiet, seclusion. Near **Cuyk:** N.B. in North Brabant, at **De Messemaker Recreation Center** (Haagsestraat 8) supervised sandplay, amusement park section, and water activities. **Delft:** Come in Aug. for the **Delft Tattoo,** a pageant of military marching. Delft porcelain and the antique fair are not of much interest to most children, but the historical morality play of *Everyman* (last 2 weeks of July) is, and so is a boat ride through the city canals. Delft is beautiful: Quaint streets, narrow canals, swans floating past weeping willows, and gabled houses may remind you of Vermeer's paintings. **Chez Vincent** (Brabantse Turfmarkt 89) is reasonably priced for lunch. **Roodenrijs Tea Room** (Brabantse Turfmarkt 81) is the local coffee-and-cakes favorite. The **Prinsenhof Museum** (St. Agathaplein 1), housed in a former nunnery, is interesting. Stay if you can at the **Hotel de Ark** (Koornmarkt 59-65), a comfortable hotel comprising three renovated canal houses. **Korft** (Korftlaan) has animals to play with, swimming pool, and the delight of all children, a trick water-fountain garden. On a Tues., Thurs. or Sat., the 48-bell carillon in the New (ha! it was completed in 1496) Church will chime a concert for you 11 a.m.–noon. The **Lambert Van Meerten Museum** (Oude Delft 199) is a Victorian mansion filled with tiles, pottery, and Delftware. You can still see the latter being painted freehand by artists at **De Porceleyne Fles** factory (Rotterdamseweg 196), whose showroom and demonstration appeals to children.

Den Bosch ('s Hertogenbosch) clusters about a beautiful market square. Market days (Wed. and Sat.) find every artist setting up his easel. The magnificent cathedral, St. John's, has a 48-bell carillon that chimes an hour concert at 11 a.m. Wed. The Town Hall (Stadhuis) has its own carillon of 38 bells and a Glockenspiel with knights that do battle hourly. The **North Brabant Museum** (Bethaniestr. 4) has eclectic collections, lovely old pewter, coins, paintings, archaeological treasures, religious art, folklore. Town ramparts; narrow and winding streets; great charm. Beach; boats for hire; pet animal farm at **Zuiderplas Recreation Park.** Farmhouse cafe-restaurant **De Pettelaar** (Gestelseweg), furnished in old Dutch style, specializes in pancakes and chicken roasted on a spit; after a meal or a snack you can rent a canoe, rowboat, or sailboat; also a fun-fair playground. A ***whole-day VVV tour*** of a 45-mile circuit, with an elaborate lunch (includes an old Brabant farm, hoop making, hand weaving, a bird park, an old smithy, a windmill, a riding school, a castle) makes the best possible use of time, plenty of variety and fun; cheers to the Hertogenbosch and the Meririj VVV (Markt 77, 's Hertogenbosch). **Deventer,** in Overijssel, has a sweet museum of mechanical toys (Noorderbergstraat 9), the **De Drie Haringen Museum** (Brink 55) with costumes, furnished rooms, jewelery, toys, changing exhibitions; the **Museum de Waag** (Brink 57) which highlights the history of this old Hanseatic town in a former weigh house. **Doornenburg,** about 15 miles south of Arnhem, is the site of an impressive castle (at Kerkstraat 25) with moat, stables, and thatched-roofed cafe in the courtyard. **Doorwerth:** Cafe-restaurant Beau Lieu at the 12th-century **Castle Doorwerth** (Fonteinallee 4) lies in a ravishingly beautiful park; riding facilities. The restaurant itself, in a 14th-century restored coach house, features haute cuisine and prices, but why not splurge a bit? Sobering **Airborne Museum** in the castle annex, a memorial to W.W. II.

Dordrecht: The story goes that in medieval times, meat brought into the city was heavily taxed. Someone trying to outwit the tax officials tried entering town with a sheep dressed in man's clothing. The deception was brought to an end with a resounding "baaa," but gave the Dordrechtenaars the amusing nickname of Sheep Heads. Rich butter cookies by this name are sold at **Van der Sluys** and **Brusse Bakery** (Bagijnhof 40), good to eat, good to send home. Dordrecht has broad canals, steep and step-gabled houses. The sweet **Simon Van Gijn Museum** (Niuwe Haven 29) is filled with children's toys, costumes, silver, tapestries, and furniture. The **Dordrecht Museum** (Museumstraat 40) is filled with paintings from the 17th-century to the present. On Fri. an hour ***carillon concert*** at 11 a.m., on Sat. at 2 p.m., from the tower of the Great Church, up whose 270 (count 'em) steps the children can climb for a spectacular view. **Wanty Park,** has a miniature zoo, tea room, and large playground. In town, an ice cream parlor is **La Venezia** (C. de Wittstr. 65, or Voorstr. 234). At the 17th-century Groothoofdspoort gate, at the junction of three rivers, let the children try counting some of the 1500 vessels that pass through daily. You might like a meal overlooking the three-rivers at the **Hotel Beelvue** (Boomstr. 37). You can also ride, swim, sail, canoe, or enjoy the facilities of the recreation park **Bruggehof.** Ask the VVV for information.

Drouwen: Recreation park (Hoofdstr. 25), with water-scooters, rowing, canoeing, a junior car-racing track, ponies, sulky rides, drive-in movies, animals, and performing birds. **Drunen:** "Autotron" (Museumlaan 1) features vintage cars, and a miniature racing circuit.

Ees: Recreation park **Het Land van Bartje. Eindhoven:** Please don't miss the **Evoluon** (junction of North Brabantlaan and the Rondweg), the free exhibition of science and progress; it will automatically up any child's grades in science and biology. Called Action-Expo; founded by the Philips Electrical people; a Gidophone gives you a taped tour in English; all aspects of man's evolution are presented in an illuminating and entertaining way. You can test your memory, determine if you are color blind, work a computer, check your reaction speed, see yourself talk on a video telephone (and I hope THAT invention never becomes popular), see heredity graphically explained. A topic of conversation for days, years. Also the **Animal and Monkey Bird Park** (Roostenlaan 303) **Van Abbe Museum** of 20th-century art; children's pet animal farm in the **Philips-Van Lennep Park. Emmen: Naber's Hof** (Noordeindezi), an old farmhouse; an arctic zoo (Hoofdstraat 18) with aquarium, children's farm and zoo. **Enkhuizen:** Love canals, old gabled houses? Fabulous **Zuider Zee Museum** (Wierdijk 18) with costumes, room settings, ships, scale models, and Holland's nautical history presented in a singularly interesting way. **Enkhuizer Zand** is the recreation center between Krabbersgat and De Ven lighthouse 2½ miles away; heated pool; special paddling pool. **Enschede: Natural History Museum and Vivarium** (De Ruyterlaan 2) is complemented with an aquarium (M. H. Tromplaan 19). **Franeker:** charming town; 18th-century **Eise Elsinge planetarium** operated by a clockwork mechanism. **Frederiksoord: Miramar Maritime Museum** (Vledderweg 25), a marine, natural history, and seashell museum.

Giethoorn: In the romantic lake district; wooded, provincial, sleepy enclave in a three-century-old peatbog where each house stands isolated on its own island in a cobweb of canals criss-crossed with bridges. Tree-mirroring canals arched over by the primitive sort of plank bridges you see in southeast Asia; everything done by flat-bottomed punts propelled by poling along: weddings, funeral processions, garbage collections; mail and food deliveries; the transport of cows to pasture, children to school, babies to their christenings. This extraordinary community includes antique shops, a **museum of Dutch tiles,** a **museum of local folklore,** costumes and artifacts, and brick-and-thatch houses. On the last Sat. in Aug., there is an illuminated punt-ride. **Boat trips** to the pretty little towns of Vollenhove and Blokzyl from here are pleasant. You can eat at **Smit's Paf** (Binnenpad 29A); cozy; on the waterfront. **Gorinchem?** Charming medieval walled city; narrow streets, gabled houses, old gateways, a grain windmill built right into part of the old walls that take one half hour to walk around. Gasthuisporrtje Gate, one of Holland's oldest, leads via walled passage to Gasthuisstr., the main shopping street, and to a gabled house called **Dit Is Bethlehem** (named for a Catholic cloister destroyed during the Reformation). It is now the municipal museum, housing also the VVV. The **Burgerweeshuis** (Molenstr.), another interesting museum, displays the chest in which Hugo Crotius (father of international law) escaped from the castle of Loevestein about a mile away (now reachable by steamer from the Water Gate). **Gouda** is where, many experts will tell you, Shakespeare is buried in the vault of **St. John's Church** with members of a friend's family by the name of Cool. St. John's stained glass windows are beautiful and special, as are recitals on its superb organ. On **market** days (every Thurs. morning) you can watch cheese being bowled through the street like hoops from the Town Hall of the Waagebouw (the Weigh House), and the old crafts exhibitions which go on in the square from 9 a.m.–noon are great fun. Among the things you can see being made are wooden shoes and *siroop-wafelen* (more wafers than waffles, more treacle than syrup), a town specialty. If Father is a pipe-smoker, he will enjoy conducting the children through **De Moriaan** (Westhaven 29), a museum of pipes. Great fun for everyone is **Het Catharina Gasthuis** (Oosthaven 10); antique toys galore, medieval surgical and torture instruments, and a medieval Dutch kitchen among other attractions. Candles and clay pipes are Gouda products the children might enjoy seeing made; the VVV (Waagebouw) will tell you where. The **Hotel De Zalm** (Markt 34) claims to be Holland's oldest hotel, offers haute cuisine in its dining rooms and pancake specialties in its restaurant, De Eenhoorn (the Unicorn). **Groningen:** Tues., market day, is a good time to go; its **Northern Shipping Museum** (Brugstraat 24) is small but significant; and a natural history museum (St. Walburgstraat 9) is fine. A state recreational park (Concourslaan) offers pony riding, a skating rink, and an animal farm. **Gulpen,** in Limburg province, has the **Foreldorado Recreation Park** (Euverem 5), where there is a trout hatchery, fishing, swimming, and mini-golf. Also, there's **Gulperberg Panorama,** a bird and monkey park.

In South Holland, at **Groot Ammers,** see and stalk the storks at their village, "Het Liesveld," open Apr. to end of Aug. **Haamstede** (near Goes) is an island resort about three miles from the beach, with a large wood, dune, and nature reserve. Fine **lighthouse** here to see and climb through.

Haarlem, a cradle of Holland's 17th-century Golden Age, three miles from a beach is charming. In spring, the Haarlem flower girls give away flowers. The last Sat. in Apr. features a **flower parade.** At Whitsuneve or Pentecost, the flower markets stay open all night and from dawn Sun. on, youngsters make a wild hullabaloo ringing doorbells and waking everyone up; a time not to stay in Haarlem! The **Frans Hals Museum** (Groot Heiligland 63) in a charming 17th-century building; an old-time pharmacy; enchanting doll's house; arts, crafts, silver. In Apr. and May on Sun. evenings, and from mid-July–early Sept. on Sat. evenings, the 17th-and-18th-century rooms are lit with candles, the inner court is illuminated, and concerts are given—let the older children stay up. The **Glockenspiel** (Wagenweg 88) swings into action at noon and 4 p.m. The **Teylers Museum** (Spaarne 16) has musical instruments, some sketches and drawings by Michelangelo, da Vinci, Raphael, and Titian along with Dutch paintings, semiprecious stones, and antique windmill models; custom-tailored for children's museum-going.

In summer, in the **Grote Markt** (a dreamily beautiful square with many outdoor cafes), there are Sat. handicraft demonstrations; barrel organ recitals, antique market. From mid-Apr.–Oct., twice-weekly **organ recitals** in the 15th-century Church of St. Bavo, dominating the Grote Markt; Mozart and Handel played the organ in St. Bavo's. The cafe restaurant **Brinkmann** (Grote Markt) is the place to eat. At Kruisstr. 37, you can buy the local *Haarlemmer halletjes,* a ginger cookie sold, to the best of my knowledge, only in this little centuries-old specialty shop. The **Droste chocolate factory** is here; so is the "Bulb district," the heart of the bulb industry. At **Vijfhuisen,** just outside Haarlem, is the **Cruquius Museum** (Cruquiusdijk 32) with working models, scale maps, to show how the Haarlemmermeer area was drained, an engineering feat that may be of interest. **Spaarndam,** in the suburbs, has the **Monument of Peter,** the mythical little boy who stuck his finger in the dike to save the polder and the town of **Haarlem** from inundation.

Harderwijk: This 13th-century Hanseatic port is *the* playground of the southern shore of the IJsselmeer. The town, with its ruins, has a ribbon of beach stretching bonnily on and on; fishing; and an ***amusement park*** with swings, merry-go-rounds, revolving barrels, trampolines, rides of every description where the young can be left to play for a pittance. Also, there's the world's largest roofed-in **Dolphinarium** (Boulevard Oost 1) and **Robariam** (sealion and narwhal pool), and the largest glass aquarium wall for close-up viewing of lovable dolphins. Performances timed so you can take in both sealions and dolphins in convenient sequence. **Heemstede:** Cafe-restaurant **Groenendaal** (Groenendaal 3) with deer to feed, a pet animal farm, duck pond, marmot house, aviary, and all of the Groenendaal woods to walk through in addition to the round-about, carousel, and slides. **Heerenveen:** The **Bicycle Museum** (Industrieweg 4) displays bicycles from 1817 to the present with posters and pictures showing how and why the Netherlands became the greatest nation of cyclists in the world (an average of two bicycles per family). **Heerlerheide:** The **Dream Castle Fantastico** (Ganzeweide 113–115), a 17th-century ruin, has hundreds of statues of people and animals of the fairy-tale world in a beautiful castle park in Limburg.

At **Hellendoorn, De Elf Provincien** (Luttenbergerweg 18)— a venue for all the elves of the provinces—has a fairy-tale Enchanted Forest, with a labyrinthine maze; an amusement center; mini-golf, electric boats, and mini-cars; a goat farm; a miniature garden; an echo chamber; restaurant; you can feed deer. The living fairy tales are wondrous to behold. Not up to the Efteling, but charming. **Hengelo:** Fine recreation park, **De Waarbeek** (Tweekelerweg 327), with amusement playground, a target-shooting hall, aerial cableway around the grounds, plus boat trips along the Twente Canal. Bungalows for rent; see "Camping." **'s-Hertogenbosch:** See Den Bosch. **Hilvarenbeek: De Beekse Bergen** (Beekes Bergen 1) features a road winding through a lion park with over 40 adult lions and a pride of young roaming free. You can see the park comfortably from a promenade train or you can play tennis or mini-golf; fish, waterski, ride a sightseeing plane; ride ponies; swim or sunbathe at the lake; canoe; row or motorboat; bounce on the trampolines. Baby animals for children to play with; a deer park; a labyrinth to get lost in; a light-water-music organ; a children's mini-car traffic park; a Brabant fun-fair; and a garden with amusement park attractions. There is a place to camp, or picnic, a health garden, mini-auto racing, mini-scooters, miniature trains, a barbecue grill, a cafe-restaurant, and, naturally, a supervised playground. Also, a pleasant pancake restaurant. What a safari, what a lion's share of pleasure! If you're near **Hilversum,** stop by "Anna's Hoeve" Playground (Liebergerweg 301) with scooter riding, underwaterland, and other diversions.

Hoek: Recreation center **De Braakman** (Middenweg), with open-air pool, fish ponds, bird park, woods, watersports on the lake, sail, motor, and row boats for hire, also canoes, a yacht basin, and plenty of sailing instruction. **Hoge Veluwe:** Special! A 22-mile forested park in Gelderland that stretches from Arnhem to Apeldoorn; middle-of-the-forest **Kroller-Muller Museum** with the world's largest collection of Van Goghs. From Easter–Oct. 31, *bicycles are available free* on the honor system on a first come–first served basis from the parking lot in the park across from the **Koperen Kop** restaurant. The village church in **Otterlo** is lovely; you can have tea at the main crossroads cafe where every table is covered with a "Turkey carpet," just as they were in the 17th century. There is also a pleasant country inn, the **Rijzenburg Restaurant,** at the S entrance to the park near Schaarsbergen. From Amsterdam, it is a 50-minute train ride to Arnhem. During the winter months, when the direct bus line isn't running to the museum, take the bus from Arnhem to Otterlo, and a taxi from the village. This is a sensational full-day roundtrip excursion from Amsterdam. **Hoorn:** A lovely old town. Ornate-facaded **Westfries Museum** (main square); dolls; Hotel Bakery doll's house built in 1910, called Juliana, is hidden away up in the attic; an old-fashioned museum; small, meriting maybe a half hour brisk-through; it's memorable. Here, on Wed., mid-June–end-Aug., the local market finds everyone in costume. Many antique stores around with inexpensive finds. Enjoy a meal at **De Waag** (Rodesteen 8), the former weigh house. On the harbor, **De Bonte Koe Taverne** (De Doelen Kade) is another old restaurant. **Huizen:** Costume village.

Kaatsheuvel (near Tilburg): A *super special park: 375-acre* **De Efteling** (Europaweg), open Easter–Oct., 10 a.m.–7 p.m.; swimming pool in a wooded setting, all amusement and recreation facilities are included in the admission charge—an unbelievable bargain. It offers shady forests, gardens, ornamental lakes; in the flowering meadows are ponies, deer, donkeys, lambs; a paddling pool into which a white statuary elephant squirts water from his trunk; rowing and canoeing; a rare steam carousel (fabulous folly of the Victorian era); picnic grounds, snack bars, and an excellent terrace restaurant; fun-grounds with pony carts, ponies to ride, miniature trains to steer, and a puppet theater. The children may want to spend an hour at the musical fountain. Goblins point the way to the Enchanted Forest, where fairy-tale figures move and speak. A mechanical nightingale sings so sweetly that flowers unfold; dwarfs live in a mushroom village with musical toadstools. Red shoes dance by themselves, and parrots repeat everything children say, no matter what language. Baby carriages and strollers for rent. Not to be missed!

Keukenhof: Spectacular **bulb fields;** daffodils, narcissi, tulips, hyacinths, and a lake filled with swans; ten million bulbs in bloom in Apr. and May; windmill, photographic pavilion, and amaryllis greenhouse. In season, a helicopter will fly you from Schiphol over 10,000 acres of tulip fields. **Koog aan de Zaan:** A restored 1620 windmill, called **Het Pink,** an old mill with ingenious machinery for extracting oil from seeds. Nearby the **Windmill Museum** (Museumlaan 18) offers fascinating model windmills.

Leek: Cafe-restaurant at **Castle Nienoord** (Bosweg), open Easter–Oct. daily. The castle houses the National Carriage Museum, a model railway for train lovers, and a cave with seashell-covered walls. The surrounding sweep of parkland encompasses an open-air heated pool (May–Oct.); a large pet animal farm; aviaries; mini-golf; deer to feed; an open-air theater—and plenty of room for camping. **Leeuwarden** (capital of Friesland): The **Frisian Museum** (Turfmarkt 24) harbors a sea of antiquities, folk art and folklore, beautiful silver and china, colorful costumes. See this museum before you invest in the delightful painted furniture or pottery for which Friesland is sought out by knowledgeable shoppers (both products interest children). Fri., the **Cattle Market** (Frieslandhal)—have a look at the bronze masterpiece of a pedigreed cow, entitled Our Mother; no statue of Mata Hari, though, who was born here! **Het Princessehof Municipal Museum** (Grote Kerkstraat 9–15) has an interesting workshop and exhibition garden.

Leyden (Leiden): Home of one of the most famous universities in Europe, birthplace of Rembrandt, a town cobwebbed with canals and narrow, winding streets from which Pilgrims progressed to the New World (a memorial service is held every Thanksgiving Day in John Robinson's church—Pieterskerk—where Robinson, leader of the Pilgrims, is buried); the **Pilgrim-Fathers** documentation center is at Boisotkade 2A. When Leyden was besieged to the point of starvation by the Spanish in the 16th century, a miraculous rescue took place; the Spanish fled and in their deserted encampment a copper kettle was found filled with a delicious stew—called *hutspot;* every Oct. 3, in commemoration, the Dutch dine on *hutspot* as we on turkey to commemorate Thanksgiving. The famous stewpot is on view at the **Municipal Museum, De Lakenhal** (Oude Singel 28), along with period-style rooms, silver, historical bric-a-brac and paintings of Jan Steen, Rembrandt, Lucas Van Leyden (where else!), and a Pilgrim Fathers' room containing spinning wheels and hand looms on which the Pilgrims wove to earn money for outfitting their ship. The **De Valk Windmill Museum** (Binnenvestgracht 2E) with interiors of millers' homes and workshops in fascinating detail along with many model windmills; The **Netherlands General Hoefer Museum** (Pesthuisiaan 7) is a military museum with uniforms, every known weapon from bow-and-arrows to machine guns; The **National Museum of Ethnology** (Steenstr. 1), important collections of art and ethnology of non-Western peoples (not as interestingly exhibited as at the Amsterdam Tropen, perhaps, but remarkable); The **Boerhaave Museum** (Steenstr. 1A), alchemist's laboratory, instruments of historical interest (Fahrenheit's original thermometer, the world's oldest pendulum clock, a 19th-century theodolite), pictures and manuscripts relating to the sciences; absorbing and educational. **National Museum for Geology and**

Mineralogy (Hooglandse Kerkgracht 17), dazzling minerals and jewels. **National Museum of Antiquities** (Rapenburg 28), with prehistoric, Egyptian, Greek, Roman antiquities; lots of mummies; handicrafts, including all the plastic arts. Also educational and interesting. You can climb up to see the **Burcht,** the fortress that defended the city, and gaze down upon the Rhine, canals, spires, the green of the **Botanical Garden** with its tropical glass houses glinting in the sun. Your children will feel they are in touch with history here, for this is a town of history. **Lunteren:** Recreation **Park De Goudsberg** (Hessenweg 85) features pony riding and swimming. **Maastricht:** This, the oldest fortified town in Holland, is a wonderful place to walk around and explore. Treat yourself to a meal at the 12th-century **Chateau Neercanne** (Cannerweg 800); Michelin-starred and of little interest to children, but a wise and money-saving choice if you are traveling with an infant. The restaurant sign that may delight you most here is **Coin des Bons Enfants** (Ezelmarkt 4), where haute cuisine is offered in a small restored medieval house. The damp and cold (52°) **caves** at Mount St. Peter are more interesting to the true speleologist than those at Valkenburg; bat-free when I was there, with graffitti dating from Roman times, some 200 miles of tunnels and 1100 crossways that must never be attempted without services of a guide. During W.W. II, the caves were used as a hiding place for art treasures and refugees. Ask the VVV (Tel: (043) 12814) for information.

Marken and **Volendam:** The people of these two costume villages (about 13 m from Amsterdam) are accustomed to being photographed and stared at by tourists and have made a going concern of tourist shops. No need to skip these towns just because they are touristy. Your children will be delighted to see Volendam on Sat., where a staged celebration welcomes the return of the fishing fleet, and at church time on Sun., when everybody is out in full costumed force. The houses at Marken with their boxed-in beds (any child who has read Hans Brinker knows these from the pictures) are entertaining, as is the herring boat in full sail that hangs from the vault of the village church. **Medemblik:** (see Hoorn). The main attraction is **Radboud Castle,** with sound and light performances during July–Sept. **Meppel:** June–Aug., the Thurs. market sees all the locals in costumes, giving displays of dancing, music, folklore and crafts; charming 19th-century coachhouse with curiosities on the wall for the children to examine; antiques for Mother; good food at economical prices for all.

Middleburg: Market Day is Thurs., when a bevy of *Beveland* women appear in enormous oyster-shell-shape lace headdresses. In the center of town is **Miniature Walcheren,** reproduced on a scale of 1/20th with over 200 buildings, ships, trains, villages, dikes, and a dredging machine, all in living action, greened with 100,000 dwarf trees and plants. Illuminated in the evening. For dinner, try the old monastery setting of **Abdij** (Abdijplein 5) next door to the **Zeeland Museum,** with a rich, eclectic collection of exhibits. **Mierlo:** A 250-acre recreation park, **'t Wolfsven** (Patrijslaan 4) including a ten-acre lake with pedalos, canoes, row boats—all very safe for the children, as the lake is 2′ deep. Open-air pool, mini-golf, large amusement park playground, and camping. **Monnickendam:** An interesting old town in North Holland, it's worth stopping to visit the **Stuttenburg** restaurant's fascinating music boxes. A strong aroma of smoked and smoking eel pervades the town, however—not my idea of a pleasant fragrance. A pancake house sandwiched between a ground-floor weighing house and a museum of Dutch tiles is also a good eating spot. **Muiden:** An impressive castle, 13th-century **Muiderslot,** on lake IJssel; massive towers, drawbridge and turrets.

At **Naarden,** an historic town in North Holland with ramparts and fortresses (including a great fortification museum [Westwalstraat]), the **Oud Valkeveen** circus and recreation park has a sparkling clean wading pool, a pool for toddlers, an amusement section, electric scooters, distorting mirrors, carousel, pond for motorboating, a **pleasure garden** for infants and toddlers, an Indian village, a miniature train, and a park with wild deer. **Nijmegen** contains a 16-sided **chapel** that once belonged to Charlemagne's palace, and has, at nearby Groesbeek, a **Biblical Open-Air Museum** (Mgr. Suyslaan 4). **Oosterbeek:** Amusement recreation park **De Westerbouwing Rhine Terrace** with swan train, cableway, observation tower, and roundtrip boat ride to Arnhem. **Oosterend:** See Texel. **Otterlo:** See Hoge Veluwe. **Oudewater:** A Dutch Renaissance river town of special interest to children, where the **Witches' Weigh Stool** is housed in the 16th-century Weigh-House—everyone knew that witches were featherweights because they rode through the skies on broomsticks, a feat nonwitches were too heavy to perform. Therefore, the Weigh Stool offered proof that one was not a witch; now operates as a scale for tourists who would like a nonwitch certificate. Storks nest on the **Town Hall** roof. **Rhenen,** in Utrecht, features the **Ouwehands Zoo** (Grebbeberg 109), pony rodeo, Western train, and aquarium.

In **Rijs, Sybrandy's Bird Park** (Schotanusweg 71), with 175 different kinds of birds, fishing ponds, an amusement park playground with a toddlers' corner, small traffic park, and deer enclosure. **Rijswijk:** Cafe-restaurant **Drievliet** (Jan Thijssenweg 16); amusement park and separate garden for children, with merry-go-round, autoscooters, funny mirrors, etc. In **Roden,** in Drenthe, the **Nederlands Museum Kinderwereld** (Brink 31) shows children's toys and games of yesteryear. **Roosendaal,** in North Brabant, features the **Recreation Centre Vrouwenhof** (Scholtensboslaan 2) with deer park, open-air theater, and a cafe-restaurant in a handsome country house in the park center. **Rosendael,** N of Velp in Gelderland, is where you'll find the **Rosendael Recreation Park** (Rosendaelselaan 15) with a drawbridge and the **Rosendael Castle,** which technically is a ruined tower now attached to an 18th-century manor house that serves as a castle museum.

Schagen: A wonderful festival here every Thurs. during July and Aug. A special **Schager markt** train departs Amsterdam at 8:55 a.m.; you arrive at 10 a.m. to be received by a band that escorts you around town. At 11:30, there's folk dancing in front of the church. The market goes on all day, with everyone in costume. Children's games; children can also watch the village women spinning and making lace. Recommended for all ages 5 and up. **Scheveningen:** see The Hague. **Schiermonnikoog:** A get-away-from-it-all-island; no cars allowed. **Schoonoord,** in Drenthe, is the site of De Zeven Marken Open-Air Museum (Tramstraat 73) which illustrates turn-of-the-century life with a clogmaker's shop, turf huts, bee farm, saw mill, and smithy. In Overijssel, at **Slagharen** (Zwarteweg 41) there's a Shetland pony park, with a water organ, bumper boat pool, amusement attractions. **Sneek:** Sample the frizzly *Drabbelkocken* confection at the **Haga Bakery. Spaarndam:** see Haarlem. **Spakenburg** is best visited on washday Mon. when the costumes are hung on clothes lines stretching across the streets; on Sat. these are worn for the market. *No photographing* allowed on Sun.

Staphorst: A Calvinist village scarcely altered since the 18th century (which moved Sacheverell Sitwell to remark that it was "one of the seven wonders of the world"); so out of touch with the times that it regards Salk vaccine as a violation of the will of God. The Sun. headdress here, a silver casque worn over two black caps and trimmed with gold spirals at the ears, is almost sinfully fetching, however. The buckram shoulder boards *(kraplap)* worn by the women are unusual. Photograph with caution and only with permission—and *never photograph on Sun.* A pleasant hotel, **Waanders,** with restaurant furnished in Staphorst style; a farm for visiting in the rear; the farmer's wife will tell you about her treasured heirlooms for a pittance. At **Stein** (N of Maastricht) is **Steinerbos** (Dieterenstraat 1), a pretty pastoral recreation park with duck pond, rustic bridges spanning swan-filled streams, deer park, trampolines, mini-golf, pleasant restaurant with outdoor cafe terrace, water-scooters, and two amusement playgrounds; an aerial cable lifts you comfortably seated for a lofty view of all activities.

Texel: Before leaving Amsterdam, check with the VVV about the ferry schedule to Texel Island so that you don't have to wait around in Den Helder (a naval base) unless you want to browse through the **Helders Navy Museum** (Hoofdgracht). The 20-minute ferry ride will take you to the port of 't Horntje. If you are driving, book transportation with the **Eigen Stoomboot** Onderneming (Elemert 8, Den Burg, Texel; Tel: 2300). Apply at the De Koog town hall for permission to visit the marvelous **bird sanctuary.** No permits needed to visit the aquarium and seal basin at the Nature Recreation Centre (Ruyslaan 92). Luxury hotel **Prinses Juliana** is at the top of the dunes with a sea view. Bungalows for rent here and in the Cocksdorp area. The water is rough and cold, but the island, with its dunes, sailboats, bicycle paths, flowers, and general charm is an escapist retreat. In De Dennen, a farmhouse restaurant, **Catharine Hoeve** (Westermeant B 142), in the woods, has yummy food and homemade bread. Den Burg, the fortress, has a Mon.-morning lambs' market from mid-May–July. **De Lindeboom-Texel** Hotel here provides excellent food and accommodation for 60 guests. Hoge Berg, formed during the Ice Age, means high mountain, and it's 45′ high. A Youth Hostel here. Bicycles and horses can be rented. Oosterend has about ten bed-and-breakfast pensions for modest prices. More than an ornithologist's paradise.

Terschelling: Another of the Wadden Islands, for quiet, solitude, bird watching; with **Boschplaat,** Europe's largest nature reserve. **Tilburg** (see also Kaatsheuvel): A modern industrial town which offers a **Craft Tour** by the VVV (Spoorlaan 440); you'll see weavers working, a cabinet-maker and a chair-bottomer, a potter who paints, and a puppeteer who will put on a performance for you. Spinning, weaving, and tapestry-making demonstrated daily at the **Netherlands Textile Museum** (Gasthuisring 23). A **missionaries' museum** (Koosterstr. 26). **Twent:** The children may be interested in the oak wood carvings, *levensboom,* placed on roofs of farmhouses to tell at a glance the number of the farmer's children and his religion. At **Uithuizen,** the **Menkemaborg** is a lovely 15th-century moated manor with boxwood maze and rose garden. Visit **Urk,** in the northeast polder reclaimed from the sea, charming, traditional village, once an island, where the villagers still wear costumes (men wear breeches).

Utrecht: a marvelous **Music Box museum** (Achter de Domiz). Also an indoor and outdoor exhibit of model trains, including one offering a simulated train journey, at the **Netherlands Railway Museum** (Spoorwegmuseum). Also the **Rijksmuseum** (Het Catharijneconvent) at Niewe Gracht 23, and the **Central Museum** (Agnietenstraat 1). Near the river Vecht, north of Utrecht, is **Zuylen Castle** housing many collections of special interest to historians and art lovers. There are many other castles in the area as well. One of the most handsome, the **Castle de Haar** at Haarzuilen, comes right out a book of fairy tales. Haarzuilen is a fine place to stop for lunch, tea, or dinner. **De Vier Balken** (Brinkstr. 3) offers pancakes as a luncheon specialty. **Vaasen:** Cafe-restaurant **'T Koetshuis** (Maarten van Rossumplein 2) in the restored carriage house of 14th-century **Castle Cannenburgh,** with period furnishings; private park with fish ponds.

Valkenburg: This May–Sept. spa-resort in Limburg has many attractions. Above the town rises a rock crowned with a crumbled **castle** over 1000 years old; an underground passage links its subbasement with grottoes hewn out of limestone by Roman construction workers that now have been developed into phony-but-fun phantom **caves** (with colored lights, rubber-wheeled sightseeing trains, and fluorescent murals with suitably mysterious electronic accompaniment). The caves (60°) require the services of a guide, and feature a subterranean lake through which children can paddle by boat. There is a miniature coal mine (Dealhemerweg 31), however, to be explored; educational. The biggest attraction for children is **Sprookjesbos Valkenburg** (Sibbergrubbe), the Enchanted Fairy Tale Forest Park (though only a reflection, perhaps, of De Efteling); a fine fun-fair playground and a miniature train making the rounds of Kabouterdorp (Gnomes' Village) with automated dwarfs. A cafe-restaurant features a *waterorgel* (a fountain with synchronized music and water jets); aquatic concerts every hour from 9 a.m.–11 p.m. On the Cauberg, a miniature **Cosmorama** (50 famous buildings from all over the world reduced to a scale of 1⁄25) makes children feel like traveling Gullivers. Also on the Cauberg: A **Grotto Aquarium.** The cafe-restaurant **Wilhelminatoren** (Oud Valkenburgenweg 44); observation tower to climb; an amusement playground. Open-air pool (Koningswinkelstr.) at the *De Valkenier* recreation park; boating on the lake; an amusement playground with an aerial sightseeing ride among its attractions. Then there is the replica of **Cape Kennedy** (Plenkerstr.) where you fasten your seat belt and take off for Saturn and the moon. At Cloisterroad 2, near the station, a panorama of stuffed animals in tableau setting. And a real coal mine, part of **The Rolduc Mine Museum** (Daelhemerweg). For details about all the things parents can do while the children are so happily occupied, consult the VVV.

Veluwe: Women wear lace caps. **Velzen:** A *gezellig* (cozy) cafe-restaurant, **Taveerne Beeckestij** (near Rijksweg 9), at the carriage house of an 18th-century mansion set in a pretty park. Main attraction: a **museum** filled with antique silver toys. **Vlieland:** One of the Wadden Islands, with seafaring villagers; no cars allowed; quiet and seclusion. **Volendam:** See Markem. **Vorden** (near Arnheim) is a little *dorp* encircled by eight **castles.** Ask the VVV how to make a four-hour, 20-mile circuit of all of them. **Vught:** Here is the recreation park **Deljzeren Man** (Boelan 43). Also cafe-restaurant **Maurick,** a drawbridge castle open to the public Mon.–Fri. **Waalwijk:** Children will gallop gleefully through the **shoe museum** (Grotestr. 148). Historical and exotic footwear, tools of the trade, prize-winning shoes of contemporary design contests. Nearby is Hoeven recreation park with open-air pool, deer park, rowing lake, and mini-golf course. **Warffum:** June folk festival, fair, and antique show. At **Wassenaar** (a hop from The Hague), 250-acre **Duinrell** has a campground; pony center; wading and swimming pool; trampolines; canoes (noncapsizable); sound light water show; fishing; riding; gondolas; rowboats; woods and sand dunes; exhibits of handicrafts in the park castle; cafe-restaurant; enchanting Fairy Tale Wood; children's super playground; an observation tower; an indoor amusement hall. See also "The Hague."

Weert: Netherlands Train Museum (Kruisstr. 6), open mid-Apr.–mid-Oct. for trolley fans. **Westerbork:** A marvelous **museum** on the art of paper cutting in the **Burg** (van Weezelplein 15), a great inspiration to children to try their hand. **Westerhoven:** See "Camping" for a description of Eurostrand recreation center. **Westkapelle:** Beach festivals and a display of **Ring Tilting.** You can take a few hints on threading a needle from the Zeeland sportsmen who ride along bareback with a sort of giant ice-pick with which they try to spear a cartridge on a string. There's a fine 15th-century **lighthouse** to climb. In summer, a sport and amusement-recreation **park** (Hogewegz) offers mini-golf; trampoline; mini-bowling; fun-fair playground; toddlers' corner; all sorts of scooters. **Willemstad:** Attractive town in heathland; sweet harbor; old fortress shaped like a seven-pointed star. **Winsum:** On the third Sat. of Aug., watch the Frieslanders pole vault across a 30′–36′ stretch of water. Houses in this flat land are often built on *terpen* (mounds). At **Wolvega** in Friesland, a mighty windmill in action grinding grain into flour serves as the local museum—displaying school desks, toys, tools, and kitchenware. **Wonseradeel** offers a *museum route* with a museum farm, arts and crafts, old shops, and an open-air museum. Ask the VVV for details. A town called **Wouw** (pronounced Wow!) has a **Brabant Gothic Church.** The main attraction for children, however, is sending postcards saying, "We're having a wow of a time in Wouw" or just "Wow! Wouw!"

Zaandam: You can sail here from Amsterdam in 1½ hours in a nice saloon boat operated by **Koppe Rederij** departing from Centraal Station. Or take a bus to the open-air museum of **De Zaanse Schans** providing a careful ***reconstruction of the 17th century.*** About 40 wooden houses, five large windmills, a grocery store, and De Walvis (The Whale) restaurant. The **Zaanland Museum of Antiquities** (Lagedijk 80 in Zaandijk, across the river) is furnished in old Zaanse style, filled with Zaan costumes, toys, handwork, and art; more houses and **windmills** are scheduled to be moved here. A miller busily makes peanut oil at The Searcher (De Zoeker) Mill; mustard is ground at The Householder; De Kat, built as a sawmill, now strains sawdust; another mill rotates to face the wind direction. Nearby, two more 17th-century mills, De Dood (The Death) and Ooievaar (The Stork) face each other on the banks of the Zaan River.

Zandvoort: A seaside resort with a **Dolfirama** (next to the Bouwes Palace), seats 1500 for daily demonstrations. Performances of dolphins and sealions, underwater viewing gallery, a sea aquarium. The **Mobilarium** is an old-time car, train, and bicycle museum, with a film auditorium, a model train exhibit, and bowling and skittles added to the happy hodgepodger. Later, dive into a covered swimming pool to rue the agility differential in human and dolphin bodies. By all means see the **car races** (Apr.–Oct.) if you and the children enjoy automobile racing; also horse-drawn carriages to drive.

Zeist: Cafe-restaurant in the cellar of **Slot Zeist** (Zinzendorflaan 1) a 17th-century castle. A children's amusement playground center at cafe-restaurant **Het Jagerhuis** (Woudenbergseweg 15) located in a forest. **Zuidlaren:** in Drenthe, stages a traditional folkloristic market every Wed. evening, 7 p.m.–10 p.m. during July. **Sprookjeshof** (Groningerstr. 10), open 8 a.m.–12 p.m., with a cafe-restaurant; Bambi Land (deer park); a very large amusement fun-fair; 1½-hour excursions on a lake cruiser on Zuidlarder Lake. The Sprookjeshof is a Fairy Tale House, not a forest, but you'll see *Doornroosje* (Sleeping Beauty), *Sneeuwwitje en de zeven dwergen* (you know them), and others. The children will recognize most of them. **Zundert:** Birthplace of Van Gogh; on the first Sun. in Sept., one of the country's most elaborate **flower pageants;** giant floats made up of millions of flowers. **Zwolle** (the provincial capital) is best on Fri. (market day) when the costumed people from Staphorst, Veluwe, and Urk come. Near the **Grote Market,** you can have a look at the town smithy at his shop (Nieuwstr. 26) if you don't mind getting smudged with soot. Also recommended: the cafe-restaurant **Urbana** (Wipstrikkeralle 213).

FUN TRIPS ***Boating.*** For Sun. sailors, international yachtsmen, kids who want to live in bathing suits, the Netherlands is a heaven and a haven of blue lakes (100 of them at least) connected with rivers and canals; one watersports center after another with all entertainment facilities near at hand; and marine, riverine, lacustrine camaraderie that is outstanding.

Holland has been a pace-setter in building boats and yachts—our word yacht is the Dutch word *jacht*. At sailing schools in the Netherlands you can intern or extern with the assurance that *Zeilen goed voor u!* (Sailing is good for you, right?!)

Cruising and Boat Rental. Sailing conditions are so good, boat-hire so reasonable, seagoing babysitters so easily obtainable, that even if you don't know the bow from the stern you may consider the possibility of literally sailing through all of Holland's 11 provinces. Zealand is recommended as a start. In a motor yacht, you might want to make a trip from Rotterdam to Arnhem, and from there along the IJssel to the IJsselmeer. Or you can go from Rotterdam to Amsterdam via Delft, Leiden, and The Hague, although a better route is via Gouda. You can sail to see the birds and beaches of Texel, to Friesland's interesting old towns, along the Rhine (spelled Rijn here). You can do it in style or on-the-cheap, and from one who has tried both, I promise you that sailing is the one mode of travel where not doing it luxuriously is more fun.

You must have clean, warm, dry clothing for all the family to change into; cozy bedding, which can include a sleeping bag on deck; and good things to eat and drink, something to read, something to write with and on, a basket for shopping and provisions, a flashlight and a couple of lanterns for security, bath towels, suntan lotion, dark glasses (if you don't want to get that crinkled look around the eyes), plastic bags for storage and garbage disposal. The rest is a matter of preference: *Crew*—do you want to go with or without; with a captain only, or with captain and hostess or cook or babysitter? *Sleeping accommodation*—how many berths, how many separate cabins?

Do you want a sailing yacht (requires experience in handling) or a motor cruiser (comparatively easy to handle and well-suited to touring canals and rivers—where independence of the wind is often essential)? Would you like a small open motor boat, a motor cruiser, a converted barge, a fishing boat, or a larger vessel with adequate sleeping accommodations: Do you want to camp aboard with sleeping bags or do you want proper bunks? Would you rather a cabin yacht, a *botter* (a sturdy fishing vessel used on the ancient Zuiderzee), a *tjalk* (a Frisian type of sailing barge), or a *Kotter* (cutter—not flat-bottomed like the *botters* and *tjalks*) in which you can cope with the tidal currents and weather of the open sea? Do you want a boat for sightseeing or for living aboard? What equipment would you like aboard? Drinking water? Head? Cooking equipment? Shower? Heating? Refrigerator? Bedding and towels? What about insurance? Guides and charts?

You can get charts from boat rental firms, or order them from the **L. J. Harri Company,** Prins Hendrikkade 90, Amsterdam. The **Royal Dutch Touring Club** ANWB (Wassenaarseweg 220, The Hague; Tel: 264–426) publishes the *Almanak voor Watertoerisme* in two volumes, Part I containing the traffic regulations which you MUST have and Part II giving details about harbors, canals, bridges, locks. Imray and Wilson Yachting Ltd. in London publishes *The Inland Waterways of Holland.* The NNTO puts out two basic informative primers: *Friesland Water Sports; Holland, Watersports Paradise,* and if you'll con these, you'll ken the sailing situation in general. For specifics about prices and types of boats, the NNTO will provide information as will the VVV, but a general source is the **Bureau Voor Watertoerisme** (Museumplein 5, Amsterdam; Tel: (020) 730–844). For cabin yachts and motor cruisers sleeping four to six people, prices depend on equipment, size, and season—high season is mid-May–mid-Oct. when prices shoot up about 25% at some agencies. If you arrive by plane, the boat rental people can meet you and whisk you to your new boat home. Be sure that your hire charge includes all risks and personal liability insurance, particularly if you hire from a private owner—since an ordinary boat policy covers only private use, and not chartering!

Sailing, you won't have to worry about hotel space and can stay as long as you want in any place that pleases you. Every water village has a water consul to give you help or advice. You can arrange to have mail forwarded, or the boat of your choice waiting for you in the canal that surrounds Amsterdam's Schiphol Airport. If you think your children will want to nap or play card games while you want to go ashore, avail yourself of a seagoing babysitter (see Magic Family Helpers).

Sailing holidays for young people 14–25? A week of canal-boat touring, or seven days of sailing instruction with full board and lodging aboard ship in the lake district of Friesland; or a week of sailing, swimming, and waterskiing in **Enkhuizen,** are possible. Parents with children over 12, particularly parents of teenagers who like privacy, why not sail through Dutch waterways aboard the luxury passenger barge *Juliana*? This super-barge, part of the luxurious **Floating Through Europe** fleet, became the new flagship in 1982, with room aboard for 24 passengers. With her sister ship the *Lys,* the *Juliana* offers an array of three to seven day cruises beginning in early Apr. for the enjoyment of the Dutch Tulip and Spring Flower festivals, and then plying Dutch waterways from mid-May–mid-Oct. **Floating Through Europe** (271 Madison Ave., New York, NY 10016; Tel: (212) 685–5600) can supply you with all the itineraries and necessaries about bookings and reservations.

The ***Mini-Trip,*** an all-inclusive, two- or three-day weekend has been dreamed up by the NNTO for the Dutch in off-season (Sept. 18–May 23). Each weekend is meticulously planned for sightseeing, antique-hunting, fishing, bird-watching, riding, bicycling, handicraft specialists, gypsying in a covered wagon, science buffs, cooking experts, lovers of art and history, all with options for children. However, there isn't an idea in it that couldn't be adapted for in-season tourism for those of us who would enjoy the Netherlands as the Dutch do. Ask the NNTO for itineraries.

Mini-tours are offered by the VVV for airline passengers traveling via Amsterdam who lack time for a full visit. These depart from Schiphol Airport and give you a canal ride, visit to a diamond cutter, museum, and other quickies. Also a choice of special tours: the Anne Frank house, Van Gogh Museum and canal ride (½ day), windmill tour (½ day), one-day bicycle tour (June–Oct.), Marker and Volendam (½ day), Marker Express coach and boat tour (½ day), one hour canal ride, Amsterdam by Candlelight (2 hrs., Apr.–Oct.), and other variations of half-day sightseeing trips of Amsterdam, or The Hague and Delft; the Alkmaar Cheese Market (½ day), the bulb fields and Keukenhoff (½ day, Apr.–May).

Covered wagon touring for a day or a week can be worked out with the **Paardensportcentrum Ryko de Jong** in northern Drenthe.

FUN AND GAMES The Dutch invented ***golf*** and have 18 good golf courses that I know of. The NNTO can tell you where to find courses from Arnhem to Wittem, all open to visitors on presentation of their local membership card from home. If you're interested in national and international golf tournaments, contact the **Nederlandse Golf Federatie** (Soestdijkerstraatweg 172, 1213 XJ Hilversum). Information on scuba diving and indoor and outdoor swimming pools may be obtained from the **Netherlands Underwater Sports Assoc.** (Nassaustraat 12, 3583 XG Utrecht). ***Fishing*** for bream, carp, pike, perch, roach, eel; no permits required for sea or coastal waters; for inland waters anyone 15 or older must have a permit issued by the police (or, in smaller places, by the town's mayor); firms and cafes renting boats can arrange for permits. For general information, contact the **Nederlandse Vereniging van Sportsvissersfederaties** (NVVS) Van Persijnstraat 25, P.O. Box 288, Amersfoort). There are as many special boat trips and cruises along rivers, estuaries, waterways routed through windmill districts, and unique natural areas. Information about all things horsey can be had from the **Netherlands Equestrian Sport Assoc.** (Waalsdorperlaan 29, The Hague).

Artificial ski runs usually go into action in Sept.–mid-Mar., but there is **summer skiing** free of charge and optional lessons you pay for at ski schools in **Bergen,** close to Amsterdam, at **Il Primo** (Duinweg 1) with lessons every month except July. In **Schaesberg** (Limburg Province) at **Ski School Sigi Moser** (Strythagen) with free skiing Sat. 2 p.m.–5 p.m., and Sun. 10 a.m.–5 p.m., lessons during every month except July; and in **Soesterberg** in Utrecht province, at **Ski School Otto Zoetelief,** in Sportpark Kerklaan, with ski lessons year round and free skiing by appointment every afternoon and evening for qualified skiers.

Tennis and bowling are other popular sports. Ask the VVV for information on these. Skating on artificial ice rinks indoor and open-air during the winter months at major cities, and on canals and waterways when these are frozen over. For details on rinks, ask the VVV or **The Royal Netherlands Skater's Association** (Stadsring 103, 3811 HP Amersfoort). Another way of zipping along on top of the water is water-cycling, a sport you can try for yourself at many watersports centers. As much fun for the children as Grandpa and Grandma! Public swimming pools may be anathema at home, but here they're sparkling clean and a pleasure. Fine open-air ones in most recreation parks, indoor and outdoor (some with warm water). Check with the VVV for the ones most convenient to you.

The Netherlands has some 200 miles of soft, broad, clean sand ***beaches***—few shells, no pebbles. The sea floor slopes very gradually, allowing plenty of wading room for little nonswimmers. In summer, most resorts have organized children's games, treasure hunts, balloon processions during the day, evening processions of Chinese lanterns; fireworks, festivals, special entertainments; horses and donkeys for hire; beach carts with wide tires for transporting toddlers and babies on the sands; beach bicycles for the sandpail set. Deck chairs, changing cubicles, beach tents, and brightly colored windbreaks can also be hired almost everywhere.

▶ **Note:** Apply sun lotion lavishly; the sea breeze may give you the illusion that the sun isn't shining as radiantly as it is. Do hire a windbreak. At no time should the children pull up the beach grass or ignore the "Keep off the Dunes" sign (the beach grass has been planted at great expense to serve as protective dikes for below sea-level terrain). On calm, windless days, there is *considerable danger* in using air rafts, life belts, or rubber animal rings owing to offshore currents; wading is fine. There are expertly guarded beaches where you can swim without danger if you keep within the limits set by the life guard. On unguarded beaches, children should wade and confine their swimming to resort pools only.

Best beaches (see Attractions for details) are at **Zandvoort** (near

Amsterdam and Haarlem); **Noorwijk aan Zee** (smaller) and **Katwik aan Zee** (larger and with more attractions for children) both with bus and train connections to Leyden, The Hague, Haarlem; **Scheveningen** (see Attractions in The Hague) crowded but great for fun-loving families; as far as children are concerned this is where the action is. **Bergen aan Zee** (family oriented; marine aquarium, leafy stretch of woodland). All of these are right on the sea. **Wassenaar** is three miles from The Hague and about two miles from the beach. To really get away from it all: **Texel; Vliesland; Schiermonnikoog; Terschelling; Ameland.**

No other country gives bicyclists as much space or as much consideration as Holland, with its six million cyclists. Everyone ***bicycles;*** mothers cycle along with children, groceries, and the family pooch. You'll find parking places for bicycles everywhere; even floating parking lots on canals. You can hire bicycles by the hour, day, or week anywhere.

A bicycle is a *fiet. Fietspad* means a bicycle track (so does *rijwielpad*). The *rejwiel* or *fiet* center for rental is usually found at the local railroad station in small towns; timetables list these stations. Bicyclist parent's delight are sturdy wicker baskets unique in the Netherlands. More or less vase-shape, you pop a child into them like a flower. Called *kinderstoeltjes,* they are rather hard to find (see Shopping, Amsterdam). ***Gliding?*** On weekends, gliding enthusiasts are at the **Terlet National Gliding Centre** (Apeldoornseweg 203, Arnhem). The minimum age is 14. For possibilities outside the weekends for gliding, telephone the gliding centre's appointment number: (085) 43–64–35.

KLM, the Dutch Air Sprayers Organization, and the Netherlands Aviation Co. will fly you anywhere you'd like a bird's eye view of. ***Sightseeing by plane*** may sound like the prerogative of millionaires, but it's a light-as-a-feather expense. Flights can be made from Amsterdam, Rotterdam, Eelde (near Groningen), Beek (near Maastricht), Hilversum, Hoogeveen, and other airports. Details from the VVV.

SHOPPING WITH AND FOR CHILDREN Generally speaking, hours are 9 a.m.–6 p.m. on weekdays, Sat. 9 a.m.–5 p.m. Department stores, clothing stores, shoeshops, liquor stores, close Mon. mornings until 1 p.m. In Amsterdam, hairdressers and barbershops are closed Tues.; in Rotterdam Wed.; grocery shops close at 1 p.m. Tues.; vegetable stores close Wed. afternoons.

The covered shopping centers for the entire family, a one-stop-100-store complex known as the **Piazza Center,** first opened in **Eindhoven,** are scheduled to appear all over the country. The prototype at Eindhoven is a four-story wonder with hip boutiques, druggists, restaurants, and coffee bars, antiques, clothing shops, home furnishings—plenty of merchandise for all tastes. Air conditioning, fountains, landscaping, ample seating, ample parking.

Department stores? **De Bijenkorf** (in Amsterdam, Rotterdam, The

Hague, Eindhoven) is outstanding for *Drabbelkoeken* (crispy, frizzly Friesian cookies) to send home; baby food; all sorts of delicacies; lace; children's clothes and toys; wooden shoes; records; nice things for the kitchen; handicrafts from all over. Services include restaurant and coffee shop; supervised nursery only in the Eindhoven branch. The less expensive **C&A** chain (in Amsterdam, Rotterdam, and The Hague), has a nursery in its Amsterdam branch, cafes in all branches, multilingual hostesses, and good children's clothes. The **Vroom & Dreesman** chain (all over the Netherlands) has good toys and hobby equipment.

For English-language ***children's books***—or adult magazines, books, and newspapers—you have but to walk along Lijnbaan in Rotterdam, Ila Donner in The Hague, and Kalverstr. in Amsterdam where bookstores abound.

Amsterdam: *Clothes* for your little prince and princess? **Maison de Bonneterie** (Kalverstr. 183); **Prenatal** (Kalverstr. 166), and **De Keizerskroon** (Nieuwendijk 79).

Model trains: **Het Treienhuis** (Bilderdijkstraat 94) 22 different makes of train; all the accoutrements for track, station, and landscape.

For ***candies, cookies, and good things to eat,*** the leading specialty food shop is **Dikker & Thijs** (Leidsestr. 82). For an old-fashioned, unique shopping experience, take the children to **'t Koffiewinckeltje** (Prins Hendrikkade 26, near Centraal Station), where scores of teas and coffees are weighed and poured for you into paper cornucopias. You can see coffee ground in the back of the store.

Souvenirs? Little brass manbakjes (money holders used by operators of street organs to collect money) are unusual and can be found in the kitchenware dept. of De Bijenkorf. *Speculaas planken,* wooden cookie molds—fun to use and to hang as wall decorations in a kitchen. **The Mill Shop** (Rokin 123) has all the usual ghastlies, but also a sweet collection of miniature copper and pewter doll-house-size furniture and accessories. **Leunstein** (Dam Square 17) has some of these too, along with a large range of sewing supplies. Wooden shoes? **A. W. G. Otten** (Albert Cuypstr. 102).

Wicker and rattan doll's ***furniture,*** grownup furniture, picnic hampers, and the vaselike bicycle baskets (see Fun and Games) into which a child can be securely and comfortably transported? A tiny shop fills the bill for these or any item you would like custom made (even a bicycle basket to hold twins) from rattan or wicker at prices that are modest for excellent workmanship: **G. Van Batenburg & Zn.** (van Baerlestr. 59). Don't forget duty-free shopping at **Schiphol Airport.** Along with discounts on everything from cameras to liquor, there are discounts on Schuco mechanical toys, Dinky super toys, and Steiff stuffed animals!

In **The Hague,** you'll want to have a gander at **Gossie** (Molenstr. 30), an outstanding children's boutique. Friesland has folk-crafts particularly suited to children's rooms. Hand-painted furniture is a specialty of **Hindelopen,** and it's worth going there just to see, buy, and ship home this delightful work which combines Scandinavian art, Oriental illustrations, and the pastoral influences of Friesland. The older hand-painted furniture—some from the 16th and 17th centuries, but mostly about 100 years old—has found its way into local (and mostly reasonable and honest) antique shops. Frisian clocks, wildly elaborate and ornate, are a bit too rocuckoo for me. Of the two types of native pottery, the better-known is Makkum ware, a Faience-like painted over glaze ware, featuring brightly colored birds and flowers. Primitive pottery, from nearby **Workum,** would look handsome in a boy's room.

DUTCH FRIENDS AND PEN PALS The VVV runs a *''Get in Touch with the Dutch''* program whereby you and your family can meet Dutch families who share your interests in boating, engineering, cookie-mold collecting, or whatever, and whose children are of an age with yours. Do take advantage of it. BBTBBA (see Magic Family Helpers) members are also good hosts. And with your HCC (see Information) you can also meet Dutch artists and fellow art lovers!

The **Stichting Voor Educatieve Reizen,** Correspondentie en Uitwisseling RQ (Statenlaan 51, The Hague, P.O. Box 9375) will supply addresses of pen friends. If you write to the *Holland Herald* c/o East West Network, Inc., 34 East 51st St., New York, NY 10022, your letter with details about the pen friend you would like will be published in the Letters Column.

CALENDAR OF EVENTS For further information on events, ask the NNTO.

From **Jan.**–Feb., Heerenveen has ***skating championships.*** **Feb.**–Mar. (including Ash Wed.), ***Mardi Gras*** is celebrated throughout North Brabant and Limburg; four-day carnival; regional costumes. Mid-Feb. features a ***flower exhibit*** at Bovenkarspel. Mid-**Mar.**–mid-May, Keukenhof has a spectacular ***flower display.*** At this time throughout the Netherlands, bulbfields are in bloom; flower processions everywhere. From Mar.–Nov. on Sun. you'll find ***horse racing*** at Alkmaar, The Hague, Hilversum, and Utrecht.

In **Apr.,** Haarlem-Sassenheim has a ***Floral Parade.*** On Apr. 30, the ***Queen's Birthday*** is celebrated throughout the Netherlands. From end-Apr.–end-Oct., Leyden holds festivities commemorating the departure of the ***Pilgrim Fathers*** from Delfshaven, 1620. On **May** 5, Liberation Day is celebrated throughout the Netherlands every five years, 1985, etc. In mid-May, Scheveningen, Katwijk, and IJmuiden have ***Flag Day;*** gaily decorated boats sail out for the season's first herring catch.

Mid-**June**–mid-July features the ***Holland Festival of Music and Drama*** in Amsterdam, Haarlem, The Hague, Rotterdam, and Scheveningen. June–Aug., every five years (1985, 1990, etc.), ***Passion Plays*** are performed by the villagers of Tegelen. On Thurs., mid-June–mid-Aug., Schagen holds its ***Folkloristic Farmers' Market and Dances.*** From end-June–end-Aug., Apeldoorn has a ***Sound and Light Lumido*** at Berg en Bos Park. Other June–Aug. events include: horse shows; automobile, bicycle, sailing, and motorcycle races; fishing contests; and tennis tournaments.

July brings to Arnhem the ***Military Tattoo;*** military parades and music. The last two weeks of July in Delft there are outdoor theater performances of ***Everyman,*** at Prinsenhof. From July–mid-Aug., Meppel opens its festive ***Folkloristic Market;*** throughout July and Aug., ***folklore pageants*** and ***shooting contests*** take place in South Holland; ***Windmill Days*** are celebrated in Kinderdijk. The end-July–early Aug. there's the ***Skutjesilen*** at Sneek, with racing of Frisian freight barges. July–Sept., Binnenhof, The Hague holds a ***Historical Pageant.***

In **Aug.,** The Hague features a ***Flower Festival;*** Middelburg has ***Ring Tilting*** on horseback, an exciting folklore event; and Delft drums up a wonderful ***Military Tattoo.*** The first week in **Sept.** there are ***Flower Processions*** and ***Festivals*** from Aalsmeer to Amsterdam to Zundert. The third Tues. in Sept., The Hague opens the ***Dutch Parliament;*** fascinating pageantry. From **Nov.** 15–**Dec.** 6, throughout the Netherlands, are celebrations for ***St. Nicholas,*** the patron saint of children and present-giving. In Leyden, Thanksgiving Day features a Remembrance Service in the Pieterskerk, commemorating the ***Thanksgiving of the Pilgrim Fathers.***

LANGUAGE AND PHRASEBOOK *I* and *J* are a diphthong that stand for *Y;* that is why you see IJsselmeer, instead of Ijsselmeer. The *'s* and *'t* you see before words are abbreviations of the Dutch for *Des* (of the) and *Het* (the). The Hague is sometimes known as 's-Gravenhage.

Hello	*Hallo*	*ha-loh*
I am an American	*Ik ben Amerikaans*	*Ikh ben amair-i-karntz*
My name is____	*Ik heet____*	*Ikh hate____*
I am____years old	*Ik ben____jaar*	*Ikh ben____yar*
Please	*Als het U belieft*	*ahl-stoo-bleeft*
Thank you	*Dank U*	*dahnk yew*
I can't speak Dutch	*Ik kan geen Hollands spreken*	*Ikh karn hayn Hollantz spray-ken*
Yes	*Ja*	*yah*
No	*Neen*	*nayn*
I am having a wonderful time	*Ik vind het hier heel leuk*	*Ikh vint het here hail lerg*
1	*een*	*ayn*
2	*twee*	*tway*

3	*drie*	*dree*
4	*vier*	*veer*
5	*vijf*	*vayf*
6	*zes*	*zess*
7	*zeven*	*zayvun*
8	*acht*	*ahkt*
9	*negen*	*nay-h'n*
10	*tien*	*teen*
11	*elf*	*elf*
12	*twaalf*	*tvalf*
13	*dertien*	*dare-teen*
14	*veertien*	*vare-teen*
15	*vijftien*	*vayf-teen*
Goodybe	*Goeden dag*	*hoo-dun-dahk*

NORWAY

Norway isn't as cold as it ought to be, considering its latitude. There are places in Europe much farther south that are a lot colder. Count on the warmest of welcomes for you and your children, and many family-oriented travel bargains.

Norway is the narrowest country in Europe, the most mountainous, has the most islands, and is sparsely populated. What's more, it is the country of the lemmings, who migrate from the mountains to the sea and swim toward England (no one has ever seen a lemming in England, however). Their migrations happen on a large scale once every 11 years or so and last one to three years. Even small-scale migrations are wondrous to watch. You can see lemmings 50 miles north of Oslo, but the farther north you go, the more you will be likely to see. In Norway, everyone from tots to octogenarians is out in furlined parkas on cross-country skis in the wintertime; natural wood takes the place of chrome and plastic; you never lose sight of mountains, trees, meadows, fjords, and turquoise lakes. Norway's northernmost county, Finnmark, referred to by Tacitus as Ultima Thule (the back of beyond) is now gratifyingly accessible for those on the track of Stone Age settlements and virgin country with both primitive and sophisticated accommodations.

Children's hotel facilities are good. If your children are from 5–15, you certainly should consider letting them join a summer camp in the fjords or the mountains, or enjoy pony trekking holidays.

INFORMATION ABOUT NORWAY There is no Norwegian Tourist Board in the U.S. However, **Scan Service** (75 Rockefeller Plaza, New York, NY 10019) will send brochures on request. Or, the **Norwegian Information Service**—facts about Norway—(825 3rd Ave., New York, NY 10022) welcome inquiries. General information is dispensed with characteristically generous Norwegian hospitality. Your most helpful sources of tourist information in the U.S. are the **Scandinavian Airlines System** (SAS Tour Department, 138–02 Queens Blvd., Jamaica, NY 11435) and your travel agent.

In **Oslo,** the **Norwegian Tourist Board** (H. Heyerdahlsgate 1) is known as Landslaget for Reiselivet i Norge, abbreviated as LRN. Its helpfulness is never abbreviated! Local tourist information offices are located in all major cities and areas: About 160 sources of information, from **Alvdal** to **Årdalstangen.** That's right, the Norwegians, in alphabetical lists, place towns beginning with Æ, Ø and Å at the end of the list. (The same is true in Denmark.)

If you would like specific tourist information, your best bet is to write to the regional tourist boards and then, if you need more local information, to contact the local tourist offices in that region. Not alphabetically, but geographically, here are your major sources for information: **RTF** for Oslo and District, Radhusgate 19, N–Oslo 1; **RRK Ostfold,** Turistsenteret, N–1600 Frederikstad; **TTK Vestfold,** Radhuset, N–3200 Sandefjord; **TTK Hedmark,** Fylkeshuset, N–2301 Hamar; **TTK Oppland,** Kirkegate 74, N–2600 Lillehammer; **TTK Buskerud,** Storegate 2 III, N–3500 Honefoss; **TTK Telemark,** Box 250, N–3701 Skien; **TTK Aust-Agder,** Box 366, N–4801 Arendal; **TTK Vest-Agder,** Box 592, N–4601 Kristiansand; **TTK Rogaland,** Box 130, N–4001 Stavanger; **TTK Bergen og Vest-Norge,** Slottsgate 1, N–5000 Bergen; **Trivelige Trondelag,** Box 2102, N–7001 Trondheim; **TTK Nordland,** Box 434, N–8001 Bodo; **TTK Troms,** Box 1077, N–9001 Tromso; **TTK Finnmark,** Box 223, N–9501 Alta. As you see, the abbreviation for the regional tourist office precedes the P.O. Box or street address; the area code precedes the town name.

For information about skiing vacations, where to stay, and baggage transport by dog sled or snowmobile; information about camping, hiking, mountaineering vacations, get in touch with the **Norwegian Mountain Touring Association** (Stortingsgaten 28, Oslo 1).

The **Norges Automobil-Forbund** (NAF) is headquartered at Storgaten 2, Oslo 1, with information services, routing service, travel counseling; branch offices functioning mostly as tourist offices are NAF Turistkontor, Torgalmenningen 4, 5000 **Bergen;** NAF Turistkontor, c/o Bennett Reisebyra, Markensgate 12A, 4600 **Kristiansand** S; Naf Turistkontor, c/o Leif Bowitz's Reisebyra, Kirkegt 34, 4000 **Stavanger;** NAF Turistkontor, Lilletorget, 7000 **Trondheim.**

Norwegian State Railways (Norges Statsbaner, Storgaten 33, Oslo) operates its service as far north as Narvik, above the Arctic Circle. The **Bergensbanen,** or Bergen Express, makes several runs daily between Oslo and Bergen (see Fun Trips).

HEALTH, WATER, AND FOOD Health standards are high, water is 100% safe, and the food is simple, delicious, and wholesome.

The national dish is fish—mostly herring, mackerel, salmon, sardines, and codfish; but it's those little, sweet, flavorsome shrimp that children like best. *Fiskegratin,* fish souffle, is another good choice. Not much chicken, but plenty of lamb, veal, smoked ham, and beef. A lamb and cabbage dish (pronounced "four-ee-kawl") is especially good. Ptarmigan, or mountain grouse, is too bony for small children to handle, but meat picked from the bone is a treat. Other food specialties include: spinach soup topped with hard-boiled egg slices; fillets of sole *Fregatten* garnished with shrimp, dill, white asparagus, and cream sauce with cognac and wine (for teenagers only!); lamb shanks with sour cream sauce; cold orange souffle; baked prune custard *(bakt krem med svisker);* sour-cream waffles, almond cake and fruit, fruit compotes or fruit "sauces" served with whipped cream, or fruit jellies. There's *multer,* an apricot-colored mountain cloudberry; red and yellow gooseberries; *solberries,* often made into a juice rich in vitamin content with a refreshing raspberry-blackberry taste; *ripsberries,* also made into delicious jam; and fruit often pureed and served with cream and cake. A cake filled with whipped cream (sounds like "flirt-a-carker") is superb. So are pancakes served with butter and sugar; the hard candies and chocolate made in Bergen; and the cookies with little scenes and figures painted on them in colored icing; ginger-nuts, large gingersnap "kisses," very crunchy; marzipan; and very licoricey-tasting licorice, the greatest virtue of which, to my way of thinking, is that the black doesn't come off.

Meal hours may seem a bit odd. A hearty breakfast at 8 a.m.; around noon, everyone eats a fast soup-and-sandwich snack; at 4:30 p.m., it's dinner time, the heaviest meal of the day. From 9–9:30 p.m., they have tea and sandwiches.

Oslo restaurants often offer special children's menus. (Alcohol is highly taxed, so you would do well to stock up in advance.)

BABY FOOD English, Swiss, and American brands of strained fruit, vegetables, meat, and fish are available in pharmacies and department stores. Highly recommended **Nestle's** foods are:

Homogenized baby food, red label:

Gronnsaker med Kjottkraft, vegetables with meat; *Gulrot,* carrots; *Epler,* applesauce; *Stuet Spinat,* spinach; *Aprikospure,* apricot puree; *Gronnsaker med Lever,* vegetables with liver; *Gronnsaker med Kalv,* vegetables with veal; *Kylling i Kraft med Ris,* chicken with rice; *Gronnsaker med Lam,* vegetables with lamb; *Fisk med Tomat,* fish with tomatoes; *Solbaerpure,* pureed solberries; *Gronnsaker med Oksekj ott,* vegetables with beef; *Torsk med Persille,* codfish and parsley.

Junior Foods, blue label:

Kalv med Gronnsaker, veal with vegetables; *Lam med Gronnsaker,* lamb with vegetables; *Lever med Groonnsaker,* liver with vegetables; *Oksekjott med Gronnsaker,* beef with vegetables; *Tomater med Oksekjoott og Skinke,* tomatoes, beef and ham; *Skinke og Kalv med Gronnsaker,* ham and veal with vegetables; *Fiskeboller i Buljong,* fishballs in broth; *Kjottboller i Buljong,* meatballs in broth; *Fruktdessert,* fruit dessert; *Eple og Aprikos,* apple and apricots.

Junior, glass jars:

Kalv med Gronnsaker, veal with vegetables; *Lam med Gronnsaker,* lamb with vegetables; *Lever med Gronnsaker,* liver with vegetables; *Oksek-*

jott med Gronnsaker, beef with vegetables; *Skinke og Kalv med Gronnsaker,* ham and veal with vegetables.

Nestle also has instant cereal (Barnemel); milks and solberry and apple juice.

DIAPERS AND LAUNDRY You can buy paper diapers, *papier bleier* (pronounced pap-yay bly-uh), in pharmacies or department stores, and almost everyone will understand "paper diapers." Pampers, Luvs, Chux, or their European equivalents are available in Oslo's pharmacies. There are no organized diaper services; regular laundry services will take care of diapers, but rather slowly—a week–ten days, as a rule—unless you pay extra for speedy delivery. Laundromats are available in larger cities only, but most resort hotels provide 24-hour laundry services.

EMERGENCIES MADE EASY ***Pharmacies*** (called Apotek) rotate night duties; check the newspaper for the closest. Your hotel can direct you to an appropriate physician or hospital. Norway's physicians are divided into three groups—public health, hospital staff, and private practice. Most hospitals are public and give every patient the same quality of care; no one gets a private room, a private nurse, or special food just by paying a higher fee. For ***doctors*** recommended by the American community, get in touch with the **American Embassy** (Drammensveien 18).

MAGIC FAMILY HELPERS ***Babysitters*** and nurseries can easily be provided in most hotels for children aged 5 and over, but they are difficult to come by for under-4's. For babysitters, nurses, household help, *au pairs,* the most helpful agencies in Oslo are **Arbeidsformidlingen,** Kongensgate 15; Tel: (02) 20–40–90; **Hjemvikartjenesten,** Akersgaten 55; Tel: (02) 20–92–10; **Contact Service,** Linstowsgate 6 (entrance in Sven Brunsgate); Tel: (02) 69–54–31. In **Bergen:** Arbeidskontoret for Bergen og Omland (Nygaten 2; Tel: 18190). Most ski resorts will supply babysitters; in **Lillehammer,** or **Sande-fjord,** consult the tourist office.

Tomm Murstad runs the popular **Tommleplassen** ((02) 148–671), a **Children's Day Nursery** at **Ovreseter,** 1300′ above sea level; open all summer; space for 240 children, supervised by ten "aunties." In the **Frognersetern** suburbs, the **Ski Centre** welcomes children aged 4–7 years between 10 a.m.–3 p.m.

Many ski resorts run day nurseries staffed with specially qualified "aunties." Examples are: **Geilo:** for 3–7s, the **Geilo Snow Nursery** (near Holms Hotel), 9:30 a.m.–4 p.m. The **Children's Centre** arranges classes with the ski school; toboggan or skate rental; reduction for more than one child. **Lillehammer: Birkebeiner Snow Nursery** (close to chairlift and ski school), 10 a.m.–1 p.m. **Oppdal:** Nursery (weekdays), open 10 a.m.–2 p.m. for ages 2–6. **Voss: Voss Snow Nursery** (at the head of the funicular), for children 3–8, is open 10 a.m.–3 p.m.; skiing lessons. Rates at all of these are extremely reasonable.

Personalized Services: In Oslo and other cities, ''tourist pilots'' (girls on motorscooters) will guide you gratis to your destination if you're driving. **Mytravel International Travelbureau** (Ruselokkveien 14–18), will solve your travel problems in Norway in a trice. An exceptionally helpful outfit.

Long-distance trains have special compartments in second-class carriages (some with hot water) for mothers with children under 2. Many stations (Bergen, Oslo East, Dombas, Fauske and Bodo) have a special room for baby care.

HOLIDAYS FOR CHILDREN ON THEIR OWN Norway has excellent children's day hotels and pensions (minimum week stays) for ages 1–12.

Oslo has 50 municipal children's day kindergarten-hotels, all supervised by experienced staff. Write to **Barneversnemndas Barnehjemsentral** (Akersgaten 55) for information.

CHILDREN'S CAMPS Real outdoor adventure in unbelievably beautiful mountain, valley, or fjord surroundings set Norwegian camps apart from all others.

The camps fill a national need: parents' holidays don't always coincide with those of their children; but there is also a high proportion of campers from other Scandinavian countries and America. All summer camps listed below are recommended especially to American children and are well supervised. All are medically supervised, and every child must produce a physician's certificate before arrival. The camp forms and clothing requirements are simple—no uniforms, thank heavens. Shorts, blue jeans, sweaters, and sneakers, are typical. Nowhere in Norway do I know of camps based on the tedious ''perfection of skills,'' the solving of ''psychological difficulties,'' or operated on a clockwork that allows 45 seconds to get from basket-making class to the archery field. Norwegian camps are the relaxed, carefree sort that boys and girls are happiest with. Camps usually run late-June–mid-Aug.

Mr. Tomm Murstad, a distinguished sportsman and ski instructor (his home address is: Lundekroken 6, Oslo), heads **Onkel Tommsfjelleir i Osterdalen,** for boys and girls 7–13, a summer camp in the hills near Oslo, with superb fishing trips, camping, riding, mountaineering; **Onkel Tommssjoleir i Oslofjorden,** a sailing camp for boys and girls 10–15 in weekly courses planned in collaboration with the Royal Norwegian Yacht Club Junior sections; rowing, waterskiing, swimming, lifesaving, and sea fishing. The administrative address for both camps is Bogstadveien 53, Oslo; or Voksenkollen, Oslo 3. For information about the **Villmarksskole,** a wilderness camp in east central Norway, close to the Swedish border, get in touch with **Norske Ungdomsherberger** (N.U.H., Dronningengsgate 26, Oslo 1), an organization which abides by the traditions of boy and girl scouting.

Among highly recommended summer camps for boys and girls 9–13: A camp for sailing instruction is **Skottevig Leitskole** (4770 Hovag). In Trofors, the **Borgefjell school** (Nedre Fiplingdal, 8680 Trofors) runs a mountaineering, nature study camp; mountain-climbing and swimming instruction at **Knutmarka Hyttlegrend og Leirskole** (Villaveien, 8300 Svolvcer) and at **Levajok Fjellstue** (Levajok 9828).

Children's Farm (Barnasgard) for boys and girls aged 7–14 near Bunnefjord gives children 8–14 the opportunity to live on a farm and learn animal husbandry. Supervised by retired schoolteachers Dagfrid and Terje Vigerust (Kirkeveien 12B, N–1400 Ski).

Riding Camps: **Bakk Riding Camp** for children 10–14; ten horses, one for each child. Weekly courses June 19–Aug. 16. Details from Ingrid and Gunnar Bakk (Groa N–7420). **Hovland Riding School** (Hovland Ridestall, Larvik N–3250), weekly courses during Easter and summer for under-18s; also weekend courses in spring and fall; 15 horses, five ponies; accommodation in the villa owned by instructor; courses (including care of animals, and horsemanship) for novices and experts (dressage and jumping); evening rides in the countryside. Weekly courses June 21–Aug. 15.

CASTLES AND OTHER HAPPY FAMILY ACCOMMODATIONS No castles in Norway, but an extraordinary range of hotels favorable to traveling families. Generally speaking, children under 3 are allowed a 75% discount and children 3–12 a 50% discount for room and food if they occupy an extra bed in their parents' room. "Mother-and-child programs"—whereby one child under 12 or under 6 (it varies with the area) gets free room and board, and other children in the family get substantial reductions (often 50% off)—is now quite common at winter resorts. Winter resorts also offer many entertainments for children (tours, competitions, fancy-dress parties) as well as instructors specialized in teaching youngsters to ski.

Dombas: Dombas Turisthotell organizes "family weeks" during the ski season; mother-and-child program; special children's skating rink, ski competition, and "Half Hour" (entertainment) every evening; other programs for children include films and a "Norwegian Evening." **Dovrefjell Hotel:** free nursery (9 a.m.–3 p.m., daily except Sun.) for 3–7-year-olds; children's dining room and children's menu; in Jan., mother-and-child rates; weekly programs include a "Norwegian Evening," national dances, children's fancy dress ball, and a torchlight procession. In **Geilo,** the luxurious **Bardola Hotel** goes all out for families with a great games room, swimming pool, sports and activities galore, and a special babysitting service. In winter, highly recommended childcare facilities at the **Vestlia-Hoyfjells Hotel** during the daytime (Tel: (067) 85611). **Lillehammer:** Several hotels offer mother-and-child programs; Lillehammer Ski School offers 50% children's discount for all charges. The **Nordseter Mountain Hotel** has an indoor pool. **Oppdal:** A rapidly expanding ski center; two ski tows a mile long; ski school has classes for all ages; curling and skating rinks, sleigh rides organized on request. Hotels welcome families in Jan. with reductions of up to 75% for children 3–12. Reductions also for children who sleep in an extra bed in their parents' bedroom. In **Oslo,** the **Scandinavia** has a fine babysitter service and indoor pool; the little **Ambassador** has a pool and apartments with refrigerators. The **Holmenkollen Park Hotel** (26 Kongeveien) is a luxury winter resort with indoor swimming pool, indoor tennis, floodlit trails for night skiing, and more. For reservations in the NY area call (212) 757–2981, or (800) 223–9868 outside NY. **Roros:** The **Bergstaden Hotel** has its own indoor pool. In **Sandefjord,** the Park Hotel, with motorboats and bowling among other activities, is a fine hostelry. **Tretten:** Gausdal Mountain Hotel offers reduced rates for children; specially favorable rates in Jan.

Vinstra: Wadahl Mountain Hotel has film and lantern-slide evenings, children's fancy dress parties, dancing, and games evenings twice a week. Outdoor activities include children's ski and toboggan races. **Gola Mountain Hotel** arranges evening dances and games; a babysitting service; easy hire of toboggans, skid lids, and *pulks.* Children's ski and toboggan races. **Dalseter Mountain Hotel** evenings feature dances, games, movies and entertainment in a games room. Children's skating rink; toboggans and skid lids. Children's ski school. Ski and toboggan races. **Fefor Mountain Hotel** has evening games and dances. Special games rooms. Nannies available. Children's ski school. Hire of toboggans. Ski and toboggan races. **Voss:** At the great snow nursery, under-12s sharing their parents' room are granted a 50% reduction on room and meals at the **Hotel Jarl, Bavallstova Guesthouse, Kringsja Guesthouse, Rondo Guesthouse, Vang Guesthouse, Vassenden Guesthouse,** and **Vossestolen. Hotel Vossevangen** offers 30% off for ages 6–12, and 50% off for under 6s. **Park Hotel Liland** offers 50% reduction for ages 4–12, 75% for under-4s. **Kaardal Guesthouse** and **Oppheim Hotel** give a 75% discount for under-3s and 50% for ages 3–12. In all cases, the child must occupy a bed in his parents' room. Voss offers package ***Snow Pack*** holidays that include ski school; hire of equipment; unlimited use of tows, lifts, and cable railway. Under 6's may use all tows and lifts free, while 6–15-year-olds are granted a 50% reduction. Special children's rates are available in the ski school for over-6s. Generally, special classes are arranged for children. Babysitters are available in the evening; and amenities include an indoor swimming pool and a skating rink.

(*Note:* In all of Norway, hotels should be booked long in advance. If, however, you should arrive in Oslo unexpectedly without a reservation, go to the East Station, where the city's **hotel-finding service,** Innkvartering, will put you up in a private house or, miracle of miracles, may produce hotel accommodations for you.)

Families who like the casual way of life will find over 170 ***youth hostels.*** To use the hostels, you must be a member of the American Youth Hostels, Inc., but while American hostels have an age limit, there is no age limit in Norway. More than 100 have "family rooms" for families with children two to fifteen; these can be booked in advance. Rates are rock bottom, with a reduction for children; in Oslo and Bergen, prices are slightly higher. For a complete list, write: **Landslaget for Norske Ungdomsherberger** (Dronningens Gate 26, Oslo). Some of the more popular hostels, all open summer and winter, are: **Oslo:** Haraldsheim YH, modern and comfortable; 260 beds in six-bed rooms. **Bergen:** Montana YH (Ravneberget, near Ulriken aerial cableway); fine views; 250 beds in four-bed rooms; modern and comfortable. **Geilo** YH: 200 beds in four-bed rooms; modern and attractive. **Gjovik:** Hovdetum YH on lake Mjosa; 132 beds in four-bed rooms, pool; tennis; ski lift. **Stavanger:** Mosvangen YH faces the lake; 130 beds in four-bed rooms. **Lillehammer:** Birkebeirnern YH; 120 beds in four-bed rooms; popular youth center; beautiful countryside. **Mjolfjell** YH; 120 beds in four-bed rooms; fine walking tours in mountains; ski lift; swimming pool. **Rjukan** YH; with 120 beds in 25 rooms; lovely surroundings.

Privately owned ***cabins,*** mostly in the southern mountain districts by the sea, offer hiking, skiing, swimming, fishing, and boating, are available summer and winter. Cabins generally contain fully equipped kitchens (pots and dishes included), open-hearthed sitting rooms, and one to three bedrooms, with accommodations for four to six people. Many are wired for lighting, cooking, and heating, but others have propane gas for cooking, and oil lamps. Not all have running water. You may have to bring water in from a well, or put up with a chemical john or outhouse. Others are deluxe, with all conveniences except towels, bed linen, pillows, and blankets. Rentals are Sun.–Sun. Interested? **Fjordhytter,** Den Norske Hytteformidling Bergen A.S., Kaigaten 10, 5000 Bergen; **Norsk Hytteferie,** Den Norske Hytteformidling A.S. Box 3207, Sagene, N–Oslo 4; **Folkeferie,** Arbeidersamfunnets Pl. 1, N–Oslo 1; **Nordisk Hytteferie,** Storgate 8, N–2600 Lillehammer.

At some hotels you may stay in a ***log cabin*** (usually accommodating at least 4 persons), having your meals at the hotel. Recommended are: Noss Mountain Farm in **Aal;** Beitostol Pension in **Beitostol;** Golaa Mountain Hotel in **Harpefoss;** Skogstad Pension in **Hemsedal;** Ostenfor Hotel in **Nesbyen;** Roros Hotel in **Roros;** Savalen Lodge in **Savalen;** Tyinholmen Mountain Hotel in **Tyin.**

Most farmers offer bed and full board throughout the year at reasonable prices (including reductions for children); many farms also have *seterbu* or *setterhytte* (small log cabins in the mountain ranges where cattle graze in summer). Lots of trout fishing, hiking. All reservations for ***farm vacations*** in the **Gudbrandsal Valley** should be made through the **Lillehammer Tourist Office** (Box 181, Storgaten 56, N–2601 Lillehammer). An example is Lunke Farm atop a steep hill overlooking the valley and river; owned by the same family since the 12th century; accommodation for 16 in the comfortable, modernized main house (with good home cooking in a dining room built on the foundations of a Viking log house) or in the annex (where family suites are large enough to accommodate a family clan). Or the Hole Gard, the family farm of English-speaking Mrs. Hole and her husband, located near the little town of Lesja, north of Oslo, also in the Gudbrandsal area which, during the summer, is a panorama of snow-capped mountain peaks and flower-filled fields. Each of the farm guestrooms has hot and cold running water, but the john is in the hall. You can picnic, fish, visit a nearby glacier, or drive to the beautiful Geiranger fjord. For other affordable farm holidays in Norway, information can be had from and reservations made with **Den Norske Hytteformidling A/S** (Box 3207, Sagene, N–Oslo 4).

Explorers, wildlife enthusiasts, campers can find accommodation in ***fishermen's wooden houses*** during Midnight Sun time in the **Lofoten Isles.** Your fishing hut or shelter, known as a *rorbu,* has electric light, a large stove for heating, often an extra hot-plate, a kitchenette which may and may not provide cutlery; most have running water and a sink. Boats and fishing tackle can be hired. For information contact **TTK Finnmark,** Tabernaklet, 9510 Elvebakken; **TTK Troms,** Box 1077, 9001 Tromse. Or, the **TTK Nordland,** Box 434, N–8001 Bodo; or for a *rorbu* on the south coast: **Korshamn Rorbuer,** N–4586 Korshamn.

CAMPING AND CARAVANING Ideal natural conditions exist for camping. Mountain and fjord sites for camping are numerous and accessible, and some 800 of the 1400 are listed in a booklet available from the LRN in Oslo. For more detailed information, the **NAF Turistavdelingen** (Storegate 2, N–Oslo 1) has an excellent inexpensive manual. Norway's youth hostels are among the best in Europe. Sheet sleeping bags are obligatory and can be hired at the hostel. If you don't have a card, international membership cards can be bought at most YHs. Family rooms, with four to six beds; guest kitchens and meals that can be provided at most YHs make Norway's YHs extremely attractive to families traveling with children. Detailed information can be obtained from LRN's Camping/YH List, or direct from **Landslaget for Norske Ungdomsherberger,** Dronningensgate 26, N–Oslo 1. Over 20 mountain areas offer a network of marked routes, with huts/lodges located a day's walk apart. These are run by local associations, with the **Norwegian Mountain Touring Club** (Stortingsgate 28, N–Oslo 1) their organizing body and publisher of detailed programs, mapped mountains, suggested tours, bus and boat schedules, in their manual *Mountain Touring in Norway*.

ATTRACTIONS FOR CHILDREN IN OSLO Museums are usually open 10 a.m.–6 p.m. in summer, but close as early as 3 p.m. in winter. Take the 1½-hour cruise through the Oslo fjord on a **sightseeing launch** that leaves every hour in the summer from a pier by the Town Hall. **Karl Johan's Gate,** the main street, has lots of sidewalk cafes, band music, and plenty of hot chocolate and pastries. The **Kon-Tiki Museum** houses the raft on which Thor Heyerdahl, five companions, and a parrot traveled 4800 miles from Peru to Polynesia. Diaries and records on display are all in English and make fascinating reading. The **Viking Ship Museum** (Huk Av. 35); Viking sea warriors and their wives were buried or burned with their ships, and here you can see three of the remarkable 9th-century oared Viking ships with their high sterns and arching prows carved like the heads of snakes and dragons. On the *Oseberg,* reputedly the burial chamber of Queen Aasa, everyday materials to carry on life after death were buried with the Queen. On the *Gokstad* and the *Tune,* the round shields, the mail shirts, the swords, bows, arrows, and javelins, bring those embattled Viking days very much to life again. The **Norwegian Folk Museum,** an open-air collection of some 150 genuine old wooden houses from all parts of Norway that have been carefully dismantled and reassembled in a large park also on the Bygdoy Peninsula; farms; an extraordinary 12th-century Stave church, uniquely Norwegian; a Lapp section is almost as good as visiting Lapland; Henrik Ibsen's study; scores of other exhibits to wonder at, and a pleasant open-air restaurant. (Owners of veteran cars have established transfer services during the summer between the Viking Ship Museum, the Kon Tiki Museum, and the Norwegian Folk Museum.) The **Norwegian Technical Museum** (Norak Teknisk Museum; Fyrstikkalleen 1, Etterstad) is marvelous; all machines can be worked by pressing buttons; Scandinavia's largest model railway; special children's parties are often arranged. The **Fram Museum** houses the polar exploration ship "Fram," and for more about boats, there is the **Maritime Museum.** The **Universitets Oldsakamling** has the best examples of Viking art. The **National Gallery** is strong on Edvard Munch and other 19th-century landscape painters. The **Akershus Fortress** is a romantic landscape in itself, and it shelters a war museum.

At least ten movie houses run children's performances. At least three theaters offer special entertainments for children. Marionette shows at **Osly Nye Theater** (Rosenkrantzgaten 10), usually after 3 p.m. on weekdays, performances run continually 11 a.m.–5 p.m. Oslo's amenities also include five indoor swimming pools, three artificial and some 50 natural ice rinks, sleigh rides, and a riding school. Take along bathing suits and go down toward the harbor of the twin-towered, red-brick Radhuset (City Hall) and from the Pipervika (wharves) behind it, take the ferry marked *Til Bygdones og Dronningen,* which leaves every quarter hour from Pier C; it's ten minutes to the **Bygdoy** Peninsula just across the harbor. You will dock in front of a pyramid-shaped building built so you can see the ingeniously designed round hull of the polar ship *Fram* that took Nansen to the North Pole and Roald Amundsen to the South Pole. Rigging and equipment all intact. At Bygdoy, there are some fine beaches; surprisingly few bathhouses—Norwegians undress in the nearby woods. Trolley cars operate on a circular route which gives one a fine look at Oslo.

Frognerseter, the highest hill overlooking Oslo, and a three-minute walk from the delightful Frognerseteren Hovedrestaurant, with a fabulous view of Oslo and the mountains. A trolley can take you to **Frogner Park.** The funicular goes above ground just before it begins to climb, so you can stop off at Holmenkollen to see in and around the famous **Holmenkollen ski jump tower.** The building is ten stories high and contains a ski museum of interest to older children, a souvenir shop and a restaurant, also with a fine panoramic view. **Changing of the Guard** at the Royal Palace; ask the Oslo Information Office for hours.

Lake Gjersio (12 m S of Oslo): **Dyreparken,** a fairy-tale land consisting of Children's Town (miniature town with toy automobiles and tricycles), Children's Country (goats, hens, sheep, and cows) and Children's National Park (reindeer and elk). Adjoining campsite. Details from, and all thanks to, its owner, Mr. Odd Fornebo (Kongsveien 90, Bekkelagshogda, Oslo). The **Henie-Onstad Museum,** at **Hovikodden,** about 20 minutes outside Oslo, is a small, fine museum of modern art. Nearby at **Sorumsand,** at Tertitten, a fun narrow-gauge railway. Day trips from Oslo might include the **royal burial mounds** at **Borrehaugerne** (near Horten), north Europe's largest collection; the **whaling museum** in **Sandefjord;** and **Tonsberg,** Norway's oldest town, with **Slottsfjellet,** the ruins of a medieval castle; or in Ostfold province, to the east of Oslo, the "Road of the Ancients" (Opdtidsveien) between **Frederikstad** and **Skjeberg,** with rock carvings from the Bronze Age, Viking burial mounds; and **Frederikstad** with its Old Town (Gamlebyen) and its 17th-century fortress; old houses; and the **Kongsten Fortress recreation park.**

ATTRACTIONS FOR CHILDREN ELSEWHERE **Alta** in the North Cape is the provincial touring center of Finnmark, with a river leaping and flashing with salmon on which you, too, can boat and fish; 2000 year-old carvings of hunting scenes; glaciers towering above the fjords; a river valley glittering with waterfalls. Stay at the **SAS Alta Vertshus.** **Bergen:** Gateway to the popular ski resorts of Voss and Geilo, Bergen is a town with medieval charm and many engaging diversions for children, including: A ride in the **funicular railroad** to the top of Floyen Mountain, with a superlative view and an excellent restaurant. The 1050′ climb, made in ten minutes, is entrancing. So is the cable car trip up Mount Ulriken, operating all year. **Old Bergen,** an outdoor museum open May 15–Aug. 31. Fascinating. You can also go to Old Bergen by horse cart, (and you can use horse carts to get around Bergen). The **Torget fish market** on the Torgalmenning, a lively and colorful spectacle. **Boat trips,** leave from the fish market jetty for outlying islands; great fun in good weather (it's not true that people in Bergen are born with umbrellas in hand, but you can almost count on a quick spurt of rain sometime during the day). For particulars about these boat trips, ask the Tourist Information Center at Torgalmenning. The **Bergenhus,** a fortress comprising other halls, towers and historical buildings, is well worth a look, although most children find more entertainment in seeing the old wooden houses at **Bryggen** along the wharf of the east, and the **Hanseatic Museum** on the quay, which is open daily June 1–Aug. 31, and on Sun., Mon., Wed., and Fri., Sept. 1–May 31. Don't miss the "Smugs," those narrow streets that often turn into old stone stairways. You'll find these on Upper Street (Ovregaten). A tram trip to Nordnes Peninsula to visit the **Aquarium.**

In summer, Bergen's famous Viking Castle, the **Haakon's Hall,** built in 1250, is the scene for concerts, and there are daily recitals at **Trollhaugen**—Grieg's home which is now a museum—where Grieg's music is played on the maestro's own grand piano. The colorful **Fana Folklore excursion** with folk music and dancing is another happy family attraction. The **Turistkontoret** (TTK) of Bergen og Vest–Norge (Slottsgate 1, N–5000 Bergen) can help you make excursions to nearby Geiranger, Andalsnes, Kristiansund, Molde, Alesund.

Bodo has an amazing Midnight Sun panorama. **Geilo** is Norway's most developed winter sports center with superb downhill and cross-country skiing from Dec. to May. More information from Turistkontoret for Geilo og Hol, 3581 Geilo. **Karasjok** in Finnmark, near Kautokeino, is a Lapp center with a **Lapp Museum** and a silversmith who specializes in old and new Lapp designs; interesting arts and crafts center; river excursions; panning for gold in Storfossen; the Levajok Riding School. Stay at the **Karasjok Gjestgiveri. Kautokeino,** in the lap of Lappland, with reindeer driving races, Lapp wedding festivities at Eastertime and spring skiing. For **Lofoten Isles,** see Fun Trips. **Narvik** has a fine cable car called a telecabin. For junior Audubon members, **Rost** has huge and fascinating colonies of seabirds. **Skien:** Telemark Canal Trip (see Fun Trips). Excursion also from here to **Lekeland Amusement Park. Stavanger** is a treat. A blend of old fishing village and modern city, it offers a dandy **hydrofoil** service to nearby islands, to Sand, Sauda, Sandeid, Bergen, Haugesund, and into the Ryfylke fjords. **The Iron Age Farm** is a reconstruction of a farmstead from the time of the migrations. Outings to the **Lyse Fjord** and other beauty spots can also be made by Fjordcruiser Clipper, a motor launch, a 3½-hour cruise that starts from the quay near the market place, Strandkaien. Best of all, at **Hafrsfjord,** about six miles out of town, you can board the *Leif Ericson,* a true copy of the Gokstad ship in Oslo, and sail off on a **Viking voyage** with a crew in full Viking regalia. For full particulars about these and other excursions, as well as Stavanger's beaches and folk dances, check with the Tourist Office in Stavanger. **Tromso** is the town of trappers and polar explorers. **Trondheim:** The **Nidaros Cathedral** is a national shrine; the **Sverresborg Folk Museum** includes a stave church, and the **Ringve Musical Museum** is lovely. **Vadso** is an outstanding trout and salmon fishing center. **Voss** is a picturesque village. In winter, it is a prime ski resort.

FUN TRIPS The charm of Norway is really not in her cities, although Oslo, Bergen, and Stavanger have much to attract adults and children alike. The real Norway in all its scenic magnificence and excitement will take you west to the **fjords**—Hardangerfjord, Sognefjord, Sunnfjord, Nordfjord, and Geirangerfjord—and north to that winter wonderland in the Arctic Circle.

The fjord country lies between Stavanger and Kristiansund. It's hard to believe that a cleft in the earth's crust, where the sea flows along rock-walled corridors that are 3000′ deep and 3000′ high, is responsible for the marvelous beauty of a fjord, with waterfalls and gleaming glaciers. A fjord is unbelievably and startlingly beautiful. A child who has seen Hardanger fjord in the spring will never forget it. The great trip is to cruise the western fjord and around the northern cape of Norway, from **Bergen** to **Kirkenes** and return. You can do this aboard a coastal express steamer in 11 days, stopping for an hour or so at 35 ports along the way. Some prefer to make the outward journey by boat and return via **Bodo, Tromso,** or **Kirkenes** by bus, train, or air. During the summer, there's also a trip from **Bergen** to **Spitzbergen,** via **Honningsvag** to **Longyearbyen** and **Ny-Alesund,** returning via **Tromso** to **Bergen.** The Honningsvag-Svalbard-Tromso stretch is covered in five days. This trip is not for children under 10! *The Bergen-North Cape-Kirkenes coastal steamship service operators* from whom you can get brochures, folders, schedules and prices include: Det Nordenfjeldske Dampskibsselskap, N–7000 Trondheim; Vesteraalens Dampskibsselskap, N–8450 Stokmarknes; Ofotens Dampskibsselskrap, N–8500 Narvik; Troms Fylkes Dampskibsselskap, N–9000 Tromso which is represented by Det Bergenske Dampskibsselskap, N–5000 Bergen. You can also order an excellent guide *2500 miles on the Coastal Express* from the LRN. RESERVATIONS SHOULD BE MADE AT LEAST SIX MONTHS IN ADVANCE! In spring and autumn, you can travel for half-price, but in summer these trips are booked far in advance. If you really want to make this North Cape Cruise in style and luxury, with the ratio of a crew member for every two passengers, travel on the **Vistafjord** (Norwegian American Cruises, 29 Broadway, New York, NY 10006) embarking from Hamburg. For the same price, I recommend making reservations with the small, select tour groups of **Joseph Edmund,** 151 East 83rd St., New York, NY 10028. Mr. Edmund's land arrangements with optional side trips, his special lectures on each port of call, his handling of baggage and details, his conscientious service, have earned him a devoted following among those who like to travel in comfort and style!

You can also literally be on top of the world, in the **Arctic Circle** where the sun shines at midnight and Kriss Kringle stables his reindeer. It's possible to hire canoes and river boats and sail through reindeer pastures, staying at immaculate, charming, comfortable mountain chalet type guesthouses along the river bank; you can seek out Sames (all the same as Lapps, one 8-year-old reported) in their migrant tent villages, in fine costumes, and fine form when it comes to trading their leather and bone handicrafts; the scenery is fantastic, rivers teem with salmon; the weather, is generally, in summer months, jacket or sweater rather than furlined-overcoat weather; and your children will have a holiday that could only be flawed if you drove the whole distance along Highway B (the coastal highway from Oslo) or if you forgot the mosquito repellent. Those 1500 and some miles of coastal highway do get pretty dreary toward the end, and the mosquitoes, in some parts, seem to outnumber the lemmings in their migratory season, although plenty of repellent will keep them comfortably at bay. But a *trip to the North Cape and the Land of the Midnight Sun should not be missed.* Your itinerary might be **Oslo-Tromso-Alta-Karasjok-Hammerfest,** or the **Arctic Adventure Tour,** or the **Midnight Sun Excursion** offered by SAS (this one is for older children only because it is a capsule junket all packed into one night—oddly enough, a 12-year-old is able to stay up during a daylit night and enjoy it).

The *Victoria,* with a cafeteria and room for 130 passengers, a romantic and elegant boat, makes the 65-mile trip along the **Telemark Canal;** like a form of mountaineering by boat, using 18 locks to gain height. Not for younger children, but preteens and teenagers adore this trip. Starting at **Skien** at 8:30 a.m. on Mon., Wed., or Fri., you reach **Dalen** (240′ above sealevel) at 7 p.m.; 37 miles of lakes, the remainder rivers, canals, and locks—often so narrow that you've only to lean over the rail to pick the flowers growing on either side. Part of the charm is the variety of landscape, from pastoral scenes to the rugged majesty of fjords. Details from TTK Telemark, Box 250, N–3701 Skien.

For a spectacular adventure beyond the Arctic Circle, the **Lofoten Isles** offer an incredible scene of peaky mountains, fishing villages, stave churches, and a real whirling and roaring maelstrom on Moskeness Island (which inspired Edgar Allen Poe's "A Descent Into the Maelstrom"). The climate is mild owing to the Gulf Stream, the largest seabird sanctuaries in Europe are found here, and the huge cod fisheries draw thousands of tourists Feb.–Apr.; Midnight Sun time is early June to early July. You can reach these remote islands by plane, helicopter, train, road, boat, ferry; further details from SAS or your travel agent. The **Bergensbanen** (The Bergen Express) between Oslo and Bergen, tunnels and rollercoasters its 292-mile cross-country route in six hours and 40 minutes. No dining car, but a refreshment trolley is in service during this 200-tunnel ride. If you take the #61 train which leaves Oslo's East Station at 7:30 a.m., you can get off at **Myrdal,** take the shuttle train to **Flam,** eat at the **Fretheim Hotel,** and either return up the mountain to catch the #63 train from Oslo to Bergen, or take a six-hour fjord boat on to Bergen during the summer months.

FUN AND GAMES Norwegians are sports-minded—plenty of sailing, swimming, windsurfing, waterskiing, tennis, shooting, hunting (reindeer, elk, stag, polar bear); and in winter, all winter sports. Some of the best ***fishing*** in Europe in 200,000 trout-filled lakes and salmon-leaping rivers. The season for rod and reel is June–Aug. There are a number of simple yet perfectly adequate and very pleasant country inns that provide room, board, free fishing, and fishing tackle for rent. ***Spring and summer skiing:*** In late Mar. and early Apr., spring skiing conditions at Kautokeino, in Finnmark, include 16 hours of sunlight a day, snow depth of 2′ and an average temperature of 25°F. The heart of Norway's late Feb. early Mar. ski country is the **Gudbrandstal Valley,** central Norway, in the **Rondane National Park area.** Reasonably priced accommodations at the **Mysuseter Hoyfjellspensjonat** on the trail to Rondvassbu Hut in the center of the park, a six-mile, 2½-hour uphill trail. An easier trail from Mysuseter is to the flat area around Furusjoen, a lake nearby. The **Rondane Hoyfjellsjotel** is more expensive. From Oslo, six trains daily to Otta, jumping-off point for Rondane and Hovringen, another good base with seven hotels, and a better choice than Mysuseter for families with younger children. **Summer skiing** at **Galdhopiggen Summer Ski Centre,** Juvasshytta in the Jotunheimen, cross-country trekking. Season July 1–mid Sept.; at **Dyrskar Ski Centre,** Haukelifjell in Telemark. Ski treks, ski school open from May–Aug. for beginners, intermediates and advanced. **Stryn Summer Ski Centre,** Strynefjell, open June to Sept.

Fishing tackle used outside Norway must be disinfected before use in Norway. The local veterinary can arrange this. Anyone *over 16* must buy a national fishing license before any angling can be done in Norway (licenses don't cost much, and are obtainable at any post office). If you're an expert and looking for a first-class salmon beat, contacts for good rivers can be arranged by **Fly-specialisten Reisebureau,** Kronprincesse Marthas Pl. 1A, N–Oslo 1.

Riding facilities for beginners and experts are some of the most interesting in Europe. Pony trekking tours can be enjoyed by parents and children alike.

Jarlsberg Riding Center (Jarlsberg Ridesenter, Nauen Gard, N–3157 Barkakor) offers continuous courses and riding tours from Nauen Farm (3 m outside Tonsberg); 18 horses and two ponies; no accommodations (you stay at hotels in **Tonsberg). Norwegian Youth Hostel Assoc.** (Dronningens Gate 26, Oslo) offers eight-day riding tours in **Hallingdal,** starting either from Skarslia Lodge near Al or Vaset Seter at Ulnes, every Sun., late-June–mid-Aug. Pony trekking on the **Har-**

danger Moors is arranged by the **Norwegian Touring Club** (Den Norske Turistforening, Stortingsgaten, Oslo) late-June–mid-Aug.; each trek lasts a week, instruction on the first day; one of Norway's most beautiful mountain plateaus. The **Oppdal Hotel** arranges one-week tours, starting every Sun. from late-June–early-Aug.; instruction on the first day; plenty of time to fish and hike en route. Seven-day riding treks in the **Ringsaker and Lillehammer mountains** are arranged every Mon., July–Aug. by the **Lillehammer Hestesenter.** At **Stord,** the beautiful island at the mouth of the Hardanger Fjord, the **Sunnhordland Rittel** organizes summer holidays on horseback; many well-stocked lakes, superb wooded and mountain terrain. A week's holiday includes riding instruction, fishing, swimming and accommodations at Ryttergarden Manor; late June–mid-Sept.

And for casual ***hiring of ponies and horses,*** a stableful of possibilities:

At **Skinnarbu** (near Rjukan), horses may be hired for long or short excursions, with a guide, during late-June–Sept. At **Kongsberg,** ¾-hour tours with guide, start daily from the foot of the chair lift. The Kongsberg Tourist Office will make arrangements for you. In the **Oslo** area, **Oslo Ridehus** (Hippodrome, Drammensveien 131) is open daily (except Mon.); Sun. riding parties to Bygdoy or Sognsvann; also try **Tveten Bruk** (Tvetenveien). The **Ekeberg School of Riding** (Ekeberg, Rideskole, Jomfrubratveien 40, Bekkelgashogda) just outside Oslo, is open daily; attractions for children include "circular rides" and driving in prairie wagons and sulkies in magnificent countryside. **Ekt Riding School** (Nygaten 2B, Oslo 1) has horses and ponies; open all year; summer course for teenagers; can also provide horse carriages for outings, including sleds for torch-light rides in winter.

Bergen: Lessons in the **Bergen and District Riding School** (Mathopen 5070). **Espedal:** At Dalseter, lessons for children in the riding school. **Geilo: The Geilo Mountain Riding Club** open June–Sept.; horses by the hour, day, or week. Rates for a guide depend on the number of persons in the party. Children are not allowed to ride on their own, but special children's sessions, generally in the afternoon include the services of an instructor, whose fee depends on the number of pupils involved. **Lillehammer:** Both **Lande Mountain Hotel** (Nordseter) and **Dalseter Mountain Hotel** (Espedalen) rent saddle horses and give instruction. Daily tours in the mountains, with guide. **Molde Equestrian Center** (5 m from Molde in Hestesportsenteret) has Islandic ponies and Norwegian horses. **Tretten: Austlid Mountain Lodge** has a good selection of hacks, fjord ponies, and thoroughbred trotting horses; instruction. Advanced pupils are allowed to ride free of charge, often in company with the instructor. **Vinstra: Wadahl Mountain Hotel** has nine horses; instruction.

Winter sports: A children's *pulk* (Lapp toboggan) weighs only 10 lbs. and may be rented either at your hotel or from the Tourist Office. At all skiing resorts, sleighs, *pulks,* toboggans, snow discs or skid lids, and *sparks* (Norway's special ski scooters), are available for children. All skiing equipment can be easily rented, and as even toddlers are put on skis, you'll be amazed by the vast array of equipment for children. Skiing instruction is inexpensive and available at most ski resorts throughout the winter. The **Norwegian Ski School** operates at Beitostolen, Geilo, Gol, Hemsedal, Hovden, Lillehammer, Mjolfjell, Nordseter, Oppheim, Oppday, Oslo, Rauland, Rjukan, Sjusjoen, Solfonn, Tretten, Tyin, Vinstra, and Voss. At other resorts most hotels have a resident ski instructor. All resorts organize ski classes for children at reduced rates. An example is the ski school at **Tretten:** special children's class daily from 10 a.m.–2 p.m.; ''children's evening'' once a week; playroom with a nanny; toboggans; skating rink. A special is **Seterkleiva** (Frognerseteren) which runs a ski school for asthmatic children; also organizes ski races for under-12s every other Sun. Sled rides (torchlit at night!) are low-cost and available in **Oslo** through Ivar Bakke (Maridalen) or Ekeberg Rideskole (Jomfrubratveien 40), or through any hotel in **Geilo, Lillehammer,** and **Voss.** Ski touring trips by dog sled are also available in wintertime.

Of special interest is **Tomm Murstad's Ski School** (Ovreseter, Oslo) where skiing is made easy by a team of English-speaking instructors; nursery slopes (just right for 2-year-olds and me), advanced slopes, and trails for short tours. Open Jan. 2–Mar.; lessons (group classes or private instruction); Sat. are reserved for English-speaking skiers; on Mon., special classes on floodlit slopes. Inexpensive; topnotch.

Mountain Craft Vacations, The Norwegian Alpine Center (Fosheim Pension, N-3560 Hemsedal) offers courses throughout the year on rock climbing, glacier walks, alpine skiing, river canoeing—for teenagers over 14 and adults. Far too demanding for under-14s.

SHOPPING WITH AND FOR CHILDREN In **Oslo,** don't miss the Forum **Permanent Exhibit** (Rozenkrantgate 7) and **Norway Designs** (Stortinsgaten 28) for sales exhibitions of Norwegian arts and crafts!

For hand-knitted wear for children, also sealskin slippers: **Husflidén** (Norwegian Home Arts and Crafts Assoc., Mollergate 4). They also stock yarn and instructions for knitting sweaters, as does **Maurtua** (Fridtjof Nansens Plass 9, opposite City Hall) where the Setesdal sweaters in the classic style with pewter clasp and embroidered borders are available. A huge variety of sweaters at the **Oslo Sweater Shop** (the arcade of the SAS Hotel Scandinavia at Tullins Gate 5); reasonably-priced sweaters at **The Sweater Lady** (Solligate 2, near the U.S. Embassy). Wonderful variety of hand-knitted winter wear at **Heimen** (Kristian IV Gate 4); also custom-made dept. and dolls in national costume. **William Schmidt & Co.** (A/S Karl Johansgate 41); cardigans, caps and handwoven jackets, gloves, and sealskin slippers, good woolen and suede things. Also, for souvenirs and dolls in national costume: **Hjordis Egelund** (A/S Roald Amundsens Gate 4) and Holmenkollen Ski Jump **Souvenir Shop** (Ski Tower Building at Holmenkrollen). For skis and skiing equipment: **Onkel Tomm** (on the platform of the Majorstuen Station); **Marius & Stein Eriksen** (Ruselokkveien 5); **A. Gresvig** (Storgaten 20); **Speider-Sport** (Stortingsgaten 12); **Sigmund Ruud** (Kirkegaten 57); and **Sport** (Karl Johansgate 27).

In **Bergen,** ***handicrafts*** Norwegian folk costumes, native dolls, and hand-knitted clothes: **Husfliden** (Vaagsalmenning 30) is your best bet. Excellent ***department stores:*** **Kloverhuset** (Strandkaien 10, **Strandgaten** 13); **Sundt and Co.** (Torgalmenning 14) for baby foods. ***Sports equipment:*** **Wallendahl and Son** (Strandgaten 17).

Skiing equipment is available in **Geilo** (at **Geilo Sport** or **Harald Joachimsen**) and in **Lillehammer** (at **Alpin Design, Brusveen Sport, Helleberg, Rustadstuen Sport,** or **Sport & Radio,** all on Storgaten). **Stavanger** is the center of Norway's ***pottery*** industry; **Bordene Pedersen** (Breigaten 5) and **Thomsens Glassmagasin** (Breigaten 11) have enchanting cups and plates. In **Voss,** try **Arne's Sporthouse** or **Voss Sports Service** for ski togs.

NORWEGIAN FRIENDS AND PEN PALS Getting to know the Norwegians is easy—simply apply in person at the **Oslo Travel Assoc.** (Radhusgate 19, Oslo). It's helpful if you write in advance giving your expected date of arrival, but no appointments are made until you show up in person. Arrangements are easy to make except during July and Aug., when most Norwegians are away on their own vacations, but it's not impossible for you to "Know the Norwegians" at this time. Similar programs are in effect in **Bergen** and **Stavanger.** For a fee of $30 **Friends Overseas** (68–04 Dartmouth Street, Forest Hills, NY 11375) will arrange three contacts between Americans and residents of Oslo to make whatever arrangements they wish about meals together, an evening of conversation, sightseeing or other activities. (See also Danish Friends and Pen Pals).

CALENDAR OF EVENTS In **Jan.,** Oslo features a cross-country ***Ski Race*** in Frogner Park. Mid. Jan. there's a ***Winter Sports Festival*** in Geilo, Voss, Lillehammer, and Dombas; skiing, sleighrides, curling, and skating. **Feb.**–Mar., Oslo holds Ski Meets and winter sports at Holmenkollen; ***winter festival.*** In **Mar.,** Rjukan and North Norway greet the Return of the Sun with ***carnivals*** and ***Lapp fairs.*** **Apr.,** Easter week, Nomadic Lapps come to Karasjok and Kautokeino to have church weddings performed in colorful traditional ceremonies. **May** 17, throughout Norway, is ***Constitution Day;*** parades; honoring of the Royal Family in front of the palace in Oslo. Late-May–June, Bergen offers ***International Music, Drama, and Folklore festivities.*** Wonderful.

June 14, in Oslo, is ***Oslo Day;*** parades and celebration. June 21–28, Harstad holds a ***Cultural Festival.*** June 23, throughout Norway—particularly Oslo, Voss, and Lillehammer—***Midsummer Eve*** is celebrated; folk dancing, bonfires, parades, and "wedding" processions. Other June events: in Tromso, ***Polar Day,*** celebrating 24-hour sunshine; ***Skiing Competitions*** in various places; and in Voss, a ***Folklore Meet*** for Children in national costumes (late June).

July 4, U.S. Independence Day celebrations in Sandefjord and Frogner Park Oslo. In July, Hanko holds an ***International Yachting Regatta.*** July 29, throughout Norway, is ***Olsok Eve;*** bonfires commemorate Norway's patron saint, King Olav. In **Aug.,** Geilo features ***Traditional Hallingdal*** (costumed) weddings, parades, and folk dancing. **Sept.** 1–3, Oslo, Bergen, and Trondheim hold ***Student Festivals.*** In mid-**Nov.,** in Skibotn, Lapps gather together for ***Fall Fair.*** In **Dec.,** throughout Norway, Christmas celebrations begin.

LANGUAGE AND PHRASEBOOK English is taught in all the schools and almost everyone speaks and understands English.

Hello	*God dag*	*Goo dog*
I am an American	*Jag er en Amerikaner*	*Yay air ayn amair-ee-con-er*
My name is____	*Mitt navn er____*	*Mitt nomm air____*
I am____years old	*Jeg er____aar*	*Yah air____oar*
Please	*Var so god*	*Vair suh goo-duh*
Thank you	*Mange takk*	*Mahng-uh tahk*
I can't speak Norwegian	*Jag kan ikke snakke Norsh*	*Yay con ikkuh snocker Nawsk*
Yes	*Ja*	*Yah*
No	*Nei*	*Nay*
I am having a wonderful time	*Jag har en deilig tid*	*Yay har ayn day-lick teed*
1	*en*	*ayn*
2	*to*	*toh*
3	*tre*	*tree*
4	*fire*	*free-ruh*
5	*fem*	*fem*
6	*seks*	*secks*
7	*syv*	*see-uv*
8	*otte*	*ah-tuh*
9	*ni*	*nee*
10	*ti*	*tee*
11	*elleve*	*all-vuh*
12	*tolv*	*tall*

13	*tretten*	*tret-un*
14	*fjorten*	*fyawr-tun*
15	*femten*	*fem-tun*
Goodbye	*adieu*	*add-yer*

PORTUGAL

Every family I know who has been to Portugal loves it. Everywhere you'll see flowers, white peacocks and moated castles, donkey-operated water wells, windmills (many whistle and "sing"!), roofs topped with ceramic birds, tile-fronted houses, houses outlined in primary colors like kindergarten drawings, and irresistible hand-crafts at allowance-size prices. Beach resorts along the sunny Coast of Kings near Lisbon and on the Algarve (where chimneys are wedding-cake-like) offer family accommodations at all price levels. Inland, away from mountains and the sea, summer can be almost tropically hot, but most hotels are air conditioned, and flies and mosquitoes are rare. The little-known northern area—aglow with regional art, with beaches and fishing villages, corn granaries on stilts, Celtic and Roman ruins, pine-forested mountains—is well worth exploring; Viana do Castelo, Guimaraes, Nazare, Evora, Vila Vicosa, Tomar, Estremoz in the cork tree and castle provinces of Alentejo and Ribatejo may not be on many people's itinerary, but I hope they will be included in yours. Prices for food and beauty salons are real bargains.

INFORMATION ABOUT PORTUGAL The **Portuguese National Tourist Office** (548 Fifth Avenue, New York, NY 10036) and their branches in Chicago (919 N. Michigan Ave., Suite 3001, Chicago, IL 60611); Los Angeles (3440 Wilshire Blvd., Suite 616, Los Angeles, CA) offer help; a free tourist guide lists hotels, restaurants, museums, events, shops, itineraries for Lisbon, Estoril, Oporto, and Madeira. In **Lisbon,** your major informational source is the **Direccao Geral do Turismo** (Palacio Foz, Praca dos Restauradores; and Avenida Antonio Augusto de Aguiar, 86). Information offices are also at the **Airport** (Tel: (1) 88–59–74); in the maritime stations of **Alcantara** (Tel: (1) 60–07–56) and **Rocha Conde de Obidos** (Tel: (1) 66–50–18); and the **Santa Apolonia Railway Station** (Tel: (1) 86–78–48).

The **Lisbon City Tourist Office** provides information by telephone in *English* (Tel: (1) 36–94–50); *French* (Tel: (1) 36–79–27); *Spanish* (Tel: (1) 36–95–10); *German* (Tel: (1) 36–96–43).

Your best source about accommodations, itineraries, and special interests is **Heyward Associates, Inc.** (Rua da Mae d'Agua, 13, 1200 Lisbon). If you want to check out other travel agencies, contact the **Portuguese Travel and Tourist Agency Association** (Rua Duque de Palmela, 2).

TRANSPORTATION *Motoring:* The **Automovel Club de Portugal** (Rua Rosa Araujo 24, Lisbon 1200) with offices also in **Aveiro, Braga** and **Oporto,** is your source for maps, routes, and information. If you have a breakdown or an accident, call the **ACP Breakdown Service:** in Lisbon; (Tel: (1) 77–54–75/ 77–73–54/ 77–54–02/ 77–54–91); in Oporto (Tel: (2) 29271/ 29272/ 20552). *Gas pumps* are open between 7 a.m. and midnight. *Service stations* aren't open on Sun. or holidays. *Garages and workshops* aren't open on the weekends or public holidays, and are usually closed weekdays from 12:30 p.m.–2 p.m. No problems about *car rentals,* which are easily available, and very reasonable. *Gas* is expensive.

▶ **Note:** Avis offers a special rate with unlimited mileage. You have to book before you leave the U.S. Warning: Traffic can reach gridlock proportions in Lisbon. The **Portuguese National Bus Line** based in **Lisbon** at Avenida Casàl Ribeiro 18, is convenient, inexpensive transport. Compared with New York prices, taxis seem very inexpensive. Radio taxi service in **Lisbon** (77–11–19 and 65–91–51); **Estoril** (26–87–095 and 26–80–067). On a *charter basis,* T.A.P.-Air Portugal, based at Lisbon's Portela Airport (Tel: (1) 244–0553) will fly you anywhere where there's an airport in Portugal, Morocco, Europe, with 24-hour service. The **Aeropiloto Lda.** (Aerodromo Municipal de Cascais, Tires; Tel: (1) 244–0553) has three-passenger planes available with pilots to serve you as convenient, timesaving *air taxis. **Telephones:*** as of press time, the area code for **Lisbon** was (1); for **Oporto** (2); for **Faro** (89); **Madeira** (90); **Azores** (966); area codes are being revised and may be subject to change elsewhere. The good news is that Portugal's hotel associations are members of Teleplan, so that you won't be hit by walloping surcharges on your telephone bills. English-language sources for current attractions are *What's on in Lisbon, What's on in the Algarve,* and *Anglo-Portuguese News.*

HEALTH, WATER, AND FOOD Health standards are fine. I think your children would undoubtedly be happier with bottled water. *Agua de Luso* is nonfizzy. Nonfizzy but "sparkling" is *Vimeiro.*

Food? There is widespread use of garlic, olive oil, tomatoes, and onions. If this is a style of cooking your children are not used to, speak up and say *Sem azeite!* (without oil!), *Com manteiga!* (with butter!), *Sem alho!* (without garlic!). Seafood is first class, chicken and duck are excellent. There is codfish *(bacalhau)* prepared hundreds of ways; octopus *(polvo);* squid *(lulas);* trout *(truta);* grilled sardines *(sardinhas)* are awfully good if the children are old enough to watch out for bones; shellfish in general *(mariscos),* crab *(santola),* clams *(ameijoas),* mussels *(mexilhoes),* shrimp *(camarao).* Veal *(vitela),* chicken *(galinha),* ham *(fiambre),* turkey *(peru),* and liver *(figado)* are almost always delicious, but the delicacy, crisp roast suckling pig, may be too fatty for your children. Chicken (galinha) is often tough, as is steak. The choice of vegetables is usually limited to asparagus *(espargos),* carrots, peas *(ervilhas),* potatoes *(batatas),* spinach *(espinafres),* squash *(abobora),* and string beans. The choice of fruit is unlimited. Delicious *maracujas* (Madeiran quinces) look like kumquats and taste like plums. *Queijo fresco,* like cottage cheese, is liked by most children. Other local cheeses tend to be too sharp or too something for unsophisticated tastes.

But the candies, cakes, pastries, and desserts, well, Portugal is a land of delight for the sweetest teeth ever. The *pudins* (puddings) are frightfully rich. *Pudim de Noses,* a name that seems unbearably funny to children, is walnut pudding. *Pudim Portugues* is orange pudding. *Pastel* can be a pie, a tart, or a pastry; and *rabanadas* is a dessert rather like French toast without eggs. Sugared almonds decorated with flowers are so beautiful you might bring them home as decorations! Every town has special candy and pastry. *Ola* brand ice creams are equivalent to our Good Humors.

In the cities, milk is fine; in the country, check to be sure it is pasteurized. Bottled fruit juices are safe and acceptable and fresh orangeade *(laranjada)* is sold everywhere.

In **Lisbon** there's a convenient snack bar in the **National Library,** or try snacks at **Pastelaria Suica** (Rossio 96); the three-story **Snack Bar das Galerias Ritz** (Ritz Galleries) has a menu illustrating the food, plus desserts decorated for children, in the downstairs snack bar, and an attractive grill upstairs; **Pastelaria Ritz** (Rua Rodrigo da Fonseca 129); **Noite E Dia** (Av. Duque de Loule); and in the Alfama area (avoid it Sun., when men go on drinking sprees). Touristy but with good shellfish is **Soomar** (Ruas das Portas da Santo Antao 108). You can eat well along the Rua das Portas de Santo Antao or in the Barrio Alta.

Near Lisbon, in **Queluz,** at **Cozinha Velha** (Palacio Nacional; Tel: 950–232) you eat in the palace's former kitchen (pillars, great copper hood, copper cauldrons, lanterns, rush chairs, smiling service); if you can't afford the deservedly high tariffs, come for afternoon tea; lovely gardens. At **Sintra,** I'd skip the **Galeria Real de Sao Pedro** as too expensive and instead celebrity watch at the beautiful **Hotel Palacio de Seteais** (Tel: 923–3200), set in tranquil gardens, and too grand to stay overnight in with children.

In **Cascais,** the tavern-style **Pescadore** (Rua das Flores 9) has delicious shellfish, a child-loving proprietor; cozy **Salinha Saloia** (Rua da Palmeira 14) has roast chicken, charcoal steaks, homemade desserts; seafood in the pleasant nooks of **Pipas** (Rua das Flores 18) where onions and peppers garland the ceiling. On the coastal road to Guincho, stop for lunch and a swim in the pool at the pine-forested **Clube de**

Campo Dom Carlos I (Quinta da Marinha). **Oitavos,** on the crest of a nearby hill, is another panoramic stop. At **Praia do Guincho** itself, **Estalagem Muchaxo** (Tel: 285–0342) has a good lunch and super pool. In **Nazare,** good fish-serving restaurants are found all along the waterfront and around the Praca Sousa Oliveira. **Mar Bravo** (71 Avenida da Republica) and **Mar Alto** (27 Praca Dr. Manuel Arriaga) are recommended.

In **Obidos,** with garden patio or cozy dining room (with brick oven and stone fireplace), I think the **Estalagem do Convento** (Rua Dr. Joao de Ornelas; Tel: 95217) is more fun and more delicious than eating at the castle. In **Oporto,** a delightful restaurant tunneled into the rocks so that you feel you're in an airy cave, is **Boa Nova** on Leca beach; good food; rock garden; rocks to climb outside. For elegant and panoramic rooftop dining, **Portucale Restaurant** (598 Rua da Alegria; Tel: 27861); for good family fare and comfort, the **Boa Vista Hotel Grill,** or the **Foz do Douro** downstairs; for ''typical'' fare, the pubs by the river, **Marina** or **Bebeovos. Varanda da Barra,** overlooking the Douro, is also good. In **Viana do Castelo,** cozy tavern-style **Os 3 Potes** (Beco dos Fornos) is a find: regional specialties; exceptionally pleasant; music at lunch and dinner; the bill (moderate) is discretely presented in a pewter box!

On the Algarve, at **Quinta do Lago,** the five-star **Casa Velha** (Tel: Faro (89) 94272) is designed for the beautiful people; too sumptuous for your children's dinner, but well worth going for lunch or afternoon tea.

For other suggestions, see sections on accommodations and attractions.

BABY FOOD All pharmacies plus many supermarkets and specialty food shops stock baby food; most common are Beechnut and Bledine, but you'll also find Mame, Fali, and other European brands.

Baby food range: carrots *(cenouras),* mixed vegetables *(legumes sortidos),* beef with vegetables *(carne de vaca com legumes),* ham with carrots *(fiambre com cenouras),* chicken with semolina *(frango com semola),* beef *(carne de vaca),* veal *(vitela),* sole with vegetables *(linguado com legumes),* pineapple and peach *(ananaz com pessego),* banana with apple *(banana com maca),* orange with banana *(laranja com banana).* Junior range: beef *(carne de vaca),* meat and spinach *(carne com espinafres),* ham with beef *(fiambre com carne de vaca)* beef with vegetables *(carne de vaca com legumes),* chicken with rice *(frango com arroz),* chicken with tomatoes *(frango com tamate),* fish with sauce *(pescada em Bechamel),* sole with potatoes *(linguado com batatas),* mixed fruit *(frutas variadas),* apple sauce *(sobremesa de maca).* Readily available are Farex cereals; Nestle's Milupa, Apramil, and many other brands of milk.

In **Lisbon** Jeronimo Martins & Filhos (Rua Garrett 17) has a wide variety; in **Nazare,** try **Farmacia Sousa** (Rua Nousinho Albuquerque, 22/30, Nazare).

DIAPERS AND LAUNDRY There are no diaper services, but laundry arrangements can be made at your hotel. The word for diaper is *fralda,* and you can get disposable diapers (*fraldas de papel*) at large pharmacies. In **Estoril, Farmacia Parque** (Arcados do Parque) stocks Chicco, Johnson's, and De Ne Nes baby products; snap-on pants, Bebe Confort diaper liners, Qurit, Wandex, and Lanitol. In **Cascais,** try **Cordeiro** (Rua Frederico Arouca and Av. Marginal). In **Lisbon,** a commercial laundry is **Texas** (Av. Almirante Reis 89D) or **Cambournac** (L. da Anunciada 11). In **Cascais, Lavanderia Cascais** (Largo das Grutas) is a self-service laundromat.

EMERGENCIES MADE EASY There's always one ***pharmacy*** (*farmacia*) on night duty in large towns—the name is published daily in the newspaper, or ask your concierge. Pharmacists will fill every type of prescription. Try: **Farmacia Azevedos** (Rossio 31–32; Tel: 327–478) or **Ducal** (Av. Duque de Loule).

For a ***doctor,*** ask your hotel or call the **American Consulate** in Oporto (Rua Julio Dinis, 826–30, Tel: 63094) or at Ponta Delgada Sao Miguel, Azores (Avenida D. Henrique; Tel: (966) 22216), or the **American Embassy** in Lisbon (Av. Duque de Loule 39; Tel: 570–102). In Lisbon, you can also telephone **Hospital Particular de Lisboa** (Tel: 539–031) or the tiny **British Hospital** (Rua Saraiva de Carvalho 49; Tel: 602–020). A pediatrician is **Dr. Campos d'Oliveira** (Av. da Liberdade 212; Tel: 46217). Special children's clinics are the Dona Estefania Hospital and the Hopital de Santa Maria; in Coimbra, the University Hospital; in Oporto, the Sao Joao and Donna Maria Pia hospital.

For ***dentists*** in Lisbon, call **Centro de Medicina Dentaria** (Tel: 684–191). An accommodating ***oculist*** is **Optique Oculista Cristal de Ouro** (Av. Republica 10; Tel: 562–663). For ***first aid*** dial 115.

MAGIC FAMILY HELPERS In **Lisbon,** for babysitters, and trained nurses, **Hospedeiras de Portugal** (Rua Borges Carneiro, 63, Lisbon, Tel: 604–353); for babysitting and kindergarten services (by the hour, day, week) for infants through age 6, **Girofle** (Passos Manuel 84; Tel: 533–308). The **Infantario O Bibe** (38 Rua Eduardo Noronha; Tel: (1) 88–68–66), close by the Queen Elizabeth School, is a recommended kindergarten for English-speaking children. Its teachers are available by arrangement for babysitting *during the day* as well as evening. **Externato Conchinha** (Praca dos Flores 31; Tel: 367–867). In **Coimbra,** babysitting and kindergarten for age 1 month to 3 years at **Infantario Arco-Iris** (Rua Eca de Queiros 7; Tel: 20570) or for infants to age 6 at **Bergo** (Rua Gomes Freire 11; Tel: 20567). Elsewhere ask your hotel concierge.

For English-speaking ***children's companions,*** the **American Consulate** in **Oporto** or in **Lisbon** the **American Chamber of Com-**

merce, the **Church of England** (Rua da Estrela), or the **Women's Club of Lisbon** (Avenida de Sintra, 3, Cascais) should be helpful. Children's playgrounds can now be found in most public gardens throughout Portugal.

For ***kindergartens*** in **Lisbon,** see Infantario O Bibe above; other choices are **Externato Conde de Monsaraz** (Av. Rio Janeiro 56; Tel: 883–974); **Externato Os Pequeninas Amigos** (Ressano Garcia 27; Tel: 557943); **Girofle** (see above). Throughout Portugal you'll find many *infantarios* (kindergartens). Those styled *externatos* are education-oriented, for children 3–7, and not too amenable to looking after visiting children. But those styled *jardims de infancia* are play schools which operate as day-care centers for infants through age 6; usual hours are 8 a.m.–8 p.m.; some board children overnight or for longer periods. Since these are organized chiefly for the benefit of working mothers, and are often connected with schools, tourist information centers have little information on them, so look in the yellow pages of the phone book. Some near Lisbon are: At Queluz, **O Coelhinho Branco** (Rua 1 Lote; Tel: 954751). At Paco d'Arcos, **O Castelinho** (Comte Tavares Melo 2; Tel: 243–5192). At Parede, **Externato A Cegonha** (Rua Octaviano Augusto 1; Tel: 247–4259) is well set up for English-speaking children, will pick up and deliver (7 a.m.–9 p.m.) or board children; kindergarten services plus primary education.

Five good ***English-speaking schools*** in the Lisbon area (charges are a fraction of fees in American private schools) from kindergarten through high school: **St. Julian's** (Quinta Nova, Carcavelos; Tel: 247–0140); **St. Columbus International American school** (Quinta Casa Branca, Carnaxide); **Queen Elizabeth II** (Rua Filipe Magalhaes 4; Tel: 886–928); **Our Lady of Bom Success** (Rua Bartolomeu Diaz 53; Tel: 610–442). **St. Anthony's International School** (Avenida Portugal 11, Estoril), **St. George School** (Quinta das Loureiras, Cascais). Also French-speaking **Lycee Frances Charles Lepierre** (Av. Duarte Pacheco; Tel: 681–101); and German-speaking **Escola Alema de Lisboa** (Av. Norton de Matos, Telheiras, Lisbon; Tel: 791–401). On the Algarve, **St. David's** (Estrada da Mexilhoeira da Carragacao, Estombar), run on English lines, takes children from three years up to "O" and "A" levels.

Personal services? Try **Interpreter Guides** (Sindicato Nacional da Actividade Turistica, Rua do Telhal 4; Tel: 367–170). Interpreter-guide-translator-courier service also in **Coimbra** (Avenida Marnoca e Sousa 35; Tel 26447); in **Faro** (Rua do Letes 32; Tel: 22083/4); in **Funchal** (Rua Dr. Brito da Camara 4; Tel: 30705) in the **Madeiras;** in **Oporto** (Rua Nova de Avilho 180, Custoias, Matosinhos; Tel: 95–29–55); in **Ponta Delgada** (Rua Engenheiro Jose Cordeiro 78; Tel 26244) in the **Azores.** Babysitters, children's companions, guides, and shipping services at **International Travel Service** (Av. da Liberdade 224; Tel: 532–511; Rua Castilho 61; Tel: 534–879). Miss Ellen Broom of **American Secretarial Services** (Rua Castilho 38; Tel: 539–650) offers translation and secretarial services. Beauty salons in Lisbon are excellent and inexpensive.

In the upper level of Lisbon's **Portela Airport,** you'll find a baby bath in the Departure Lounge john, and an attendant not averse to babysitting for short periods of time. **Apolo 70 Drugstore** (Av. Julio Dinis 10A; Tel: 763–233), has a playroom-nursery in which to leave the children while you shop; also snack bar, bowling alley. Hairdressers are generally delighted to take on boys as well as girls and to mind the children while you're under the dryer. Chiropodist: **Salao Rossio** (Pr. Dom Pedro IV, 1; Tel: 326–631). At **Descansauna** (Av. da Republica 83; Tel: 779–602) you can have a sauna and massage while the kids exhaust themselves in the gym.

English-language magazines, newspapers, books at the **American Embassy Library** (Av. Duque de Loule 39) and the **British Institute Library** (Rua Luis Fernandes, 3).

HOLIDAYS FOR CHILDREN ON THEIR OWN The **International School of the Algarve** (Escola Internacional do Algarve, Burros Branco, Porches) for children 7–12, operates as a children's hotel during July, Aug. and Sept.

CASTLES AND OTHER HAPPY FAMILY ACCOMMODATIONS The Portuguese government has developed 30 or so hostelries called **pousadas** (resting places) perched on promontories, and snuggled in villages, all styled as showcases of regional cultural, culinary, and folkloristic heritage. Children under 8 sharing your room are given a 50% discount. Because pousadas are relatively small, rarely with more than 25 rooms, some with as few as six, be sure to book well ahead. The tourist offices in New York or Lisbon will provide you with a complete list. Recommended for reservations and information is **Marketing Ahead** (515 Madison Avenue, New York, NY 10022). Or, you can make arrangements directly with the pousadas, through your travel agency or through the Portuguese travel agency, **ENATUR** (Avenida Santa Joana Princesa, 10–A, 1700 Lisbon). **Estalagens** are almost the same as pousadas, but privately owned, and often somewhat more expensive. Bed-and-breakfast accommodation or longer stays in private houses, manor houses and farms throughout Portugal are another possibility. For further information contact the Directorate-General for Tourism in Lisbon or the PNTO.

It's possible to rent furnished ***villas*** for a week, a month, or longer in the Algarve, Estoril, Cascais, and other seaside areas. They often come complete with an English-speaking staff. *Warning!!!!* Beware of real-estate sharpies! Deal only with recommended agencies, such as **Agencia Oasis** (Arcadas do Parque, Estoril); **Ritta & Ritta Lde.** (Av. Visconde Valmor 15, Lisbon; branch in Paris); or any of the real estate outfits mentioned in Ch. 7. On the Algarve, by far the most attractive villa villages are the privately owned **Vale do Lobo** and the **Luz Bay Club.** About 15 miles from Faro Airport, **Vale do Lobo** encompasses the luxury hotel **Dona Filipa,** under separate British management, but far kinder to your bank account are the Moroccan-style rentals, tastefully designed villas, which come in all sizes and prices. All share a lovely beach; 18-hole golf course; mini-golf; heated swimming pool; and the Roger Taylor Tennis Center with 12 lighted championship courts. If you are considering a long-term lease, there are excellent catering, shopping and school facilities. To book a holiday, rent or buy a property, contact **Vale do Lobo do Algarve, Lta;** Vale do Lobo, Almansil, Algarve. At the **Luz Bay Club** at Praia da Luz (for details write Rua Diretta 102, Praia da Luz, 8600 Lagos, Algarve) some garden-set villas cluster on the hillside while others are closer to the beach—small, quiet, simple, lovely, very reasonable; clubhouse; two swimming pools; tennis, indoor and terrace restaurant; magnificent garden; beach safe for children; nearby watersports, golf, riding. Away from it all in comfort, yet close (by taxi or bus) to Lagos. Still unfinished, the 1600-acre **Quinta do Lago** development, lavish in price and concept, is in the process of reorganization. For details, write: Administrative Mgr., Planal SARL (Quinta do Lago, Almansil, Algarve, Portugal; Tel: 94271). (**Tip:** When dealing directly with a development, you'll receive more information than is usually given lessees if you say you are renting as a potential buyer.)

Simple accommodation in ***pensions*** or breakfast-only boarding-houses at tiny prices? Many too many to describe here; consult the PNTO.

If you are venturesome and don't mind camping out indoors, you'll find ***cottages*** for rent in summer in almost every fishing village. Prices range from rock bottom to very reasonable, but since rental agents don't even consider these, and furnishings and desirability vary so much, it's mandatory to make your own thorough on-the-spot check and to make your own arrangements with the owner for some mutually agreeable advance date (not always easy, since few fishermen speak English). Maybe I'm overcivilized, but if I were going to do this I would pick a village used to foreign visitors (such as Nazare) rather than one where I might feel out of place or find living arrangements difficult to cope with.

Hotels on the Algarve: At **Albufeira,** hotels courting the family trade are mostly in the hills. **Hotel Boavista** has suites with kitchen; pension-basis restaurant; swimming pool with moat for paddlers; moderate rates. **Hotel da Balaia** (3 m E) is a five-star monster (some cottages for 2–6 occupants available) with its own beach, all watersports, heated adult pool, children's pool; babysitters available. **Alijo: The Pousada Barao de Forrester,** in north central Portugal, is based in a 750-year-old village in the heart of the Douro wine-producing area. **Alvor:** If you can afford it, my first choice on the Algarve would be **Hotel Alvor Praia** above the beautiful Praia dos Tres Irmaos; spacious lawns and flower beds; lily pond; pool with moat for toddlers; poolside lunch buffet and snack bar; watersports; tennis (lessons for children); babysitting and supervised playground; early-evening folklore entertainment suitable for children; full complement of boutiques and services; golf privileges at Penina Golf; meals exchangeable with selected other hotels. **Faro: Hotel Eva,** on the harbor, is simple, modern, functional; rooftop pool; restaurant; free bus to beach. Nearby is **La Reserve,** with 20 rooms, each with fireplace; swimming pool and tennis, also. **Monte Gordo: Hotel Vasco da Gama** seems popular with English families; on the beach; pool; tennis, bowling; playground; babysitters; casual dining room atmosphere at lunch. **Praia da Rocha:** The **Algarve Hotel,** atop a cliff, cantilevers its pools (adult and children's) on a terrace; all watersports; babysitting; its costly pleasures include a social director who plans barbecues, sports competitions, excursions, and parties and picnics for children. Far simpler and far less expensive is the old-fashioned **Bela Vista,** once a Victorian summer house, now a guesthouse with only 27 rooms (suites facing the sea are best and costliest); babysitting on request; private sand cove for waders and junior swimmers; book well ahead.

Aveiro: Pousada da Ria has a fish pond in its lobby, a lagoon outside, and terraces from which to watch the *moliceiros*. **Azeitao: Quinta dos Torres** (Estrada Nacional 5; Tel: 228–001) is a secluded stone manor; lovely gardens; good for a lunch stop too, in its handsome dining room or garden gazebo, with an after-meal dip in the pool. **Barcelos:** Albergaria Conde de Barcelos, with modern decor and family suites, is the *only* comfortable place to stay or have a meal. **Berlenga Islands: Abrigos dos Pescadores** is a 17th-century castle fortress, open only during the summer, irresistible to young families, fishermen, and those who just like to laze in the sun—you can't go anywhere until the next boat!—14 delightful rooms on a great rock island in the Atlantic. Nearby restaurant, **Pavilhao Mar e Sol. Braga:** Attractive **Hotel do Elevador** (comfortable, moderate rates, villa-style), with easy prices for lunch or dinner; old-fashioned **Hotel Parque** minus dining facilities; second-class **Hotel Sul Americano** for the determinedly thrifty. Or the **Pousada de Sao Bento,** high in the mountains in a nature reserve. **Braganca: Pousada de Sao Bartolomeu** is pleasant as can be. **Bucaco:** the **Palace Hotel** (Mata do Bucaco; Tel: 93101); its preposterous pomp and splendor will enchant you. On the edge of a forest that children can explore by donkey. Donkeys wear blue jeans to protect their legs from flies and gnats! Moderate rates. **Canicada: Pousada de Sao Bento** offers swimming pool, tennis, and gorgeous countryside one-half-hour from Braga. **Cascais: Hotel Citadela** (Ave. Jose Frederico Ulrich; Tel: 282–921) has suites and duplexes (with kitchenette) ideal for families of three to six; verandas overlooking swimming pool and wading pool; supermarket nearby, or eat in the hotel dining room. Moderate prices. The **Estoril-Sol** is a luxury hotel with a swimming pool. About five miles N of Cascais is the **Hotel do Guincho,** a converted 17th-century fortress with balconied rooms overlooking the Atlantic. **Esposende:** Semimodern **Hotel Suave Mar,** with swimming pool and tennis, is for campers and budgeteers.

Estoril: The deluxe **Hotel Palacio** (Parque; Tel: 268–0400) is *the* place to stay; air-conditioned duplex suites overlooking the swimming pool; poolside snack bar; tennis, mini-golf, golf, babysitting; by far the best hotel, I think, in the Lisbon area; within walking distance of Tamariz beach. **Estremoz: Pousada da Rainha Santa Isabel,** within the walls of the 15th century castle, is a showpiece, lavish furnishings in 23 exquisite rooms; sumptuous bathrooms; lovely dining room, good food, excellent service. **Evora: Pousada dos Loios** is a 15th-century monastery, restored and enlarged in the 18th century, with 28 luxury rooms. Carved doors; vaulted ceilings; fireplace large enough to roast an ox in; dining garden. The nearby **Estalagem Monte des Flores** is said to be on a large estate with horses and carriages for rent, a swimming pool, a castle. **Guimaraes: Pousada de Santa Maria da Oliveira** (4800 Guimaraes): Here in the Cradle of Portugal, 38 miles NE of Oporto, nearby the neolithic remains of Briteiros, with handicrafts and folklore galore, this pousada, comprising six 16th-century houses, luxuriously put together as ten bedrooms and six suites, is the perfect base from which to tour Guimaraes, Braga and environs.

Lisbon: The **Sheraton** has a rooftop pool, but I'd recommend staying at the nearby seaside resorts of Cascais or Estoril. **Madeira:** The deluxe **Palacio** (Funchal; Tel: 30001), with tennis and heated pool, features breathtaking fireworks New Year's Eve and an Easter egg hunt for children. **Nazare: Hotel da Nazare** (Largo Afonso Zuquete; Tel: 46311), modern, comfortable, and functional, offers suites for two. **Pensao Central** (Rua Mouzinho de Albuquerque; Tel: 46100) is managed by a man you should meet, helpful Mr. Guilherme Ramos, the encourager and preserver of Nazare's folklore and dances; accommodations in 20 rooms are simple, old-fashioned, immaculate, and very reasonable! Also budget-priced, immaculate, and simple is **Pensao Ribamar** (Rua Gomes Freire 9; Tel: 46158) on the waterfront; good village-inn-style restaurant; from the balconied rooms you can watch fishing boats drawn onto the beach. Many inexpensive pensions and fishermen's houses to rent too.

Obidos: Pousada do Castelo is a fabulous castle dominating the 12th-century walled city—glistening cobbled streets, whitewashed houses with lichened roofs, windmills in the distance; six rooms only. **Estalagem do Convento** (Rua Dr. Joao de Ornelas), formerly a nunnery, has 13 charming rooms, delicious food. **Ofir: Hotel de Ofir** (Tel: 89383) has babysitting; playground; on the beach; watersports; bowling; tennis; mini-golf; riding; bicycle rental; an aviary in the lobby; hairdresser; boutiques; excellent manager and service. **Palmela: Pousado do Castelo de Palmela,** a castle in the clouds 45 minutes S of Lisbon via the autostrada, with the pousada built around the marble cloisters of a monastery on the castle grounds; mixed modern and traditional interior. You can actually see this pousada from the acropolis of Lisbon's Castelo de Sao Jorge. **Penela: Pensao Gloria** is simple, clean, and cheap for campers and true budgeteers. **Santiago do Cacem: Pousada de Sao Tiago;** site of Mirobriga ruins, the largest Roman hippodrome in the peninsula. **Sao Martinho do Porto: Parque Hotel** for budgeteers. **Setubal: Pousada de Sao Filipe** built into an exceptionally handsome 16th-century fortress on a mountain spur overlooking the sea; **Casa de Sao Joao** (Rua Garrett 18; Tel: 22681), installed in a 16th-century monastery, serving only breakfast; a maze of interesting antique-filled rooms opening onto an inner cloister. **Tomar:** The charming **Estalagem de Santa Iria,** beautifully sited in a tree-shaded park, lacks the comforts, services, and facilities of the big, modern **Hotel dos Templarios** (Largo Candido dos Reis; Tel: 33121) with balconies for viewing the castled hill, swimming pool, tennis, hairdresser, river boating.

Valenca: Pousada de Sao Teotonio. Charming interior belies exterior. **Viana do Castelo: Hotel Afonso III,** catering to British package tours; **Parque,** with swimming pool; **Santa Luzia** on Monte de Santa Luzia, with fabulous views of river, sea, and countryside; swimming pool and tennis; the remains of a Celtic-Roman castro (watch out for the prickly broom) just off the entrance driveway; funicular to its summit (wonderful for a meal or a picnic)—but I unfortunately found poor service, indecently thin walls, seedy bathrooms. Many inexpensive pensions in town. **Vila Nova de Cerveira: Pousada de Dom Dinis** is plush, with three suites, 26 rooms; one half-hour from beaches. **Viseu: Hotel Grao Vasco** (Rua Gasper Barreiros; Tel: 23511) is lovely, comfortable; swimming pool.

Special: for discriminating travelers in search of the unusual, there's a singularly enchanting crenellated castle, with a history that dates back to the Carthaginians, overlooking the sea and a delightful fishing village. This privately owned gem has only eight bedrooms with bath. For reservations, get in touch with the owner, Luiz M. de Castro e Almeida (Castelo de Vila Nova de Milfontes).

CAMPING AND CARAVANING Over 50 campsites are listed in a booklet called *Roteiro Campista,* available from the tourist office, giving all the facilities, plus details about caravan and camping supply rental firms. Near **Lisbon Parque Municipal de Campismo de Lisboa** (Monsanto) has everything from pools to grocery; in **Tomar,** the **Parque Desportivo** also has a pool; in **Oporto,** head for **Prelada** (Rua Monte dos Burgos); near **Angeiras, Matosinhos** has access to several beaches; good restaurant, lovely park, a nearby pool. Camping is forbidden outside authorized parks, but there are campsites all along the coast from **Caminha** down to **Faro,** with scattered sites in the interior and along the Spanish border. For further information, contact **Federacao Portuguesa de Campismo e Caravanismo** (Rua Voz do Operario 1, 1100 Lisbon).

Orbitur, Intercambio de Turismo, SARL (Av. Almirante Gago

Coutinho 25D, Lisbon; Tel: 892–938), has set up a camping-and-bungalow, mountain-and-seaside park with restaurant and micro-market; bungalows for four, fully equipped kitchens, john and shower, for extremely reasonable prices, including maid service! That's what I call camping out in style!

Motor caravans are outnumbered by trailers in Portugal, but some may be found in **Lisbon** at **Marcamp** (Av. Almirante Gago Coutinho 56A). Or perhaps **Contauto/Eurocar** (Av. Antonio Augusto de Aguiar 24C; Tel: 535–115) can help you out. For information about youth hostels in Portugal, contact the **Portuguese Youth Hostels' Association,** Rua Andrade Corvo 46, Lisbon.

ATTRACTIONS FOR CHILDREN IN LISBON All year round the city blooms with special smiles for children. Most museums and attractions are open 10 a.m.–5 p.m., and closed Mon. The waterfront section from the old Alfama quarter east of Praca do Comercio (known as Black Horse Square because of the equestrian statue in its middle) westward to Belem is all up and down, with narrow cobbled lanes, chanted, sung, and shouted through with vendors and hucksters. High overhead, the washing strung between balconies flaps like little flags. The Thieves' Market, **Feira da Ladra,** has masses of stalls dispensing everything from bathtubs to paper flowers. Lisboans enjoy this slice of ''local color'' and most children do too.

Take a double-decker bus, open-air trolley, or a taxi (far from dull, because the drivers drive like Keystone Cops) to the railway station west of Black Horse Square. Between the station *(Cais do Sodre)* and the Tagus River front, you will see a stream of women fish-sellers jogging off to sell their wares (balanced on their heads); early morning is liveliest.

Daily programs and guided tours for children are offered by the following museums: **Ancient Art Museum** (Museu Nacional de Arte Antiga, Rua das Janelas Verdes 95); the **Royal Coach Museum** (Museu Nacional dos Coches, Praca Afonso de Albuquerque, Belem); **Costume Museum** (Museu Nacional do Traje, Parque do Monteiro-Mor, Largo San Joao Baptista 4); **Philatelic Museum** (Museu dos CTT, Rua Dona Estefania 173); **Numismatic and Philatelic Museum** (Casa da Moeda, Avenida Dr. Jose de Almeida). Changing of the Guard at Belem Palace takes place daily at 11 a.m. and 3 p.m. For boys, an artillery museum with a courtyard filled with cannon, and inside, a vast collection of uniforms and weapons, **Largo do Museu de Artilharia** (off the Av. Dr. Jacinto Nunes). The **Aquarium** (Av. Marginal). **Museu de Arte Popular,** a folk-art museum with exhibits or regional costumes and crafts. **Museu de Arte Decorativa** (Largo das Portas do Sol) is of interest to children chiefly for the adjacent craft schools—gold-beating, book-binding and others—at the Fundacao Ricardo do Espirito Santo Silva (#90), open weekdays. Don't miss the tiles at the church of **Madre de Deus**

(Rua Madre de Deus 4), especially those painted by children in the museum in the cloisters. **Jeronimos Monastery** has a magpie collection most people skip but which my children found fascinating (handcrafts, ethnology, etc.); nearby are a **Naval Museum, Fonte Luminosa** (floodlit every evening), and the **Tower of Belem** (for a panoramic view, cross the drawbridge and climb to the ramparts). The **Calouste Gulbenkian Foundation** (Av. da Berna 45) houses one of the world's great private art collections, eclectic and beautiful; children top-rate Manet's soap-bubble-blowing boy, Greek coins, and bronze Egyptian cats; music and dance recitals; restaurant; comfortable chairs.

There are parks and viewing places *(miradouros)* scattered about the city, and funiculars or cable cars will take you effortlessly to the top of Lisbon's seven hills. The children's favorite may well be the view over Alfama and the Tagus from the Santa Luzia belvedere. There is a ***boating lake*** at Campo Grande Gardens; also a swimming pool, rollerskating rink, tennis, a good zoo at the **Jardim Zoologico,** where the gentle elephant Rosie rings for a snack when a one-half-escudo coin (she rejects any others) is placed in her trunk; gardens, boating, roller skating (skates for hire), and driving school for children. Next to the zoo is a new amusement park—**Luna Park.** A special is **Edward VII Park:** Take the extraordinary Santa Justa elevator (at the top of which you'll find a fine restaurant) from the lower to the upper city; or take a funicular from Av. da Liberdade. The park has lots of *miradouros;* goldfish ponds; a veritable Garden of Eden; music; and a lovely cool-hothouse *(Estufa Fria).* Also see the **Castle of St. George.** For relaxing, try **Estrela Garden** (Largo do Estrela), with enclosed playground; or Parque Infantil at **Montes Claros Park,** with playgrounds, supervised swimming pools, picnic areas, gardens. Circus performances in season at **Coliseu dos Recreios.**

A whooping carnival featuring an amateur bull ring, fireworks and marionette shows goes on merrily from June–Sept. The bullfighting season is May–Oct., and generally, there is a bullfight on Sun. and most Thurs. There are ***bull rings*** at Campo Pequeno, at Cascais, staging bullfights on some summer Sun. and Vila Franca (about 19 m) where bulls run loose in the streets in July and Oct. Get your concierge to buy tickets for seats in the shade *(sombra).* They cost a bit more, but are worth the difference.

Discotheques for teenagers are **Ad Lib** (Rua Barata Salgueiro 28), **Pop Club** (Av. Estados Unidos da America 129 a), **Van Gogo** (Alfarrobeira 9). The celebrated *fado* may not turn on your younger children, but all ages find folk dancing and music lively (if you're not a stickler about bedtime—most performances begin about 10 p.m.) at **A. Severa** (51 Rua das Gaveas); and **Lisboa a Noite** (60 Rua das Gaveas), and others your concierge can tell you about.

The following ***movie houses*** have children's performances: **Cinema Vox** (Av. Miguel Contreiras); **Cinema Berna** (Av. Marques de Tomar). Movies are classified A for children over 6; B for over 13s; C for over 18s. In **Estoril,** the theater runs special children's matinees every Sat. afternoon. ***Excursions*** you'll want to make: Cascais, Estoril, Sintra, Queluz, Setubal, and Palmelá—all within about 20 miles. Take the train from downtown Lisbon rather than a taxi; departures every 20 minutes.

ATTRACTIONS FOR CHILDREN ON THE ALGARVE The Algarve—100 miles of tawny-rose cliffs sheltering great crescents of soft, clean sand beaches, and protected on the north by the Monchique mountains one-half hour by air from Lisbon, or a five-hour drive—is beautifully unspoiled by its comparatively recent success. Because of government-controlled building and lack of coastal road (which means villages lie at the end of 1–3-mile lanes to the beaches) it's likely the Algarve will be spared the Miami-high-rise fate of some Spanish and Italian coasts. For centuries in Moorish hands, separate from the rest of the country, its name derives from the Arabic *Al Gharb,* which means "the land beyond," and it *is* beyond compare. The Sotavento coastline east of Faro is hotter and flatter than the Barlavento coast west of Faro—which has cliffs and fantastic, colorful rock formations hollowed by wind and time into archways and tunnels, creating little rock-ringed pools children can claim as theirs. Inland are agreeable whitewashed villages, discreet housing developments, luxurious hotels, simple villa-style pensions, Roman ruins, orange groves, almond orchards, beautiful gardens, golf courses, a complement of other easily accessible things to do and see. Check with the tourist office for the many fascinating fairs and festivals; monthly markets, where animals are auctioned and handcrafts sold, are fun at Albufeira (3rd Sun.), Estoi (2nd Sun.), Lagos (1st Sat.), Loule (every Sat.), Portimao (1st Mon.), Silves (2nd and 3rd Mon.), Tavira (3rd Mon.), Vila Real de Santo Antonio (every Sat.).

In geographical sequence going west from the Guardiana River (where a car ferry to Ayamonte links Portugal with Spain) to the final southwesterly jut of Europe at Cape St. Vincent, here's my selection of highlights: **Monte Gordo** comprises a cluster of hotels, a casino, and a wide beach. **Vila Real de Santo Antonio** is a convenient shopping center with open-air cafes; yacht club; horse-drawn carriages transport you to the lighthouse and to bullfights in July and Aug. Do make a side trip to **Castro Marim,** a 12th-century fortress, walled and wonderful, with a small archaeological museum run by Count Victor Veiros (Rua do Brasil 46), who is most helpful about the Algarve (he can show scuba divers where the remains of a Roman city lie only 1000 feet off Praia Verde or direct you to a stretch of Roman road or to hangman's block in a tiny 200-year-old fortress above a lovely lagoon). Through the center of **Tavira,** the loveliest town in the Algarve, the River Gilao runs quietly under the Roman bridge, its banks edged with balconied houses; palmy parks; a 13th-century castle fun to explore; several fairs Aug.–

Oct.; the tourist office (Praca da Republica) can arrange a full-day trip on a fishing boat (bring a picnic, and sweaters for dawn and early evening).

If you fly from Lisbon to the Algarve, you'll land at **Faro,** the provincial capital. Try to come in mid-July for the **fair** of Our Lady of Carmel. Next to the Eva hotel, the former office of the port captain houses a small **maritime museum** (model boats, fishing tackle, a portrait gallery of fish). If the kids feel ghoulish, trot them off to the **Chapel of the Bones** (Capela d'Ossos), entered through a courtyard behind the Church of Our Lady of Carmel (Largo do Carmo), where the interior decor is artistically worked out in skulls and bones. The best view in town is from the belfry belvedere of the Church of **Santo Antonio do Alto.** Ferries frm the Arco da Porta Nova landing stage will take you to the **S.K.I. Faro Beach Club** (Tel: 25339) which offers ski-boat and sailboat hire and lessons, plus fishing; good food. Side trips for romantics: to **Milreu** (6 m) for the modest, untended, as-yet-unexcavated remains of the Roman city of Ossonoba among the grass and trees of someone's farm; to **Estoi** (6 m) for an abandoned pink house on the ancestral property of the Counts of Estoi, strangly appealing (Victorian statuary, bandstand, twin gazebos, overgrown orchard, beds of roses); to **Olhao,** where there's a great fish, meat and fruit market dockside; to **Tevira,** with its Roman bridge across the Gilao river; or inland to **Loule,** a hilltop town about ten miles NW of Faro, with craftspeople working on leather harnesses, brass, copper and straw articles at the foot of medieval castle walls.

Albufeira's main street culminates in a huge whitewashed archway to the beach; hilly cobbled streets; white cottages cascading between tawny cliffs to the honeyed sand of the bay, which offers safe swimming for children; lively with discos, restaurants, shops, activities; entertaining festivals in late Aug. A rock tunnel separates the sunning beach from the fishermen's beach where painted boats are drawn up on the sand. The ruling crowd are swinging singles, fun-in-the-sun-on-bread-crumbs adventurers, childless couples. Nearby **Rancho Orada** (Tel: 52196) has a playground, restaurant, donkeys to ride; about four miles out, **Algarve Riding Centre** (Quinta da Saudade; Tel: 56178), run by two English girls, has a jumping ring and many ponies. Inland **Alte** (about 20 m), bypassed by progress, is a white and lovely gem, splendid for a picnic. The tourist office at **Armacao de Pera** (Edificio do Casino; Tel: 55145) can arrange a boat for you to see the **Sea Grottoes,** cathedral-size caves entered through arches, nested in by pigeons (not bats, happily), a fairy-tale world of dazzling green water, stalactites, and echo chambers beneath the jutting headland of Our Lady of the Rock (a desolate chapel here—but children prefer the Chapel of the Bones in the Parish Church of **Alcantarilha.**). **Porches,** mid-coast, is where you'll see the best pottery in the Algarve at a studio located along Route 125, **Porches Pottery.**

In **Portimao**—a fishing port, fish-canning and boat-building center—the Algarve's two-wheeled ox carts are joined by brightly painted *carrinhas* drawn by mules, and you'll find good local handicrafts. The local ferry *(Pirata Azul)* can take you across the Arade River ("fun to go just to see there isn't anything to see," my daughter said). The bakery **Panificadora** (on the Silvas–Monchique road) will make bread into any shape you wish; these make permanent decorations if you specify hard bread *(pao duro)* without yeast *(sem fermento)* and then brush them with clear lacquer; draw a picture of anything complicated but, as the bakers render their own interpretations, don't expect fidelity to your design; they're best at human and animal figures, and letters. It's fun to eat at the alfresco charcoal grills beneath the bridge along the promenade of the Arade estuary. **Praia da Rocha**—a covey of hotels, villas, and boarding-houses above tawny red cliffs, fantastic rock formations, caves, and rock tunnels massed on a beautiful beach—was the Algarve's first resort and has remained popular and beloved. For a private picnic, try the little beach of Van (about 3 m), with a trio of glorious rock formations, just off the Praia da Rocha–Alvor road. Praia dos Tres Irmaos (Beach of the 3 Brothers) at **Alvor** is the most beautiful, it seems to me, of all the beaches, circled by giant red and gold rock formations keyholed with tunnels and passageways. Riding? Mrs. Jennifer Townson, M.B.H.S., R.A.N.A. (Quinta dos Kelpers, Caldas de Monchique; Tel: 92219) has a stable at nearby **Alfarrobeiras** (Via Chao dos Donas); lessons for children; dear little ponies for very small children, trail rides for older ones. A pleasant excursion is to **Silves,** to its 10th-century Moorish castle and gardens; pigeons to feed; the caretaker's wife earns extra money by making sweet little doll's-house chairs. Archaeology buffs might like to know about the few uncovered mosaics (not as interesting as those at Milreu) and a Roman city yet to be excavated at **Abicada** (on someone's farm; not easy to find). At **Alcalar,** in a sunbaked field just before the Penina Hotel (children are *not* admitted to its casino), are the remains of a Neolithic necropolis; most of the findings are in the museum at Lagos.

Lagos—with lovely old sections, ancient city walls, narrow streets, tile-faced houses—was Prince Henry the Navigator's principal maritime base. If you'd like it to be yours, check in at the **Lagos Sailing Club** (Clube de Vela de Lagos) where you can hire sailing dinghies. Walk along the broad esplanade and look at the fishing boats until you come to the **Church of Santo Antonio** (Rua Silva Lopes); the chapel lined with blue-and-white tiles is a golden masterpiece of baroque carving, plumped out with smiling cherubs. Right of the Church is the **Museu Regional de Lagos** with stuffed birds, local crafts, coins, opium pipes, farm implements, ouch-looking ancient medical kits, filigree chimneys, bells, pictures made out of cork, an archaeological wing with findings from all over the Algarve—assorted curiosities of the sort children adore and learn a great deal from. **Alpendre Restaurant** (Rua Antonio Barbosa Viana 17) is open for lunch and dinner; excellent mixed grill; typically Portuguese decor. **Praia Dona Ana** is sheer enchantment: tiny cove amid fantastic grottoes, arches, caves sculptured and colored red and gold by wind and weather, with clear greeny-blue water. You can rent boats here and be rowed around the promontory and through the grottoes and tunnels, a delectable trip. There's a small cafe at the top of the steps to the beach. **Praia da Luz** is a large beach, site of the Luz Bay Club development (with swimming pool, restaurants, windsurfing). Fisherman will take you out in their boats; the water is quiet and calm for family swimming. On the beach, **A Concha** restaurant has delicious waffles, chopped beef, spare ribs, chicken in the basket, just what the children wanted! **Sagres,** a rocky escarpment jutting out into the Atlantic, was where Henry the Navigator founded his School of Navigation, the first in the world; you can see his great stone compass rose, chapel, and house (you must ask the tourist office to let you in) and, in the Sagres Auditorium, a 3:45 p.m. daily film tells his story. At the promontory of **Cape St. Vincent** (3 m) is a lighthouse (the caretaker will be delighted to take some small gratuity for showing you around); on the way stop off at the **Fortelezo do Beliche** (fortress of the cabin), an old fort turned into a pleasant place for a snack. Or, eat at the **Sagres Pousada,** or at the seaside restaurant, **Tasca do Rolim.**

ATTRACTIONS FOR CHILDREN ELSEWHERE Abrantes: Worth a stopoff for the massive hilltop fortress with museum in the chapel. **Alcobaca:** A **pottery** center; its famous peaches are sold in the Fri. market under the walls of the **Monastery of Santa Maria** (where King Pedro the Cruel is entombed); once the richest monastery in Portugal, it's an interesting combination of Cistercian austerity and culinary extravagance (the stream flowing through the kitchen provided fresh fish and served as a dishwasher!). **Amarante:** Children will delight in the local confectionary. Outside of **Atouguia da Baleia** at Casais Brancos (between Peniche and Obidos) are many cylindrical **windmills** with conical tops, their besailed arms strung with clay pots that whistle and sing in the wind, none more beautifully than that owned by Joao Firmino, cited by the Portuguese Society of Friendship to Windmills as having a particularly handsome windmill; he is delighted to show tourists how it works. The musical pots *(buzos)* are unique small souvenirs your child might like to exhibit at school. No signs, but Lisbon's Turismo Cruzeiro can direct you. **Aveiro:** A city of water; immense **lagoon** traversed by *moliceiros* (curving-prowed, brightly painted craft used for gathering eels, and seaweed for fertilizer). The tourist office (Av. Dr. Lourenco Peixinho) will arrange four-hour **motorboat trips** from the city's canals through surrounding saltpans, islands, and bayou-like waterscape. The **Vista Alegre Porcelain Factory** (near Ilhavo, 3 m away), open weekday afternoons, has a museum explaining history and techniques. **Azenhas do Mar:** Seaside resort; a charming hillock of houses above a lovely bay and the sandy sweep of **Praia das Macas,** a safe beach for children; swimming pool, riding, hotel, and campsite.

Barcelos: Local **handcrafts** sold in the Torre da Porta Nova *underneath* the ruins of a Braganca palace; Thurs. market (Campo da Feira) is splendid for handcrafts. **Batalha: Abbey of Santa Maria de Vitoria,** undoubtedly the most beautiful Gothic building in Portugal, has a royal cloister in which stone is transformed into lace. **Beja:** A walled city with orange trees and shady squares, has (1) **Museu Rainha D. Leonor** (in the 15th-century Convent of the Conceicao) with engaging artifacts ranging from Roman lamps and Victorian medicine cases to the grille through which a nun and her French lover exchanged kisses recorded in *Lettres Portugaises d'une Religieuse,* an 18th-century best-seller; (2) a **castle** with ramparts to climb and a small military museum. **Berlenga Islands:** See "Fun Trips." **Braga:** To emphasize age, the Portuguese say that something's as old as the **cathedral** in Braga. It is 13th-century and somber, but children head for the sunlit cloisters and are transfixed by the ex voto offerings in the chapel—explain beforehand so they won't make embarrassing remarks about all the white wax hearts, pigs, cats, legs, ears, and paper-wrapped packages surrounding the carved figures of saints; upstairs is a museum treasury (and a guide who knows nothing interesting about it). Outside the church, you'll usually find women selling pinwheels. You can lunch at **Restaurante Regional Inacio** (Campo das Hortas 3), cheap, filling, good, or you wait until you get to the cafes around the hilltop **Bom Jesus do Monte,** a popular pilgrimage site three miles southeast of town reached by funicular, by car up a steep hairpinny road, or on foot by a dazzling baroque staircase with crossed balustrades designed as a way of the cross (chapels at each landing contain startlingly realistic scenes from the Passion). Devout pilgrims make the climb on their knees and, though you'll also see paid and proxy penitents, it can be a touch-the-heart sight.

At the snack bar at **Cabo da Roca** (off the Cascais-Sintra road) you can get a certificate stating you have been to the most westerly point of Europe; terrain of golden broom, wild canaries, X-winged windmills; a lighthouse to climb. **Cascais:** A paradise for boat lovers and water skiers; the harbor is colorful, the village pleasant with citadel ramparts. Visit the **Museu Castro Guimaraes** (on the Guincho road just before the wave-dashed Boca do Inferno), a tiny fortress moated by the sea, with a lovely park, gardens, and library. Its **Clube de Campo Dom Carlos I** (Quinta Marinha; Tel: 289–220), in a pine forest, is a private club willing to accept visitors for a meal, sauna, swim in the pool, picnic, tennis (lessons, rental of rackets and balls), and riding (see also Fun and Games).

Citania de Briteiros is a virtually unheard of (even in nearby cities) but exceptionally rare and interesting archaeological discovery accessible if you follow the Guimaraes–Braga road to the thermal resort of Taipas; there you take the Povoa de Lanhoso road as far as the church of St. Estevao de Briteiros, branch left to Salvador de Briteiros to Citania (altogether about 10 m from Guimaraes). Begun as a Bronze Age settlement of autochthonous pre-Celtic people, it reached its zenith about 300 B.C. under the cultural influence of Celtic invaders, and was abandoned about A.D. 300 when the peace of Rome no longer compelled the locals to seek shelter in the rocky hills. You and the caretaker's family may be the only people around this unique *oppidum* or *castro;* you can walk freely, undisturbed by tourist claptrap, through the 150-family settlement and ruined round huts (2 reconstructed) for an experience as engrossing and educational as you could wish for. The pottery, jewelry, carved figures and other artifacts found here are in the Martins Sarmento Museum in Guimaraes. There are possibly close to a hundred more such settlements unexcavated up in the hills; **Sabroso** (from Taipas follow the Santa Christina de Longos road to Cancela where you'll have to ask which tiny dirt road to take to the rocky hill site) was once excavated but is now so overgrown and remote I can suggest it only as a picnic site for romantic pioneers.

Coimbra: This university city is serene (except during the May student carnival) and beautiful. **Portugal dos Pequenitos** (Portugal of the Little Ones) playground contains miniature buildings and monuments representative of Portugal's provinces and territories, a delight for the 4–14 set. Romantic **Quinta das Lagrimas,** a little flower garden with fishpond and forest walks, is ideal for a picnic. Be sure to go to **Conimbriga,** Portugal's finest archaeological find, with almost perfect, brilliantly colored mosaics; gardened pools and piping system plus three Visigoths' skeletons in a glassed-in pit are open daily to sunset; museum-restaurant-bar near the entrance; bus from Coimbra lets you off at Condeixa a mile away (taxis can then transport you). **Esposende:** Calm beaches, pinewoods, quiet fishing-village life, and the site of a Roman city and necropolis (villagers use the jagged stones as pointy-toothed property walls). **Estoril,** playground of the rich and noble, is an easy commute from Lisbon (via electric train to Cascais). Its **Tamariz beach** is the best in the area, with rentable canoes, rowboats, motorboats and skis, paddleboats, umbrellas, tents, sun cabins, changing rooms. A number of hotels have swimming pools and all major sports (see Fun and Games). Medieval **Estremoz,** a national monument, rises white and dazzling from the Alentejo plains; its ancient walls, marble and stucco houses, narrow streets are crowned by the **Castle of Dinis** which enfolds the luxury Pousada da Rainha Isabel. What my children liked best were the *bonecos de Estremoz,* the little painted clay creche figures and figures of peasants at their daily tasks for which Estremoz is famous, sold at stalls in the market square and in a few shops (nowhere else in Portugal can you find these beguiling figurines), and displayed at the attractive small **Regional Museum** (Rossio 62B). Also see the **Castle Chapel** (walls covered with *azulejos* showing scenes in the life of Queen Saint Isabel of Aragon, wife of King Dinis). Stop for a meal at the Pousada da Rainha

Isabel or at Aguias d'Ouro (Rossio do Marques de Pombal 25), but be sure to allow time to visit the **Museum of Crist** (Villa Lobos, on the Estremoz–Vila Vicosa road, near Borba; Tel: Borba 94412), displaying 3000 crucifixes and figures of Christ dating from the 8th to the 20th century from 36 countries, as well as antique mortars and pestles and regional artifacts of exceptional interest. The owner, Manuel Lobo, who paints, carves designs in powderhorns that are sold at Williamsburg, is an expert on Portuguese heraldry and landscape design, and encourages his neighbor to make weather vanes in animal and bird silhouettes (if you would like one made to your own specifications Manuel will see that it is sent to you). Down the road, he has hand-built a small house (with 2 bedrooms, attic dormitory for 4, small orchard, mite-size pool) and he extends an open invitation to teenagers or students (even a family) to stay on this farm, paying him nothing if they are willing to work around the place or arranging with him whatever terms they wish. Anyone interested in western Portugal's handicrafts or antiques will find him delighted to act as a guide. His offer is friendly, hospitable, and made out of his gratitude for his many American friends. **Evora,** a museum town with the **Roman temple of Diana,** has historical monuments, masses of flowers, the claim to the "cleanest streets in Europe," and, in the **Church of Sao Francisco,** a chapel adorned with the bones and skulls of men and women of holy orders. Once children realize that the lattice work is made of rib bones and that the sunburst is of thighbones, they can hardly be winkled away from columns whose capitals are composed of human skulls. Walk around the **Praca do Giraldo** and the shops that line its arcades to see extraordinary cork, tin, leather, pottery, and silver crafts. The cedar-scented **Regional Museum** houses church treasures, tile-faced stairway, primitive paintings, and an ivory virgin who opens up like a medical model to show scenes in her life. The interior of the **Espiritu Santo Church** is very special. **Taxidermy** is a local art, and the leading *embalsamador* displays stuffed birds and animals at the bus-stop marketplace. On the outskirts of town is a superb complex of **swimming pools.** The place to eat is Giao. Fun fair and huge market of regional goods at June's **Feira de Sao Joao.**

At **Fatima,** the shrine of **Our Lady of Fatima** has special pilgrimages on the 13th of May, June, July, Aug., Sept., and Oct., the May and Oct. pilgrimages being the most important. On these dates, Fatima is jammed. **Guimaraes:** The impressive empty shell of the 10th-century castle is attractive to children, wild rabbits, and stray goats; its Church of Our Lady of the Olive Trees (Largo da Oliveira) houses the **Museum of Alberto Sampaio;** on Fri. a **linen market** in the handsome square; the **Martins Sarmento Museum** in the church of Sao Domingos (Rua da Paio Galvao) tops on my Must-See list, contains all the finds from Citania, Sabrosa, and Penha plus a spellbinding Celtic fertility statue known as the Colossus of Pedralva. The **Palace of the Dukes of Braganca,** heavily restored, contains tapestries, antique furniture, paintings, porcelains. If at all possible, go to nearby **Penha,** not to see the shrine of Fatima, but to discover the historic, dramatic, romantic park of huge boulders, giant caves, and forest pathways behind the inn: a former pre-Celtic, Celtic, and Roman stronghold ingeniously landscaped with belvederes and walkways into one of the most memorable small natural parks you can imagine. The children will go wild and so will you. Take a picnic lunch (you can get coffee or cold drinks at a small cafe by the inn). **Leiria:** It's a huffing and puffing climb to the 14th-century fortress and summer palace, but what a site for a picnic! **Nazare** is an extraordinarily charming, don't-miss fishing village whose fishermen are costumed in handsome tartan outfits. The *lota,* the mid-afternoon fish auction, is the daily big event. Vasco da Gama prayed here before he went to India. Take the funicular to the **Sitio** (upper town), with a lighthouse to explore. Mr. Guilherme Ramos (Pensao Central), guiding light behind the **Ta-Mar folkdancing group,** will arrange a 45-minute, fast, spinning *corridinho* with four dancers and three musicians just for you; on Tues. and Fri., you can watch rehearsals at the Casa do Pescadores (Avenida Vieira Guimaraes).

Obidos, a walled city which is a national monument, may be self-conscious in its charm but is a delight for those who like their medieval manicured. Take the sentries' walk on top of its walls. Nearby is **Caldas da Rainha,** the production center for amusing glazed pottery. **Ofir:** With a pine-fringed beach and good accommodation, this is an ideal base for touring the fascinating, little-known Minho. **Oporto,** where the industry is port wine, stands on the site of a pre-Roman settlement called Portucale, from which the name Portugal is derived. **Quinta de Conceicao,** the municipal park in the suburbs, features lovely gardens, swimming pool, recreation area and pleasing playgrounds. **Palacio de Cristal** (Rua Dom Manuel 1), another park, is the site for a winter circus, a summer amusement ground; a year-round sports pavilion. Mini-golf and lovely gardens at the **Passeio Alegre Gardens** in the Foz do Douro section. The **National Museum of Soares dos Reis** (Rua Dom Manuel 11), housed in a neat but not gaudy palace embracing a pooled and beflowered courtyard, is a nerve-soothing collection of religious sculpture—my children's favorite was Cain as a boy—ceramics, silver, glass, jewelry, Portuguese and Flemish paintings; a refreshing half-hour. In contrast, the **Ethnography Museum** (Largo de Sao Joao Nova 11) has the fascination of an attic filled with toys of a bygone era, its dolls, bucolic valentines, folk pottery, nutshell airplanes, miniature furniture, puppets, baptismal candles on display in a style all parents will recognize as Middle School Exhibit Day. In the same square is the **Sao Francisco Church**—wild gilded wood carving in the interior; spooky subterranean museum of liturgical oddments; crypt overflowing with bones and skeletons; terrace overlooking the Douro River. I'd skip the Stock Exchange (Praca Infante Dom Henrique), boasting a Moorish Hall inspired by the Alhambra. The Tourist Office will arrange for you to visit the **Sandeman port wine lodges** in Vila Nova de Gaia on the river front, some 250 yards beyond the Porto bridge; also **Gondomar,** across the Douro, where you can watch artisans whipping up gold and silver filigree jewelry. Do have a meal at the Boa Nova (see Food). Comfortable *launches for excursions* along the River Douro leave **Cais da Ribeira** daily except Mon. Ask the Tourist Office (Praca General Humberto Delgado). In the old fortified village of **Ourem** (outside the charmless modern town of Vila Nova De Ourem, close to Fatima) a fountain and flowers cluster around its 15th-century **castle;** hardly changed since the Middle Ages and a national monument, it's an enchanting place for a picnic lunch; the tourist office in your hotel can arrange for you to attend the medieval banquets and pageants here. **Palmela:** If you're in the area, you might stop briefly to see the medieval fortress-castle and Roman road behind it. **Penela:** This hilltop village, with the beautiful shell of a 12th-century castle rising from the rock, is a photographer's delight. **Peniche,** a Roman-walled town on a promontory, is a fishing village with net mending and boat building to watch; **Cabo Carvoeiro lighthouse** to explore (tearoom here); excellent fish at A Gaivota restaurant on the wharf; miles of white sand beach and dunes, but offshore swimming is dangerous. **Portinho de Arrabida:** backed by pine-forested hills, with a lovely scimitar sweep of sand, has a pleasant inn and restaurant, a convent with shrines of the stations of the Cross above it in the hills, nearby grottoes that you get to by boat, the scent of thyme and pine in the air; *very* crowded in the summer.

Queluz: The pink **palace** isn't much to look at, but its gardens are bewitching, and its Conzinha Velha restaurant is one of Portugal's best. **Sao Martinho do Porto,** an away-from-it-all village priced for budgeteers, has a fine, safe, soft-sand **beach** sweeping around a scallop-shape cove; easy boat hire; good meals at Estalagem Concha. **Setubal:** A fishing port with beautiful **beaches;** do see the **Church of Jesus,** with twisted taffy-like marble columns and lovely blue-and-white tiles (one of an elephant trampling a lion). From here take the hovercraft to the Troia peninsula (see Fun Trips). **Sintra,** which Byron called a little Eden, is a beautiful drive from Lisbon; magnificent *quintas* (country estates) along the way have wrought-iron gates and chimney tops surmounted with ceramic birds. Brisk through the Royal Palace (closed Tues.). Take a horse-drawn carriage from the square to the **Castle of Pena** (closed Mon.), a whimsical mixture of Snow White and Rhineland fortress which Richard Strauss considered the loveliest thing he had ever seen. Or take a horse-drawn carriage to the old Moorish **Palacio de Sintra** with its ramparts, gardens, fountains, tile mosaics. On the second and fourth Sun. of every month, there's a **market fair** at Sao Pedro de Sintra; always fun. Try the *doce regional* (regional sweetmeat) *queijados*—small, sugary cheese tarts. At **Sobreiro** (between Mafra and Ericeira), make a detour if you possibly can to watch farmer-ceramicist Jose Silos Franco (Tel: 52420) at work. Single-handedly, he has created a little **open-air**

museum around his studio workshop incorporating farmhouse accommodations furnished as they used to be, a real windmill, a model pottery village, many working-model windmills, a wine press. There's even a swing and a whirligig for small children. Mr. Franco loves to have families visit him.

Tomar is outstanding. In the center of town is a three-acre island of trees and flowers, encircled by the Nabao River in which turns a creaking waterwheel (its sound romantically evocative of a sailing schooner). High on the hill, illuminated at night, is the glorious **castle** built by the Knights Templar; Henry the Navigator added the Gothic cloister; later it became the Convent of Christ—a hauntingly beautiful structure that some call Portugal's history in stone. At the foot of the hill is a lovely municipal **park,** all forest and gardens, with a playground. The arcaded Town Hall, the central square diamonded with black-and-white mosaics, the gentle Nabao overhung with willows (rowboats for rent at the hotels), on whose banks is the very reasonable Bela Vista Restaurant with a vine-covered trellis. Frequent **market fairs** with processions. Sept. fairs (traceable back to Sumerian origins and Greek and Roman harvest rites) are marvelous fun, with fireworks; check dates with the tourist office. Make an excursion from here to Ourem. **Viana do Castelo** is northern Portugal's center for pottery and regional handicrafts (for sale in its shops or Fri. market). Praca da Republica, the town square with a fountain and cafes in the arcades, is a photographer's delight. Antonio Cunho's **AVIC** (Avenida dos Combatentes; Tel: 23432) is a travel agency that operates boat trips for fishing and picnicking at Barco do Porto (a lovely river site on the Lima) and Quinta Santoinho (a farm-style restaurant with corn threshing, folk dancing, fireworks, bonfires, barbecues, and other programs); for details contact AVIC's Barbara Andrews. If you'd like to see rugs being made (you can have one made to order), if you're interested in local handicrafts, or if the children want to ride an amiable horse, head for **Somartis** (Rua de Monserrate; Tel: 22413) just north of town; run by beautiful people (they have children, naturally). **Vila Cova** (on the Curvos road, branching off from the road between Ofir and Barcelos) is a dream spot of vineyards, camellias, orange groves, where villagers are curious about cars and visitors; near the village of Perelhal, I explored a broad path leading into the pinewoods and uncovered wheel-rutted stone, an unlooted section of the Roman road tying in with the Via Romana from Braga to Madrid, so there well may be remains of a Roman settlement near by. **Vila Vicosa** is an old dominion of the Dukes of Braganca, dominated by the **Ducal Palace** (contains arms and armor, 17th-century coaches, furnished personal apartments) set on a huge square once used for bullfights. Have a look at the **Pantheon** (opposite the Palace) and the **Museum of Sacred Art** (Rua Doutor Oliveira Salazar) with amazingly realistic polychrome statues (Santa Rita de Cassia, whose black-and-gold dress has to be touched to discover it isn't fabric, is the saint who saves the lives of children). The rosy stone **castle** has a very deep moat (no guardrails, so be careful) where at twilight white fantail pigeons, ducks, and white peacocks come to roost; the castle interior, with first-floor archaeological museum, is open daily. Don't miss the **Church of the Conceicao** also enclosed by the walls, its interior completely covered with *azulejos* (blue-and-white tiles).

ATTRACTIONS IN THE AZORES This archipelago, 900 miles from Europe and 2000 miles from America, only a two-hour flight from Lisbon, comprises nine islands, on which **Ponta Delgada** on San Miguel Island, is the largest town. There is a **toy museum** in Ponta Delgada; there are little local museums, volcanic cones, extinct craters, thickets of flowers, caves to explore, soft sand beaches, and an abundance of opportunities for fishing. The **Terra Nostra Hotel** (Rua Padre Jose Francisco Botelho), in the botanical gardens of the same name, is located in the Furnas Valley on San Miguel. Golfing, swimming, boating, sailing, tennis, hunting; handicrafts; folklore and festivals; car rentals. For further information: **Delegacao de Turismo dos Acores em Lisboa** (Rua dos Navegantes 21, 1200 Lisbon); **Delegacao de Turismo de Ponta Delgada** (Avenida Infante D. Henrique, 9500 Ponta Delgada, Azores).

ATTRACTIONS IN MADEIRA Ideal for relaxing, a land of perpetual summer. Porto Santo and Madeira are the only settled islands of the eight isles. **Porto Santo** has five miles of sandy beach, windmills, a tiny village, an ancient fort, fossil beds, and looks quite like the Sahara. **Madeira** is brilliant with flower and fruit, lush plains, and mountains. It offers boating, watersports, fishing, golf, tennis, hiking, and wonderful excursions. Try to see the New Year's Eve fireworks at the **Savoy** in **Funchal,** the capital, the greatest display imaginable. The **Savoy** and **Reid's** are the old-time hotels; **Casino Park** is ugly on the outside but, as Wilfrid Sheed remarked, "I'd rather be inside it (it's superbly run) looking at Reid's than the other way 'round"). Fascinating Funchal has cool mosaic pavements and jacaranda trees; terrific markets; if you have only one day, include a pull around town in a **bullock car**—a cross between a canopied four-poster and an old-fashioned sleigh on greased wooden runners that slide leisurely over the cobblestone pavement. Stop and look at the flower and fruit markets, the embroidery shops, displaying charming children's clothes; all that delicate-looking handwork can survive years of wear and washing. Try the toboggan or **running car ride** from the hill resort of Monte, or the restaurant **Terreiro da Luta.** Here you will find a lively assembly of sturdy men (in white, with ribboned boater hats) ever ready to provide a three-passenger wicker chaise on runners and race down a half mile, guiding the wicker chaise with ropes. Sample the pastries at **Mimo** (Av. Zarco); **Iris** (Rua das Pretas); **Felisberta** (Rua das Pretas); or **Minas Gerais Tea Room** (Av. Infante).

To hire a car, check with the Tourist Bureau (Av. Arriaga; Tel: 20156). These are other ***excursions:*** Try **hammock-riding.** A hammock, called a *rede,* is slung between two poles. You are carried by two porters who have remarkable endurance. (It's the greatest form of locomotion ever devised for putting your children to sleep.) The porters carry you along mountain paths or anywhere you want to go. Conceivably, you could cover the whole island, but a half day of this is enough for most children and their parents. For details, check with the Tourist Bureau. If you are driving, there are little country inns to stop at. Very little English is spoken, so you may want to take a guide. Bring along a picnic basket because, without advance notice, you can't just pick up a good meal along the way. Places to head for are **Camacha,** an upland village apprenticed almost totally to the art of wickerwork and basketry, **Sao Roque do Faial,** a fantastic-looking little village; and farther on, **Faial,** with a nice little restaurant, **Casa de Cha,** where you can have a hot meal *if* advance arrangements have been made; and **Camara de Lobos,** a lovely locale. Check with the Tourist Bureau in Funchal before you set off; they can tell you where and when markets or *festas* will be held, and give you excellent maps and guidance.

FUN TRIPS Boats and donkeys are often available throughout Portugal. (See Madeira for bullock cars and hammock riding, and the running car ride which is the closest thing to a rickshaw ride in Europe.) For short trips, most children will find the old-fashioned coalburning and even wood-burning choo-choos in the country lots of fun. The Portuguese Railways operate the **Historical Train,** a steam locomotive circa 1881–1908, on the narrow gauge track of the **Tamega Line** *(Livracao-Amarante-Arco de Baulhe).* You can see the locomotive at the Livracao station; the carriages and memorabilia are at the Arco de Baulhe station. The Portuguese Railways also operate the **19th-Century Train** on the wide gauge track mostly on the **Minho** line, between Oporto and Valenca. This steam train's British locomotive is housed at the Nine station, and its carriages, saloon cars, luggage van at the Valenca station. Check with the **Amarante Tourist Office** (Rua Candido dos Reis) and the **Oporto Tourist Office** (Praca General Humberto Delgado) to find out if you can schedule a ride aboard these beauties.

From **Lisbon,** the two-hour ***boat trip*** on the Tagus (leaves Terreiro do Paco, also known as *Praca do Comercio,* twice daily at 10:30 a.m. and 2:45 p.m. The 15-minute ***ferry*** (car and passenger) across the Tagus will take you to the towering Crist the King monument, where an elevator lofts you 732 feet for a 12-mile panorama. At **Caparica** a tiny ***narrow-gauge railway*** with open coaches runs along a fine stretch of beach (but the coast here is inclined to be windy, the water rough, and you might find the people too Coney-Island-like).

From **Setubal** take the ***hovercraft*** that skims all day during the summer to the sandy isthmus of Troia for a beach picnic, a snorkling survey of the remains of the Roman city Cetobriga that has crumbled into the sea, or a look at the giant Torralta hotel complex; this trip can be made by car via Grandola. Car ferry and regular ferry service year round.

From **Peniche** a one-hour ferry (exciting when the sea is choppy) leaves 10 a.m. for the rocky Berlenga Islands for a day's fishing (equipment available in Peniche), sunning, and eating at a fortress inn; take books and games, as the launch doesn't return until 6 p.m. and there's nothing else to do except watch wild hares. In July and Aug., ferries leave at 9 a.m., 11:30 a.m. and 5 p.m.

The yacht club in **Vila Real de Santo Antonio** arranges ***boat trips*** up the Guardiana River.

FUN AND GAMES In Portuguese ***bullfights,*** bulls are not killed. Very exciting is a bull-run—led by herdsmen on horseback, a herd of bulls run through the village streets while every able-bodied man tries his skill as amateur bullfighter (try to get the children up on a balcony looking down on the street—otherwise the crush is unbearable). In the Algarve, bullfighting can be seen in **Vila Real de Santo Antonio,** Albufeira, Lagos, and Portimao, in July and Aug., a traditional and colorful spectacle.

Swimming is great. In the **Lisbon** area you'll find pools in Lisbon (Sheraton Hotel roof) where you can have lessons and enjoy many beach attractions; Hotel Palacio in Estoril; Atlantico Hotel in **Monte Estoril;** Estoril Sol Hotel in **Cascais;** or at the great Muchaxo Hotel at **Guincho.** Although the greatest beaches *(praias)* are of course in the Algarve (see Attractions), good beaches also stretch from Lisbon to Cascais; I'd recommend swimming *only between Carcavelos and Cascais* (the water between Oeiras and Lisbon is dubiously keekee in my opinion, and at Guincho the sea is not safe for children because of too many currents and a strong undertow). The beach with the mostest is Tamariz (Estoril); the sandy coves at Cascais are quieter.

Watersports near **Lisbon?** Waterskiing and motorboat rental are available at Estoril Sol Hotel in Cascais. Sailboat, fishing-boat, and motorboat rental at the Cascais yacht club (Clube Naval; Tel: 280–125); just show your membership card from your home club and pay a small fee (club services include fencing, ice skating, roller skating, swimming). Elsewhere such rental tends to be spur-of-the-moment through yacht clubs or shipping yards *(estaleiros).* In Setubal, try Americo Esteves T. Cirne (Estaleiro, Praia Saude; Tel: 22863).

The local tourist office or your hotel can make ***fishing*** arrangements for you. Sagres and Carrapateira have the best fishing grounds. Underwater fishing centers are the Berlenga Islands, Sesimbra, Sines, and Lagos. Enthusiasts should contact **Centro Portugues de Actividades Submarinas** in Lisbon or the **Clube dos Amadores de Pesca de Portugal** (Rua do Salitre 105).

Riding? Check with the **Centro Hipico de Cascais** (Quinta da Guia, Cascais) and **Centro Hipico da Marinha** (Quinta da Marinha). **Centro**

Hipico da Costa do Estoril, Lda., located on Estrada da Charneca, Cascais, is another outstanding riding school. Estoril also offers a hunt club with a good fox-hound pack.

Coursing (chasing rabbits with greyhounds)? The concierge at the Palacio Hotel in Estoril, can arrange this for you.

In Cascais, you can ***bowl*** at the Hotel Estoril Sol or, if you are over 14, play pinball and other mechanical solo games at the boutique-amusement center of Pompadour Saint-Louis (Rua Frederico Arouca). ***Go-karting*** (Tel: 268–0965) near Estoril's Casino.

Itinerant ***circuses*** play in rural areas with no fixed dates. In **Lisbon,** the circus plays at the Coliseu dos Recreios (Rua P. Santo Antao; Tel: 361–997).

Tennis? **Estoril Tennis Club** (Estoril Park; Tel: 268–1675), with temporary membership, ball but not racket rental; bar and terrace. In the **Lisbon** area also: **Clube de Tenis do Jamor** at the National Stadium, Cruz Quebrada; **Clube Internacional de Futebol** (CIF), Avenida Dr. Mario Moutinho; **Clube Internacional de Tenis** Rua Prof. Sousa Camara 193. In the north: **Clube de Tenis do Porto,** in **Oporto;** also, Lawn Tennis Clube da Foz; in **Miramar,** Clube de Tenis de Miramar; in **Viana do Castelo, Clube de Tenis de Viana.** There are courts at most leading hotels. But nothing in Portugal can compare with the tennis complexes in **the Algarve** at **Vale do Lobo,** and **Albufeira.**

In Estoril, an 18-hole ***golf*** course at Clube de Golf do Estoril open to nonmembers except weekends, where children can have lessons; mini–golf behind the Palacio Hotel. Other championship courses are: **Estoril-Sol Golf Club** at **Linho** on the Estoril-Sintra road; **Lisbon Sports Club** at **Aroeira,** Fonte da Telha (on the left bank of the Tagus river); the **Oporto Golf Club** at **Espinho;** Miramar Golf Club at **Praia de Miramar; Vimeiro Golf Club** at Praia de Porto Novo, Vimeiro; in **the Algarve** at **Quinta do Lago Golf Club** at **Almansil; Dom Pedro Vilamoura Golf Club** at **Vilamoura; Palmares Golf Club** at **Meia Praia, Lagos.**

Bicycles can be rented almost anywhere (look in the yellow pages under *''Bicicletas–Aluguer'')*, but motorcycles, motor bikes, and scooters are hard to find.

SHOPPING WITH AND FOR CHILDREN Shops open at 9 a.m., close two hours for lunch, some noon–2 p.m., others 1–3 p.m. All shops close at 7 p.m. but are open on Sat. June–Sept., many shops close Sat. at 1 p.m.

Among the most interesting buys are handicrafts: pottery from Caldas da Rainha, Alcobaca, Barcelos, Estremoz; fishermen's sweaters and crocheted shawls; hand-woven textiles; embroideries; lace; dolls in regional costume; painted furniture from Alentejo; decorated baptismal candles; baskets. These can all be found in Lisbon, Cascais, Estoril, but are less expensive and in greater variety in the provinces of their origin.

Lisbon: for infants' and young ***children's clothes:*** **Castro** (Rossio 71) delectable baby things. **Pre-Natal** (Largo do Carmo 4) has everything for infants to 4-year-olds. Enchanting embroidered hand-made dresses; feeding dishes, baby toys, bassinet sheets and coverlets, and christening dresses. **Principe Real** (Rua da Escola Politecnica 12), with luxury linens, and hand-knit baby things at surprisingly reasonable prices. **Melanie** (Rua Capelo 8) offers christening dresses, charming smocked and embroidered poplin dresses, underwear, coats, hats, sandals, linen and cotton suits, sun dresses; for girls up to 5, boys up to 4. **Casa Xangai** (Av. da Republica 19A), hand-made, hand-embroidered clothing for boys and girls up to age 6. Complete line of baby accessories. Christening dresses and dear little shirts. Knitted things tend to be a bit overberibboned, but the baby dresses are dreamy. All of the following carry embroidered place mats, linen, handkerchiefs, blouses—plus fairy-tale christening dresses: **Casa Regional da Ilha Verde** (Rua Paiva de Andrade 4); **Madeira House** (Rua Augusta 131–133); **Madeira Superbia** (Av. Duque de Loule 75A); **The Ritz Hotel Shop; Principe Real** (Rua da Escola Politecnica 12–14); **Leacock's** (Rua do Ouro 157, Av. 24 de Julho 16).

Old England (Rua Augusta 100) has ready-made and custom clothes for boys 10 up; **S–3** (Barata Salgueiro 31A) has sizes 0–16, milk bar, hairdresser, discotheque, books, toys, and shoes; **Materna Maxi** (Barata Salgueiro 28) is for preteens and teens; for teens too: **Pitaxo** (Rua Serpapinto 16), **Rosa e Azul** (Rua Garrett 27), **Tara Boutique** (Rua Ivens 68), **Sopal** (Rua Ivens 62). Department stores are: **Armazens Grandella, Lda.** (Rua Aurea 205), **Grandes Armazens do Chiado** (Rua Nova do Almada 110); **Casa Africana** (Rua Augusta 161). The first also carry toys.

For toys, try: **Pinoquio** (Praca dos Restauradores 79–80), **Casa Bernard** (Rua Garrett 84), **Estudio Tom** (Rua Ivens 34); little wooden dolls with hand-painted folklore costumes; three flights up, but well worth the climb. **Kermesse de Paris** (Rua 1 de Dezembro 127), and toy-shop **Rosarinho** (Rua Augusta 260). **Casa Senna** (Rua Nova do Almada 50), and **Spril** (Rua do Carmo 21); feature sports equipment, games and puzzles; **Casa das Corticas** (Rua da Escola Politecnica 4–10); dominoes and chess sets made from cork. For toy soldiers and puppets, **Cutileiro** (Rua das Furnas 30).

For ***camping supplies*** and ***sports equipment,*** **Vieira Campos** (Rua da Prata 215).

For dolls and souvenirs, try: Gift shop at the **Ritz Hotel; Caniche** (Rua Borges Carneiro 11B); **American Tourists Service** (Rua Castilho 61); **International Travel Service** (Av. da Liberdade 258); **Casa Regional dos Acores** (Rua da Misericordia 94–98). Folk music, fado, and other recordings at **Centro de Artesanato** (Rua Castilho 61). For rugs (custom-made too!), **Somartis** (Rua Joaquim Antonio de Aguiar 29). For tiles made to order (with your name or other lettering), go to **Sant'anna**

(Rua do Alecrim 95); you can watch their wares made at the factory (Calcada da Boa Hora 96).

You can buy marvelous fireworks at **Almeida & Oliveira, Lda.** (Trav. Nova de S. Domingos 8–10). During the Christmas season, this little shop also carries *presepios* (nativity scenes made with little terra-cotta figures, moss, and colored paper).

Bookbinding is an unbelievably beautiful and inexpensive art in Portugal. The workmanship is superb. You can bring a book to be bound, or you can select the bindings and then send on the books to be bound by the dealer of your choice. Remember that bookbinding is an art and takes time. It may take two weeks or two months, but in this case I wouldn't mind waiting two years because the result is breathtaking. Suggested bookbinding establishments are: **Frederico d'Almeida** (Rua Antonio Maria Cardoso 31); **Fundacao Ricardo Espirito Santo Silva** (Largo das Portas do Sol 90); and **Oficinas de Sao Jose** (Trav. dos Prazeres 34). At the latter you can watch work done by apprentices aged 11–17, under the supervision of elder craftsmen.

Suggested ***bookshops*** in Lisbon are: **Bertrand** (Rua Garret 73), and **Diario de Noticias** (Largo do Chiado 6). Both places sell English books and magazines. If you want to start your child off with a library of rare books and bindings, try **Livraria Coelho** (Rua da Misericordia 27), or **O Mundo do Livro** (Largo da Trindade 12).

Cascais: Fishermen's sweaters at **Peter's Shop** (Rua Regimento 19 Infantaria 12/14A); baby clothes and toys at **Botinha Azul** (next to S. Jose theater) or **Materna** (Rua Frederico Arouca 51); baptismal candles at **Agencia Magno** (Rua Frederico Arouca 62A). **Estoril:** Head for the excellent shops in Arcadas do Parque; **Huimberto R. Duarte** (toys, sailboats, beach hats for small fry, dolls); **Madeira House** (children's sweaters and embroideries); **Galadouro** (food, candies, snacks); **Tabacaria do Parque** (English books, crayons, paints). **Estremoz:** You can buy *bonecas* in stalls in the market square or at **Jose Marcelino Moreira** (Rua da Nina 12). **Nazare:** Recordings of the Ta-Mar folksingers at **Casa Souslinha** (Rua Alexandre Herculaneo); ask for *Vira da Nazare* and *Nao Vas Ao Mar, Tonio* (Don't go to the sea, Tony!). For regional articles, **Jorge Goncalves** (Rua Mousinho de Albuquerque 89); the fishermen's stockings are great for winter. **Obidos:** beautiful handwoven materials, baskets, loom in operation in **J. Ramos** on the main shopping street.

PORTUGUESE FRIENDS AND PEN PALS There are no organized facilities for meeting the Portuguese at the moment, so see Chapter 2 for general recommendations.

CALENDAR OF EVENTS No country has more folk festivals and fairs and *romarias* (religious festivities combined with fun and games). Whenever you see a crowd of people, follow them. They are almost always heading for a market fair or festival. I have not gone into full descriptions because they all feature the same basic attractions with regional variations—brilliant folk costumes, fireworks, flowers, singing, music, dancing, usually bullfights, all the county-fair attractions of farm animals and poultry, stalls of charming things to buy and good things to eat and drink. The Portuguese National Tourist Office in New York will supply you with a basic list of the major fairs and festivals, and once you are in Portugal, consult the SNI for local events. Market fairs, for instance, take place every Thurs. at Barcelos and Malveira, and on the second and fourth Sun. at Sintra, and on the 29th of every month at Leiria. These market fairs, though far less elaborate than *romarias* or festivals, are a delight too.

In **Jan.,** Obidos celebrates the ***Festival of St. Anton;*** Feira, the ***Fogaceiras Festival,*** in honor of St. Sebastian; and the northern provinces, ***Festivals*** in honor of St. Sebastian and St. Vincent. **Feb.** brings to Evora the ***Festival of the Little Jars*** in honor of Our Lady of the Candles. Abrantes holds its annual ***Fair of St. Matthew;*** Guimarais an annual ***Fair of St. Torquatus.*** Outstanding ***Carnival*** celebrations at **Estoril** near Lisbon; **Loule** in the Algarve; **Ovar** near Oporto; **Torres Vedras** in central Portugal. In **Mar.,** Loule and Portimao hold ***Festival.*** Mar.–Apr., Aveiro features an annual ***Boat Fair.*** Leiria opens its annual ***Fair.*** Mar.–May, all over Portugal, ***Children's Concerts*** are given under the auspices of the *Fundacao Musical dos Amigos das Criancas.* All information is supplied by this organization at Travessa de Sao Placido; 50; Lisbon (Tel: 667–545). **Apr.,** ***Religious Festivals*** at Mafra. You'll find them throughout Portugal, during Easter week. The ones in Braga, Penacova, Alcochete Constancia, Santarem, Serpa, and Almeirim are special. Great Easter festivities at **Braga.**

In **May,** Santarem celebrates the annual ***Fair of the Ribatejo.*** Matosinhos features a ***Pilgrimage*** of Senhora de Hora—important in northern Portugal. Other May events include: ***Festival of Crosses*** (Barcelos); ***Festival of the Burning of the Ribbons*** (Coimbra); ***Religious Festival*** (Sesimbra); ***Festival of the Roses*** (Vila Franca do Lima). May 12–13, the ***First Annual Pilgrimage*** takes place in Fatima; less important pilgrimages on the 13th of June, July, Aug., and Sept. May–June, Lisbon holds its ***Annual Horse Show.***

In **June,** Amarante celebrates ***Festival of St. Goncalo;*** Lisbon holds its ***Festival of St. Anthony*** and popular saints. On June 24, the ***Festival of St. John*** is featured in Lisbon, Braga, Evora, Figueira da Foz, Fontainhas, throughout the province of the Alentejo, and in Sobrado and Valonga. In **July,** the ***Red Waistcoat Festival,*** with marvelous bullfight, at Vila Franca de Xira; the ***Fair of St. Santiago*** at Estremoz; and a Village Festival at Sao Joao da Madeira. **Aug.,** the ***Green Cap Festivals*** at Alcochete; the ***Aljubarrota Fair*** at Batalha; and the ***Festival of Nossa Senhora da Agonia*** at Viana do Castelo. Aug–Sept., there are ***Regattas*** in Cascais Bay.

Sept., at Viseu, the annual ***Fair of St. Matthew;*** horse market and cattle fair. Benavente holds its ***Annual Fair;*** Moita celebrates the annual ***Festival of Our Lady of Good Voyage;*** Cascais holds its International Horse Show; and Sintra opens its ***Festival of Our Lady of the Cape.*** Nazare, ***Our Lady of Nazare procession.***

Oct. 5, throughout Portugal, is Portuguese ***Republic Day;*** military parades and festivities. Oct. 12 and 13, Fatima features its second Annual ***Republic Day;*** military parades and festivities. Oct. 12 and 13, Fatima features its second Annual ***Pilgrimage.*** Other Oct. events are: the annual ***Fair*** at Vila Franca de Xira, highlighted by bullcatching in the streets; the ***Festival of St. Iria*** and the ***Fair of the Dried Raisins*** at Tomar; the annual ***Fair*** at Monchique; the ***Fair of Piety*** at Santarem; and the Fair of ''Our Lady of Mercy'' at Sintra. In **Nov.,** Penafiel, Portimao, Golega, and throughout Portugal, ***St. Martin's Fair*** festivities are held. The ***Fair*** at Golega features a horse show. At Mafra, is the ***Festival of St. Andrew;*** at Cartaxo, is ***All Saints' Fair,*** including a bullfight.

In **Dec.,** Feira opens the ***Beekeepers' Honey Fair.*** Throughout Portugal, every house and shop window sets up a *presepio* (Nativity scene) and a Christmas tree. On Dec. 31, Funchal, Madeira holds the ***Feast of St. Sylvester;*** magnificent fireworks.

LANGUAGE AND PHRASEBOOK In principal centers you can get along with just English, but be sure to have your hotel porter write your destination or needs on a slip of paper, and take along a two-way phrasebook. Many names derive from trees and occupations—Ferreira (iron worker), Oliveira (olive tree), Pereira (pear tree), Silva (blackberry). On bathroom doors, ***S*** stands for women, ***H*** for men. *Crianca* means child.

Hello	*Ola*	*oh-lah*
I am an American	*Sou Americana (girl)*	*so ameri-con-nuh*
	Sou Americano (boy)	*so ameri-con-noh*
My name is——	*Chamo-me——*	*Sheh-moo-mair*
I am——years old	*Tenho——anos*	*Ten-you——anoosh*
Please	*Se faz favor*	*soo fash fah-vor*
Thank you	*Obrigada (girl)*	*oh-bree-gah-duh*
	Obrigado (boy)	*oh-bree-gah-doh*
I can't speak Portuguese	*Nao sei falar Portugues*	*now say fal-are port-oo-gaysh*
Yes	*Sim*	*seem*
No	*Nao*	*now*
I am having a wonderful time	*Estou tendo um tempo maravilhoso*	*Shtoh tyen-doh oom tem-poh mara-veel-yo-soh*

1	*um*	*oom*
2	*dois*	*doy-aysh*
3	*tres*	*tray-sh*
4	*quatro*	*kwot-troh*
5	*cinco*	*seenk-oh*
6	*seis*	*say-sh*
7	*sete*	*set*
8	*oito*	*oy-toh*
9	*nove*	*narf*
10	*dez*	*dash*
11	*onze*	*orns*
12	*doze*	*doze*
13	*treze*	*trayz*
14	*catorze*	*cat-tawz*
15	*quinze*	*keenz*
Goodbye	*adeus*	*ah-day-oh-sh*

SCOTLAND

The Scottish people may have earned a reputation for being thrifty with money (and you'll find prices reasonable), but they are extravagant with courtesy and hospitality. Children are welcomed everywhere—except, of course, in pubs. Remember that in Scotland "Scotch" is an adjective that applies correctly only to whisky, broth, and other American colloquialisms. It's the home of Scots and the Scottish (but not Scotland Yard which is in Victoria St., London, its name deriving from a mansion once occupied by the kings of Scotland during their visits to England). While Scotland is more church-going than most of Britain, gas stations are usually open on Sun. as a concession to visitors; although some restaurants shut down, there are always plenty of hotels and cafes where meals can be had. Scotland is becoming more relaxed about observation of the Sabbath, and only in the far northwest is it hoped the visiting family will not disport themselves too much on that day.

Pony trekking is very popular. You frequently see families carrying golf clubs, the smallest toting a sawed-off niblick, for the Scots often play golf as part of a family walk. The lucky child whose father is an ornithologist, geologist, or archaeologist will get to explore Islay and Jura, or help search for sea-buried treasure in Tobermory Bay. The child of the golfer, fisherman, and hunter will spend most of his time in the Highlands. Fascinating but far from the beaten track are the Orkney Islands, where the summers are nightless and the brown-trout fishing spectacular; the small Fair Isle, where those beautiful patterned sweaters are knit; and the wild Shetland Islands, where the ponies and wool come from; the Inner Hebrides, wet, wild, bleak, but fascinating for naturalists.

INFORMATION ABOUT SCOTLAND Information about Scotland is available from British informational sources (see England), or from the **Scottish Tourist Board** (23 Ravelston Terrace, Edinburgh EH43EU; Tel: (031) 332–2433). Most cities and islands have marvelous local tourist information offices. The BTA or STB will provide a full list of these. ***Reference books and booklets?*** British Tourist Authority publications, AA guides, the Egon Ronay food and hotel guides that cover England, also cover Scotland. Also useful are Scottish Tourist Board's accommodation guides and such books as STB's *Scotland—1001 Things to See*. Special interest books are also available from **British Travel Bookshop** (40 W. 57th St., New York, NY 10019). Campers, adventurers, nature-lovers, geologists, archaeologists, and those who wish to sample the life of a lordly laird, should get *Getting Around the Highlands and Islands*. *Scottish Island Hopping* by Jemima Tindall (Hippocrene Books) is a detailed guide, mixing history and practical advice.

Godfrey Davis Europcar rental car offices at Aberdeen, Edinburgh, Glasgow, Inverness and Prestwick airports, Rail Drive locations and many cities. Look in the Yellow Pages for nearest agency, or call their Central Reservations office in London.

For the Edinburgh International Festival, late Aug.–mid-Sept., full details about schedules and accommodations are available from the **Edinburgh Festival Society** (Dept. 33, 21 Market St., Edinburgh EHI IBW).

HEALTH, WATER, AND FOOD Health standards and water quality are tip-top. Hotel managements will try to produce hot dogs, hamburgers, and milk shakes. But as one puzzled child rightly said, "Maybe we should stick to Scottish food. It's more American than American food."

Scotch broth (a hearty vegetable soup); the joy of fresh-caught salmon and trout; oatcakes, scones, heather honey, Dundee marmalade, barley broth, are specialties children will enjoy. Cheeses are delicious, and there are many of them. The haggis is not an animal to be shot as the old joke goes, but a special dish of chopped meats, onions, oatmeal, and spices. Scots take it with what they euphemistically refer to as "gravy"—very groovy gravy—straight whisky! One sip between each bit is customary. (Children forego the gravy!) Haggis is not always on the menu; you order it a day in advance. The whisky will always be available. Bannocks (flat griddle cakes) are filling and good.

Other specialties include: roast haunch of venison with rich brown sauce; game pie; scallops of salmon; haddock mousse; partan bree (delicious pureed crab with cream sauce); cock-a-leekie (boiled chicken with leeks, prunes, onion, rice, and carrots); pigeon pie; wild rabbit stew; beef galantine; salmi of pheasant (divine); clootie dumpling (suet-cidally fattening dessert with raisins, spices, apple, and dredged in sugar); orange and banana flummery (with whipped cream, nuts, and brandy—not too much for the children!); auld kirk pudding with butterscotch sauce (a fluffy steamed pudding); scotch trifle (sponge cake, custard, jam, glaceed cherries, and strips of angelica plus nuts); Dundee cake is a teatime standby.

In **Edinburgh** for morning coffee and afternoon tea, **Jenners, Macvittie's, Guest**—all on Princes St. Good chain restaurants, **Crawfords Ltd.** (off Princes St. and throughout city). The great find for lunch, just outside Edinburgh, is a beautiful manor house—where children ask to be taken as a treat—or a festive dinner just for parents: **Prestonfield House** (9 Priest Field Rd). Fine for children is the **Farmhouse Restaurant** (121 Princes St.). Outstanding and different: The **Beehive Inn** restaurant (18 Grassmarket) in the old part of town; children will appreciate the Omelette Royal Swan and the Steak Diane; delicious gourmet fare, but no children under 8 allowed. A good fish restaurant is **Merman's** (8–10 Eyre Pl). Also popular is **Laigh Kitchen** (117A Hanover St.).

BABY FOOD (See England Baby Food section). The chain of **Boots Chemists** has a terrific selection; stunning quantity in Edinburgh: **Cow & Gate** line of soups, cheese savouries, beef and tomato dinners; a full line of **Heinz;** baby and junior foods; a few British specialties like rose hips puree; Robinson's egg custard and full cereal milk foods; Farex cereals; SMA milk, Ostermilk, Cow & Gate milk; Ovaltine teething rusks, Farley's rusks, Chuckles rusks; variety of fruit and vegetable juices. **Milupa** and Boots' own brand of baby food are excellent.

DIAPERS AND LAUNDRY Chemist shops stock disposable diapers (nappies), diaper liners, and waterproof pants, as do department stores and baby specialty shops. At **Boots Chemist** (101 Princes St., Edinburgh; Tel: 225–8331), and other branches. All-in-one disposable diapers such as Snugglers, Peaudouce, Robinson's Cosi-fits, Pampers, Boots' own brand are good. Paddipads and Boot's own brand disposables fit into plastic pants which are also available.

No diaper services that I know of, but many laundromats and laundries will take on the chore.

BABY EQUIPMENT FOR HIRE In Edinburgh, strollers can be hired at the Zoo. **Scott Brothers** (40 Cockburn St.) rents cots, strollers (pushchairs) and carriages (prams).

EMERGENCIES MADE EASY Everyone knows that a doctor graduated from Edinburgh University is one of the best there is. Graduates from the Edinburgh Dental Hospital are considered tops too.

Hospitals in Edinburgh: **Bruntsfield Hospital** (1A Whitehouse Loan 10; Tel: 447–4745); **Dental Hospital** (32 Chambers St. 1; Tel: 225–5261); **Royal for Sick Children** (9 Sciennes Rd. 9; Tel: 667–1991); and many others. For ***Doctors and Dentists*** recommended by the American community, check with the **American Consul General** (3 Regent Terrace; Tel: 556–8315). For trained nurses, male and female, a 24-hour service, call **British Nursing Assoc.** (50 George St.; Tel: 225–7840); or **Brunsfield Helping Hands Agency** (See Magic Family Helpers).

MAGIC FAMILY HELPERS ***Babysitters:*** It's not to worry in Scotland. Jolly lassies can be acquired at any hotel to mind your wee bairns. In **Edinburgh,** the **Bruntsfield Helping Hands Agency** (45 Barclay Pl.)

will provide babysitters, housekeepers, family helps and trained nurses. **Guardian Babysitting** (28 Sthalmond) will find you a babysitter.

Kindergartens: The following have been recommended to me, but, as I haven't used any of them, I cannot give a personal appraisal:

Murrayfield Kindergarten (76 Murrayfield Gardens); **St. Ann's Nursery and Kindergarten** (14 Strathearn Pl.).

Instruction: The **Scottish Youth Hostels Assoc.,** National Office, (7 Glebe Crescent, Stirling, Tel: Stirling 2821), offers summer courses in canoeing, field studies, pony trekking, climbing, gliding, highland safaris, riding, sailing, and Try-a-Sport (see Children's Camps). In winter (Jan.–Apr.), courses in snowcraft at Glencoe.

For nature lovers, the **Scottish Field Studies Association** (Kindrogan Field Centre, Enoohdu, Blairgowrie, Perthshire) runs field studies courses for 14s upward at several of their centers. The Orkneys are a naturalist's paradise, and courses in botany and bird-watching are run by **Orkney Field and Arts Centre** (Links House, Birsay, Orkney). **Holiday Fellowship** (142–144 Great North Way, London N.W.4) runs a host of holidays which include archaeology, country life, sport.

Supervised residential riding courses or holidays are offered by **Wright's Riding Academy, Ltd.** (Sandhill Estate, Southwood Monkton By Troon, Prestwick; Tel: Prestwick 77979). Residential centers for riding holidays, and local riding schools, are listed in *Where to Ride,* covering the entire British Isles. All information and booklet from the **British Horse Society** (British Equestrian Center, Kenilworth; Warwickshire).

Scotland is world-famous for its fishing waters and facilities. Courses in fly fishing techniques are offered by the **School of Casting** (P.O. Box 10, Inverness IV1 ITP) for adults and juniors. Salmon/trout fishing is also included in the program of the **Loch Insh Sailing School** (Insh Hall, Kincraig, Invernessshire), an organization which also operates courses in sailing and watersports.

Personalized Services in **Edinburgh**? For *au pairs* and mother's helpers, Scotland's oldest agency, **Mackay's** (30 Frederick St.; Tel: 225–3530) can supply you with someone helpful and pleasing.

You can hire a bagpipe player from **West of Scotland Pipers & Ceilidh Group** (24 Campbell St., Darvel, Ayrshire). For the ultimate to celebrate a child's birthday, **Mr. W. Hamilton** (106 Netherby Rd., Edinburgh) will supply you with eight dancers, a piper, an accordion player and a solo dancer to perform Scottish dances for you.

Any form of guided, chaperoned, or specialty tour in a chauffeur-driven car can be arranged by **Ghillie Personal Travel** (64 Silverknowes Rd. East, Edinburgh). A chauffeur-driven touring service, extremely special, is **Newington Chauffeur Drive** (8 Merchiston Mews; Tel: 229–8666). They do everything for children, put in car beds, extra luggage racks, kiddy-car chairs, go to all lengths to satisfy you and make your journey happy. The cars will go anywhere, pick you up anywhere;

morning or extended tours; they can work out individual itineraries for whatever your interest is.

HOLIDAYS FOR CHILDREN ON THEIR OWN There used to be guest-houses and holiday accommodations for unaccompanied children, infants to teenagers, but these have given way to resident nannies, *au pairs* and mothers' helpers for the little ones, and to the popularity of riding and trekking centers for older children, and the prevalence now of multi-activity camps.

A list of riding establishments recommended by Ponies of Britain and the British Horse Society is available from the British Tourist Authority, but here are a few suggestions: The **Scottish Centre of Equitation** (Greenloaning, Dunblane) accepts children from age 7, year round, but preferably during Christmas and Easter holiday specials for ages 10s up. **Ayr Riding School** (Castlehill Stables, Ayr) open year round, accepts children from age 9. **Drumbrae Riding Centre** (Bridge of Allan, Stirlingshire). **Drumstinchall Pony Trekking** (Brow Hill, Drumstinchall, Dalbeattie) accepts children from 10 years during July and Aug. **Highland Riding Centre** (Borlum Farm, Drumnadrochit) takes 10s and over. **Nethybridge Riding Centre** (Nethybridge, Invernessshire) takes over 7s, and operates May–Oct. (See also Children's Camps)

Agencies able to arrange for unaccompanied children from 8 to enjoy home stay with Scottish families are listed in BTA's free guide *Meet the British: En Famille and Paying Guest Agencies*.

CHILDREN'S CAMPS **Ru'a Fiola Island Exploration Centre** (Cullipool, Oban, Argyll) is an adventure camp for 8–16 year olds, with sailing instruction, campouts in tents, and more. **Carnoch Outdoor Centre** (Glencoe) offers multi-sport adventure holidays for over 10s and single activity courses in sailing and hillclimbing during the summer. **Highland Guides** (Inverdruie, Aviemore) takes 12- to 16-year-olds for year-round multi-activity, walking and cross-country skiing holidays. For over 12s, **Try-A-Sport Holidays** are offered at Aviemore Centre that encompass sailing, canoeing, pony trekking, and skiing courses in winter. **John Ridgway School of Adventure** (Ardmore, Rhiconich, Sutherland) offers adventure holidays for 12– to 30-year-olds during the summer, including sailing, canoeing, climbing. Courses for the over 14s in mountaineering, sailing, orienteering are run by **Outward Bound Loch Eil** (Achdalieu Lodge, Fort William).

CASTLES AND OTHER HAPPY FAMILY ACCOMMODATIONS Hostels feature children's playrooms, nurseries, resident nannies. Scotland specializes in thrifty accommodations and in hotels that are casually referred to as Country House hotels, but which actually are magnificent manor houses and castley-castles. Available from bookshops or from the STB is a paperback listing hotels, guesthouses, farmhouses (with babysitting facilities, cots and high chairs, washing and drying facilities), and hotels with family suites. Free is *Hotels in Scotland with Facilities for Young Children,* detailing child care, food, amusements. See England for the many helpful publications from the BTA and other sources on castles, farmhouses, and other accommodations. STB's **Self-Catering Accommodations** (available from the British Travel Bookshop—See Information for address) lists *cottages and other holiday homes to rent all over Scotland.* Excellent agencies for cottage rentals are: **Scottish Country Cottages** (Suite 2d, Churchill Way, Bishopbriggs, Glasgow); **Scottish Highland Homes** (26 Station Square, Inverness).

Vacation cottages can be rented from the Laird of the Isle of Muck, a small isle in the Inner Hebrides (See The Inner Hebrides), and on Eigg (pronounced egg)NE of Muck, 15 crofters' cottages, somewhat booth-like, to be sure, basic, simple, with primitive to modest bathroom facilities, can be rented; high season is Aug., and accommodations and prices vary widely. Information from the Estate Office (Isle of Eigg, Inverness) or **Eigg Holiday Bookings** (Maybank, Udny, Ellon, Aberdeenshire).

Aviemore: The **Strathspey Hotel** includes sauna, children's playroom; the **Badenoch Hotel** has a children's nursery, a ski store, and 18 economy rooms; the **Aviemore Chalets Motel,** designed to meet the needs of young people and families, has four-bed rooms. **Post House** is a modern hotel with games room and resident nanny. **Edinburgh:** Elegant **Prestonfield House Hotel** (Priestfield Rd.) has peacocks on the lawn and golf course adjacent. **Fort William: Inverlochy Castle** has billiards, trout fishing, and tennis. It's worth going to **Gatehouse-of-Fleet** just to stay at the sumptuous **Cally Hotel** (Castle Douglas) with swimming pool, tennis, nursery, and playground. **Gullane: Greywalls** (Muirfield) in a lovely private manor near Edinburgh, is for golfers; I would suggest you consider this *only* if your children are at least 12. **Huntly: Huntly Castle** (Tel: 2696), in 10 acres of sheltered grounds, has 24 rooms, six with private bath; a putting green, fishing in the River Deveron. **Isle of Eriska: Isle of Eriska Hotel,** with 28 guestrooms with private baths, is much like a private mansion. Peace, quiet, pony trekking, a seven-ton yacht guests can charter, country houseparty atmosphere. **Kildrummy: Kildrummy Castle,** built at the turn of the century, was visited by Queen Victoria and is located by the River Don at the foot of the Cairngorm mountains; salmon and trout fishing; open Mar.–Dec.; 13 rooms, 9 with private bath. **Ladybank: Fernie Castle** dates from the 14th century; once the home of the Earl of Fife; has 16th-century slit windows, watchtower, and an original lead bath in the East Wing. It offers fishing. **Lasswade: Melville Castle** reservations should be made through Norway House (West End, Edinburgh; Tel: 255–2881), but check to be sure whether this comfortable house on the banks of the North Esk outside of Edinburgh is still accepting children. **Melrose: Waverley Castle** (Tel: 2244), built in the 19th century, sits in eight acres of woodland overlooking the River Tweed in Sir Walter Scott country; over 70 rooms; fishing. **Peebles: Venlaw Castle** (Edinburgh Rd): a towered, turreted, 18th-century mansion standing on the site of a much older castle; 12 rooms; closed in winter; offers tennis, golf, fishing, shooting. Just outside Peebles is **Cringletie House Hotel** (Tel: Eddleston 233), a beautifully furnished mansion serving excellent food, with tennis court, croquet, and a putting course. **Isle of Skye: Skeabost House** has excellent food with Scottish specialties, salmon and trout fishing. In Portree, the **Royal Hotel** has a program of entertainment and dancing.

Strachur: In this tiny hamlet on the shores of Loch Fyne on Scotland's west coast in Argyllshire, is **Creggans Inn;** 23 bedrooms in a long, low, white country-house hotel with 98 different dishes on the weekly dinner menu. In **Stranraer,** is **North West Castle** built by Arctic explorer Sir John Ross in the early 19th century; overlooks Loch Ryan; fishing, putting, swimming, water-skiing; all comforts in its 30 rooms, 17 with private bath. Just where the ferries embark for Northern Ireland, 15th-century **Lochnaw Castle** (Tel: Leswalt 227) standing on the edge of its own loch, is surrounded by acres of rhododendrons and beechwoods, beyond which heather-covered moors stretch to the coast. Attractively furnished with antiques; very comfortable; only six rooms, but several cottages—fully serviced—on the property are desirable family accommodations. Squash court; two golf courses nearby, trout fishing, sandy beaches nearby, and an ideal picnic spot on the Isle of Lochnaw in the middle of the loch in the shade of an 11th-century ruined castle. The island, a santuary for water birds, is a lovely spot.

CAMPING AND CARAVANING For information on campsites, tent or gear hiring, see England, "Camping and Caravaning," the STB, or the Scottish Youth Hostels Assoc.

Motor caravans are for hire at **Halley Caravans Ltd.** (Halley Hire, Glasgow Rd., Milngavie, Glasgow); **Sharp's Motor Homes** (11 Queensgage, Inverness); **Abcar Hire Drive** (Stirling Ltd., 17 Wallace St., Stirling).

ATTRACTIONS FOR CHILDREN IN EDINBURGH Most attractions are open daily 9–10 a.m.–5–6 p.m., plus Sun. afternoon. Edinburgh is one of the world's loveliest cities and the least frustrating, because it is simple to find your way around and it is small enough to be seen without exhaustion. In a wee nutshell, attractions of special interest to children are: **The Castle,** on the Castle Rock overlooking the city. Every weekday at 1 p.m., a 25-lb. howitzer is fired from the Half Moon Battery. Children are equally fascinated with the silent Mons Meg, the huge 15th-century cannon that shot giant stone balls over 1½ miles. See the Royal Apartments and the Crown Chamber, where the Scottish Regalia or Honors of Scotland are kept; a museum of armor in the Great Hall. The **Royal Mile,** from the Castle to Holyrood Palace through the Old Town, comprising the Esplanade, Castle Hill, Lawnmarket, Parliament Square, High St., and Canongate. Have a look at Edinburgh in the Camera Obscura, a sort of periscope in the **Outlook Tower,** Ramsay Lane. The museum of Edinburgh's history in **Huntley House,** and the **Royal Scottish Museum** (Chambers St.). The 200′ tower of the Scott Monument with a statue of Sir Walter Scott, a landmark, in East Princes St. Garden, where you can also see the first clock in the world planted with flowers, built in 1903, and replanted every spring. **Greyfriars Bobby,** a statue of a Skye terrier sitting on top of a drinking fountain near Greyfriars Churchyard, a faithful dog who lingered close to his master's grave for 14 years until its death. South end, **George IV Bridge. Edinburgh Zoo** (Corstophine Rd.); marvelous penguins, the largest captive colony in the world; they parade at 3:30 p.m. every summer afternoon. A Children's Farm, a miniature farmyard—farmhouse, stables, pig and kid pens, duck pond, dovecote, free-running (and they do run) rabbits; working miniatures of implements, from hay wagon to plough; strollers can be hired; restaurant.

Princes St. Gardens are lovely, overlooked by that beautiful castle; June–Sept., open-air entertainment here includes morning shows for children, afternoon and evening band and variety performances. The best British and continental bands compete in an annual contest held on a Sat. afternoon during the Festival season. Go out to the **Hillend Ski Centre** (Pentland Hills just outside of town); artificial ski slopes; a two-seated chair lift for a panoramic view.

The **Royal Scottish Academy of Painting** (Princes St.), also the **National Gallery of Scotland** (at the foot of the Mound), one of the more important of the smaller galleries of Europe. I also love the little **Scottish National Gallery of Modern Art** (Inverleith House in the Royal Botanic Garden). It stands on a rise and commands a view of Edinburgh, and it's free, lovely, and small enough so you can go through it all with great pleasure; some of the contemporary Scottish artists are exceptionally good; several American painters represented. Children will adore the **Botanic Gardens,** whose hanging greenhouses (with fish tanks for good measure) are unique; friendly birds will almost feed from your hand if you are patient enough—most children are. The absolutely enchanting and unique **Museum of Childhood** (Hyndford's Close, High St.), some 100,000 toys, costumes, children's memorabilia, collections and artwork, mostly from 1850–1945, but a few items going back to about 2000 B.C.; a great rocking horse; tea sets of all sizes; endearing doll-houses with perfect scale furniture and ornaments; puppets; toy soldiers; clockwork motor cars; savings banks. Nothing seems to have been left out; a juvenile theater will interest you, so will the classic story books. **Roslin Chapel,** with its incredible stone carving, is approximately seven miles south of town.

If it's warm enough, have a swim at the open-air pool at **Portobello** which has a wave-making machine or swim in the **Royal Common-**

wealth Swimming Pool (21 Dalkeith Rd.; Tel: 667–7211 (restaurant; swimming lessons; towels and suits for rent). You can hire rackets and tennis balls and play at any of the two dozen municipal courts. For ***fishing,*** permits are available from the Lothian Regional Council (New County Buildings, George IV Bridge); if the children want to fish in the city's reservoirs, on the banks, or by boat, obtain permits from the Lothian Regional Water Supply Services (Comiston Springs, 55 Buckstone Terrace). On Thurs. and Sat., there is Greyhound Racing at the **Powderhall Greyhound Stadium.** There are stables in Edinburgh where riding classes are held and treks organized over the hills, from Redford, Colinton.

If you go to Edinburgh for the **Festival** (late Aug.–mid Sept.) a computerized **Accommodation Bureau** (5 Waverly Bridge; Tel: (031) 225–8821/226–6591) can find space for you within a two-mile radius of the castle. Opt for guest house and bed-and-breakfast accommodations rather than what's available in the less-than-grand city hotels. The children will go wild over the **Edinburgh Military Tattoo,** an international marvel of massed pipes and drums, precision drill and pageantry on the Castle Rock. The Tattoo ticket office is located at 1 Cockburn St. (Tel: (031) 225–1188). Other official Festival Events can be booked by calling 225–5766 during office hours; festival ticket office is located at 21 Market St.

ATTRACTIONS FOR CHILDREN ELSEWHERE **Aberdeen** is a bustling seaport; special junior programs on its extensive beaches, with lots of paddling pools and playgrounds. Just a short cast from the harbor is the **Farlow Sharpe workshop** making some of the world's finest split-bamboo fly fishing rods 8′–15′ in length, weighing 5–10 oz. Birds and animals in natural surroundings are a great **zoo** attraction. Near Royal Deeside country, it's fine for an excursion to **Balmoral,** the Queen's country residence; not open except for the grounds (on which Prince Philip has done so much fine work). **Arbroath:** A large seaside resort, a busy fishing port, with many attractions for children, among them miniature railway and coaches plus paddling pools. **Arran** island has a country village atmosphere, lovely scenery, nice beaches, but no special organized attractions for children.

For outdoor and indoor sport, **Aviemore** is the focal point of the Central Highlands. It features an international-size indoor ice rink (skates for hire); seven lanes for curling; a 25-meter heated indoor pool (instruction given in swimming and diving; suits and towels rented); artificial ski slope (instruction given); trampolines, crazy golf for laughs, 18-hole golf course, tennis, shooting, gliding, fishing, sailing, a splendid playground, pony trekking, shopping center, ski school, highland wildlife exhibition; a nature study and photography course; complete range of sporting life at prices for every purse. The **Tourist Information Bu-**

reau (Tel: 810–363) can provide details. **Ayr:** In the heart of Robert Burns country, has an ice rink, and a boating pond. The birthplace of Robert Burns is in **Alloway,** two miles distant, where there is an interesting museum about the poet. His birthday (Jan. 25) is not celebrated here but at the Globe Inn in Dumfries. **Culzean** (pronounced Cullane) **Castle Park;** interior and exterior of the castle created by 18th-century architect Robert Adam; a suite was set aside for life for Gen. Eisenhower; armory; wonderful 500-acre park, swan pond, and walled garden. **Balloch: Loch Lomond Bear Park** (has bus service if you have no car); wildlife park and boatrides on the loch. **Blair Atholl: Blair Castle** has armor, costumes, toys, stuffed animals. **Blair Drummond:** At Sir John Muir's imposing manor house, over 100 acres have been made into a **Safari Park.** You can drive or take a safari bus through lion and baboon areas; at the giraffe and zebra reserve you can get out of your car; boat safari (amid dandy sealions as one child called them—I think they're seals) to a Chimpanzee Island; performing dolphins; pets' corner. **Island of Bute:** Rothesay is a well-known beach resort with many family attractions. **Caerlaverock: Wildlife Bird Sanctuary.** Best in autumn before dusk when the wild geese wing home to winter. **Carnoustie:** five miles of golden beach with children's playground. **Comrie** is the site of the **Museum of Scottish Tartans,** with a large collection of tartans, reference library and information service. **Culloden** is the site of Bonnie Prince Charlie's defeat at the famous battle of 1746. Audiovisual presentation of this historic battle at the Visitor Centre; a spell-binder. On the tiny island of **Cumbrae,** Millport has **donkey rides** on the sands, safe bathing, and a host of events planned for children. Bicycles are rented here and everyone rides them. Many people take summer cottages here. **Doune:** Motor Museum with 40 cars on display.

Specially attractive is **Drumnadrochit** (See Fun and Games), a **pony trekking** center which caters to children; and the farm life is heavenly. **Dumfries:** Scholars and admirers of Robert Burns flock here to celebrate his birthday (see Ayr; Alloway), and you can visit his tiny house in town kept exactly as it was in his day. The **Dumfries Museum** is noted for its dragon lore. Just south is the **Castle of Caerlaverock,** a favorite place for picnics. **Dunbar:** small, lively resort; children's pools and playgrounds, well-organized games and entertainment; pony trekking; all the attractions of a fishing port, with many interesting **boat trips** (including one to Bass Rock, teeming with birds). **Glasgow:** art gallery in Kelvingrove Park; Museum of **Transport** (Albert Rd.) with sailing vessels, old trains, streetcars, with gift shop and tearoom; the **Burrell Collection** of art and antiquities; **Haggs Castle** (100 St. Andrew's Dr.) which houses a history museum for children. **Rouken Glen Park. Innerleithen:** Search out **Traquair,** the oldest inhabited house in Scotland. **Inveraray:** The lived-in **Castle** is the ancestral home of the Campbells and Argylls; particularly good armor collection; teas; don't miss the museum-room of Princess Louise, daughter of Queen Victoria. Nearby, at **Auchindrain** is an open-air folk museum comprising 18th- and 19th-century houses and farm buildings.

The **Inner Hebrides** comprise more than 600 islands off the jagged coastline of western Scotland, accessible by boat and the ferry company of **Caledonian MacBrayne** based in Mallaig, Inverness. Private charters can be arranged with Bruce Watt (Arisaig, Inverness Tel: (06875) 224). (See Fun Trips). **Skye** is the most dramatic, tourist-oriented, with the most accommodations (See Castles and Other Happy Family Accommodations). Accommodations are also plentiful on **Mull,** with recommended choices of the **Western Isles Hotel** or the seven-room **Craig Hotel.** On tiny **Canna,** you'll find a fine example of a Viking ship burial, a tower, and a Celtic cross. Information and accommodations arranged through the **National Trust of Scotland** in Edinburgh. **Rum,** nine miles SW of Skye, is a wild and magnificent nature reserve with peaks to climb, sea and trout fishing, wild-flowers, free-ranging ponies, and a diversity of bird-life; lodging available at **Kinloch Castle,** providing both grand and hostel-type accommodations. In the Mar.–Sept. season, reservations can be made by calling Mallaig, Inverness, on the mainland (Tel: (0687) 2038) or by writing to the **Nature Conservancy Council** (12 Hope St., Edinburgh) who own the island. Groups must obtain prior permission to visit Rum from the Chief Warden (White House, Kinloch, Isle of Rum). Ferry service from Mallaig and helicopter service is available. **Eigg,** about four miles SE of Rum, volcanic in structure, has "singing" sand beaches whose grains of black and white quartz can be squeakily scuffled. A landrover and bus provide transport from Galmisdale, the main village, and the beach. Bicycles and ponies can be hired. There is a guesthouse cum teashop-restaurant. You're in luck if you can secure accommodations in **Muck** at **Port Mhor House** from Lawrence MacEwan (Gallanach, Isle of Muck, Inverness) who also can rent vacation cottages. A boat is available for exploring or deep sea fishing. **The Highlands and Island Development Board** (27 Bank St., Inverness, Scotland 1V1 QR) publishes a guide to the area and its transport system, available at all of the Scottish TICs.

Don't miss the **Highland Folk Museum** at **Kingussie,** or the **Highland Wildlife Park** with native animals at nearby Kincraig. **Kirriemuir:** J.M. Barrie, who wrote *Peter Pan,* was born here. Manuscripts and mementoes displayed in his house, but there's no nice doggy Nana for the children to play with, so it's no great, groovy place for the children. Princess Margaret was born nearby at **Glamis Castle;** its garden was laid out by Capability Brown. **Leven:** Trampolines, organized entertainment, a pets' corner, fairground, and safe bathing. **Lossiemouth** on Spey Bay; **castle ruins;** a fishing port older children will [illegible]. In the Isle of **Mull,** the **Little Theatre** (at Dervaig) plays through[illegible] summer. Live actors and puppets are both used in highly indi[illegible]rpretations of classics by Shaw, Shakespeare, Barrie. **Nairn** has two sandy beaches, indoor pool, playground, beautiful parks, lots of boating. **North Berwick** has a busy, attractive harbor. **Paisley Museum and Art** Galley (High St., Paisley, Strathclyde) has the world's best collection of paisley shawls. **Pitlochry:** attractive inland resort; Apr.–Oct. Festival Theater. **Ruthwell:** Pronounced Ruffle, a village on the Solway coast, enfolds in the apse of its parish church the **Ruthwell Cross,** ancient and awesome, carved with miniature sculptures of the Gospel stories and imprinted in runic script with Caedmon's "Rood Lay," the lament of the Cross on which Christ was crucified. **St. Andrew's,** with the famous golf course, combines sandy Fifeshire beaches with a ruined **castle** that has secret passages and dungeons to explore. **Isle of Skye: Dunvegan Castle,** built on a bleak overlook in the 9th century; terriers come from this largest and most northerly of the Inner Hebrides. Skye was ruled by Norsemen until the 13th century; archaeologically interesting; **Portree** is the main tourist center; read James Boswell's *Tour to the Hebrides* before you go. **South Queensferry: Hopetoun House** is a fine example of Robert Adam's Neoclassical architecture; there is a deer park, nature trail, stables museum (open May–Sept.). **Stirling:** Benjamin Franklin, puffing his way, even as you and I, along the battlements of **Stirling Castle,** pronounced it "awesome." Landmark Visitor Center has an audiovisual documentary.

FUN TRIPS Interested in ***cruising?*** The **Caledonian Canal,** connecting coast to coast is one of the loveliest waterways in Europe. It runs southwest across the Highlands through the Great Glen from Inverness to Fort William, runs into the great lochs, including Loch Ness, and connects with short lengths of canal with Loch Oich and Loch Lochy. For information, consult the **British Waterways Board** (Canal Office, Ardrishaig, Argyll). The **Crinan Canal** connects the Firth of Clyde with Crinan on the Sound of Jura; for information, consult the **British Waterways Board** (Glasgow Area, Old Basin Works, Applecross St., Glasgow; Tel: 332–6936). Island cruises are the best way to visit the Inner Hebrides, and **West Highland Cruises** (10 Clairmont Gardens, Glasgow G37LW) offer six-day cruises or longer from Apr.–Sept. aboard a six-cabin converted fishing boat and a luxurious motor yacht.

You can cruise on beautiful **Loch Lomond. Caledonian Macbrayne Ltd.** (Ferry Terminal, Gourock, Renfrewshire) run a.m. and p.m. cruises from **Balloch, Luss, Rowardennan** and **Inversnaid** during the summer. **Jacobite Cruises Ltd.** (26 Inglis St., Inverness) run cruises on Loch Ness that depart from Inverness.

For cruising on Loch Lomond, you can rent your own boat from **Cuillins Yacht Charters (The Flat a-Float,** Ardlui Arrochar, Dunbartonshire) who have three-to-four bunk yachts available from Easter–Sept. Or, try **Loch Lomond Cruisers** (The Inverbeg Inn, Luss, Loch Lomond, Dunbartonshire) who can set you up with two-to-six berth cabin cruisers all year round. **Blakes** (Wroxham, Norwich, NR 12 8 DH) lease two-to-ten berth cruisers and yachts for sailing on Loch Ness and the Caldonian Canal. **Caley Cruisers Ltd.** (Canal Rd., Inverness) whir two-to-eight berth cabin cruisers into action along the Caledonian Canal for reasonable fees.

Steamers for day or overnight trips to Mull, Skye, and other western isles, plus car and passenger ferries to Arran and Bute, **Caledonian MacBrayne Ltd.** runs excellent services with scores of choices.

Hunting, shooting and fishing holidays are managed by the **Tourist Promotion of Scotland** (36 Castle St., Edinburgh). The **SSC** (see Fun and Games) can tell you about other fun trips.

FUN AND GAMES British Tourist Authority can supply you with the invaluable *Activity Holidays* covering sport holidays on land, sea and in the air; information sheets on fishing waters, and fairways for golfers. STB's *Adventure and Special Interest Holidays in Scotland* is an anthology of ideas from Antiques to Yachting. The **Scottish Sports Council** (1 St. Colme St., Edinburgh) is informative.

Angling. Fishing schools are associated with the River Tweed (salmon and trout); Tay (salmon); Spey (salmon and trout); game fishing and sea angling. Fishing equipment and boats easily hirable. The BTA sells *Scotland for Fishing,* a guide to angling areas; hotels; clubs; with rivers and lochs indexed, plus maps.

Sailing: Sailing schools and holiday centers for adults and teenagers, novices and experts, both coastal and inland sailing.

Recommended ***sailing schools:*** **Lochearn and Coastal Sailing School** (Dalvreck House, Crieff, Perthshire) takes 10 year olds up; **Tighnabruaich Sailing School** (Tighnabruaich, Argyll) offers basic, junior, intermediate, advanced and racing courses for unaccompanied 12s and up, and accepts 8-year-olds when accompanied by their parents or guardians; **North Channel Yachts** (Stroul Bay, Clynder, Dunbartonshire) offers courses from Mar.–Oct. and will accept unaccompanied children 14+.

Scotland is ideal for ***canoeing,*** and many canoeists test their skill on fast-flowing rivers such as the Spey and the Tay on which leading canoe clubs run their championships.

The **Scottish Canoe Association** (18 Ainslie Pl., Edinburgh) can provide information on this sport. **Loch Insh Sailing School** (Insh Hall, Loch Insh, Kincraig) has a basic canoeing course that is simple and thorough.

Pony trekking and riding holidays: You have the option of staying at a pony trekking center and touring from there, or living at a hotel and trekking by the day.

The **Tweed Valley Hotel** (Galashiels Rd., Walkerburn), is specially recommended, and offers riding and fishing. The **Craiglynne Hotel** (Grantown-on-Spey) provides wonderful riding country with magnificent scenery; families especially welcomed. **Tobermory Trek-**

king Centre (Erray, Isle of Mull) takes children from 5 with the option of hotel accommodation or tent-camping. Unaccompanied trekkers 13 and over are specially catered to in local hotels and guesthouses at the **Dunbar Pony Trekking Center** (Braidwood, by Innerwick, Dunbar; Tel: 3258). A children's playground, a warm welcome for families on a 300-acre farm where shaggy Highland cattle graze, a blacksmith shoes the "canny beasts," and where children may cuddle the donkey, play with the goatlings, or discover the latest family of kittens, is offered at the **Highland Riding Center** (Borlum Farm, Drumnadrochit; Tel: 220). See also listings under England and the STB's free booklet on riding and trekking.

Golf: *Scotland, Home of Golf* lists over 400 golf courses with details on applications to play, telephone numbers, greens fees. British Travel Bookshop has it. Information and maps may be obtained directly from the Scottish Tourist Board in Edinburgh, who will also send on request, brochures from regional councils. **Gleneagles Hotel Golf Course** (Auchterarder, Tayside PH 3 INF) is a five-star hotel and resort with four golf courses and a myriad of other sports and nonathletic amenities. **Turnerry Hotel** (Ayrshire KA26 9LT) offers packages of golf holidays, as do many smaller hotels. Information from tour operators of International Golf (for both Scotland and Ireland) 1650 Maisoneuve W., Montreal, Canada H3H 2P3); **David Begg Sports Promotions** (112 Cornwall St., Glasgow); **Fairway Tours** (9 Roseberry Place, Gullane EH 31 2 AN); **Go-Scot Tours** (Doonbank House, Patna, Ayrshire KA 6 7JD). The STB or BTA will send you on request masses more information. ***Bicycling:*** See "Fun and Games" in England. ***Mountaineering:*** The SSC can send you more information on this as well as on hill-walking, summer skiing, and climbing courses for beginners. ***Gliding:*** Holiday courses have added greatly to its popularity; information from the **Scottish Gliding Union** (Portmoak Airfield, Scotlandwell, by Kinross). ***Hunting*** is arranged by a select number of hotels; full list from the STB.

Skiing: Ski schools, ski hire, ski centers (mid-Dec.–May) and year round centers with plastic slopes (such as Hillend in Edinburgh, Aviemore, Glasgow's Bellshouston Park, and Aberdeen) are covered in *Winter Sports in Scotland,* also available from BTA. Try Aviemore and Glencoe for inexpensive packaged holidays that include hotels with playrooms and childminding services.

SHOPPING WITH AND FOR CHILDREN Do invest in a sporran—it makes a great purse for a teenager. Silver Celtic buttons are wonderful to buy now, use later. Wet-weather footwear for children are Baby Deer; they range from wash-n'-wear, warm-lined, machine-washable boots, to sandals, sneakers, and slippers. Scottish woolens (woolen and cashmere sweaters, tweeds, tartans) are world-famous. You can visit some of the mills to see how these are made, often finding a mill outlet shop where prices are lower than in the stores. In **Inverness,** you can visit **James**

Pringle Ltd. (Holm Woollen Mills, Dores Rd.). In the 12th-century border town of **Selkirk,** the **Dalgleish Mill,** family-owned, also weaves silk tartan scarves. STB's booklet *See Scotland at Work* lists others.

In **Edinburgh: William Borthwick** (1 Cockburn St.) has a fine selection of baby carriages. Also carriages at: **Marmet (Scotland) Ltd.** (Lower London Rd.); **Nurseryland** (11 Clerk St.); **Pram Economics** (4B Downfield Pl.); **Raeburn Pram Centre** (48 Raeburn Pl. 4); **Scott Bros.** (40 Cockburn St. 1). A marvelous children's barber: at the department store of **Patrick Thomson** (South Bridge). **Boots Chemist** (see Baby Food) also has records, stamps, books, teddy bears, picnic flasks, umbrellas, crayons, wine-making sets, and just about everything handy and useful for children and motoring. A bagpipe maker is **J. & R. Glen** (497 Lawnmarket). Best kiltmakers are the following, who also have Scottish knitwear and accessories: **Kinloch Anderson & Sons, Ltd.** (4–14 George St.) outfit for daytime wear (coat, Lovat stockings and tie, shirt, sporran, garters and flashes, skean dhu, and Ghillie brogues) or evening wear (coat and vest, shirt with jabot and ruffles, tartan stockings, black bow tie, sporran, garters and lashes, skean dhu, and Ghillie brogues). Can deliver daytime outfit in four weeks, evening wear in six weeks without fittings. Normally, two fittings are offered. Large selection of materials by the yard. **Hugh MacPherson (Scotland) Ltd.** (17 W. Maitland St.), no fittings necessary; in an emergency, delivery can be made in two days; normally, two weeks; bagpipes too. **Highland House** (328 Lawnmarket); kilts in worsted only; no fittings required; 24-hour delivery possible in an emergency; normally seven to ten days. Also bagpipes, drums (!), tweeds, jewelry, tams, sporrans, purses. The **Kilt Shop, Ltd.,** (21 George IV Bridge); two grades of kilt; no fittings required; two week delivery.

Excellent skirts in flattering styles at **John Morrison** (461 Lawnmarket); good highland dress; super sporrans. For sweaters and wools, **R. W. Forsyth** (30 Princes St.); kilts, plaids (over-the-shoulder lengths in colorful tartans); good selection of cashmere and Fair Isle sweaters. **Jenner's** (Princes St.); knitwear and sweaters. **Romanes and Paterson** (62 Princes St.), more wonderful cashmeres. **Roderick Tweedie** (7A Frederick St.) for tweeds and knitwear, coats, skirts, suits. For Fair Isle and Shetland socks, mittens, scarves, sweaters, **Highland Home Industries** (94 George St.) and the **Scottish Craft Center** (Acheson House, Canongate); knitwear, pins and bracelets, and other regional products. Sporting equipment: **Lillywhites** (129 Princes St.); **John Dickson and Son** (21 Frederick St.) **Galt Toys** have an in-store boutique at the **Scotch House** (Princes St.). **The Toy Tub** (100A Raeburn Pl.) stocks a cornucopia of quality toys. For model railways, the place to go is **Wonderland** (97 Lothia Rd.; branch at 116A Rose St.); for tartan traveling rugs, mohair rugs, knitting wools, and a truly quaint old-fashioned establishment your children will like, head for the **Edinburgh Woollen**

Mill (9 Randolph Pl.), in a dear little enclave of exclusive antique shops that any husband in his right mind will try to steer you away from, but find this place out! Antique pieces that would be nice if you can afford them, such as super dolls' furniture. For junk shops to browse around for finds like mechanical pennybanks and porcupine quill baskets, try the fascinating Grassmarket section. For books and magazines, **John Menzies** (138 Princes St. or 9 Castle St.).

In **Gleneagles,** best store for kilts, tartans, sheepskin coats is **R. Watson Hogg** (Auchterarder). In **Glasgow,** a permanent display of well-designed, modern British consumer goods, ranging from toys to furniture, similar to the Design Centre in London, is the **Scottish Design Centre** (72 Vincent St.).

SCOTTISH FRIENDS AND PEN PALS: See English Friends and Pen Pals. For adults and children over 8, **Travel at Home Family Bureau** (Craighall, Huntley, Aberdeenshire) arranges home-stay accommodations throughout Scotland and the rest of Britain. **Welcome Homes Organization** (2 Strathalmond Green, Barnton, Edinburgh) arranges for visitors over 16 with special and professional interests to stay with Scottish homeowners who share their pursuits and passions. **Welcome to Scotland** (42 Heriot Row, Edinburgh) will tell you of hosts throughout Scotland who offer hospitality and a chance to meet local people. TICs have details of the Welcome to Scotland local representatives. Lunches and teas are offered in Culcreuch Castle, Fintry, Stirlingshire, by Baron Hercules of Culcreuch (Tel: Fintry (03686) 228) to interested individuals on Sundays only.

CALENDAR OF EVENTS Highland games are exciting, colorful events, with piping, dancing, tossing the caber and other athletics. Big days include the Royal Highland Gathering at Braemar, early Sept. and the Cowal Gathering at Dunoon, with 1000 pipers playing and parading, in Aug.; but there are Highland Games somewhere in Scotland every Sat. in season.

In **Jan.,** Lerwick, on the Shetland Isles, celebrates ***Up-Helly-A',*** a fire festival of Viking origin. ***Skiing and Curling Championships.*** **Mar.–Apr.:** The **Edinburgh Folk Festival** with ceilidhs (dances) and concerts. **Apr.–Sept.** The Royal Scottish Academy holds its Annual ***Exhibition*** in Edinburgh. **Apr.:** The ***Scottish Grand Racing Event*** is held at Ayr. **Apr. –Oct.** ***Pitlochry Festival Theatre,*** drama and music.

May: ***Perth Festival of the Arts*** with concerts, ballet, opera performances. **May–**Nov. Highland Games. May.–Nov., ***Highland Games, Athletic Events,*** and ***Dancing*** take place throughout Scotland. **June:** ***Royal Highland Agricultural Show*** at Newbridge, Edinburgh. From **June–**Nov., almost every town and village holds ***Sheep-dog Trials, Folk***

Festivals*, and *Fairs; usually on Sat. Riding the Marches horseback procession in Hawick.

In **July,** St. Andrews has ***Golf Championships*.** **Aug.** brings a ***Festival*** to Edinburgh; music, drama, dancing, and wonderful military tattoos. In **Dec.,** Christmas is celebrated throughout Scotland. **Hogmanay** or New Year's Eve day prompts a flow of whiskey and exuberant Scottish country dancing.

SPAIN

"I have never seen so many friendly and eager-to-help people anywhere," my teenage daughter said. "Couldn't we live here?" For teenagers, Spain is an Eldorado, but you simply are not going to find the range of child-care facilities that other countries offer. If you are a first-time traveler, you will probably find a baby or a young child a burden unless you are the marvelously organized sort who can always "manage," and stay only in modern hotels in tourist centers.

If you travel by car and with a baby, you might as well know the worst: service stations are few and far between; the restrooms seldom provide towels or soap. In Madrid, along with high-rise buildings and supermarkets, facilities for children are increasing rapidly.

Many young Americans backpack their babies, but my advice is to only bring over-8s with you. Children of that age will truly enjoy Spain. People still have time to tell folk stories—about Perez the Mouse, or *Ratonperez,* a timid little creature who exchanges baby teeth tucked under children's pillows for some small present; *pícaro* tales about rogues and rascals; about Halfchick *(Mediopolo* or *Mediogallo),* a chicken with one wing and one leg; about Carlanco the Terrible, the bogeyman; plus many variants on familiar stories. Storytellers narrate with such pleasure that the tales always sound new. Try to find someone to translate folk stories they know. Gypsies *(gitanos)* are adroit at improvising *coplas* (couplets) about local traditions or, more often, to flatter you in return for a well-greased palm. You need to know Spanish pretty well to appreciate the cleverness of these, but after hearing gypsy experts, children are usually inspired to give this sort of rhyme a whirl.

Life is simpler if you don't follow Spanish family conventions: i.e., go to zoos and amusement parks on weekdays, not weekends when the crowds are worst.

INFORMATION ABOUT SPAIN The **Spanish National Tourist Office**—SNTO—(665 Fifth Ave., New York, NY 10022), in Houston, St. Augustine, Chicago, San Francisco, and Toronto are all sources of excellent information. In Spain, the SNTO maintains over 60 offices. Just ask for the Oficina Municipal de Informacion y Turismo wherever you go. A list of national tourist offices is available from the SNTO free for the asking.

Almost all major towns have guides that list the local entertainments in English; available at the local tourist offices or at your hotel. Consult also *Iberian Sun* and *Guidepost,* weekly publications for American residents of Madrid, and similar English-language papers in other areas. For lengthy visits get *Bear Facts* (the bear is a symbol of Madrid) from the American Women's Club (see Magic Family Helpers). ***Motoring:*** Because of the network of government-organized and operated *paradores,* roadmaps and routes are excellent. Consult the **Real Automovil Club de Espana** (Gen. Sanjuro 10, E-Madrid 3).

HEALTH, WATER, AND FOOD Spanish kitchens, homes, restaurants, hotels, are all spotless, but in summer there are flies (the Spanish don't use screens, as they feel screens block the view and cut off the circulation of air). Bring along your favorite repellent. For small babies, a mosquito net while sleeping is essential.

Unless you want to boil milk on a portable stove, I strongly recommend that you either give the younglings powdered milk or just forget all about drinking milk. *Leche esterilizada,* milk that doesn't need refrigeration until opened, is poor nutritionally. Airbase personnel at Torrejon advise avoiding all ice cream sold on the street. Stick to bottled water. Ask for *agua minerale* if the children like the fizzy kind (Mondariz and Vichy-Catalan are best) or for Solares (nonfizzy). Tap water in Madrid and Barcelona is fine and pure but I would give the children bottled water just the same. The frequent change in mineral content in Spanish water can cause intestinal havoc!

Food? Spanish food is not stoked with spices the way Mexican food is. Traditional seasonings—paprika, pimentos, sweet peppers, tomatoes, and saffron—may be flaming in color, but the taste is not a burning one. The basis of most cooking is olive oil, and for children the effect is often as drastic as if the food were cooked in mineral oil. To sidestep this laxative special, insist that everything be cooked without oil, cooked in butter *(sin aceite, preparado en mantequilla!)* If your children do not like garlic, you can also add, without garlic *(sin ajo).*

Favorite vegetables are onion, garlic, artichokes, peas, eggplant, and asparagus—the Aranjuez asparagus in May and June is superb. Salads, fresh vegetables and fruit are safe wherever you go. Fruit is stupendous. Raspberries *(frambuesas);* small sweet strawberries *(fresas)* and large delicious ones *(fresones),* both generally served with orange juice or whipped cream; small, sweet bananas *(platanos);* watermelon *(sandia)* in late summer; grapes *(uvas),* lemons and oranges *(limones* and *naranjas),* the latter being exceptionally good. There's no trouble getting fresh orange juice *(jugo de naranja).* A good drink for children is *horchata,* a milky-looking beverage made with crushed chufa nuts, served ice cold; tastes almondy and nice. *Naranjada* and *limonada,* orangeade and lemonade, are always available, always good.

Gazpacho (a cold soup of oil, tomatoes, garlic, cucumbers, and green peppers) is a bit exotic for most children. *Paella*—saffron-flavored rice with tidbits of seafood, meat, or chicken, decorated with strips of pimento and green peas—is a hearty dish (a specialty of Valencia) that most children enjoy. In Spain, a *tortilla* is an omelet. The *tortilla de patatas,* a potato omelet, is practically three-meals-in-one, and there are mushroom omelets generally called *setas* or *champinon.* A characteristic is the mixture of apparently ill-assorted ingredients to make a harmonious ensemble. *Huevos* (eggs) *a la Flamenca,* for instance, combines eggs, tomatoes, peas, string beans, potatoes, sausages, asparagus, pimentos, ham, onion, and soup stock. If your children prefer one thing at a time, the baby lamb chops, a dozen to a plate, are always good—ask for *chuletillas.* If your children don't eschew mixtures, *cocido,* or *olla podrida,* a vegetable and meat stew, can be found almost anywhere. *Cocido madrileno* is made with red and black sausages, chick peas, chicken, other meats, and goodness knows what else, a better choice than the *fabada,* a stew made with different kinds of sausages, beans, ham, and pigs' ears. Roast lamb *(cordero asado)* and roast suckling pig *(cochinillo)* are almost always the best meat choices. *Perdiz,* a small partridge, generally has too many little bones in it. *Solomillo* is a thick, juicy filet mignon; delicious. Ham, *jamon serrano,* is good, and nuttier-tasting than the similar Italian prosciutto; like the latter, it's often served with melon.

If your children like seafood—which is varied and abundant—the best choices are *lenguado* (filet of sole), crabmeat *(centollo),* and for high vitamin content, *angulas* (baby eels), often called the spaghetti of the sea; if a child has no preconceived notions about eating eels, they are a treat. Squid or baby octopus *(calamares)* and octopus *(pulpo)* are much better eating than they sound. *Percebes* (goose barnacles, a shellfish much like our Long Island scallops) are delicious; most children, even if they are not great fish-eaters, seem to like them because they are not "fishy" in taste. Caution: *percebes* must be fresh and firm. Of cheeses, only *Burgos,* a mild cream cheese, is appealing to children as a rule. Most restaurants in tourist centers offer an international menu. Traditional dishes are mostly specialties you will find in the country.

As far as children are concerned, the best of Spanish cookery are the sweet things—fruit; *flan,* an egg custard, very good; orange-blossom honey (honey scented with rosemary and marjoram is not as much of a favorite among diminutive gourmets); *pena Santa,* rather like Baked Alaska; the cakes and pies for which *tarta* is the generic name; all the nougat *(turron)* specialties; caramel custard, called *crema cremada* (do not let the children eat this or any custard except at the best places, to be sure it has been properly refrigerated); the Catalan specialty, cake a la Domenech *(Bizcocho de Patatas Domenech);* and all the traditional buns, fritters, cakes, crystallized fruit sweetmeats, candies and pastries associated with religious and historical feast-days throughout the country. As for *churros,* a kind of fried doughnut and *porras,* which are larger and twistier, nothing could be more delicious except *porras* and *churros* dipped in hot chocolate, a dunking custom approved of at all churrerias, of which the coziest is the **Churreria San Gines,** on the Pasadizo de San Gines, not far from Madrid's Plaza Mayor. Churrerias open their doors at 4:30 a.m. on weekends, close at 10:30 a.m. and re-open in the late afternoon.

Breakfast is any old time in the morning. Lunch is served from 1:30 p.m. on, followed by a lengthy siesta. Children may be happier about taking naps if they realize that nap-time, or siesta time, is a national custom. Since dinner is not before 9:30 p.m. and usually around 10 p.m. the best thing is for children to have a good breakfast, a substantial lunch, and then have supper at 6 p.m. in a teashop. Or, you could take them for hot dogs, sandwiches, and hamburgers to a Burger King or McDonald's. Your hotel may or may not be obliging about providing sandwiches for the children's supper. Many supermarkets have sections where you can get delicatessen foods. The **Castellana** (49 Paseo de la Castellana) has a coffee shop that serves food all day.

Parents with children along are expected to sit outside *bares* or *tascas* where snacks are served with liquor.

In **Madrid,** there are adequate luncheonettes: **California** (Goya 21, Goya 47); **Texas** (Montera 46); but **Club 31** (Alcala 58) is a much nicer place, where you can get regular meals and snacks noon–2 a.m. daily and Sun. The **Embassy** (Paseo de la Castellana 12) is a tea room with delicious sandwiches and pastries. **Prince's** (cor. Alcala and Caludio Coello) is an English bakery. Major department stores also have snack bars (see Shopping). Children delight in **La Masia** (Hileras 4), specializing in roast chicken; Paella at **La Barraca** (Reina 29); a lobster tank at **Bajamar** (Jose Antonio 78); **Pizzeria Vittorio** (Felix Boix 7). **Drug Store Good Lunch** (Ramon de la Cruz 5) and **Hollywood** (Magallanes 1) have American food, and American residents rave about **VIPS** (cor. Velasquez and Lopez de Hoyos; Julian Romea 4) For crackling, crisp-skinned *cochinillo* (roast suckling pig) go to **Casa Botin** (Cuchilleros 17, a block from the SE gate of the Plaza Mayor). *Bonbonerias* sell candies of all kinds—**Palacios bonboneria** and **Bonboneria Casa Mira** (San Jeronimo 30) are two of hundreds. ***Health foods*** at **Casa Santivieri** (Plaza Mayor 24). Good moderately-priced family dining at **El Meson de San Javier** (3 Calle Conde).

Barcelona: eat at the **Hostal de la Gloria** (Escudillers 14). Two large typical restaurants: **Siete Puertas** (near the port), for *paella* and suckling pig; or **Los Carcoles,** which specializes in spit-roasted chicken. In **Benalmadena, Bodegon del Muro** in front of the church has regional decor. In **Cordoba,** try **Meson del Conde** or **Meson el Caballo Rojo.** In **Granada,** the great dinner treat is the rooftop grill of the **Ho-**

tel Luz de Granada. In **Malaga, Ebano** (Granda 11), specializes in sandwiches and salads; the supermarket **Supermercado Maroto,** next to the bull ring, has delicatessen foods. Lunch spots in **Marbella: Hosta Mena** (Plaza General Franco); **Restaurante La Reja** (cool courtyard off Plaza Iglesia); topnotch **Antonio's** or **Don Benito** at Puerto Banus; **Le Grillon** next to the Marbella Club; **7 Puertas** (Ricardo Soriano). For succulent roast pig go to **Meson de Candido,** next to the Roman Aqueduct at the entrance to **Segovia.** In **Seville,** the pleasant **La Raza** is just at the entrance of Maria Luisa Park. Outside **Tarifa,** stop at **Meson de Sancho** for Picadilla Soup and a look at the young bulls. **Salon de Te Bagatelle** (La Nogalera 108) is a tearoom in **Torremolinos; Chez Lucien** (Carretera de Cadiz) is good for quiet, civilized French meals.

BABY FOOD Wide variety of international baby foods—**Nestles, Heinz, Gerber, Beechnut,** and almost all European brands—are found in supermarkets *(comestibles)* and pharmacies *(farmacias)* of all major towns and resort areas. Formula **SAM, Nestles, Milupa,** and **Pelargon** milk preparations are widely available in pharmacies. Some pharmacies and supermarkets have powdered milk, baby foods, the junior chopped preparations. In **Madrid,** try **Farmacia Hamburgesa** (Jose Antonio 39) and **Supermercado Aurrera** (Doctor Fleming and Arapiles; Goya 79; Velasquez and Plaza Peru).

A few common varieties of baby food *(alimentacion infantil)* are: *pure de verduras* (vegetable puree), *verduras surtidas* (mixed vegetables), *zanahorias* (carrots), *pollo con semola* (chicken and semolina), *higado con verduras* (liver and vegetables), *ternera* (veal), *vaca* (beef), *albaricoque-manzana* (apricot and apple); for juniors, *carne con espinacas* (meat with spinach), *pollo con arroz* (chicken and rice), *merluza en bechamel* (hake in cream sauce), *lenguado con patatas* (fillet of sole with potatoes), *melacoton* (peaches), *peras* (pears), *frutas variadas* (assorted fruit). See "Health, Water, and Food" for translations of other food names.

DIAPERS AND DIAPER SERVICES The word for diapers is *panales.* Disposable diapers *(panales disponibles),* or paper diapers *(pinales de papel),* come in rolls **(Mon Cheri, Bebe Confort, Dodo, Famosette,** and **Zig-Zag),** or separately packaged in either the cellulose variety **(Mimosan)** which I found useless, or in cotton *(algodon)* and cheesecloth **(Bebesan)** which are adequate. Pampers, Chux, Luv brands and such are becoming more available. Waterproof pants are *picos* (peekos). Baby supplies available in major stores, supermarkets, large pharmacies. There are no organized diaper services, but getting diapers laundered quickly at your hotel by the maid is no problem.

EMERGENCIES MADE EASY In large cities, most hotels have a reputable physician but not always an English-speaking one. In Madrid and

Barcelona, hospitals have English-speaking staff. Pharmacies in Madrid and other large cities often stay open 24 hours. Your hotel concierge can tell which one is nearest to you. In **Madrid,** you have the services of the **British-American Hospital** (Calle Isaac Peral and Calle Limite; Tel: 234–6700) and a U.S.-trained physician group (Tel: 276–4238) 10 a.m.–2 p.m., 4–8 p.m. Outside of town is **Torrejon Air Base Hospital** (Tel: 222–8390, 222–1190, 232–3148). For doctors and dentists recommended by the American community, contact: in **Madrid,** the **American Embassy** (Serrano 75); or consular offices in Barcelona, Bilbao, Seville.

MAGIC FAMILY HELPERS ***Babysitters:*** With the exception of Madrid and Mallorca, there are no babysitting agencies per se in Spain. Nursemaids are readily available, however, although few are English-speaking. Your concierge can recommend one. In **Madrid,** you can also try calling the American Embassy; the **American Women's Club** (Plaza de la Republica del Ecuador 6; Tel: 259–1082); **Family of Babysitters** (Tel: 223–6963) available anytime; or, doubling as a child-care center, children's hotel, and kindergarten, **Baby Parking** (Carbonero y Sol; Tel: 261–1657). **Father Raymond Sullivan** (Vina 3; Tel: 233–2032, 233–7700), available days, runs a summer babysitting group of 80 American students who double as part-time guides. **Mayfair English School** (Pintor Ribera 31; Tel: 250–1496) will take young children by the hour, day, week, or month, providing toys, love, attention, and transportation. Both the major department stores, **Corte Ingles** and **Galerias Preciados** have free supervised playrooms *(guarderias)*. Nursing services for infant and child care are **Salus Infirmorum** (Joaquin Garcia Morato 18; Tel: 223–0101) and **Parroquia San Fernando** (Las Adoratrices, Padre Damian 50; Tel: 259–8229). In **Mallorca,** almost any first-class hotel will arrange an English-speaking babysitter for you. The deluxe Fenix offers its clients the personalized services of "Miss Fixit."

Kindergartens: Among the ones favored by the American community in **Madrid** are:

International Primary School (Madre Carmen del Nino Jesus 3; Tel: 259–2121), 4–8 years, daily Spanish classes; **Hill House School** (Av. Alfonso XIII 34), age 3–8, kindergarten and elementary school, Montessori method; enrollment throughout school term, special summer course; **Mayfair English School** (Pintor Ribera 39; Tel: 250–1496), age 3–8, also first grade; lunches, school bus; **San Isidro Montessori School** (Serrano 196; Tel: 259–0920), 2–6 years, bilingual elementary school, first and second grades (remaining grades to be added), bus, lunch; **Hastings School** (San Amaro 7, off Peron; Tel: 270–1179), age 3–7; **Madrid American Kindergarten** (El Viso; Tel: 261–5012), American curriculum. An afternoon play group for 5–12s is **Kindergarten La Salle** (Alfonso Rodriguez Santamaria 23; Tel: 250–5488, 457–0770), run by

Miss Ellen Conway. In **Barcelona,** try the **Anglo-American School** (Paseo de Garbi 152; Castell de Fels; Tel: 365–1584). In the **Costa del Sol** area, **Jardin de Infancia San Jose** near Estepona offers 3–7s play, swimming, and riding; kindergartens also in Torremolinos (Colegio La Milagrossa) and Las Chapas.

Instruction: Among the many schools recommended for Americans in **Madrid: Runnymede College** (Calle del Arga 9; Tel: 250–1891) ages 10 and up, British secondary school; **Numont PNEU Preparatory School** (Calle Olimpo, corner Calle Palma; Tel: 200–7179) all enquiries, Mrs. Ann Swanson, Principal; King's College, **The English School** (Cuesta del Sagrado Corazon 10; Tel: 259–0845) boarders and day pupils, elementary and secondary; **St. Michael's Preparatory School** (Agustina de Aragon 10; Tel: 401–6421; branch at Henares 6; Tel: 259–0124), age 3–11, English syllabus; the **American School of Madrid** (Carretera de Humera, km. 2 Aravaca; Tel: 270–8643), grades kindergarten–12, accredited by Middle States Assoc. of Secondary Schools, emphasis on Spanish language and culture, Spain's largest American school. Near **Barcleona,** the **Anglo-American School** (see above), kindergarten–9th grade, small classes, first-class boarding facilities and supervision; also **American School** (Plaza Eusebio Guell 8; Tel: 203–7901). In **Palma,** Mallorca, **American Community School of Palma** (Camino Vecinal de Genoa 87, San Agustin; Tel: 237–809); also **Baleares International School** (Calvo Sotelo 599; San Agustin; Tel: 234–131), students 13–18; special summer program featuring language study; boarding and day pupils. There are military schools in Spain for dependents of U.S. forces. The **Instituto de Cultura Hispanica** (Avenida de los Reyes Catolicos, Ciudad Universitaria, Madrid 3) has a list of many classes.

Would you and your children like to learn to speak Spanish? In **Madrid,** try **Centro de Estudios** (Puerta del Sol 11; Tel: 232–2000); home classes at all levels (Tel: 256–4756); **Lenguas Attika** (Plaza Isabel 11; Tel: 241–1458).

Personalized Services: For shopping, shipping, packing, and guide services, try the **American Visitors Bureau** in **Madrid** (Jose Antonio 68; Tel: 247–0333) or in **Barcelona** (Jose Antonio 591; Tel: (93) 232–0658); they also have great bullfight posters. Anglo-American team Tessa Hubbell and Barbara Fulford run **Viajes Valesa** (Nune de Balboa 46) specializing in offbeat trips for families. **ATESA** (501 Madison Ave., N.Y. 10019; Tel: 751–2410; Gran Via 59, Madrid) has car-rental services throughout Spain; their English-speaking chauffeurs are extremely helpful.

If you want a house, a babysitter, a cottage, a villa, anything at all, just write to *American Weekly Guidepost* (Guidepost Publ., 5th Floor, Group 2, Edificio Espana, Madrid). In its extremely efficient personal advertising section classified ads can be placed at modest cost.

Hairdressers all over Spain will do children's hair.

In Madrid, to hire a magician for a birthday party, call (1) 266–0860. Rent films and projectors for children's parties from **Cines Familiares** (Manuela Malasana 19; Tel: 257–6425).

HOLIDAYS FOR CHILDREN ON THEIR OWN No children's hotels that I know of, with the exception of **Baby Parking** in **Madrid** (see Magic Family Helpers and the Club Mediterranee section).

CHILDREN'S CAMPS Scattered across the country are about 20 excellent international "summer colonies" for 7–12-year-olds which are state-run, with high standards of food, lodging, and activity. Some are for boys, some for girls, and some co-educational. They offer swimming, many sports, arts and crafts, and an opportunity for children to learn Spanish rapidly, since most of the campers are Spanish-speaking. Camp periods are from mid-July–early-Aug. and from early–late-Aug. The camps are simple, outdoorsy; for the adventurous, independent, mature child, they might be educational and a great deal of fun. For details on camps listed below, get in touch with **Servicio de Centros de Vacaciones Escolares Internacionales** (Alcala 36, Madrid) or the SNTO.

Alicante: El Castillo, coed. **Almeria:** Madre de la Luz, coed. **Blanes:** Joaquin Ruyra, coed. **Coruna:** Puentedeum, coed. **Gandia:** Cervantes, girls. **Grao de Gandia:** Juan XXII, girls. **Hecho:** Nuestra Senora de Escabues, boys. **Jaca:** Nuestra Senora de las Nieves, girls. **La Escala:** Tramontana, girls. **Los Urrutias** (Cartagena): El Carmoli, boys. **Nerja:** XXV Anos de Paz, girls. **Oliva:** Santa Ana, boys. **San Feliu de Guixols:** Pedralta, boys. **Santiago de la Ribera** (San Janvier): Mar Menor, girls. **Sierra Espuna:** Escuela Hogar, coed. **Tarragona:** Saavedra, girls. **Torre del Mar:** Virgen del Carmen, boys. **Valencia:** El Cabanal, boys. **Vinaroz:** San Sebastian, girls.

In summer, the "fun camp" at **Torrejon Air Base** outside of Madrid invites all American children. For students interested in French and Spanish courses that can be taken through summer-in-youth-homes with families in Avila, Caceres, Ciudad Real and other places, write to the **Instituto de la Juventud y Promocion Communitaria,** 71 Calle Jose Ortega y Gasset, Madrid. The Ministry of Culture runs a program of work camps for age 18 and over, primarily in archaeology, operated as exchange programs, about which information can be obtained through the **Council on International Exchange** (205 East 42nd St. New York, NY 10017).

CASTLES AND OTHER HAPPY FAMILY ACCOMMODATIONS SNTO will send you a list of government-constructed *paradores*—highly recommended accommodations at places that are scenically and historically interesting. Some of these are converted estates, castles, monasteries, palaces, and convents. Others are new. All offer large rooms, plenty of storage space, and nice bathrooms. Most of the *paradores* fall into three to four star categories, just below the "luxury" level. Often they are the area's most attractive accommodations and offer in their dining rooms regional specialties and other fare that is generally very good; and available to all visitors and not just in-house guests. You should book one to two months ahead, sometimes six months ahead for particularly desirable *paradores* like the **San Francisco** in Granada. **Marketing Ahead** (515 Madison Ave., New York, NY 10022) is the agency representing *paradores* in the U.S. The ***albergues*** are all new, more like motels than hotels, more modest in cost than the paradores. ***Albergues de Carretera*** are motels, and provide food and lodging, gas, and garage, at any hour of the day or night. ***Refugios*** are simple but adequately equipped shelters in remote or mountain districts, bases for walking or mountain climbing. Finally, the SNTO will also provide addresses of ***Casas de Labranza,*** simple accommodations for nature lovers, not luxury lovers, in mountain or seaside villages. Also ask about the breakfast-only ***residencias,*** which are cheaper than hotels.

Villas in Spain? Everywhere, more villas for rent than anywhere else, and the SNTO can give you a list of rental agencies for all areas. In the White Town of **Arcos de la Frontera,** Parador **Casa del Corregidor** is a romantic-looking castle about 65 miles from Cadiz. In **Avila,** the **Parador Raimundo de Borgona,** a former palace on a ridge overlooking town, with 26 double rooms, garden, is conveniently situated and about 85 miles from Madrid.

Balearic Islands: Accommodations to satisfy every taste and purse. **Hotel Son Vida,** 15 minutes from Palma, is the only five-star luxury hotel in the Balearics, with 18-hole golf course, riding, heated pool, children's pool, tennis courts, barber shop, hairdresser.

Barcelona: Expensive, modern, with a swimming pool and air-conditioning, 15-minutes from city-center, with TV and refrigerator in every room is the **Princesa Sofia.** Midcity, modern, air-conditioned, with tiny pool, TV in suites and double units is the **Diplomatic.** Air-conditioned, modern, with suites and rooftop swimming pool, good value is the **Gran Hotel Calderon.** A converted Belle Epoque residence with rooftop solarium, small pool, air-conditioning, great accommodations on the sixth and seventh floors with dining terraces, the **Regente** (76 Rambla Cataluna) is excellent value. If it's space you crave, rather than air-conditioning, the **Gala Placidia** (112 Via Augusta) has 28 suites of one or two bedrooms with convertible sofas and/or queen-size beds, with serving pantries, refrigerators, ample storage; a friendly cafeteria on the ground floor with fast-food counter, table service for breakfast and light meals, and a restaurant.

Ciudad Rodrigo: a glamorous walled town, has **Parador Enrique II,** Henry II's imposing 14th-century castle with towers and battlements, but with modern comforts. **Cordoba: Parador de Arruzafa,** in the mountains overlooking the city. Swimming pool; tennis, nearby golf course; suites with private terraces; a children's dining room; all rooms with telephone and bath. **Residencia Marisa** (Cardinal Herrero 6) has only 16 rooms. Cordoba is heavenly both for esthetic appeal and for comfort. Near the Alcazar is **Hotel Melia Cordoba** (Jardines de la Victoria) new and surrounded by gardens. **Hotel Maimonides** (Torrijos 4) with 61 rooms, next to the great Mezquita is the budget special. **El Escorial:** Overlooking the enormous structure of the Escorial is the **Felipe II Hotel,** attractive, with a terrace-dining room. **Fuenterrabia: Parador del Emperador,** a converted castle, is superb. **Granada:** To enjoy to the fullest the Alhambra, stay there, in the garden park, at the **Parador San Francisco,** a 26-room villa, once a convent, now delightfully furnished, comfortable, and extremely popular. If you can't get in here, try the top hotel, the **Alhambra Palace,** which will give you the sensation of living in a Moorish castle. Also, **America Hotel** (Real de la Alhambra 53) formerly an Andalusian-style private house with patio, is extremely pleasant. **Gredos:** Off the beaten track, in the mountains, adjoins a national game preserve where you can hunt ibex; the River Tormes teems with trout; horses provided to explore the lovely surroundings.

Jaen: Parador del Castillo de Santa Catalina has a fabulous vaulted-ceilinged living room in its 13th-century interior. **Jarandilla: Parador Carlos V**—so named because it was once the castle of Charles V—is at the foot of the pine-forested Gredos mountains; massive crenellated walls, turrets, and battlements enclose a fountained courtyard off which the rooms open; four poster beds; armor; medieval furniture. **Javea: Parador de la Costa Blanca** is wonderful, with pool and nearby beaches. A real bit of Spanish heaven is the triangle between Gandia and Benidorm with Javea as its center—a land of baby-size farms, groves of oranges and lemons, moderate-size hotels, and an air of simple living which is most appealing. **Madrid: Wellington Hotel** has attractive suites, pool, roof garden, good restaurant, excellent service; Manager Losada is father of six! Good inexpensive apartments (kitchenettes) on a daily basis at **Castellana Sesenta** (Paseo de la Castellana 62). The **Gran Hotel Victoria,** is in the heart of old Madrid, close to the Prado and the Plaza Mayor. Many *tascas* (bistros) in the area, of which **La Trucha** (Calle Manuel Fernandez y Gonzales, at the NE corner of Plaza Santa Ana) is a top recommendation. Double rooms at the hotel, with balconies facing the plaza, are moderately priced. The grandest hotel in town is the **Ritz** (5 Plaza de la Lealpad) with great style and grace, smaller, more formal, more elegant than the **Palace** (7 Plaza de la Cortes) across the way on the other side of the Neptune Fountain, which is less expensive. **Malaga: Parador Gibralfaro,** a bit out of town. **Marbella:** A wonderful place to stay with children. The chic **Marbella Club Hotel,** which has donkeys, burros, marionette shows in the summer, its own bullring, mini-golf, pool, heavenly bungalows, a beach, its own mixed shooting, and excellent golf courses. The gardens are beautiful, the

Marbella Club is beautiful, and everyone was wonderful to my children; deluxe prices, but not steep for the value offered. **Puente Romano,** located on Marbella Beach, is more expensive, more luxurious with 150 rooms, 45 suites; Bjorn Borg tennis center; three freshwater pools, one heated in winter. The **Guadalmina Golf Hotel** with seaside golf links and a pool in which you not only can swim but also eat (to the great delight of children who like their lunch "chairs" being underwater).

Merida: The **Parador,** converted from a 15th-century convent, has an arched patio with columns that are thought to have been part of a Roman temple. **Mijas:** Wonderful **Hotel de Mijas** has refrigerators in every room, swimming pool, gym, games room, tennis—a secluded eyrie within easy reach of beach life below; reasonable rates. **Nerja:** The **Parador** on the Mediterranean has a pool. **Olite: Parador del Principe de Viana,** a converted palace, has glorious views. **Oropesa:** The **parador** is a "real" castle with walls and crenellated towers, baronial reception hall. Comfortably modernized with eight double rooms (4 have private bath) and one single; mellow furnishings; fine medieval surroundings; excellent food.

Ronda: The **Reina Victoria** in the mountains; courteous management; distinguished air of elegance and old-world charm; large garden; pool; tennis; exceptional views of the unique town and the Tajo canyon—older children only, you'll get nervous with toddlers here! **Santiago de Compostela: Hostal de los Reyes Catolicos** is in a class by itself. Built by Ferdinand and Isabella in 1499 as a shelter for pilgrims, it has been converted to a multimillion-dollar hotel. It has an arched stone doorway worthy of a cathedral; authentic antique furnishings, coffered ceilings, sculpture, hundreds of paintings, balconies, a cloistered courtyard; canopied beds; 200 rooms including royal suites; dormitory accommodations; everything from concert hall to oyster bar to bowling alley; rates reasonable. **Santillana del Mar: Parador of Gil Blas** is a base for excursions to good beaches, the mountains, and the cave paintings of Altamira; 16 double rooms; formerly a large private house, much of the old furniture and decoration remains. **Seville:** A memorable Andalusian palace, an immense polished Victorian masterpiece, has been converted into the 250-room **Alfonso XIII Hotel** (San Fernando 2) with masses of paintings, tiles, tapestries, and other mellow treasures. Charming garden. **Hotel Dona Maria** (Don Remondo 19) in a converted 18th-century building, has a roof terrace with a swimming pool in a beflowered setting; all rooms differently furnished and named in honor of celebrated women. In the marvelous medieval town of **Siguenza,** about 100 miles from Madrid, the **Parador Castillo de Siguenza** is truly special! **Sotogrande: Tenis Hotel** attracts younger types; pool; movie matinees twice a week for children; tennis; riding; close to beach club, golf.

Toledo: If you do not want to stay at the **Carlos Quinto,** and the magnificent 22-room **Parador Conde de Orgaz** is booked solid, try the

Cigarral Monte Rey, a country house two miles outside of town converted into an inn with lovely gardens, pool, and 20 pleasant rooms; reserve in advance. **Torremolinos:** I think **El Pinar,** a little way out of town, with cottages and swimming pool, might be a happier choice for younger children than on the beach, with nightclub, arcaded shops, and everything "moderne" as all get out. **Ubeda: Parador del Condestable Davalos** is installed in the 16th-century palace of Dean Ortega; impressive; beautiful. **Villalba: Parador Condes de Villalba** is an ancient castle, elegantly modernized. **Zafra: Parador Hernan Cortes** is in a marvelous castle. **Zamora:** The cloistered, handsome retreat of the Counts of Alba and Aliste, is the **Parador de los Condes Alba y Aliste,** a 15th-century monastery, about 50 miles from Salamanca.

CLUB MEDITERRANNE At **Marbella** is **Don Miguel,** with a Baby Club for infants from 4 months to 4 years; a Mini Club for those 4–8; a Kid's Club during school vacations; children's own supervised swimming pool; instruction in tennis, sailing; games, walks; manual arts workshops. Accommodation is in a luxury hotel with air conditioning and fine facilities. Write to Club Mediterranee Don Miguel, Marbella, Province of Malaga.

For young, active parents with children 12 and over, Club Med has a Catalonian retreat on the **Costa Brava** where the specialty is snorkeling, instruction in scuba diving, in superb location and conditions; with additional diversions, such as boat trips, archery, sailing, yoga. You live in tile-roofed little white bungalows without electricity or running water, share communal bathing facilities; nightclub, dancing, concerts, library, underwater photography laboratory. Open from the end of May to mid-Sept. Write to Club Mediterranne, Cadaques, Province of Gerona.

Club Mediterranee Puerto Maria (Puerto Santa Maria, Cadiz) accepts children over 8, for whom there's a Kid's Club. Accommodation is in comfortable two-bed bungalows with shower and lavatory. The breeze from the Bay of Cadiz is your only air conditioning. Bicycling, sailing, tennis, swimming pool, yoga, archery, mini-golf; concerts, nightclub, dancing, rental cars. The main attraction here is the excursion program which takes you to Cadiz, the White Towns, of Andalusia, Seville, while providing a pleasant base. Longer trips also available. Open late May to end of Sept.

Club Mediterranee Porto Petro (Santanyi, Mallorca, Balearic Islands) accepts parents with children 12 and over; two-bedded bungalows with shower, lavatory, basin, but no air conditioning. Pinewood, palmy tropical flower setting by the sea, with the usual Club Med facilities, plus riding stable with two dozen horses, kayaking, beach picnics, excurisions. Open mid-May to early Oct.

CAMPING AND CARAVANING Along the Costa Blanca there is an almost unbroken chain of campsites, all on private farmland; hundreds more along the Costa del Sol, north coast, and scattered throughout the interior. You can buy bed rolls or blankets in any large town and save enough by camping to pay for them. Almost all campsites have a washing machine. The SNTO will supply you with infinitely more details. In Madrid, camping equipment and English spoken at **Gonza-Esport** (Ribera Curtidores 10).

Caravans and campers? Volkswagen Campmobiles offices, where you can buy and often rent a happy house on wheels: **Talleres Hispano/Aleman** (Generalisimo 38, Madrid; Tel: 457–3549); **Ciadasa** (General Mola 96, Madrid; Tel: 262–4695); **Motor Repris** (Gran Via, Barcelona; Tel: 250–3076); also in Malaga, Rota, and Zaragoza.

ATTRACTIONS FOR CHILDREN IN MADRID Comfortable, convenient, bright, and spacious, Madrid is the bull's eye in your Spanish target. Between Aug. 1–Sept. 15 many stores, service institutions, and attractions close. May and Oct. are ideal. Midwinter can be very chilly. Some of the following attractions are appealing to 8-year-olds, but the majority are recommended for older children. Most museums are open only 10 a.m.–1:30 p.m. and odd hours afternoons.

First and foremost, the **Museo del Prado** (Paseo del Prado), one of the great museums of the world, is open all day (least crowded during the siesta). An excellent guidebook in English is available at the entrance. The Velasquez pictures are the children's favorites—the royal children, the dwarfs, and the famous *Las Meninas;* also "spooky" Goyas; boys blowing up pigs bladders *(Ninos Inflando Vejiga);* Carreno de Miranda's horridly fat adolescent forerunner of Goya's *Maja.* Wonderful art objects at **Lazaro Galdiano Museum** (Serrano 122). **El Retiro park;** 350 forested acres, large artificial lake, the *Estanque,* where you can hire a boat or sit at cafe tables along its marble borders. On Sun. in spring and summer, the Teatro Guinol, or marionette theater, puts on performances. There are also band concerts. Check with the SNTO for times and exact location. The **Casa de Campo** has a *Parque de Atracciones* with weekend festivities and all manner of entertainment for the little ones; zoo; boatrides on the lake; apprentice bullfighters work out here (sometimes with a wickerwork bull's head) at Camino de los Pinos. Check the best time to go with the hotel concierge or the SNTO, but go there via the 20-minute teleferico (Pintor Rosales 42). Another pleasant park is **Plaza de Espana,** with bronze statues of Don Quixote and Sancho Panza that form part of the monument to Cervantes. The **Botanic Gardens,** next to the Prado, is cool and pleasant. Free samples of medicinal herbs are handed out from 11 a.m.–noon daily, in accordance with a royal decree of Charles III. The **Royal Place** (Plaza de Oriente) is immense, with geometrically formal gardens. Head directly for the Armeria Real (Royal Armory) to see marvelous arms and armor—the armor, to the interest of children, is sometimes child-size. Then see the Farmacia Real (Royal Pharmacy) and the carriage museum. There is a playground right at hand in the Plaza de Oriente, and a charming little parklet, the Sabatini Gardens, to the north of the Palace. **Army Museum** (Museo del Ejercito; Calle Mendez Nunez 1); weapons from the harquebus to the rifle, and stunning array of model soldiers. Bullfighting artifacts at **Museo Taurino** (Alcala 231); trains at **Museo del Ferrocarril** (San Cosme y San Damian). The famous cave paintings of Altamira are reproduced in the **Museum of Archaeology** (Serrano 13). The small waxworks **Museo de Cera** (Plaza Colon) may make someone wax ecstatic—not me. More interesting than one might imagine is watching fine tapestries made at the **Real Fabrica de Tapices** (Fuenterrabia 2); plus a train ride through the gardens. Folk art at the **Museum of Decorative Arts** (Museo de Artes Decoratives; Calle de Montalban, 2). The **Maritime Museum** (Museo Naval; Calle de Montalban 12), ship models and other things of nautical interest. The **Rastro** (Thieves' Market) at the Plaza de Cascorro, due south from the Plaza Mayor, takes place on Sun. mornings, and you must haggle like mad. **Stamp Exchange** every Sun., 11a.m.–1 p.m., in the Plaza Mayor. **Flamenco dancing** should be seen by the older children at Zambra, Corral de la Moreria or whichever place currently has the best performances. Take in the mixed bag of musical attractions at **Teatro Zarzuela** (Jovellanos 4). **Zarzuela,** the musical theater of Spain, offers performances every evening at 7 p.m. and 10 p.m., *except* Mon., at the **Monumental Theater** (65 Atocha). Movies in English at **Cine Pompeya** (Jose Antonio 70), **Galileo** (Galileo 100), **Penalver** (Conde Penalver 59). Older children may enjoy Spanish ballet performances during the summer at the **Cultural Center** (Plaza Colon).

A walk around medieval and 16th- and 17th-century Madrid. Just wander around Puerta del Sol, Calle Mayor, Plaza Mayor, Plaza de Santa Cruz, Calle de Toledo, Calle del Sacramento, Plaza de la Villa, and Plaza de la Paja. A circus, the **Circo Price** (Plaza del Rey 3), runs from Oct.–Apr.; occasionally also small traveling circuses. Check with the SNTO for exact dates. Throughout the summer there are night festivals, called *verbenas,* on the eves of religious holidays. Music, food, gaiety, side shows, great fun for all the family. One-day ***excursions*** can be made from Madrid but these are exhausting. Busloads of excursionists endure these grueling junkets and live to tell the tale—but I would suggest a more leisurely program combined with an overnight stop at a parador. Interesting targets include El Escorial, Toledo, Avila, Segovia, La Granja, Pedraza de la Sierra.

ATTRACTIONS FOR CHILDREN IN BARCELONA Before you do anything else, check in at the SNTO for a good map, the rundown on museum hours (which vary), transportation information, and other practical hints.

At Montjuich, a hill in southwestern Barcelona, you will find the **Pueblo Espanol,** an outdoor museum; a good place for children to buy souvenirs. The entrance, at the base of the hill, is through the Puerta de Avila, a replica of a postern in Avila. Don't miss the **Museum of Pop-**

ular Arts, with toys, costumes, Christmas creches, and regional crafts. On top of Montjuich is the **Parque Attraciones,** an amusement park with waterfalls, fun rides, fun house, trampolines, Ferris wheels, go-karts. From here, you can wander through the hill's parklands, flowers, and statuary to the Greek Theater, where classical plays are performed in summer; to the Stadium, where sports events are held; to the outdoor restaurants for roast or barbecued chicken; or, back of the huge fountains that look so delicious at night lit with colored lights, to the **Museo de Arte de Cataluna,** with Romanesque, Medieval, Rennaisance, and Baroque murals, paintings, sculpture, carvings, and religious primitives. A hop away are the **Ethnological and Colonial Museum** and the **Archaeological Museum** (prehistory–18th century plus many good paintings).

Southeast of Montjuich, at the very end of Calle del Marques del Duero, you will find the **Maritime Museum** in the Reales Atarazanas, a 15th-century Gothic arsenal that now contains ship models and nautical lore. In front of the entrance, on Paseo de Colon, is the Plaza Puerta de la Paz, with a monument to Columbus; elevator inside will carry you to a lofty lookout for a fine view of the city and the harbor. Moored along the water's edge here is a replica of the *Santa Maria,* in which Columbus discovered America. You're welcome aboard. You can hire a *golondrina* (swallow) or a *gaviota* (sea gull)—motorboats—to putt-putt you around the harbor or even along the coast. The **Parque de la Ciudadela,** the town park, adjoining the main railroad station, is laid out where the Castle of Barcelona once stood; it contains the **Botanical Gardens;** marionette theater; and up-to-date **zoo;** the **Natural History Museum;** the **Martorell Museum** (for young geologists and paleontologists); and the **Museum of Modern Art.** Tibidabo (its name, "To Thee I Give," refers to the Catalan legend that Jesus stood on this hill when exhorted by the Devil to worship him in exchange for the kingdoms of the world) is the highest hill close to Barcelona, and offers an open-air restaurant with a fine daytime and after-dark view. Adventures offspring may find the funicular ride to the top shriekingly amusing.

In the **Plaza de Cataluna,** the enormous, main fountained square, on a Sun. morning—and often in the evening—you will probably find a group of people, hand in hand in a ring, dancing the *sardana,* the most popular regional dance. Generally, the dancers are accompanied by a cheery little band. From here, Avenida Puerta del Angel leads into the Plaza Nueva, with bits and pieces of Roman remains, including the Roman city wall; walk past the **Historical Archives,** with its lovely courtyard, and to the Cathedral, which has a museum. Tradition has it that the first American Indians brought to Spain by Columbus were baptized here. On Corpus Christi day, an empty eggshell is balanced on the spray of the main fountain in the cloister, where it bounces about all day. The fountain is decorated with fruit and flowers, and sometimes the geese who live here are garlanded with flowers. Geese appear on the Barcelonese coat of arms, a carryover from the time of the Romans, when the goose was a symbol of providence and vigilance. Geese also appear on a tapestry picturing St. George in the Chapel of St. George in the **Diputacion** (Provincial Council), a building you should visit; on St. George's Day, Apr. 23, roses are sold in the patio for boys and men to give to their loved ones. Leave via the narrow street of the Condes de Barcelona, facing the **Great Royal Palace.** If you have time, see the **Museo Mares** with wonderful wooden religious statuary. Right at hand is the Plaza del Rey where Columbus made his triumphant return after discovering the New World. Under the plaza you can visit **Roman ruins** of the original city of Barcino. To see more of the old quarter, where streets still bear the names of the trades that used to be practiced along them, walk along Calle Plateria, which leads out of the Plaza del Angel (more Roman walls here). If you keep on walking to Plaza Santa Maria del Mar (St. Mary of the Sea), the back door of this lovely church leads into a square that in turn leads into Calle Montcada, inhabited by the Spanish nobility until the 19th century, a beautiful quarter. The old palace of **Berenguer de Aguilar** (Calle Montcada at 15) has been turned into a Picasso museum (800 paintings). See a **bullfight** at the *Plaza de Toros Monumental,* or the *Plaza de Toros Las Arenas.* To enjoy the atmosphere of modern Barcelona, stroll along the Ramblas, the main social arteries that arrow from the Plaza de Cataluna down to the Plaza Puerta de la Paz (horse-drawn carriages for rent). Be sure, as doors open for you, to check the imaginative doorknobs, which can be animals, corkscrews, funny faces, or even barometers. **Safari Park** close by.

ATTRACTIONS FOR CHILDREN ON THE BALEARIC ISLANDS These islands are a mecca for budget-minded young families, and German and British two-week package trippers. To avoid the tourist crush, go in May, Sept., or Oct. From May–Oct., the weather in Mallorca is perfect for swimming and watersports; beaches are all good, but the top ones are **Formentor; Cala d'Or; Paguera;** and **Camp de Mar.** In **Palma,** fishing equipment can be rented from **Fishing Sport** (Plaza de la Lonja 13) and any kind of craft from a motorboat to a yacht from the **Yacht Club. Bullfights** on Sat., Sun., and holiday afternoons in the Palma Plaza from late spring to early fall. Explore the 14th-century **Bellver,** and have a look at the **cathedral** (Palma's landmark) and the **Lonja** (the medieval Exchange building). The Drach (Dragon) **Cave Trip:** The highway leads to Manacor through the windmill region and almond orchards to Porto Cristo, the little port close to the illuminated stalagmite, stalactite caves. After a tour through the caves, you are treated to an underground concert staged on lighted barges floating on an amphitheatered subterranean lake; then gondolas ferry you ashore. There are other stalagmite and stalactite caves at **Hams, Campanet,** and **Arta,** but music days at Drach are the choice excursion. A trip to **Selva,** where Mallorquin dancers perform on certain days; full particulars from the SNTO. Have a look at the **windmills** east of Palma; the four-masted Spanish schooling-schooner *Juan Sebastian de Elcano* (ask the SNTO for time). On a day's auto trip out of Palma, you follow hairpin turns into the mountains to **Valldemosa** and the **Carthusian Monastery** where Chopin and George Sand lived; Chopin's piano in one room, folk-dancing in the next. Not far from Valldemosa is the former Moorish estate called **La Granja;** olive-pressing and weaving techniques are demonstrated; caged peacocks and a small natural geyeser to see. Beyond Valldemosa is Deya. Then comes **Soller,** a village of fishermen's fleets and souvenir shops, with launch trips to the cliffs of Mallorca's Costa Brava. Or visits to the interior towns of **Inca,** for its Thurs. market, **Santa Maria** for its Sun. market.

Ibiza is the new paradise discovered by the Scandinavians, who fill many tour buses in the summer, and young Europeans, who are wild about **Ku,** a huge discotheque-cum-glass-enclosed swimming pool. This extravaganza is about 1½ mi. out of **San Antonio,** the main town. In the old town of **Ibiza,** there are still donkey carts to be seen, a treasure-filled **archaeological museum,** Ibicencos cordial to children, and women wearing long skirts, shawls and a braid down their backs. Every Wed., there's a **Hippie Market** dispensing irresistible bangles, clothes, pottery made or acquired by the hippies who have frequented Ibiza for years, and who have now organized a tourist-oriented market just outside of **Santa Eulalia,** a charming small town. There are a number of hotels, inns, pensions; few private telephones; an organized Vespa or Moped rental service; few cars, but many buses that negotiate the hilly roads. **Minorca** is a simpler cousin of Mallorca, and *infinitely* preferable if you like "unspoiled" islands where tourists aren't abused and there's nothing much to "do" except at each town's yearly festival. **Ciudadela** is the most Spanish town on the island, with a strong Moorish influence visible in its arcades, vaulted passageways, narrow streets. **Porto Mahon,** on a plateau above the port, is the capital, with superb free admission organ concerts in the Cathedral of Santa Maria during its Sept. Music Festival. Large resort hotels with such amenities as swimming pools, saunas, air conditioning are everywhere; scores of small inns and "*casas de huespedes*" (boarding houses) listed by the CTO (13 Plaza de San Parroquia, Mahon); also from the **Formento del Turismo** (25 Gral Goded, Mahon). **"Biniali** just outside **San Luis** on the road to seaside resort **Binibeca,** is a renovated farmhouse converted to a hotel furnished with Spanish antiques; double rooms, bath and terrace are moderately priced. Villa rentals can be arranged by most travel agents. Some 120 beaches; major ones have windsurfing equipments and instructional facilities; boat rentals from the Club Maritimo in Mahon; Club Nautico in Ciudadela; Club Nautico in Fornells; Club Nautico in Villacarlos. For day and night tennis, go to Las Dunas at Santo Tomas, S'Algar at San Luis, or Club Tenis in Mahon. N.B. Don't take your car with you. Cars are transported from Barcelona to Minorca via the **Transmediterranea Co's** passenger and car ferry for the price of a one-way air fare from Madrid to Minorca, and cost more to transport than you. There are dozens of car rental companies in Minorca, good bus service, taxis. You can also get a cheap roundtrip charter from London for about 25% less than the price of the roundtrip fare from Barcelona.

ATTRACTIONS FOR CHILDREN ELSEWHERE Everywhere business hours are geared to the afternoon siesta. Food shops and restaurants are almost always open, but almost everything else shuts down from 1–4 p.m. Closing hours for shops are between 7–8 p.m. Museums are usually open only in the morning. Hotels and apartment houses lock their doors at night. If you find yourself locked out, clap your hands. This will summon the *sereno,* or night watchman.

Aigua Blava is a small family resort on the Costa Brava. **Almunecar,** once a Roman town called Sexi, has archaeological and architectural treasures. **Andalusia's "White Towns,"** located between **Jerez** and **Ronda,** are hilltop eyries, Iberian-North African in ambiance and style. **Arcos de la Frontera,** a one half-hour drive east of Jerez, is the most spectacular. Stay there at the **Parador Casa del Corregidor.** Rooms with the greatest views from their balconies cost extra, but are worth it. **Zahara** and **Grazalema** are the other two major wonders on the route, although there are some 30 others along the way.

▶ **Special:** Spain, once a province of Rome, is rich in Roman ruins, and two of the most spectacular are the recently-made-accessible **Acinipo** (pronounced Ah-thee-NEE-po), about 10 miles NE of Ronda, to be astonished by after a turn-off from the Seville road and a little hike into what looks like hill country with a blank blob up on a hill crest. This reveals itself as a 15,000-seat theater with extraordinary acoustics, bleacher seats with a sheer cliff-drop behind, and a fabulous vista beyond the stage backdrop. Children will be fascinated by the acoustics. (You can hear a normal speaking voice carrying from the stage up to the topmost, tip-back-into-the cliff-most bleacher seats.) The other wonder is **Baelo-Claudia,** a former tuna-packing town about 10 miles drive along the coast W of Tarifa, with 2-storeyed Roman buildings, theater, forum and extraordinary statuary. The only statue of Claudius was found here (now in a museum in Paris, I'm told). This is the occasion to explain to the kids that not only did the Romans sculpt their statues with removable heads (the body of Claudius' sculpture was thought to be that of Trajan or possibly Hadrian, although the head was unmistakably that of Claudius), but also removable *wigs,* so that women could always have their stone portraits updated, because you'll see a lot of fascinating statuary here that you are unlikely to see anywhere else. **Aranjuez,** the strawberry and asparagus center, has a handsome summer palace with lush gardens, a royal boathouse filled with royal barges, and the *"Casita del Labrador,"* literally the Farmer's Cottage, but actually a little palace jampacked with clocks, porcelain, and lavish furnishings, including a gold-walled john. On May 30 there is a riproaring bullfight in honor of San Fernando.

Avila, dedicated to St. Teresa, is a medieval and Renaissance museum, surrounded by spectacular battlemented walls with 88 towers, 9 gates, and subterranean passages. From a distance, the city is enchanting. In the day, with the sun shining on the crenellated towered walls, it is breathtaking. On Oct. 15, there are fairs, fireworks, bullfights, costumed floats, and parades during the **festival of St. Teresa.** There are religious processions during Easter week and on the first and second Sun. in Oct. A dozen churches and convents, palaces, and a cathedral; the tomb of Torquemada, the Scourge of the Inquisition, can be found in the **Convent of Santo Tomas,** a little way out of town. **Burgos,** where the Cid was born, has one of the finest cathedrals in Spain. The Cid and his wife are buried beneath the transept. On June 29, the lively Burgos fairs begin and go on for about a week—fireworks, dancing, bullfights, and general merriment. Children like going to **Caceres,** a walled town with Roman and Arabic towers. Along the Costa Brava, **Cadaques** deserves a bravo; red tiled roofs, white-facaded houses, wonderful weekly market; Salvador Dali chose this above all fishing villages as a place to live. **Calella de Palafrugell** is a family resort on the Costa Brava not yet in the tower-block hotel range.

The **Canary Islands:** Of the seven islands, **Tenerife** is the most popular and attractive. It's mobbed in winter, mostly by European trippers out for fun-in-the-sun. Lanzarote has camel riding. Gomera was the last landfall of Columbus on his first voyage to the New World; a mountainous island with a parador to stay in. It's unique because many of its inhabitants have acquired the art of talking by whistling and are able to produce rhythmic, birdlike sounds that can be heard far beyond shouting range (9 miles, I believe, is the record); goatherders communicate not just with various tones, sounds, and trills, but with a vocabulary of whistle-sounds. You can rent paddleboats; swim, snorkel, take a cable car ride to the top of Tenerife's peak. Useful contacts: **Provincial Tourist Office** (Leon y Castillo 17, Las Palmas, Gran Canaria) also in Las Palmas, **U.S. Consular Agent** (Franchy y Roca 5). **Island Tourist Office** (Palacio Insular, Santa Cruz de Tenerife, Tenerife); **U.S. Consulate Information Office** (Alvarez de Lugo 10); **Tourist Office** (Parque Municipal, Arrecife, Lanzarote).

Cordoba is a favorite of many children. The **Mezquita,** a fantastic Moorish mosque with colored inlaid columns, wonderful double keyhole arches, prayer recesses (be sure to see the mihrab, or recess, at the southern end where the Koran was kept), and patio of orange trees and fountains, is a glory to add to your child's memories. Cordoba itself is a Moorish-looking town with twisting streets, quiet squares, and many convents, churches, and beautiful old houses set in walled patio gardens shut off from the street by massive wrought-iron gates. The **Zoco,** the municipal market, is fun as are the small zoo and Flamenco shows. Have a look also at the **Casa de los Paez** (the Archaeological Museum), the **Fine Arts Museum,** the **Synagogue,** the **Alcazar,** and the **Casa de las**

Bulas, a museum of Cordobese art and bullfighting souvenirs. Sample the homemade pistachio ice cream at **Caballo Rojo** restaurant (Cardenal Herrero 28). To see the embossed leatherwork of Cordoba at its best, visit the **Palacio de Viana** (Plaza de don Gomez), a former palatial residence now opened as a museum (mornings only, small admission), **Meryan** (2 Calleja de las Flores), is a leather workshop and commercial outlet. Don't miss the **Monastery of San Jeronimo** back in the mountains next to a ruined palace, filled with skulls, some bearing the approximate message, "As you see me now, I saw myself. This is all you are in the end. Think, don't sin." This might seem awfully macabre, but children find it fascinating. Outside of town is the **Medina Az-Zahara,** an archaeological dig. **El Escorial,** an attractive resort in the foothills of the Guadarrama Mountains. *The* sight is the immense **Royal Monastery of San Lorenzo,** the most ambitious Renaissance edifice in Spain, a 16th-century palace-monastery-mausoleum of vast proportions built by Philip II and containing suites of furnished rooms, sacred relics, medieval books, and beautiful paintings and frescoes (including Durer, Bosch, Titian, Tintoretto, Velasquez). Nearby are two smaller museum-palaces. The best time to go with children is **fiesta week** of San Lorenzo (Aug. 10–15), when all sorts of entertainments go on, including bullfights. As San Lorenzo (St. Lawrence) was burned alive on a gridiron—for refusing to give up to the Romans church treasures in his possession (he is reported to have said, "I am roasted enough on this side; turn me and eat.")—the Escorial is built in the shape of a gridiron. During Easter and on the second Sun. in Sept., the religious processions are well worth seeing. Whenever you go, be sure to bring sweaters for the children. It's always chilly inside the Escorial.

Estepona remains an old-fashioned fishing village, but its yacht club rents boats and equipment for game fishing, scuba and spear fishing. **Fuengirola:** Zoo. **Gerona,** a lovely old town; pottery shops offer exceptionally nice things for children's collections. **Granada:** You come here to see the most celebrated monument left by the Moors—the citadel pleasure-dome of the **Alhambra** open 9 a.m.–7 p.m. Its galleries, colonnades, filigree walls, arches, domes, trellised windows, tiles, fountains, courtyards, pools, gates, and pavilions sweeten your memories for life, so go through it slowly and do your best to lag behind the guide and the group. You cannot visit the interior unescorted and the droning of the guide may diminish your pleasure. Encourage your children just to look about them and listen to the splashing water rather than the guide's mumblings. The **International Music and Dance Festival** takes place every year from June 20–July 2 or 4, and the world's great soloists and ensembles can be seen and heard in the incomparable setting of the pomegranate-colored Court of the Lions or in the gardens. Up the mountainside, you can also see the **Generalife,** the summer palace of the luxury-loving caliphs, with terraced gardens of cypresses and jasmine, roses and yew. Combine this with a picnic or a trip to the Sacro Monte and the **gypsies' caves** (electrically lit and rather garishly furnished); the gypsies sing, dance, and behave in the pat, phony way of performers rather than like just plain folks, but if you join in and pretend they're real, it can be fun. They are fond of the five-fingered discount, so keep track of your possessions. Also worth seeing are the **Cuarto Real de San Domingo,** an admirably preserved 13th-century villa set in a lovely garden; the **Cartuja** (or Charterhouse) on the edge of town; the **Royal Chapel,** opposite the Cathedral, containing the tomb of Ferdinand and Isabella; and Flamenco at Neptuno.

In **Illescas,** El Greco paintings at the Hospital de la Caridad. **La Granja,** the summer palace of Philip V, known as the "Spanish Versailles," houses magnificent tapestries, some by Goya, and is surrounded by impressive gardens and fountains—the water is turned on twice a week Apr.–Sept., check with the SNTO for exact dates. Puerto de Navacerrada and the villages nearby are summer resorts as well as winter skiing stations complete with funicular, a teleski, several adequate inns and restaurants. **Llafranch:** Hotels are very much family businesses; red rocks, sandy beaches, dense pines, cliff paths, cactuses, brilliant flowers. **Malaga:** Founded by the Phoenicians, with flower-filled parks and plazas, a luxuriant orchard and vineyard setting—famous for its muscatel wine—an almost tropical climate and a busy harbor that twinkles at night with the firefly light of hundreds of little fishing boats. Special **bullfights** on Easter Sun. and on Corpus Christi; also daily *corridas* during the Aug. Festival, and on most Sun. and holidays during the summer. Hot and crowded in summer, pleasant in winter (particularly during the festival held Jan. 15–Feb. 15, at which all sorts of folklore and sporting events take place). Plenty of golf, tennis, swimming, and local fiestas. The main sights are the **Cathedral** and the **Alcazaba,** a restored Moorish castle now a museum—with more battlements, passageways, towers, palace rooms, and dungeon space than one thinks possible; it is best to go with a guide the first time around. Up on the hill of El Gibralfaro (the lighthouse) are unattended **ruins.** The Parador Gibralfaro is a marvelous lunch stop; the children can then explore the ruins of the castle fortress of **Las Ruinas,** wandering about the watchtower, sentinels' walks, dungeons and stairs. From the tourist office, you might arrange a trip out to a bull-breeding ranch where you can hire horses and ride with the trainers. Bulls are placid as Ferdinand in herds. You can also watch the *novilleros* (apprentice matadors) working out. Motorboats for hire to go underwater fishing. **Marbella:** The liveliest, most fashionable resort on the Costa del Sol. If the children like Roman ruins, the best preserved are at **Merida,** with a superb Roman amphitheater in which classical plays are performed, an aqueduct, a bridge that is still in use, and a triumphal arch. **Mijas:** This self-consciously charming village has an attractive hotel, donkey taxis, arts and crafts, and **Carromato de Max,** a museum housed in a covered wagon featuring miniatures carved and painted on pinheads, matchsticks, seeds, buttons, thumbtacks, a shrunken head, and the Lord's Prayer written on the edge of a calling card! **Monserrat:** The **monastery** is worldfamous for its history, sanctity, spectacular view, liturgy, and Gregorian plainsong. The boys' choir sings at 1 p.m. and 6 p.m. daily. The Fiesta of the Black Virgin draws pilgrims on Christmas Eve. An aerial cableway carries visitors up some 4000′ to the **Hermitage of St. Jerome. Nerja,** the site of **caves and mural paintings** almost as good as those at Altamira, is a must; fascinating.

Pamplona: The *Fiesta de San Fermin* (July 6–July 15) a time of general high jinks climaxed by the running of the bulls. All cross streets are shut off, and the bulls for the *corrida* are let loose on the main street that leads to the bull ring. The bulls come snorting and galloping along, and ahead of them run the young men of the province, showing off their bravery to their girl friends who watch—as you do—from windows and balconies. This is a hilarious and exciting chase that all children love. Hemingway wrote a book about this—*Fiesta*—and also wrote about Pamplona and the fiesta in *The Sun Also Rises.* **Pedraza de la Sierra:** Please treat yourself to this medieval town with a castle, walls, colonnaded Plaza Mayor, a pewter factory, and tremendous atmosphere. **Ronda:** A mountain village straddling a gorge, an alternate choice to **Arcos de la Frontera** as a base for touring the Andalusian "White Towns." Stay at the restful **Hotel Regina Victoria,** the **Hotel Polo,** or the **Hostal Residencia Royal.** *Be sure* to make the trip to see the **Pileta Caves,** about an hour away on the road to **Seville,** where the pottery and cave drawings are said to attest to 25,000 years of occupation. The **Plaza Mayor** of **Salamanca** has been cited as "the finest in Spain and one of the four best in the world," and it's worth driving 2½ miles from Madrid to see this beautiful twin-cathedral city. **San Roque: Auto Safari Park Andaluz. Santiago de Compostela:** This National Monument is a pilgrim city of surpassing glamour with an extravagant cathedral, central square, and fiesta on July 24. **Segovia:** Famous for its Roman **aqueduct,** giant **Alcazar,** and **cathedral. Seville:** Famous as the site for *Don Giovanni, Carmen,* and the *Barber of Seville,* this city attracts vast crowds and wild cram-jammed confusion during **Holy Week** (spectacular!) and the **April Fair** (extravagant festivities). See the **Cathedral** (where Columbus is buried), **Giralda Tower** (climbable in easy stages), beautiful Maria Luisa Park, the **Alcazar** and its gardens, the enormous **Plaza de Espana** ringed with a canal (fun to have yourself rowed around), the Virgin beloved by bullfighters in the Basilica de la **Macarena** (even though she is less impressive in reality than in photographs), the bull ring; see too the **Columbus Library** (in the orange-tree-filled courtyard next to the Cathedral) with maps, books, fascinating marginalia, and manuscripts by our discoverer. The **Casa de Pilatos** is a lovely Mudejar-style palace, open 10 a.m.–1 p.m., 3 p.m.–7:30 p.m.; top floor closed Sat. eve. and Sun. The **Torre del Oro,** the Golden Tower overlooking the Guadalquivir River is now a **Naval Museum,** open 10 a.m.–2 p.m., closed Mon. Also overlooking the Guadalquivir is the **Rio Grande restaurant** (Betis 70), open 1:30 p.m.–5 p.m., 8:30 p.m.–1 p.m. Discover documents about the Spanish colonization of

America at the **Archivo General de Indias,** open 10 a.m.–1 p.m. Discover the joys of glorious food at **Enrique Becerra** (Gamazo 2), a few blocks from the Cathedral, closed Sunday evening, and eves. Sat. and Sun. in summer; otherwise open 1 p.m.–5 p.m., and 8 p.m.–midnight. **Rincon de Curro** (Virgen de Lujan 45) is another restaurant recommendation, closed Sun. eve., open 1:30 p.m.–4 p.m., 9 p.m.–midnight. ***Flamenco dancing*** at the **Tablao de Curro Velez** (Rodo 7), an untouristy place. Recommended for picnic foodstuffs is **Marciano** (Linares 6). Walk around the **Barrio de Santa Cruz,** the former Jewish Quarter. Young archaeological buffs will enjoy the necropolis of **Carmona** and the ruins of **Italica** in the suburbs. Early Sun. morning the stamp (Plaza de Santa Maria) and bird (Plaza de la Alfafa) markets are entertaining.

Toledo: This tourist-trodden ancient capital, instantly recognizable from El Greco's *View of Toledo,* is a National Monument; top sights are the **Cathedral, Fine Arts Museum, Archaeological Museum,** but all of Toledo is interesting to explore. Ferry across the Tagus on an unexpectedly small boat for fun, a great view, and to see the Chapel of the Virgin of the Valley on the other side. **Torremolinos:** Target of cheap package tours—with high-rise warrens, a bullring, a **Reptile Park** (Malaga side of town), and a **London Wax Museum** (Carretera de Cadiz 17) with a grisly Chamber of Horrors—this resort redeems itself completely with **Tivoli Amusement Park** (Benalmadena); exceptionally easy and untiring route through over 100 amusement rides and attractions; dolphinarium; open-air theater; boating lake, donkey rides, gardens; free baby-minding playroom (no beds) for children over 2; over 30 restaurants feature just about every national cuisine; open daily except Mon. at 4 p.m. and Sun. at 11 a.m. (with children's gala party at 5 p.m.); midnight fireworks Fri. **Valladolid:** Home of Cervantes, a city of churches, monasteries, palaces, colleges, with the great **Museo Nacional de Escultura** (in the Colegio de San Gregorio, Cadenas de San Gregorio) with its extraordinary, lifelike, polychrome wooden sculptures which alone make a trip here worthwhile.

FUN TRIPS At **Lanzarote,** an island in the Canary group, visit the **Timanfaya National Park,** not so much for the volcanic craters and lava-covered hills, as for the ride in deck chairs on the backs of camels that will sway you like desert chieftains through the **Montanas del Fuego** (Mountains of Fire). The **Costa Brava,** the 70 miles of shoreline north of Barcelona dotted with a score of famous resorts (Tossa de Mar, San Feliu de Guixols, S'Agaro), has water taxis that ply from Blanes to Tamariu. Up a spaghetti-thin gangplank, into a hot little wooden ferrylike boat to settle down on hot little wooden benches for a passage that costs from 50¢ to $5 (depending on the distance) is many children's idea of sheer heaven.

In **Mijas,** burro taxis—donkeys drawing wheeled carts for two—are transports of delight.

You can take a two-night cruise aboard a car-ferry with swimming pool from **Malaga** to Genoa through **DFDS Seaways** (Alameda de Colon 9, Malaga; Tel: 218–857).

FUN AND GAMES ***Bullfighting:*** The season is Mar.–mid-Oct. Technically, bullfighting is not a sport. The adversaries are not equally matched. The outcome is never in doubt. What you are actually seeing is the solemnization of a death and resurrection ritual that has been practiced for so long that its origins have been forgotten.

If you don't know about bullfighting and don't know whether or not you'll like seeing a fight, it's far better to buy a cheap seat in the sun, way up high, than to spend a lot of money for the *barrera* (ringside), *sombra* (in-the-shade) seats which, of course, are always recommended, but often cost $20 more than the cheap seats. Being high up in the bleachers puts distance between you and the graphic realities of the fight. Most people who believe they, or their children, won't be able to stand the sight of blood and gore, find that from the inexpensive seat areas—called *grada* and *andanada* in *sol* (in-the-sun)—they enjoy the pageantry immensely. They are also *grada* and *andanada* sections on the *sombra* side which are somewhat more expensive than their *sol* mates. Another advantage for families who opt for the inexpensive seat areas is that it's much simpler to make a rapid, unobtrusive exit from them than it is from the prestigious *barrera* and *sombra tendido* areas.

Whether your children are horrified or think it is enormously exciting, I think a bullfight is a fine addition to a child's education, and I can't imagine going to Spain and not seeing a bullfight. Seats should be reserved in advance through a travel agency or through the concierge of your hotel. Every town has its Plaza de Toros; in Madrid, you have a choice of Monumental de las Ventas, Vista Alegre, and (12 m out) San Sebastian de las Reyes.

You can watch ***jai-a-lai (pelota),*** a Basque invention often played with an armlong basket scoop, in a great hall called a *fronton*—in Madrid at **Fronton Madrid** (Doctor Cortezo 10), **Fronton Recoletos** (Villanueva 2), or at **Casa de Campo.** You can get tickets and schedules from your concierge. The uproar of cheering and betting, barely tolerable to me, is thrilling to some people.

Tennis: Among the many tennis courts and clubs, the **Bjorn Borg Tennis Center** in Marbella is in the most luxurious of settings.

Golf: Most major resorts and cities have at least small courses, and there are good courses in the **Canary Islands,** but the **Costa del Sol** has been nicknamed The Costa del Golf because it scores all birdies with **Golf Hotel Guadalmina, Nueva Andalucia, Los Monteros,** and **Atalaya Park Hotel.**

Fishing: Salmon fishing is excellent in the province of Galicia. Fine brown-trout fishing in the Sierra de Gredos region. Good sea fishing in the Canary and Balearic islands. Bait, tackle and boats can be rented.

Hunting: Excellent game in the mountains—bear, wolves, deer, boar, chamois and ibex—particularly around the Santander area. Hares, rabbits, partridge, grouse and snipe are also plentiful around this district. With an owl as a decoy, eagle hunting is also practiced. Ask for the SNTO booklet on hunting and fishing. In Madrid, information is available from the **Direccion General de Montes, Caza y Pesca Fluvial** (General Sanjurjo 27; Tel: 254–7527 (hunting); 254–8869 (fishing).

Swimming and Sailing: From May–Oct. in Mallorca, Minorca, Ibiza, and all along the Costa Brava, Costa del Sol, and Costa Blanca. From mid-June–mid Sept., the Costa del Sol and the Costa Brava are crowded. The Costa Blanca is the least crowded. Other attractive beach areas are Sitges and Tarragona, Santander, San Sebastian, and La Coruna. Many opportunities for waterskiing, skin-diving, underwater fishing, and many outdoor pools in large tourist centers and beach resorts. In Madrid, outdoor pools at **Castilla** (Habana 187), **El Lago** (Valladolid 37); indoor pools at **Vallehermoso** (Santander); the Municipal pool at **Casa de Campo.**

Skiing and Winter Sports: Feb. is the season, and teaching methods at ski schools have been adopted from the French. Adult equipment is rentable, but you must bring the children's boots and skis. Most popular family resorts are in the Pyrenees at **La Molina** (ski school, lifts, day nursery, ice rinks), **Nuria,** and **Valle de Aran;** near Huesca, **El Formigal** with ski school for children plus playground and heated pool; near Jaca, **Candanchu,** with ski school and child-care centers. Near Madrid there is skiiing at **Puerto de Navacerrada** in the Guadarrama range, with ski school and sled rental. In the Sierra Nevada you can ski **La Veleta** and then take a one-half-hour helicopter ride to a seaside resort. Additional information from SNTO or **Federacion Espanola de Esqui** (Modesto Lafuente 4, Madrid; Tel: 224–6758). Ice skating (with skate rental) in Madrid at **Ciudad Deportiva** (Generalisimo 175).

In **Madrid,** ***bowling*** at **Club Stella** (Arlaban 7), at the **Stadium** (Alcala 106); **Carlos III** (Goya 5); **Hollyday** (Jose Antonio 78); **Montesol** (Montera 25). ***Fencing*** at **Club Esgrima de Madrid** (Alcala 120). ***Flying*** lessons, model airplane flying, parachute jumping and skydiving at **Real Aero Club de Espana** (Carretera de Jeronimo 19 at Cuatro Vientos Airfield).

Riding is extremely popular, horses are good and easily rentable at most resorts, and hourly fees are modest. In Madrid, check with the **Real Sociedad Hipica Espanola Club de Campo** (Fernanflor 6; Tel: 222–9226), or **Trebol** (Pozuelo/Somosaguas; Tel: 291–0298). There are **Royal Equestrian Societies** in San Sebastian, Granada, Valencia, Valladolid; riding clubs in Barcelona, Burgos, Seville.

Bicycles are difficult to rent; for information, contact **Federacion Espanola de Ciclismo** (Alfonso XII 36, Madrid; Tel: 230–9088). On the Costa del Sol, ***scooters*** are rentable by the day, week, month from **Autos Miranda** (Nueve Marbella 35; Tel: 823–486). In Madrid, ***horse-racing*** at **Hipodromo de la Zarzuela** (Carretera de la Coruna, Km. 6.5).

Greyhound racing in the **Canodromo Madileno** (Av. de las Animas; Tel: 228–8458) in Madrid. Restaurant and attractive stadium.

SHOPPING WITH AND FOR CHILDREN Invest in several packs of Spanish playing cards. These are printed with pictures of bullfights or of scenic interest and, as a diversion, as souvenirs or presents, they couldn't be more welcomed by children. Spanish soap, sugar cubes, candies come artistically packaged. Even Bisonte cigarettes come with a picture from Altamira on the wrapper. Sugar-coated almonds in the guise of eggs nestle in baskets perfect for saving to hang on the Christmas tree. Wonderful miniature painted furniture for decorations and dollhouses, metal bulls with Toledo-bladed swords meant to do battle as cocktail sausage holders but much more fun for children; all sorts of miniature paintings, tea sets, wooden and ceramic dollhouse furniture, are all well within the range of childrens' allowances. Excellent childrens' shoes are about half the American price (but some of them may squeak) at department stores. Charles Jourdan made-in-Madrid shops at 6 Serrano and 1 Gran Via offers shoes at ¼ the price of similar shoes in New York. For the exceptionally interesting and well-made regional handicrafts, SNTO lists artisans specializing in every craft from ceramics and wrought iron to guitars and fans; in Madrid, the government-sponsored **Official Handicraft Exhibition** (Floridablanca 1) has tasteful selection, low prices, and will ship anywhere. The government-owned **Arte Espana** sells work crafted by the hands of Spain's fine artisans at branches throughout the city including those at 32 Gran Via, 33 Don Ramon de la Cruz, 14 Hermosilia, and 3 Plaza de las Cortes, and across the street from the Palace Hotel. Bullfight and flamenco posters, on which children's names can be printed, are sold by almost every hall porter and souvenir shop.

In **Madrid,** the main street is the Gran Via. For dolls and doll clothes: **Mariquita Perez** (Gran Via; Serrano 8; Calle Nunes de Balboa 52), with matching clothes for girls 2–10. **Casa Zato** (Peligros 10), dolls for younger girls, double dolls that change faces, clothes, and personalities when you turn them upside down. **Ramon Calvo** (Gran Via 85), handmade dolls in regional costumes. **El Paraiso de los Ninos** (Serrano 48), toys and games, dolls. Antique dolls and accessories (12 Ribera de Curtidores) shop #13 in the area near Plaza Mayor. For baby clothes: **El Bebe Ingles** (Gran Via 36), **Lenceria Nieves** (Gran Via 55), **Aralena** (Conde de Aranda 19) which also has party clothes and practical viyella outfits for boys up to 8 and girls up to 12, **Dodo** (Ayala 11) with sweet confections up to 10s, **La Ciguena de Paris** (Serrano 3), **Nanette** (Recoletos 21) which also has maternity clothes, and **Mendivil** (Recoletos 19) which features classic wear sewn by seamstresses from San Sebastian. For girls' and women's knitwear try **Boutique Mitzou** (Serrano 27); custom-made dresses at **Linkaya** (Espartinas 4); custom-made shirts and suits at **Mariano Valdivia** (Gran Via 86). Splendid Spanish capes at **Sesena** (Cruz 23).

Department stores, such as **Sears** (Paseo de la Castellana 86) and **Woolworth** (Arapiles 11; Juan Hurtado de Mendoza 4; plus branches in Malaga, Palma, Santander) feature European merchandise and snack bars; but you'll find baby-minding services at **Galerias Preciados** (Preciados 28–30; Arapiles 10–12) and **El Corte Ingles** (Preciados 3; Goya 76)—the latter has good bargains in children's skis and boots, camping and sports goods. The **Annex of Galerias Preciados** carries examples of ceramics from most towns in Spain.

For everything under one roof, high fashion in all sizes, children's suede and wool pants, skirts, sweaters, coats, for perfume, soap, rugs, brass, iron, wood, copper, pottery, toys, **Casa Bique** (Paseo de la Castellana 64). Prices may be somewhat higher than elsewhere, but the selection is good, service so excellent that it's worth it. Everything guaranteed. For life-size religious statues from back-country churches disposing of their treasures, there's no place like the **Rastro** (Plaza de Cascorro), the flea market. Spanish costumes: **Menkes** (Calle Mesonero Romanos 14), plus ballet and bullfight outfits. Children's sportswear: **Montana Blanca** (Av. Jose Antonio, 65).

Everything for the equestrian at **Moises Sancha** (Travesia Arenal 3). Sporting equipment at **Deportes Diez** (Paseo de la Habana 5). Custom-made leather and suede at **Boutique Shalom Leather Factory** (Gran Via 45, 3rd floor). Guitars at **Casa Garrido** (Valverde 4). For toys, try **Minon** (Serrano 4) or **Bazar Chamberi** (Eloy Gonzalo 28); large leather animals at **Kreisler** (Serrano 19); charming straw animals at **Enrique del Val** (San Bernardino 3); baskets at **Cesteria Pleite** (Cascorro 1); extraordinary masks, party favors, costumes, bombs that explode with party favors, and a fascinating catalogue at **Vicente Rico** (Conde de Aranda 3). English books at **Miessner's** (Ortega y Gasset 14); children's books at **Talentum** (Nunez de Balboa 53).

Barcelona: English-language books, magazines and newspapers: **Occidente** (Paseo de Gracia 73). For children's wear, try **Santa Eulalia** (Paseo de Gracia 60 and 93), or **Asuncion Castaner** (Calle Petritxol 11)—Spanish costumes made to order. **Morinigo** (Via Layetana 70) for boys' and children's wear. For toys and children's wear: **Tic Tac** (Av. Generalisimo Franco 550) and **Bebelin** (Paseo de Gracia 39 and Consejo de Ciento 298); boys' clothes in both these shops are mostly party things for boys under 5; little girls' clothes are sweet. For toys, clothes, wind-up plastic flying birds children of all ages like (and instantly lose—but what a blissful 15 min. before they do!), for just about anything, try **El Corte Ingles** (Plaza de Cataluna). More toys at **Paque** (Diputacion 254)—Mariquita Perez dolls dressed in marvelously detailed clothes; and **Chiquito** (Paseo de Gracia 90) for assorted toys for all ages. Children's and young people's shoes: **Torrens** (Jose Antonio 630). If your children's feet are narrow, try here. Or ask your concierge to recommend a good place to get custom-made children's shoes.

In **Estepona,** ask where you can buy a kite *(cometa de tela).* Sports equipment at **Deportes Safari Armeria** (Carretera de Cadiz & Queipo de Llano). In **Marbella,** model boats, bullfighting costumes for dolls, souvenirs at **Juan C. Reina Lozano** (Gonzales Badia 1); children's clothes and flamenco dresses at **Cristina** (Jose Antonio Giron 12); baby things at **Mame** (Galeria San Cristobal). In **Mijas,** interesting buys everywhere; shawls and shirts at **Casa Pepe** (Ramon y Cajal 11). Just outside **San Pedro de Alcantara,** seek out **Ceramica Galeria San Pedro** (Carretera de Cadiz, km 176) which has pottery, straw, fur, suede, leather, plus snack bar. In **Seville,** Calle Sierpes is one of the wildest pedestrian malls in Spain; children's flamenco costumes at **Galerias Sevillanas** (Sagasta 20); fans in many shops; mantillas at **M. Adarve** (Queipo de Llano 28). In **Torremolinos,** you can't miss **Bazar Aladino** (Carretera de Cadiz), an eclectic souvenir shop built like an aircraft carrier.

SPANISH FRIENDS AND PEN PALS No organized hospitality service exists. If you would like to meet a Spanish family, the SNTO might be able to arrange such a meeting, but as this would be an entirely voluntary service, you would just have to take a chance on how things would turn out. In **Madrid,** you might be able to round up either Spanish or American playmates for your children by inquiring at the **American Women's Club.**

CALENDAR OF EVENTS In addition to these listings, there are countless *verbenas,* night festivals on the eve of religious holidays; *romerias,* or picnic excursions to religious shrines, accompanied by processions of brilliantly costumed participants, horses covered with richly ornamented blankets and harness, floats and decorated carts, sacred relics displayed in magnificent silver and gold monstrances; *fiestas* in honor of local saints' days with fireworks, dancing, merrymaking, and bullfights following the special mass in the church or the cathedral; local fairs, called *ferias;* and giant bonfires, or *fallas,* in which giant effigies are burned while everyone dances around in their best regional finery. Often there are folk dances—the *sardanas, fandangos, jotas,* and *flamencos*—in the evening or on Sun. and holidays in village plazas and streets. For full particulars, check with the local SNTO.

Jan. 6 throughout Spain, is ***Epiphany;*** presents are given to children. From Jan. 15–Feb. 15, Malaga holds ***Winter Festival;*** folklore exhibitions, horse show, and sports events. In late Jan., Alicante also has a ***Winter Festival*** and ***regatta.*** **Feb.** 5, Segovia and other cities celebrate ***St. Agatha's Day;*** folk-costume processions and folk-dancing. **Mar.** 11–19, Valencia has the ***Fallas de San Jose*** (St. Joseph's Day Bonfires); wonderful festivities, bullfights, huge statues exhibited and then burned; a top fiesta you shouldn't miss.

In **Apr.,** ***Holy Week*** (Semana Santa) is held throughout Spain; particularly impressive in Seville, also in Malaga, Granada, Toledo, Cordoba, and Valladolid. Some 3000 religious processions take place between Palm Sun.–Easter; floats depicting scenes from the Passion. Late-Apr. events include: ***Spring Festival*** in Murcia, ***Battle of the Flowers*** and bullfights; ***Fiesta of St. George*** in Alcoy, featuring the Battle of the Moors and Christians, cavalry attack and capture of the castle, and bullfights; and Seville's week-long ***Feria*** (Spring Fair), Spain's best-known fiesta, about three weeks after Holy Week. Folklore exhibits, costumes, dances, bullfights, and parades; a must if you are anywhere near this area.

In early **May,** Selva celebrates the ***Fiesta de la Santa Cruz*** with folk dancing. Madrid holds its ***Feast of St. Isidro,*** patron saint of Madrid; sporting and folklore events; bullfights; wonderful fun. Jerez celebrates ***Spring Festival;*** processions of floats, bullfights, and dancing. Outstanding. In late-May or early June, Cordoba's ***Fair and Festival*** includes bullfights, dancing, and costumed parades.

In **June,** ***Corpus Christi*** is celebrated throughout Spain. Religious celebrations and processions; week-long festivities in Granada. Sitges is charmingly garlanded with flowers and pictures made with petals. Special celebrations also in Toledo, Seville, and Cadiz. June 29, throughout Spain (especially in Segovia, Tarragona, and Alicante), there's the ***Feast of St. Peter and St. Paul;*** bullfights, parades, dances, and fireworks. On June 30, Irun holds the ***Festival of San Marcial;*** medieval costumed parade and floats. The last week in June–first week in July, Granada features an ***International Music and Dance Festival;*** performances in the courts and gardens of the Alhambra. Outstanding.

July 6–15, in Pamplona, brings the ***Running of the Bulls.*** In late July, sometimes lasting until mid-Aug., all Spain holds festivities in honor of ***Santiago*** (St. James), its patron saint. Valencia features flower battles, bullfights, fireworks, parades, dances, folklore exhibits, and music competitions. Costumed ***religious mystery plays*** in Elche, La Alberga, and Santiago de Compostela; special pilgrimages in the latter. The end of July–mid-Aug., Malaga holds ***Sporting and Folklore*** events; parades and bullfights honoring the reconquest of Moorish Spain by the Catholic kings; lots of fun.

Around **Aug.** 10, a fair and bullfights in honor of ***St. Lawrence*** at El Escorial. Aug. 12–19 is ***Semana Grande,*** the height of the summer social season at San Sebastian; bullfights, fireworks, concerts, the works. Aug. 15, the ***Feast of the Assumption*** is held throughout Spain; religious pageants, festivities, special bullfights, feasts, and fairs.

Sept. 5–22, in many places, fairs and festivals honor the ***Virgin Mary;*** on the 8th (her Nativity), Salamanca holds processions in folk costumes at nearby monastery; festivities elsewhere, especially Murcia, on this date. In mid-Sept., around St. Matthew's Day (the 21st), Logrono holds a ***Village Festival.*** Sept. 23, Tarragona has ***Fiestas*** with costumed folk dances. Around the last week, Barcelona celebrates the ***Feast of Our Lady of Mercy;*** *sardanas* street dancing, bullfights, and music festival. Oct. 11–22, Zaragoza features the ***Festival of Our Lady of the Pillar;*** fireworks and parades of marvelous figures of giants and dwarfs dancing in the streets; bullfights; marvelous costumed parade, folklore events, music competitions. One of the top fiestas. **Dec.** 24, at Montserrat, is the ***Christmas Eve*** religious festival in the Monastery. Beautiful boys' choir.

LANGUAGE AND PHRASEBOOK You can skimp along with English only in major tourist targets like Madrid and Barcelona. Otherwise, you will have to rely on sign language, phrasebook, and dictionary. The Spanish will do everything possible to understand you or to make themselves understood. The term most in usage for a public lavatory is *servicio*.

Hello (Good morning,	*Buenos dias*	*bweh-nohs dee-ahs*
Good evening)	*Buenas noches*	*bweh-nahs noh-chehs*
I am an American	*Soy americano (boy)*	*soy ah-may-ree-kahno*
	Soy americana (girl)	*soy ah-may-ree-kahna*
My name is____	*Mi nombre es____*	*me norm-bray ess____*
I am____years old	*Tengo____anos*	*Teng-goh____ah-nyohss*
Please	*por favor*	*por fah-vor*
Thank you	*muchas gracias*	*mooch-us grah-thee-ahss*
I can't speak Spanish	*No hablo espanol*	*noh ah-blo ess-pan-nyawl*
Yes	*Si*	*see*
No	*No*	*no*
I am having a wonderful time	*Me estoy divirtiendo mucho*	*may ess-toy dee-ver-tyen-doh moo-choh*
1	*uno*	*oo-noh*
2	*dos*	*dose*
3	*tres*	*trayss*
4	*cuatro*	*kwah-troh*
5	*cinco*	*theen-koh*
6	*seis*	*sayss*
7	*siete*	*syeh-teh*
8	*ocho*	*oh-choh*
9	*nueve*	*nway-bay*
10	*diez*	*dee-eth*
11	*once*	*ohn-thay*
12	*doce*	*doh-thay*
13	*trece*	*tray-thay*
14	*catorce*	*kah-tor-thay*
15	*quince*	*keen-thay*
Goodbye	*adios*	*ah-dyohss*

SWEDEN

The world knows Sweden for its contribution to science, literature, filmmaking, and smorgasbord. Children know it for its trolls. You can tell a lot about the attitude toward children in Sweden by the slogan of her preschools, kindergartens, and daycare centers: For Children's Minds, Not Just to Mind the Children. There are loads of summer camps, babysitting services, supervised playgrounds, and other child-care aids. Sweden offers sunshine, magnificent countryside, arts and crafts, festivals. Fishing and hunting are fabulous; winter sports are superb; and riding, sailing, and golf are excellent. Camping facilities are extraordinarily good. Many hotel reductions and travel plans make family travel easy and inexpensive. Sweden enjoys a high standard of politeness as well as a high standard of living. Everything is clean and comfortable.

Dalarna, known as the heart of Sweden, is the province of folklore and fantasy, carpeted with cornflowers, with thatched farmhouses with handcarved gables, Midsummer Eve maypoles, blue lakes, colorful costumes. Don't miss it. You'll also like the Skane chateau country.

INFORMATION ABOUT SWEDEN The **Swedish Tourist Board** in New York (75 Rockefeller Plaza, New York, NY 10012). In Sweden, the Swedish Tourist Board (Sveriges Turistrad) headquartered in Stockholm (Kungstradgarden, Sverigehuset), maintains 200 branch offices, identifiable by the international "i" sign, in all major cities. The Tourist Center at Sverige Huset (Sweden House) in the same location as the Swedish Tourist Board, can also sell you the key to Stockholm, the "Stockholmskortet," a three-day minimum pass which provides you with free entrance to the 46 museums of the city, a free boat trip, free sightseeing bus ride as well as *unlimited* free public transportation by bus, tram, and subway throughout the city and county. Children under 18 (!) pay half-price. Swedish radio stations broadcast English and other foreign language programs with the news, plus commentaries and information about Sweden. Broadcast schedules are available at most hotels, or telephone (08) 784–0000 for information. For daily attractions in Stockholm, just call "Miss Tourist" (Tel: 221–840). The publication *This Week in Stockholm* is also most helpful.

The best book about Sweden that I have ever read is *The Wonderful Adventures of Nils* (Pantheon Books), by Selma Lagerlof (the Swedish novelist and short-story writer, and the first woman to win the Nobel Prize for Literature), one of those rare, beautifully written classics that appeals to both genders and all ages from 8–80.

Available at newsstands and bookstores is *The Scandinavian Times,* in English, with news of entertainments and attractions.

Telephone facilities in Sweden are located at Telegraph offices instead of post offices as in other European countries.

▶ **Note:** Alcohol and tobacco products are extremely expensive, so take all you will want with you.

HEALTH, WATER, AND FOOD Everything is immaculately clean and tidy in Sweden. The water is pure. The milk is pure. Food-handling is supervised with scrupulous care—fresh produce, canned products and food preparation alike.

Food specialties that children will enjoy? Strawberries, raspberries, lingonberries, bilberries, and cloudberries. Imported fruits are available also. Turkey, goose, chicken and ham are always good. The best cuts of beef are turnedos and chateaubriand (Swedish cuisine in tourist centers and large towns leans heavily on international fare). Your children might like *renstek,* roast reindeer meat, as a novelty; it is, after all, just venison. Delicious little meatballs are *kottbullar;* hamburgers, *kottfars.*

Lots of fish: *stromming,* a cold-water herring, is the same as smelt; *lax* is salmon; *laxforell,* is salmon-trout, tuna, perch, sea trout, and grayling, all locally caught. Crayfish or *kraftor* in season (Aug.–Sept.) is superb. Boiled potatoes, mashed potatoes, potato salad, cucumber salad, green salads, but nothing exciting in the way of vegetables.

Dreamy desserts, pastries, cake-breads and pancakes *(pannkakor)* usually served with lingonberries; butter-rich cookies and tarts, sour-cream waffles served with sugar and jam; *limpa,* a sort of coffee cake, are all specialties. Desserts such as apple cake, shortbread, brandy rings, and *limpa* have all proved too delectable not to eat at home. If you feel like a snack, you can enjoy any of these at a *konditori,* or coffee shop, which usually also serves sandwiches and nonalcoholic beverages. Coca-Cola is available; so is *Loranga,* an orange drink; *Saft,* a sweet mixture of water and fruit syrup; *Grappo,* carbonated grapefruit juice which isn't sweet enough for sweet-toothed children as a rule; excellent milk; and a type of ginger-ale called *Sockerdricka* that tastes like gingery, faintly soapy water to me, but some children look upon it as pure nectar.

The famous *smorgasbord,* literally bread-and-butter table, which consists of dozens of platters of cold meats, salads, aspics, eggs, fish and hot dishes, is featured at the **Solliden** restaurant at **Skansen;** the **Stallmastaregarden, Nortull** near **Haga,** and the **Grand Hotel** in **Saltsjobaden** (Sun. only) as a lunchtime specialty in the Stockholm area; but in general, it has been replaced in most restaurants by the *de-*

likatessassietter or the *assietter* (fewer selections). The true gourmet version of the smorgasbord can be found at any of 24 towns in the province of Skane featuring *Gastgiverier* (ask any Swede to explain what this term means—it's a great conversational gambit).

Meal hours are the same as ours except for an earlier dinner, supplemented by midnight snacks. Lunch is served from 11 a.m.–2 p.m., dinner from 5 p.m. on, but restaurants are more or less continuously open. In every restaurant, snack bar, cafe in Sweden, children can have chocolate, pastries, sandwiches, fruit juice; they usually also can order from a children's menu.

Children should enjoy lunching on the **Af Chapman,** a three-masted sailing ship moored at Skeppsholmen. Open year round as a youth hostel, bright tables are placed on deck in sunny weather. Operated by the Swedish Touring Club, this is a happy idea for a light lunch or between-meal snacks. Department stores such as **Domus** and **Tempo** offer self-service cafeterias, the **ICA** and **Tre Snackor** eateries offer fast food, as do **Clocks** and **McDonald's.**

On weekends, folk dances and folk operas as well as occasional firework displays take place in front of **Solliden Restaurant,** where the food and the view are very pleasant.

BABY FOOD No trouble at all. American and European varieties are imported. A local variety, **Findus,** is wonderful. **Semper** is also a producer of locally manufactured baby food. You'll find strained fruits, vegetables, meats and fish. Swedish children thrive on strained fish. Check with your doctor to find out if it's advisable to add fish to your baby's diet. You can get prepared baby cereals and all varieties of local, European and American baby foods at department stores, such as **N.K.** *(Nordiska Kompaniet)* in Stockholm, groceries, and almost any pharmacy *(apotek)* or the Swedish version of our 5-and-10, such as **Tempo** in Stockholm and other cities.

DIAPERS AND LAUNDRY Disposable diapers are now in general use. You can buy them at the local pharmacy *(apotek),* or in the children's department of any general store. They are known everywhere by their brand-name—*Cellstoff. Bloja* is the word for a regular cloth diaper, but this is used far less frequently than *Cellstoff,* which comes packaged with or without a separate outer holder-covering. There are no organized diaper laundry services, but the laundering of cloth diapers can be done easily and quickly by hotel or commercial laundries.

EMERGENCIES MADE EASY In **Stockholm,** *pharmacies* open day and night include: **C. V. Scheele** (Vasagatan 12; Tel:109–045, days; 109–055, nights); **Lejonet** (Regerinsgatan 55; Tel: 249–400); **Salen** (Gotgatan 79; Tel: 434–801, days; 415–601, nights); and **Svanen** (Stureplan; Tel: 230–235).

In **Goteborg,** pharmacies open nights are: **Vasen** (Drottningtorget); and **Biet** (Engelbrektsgatan 34 C).

English-speaking ***doctors*** are readily available. You can call the Tourist Information offices or the **American Embassy** (Strandvagen 101, Stockholm; Tel: (08) 630–520), or ask your hotel for recommendations. Hospital care is free to Swedes but not to travelers. In **Stockholm,** the **Southern General Hospital** (Sodersjukhuset Ringvagen 52; Tel: 237–000) is topnotch; every facility, including ambulance heliport. In **Goteborg,** there's an excellent hospital at Sahlgrenskasjukhuset Anggarden (Tel: 172–080). To call the EMERGENCY number (90000) from a public telephone, no money is necessary.

MAGIC FAMILY HELPERS ***Babysitters and children's companions*** are no strain at all. Simply call the **Tourist Information** center and they will make arrangements for an English-speaking babysitter, children's companion or guide to be at your side within the hour. You can arrange for a student or other companion to take your child sightseeing; they go all-out to supply sitters and companions ideally suited to your needs. Outside of Stockholm, regional tourist offices perform the same service with the same happy results; ask the Stockholm Tourist Board for a complete list.

In Stockholm you can leave your children (below 15 years) in any of 150 ***parks,*** where they are taken care of by nurses, free of charge!

About a third of these parks are open year round, and all are open for the five-month summer season. Each playground has two or three playleaders, many different group games, competitions, theater shows, and singing groups are arranged from time to time; road safety games are taught. Outings are made to Haga Park, gardens, and castles. Some playgrounds have paddling pools. All have indoor play areas for bad weather. During the winter, ice rinks, sledge runs, and slides are set up. Children aged 1½–4 can be left for an hour or more. Buckets and spades are provided, and they *should not* bring their own toys. No previous appointment is necessary; open daily 9:30 a.m.–12:30 p.m. and Sat. 9:30 a.m.–12:30 p.m. For older children, supervision every weekday 9 a.m.–5 p.m., to 1 p.m. on Sat.; certain playgrounds shut at lunch time, and a number are open until 8 p.m. All details and addresses of parks can be had from the **Parkleken** (Fleminggatan 8; Tel: 224–080).

Elsewhere in Sweden, most town parks offer similar supervised playground areas where children may be left. In **Goteborg,** the main playground (same hours as in Stockholm) is **Tradgardsforeningen** (near the Central Station).

Kindergartens. Swedish preschools are classified as either day nurseries which look after children (6 mos.–6 yrs.) for five or more hours, or nursery schools that take children (usually 3–6 years) in groups for three hours. In both, children are grouped by age. All are well equipped with big wooden toys (a Swedish specialty), imaginative and marvelous play materials, and are staffed with nurses and nursery school teachers. Staff, space, play, and meal requirements all have to conform to high standards regulated by the state. The results are spectacular child-care centers in Stockholm, Goteborg, Malmo, and the rest of Sweden. The tourist centers can direct you to these, or, for more information, get in touch with the **Swedish Institute** (Hamngatan 27, P.O. Box 7072, S-103 82, Stockholm).

Personalized services? For children's tours in Stockholm, try **Swedish Student Guide Service** (Tel: 600–836).

In Stockholm (Tel: 220–400) and Goteborg (Tel: 173–000) you can hire **taxi-drivers** who have been trained as guides to the city, and who can speak English. The fare is the same as for a regular cab! It's advisable to book a taxi-guide in advance.

The tourist offices can find you guides, interpreters, secretaries, companions to go on shopping tours and can even let you know where to locate domestic home help services, maids, mothers' helpers and the like. For these services in Stockholm, try **Contact Service** (Gamla Brogatan 29; Tel: 208–181).

On trains, children get a 75% reduction when three or more members of the same family travel together on a trip of at least 30 miles. Most long-distance trains have restaurant cars. A number of second-class carriages are fitted with special children's compartments *(Barnkupeer)* for mothers with children under 2, which have their own johns. All carriages have closets, drinking water, and plastic cups. Hurray!

For children under 12, entrance fees and transportation costs are usually halved. Under 6s are generally admitted to museums and other attractions and allowed local transportation free. For parents and older children, costs for Stockholm sightseeing may be whittled considerably by buying a "Stockholm kortet." (See Stockholm.)

HOLIDAYS FOR CHILDREN ON THEIR OWN None that I know of.

CHILDREN'S CAMPS Several camps are operated by the Society for the Promotion of Skiing and Open-air Life. **Course Westward,** for boys and girls 14–17, offers ten days aboard a rescue ship sailing along the west coast; a Gota Canal trip, exploring uninhabited islands, hiking, swimming, and marine research. For children interested in horses, a ten-day program operated in cooperation with the **Arvika Riding Academy.** Another ten-day program offers camp life with Laplanders at their summer quarters on the lakes in northern Jamtland.

A list of summer riding camps and courses for children is published annually by **Ridframjandet** (Society for the Promotion of Riding; Ostermalmsgatan 80, Stockholm). Two examples are: **Storliens Hogfjallshotell** (Storlien) and **Radmundbergets Ffallgard** (Harjedalen Province), which offer riding, riding tours, and instruction for all classes of horsemen, including beginners, July 1–Sept. For information on sailing, biking, hiking, and canoeing programs for children, write to **The Swedish Touring Club,** Box 25, S–10120 Stockholm. For information on riding camps, get in touch with **Sveriges Ridlagerarrangorers Riksforbund,** Taffnas Gard, S–15400 Gnesta, Sweden.

CASTLES AND OTHER HAPPY FAMILY ACCOMMODATIONS The Tourist Board can give you a list of *Family Accommodation hotels* where you can get large family rooms at bargain prices. Operative throughout Scandinavia is a money-saving *Hotel Bonus pass,* for both quality and budget accommodations, with 15%–40% reductions. You must book the first hotel in advance, but when you check out the desk clerk will make a reservation for you at the next stopover. A book of checks can be bought through a travel agent. A great many *guest rooms in private homes* are available. Ask the local tourist information office *(Turistbyra)* about these. There is usually a hotel-booking service *(Rumsformedling)* or *''Hotellcentral''* attached to a tourist office where you can get help in finding overnight accommodations in a hotel, Pension or in a private house, or find out about renting a chalet or *''stuga.''* If you arrive in Stockholm without a hotel reservation, go to the *''Hotellcentralen''* at the Central Railway Station, which is staffed with English-speaking aides. The local tourist offices can also offer you a considerable number of plain, simple little *cottages,* furnished with all the necessities in **Vacation Villages,** for modest prices. These Vacation Villages, in beach and other resort locales, are geared for strictly budget-level trade, but facilities and activities are oriented for the pleasure and comfort of families with children.

In Sweden, a *cottage* is a *chalet* is a *stuga,* which can range from a reconverted barn to a cattle-herder's functional hut to a small modern house. A *stuga* is usually rented by the week, and some cottages have a two to three week maximum stay. Most are very reasonable. Information about them can be obtained from the regional tourist boards who can also give you a complete list of English-speaking farmers who are willing to take guests in their area. Children aged 2–11 get 50% reductions. For a list of farms, write to Land, 10533 Stockholm, Sweden. Bookings can be made through local tourist offices. If you are a youth-hosteling family, about 220 ''Hikers' Homes'' provide special accommodations in summer for families with children up to 16. Stays are limited to three days and nights; International Youth Hostel Cards are valid, but nonmembers are also accepted. Prices are rockbottom. Write to the **Swedish Touring Club** (Svenska Turistforeningen, Box 7515, 10394 Stockholm, Sweden) or to the Swedish Tourist Board for a handbook and map listing all hostels. About 70 hostels are open year round, but some of them only take groups. There is no age limit. Children under 6, however, are only accommodated in family rooms that have four to six beds. Sheets and sleeping bags can be hired; cooking facilities are usually provided. Youth hostels the world over can be bleak and, in the case of Sweden, surgery clean, but nice ones are the **Af Chapman sailing ship** in Stockholm; in the medieval castle **Glimmingehus;** in a merchant's house in Visby; and in an old mill at the **Orrefors glassworks.**

Herewith the list of tourist boards to contact, from the south of Sweden to the north. The Swedish classifications and listings by provinces may be easier to deal with if cross-referenced alphabetically as follows: **Blekinge** Tourist Board (Box 506, 371 23 Landskrona); **Dalarna** Dala Tour (Tullmakaregatan 1, 791 31 Falun); **Dalslands** Tourist Board (Box 181, 662 00 Amal); Turism och **Fritid** i **Jonkopings** lan (Box 1027, 551 11 Jonkoping); Turism och **Fritid** i **Kronoberg** (Box 36, 351 03 Vaxjo) **Gastriklands** and **Halsingland** (Kommungruppen, Fritid, Gavleborgslan (Brunnsgatan 63 A, 802 22 Gavle); **Goteborg** and **Bohuslan** Tourist Board (Kungsportsplatsen 2, 411 10 Goteborg); **Gotlands** Tourist Association (Box 2081, 621 02 Visby); **Halland** Vastkustens Tourist Board (Kungsportsplatsen 2, 411 10 Goteborg), **Harjedalen** and **Jamtlands** Tourist Association (Box 478, 831 26 Ostersund); **Medelpad** and **Angermanland** County Council, Vasternorrland Turism (Box 1010, 871 01 Harnosand); **Narke** and **Bergslagen** Orebro Tourist Association (Box 1816, 701 18 Orebro); **Norrbotten** and **Northern Lappland,** Norbotten Turisttrafikforbund (Box 76, 051 21 Lulea); **Oland** Kalmar lans Tourist Association (Turism och Fritid i Kronoberg (Box 36, 351 03 Vaxjo); **Ostergotlands** Tourist Association (Box 325, 581 03 Linkoping); **Skanes** Tourist Board (Stora Sodergatan 8 C, 222 23 Lund); **Smaland,** Kalmar lands Tourist Association (Box 86, 391 21 Kalmar); **Sodermandlands** Tourist Association (Turist och Friluftsnamnden, 611 88 Nykoping); for **Stockholm** and surrounding area, write to **Stockholm Information Service,** Sweden House (Kungstragarden, Box 7473, 103 92 Stockholm); **Uppland** Uppsala County Council, Turist och Fritid (Box 602, 751 25 Uppsala); **Varmlands** Tourist Board (Box 323, 651 05, Karlstad); **Vasterbotten and Southern Lappland** Vasterbotten Tourist Association (Box 337, 801 07 Umea); **Vastergotlands Tourist Board** (Box 237, 514 24 Skovde); Vastmanland County Council, Turistavdelningen (Hallgatan 2, 722 11 Vasteras).

Hotels at most ski resorts have day nurseries. From cots for tots on to castle accommodations, for a list of which you can contact the **Skanes Tourist Board** (Stora Sodergatan 8 C, Lund).

Bastad: Hemmeslov Manor Pension is really very good for families; specially recommended. **Filipstad: Hennickehammar** (Tel: 12565), is typical of the manor houses (surprisingly like our own pillared plantation houses in the South) scattered through this wooded lakeland province. Accommodates 50 guests; comfortable and pleasant; lake on the property; good swimming, fishing, and tennis. Outstanding sports center in winter. Excursions to nearby Rottneros and Marbacka, home of Nobel Prize-winning author Selma Lagerlof, whose work is filled with descriptions of Varmland's lovely countryside. If your children have studied the Civil War, they will be interested that Filipstad is the birthplace of

John Ericsson, who built the *Monitor*. Or what about less conventional accommodations? **Circus wagons,** for instance? A little bit south of Gavle, there is **Furuvik,** a great big public park that has the ordinary attractions of a zoo, amusement section, and children's playground, open-air theater, restaurants, swimming, and the extraordinary attraction of a children's circus where all the performers are under 16. Here you'll find a motel where you will be housed in a gaily decorated circus wagon at youth-hostel prices!

Granna: Gyllene Uttern (Golden Otter) Inn, two miles south of town, has a main building and about 20 guest cottages scattered (to insure privacy) through the wooded grounds terraced above the lake. Open May 15–Sept. 15; an idyllic spot, a lakeside resort where there is plenty to do for children and energetic parents and the chance for complete and blissful peace. **Hok: Hook Manor** (Tel: 21080). An 18th-century manor surrounded by lovely parklands; all rooms with private bath; accommodates as many as 120 guests; wonderful for children. International clay pigeon shooting range, practice shooting ranges for elk and deer, tennis, badminton, croquet, boccia, golf, marvelous pool; row-boating and sailing; playground with splendid equipment; bathing beach nearby. In winter, curling, skiing, and skating. Prices for all this comfort and joy are very reasonable and the food is excellent. **Jonkoping: Grand Hotel. Kalmar** is good as a base for visiting the Orrefors glassworks, or just for itself. Stay at the **Slottshoteller** for bed and breakfast. A fine restaurant is Stadsparkrestaurangen (Byttan, Slottsvagen).

Six miles east of **Kristianstad: Backaskog Castle,** a 700-year-old gem centered around a medieval cloister, was a favorite stopping-off place for Swedish royalty back in the days of stagecoach travel, and it is now a favorite for motoring families. Situated between two lovely lakes, it offers swimming, boating, fishing, and beautiful woodland and garden setting; nightingales; riding horses, folk-dancing performances in the courtyard every week; and the opportunity to have a textile-weaving lesson. Accommodations for 100 guests; moderate rates. **Linkoping: Frimurare** hotel is very pleasant. **Motala:** Mr. and Mrs. Hildebrand, who run the excellent **Stadshotellet,** have a big motorboat to take their guests on cruises on Lake Vattern and the Gota Canal. **Persberg: Hotel Lerdalshojden,** on a slope overlooking the lake, has an excellent rope-lift to one of Dalarna's finest views. Comes winter, there is plenty of skating, old-fashioned sleighs, curling, skiing, and a ski lift. **Stockholm:** If you would like to stay in the only hotel that ever fought enemy submarines during WW II, you can bunk in a yacht formerly owned by Woolworth heiress Barbara Hutton, the **Malardrottningen** (Riddarholmen, 1128 Stockholm), moored by Gamla Stan, the old town, and featuring 59 compact cabins complete with color TV, radio, direct-dial telephones. Rates are reasonable; the front desk is the purser's office, and the dining-room is excellent. **Storlien: Hogfjallshotell,** Scandinavia's largest mountain resort hotel, has nurses and nurseries to look after children.

Make **Tallberg** your base for Dalarna Province. You'll be met at the station by a horse-drawn carriage that will taxi you along a pine-bordered road to one of three hotels. **Romantil Hotel** (Tallbergsgarden), overlooking Lake Siljan, which Hans Christian Andersen called "The Blue Eye of Dalarna." Rustic architecture; sweet young hostesses in national costume; tennis; swimming; mini-golf; gay decor. **Dalecarlia Turisthotell,** a converted private house surrounded by parklands, near the lake; big modern rooms in the new wing, smaller country-style rooms in the old wing. **Langbersgarden Pension,** a delightful country-house atmosphere; flowers, not numbers, on guestroom doors; yummy food; lovely lake views. **Visby:** Stay at the **Snackgardsbaden,** 2½ miles north of Visby. The hotel, long and low, crowns a cliff, with gardens sloping seawards and woods behind. Open only mid-June–mid-Aug. Only a dozen accommodations come with private bath, but if you get a room with a balcony facing the sea and sunsets, or take one of the ten cottages by the sea, you could hardly feel other than that this is one of the most delightful spots to stay in. Bathing beach at the foot of the cliff; swimming pool; badminton and mini-golf; serene and lovely.

CAMPING AND CARAVANING Thanks to the law of "Allemansratten," you may put up your tent anywhere, provided it isn't too near a house or fenced land. Before camping on private land it is only polite to ask permission of whoever owns it. This is not necessary in mountain districts and other thinly populated areas. However, there are also about 500 private or publicly owned campsites approved by the **Swedish Tourist Board** which sells an annual detailed list on these, with maps, text in Swedish and English. Most campsites are open June–Aug., but a few remain open all year. Some campsites have two to six bed cottages equipped with electricity, kitchen utensils, and hot plate for cooking.

ATTRACTIONS FOR CHILDREN IN STOCKHOLM **Djurgarden** (Deer Park), first and foremost, is an absolute must; on this island you will find the marvelous pleasure park and open-air museum (oldest in the world) of Skansen, where Old Sweden is authentically reproduced, with whole estates, villages, churches, and rune stones, moved here, complete with representative Swedish livestock and fauna. Lapp Camp and reindeer enclosure; seal pond; beaver pond; swan pond. Peacocks and pheasants decorate village greens. Old-time crafts—printing, weaving, pottery-making—are demonstrated, and you can wander into houses furnished and peopled as they were centuries ago. An intriguing goldsmith shop, a glass-blowing factory, and a pharmacy are of special interest. Meeting halls, 16th-century churches, windmills, bell-towers, and farmhouses can be explored on foot, spelled by a tour in a child-size electric train. Open daily to 11:30 p.m. all year; very small admission fee. In summer, a daily entertainment program includes folk dances, games, special celebrations including a handsome firework display on July 4 and attractions such as the Yale Glee Club. For information on the day's events and on guided tours, call Miss Skansen (Tel: 670–020) or the Tourist Information Center. The **Zoo** and the **Aquarium/Terrarium** have a 2 p.m. daily animal feeding time. Near the 508′-high **Kaknastornet,** with open air and glassed-in lookout platforms, there is a **Children's Zoo** (Lill-Skansen) where children can ride ponies, pet and feed cuddly animals, and more. Close to Skansen is the **Grona Lund** amusement park (open May–Sept.) with Ferris wheel and all the fun-fair attractions. The **Nordic Museum,** (north gate entrance) is one of the best-arranged museums in the world and contains costumes, furniture, and other artifacts from the Middle Ages to modern times. The Dalarna and Lapland exhibits are particularly interesting. The **Royal Armory** is housed in the same building; century costumes, coronation robes, pearl-embroidered saddles, armor. A must.

Down by the harbor is the **Royal Flagship** *Wasa.* Capsized and sunk right after her launching in 1628, the 200′ galleon was recovered in 1961. The crewmen's possessions are displayed in the "Life on Board" presentation; skeletons, wood carvings, sculptures that were part of the man-of-war's superstructure are in the "The Power and the Glory" exhibit.

Other museums of interest to children at Djurgarden are:
Biological Museum, exhibits of Scandinavian animal life. **Technical Museum** (Museivagen; Norra Djurgarden), open afternoons only; machine models and all sorts of exhibits that mechanically inclined and nuclear-minded youngsters will find utterly absorbing. Push-buttons start things whirling, gyrating, pulsing, and working in all sorts of wondrous ways. An iron mine somewhere down in the subbasement level is shown off with justifiable pride every half hour. A remarkable museum, even if you are not mechanically minded! **National Maritime Museum** (Sjohistoriska Museet; Djurgardsbrunnsvagen, Norra Djurgarden). Collections illustrating the history of the Swedish Navy and merchant marine. Not to be missed if your children love the sea and ships.

Stockholm has scads of other museums for specialized interests: Illuminated manuscripts: **Royal Library** (Humlegarden), one of Stockholm's most charming parks. Trains: **Railway Museum** (Torsgatan 19). Particularly fine push-button exhibits. Locomotive and Carriage Hall (Tomteboda). The **Tramway museum** (Odenplan Underground station) children can drive a bus or a tram themselves. Music: **Music Museum** (Sibyllegatan 2). Dance: **Dance Art Museum** (main entrance Royal Opera House). Sports: **Ski Museum** (Fiskartorpet). **Sport and Gymnastics Museum** (Gymn. Centralinstitutet, Lidingovagen 1). History of Stockholm: **City Museum** (Sodermalmstorg). Also **Kulturhuset** (Sergels Torg), with information about Stockholm's varying exhibits. History of Sweden: **National Museum of Antiquities** (corner of Narvavagen–Linnegatan). You'll also find coins here. **Cells of the Dominican Friary** (S. Benickebrinken). Stamps: **Post Museum** (Lilla Nygatan 6). Schools: **School Museum** (Hantverkargatan 29). The **AGA factory,** which makes electronic equipment, has a delightful museum-showroom with push-button exhibits to demonstrate all sorts of lighthouse equipment; very special, most unusual, and highly entertaining. The factory is on Lidingo Island in the eastern section of Stockholm, reachable by bridge and easy to get to. (Millesgarden, in the same island suburb, is just another park as far as the average child is concerned.) Paintings: **National Museum,** Sodra Blasieholmhamnen. Toys: the **Toy Museum** (Mariatorget) has over 7000 toys.

Try your luck at the crank of a **hoop-net fishing** boat in Stockholm's canals and bays. For this 300-year-old style of fishing, you'll have to divide the family into teams because only two passengers are allowed in each boat. You can arrange for a special one-day tourist fishing ticket for a modest fee. Fishing equipment and fishing tackle can be rented.

Have a look through Gamla Stan, the Old City, where many streets are too narrow for cars. Old gabled houses, charming old courtyards and the **Royal Palace** itself, with most of its 700 rooms open to the public on weekdays and Sun. afternoons in summer. (In winter, hours are shorter.) A lot of walking to do if you are going to take in the Royal State Hall and the Chapel Royal, May–Sept. 15. Magnificent palace, filled with priceless things: be sure to time your visit if possible to include the **Changing of the Guard.**

For lovers of tower views, **Kaknastornet** (in the Djurgarden) is great. **Fjallgatan** (at Sodermalm) provides a splendid view, as does Stockholm's **Stadshus,** or Town Hall. The Town Hall is open daily during summer from 11 a.m.–3 p.m.; guided tour at 10 a.m.; certainly worth seeing. It is here, in the Gold Hall, that the Nobel Prize dinners are held.

Drottningholm Palace, a royal winter residence on the shore of Lake Malaren, is, no matter how jaded you may feel about palaces, particularly impressive and beautiful—the building itself, the magnificent apartments, the gardens and the fountains (the water is turned on only from 1–6 p.m.). Completed in the late 17th century, a few years after Versailles, which it somewhat resembles; has Trianon-like pavilion, the China Palace, where in one room (much to the pleasure of Mandrake the Magician fans) a device enables a fully set table to come up from the kitchen beneath and to disappear when the meal is finished. The Court Theater (in a separate building next to the palace) has been restored with all stage apparatus in working order, and you can even see and hear the workings of the earliest thunder-making machine roar into action; enchanting; in summer, 18th-century plays are performed and costumed exactly as they were for court entertainment 200 years ago. Take the children if you possibly can. There are performances two or three times a week. Scarlatti, Handel, Gluck concerts, too. Inn-restaurant nearby.

From Jan.–mid-June, and from end-Sept.–Dec., performances are given every night, except Sun. and Mon., by the **Marionette Theatre,** Fredsgaten 12. This is for the entertainment of adults primarily, but performances leave most children 8 and older pink-cheeked and starry-eyed. In summer, there are also daily concerts, open-air stages with entertainment programs going on every evening at Skansen, on the grounds of Grona Lund, and in the metropolitan park, Kungstradgarden.

Sigtuna, Gripsholm Castle, Skokloster Castle, Uppsala and **Old Uppsala** are all pleasant excursions, but not of the same stripe as Visby and the Island of Gotland.

ATTRACTIONS FOR CHILDREN ELSEWHERE **Arilid:** seaside resort; enchanting. **Bastad:** enchanting seaside resort. **Falsterbo.** The summer resort of the Social Establishment, reminiscent of Newport and Southampton. Conservative gaiety, excellent swimming on white sand beaches, tennis, and in summer a midday goose parade—flocks of geese conducted by children—through the main streets of town, a sight you often see in the south of Sweden. **Falun:** the cradle of Swedish industry; its great copper mine has been in operation for almost 750 years, a source for the red paint that is used throughout Dalarna. A section of the mine is open (May–Aug.) to visitors; you get carried down what is probably the world's highest shaft. "But it's just a wooden wall," a child said. My feelings exactly. Unless your children are mining aficionados, who might find all the gadgets in the mining museum of mesmeric appeal, forget Falun. **Gavle:** At the **Furuvik,** a large public park, there is a children's circus; all performers under 16; open May–early-Sept.

Goteborg: Liseberg Amusement Park, with daily concerts, open-air theater, restaurants, entertainment programs of folk dancing, and fun-fair attractions in a lovely setting that is illuminated after dark. A treat for everyone. Open mid-Apr.–Sept. If you get up at the crack of dawn, you'll be in time to see the fishing boats unload their morning catch for sale at the harbor market, known as "Feskekyrka." **Slottskogen,** a beautiful natural park, and **Tragardsforeningen,** the site of the horticultural gardens, a delightful open-air restaurant, and a supervised playground for children. **Maritime Museum** (Sjofartsmuseet); nautical instruments, ship models from Viking days to the present. Lighthouses, harbors, fishing techniques, plus an aquarium. One of the finest museums of its kind. The nearby tower, with Ivar Johnson's statue of the "Sailor's Wife," is fun to climb—elevator part way. **Rohsska Arts and Crafts Museum;** exhibits to illustrate the development of pottery, textiles, and furniture in Sweden; exceptionally interesting book bindings.

Day ***excursions*** from Goteborg that are fun for children are: **Langedrag** a seaside suburb with the pleasant Langedrag restaurant, fine for sunny days when you can eat on the terrace and watch all the boating in the island-dotted inlet. **Kungalv,** little 1000-year-old town with a charming inn where you can enjoy lunch or a snack while fishing in the river from the inn's porch. **Bohus Castle** dominates the town, and the ruins of this 14th-century fortress are sort of fun to see.

A two-hour ferryboat ride to **Marstrand,** a center for sailing buffs who go in for ocean racing, deep-sea fishing, and an all-round popular resort with an international sailing regatta as the star of its summer attractions. To the north, there is **Bohuslan,** the summering mecca for German and Swedish junior clerks, who flock here to bask on the granite cliffs or fly-cast for cod. From the Norwegian border down to Marstrand—Stromstad, Fjallbacka, Bovallstrand, Smogen, Lysekil, Fiskebackskil and Gullhomen, one picturesque fishing village after another is taken over by swarms of vacationers, making it almost impossible to find accommodations. It's attractive to drive through, however, and may put you in mind somewhat of our Maine coastlands. Unless you have lots of time, I'd skip the rocky coast of Bohuslan.

Gotland island: see Visby. **Granna:** A dear little orchard town (famous for its pears) on Lake Vattern, along one of the most beautiful stretches of road in Sweden; good **museum** illustrating local life in olden times, and at Uppgranna the ruins of **Brahehus Castle** are fun to explore and picnic near. Delicious red-and-white-striped candy is made in Granna, for sale along the section of the main road; lots of ***excursions*** to make from here. Several times a day, boats make a half-hour run to **Visingso;** you can make connections to join the Gota Canal cruise at Motala or at Vadstena. **Hallands Vadero:** seaside resort; lovely. **Halmstad,** in the province of Halland, is the site of a miniature Sweden, with radio-controlled boats cruising over lakes and sea, models of notable buildings, and more. **Halsingborg:** the tuna center for sports fishermen; open-air **museum** with old buildings and farmhouses. The **Karnan,** or Keep, all that remains of the city's fortifications, is definitely worth a look. The interior of the tower has been restored and furnished as it was in the 12th century. **Jonkoping** is the match kingdom of the world, with a **Matchstick Museum** open in summer. Driving here from Granna, the scenery is incredibly lovely. Have lunch at the restaurant in Stadsparken municipal park; **open-air museum** with great churches and old timber buildings, and, for birdlovers, a marvelous open-air **ornithological museum;** also, an **archaeological museum** in the Town Hall is a delight. ***Boat trips:*** **Jonkoping-Visingso-Granna;** also one of the best one-day trips is the steamer between **Jonkoping-Vadstena-Berg,** where 15 locks lead your little white steamer down some 130′ of water to Lake Roxen; with sailing, swimming, fishing or making a steamer excursion along the lovely **Kinda Canal.**

Kalmar, is the ancient "Lock and Key to Sweden." **Kalmar Castle** is vast, with dark dungeons, moat, courts, round towers, and battlements. The interior is completely furnished and exceptionally interesting.

An hour's drive west of the city is the exciting **Orrefors Glass Factory,** where you can watch artists who have served a 20-year apprenticeship blowing exquisite glass products. Kalmar Hemslojd is one of the best of Sweden's topnotch craft centers. Its Old Town, with ancient houses, is absolutely charming. Both old and new Kalmar can be seen by the *Kalmar Flounder,* a very comfortable sightseeing boat; a particularly nice trip.

You can get to the heart of **Lapland**'s mountain wilderness on your own, and for adventurous, sportsminded families, there are all sorts of possibilities, with surprisingly comfortable accommodations in good hotels, simpler but adequate rustic chalets, and mountain and rest huts that come under the roughing-it category. Transportation in remote sections away from railroads is supplied by mail buses equipped with post-horns, air conditioning, radio and, in some instances, with plastic glass roofs. Modern mountain resorts? Try Tarnaby, the village where Ingemar Stenmark was born; or Riksgransen where you can ski in the light of the midnight sun.

Leksand, at the southern tip of Lake Siljan, has a lovely old onion-domed **church**—white-walled and black-roofed with a blue and white countrystyle interior. The women have seven elaborate costumes that they wear on different occasions, and on Sun. it is quite a thing to see this brilliant contingent walking up the avenue of birches leading to the church door. The bells that summon churchgoers are too heavy to be hung in the church steeple, and are hung in a separate belfry. If you possibly can, do take the children with you to church here. Leksand also offers races in miniature Viking ships, garlanded with greenery, across Lake Siljan. These long boats, which hold 20 oarsmen plus passengers, used to transport people to church, are called Church boats. **Church boat races** are usually held the first week in July. Because of its events Leksand attracts a good deal of the summer tourist trade, although Rattvik is the main resort in Dalarna. Tallberg, between the two, would be my choice as the nicest base for all the local attractions. **Linkoping:** a lovely old cathedral city with a most attractive **open-air museum,** an outstanding provincial and **city museum.**

Lund is a pleasant university town, with a cathedral best seen at noon, when the mechanical figures of the cathedral clock whir into action. The outdoor museum of peasant culture under the direction of the **Kulturhistoriska Museum** is a delight.

Malmo: Malmohus Castle museum and the **Folkets Park,** the largest and oldest of the municipal recreation parks in Sweden, with open-air theater, restaurant, and attractive fun-fair. Take a 45-minute canal boatride through the Old Town.

Molle: A popular and beautiful seaside resort. **Mora:** Thousands of spectators come here the first Sun. in Mar. for the **Vasa ski race** from Salen to Mora over a 55-mile course commemorating the trip that two skiers made back in 1521 to bring Gustav Vasa to Mora so that he could rally the dalesmen in the war of liberation against the Danes. Also in Mora is the dragon-beaked roofed house of painter Anders Zorn and the adjacent **Gammelgarden** that he founded, an **open-air folk museum** where timbered buildings have been reconstructed in a natural outdoor setting with costumed guides to show you around. One other attraction is an **excursion** by car to **Frykas.** You follow the lakeshore road to Orsa and start driving up forested slopes past Oljonsbyn until you come to the gray-log saeter huts used in the summer by Swedish cowgirls; lookout tower here; and a little inn, **Frykasen's Pensionat,** where you can enjoy the local trout. Picnic lunches are also supplied by one of the local farm cottages. You might be able to cajole someone here out of a birchbark horn used to call home the cows, an artifact of great delight to children! About six miles N of **Norrkoping** in Ostergotland is **Kolmarden Zoo** with a delphinarium, safari park. **Odeshog:** An **open-air museum** exhibiting a collection of old-timer buildings. Interesting! **Oland Island** has a four-mile bridge, Europe's longest, connecting it to Kalmar on the mainland. A narrow, rugged island of windmills, wild ponies, and a paradise for birds, including nightingales. The main town is Borgholm, near which is the ruin of one of the grandest castles Sweden ever had. Near **Borgholm Castle** is **Solliden,** a beautiful chateau in which Sweden's royal family spend their summers. Geologists, botanists, zoologists, and archaeologists find Oland of particular interest. **Gettlinge Gravfalt,** an Iron Age burial ground of standing stones arranged in the form of a ship; **Eketorps Borg,** a massive fortress with reconstructed dwellings; **Ismantorps Borg,** another huge ancient fortress, are special. **Rattvik:** The main winter and summer resort in Dalarna, with a number of hotels offering tennis, golf, fishing, swimming, boating. The **Nittsyo** pottery works are nearby; visitors always welcomed. In **Gammelgarden** (open-air folk museum), handloomed textiles, blocked linen, jewelry, pottery, topnotch knives, are all beautifully made, but perhaps of most appeal to children are the brightly painted wood carvings. All the homecrafts are sturdy and handsome, and Rattvik is the center for the Dalarna branch of the Swedish Hemslojd (Homecraft) League. Rattvik's pleasure park, **Sorlin Summerland,** has the highest aquaslide in Europe, as well as boating, tennis, and more.

Skane, Chateaux Country, an exquisite countryside filled with great mansions, magnificent estates, and gardens of extraordinary loveliness, all beautifully maintained. There are hundreds of these castles and chateaux, but unless your children are serious students of architecture, gardening, and Swedish history, I would advise seeing only one or two of the grandest, or whichever ones are the easiest for you to get to. Some possibilities are: **Vittskovle,** south of **Kristianstad,** with more than 100 rooms, secret passages and speaking tubes in the walls. Very grand indeed. **Glimmingehus,** south of **Kivik,** now housing a youth hostel in its splendid interior. If you are in the area, do try to see the great prehistoric burial mound of stones in the form of a ship pointing out to sea at

Kaseberga. **Ostarp:** Interesting **open-air museum** of farm and peasant culture, and one of the nicest inns to stay in or have lunch at, the Gastivaregard. **Skabersjo, Borringekloster, Svaneholm, Marsvinsholm** and **Torup** are all noteworthy chateaux. Skabersjo and Svaneholm are the most interesting. **Trollenas and Trolleholm** (special) are the castles to see near **Lund. Sofiero Chateau,** the summer residence of the King of Sweden, with perfectly lovely park and gardens, described in a guidebook written by His Majesty himself! **Kulla Gunnarstorp,** just south of Sofiero, is surrounded by a moat; outstanding. The ancient castle of **Krapperup** is another. Between the two castles is a little town called **Hoganas,** where you can watch pottery being made. **Kullaberg:** a mountain about ten miles long and less than 700′ high, with a lighthouse built on the spot of Sweden's first lighthouse in the 16th century. The caves all around used to be the homes of early men, and all sorts of pots, tools, and weapons have been recovered from this region. In Feb. or Mar., the cranes come to dance on Kullaberg.

Skokloster is a more interesting castle than **Gripsholm,** but if you've seen Drottningholm you've seen something with immensely more appeal. **Sigtuna** is a sweet little place, but there are scores of places in Sweden more interesting. Close to Vadstena, **Takern Lake,** thicketed with green reeds, is the choicest bird lake in Sweden. Right near Takern, at Rok, is one of the largest and most remarkable **runic stones** in the world—the best known of Sweden's multitude of rune stones. Runes are the earliest form of Germanic writing, and were used for inscriptions and magic and secret purposes—erected by a father in memory of his son in the hope of wreaking vengeance upon his son's slayers. On the slopes of Mt. Omberg, you might want to combine a picnic with exploration of the caves and ruins of a 12th-century **Cistercian abbey** building at Alvastra. **Tallberg** is entrancing. The local sights are some Viking burial mounds and **Holen** or Ankarcrona's Farm up on the hill. Gustav Ankarcrona was a 19th-century painter, and his rugged loghouse is now an art gallery-museum with a collection of musical instruments, grandfather clocks, household furniture and utensils. **Uppsala** is rich in associations, not only of the famous botanist Carolus Linnaeus, but also of Thor, Odin, Freya and Tyr. Cultural interests, certainly for the **Cathedral** and **University** are here, and so is the Library and the **Castle of Uppsala.** But do you know what children invariably remember most clearly? Drinking mead (nonalcoholic) out of cow horns in **Odinsborg Inn.** In **Vaxjo,** visit the **Smalands Museum** for an interesting collection of glass and weapons.

Visby, on Gotland island, is a treasure you just shouldn't miss. Visby is a heavenly vacation center—fine beaches, tennis and bicycling, beautiful scenery, marvelous roses and at Lummelunda, a handspring away, a series of stalagmite and stalactite **caves** that are pristine in their freshness, certainly worth seeing, as is the prehistoric Maze (Trojaborg). Most of the beaches sprout curiously eroded tall limestone columns called *rauker* that children can climb and play around. The city is encircled by 13th-century walls without counterpart in Northern Europe. There are several dozen towers from 50–70′ high along the walls, and the town rises in tiers of narrow streets, stepped-gable houses and the ruined churches and convents of what was once the richest and greatest Baltic city in the days of the Hanseatic League. From mid-July–mid-Aug., an **opera-miracle play** is staged in the roofless nave of the St. Nicholas Church, a lovely pageant called *Petrus de Dacia* that tells the story, with music, of a long-ago abbot of the Dominican monastery of which this church is a part. On the first Sun. in July, there is a children's race on the Shetland-like Gotland ponies that still roam the island. Toward the end of July, there is a traditional "Ball of Roses" and a Children's Day Carnival at the same time.

Gotland has been a center of trade and shipping since the Stone Age. Thousands of Roman, Byzantine, Anglo-Saxon, and Arabic coins have been dug up; Chinese cups; seashells from the Indian Ocean; Viking remains are here as well. Every July at **Stanga,** the men compete in local games—rather like shotput, pole-hurling, and bowls—that date back to pre-Christian times. In many little villages, customs and music of the ancient Goths have been preserved. The **Gotland Museum of Antiquities** is strangely thrilling, because you realize that the soil you are walking on yielded most of the evidence of this astonishingly rich past. One day in Visby, is just not enough. If you spent one day, you'll want to spend two, and if you spend two, you'll want to stay a week. It's that sort of place. A special ***excursion*** for nature-lovers, and for those who like the feeling of adventure, is a daily-except-Wed. trip to **Stora Karlso,** rocky bird-sanctuary islands where you can swim, explore caves, and picnic while you watch the snipe, gannets, loons, curlews, and grebes assembled there. You go by boat to these islands, which used to be piratical hangouts; you have lunch and dinner and are back in Visby after a nine-hour safari.

Visingso Island: At the landing place, you'll find typical Visingso transport—strong carts drawn by a pair of strong horses. Passengers sit back to back on cushioned planks running the length of the cart. Bumpity-bump ride to **Kumlaby church,** where there are great 12th-century murals and a belfry tower to climb for the wildly energetic. At the ruins of fire-swept **Visingsborg Castle** and the **Brahe Church** there is a museum of 16th- and 17th-century ecclesiastical art and the bridal crown of Ebba, which is worn by all brides on Visingso. The story of Ebba Brahe is as romantic and complicated as any in Swedish history, too long to go into here. From Visingso, there are boat connections with Jonkoping. **Ystad.** Magnificent curving stretch of white sand beach on the south coast of Skane. Picturesque town with quaint streets, a good town **museum** and some 400 medieval half-timbered houses. A popular resort, with one of the world's last remaining town criers calling out the hourly news from the main church tower.

FUN TRIPS From **Stockholm** the **Around Djurgarden** boat tour takes you past quays, wharfs, around the Deer Garden; and alongside the *Wasa;* tour lasts one hour and is the most fun of all the sightseeing tours for children; boats cast off from a dock diagonally in front of the Grand Hotel every hour on the hour from 11 a.m.–7 p.m. in summer. **Saltsjobaden** has fine swimming, tennis, 9-hole golf course, riding stable, mini-golf, sailing and motorboat excursions. Skiing, good ski lift, ice-skating and ice-boating in winter. Plan to have lunch at the Grand Hotel, very nice indeed, or get off the train at **Igelboda** and get on the local train for the **Erstaviksbadet** section, where the beach is quieter and wooded and the swimming is great. Visitors to Stockholm who like to spend a lot of time at the beach make Saltsjobaden headquarters for their stay. It's a lovely place, not to be missed. **Sandhamn:** If you are a sailing family, you'll want to come to this popular sailing center. Sandy beaches, wonderful swimming. **Waxholm** is a charming little town. To get there, take a ''Waxholm boat'' from Stockholm.

The beautiful Stockholm Archipelago is also serviced, by SAAB-built MEFA craft, the same thing as a ***hovercraft.*** Another way of seeing the Archipelago is the *Sirena,* a fast ***hydrofoil*** that can zoom you between Stockholm and the Finnish Aland Island in just over two hours. You land at the fishing town of **Mariehamm.** Swimming, picnicking, and fishing in an area that looks very much like Nantucket.

Typical of Sweden are the ***archipelagoes.*** The largest of these lie just outside Stockholm and Goteborg, but others, also attractive, lie along the Blekinge coast, off the little town of Vastervik in Smaland, St. Anne's archipelago off the coast of Ostergotland. These islands are serviced by regular boat traffic. Detailed information from the local tourist offices. In the north of Varmland, you can hire a raft at **Munkfors** and sail down the river Klaralven.

Other ***boat tours:***

From Goteborg (Skeppsbrokajen) daily boat tours go to the skerries, Vinga and elsewhere. From Uddevalla the archipelago boats go to Lysekil-Karingon (4½ hours) three to four times a week and to Stenungssund-Marstrand (4 hours) twice a week. Meals served on board. On inland lakes and canals passenger boats ply: **Lake Vanern,** tours from Karlstad, Kristinehamn, and Saffle; **Lake Vattern,** tours from Granna Visingso and from Motala; **Lake Malaren,** tours from Stockholm (Klara Strand) to Mariefred, Sigtuna-Skokloster, Drottningholm and, on some days, to the prehistoric capital (archaelogical remains) on the island of Bjorko; **Lake Hjalmaren,** sightseeing tours from Orebro; Lake Siljan, daily sight-seeing trips and evening tours from Sunne; and **Helgasjon Lake,** tours leaving Vaxjo going through locks at Aby. A unique boat service goes through the lakes along the **Stora Lulealv river,** in Lapland, the so-called Sjofallsleden. This is arranged by the Swedish Touring Club (STF). Starting at Suorva, the boat goes to Ritsemjokk and

Vaisaluokta, 36 miles into the heart of the mountains. Daily tours also go to STS's mountain station at Saltoluokta and the Stora Sjofallet, Sweden's greatest waterfall. In summer, STF operates boats along the **Sitajaureleden** and around **Lake Tornetrask** in northernmost Lapland.

Dalslands Canal, 151 miles long, goes through a province which is often called "Sweden in Miniature." Regular trips from Bengtsfors and Kopmannebro. The whole trip takes six hours. Meals served on board. The **Kinda Canal** tours from Linkoping to Rimforsa (7 hours) leave three times a week. Also shorter trips like Linkoping–Sturefors (2½ hours), evening trips (2½ hours), and tours through the Rimforsa-Horn.

Sight-seeing flights: **Midnight Sun:** The SAS flight gives half-fare to under-12s and is free for under-2s, but my feeling is most children would sleep through the midnight sun—the whole point of the trip. Sightseeing flights in mountain areas can be taken at **Ostersund,** Funasdalen. From the helicopter station at **Valadalen** there are flights to Sylarna, Helags, and other places, and to highland fishing waters. Further information from **Jamtlands Aero** (Ostersund; Tel: 15162) or from **Jamtlands Resor** (Ostersund; Tel: 24590). For private flying, light aircraft may be chartered for sightseeing and fishing flights all over the country.

The **Gota Canal** runs right across Sweden from Goteborg to Stockholm, a three-day, two-night trip along 347 miles of lakes, woodland, and villages; pauses long enough for a stroll as the steamer goes through some 60-odd locks; at principal points of interest, pauses long enough for brief, guided tours that you can take or leave. Many stretches, where the waterway narrows, you will find yourselves—for example, at Toreboda—with cows so close you can almost pat them. For 100 years, this has been a delight. The steamers are small, attractive, spotless, and serve excellent food. Probably the most appealing stretch is around the province of Ostergotland. Takern, Granna and the island of Visingso in this area are the most fun for children. South of Lapland in the province of Jamtland, ***sightseeing flights*** above mountain areas are available at Ostersund and Funasdalen. Or, take the chopper from the heliport at Valadalen to Sylarna, Helags or to the fishing waters of the highlands. For more information, contact **Jamtlands Aero** (Ostersund). Sweden's canal and lake system are ideal for boating or canoeing holidays of a day or longer. Ask the nearest Tourist Center.

FUN AND GAMES *Sailing:* The Stockholm Archipelago is a Sun. sailor's heaven, and you can hire sailboats and motorboats with or without a guide very cheaply; try **Rent a Boat** (Sturevagen 7, Saltsjobaden). The east, west, and south coasts all offer excellent boating, which can also be done in the inland lakes. Goteborg has many regattas and races. Sail and power charter boats can be hired at the highly recommended **Scandinavian Charter Boat AB** (Bergsgarden, Goteborgsvagen 55, Uddevalla).

One of the most typical Swedish sports is ***orienteering,*** a cross-country race through woods and fields on an unmarked route; runners must find their way with map and compass; competitions are held in spring, summer, and autumn.

All along the south coast are fine beaches and attractive bathing resorts.

As for ***spectator events,*** the racing season is Mar.–Dec.—both trotting and flat races—with the main events taking place in June–Aug. If you are in Halsingland around July 1, don't miss the ''Halsingehambon,'' a folk dance festival with 3000 costumed participants performing on stages at Arbra, Bollnas, Harga and Jarvso.

Riding stables can be found in many Swedish cities. Riding schools and camps flourish at Falkenberg, Goteborg, Halmstad, Kungalv-Gullbringa, Laholm, Lysekil, Kungsbacka-Alekarr, Uddevalla, Varberg. Details from the local Tourist Centers.

To hire a horse for an hour try: **Stockholm Riding Stables** (Stockholms Ridhus) at Valhallavagen (Tel: 606–179), or **Djudgarden's Riding School** at Djugarden (Tel: 622–147). (See also Children's Camps.)

If you're an all-season athletic family, the year-round resort of Are and Duved (W of Ostersund in Jamtland) will sell you a multi-purpose card, valid for a week, entitling you to *unlimited* use of ski-lift, cable-car; windsurfing and canoeing and fishing facilities; free bicycle hire.

Fishing: Sweden, with 4,300 miles of coast and 96,000 lakes, has excellent fishing.

Grayling, trout, salmon, pike, perch, and cod fill the rivers and streams during May and August. From Aug. 15–Sept. you can charter a specially equipped boat or helicopter and have the thrill of fishing in the Oresund for tuna. In Lapland, seaplanes will ply you to fishing camps. Halsingborg is the center for deep-sea fishermen. The Morrum River, the Atran, the Dalalven River at Alvkarleby, and Kalix and Torne Rivers in Lapland are great for salmon. All specifics on permits are available from the tourist offices. The most comprehensive guide (with maps) is *Fiske,* written in English, available from bookshops or from the **Swedish Anglers' Assoc.,** Fiske-framjandet (Box 14114, 10441 Stockholm). In winter, Swedes are fond of fishing through a hole in the ice, known as ''pimpling.'' Pimpling competitions are festive occasions; the largest, held at Rissna (end of Mar.) attracts 5000 participants. Many resort hotels in the northern mountains specialize in fishing and arrange tours and courses. Sea-fishing tours are also specialties of Stockholm (Strandvagen quay), Halsingborg, Landskrona, and Varberg. In Aug., fishing festivals are held at Varberg, Lysekil, Stromstad, and other towns along Sweden's west coast.

Hunting: For information on licenses, seasons, and tours, contact the regional Tourist Assoc. in Dalsland, Gotland, Harjedalen, Jamtland, Vasterbotten, and Vasternorrland.

For every activity mentioned, plus winter sports, archery, bowling, and bicycling, there are clubs and assoc. in Sweden that can fill you in on details. Write to the STB.

SHOPPING WITH AND FOR CHILDREN Watch for *hemslojd*—Swedish Cottage industry handicrafts. Children's clothes are particularly good investments for hand-knit sweaters, durable reindeer-skin slippers, textiles for home-sewing. In Stockholm, shops are usually open from 9 a.m.–6 p.m., Mon. through Fri. On Sat., closing time varies between 1 p.m. and 4 p.m. Department stores and many other shops stay open until 8 p.m. one evening a week for late shopping (usually Mon. or Fri.) In Stockholm, food stores at the underground stations of Fridhemsplan, Hotorget, T-Centralen, and Ostermalmstorg remain open until 10 p.m. every evening. On Sun. they open at 1 p.m.

In **Stockholm,** for everything, including Swedish costumes and costume dolls, try **Nordiska Kompaniet** (NK for short, Hamngatan 16). English-speaking clerks, a roof-garden restaurant, personal shoppers, shipping office. The finest of Swedish regional and national products plus the best from all over Europe. For a choice selection of the very best of Sweden's handicrafts, and the best dolls, try **Svenskt Hemslojd** (Sveagagen 44), and also **Stockholms Stads Och Lans** Hemslojdsforeningen (Drottninggatan 18–20). Wooden horses and bowie knives from Dalarna. For a wide range of traditional toys, sturdy and well designed, exceptional in every way, try: **Gamlaleksaker** (Lilla Nygaten 9). Sweden is the home of the Hasselblad camera. You can find these at **Hasselblad Camera and Foto Shop** (Hamngatan 16).

In **Goteborg,** for toys: **Alida Soderdal** (Norra Hamngatan 30), all Swedish-made; also **Pinocchio Sagoland** (Kungsgatan 58–60). For Swedish children's costumes: **Polarn & Pyret** or **Femman** department store, both on Norstadstorget. For hand-knit apparel and the finest handicrafts, great sources are **Bohusslojd** (Kungsportsavenyn 25) and **Konsthantverkhuset** (Brogatan 3). For foreign magazines: **Presscenter (Nordstatstorget) and Turisten** (Kungsportsplatsen); books and magazines at **Gumperts** (Norra Hamngatan 26).

SWEDISH FRIENDS AND PEN PALS If you apply in person at the information Tourist Center in Stockholm, Goteborg, Vaxjo (Oland), Karlstad or Sunne (Varmlands), you can participate in the ''Sweden at Home'' program, whereby you are invited for a morning, afternoon or evening to the home of a Swedish family sharing similar interests to those of your own. Just fill in a form indicating the pastimes, talents, professional and other interests of you and yours, and then be prepared for heartwarming Swedish hospitality. If you have older daughters who would like to meet Swedish boys, or sons who would like to meet Swedish girls, or if you don't know much about sailing and would like to meet a yachting enthusiast, even this can be arranged. No fees are involved, no obligations.

CALENDAR OF EVENTS For additions, special events, and local attractions that vary in place and time, ask the STB.

In **Jan.,** usually the last week, Orebro features ***Hindermassan;*** lasting three days; the largest market fair in central Sweden; medieval traditions. From **Feb.**–Apr., Dalarna, and Jamtland provinces, and Lapland hold ***skiing championships.*** The major event is the ***Vasa Ski Race*** from Salen to Mora (the 1st Sun. in Mar.). **Apr.** 30, all Sweden (especially Lund, Uppsala, Stockholm, Goteborg, Umea) celebrates ***Walpurgis Night;*** a salute to spring's arrival; bonfires, torchlight processions, songs, and merrymaking.

From late June, Stockholm ***Festival.*** Gala performances of opera, ballet, concerts, and theater. The Drottningholm Court Theater stages performances of ***18th-century plays;*** festivities galore. **June** 6, throughout Sweden (especially Stockholm Stadium) is ***Swedish Flag Day,*** commemorating the crowning of Gustav Vasa, unifier and liberator, in 1523; and the adoption of the Constitution (1809). Parades and other celebrations. The Fri. and Sat. nearest June 23, all Sweden (particularly Dalarna) celebrates ***Midsummer Eve;*** flowers and ribboned maypoles are raised; games for children and all-night dancing around the maypole; much fun. Late-June–early-Sept., in Stockholm, ***Opera Performances*** open at the Drottningholm Court Theater.

Late June at Leksand features ***Church Boat Races*** across Lake Siljan; costumes, music, and excitement. During the second weekend in July Stanga holds its ***Competition of Traditional Games;*** pole-hurling, stone tossing, and the like. July 10 or 11–Aug. 11 or 12, Visby holds its ***Festival;*** frequent performances of a miracle play with music; not to be missed; *Petrus de Dacia* performed in the ruins of St. Nicholas Church. Around the last ten days of July, Leksand has open-air performances of *The Road to Heaven,* an allegorical play with music; highly recommended.

Late-**Aug.**–early-Sept. in Stockholm is the time of the ***St. Erik International Trade Fair.*** Throughout **Sept.,** you'll find the ***Scandinavian Design Cavalcade;*** chiefly in Stockholm, but with exhibits throughout Sweden's provincial capitals; Swedish crafts and special tours to workrooms and factories where products are created.

Late Nov.–mid-Dec., Stockholm features ***Skansen Christmas Fair.*** Held in authentically restored guild houses in which craftsmen work; open-air booths, food, decorations, handicrafts. Dec. 13, all Sweden celebrates ***St. Lucia's Day,*** a festival of lighted candles heralding the beginning of the Christmas season; ***processions*** with young girls crowned with candles; other ceremonies; lasts until Jan. 13. ***Christmas celebrations*** throughout Sweden.

LANGUAGE AND PHRASEBOOK In hotels, restaurants, shops, and tourist centers, English is spoken. In the countryside, you'll have to rely on phrasebooks. Most Swedes know English. The one phrase you should know, and will find yourself saying over and over again, is *tack sa mycket,* pronounced tahk-sah-mick-it and meaning "Thank you very much." The plural of krona is kroner, abbreviated Skr.

Note: å=the sound of *aw* as in law; *ä*=the sound of *e* as in met; *ö*=the sound of *u* as in fur; g, when followed by *e, i, y, ä* or *ö*=the sound of *y* as in yes; g, when followed by *a, o, u,* or *å*=the sound of g as in go; *k* sounds like the *ch* in church before *i* or *ö;* otherwise it sounds like the *k* in kick.

Hello	*God dag*	*Goo dah*
I am an American	*Jar ar amerikan-are (boy)*	*Yog air ah-mer-i-kah-nahray*
	Jag ar amerikan-ska (girl)	*Yog air ah-mer-i-kahn-ska*
My name is____	*Jag heter____*	*Yog hee-uh-tuh____*
I am____years old	*Jar ar____ar*	*Yog air____or*
Please	*Var snall och*	*Var snell ohk*
Thank you	*Tack sa mycket*	*Tahk sah micket*
I can't speak Swedish	*Jag talar inte Svenska*	*Yog tah-lahr een-tuh svenska*
Yes	*Ja*	*Yah*
No	*Nej*	*Nay*
I am having a wonderful time	*Jag har trevligt*	*Yog hahr tray-uh-vleekt*
1	*ett*	*et*
2	*tva*	*tvoh*
3	*tre*	*tray*
4	*fyra*	*fee-rah*
5	*fem*	*fem*
6	*sex*	*sex*
7	*sju*	*shoo*
8	*atta*	*awt-tah*
9	*nio*	*nee-yoh*
10	*tio*	*tee-yoo*
11	*elva*	*el-vah*
12	*tolv*	*tawlv*
13	*tretton*	*tret-tawn*
14	*fjorton*	*fyoor-tawn*
15	*femton*	*fem-tawn*
Goodbye	*adjo*	*ah-yer*

SWITZERLAND

The Swiss gave us the kindergarten, but its corollary, the *kinder-paradies*—a super-playground-recreational area—is a kind of paradise few children living outside of Switzerland have been privileged to know. And I know of no kinder paradise than Switzerland for the entire Europe-bound family. Switzerland has a soothing babysitting-kindergarten-playground-ski school system operative everywhere. For families who wish to enjoy medieval cities and stunning landscapes while retaining luxury in surroundings as spotless in town (no soot, smog, or cinders) as in the headily oxygen-filled countryside, Switzerland is *the* place!

For children there are also folk plays, fairs and festivals, Roman ruins, hot chocolate and pastries, fascinating exhibits, bears to throw carrots to, cows, goats, ponies, seagulls, peacocks, and castle deer to pet and feed. The Swiss are wonderful with children. Swiss toys are wonderful for children. And you and your children will feel wonderful in Switzerland.

INFORMATION ABOUT SWITZERLAND You will be sent a veritable *Jungfrau* of artistic brochures if you get in touch with the SNTO, **Swiss National Tourist Office** (608 5th Ave., New York, NY 10020; Tel: (212) 757–5944) in Chicago, (104 South Michigan Ave., IL 60603; Tel: (312) 641–0050) or in San Francisco (250 Stockton St., CA 34108).

Every Swiss town has its tourist office *(Office du Tourisme, Associazone per il Turismo,* or *Verkehrsverein).* Basic hours are 8 a.m.–noon; 2–6 p.m. weekdays. During peak season, some offices remain open evenings and weekends.

In **Zurich,** Mr. Walter Bruderer is the fabulous Press and Public Relations Director of the SNTO (Bellariastrasse 38; Tel: (01) 202–3737). If you have any trouble about anything—a car breakdown, the teddy-bear left in the station—just call SNTO. **Tourist Information Offices,** heralded with a green sign with a centered lower-case ''i,'' provide capital information about everything: **Arosa** (CH–7050 Arosa; Tel: (081) 31–16–21); **Basel** (Blumenrain 2; CH–4001 Basel Tel: (061) 25–38–11); **Bern** (Hauptbahnhoff, CH–3001 Bern; Tel: (031) 22–76–76); **Davos** (CH–7270 Davos Platz; Tel: (083) 35–135); **Geneva** (1 Tour-del'Ile, CH–1211 Geneva 11; Tel: (022) 28–72–33); **Grindelwald** (CH–3818 Grindelwald; Tel: (036) 53–12–12); **Interlaken** (Hoheweg 37, CH–3818 Interlaken; Tel: (036) 22–21–21); **Lausanne** (60, Avenue d'Ouchy, CH–1006 Lausanne; Tel: (021) 27–73–21); **Lucerne/Luzern** (Pilatusstrasse 14, CH–6002 Lucerne; Tel: (041) 23–52–52); **Montreux** (Grand-rue 42, CH–1820 Montreux; Tel: (021) 61–33–84); **St. Gallen** (Bahnhofplatz la, CH–9001 St. Gallen; Tel: (071) 22–62–62); **St. Moritz** (Via Maistra, CH–7500 St. Moritz; Tel: (082) 33–147); **Zermatt** (CH–3920 Zermatt; Tel: (028) 67–16–25); **Zurich** (Bahnhofplatz 15, CH–8001 Zurich; Tel: (01) 21–14–000). You can also request a colorful booklet that depicts 19 regional Swiss costumes; your kids will love the illustrations.

Tri-lingual (German-French-English) weekly magazines, free for the asking, with city maps, hours of attractions, events, and suggestions for sightseeing, are available at your hotel or at tourist offices. For ***special reports,*** given in the language predominating in the area you happen to be in, dial 161 for the time; 162, weather; 163, road and snow conditions; 164, sports results; 167, 168, and 169 for news reports. Dial 120 for tourist information. Substantial service charges are levied when you make a call from your hotel. If you're calling the U.S., it's best to place your call and ask them to call you back.

HEALTH, WATER, AND FOOD Cleanliness is a Swiss obsession. Swiss mountain air is celebrated for its tonic effect, and since your great-grandfather's time Switzerland has been the place to go when you're feeling out of commission. However, be careful about overexposure, particularly in winter, to the brilliant sunshine; combined with dry air and snow, ice dazzle (a form of temporary snow blindness) and a whopping sunburn can result.

If water is not divinely pure, there'll be an occasional sign in bright red letters notifying you.

The Swiss take great pride in their cattle and modern dairies. Milk is drunk in the country right out of the milk pail, or boiled for urban consumption. The taste of unpasteurized milk is hard to get used to, but it makes a wonderful base for hot or iced chocolate capped with whipped cream or mixed with Ovaltine (called *Ovomaltine).* Pasteurized milk is generally available. For children who prefer hot chocolate to Ovomaltine, **Caotina** is an excellent brand. Children who have read *Heidi* sometimes develop a passion for drinking the hot milk served with the breakfast *cafe au lait* out of a bowl (but it's not polite in public).

What children know as "Swiss cheese" is an Americanization of Emmentaler. Emmentaler (with larger holes) will probably appeal to children more because it's milder. *Gruyere* and *Appenzeller* are also among Switzerland's greatest cheeses that children like. Around Geneva and Lausanne, regional dairy products are prepared with a French touch—*ramequins* (little cheese pies).

Traubensaft is like grape juice; it comes in *rot* (red) or *weiss* (white); Merlino or Virano are excellent brands. *Apfelsaft* is the cider my children preferred.

You can have the French or Italian continental breakfast *(croissants* with butter and jam). The German Swiss go in for hearty breakfasts—the Swiss *Zmorge,* or country breakfast—including cheese, ham, bacon, eggs, and sausage. Omelets are delicious. Dr. Bircher-Benner of Zurich concocted the cereal mixture of oatflakes, cream, nuts, and fruits called *Birchermuesli,* which is delicious and nutritious.

Railroad stations and zoos sell *Wienerli* (hotdogs), the best in Europe. *Bundnerfleisch* (air-cured beef) is a snack some children like. Standard hotel fare offers a raft of fresh, wholesome, attractively prepared dishes that suit most children to a T-bone. *Fondue Bourguignonne* is as much fun to do as it is good to eat. Let the children make merry with this nonalcoholic fondue rather than the wine and cheese mixture, which can knock them for a loop. *Roschti* (golden hashed brown potatoes) are a great favorite, as are *Spatzli* (dumplings sauteed in butter). *Raclettes,* a pool of fresh melted cheese surrounding a pile of baked potatoes is another favorite.

For pick-me-ups, children familiarize themselves speedily with *Lebkuchen,* a spiced honey cake with white icing (in Bern, they're decorated with a white sugar bear), and *Leckerli,* a Baseler specialty, like *Lebkuchen,* but smaller and harder. Watch out for *Kirschtorte;* it's not just flavored with cherry brandy—it's generally soaked in it.

The word for herbs may be *herbes, erbe,* or *Krauter,* and both Klaus' Alpine herb-flavored toffees and Ricola's aromatic herb-flavored hard candies (prettily packaged), proclaimed as cough remedies, appeal to children. Everywhere, children will find scrumptious Swiss chocolates made by Lindt, Tobler, Suchard, and Cailler; Swiss law demands that the sugar content not exceed 68%, so chocolate contains a high content of cocoa and cocoa butter. Candy, cake, bread, and meat specialties sold in markets and during festivals are chemical and preservative free, and appetizing.

For restaurants in **Zurich,** try the rustic **Doltschistube** at the Atlantis Sheraton; lunch and supper are casual and cozy; steaks, fresh fruit, cheese, and desserts; hearty breakfasts too. **Opfelchammer** (Rindermarkt 12; Tel: 251–23–36) is a student favorite by night, a businessman's gourmet lunch spot by day; a great treat; romantic atmosphere and setting; reservations necessary. Among the Movenpicks, try Sun. mornings at the **Grut Farm** (enormous buffet and the fun of helping prepare one's own eggs beneath raftered toy hens); try brunch also at the zoo's **Outpost** (the Swiss version of the Wild West with a children's menu printed on lion's masks) rather than the zoo's steamy cafeteria. Other Movenpicks: **Locanda's, Il Giardino** (open-air lunch; special Sun. lunches for children); and the one on Talacker and Sihlporte. You can get the best fondue in town at **Le Dezaley** (Romergasse 7; Tel: 251–

61–25); other Vaudois specialties. Combine a steamer or pedalo trip on the lake with a snack at **Bauschanzli's Cafe,** a remnant of an old ring of fortifications, jutting out from Stadthausquai into the Limmat. Or snack at the **Cafe Odeon,** across the Quaibrucke; the former rendezvous of James Joyce, Mata Hari, and radical politicians is now a meeting-place for students, hippies, and the avantgarde. Along Bahnhofstr., **Jelmoli's** or **Globus's** have cafe-restaurants. The tea room, where the medium is coffee and pastry, is a civilized Swiss institution usually located above shops or restaurants—a great place to relax. Try **Sprungli** (Paradeplatz), one of the best tea rooms in the world; at the upstairs marble-topped tables Father won't feel out of place. **Durisch Confiserie** (Strehlgasse 9) has yum-yums.

Basel: Try the **Goldener Sternen** (St. Alban Wheinweg 7) near the old city wall; and the **Broetlibar** at the Stadthof (Barfuesserplatz), which features many varieties of open-faced sandwiches. Try a meal at **Schloss Bottmingen** (Tel: 541–131), a baroque lake castle about two miles from Bottmingen; you can eat outside on a sunny day; lovely; low-walled courtyard garden, bridge, and two round towers. **Bern: Movenpick** (Bubenbergplatz 5) or the **Kornhauskeller,** a huge, vaulted-ceilinged granary converted into an agreeably roistering restaurant. Yummy confiserie tea rooms where fathers are well-represented: **Abegglen** (Spitalgasse 36); **Figaro** (Neuengasse 45); and **Au Litteraire** (Marktgass-Passage, upstairs). **Geneva:** Everyone should be treated to a festive evening at **Au Chandelier** (Grand' rue 23), where the specialty is *Fondue Bourguignonne*. **La Bergerie** (Mont Blanc 3) is good for sandwiches, and yes, there is a **Movenpick** (Cendrier 17). **Lausanne:** Try fondue at **Cafe du Jorat** (pl. de l'Ours); yummy. **Movenpick** (pl. de la Riponne 1) will go all out to make your child's birthday festive. **Lucerne:** The **Stadt-und-Rathauskeller** (Sternenplatz 3) features Swiss costumes, music, and yodeling. **Movenpick** (Schwanenplatz) has special features for children. **Muerren,** a car-free resort in the Bernese Oberland, is the access point, via the longest cableway in Europe, to the top of the Schilthorn, and on top of the Schilthorn is the revolving **Piz Gloria** restaurant, making a complete circle every 60 minutes, with views of the Jungfrau, rock passes, glaciers and a vast Alpine panorama. **St. Moritz: Caleche** is a teenage bar where only cakes and Shirley Temples are served.

BABY FOOD Zurich's department store **Jelmoli** carries a sizable array of **Heinz** baby and junior foods, including hard-to-find fruit and dessert preparations. The supermarket chain of **Migros** is sole distributor of **Gerber** baby foods (8 varieties) and Junior foods (9 varieties). **Galactina,** highly recommended Swiss pureed vegetable, cereal, meat, and fruit for babies, is most widely distributed; you'll also find limited but excellent Swiss-produced Wander Veguvit products, the French Bledine, the Italian Buitoni, and the German Hipp line, plus a considerable selection of milk formulae and cereal products made by Humana, Wander, and Guigoz; all in *apotheke,* pharmacies, *drogeries,* supermarkets and the food depts. of department stores.

In general, only *apotheke,* pharmacies, and *drogeries* stock milk and Pablum-like cereals for the new-born—of which the most easily available are Humana's dried milk, Guigoz (medium), Ovaltine and Ovomaltine producing Wander's Adapta, and others. Guigoz' Vollfett, Wander's Lactovegura, and the French Bledine milk products are tailored to the requirements of the 3- or 4-month-old. In the cereal line for infants, try Zwieback cereal. Wander has Ceral. For 4-month-and-older appetites, Nestle suggests *Milchbrei* (a creamy porridge), *Apfelmilchbrei* (an apple cream cereal), and *Vollkorn* (whole grain in flake form). In pharmacies, the word baby food is understood. In supermarkets and department stores, ask for the baby corner.

DIAPERS AND LAUNDRY The word for regular diaper is *Windel* (plural *Windeln),* for disposables, *Papier Windeln* in German-speaking areas; *lange* and *lange a papier* (French); *pannolini* and *pannolini di carta* (Italian). Cloth diapers and disposables are available at all baby specialty shops and in the children's depts. of all large department stores.

The two largest-selling brands of disposables are supermarket chain Migros' **Mimi** and Co-op's **Hyganella. Pampers** are available at discount house Denner. Elsewhere (at *apotheken* and *drogeries*) **Dolly** and other brands of disposables—and rubber pants—are also widely available. **Jolyponge,** the boilable, long-lasting super-special French rubber pants that outwear all others, can be found at **Handar** (Banhofstr. 83, Zurich; Tel: 221–08–33).

There are no diaper services; give the diapers to your hotel or nearest commercial laundry.

BABY EQUIPMENT FOR HIRE Backpacks, prams, strollers, playpens, folding cots, traveling johns are delivered with a day's notice (any day except Sat. or Sun.) by **Bebehaus Wehrli** (Schaffhauserstr. 95, Zurich; Tel: 363–12–12) for a deposit of about one-half of the retail price of the item. Rental is extremely reasonable.

EMERGENCIES MADE EASY *Pharmacies* alternate night duties, and those on 24-hour duty are noted in the newspaper. Your concierge will tell you which pharmacy to call for midnight delivery, or will see that someone picks up your order for you. In **Zurich** try **Sammet Apothek** (Bahnhofstr. 106; Tel: 221–31–33).

In **Bern, Apotheke A. Horning** (Marktgasse 58; Tel: 224–019); also **Schwanen-Apotheke** (Bubenbergplatz 12; Tel: 223–411). In **Lucerne, Rigi-Apotheke** (Grendelstr. 2; Tel: 220–139). In **Klosters, Perroco** (pl. Hotel-de-Ville 5); **Droz** (rue Jardiniere 127); and **Pillonel** (rue Balancier 7). in **St. Moritz, Drogerie Steiner** can provide for baby needs. In **Winterthur, Drogerie Meier** (Marktgasse 19).

Swiss ***doctors and hospitals*** are generally excellent, as you would expect in a country that is Europe's sanatorium; CIBA-Geigy and Hoffman-La Roche are world leaders in pharmaceuticals and vitamins. Most large hotels have house physicians, and can also recommend English-speaking physicians. In **Zurich,** American mothers recommend pediatrician **Frau Dr. Forster** (Schaffhauserstr. 188; Tel: 362–70–80); 700 other Zuricher doctors are also at your disposal. In **Basel,** there's an excellent children's hospital at Romergasse 8 (Tel: 26–26–26).

English-speaking doctors and dentists can be recommended by the **U.S. Embassy** (Jubilaeumstrasse 93, 3005 Bern; Tel: (031) 43–70–11); by the U.S. **Consulate General** (Zollikerstrasse 141, 8008 Zurich; Tel: (01) 55–25–66); by the **U.S. Embassy Branch Office** (11, Route de Pregny, 1292 Chambesy/Geneva; Tel: (022) 34–60–31).

You can also ask for the services of a *Hauspflegerin,* a nurse subsidized by the state; she is trained to look after infants, children, your living quarters, and any cooking that has to be done.

Emergency numbers for the ambulance or the police, dial 117 throughout Switzerland. Although some cities have a special number to summon a doctor; dial 111 day or night and ask for an English-speaking operator; she'll give you the name of a doctor, dentist, or pharmacy open after hours, advise you where to get information about roads, hotels, or train schedules if the tourist office is closed.

MAGIC FAMILY HELPERS You will be delighted to find out that child-care facilities amount to a sort of national cult. But, because the Swiss take this all so much for granted—and because tourist offices assume that you will instantly sort out *Kinderaufsicht* (nurseries), *Kinderhutedienste* (babysitting services), kindergartens, *Kinderheime* (children's homes away from home), *Kinderbetreuung* (child-care), *Kinderparadiese* (supervised playgrounds), *Kinderspielplatze* (unsupervised playgrounds), and all the French and Italian equivalents thereof—you may find yourself in a land of plenty without even a vague idea of the quality and extent of services.

The basic precept of Swiss child care is that there should be order and respect for the authority of grownups who in turn regard the body, soul, and brain of a child as a sort of sacred trust to be diligently nurtured. Therefore, all child-care personnel and services meet such exacting government standards that you can rely on them to be utterly conscientious about encouraging the virtues of early bedtime; afternoon naps, nutritious food, the pleasures of nature and out-of-doors play; educationally wholesome toys, TV and reading matter; and abiding by the strictly enforced law of non-movie attendance for children under 16. Don't be put off by this serious mien—children aren't. They're the first to sense the respect for individuality, the kindliness, thoughtfulness, and concern behind that rather sober public Swiss mask.

Babysitters. Almost every hotel and local tourist office has a standby list of mother's helpers waiting to be summoned within a few hours' notice. In **Zurich,** for babysitting and for everything from shopping and packing to catering, call **Kady** (Pfalzgasse 6; Tel: 211–37–86).

In **Basel,** call **R. Gafner,** (Florastr. 8, Binningen; Tel: 475–834). In **Bern, Babysitting Alther** (Schlosshaldenstrasse 206; Tel: 44–30–31 and Laubeggstrasse 27; Tel: 44–30–37) and **Babysitting-Agentur Tupf** (Munstergasse 6; Tel: 226–001); in **Lausanne, Garderie A.P.E.F.** (Tel: 220–980); and in **Lucerne, Baby-Sitter Service "Ursula"** (Horw 6048; Tel: 413–738) can send a sitter to your hotel or look after your toddler for an hour, day, or week. In Gstaad, Vevey, and Zermatt, telephone the tourist office.

Department stores with nurseries? You don't even have to be a customer. In Zurich, **Globus** (Schweizergasse II) has hidden away its fifth-floor children's dept. the *Spatzenturm* (Sparrow Tower), a small but charming playroom for children 3–7. Your youngest (2–4s) might be happiest here, but your 5–10s might prefer the whoop-de-doo **Jelmoli's** (Sihlstr.) with space for 480 (including babies). Your baby will be watched over, but not fed. Older children get a snack, a run in a model train, a marionette show, a carousel ride. The teeny-tinies can be sequestered in a world of their own. In **Bern,** the toy-store, **Franz Carl Weber** (Marktgasse 52–54) has a supervised playroom for 3–7-year-olds; open daily 1:30–5:30 p.m. Fees at all are minuscule.

Zurich's **Kloten Airport** has excellent part-time nursery facilities where you can safely leave the baby and tiny tots. If you and the baby both feel like stretching out and having a nap, there is a nice quiet room set aside for this. Also the **Pro Juventute,** a private child and youth organization, has set up 20 remarkable recreation complexes *(freizeitanlagen)* called Robinson playgrounds, comprising open-air theaters, swimming pools, pottery, photography, boat-making, ham radio, handicraft workshops, tennis courts, rifle ranges, picnicking facilities—all are standouts. For information, contact their offices (Seefeldstr. 8; Tel: 327–244). In supermarkets, you'll often find a *Kinderhutedienst* or a *garderie* where your child can be looked after for not more than two hours while you shop.

All major cities and resorts have supervised indoor-outdoor ***kindergartens,*** with and without meals and sleeping facilities, in general for children 1–10. Some are open year-round, some are seasonal; age range and hours vary but usually you can bring your little one around 9 a.m. and pick him up around 5 p.m.; all are very reasonable.

Check with the local tourist office about details of the best *garderie, kindergarten,* or *hutedienst,* usually to be found also under these listings in the yellow pages of your local telephone directory. In some cases, the local tourist office will operate its own *garderie* or *hutedienst.*

All the hotels mentioned that belong to the association of **Happy Swiss Family Hotels** (See Castles and Other Happy Family Accommodations) provide services which are open to non-guests as well. Here is just a sampling of other facilities. In the Grisons: In **Arosa** Kindergarten "Churer Sage," Tel: (081) 31–16–21, for ages 4–8; **Chur:** Kinderhort, Reichsgasse 1, Tel: (081) 22–78–29, ages 3–7; **Davos:** for ages 3–10, Kindergarten Bolgen, Tel: (083) 3–40–48 and Kindergarten Pinocchio, Tel: (083) 3–71–71; **Lenzerheide:** a kindergarten for children up to 7 at Hotel Valbella, Tel: (081) 34–01–31; **St. Moritz:** Kinderparadies bei Hallenbad, Tel: (082) 3–66–37, for ages 2–12. In eastern Switzerland (Ostschweiz/Suisse orientale) at **Unterwasser,** for children up to 10, Chinderhus Maria Theresia, Tel: (074) 5–16–37. In **Winterthur:** "Junge Altstadt," Obere Kirchgasse 3, Tel: (052) 22–41–68, ages 2–10; in **Zurich:** Kady Kinderhutedienst, Pfalzgasse 6, Tel: (01) 211–37–86, ages 1–6. In central Switzerland, in **Rigi-Kaltbad,** Hostellerie Rigi, Tel (041) 83–16–16, for ages 3–12. In Northwest Switzerland, at **Baden,** Kinderhort, im Graben 2, Tel: (056) 22–37–76, ages 1–6; in **Basel,** Basler Bastelstube, Schutzengraben 9, Tel: (061) 25–28–87, ages 4–12, and "Gygampfi," Drahtzugstrasse 55, Tel: (061) 33–79–51, for ages 3–7. In the Bernese Oberland, in **Gstaad,** Hotel Gstaaderhoff, Tel: (03) 8–33–44, for ages 4–15. In the Valais, in **Champery,** Home Joli-Nid, Tel: (025) 79–12–40, ages 3–15; in **Montana Crans,** Centre Commercial, Tel: (027) 41–58–44, for ages 2–7; in **Sierre,** Creche de Beaulieu, Place Beaulieu, Tel: (027) 55–05–95, for ages 1–6; in **Zermatt,** Kinderheim Theresia, Tel: (028) 67–20–96, for ages 2–8. In Ticino, at **Ascona,** Hotel Losone has pleasant facilities for children from 2–8, Tel: (093) 35–01–31; in **Lugano,** Centro Assistenza Bambini, Via Treveno 13, Tel: (091) 23–33–13, for ages 6–12. In the Jura-Neuchatel area, in **Neuchatel,** you'll find La Creche, rue des Bercles 2, Tel: (038) 25–33–27, for ages 2–6. In the **Lake of Geneva** area, at **Les Diablerets,** there's La Cottetaz, Tel: (025) 53–14–46 for ages 1–12; in **Geneva,** the tourist office has many suggestions, Tel: (022) 28–72–33; in **Lausanne,** Vallee de la Jeunesse, Tel: (021) 27–97–01, for ages 2–9; in **Montreux,** La Coccinelle, 21 rue Industrielle, Tel: (021) 62–15–55, for ages 2–5.

During the winter season, ***ski schools,*** instruct children 3–14 in cross-country and downhill skiing. You can be sure of finding children's ski schools—and nurseries, babysitters, kindergartens for summer childcare—at the following resorts: Adelboden, Anzere, Arosa, Beatenberg, Bettmeralp, Blenio, Champery, Chateau-d'Oex, Crans-sur-Sierre, Davos, Disentis, Engelberg, Flumserberge, Grindelwald, Gryon-Barboleusaz, Gstaad, Klosters, Lausanne, Lenk, Lenzerheide, Les Diablerets, Les Marecottes, Les Mosses, Les Pleiades, Leysin, Locarno, Oberageri, Pontresina, Saas Fee, Savognin, Scuol-Tarasp-Vulpera, Sedrun, Sils, Silvaplana, Stoos, St.-Cergue, St. Moritz, Verbier, Villars, Wengen, Wildhaus, Zermatt, Zweisimmen. At **Badrutt's Palace Hotel** in St.

Moritz, in addition to the ski school, there is an all-day full-service kindergarten for young guests 9 months and up (See St. Moritz).

Instruction? For courses in French contact the **Secretariat des Ecoles-Club Migros** (Kanalgasse 38, Biel-Bienne branch in Interlaken), and in German the **Sekretariate der Klubschulen Migros** (Marktgasse 46, Bern) branch in Thun. In addition to much-heralded Le Rosey and the American School, Switzerland has so many good schools for American children that I cannot detail them all here; the SNTO can supply you with information; see also ''Holidays'' (below) and Chapter 8.

Personalized services? For a chauffeur-driven car or car rental, a matchless firm is **Welti-Furrer** (Zurich; Pfingstweidstrasse 31a; Tel: 42–14–42; branches in Geneva and New York). They'll provide car chairs and car beds for infants and toddlers, meet you at airports, transport anything anywhere, pick up luggage sent ahead by train.

HOLIDAYS FOR CHILDREN ON THEIR OWN Switzerland offers a galaxy of *Kinderheime, Homes d'Enfants, Kinderheim Schulen,* and *Homes Ecoles*. Some, stressing convalescent care and cures for asthma, are specialized health resorts. In others, the atmosphere is more like a nicely chaperoned house party, and the accent is on year-round fun. During the school year many are boarding schools. During vacation periods, these function as holiday camps offering language and music courses at kindergarten and primary levels for an hour or so a day to hold on to the educational franchise grant by the government. These facilities are superb. You can count on all of them being spotless, well-supervised, meticulous about the preparation of good, simple food, and staffed with trained, dedicated personnel. However, since I have not visited any of these facilities recently, please ask the SNTO for detailed information about them.

Club Mediterranee's **Valbella Summer Camp,** is a splendid possibility for children 4–13. See Children's Camps.

CHILDREN'S CAMPS In Clarens-sur-Montreux, there's an **International Junior Camp,** organized by Mrs. Charlotte Barnett, for boys and girls 6–13, and under the same management, an **International Teen Camp,** at the Ecole Nouvelle, for co-ed campers 13–19. For information and details, contact Mrs. Barnett, Case Postale 122, 1012 Chailly-sur-Lausanne; Tel: (056) 22–67–78 (Sept.–June) and (021) 32–11–22 during July and Aug. when the camp is in session. **Summer Camp Montana** (La Moubra, CH 3962 Montana; Tel: (027) 41–23–34 or (027) 41–18–97) accredited by the American Camping Association, is for boys and girls, divided into groups—Juniors, 8–10; Pioneers, 11–13; Seniors, 14–17—drawn from a wide circle of international families. The climate is superb, the facilities excellent. Mr. Rudy Studer (who has a doctorate in physical training and education), his wife Erica (a professional dietician) and a staff of over 100, oversee activities as varied as riding, mountaineering, archery, photography and sailing. Excursions and optional courses in French, German, English. My children loved the summer they spent here. During the winter, this is the site of the **International Ski Camp,** for boys and girls 8–17; beginners, advanced, and expert skiers, with ice-skating, parties, and a varied program of entertainment. In Leysin, during the summer, Mr. Robert F. Gilbert, an associate of Mr. Studer has organized the **International Hockey Camp** for ice hockey enthusiasts aged 11–17, directed by top National Hockey League professionals from teams such as the N.Y. Rangers, the Toronto Maple Leafs, and the Edmonton Oilers. For further details and information about the International Summer Camps in Montana and Leysin, your best source of information is Mr. Robert F. Gilbert, International Summer Camps, Inc., P.O. Box 543, Scarsdale, NY 10583; Tel: (914) 725–1818 (after hours, Tel: (914) 723–1141).

For boys and girls 8–16, from June–Aug., **Village Camps** (1296 Coppet (Vaud); Tel: (022) 76–20–59) offers two-week camping sessions with instruction in French and English, plus excursions and a variety of sports and games. The same is offered for boys and girls 12–18 by **Anglo World Summer School** in Villars, in the Vaud region. For information and details, contact Anglo World Travel, Blumenstrasse 1, 8820 Wadenswil; Tel: (01) 780–79–79.

In the Grisons, the little village of Valbella is **Club Mediterranee Valbella** (7078 Lenzerheide), a summer camp, from the end of June to early Sept., just for children 4–13—one big happy Mini Club and Kid's Club with excellent 24-hour supervision. Children are housed in two- and three-bedded rooms in a handsome hotel; sports, manual arts workshops, dancing, and photography, and much more; overnight camping trips in the mountains; plus library and movies.

CASTLES AND OTHER HAPPY FAMILY ACCOMMODATIONS The Swiss have recently developed Happy Family Swiss Hotels *(Klub kinderfreundlicher Schweizer Hotels/ Club des hotels suisses "enfants bienvenus"),* an association of hotels that offer supervised nursery/playroom for young children, 3s and older (by arrangement, for younger children); open-air play areas; organized picnics and walks; comprehensive information service for family activities in and around the hotel and elsewhere in the area; kitchenette for the preparation of baby food; children's menus; children's evening meal served from 6 p.m.; highchairs in the dining room; cots; price reductions for children (1 child per adult in parents' room)—up to age 6, free; 6–12, 50%; 12–16, 30% (not applicable to hotel suites or apartments); minimum three-day stay. The hotels are located in resort areas, and range in quality from two-stars to five-stars. Most have their own indoor swimming pool; many have a sauna, solarium, gym; all offer a varied palette of indoor and outdoor activities during the summer and winter. In **Adelboden,** you'll find the **Parkhotel Bellevue; Beatenberg,** the **Bluemlisalp;** in carefree, car-free **Braunwald,** the **Bellevue; in Brienz,** the **Lindenhof; Champex-Lac** has the **Alpes & Lac; Davos-Dorf** offers the **Derby,** open only in the winter; **Disentis** has **La Cucagna** with sound-proofed rooms and babysitting services; **Laax-Films** offers **Happy Rancho; Les Marecottes** offers **Aux Mille Etoiles; in Lugano-Paradiso,** the **Nizza,** has its own farm for dairy and produce; in **Melchsee-Frutt,** the **Glogghuis** has its own sports counselor and Alpine guide. In **Montreux-Territet** is the **Bristol,** a two-star budget hotel, a good base for many tours in the area; in **Morcote-Lugano,** the **Olivella au Lac** has all the luxury of a five-star establishment; in **Pontresina,** the **Atlas** offers a private park; **Saas-Fee** has the **Alphubel; San Bernardino** has the **Brocco E Posta;** in **Stoos,** where no cars are allowed, there's the **Sporthotel; Trubsee-Engelberg** offers a smaller **Sporthotel,** also a four-star gem, with its own ski-lift and children's ski school; **Via-Gambarogna** has the **Viralago,** with all rooms equipped with baby-minding acoustics; in **Vulpera,** the **Schweizerhof** has, among other facilities, a children's club; in car-free **Wengen,** the **Belvedere** is a paradise for walkers and hikers; also car-free, **Zuoz** has the **Castell.**

The supervised toy-filled nursery, a courtesy usually free of charge to hotel guests' children, is as much of an institution in luxury hotels as bowling or Ping-Pong; nurseries are generally open 9 a.m.–noon and 2–5 p.m.; during off-hours, the concierge will provide babysitters. For older children who can be trusted to play alone with minimal supervision, many hotels have playrooms. For a lengthy list of hotels and motels, contact the SNTO.

Brestenberg: Hotel **Schloss Brestenberg** (Tel: (064) 54–22–12), overlooking Lake Hallwil; beds for 40 guests; lovely garden, beautiful countryside; lake swimming and boating; fine food. **Burgenstock Hotel Estate** (Tel: 041) 641–331) is one of the greatest, grandest hotel resorts in the world, 1500 feet above Lake Lucerne, with limousine and helicopter transportation service, heated pool, beach, tennis, golf, hiking trails, sports club, disco, 20 minutes by car, 40 minutes by lake steamer from Lucerne. **Chateau-d'Oex:** The **Chalet Hotel,** with charm and character, has special terms and facilities for families. **Klosters: Chesa Grischuna** (Tel: (083) 42222); decorated in regional style; very pleasant; bowling alleys; marvelous food. **Lausanne:** Historic **Chateau d'Ouchy** (Tel: (021) 26–74–51) has been converted to an up-to-date lake resort. **Lucerne/Luzern:** A "fairytale castle," **Chateau Gutsch,** (Tel: (041) 22–02–72), dominates the town and offers a funicular, an outdoor swimming pool, great food at its restaurant with panoramic view. No playrooms, nurseries, or anything special for younger children; neither an authentic castle nor even a historic building, but a four-star hostelry that you and your teenagers may find happily accommodating. At **Meyriez,** just outside of Murten (a medieval gem): **Le Vieux Manior** accommodates 40 people. Rustic-style country house; 27 rooms are commodious and charming. Oak-beamed dining room with wrought iron chandeliers. Delicious food. Private beach on Lake Murten; tennis, riding, fishing, and all watersports. **Rigi: Hostellerie Rigi,** halfway up Mt. Rigi, could be ideal for young fun-loving families; view of Lucerne and its surrounding lakes is beautiful from your flower-sprigged mountain eyrie; sparkling indoor, glass-windowed pool; interconnecting family rooms, all furnished in a cheerful, contemporary way; supervised playroom nursery; special children's menus; a ski school for pint-size piste lovers; and an all-out effort by the manager to make family vacations fun. Children feel right at home from the moment they arrive at the reception desk, where there is a measuring stick to see if they are the right size to stay for free, until the time they leave with all their souvenirs.

For **St. Moritz** See St. Moritz on p. 731. **Soglio:** Off the Maloja Pass highway above the Valley of Bregaglia, and far off the beaten track, there's a tiny hidden mountain village, the retreat of the de Salis family who built three castles there, one of which is now the **Palazzo Salis** (Tel: (082) 41208); open May–Oct. I'd feel sneaky if I didn't tell you that none of the rooms have private baths, or didn't when I was there last. If this doesn't faze you, then the clean but faded splendor of the nice antique furnishings, the old garden, and the utterly unspoiled, high-perched village add up to a romantic and lovely adventure. **Splugen:** At the **Posthotel Bodenhaus** (Tel: (081) 621121), Napoleon, Queen Victoria, the Hohenzollern princes and kings of Wurttemberg have slept before you.

Zermatt: The **Seiler Hotel Mont Cervin,** (Tel: (028) 66–11–21) right in the center of this car-free village, is the leading hotel, comfortable and friendly, with an indoor pool, sauna, summer skiing, tennis, hiking, mountaineering, and in the glorious winter, a children's nursery and winter sports. Many less expensive and charming choices are also available (see Zermatt).

Zurich: The 235-room **Atlantis Sheraton** Doltschiweg 234; Tel: (01) 463–00–00) is streamlined, contemporary, spacious, shaped like a Y. Among reasons you'll love this five-star giant (and I usually avoid hotels this expensive and this sizable): three of the best family suites (#208, #308, #408) I've ever come across for accommodating mother, father, two children, and a baby; a terrace balcony, picture window, mountain view. A luggage rack converts into a niche for a travel-cot; bedside control for radio and TV; eiderdown quilts; teak furniture in the bedroom, plus comfortable chairs; bathroom featuring thermal controls, and heated by infrared light. The children's room, though, is the real inspiration—curtained bunk-beds; bathroom minus tub; radio; sofa and child-size furniture with plenty of storage space; balcony with table and chair. Exceptionally pleasant indoor pool, gymnasium, sauna, massage complex; cheery playroom; transportation to town; tennis courts; outdoor pool. Mini-golf five minutes away; wine press; cow barn. Children can play in the wooded meadows.

Swiss inns are charming and comfortable, and *Switzerland, The Inn Way,* by Margaret Zellers, describes more than 100 small inns in the farmlands, mountains, and by the lakesides. If you're interested in simple, inexpensive country accommodations, a furnished flat, bed and breakfast accommodations, or a farm accommodation, ask the SNTO for their illustrated booklet called *Country Holidays,* available also from **Federation du Tourisme Rural de Suisse Romande** (Office du Tourisme, CH 1530 Payerne, Switzerland). The booklet is in French, with a brief English and German gloss of the more common terms. Most of the chalets for rent seem kindly disposed toward making reductions for children up to 12.

If you can imagine yourself on an adventure tour, contact **Directions Unlimited Travel Service,** 344 Main St., Mount Kisco, NY 10549; Tel: (914) 241–1700, or (212) 828–8334. Bicycle tours of the Swiss Jura and of Eastern Switzerland, leaving from Zurich from early June to Oct., with overnight accommodations in standard class hotels are organized by **Adventure Center,** 5540 Colege Ave., Oakland, CA 94618; Tel: (415) 654–1879. For information about biking around Lake Geneva, from late Apr. to Oct., staying overnight in tourist class hotels, get in touch with **Swissair.** Hiking tours, with overnights in country inns, tourist hotels, mountain huts, are also offered by Directions Unlimited Travel Service, Adventure Center and Swissair. Hiking tours with stays in standard class hotels are offered by **Chappaqua Travel, Inc.,** 24 South Greely Ave., Chappaqua, NY 10514; Tel: (914) 238–5151; the **Chima Travel Bureau, Inc.,** 1650 West Market St., Akron, OH 44313; Tel: (216) 867–4770; and **Thru the Lens Tours, Inc.,** 12501 Chandler Bd., P.O. Box 45 16, North Hollywood, CA 91607; Tel: (213) 877–0181.

CLUB MEDITERRANEE There are summer villages, winter villages and year-round villages; Baby Clubs, Mini Clubs, Kid's Clubs, and children's ski schools; all attractive, all with mountain views. There's the Club Med, about eight miles from St. Moritz at **Pontresina** (7504 Pontresina, Engadine, Canton des Grisons); lodging in a schloss-hotel; with a Mini Club and a Kid's Club during school vacation times in the summer and winter, and a winter ski school for children from age 6. Cross-country skiing only at the club. Also in the Engadine is the **Club Mediterranee Reine Victoria,** 7500 Saint-Moritz-Bad; accommodation in a schloss-hotel during the summer and winter when, along with the Mini Club and Kid's Club, there's also a ski school for children from age 6. In the Bernese Oberland, fronting the Jungfrau, close to Interlaken, there's **Club Mediterranee Wengen** (3823 Wengen), open summer and winter, with Mini Club, Kid's Club, and ski school for children from age 6; schloss-hotel accommodation. Fond as I am of the town of Wengen (see Wengen), of all the Swiss Club Meds, Wengen is least appealing to me. I much prefer **Club Mediterranee Zinal** (3961 Zinal, Canton du Valais) about 5000 feet up, with a Baby Club, Mini Club, and Kid's Club *and* ski school open in the winter season for children from age 6; accommodation in a hotel. Villars/Orlon (1884 Villars-sur-Orlon) near Montreux, in the Vaudois Alps has splendid summer and snowtime activities as well as leisurely pleasures; Mini Club and Kid's Club; and, in winter, a ski school for children from age 5. Wintertime ski schools for children from age 5 up are also at **Valbella** (see Children's Camps) in the Grisons, and at Club Med wintertime retreats at **Leysin** in the Vaudois Alps and in central Switzerland's **Engelberg;** all with Mini Clubs and Kid's Clubs. **Zinal** is the only Swiss Club Med resort with a Baby Club, for children 4 months–2 years.

ATTRACTIONS FOR CHILDREN IN ZURICH I would unhesitatingly choose this cultural and shopping center as a point of departure for touring with children. Most entertaining during its June music, ballet, and theater festival. It is quintessentially contained in the Bahnhofstr., an avenue with shops (toys, clothes, cakes) that leads from the Haupt Bahnhof (train station) to Burkliplatz (where the lake steamers leave from); lots of swans (bring bread for them) along the river; lots of seagulls (throw bread into the air and they'll catch it) above the five bridges. Almost everything you'll want to see and do is here, within walking distance. Walk along Stadthausquai and across Quaibrucke to Bellevueplatz, near the landmark cathedral, **Grossmunster,** its double towers crowned with spires and tipped with gold; and Niedendorferstr.'s student youth; wend your way along Augustinerstr. (with oriel-windowed houses), Munzplatz, Widdergasse, Glockengasse. Off Bahnhofstr. you'll find the single-steeped **Fraumunster** and **St. Peter's** (its clock face, 28′ wide, so big even those just learning can tell time). Up the stairs, behind a fountain where busy Rennweg winds into narrow, curving Strehlgasse, is secret, hidden **Lindenhof park** that seems to rest on rooftops. Save some time for evening walks around St. Peter's, Fraumunster, and Grossmunster.

At Paradeplatz, take the #5 Tram (*much* cheaper than a cab) to the **Zoo,** a 15-minute ride up into the hills of Allmend Fluntern, overlooking the city and the lake. You disembark at a rather drab little tram station and on the way to the zoo is a mini-golf course and then the **Paradies der Alpenbahnen**—a miniature alpine railway directed by Robi Otter, an electronic robot stationmaster who talks, moves his hands and head; hailed as a technological wonder, it's a letdown unless you go expecting nothing; continuous 15-minute performances; the track (to 1/45th scale) winds through typical Swiss scenery, while church bells ring, lights twinkle, trains huff and puff. Outside is a child's carousel swing. The Zoo is a charming garden-park with more park than zoo atmosphere, but highly regarded in zoological circles for its scientific bent and admirable role in the community's educational system; animals in enclosures, with and without bars; forest in the background; flowers and pleasant paths for strolling; rare and beguiling baby animals; a lot of peacocks wandering across the paths.

Landesmuseum (the Swiss National Museum) is a blue-gray, enormous castlelike building, its roof pricked all over with delicate copper green turrets; cannon in the cobbled courtyard; make your way to the top floor costumes and costumed tableaus; lovely view of the city from the mullioned windows here; collection of old toys, dolls, doll kitchen, books and trains of 10th-century Swiss children. Smaller collection of toys on the third floor; more costumes; weapons hall; on the second floor, a marvelous apothecary's shop, very Charles Addamsish, with a crocodile hung from the ceiling; in the basement, reconstructed kitchen, prison cells, wine-making instruments; impressive Romanesque art on the first floor, paintings, goldsmith's art, stained glass, carvings, coins, and seals. Easy to go through, interesting, restful layout; will give the children an excellent resume of 12th–19th-century Switzerland. Several other outstanding museums—**Kunsthaus, Rietberg,** the archaeological museum at the university, even a **North American Indian** museum, graphic arts and an applied arts museum—may interest parents more than children.

For Sun. excursions, the **Botanical Garden** (Pelikanstr. 40) is surprisingly pleasant. From here you can make the teleferique aerotramway trip from Adliswil to the summit of Felsenegg, which has a happy carousel swing for children on top, and return via cogwheel train to the main station. Don't forget to go to the Dolder Grand **swimming pool** to watch the breakers churned up every half hour by electric motors. A cogwheel train goes up to the Uetliberg; cafeteria on the summit. A walk in the woods is extremely pleasant; buy food at the restaurant for a picnic, or bring lunch with you. The **Beyer Museum** of antique clocks and watches (Bahnhofstr. 31) is great for a half-hour visit; a must. Above the jewelry shop of **Armin Kurz** (Bahnhofstrasse 80) there is an enchanting *glockenspiele* with carillon chimes, daily at 11 a.m., 4 p.m. and a continual parade of costumed residents of Basel or St. Gall. (See also Information, and send for booklet.) The **Johanna Spyri,** of *Heidi* fame, archives (3rd floor, Predigerplatz 18) is open Wed. only, 4–6 p.m.; entrance free. The **Univ.** has a collection of historical medical books and apparatus (4th floor, Ramistr. 71) of special interest to doctors' families—also a wonderful way to enlighten children about the wonders of science. Check on hours. The **Kronenhalle,** where James Joyce wrote part of Ulysses, houses a fine selection of 20th-century painting. Wander along the Limmatquai's guildhalls; try sampling their restaurant fare (Limmatquai #40, #42, #54 and, in the Grossmunster area, guildhalls at Munsterhof #8 and #20).

Highly recommended are ***excursions*** to Rapperswil, Stein am Rhein, Schaffhausen, Winterthur, St. Gallen, and Lucerne—all easy, pleasant, rewarding.

The children's parade and the egg-knocking contests in Apr. are glorious (see Calendar of Events). The ''Knabenschiessen'' is a rifle shooting contest in which over 6000 boys from 12–16 take part annually (on a Sat. in Sept.); competition ends Mon. with a huge public fair.

ATTRACTIONS FOR CHILDREN IN BERN Switzerland's capital looks like a storybook illustration, with turreted buildings, arcaded streets, decorative fountains wreathed with geraniums and crowned with statues, rose gardens, ramparts, and emblematic bears (the city's heraldic device, they appear everywhere, sculptured in stone, even baked in cake form). Obligatory is the famous **Bear Pit;** you hang over the wall above and toss carrots and bread to these town totems, which you'll find just across the Nydegg Bridge over the Aare River. Cubs, first displayed about Easter, are at their sweetest in June. The other obligatory sight is the **Zeitglockenturm** (clock tower), whose mechanical crowing rooster, bell-ringing jester, lumbering bears, Father Time, and a knight in armor sound out the hour. Other things to see are: The **Zoo,** where the animals roam around in enclosures without bars; pleasant restaurant; playground; pony and donkey rides on Sun.; Aquarium; aviary; and reptile house. The **Swiss Alpine Museum** (Helvetiaplatz 4); unique exhibits of mountaineering, rescues, glaciers, animal and plant life, folklore, art and geology; an entertaining way to learn about the Alps. The **Postal Museum;** stamps and exhibits of electric communication systems. The **Natural History Museum** (Bernastr. 15); wonderful minerals and rock crystals, interesting dioramas of animals and birds, a live honeybee exhibit. Barry, the most famous St. Bernard dog of all, credited with saving 40 lives, can be seen 150 years after his death, stuffed, and looking alive and friendly, here. In the same building are the **Rifle Museum** (portable firearms and marksmanship trophies) and the **Historical Museum** (guarded by a bear statue) with Bernese handicrafts, farmhouse rooms; statue of William Tell and his son; medieval weapons and armor; tapestries; and a section devoted to books and printing (Swiss Gutenberg Museum).

Chindlifrasserbrunner (Kornhausplatz), a "child-eating" ogre, is one of the most colorful of Bern's 21 painted medieval statues mounted on fountain-bases; a warning to children not to fall into the moat which used to be here. By "collecting" ***fountains***—a runner (immortalizing the guild of messengers); a bagpiper (immortalizing the musicians' guild); the town's oldest hospital's founding mother decanting water from a jug—you'll see all the most interesting gargoyles, oriel windows, guildhalls, stone sculptures, arcades, and ornamental doors of the old city.

From June–Sept. ***organ music*** is played in the Munster one evening a week; beautiful and moving. **Jegenstorf Castle** offers interesting exhibits and historical collections. The June **Festival of Youth** for teenagers, centering around the Munster, offers horsedrawn carts and a variety of puppet shows for the younger ones. An authenticated **haunted house** is at Junkerngasse 54. The **Rose Garden** is a delicious spot, with public chessgames (semi-lifesize figures); spectacular during summer and fall evenings when the old part of the city is illuminated (an even more spectacular view is from the steeple of Munster). The **Marzilibahn** (shortest railway in Europe, the only one left in Switzerland operated by water) connects the Marzili area with the center of town; in operation during summer. **Boat trip:** on Fri. evenings, starting from the Schwellenmatteli restaurant at 6:30 p.m., you can motorboat around the Aare river to the Kappelen bridge at Lake Wohlen; a bus will take you back to the center of town by 9 p.m.; book through the tourist office.

Vegetable, fruit, and flower ***markets*** every Tues. and Sat. can be found along Bundesgasse, Gurtengasse, Schauplatzgasse, Bundesplatz, Barenplatz, Waisenhausplatz, Kramgasse, and Gerechtigkeitsgasse; on Munstergasse, meat, cheese, and dairy products are sold. Gerechtigkeitsgasse's arcaded street is the nearest thing to a ***flea market,*** the teenagers' poster and pop hangout. **Schloss Landshut,** a moated 17th-century castle in a lovely park, contains a museum of hunting and wildlife preservation from the Stone Age to the present; open May–Oct. The **Kursaal,** perched on a green hill in the center of town, offers orchestral concerts every afternoon and evening; children free on weekdays. Children get reduced rates on fishing licenses in nearby lakes and rivers. For trapshooting, clay pigeon-shooting, skeetshooting aficionados, one of the most modern and attractive **shooting grounds** in Europe, is open daily except Mon., modest fees, a few minutes from city center (Tel: 566–552). At Wabern, the fastest cable railway in Europe will take you up to the **Gurten,** a mountain park recreation center, 25 minutes from the center of town; spectacular view of the Alps; Lilliputian railway, a miniature road with peddle cars, a go-cart; exceptionally nice playground; woodland walking paths; and no cars allowed. On Aug. 1, **Swiss National Day,** the fireworks display here is sensational. Don't miss the confetti-throwing, good-natured **Onion Festival** in Nov. Easy ***excursions*** can be made to Thun, Spiez, and Interlaken.

ATTRACTIONS FOR CHILDREN ELSEWHERE **Arosa:** A ***summer and winter resort*** most active mid-Dec.–mid-Apr.; offers every possible winter sports facility, including one of the three largest ski schools in Switzerland, horse races on show, and horse-drawn sleighs for excursions; aerial cableway to the 7000′ Weisshorn. During the quiet summer season (mid-June–mid-Sept.), take the children on tranquil picnics in the woods; swim at the lido; play tennis or golf, skate on the artificial rink, fish or ride. **Basel:** The **Zoo** small in size but zoologically major, is remarkable for its animal breeding; Wed., Sat., and Sun. afternoons there are elephant and pony rides. The Sun. carousel at **Erlenpark** (Fasanenstr.), an animal preserve—with a lively playground, ponds with daily regattas of model boats—is a highlight for children. Other attractions for children are: Climbing the **Cathedral tower** for a fabulous view of the Rhine, where France, Germany and Switzerland meet. **Motorboat tour** around the port (which gives a child the novel experience of biting an apple in

France, chewing it in Germany, and swallowing it in Switzerland), and the **riverboat trip** (end-Apr.–end-Oct.) leaving three times daily from Schifflande, near Mittlere Brucke behind the Drei Konige Hotel (whose terrace is a traditional eating place). A **ferry ride** across the Rhine is also amusing, as the boats are attached to cables and are current-propelled. From Sept.–Apr., the **Zehntenkeller** in the Cathedral features puppet plays; tickets should be bought in advance at Hug, House of Music (Freie Str. 70; Tel: 233–390). Museums (open daily; but usually closed Wed. morning and open Wed. evening) are special: The **Kunstmuseum** (St. Albangraben 16) is more riveting to children than you might suppose with the best art collection (and Holbeins) in Switzerland. Visit the **Haus zum Kirschgarten** (Elisabethenstr. 71) with glorious antique toys, 25 fully furnished rooms, an interesting kitchen, timepieces, and tapestries. The lake dwellers' structures are interesting in the **Ethnological Museum** (Augustinergasse 2). The **Historical Museum** (Barfusser Church, Barfusserplatz) has prehistoric and Roman things, wonderful jewelry and ornaments in the Treasury section, and lots of armor. There's a **museum of sports and gymnastics** (Missionsstr. 28); **Swiss Pharmacy Museum** (Totengasslein 3) with two old drugshops completely restored, an alchemist's kitchen, and science labs. You might make an excursion to the **Roman House** at **Augst** (theater, temple, and walls, and a model Roman house) or to the ruins of **Pfeffingen, Dorneck,** and **Landskron** castles. In nearby **Riehen,** the former summer residence of a rich Basel family has been converted into Europe's first **Cat Museum** (*Katzenmuseum,* 101 Baselstrasse) with a library and extensive archives; collections range from Egyptian mummified cats to contemporary cats in print. Also, you'll find a museum of toys in the stately Wettstein Haus. Best of all is the three-day **carnival** beginning the Mon. following Ash Wed.—costume balls for children, processions, and an entire city turned out for costumed merrymaking. *Fantastisch!* In Jan., there's also the old guild pageant of **Vogel Gryff** when the Wilder Mann (the savage from the woods) comes floating down the Rhine on a raft to be welcomed by a griffin and a lion who dance with him on the Mittlere Brucke at noon.

Bellinzona: Three massive **medieval castles,** referred to as Uri, Schwyz, and Unterwalden and, alternately, Castello Grande, Castello di Montebello and Castello Corbaro. **Brig:** A comfortable base at the site of the Simplon Pass for exploring nearby glaciers and small towns in the valleys of the Upper Valais, and linked with Zermatt by a narrow-gauge railroad. (See Fun Trips). Squaretowered **Stockalper Castle,** with gilded domes and arcaded courtyard was the folly of a 17th-century merchant and fun to visit. **Burgenstock:** The Swiss "Gibraltar," overlooking the Lake of Lucerne. Don't miss this ***luxury resort*** with its three wonderful hotels. Try the fastest and highest elevator in Europe, the glass-enclosed job that will take you up the Hammetschwand cliff to the Mountain Inn for light refreshments! This very special hotel complex, created by art-collector Fritz Frey, offers tennis, pool or beach swimming, 9-hole golf course, and a 100-passenger yacht for trips around Lake Lucerne, church, resident doctor, drugstore, movie theater, shops, everything. The season is May–Oct.

Chur: A charming little medieval town in the Grisons to have a look at. **Coppet:** Just off Highway 1 on the lakeshore road from Geneva to Nyon is the castle which formerly belonged to Madame de Stael. **Crans/Montana/Vermala:** Three neighboring **ski-resorts,** all sharing the same sports facilities. The ski-bob was first introduced in Montana and there are two newer pistes at Chezeron. Crans is more luxurious than family-holiday Montana.

Davos: Every imaginable facility for ***winter sports,*** including a seven-acre skating rink. In summer, golf, riding, trout fishing, tennis, rowing and sailing; indoor and outdoor pool; mountains just as fabled as in song and story. Even if you don't like walking, geology, alpine flora and fauna (or think you don't or won't) you might as well invest in a map from the tourist office (or a bookshop) showing walks, plus a guide to Alpine flowers. Check into the July–Sept. bargain ticket for unlimited travel on the Schatzalp-Strela, Bramabuel-Jakobshorn, Pischa, and Parsenn funiculars. Restaurants at Parsenn and Schatzalp are a joy; so is the mountain inn at Strela Pass. The children may see, if they're lucky, a marmot, an ibex, or a chamois. Do let the children try the saunas with you. If you prefer them to do their climbing on **guided tours,** there are weekly summer trips (Tel: 36494). **Ermatingen: Arenberg Castle;** Empress Eugenie and Napoleon III once lived here. Two medieval fortress castles close at hand. **Essert: Champvent Castle,** a magnificent four-tower, 13th-century castle. Ask the tourist office about permission to see it. **Geneva:** boat trips from the Quai du Mont Blanc from morning to night; a bathing beach, Botanical Garden, the world's tallest fountain. The north tower of the Cathedral of St. Peter is where Calvin preached on a hill south of Lake Geneva (Lac Leman). The most important museum is the **Museum of Art and History** (Musee d'Art et d'Histoire, Rue Charles Gallard), with a good collection of Dutch and Italian paintings of the Renaissance, Islamic ceramics, and notable archaeological finds unearthed around the city; open 10 a.m.–5 p.m.; closed Mon. The **Ethnographical Museum** (Musee d'Ethnographie, 65–67 Boulevard Carl Vogt); open Wed.–Sun., 10 a.m.–noon, 2 p.m.–5 p.m.; a fine collection of musical instruments, and a new Amazon Hall. The **Natural History Museum** (Musee d'Histoire Naturelle, Route de Malagnou) is open daily except Mon. 10 a.m.–5 p.m. Nearby is the **Clock and Watch Museum** (Musee des Horloges et des Montres), open Tues.–Sun., 10 a.m.–noon., 2 p.m.–6 p.m.; Mon. 2 p.m.–6 p.m. The **Palais des Nations,** the United Nations Center is about five city blocks long, and the **Bibliotheque de Geneve** has a Jean-Jacques Rousseau room filled with books, manuscripts, memorabilia. The **Place du Molard** is the relaxed el cheapo quarter with a flower market and cafes. For details about the **Russian Orthodox Church** with superb icons, the flowerbed clock, the *Petit Palais,* and current attractions of interest for children, consult the **Geneva Tourist Office** (Tour de l'Ile, 1211 Geneva 11; Tel: (022) 28–72–33). **Grandson: Museum of old cars.** Near Yverdon on Highway 5 (the shore road of Neuchatel Lake) stands the Counts' 13th-century, four-towered **castle. Grindelwald:** A year-round resort; sleigh rides in winter, swimming in summer. Bliss. Surrounded by mountains; marvelous scenery. Children love the breathtaking **chairlift** (4 stops along the way) to a vantage point called First, 7200' high, where you can snack before returning. Thank heavens you have platforms so that your legs don't dangle—and you are provided with fleece-lined coats before you start. The trip takes one-half-hour, one-way. Take the 50-minute ride on the narrow-gauge Jungfrau cog rail line to the Jungfraujoch lookout station high in the Bernese Oberland, beginning at Kleine Scheidegg. (See Interlaken, also Fun Trips). The chalet-style addition to the **Grand Hotel Regina** features ten de luxe apartments for two to six people, each with kitchenette, balcony; indoor and outdoor pool; tennis courts, sauna.

Gruyeres 70 miles northeast of Geneva, is a storybook village of fountains, cobbled streets, a castle, old eave-shaded houses. You can eat the best fondue you ever tasted at the tiny, simple **Cafe de la Halle;** explore the ramparts and fortifications and 15th-century castle open to visitors (Tel: (029) 62178/62102). Then down in the town, watch Gruyere being made at the **Cheese Dairy,** 8 to 10:30 a.m. every morning, and again from 1 to 3 p.m., Mon.–Sat. In nearby **Bulle,** there is an exceptional provincial and folk art museum concerning this area (**Musee Gruerien,** Place du Cabalet, Bulle; Tel: (029) 27260), open year-round, 10 a.m.–noon, 2 p.m.–5 p.m., Tues–Sat., Sun., 2 p.m.–5 p.m. Closed Mon. **Gstaad:** A charming winter and summer ***ski resort.*** In summer, mini-golf, tennis, golf, fishing, a riding school, abundant flora and fauna, swimming pools. In winter, a card entitles you to unlimited runs on lifts and reductions on aerial cableways. Helicopter service for skiers; air taxi rides to the glacier; parties for children; a **ski school** (Tel: 41865) offering half-day instruction and practice for children; also a skating school. Ask the tourist office about the weekly special events for children. **Interlaken: Jungfrau**—have the concierge check weather conditions at the summit before you go. If all is sunny, outfit the children with comfortable rubber-soled walking shoes, extra sweaters, a coat, and sunglasses. A train takes you to Jungfraujoch (Kleine Scheidegg), where you begin to climb in earnest on the Jungfrau railway. A 4½-mile tunnel at Eigergletscher; at Eigerwand, you see Grindelwald and the Lake of Thun through windows in the rock. At Jungfraujoch, an elevator lifts you 370′ to the highest **Observatory** in Europe; or you can cross the glacier by dogsled, skate on the rink of an **ice grotto** that looks like a room in an ice palace. You can stay overnight at the **Berghaus Hotel** to see the sun set, but the high altitude can give you mountain sickness if you overeat or overexercise. I think it's wiser to spend a couple of hours at Jungfraujoch and then return by way of Grindelwald (you change at Kleine Scheidegg). Unforgettable. To mention any other excursion in the same breath seems absurd, but if you are interested in beaches, watersports, and castles to be enjoyed all in one fell swoop, remember Spiez and Thun. From the end-June–early Sept., every Sat. and Thurs. evening, there is an outdoor performance of *William Tell*. This is all acted out by a cast of 250 plus a lot of horses against a backdrop of trees and specially built chalets. The performance is in German, but for children this is no hindrance. The tourist office will get you tickets. An anticlimax for you, but not the children, are daily shows at the **Casino Kursaal** of folk dancing, yodeling, fancy flag-swinging, and alphorn blowing. In the mountains, alphorn experts can achieve a strangely beautiful counterpoint of horn sound and echo. The Casino alphornists are definitely not in this class, but the children will have a lot of fun watching these Swiss shenanigans. The **Flower Clock** is here, a lesson in humility to all green-thumb experts. **Kiesen,** between Bern and Thun, is worth a detour to see the **National Dairy Museum,** open Apr. through Oct. and part of a 19th-century cheese dairy displaying great-grandpa's farm implements; audiovisual presentations to show how cheese is made and how *fromage* from age to age endures.

Klosters: Lovely summer and winter resort. **Nuthusli,** a peasant and **folklore museum,** open Mon., Wed., and Fri. afternoons. Kindergarten, a children's hotel, and Chesa Grischuna all are here. And, of course, one of the best **ski schools** in the world for children. **La Chaux-de-Fonds:** An industrial town and watch-making center; most Swiss watches are made here. Also here, in Switzerland's Wild West, is a **Youth Festival,** the first Sat. of July every odd-year; the lovely **Bois du Petit-Chateau** (children's playground, flower garden, and little zoo); the **watch museum;** a swimming pool-skating rink (Melezes). A watch festival on the first Sun. in Sept. **La Sarraz:** Midway between Cossonay and Orbe, on Highway 9 between Lausanne and Vallorbe; good **castle museum,** nice to see if you have time, check hours. **Laufen: Schloss Laufen,** a restaurant in a manor house overlooking the Rhine Falls; fine view, good food. By all means, cross the Rhine by motorboat to the smaller castle of **Worth,** which has a little fishing museum. I think the view from Worth is better, and the **motorboat trip** is wildly exciting but completely safe.

Lausanne: A delightful city laddering up to its top-tipped **Cathedral.** Sat. evenings all the other church bells chime in tune with the Cathedral carillon. The lakeside esplanade of Ouchy, the old port, is beautiful. All the lacustrine attractions of Geneva. The **Bellerive beach** is splendid with three swimming pools. The museums aren't to be compared with others elsewhere. Pleasant things to do include (1) an inexpensive ride on the **P'tit Train de Vidy** which makes about a one-half-mile, ten-minute trip afternoons if the weather is good; departing from a little station at Vidy, Ouchy. (2) **Chateau St.-Maire.** The Bishops' Castle, not the seat of the Cantonal government. The library, Natural

History Museum and prehistory and Roman collections are all housed here. A 12-lane **bowling alley** open 2 p.m.–midnight every day at Montbenon-Richemont (Tel: 222–304). Two riding stables are **Chalet-a-Gobet** (Tel: 916–434) and **Manege de la Maison-Blanche** (Tel: 343–360). ***Excursions*** to Montreux, Gruyeres, lake and motor tours, wine-tasting are offered by the tourist office. **Lenzerheide-Valbella,** with an Alpine lake, six peaks, above-timberline terrain suitable for intermediate skiers, has excellent ski schools with small classes, daily from 10 a.m.–noon, 2 p.m.–4 p.m., for children and grownups, with multilingual instruction, including English, of course. For further information, contact **Verkehrsburo Lenzerheide-**Valbella, CH-7078 Lenzerheide; or the SNTO **Locarno:** A resort on Lake Maggiore; serene, extremely pleasant, except during Jan. and Feb., when it may be cold and rainy. Many water sports; an outstanding chiller-diller **funicular ride** 4500′ up to the Cardada Hotel for a meal should entertain the children no end. **Castello Rusca,** good museum inside if you have time, an interesting fortress castle. Subtropical gardens of the Brissago islands.

Lucerne: This medieval town and its romantic lake attract more foreign visitors than any other resort in Switzerland. Handsomely provided with facilities for watersports, tennis, golf, riding, and lake excursions (the one you must take is the steamer to **Burgenstock,** a 25-minute ride). Other attractions: Two elaborate **miniature railways**—one electric, with 3500′ of track, on top of 2000′-high Dietschiberg (reached by funicular) where there is a dream of an 18-hole golf course and a restaurant; the other a steam model on Bruelmoos. The fabulous lake festival. The famous covered wooden **Chapel Bridge,** dating from the 14th century, across the Reuss River giving access to the even older octagonal water tower with conical shingled roof, a former prison and torture chamber, now a popular meeting place for Lucerne's young people; the bridge is about 560′ long; decorated with paintings on wood that tell the early history of Lucerne and the story of Willam Tell among other things. The **Mill Bridge** (Spreuerbrucke) with very spooky murals showing the dance of death. The **Swiss Institute of Transports** with old and new locomotives, cars, airplanes, many working models; the old Rigi steamer (children will have a sensational time operating its machinery and steering mechanisms), which also serves as a restaurant; antique coaches and cars cheek by jowl with space-age exhibits including space shuttle, lunar roving vehicle and audiovisual presentations. The **Glacier Garden,** Lowendenkmal, with its potholes or giants' cauldrons, exhibits of a glacier grinding away as it did in the Ice Age, lots of prehistoric skulls and fossils, and a relief map explaining all the eccentric phenomena of glaciers. Adjoining is a pleasant **regional museum** plus the Labyrinth, a **maze of mirrors** which all over-8s love. The **Alpine Museum** is close by, with pictures of Alpine landscapes; lake dwellers' relics; alpine plants, animals, and geology. The famous sculpture of the lion of Lucerne. The Lucerne **Art Museum** is a lulu.

Have a look at the **Musegg Towers,** medieval towers joined by a fortified wall, and then try out the suspension **cable car** to the top of Mt. Pilatus or the **cog railway** from Alpnachstad—a mighty steep climb of 7000′. From mid-Aug.–mid-Sept., an annual music festival. If your children have never been to a planetarium, see the **Longines Planetarium** offering an entertaining program wherein vast dimensions of time are reduced to minutes and seconds. **Museum of Swiss Folk Costumes and Folklore** (Untenberg, Lucerne) is reachable by bus #14, the Dietschiberg funicular, or by foot. Little boys will probably find it a yawn except for the surrounding park, and, of course, the ride up there. **Kursaal Casino** (Haldenstr. 6) with afternoon and evening concerts, folklore performances daily Apr.–Nov., with alphorn-blowing, flag-throwing, yodeling, folkdancing (also nightclub, cabaret, dancing, gambling in another section). Children may want to investigate riding and a mountain climbing school, for which arrangements can be made by the **Lucerne Tourist Promotion Board** (Pilatusstraasse 14, CH-6002 Lucerne) who can also give you details and get seats for you at classical music and other special performances during the **International Music Festival.** The ***excursion*** to the **Stanserhorn** from Stans up to the sunny lunching terraces of the hotel and a ramble in the Alps is simple, inexpensive, and fun. You can do it by train or by bus and steamer.

Lugano: Enormously popular, rather crowded, but children love it. All water sports, including pedal-boats. **La Villa Favorita,** has a private museum (check hours) housing fabulous Holbeins, Titians, Murillos, and Rembrandts among others, owned by Baron von Thyssen-Bornemisza. The **Lake Festival,** end-July–Aug. features glorious fireworks; a **Grape Harvest Festival** in Oct., with flowers, costumes, music and processions. The lake steamer ***excursion*** to the idyllic fishing village of **Gandria.** Any or several of at least two dozen funicular, cableway, boat, chair-lift, cog-railway or electric-railway excursions. Do make the excursion to Melide. **Melide: Switzerland in Miniature** exhibit of towns, castles, mountains, railways, monuments representing the most beautiful spots of Switzerland, all built on a scale of 1:25 (castles are taller than 10-year-olds, 5-story houses just right for a 5-year-old to lean an elbow on), with everything that is supposed to locomote doing so. A very winning spectacle indeed; open daily (Nov.–Mar. Sun. only). **Montreux:** Beautiful year-round resort, with the **Castle of Chillon** 3½ miles away; an obvious must, it's just as lovely as it looks on all the postcards. Rising from the water, towered and turreted, it was great subject matter for Byron, Rousseau, and Victor Hugo. The children will have delicious thrills from the torture chamber and prisons down deep in the rocky foundations (satisfactorily damp, of course). Cog-railway and lake steamer ***excursions.*** Visit to the Nestle chocolate factory in nearby Vevey—a vision of chocolate lakes, hills of butter, and flowing glaciers of sugar—can be arranged by the tourist office (as can a tour of how baby food is made). You can also see the equivalents of America's eastern seaboard boarding-finishing schools by the dozens (a chance to decide about your own child's schooling). **Murren:** Summer and winter sports center; no cars; an entrancing medieval town with arcaded streets, a covered bridge, ancient ramparts, many fountains. If a **balloon excursion** in the Alps seems romantic and adventurous, this is where to make your dreams come true. The tourist office will let you know the June–July dates for High Alpine Ballooning week. **Murten,** 16 miles from Bern, a medieval town surrounded by towers and ramparts, is a delight. Have afternoon tea at the rustic **Stube** of **Channe Valaisanne** on Grand' Rue, with fine French fodder upstairs. Stay at the lovely small lakeside manor house by the lake, **Le Vieux Manoir au Lac.**

Neuchatel: On the first Sun. of the month, the **Musee d'Art et d'Histoire,** life-size mechanical dolls write, draw pictures, and play the harpsichord (a private showing is worth it!). Enchanting too is the **Suchard Chocolate Factory** (the tourist office can arrange a visit). A boat ride in the fjordlike **Bassins du Doubs** is exciting. A children's costume procession heralds the **Fete des Vendages** on the first Sun. in Oct. **Neuhausen:** Europe's Niagara and largest **waterfall;** be prepared to get wet; a boatman can take you in a gondolalike boat right into the **Rhine Pool** (immensely exciting and not as dangerous as it looks and feels). The Schloss Laufen restaurant is a dreary cafeteria (Schlossli Worth, ½-mile away, might be nicer); the ruins of Laufen provide a nice setting for a deer park. **Nyon:** A five-towered castle housing a **museum of Roman and Celtic remains,** plus a collection of Nyon china.

Pontresina: If you are an energetic, outdoors, nature-loving family, this village is heaven-on-earth. In June, alpine flowers are most beautiful; by Sept., the leaves are at their best. Village of fountains; typical white-plaster houses with wrought iron grills, painted decorations; frescoes in the chapel; horse carriages; golf, tennis, swimming and fishing; orchestral concerts in the woods, cafes, hotels. Playground adjoins the Roseg Ice Rink. Bookings for **horse-drawn carriage excursions** into the Roseg Valley can be made through the tourist office. At the Piz Lagalb aerial railway, there's an Alpinarium. Guided excursions daily by Postal Motor Coach; on Mon. and Wed., trips to the **Swiss National Park.** *Specials:* The **Mountain School** offers training and conducts daily four-hour tours on the Diavolezza glacier. Wed. sunrise **aerial cableway** trip. In summer, ***excursions include:*** **geology,** by a top-notch geologist who'll have even a 10-year-old fluently conversant with rhyoliths, carbon conglomerates, and the Triassic; **photography; botany** (June–mid-Aug.). From June, mountain hunters escort wild game trips in the park; overnight stays in alpine huts. Trout fishing in the lakes.

Rapperswil: You can come from Zurich by car via **Wildpark Langenberg** near Langnau (alpine animal garden and wild game preserve), by train, or by boat (enjoyable excursion along the lake of Zurich). A town of roses; see the **castle** (closed Nov.–Feb.), impressive round towers and battlements plus armor, weaponry, models of fortress castles, plus an exhibit of falcons and the accouterments of falconry on your climb up to the tower. Be sure to feed the deer in the park. Lovely rose garden. See the **Children's Zoo,** extraordinarily nice, sized just for children; owned and managed by the famous Knie Circus, it is coupled with a **Dolphin Show.** Pony and elephant rides; the "Pony Express" train; a maze to get lost in; a whale to scramble into to see a small aquarium; a gypsy caravan in which to picnic, an old boat to climb into, rides on donkeys. Outside the zoo proper, there's an aquarium. Alderman Hans Rathgeb, former president of the Rapperswil Tourist Office, has supplied the text for an outstanding book of photographs by Otto Eggmann, *Rapperswil-Stadt und Land*.

Regensberg: A medieval hilltop town; 13th-century **Regensberg Castle** tower to climb; Haus Rote Rose (house of the red rose) in the diminutive **Swiss Rose Museum** with watercolors by Lotte Gunthart. **Rhine Falls:** See Stein am Rhein. **Rigi:** A summer and winter mountain resort. From Lucerne, you go by steamer to Vitznau, a little red-roofed resort town filled with flowers and promenades, then by cog-railway (Mark Twain rode this first-built-in-Switzerland cogwheel before you!) to Rigi. In winter, fine skiing, horse-drawn sleighs (no cars), and ski school; even more popular in summer with young Swiss families.

Saas-Fee: Summer resort, winter sports; no cars (horse-drawn carriages and sleighs). You can take a bus in from Brig or leave your car in a garage at the edge of town. Skiing is good for beginners and advanced; not much for fledgling intermediates. The Nursery slopes at the village outskirts are wide, long and served by T-bars and rope tows. Ask the Saas-Fee Tourist office for more details (Saas-Fee Tourist office, 3906 Saas-Fee; Tel: (028) 57 1457). Encircling mountains. Chalets (there are 300), completely furnished, available for two to ten occupants. **St. Gallen,** built around a monastery named for Gallus the Gael, an Irish monk. Come for the **Children's Festival** held every three years (late June or early July); 10,000 children participate in a costumed procession, folk dancing, games, gymnastic demonstrations, and a tent fair displaying the beautiful embroidery and lace for which St. Gallen is famous. Everyone consumes vast quantities of sausage, the regional specialty, listens to band music, and has an utterly marvelous time. Little girls wear flowers in their hair and unbelievably pretty dresses. A textile and fashion center (the handwork on Swiss handkerchiefs is done in the outlying Appenzell rural communities), a university and cultural center. The **Industrial Museum** (Vadianstr. 2) features contemporary and antique fabrics, lace, and embroidery. What you really must see is the richly decorated **Cathedral** and the **Abbey Library** with its spectacular illuminated manuscripts (very special indeed!); the Klosterhof Square; Spisergasse (with marvelous oriel-windowed houses). See Schmiedgasse, Kugelgasse, Gallusstrasse, Gallusplatz and you'll see all the old parts of town. **St. Katherinenhof,** a serene cloistered spot, has Mon. evening concerts in summer. The **marionette theater** (if the libretto is familiar or in English); Peter and Paul Hill (ibex, chamois, deer, wild boar, marmot; restaurant with lake view); the **recreation center** (Goliathgasse 18); and a meal at **Set's** restaurant (Tel: 229–848) on Blumenberg, where the decor is a train car, should also keep the young happy. If you would like to visit an Appenzeller cottage industry or the unique Pestalozzi Children's Village at Trogen where orphaned and needy children are settled in 20 cottages, call on the tourist office in St. Gallen. (See Urnasch.)

St. Moritz: Smartest and grandest of all Alpine winter resorts, with the world's first chauffered hang-glider taxi-service and winter golfing with bright red golf balls; it's lovely in summer for children; summer skiing; tennis; lakes; boating and swimming; golf; all the amenities; escorted tours to the **Swiss National Park,** mudbaths too; famous **Hanselmann's** for cakes and goodies; the famed **Palace Hotel** with waiters on skates; dawn heli-skiing on nearby glaciers; bobsledding, ice skating, horseracing; people come here as much for the skiing as the rich and full apres-ski life with the international rich, royal, and *glitterati* during the winter season. There's the ultra-exclusive **Corviglia Club** on the best of St. Moritz's six ski mountains and, far kinder to your budget, two local Club Mediterranee villages!!! (See descriptions earlier in this chapter.) Although Christmas and February are jet-setter expensive times, after March 27, hotel rates are reduced, and a sweet, simple hotel like the **Aurora** has prices including meals that are ⅙ the rates at **Badrutt's Palace** without meals. But the Palace, in addition to its ski school for children of all ages, has a full-service kindergarten with a full range of activities for children from 9 months up, open from 9 a.m.–6 p.m. daily; crafts, toys, ice skating or swimming depending on the season; and multilingual trained child-educators in charge. **Schaffhausen:** With houses whose doors are trellised with grapevines; the massive Munot tower fortress that commands the town (but shouldn't command too much of your time); **Abbey Cloisters Monastery** and **Museum of All Saints.** See **Zum Ritter** with its frescoes (Fronwagplatz 63), **Schmiedstube** (Blacksmiths' Guild) and **Gerberstube** (Tanners' Guild) down by the boat dock. **Sierre:** This is a landscape dotted with castles. **Sils-Maria:** Ravishingly beautiful; heated pool; even Nietzche thought it was peachy. **Sion:** In the Valais region, clustered about the two hills of Tourbillon and Valere, this medieval town is a little jewel. Valere is crowned with the restored **Valere Castle** and the 800-year-old fortress church of **Our Lady of Valere** with a 600-year-old organ jutting like a prow from its rear interior wall. You can hear concerts played on this organ, believed to be one of the, if not the oldest functioning organs in the world, and visit an adjoining museum open 9 a.m.–noon, 2 p.m.–6 p.m., Tues.–Sat. The church contains beautiful frescoes, and the museum holds carved and painted wooden chests, Christian relics, farm implements. The **Cantonal Archaeological Museum** holding exhibits from the neolithic area and Roman antiquities is nearby; also the **Majorie Fine Arts Mu-**

seum, with the same hours as above; **Roman ruins** also nearby. Tourbillon is crowned by a crenellated castle and the ruins of the old city's walls; summertime **Son et Lumiere** performances; absolutely wonderful and a must, no matter how steep the climb appears! Year-round swimming, skiing, skating; mini-golf in summer. Market day (Sat.) welds the past centuries together. All splendid, charming, well worth making a detour to see. Helicopters and little planes available for charter. (See Fun Trips). **Stein am Rhein:** A storybook town with houses that are deliciously ornamented, it is very special. If you make an excursion to the **Rhine Falls,** don't miss this gem. Combine it with a trip to Schaffhausen. Head for the Rathausplatz and the **Hotel Sonne** (sun-rayed gilt sign) and the **Alder Hotel,** where you could spend the night. Most of the frescoes on the houses refer to myths, legends, the Bible, and folklore. The **museum** is amazingly rewarding. **Spiez:** Medieval castle with only a Romanesque castle-church between it and the beach with water sports.

Tarasp: Beautifully picturesque, 11th-century castle, handsomely restored, privately owned, and a landmark that can be seen from a distance. **Thun,** an attractive town and beach, has a four-towered castle that houses the rich **historical museum;** exhibits of prehistoric lake dwellers and of the Romans who first settled Thun. **Urnasch** has the riveting **Museum of Appenzell Customs,** a showcase of regional life. **Vevey:** See Montreux. **Wengen:** No cars allowed in town. You have to leave your car in Lauterbrunnen below and board a cog railway for a 15-minute trip to get here where, in winter, children skate, ski on the "baby hill," toboggan, and sled happily in the town center, or get towed through the streets in brightly decorative buggy-sleds. Near Grindelwald, not far from the Matterhorn, extraordinarily beautiful. More information from the **Wengen Tourist Office,** 3823 Wengen; Tel: (036) 55–14–14. **Werdenberg:** On the outskirts of Buchs (not to be confused with other towns named Buch and Buchs), this quaint little town stands on the shore of a tiny lake; overlooked castle. **Wildegg:** On Highway 5 from Baden to Aarau, you'll find **Schloss Wildegg,** property of the Swiss National Museum in Zurich, up on a ridge that looks over the Aare Valley. Along the same ridge are four other castles. **Winterthur** also has four castles in its vicinity: Hegi, Kyburg, Norsburg and Wulflingen. At Kyburg, reachable from Thun or Spiez, furniture and armor can be seen at their best; complete with chapel and torture chamber (an Iron Maiden at its most wincingly memorable); the nursery, cradle and all, is directly above the torture chamber.

You will be bowled over by the art collections: the Oskar Reinhart collection "Am Romerholtz" (a connoisseur's choice); **Kunstmuseum** (art) and **Heimatmuseum** (regional) are both worth seeing; **Schloss Hegi,** with games and toys is nice. But the plum for children is the Konrad Kellenberger collection of clocks in the **Rathaus** (Stadhausstr.). Masterworks of master craftsmen, all working; clocks with heads like ventriloquists' dummies that open and snap shut their mouths to tell the bonging hours; clocks in Braille; a 12-faced astronomical-calendar-horoscope clock; all assembled by Herr Kellenberger, a teacher in the local high school. The Town Hall features summer evening concerts—and then proceed to the tavern of **Castle Wulflingen** for your meal and a look at its interesting rooms with tile ovens, woodcarvings, and old furniture.

Zermatt: The **Matterhorn** towers above this famous winter resort with its seven-mile Piste Nationale plunging down the steep north face of the Rothorn; its sunny slopes for beginners, intermediates, and the experts; its cozy horse-drawn sleighs and car-free streets; and its subway that whisks skiers from the village to the upper lifts. Take the highest **cog-railroad** in Europe to Gornergrat, a thrill for children of all ages! Getting to Zermatt is a steep climb by narrow-gauge railway, but the cog train that climbs to Gornergrat is sensational. Just before you get there, you can get off at Riffelberg and have a go at safe but exciting mountaineering. Zermatt has managed to keep its rustic charm despite thousands of enthusiastic travelers. Plenty of hotels: five-star pastel palazzos like the **Monte Rosa,** gingerbread chalets; the three-star **Gornergrat,** an ideal budget-class hotel; a wide choice of economical and elegant places, including the smaller inns down among the trees at the edge of the hiking trails near town which are particularly charming. Skating and swimming in indoor pools. Linked by Glacier Express train with St. Moritz. June is alpine flower time; in Sept. and Oct., the autumnal foliage is even more brilliant than that in New England. The ascent to the Matterhorn was first made from the Zermatt side, and the **Alpine Museum** is a must, the relics of that first ascent seen in this indigenous setting singularly touching. To round out the picture, you could make an excursion to the **St. Bernard Hospice,** home of hospitable mountaineering monks and the obsolescent, but friendly-as-ever dogs, now superseded by helicopters as mountain rescuers.

FUN TRIPS The **Kleine Scheidegg Jungfraujoch narrow-gauge cog rail line** tunnels deep within mountains that have rock-cut windows to a summit station where you can stroll about inside a glacier, with ice sculptures. Wear whatever foot-gear you don't slip in. A 25% discount on this excursion if you have a Swiss Holiday Card. (See Interlaken, Grindelwald.) The 12-day **Heidi's Fairyland tour**—more sophisticated than it sounds—is a flexible, easygoing way of seeing Switzerland's highlights by train or bus. Offered year-round, the tour whisks you up in a narrow-gauge railway on the two-hour climb from Visp to Zermatt; from here, a spectacular trip up the face of the Matterhorn to Gornergrat; through the Simplon tunnel from Zermatt to Lugano and the Switzerland in Miniature exhibit at Melide; then to Lucerne, medieval Bern, Basel with its wonderful garden-zoo, St. Gall, and the Rhine Falls at Schaffhausen. And don't forget the special trains mentioned under ''Attractions''; the SNTO can fill you in on details.

Air-Glaciers, operating out of Sion, offer glacier flights for photography, sightseeing, or summer skiing, eight planes, seating from three to eight people, plus the pilot; also two six-passenger helicopters. They'll fly you anywhere from Amsterdam to Vienna, and can land on glaciers.

More than 1200 fixed ski lifts in operation during the winter, and more than 450 cog-railways, funiculars, aerial cableways, and chair lifts to loft you to alpine heights or just up a slope I'd rather not climb!

The **Alpine Postal Buses,** the color of goldfinches, with three-toned horns and incomparably good drivers, will take you to off-the-beaten-track mountain villages, but you have to get your ticket endorsed for all stopovers at the starting point of the trip.

Graceful swan-white **lake steamers** will take you for brief excursions on some of Switzerland's 1484 lakes, or across Lake Maggiore to Italy, Lac Leman to France, or Lake Constance to Germany or Austria. Or you can take a steamer from Lucerne to the foot of the Burgenstock, a great rocky promontory thrusting into the lake, where you can ride a glass-enclosed elevator built into the side of the Hammetschwand cliff to carry you the last 550′ up to the top of the mountain.

Children delight in rides in spotless trams for which, in Zurich and other major centers, you are on your honor to buy a ticket for the correct amount.

In winter ski resorts, you owe it to yourself and your children to call the tourist office and book a **horse-drawn sleigh,** guaranteed to put any child or parent in good spirits. From Dec. or Jan.–Mar. or Apr., you'll find these at Davos, Pontresina, Klosters, Adelboden, Arosa, Zermatt (best of all, summer and winter), and other resorts.

The **Glacier Express,** of the world's longest narrow-gauge railway, makes the 150 mile Zermatt-Brig-Andermatt-Disentis-Chur-St. Moritz trip in 7½ hours, crossing 291 bridges, whizzing through 91 tunnels, including the eight miles long Furka tunnel, and climbs to an altitude of 6669′ as it crosses the Oberalp Pass. From late Sept.–mid-Oct., from mid Dec.–early Apr. splendid meals are served with wine as well as milk and other drinkables. At the end of the trip, each passenger receives a souvenir bent-stem glass (to keep the liquid from spilling on high climbs) along with a certificate signed by the stationmaster confirming that he or she has made this fabulous journey, an unforgettable experience. Shorter, but also with magnificent scenery, is the Montreux-Zweisimmen-Spiez-Interlaken-Lucerne run, the "Golden Pass" route which you can travel in luxury aboard the Montreux-Bernes-Oberland Railroad's "Panoramic Express."

FUN AND GAMES Bicycles can be rented at stations of the Swiss Federal Railways and some private railroads and returned at any other station. ***Skiing:*** During the winter season (Dec.–end-Mar. or, at resorts above 5000′, to May) the ski school is a great institution. There are over 100 ski schools and over 1000 ski instructors licensed by the government. Skis and equipment, as well as sleds and skates, can be rented from the local sports shops. Morning ski classes 10 a.m.–noon; 2–4 p.m. afternoon sessions are given over to conducted ski excursions. Chamonix, Davos, Flims, Klosters, Les Diablerets, St. Moritz, Verbier, Zermatt all have good family facilities.

For your teenagers, magnificent skiing terrain and a whiz of an aerial cableway at **Andermatt** (skiing until July); skiing June 1–mid-Sept. via summer ski lift at **Engelberg. Saas-Fee** has skiing at glacier altitudes via aerial cableway and ski lift, June through the summer. Skiing on the glacier of **Piz Corvatsch** from mid-June–mid-Oct.; at **Gstaad** and **Jungfraujoch,** reachable by ski lifts and towing lift; at **Les Diablerets** on the glacial terrain (reachable by ski lifts) are all fine for adult canone, not recommended for younger children. **Zermatt,** with ski lifts, aerial cableway, skiing school, private ski instructor is a possibility, but not really children's skiing terrain in summer. **Pontresina,** with a summer ski lift and skiing school at Diavolezza (lessons from 8:30–11 a.m.; Tel: 66419, station; 66415, instructor) is great for kids also at **Crans/Montana**—skiing year-round on the Glacier de la Plaine Morte via four-passenger gondola lift, then up from the station of Les Violettes by an 80-passenger teleferique that nonskiers can also use; from here, there are two ski lifts for the experts. Skiing school open 9:30–11:30 a.m. Restaurants at stations Les Violettes and on the glacier of Plaine Morte (which, in spite of its name is safe and sunny) make life easier for the skiing and nonskiing members of the family.

Skibobbing, the nearest thing to bicycling on skis, is easy to learn and great fun. There are indoor skating rinks at nearly every major town, from Aarau and Adelboden to Yverdon and Zurich.

Watersports: Bathing beaches and lidos have been set up along nearly all rivers and lakes. From June–Sept., the children can swim, dive, waterski, canoe, or sail. The Sailing School at Lake Thun also has centers at Geneva, Neuchatel, Lugano, and Lake Constance (Bodensee). There are many indoor pools open year-round in all major cities, and almost all resort hotels have pools. **Ka-We-De** (Jubilaumstr. 101, Bern) has a swimming pool with artificial waves in summer which converts to an ice rink in winter.

Tennis courts can be found at all resorts and almost all hotels. ***Riding schools*** with excellent horses are in all major towns. Zurich's **Kolbenhof Reitschule** (Bachtobelstrasse Tel: (01) 33–84–00). There are 28 ***golf*** courses, 11 in the Alps. Miniature golf courses flourish as abundantly as Alpine roses. There's lots of trout ***fishing,*** but you'll have to check with the local tourist information office about local licenses and regulations and for the special booklet *Fishing in Switzerland.* ***Bicycles*** can be rented very cheaply at all railroad stations and turned in at any other station, and railway transport for them is cheap. It's a great idea to rent a bicycle if you're going to be in rural areas. Clay-pigeon shooting? There are lots of possibilities particularly in the Engadine and Bernese Oberland areas.

For ***hikers*** and campers, the **Swiss National Park** at Zernez offers a rustic hotel and a network of trails over 50,000 acres. Consult the SNTO. Mountaineering? The **Rosenlaui Mountaineering School** near Meiringen may be a bit much for beginners and children; but there is no-risk mountaineering near **Zermatt.** You take the funicular to Riffelberg with your hired guide, picnic lunch, rented shoes with the special soles if you want them, and climb up the 1000′ or so to the Riffelhorn. ***Hang-gliding?*** The **Deltaflugschule** of **St. Moritz** has relatively inexpensive hang-gliding carriers that carry both instructor and passenger.

SHOPPING WITH AND FOR CHILDREN Shops are usually open 8 a.m.–12:15 p.m. and 1:30–6:30 p.m. weekdays. If they don't close on Sat. at 1 p.m., they will probably keep going until 5 p.m. Food stores take a one-half-holiday on Thurs. afternoon; if you need baby food then, go to pharmacies or department stores. Department stores, hairdressers, and barbers usually take Mon. morning off. Except for railway station kiosks and a souvenir shop here and there, Swiss shops provide quality and value (I'm assured that even all those delicate, lacy little baby things are made to be boiled). Window displays are uniformly attractive, sales people helpful and polite even if you buy nothing; Swiss sport clothes for the entire family are *the* best, and last forever.

Zurich: Sprungli's confectionery (Paradeplatz, Bahnhofstr. 21) will ship yummies home—ask that *lebkuchen* hearts and *klauses* (jolly little raisin-eyed *lebkuchen* men) and Christmas and St. Nicholas specialties be sent to you for Christmas.

Toys: Have a look at **Franz Carl Weber's** (Bahnhofstr. 62; branches all over Switzerland); antique toy museum on the top floor is open on Thurs. (3–5 p.m.); floors of dolls, doll houses, paintboxes (hard to find elsewhere), games, hobbies, books, rocking horses, hobby horses, skis, bicycles, party favors. The dolls are remarkable (Wilma sings and speaks French, German, or Italian); the Steiff menagerie for every age; the car and train models (Marklin, Fleischmann, Arnold Rapido) with every known gadget and accessory; marvelous. Toys not to be found in America, such as a supermarket stocked with European brands and a bright red wooden doll's cradle on a stand (with red-checked canopy, eiderdown quilt and matching pillow) are eyecatchers; the novelty of European doll houses furnished with reproduction antique or rustic-style furniture; the Ravensburger games, puzzles, crafts, ladybugs converted into dominoes. Write for catalogs; they have several, so specify your interest. In addition to the Bahnhofstr., the St. Peter's area is also a children's paradise. **Pastorini** (Weinplatz 3) offers the best in wooden toys for the young and the *very* young; catalog (best age guide for choosing children's toys I've seen). Shaping and workmanship is, in many cases, worthy of contemporary museum quality—solid, safe, satisfying; dolls (English Sasha and her brother, Gregor), the Kathe-Kruse dolls

(Claudia, Bettina, and Nils) are particularly nice for children 5 and older. Sturdy wooden wagons, beach and bath toys, abacuses, Noah's arks, learning and educational toys; a game of cards called Swiss Folklore is imprinted with pictures of folklore festivals; books. Write for catalog. **Schweizer Heimatwerk** (Rudolf Brun-Brucke 2), the center for Swiss handcrafts—with branches in Basel, Bern, Lucerne, St. Gallen, and several outlets in Zurich—managed by Director Albert Wettstein; some very sweet wooden toys, blocks, hobby-horses, doll's house furniture, animals, a wonderful Noah's ark, fur animals, appealing music boxes; crystals and rock samples. Beware of the bunches of alpine flowers (they disintegrate); a better buy is an illustrated book about them. Swiss army pocket knives for boys; for birthday children, wooden circular candleholders (but buy the candles here because American candles to fit are hard to find); miniature wooden tea sets; an orchestra of small angelic instrumentalists; painted wooden hangers for children's clothes; a painted frame with five hooks (decorative and useful); straw caps for boiled eggs; hand-embroidered, flowered ribbons; pad-lined basket for little treasures; play aprons.

Music boxes, wood-carving? The **Old City Souvenir Shop** (Rennweg 2) has by far the best selection; the feather bird music boxes which move and sing may be an extravagance, but once you've seen and heard one in action, you may succumb; dear little wooden angels; skillful woodcarvings. I have always found cuckoo clocks particularly trying, but for those who like them, they're here also.

Children's shoes? Fine selection downstairs at **Bally Capitol** (Bahnhofstr. 66). Children's ***clothes?*** **Handar** (Bahnhofstr. 83) has durable leggings for little boys; also Tyrolean dirndls and silver-buttoned jackets; **Gassman** (Poststr. 7) is also good. **Prema** (Kappelerg 11/13), good maternity clothes and infants' wear. **Modelia** (Bahnhofstr. 92) and **Modissa** (Bahnhofstr. 74), excellent preteen and teen sizes. If you just need to replenish socks and underwear, ask for the nearest **Au Bon Marche,** the Swiss equivalent of Sears Roebuck. **SPA** (Sihlporte and Talacker) is similar and may be more convenient. For the practical necessities of baby and toddler wardrobes, there's **Mothercare** (Rennweg 57).

Department stores: **Globus** is elegant and fashion-conscious for babies, children, and teenagers; children's clothes are imaginative and durable; attractive restaurant; playroom (see Magic Family Helpers). Globus is the home of Globi, a black-bereted bluebird with red and black checked pants, whose fun-making has made him a European children's hero for almost 40 years, giving rise to hundreds of Globi fan clubs and some three dozen Globi books. **Jelmoli's** is all hustle and bustle, fun for older children because something new is being demonstrated on every floor with opportunities for tasting and sampling. I think merchandise here is less expensive and more ordinary in styling than Globus; sport and utility clothes for children excellent. From baby food to luggage (such as the Caddie), everything is findable here. Stationery available at **Zum-**

stein (Uraniastr. 2) where you can find zippered pencil cases fitted with compass, ruler, pocket-knife, pen, pencil sharpeners ($3 to $22). Ask for an *etui von Funke!*

Bern: For children's and baby clothes, **Bebehaus** (Kramgasse 65). Sturdy, decorative, useful baskets for carrying children's toys, good to have shipped home, at **Korbwaren** (Kramgasse 17). **St. Moritz: Ender-Sport** rents children's sport clothes. **St. Gallen:** embroidery, appliques, lace, and organdy specialties featured by the **Sturzenegger** stores (St. Leonhardstr. 12); branch in **Lucerne** (Haldenstr. 5) especially recommended; others in Basel, Bern, Davos, Gstaad, Interlaken, Ontreux, St. Moritz, Zermatt, Zurich.

In **Basel,** besides **Franz Carl Weber** (Freie Str. 17), toys to be treasured are found at **Warenhaus Cardinal** (Freie Str. 36); **M. Beltrami** (Spalenvorstadt 22); **Wyni Grob** AG (Steinenvorstadt 73); **Magazine zur Rheinbrucke** AG (Greifengasse 22); and at **Globus.** Children's clothes: **Bambino** (Guterstr. 219); **Le Vaillant** (Leimenstr. 76); and **Nuggihaus** (Feldberg 42). In **La Chaux-de-Fonds, Au Berceau d'Or** (av. Leopold-Robert 84) and **Jouets Weber** (rue Neuve 18) having charming toys. Children's clothes: **Chez Arlette** (rue Balance 14). Nice children's clothes and toys can be found in the department stores: **Uniprix** (av. Leopold-Robert 19); **Gonset S.A.** (rue Neuve 16); and **Au Printemps** (av. Leopold-Robert 54).

SWISS FRIENDS AND PEN PALS The SNTO in the Main Station Bldg. in Zurich is in charge of the ''Don't Miss the Swiss'' program, which focuses attention on young people (with recreational facilities and youth centers). Unofficially, the **American International School** in Zurich is also helpful.

CALENDAR OF EVENTS These are some of the main events. Check with the SNTO for more information on these and other events. In **Jan.,** Basel features the ***Vogel Gryff Festival;*** folklore festival with costumed parades, drums, and cannon salutes. Jan. or Feb. at Flims, Pontresina, St. Moritz, and Davos you'll find Costumed Sleighing Teams taking part in the folk festival of ***Schlitteda.*** Jan. 13 is the time the New Year is heralded with masked ***Silvesterklause*** dancing processions in Appenzell, Glarus, and Grisons. Winter resorts hold ***Ski Events*** Jan.–Mar., plus ***Curling Championships*** and ***Horse Racing*** on snow.

In late **Feb.,** Basel and Lucerne have ***Carnival;*** a three-day celebration; processions, costumes, masks, and drums; special in Basel. Various districts hold Carnivals and processions in Feb. or Mar. (Thurs., Sun., Mon., and Tues. before Ash Wed.). In **Mar.,** ***Chalanda Marz*** is celebrated in the Engadiner; processions of children singing traditional spring songs. In **Apr.,** Zurich, Appenzell, and Glarus celebrate ***Spring Festival;*** burning of the Boogg or Old Man Winter, an effigy stuffed with fireworks; general pageantry. During Easter, northeastern Switzerland features children's ***Egg-Knocking Contests.*** **May**–June, in Gstaad, cattle are driven to Alpine pastures; much fanfare; cow fights. On Whitsun, Locarno has a flower festival.

June brings the ***International Music Festival*** to Zurich and Lausanne. ***Corpus Christi*** processions in Catholic towns (especially Appenzell). Geneva celebrates ***Rose Week Festival;*** Murten holds a ***Children's Procession*** and ***Commemoration of the Battle of Morat; Marksmanship Meet*** held about the same time. From June–early Aug., Lugano and Lucerne hold a ***Lake Festival.*** June–Oct., Sion features its ***Sound and Light*** spectacle; dramatic pageantry; wonderful. In early **July,** many districts hold ***Children's Festivals.*** Chatel-St.-Denis holds a ***Midsummer Festival.*** Through Sept., Interlaken performs ***William Tell.*** **Aug.** 1, all Switzerland celebrates ***Swiss Independence Day;*** bonfires and dancing in the streets. In mid-Aug., Geneva holds its ***Festival;*** flower battles, parades, fireworks.

In **Sept.,** a ***Shooting Competition*** for boys 12–16, in Zurich; La Chaux-de-Fonds has ***Braderie,*** traditional fair and autumn festival; and in mid-month, Eastern Switzerland and Bernese Oberland feature their ***Ceremonial Cattle Drive*** from Alpine pastures to the valley for winter. Late Sept. or early Oct., Neuchatel holds its ***Grape Harvest Festival.***

Early **Oct.** is the time of the ***Fulehung Festival*** in Thun; Lugano holds its ***Wine Festival;*** and St. Gall has its ***Swiss Farm and Dairy Fair.*** A **Nov.** special is the ***Onion Market*** in Bern; tons of confetti thrown; great fun. The Sun. before or on Nov. 11, the Canton of Zurich celebrates ***Rabeliechtli;*** much like Halloween, with turnip lanterns in children's procession.

Dec. 4–6, central Switzerland features ***Klausjagen;*** traditional appearance of Santa Claus; elaborate processions. On the 6th, Zurich's "Klaus" procession includes costumed children wearing lantern hats. **Dec.** 11–12, Geneva commemorates the ***Escalade;*** patriotic festival. The fourth Sun. in Advent, Lucerne has ***star-singing processions.*** On the 25th, all Switzerland celebrates Christmas with pageants and carols.

LANGUAGE AND PHRASEBOOK Just to keep everyone on his toes there are four official languages: German (spoken by 73%); French (21%); Italian (5%); and Romansh (1%). *Gruezi* (pronounced like grew-at-sea said very quickly), *salut, gruss gott* are the standard salutations. Thank you is *merci, vielmals,* or *danke vielmals;* goodbye may be *ciaou, 'bye,* or *f'wiedersehen.* Odd combinations, such as *pomme chips* (potato chips) and *halbe grapefruit* (½ grapefruit) are a result of linguistic democracy. This leads to confusion, such as the town Friedegg (pronounced free-deck), which translates as "peaceful corner." Pictorial signs bridge all communication problems, however. If you falter, don't worry, there's always someone nearby who can speak English!

THE HOMECOMING PARTY

A homecoming party reinforces your children's feeling of being specially privileged to travel and gives them the good feeling that everyone is glad to welcome them home. It's also a reciprocal gesture to those who gave your family going-away presents or bon voyage parties. The party is best if it is informal, with family and close friends, with friends of your children—and possibly you may feel as I do that this is a splendid time to invite your children's teacher, librarian, and head of the school (which will really make this an event for your children).

I mail back food parcels to myself—Scandinavian fish specialties, Scottish shortbread, sugared flower petals from France, attractively wrapped and packaged candies, chocolates and cheeses from everywhere—and the children keep on the lookout for additions. The children also should be asked about records to send home for the occasion—Bavarian yodeling and Dutch hurdy-gurdy tunes might seem a bit corny to you, but let them buy and collect what they want. This is the time when beach pebbles, potshards, Greek sponges, foreign-language comic books, European kitchenware, and other personalized remembrances are wonderful presents. Decorations can certainly include yours and your children's purchases, your children's albums made while traveling, travel posters, or maybe drawings made by your children (either as place cards or as posters).

The time to have your party is after all your food and record parcels have arrived, when your slides and photographs have been developed and set up on a carousel or arranged in albums for looking at (ever the optimist about that!) and when you've had about a month to get used to being home again. If you feel like laying on a giant smorgasbord or Italian festa food, fine. A mother of four got away with TV dinners by enlisting her children's help in skewering the foil plates with signs saying FASTEN YOUR SEAT BELTS to simulate air-travel fare, complete with plastic eating utensils!

INDEX